ARCHITECTURE | GLASS | ART

FRANZ MAYER OF MUNICH
MAYER'SCHE HOFKUNSTANSTALT

edited by
Gabriel Mayer

with contributions by
Brian Clarke
Bernhard Graf
Martin Harrison
Gottfried Knapp

HIRMER

CONTENT

Foreword

Brian Clarke

Stained glass has a simple nature. It is an apparently solid liquid. It is at times transparent, opalescent, diffused, striated with lines or alive with bubbles. Light passes through it, pauses at it or at times simply diffuses it. It is traditionally held together with lead and painted. Limited applications of color can be added to or etched away from its surface.

In the last few decades it has also become a different but analogous experience on commercial float glass. The marriage of technologies and experience gained over a millennium of stained glass is today informing the application of art digitally generated on mass-produced commercial float glass.

Art develops and alters as a human means of expression, it has always been so and technologies are created to meet contemporary needs. The creation of the one does not preclude the use of the other nor indeed combining them. Without the knowledge of the medium and its history it is impossible to use the medium to its greatest and widest ranging impact. There are but a few stained glass studios or factories that embrace both the history and the contemporary potential of the medium. The Mayer'sche Hofkunstanstalt or Franz Mayer of Munich as it is known in the English speaking world has been at the cutting edge of this investigative marriage for five generations. The creation of art, whether in the written or spoken word, the composition or performance of music or painting, sculpture, architecture or stained glass needs the constant nourishment of original thought. The radical and the original are frequently one and the same. We are used to seeing the avant-garde in the visual arts rise out of the swell of painting or the younger mediums of cinema, photography or conceptual investigations. That it should also be the product of a medium historically bound by craft, tradition, religion, and dogma is on the whole considered as nonsense and the conventional art world thus dismisses the medium of stained glass without thought or serious consideration on the basis that it is ipso facto, redundant. Armed with the ruthlessness of convention and the violence of orthodoxy the art world has summarily consigned stained glass to a place in history from which they refuse to release it. It is imprisoned in a cultural Guantanamo from which it seems there is neither release nor reprieve.

Yet, for the past two hundred years the medium has confounded its detractors by generating some of the most significant works of art of those two centuries. It has also been the fertile ground upon which have grown ideas and concepts that have permanently altered the way we see the visible world. The achievements of Burne Jones, Morris, Thorn-Prikker, Matisse, Albers, Cocteau, Knappe, Meistermann, Schaffrath, and Schreiter have fundamentally enriched and increased the languages at the disposal of the contemporary artist and architect broadening the range of experience immensely. The critics dismiss it, the historians mention it in passing if at all, and the architects view it as a medieval expression unsuited to a language that views art and decoration as a placebo to clients and a public who ought to know better. However, every now and again, despite the great efforts of the orthodoxies of the mediocre and an art world obsessed with commercial portability and re-sale potential, works in stained glass thunder through the ignorance of the ordinary and make a difference. These differences when they occur are what keep the medium alive and viable. Artists cannot make these leaps alone. To push the medium into a position from which it is capable of speaking truth to contemporary power it needs a symbiotic allegiance with the craftsmen who make it. They alone can generate the excitement needed to change thinking and find ways to effect these changes legitimately and with the delicacy of translation needed to produce poetry. Neither artist nor craftsman need fear these changes, indeed, it is only by positively embracing them that the medium has any hope of survival. It is not only the message that changes but also the medium that expresses it.

At times artists seek to bend and force the nature of stained glass towards characteristics more appropriate to easel painting or cinema. The rise of digital technology and printing have made it possible to introduce figuration at immense and complex scale giving a superficial impression of compositional complexity and thoughtful image making, however, on the whole this has only resulted in a sort of large-scale cinematic freeze-frame 'movie grabs' without architectonic substance or a respectful acknowledgement of the liquid and transilluminate nature of the medium. On such occasions this renders the resulting work vapid and banal. At other times when the artist leaps and dives with the givens of the medium and the material new opportunities are revealed that make the medium of stained glass a vital and thrilling reinvented language of the sublime.

Mayer'sche Hofkunstanstalt provide artists and architects with the knowledge of history and the enthusiasm for the future that is essential to the making of stained glass and indeed mosaics that are relevant to our own times.

The medium carries within its nature the simple joys of the well made treasured by our species for millennia and the profound complexities of poetry without which we cannot hope to appreciate the nature of the human condition. Unlike other mediums it is inexorably linked to architecture and uniquely positioned to contribute once again to the beautification of the built environment. The role the Hofkunstanstalt plays in this drama cannot be overestimated. As an artist who has benefited from their patient forbearance and technical expertise I raise my hat to them with respect and with affection.

On a personal level as an artist I have shared victories, lamented losses, been bold, been humbled, allowed and encouraged to do my best by Mayers'. My relationships with both Gabriel and Michael Mayer have taught me much and kept me laughing for many years. Franz Mayer of Munich is a great European treasure and part of our culture. We must do all we can to deserve them.

Brian Clarke

HISTORY

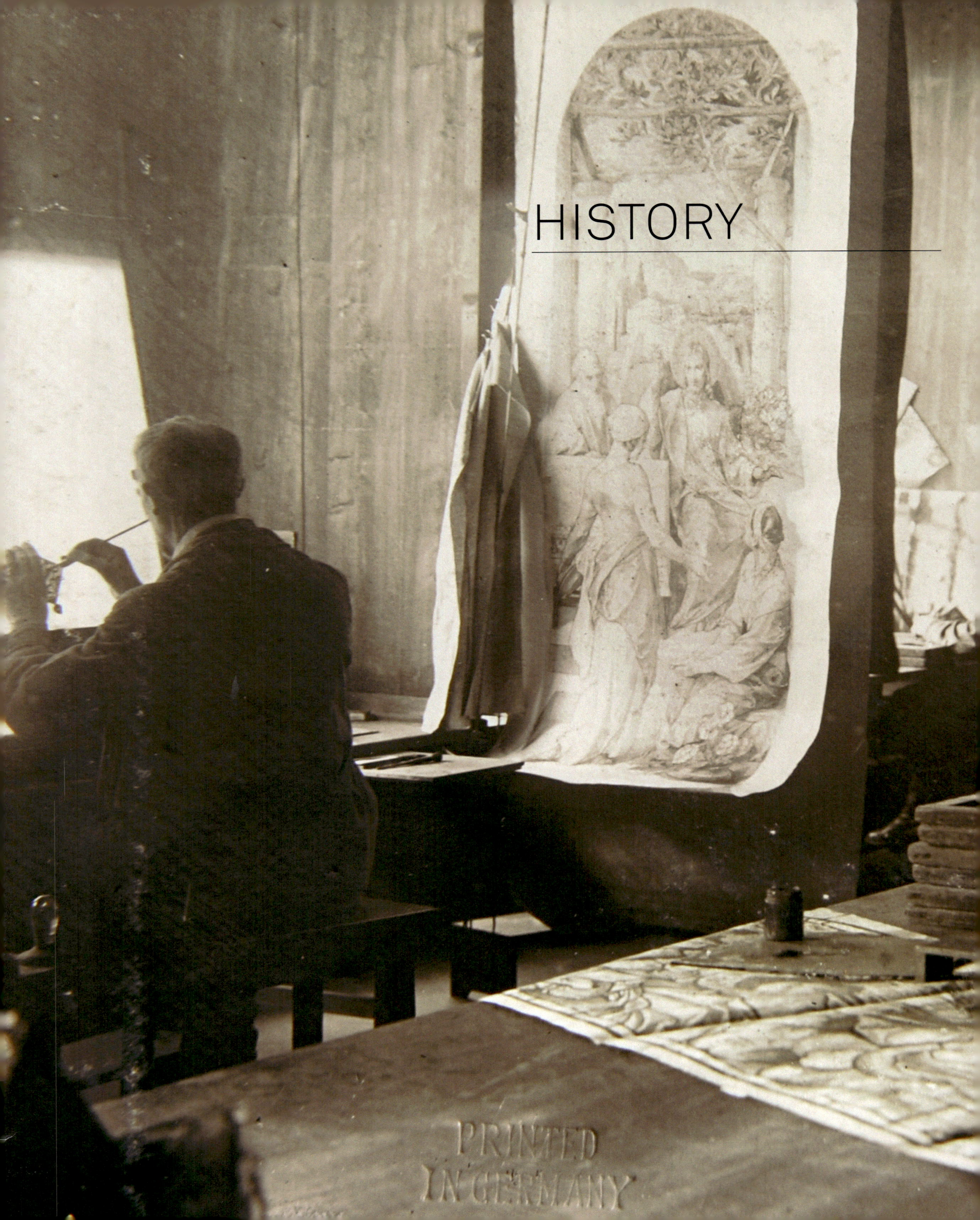

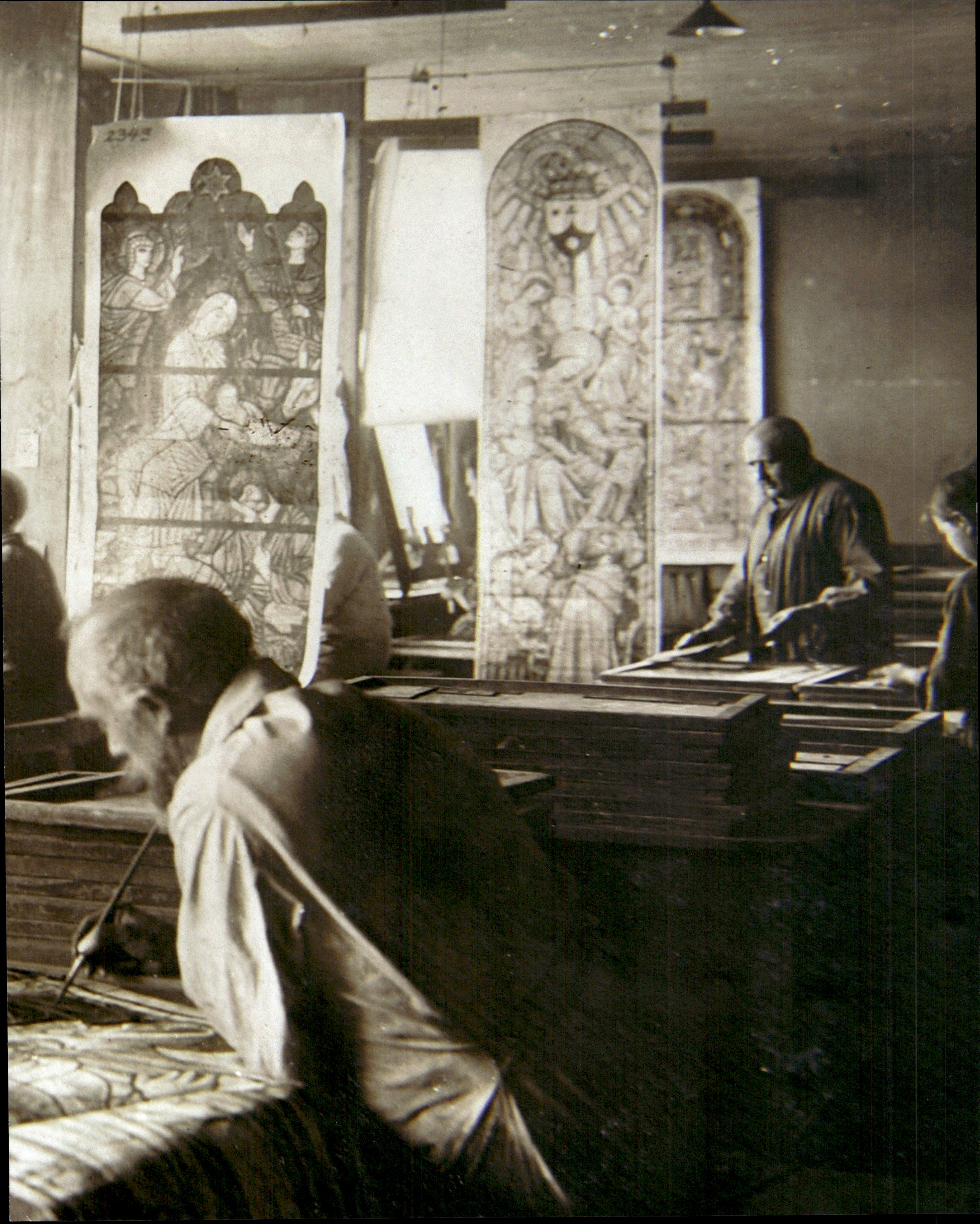

FIG. PAGES 6 + 7 Interior view of one of the stained glass workshops, circa 1910

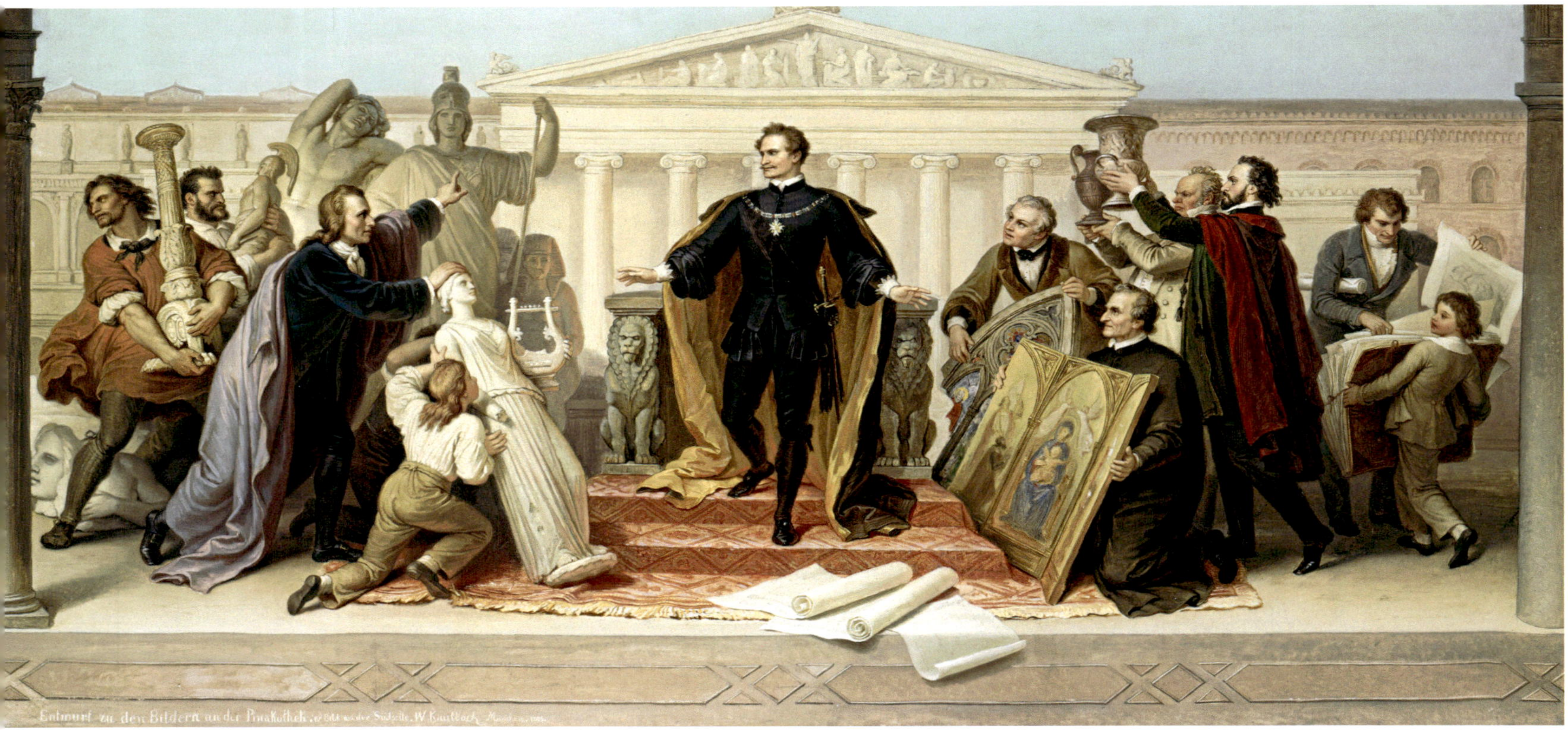

1
KING LUDWIG I SURROUNDED BY ARTISTS AND SCHOLARS, Wilhelm von Kaulbach, 1848

History

Bernhard Graf

Founded in Prerevolutionary Times

Times were restless in Bavaria: The people hated the reactionary politics of their king, Ludwig I (ruled 1825-1848), who offered censorship instead of freedom of press. They rejected their ruler's dictatorial concept of art, detested his escapades, his perpetual affairs, his erotic trips to Italy, and finding his provocative love poems printed in newspapers.[1] Increasing prices for bread and beer ultimately led to the so-called Munich Beer Revolution. Even Ludwig's Secretary of the Interior, Karl von Abel, rebelled against him. The monarch discharged him in disgrace when he refused the naturalization of the king's new mistress, Lola Montez.

In these uncertain times, Joseph Gabriel Mayer (1808–1883) *(fig. 4)* founded the "Mayer'sche Kunstanstalt für kirchliche Arbeiten" (i.e. Mayer's Art Establishment for Ecclesiastical Works). Born in Gebrazhofen in the Allgäu region of the Alps, this academy-trained artist and sculptor was a deeply religious man who served on the board of the State Education Institution for Physically Handicapped Children. He stated: "With the approval of my estimated superiors, I thus decided that I would carry out these massa works on my own account for the time being. I would do my work in a specially rented shop and solicit a special privilege from His Royal Majesty to execute the stone massa shaping I had invented. This was granted in September 1847 whereupon I soon began to set up the Art Institution."[2] His vision was going to revive organizational principles and working methods of Gothic masonry workshops.[3] Based on his idealized view of the Middle Ages, he initially produced religious stone figures and altars *(fig. 5)*.[4] He had not yet discovered the

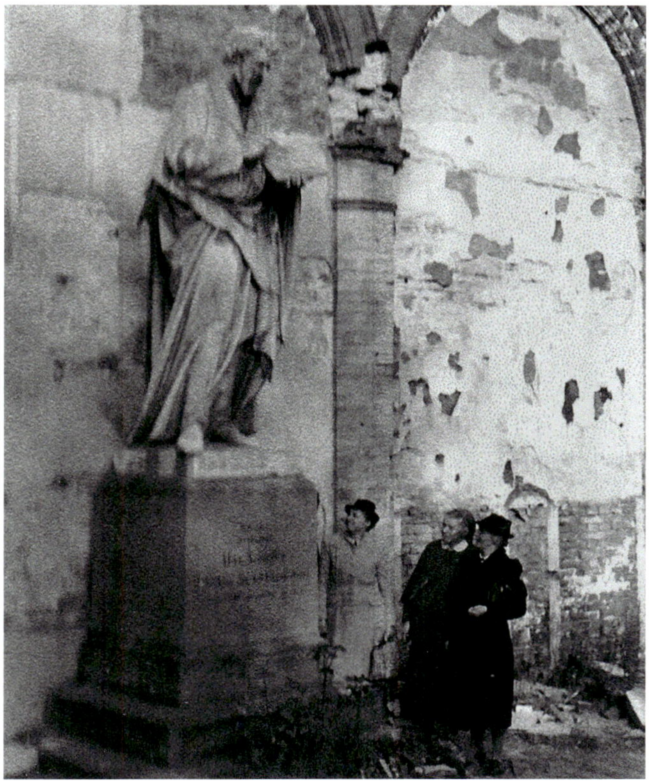

2

TOMB OF MAX EMANUEL AINMILLER (1807–1870), co-founder and director of the Königliche Glasmalereianstalt (i.e. Royal Institute for Glass Painting), Südlicher Friedhof, Munich, visited by members of the Mayer family, 1948

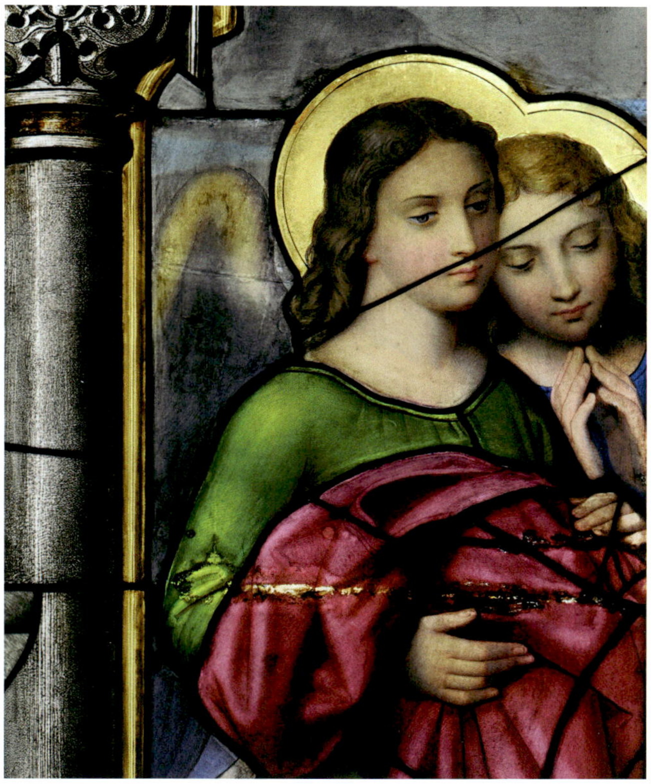

3

Glass panel from **THE WINDOW CYCLE FOR THE MARIAHILF-KIRCHE,** Munich, by Königliche Glasmalereianstalt, circa 1838

art of glass and mosaic for himself. The studio chronicle describes his motivation as follows: "the entrepreneur J. G. Mayer concentrated [...] on Christian art. He was indeed acutely aware of the sad state Christian sculpture had reached at the time. He was determined – and this was the core of the founder's struggle – to improve this sad situation by decorating the churches with artistically superior, truly worthy artifacts to enhance the Christian art and to raise sensitivity for the latter."[5]

However, Mayer's vision appeared to fail and he desperately noted: "But the following revolutionary year 1848 was demoralizing if one wanted to create an art institution of any type, let alone an ecclesiastical one. The danger of demise was inherent."[6]

At the same time, King Ludwig I of Bavaria wrote to his mistress Lola Montez: "I shall not give in. Just stay calm. Everything will be fine."[7] Yet the monarch had underestimated the situation. On March 20, 1848 the revolution was over and he had lost everything: His crown, his honor, his mistresses, and his much-adored glass art. And it had all started so well thirty years earlier.

You Do Not Know Germany Unless You Have Visited Munich.

In Munich 1818, only three years had passed since Emperor Napoleon I's final abdication. For some, this was the end of a triumphant era of victorious cooperation between Bavaria and France. For others, it meant liberation from suppression, grief, and death. Crown Prince Ludwig of Bavaria shared the latter view, refusing the politics of his father, King Max I Joseph (ruled 1806–1825): "We were opposites on too many counts."

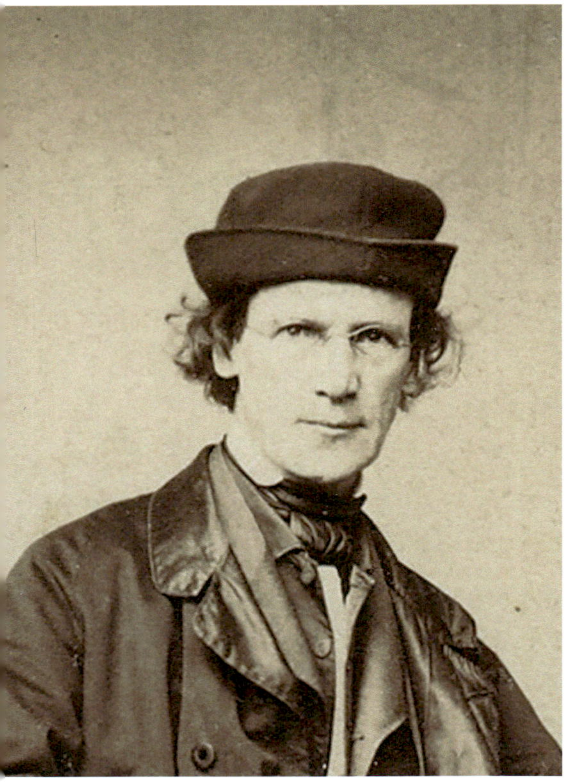

4

FOUNDER JOSEPH GABRIEL MAYER (1808–1883)

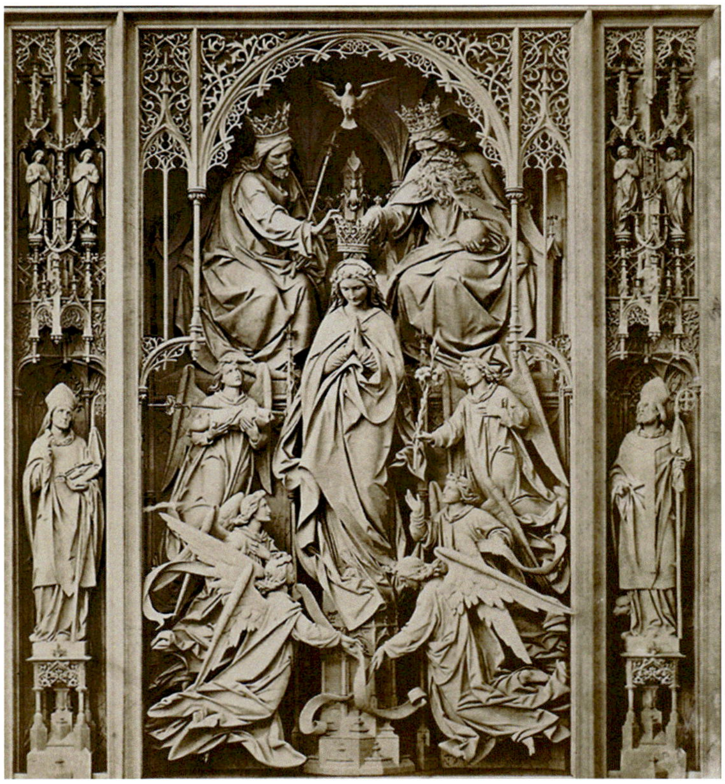

5

CORONATION OF THE VIRGIN, Neo-Gothic main altar, Dom zu Unserer Lieben Frau, Munich, Joseph Knabl, 1862

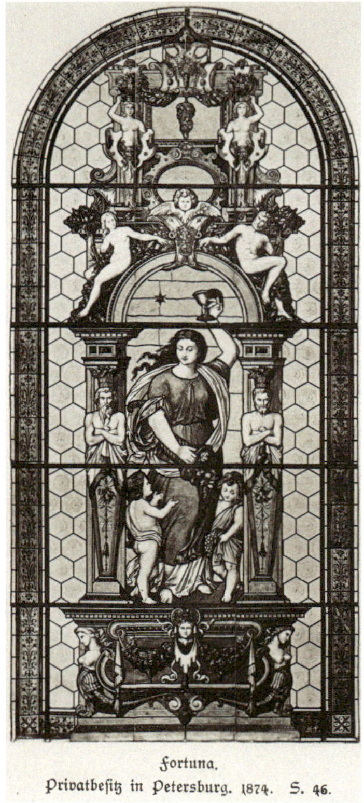

6

"FORTUNA," STAINED GLASS, Private Collection, St. Petersburg, Russia, Zettler 1874

He had a preference for the French, the Tricolore, the Republic, Napoleon, and he was very much their friend "… I violently hate the French … am full of Germanic feelings – utterly alien to him. I favor historic things, I want to preserve. He is for innovation, has no sense for the former."[8]

The crown prince owed his preference for tradition, antiquity, and the Middle Ages to the contemporary poets Wilhelm Heinrich Wackenroder and Ludwig Tieck, whose works he encountered through the Nazarenes, a Rome-based association of artists. "In Munich the crown prince felt that all was stale and cold."[9] Therefore he was determined to drastically alter cultural activities. Wilhelm von Humboldt wrote to his wife: "One of Ludwig's declared aims is to turn his residential city into a place that does honor to Germany, so that if you have not visited Munich you do not know Germany."[10] Hence the crown prince asked his father to appoint the Nuremberg porcelain and glass painter Michael Sigmund Frank (1770–1847) to Munich.[11] His tenure with the Royal Porzellanmanufaktur began on July 5, 1818. This was also the beginning of Munich glass art, which became world famous under its American name, *Munich Style*.[12] Initially, glass art attained greater importance when the Bavarian Crown Prince Ludwig succeeded his father as king and in 1827 founded the "Königliche Glasmalereianstalt" (i.e. Royal Institute for Glass Painting) as a state institution. Until then, Frank had produced predominantly small size panels – mostly of white glass. Now, the first larger panels were created for the west facade of Regensburg cathedral.[13] Shortly thereafter, the Porzellanmanufaktur's director, architect Friedrich von Gärtner, who was also in charge of the "Königliche Glasmalereianstalt," was no longer satisfied with Frank's production of col-

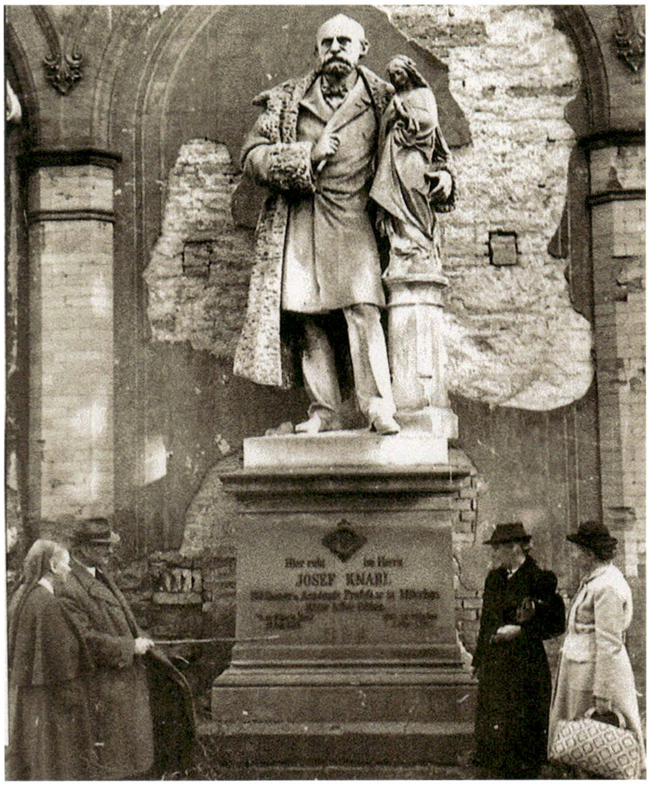

7
TOMB OF JOSEPH KNABL (1819–1881), Südlicher Friedhof, Munich, design: Joseph Leonhard Mayer, visited by Anton Mayer with sisters and sister-in-law, 1948

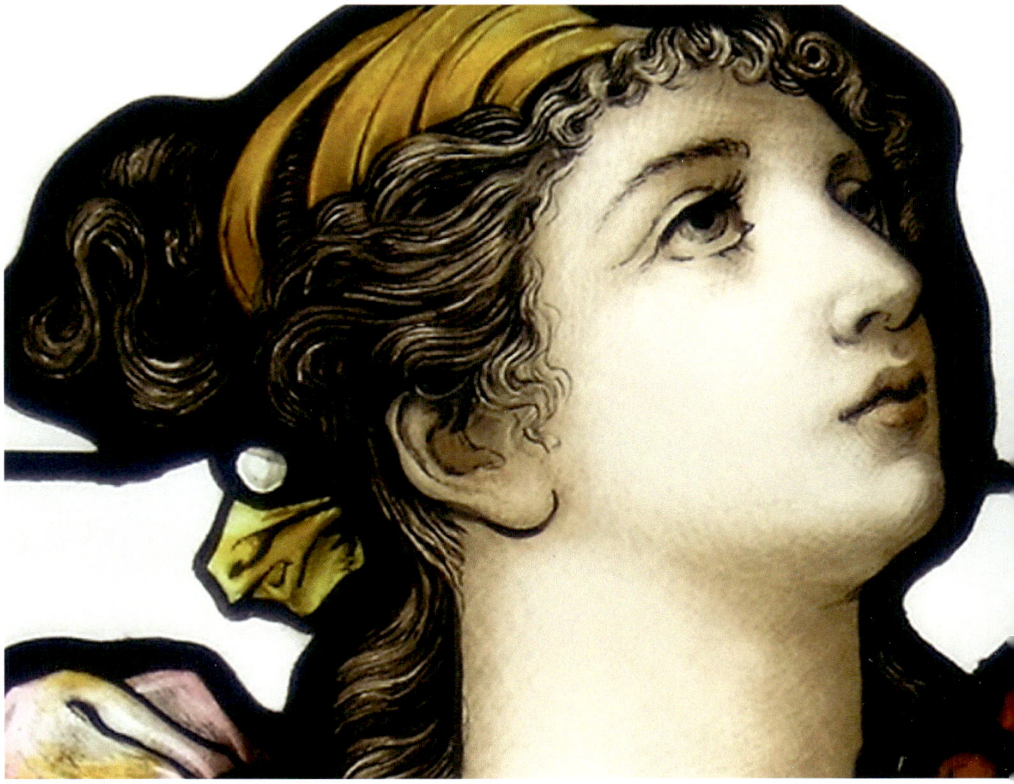

8
SCHLOSS DRACHENBURG/RHINE, detail of the many stained glass windows: Head of Diana, Johann von Schraudolph, Mayer circa 1878

ored glass. He entrusted the glass and architectural painter Max Emanuel Ainmiller (1807–1870) *(fig. 2)* with this function in 1833. Under his leadership the "Königliche Glasmalereianstalt" became an internationally recognized institution. This is considered the beginning of *Munich Style stained glass*. The realized works encompass the brilliantly colored windows for Munich's Maria-Hilf-Kirche,[14] Schloss Hohenschwangau,[15] the cathedrals of Regensburg[16] and Cologne[17] as well as the glass decoration for the Church of Our Saviour at Kilndown in Kent and the cathedrals in London, Glasgow, St. Petersburg, and Zagreb.[18]

However, when the revolution broke out and after his abdication, Ludwig I faced limitations as sponsor. The great success of Munich's first Glasmalereianstalt was suddenly called into question, followed by massive problems regarding production and sales. At times, business operation stopped. Moreover, Ludwig's son and successor, King Max II Joseph (ruled 1848–1864), had no interest in the institution. In1851 he accepted the Finance Ministry's petition to transform it into a private enterprise. His position as administrative director not only enabled Ainmiller to continue the workshop, he also extended its international reputation to the New World when he accepted the first church commission for St. John's in Boston.[19] When Joseph Gabriel Mayer and Franz Xaver Zettler took over after his death, the history of the "Königliche Glasmalereianstalt" was largely in the past.

Inspired by Ainmiller's success story, more than thirty glass firms were founded in Munich,[20] and the "Königliche Glasmalereianstalt" also served Joseph Gabriel Mayer as prototype[21] only fifteen years after its formation. Mayer was to remain the only artisan whose

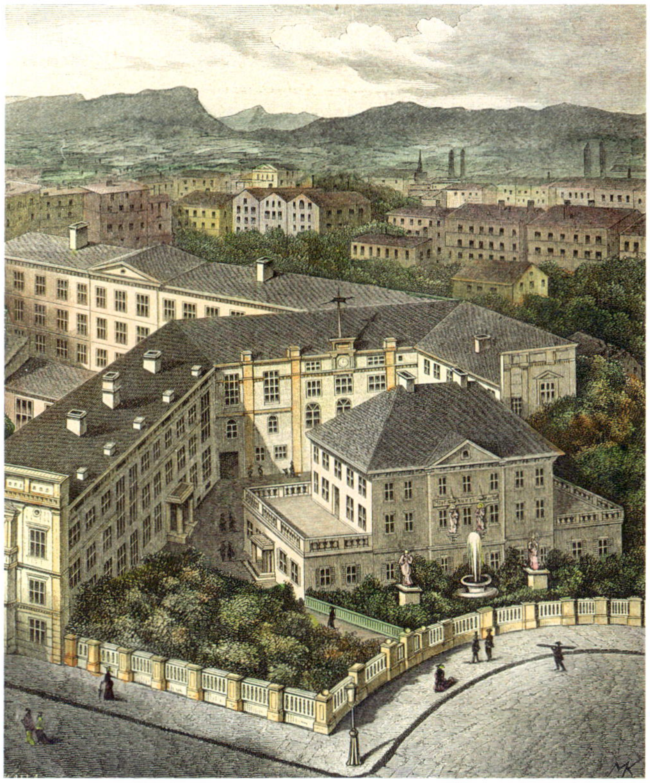

9

EXTERIOR VIEW OF THE MAYER'SCHE HOFKUNSTANSTALT, CIRCA 1880

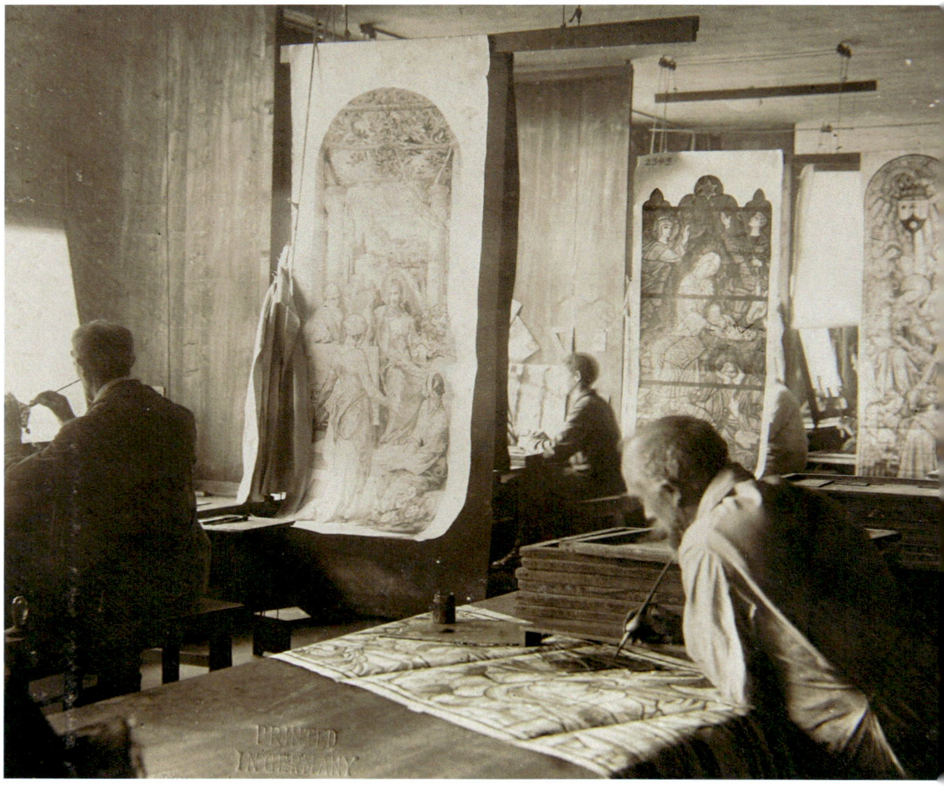

10

INTERIOR VIEW OF ONE OF THE STAINED GLASS WORKSHOPS, CIRCA 1910

successors still work to this day in the same field to the highest international acclaim. Johann Nepomuk Bürkel was the master builder who had renovated Mayer's workshop, located for a long time on the outskirts of Munich's Maxvorstadt *(fig. 9)*. "Among the many houses on offer, I purchased the one on Stiglmaierplatz Nr. 1 (then still called Luitpoldplatz). Unfortunately, it was very run down."[22] In 1862, he commissioned his later son-in-law, Franz Xaver Zettler (1841–1916), to set up a glass studio in the building[23] *(fig. 10)*. This meant that he was no longer obligated to pass church window commissions on to other workshops.[24] Six years later, this department was housed in the eastern portion of the new edifice,[25] enabling him to make the following offer to Cologne's Dombaumeister Karl Eduard Richard Voigtel: "It is with great pleasure that we recommend our newly-established stained glass studio to you."[26] From this point on, the firm prospered. Joseph Gabriel Mayer opened branches abroad: In 1865 at 70 Grosvenor Street, London[27] and four years thereafter at 23 Rue St. Sulpice, Paris.[28] It was no disadvantage that Franz Xaver Zettler, husband of Mayer's daughter Therese, founded his own stained glass studio in 1870.[29] In the early 1870s Joseph Gabriel established yet another studio for stained glass with his son.[30] Both enterprises[31] were fierce competitors for well over six decades and ultimately merged in 1939, when the Mayer'sche Hofkunstanstalt bought back the establishment F. X. Zettler. When the Bavarian "fairy tale" King Ludwig II (ruled 1864–1886) bestowed the title "Königliche Hof-Kunstanstalt" upon his company in 1882, Mayer must have felt at the zenith of his career.[32]

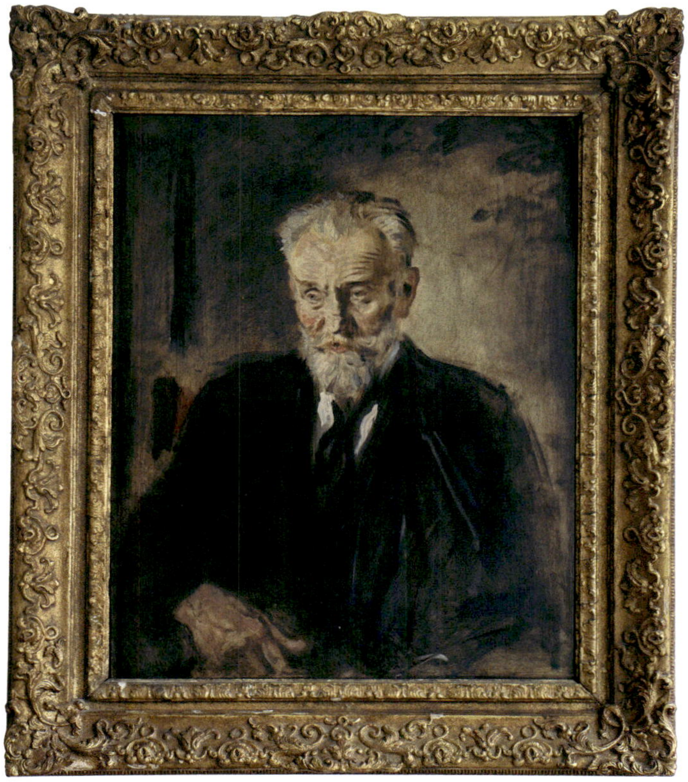

11
PORTRAIT OF FRANZ BORGIAS MAYER (1848–1926), Leo Samberger, early 1920s

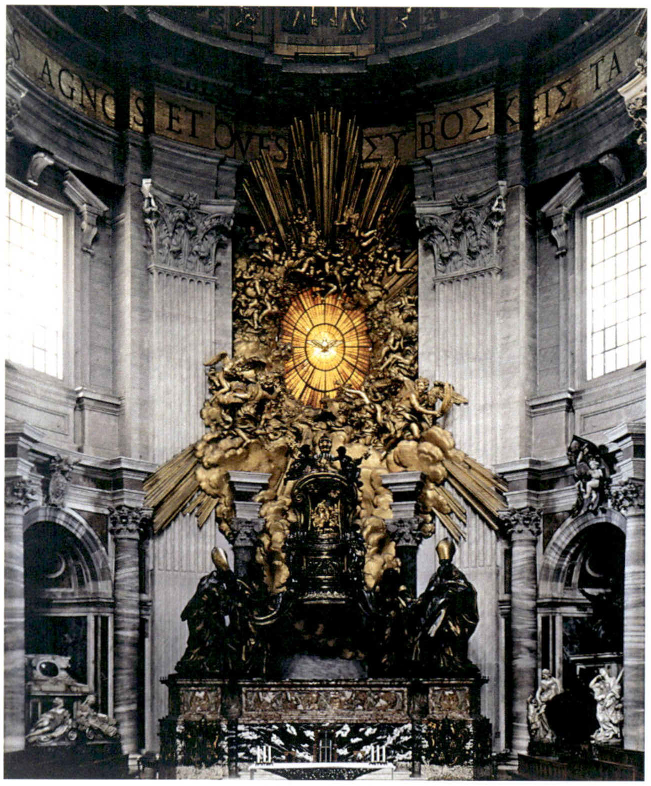

12
RECONSTRUCTION OF THE HOLY SPIRIT WINDOW OVER THE "CATHEDRA PETRI" ST. PETER'S BASILICA IN ROME, Mayer'sche Hofkunstanstalt and Martin Feuerstein, 1910

No Success without Diligence, Frugalness, and Thriftiness

"Anyone who says that you can become successful and wealthy without diligence, frugalness, and thriftiness, is a cheat."[33] Prelate Dr. Huhn used statesman Benjamin Franklin's quote in 1883 when burying Joseph Gabriel Mayer. It was not the elder son, Joseph (1846–1893), who soon withdrew from the management, but his like-minded, English-trained son, Franz Borgias (1848–1926) *(fig. 11)*[34] who continued the father's work. Under his strict regime, the Hofkunstanstalt attained the highest reputation, especially after opening its New York branch at 52 Barclay Street in 1888. In New York City alone until the 1930s, close to one hundred churches were furnished with glass paintings by Mayer (and Zettler). In her 2002 publication entitled *Stained glass in Catholic Philadelphia*, Jean M. Farnsworth states: "Mayer produced more windows for the Archdiocese of Philadelphia than any other single studio, fulfilling its first commission in an Archdiocesan Church in 1883 ... ."[35] This assured his international recognition. He also avoided the immense import duties on colored glass into the USA that affected his brother-in-law.[36] Since the cheaper European workforce posed a threat to American art institutions, they torpedoed regular customs on imported colored glass and demanded trade protection. The Munich firms hired American lawyers to fight for their rights. Even the Catholic Church supported this battle, because it wanted to continue to purchase duty-free imported glass. However, in 1888, two hundred American glass painters filed a petition to prohibit the duty-free import of foreign church windows – to no avail. Two years later, a 45% markup on all

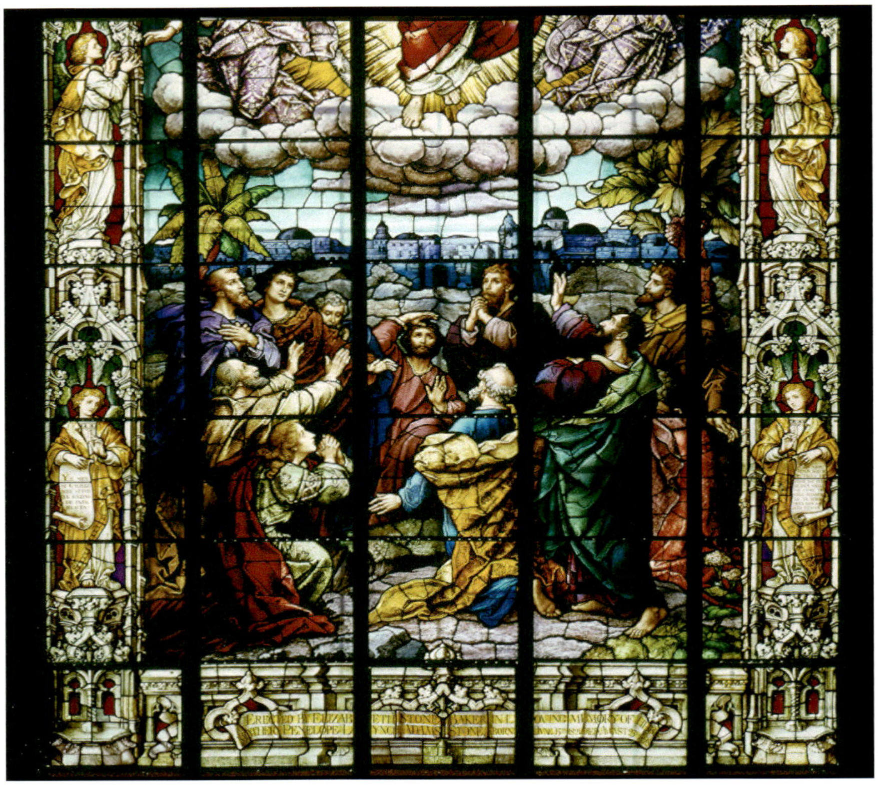

13
ST. PAUL'S EPISCOPAL CHURCH, NEW ORLEANS, LA, USA, detail of the Ascension Window, 1907, restoration/conservation Mayer 1967

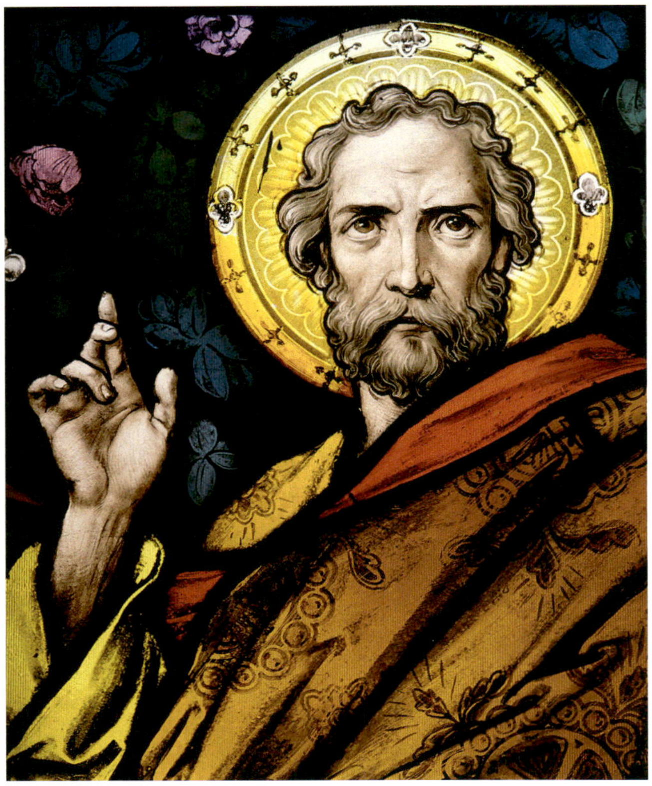

14
FORMER ST. MARTIN'S CHURCH, CHICAGO, IL, USA, all windows Mayer and Zettler 1903–06, detail: St. Peter

imported glass was implemented, resolving the conflict in favor of the American firms.[37] This was particularly bitter since at the turn of the century about 80% of the glass production by the Franz Mayer of Munich studio was sold abroad.

But there was also good news for Franz Borgias: In 1892, Pope Leo XIII bestowed upon his firm the distinction "Pontifical Institute of Christian Art."[38] It was not by coincidence that a few years later he was commissioned to reconstruct the Holy Spirit window in the western apse of St. Peter's Basilica in Rome *(fig. 12).* In addition, he and the Mayer-Zettler workshops worked on thousands of other church buildings, fifty cathedrals in the USA and Canada as well as fifty additional cathedral projects on other continents. During this phase of the Munich Glass Works, the Roman Catholic Church became its most important client. As a result, Mayer and Zettler employed as many as five hundred artists and glass painters around the turn of the century, and three hundred worked for Franz Borgias alone.[39] The situation remained virtually unchanged until World War I. Apart from the many other Munich stained glass studios, the sister enterprises Mayer and Zettler with their huge global volume of orders, were among the most important contractors for artists, artisans, and painters in the residential city and art metropolis of Munich and in the kingdom of Bavaria. Thanks to the two major corporations, the *Munich-style* trademark was on the tip of everyone's tongue. It was considered the epitome of precision and quality – not just in the US but worldwide.

Like his father before him, Franz Borgias's approach to art combined bygone aspects with innovative techniques. Romanticism inspired all of his depictions and the historic renderings glorified the Middle Ages.[40] Yet,

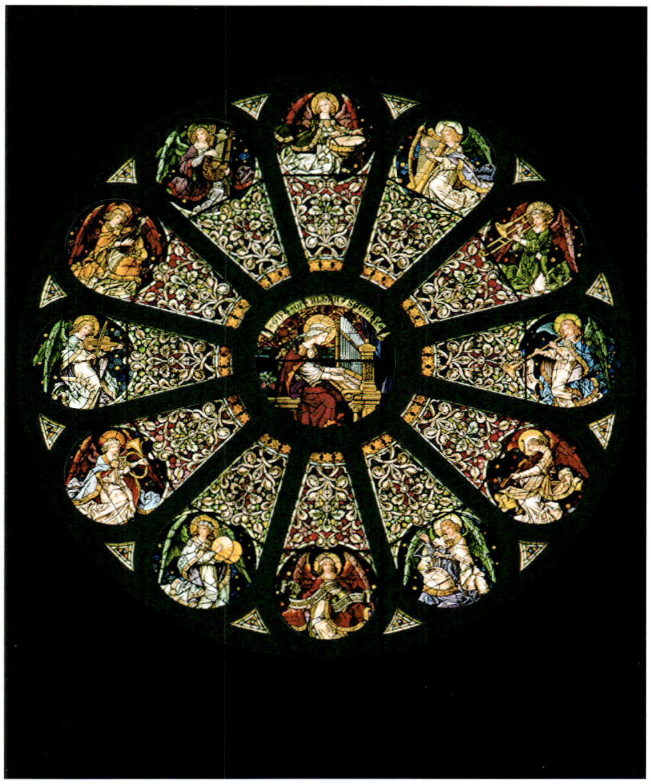

15

CATHEDRAL OF THE MADELEINE, SALT LAKE CITY, UT, USA, rose window over the organ, St. Cecilia surrounded by angels with musical instruments, all windows Zettler 1906

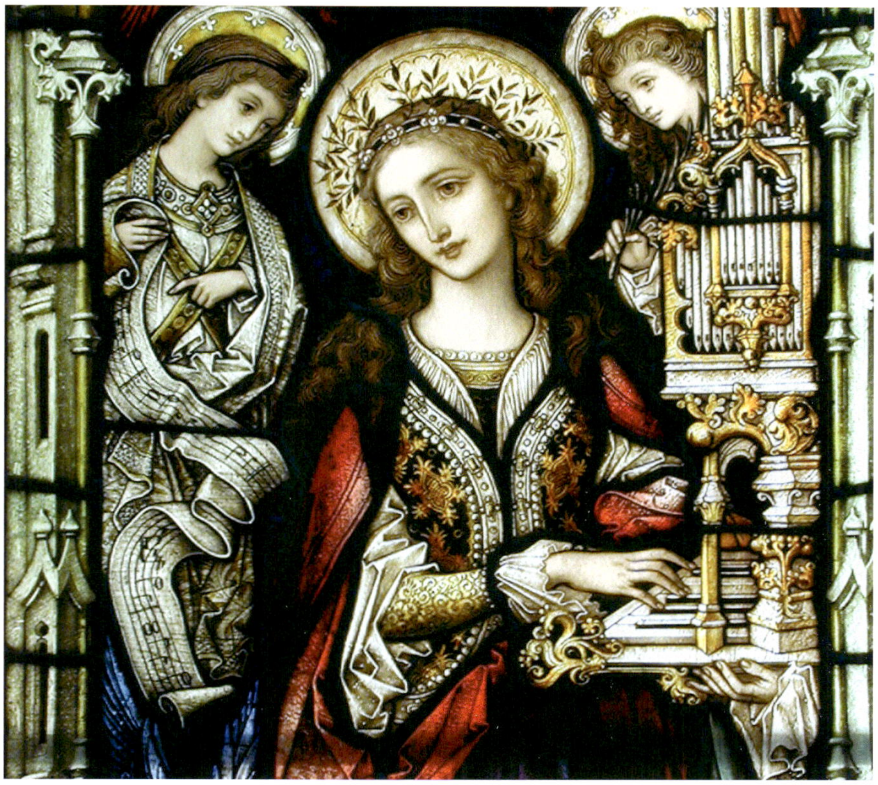

16

ST. ROCH CHAPEL, BINGEN/RHINE, St. Cecilia with angels and organ, detail, William Francis Dixon, Mayer 1905, this copy is from the archives of the Mayer'sche Hofkunstanstalt

he distanced himself from the general characteristics of the Nazarenes and the Pre-Raphaelites which Michael Sigmund Frank and Max Emanuel Ainmiller and their teams had transferred to glass art. Franz Borgias encouraged domestic and English glass painters alike to take the style of the Alsatian Master Peter Hemmel von Andlau (circa 1420 – after 1501) or the Augsburg panel painter Hans Holbein the Elder (circa 1460/65–1524) as their point of departure. It had been a 'musivic' glass technique and in contrast to British stained glass characterized through intense painting with matting colors and equally intense erasing and rubbing processes. Between 50 and 65% of the overall 'painting' work was committed to erasing.[41] Such stained glass resulted in both very colorful and very translucent stained glass windows with proportionally correct figural renderings, well-balanced compositions, and excellent design (see fig. 8, 13–17).«

This was only possible because Franz Borgias could engage a good number of the historical and monumental painters from Munich's Art Academy, utilizing specialists for each branch. Job titles at the firm included "preparer (color and glass selecting,)"cutter (glass cutting,)" "leader (leading,)" "fettler (zementing,)" "packer", "book binders", "draftsmen", and "colorists" as well as "painters of flesh, draperies, and ornaments". Teamwork was of utmost importance and was even propagated outside the firm. Although there were no stars within the applied arts at the time, artists who established themselves included Martin von Feuerstein (1856–1931) *(see f.i. fig. 12, 14)*, professor at Munich's Art Academy, Burne-Jones's student William Francis Dixon (1848–1928) *(see f.i. fig. 16)*, and Englishman George Daniels (1854–1940), making designs that were particularly popular in the US. These included the glazing of the cathedrals St. Madeleine in Salt

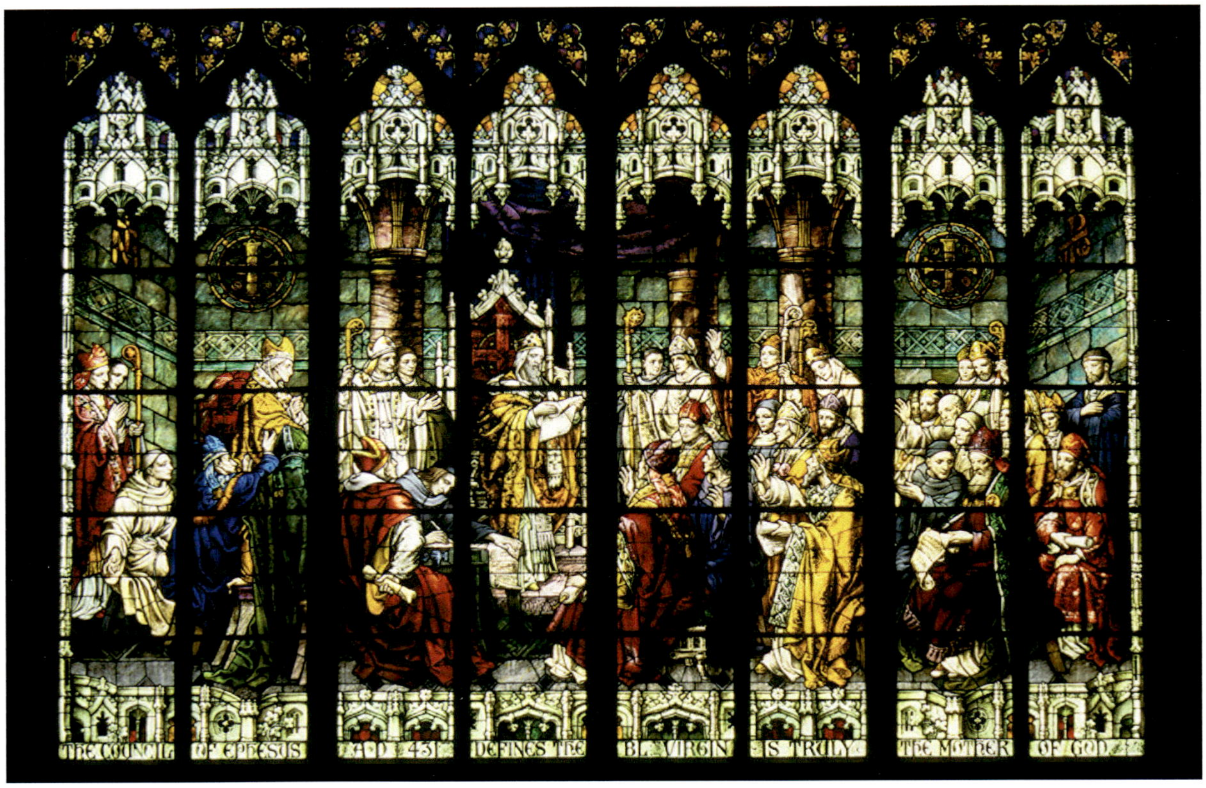

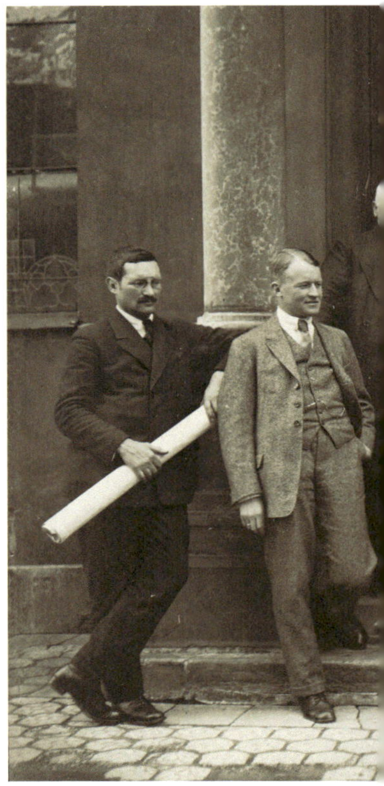

17
ST. MARY'S CATHEDRAL BASILICA OF THE ASSUMPTION, COVINGTON, KY, USA, all windows Mayer 1905–22, lower part of the northern transept window, Council of Ephesus

Lake City, Utah, circa 1906 *(fig. 15)*, St. Mary in Covington, Kentucky, circa 1909 *(fig. 17)*, or St. Joseph in Buffalo, NY, dated 1912.[42] The long-lived success and the extreme popularity of the *Munich Style* resulted in US companies opening smaller branches ("stained glass studios") in Munich, justifying the term *Munich Style* and enabling them with access to appropriately trained glass painters. In addition, there was an inferior studio in Chicago that called itself the "Munich Studio" but had no actual connection to Munich.[43]

A Studio for the Artists (since 1918)

At the beginning of the 20th century, the importance of *Munich Style* stained glass declined, and it was often looked down upon (at home). Although Emperor Wilhelm II supported Neo-Romantic art as the new "Reichsstil" (i.e. imperial style)[44] in unprecedented ways and Mayer delivered the glass windows for his Gedächtniskirche (i.e. Emperor Wilhelm Memorial Church) in Berlin, this type of historicist approach was definitely unfashionable by then. One of the most outspoken critics of applied arts was the architect Adolf Loos (1870–1933) who strictly refused the connection between the everyday life and art. His 1908 article entitled *Ornament and Crime* states: "There is certainly no connection between civilized products of our time and art. The Barbaric times, when works

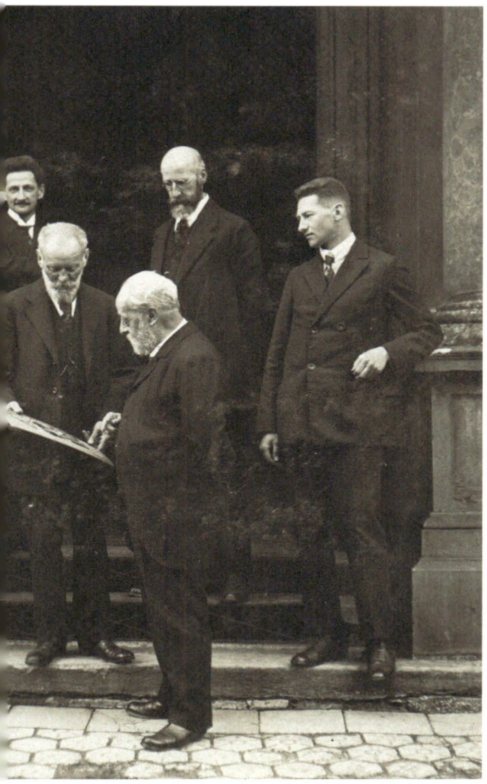

18

THE THIRD GENERATION with their father Franz Borgias and members of the Hofkunstanstalt's executive board in front of the old stained glass building, early 1920s (first left: Anton, second left: Karl, center: Franz Borgias with US-representative Patrick Kelly, right: Adalbert Mayer

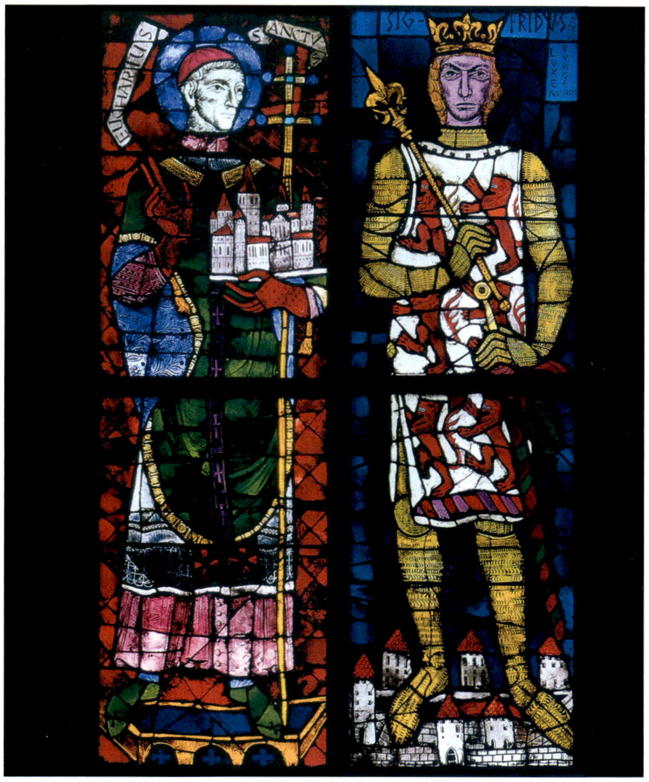

19

CATHEDRAL OF NOTRE DAME, LUXEMBOURG, two saints, detail from the four triple lancet stained glass windows for the Prince's Gallery, Josef Oberberger, Mayer 1938

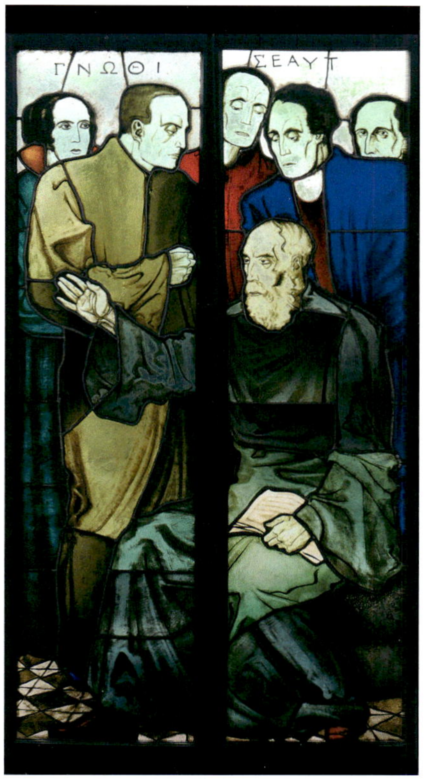

20

PHILOSOPHERS WINDOW, Sepp Frank, late 1920s, archives Mayer'sche Hofkunstanstalt

of art and utilitarian objects were amalgamated are definitely over."[45]

When Franz Borgias handed over the firm to his sons – and thus to the third generation – after World War One and at the end of the monarchy, he said: "I have always only loved beauty for its own sake, never because I intended to own it."[46] As the eldest son, academy graduate Anton (1886–1967) became the artistic leader, whereas his younger brothers Karl (1889–1971) and Adalbert (1894–1987) turned to the large firm's entrepreneurial and business sides.[47] Their work was to be overshadowed by another world war, inflation, decline, dictatorship, and destruction *(see fig. 18)*.

In keeping with the Roman Catholic Church's conservative stance, after 1918 many glass windows for this client continued to be fabricated in the traditional *Munich Style*, especially in the US. Back then, a stricter "old style"[48] prevailed, wherein the leading glass artists sometimes combined Early Gothic forms with Art Nouveau or Art Deco elements. More abstract designs were still inconceivable in the North American church.[49]

Onset of Modernity

Thanks to Bauhaus and Deutscher Werkbund ideas, things took a totally different turn in the Weimar Republic and Europe.[50] Now "modern" at times even "avant-garde" artists joined Franz Mayer of Munich with inventive ideas; albeit with primarily minor commissions, and the firm eventually began to develop into the "studio for the artist". Franz Mayer of Munich no longer represented and dictated the "style." Instead, it made available to the "free artist" all its knowledge and experience, the

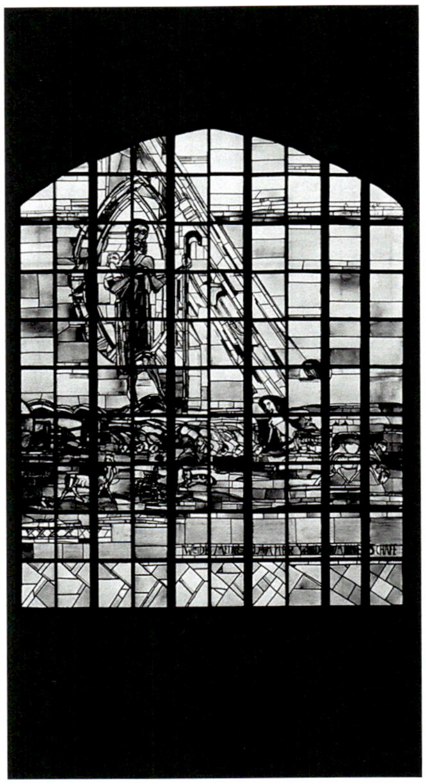

21
LUTHERAN ST. PAUL-KIRCHE, CONSTANCE, altar window with Last Judgment, Karl Knappe, Mayer circa 1928

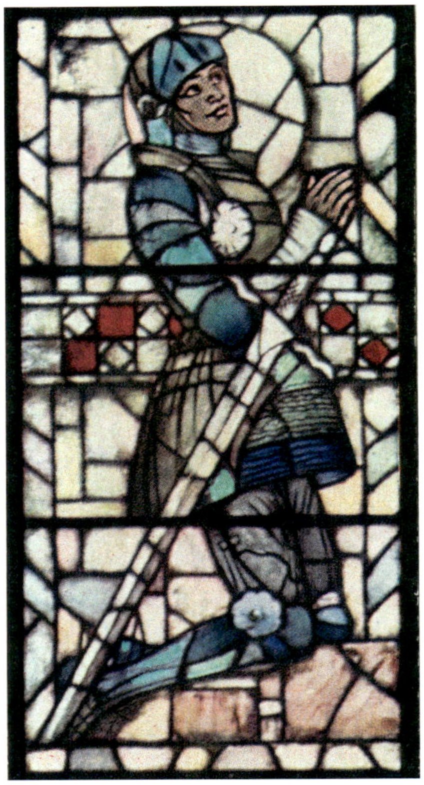

22
EXPOSITUR-KIRCHE ST. JAKOBUS D. Ä., DÖLLNITZ/OBERPFALZ, 1928

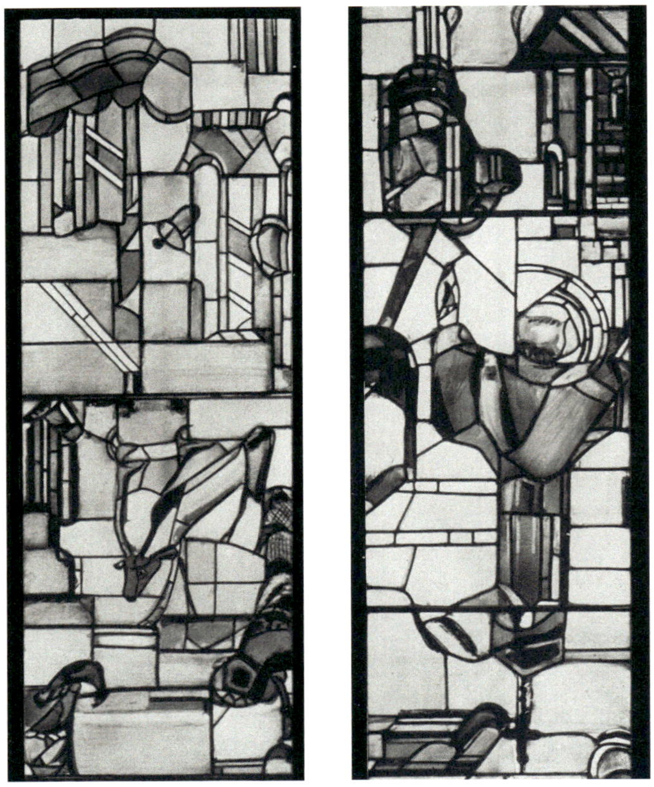

23
CANTICLE OF THE SUN, ST. FRANCIS, Karl Knappe, Mayer circa 1930

abundant supply of materials, tools, and studios – thus slowly evolving into an assisting entity. This also explains how artists such as Karl Knappe (1884–1970), Paul Thalheimer (1884–1948), Wilhelm Rupprecht (1886–1963) Albert Figel (1889–1955), and Joseph August (Sepp) Frank (1889–1970) made a name for themselves within the realm of the applied arts.[51]

Karl Knappe – The New Beginning of Stained Glass

Born in Kempten (Allgäu), the sculptor and teacher Professor Karl Knappe is paramount when addressing the dominant characters of 1920s stained glass (later also mosaics). Knappe was to remain with the firm for more than fifty years.[52] In 1918, he submitted his first window design to Anton Mayer. The Mayer'sche Hofkunstanstalt immediately offered him a free studio, which he used until his death and which enabled him to work and to experiment. At first, he created small panels that could be admired in an exhibition of the Kunstgewerbeverein in 1920. His first commission followed in 1921/22: Six windows with a connection to architecture for a war memorial chapel in Hindelang (Allgäu).[53] Contemporary witness Otto Fischer was full of praise for this new ap-

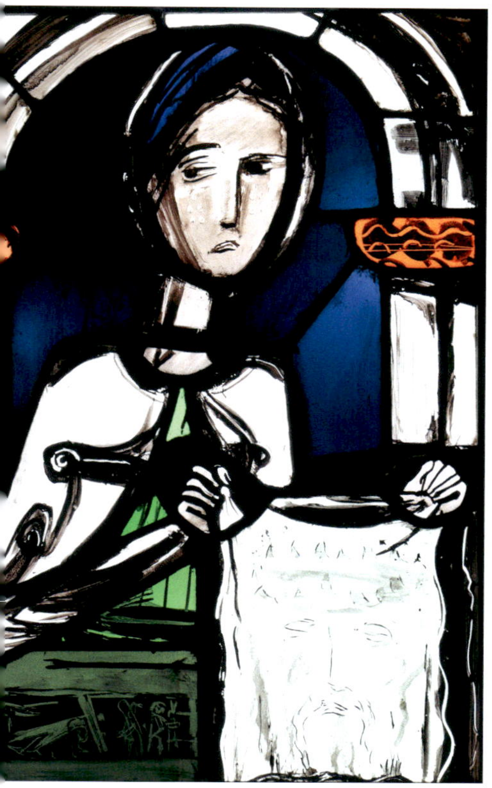

24
ST. VERONICA'S VEIL, Karl Knappe, engraved stained glass panel, still painted with Schwarzlot, Mayer late 1930s

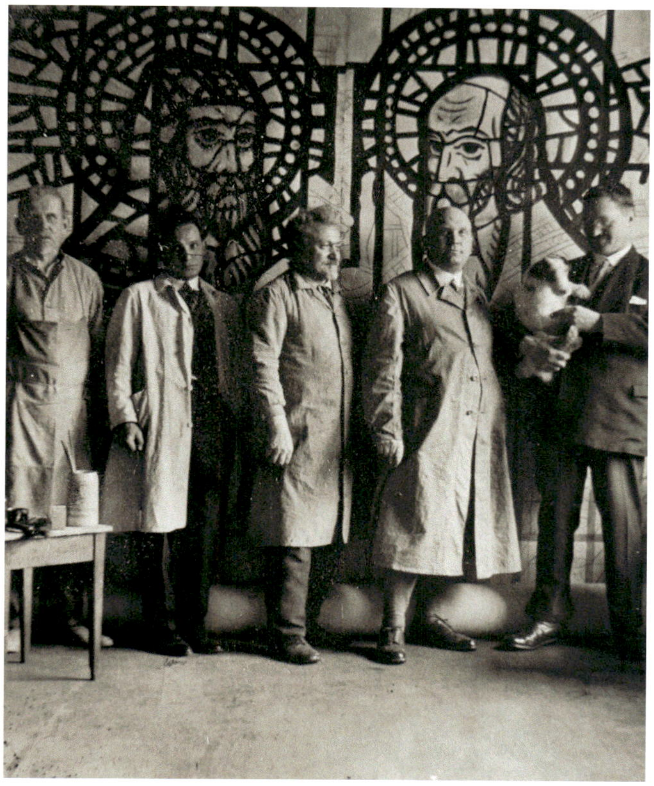

25
BULGARIAN ARTIST IVAN PENKOV AND ARTISANS IN FRONT OF CARTOON DRAWINGS, full scale, shot in the studio, circa 1930; the head depicted on the right in the cartoon is part of the window *fig. 26*

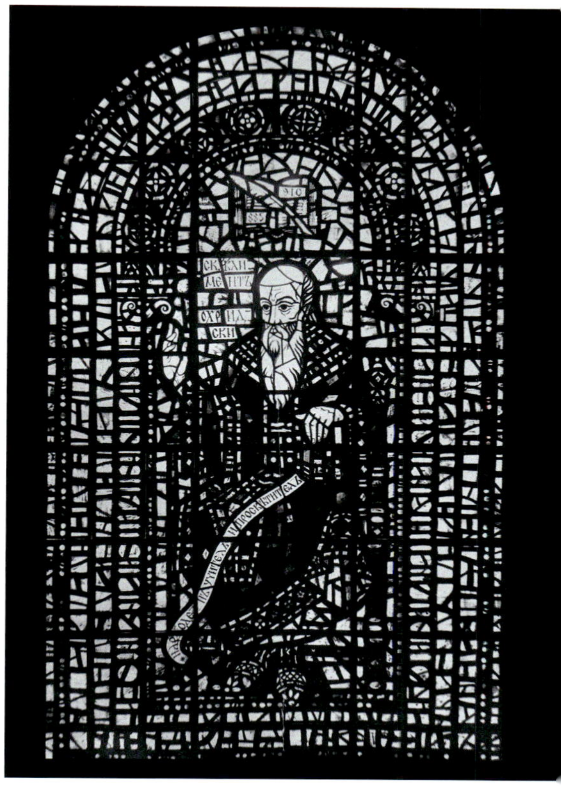

26
UNIVERSITY CHURCH SOFIA, Bulgaria one of Ivan Penkov's (1897–1957) Mayer windows

proach to art: "A depth of burning colors magnificently articulates atmospheric creatures, like a blazing, inner ember, expressing their tight movements by the most simple outlines. ... A new language is born for the super-real, the deeply meaningful. A task, similar to the Old Masters' one, is rediscovered and dissolved into a new experience."[54] Additional early Knappe creations for Mayer included glass for Munich's Gewerbeschau (1922), the Altöttinger Chapel at Munich's Gasteig, the Expositur Church of James the Elder in Döllnitz (Upper Palatinate) in1928,[55] *(fig. 22)*, and the Funerary Chapel (1931) for the cemetery in the Perlach woods. Aided by the Hofkunstanstalt, Knappe also designed an expressionistic altar window for St. Paul in Constance depicting the Last Judgment *(fig. 21)*.[56] With regards to his work for Mayer he stated: "The fact that glass moves me is related to my gift as a sculptor who loves the true material."[57] Thus, the first truly "modern" windows after World War One were created in the Mayer'sche Hofkunstanstalt *(fig. 21 – 24)*.

New Construction in Times of Inflation

Despite severe economic obstacles during the Weimar Republic, the Mayer brothers managed, thanks to their export surpluses, to erect a new commercial building. Due to income derived from their US exports in stable dollars, the firm could even use their own "banknotes." Nearby shops, craftspeople, and construction firms accepted these secure bills because the owners knew their value and that the Hofkunstanstalt would always back them.

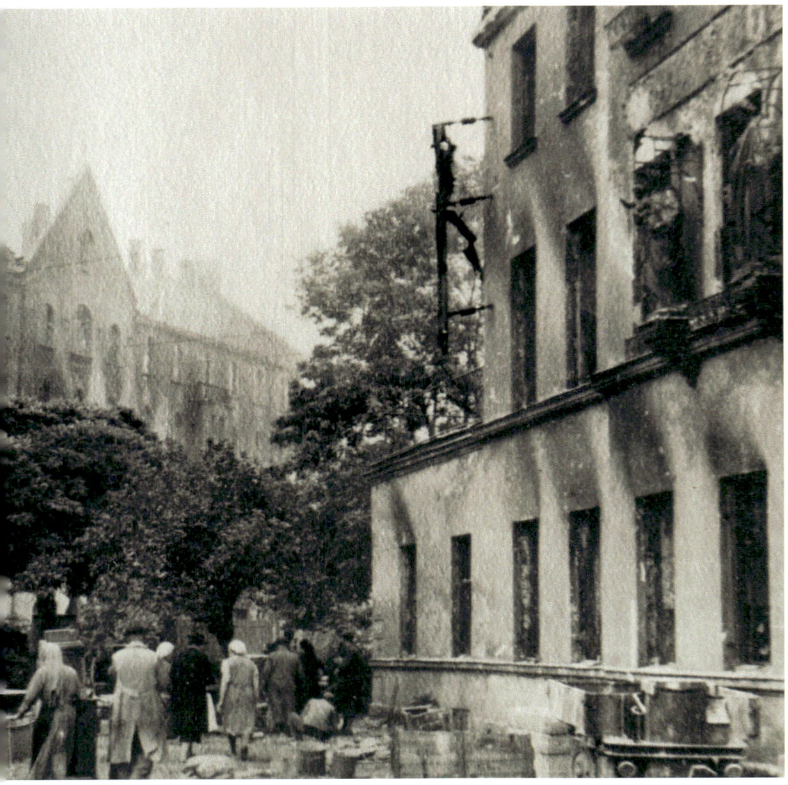

27

DESTROYED BY BOMBS IN 1944, on the right the totally burned-out old business structure

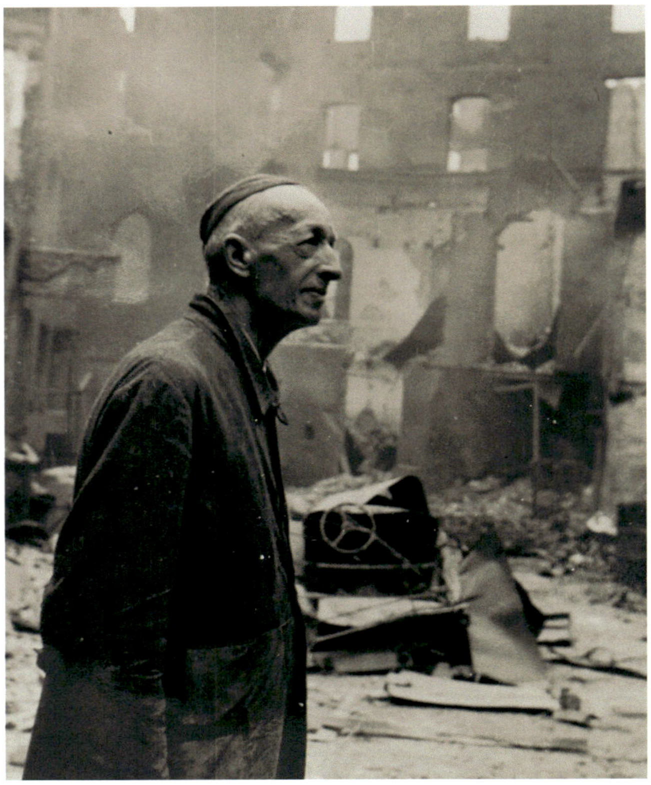

28

WORKSHOP MASTER FICHTMÜLLER in front of the ruins of the old stained glass building.

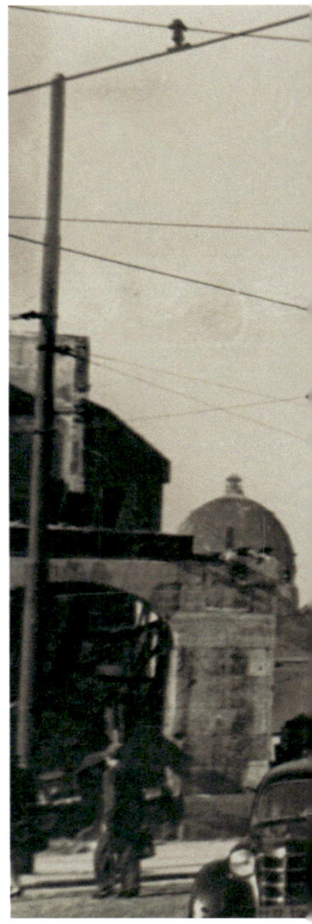

In 1922, the Mayer brothers appointed Munich-based city planner Theodor Fischer (1862–1938) as architect-in-charge of the new edifice.[58] Based on his plans, Mayer erected the prestigious main building on the newly built Seidlstraße. Fischer paid special attention to the firm's centerpiece, the triangular exhibition space with balcony and unobtrusive wall decoration. To this day, the utilitarian architecture reveals to what degree the "Franz Mayer'sche Hofkunstanstalt" had become a workshop for artists; enabling them to contemplate and to judge, if need be corrected, or simply admire their work on a multistory glass wall *(see fig. 530, 531)*.

But on October 24, 1929, one blow terminated the "Golden Twenties." Also known as "Black Friday," the crash on Wall Street led to a collapse of the world economy, inflation, and mass layoffs. In Munich, too, life consisted of being on the dole and begging, poverty and hunger pervailed. Since the Mayer'sche Werkstätte was engaged in long-term projects, the consequences of the crisis only began to take effect a few years later, yet with double impact: On top of the economic crisis, 1933 marked the rise into power of the National Socialists.

"A Vision Like Nero's"

In compliance with Hitler's reactionary concept of art, the entire cultural sector was brought into line by introducing the Reichskulturkammer on September 22, 1933. Henceforth, Modern Art was considered "entartet" (i.e. degenerate). Many artists were banned from their profession, went into exile, or fled – a catastrophe also for the Hofkunstanstalt. At the same time sales plummeted

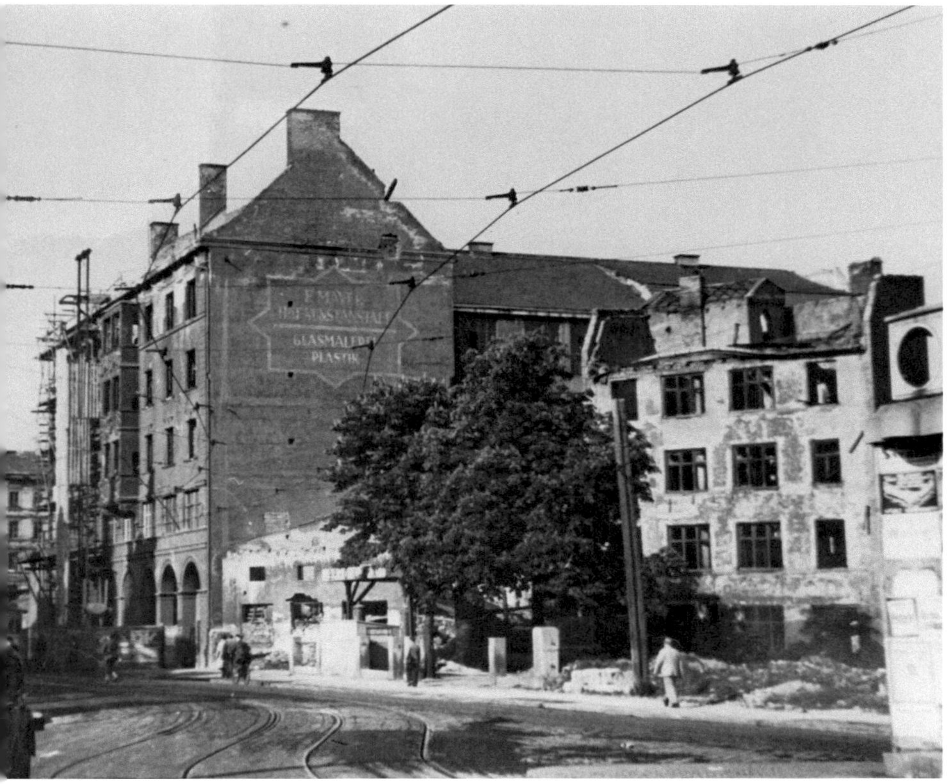

29
VIEW OF THE STUDIO BUILDING FROM 1923 ON SEIDLSTRASSE DURING RECONSTRUCTION, circa 1948; the front building was burned out from the roof to the ground. On the right the south part of the old workshop building – to be demolished slightly later

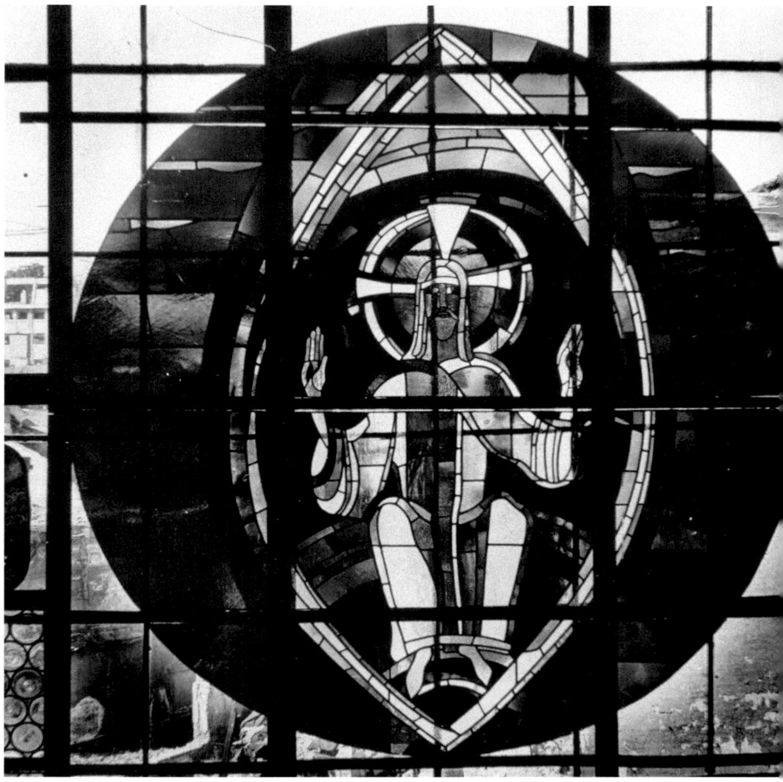

30
ST. BENEDIKT, GAUTING/MUNICH, Christ in the Mandorla, recorstruction of the pre-war window, Karl Knappe, 1947
(now without Schwarzlot painting)

both in the German Reich and the US. While the Mayer brothers were not members of the Nazi-party, director Clemens Spengler joined the party so the firm could at least continue to exist. This sufficed for the rare orders coming from the administration. When the boycott of German goods began in 1935,[59] the studio's revenues did not recover. Among the by now rare commissions, were four windows in 1938 for the duke's gallery at Luxemburg Cathedral *(fig. 19)* by Josef Oberberger (1905–1994), some larger glass paintings for German industrial plants by Sepp Frank such as the illustrated *Philosophers (fig. 20)* with their expressionist faces, as well as the large window with net-like structures that Ivan Penkov (1897–1957) executed for Sofia's University Church *(fig. 25, 26)*. The number of employed artisans declined drastically.

When the US entered the war in 1941, production came to an end, despite the prior purchase of the firm "Glasmalerei F. X. Zettler."[60] While his brothers were in the war, Anton Mayer was unable to prevent the company's collapse and destruction *(fig. 27–29)*. By 1944, the number of employees was down to less than 20 compared to the original 500.[61] In a letter to his mother, Karl Mayer describes the situation in Munich: "The apocalyptic silver birds kept coming from Italy, always flying across the Tegernsee: divinely beautiful. Equally unforgettable the view of Munich burning the night after the April '44 attack. Seen from the Zeugamt's highest roof. A vision like Nero's."[62] The structures of the united Mayer and Zettler firms shared this fate. Anton Mayer states: "By 1944, it also began to get bitterly serious for the Stiglmaierplatz area. It was, as usual with grand horror, that we saw fire and wads of smoke over the tortured city from the roof of our house." [63] "In 1944, Zettler's old business structure at 23 Briennerstraße fell victim to bombs ... Added to this

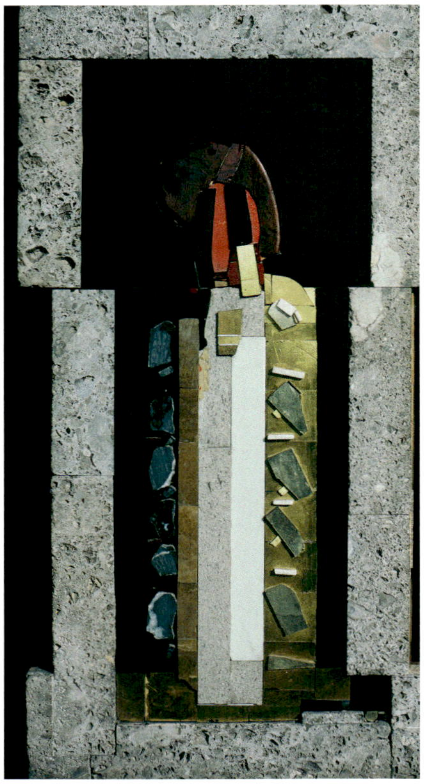

31

LAST SUPPER, Karl Knappe, mosaic-collage, circa 1960

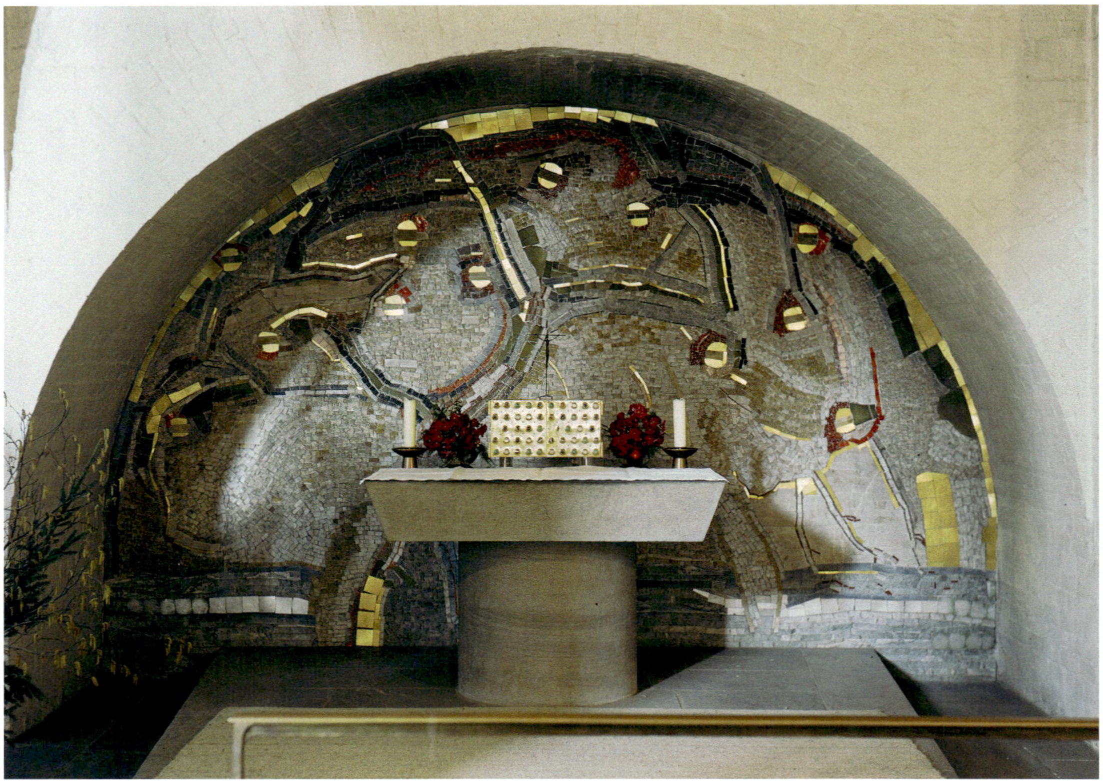

32

TREE OF LIFE MOSAIC, MUNICH, Laurentiuskirche, Karl Knappe, 1957, architects: Emil Steffann and Siegfried Östreicher

were, in July, heavy strikes of our edifice. On July 11, the front building's five stories burned out entirely. On July 13, the roof and the two top floors of the workshop building were hit by explosive bombs."[64]

When the US troops marched into Munich on April 30, 1945, the "Franz Mayer'sche Hofkunstanstalt's" absolute nadir had been reached: The firm's chronicle reports: "The front building: burnt out to the ground floor. The workshop building: roofless. Destroyed: the glass basement, the basement below the courtyard, the carpenter shop in the court, the photo studio with appliances and all. Almost all cartoons and sketches burnt. Most business papers, the old correspondence, all advertising materials and all records plus the entire equipment. Lost for the unforeseeable future: Our best German markets Silesia, the Sudeten territories and the Saar."[65]

In the Middle of Reconstruction

"After all of this, we will really begin to build: The third and fourth floors of the workshop building will be reconstructed; the exhibition gallery, where our first show will take place in early April 1946, will be rebuilt. This chapter is entitled reconstruction. All financial efforts and the mental power of the leader, Bertl [Adalbert], will be dedicated to this end."[66] Adalbert Mayer was the youngest of the brothers. From 1922 until 1936, he had worked almost exclusively in New York and the USA. Now his special project was the firm's reconstruction. Encountering the inherent challenges was his nephew Konrad Mayer (born 1923), son of his older brother Karl,[67] who entered the firm as a glass apprentice. By 1946 Adalbert had almost managed to reach the 1932 national revenue, though with a devalued Reichsmark. Many German inner

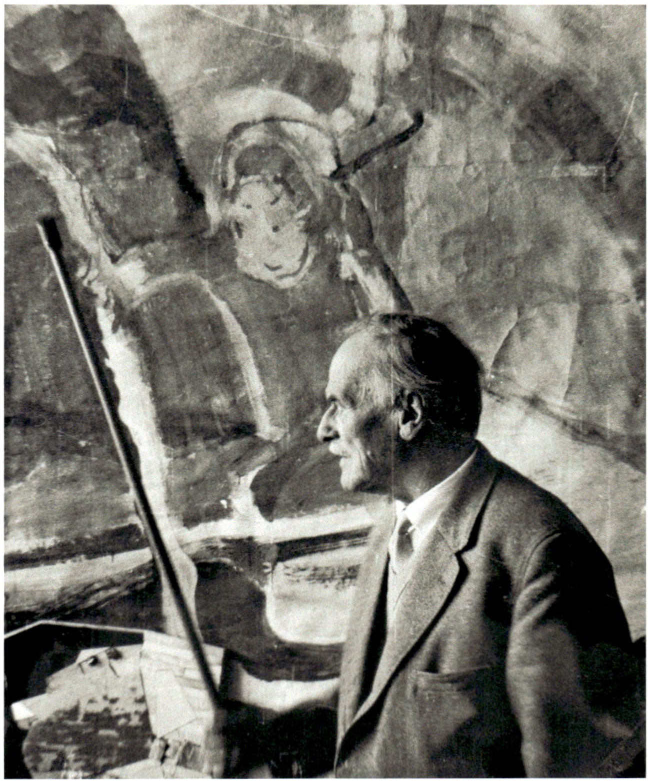

33

KARL KNAPPE, circa 1960

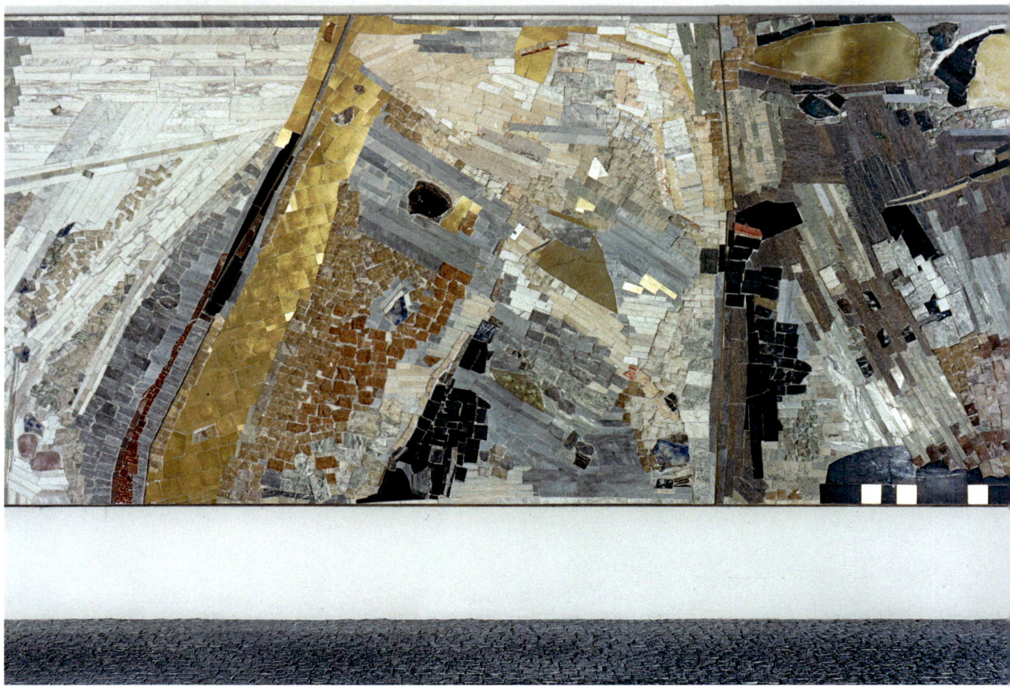

34

ABSTRACT MOSAIC COLLAGE IN POSITIVE SETTING, made of stone, semi-precious stones, gold, and silver, for the German Pavilion at the Brussels's World Fair, Karl Knappe, 1958, today kept at Munich's Oberste Baubehörde, architects of the pavilion: Sep Ruf and Egon Eiermann

city glass windows had been destroyed by the World War Two bombardments. Adalbert and his brothers attempted to combine continuity with modern expressive means. Those participating from the first moment included Felix Baumhauer (1876–1960), Hermann Kaspar (1904–1986), newly appointed professor at Munich's Art Academy Josef Oberberger, and, once again, Karl Knappe.

Karl Knappe and Mosaic Art

"At my work in glass it took me a long time to decide not to paint on it with *Schwarzlot* (i.e. black ceramic melting color) any longer, which meant to build the window with pure glass, only then I dared to approach the field of mosaic," remembers Karl Knappe.[68] Apart from stained glass windows, experimental and innovative mosaics of the highest artistic caliber were now being created at Franz Mayer of Munich: Mosaics from the 1940s include *St. John on Patmos*, the *Crucifixion* (today in the workshop building's exhibition gallery), and the *Entombment Angel* mosaic for the Stuttgart collector Beck; 1955: the *Crucifixion* mosaic for architect Alexander von Branca's monastery church Herz-Jesu located on Munich's Buttermelcherstraße, 1957: the *Tree-of-Life* mosaic in the St. Lawrence Church, Munich *(fig. 32)*, 1958: the great

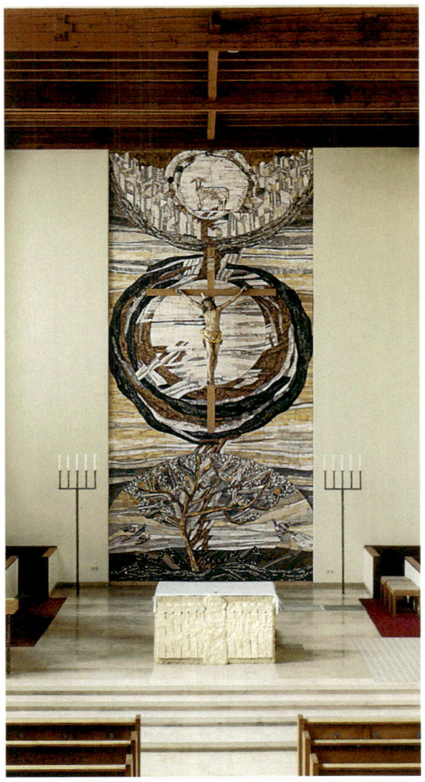

35

ST. MARGARETHA, REICHERTSHOFEN, mosaic on the altar wall, natural stone and gold mosaic form the background for a Baroque wooden cross, Benedict Schmitz OSFS, 1977

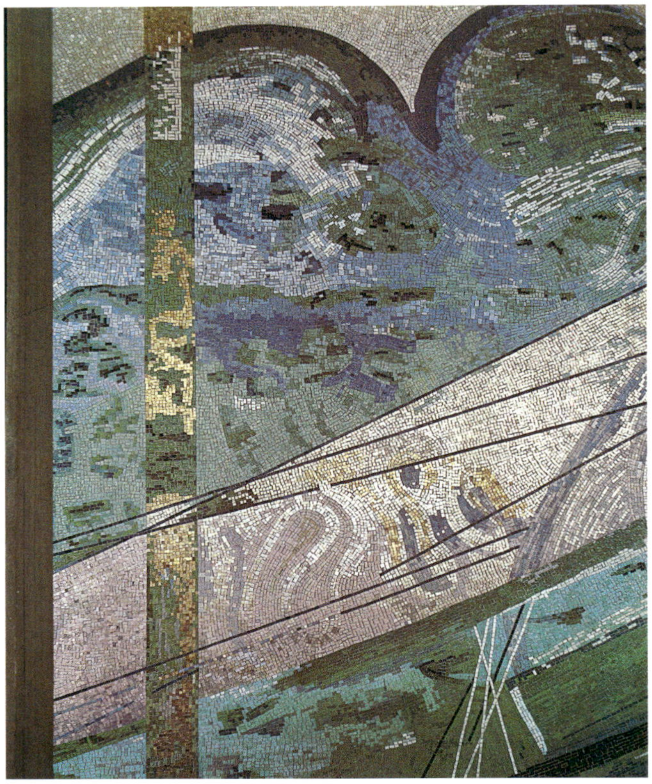

36

CASINO IN THE LVA BUILDING, MÜNSTER, detail of a glass mosaic made of Italian glass and silver smalti, Blasius Spreng, 1973

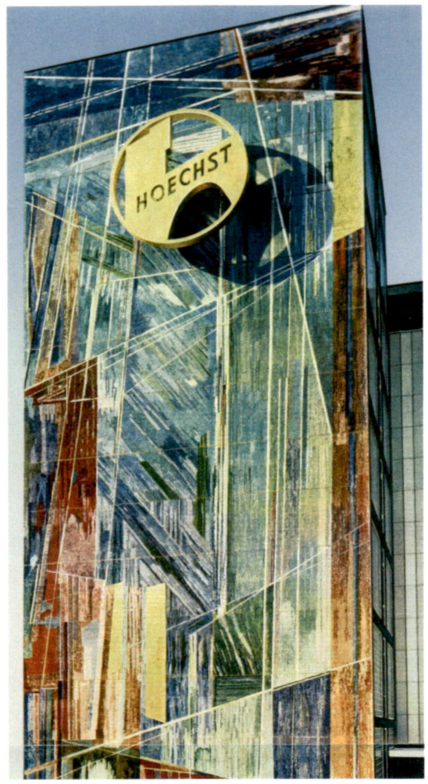

37

FACADE MOSAIC FOR FARBWERKE HOECHST AG, FRANKFURT/MAIN, colorful glass mosaic, circa 5400 square feet, Blasius Spreng, 1960

abstract mosaic for the German Pavilion at the Brussels World's Fair, today kept at the Oberste Baubehörde in Munich *(fig. 34)*. And finally the big altar wall mosaic from 1961 depicting the *Resurrected Christ* for Hiroshima's World Peace Church.

Knappe and Franz Mayer of Munich thus became innovators in the ancient art of mosaic, thereby serving as a role model for many contemporary artists who looked at similar tasks. Knappe only made rough sketches for his mosaics, developing the works mostly from the material itself. The basis of his mosaic collages consisted of varied substances including hewn stone cubes, stone slabs (either rough or polished), gold and silver "smalti," later also glass "cake," and industrial Detopak glass. The traditional 'negative' setting technique no longer satisfied Knappe; thus Franz Mayer of Munich developed the 'positive' setting technique towards the late 1950s, an important innovation at the time, which is now almost globally applied. Franz Mayer of Munich received Knappe's last and maybe largest mosaic commission at the artist's grave: The city of Munich's Kulturreferent ordered a mosaic to be executed posthumously for the Odeonsplatz subway station. The collaboration between the workshop and this important artist made Franz Mayer of Munich the leading and seminal modern mosaic studio. During the first half of the 20th century, the "August Wagner Vereinigte Werkstätten für Mosaik und Glasmalerei" in Berlin was Germany's largest and internationally most important mosaic studio. When it was forced to close down in 1969, Jucunda Wagner-Weinmeister wrote to her clients and artists: "The loss of this studio's artistic accomplishments ... would be irreplaceable for many if it were not for the Mayer'sche Hofkunstanstalt in Munich ... I am convinced there is no better studio in Germany."

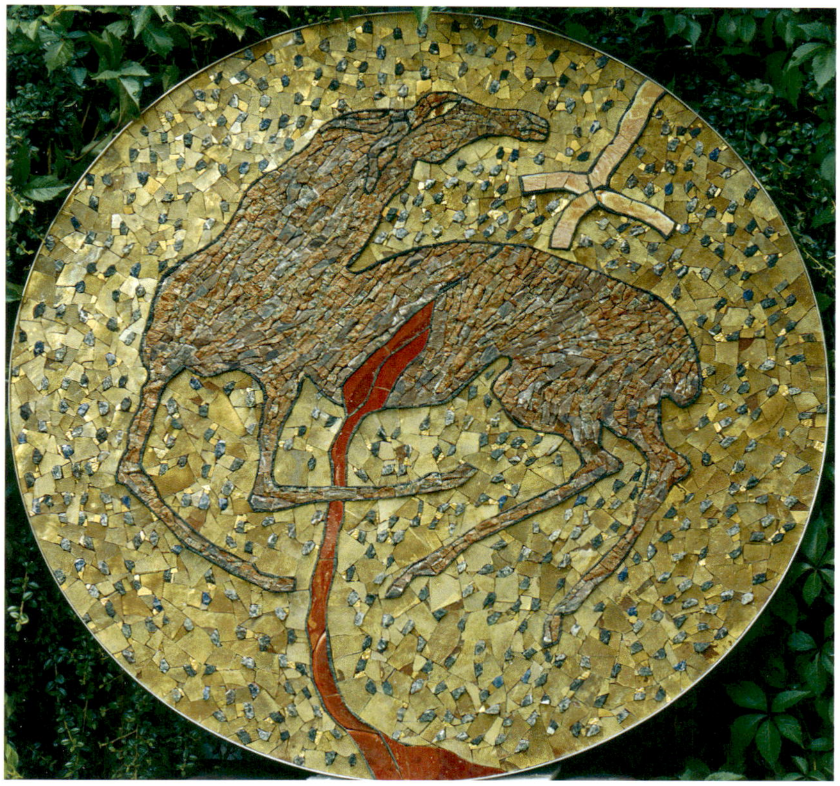

38

ST. THOMAS MORUS, NEUSÄSS, circular gold and stone mosaic, *Agnus Dei*, Georg Bernhard, 1989

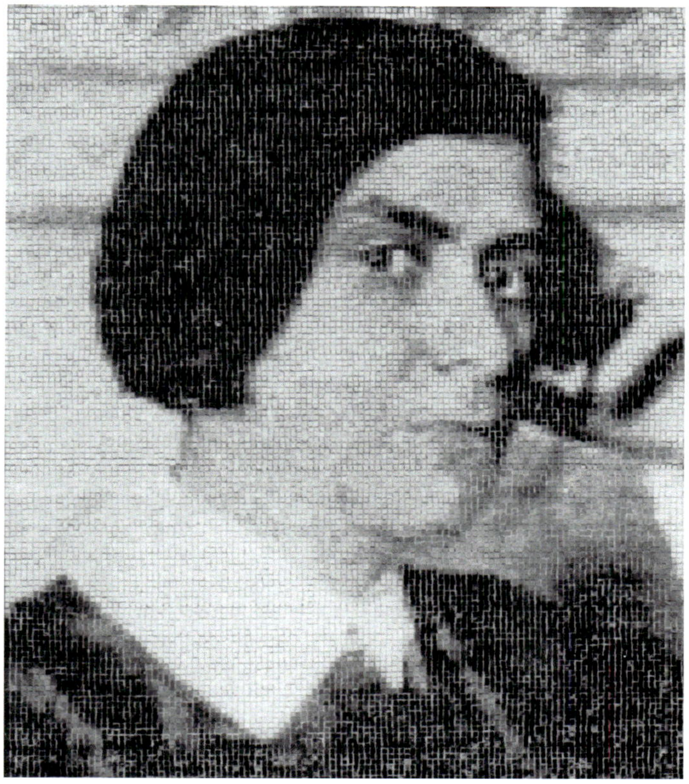

39

MEMORIAL FOR ELSE LASKER-SCHÜLER, WUPPERTAL, glass mosaic made of ¼ inch hand-hewn Italian glass smalti, Stephan Huber, 1989

Karl Knappe's influence on other artists was considerable. Among them was, for example, Benedict Schmitz OSFS (born 1935), who began to design many church mosaics starting in the 1970s, such as the one in Reichertshofen *(fig. 35)*, JoKarl Huber (1902–1996), Edeltraud Braun-Stransky, Roland Peter Litzenburger (1917–1987), Kurt von Unruh (1894–1986), Leo Müllenholz (born 1921), Bengt Olof Kälde from Sweden (born 1936), and the American Peter William Gray. Knappe's influence even extended to artists like Hubert Distler (1919–2004), Georg Bernhard *(fig. 38)*, Ludwig Schaffrath (1924–2011), and Hermann Schardt (1912–1984) from Essen. Anton Wendling (1891–1965) reverted to natural stone, glass, and gold in his large altar wall mosaic for the St. Peter in Chains Cathedral in Cincinnati, OH, which was executed by Franz Mayer of Munich.

Those in the Mayer studios who pursued entirely different approaches than Knappe were especially Blasius Spreng (1913–1987) from the 1960s on *(fig. 36, 37)* and, later, StephanHuber (born 1952) *(fig. 39)*. When the Hofkunstanstalt opened its US branch in 1988, it was an artisans' studio especially dedicated to new and modern mosaic.

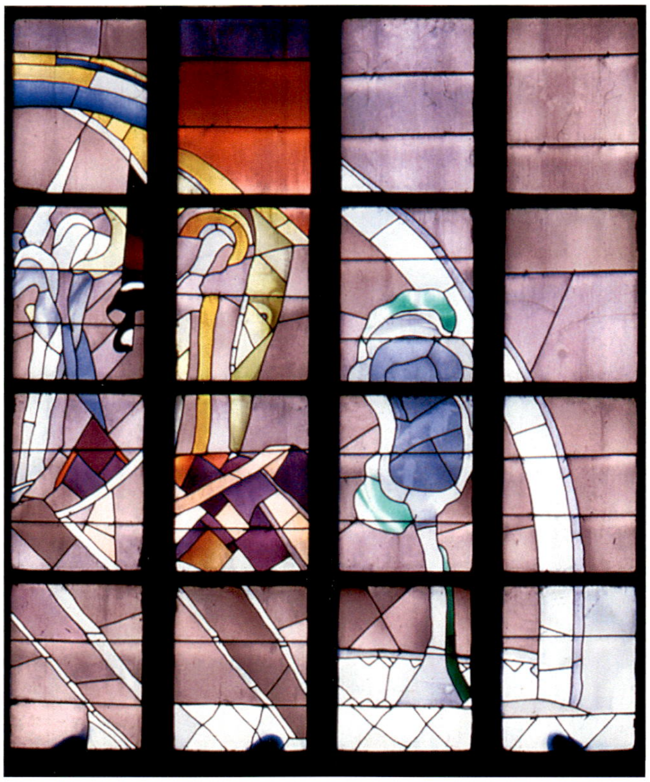

40

ANGELS PROTECT THE EARTH FROM THE ATOMIC BOMB, detail from a stained glass window over the Sixtus Portal, north side, Dom Zu Unserer Lieben Frau, Munich, Karl Knappe, 1961

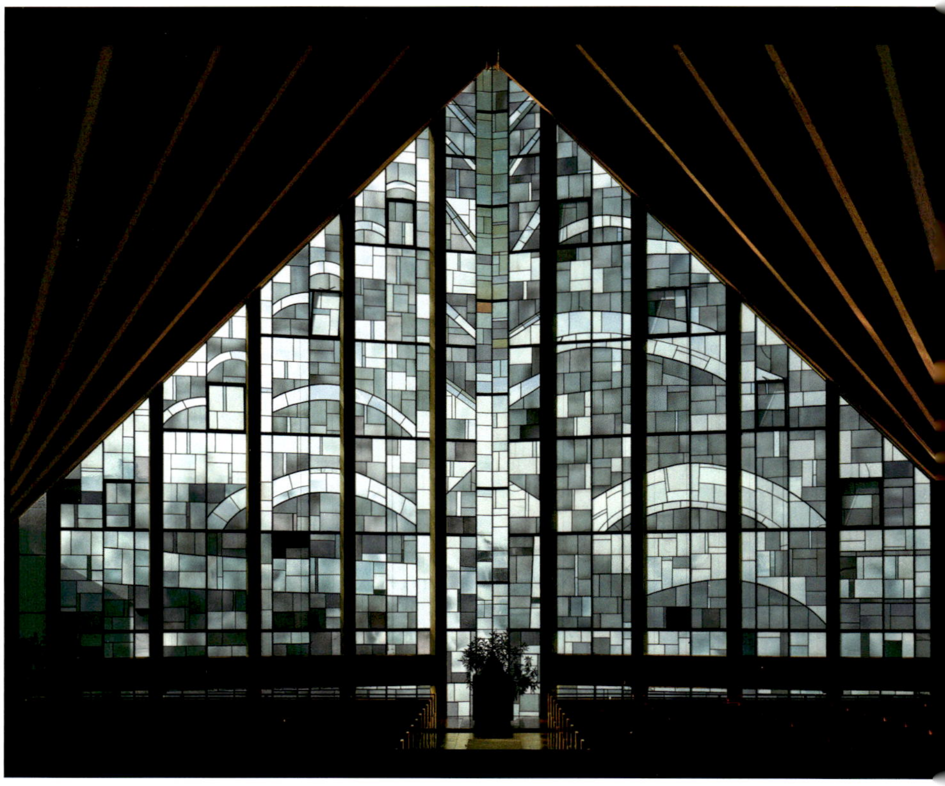

41

LARGE SOUTH FACADE WINDOW, ST. JOSEPHS KIRCHE, HOLZKIRCHEN, Karl Knappe, 1961, architect Franz Ruf

Stained Glass from the 1950s to the 1970s

In West Germany, the end of the Nazi regime and World War Two as well as the economic miracle led to a departure towards Modernism. The work of the Munich studio was characterized by multifaceted, lively, and at the same time modern artists expressing their individual styles and personalities. Once more, the most important name in this context is Karl Knappe's, who no longer used *Schwarzlotmalerei* ("tracing color") and began "to build a window using pure glass." Early examples are the reconstruction of a stained glass window, partly destroyed during the war, for church of St. Benedict in Gauting, dated 1947 *(fig. 30)*, and the Funerary Chapel for the Perlach Cemetery (1949–1951). His most important and seminal glass paintings are without doubt the window *Angels Protect the Earth from the Atomic Bomb* for Munich's Cathedral, *(fig. 40)* dated 1961, the windows for St. Gertrud's in Aschaffenburg, 1960, his work for the St. Pius Church in Hausen (1966), as well as the totally minimalist *Tree of Life* window *(fig. 41)* for the large south wall of St. Joseph's in Holzkirchen, dated 1961. There was a plethora of other artists creating glass works for the Mayer'sche Hofkunstanstalt. The list is far from complete and only lists some of the typical personalities: Albert Burkart (1898–1982) came from Riedlingen. First a professor (1949–1963) and then the director of the Städelschule in Frankfurt/M., he taught realistic painting, mural painting, painting in space, and glass painting. Apart from numerous monumental paintings for churches, he also created an impressive number of stained glass windows. The latter were mostly done in collaboration with the Mayer Studio and executed in the

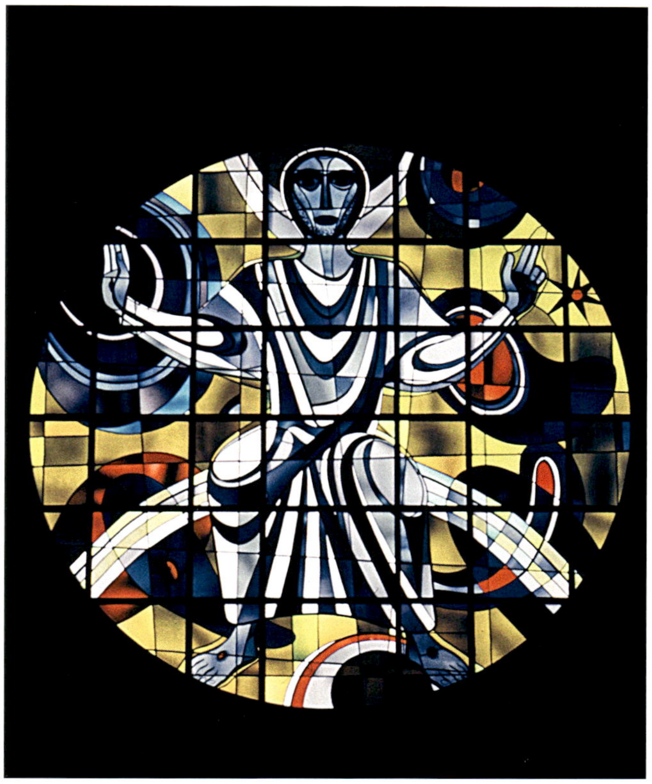

42
ST. JOACHIMSKIRCHE, MUNICH-NEUAUBING,
Christ Pantocrator, Albert Burkart, 1956

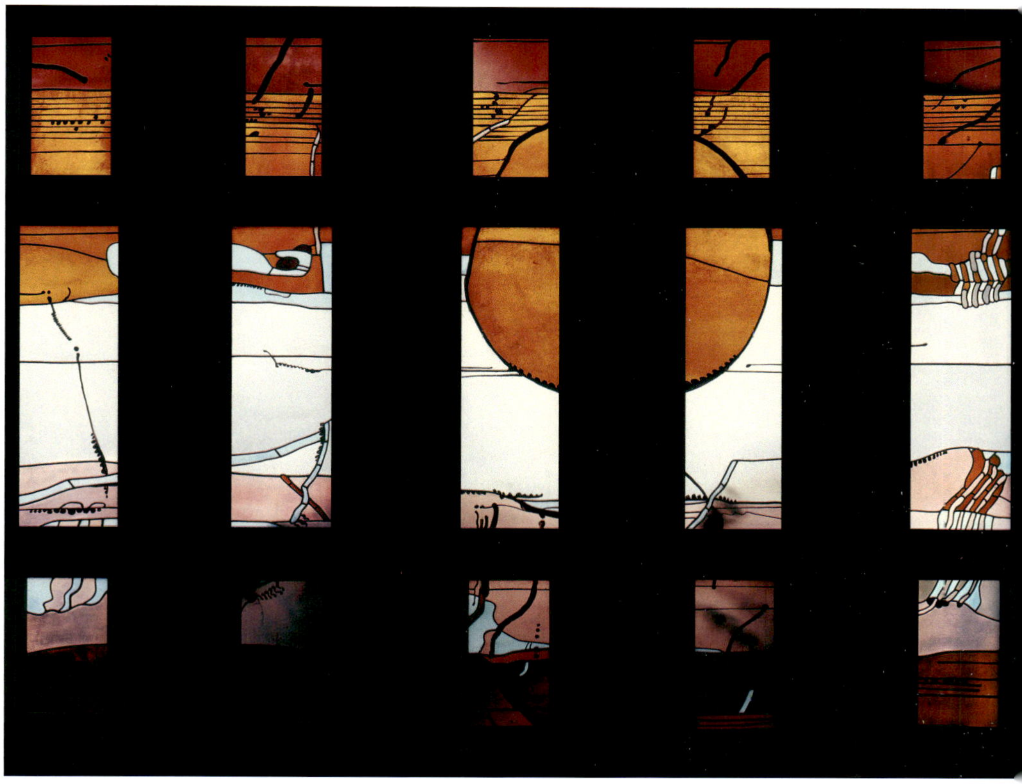

43
SENIOR CITIZENS' HOME, CHAPEL, MUNICH-PASING, Hubert Distler, 1977

1950s and 60s. He made his first larger post-War piece in 1953 for St. Peter and Paul in Brühl. In Munich alone, Burkart created stained glass windows for four Catholic churches: Zu den Heiligen Engeln (1955), St. Joachim in the suburb of Neuaubing (1956) – with the powerful Pantocrator window above the organ gallery, *(fig. 42)* – St. Willibald (1958), and the church Königin des Friedens (1962).

Hubert Distler (1919–2004) chose a completely different approach. A graphic artist, church painter, and glass designer, Distler conceived most of his glass windows in conjunction with ceiling paintings or murals and worked both in southern and in northern Germany, predominantly for Protestant churches. His first window project in collaboration with the Mayer'sche Werkstätte was for the Athanasius Church in Hanover (1964). Included are two of his four Munich projects: For the Lutheran Philippus Church he created – in tandem with the architect Lichtblau – a bright openwork altar wall with inlays of faceted glass. A particularly beautiful stained glass window may also be found at the back of the church. Good examples of Distler's glass windows – almost always revealing the graphic artist – are the small panels located in the Altenheimkapelle in Munich-Pasing *(fig. 43)*.

The other personality who shaped the art of stained glass design beside Karl Knappe was Hans Gottfried von Stockhausen (1920–2010). A fine, learned, and sensitive artist deeply rooted in tradition, he later went to the Stuttgart Art Academy (1969–1985), succesfully teaching both ecclesiastical and secular contemporary glass design.[69] He was considered one of the great proponents of 'musivic' and narrative stained glass. Like the old masters, he discovered for himself the technical and

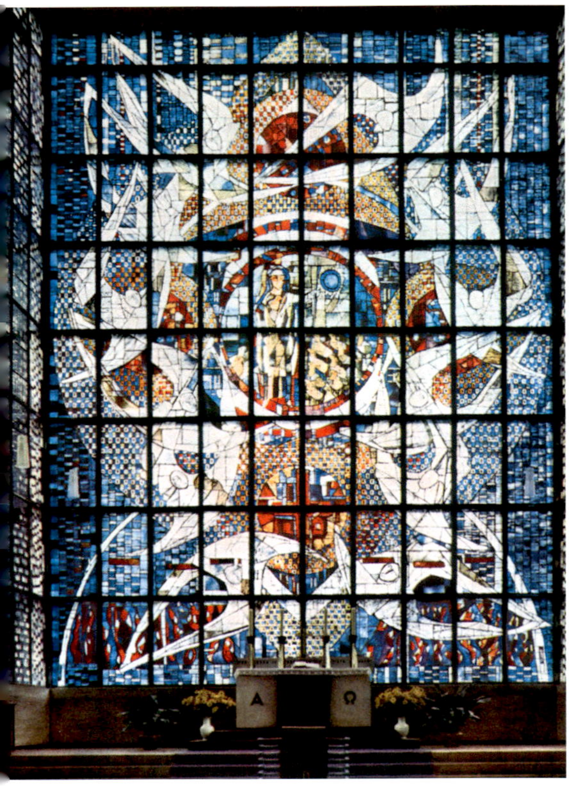

44

LUTHERAN ST. NICOLAIKIRCHE, DORTMUND; circa 6500 square feet of glass design for lateral and choir walls of this early Lutheran concrete church; in the center: *The Good Shepherd,* Hans Gottfried von Stockhausen, 1963

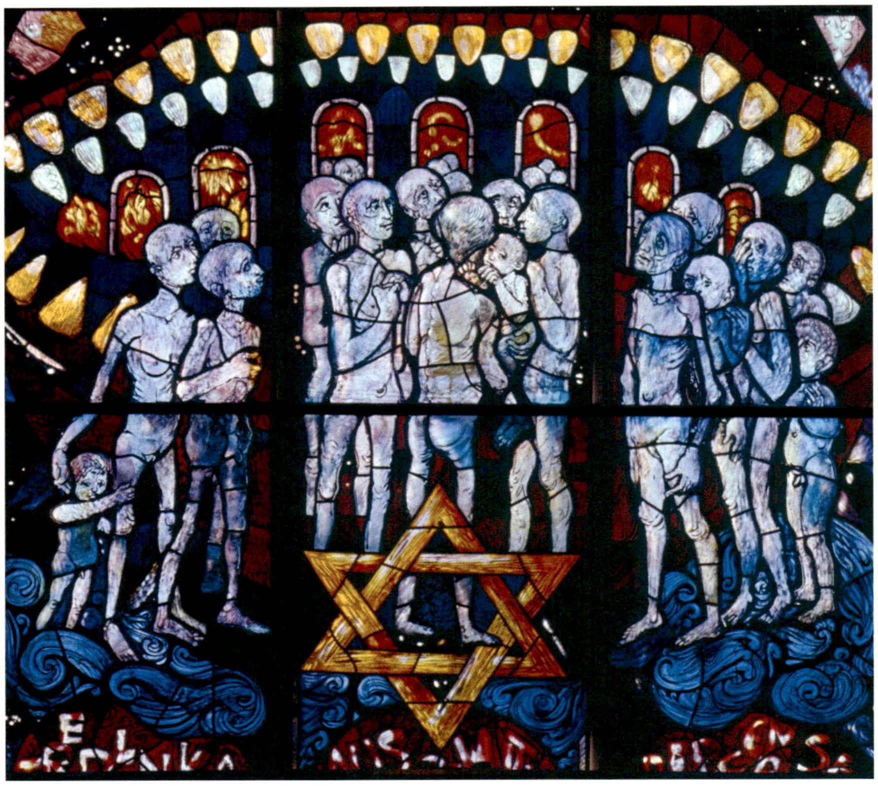

45

MÜNSTER, ULM, *ISRAEL WINDOW,* vision of the prophet Elias; detail of the two lower rows depicting the mouth of hell/Auschwitz, Hans Gottfried von Stockhausen, 1986

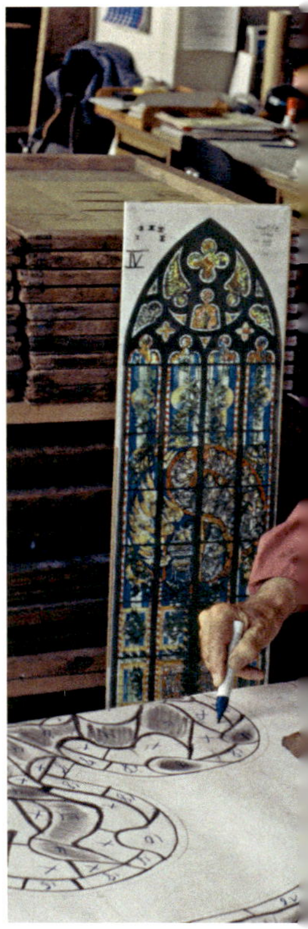

aesthetic merits of – one could say - 'functional' leading. This did occasionally lead to conflicts with Karl Knappe, who had largely abandoned *Schwarzlot*.[70] The charges of conservatism did not faze Stockhausen: "According to my understanding, terms like 'conservative', 'progressive' and such have turned into questionable buzzwords. I am the only one who can determine my artistic means ... What counts is the result, the spiritual essence alone. After all, time will be revealed in everything." [71] The Mayer'sche Hofkunstanstalt supported the realization of his designs and visions for more than five decades. The windows for the Ulm Münster are a particularly wonderful mark of the shared success story. It began in 1955, when the Gothic glazing was to be enhanced by appropriately regulating the light and sensitively adding corresponding hues of color, and it continued for three decades: In 1986 Stockhausen and Mayer realized the so-called *Israel Window (fig. 45)* for the Münster. A broad color palette, symbolism, and protagonists using expressive gestures characterize this piece. Stockhausen's vast oeuvre documents how strongly the Hofkunstanstalt and its team respected his requests and supported his development. His work includes the four sixty feet high ornamental windows for St. Maria zur Wiese in Soest 2002, the enormous glass assignment with the central scene of the *Good Shepherd* (1963) *(fig. 44)* for the entire lateral and choir walls of Dortmund's St. Nicolai Church, begun in 1929/30 by the architects Karl Pinno and Peter Grund as an iron, concrete and glass structure, the circa 750 square feet glass painting, *Stuttgart Glass Screen,* dated 1985 and generously given to St. David's Hall in Cardiff, Wales, by its partner city of Stuttgart, and the *Divine Quaternity* for the chapel of St. Joseph's University in Philadelphia (1991) *(fig. 47)*.

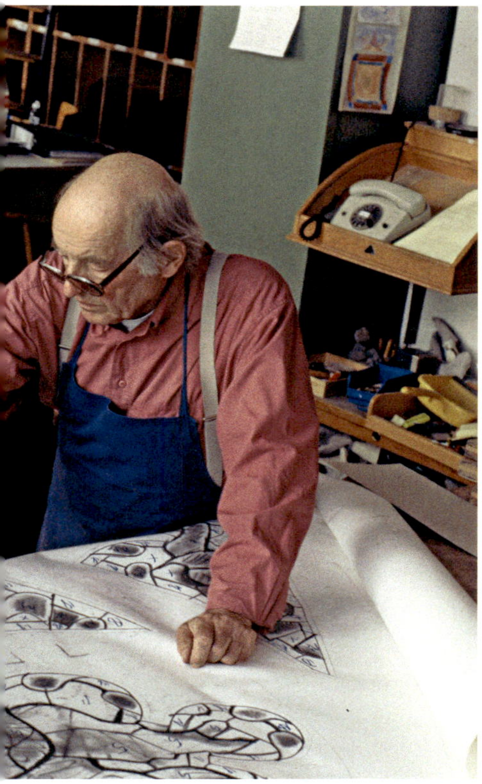

46
HANS GOTTFRIED VON STOCKHAUSEN, circa 1995

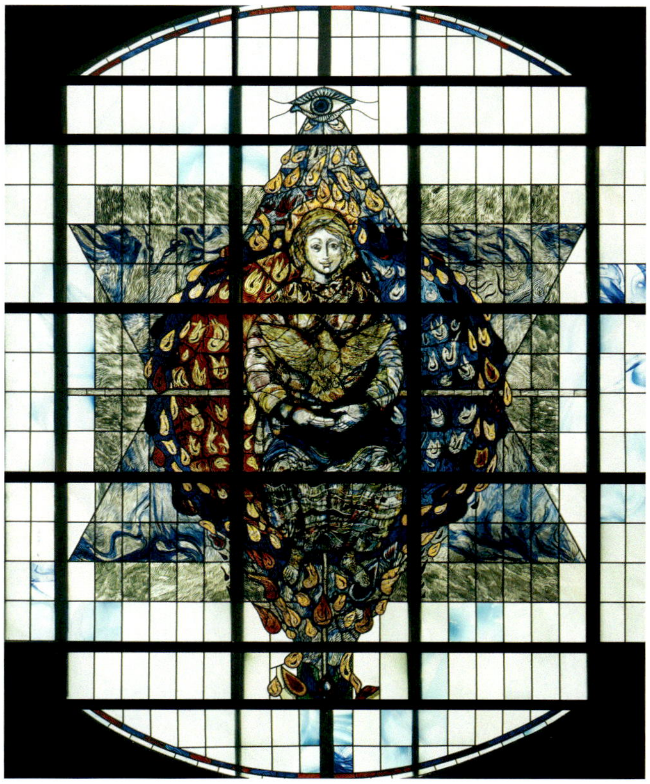

47
SAINT JOSEPH'S UNIVERSITY, PHILADELPHIA, PA, USA, CHAPEL; *Divine Quaternity,* altar window, Hans Gottfried von Stockhausen, 1991

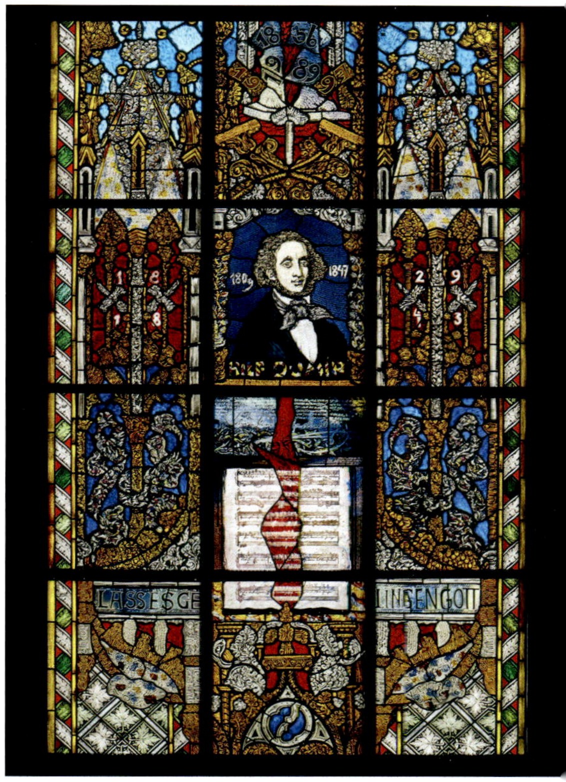

48
LUTHERAN ST. THOMASKIRCHE, LEIPZIG, *Mendelssohn window,* south nave, detail, Hans Gottfried von Stockhausen, 1997

Raised in Marseille and a student of Riemerschmid's, Carl Fritz David Crodel (1894–1973, called Charles), was someone of great importance to Adalbert Mayer during the 1950s and 60s. A professor at the Akademie der Bildenden Künste in Munich (1951–1962), he won a glass window competition for Frankfurt's Katharinen Church, painting Old- and New Testament scenes in tandem with his wife (1953/54). Aided by the Hofkunstanstalt, he created glass characterized by a fresh and lively narrative style full of movement.[72] The Mayers helped him on most of his glass projects until his death, among them the numerous brilliant apse windows he designed for the St. Jakobi Church in Hamburg (1957/1961).[73] Other examples documenting that the Hofkunstanstalt had become this artist's workshop-home are the Schlosskirche in Pforzheim (1959/60), the Catholic parish church in Fulda-Horas (1959), the St. Andreas Church in Brunswick[74] (1964), and St. Kilian's in Heilbronn (1965/1968). Glass painter Josef Karl (JoKarl) Huber (1902–1996) was Karl Caspar's master student at the Munich Academy. Between 1954 and 1967, he created, in collaboration with the Hofkunstanstalt, fascinating abstract and extremely colorful stained glass, for example for the Gothic city church in Weil der Stadt (1954), St. Martin's in Malmsheim (1962) *(fig. 49)*, and for the Catholic church of St. Elisabeth in Stuttgart (1967). A professor of graphic art and painting since 1947, Franz Nagel (1907–1976) was the president of the Akademie der Bildenden Künste in Munich from 1960 until 1963. During his cooperation with the Mayer'sche Werkstätte, he created numerous important "modern" stained glass works and also encouraged some of his students to work on church windows. Gabriel Mayer points out that Josef Oberberger (we will turn to him later; like Nagel, he also

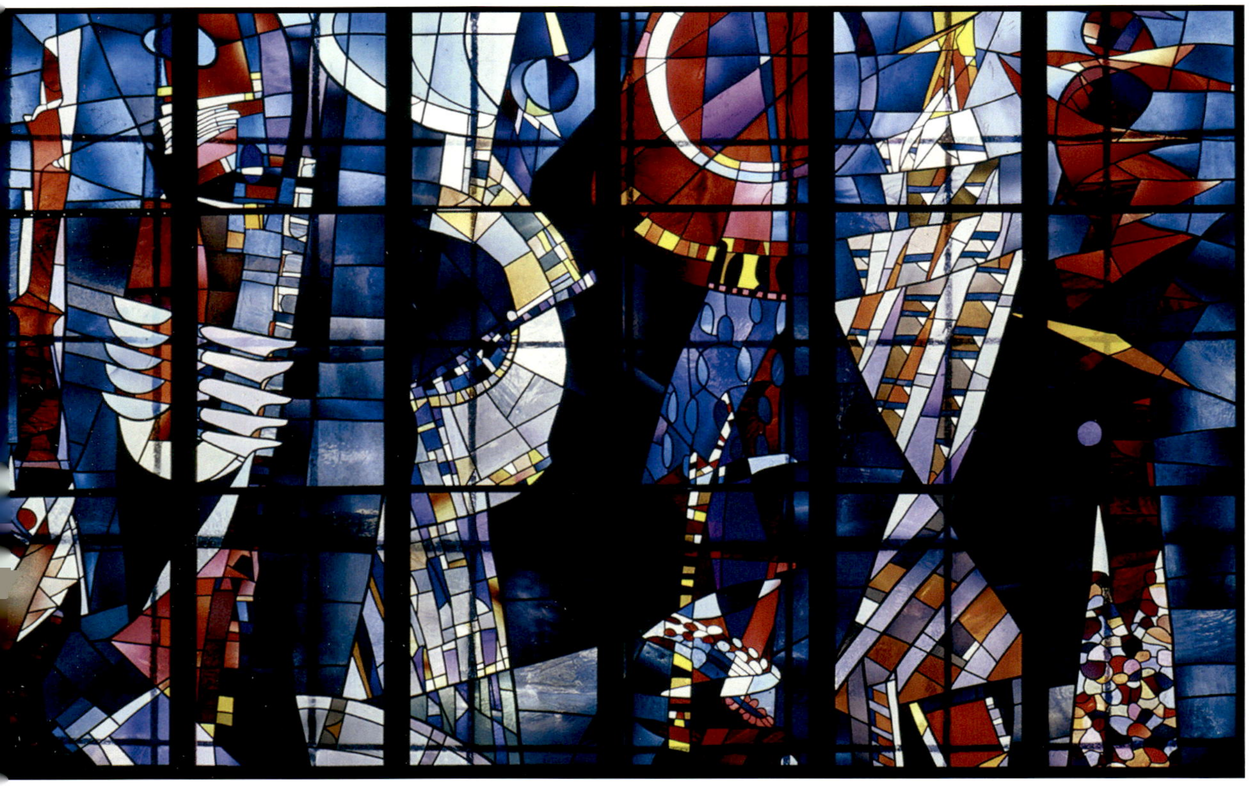

49
ST. MARTINSKIRCHE, MALMSHEIM, BADEN WÜRTTEMBERG, *Jubilate window*, detail, J. K. Huber, 1962

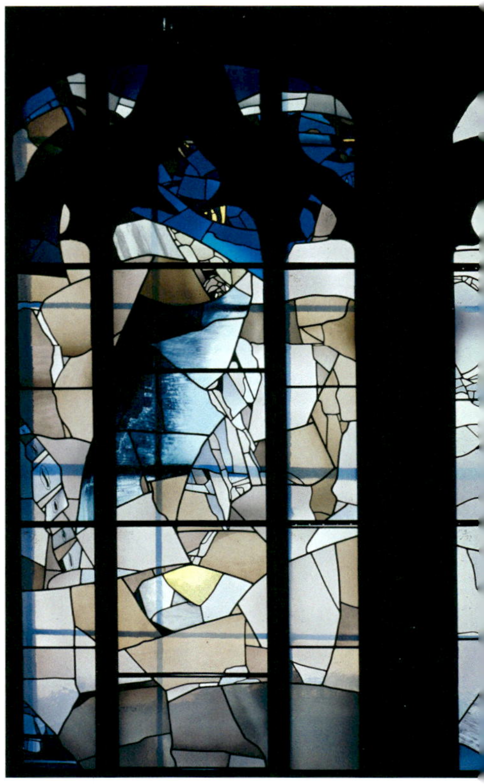

50
ST. KILIANSDOM, WÜRZBURG, two triple lancet stained glass windows from the cycle in the nave, Franz Nagel, 1966/67

collaborated with the Mayer'sche Werkstätte) supposedly fought some type of "religious war" against Nagel and his students concerning issues pertaining to 'modern' and 'old.' Nagel and Oberberger were professor-colleagues and antipodes at Munich's Academy at the same time. Nagel's point of departure was based more on graphic thoughts, with at times powerful and mostly solemn color. Among his most important works are his stained glass windows for the Catholic churches St. Albertus Magnus in Regensburg (1964), St. Pius in Haunstetten near Augsburg (1966), and the nave windows for the St. Kiliansdom in Würzburg (begun in 1966) *(fig. 50)*.

The project for St. Michael's in Hildesheim is of particular importance. This church is one of the large and most important Romanesque churches in Germany. Gerhard Hausmann and the Mayer'sche Hofkunstanstalt created concrete thick glass windows for the three east choirs *(fig. 51, 52)*. Windows made of concrete were certainly daring for such a historically eminent edifice. Hausmann carved graphite forms to create smelt glass pieces, which offer marvelously clear yet subdued light. It appears that to this day these windows still present an excellent solution. They are timeless (even in the technique of concrete glass, which in itself is really time-related).

German Post-War Stained Glass Becomes "World Famous"

There appears to be a parallel between the enormously popular *Munich Style* from around 1900 and the modern approaches of post-War German stained glass. No matter whether they were more painterly like the works by von Stockhausen, Crodel, or Oberberger or more graphic

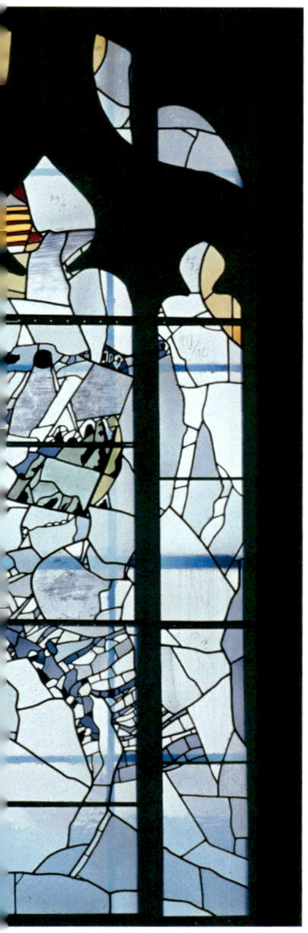

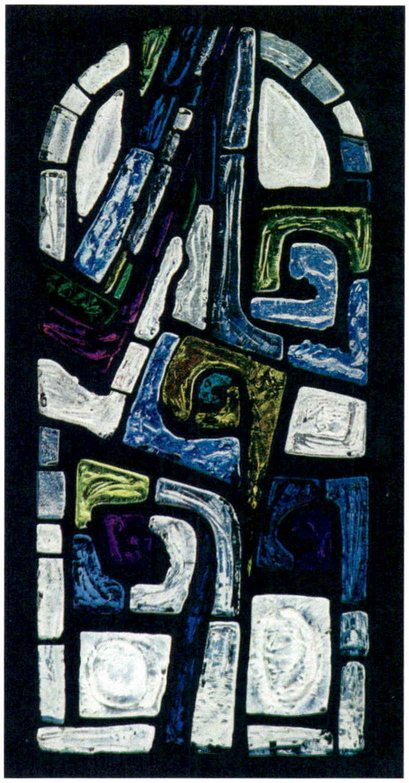

51

LUTHERAN ST. MICHAELISKIRCHE, HILDESHEIM, one of 17 concrete and melted glass windows, east choir and sides apses, Gerhard Hausmann, 1966 and 1969

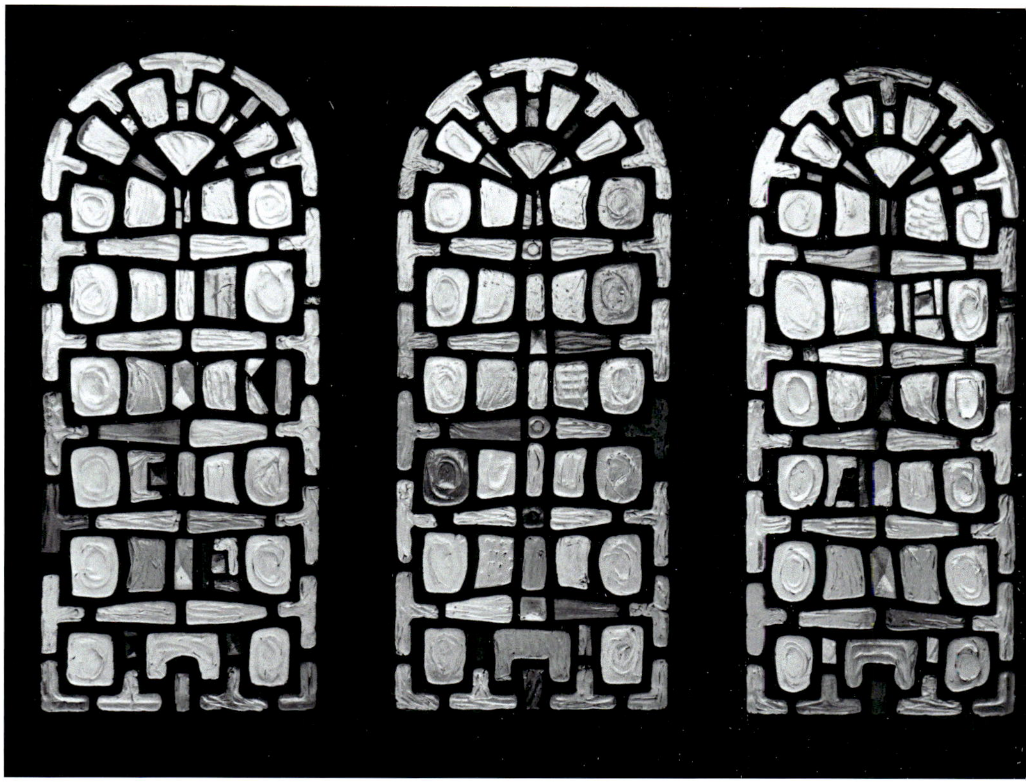

52

LUTHERAN ST. MICHAELISKIRCHE, HILDESHEIM, three of the choir windows of the Romanesque church, colorless glass, Gerhard Hausmann, 1966 and 1969

works reduced to aspects of pure color or leading, same modern German stained glass slowly became "world famous" among experts and artists.

These works of glass painting represented a real breakthrough, both for new churches and for the many old and medieval churches. In the post-War era, constructing churches was of great significance for architects. Some architects who ought to be remembered here include Rudolf Schwarz, Dominikus and Gottfried Böhm, Alexander von Branca, Emil Steffann, or Hansjakob Lill. Artists made their very own contributions with regards to windows (and mosaics as well.) Their works were ambitious. It was not until the mid-1970s that this was recognized abroad. However, it can be said that at this point artists from England, Australia, and North America began "pilgrimages" to Germany, visiting leading German artists from the stained glass scene and the relevant studios. It was only natural that they also wanted to see the projects in the churches.

Josef Oberberger Holding Court at the Kunstanstalt

Josef Oberberger (1905–1994) was appointed successor to Olaf Gulbransson as professor for glass painting at Munich's Academy. He worked with the Hofkunstanstalt for many decades – or, more appropriately and figuratively speaking: He held court. The craftspeople and most especially Adalbert Mayer, his friend for many years, had the highest regard for Oberberger. Beginning in the 1950s, Oberberger and Mayer also repeatedly and intensely worked for the cathedrals in Augsburg *(fig. 56)* and Regensburg *(fig. 57–61)*, where

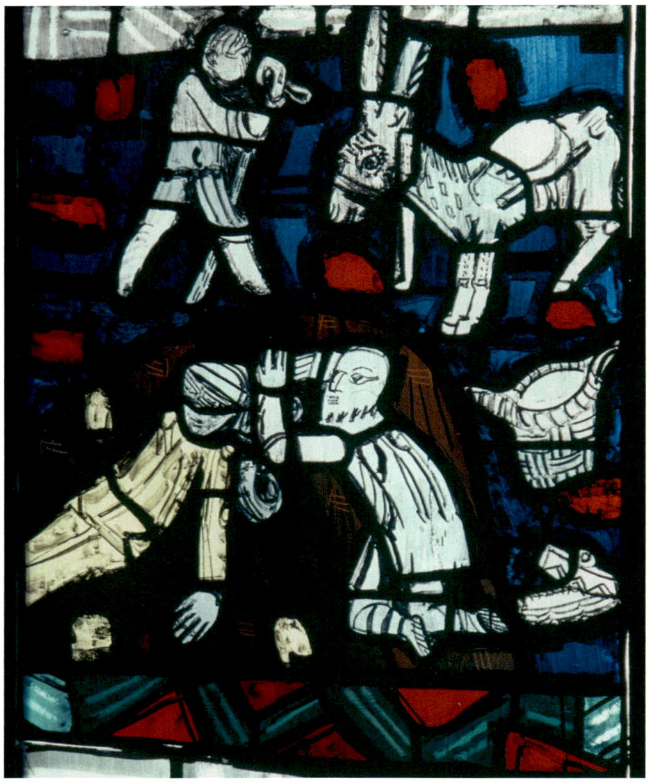

53
THE GOOD SAMARITAN, Charles Crodel

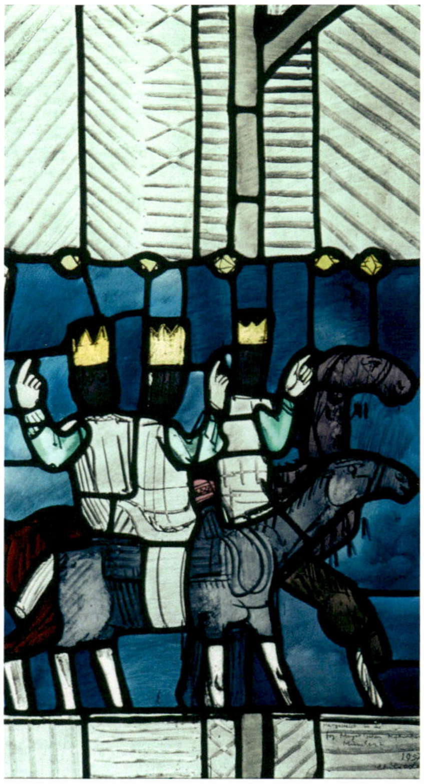

54
DREIKÖNIGSKIRCHE, FRANKFURT/MAIN, *Journey of the Three Magi,* Charles Crodel, 1957

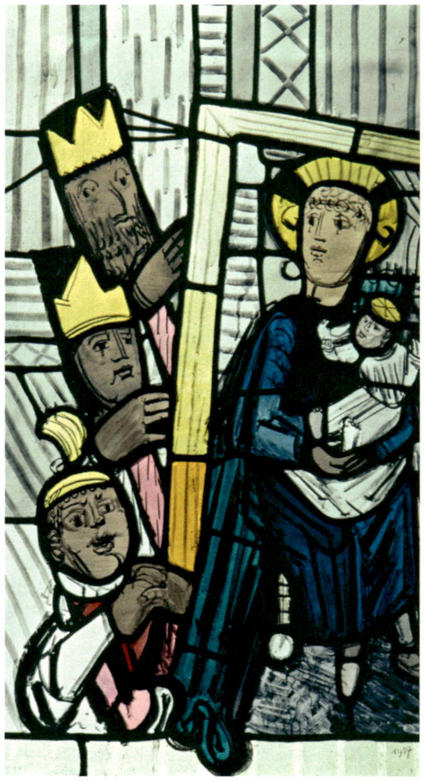

55
DREIKÖNIGSKIRCHE, FRANKFURT/MAIN, *Adoration of the Magi,* Charles Crodel, 1957

their predominantly abstract creations developed in a technique of free glass cutting and leading. Paramount to Oberberger was the impression of colored light breaking through mystical darkness. Studio and artist achieved this effect by coating the glass with a patina on both sides. Reinhard Müller-Mehlis wrote of his first work for the Regensburg Dom's north choir chapel (1966)[75]: "Oberberger's attunement to spatial and thematic connections reached a high degree of empathy, making it almost impossible to date these four windows and leaving them in utter anonymity, which Oberberger uses to place himself beside the ancients." [76]

The Fourth Generation Takes Over

Despite its success during the two decades following World War Two, in the late 1960s the Hofkunstanstalt was pulled into the economic depression, accompanied by fifteen years of reduced exports. After the Second Vatican Council (1962–1965) there were only very few orders for modern windows in Europe. This was most severe in southern Germany with its strictly Catholic and Baroque traditions. Traditional windows were hardly in demand in the US, and the clergy did not really appreciate challenging modern solutions. While there was little demand in the US for artistically ambitious works in secular architecture and in public spaces, these kinds of commissions all but perished in Germany. In these troubled times the young Dr. Gabriel Mayer (born 1938) entered the firm. His father Adalbert Mayer began, around 1965, to withdraw from

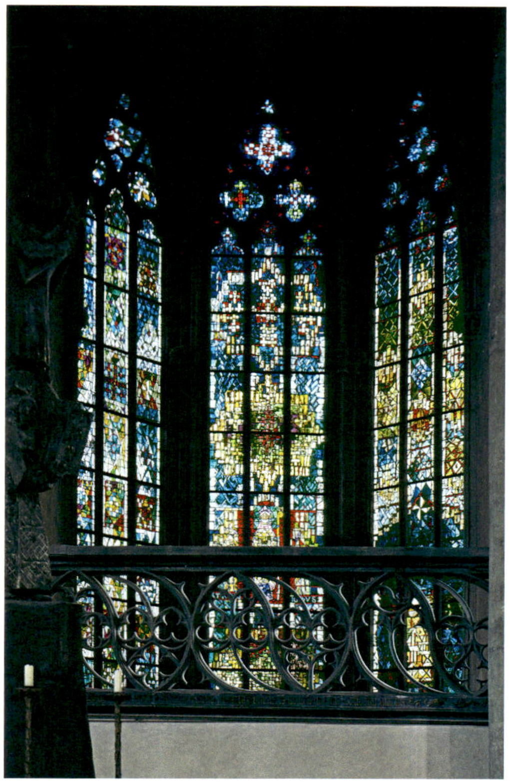

56

DOM, AUGSBURG, stained glass windows for the east choir chapels, with the central medieval window of the Medallion Master as point of reference. Here the windows in the right choir chapel, Josef Oberberger, 1962–66

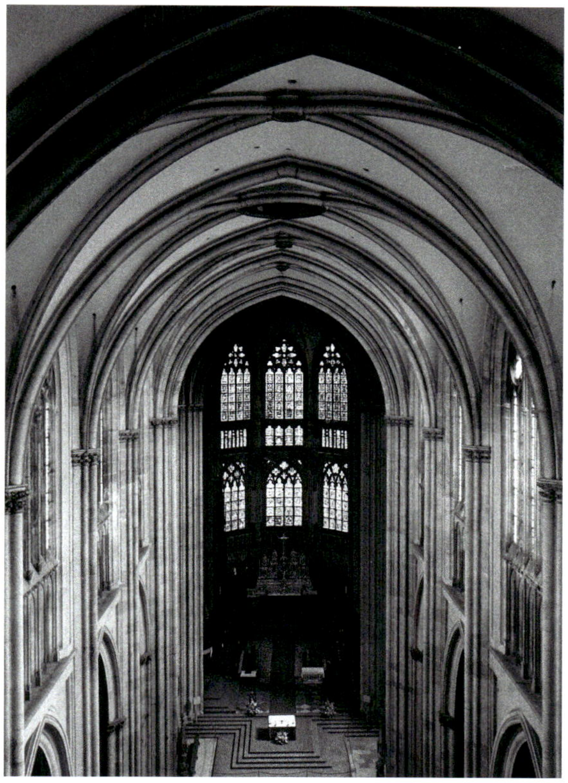

57

DOM, REGENSBURG, interior view. New stained glass by Josef Oberberger and Mayer, 1966–1989, among others all windows for the south and north nave clerestory. Mayer performed also preservation work on a substantial part of the numerous outstanding medieval windows.

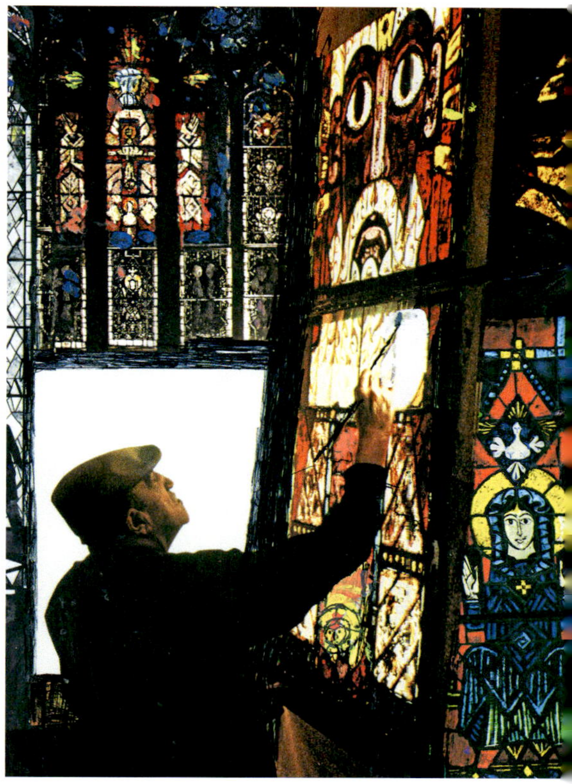

58

JOSEF OBERBERGER paints in the studios of the Mayer'sche Hofkunstanstalt

management and from a long work-life characterized by two world wars and incredible turbulences.[77] Gabriel's fifteen years older cousin Konrad Mayer had already joined the company in early 1954. At the end of the 1960s, the fourth generation was solely responsible and the times were all but rosy. At the time, conservation work formed the economic base of the workshop operation.

The Beginning of a New Era

In the early- to mid-1980s, the situation changed dramatically: Taking the slowly changing circumstances into account, Gabriel Mayer began to concentrate once more on the values of artistic and technical quality, while he always operated at the highest level. This approach had been the foundation for early successes. Therefore, he contacted the best artists and architects of the day, also and especially again in the USA, and explored, experimented with, and tried out innovative forms and techniques. A milestone had been in 1982 the first collaboration with the genius and "glass possessed" British artist Brian Clarke (born 1953). From the early 1990s onward, a close and trusting friendship began to evolve. Also worth mentioning is the fascinating *Artistic Glass Tent*, realized in 1984/85 with Frei Otto (born 1925) and his daughter Bettina. This was the first successful major work executed in a technique Mayer called "float glass painting." Equally important were the increasing numbers of contacts with the US and Canada and finally, in 1988 (100 years after the first branch opened in New York), the creation of a mosaic studio in Fairfield, NJ. Another cornerstone was the intense and renewed study of the *Munich Style*, in every respect a high-quality

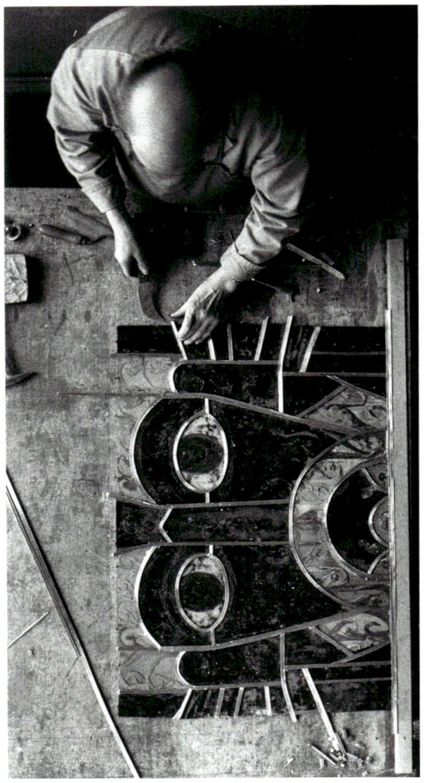

59
LEAD SPECIALIST AT WORK: leading the head of God the Father, *Pentecost window*, Josef Oberberger, Dom, Regensburg

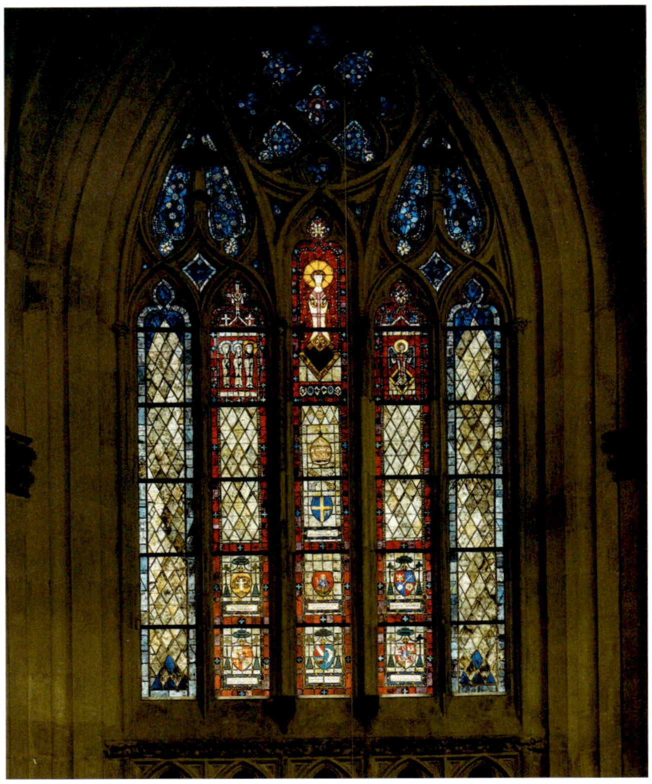

60
DOM, REGENSBURG, Window No. 7, north clerestory, *Resurrection* and heraldic panes, 1989

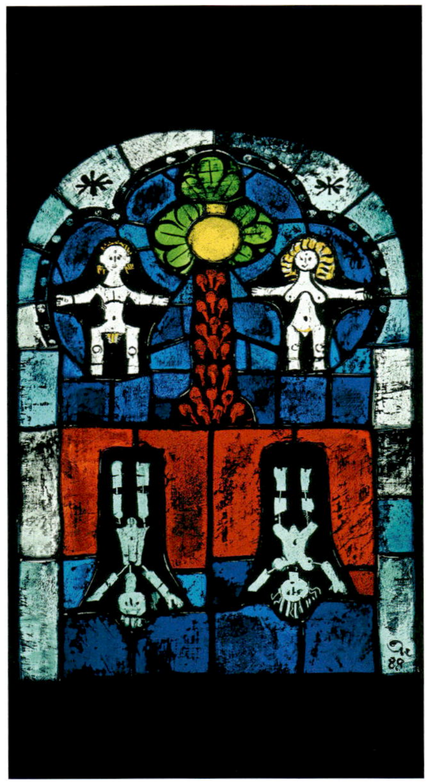

61
DOM, REGENSBURG, Detail Adam and Eve, *Pentecost window*

painting and drawing technique, which had established the works of Mayer and Zettler in circa 1900. In 1997, the entire workshop building in Munich was restored on the occasion of the firm's 150th anniversary. 2001 saw the inauguration of the newly-established float glass department, whereby the Mayer studio transferred the brilliant invention of the Englishman Sir Alastair Pilkington (1920–1995) to their firm.

The Breakthrough of Float Glass Art

The float glass process was introduced to the public on January 20, 1959. Pilkington's innovation pours the glass at circa 1000° C over a tub filled with liquid tin, facilitating the production of glass panels with highly precise surfaces in any size. They look flawless even before sanding and polishing.[78] The effect of Pilkington's discovery was a revolution in the glass industry.

With the further development of float glass painting, the industrial glass, flawless in every way, fundamentally changed the Kunstanstalt's business. The emphasis was no longer on hand-blown "real antique" glass, based on medieval processes. Now, Gabriel Mayer and his team began to shape and burn the disembodied industrial glass by sand blasting and etching, by applying and burning-in of the most diverse types of enamel colors. They attempted to return body and a translucid surface for their designs to the all-too-perfect glass.[79] The clear, neutral glass contains very few flaws, allowing for a highly differentiated, versatile treatment without the disruption of lead lines. Float glass painting offers the possibility of overcoming old traditions to pursue other means of de-

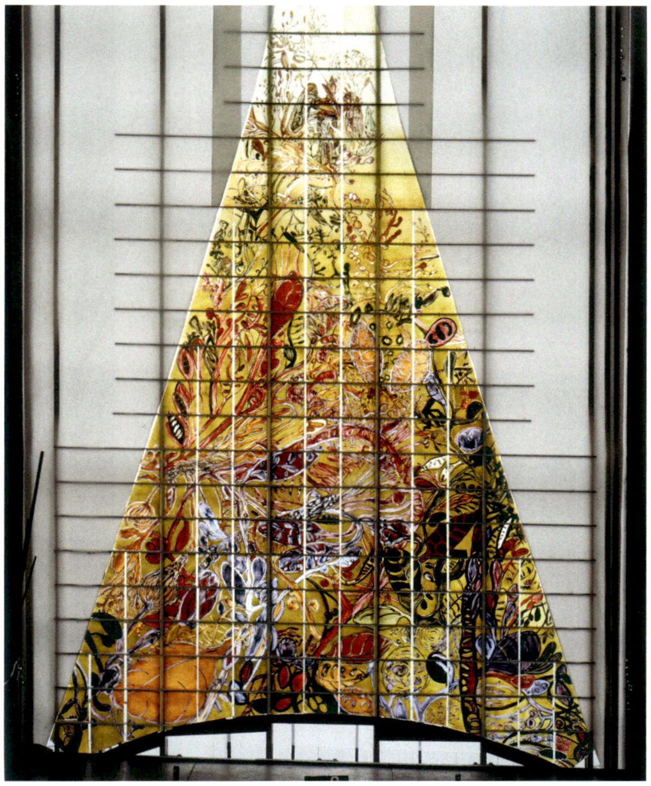

62

ARTISTIC GLASS TENT, DQDC, RIYADH, SAUDI ARABIA, architect and artist: Frei and Bettina Otto, 1984–86; the first monumental work executed in float glass painting technique, one of ten segments set up in the exhibition gallery of the Hofkunstanstalt

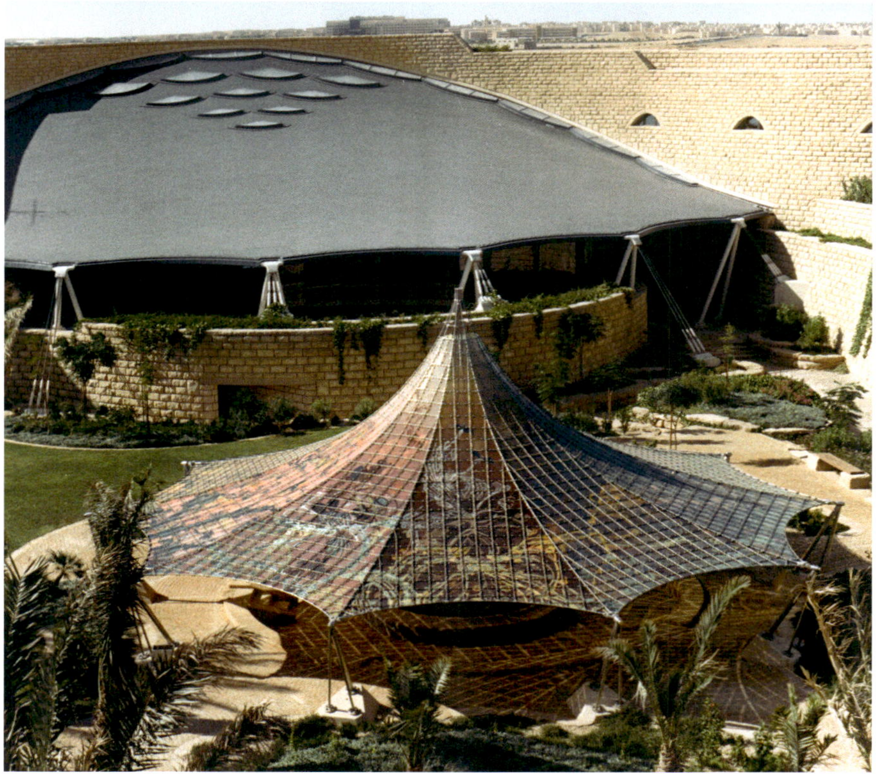

63

***HEART TENT,* ARTISTIC GLASS TENT, DQDC, RIYADH, SAUDI ARABIA,** seen from above

signing windows.[80] Artists must no longer deal with lead cames or the relatively small pieces of hand-blown glass.

Between 1984 and 1986, Gabriel Mayer accomplished the launch and the breakthrough of this extraordinary development, working together with architect Frei Otto and his daughter Bettina on the *Artistic Glass Tent (fig. 62, 63).* The ministers and commissioners from Saudi Arabia were delighted when they saw Bettina Otto's plants, tendrils, and flower designs. This was just the solution they wanted for the *Heart Tent*, the artistic centerpiece of a nature garden in a complex of the Diplomatic Club that was to be erected in Riyadh's modern diplomatic quarter. Owing to the extreme fluctuations in local temperatures and the innovative steel rope construction, this was a massive challenge. Everyone felt that a glass design would be the best solution. Yet, there had never before been a comparable project within the realm of glass painting. The Hofkunstanstalt experimented for more than six months, collaborating with material testing firms, Munich's technical university, and contributing its own experiences with glass painting. In the end, the studio managed to realize this project, an immense stimulus to "architecture art," with the aid of uncounted translucid glass shingles onto which ceramic enamel paints were applied, using painting and etching techniques. It was the first major project worldwide executed in this new type of float glass painting.[81]

In 1985, disregard for stained glass was by no means over. The art-world still regarded it as nothing but craft, although as an artistic media, glass and stone offer inexhaustible possibilities. In an attempt to restitute its major role, Gabriel Mayer and his studios used all their energy to reestablish this art form in architecture, public spaces, and buildings.

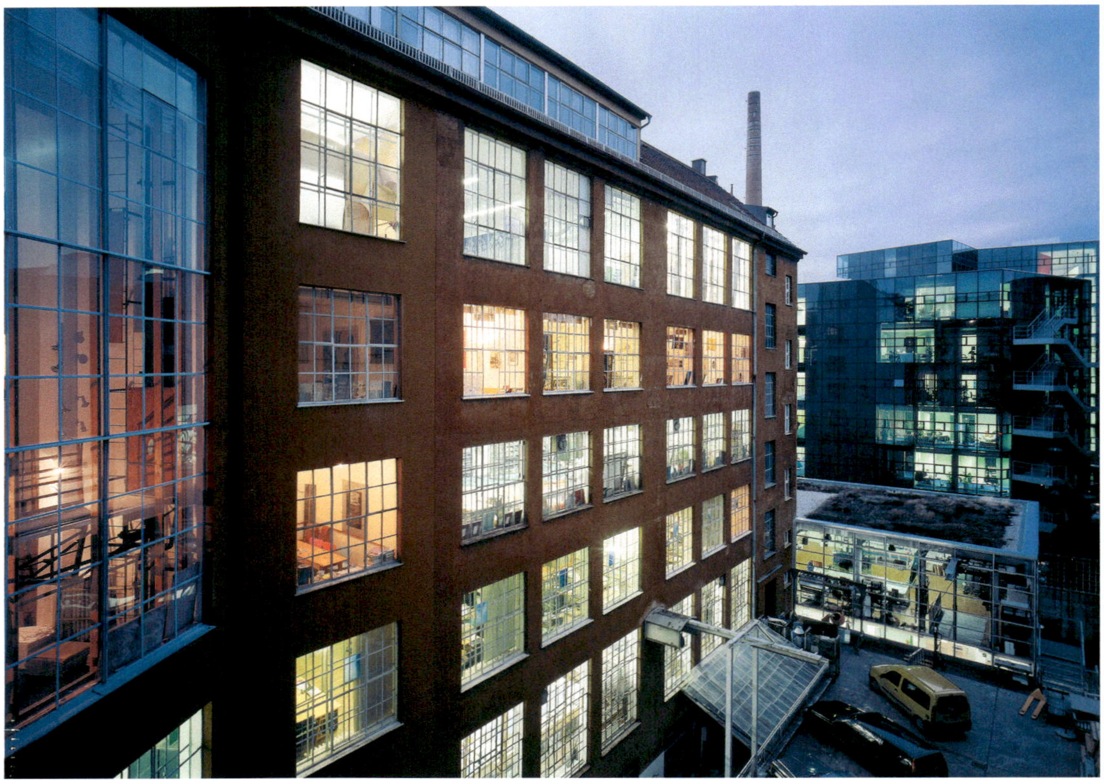

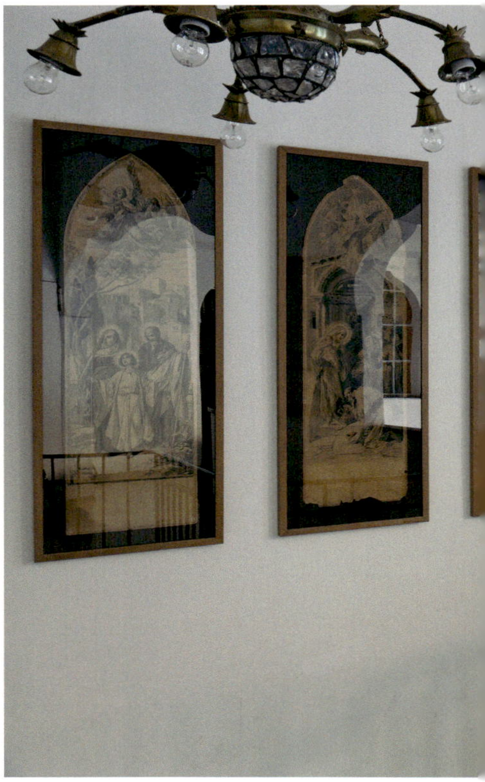

64
THE STUDIO BUILDING TODAY, view of the facade facing the courtyard and the new pavilion for float glass painting

At this point, the fifth generation had long since entered the scene. In 1990, Gabriel's son Michael C. Mayer, (born 1967), began an apprenticeship in the field of mosaics in Italy; he collaborated on such challenging tasks as the conservation of the stone inlays of Frederick II's ('the Great') Picture Gallery at Sanssouci as well as conserving and reconstructing the Roman Tethys mosaic at Harvard.

From then on it was paramount for father and son to further modernize the workshops and to elevate them to high-tech standards while retaining the age-old handicraft technologies. The Hofkunstanstalt was to become even more of an equal and up-to-date partner for the artists, who were taken seriously on all counts. As the carriers of ideas, visions, and concepts, they need support for their tasks, especially since they often lack technical and practical knowledge or experience to apply sustainable technologies to architecture.

Continuous research and experiments enabled the Munich studio to furnish artists with the latest glass handling technologies: Sand-blasting, etch engraving, digital print, airbrush, hand painting, and all types of computer design. They may all be combined with existing glass painting techniques such as adhesive bonding, slumping, or fusing. Added to this were all the possibilities of large-scale design, light and heat regulation, as well as all security elements glass techniques can offer. This virtuoso and fascinating palette of technical innovations was geared towards pure architecture.

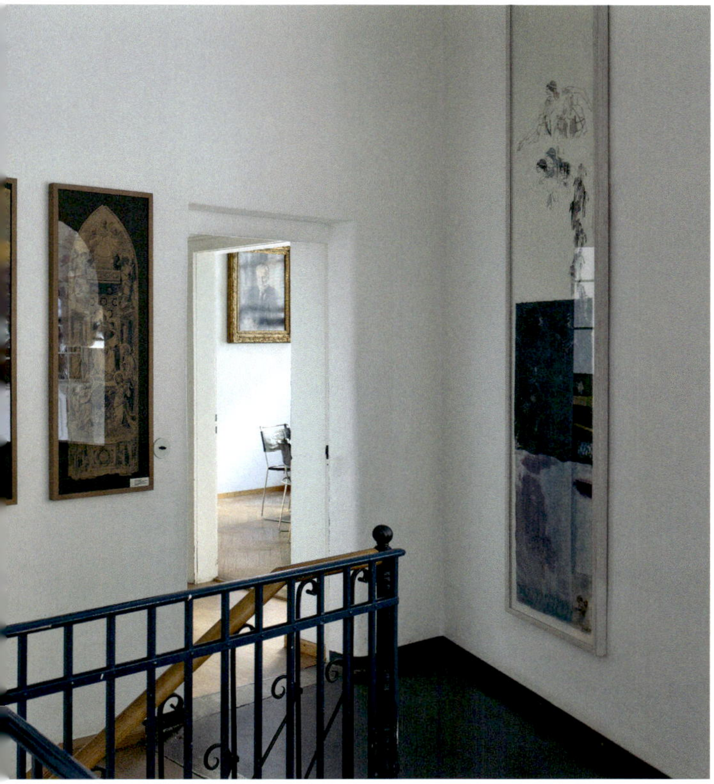

65

INTERIOR VIEW OF THE STUDIO BUILDING TODAY, 4th floor with view to the office floor from the exhibition gallery (Nancy Spero picture and original sketches from circa 1900)

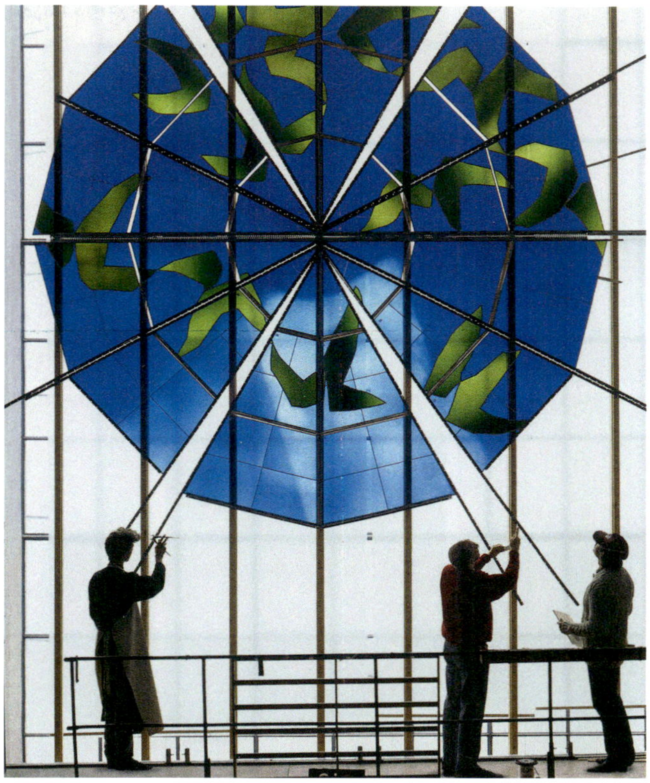

66

ONE OF THE SKYLIGHT WINDOWS, NORTE SHOPPING MALL, Rio de Janeiro; Brian Clarke and craftsmen on the hoist of the exhibition window, 1995

Innovative "Public Art" Instead of "Kunst am Bau" (i.e. Percent for Art Program)

Starting in the 1980s, the concept of "Public Art" evolved into an important movement, especially in New York City, the new metropolis of modern art. NYC's MTA Arts for Transit became very active, turning the subway system into a platform par excellence for high-caliber artworks. One could appropriately refer to a "Public Art Museum" in New York City's underground. The MTA's AFT managed to attract stars from New York's art scene, as well as emerging and not very well known local artists to design the individual stations, resulting in an appealing public art image. In the US, "Public Art" is often required by law and is generally positively regarded. Investors were increasingly approached to realize works of art where their projects affected the public. The principle is to set aside fees for artists and implementation from the overall project cost. Generally, the ratio (20% artist fee to 80% fabrication costs from budget) applies to all artists regardless of their popularity. Many of the great stars were even proud to be asked to design art for their city. This particular environment became the breeding ground for Mayer's innovative mosaic and float glass art. Within the last fifteen years, Munich's Hofkunstanstalt, known in the US as "Franz Mayer of Munich," realized over two-dozen predominantly large glass and mosaic architectural projects in New York City alone. Some of these works will be discussed in our chapter, "projects."

Based on the idea of forming first-rate, professional and fantasy-filled partnerships with the artist, over the last two decades numerous large projects evolved in the US and across the world. The prestigious list of contem-

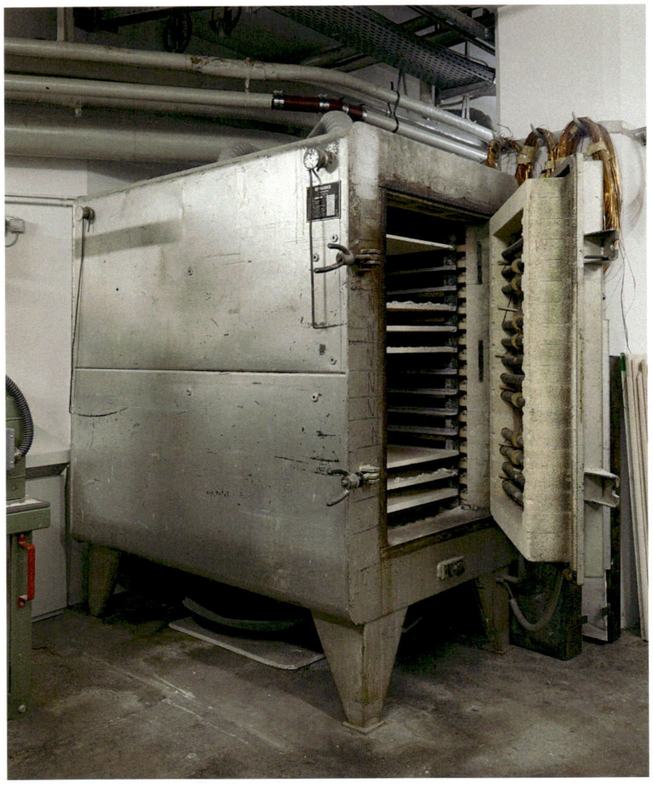

67
BETWEEN THEN AND NOW: An old Riedhammer kiln, dated circa1948

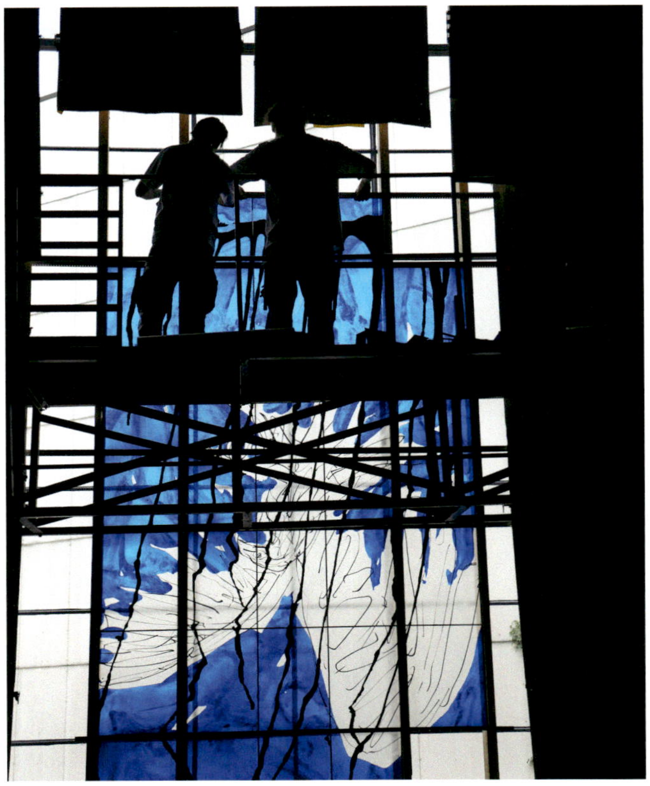

68
ART TODAY, stained glass window by Georg Baselitz during set up in the exhibition gallery, 2012

porary artists includes: Brian Clarke, Julien Opie, Robert Mangold, Alyson Shotz, Martha Schwartz, Eric Fischl, Mel Bochner, Kiki Smith, and Robert Wilson; and for Germany Imi Knoebel and Georg Baselitz, to name but a few.

British artist Brian Clarke is a wonderful example to illuminate how much famous artists appreciate the Hofkunstanstalt's expertise and knowledge of modern technologies. By now, he has collaborated with Gabriel and Michael Meyer, exclusively, for almost two decades: "In the small … churches around Lancashire, where I was born and grew up and which I visited regularly, I became aware of a stained glass, that came from something called Mayer of Munich. And they were mostly by an English artist called Francis Dixon. So from a very early age, from the age of let us say 15 years old, I was aware, that there was this studio in Munich. I wasn't quite sure, where Munich was, but I knew, it wasn't in Lancashire. 1974 I visited Munich and met Mr. Michael C. Mayer's grandfather and father and I was profoundly conscious, that this was more than a commercial operation. And so when I come here, I feel, I'm coming home and I'm coming to join with friends and colleagues, who have the same focus as me." [82]

Enthusiasm and shared interests have increased since 1982, when Brian Clarke and others worked with the Hofkunstanstalt on the mosque of King Khaled International Airport in Riyadh. Starting in 1993, big projects followed almost annually: The synagogue in Heidelberg (1993), *The Glass Wall* (dedicated to Linda McCartney) for the Corning Museum of Glass in Corning, NY (1994), the Norte-Shopping Center in Rio de Janeiro (1995/96), the monastery church of the Cistercian nuns in Romont, Switzerland (1996), the headquarters of the pharmaceutical company Pfizer in New York (from

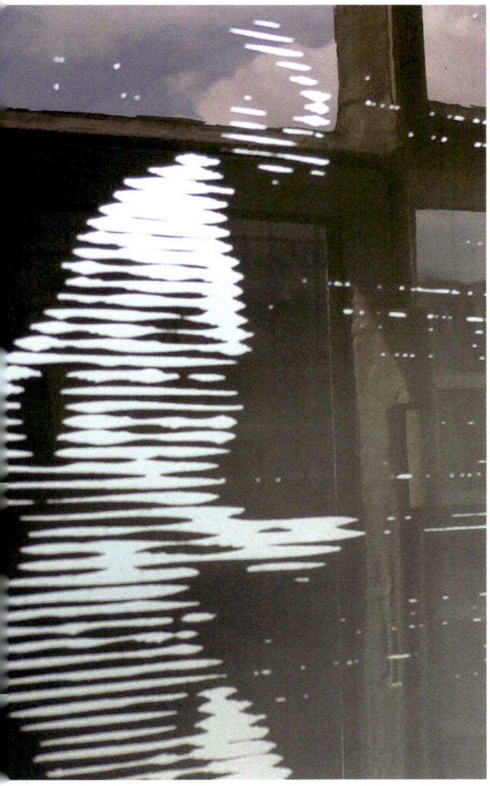

69

TODAY: detail from a float glass painting design for a private home, Felix Weinold, 2007

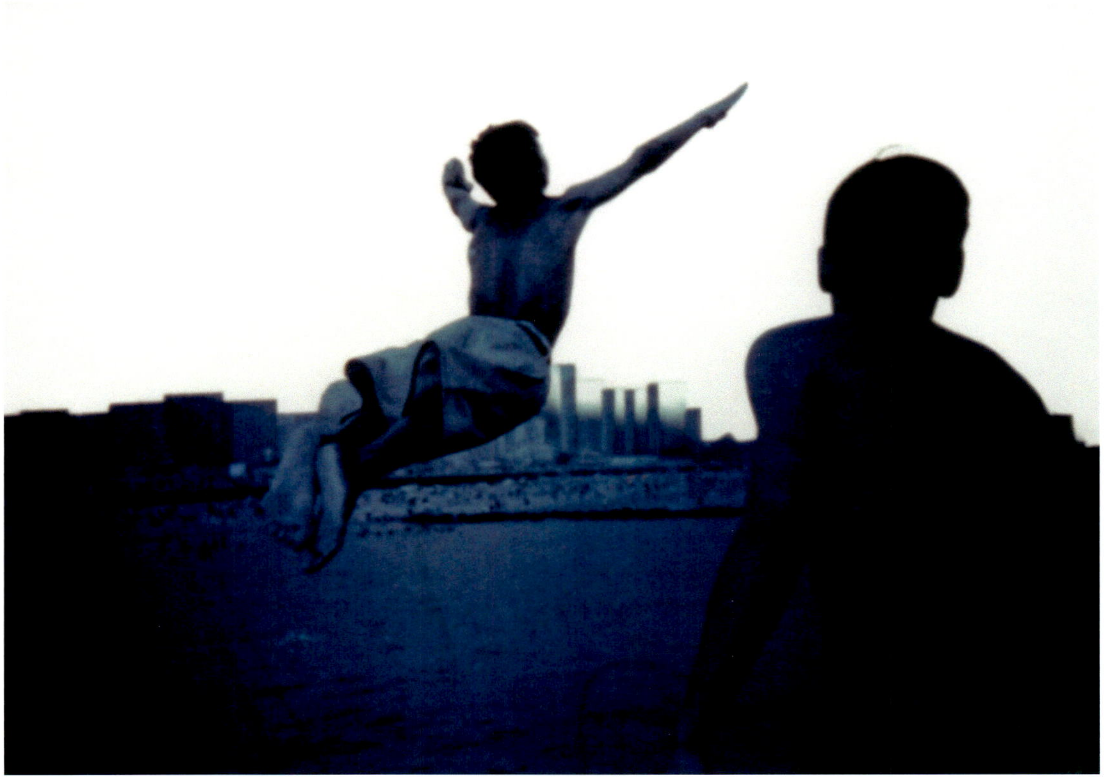

70

BETWEEN YESTERDAY AND TOMORROW: glass panel of an unknown photographer with a LOMO camera, LOMO exhibition, Mayer'sche Hofkunstanstalt, 1995

1996), the Sinai Synagogue in Chicago (1997), *Stamford Cone* in Stamford, CT (1998), and many more. In 2008 Clarke noted: "Over the years we worked on a variety of projects and I suppose principally I'm best known in this field for the very big grand, big scale projects, like the King Faisal-Foundation in Riyadh or the Pyramid of Peace in Kazakhstan, which we did last year, which is a great pyramidical structure, that was designed by Norman Foster. The apex of the structure contains images of a flock of doves swirling around to the apex and that creates an environmental atmosphere. So the stained glass in that context creates an entire environment. You are not then going into a building to look at a window, but you are consumed and surrounded by it. And so basically I suppose the criteria for choice is, when we are asked to do a project: Is this project something, where we can extend our artistic language? Is this project something, where we can at least hope to create an experience, that might be engaging or entertaining or perhaps even sublime?" [83]

The equivalent to the US concept of "Public Art" in Germany is "Kunst am Bau" (i.e. Percent for Art Program). The latter developed after World War Two and was closely connected to the democratically structured society. Its foremost intention was to offer social assistance and commissions for creative individuals. This explains why a certain percentage of the total cost was legally stipulated for "Kunst am Bau," which, until the 1960s, was practiced in West Germany with some consequence and a certain degree of success. However, the effect was the specialization of a few building-artists and inevitably a severe restriction of artistic diversity and quality. In the late 1960s, "Kunst am Bau" drifted off, due to a lack of creativity and enthusiasm. Apart from the few prestige projects, today the "Kunst am Bau" movement has degenerated into an

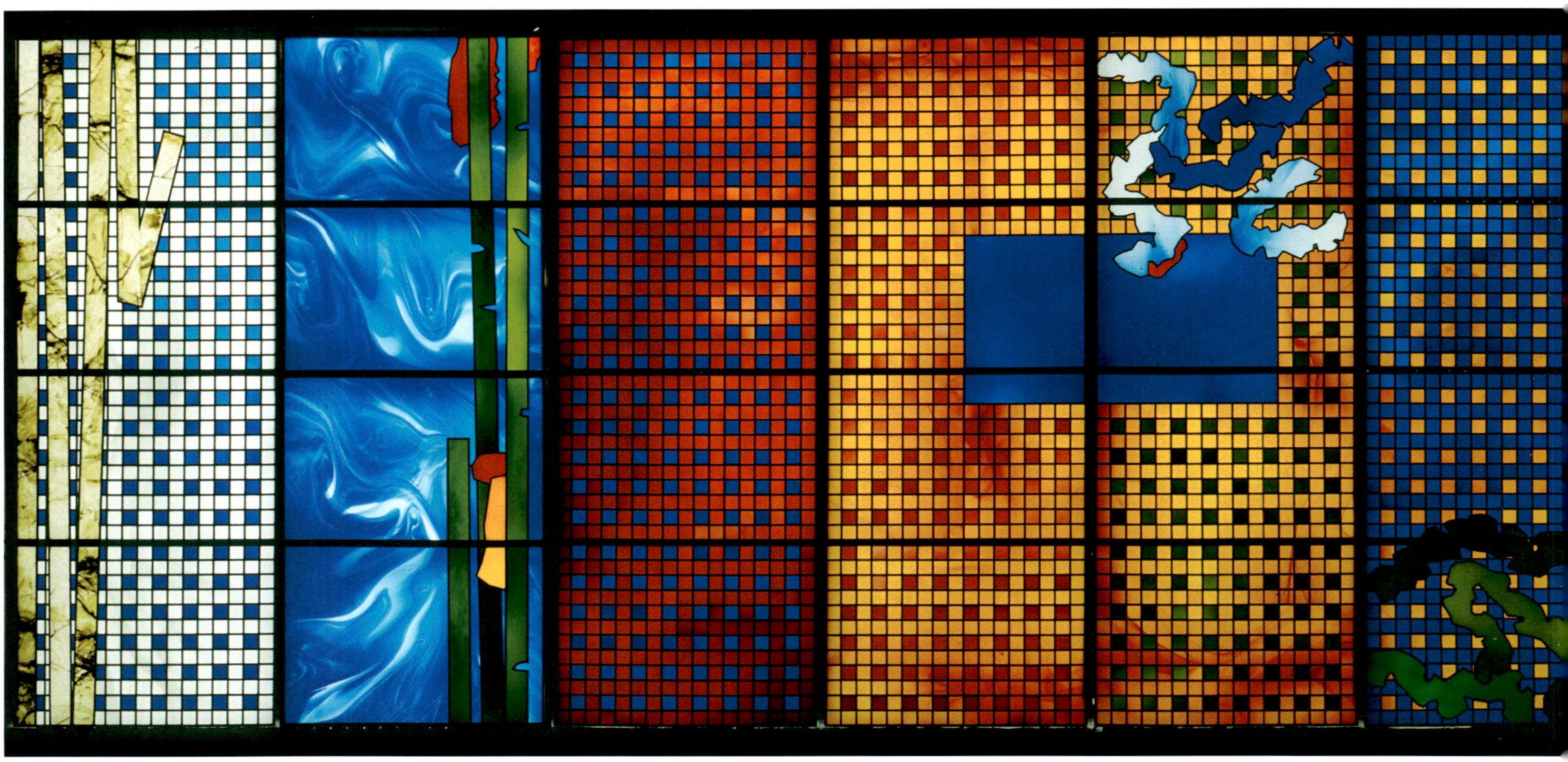

71
GLAXO HEADQUARTERS, LONDON, curved stained glass wall with hand-blown glass and onyx from Pakistan, Brian Clarke, 1990/91

unloved administrative act. In many places, art, decoration and embellishment are considered superfluous. Instead of seriously striving for quality in accord with art and architecture we are often confronted with regulations, limitations, and doubts. The Mayer'sche Hofkunstanstalt's international activities enable it to show its work in splendid ways, pointing out just how well it can be done. Like no other company, it ennobles mosaic technologies through innovation and, even more importantly, thanks to the multiple possibilities of applying the new float glass technique, to the arts of glass and mosaic. The term "Kunst am Bau" does not do justice to its large-scale projects. Instead, the Hofkunstanstalt is the place where an eminent and innovative architectural art points the way to the future.

The firm has thereby attained a deep understanding vis-à-vis the needs of the present. Its high degree of empathy and respect for traditional as well as innovative solutions are among its distinguishing characteristics, culminating in the joy of experiments and the mutually beneficial cooperation with exceptional artists. May Gabriel Mayer's apodictic motto come true:

"We need art in architecture like our daily bread. But it must be good!"

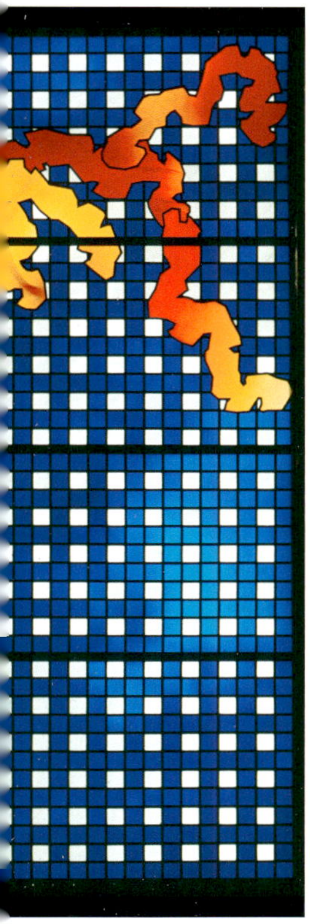

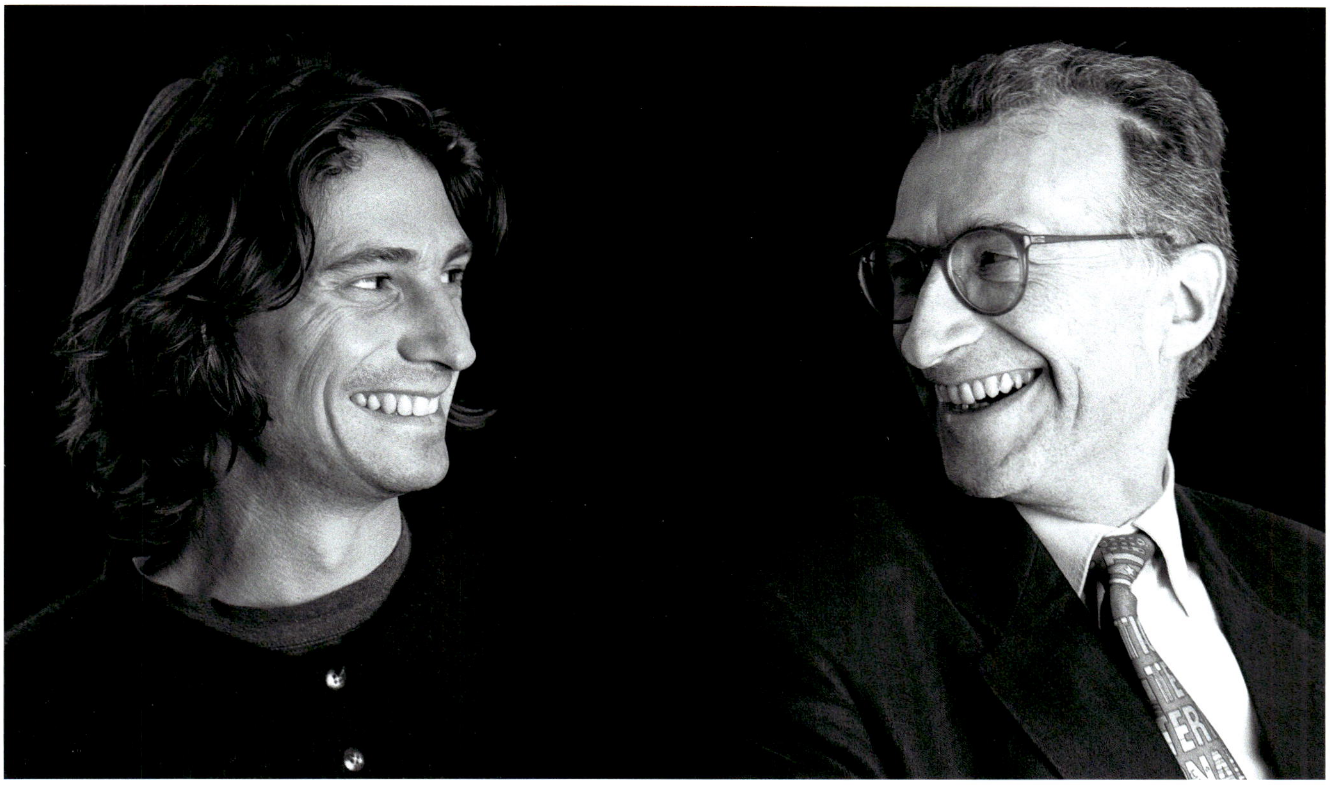

72

MEMBERS OF MAYER FAMILY CURRENTLY ACTIVE: right Gabriel Mayer, 4th generation (born 1938), left Michael C. Mayer, 5th generation (born 1967), 1998

Trained as an Art Historian, Historian, and in German Studies, Dr. Bernhard Graf was born in 1962 in the Lower Bavarian town of Landshut. He is an adjunct professor at the universities of Munich and Darmstadt. His international fame is based on scholarly books and articles, on conceiving reknowned exhibitions and on his work as screenplay writer and director for the Bayerischer Rundfunk, where he created numerous historic, art, and cultural documentaries. In his documentary film, 'Munich's Stained glass Conquers the World' (2008), he stressed the global importance of Mayer of Munich.

[1] Cf. Rudolf Reiser: König Ludwig I. in Rom. Im Paradies zwischen deutschen Malern und schönen Mädchen, Munich 2005, p. 17–86

[2] Quoted after Konrad Mayer: Franz Mayer'sche Hofkunstanstalt, gegründet 1847. Eine Münchner Unternehmensbiographie, part I: Die 1. Generation, 1847–1883, Munich 2001, p. 15

[3] Cf. Mayer, like fn. 2, p. 93: "The big challenge I envisioned was to unite the fine arts – architecture, sculpture, and painting – to connect them with technology and then to reintroduce the medieval masonry workshops, which created so many great things, especially in the ecclesiastical realm."

[4] Suzanne Beeh-Lustenberger: Dem Licht Farbe gegeben. 150 Jahre Franz Mayer'sche Hofkunstanstalt 1847–1997, in: Das Münster, vol. 51, issue 1, 1998, p. 36

[5] Quoted after Mayer, like fn. 2, p. 21

[6] Quoted after Mayer, like fn. 2, p. 21

[7] Quoted after: Egon Caesar Conte Corti: Ludwig I. von Bayern. Ein Ringen um Freiheit, Schönheit und Liebe, nach dem schriftlichen Nachlass des Königs und zahllosen sonstigen unveröffentlichten Dokumenten, Munich 1937, p. 541

[8] Quoted after Hubert Glaser: in: Wittelsbach. Kurfürsten im Reich – Könige von Bayern, eds. Hubert Glaser and Reinhold Baumstark, Exhib. cat. Bayerisches Nationalmuseum, Munich 1993, p. 56–58

[9] Quoted after Wilhelm und Caroline von Humboldt in ihren Briefen, vol. III, Berlin 1909, p. 7

[10] Quoted after Winfried Nerdinger (ed.): Romantik und Restauration. Architektur in der Zeit Ludwigs I. 1825–1849, Munich 1987, p. 122

[11] Cf. the critical acclaim when a memorial plaque was installed in 1890 in the Upper Bavarian chronicle volumes and the annual reports of the Chamber of Commerce for Upper Bavaria

[12] Elgin Vaassen: Bilder auf Glas, Glasgemälde zwischen 1780 und 1870, Munich, Berlin 1997, p. 178

[13] Elgin Vaassen: Notizen zu Leben und Werk des Glas- und Architekturmalers Max Emanuel Ainmiller (1807–1870), in: Schriften des Historischen Vereins Murnau am Staffelsee e.V., vol. 8, issue 12, Murnau 1987, p. 7

[14] Cf. extensively Vaassen, like fn. 12, p. 191 f.

[15] Cf. extensively Vaassen, like fn. 12, p. 195

[16] Cf. extensively Elgin Vaassen: Die Glasgemälde des 19. Jahrhunderts im Dom zu Regensburg, Stiftungen König Ludwigs I. von Bayern 1827–1857, Regensburg 2007, p. 9–122

[17] Cf. Vaassen, like fn. 12, p. 192–195

[18] Vaassen, like fn. 12, p. 195, 219

[19] Vaassen, like fn. 12, p. 219

[20] Extensively in Vaassen, like fn. 12, p. 249–269; among them Josef Peter Bockhorni, Heinrich J. Burmester, Gottlieb and Karl Hildebrand, Ignaz Hirschvogel, Ignaz Neumair, Josef Lechenbauer, Friedrich Dorn, Wilhelm Götz, Julius Kühn, Nathan Prager, Karl Eduard Rederer, Carl de Bouché, Franz Emil Gnant, Josef Hannes and Anton Wieninger, Joseph Gabriel Mayer, Johann Baptiste Rossmann, Otto Friedrich Wörner, Georg Boos, Gustav van Treeck, and Franz Xaver Zettler

[21] Cf. Franz Mayer of Munich and F. X. Zettler: A Short Historic Survey, ed. by the Mayer'sche Hofkunstanstalt GmbH, Munich 2009, p. 6

[22] Quoted after Mayer, like fn. 2, p. 15

[23] Mayer, like fn. 2, p. 84

[24] Mayer, like fn. 2, p. 85

[25] Joseph Gabriel Mayer: Meine Biographie, Munich 1872: "In 1867 our space turned out to be too small once more due to the increased number of workers. Therefore, we proceeded to construct an adequate new edifice in 1868/69. At the same time we introduced a workshop for glass painting."

[26] Quoted after Vaassen, like fn. 12, p. 259

[27] "In 1865, we founded a branch in London to serve England. I first had the opportunity to introduce my art products there in 1851, when there was already quite some demand for them." Mayer, like fn. 25

[28] Cf. Mayer, like fn. 2, p. 95; the inscription on the plaque (translated): "Statues, Altars, Paintings, Bronze & Zink-Foundry, Mayer'sche Kunstanstalt for ecclesiastical works in Munich Stiegelmeier Platz N.° 1, New York 52 Barclay Street, London 70 Grosvenor-St., Paris 23 rue St. Sulpice, Jos. Gab. Mayer, Knight of the Papal Order of St. Gregory, Director."

[29] Cf. extensively Joseph Ludwig Fischer: Vierzig Jahre Glasmalkunst, Festschrift der Kgl. Bayerischen Hofglasmalerei F. X. Zettler zum Gedächtnis ihres vierzigjährigen Bestehens, Munich 1910, p. 35–39; Jean M. Farnsworth, Carmen R. Croce, and Joseph F. Chorpenning O.S.F.S: Stained Class in Catholic Philadelphia, Philadelphia 2002; Vaassen, like fn. 12, p. 262–266. "In the spring of 1870 my son in law, F. X. Zettler, left our institution. As a consequence, I gave him the glass painting for himself, thereby following his wishes. Yet glass painting remained closely connected with the institution." Mayer, like fn. 27

[30] Beeh-Lustenberger, like fn. 4, p. 36

[31] Extensively on the Zettler enterprise see Farnsworth et al., like fn. 29, p. 27: in the US, Franz Xaver Zettler was represented by the Draprato-Statuary-Society in Chicago und New York City

[32] Mayer, like fn. 2, p. 94

[33] Quoted after Mayer, like fn. 2, p. 9

[34] Cf. Karl Mayer: Die Aera Franz Borgias Mayer, Munich 1950 (manuscript)

[35] Farnsworth et al., like fn. 29, p. 27

[36] Cf. Die F. Mayer'sche Hofkunstanstalt und Firma Zettler; quoted after the chronicles of Upper Bavaria and the annual reports of the Handels- und Gewerbekammer für Oberbayern for the year 1892 at Munich's Stadtarchiv

[37] Farnsworth et al., like fn. 29, p. 27. The 1899 annual report of Zettler states: "The expenses for US-customs are, as the firm decries, still as high as before (45 %), making all exports second to impossible."

[38] Farnsworth et al., like fn. 29, p. 27

[39] Mayer, like fn. 2, p. 91

[40] Cf. Franz Mayer of Munich, like fn. 21, p. 13

[41] Franz Mayer of Munich, like fn. 21, p. 42

[42] Beeh-Lustenberger, like fn. 4, p. 38

[43] Cf. Franz Mayer of Munich, like fn. 21, p. 40

[44] Cf. Michael Bringmann: Gedanken zur Wiederaufnahme staufischer Bauformen im späten 19. Jahrhundert, in: Die Zeit der Staufer. Geschichte, Kunst, Kultur, exh. cat. Württembergisches Landesmuseum, vol. V, Stuttgart 1977, p. 581–620

[45] Adolf Loos: Ornament and Crime, 1998

[46] Cf. Karl Mayer: Epilog zur Aera der Franz Mayer'schen Kunstanstalt unter Franz B. Mayer, Munich circa 1950 (manuscript)

[47] Cf. Franz Mayer of Munich, like fn. 21, p. 54

[48] Cf. the term Alt-Stil-Fenster (i.e. old style windows) in Beeh-Lustenberger, like fn. 4, p. 38

[49] Cf. Franz Mayer of Munich, like fn. 21, p. 54

[50] Cf. Franz Mayer of Munich, like fn. 21, p. 41

[51] Cf. Clemens Spengler: Die Franz Mayer'sche Hofkunstanstalt in München, Munich 1945; Beeh-Lustenberger, like fn. 4, p. 40

[52] Konrad Mayer: Speech at Karl Knappe's grave on March 24, 1970: "We from the Mayer'sche Hofkunstanstalt are standing at the grave of a man with whom we have collaborated for over 50 years. We had the privilege to follow the artistic path of the deceased, accompany him and help realize his visions for more than three generations."

[53] Beeh-Lustenberger, like fn. 4, p. 39

[54] Quoted after Otto Fischer: Karl Knappe, Münchner Kunstzeitschriften, Augsburg 1929, p. 11 f.

[55] Cf. Marianne Mayer: Chronik der Franz Mayer'schen Hofkunstanstalt München, Munich 1960–1978, p. 84

[56] Beeh-Lustenberger, like fn. 4, p. 39

[57] Quoted after Alfred Zacharias: Karl Knappe 80 Jahre, in: Das Münster, vol. 17, 1964, p. 399 f.

[58] Winfried Nerdinger: Theodor Fischer, Architekt und Städtebauer, Berlin and Munich 1988, p. 293 f.; Ulrich Kerkhoff: Eine Abkehr vom Historismus oder ein Weg zur Moderne. Theodor Fischer, Stuttgart 1987, p. 224 f. and 253

[59] Beeh-Lustenberger, like fn. 4, p. 39

[60] Farnsworth et al., like fn. 29, p. 27

[61] Marianne Mayer: Chronik der Franz Mayer'schen Hofkunstanstalt München, beginnend mit ihrer Zerstörung 1944 und ihrem Wiederaufbau nach Kriegsende, Munich 1955, p. 5, 14

[62] Karl Mayer: Bericht, in: Mayer, like fn. 61, p. 7

[63] Anton Mayer: Bericht, in: Mayer, like fn. 61, p. 16 f.

[64] Mayer, like fn. 61, p. 16

[65] Mayer, like fn. 61, p. 25

[66] Mayer, like fn. 61, p. 48

[67] Mayer, like fn. 61, p. 32: In September 1945, Konrad Mayer began to work at the Hofkunstanstalt, replacing glass painter and mosaicist Johannes Kern, who had left.

[68] Quoted after Zacharias, like fn. 57, p. 399 f.

[69] Extensive biography in Peter Schmitt: Hans Gottfried von Stockhausen. Das Glasbild, Munich 1987, p. 49 f.

[70] Beeh-Lustenberger, like fn. 4, p. 44

[71] Cf. Bert Hauser in a conversation with Hans Gottfried von Stockhausen, in: Hans Gottfried von Stockhausen, like fn. 69, p. 25

[72] Doris Schmidt: Glasmalereien von Carl Crodel in der Frankfurter Katharinenkirche, Frankfurt am Main 1956, p. 8; Beeh-Lustenberger, like fn. 4, p. 46

[73] Thomas Ehlert: Hauptkirche St. Jacobi zu Hamburg, Hamburg 1988, p. 18

[74] Robert Slawski: St. Andreaskirche Braunschweig, Kiel n.y., p. 1 f., 9 f.

[75] Cf. Hans Habermann: Zur Durchführung der Maßnahme, in: Dom zu Regensburg. Neue Glasgemälde von Prof. Josef Oberberger, Regensburg 1990

[76] Reinhard Müller-Mehlis: Neue Arbeiten. Aus der Mayerischen Hofkunstanstalt München, offprint from: Das Münster, vol. 22, issue 3, 1969, p. 149 f.

[77] After years of practical experience, he took over; cf. Mayer, like fn. 61; Munich, August 1962: "August 1; Gabi begins to work at the firm. At first in the glazier's shop. He is supposed to learn the technical side from scratch."

[78] Extensively in Theodor C. Barker: The Glassmakers: Pilkington, the Rise of an International Company, 1826–1976, London 1977, p. 75; the same: Pilkington Brothers and the Glass Industry, London 1961

[79] Cf. Michael C. Mayer: Franz Mayer'sche Hofkunstanstalt, Munich 1994, p. 29

[80] Beeh-Lustenberger, like fn. 4, p. 51

[81] Cf. Franz Mayer of Munich, like fn. 21, p. 70

[82] Brian Clarke's statement, in Bernhard Graf: Die Münchner Glaskunst erobert die Welt, Munich 2008, p. 2

[83] Clarke, like fn. 82, p. 16

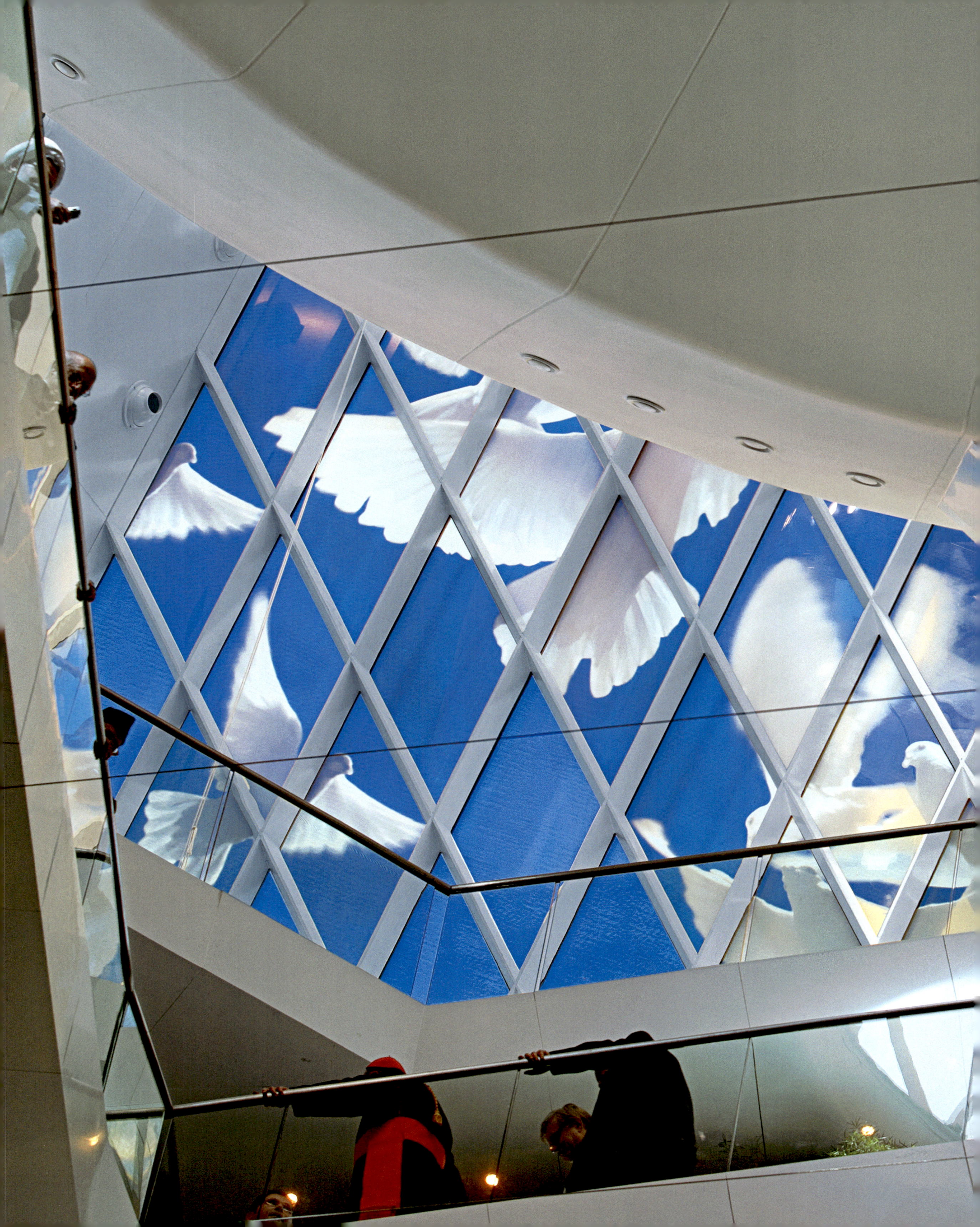

PROJECTS

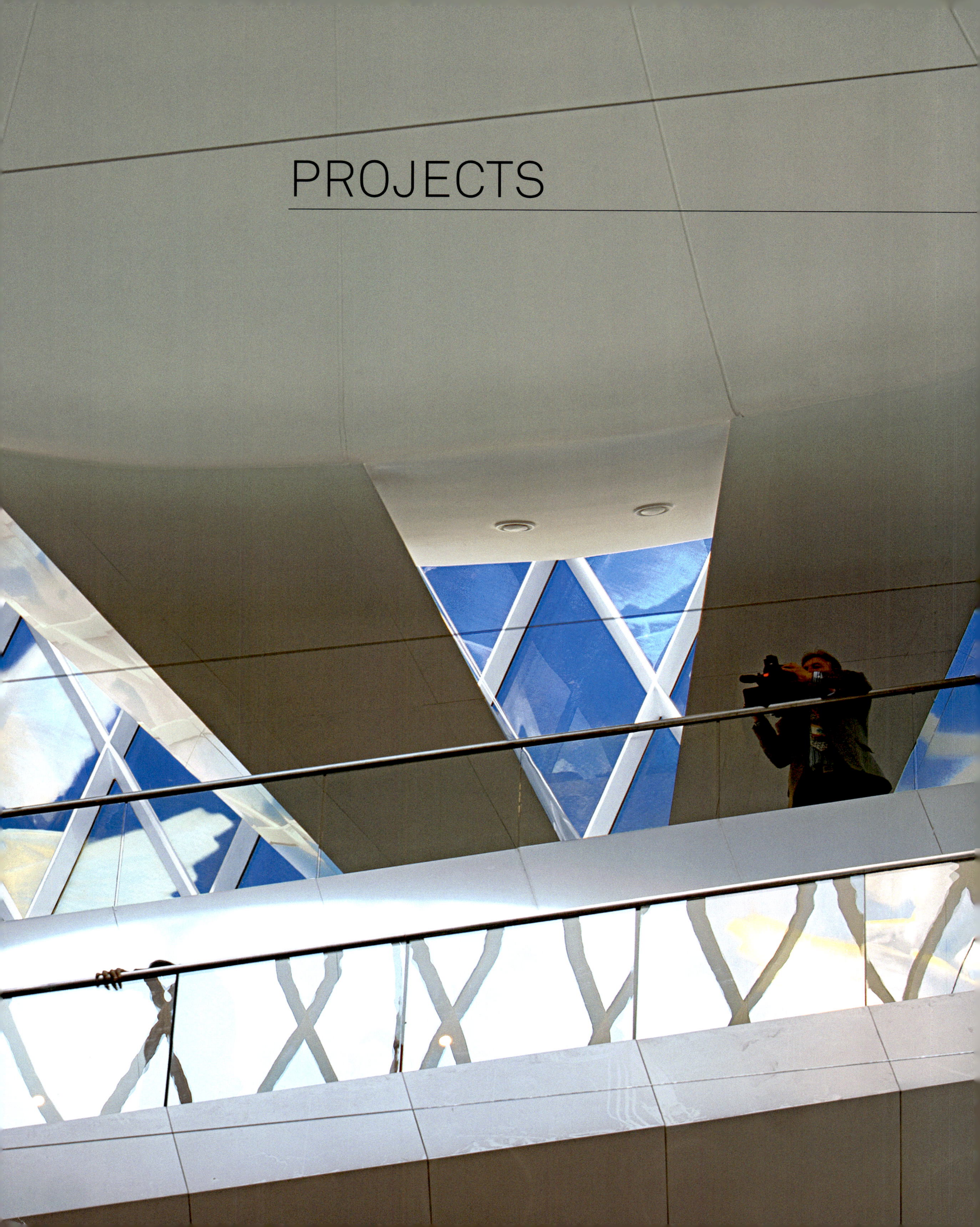

An Avant-garde Studio

The Mayer'sche Hofkunstanstalt as a laboratory for new technologies

Gottfried Knapp

Anyone familiar with the often depressing quality of "mandatory artworks" realized through the German Percent for Art Program will be amazed by catalogues of the Mayer glass studios, which show a collection of decidedly modern art objects. This is especially astonishing since the latter's works are executed using the ancient techniques of mosaic or stained glass, art forms declared dead during the course of history and especially in most recent times. Some of these secular works of art are gigantic: Occupying public spaces with great ease, only very few of them were intended to remain in Germany.

It appears that people in major cities like New York or London are much more at ease with playful images in public spaces. There, one encounters shiny and colorfully patterned walls populating central public transport hubs, giving a face to neutral interiors. Some of the areas one comes across are overwhelmingly large and cannot be designed using traditional technologies. One discovers colorful compositions filling multi-storey stairwells; virtuoso collages made of photographs and fragments from reality give structure to overlong hallways; some pieces even convey narrative qualities.

You really must visualize such impressive, aesthetically dominated spaces as your goal if you want to comprehend what is customarily commissioned from and created by the Mayer'sche Hofkunstanstalt's studios. In principle, nothing has changed since the 19th c. when creative glass painter geniuses and uncounted copyists once again began working in the revived technique. As is the case in all the arts, there is a distinct difference between the high aspiration of innovative artistic dimensions demanding creativity and routinely produced mediocrity.

The old art of glass painting, making images from translucent colored glass, was revived in the first third of the 19th c. as part of rediscovering forgotten arts. In Munich, King Ludwig I of Bavaria took the crucial step into the future: Passionate about the great epochs of the past, in 1827, the art enthusiast founded the "Königliche Glasmalereianstalt," a highly successful institution for research into the redevelopment of ancient art. Before too long, the workshops began producing painted and leaded glass windows for such famous Gothic cathedrals as Cologne and Regensburg.

Founded in 1847 by Joseph Gabriel Mayer in Munich, the "Institut für christliche Kunst" (i.e. Institute for Christian Art), was a successful family enterprise from the beginning, creatively enhancing the traditions of the Königliche Glasmalereianstalt. During the decades of Historicism the studio – retaining its name Mayer'sche Hofkunstanstalt to this day – was one of the international leaders in the field of stained glass. Today, the institute

FIG. PAGES 44 + 45:
VIEW INTO THE INTERIOR OF THE PYRAMID'S APEX WITH THE ART GLASS PROJECT. Architects Foster + Partners, glass design Brian Clarke and Franz Mayer of Munich (see artist portrait Brian Clarke, p. 234)

is considered one of the leaders in the realm of Gothic and Neo-Gothic glass conservation.

The daring steps, however, the studio took towards Modernism during the course of the 20th c. were directed towards future success. To this day, the firm's workshops offer a plethora of innovative technical possibilities, giving full justice to the multiple requirements of the even youngest generation of artists. What was once a venerable old studio for stained glass and mosaics, where highly specialized craftspeople recreated images empathizing the old styles, now has turned into a modern studio-laboratory of technically commanding caliber. Here, artists interested in the medium glass or in mosaic technology can become active themselves and collaborate with the studio and master craftsmen who work there.

Recent developments in the field of stained glass and glass painting result in radically new design possibilities. Comparatively speaking, to this day, mosaic art tends to be fabricated largely based on the traditional artisanal principles. There is a fundamental difference between ancient mosaics – they tend to emphasize the outline and are intended as more graphic than painterly – customary during the early flourishing of this art type, and the highly abstract informal wall paintings composed after World War Two or painterly images, lately executed by painters in love with *peinture.*

Today, artists like to turn to the medium's astonishing illusionistic possibilities: Mayer employees produced Eric Fischl's atmospheric views of light-drenched beach scenes from thousands of colored tesserae. Ellen Harvey had her eleven huge and lofty images of clouds located on a 250 feet long wall within a busy New York subway station. These examples demonstrate most impressively how colored stone fragments may be used to create huge photographic or painterly images. While robust, these works permit the finest painterly effects to surface, making quasi-impressionistic, subtle effects possible. Due to technical reasons, this is a new type of Pointillism that invites experimentation with colors and shapes.

As in antiquity, mosaics still need a firm wall or ground behind or below them, thus limiting their public applicability. Thanks to multiple possibilities that have surfaced during the last few decades, glass painting offers an abundance of possibilities, far surpassing the potential of mosaics. When stained glass was at its peak during the Middle Ages, it was mostly restricted to a supporting role within the architectural Gesamtkunstwerk. The stress was on the translucent effects of the church window's colored glass membrane, concentrated on transmitting the light from the outside to the inside. Today, glass painting may be applied almost universally, both within and outside an architectural context.

73
***PYRAMID OF PEACE*, ASTANA, KASACHSTAN.**
Looking at the building with Brian Clarke's glass design. Architects Foster + Partners (see artist portrait Brian Clarke, p. 234)

After obtaining an overview of the pictorial opportunities available to artists working at the Mayer'sche Hofkunstanstalt's glass studios, one might feel tempted to suggest that within the field of applied arts, no material at this point offers a wider range of artistic applications than industrially fabricated float glass, produced in all conceivable grades. Float glass is the basis for all glass panel options: Thanks to the latest printing and duplication technologies and with the aid of traditional methods such as painting or drawing, it is possible to render images, colors, and designs of all conceivable types on float glass.

Artists can spontaneously apply glass melting colors to float glass, comparable to painting with a brush or using a spatula on canvas. Even the finest lines can be drawn, transposed to the glass ground with finesse and without any complications. American artist Kiki Smith has produced numerous seminal examples of this type. For his Stations of the Cross cycle at the St. Florian Church in Munich-Riem, German painter Horst Thürheimer produced 14 glass doors. They form the back of the church and lead to the courtyard. He utilized the same complex mix of techniques – painting, drawing, rubbing, wiping, burnishing – that he would use when working on paper or canvas. The result is of high painterly quality, taking advantage of the light's wide range of translucent qualities.

The glass that serves as the foundation of an image can of course be pre-dyed a certain color. Another possibility for a colored priming layer is the application of flashed glass onto the working surface. This color coat can be acid etched or sanded as desired, returning it to neutral white, rendering it translucent, or transparent. Baselitz's *Falling Eagle,* for example, with its strong white-blue contrasts, was made with blown flashed glass using this method.

Glass as base material can be handled using many additional processes. Entire panes can be sandblasted, or, if templates are applied, clearly defined areas can be sanded and made matte, roughened, or etched into the surface. Most of the modern variants of mechanical, analogue, or digital printing techniques can be applied to glass – virtually without limitations. This enables artists to work at their own leisure with pre-existing images, using their own or other's photographs, typefaces, texts, newspaper and book quotes, or abstract designs.

When exhibiting glass painting in spaces like museums, galleries, administration buildings, or transit hubs, there are plenty of options to choose from. Different color and depth effects arise according to the way in which glass objects are mounted: in front of a firm wall or a hollow space, in a window or freestanding. It is also crucial whether the partly transparent, translucent or

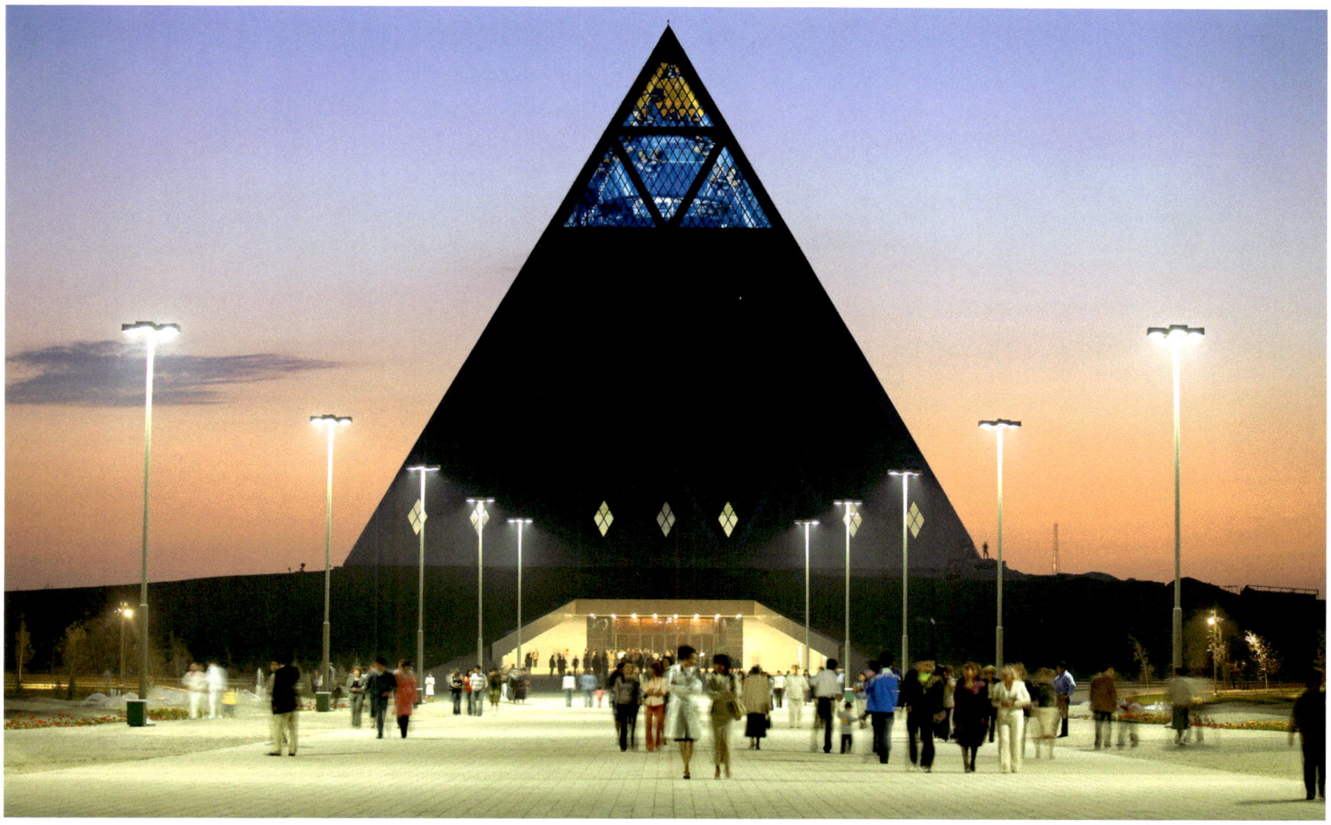

73

opaque color surface is lit from the front or from behind. It is almost impossible to conceive of a more versatile material for creating images. Hence, it appears logical to address the question of why still relatively few artists take advantage of these fabulous possibilities.

Between 1979 and 2007 Dr. Gottfried Knapp was editor for art and architecture for the Süddeutsche Zeitung. He has published numerous papers on architects, painters, sculptors, and draftsmen, as well as monographs on individual buildings. Knapp twice received the 1st prize of the German Chamber of Architects' competition among journalists as well as the journalism prize of the German National Committee for landmark preservation and the Hausenstein-Ehrung of the Bavarian Akademie der Schönen Künste, whose member he has been since 2009.

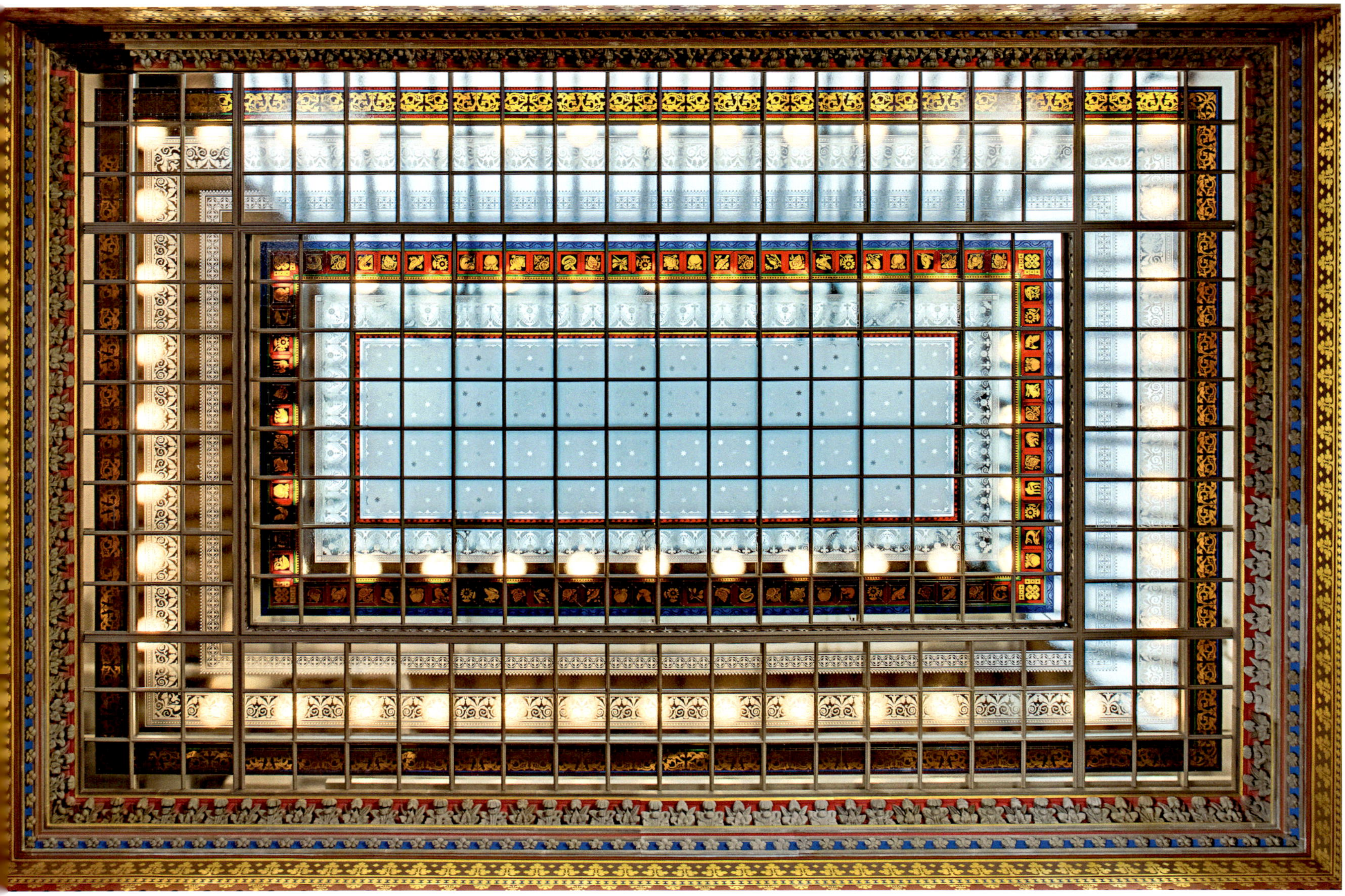

74

Albany – NYS Capitol Design Team / ornamental glass ceilings

75

50

location: New York State Capitol, Albany, NY, USA / Historic Building / **year:** 2011–12 /
technique: leaded glass, stained glass, slumped glass

The special challenge of the glass ceiling "Assembly" was the sandblasting on extremely rough glass surfaces. The design and execution of the slumped glass segments for the Senate ceiling were of paramount importance. The entire area measures approximately 3500 square feet.
The design team has been working on the conservation and the reconstruction of the two lusciously decorated stairwells in Albany's New York State Capitol for over ten years. The central task is the two glass ceilings in the stairwells of the Senate and the Assembly, planned in the early 20th century but never designed or executed.

STATE CAPITOL

74
Glass ceiling in the "Assembly" stairwell. The central portion is elevated. The sandblasting on some very rough glass surfaces required skill and diligence. Designing the stylized Flora and Fauna motifs was a great challenge.

75
The "Assembly" stairwell: red, richly worked sandstone, using templates for painting the walls, crowned by the glass ceiling.

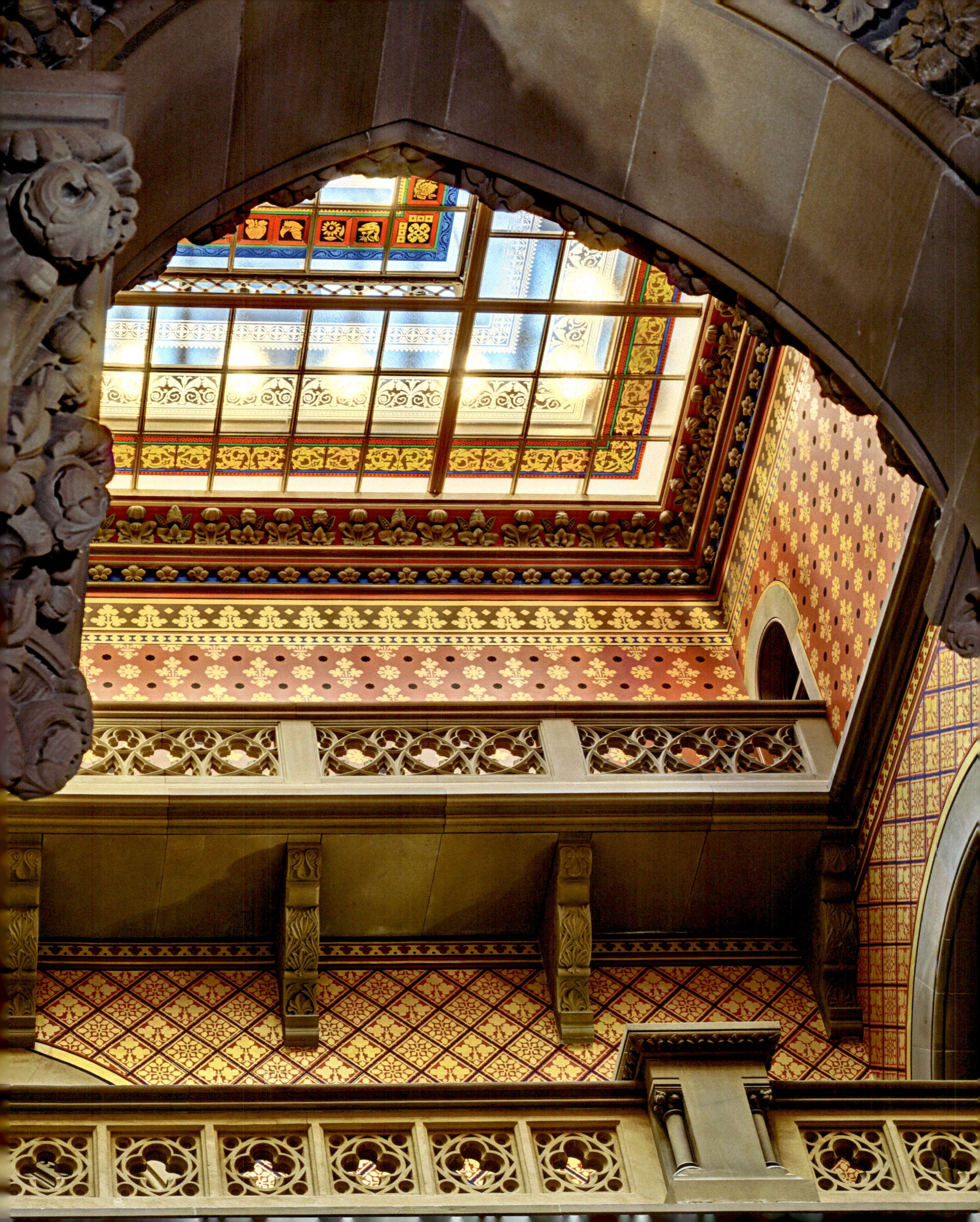

76
The north nave of the Neo-Romanesque church with new windows. The lateral windows are historic.

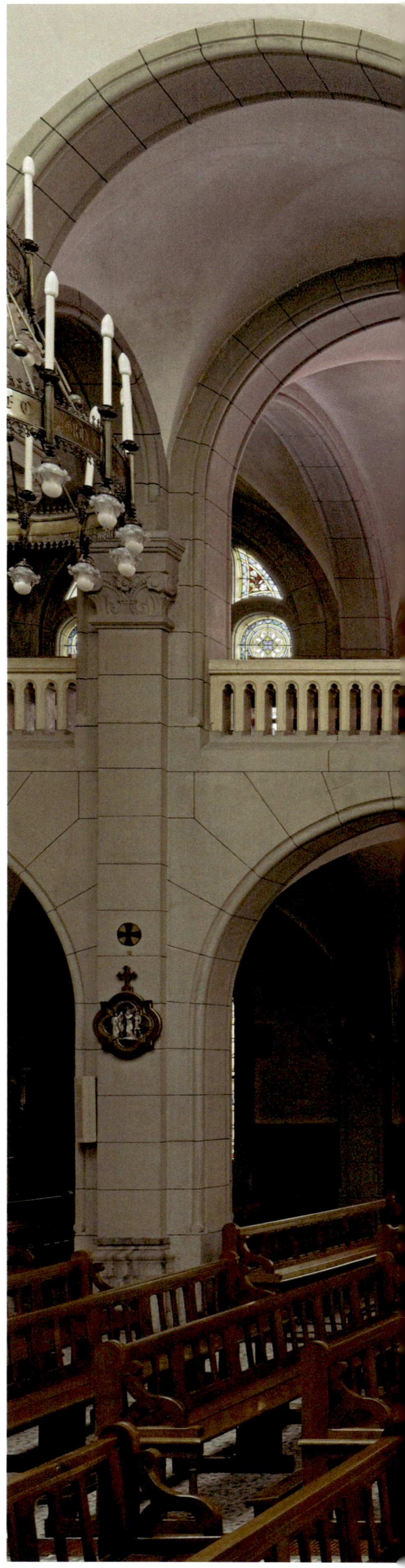

Judith Albert & Gery Hofer / "Heaven"

location: Sacré-Cœur de Montreux, Montreux, Switzerland / Historic Building / **year:** 2008–10 / **technique:** leaded glass, digital print, transparent enamel paint

Genuine antique glass, digitally printed twice with transparent glass melting colors. Cut and leaded.
The artists won a competition. The concept attempts to create a new interpretation of the 19th-century stained glass windows that were destroyed during a hail storm in 2008: "Shadow Figures" from the original windows "in front of an evening sky over the lake." They were newly created in modern glass technique and in "contemporary" Neo-Romanticism.

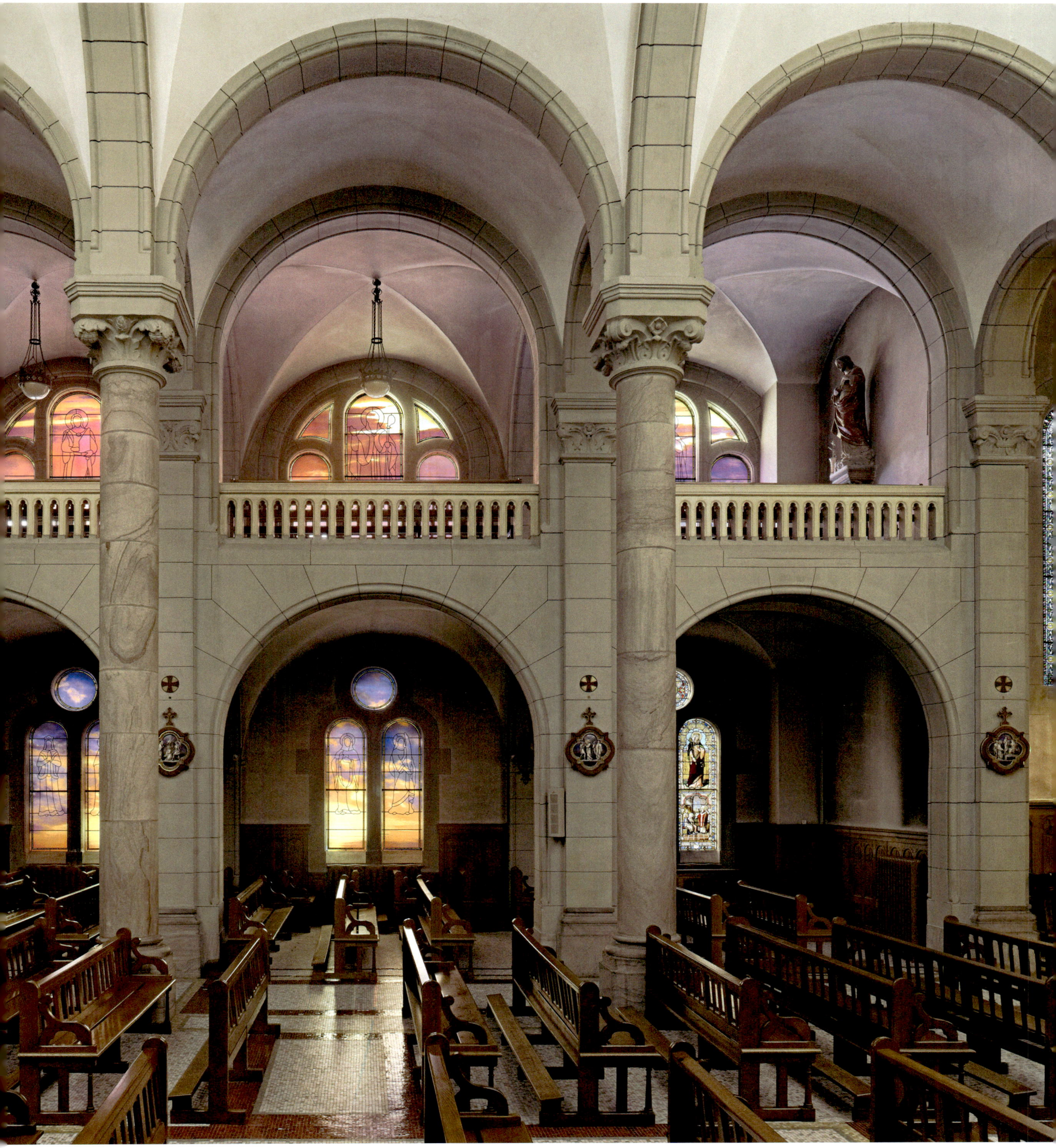

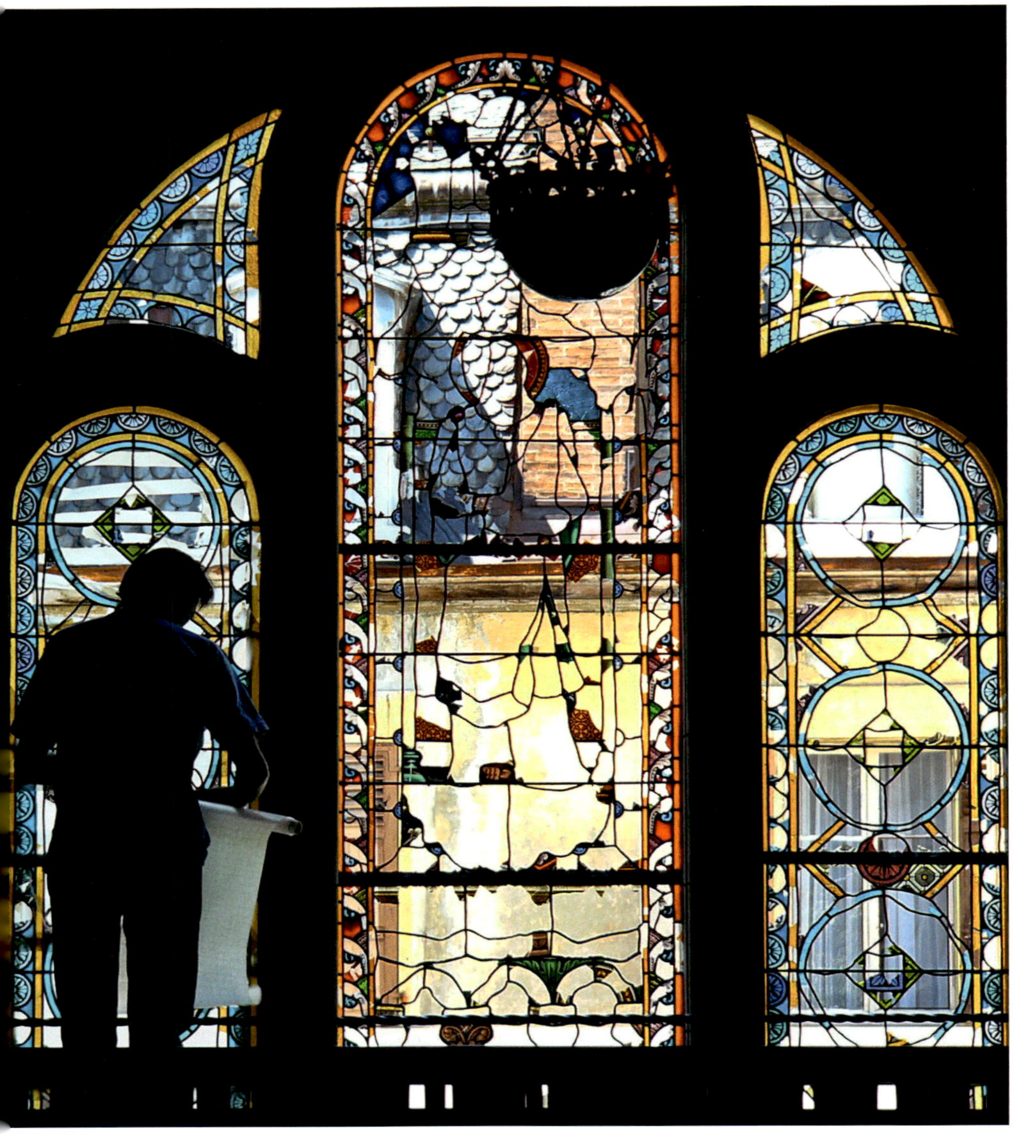

77

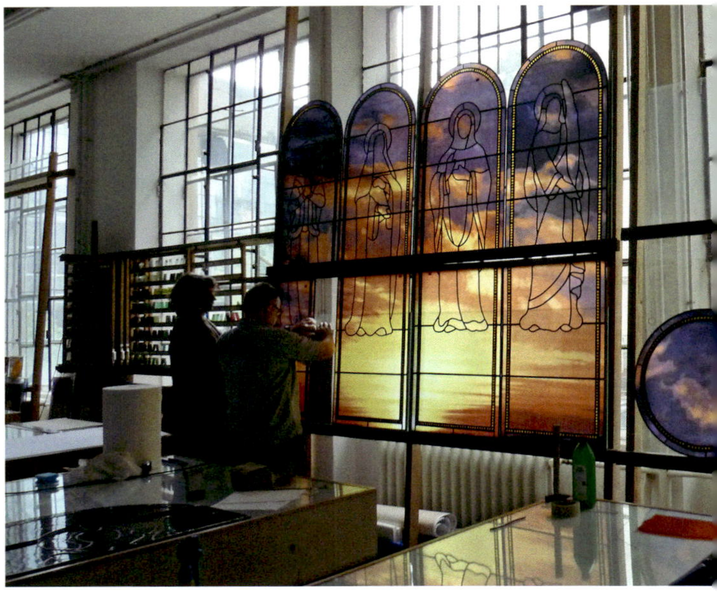

78

HEAVEN

77
The remaining net of leads after the hailstorm with remnant glass shards. Inspiration for the artists and begin of the work on site.

78
Four semicircular panels are ready to be examined.

79
The cut, painted, and fired antique glass is prepared for leading.

80
The cut glass, corresponding to the original leading pattern is affixed to the glass support and sprayed with transparent melting colors at the digital printing device, visible in the background. The utmost care is required to wax the glass for the 600° C firing process.

81
The first experimental glass panels.

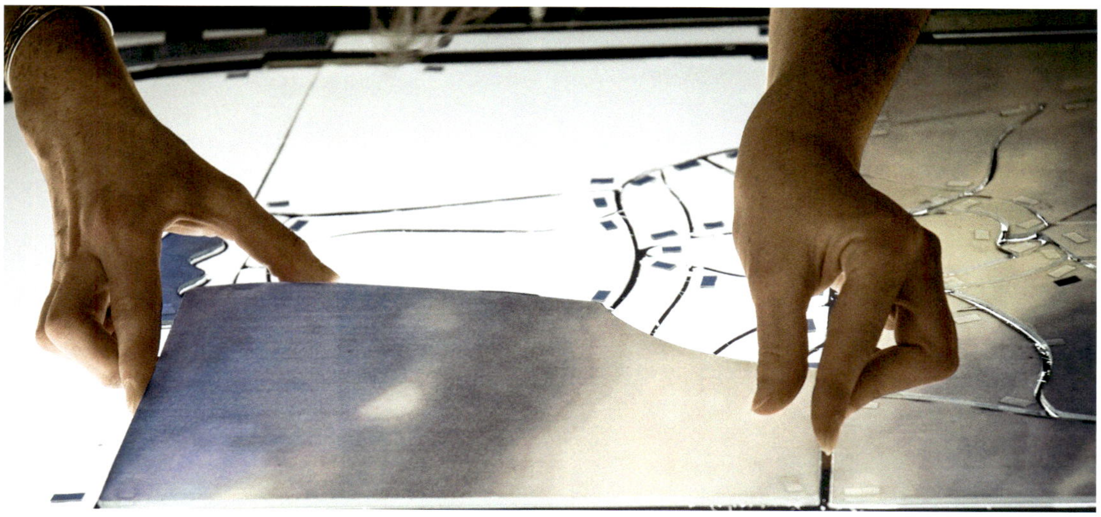

79

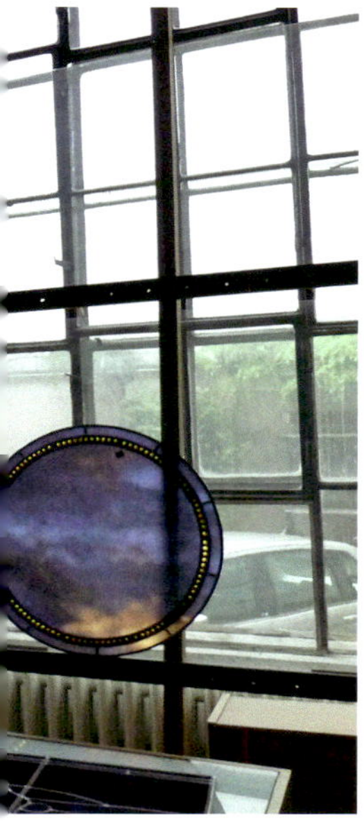

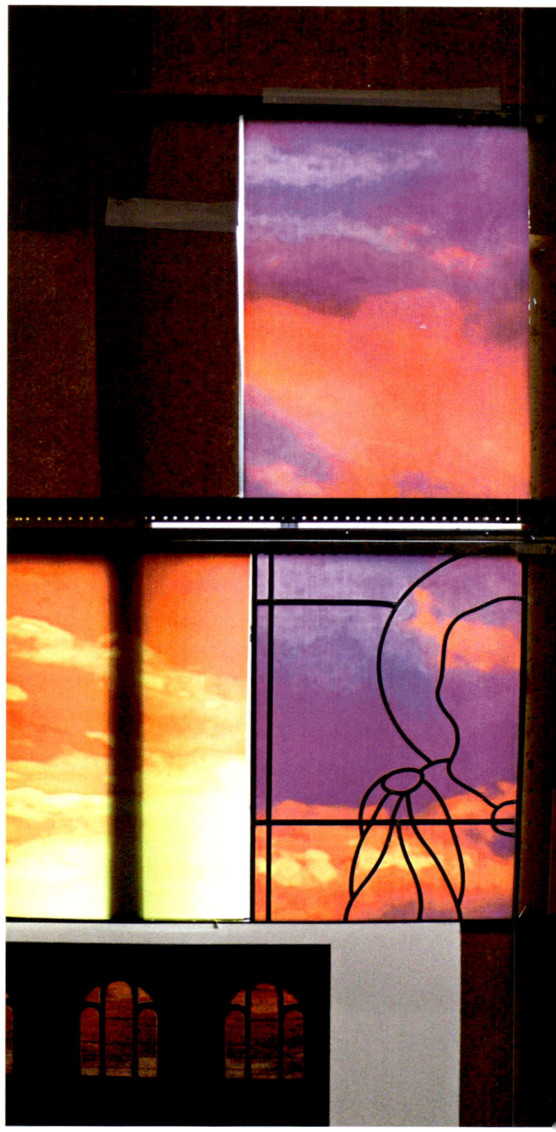

80

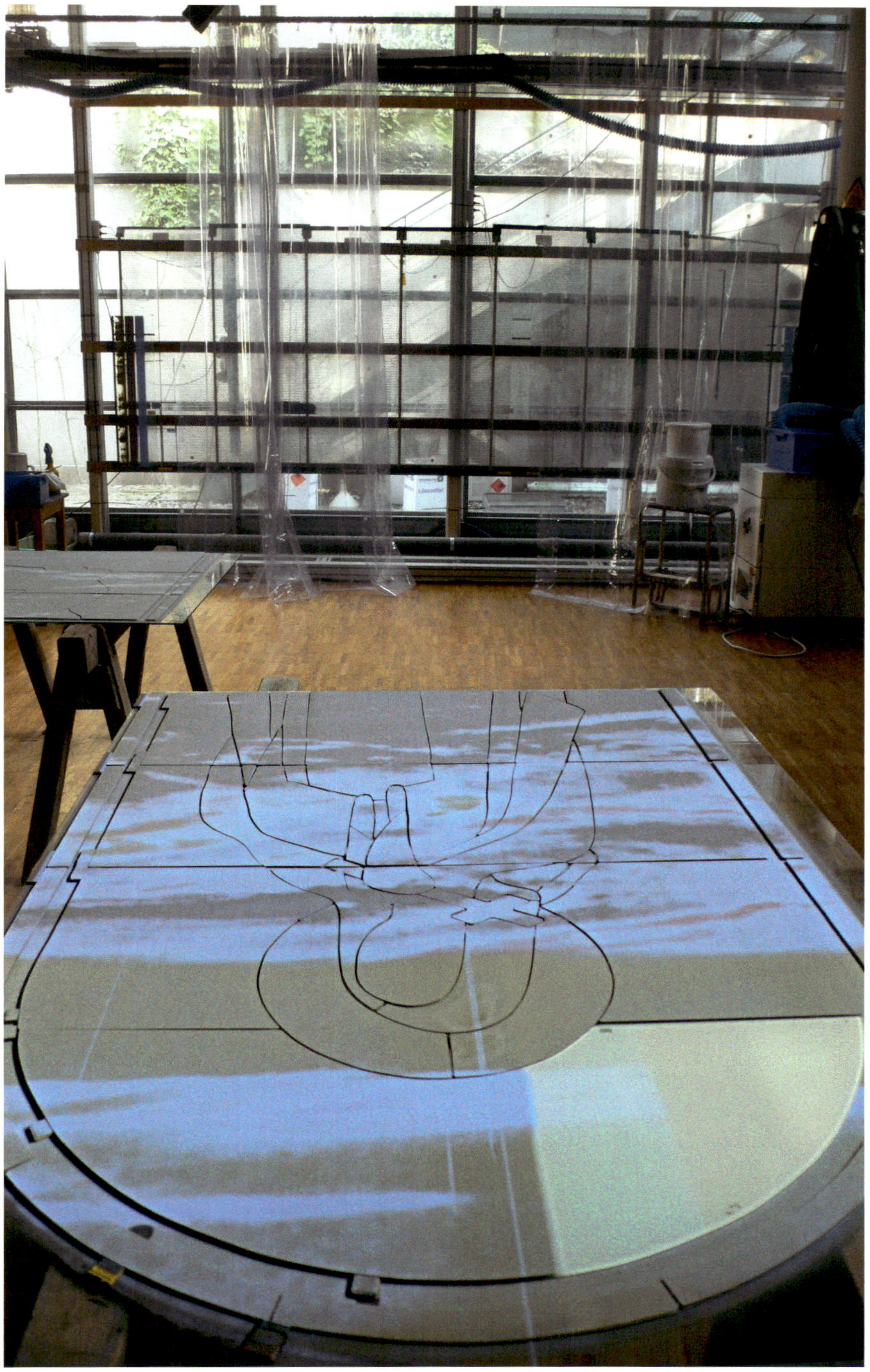

81

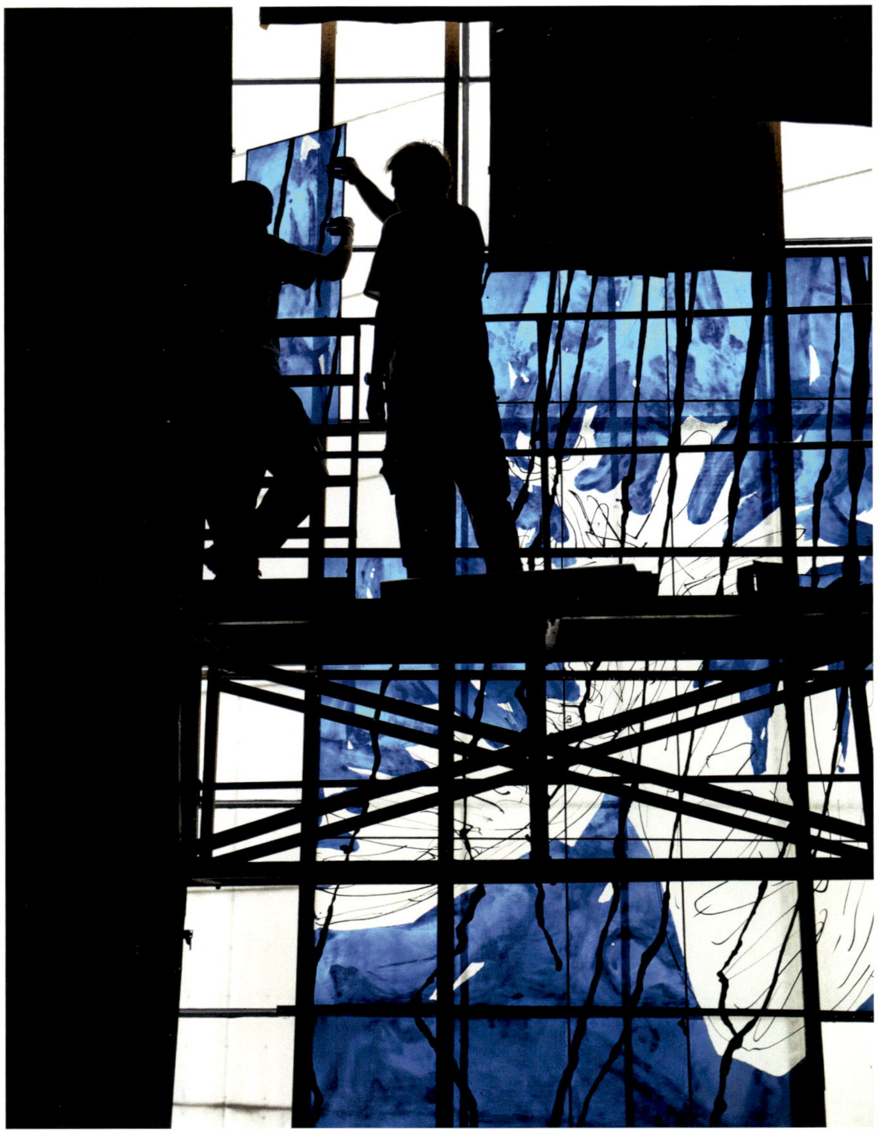

82

EAGLE 2011 STAINED GLASS

82 The almost completed glass window during installation at the Hofkunstanstalt's exhibition gallery.

83 The glass window, mounted and framed for the detailed examination in the workshop with the artist, the gallery owner, the painters, and craftspeople. Changes are still possible at this state.

Georg Baselitz / "Eagle", Stained Glass 2011

location: Private Residence, Italy / **year:** 2011 / **technique:** stained glass

Executed in traditional stained glass technique. Hand-blown antique flashed glass, carefully assembled, etched and coated with ceramic glass melting paints.
In preparation for his first glass piece, the internationally acclaimed artist frequently visited the Mayer'sche Hofkunstanstalt studying and directing the work intensely. Yet, he left the hand painting to the glass painter in the studio. Georg Baselitz signed the glasswork.

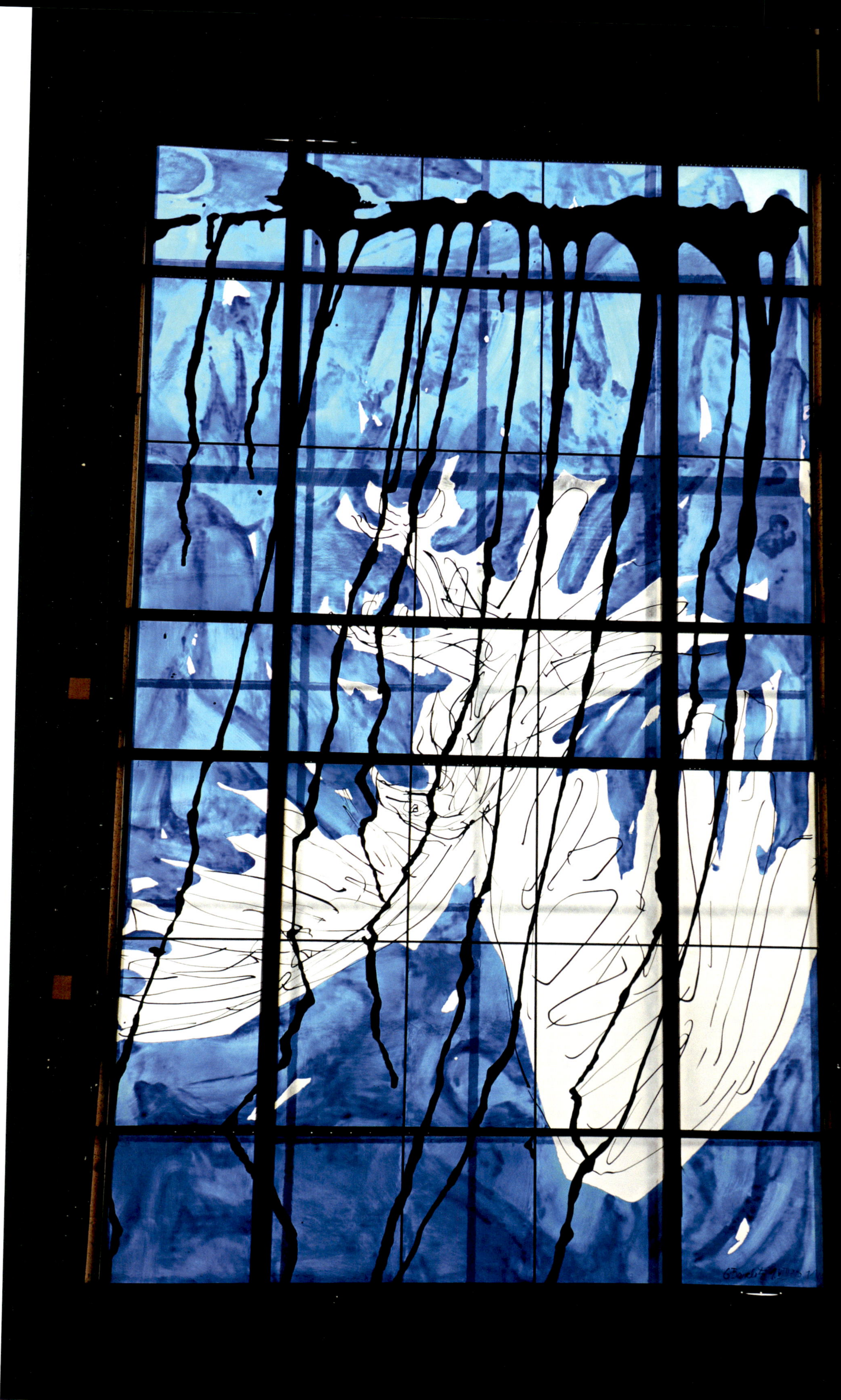

84 Partial section of Baumgarten's glass ceiling above the Sculpture Hall of the museum.

Lothar Baumgarten / "The Tongue of the Cherokee"

location: Carnegie Museum of Art, Pittsburgh, PA, USA / Historic Building / **year:** 1988 / **technique:** float glass painting

Pittsburgh, PA, is the US steel city. From here, with trains, began the colonization of the West. It is into the skylight over the Parthenon freeze located in the Hall of Sculpture, where Baumgarten places Sequoyah's Syllabary, the 85 letters of the Cherokee language.
Artistically, this work was the most important one from the "early phase" of float glass painting. *After multiple experiments with glass melting colors Baumgarten decided for a simple and factual color- as well as painting-solution, executing the work himself.*

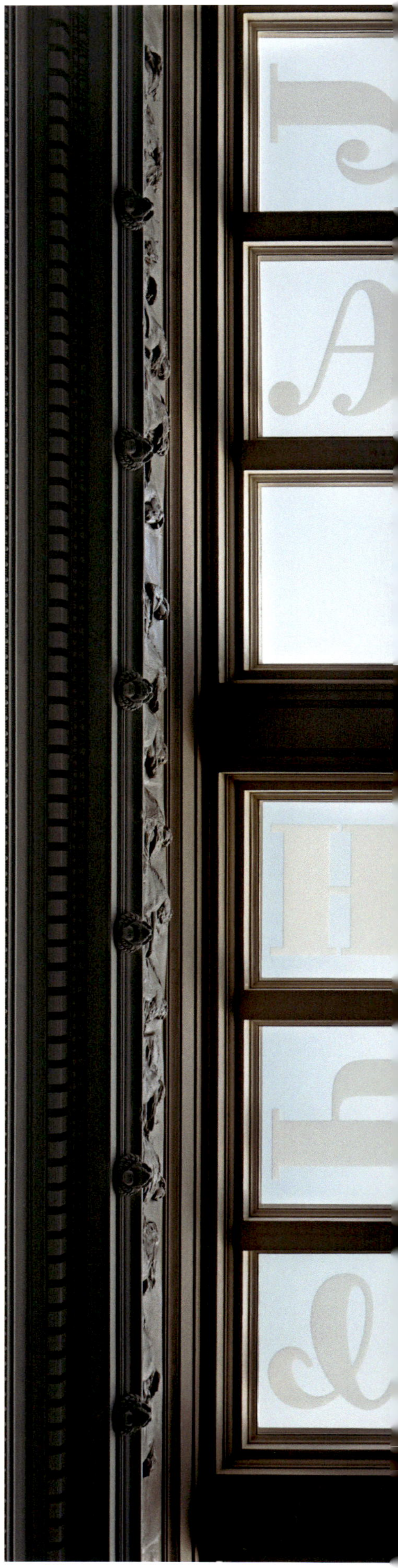

84

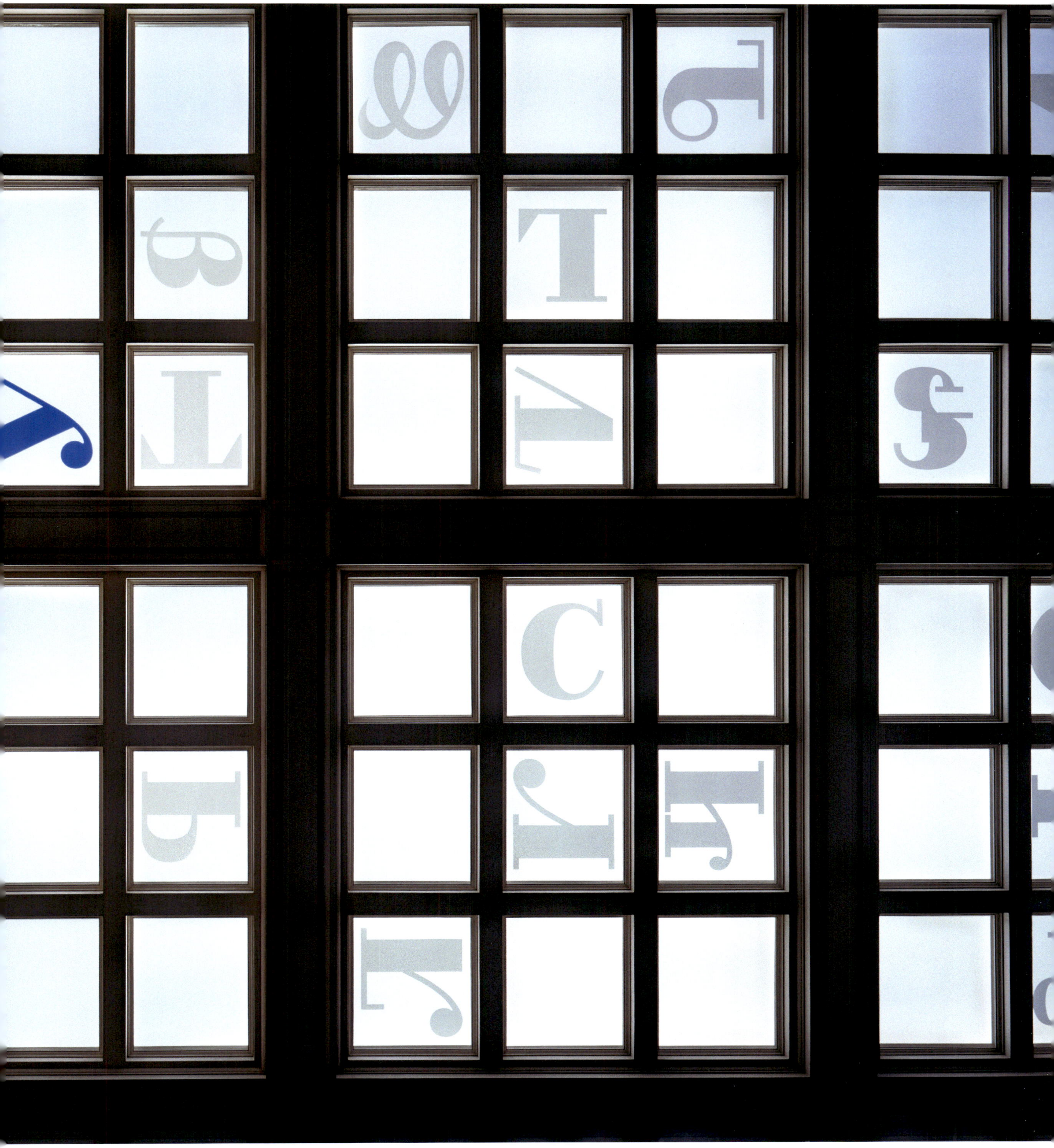

CODED TEXT

85
The open doors with the blue glazing. An encoded text – the Passion from the Gospel of St. John – runs across all window panels.

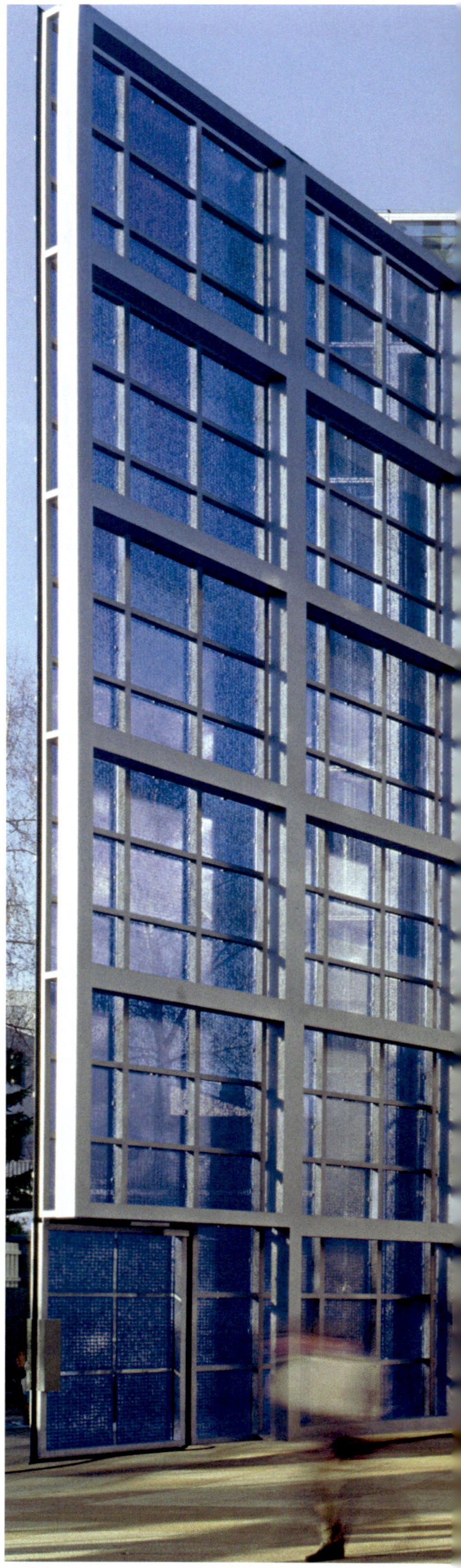

85

Alexander Beleschenko / "Coded Text"

location: Herz-Jesu-Kirche, Munich-Neuhausen, DE / Architects Allmann Sattler Wappner / **year:** 2000 / **technique:** float glass painting

Designing the blue glass from the entrance portals and participating in the development of the remaining white glazing of the church. Transparent ceramic colors, indirect elevated print, partly on both glass panes of the IGU glazing.

A millennium church for the year 2000, a thriving and active parish. To this day a pilgrimage site for architecture and art aficionados, Mayer suggested the British artist to the archdiocese for this task. Beleschenko created a first-rate artwork in tandem with the studio: This is where glass art is architectural art.

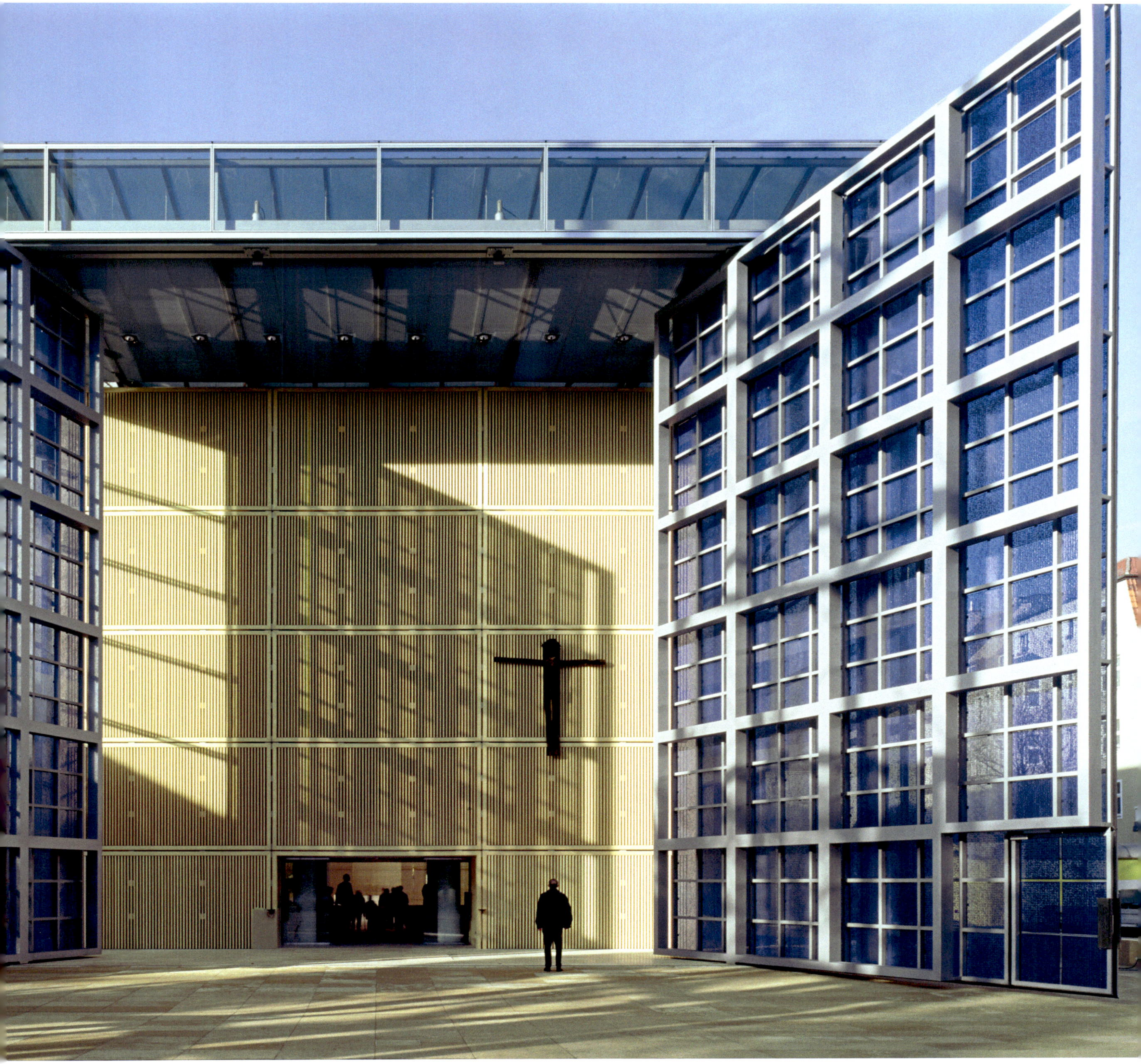

Glass artist Alexander Beleschenko created an alphabet using nails to remind us of the crucifixion and Christ's wounds. The alphabet is formally based on the Ugarit cuneiform.
He developed an individual nail symbol for each letter of the Latin alphabet, which he used to "print" on the square glass panels. Assembled together, they spell out the text of St. John's Passion.

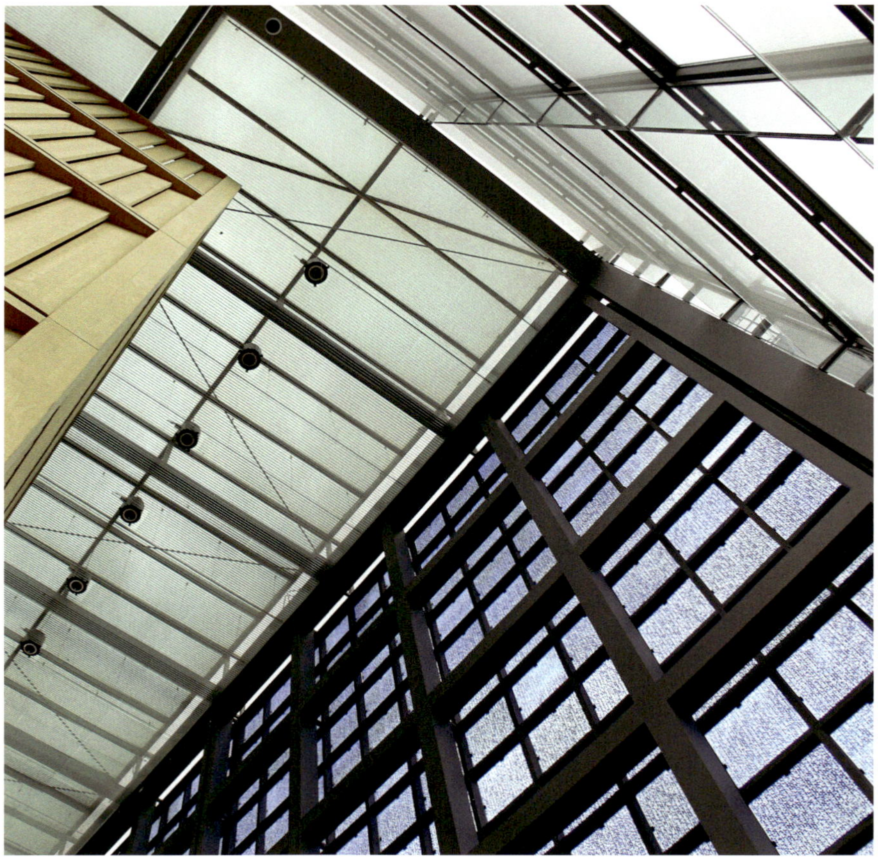

86

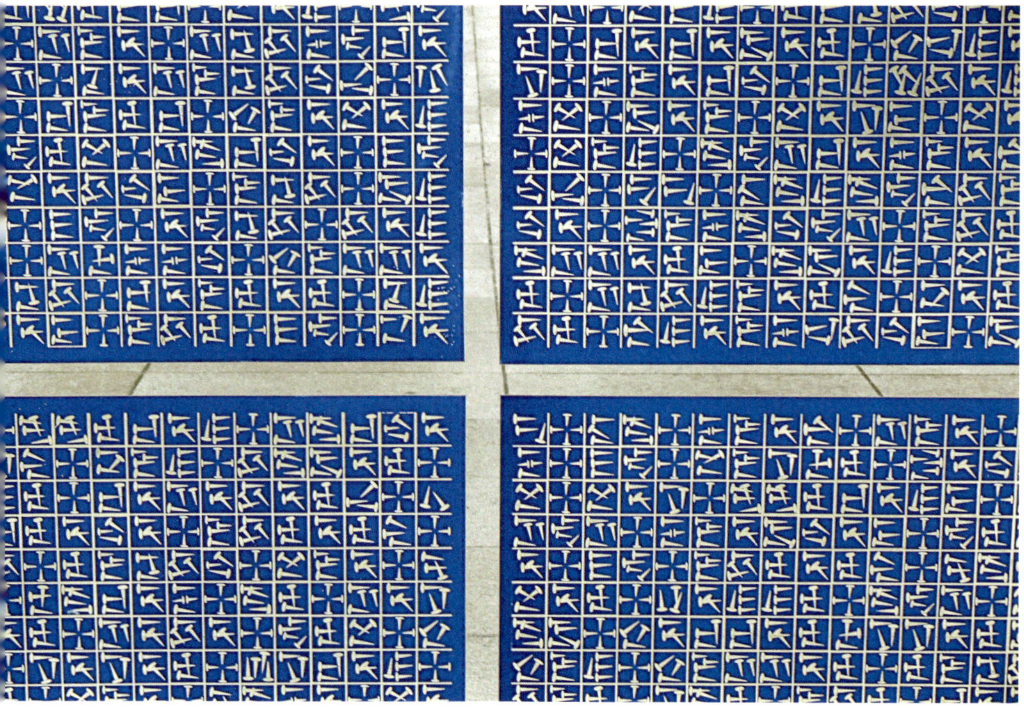

87

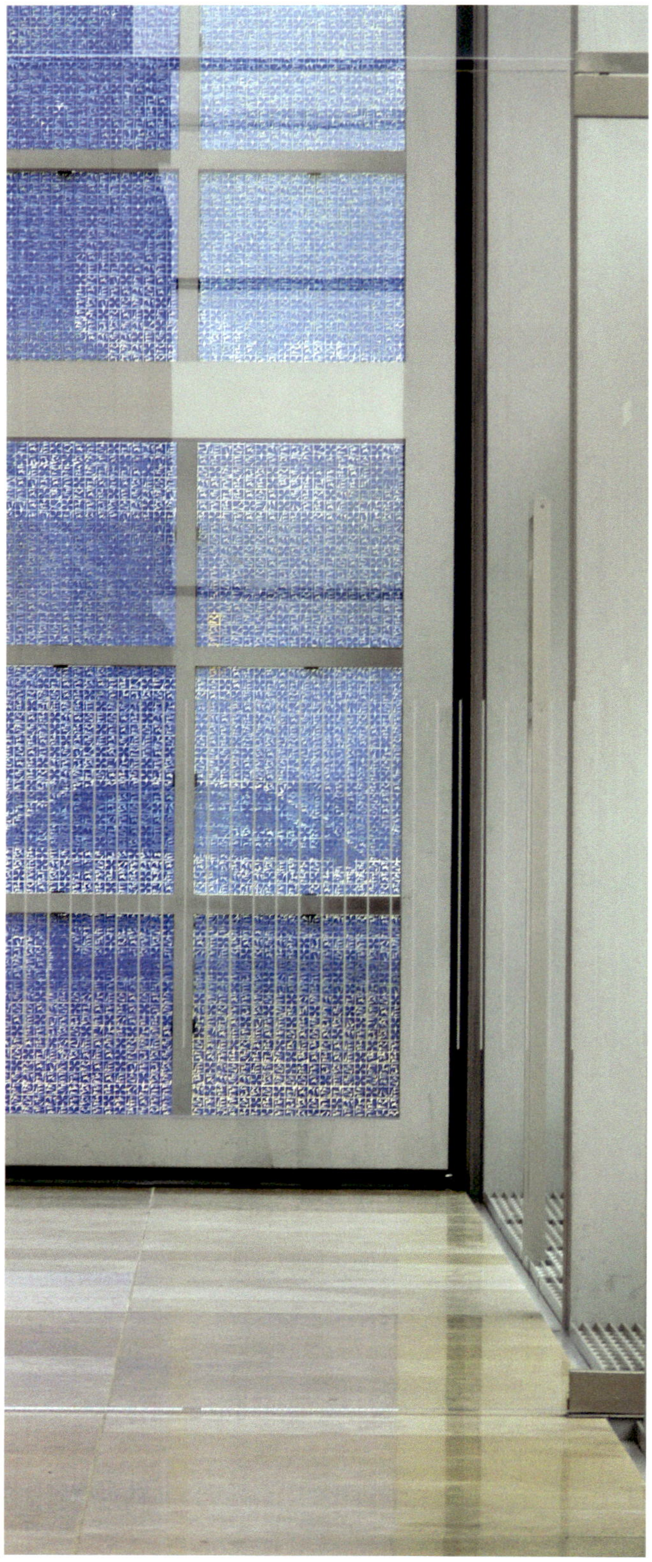

88

CODED TEXT

86

Looking up: wooden core, glass ceiling, glass gate, lateral facade.

87

The detail reveals the letters the artist made from nails – symbols of the passion.

88

View from the inside to a detail of the glass gate.

89

Lateral view of the vestibule: The glass gates on the right, the glass ceiling, and the outer glass walls form the outer glass shell. The openwork wooden wall on the left forms a casing for the interior. An extraordinary concept of material and space.

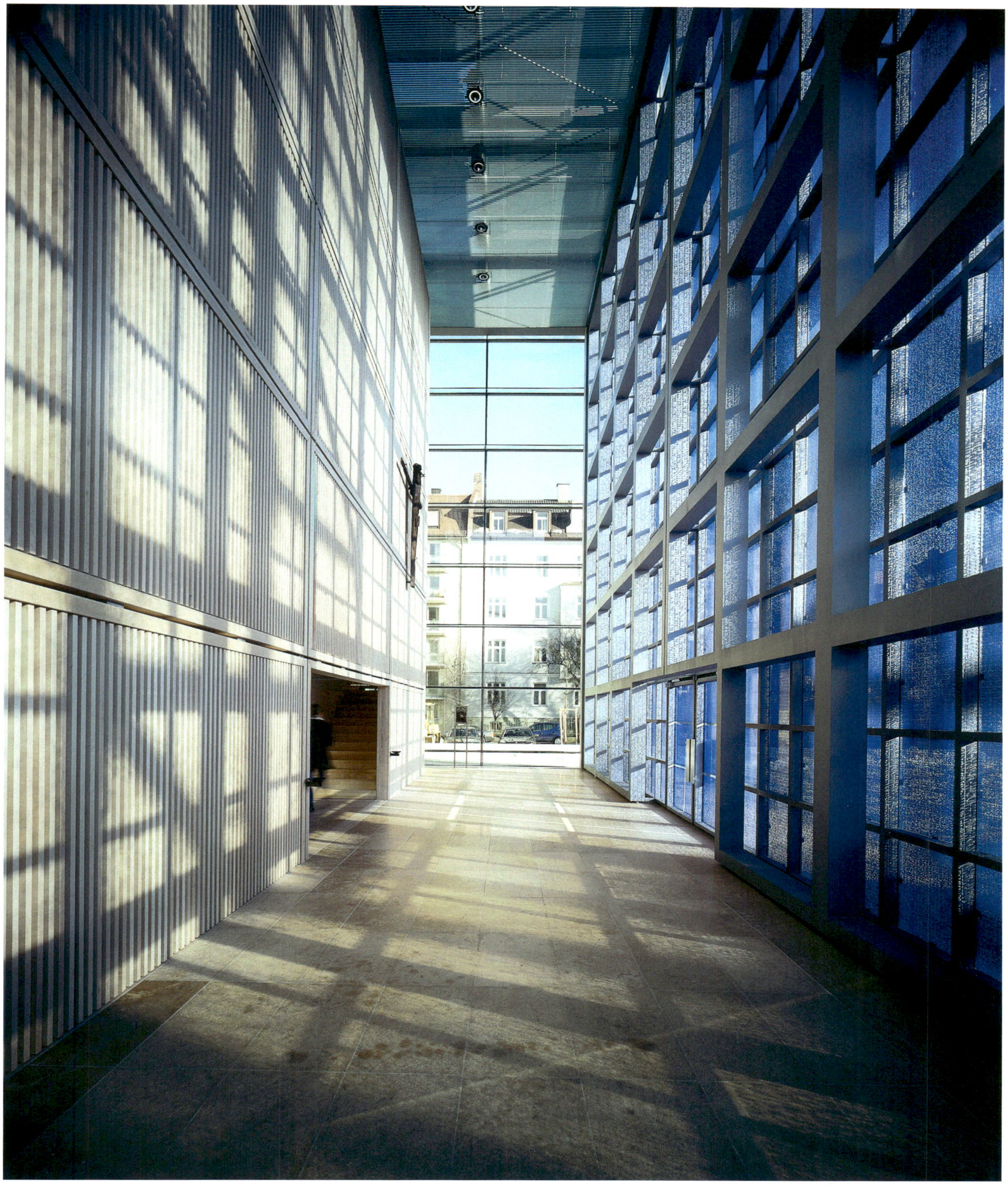

89

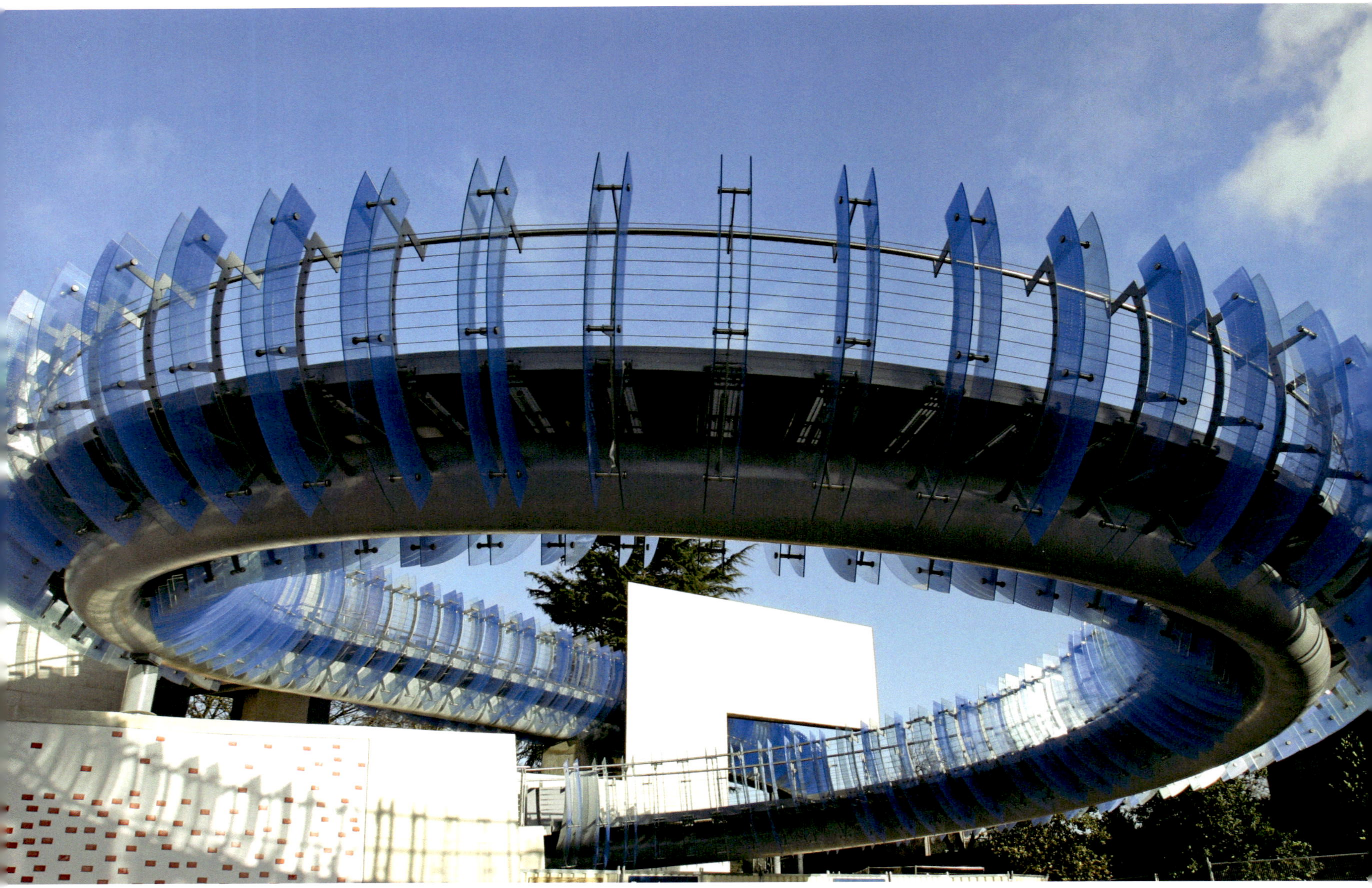

90

Alexander Beleschenko / "The Bridge"

64

location: Millennium Place, Coventry, GB / MJP Architects / **year:** 2003 / **technique:** ceramic glass melting color print

More than 800 "glass swords," silk-screen print in very fine grid gradations.
As part of Coventry's Phoenix project new public spaces were created. One of them, Beleschenko's "The Bridge" rises in a spiral to take pedestrians up and over a medieval city wall arriving in the garden of International Friendship. The bridge and ramp structure consists of an intricate steel deck and balustrade system with colored glass fins. The Glass Bridge received many awards.

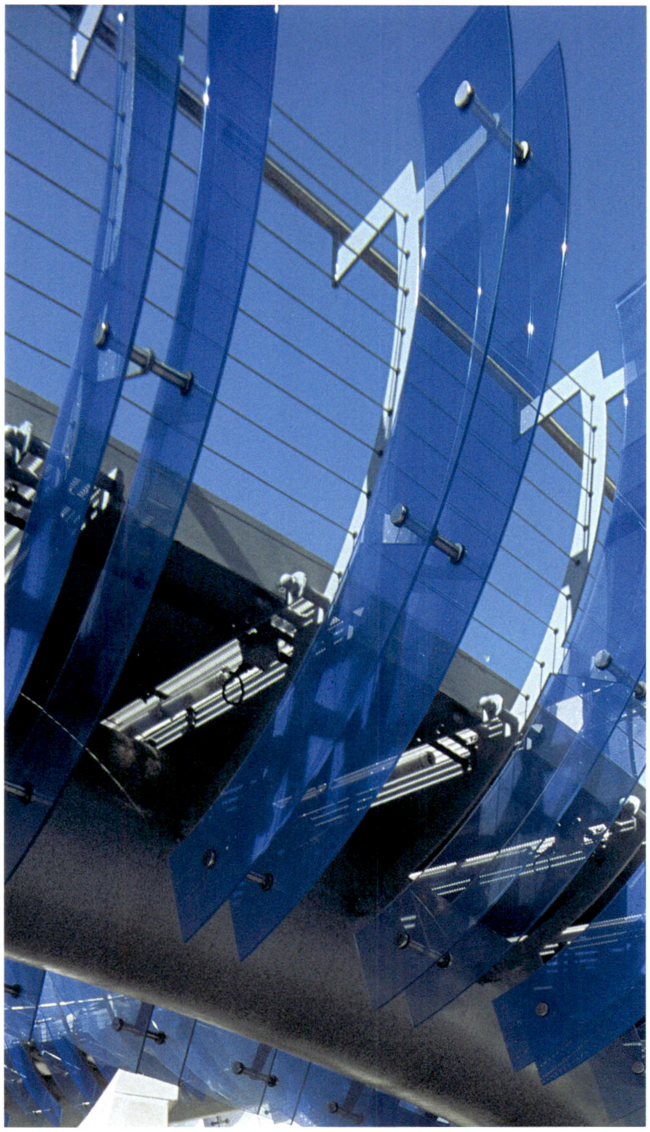

91

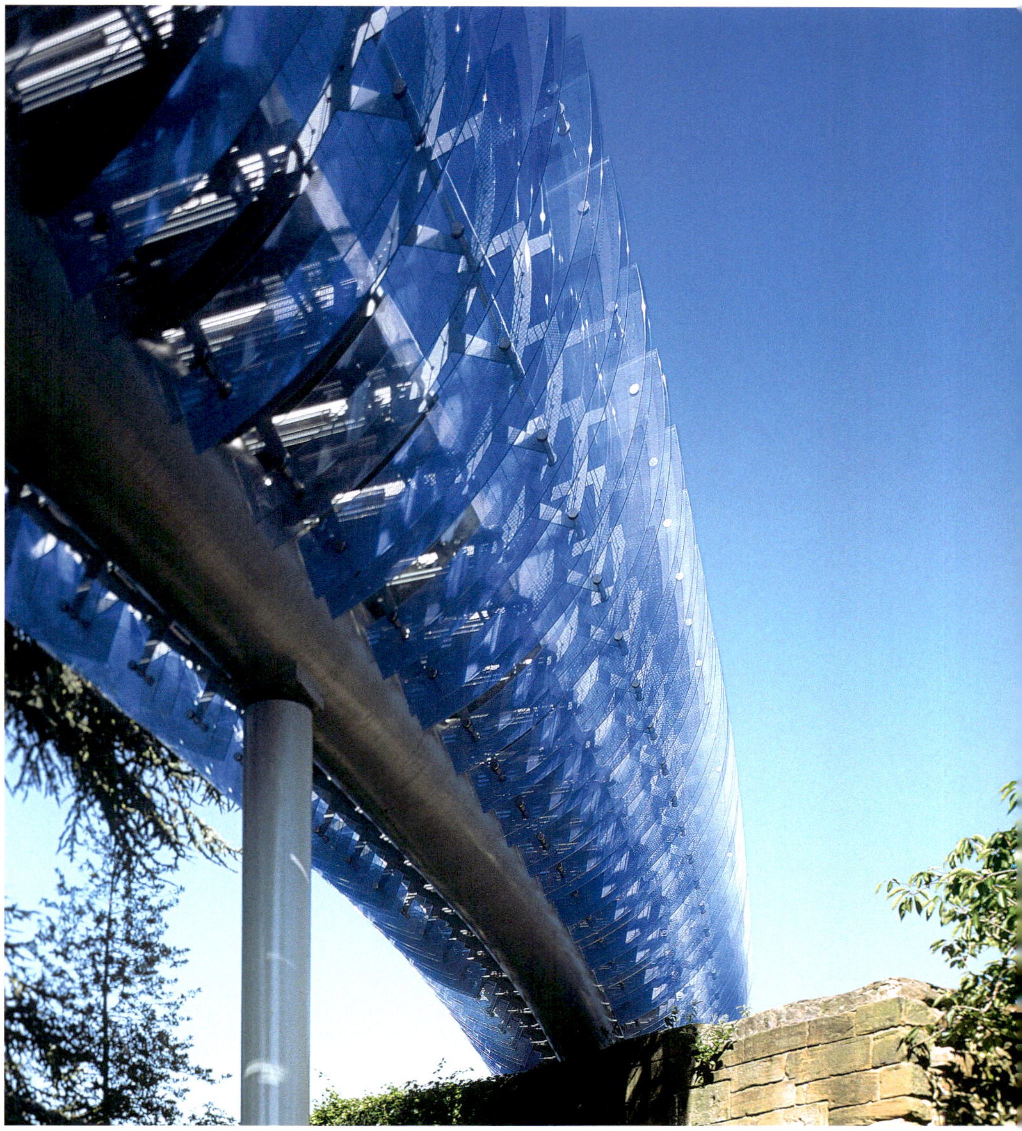

92

THE BRIDGE

90
The spiral ascent from the entrance of the "Coventry Transport Museum" towards the adjoining museum garden.

91
Details of the steel construction with double glass fins and steel ropes.

92
The descent into the adjacent museum garden ("Lady Herbert's Garden").

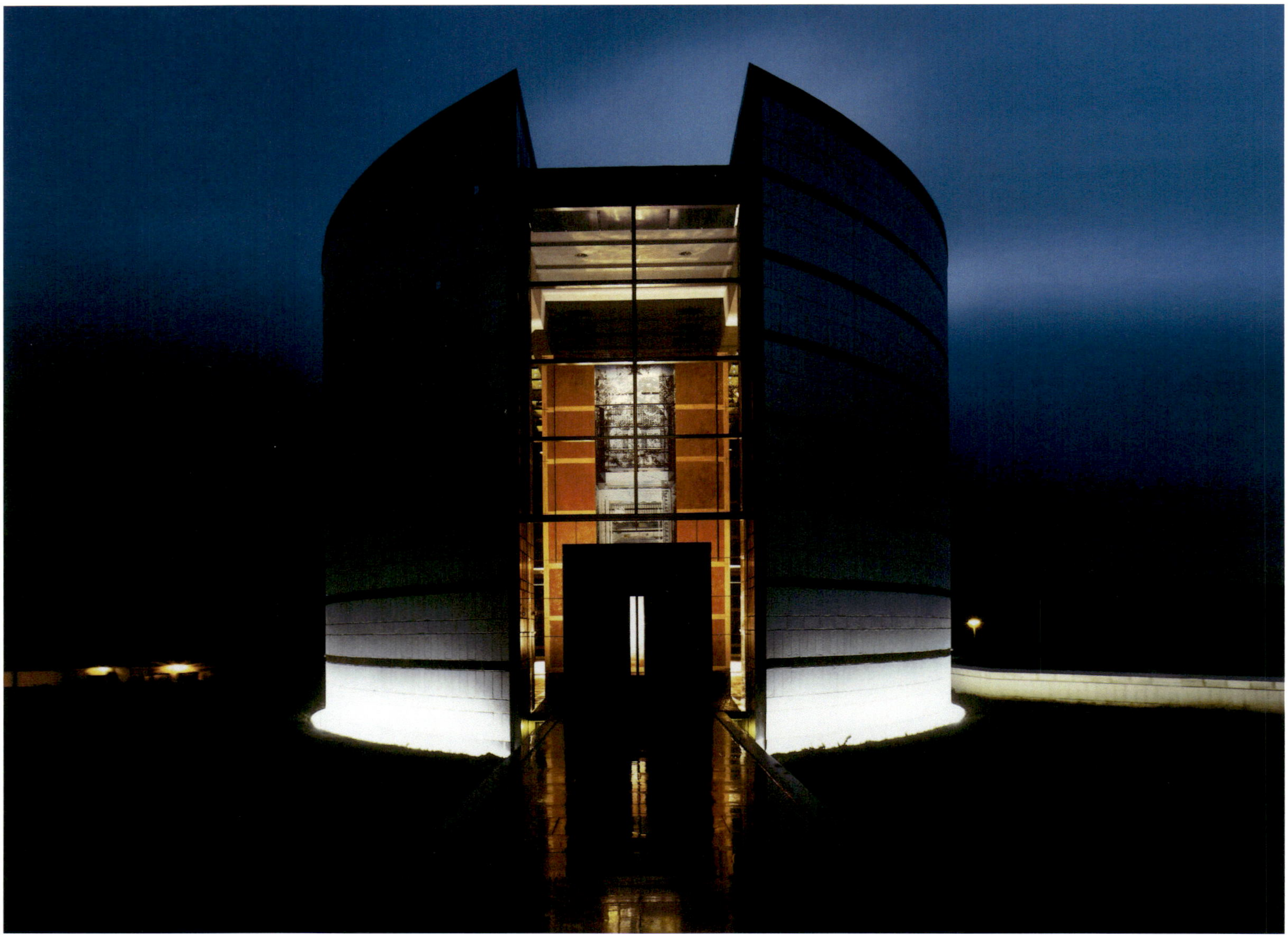

93

Alexander Beleschenko / "Screen"

location: Ruskin Library, Lancaster University, Lancaster, GB / Richard MacCormac, MJP Architects /
year: 1998 / **technique:** float glass painting

The Library Building of the University of Lancaster had been named after John Ruskin, one of the great writers, art critics, draughtsmen, and thinkers of the Victorian era in England. Alexander Beleschenko took reference to Ruskin's "Stones of Venice" and his very early Daguerreotype photos and he wanted them to be made permanent and of architectural scale. Beleschenko and Mayer found ways to realize such project.

SCREEN

93

Nocturnal exterior view.

94

Glass design after one of Ruskin's original daguerreotypes of St. Mark's Basilica in Venice. Interior view with depictions of a Gothic window arch and a stone doorway.

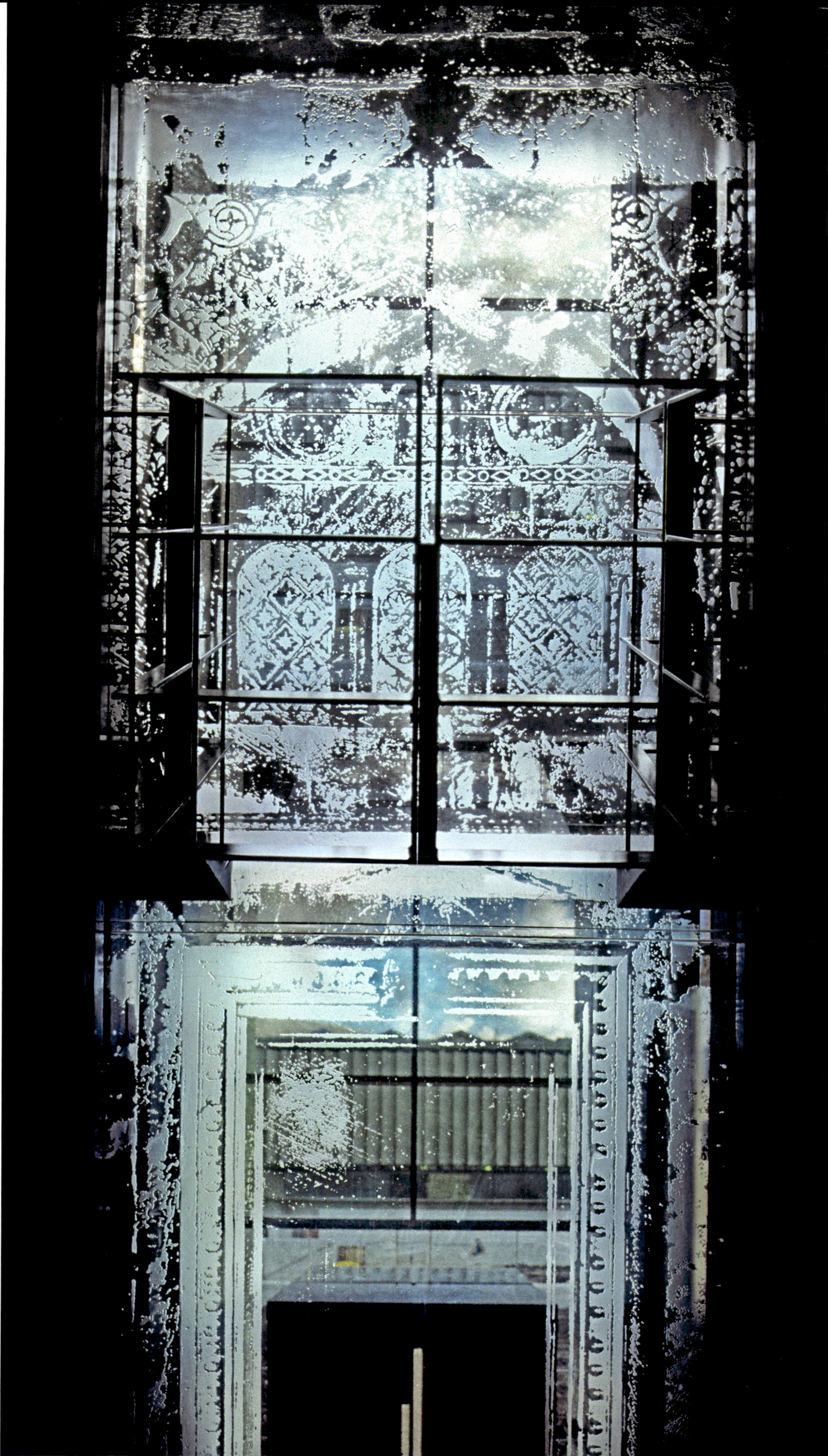

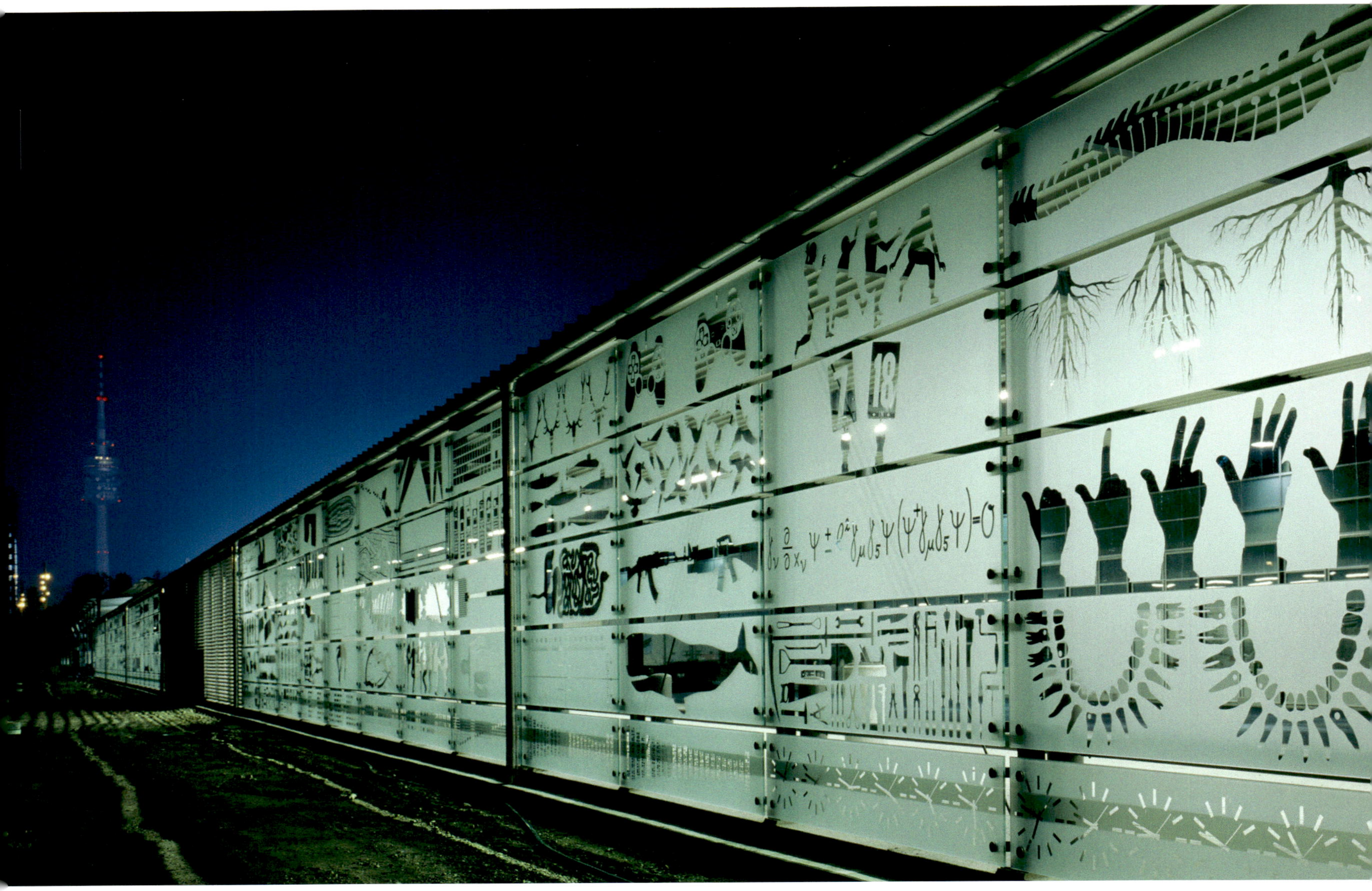

95

Heiner Blum / “Lexicon”

68

location: Waste Company, Munich, DE / Architects Ackermann und Partner / **year:** 1998 / **technique:** float glass painting, sandblasting

Commissioned by Munich’s Waste Company, Heiner Blum created a 550 feet long glass wall (approximately) entitled “Lexicon”, with pictograms representing objects, terms, and humans: a dictionary of transience and decay. The orange garbage trucks are parked behind the glass wall.

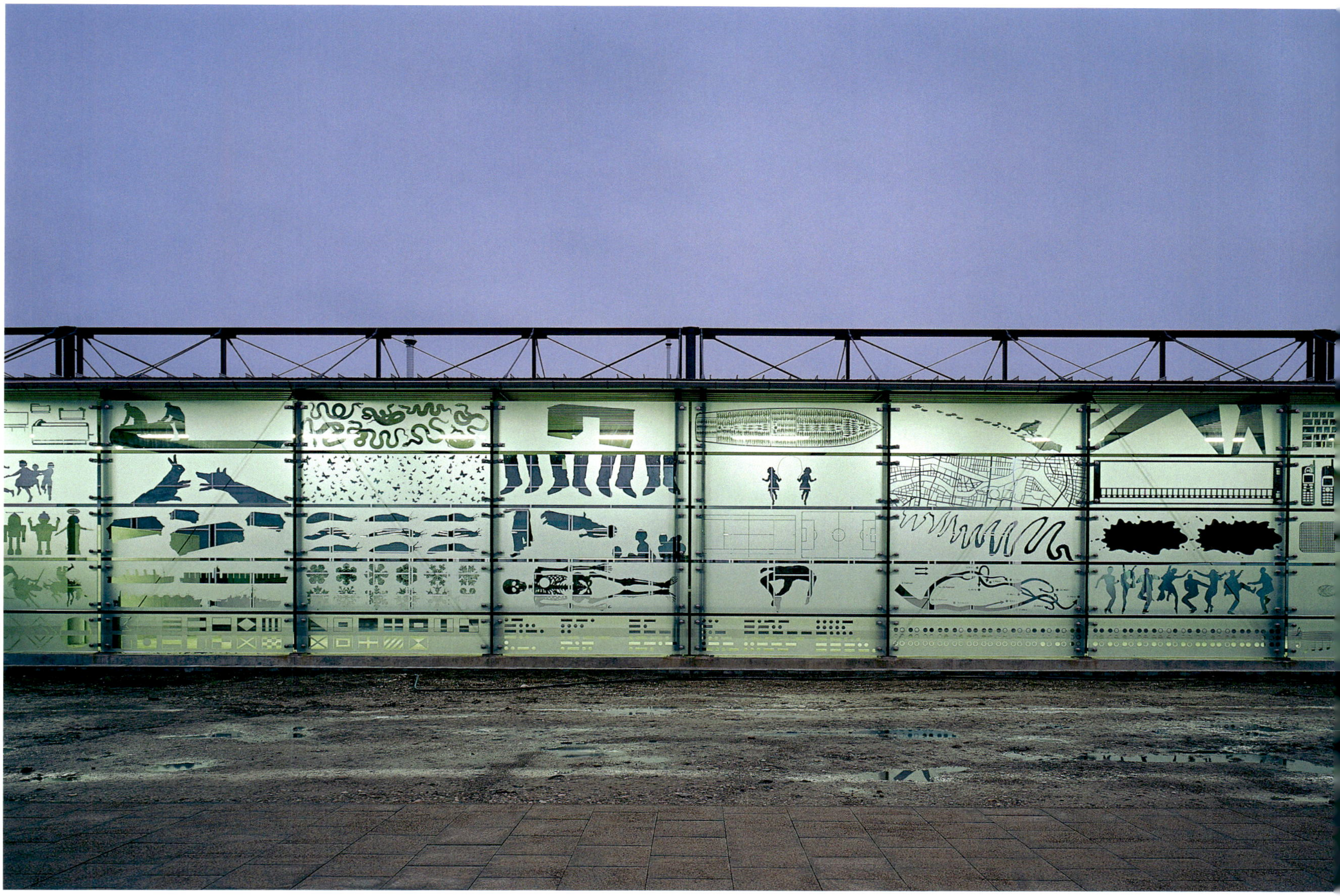

96

LEXICON

95
The western end of the glass wall and the dictionary – of course placed in alphabetical order of the German words: Zähne, i.e. teeth, Zahlen, i.e. numbers, Wurzeln, i.e. roots ... Nocturnal atmosphere with a view of the TV tower.

96
A violet evening sky. View from the street.

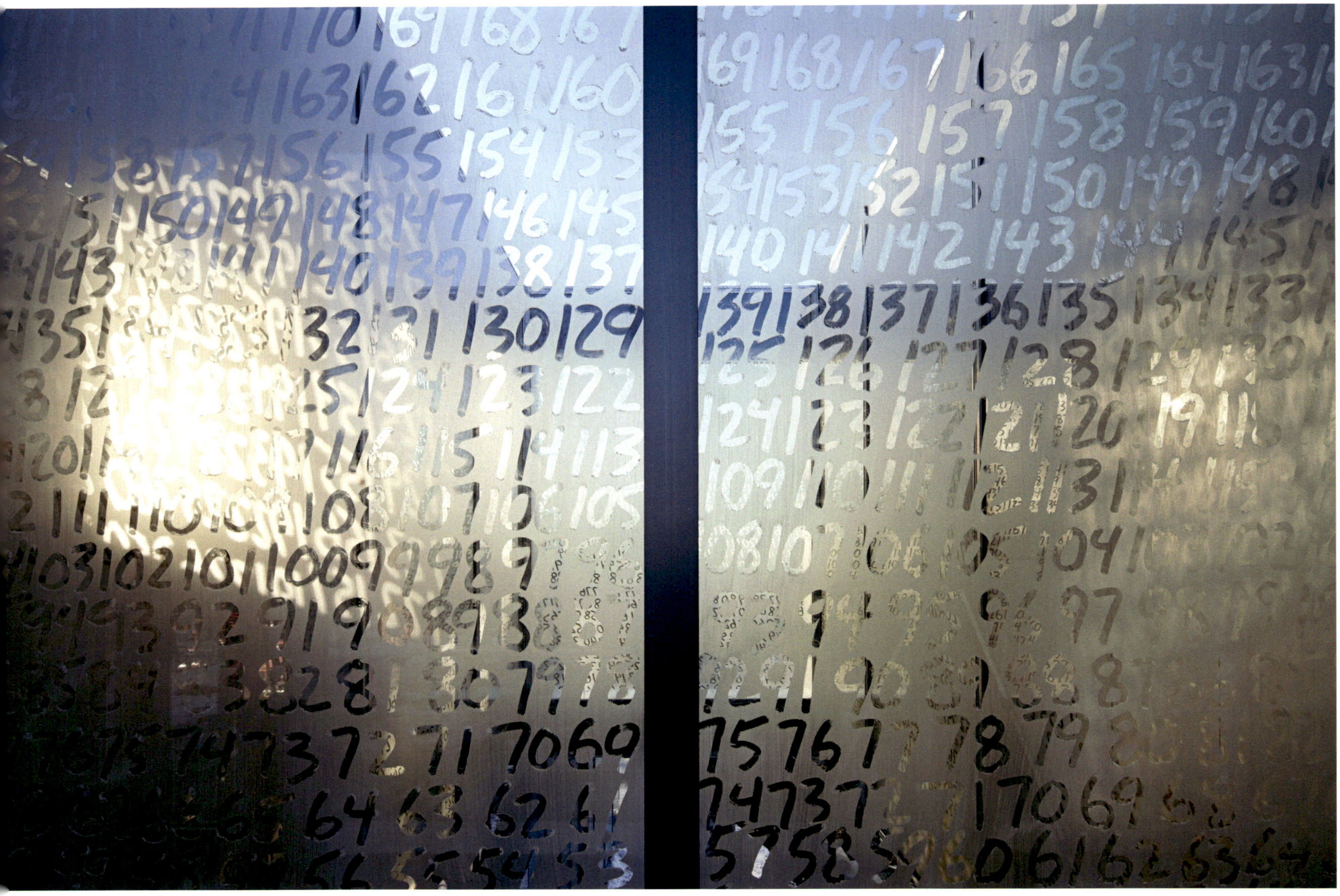

97

Mel Bochner / "To Count: INTRANSITIVE"

98

location: Private Residence, Dutchess County, NY, USA / Allied Works Architecture / **year:** 2011 / **technique:** float glass painting

Ten IGU panels made of white glass, painted with ceramic glass melting colors and "erased" by the artist.

This art glass piece bears the hand of the New York concept artist and was made for a collector's private residence. The 12 feet high glass panels enclose a "void" between bedroom, hallway, staircase, and the exterior glass panel on the second floor. From the garden patio on the ground floor, one looks up to the glass panels and the open sky.

TO COUNT: INTRANSITIVE

97 Details and light reflections: A view from the corridor through Bochner's glass into the outer "void" and onto the glass from the outside.

98 View from the lower patio to glass art and towards the sky.

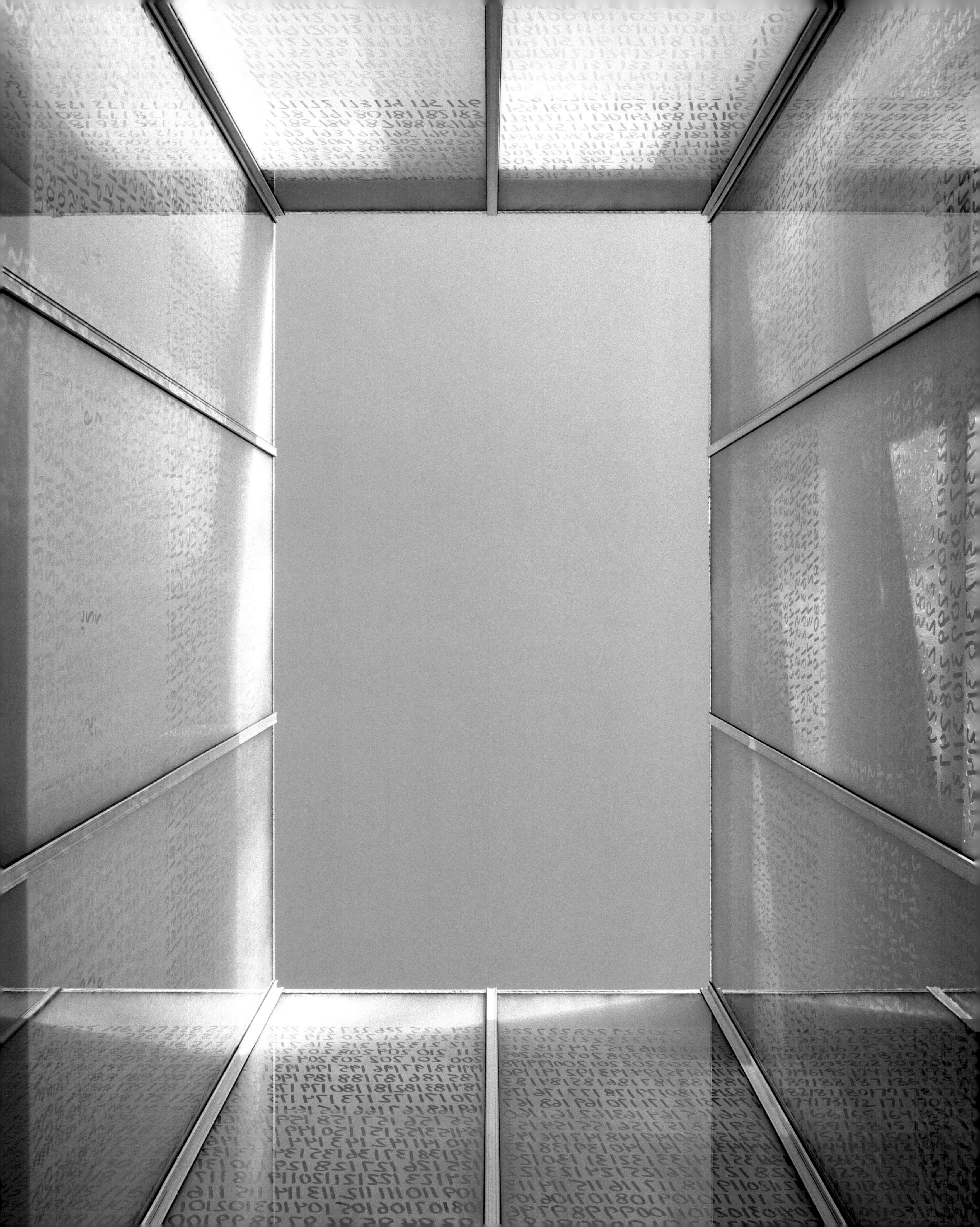

MEL BOCHNER – STUDIO

99
Palette knife and color, a still life.

100
First color and wipe patterns.

101
Mel Bochner "writing numbers."

102
Beginning "to write" the number columns from the bottom.

103
A creative break beside a 12 feet high glass panel painted white and still unfired.

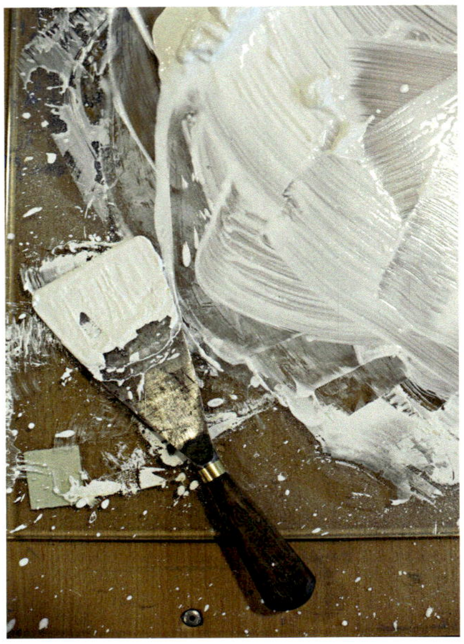

99

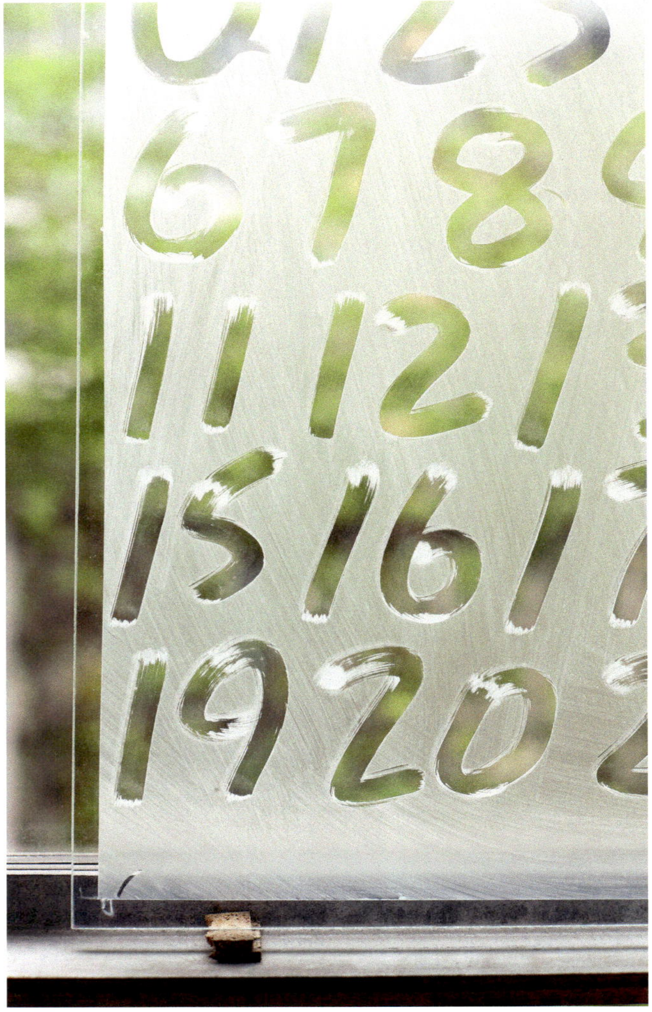

100

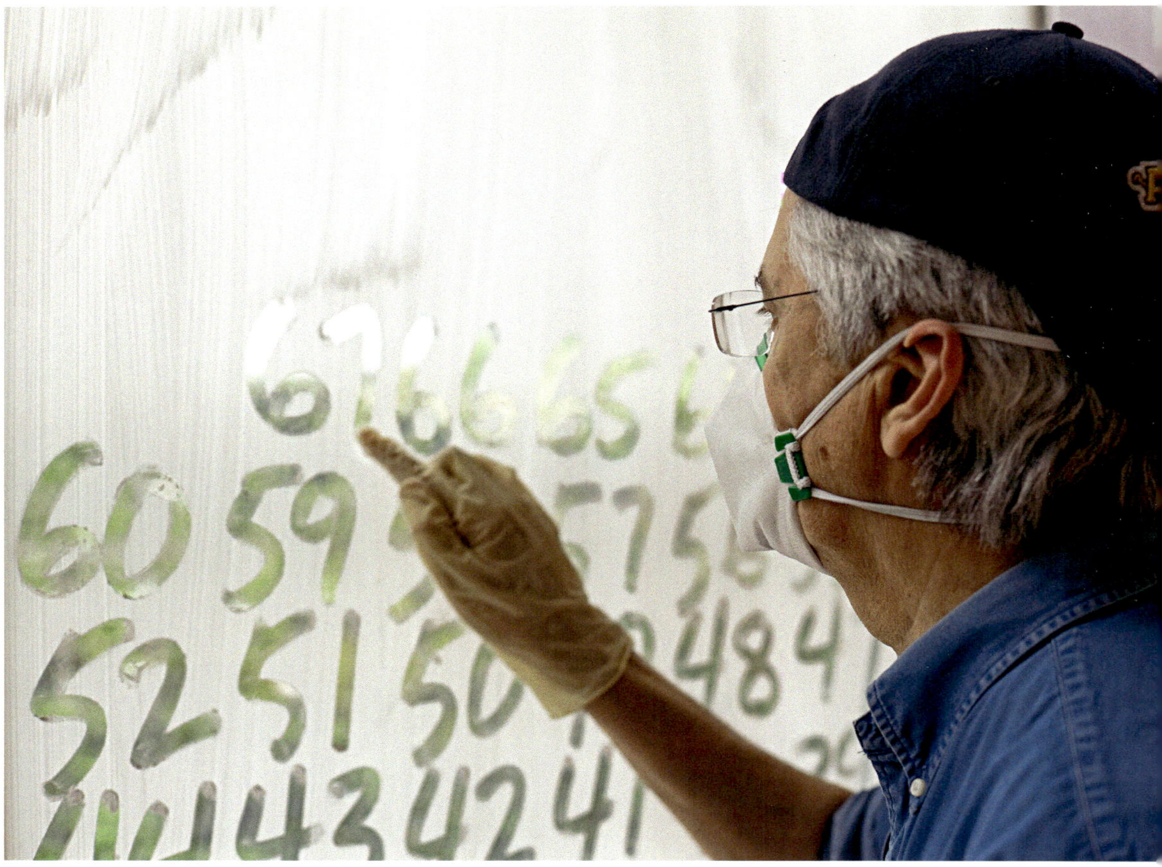

101

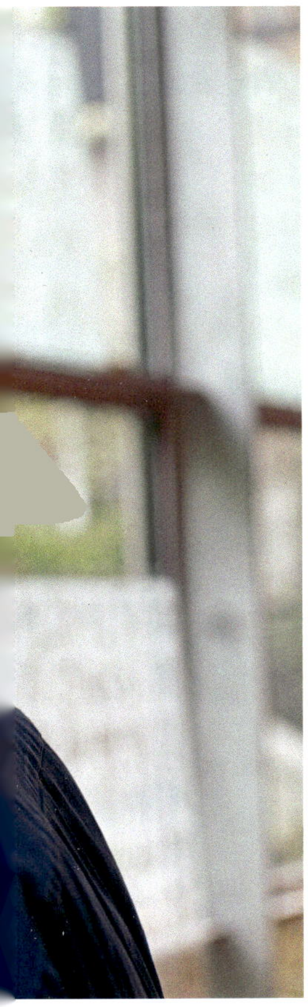

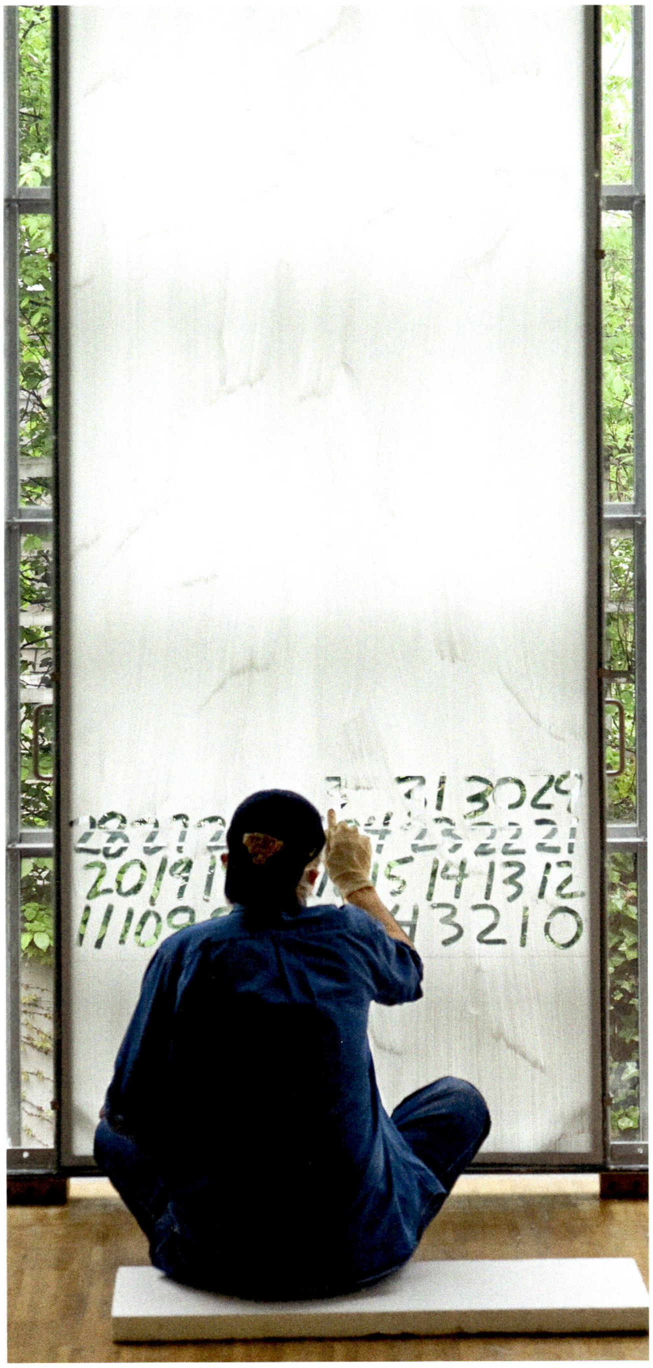

20 19 1 15 14 13 12
11 10 9 3 2 1 0

102

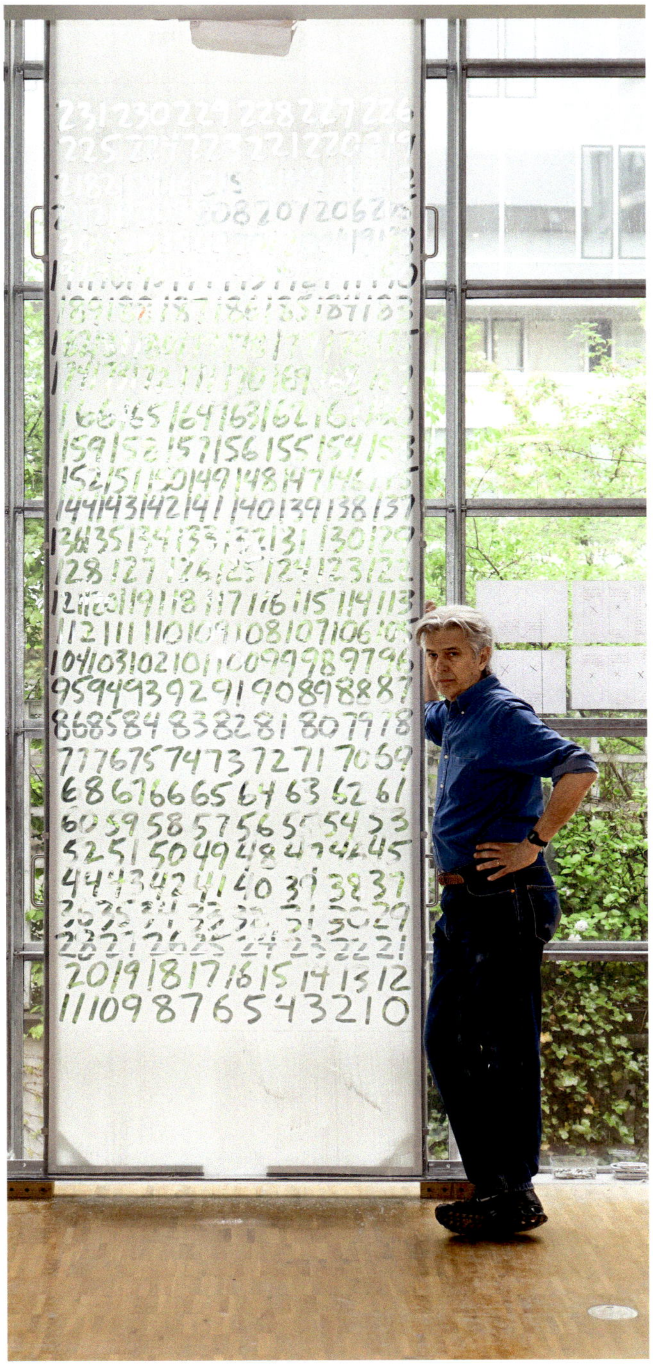

20 19 18 17 16 15 14 13 12
11 10 9 8 7 6 5 4 3 2 1 0

103

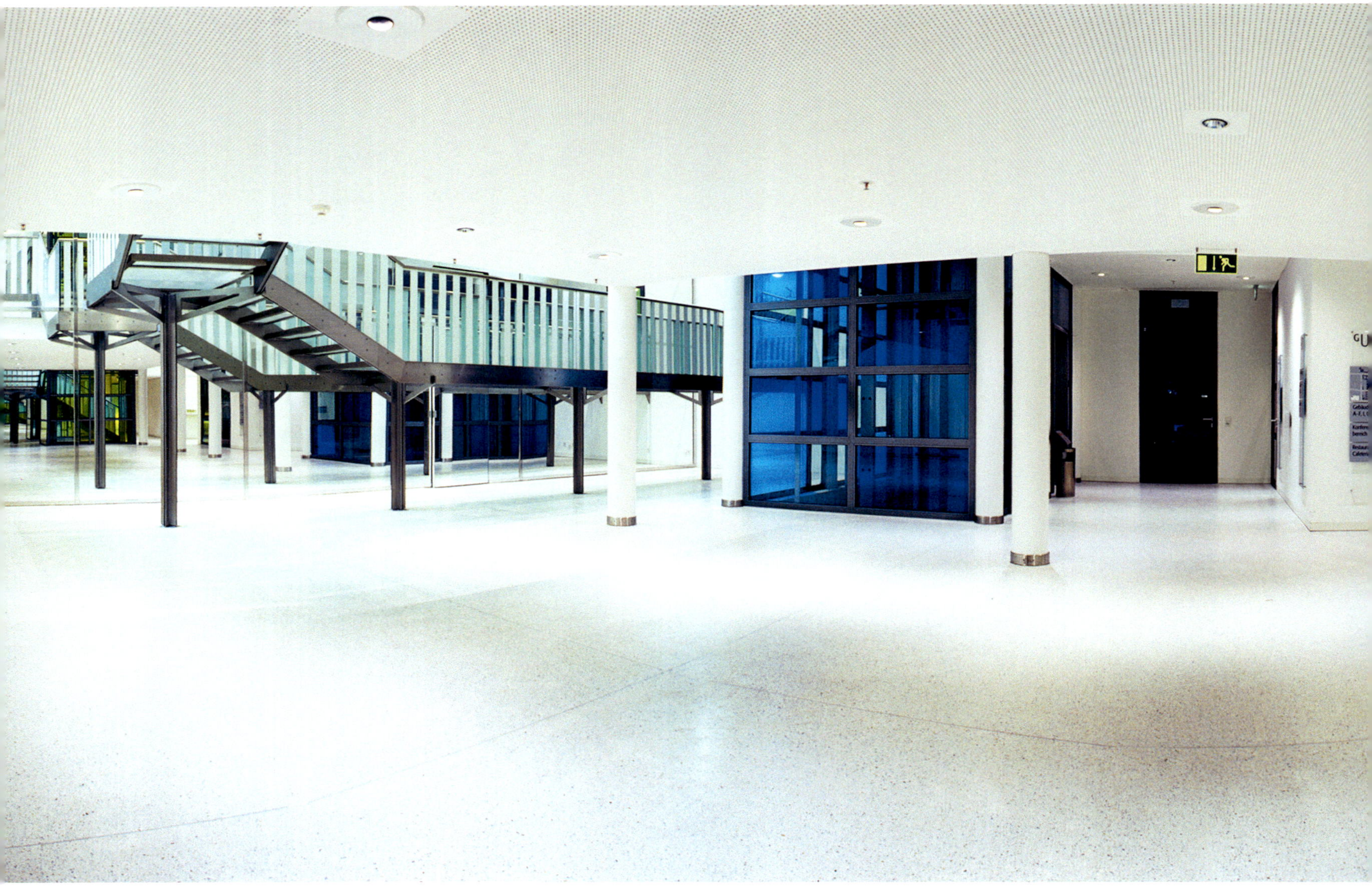

104

Daniel Buren / "Colorful Transparency"

74

location: Architectural glass design Entrance Lobby Allianz Headquarters, Building G, Munich, DE / LAI Architects. Achenbach Art Consulting / **year:** 2001 / **technique:** float glass painting

It had been important to Daniel Buren, the internationally acclaimed artist, to visually enlarge the relatively compact entrance lobby of Building G of the Allianz Headquarter complex. He therefore based his artistic concept on "mirror galleries" (Helge Achenbach) with reflecting and transparent color glass. The work is titled "Transparences Colorées", i.e. colorful transparency.

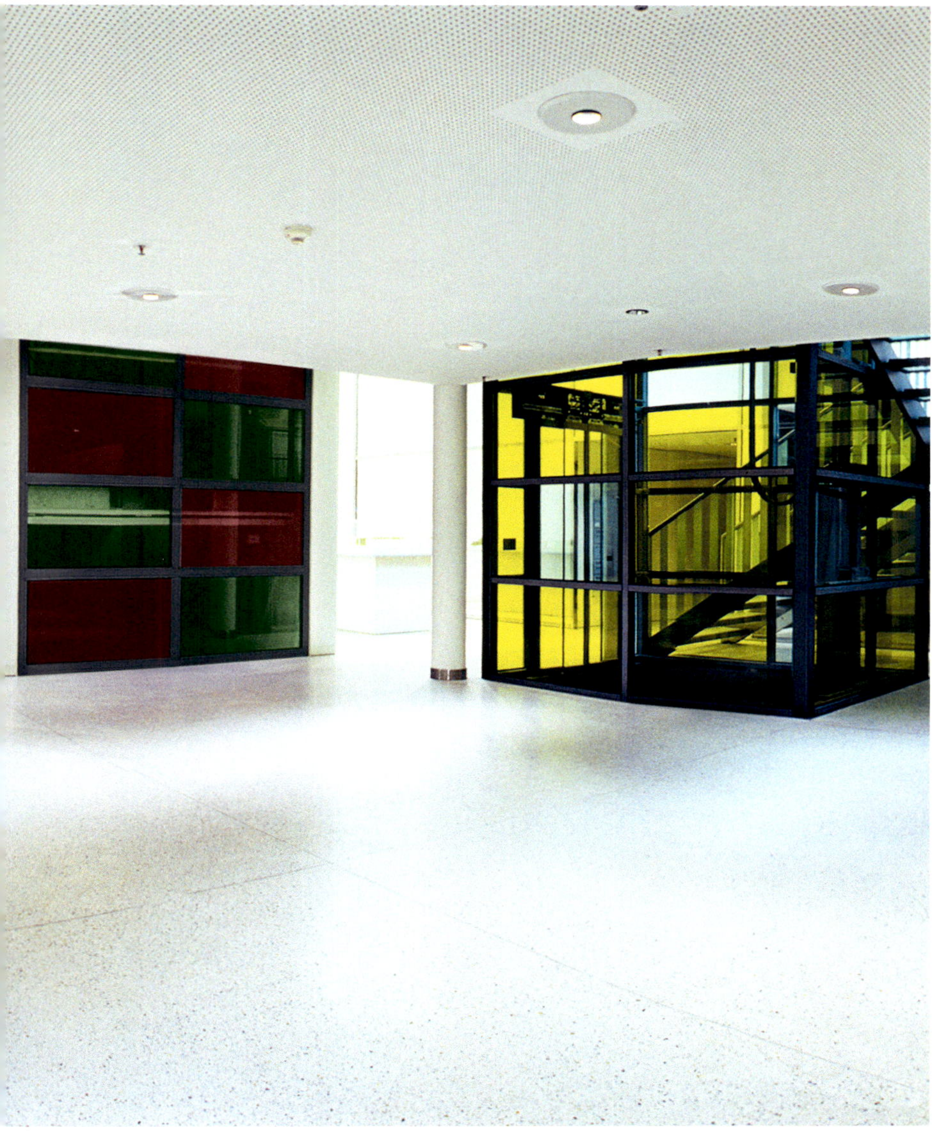

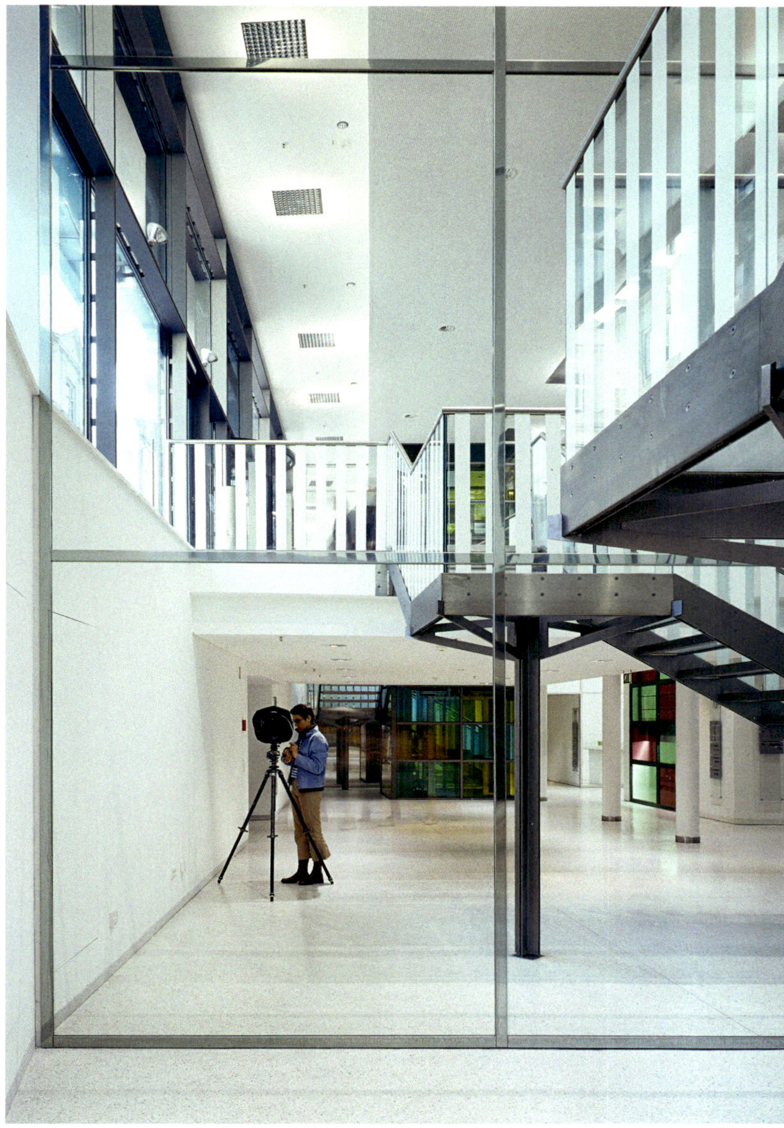

105

COLORFUL TRANSPARENCY

104
Panorama view of the entrance space with striated white, blue, yellow, and other colors in the glass.

105
Looking into the mirror wall of the lobby.

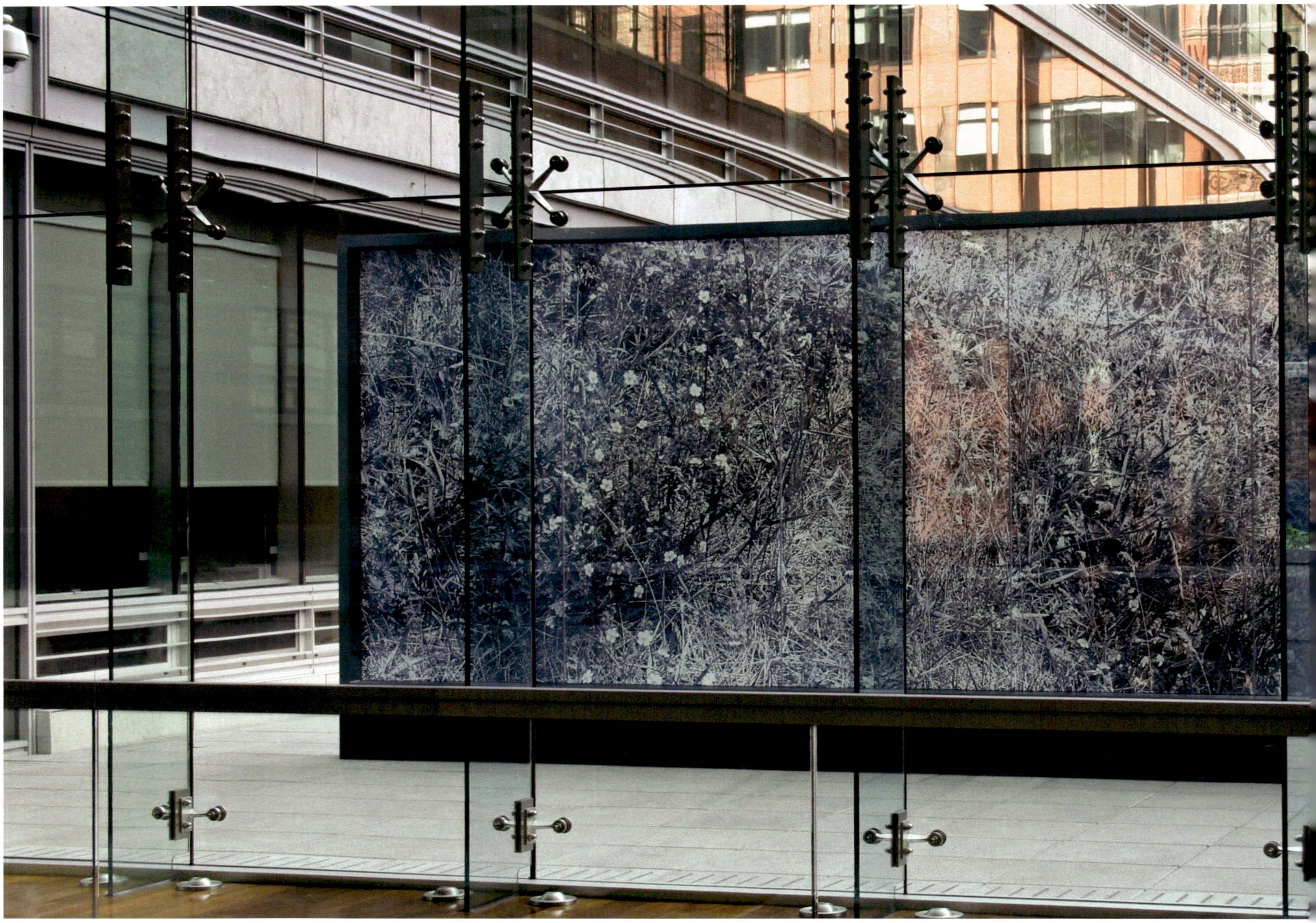

106

Geneviève Cadieux / "June"

76

location: Caisse de Dépôt, Montréal, CAN / Daoust Lestage, FABG, Lemay & Associes and Hal Ingberg, Architects / **year:** 2003 / **technique:** float glass painting, metal, granite

Freestanding glasswall with black and white photography of a blooming summer lawn. Stained glass, different from the traditionally expected. Stained glass, based on the artistic approaches of our time. Conceptual art, realized on large glass panes in the technique of "float glass painting" and brought into an architectural context.

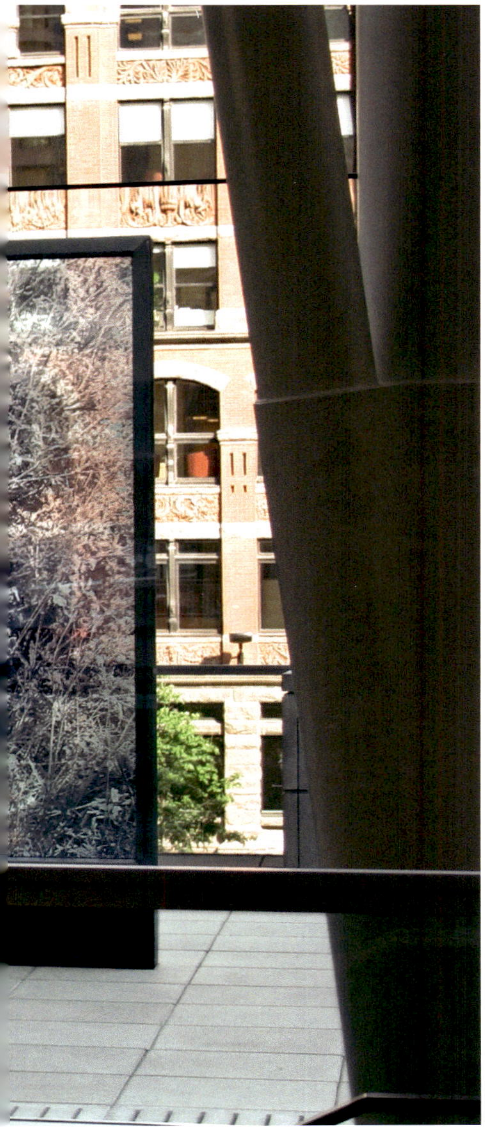

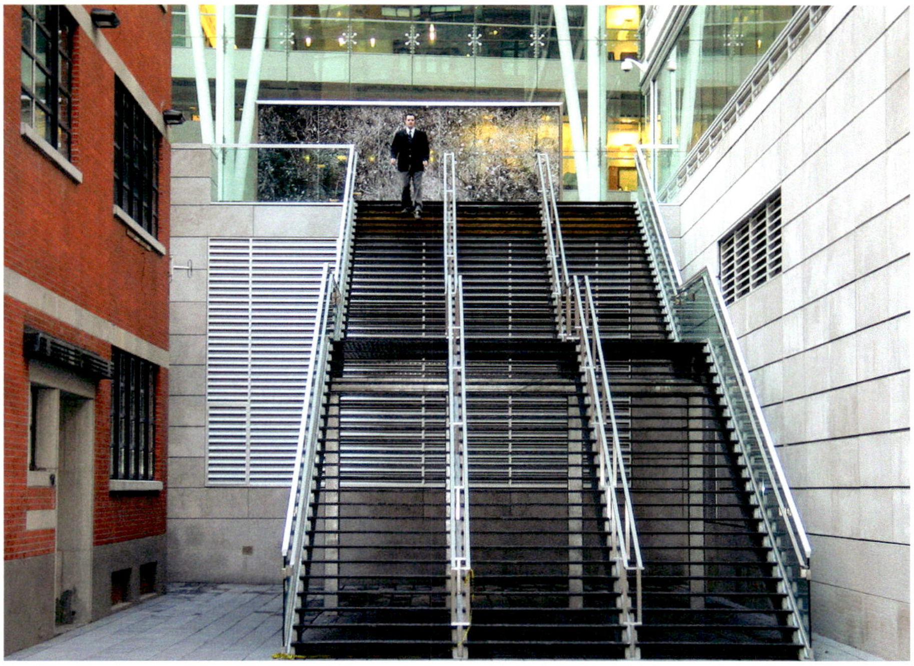

107

JUNE

106
The exterior glass wall as seen from the inside of the lobby.

107
The glass wall from below the outer stairways against the building.

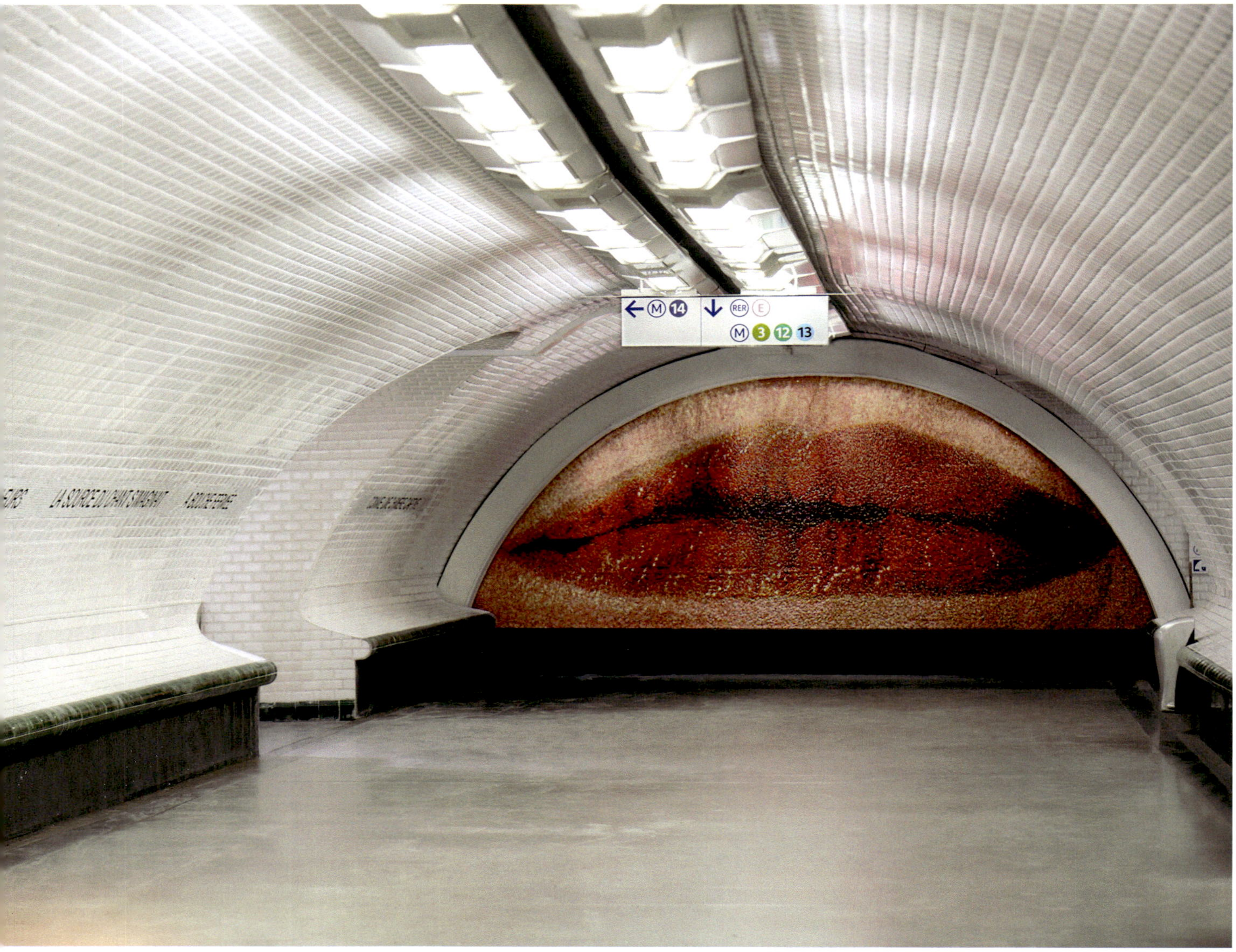

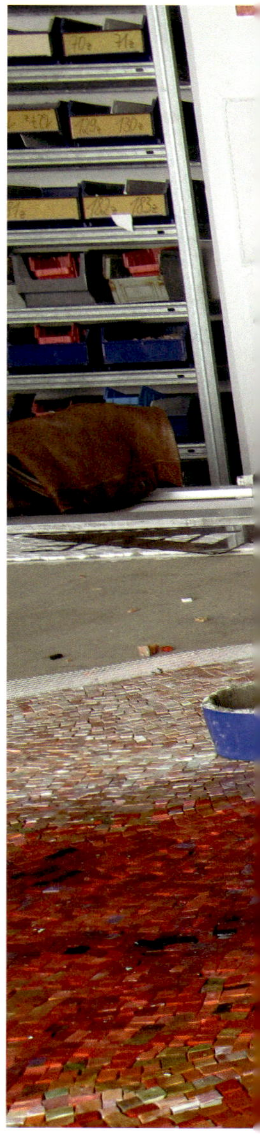

108

78 Geneviève Cadieux / “La Voix Lactée”

location: Metro Station Saint-Lazare, Paris. F / Sami Tannoury. Société de Transport de Montréal / **year:** 2011 / **technique:** Glass mosaic

The mosaic artwork is a present from the city of Montréal to her partner city Paris. Cadieux won the artist’s competition with numerous participants and became entrusted with the work. Her proposal, based on a work of hers from 1992 for the “Musée d’Art Contemporain de Montréal,” which is a backlit color photo on the roof of the building, had become an icon of the culture of Montréal and which can be seen from far away.
A band of text runs alongside the longitudinal wall on the left side, which quotes Anne Hébert, *Une fois seulement* in Œuvre poétique 1950-1990, ©Boréal/seuil 1992.

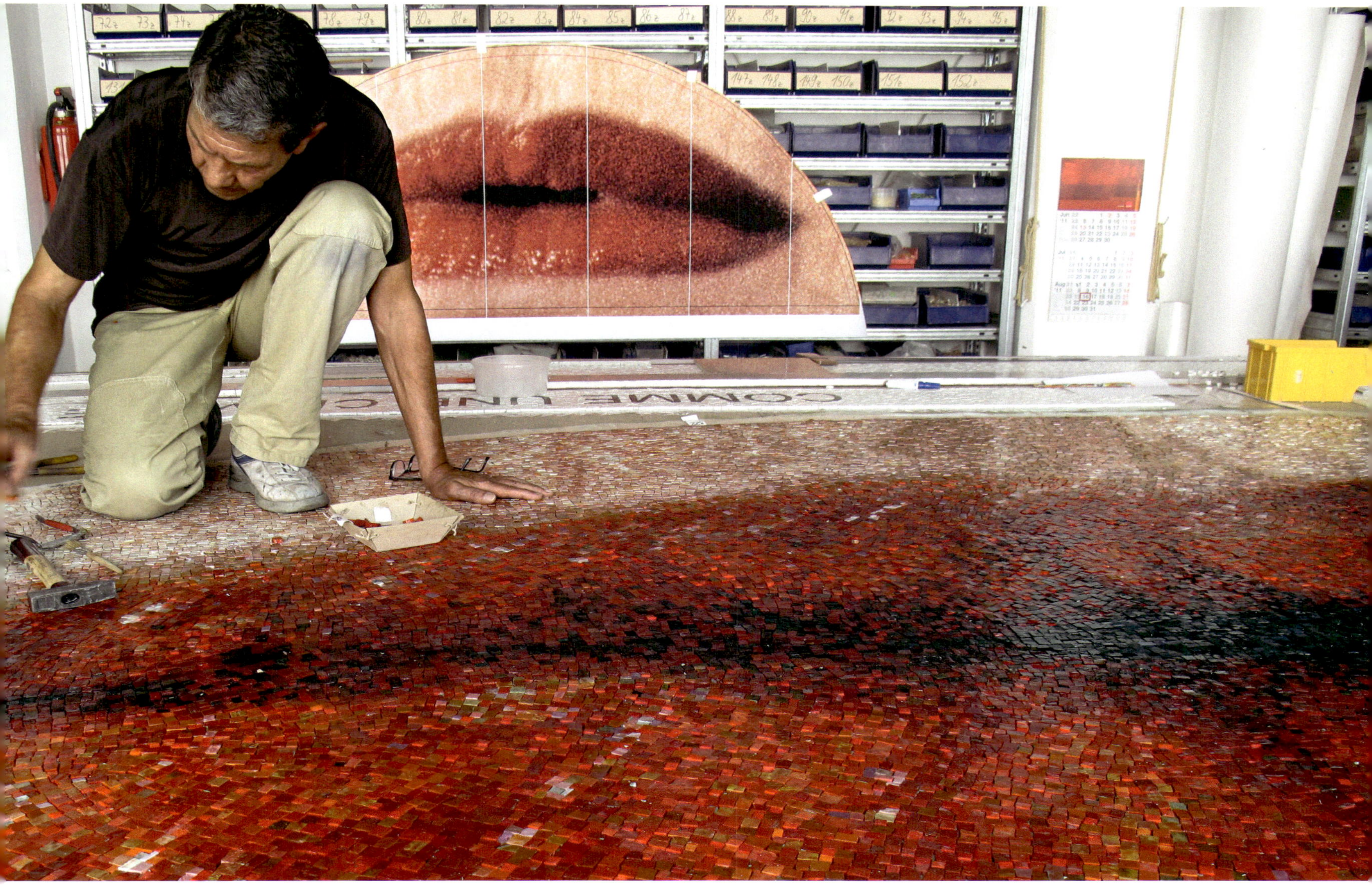

109

LA VOIX LACTÉE

108
The large mosaic covers the entire front wall. The writings on the left wall are part of the mosaic.

109
Looked at from close-up, the mosaic is impressionistic and lively. The photograph from the studio shows the dimension and the artistic challenges of the mosaicists.

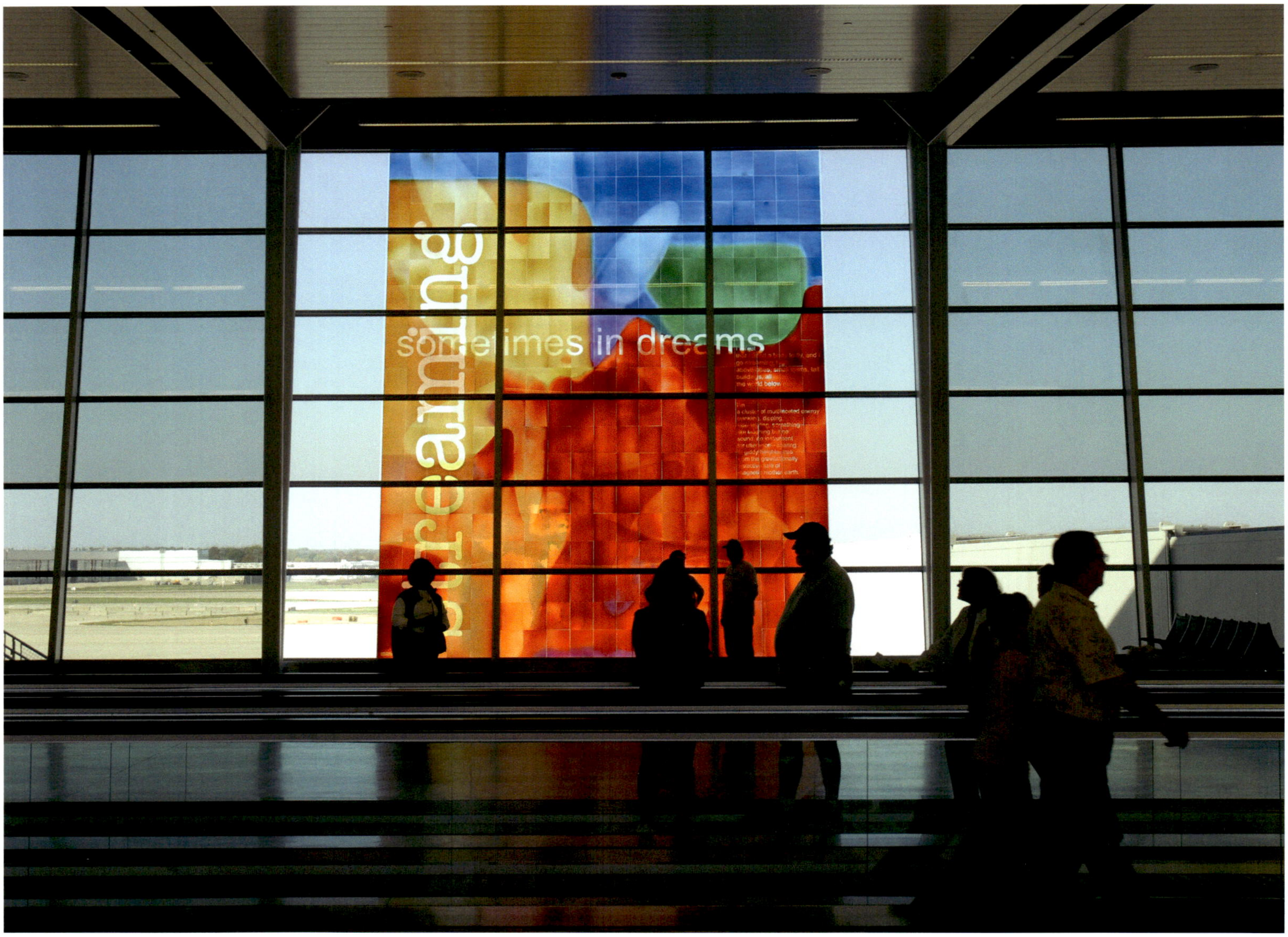

110

Martin Donlin / “The Indiana Windows”

location: Indianapolis International Airport, IN, USA, Concourse A und B / HOK Architects, Blackburn Architects - Public Art Administrator. Indianapolis Airport Authority / **year:** 2007 / **technique:** IGU – stained glass gluing

114 glass panels, 3200 square feet, hand-blown glass, etched, painted, fired, glued to laminated glass panes and worked into IGU. 14 windows, four of them 24 feet high, ten 12 feet high.
The work is based on texts about the longing for far-away places and dreams of coming home. Donlin asked poets from Indiana to contribute to this project.

THE INDIANA WINDOWS

110
“Streaming,” one of the four large glass pictures, each 24 feet high and 27 feet wide.

111
“Midnight Flight,” another one of the large glass pictures alongside ten of the medium-sized and small glass pictures, each 12 feet high.

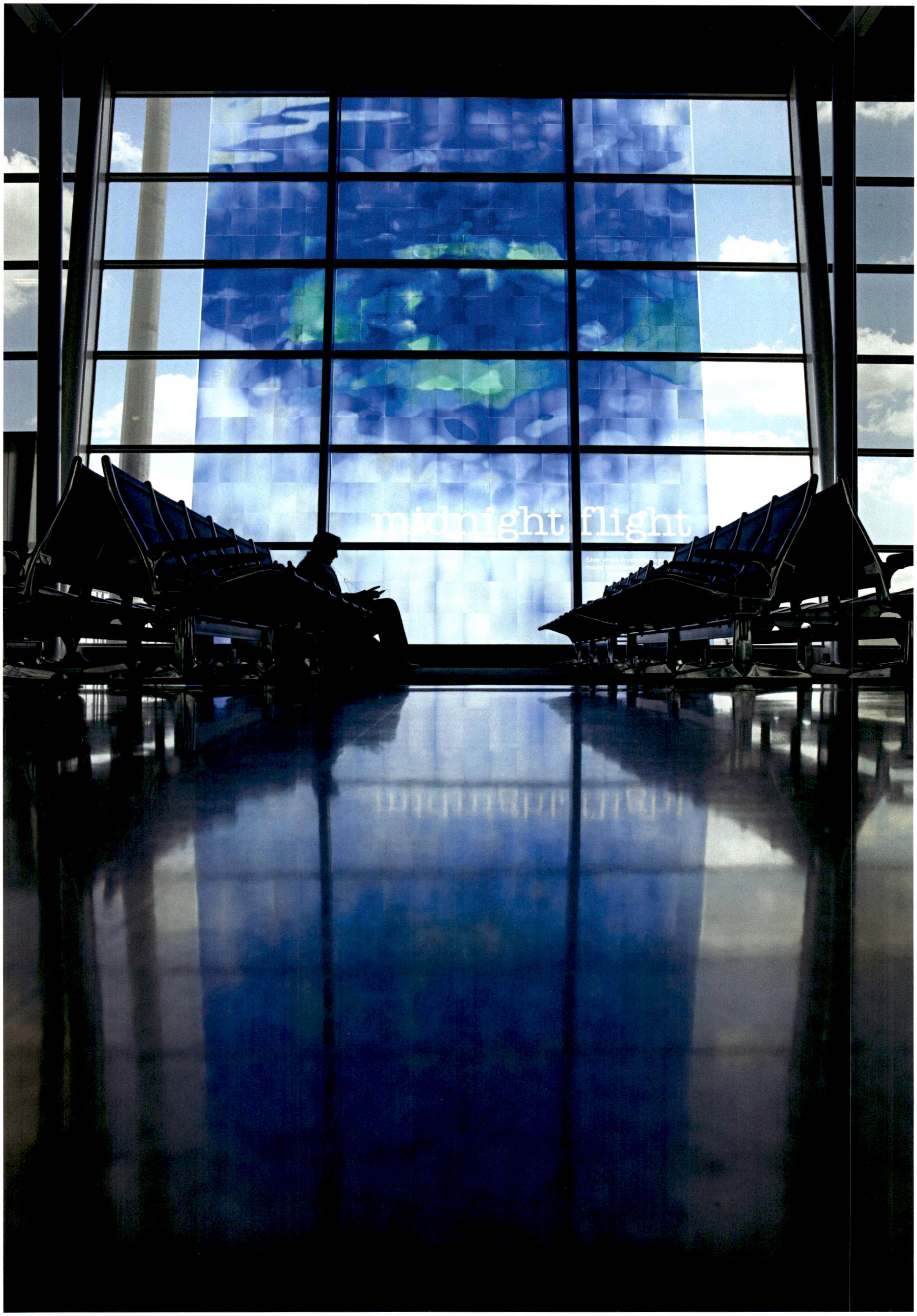

111

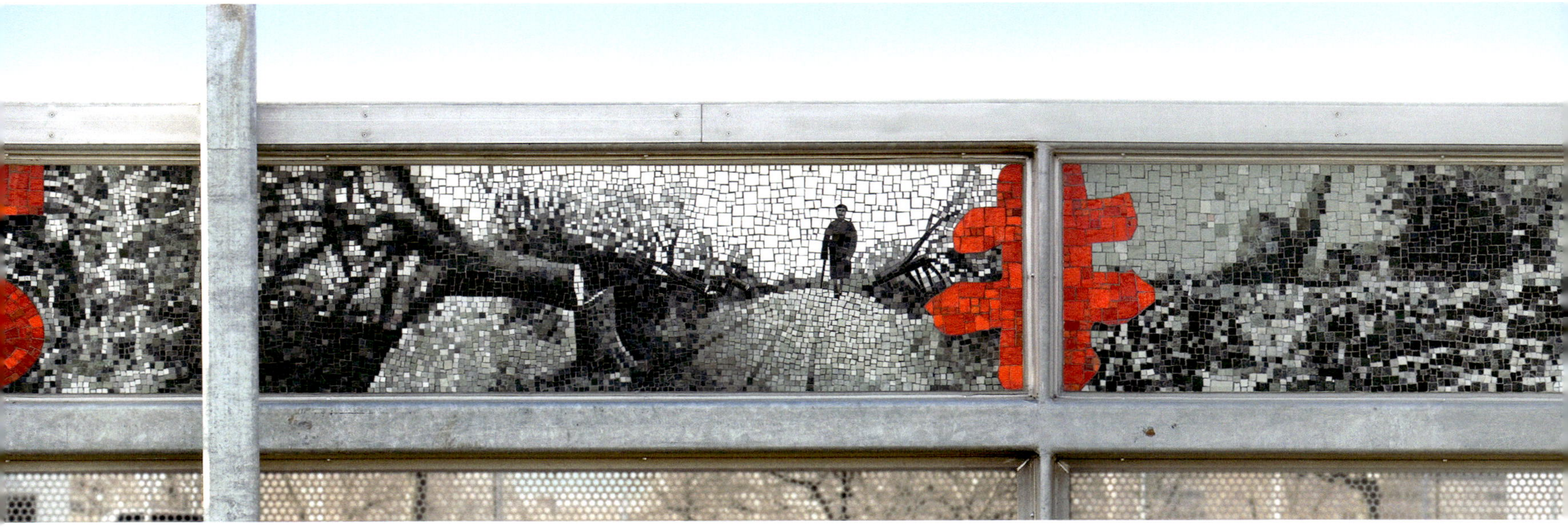

82

Ellen Driscoll / "Pro Patria Mori"

location: Liberty Memorial, Kansas City, MO, USA / Kansas City Parks & Recreation / **year:** 2006 / **technique:** mosaic, placed on either side of boards

Liberty Memorial is a spacious park ascending to a memorial for US soldiers who fell during World War One. When Ellen Driscoll designed the 80 feet wide gate to this park with metal punchwork and mosaic bands on the interior and exterior, she used her own as well as found materials such as old photographs, military plans, and drawings. This work won the Public Art Award in 2007.

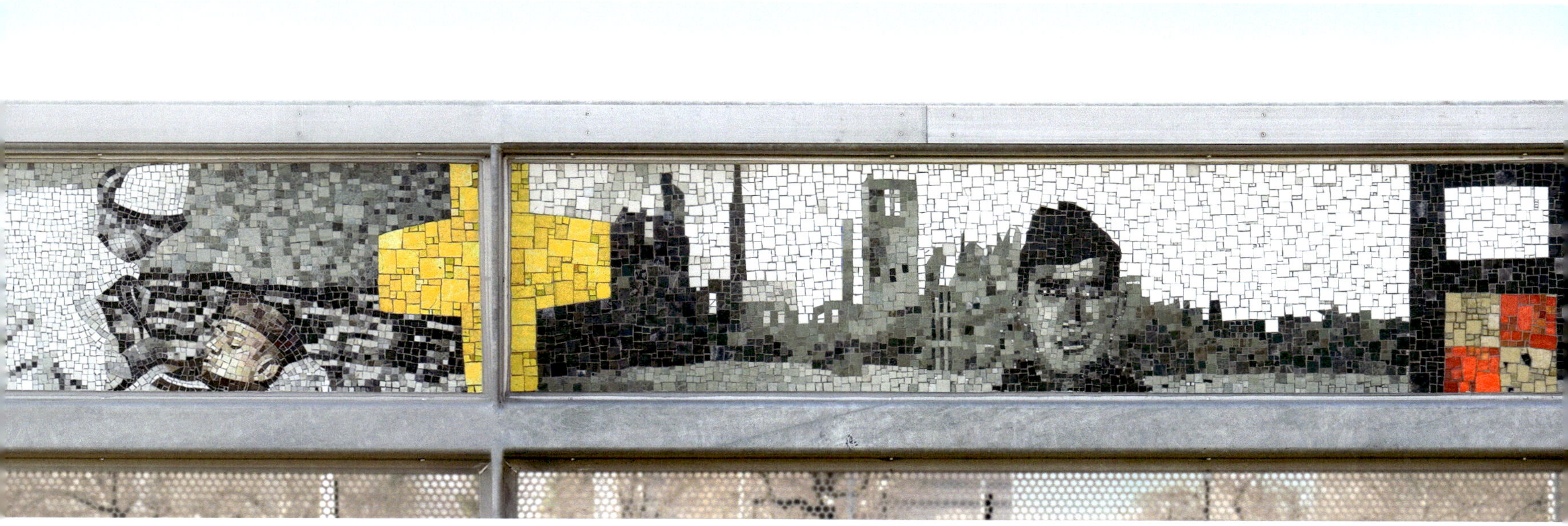

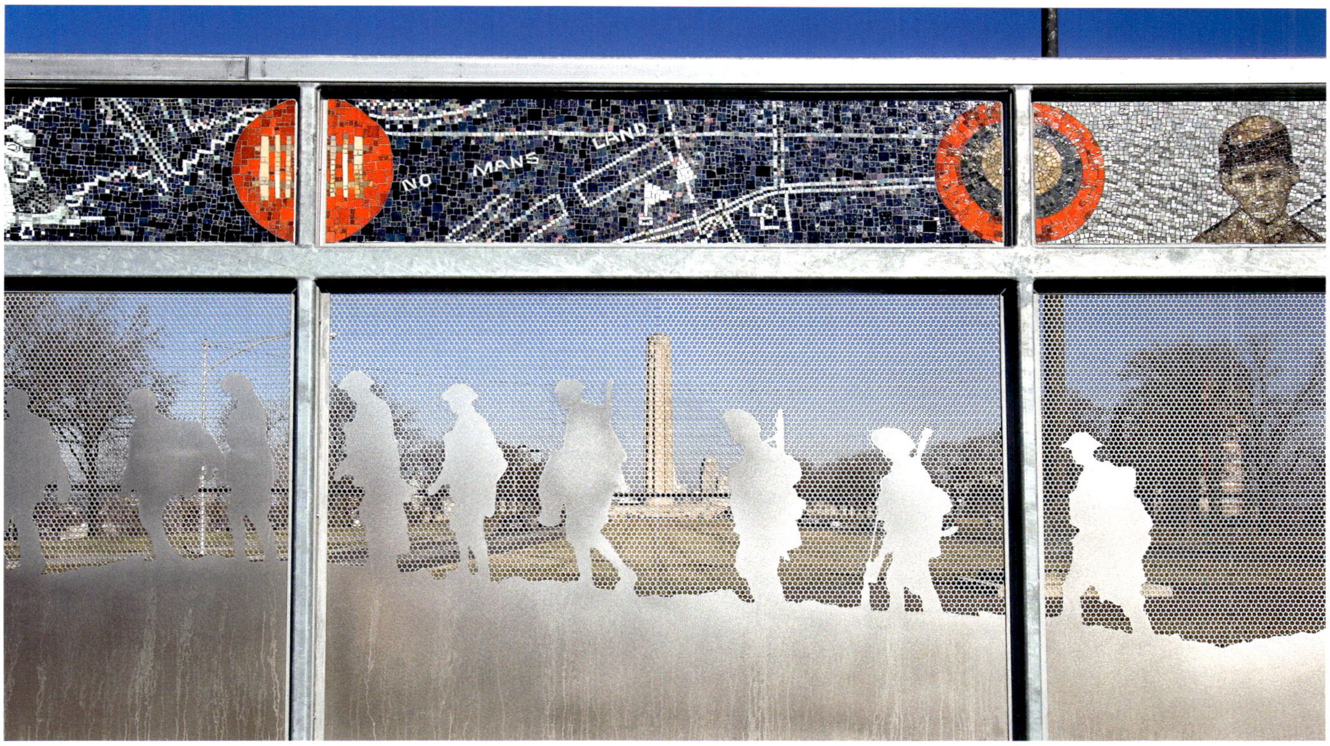

113

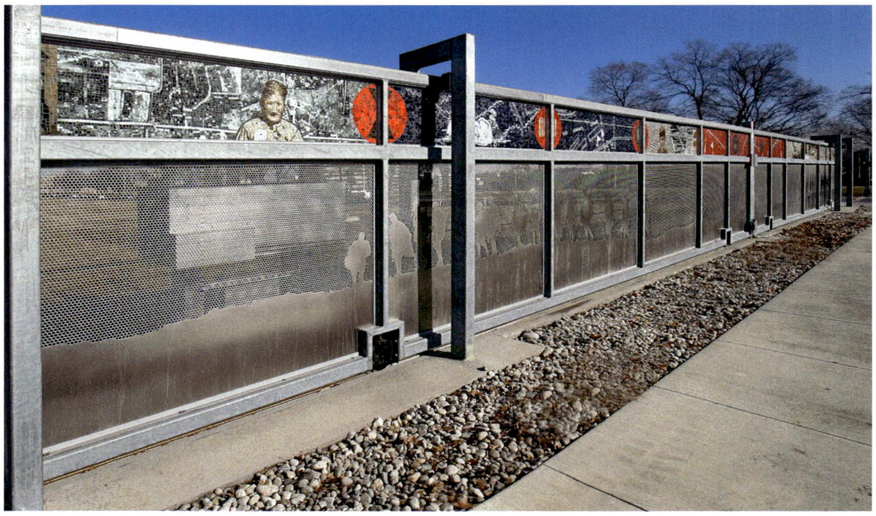

114

PRO PATRIA MORI

The mosaics on the exterior of the gate.

112
Details of the continous mosaic bands.

113
Detail of a gate seen from the outside with stenciled metal sheets and mosaic, looking towards the ascending park and the memorial with its impressive tower in the far background.

114
Diagonal view from the exterior.

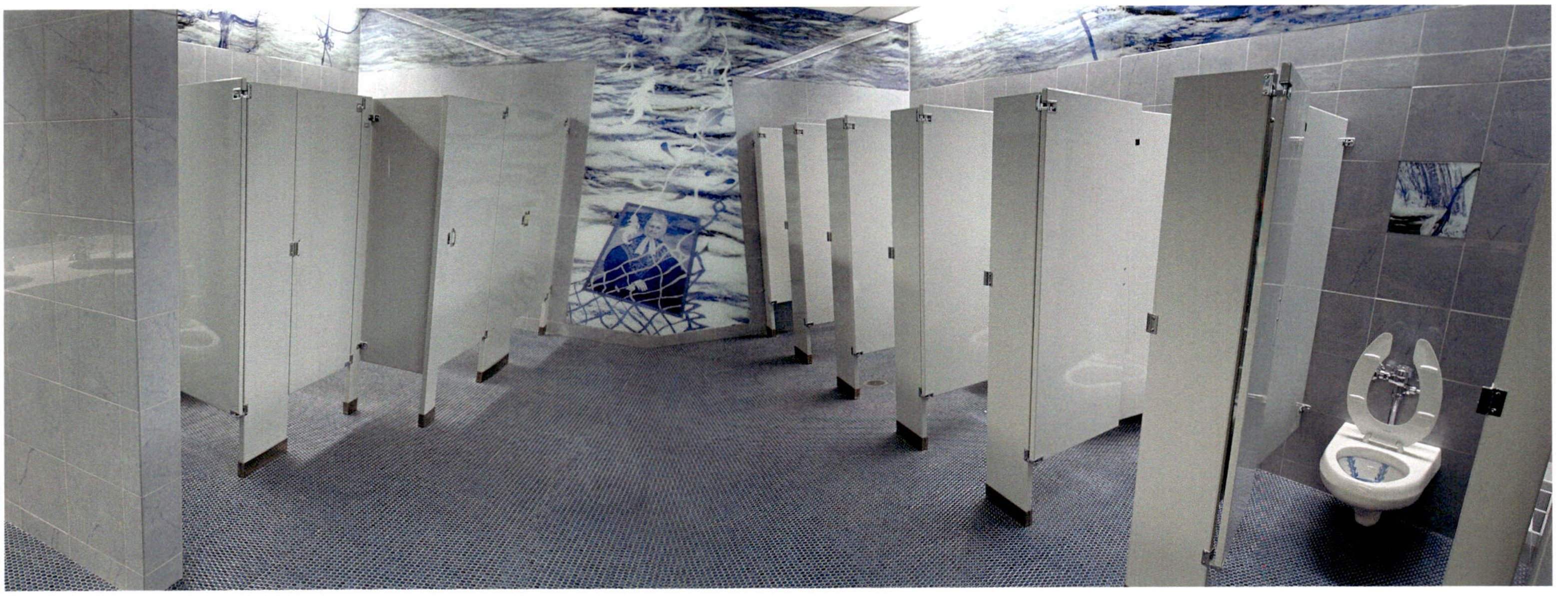

115

CATCHING THE DRIFT

115
View of the museum's Ladies' Restroom.

116
One of the bigger glass panels and part of the surrounding glass band: underwater marine life, a fishing net, and an image from the museum collection.

Ellen Driscoll / "Catching the Drift"

116

location: Ladies Room, Smith College Museum of Art, Northampton, MA, USA / Polshek Partnership Architects / **year:** 2003 / **technique:** float glass painting

Engraved float glass painting with color fill, silk-screen, hand painted and laminated; affixed to the walls in tile technique.

Driscoll's installation for the womens' room of a college's Art Museum includes a horizontal band and larger and smaller wall pieces of glass panels on which are sandblasted original drawings of underwater sealife. Around the room – on the walls, in the sinks, in the toilets – are painted images of fishing nets, hooks, and various flora and fauna relating to the sea. She incorporated four images of women that she culled from the museum's collection, the largest two face off across the space. The idea, Driscoll says, was to play with the concept of private space and public art. From "Flush with Art," Smith Alumnae Quarterly.

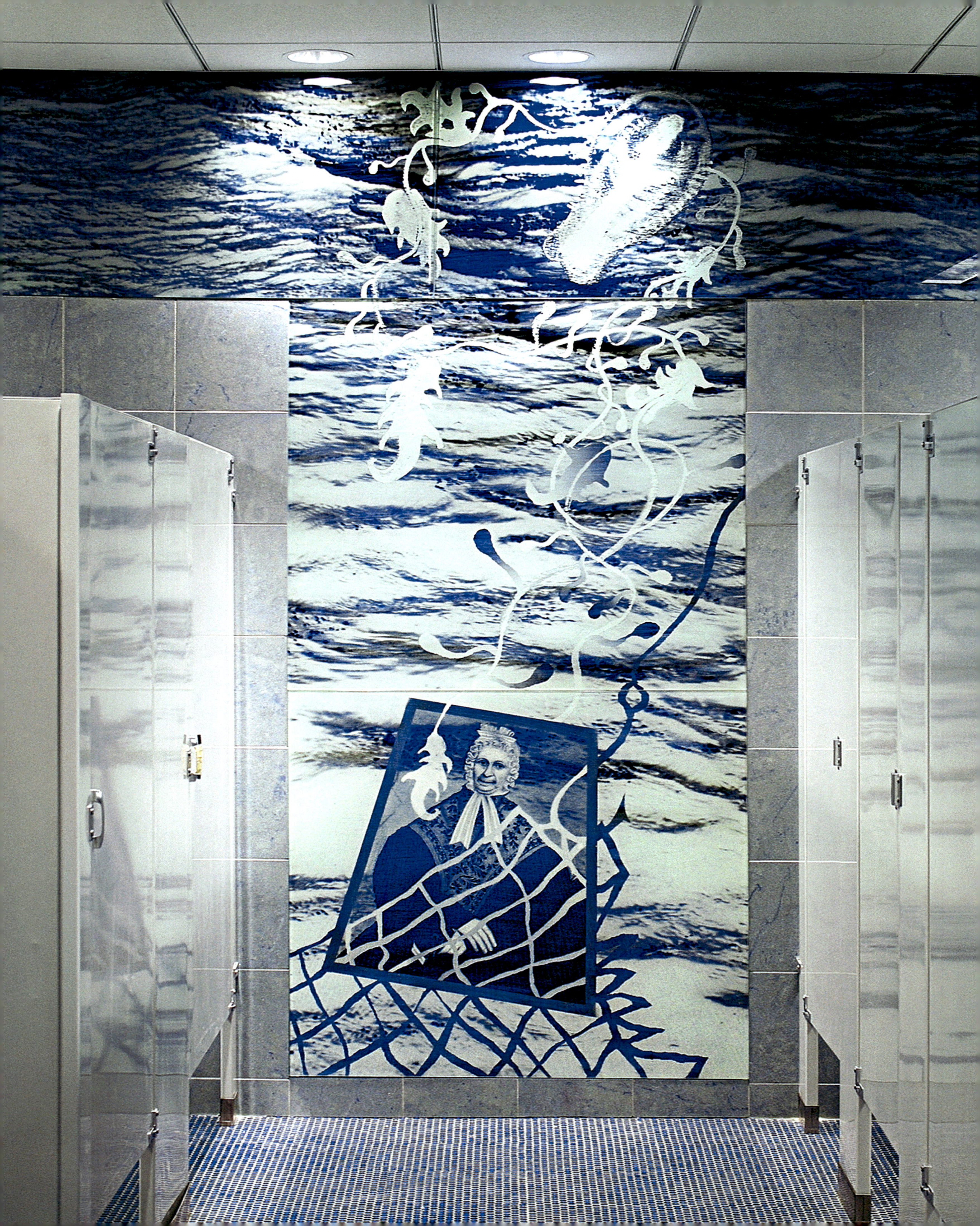

LIGHT-BOX

117
The glass sculpture, lit at night, in front of the buildings around the “Münchner Tor” complex.

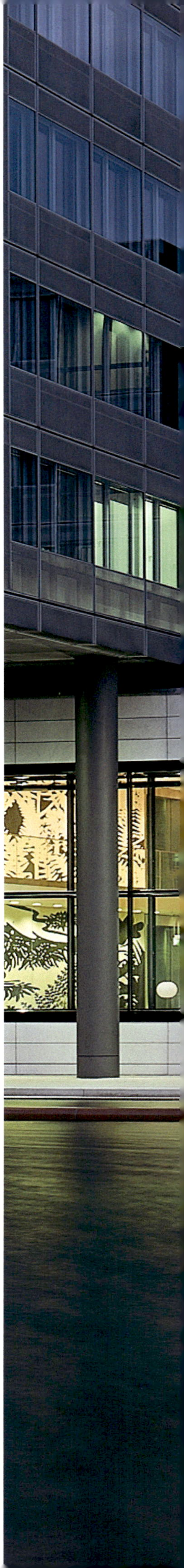

Roland Fischer / “Light-Box”

location: Air siphoning works on the lake near the Munich office building at “Münchner Tor,” Munich, DE / Allmann Sattler Wappner Architects / **year:** 2003 / **technique:** float glass painting

Roland Fischer took close-up images of skyscraper facades around the world. Details that interested him may be found as motifs on this glass block. Somewhat removed from the world by water, the object becomes a sign for architecture. (SkulpTour Munich)

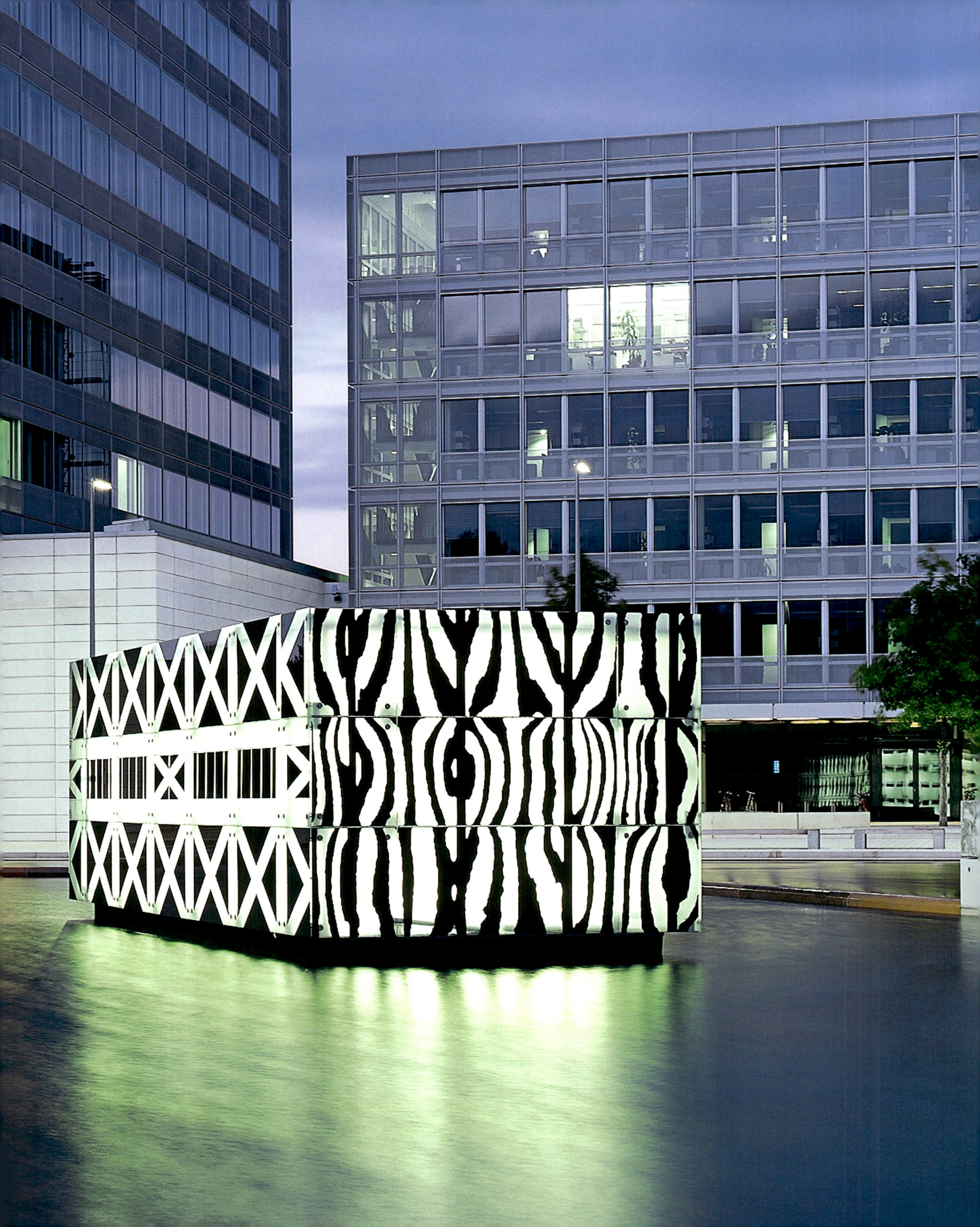

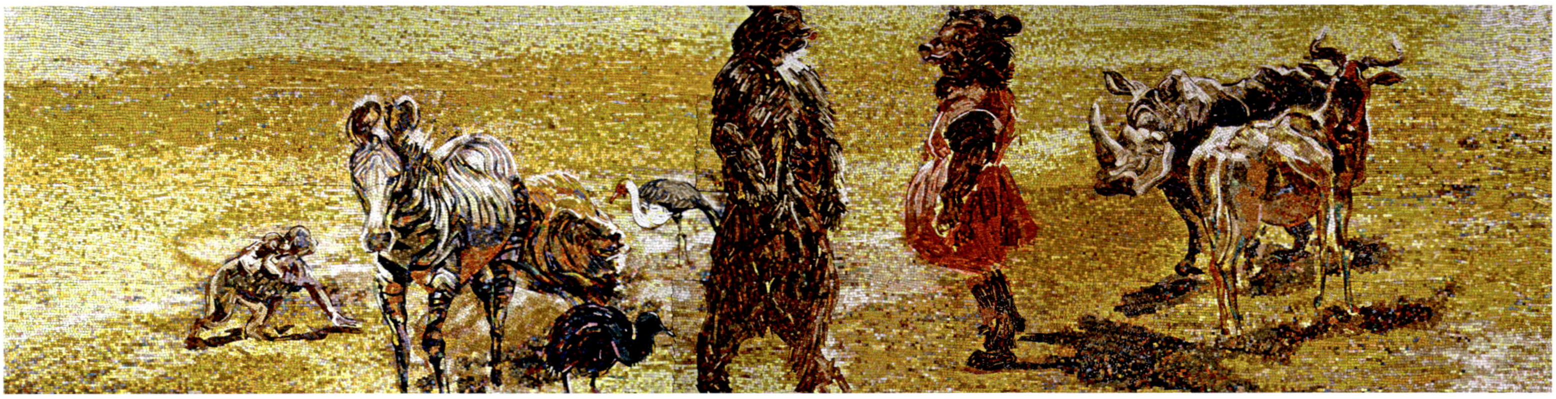

118

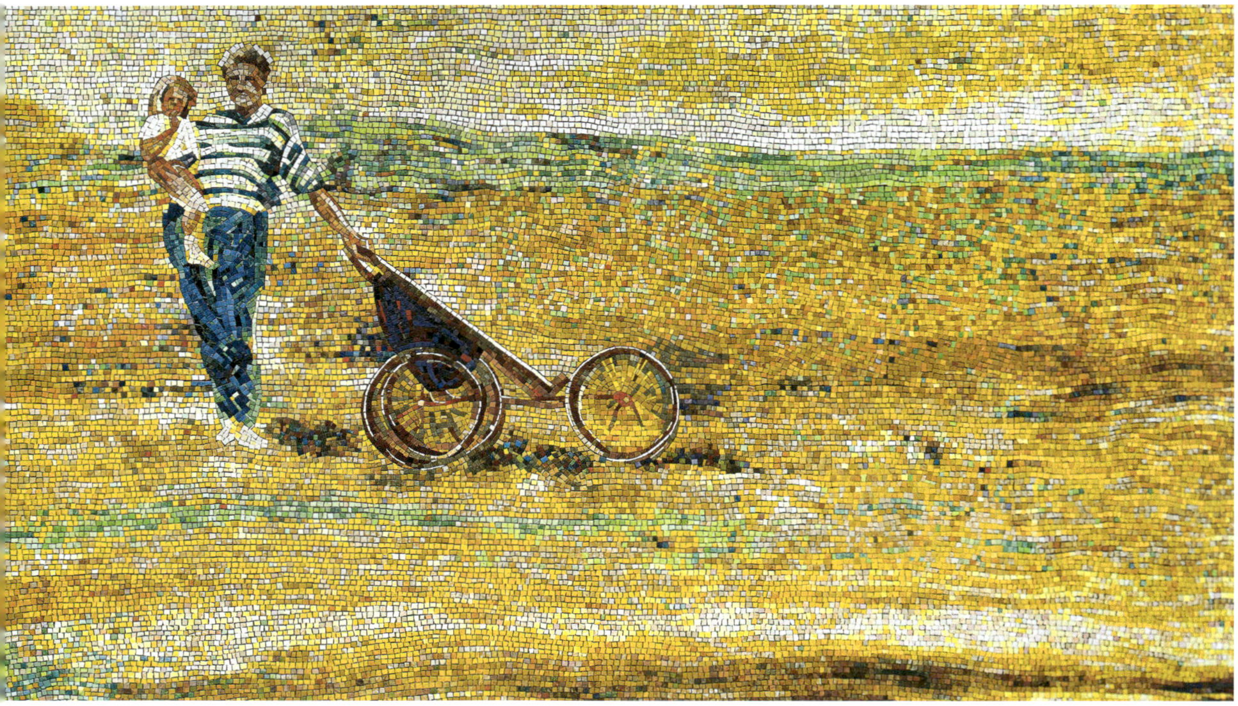

119

THE GARDEN OF CIRCUS DELIGHTS

118
A larger segment of the fairytale-like animal picture.

119
Detail from image showing a woman, a child, and a stroller.

120
The businessman returns to the light from the darkness of the circus, a small detail from the circus mosaic.

Eric Fischl / "The Garden of Circus Delights"

120

location: 34th Street-PennStation (subway), New York, NY, USA / MTA Arts for Transit / **year:** 2001 / **technique:** glass mosaic

"Gabriel, the job is just about finished. They are grouting the final pieces. I want to let you know how extremely pleased I am with our collaboration. The work done surpassed my wildest dreams. Your men brought my design to life in such an exciting way. ... I'm sure we will be in contact soon but I just wanted to thank you now while I am still so excited. Warm regards, Eric" (Eric Fischl April 9, 2003).

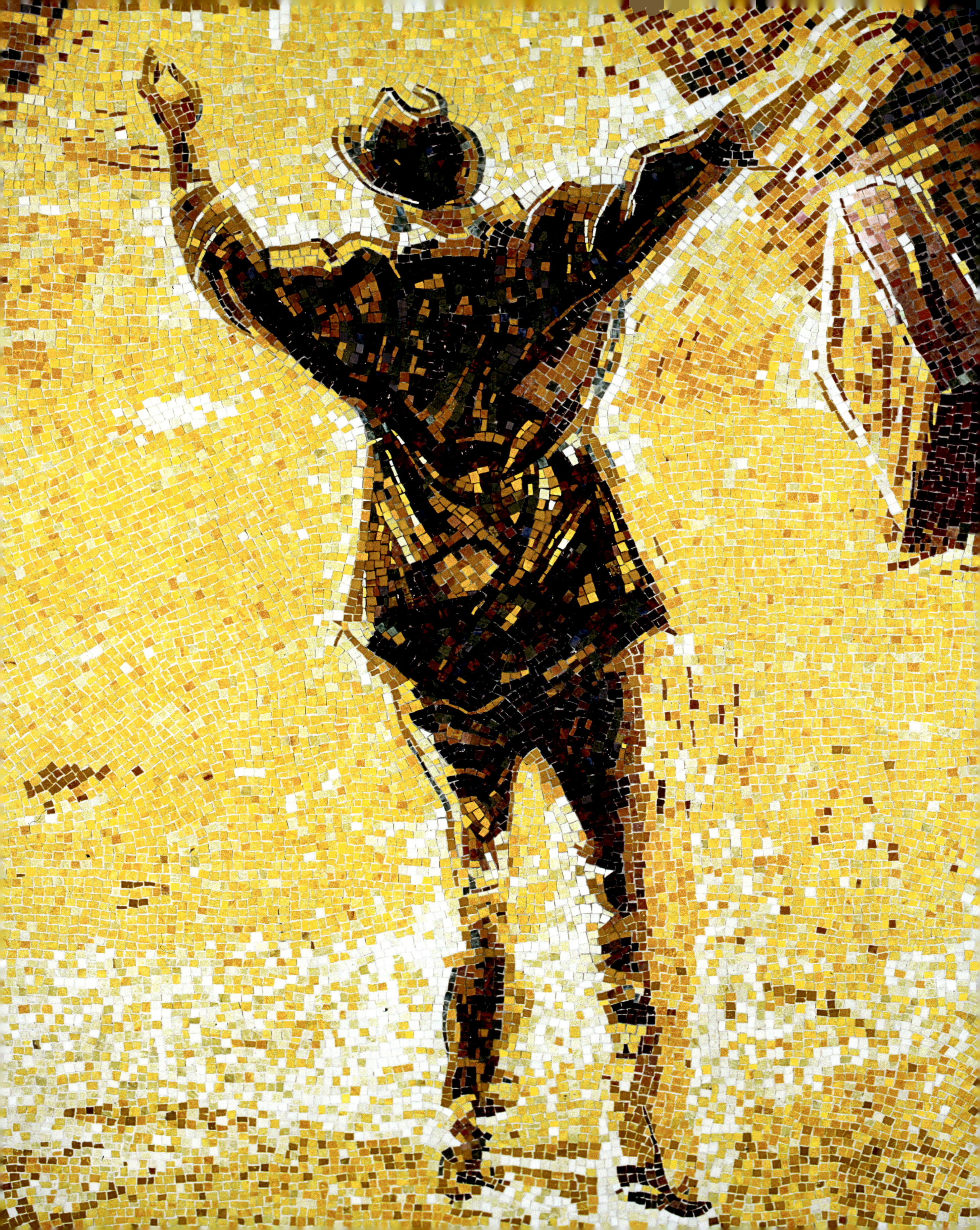

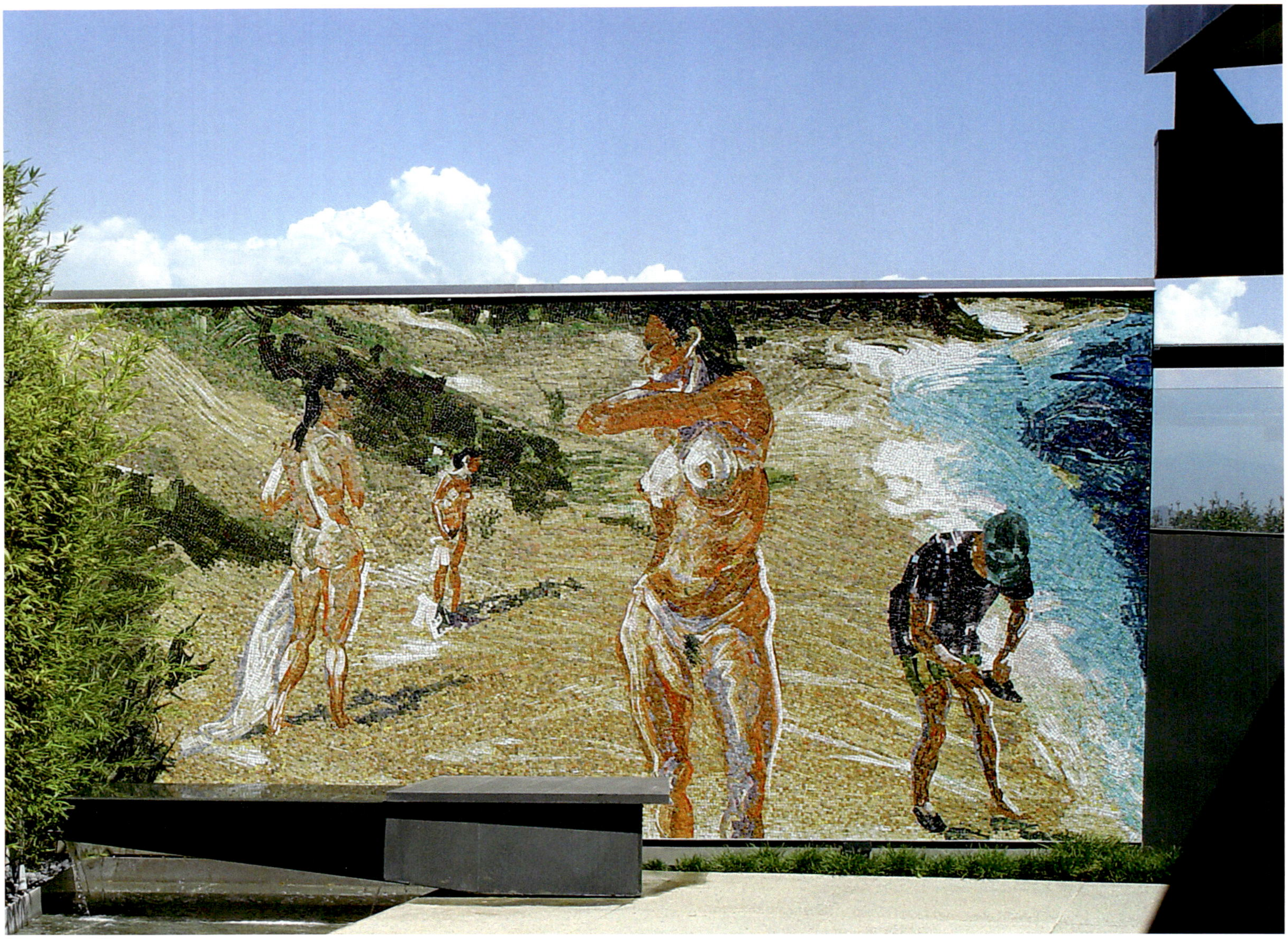

121

Eric Fischl / Untitled (Girls at Beach with Man in Green Hat)

location: Patio mosaic, Private Home, Los Angeles, CA, USA / Achitects Smith Miller + Hawkinson /
year: 2006 / **technique:** glass mosaic

In this mosaic, one senses the artist's ease and liberty. There is an obvious difference between "public" (see previous page) and "private" art, the latter influenced by collectors.

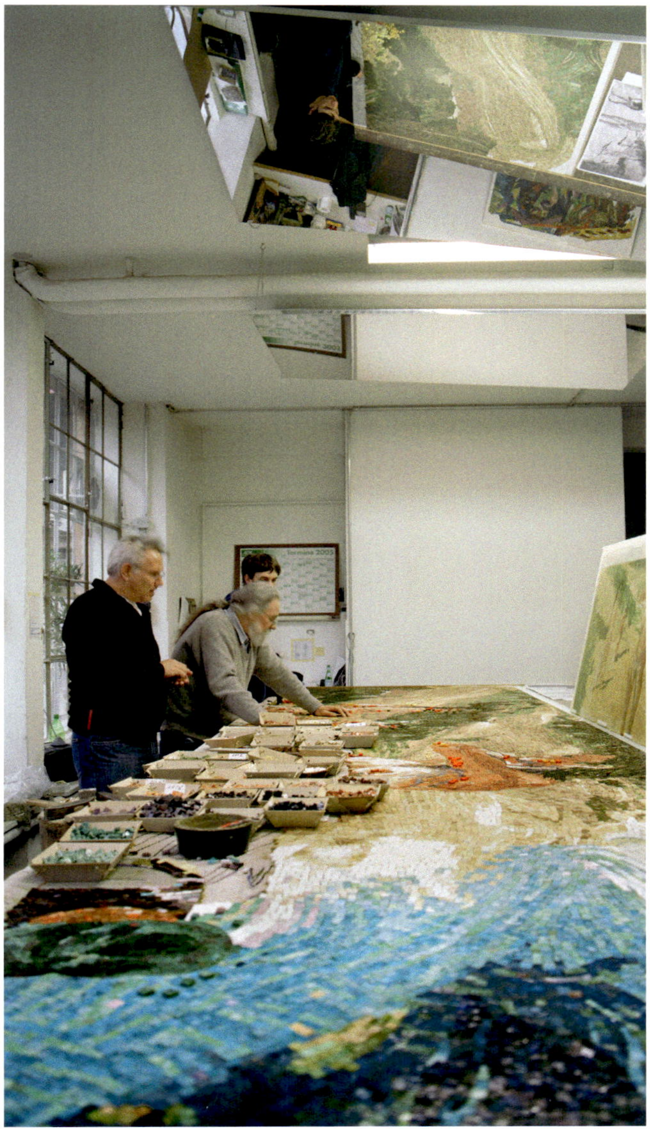

122

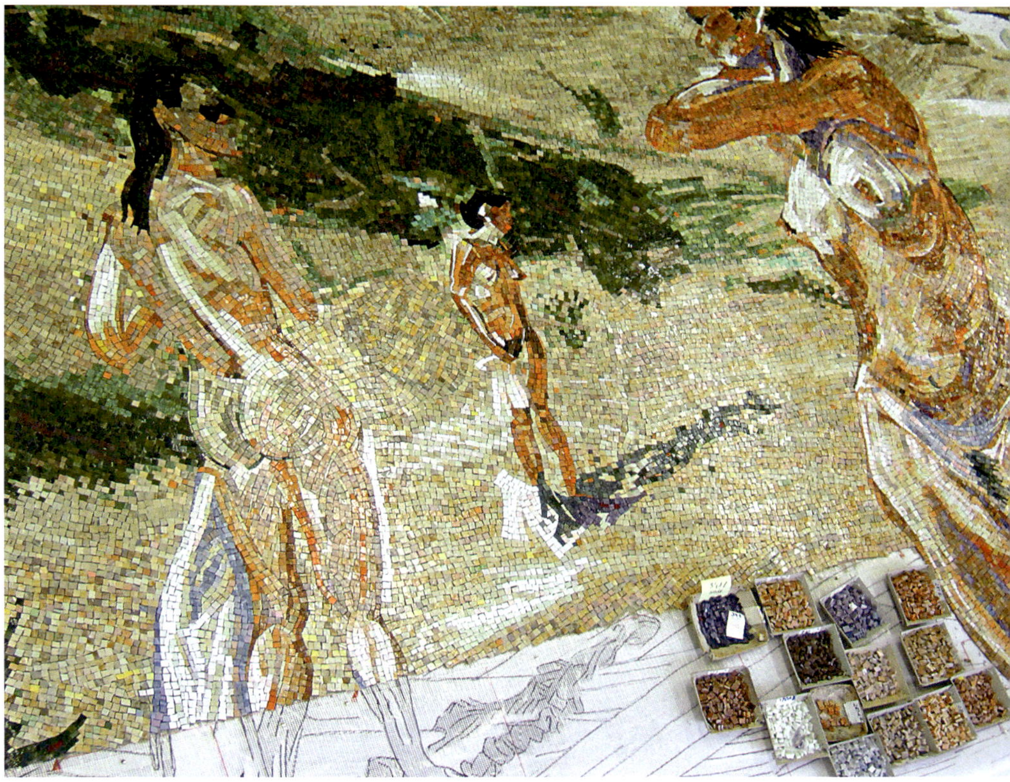

123

UNTITLED (GIRLS AT BEACH WITH MAN IN GREEN HAT)

121
The completed mosaic, installed.

122
Eric Fischl during one of his numerous visits to Munich with the mosaicists.

123
Detail: at the worktable in the studio.

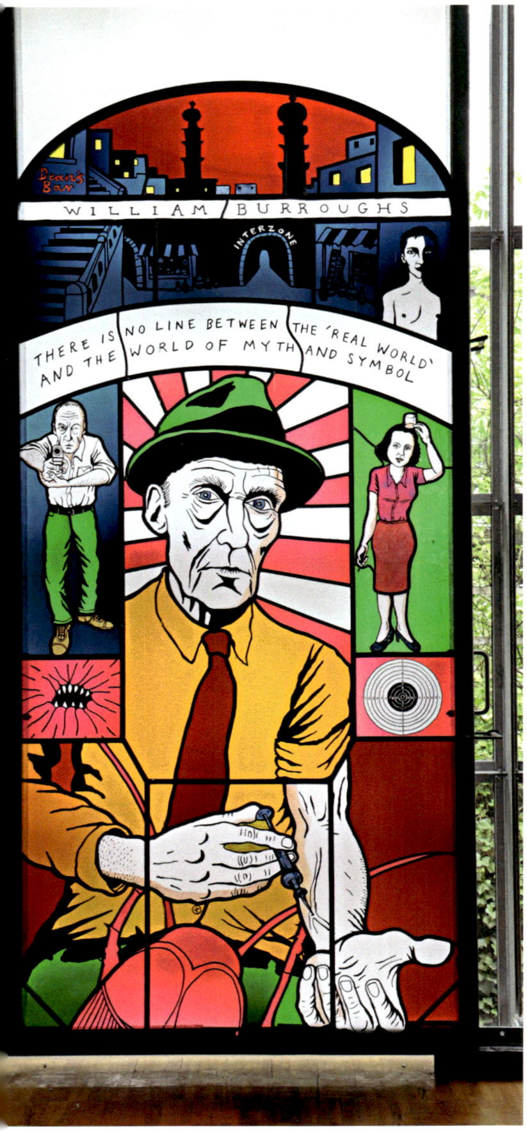

124

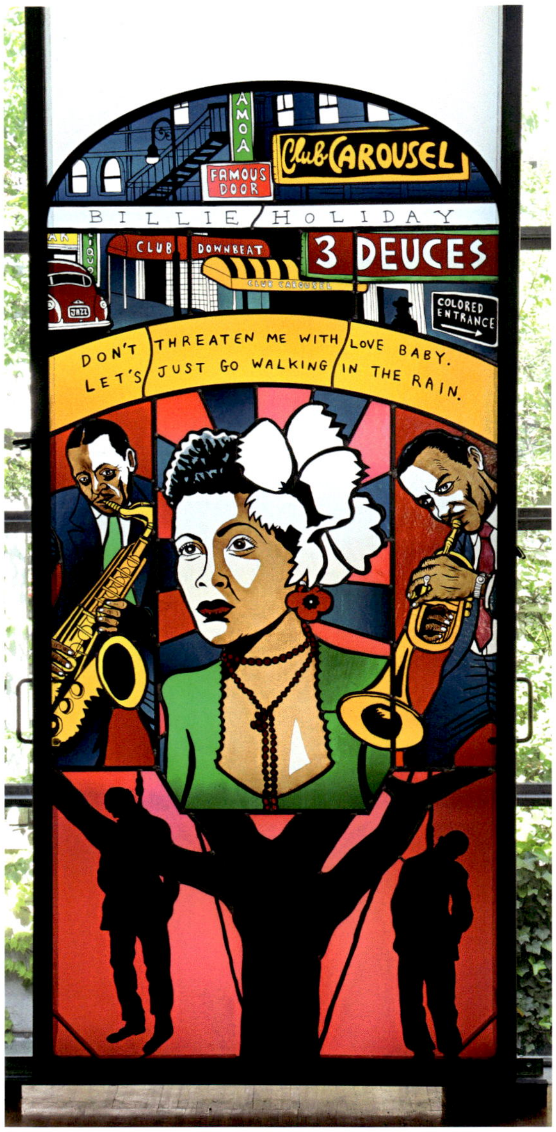

125

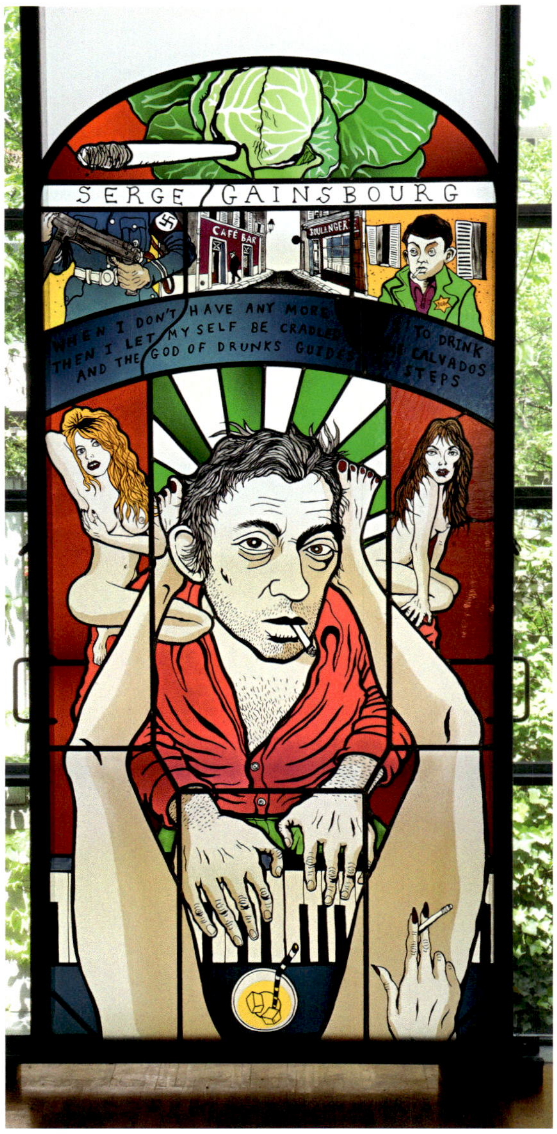

126

Neal Fox / "Beware of the God"

92

location: Daniel Blau Gallery, Munich and London / Courtesy Daniel Blau Gallery / **year:** 2011 / **technique:** stained glass, framed

Twelve windows in steel frames, each 250 × 114 cm, fabricated in the traditional technique of stained glass, genuine antique and flashed glass, acid etched, painted, fired, and leaded.
"Fox's drawings depict a phantasmagoric journey through the detritus and mythology of pop culture ... celebrations of the debauched and iconoclastic characters whose ideas have helped shape our collective consciousness.... Working with traditional methods at the renowned Franz Mayer of Munich manufacturer, Fox has produced a set of twelve 2.5 meter high stained glass windows; exhibited in a single room – an alternative church of alternative saints." (Daniel Blau Gallery)

BEWARE OF THE GOD

124
William Burroughs – "There is no line between the 'real world' and the world of myth and symbol."

125
Billie Holiday – "Don't threaten me with love Baby. Let's just go walking in the rain."

126
Serge Gainsbourg – "When I don't have any more places to drink then I let myself be cradled by the calvados and the god of drunks guides my steps."

127
Picture Aleister Crowley – "Do what thou wilt shall be the whole of the law."

128
John Watson – "Smell the roses on the way along. Hold tightly when you're strong, and when you have to, let go gently." Detail from the lower part.

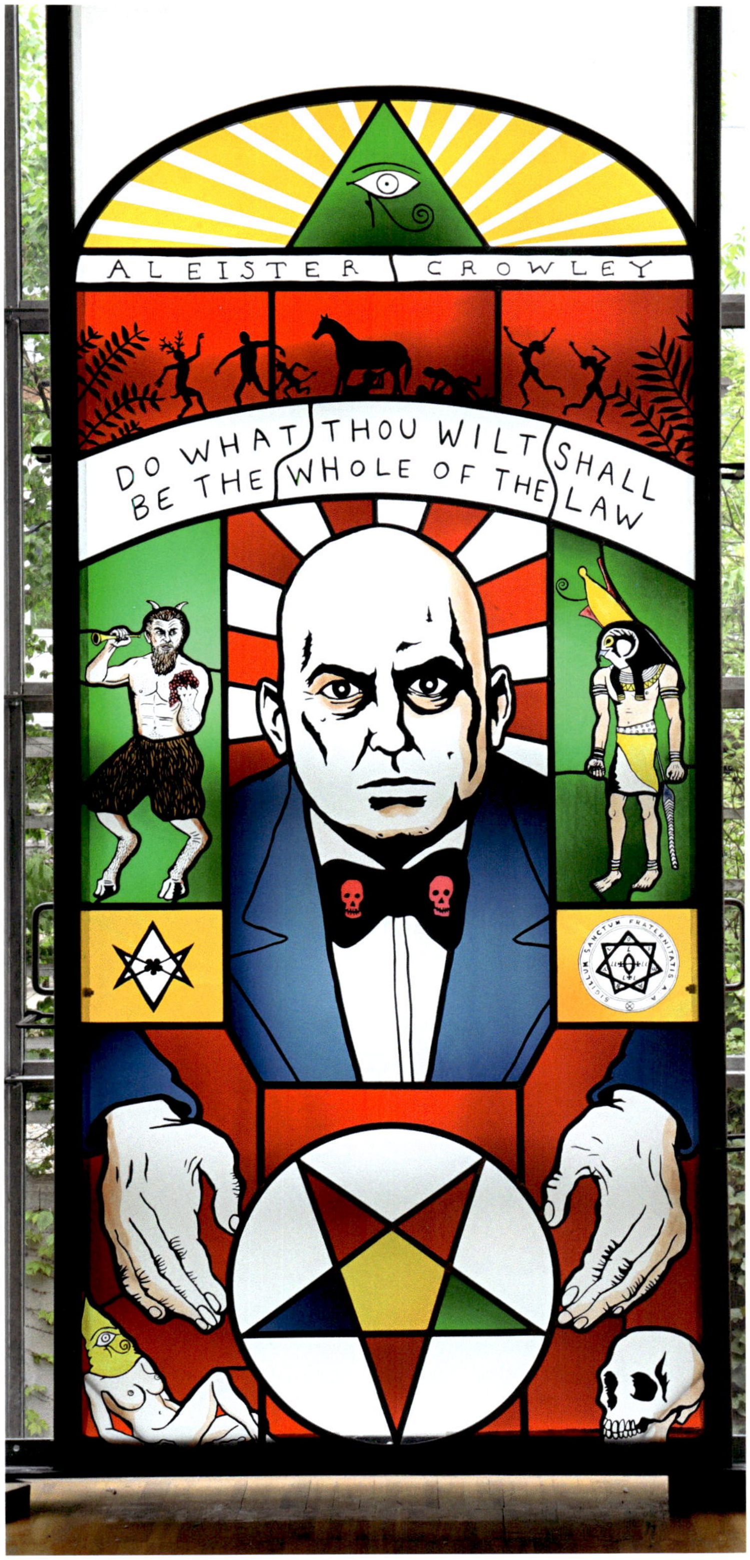

127

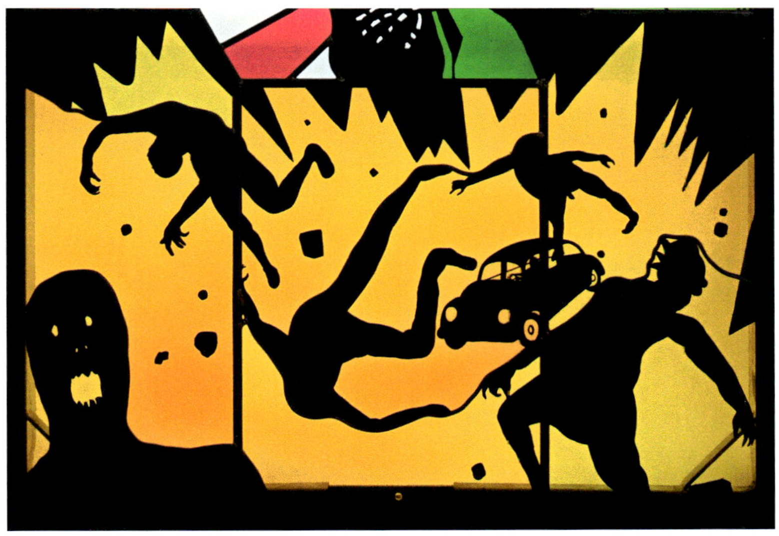

128

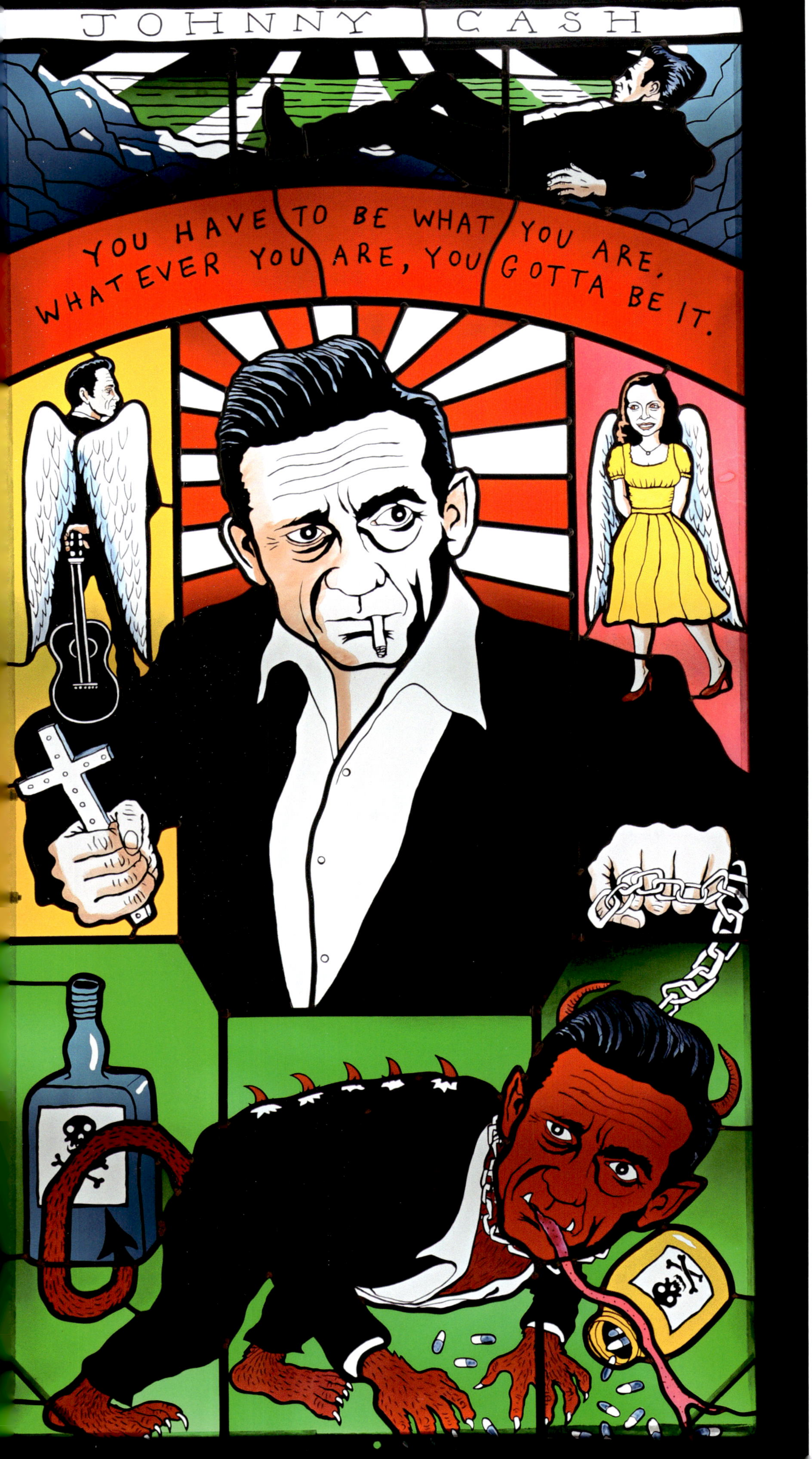
JOHNNY CASH
YOU HAVE TO BE WHAT YOU ARE.
WHATEVER YOU ARE, YOU GOTTA BE IT.

BEWARE OF THE GOD

129
Jonny Cash – “You have to be what you are – whatever you are, you gotta be it.”

130
Neal Fox in in the Munich studio.

131 +
132
Neal Fox’s leading collaborators at the Hofkunstanstalt.

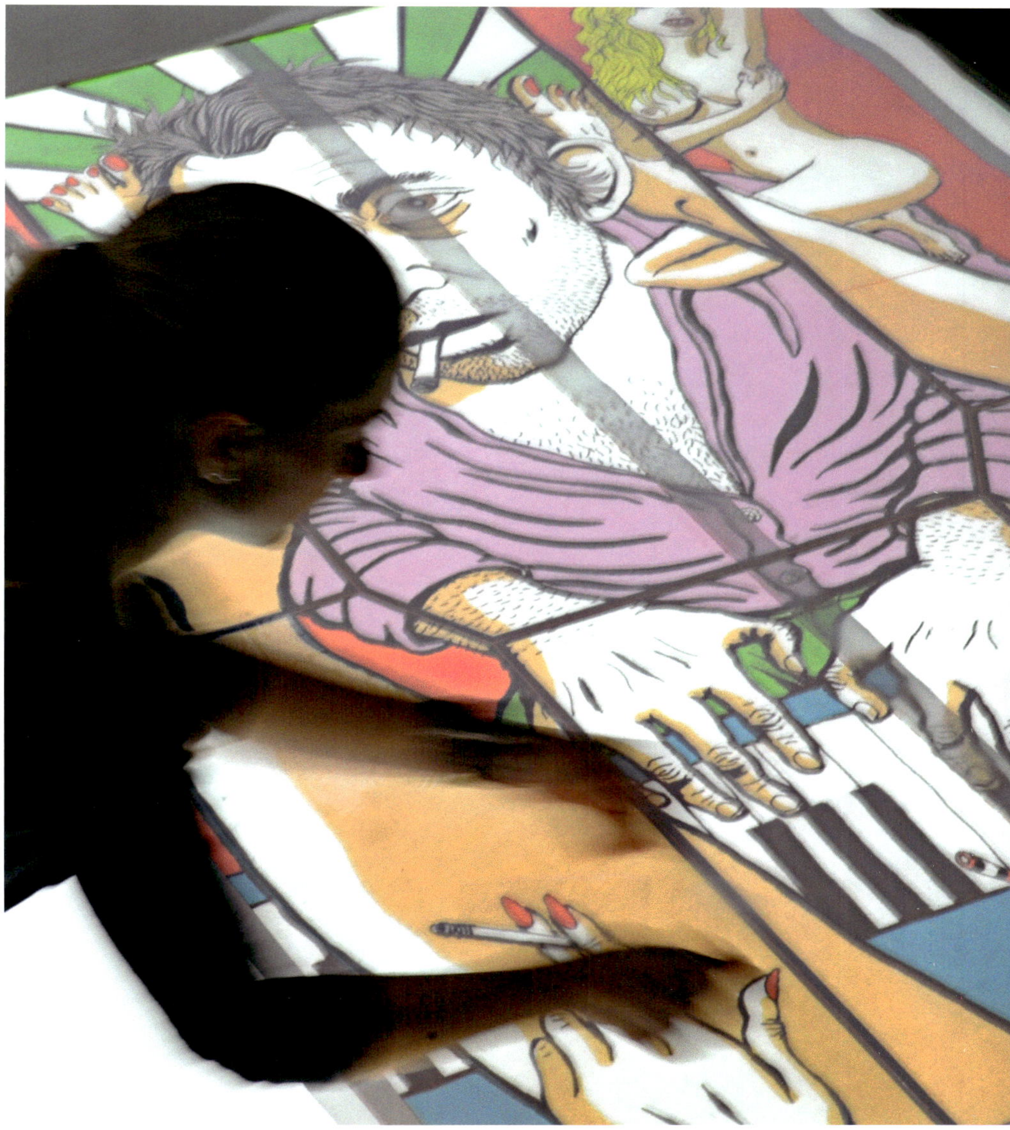

131

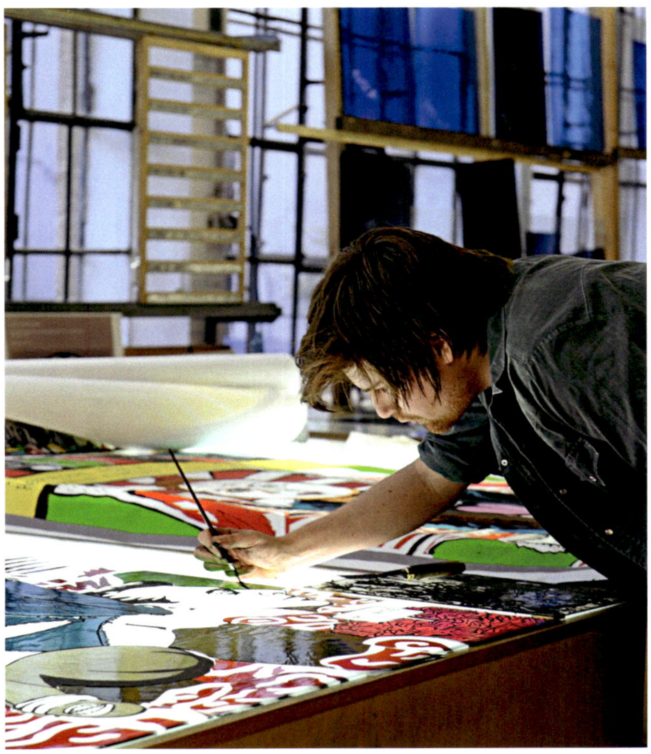

130

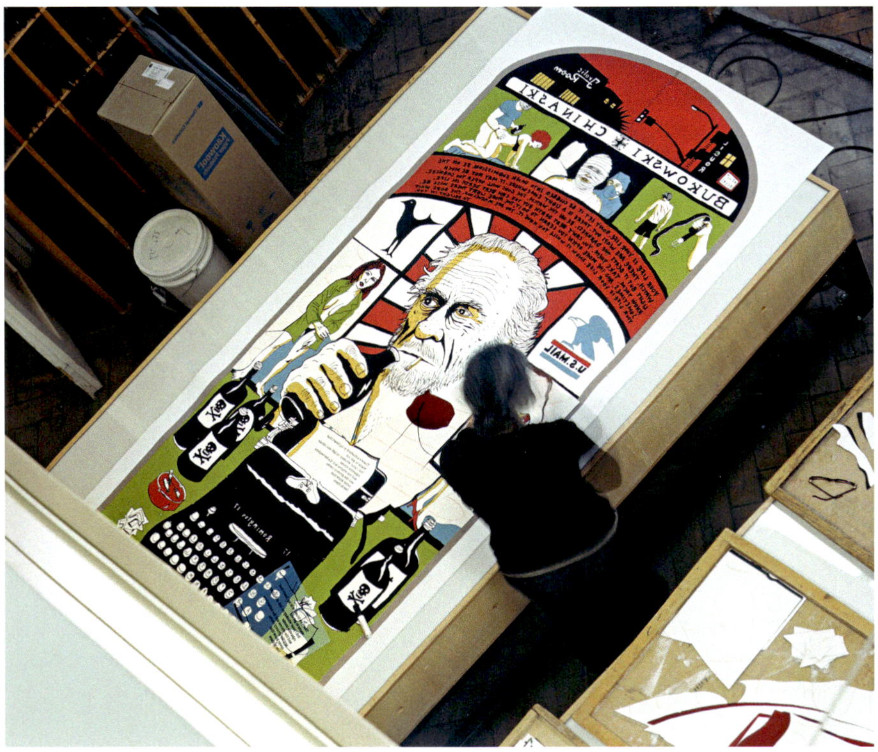

132

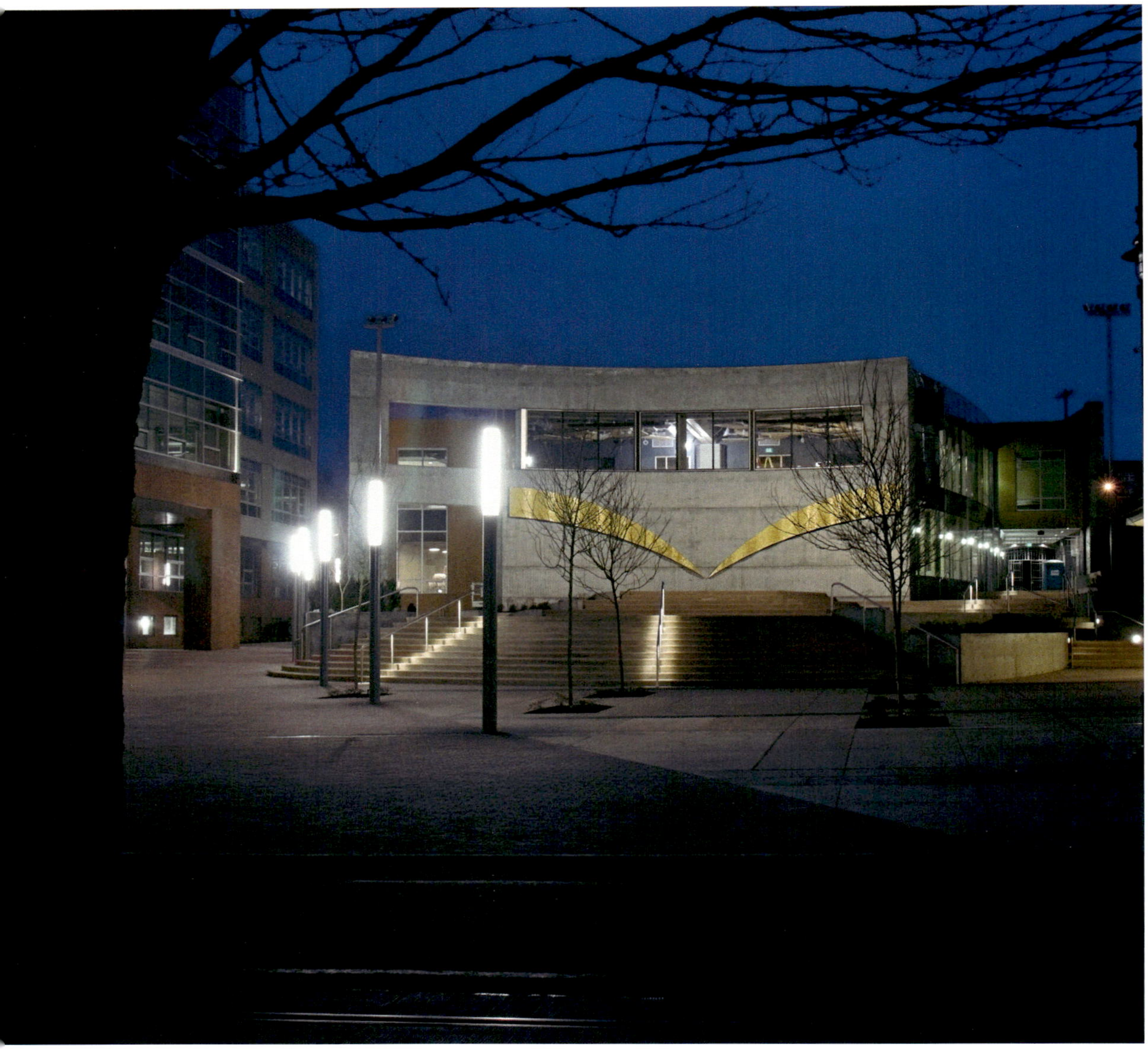

133

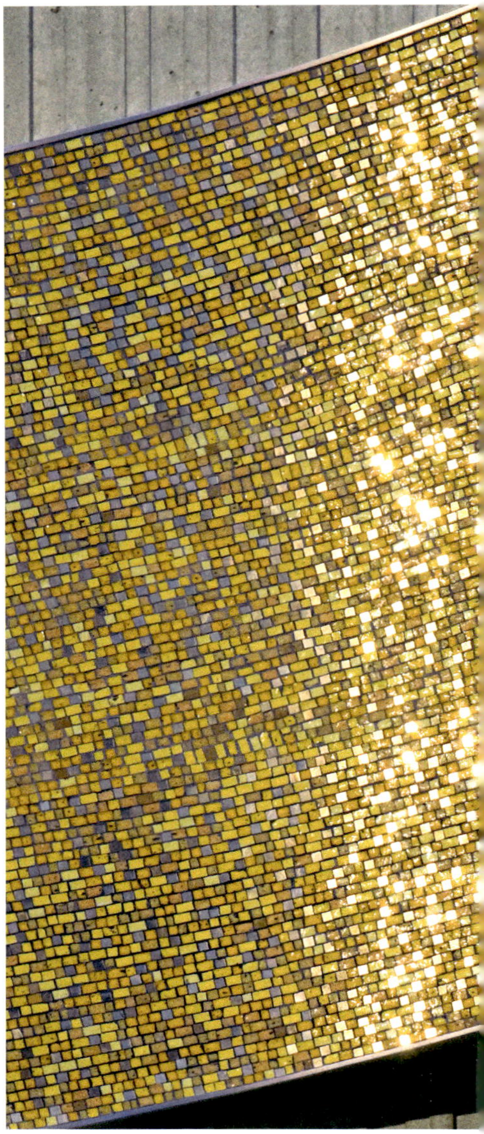

134

Ann Gardner / “Convergence”

96

location: Terry Ave. N, Seattle, WA, USA / Schnitzer West, Vulcan Real Estate / **year:** 2009 / **technique:** glass and gold mosaic

This piece is installed in a plaza between two buildings in the South Lake Union neighborhood of Seattle. The two yellow arcs that form Convergence curve down and inward toward an intimate point on the wall. The small yellow/gold glass tiles become more intense toward this point, seemingly gathering the light and energy of the plaza in this one particular place.

CONVERGENCE

133
Nocturnal view towards the plaza and the building with the mosaic bands.

134
Detail of the mosaic surface with color and gold smalti.

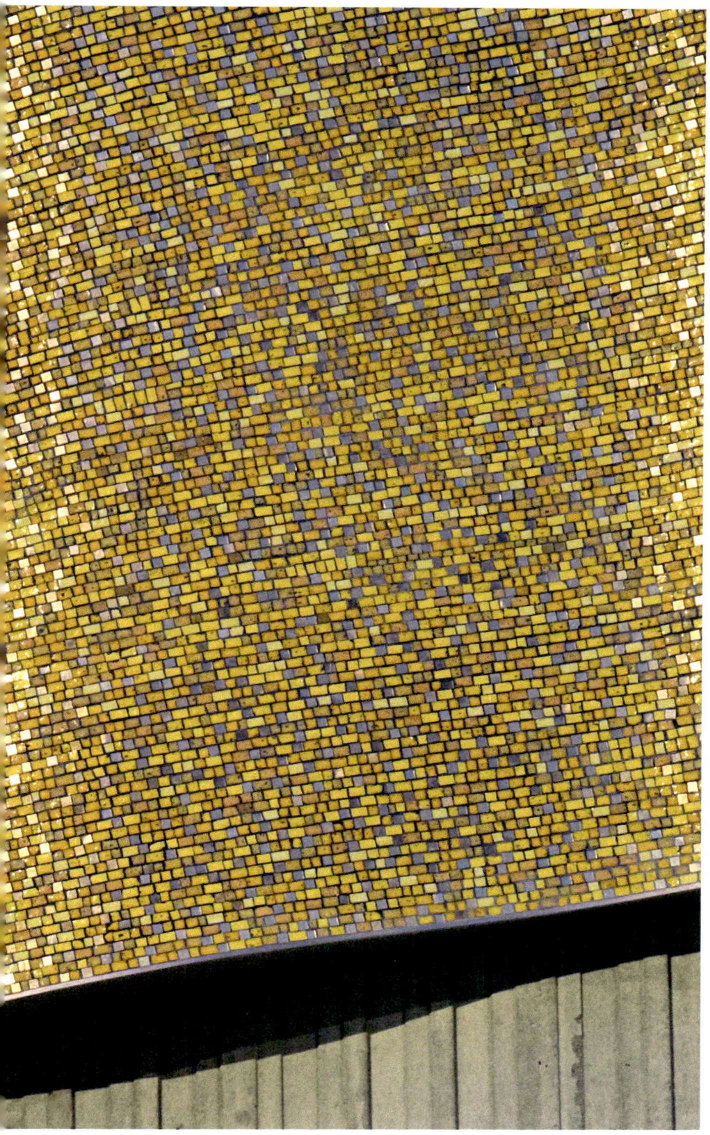

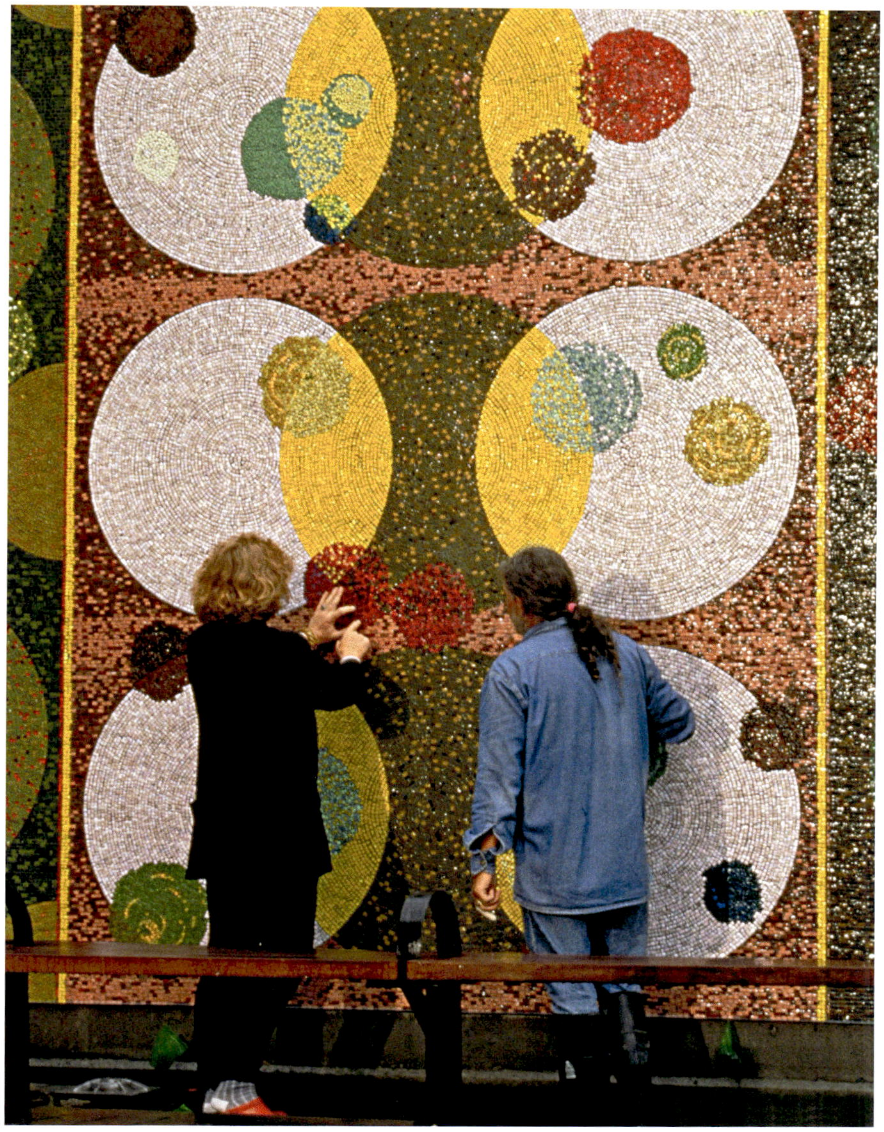

135

“Danza del Cerchio”

location: Pier 66, Port Seattle, WA, USA / **year:** 1996 / **technique:** glass mosaic

Venetian glass smalti, in Byzantine cut.
Approximately 12 feet high and 40 feet wide glass mosaic at the feet of stairs towards the harbor.

DANZA DEL CERCHIO

135 The artist and the mosaicist from Munich after completion of the installation.

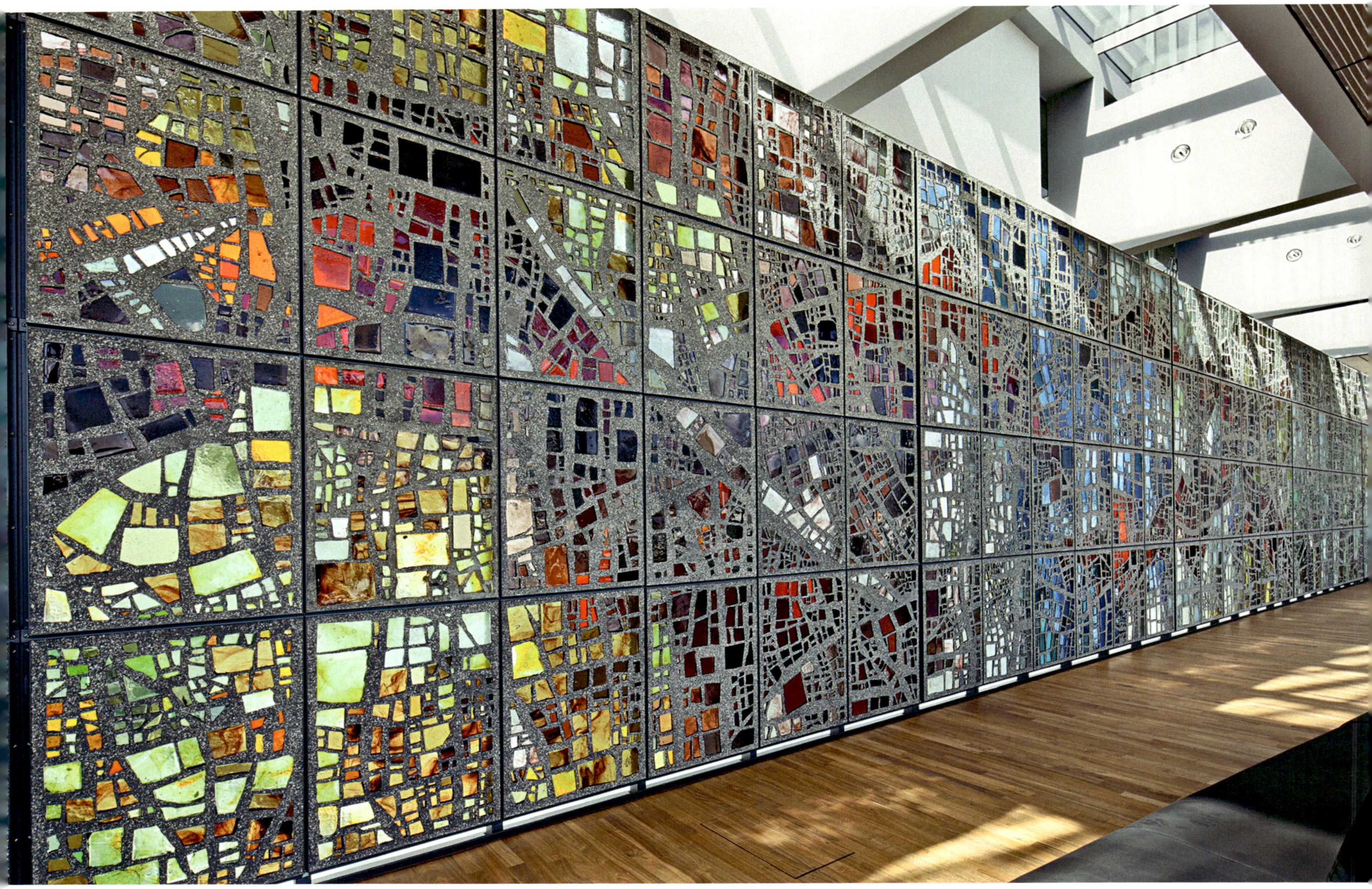

136

François Gillen / Faceted Glass Wall

98

location: European Conference Center, Place de l'Europe, Luxemburg, LU / Schemel/Wirtz Architects, J. Müller PAS / **year:** 1963/2010 / **technique:** faceted glass reconstructed / **metal**: Peter Reich

The panels of faceted glass by Luxemburg artist François Gillen (1914–1997) were made in 1963 for the lobby of a former Conference Center. In 2010 the Hofkunstanstalt recreated the windows using the original design and old glass, yet with improved technology. Meanwhile, they are integrated into the new extension of Luxemburg's European Conference Center.
It was a remarkable endeavor: to take the artwork from the old structure – typical of a previous era – and recreate it for the new one using the old work of art. It seems that conference centers, with their "most up-to-date" architecture and technical equipment, are soon "out of date."
In the present center, the "old" piece turns out to be timeless, part of a new generation of architecture. This was a great challenge for the Hofkunstanstalt, offering the opportunity to install a much superior faceted glass technique.

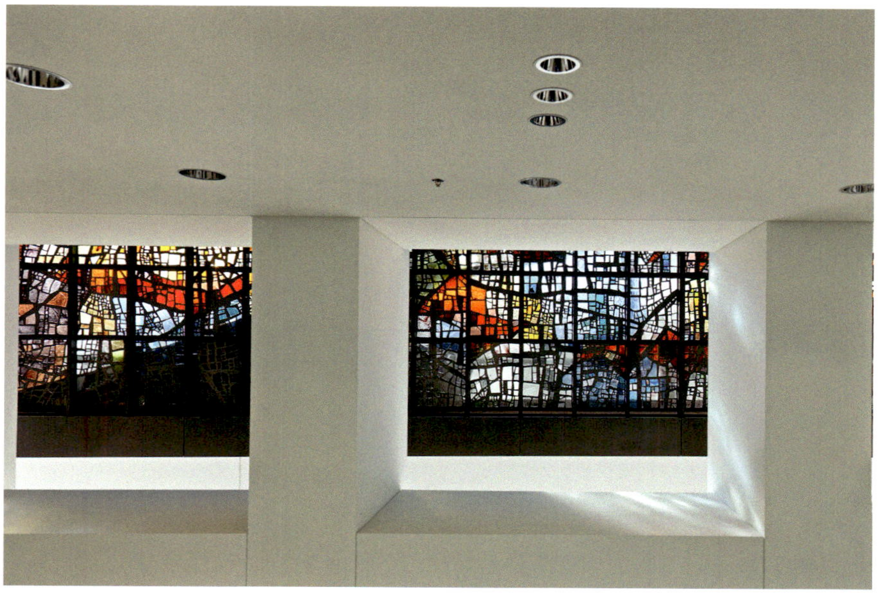

137

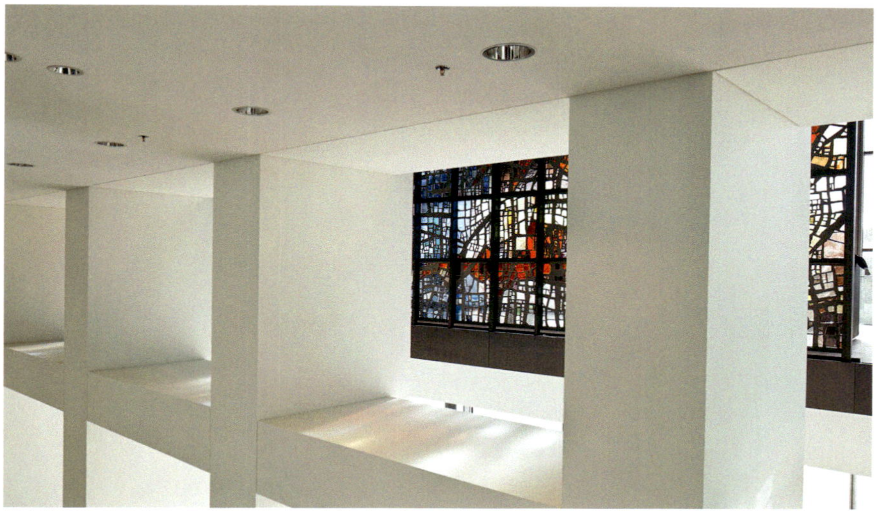

138

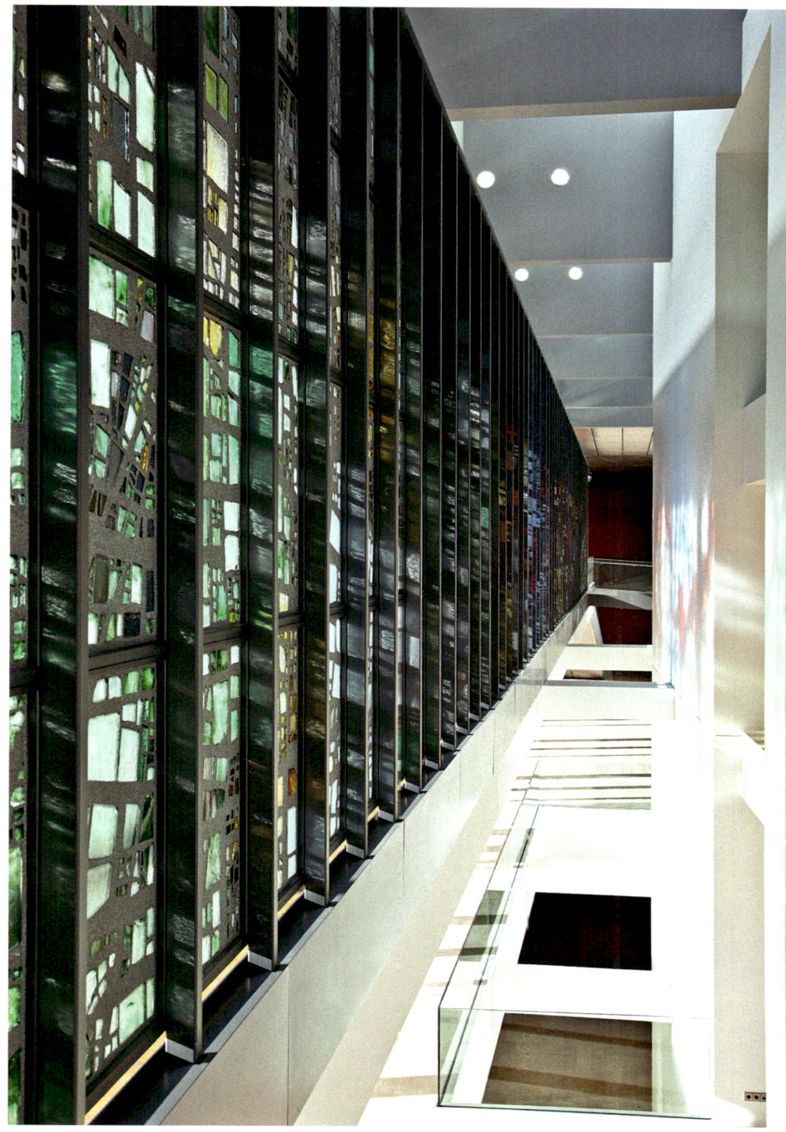

139

136
The reconstructed faceted glass wall, seen from the wide hallway, almost in its entire length of some 130 feet.

137 + 138
Two views from corridors behind.

139
A lateral view of the backside of the glass wall.

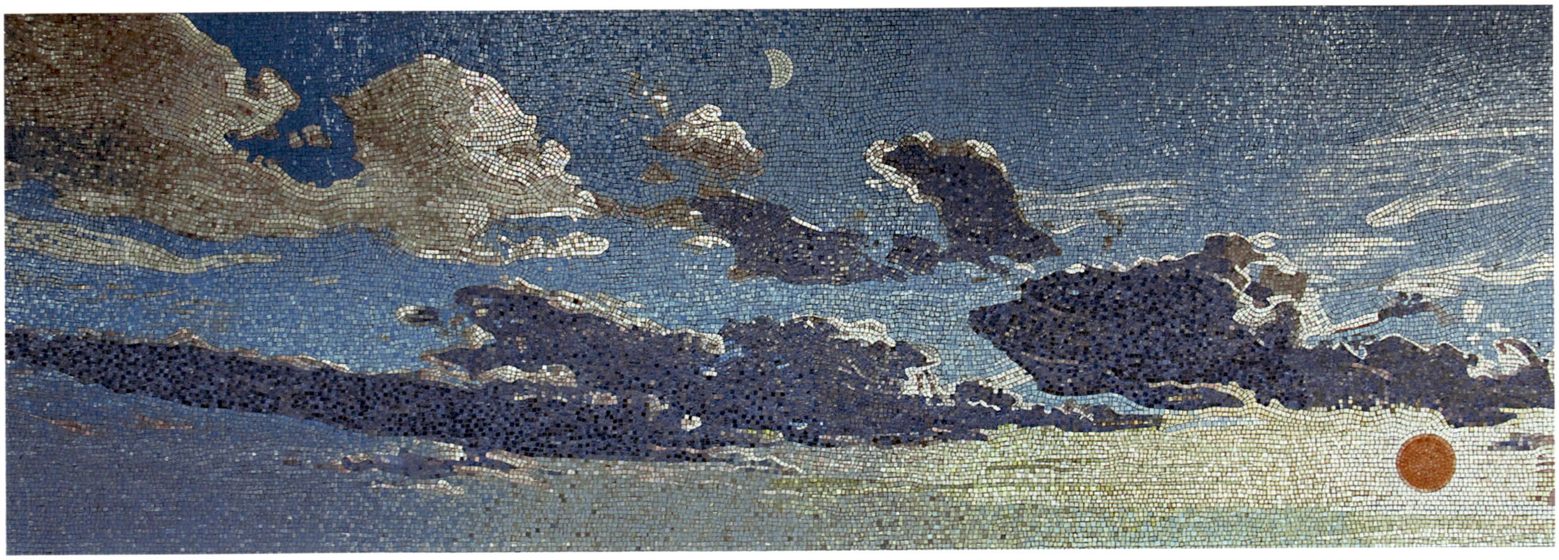

140

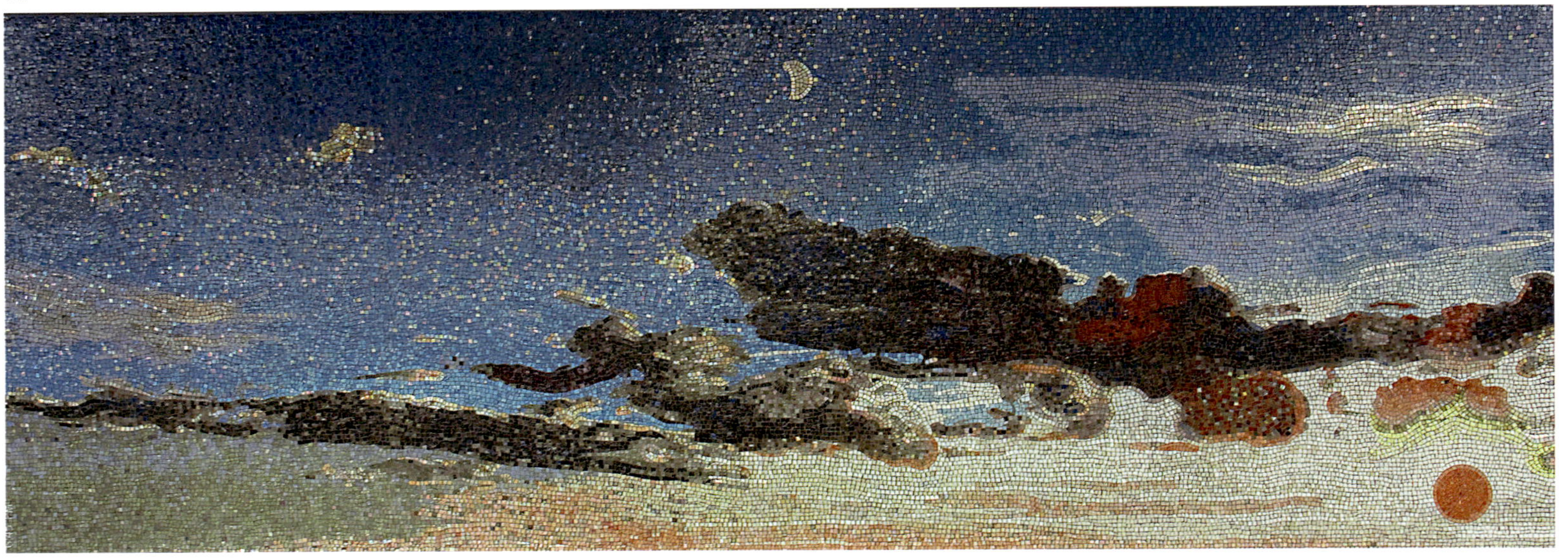

141

Ellen Harvey / "The Home of the Stars"

location: Bridge from Metro-North Railroad, 153rd St. Station to Yankee Stadium, New York, NY, USA / MTA Arts for Transit / **year:** 2009 / **technique:** glass mosaic

An artistic mosaic wall, 200 feet long, in 11 panes and pictures.
The overall concept is the evening sky over the Bronx, which develops into the night, photographed by the artist every 15 minutes, beginning at 6.30 p.m. Color and iridescent hand cut glass and silver tesserae.

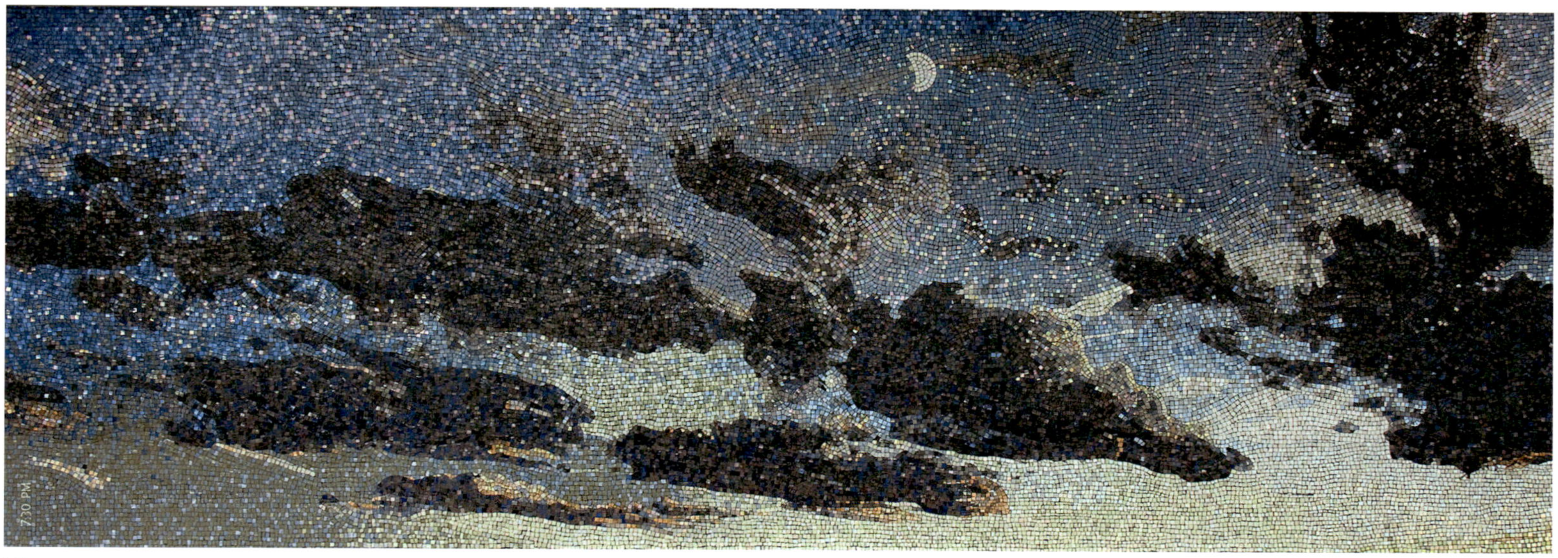

142

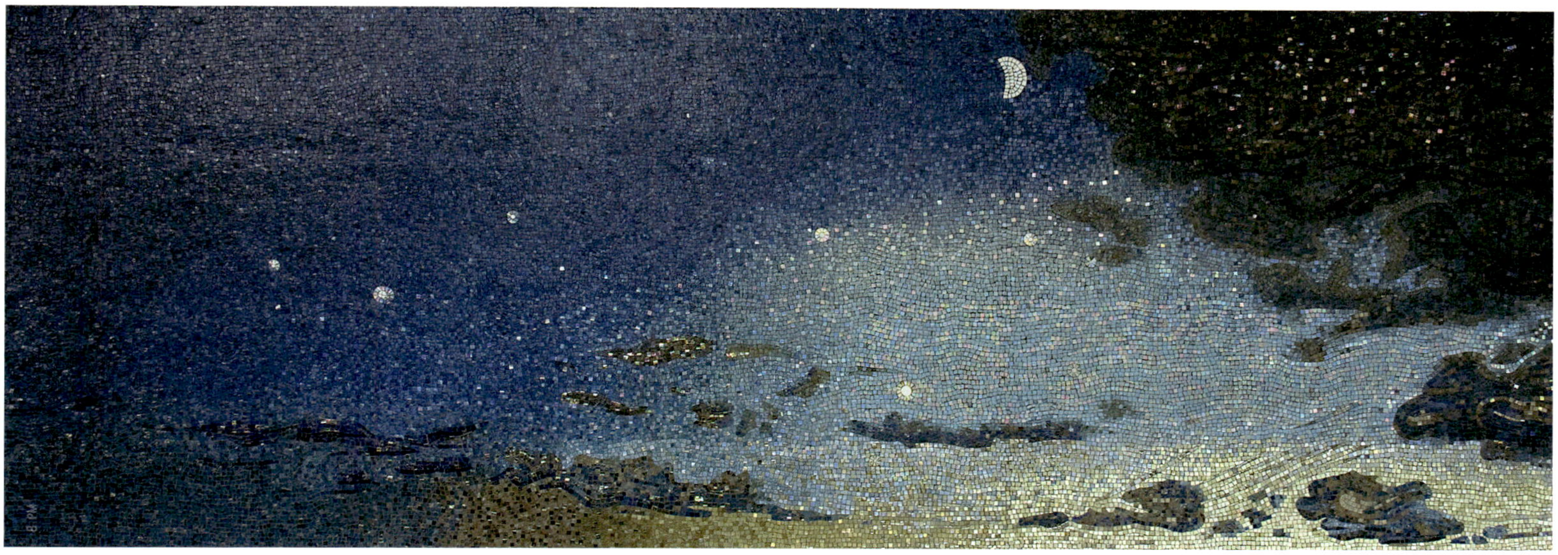

143

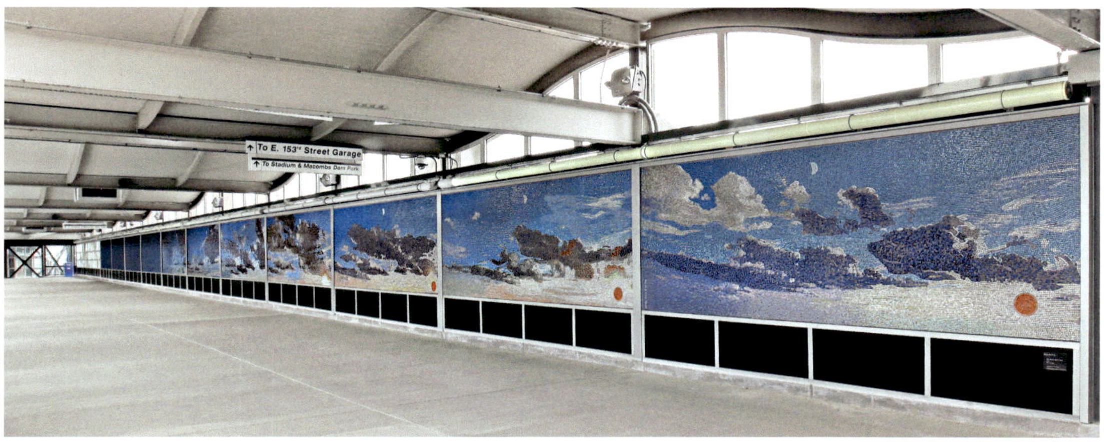

144

THE HOME OF THE STARS

Each one of eleven mosaic pictures of the early evening and night skies over the Bronx.

140
6.30 p.m.

141
6.45 p.m.

142
7.30 p.m

143
8.00 p.m.

144
Overall view of the 11 mosaic pictures on the south side of the bridge. At the right: 6.30 p.m. the day is still there, twilight begins. Towards the left the pictures become increasingly darker; at the left end we find the early night picture at 9.00 p.m.

"How exciting that the Home of the Stars has been selected as one of this year's best public artwork in PAN's Year in Review!" (MTA Arts for Transit Jun 25, 2010)

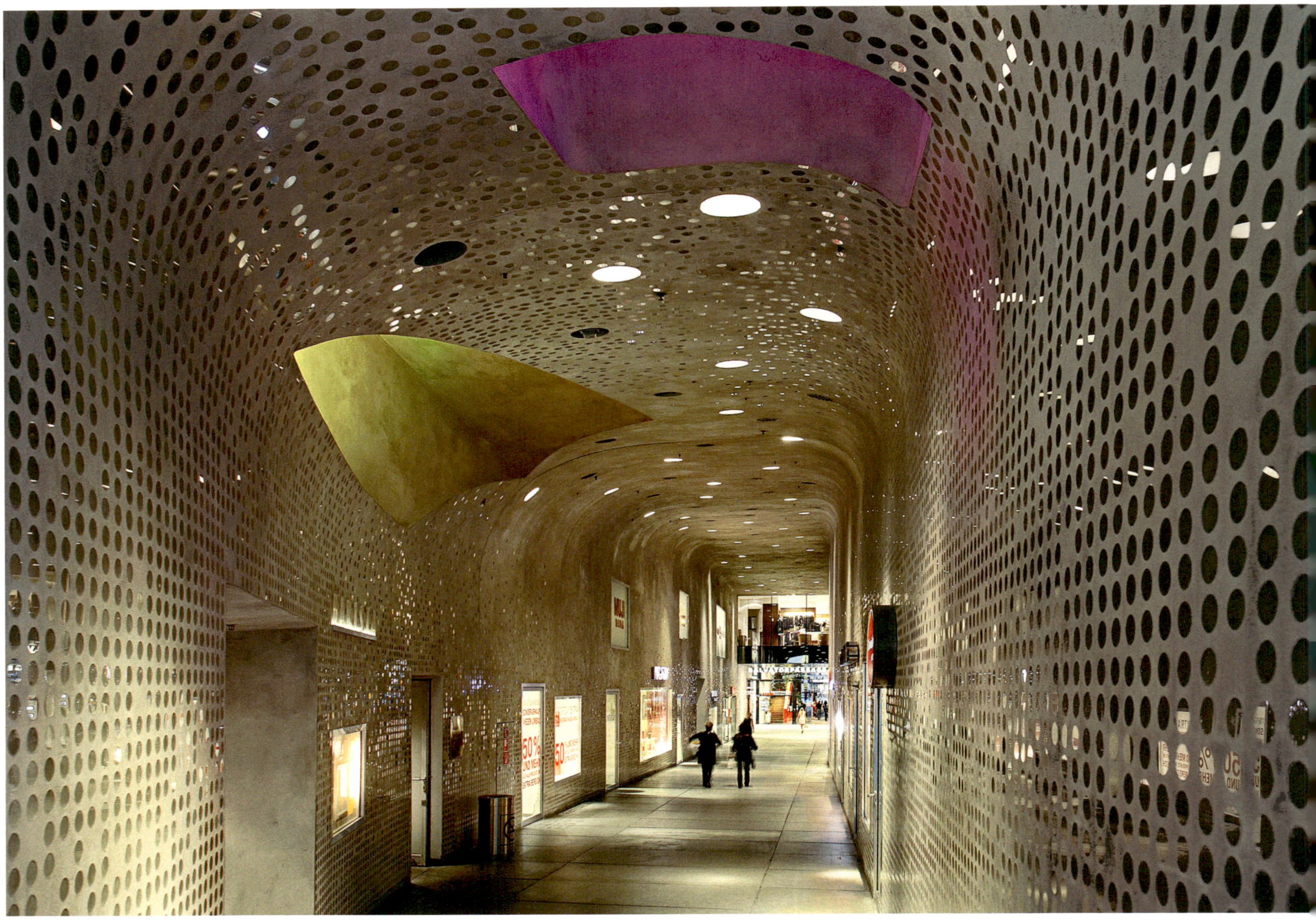

145

Herzog & de Meuron / Sequin Mosaics in the Five Courtyards

location: Five Courtyards in the Theatinerblock, Munich, DE / Fünf Höfe GmbH & Co.KG / **year:** 2001 /
technique: mosaic made of industrial clear glass

Pierre de Meuron called the Fünf Höfe in Munich "the counterpoint of the historic courtyards of the Residenz and a European answer to the US shopping malls." Historic buildings, modern architecture, varied passages, imaginatively designed interior courtyards ... – The Hofkunstanstalt's contributions include the 3400 square feet glass sequin mosaics made of circular-cut, clear window glass, images inserted into the concrete floor (based on Thomas Ruff's photographs), Remy Zaugg's floor inscriptions, and finally a glass ceiling and glass script for two stores.

SEQUIN MOSAICS IN THE FIVE COURTYARDS

145 + 146

Views from different directions into the passage of the western part – with the sequin mosaics.

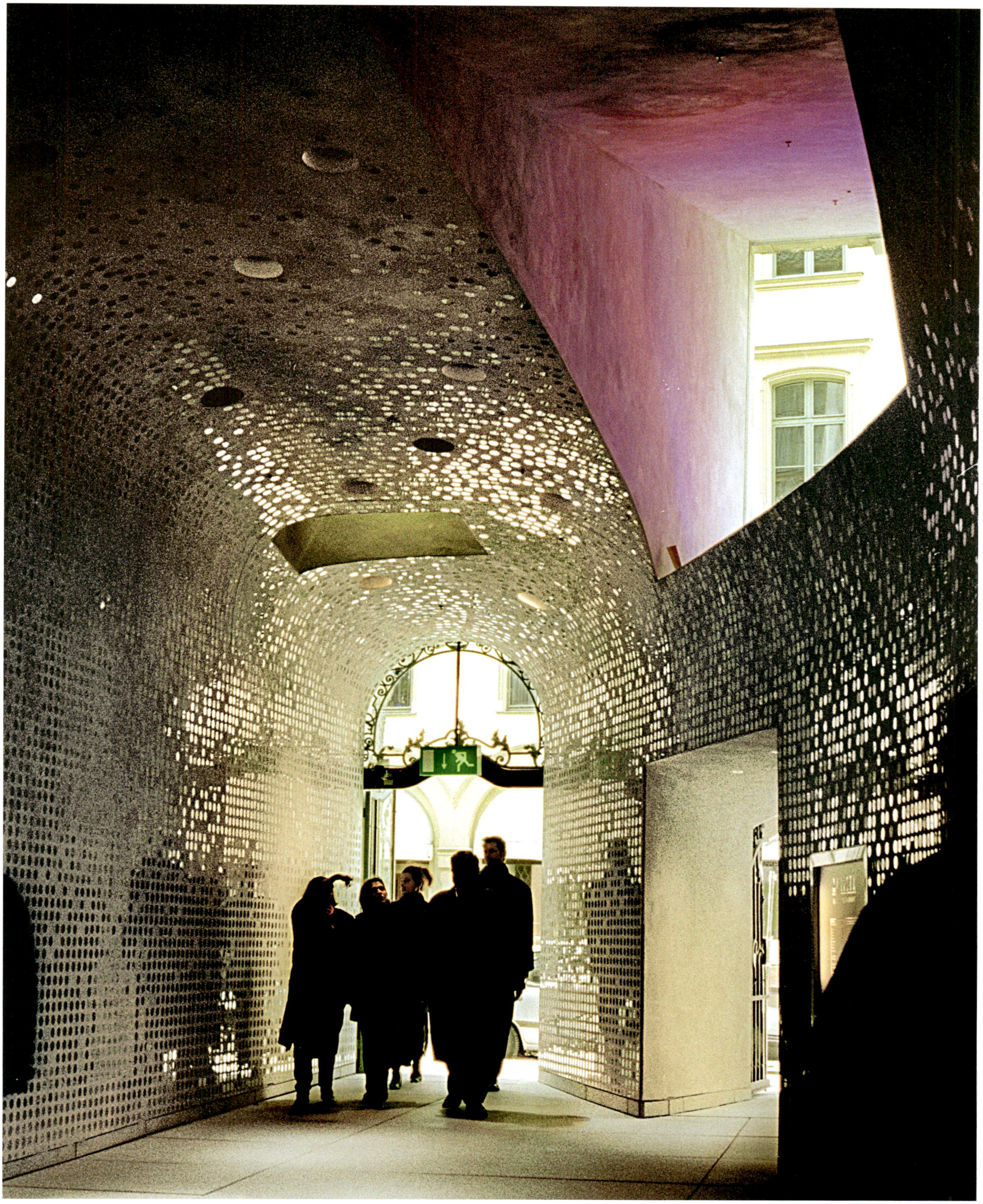

103

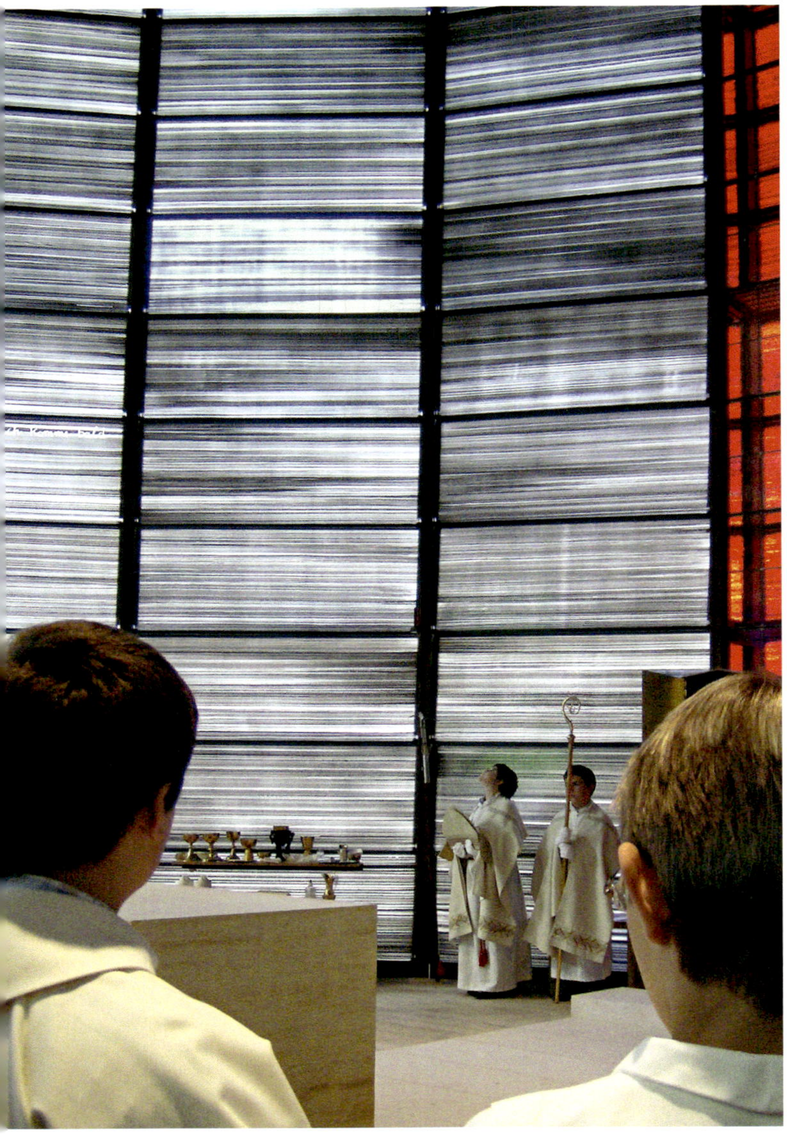

147

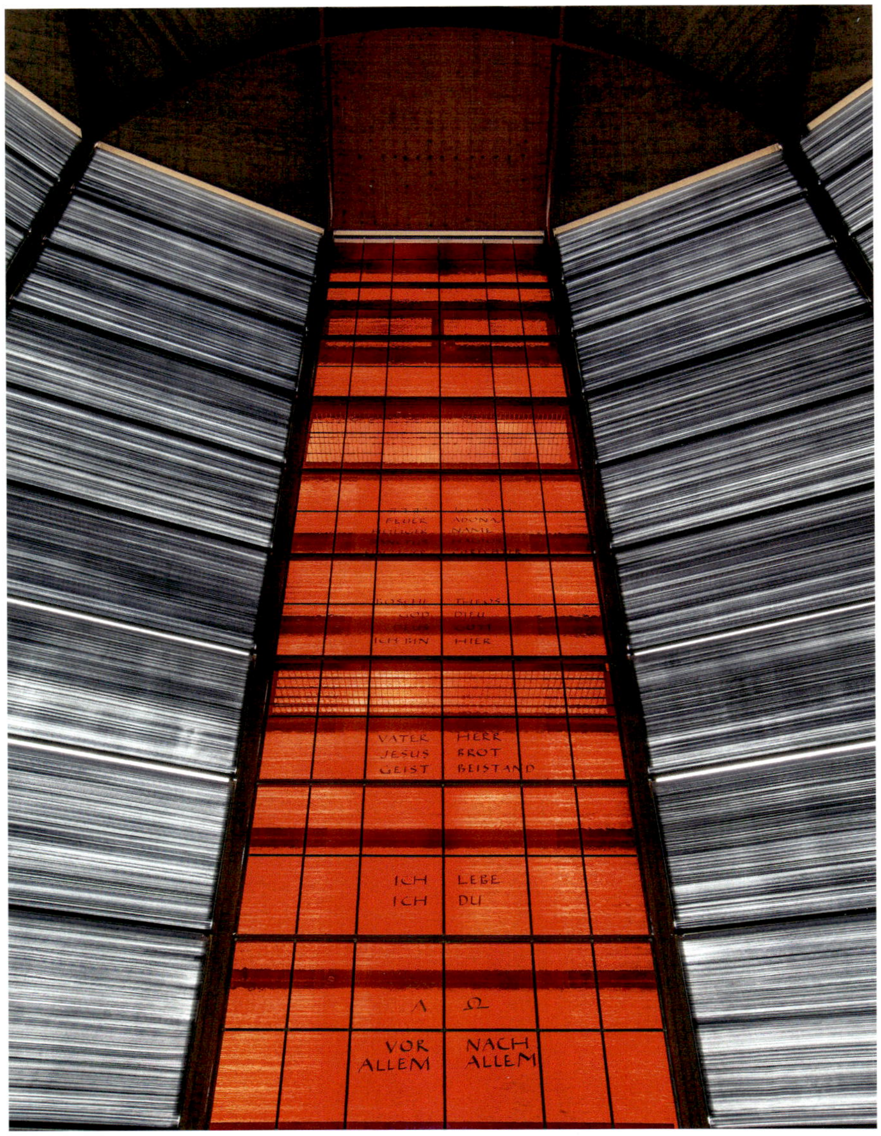

148

Godi and Lukas Hirschi / "Light Space Beyond Images and Symbols"

location: St. Bonifatius Church, Dietenhofen, DE / Karl Frey, Architect, and Building Authority of the Eichstätt Diocese / **year:** 2009 / **technique:** float glass painting and lead glazing

Artist, architect, and studio all contributed to the decision in favor of float glass panels, hand-painted with black ceramic glass color, facing the risk of being condemned and chased away by the congregation. No one wanted to create a house of mourning, but in the design and preparatory process, this could not yet be seen enough. The result is – together with the primary colors of the hand-blown glass – a wonderfully subdued, natural light.

LIGHT SPACE BEYOND IMAGES AND SYMBOLS

147 + 148
View of the sanctuary with altar boys and girls and with the strong red glass. The grey areas are stripes, hand-painted in black tracing color on float glass.

149
The green and blue windows behind the baptismal font. All colored areas are made of hand-blown glass from Waldsassen.

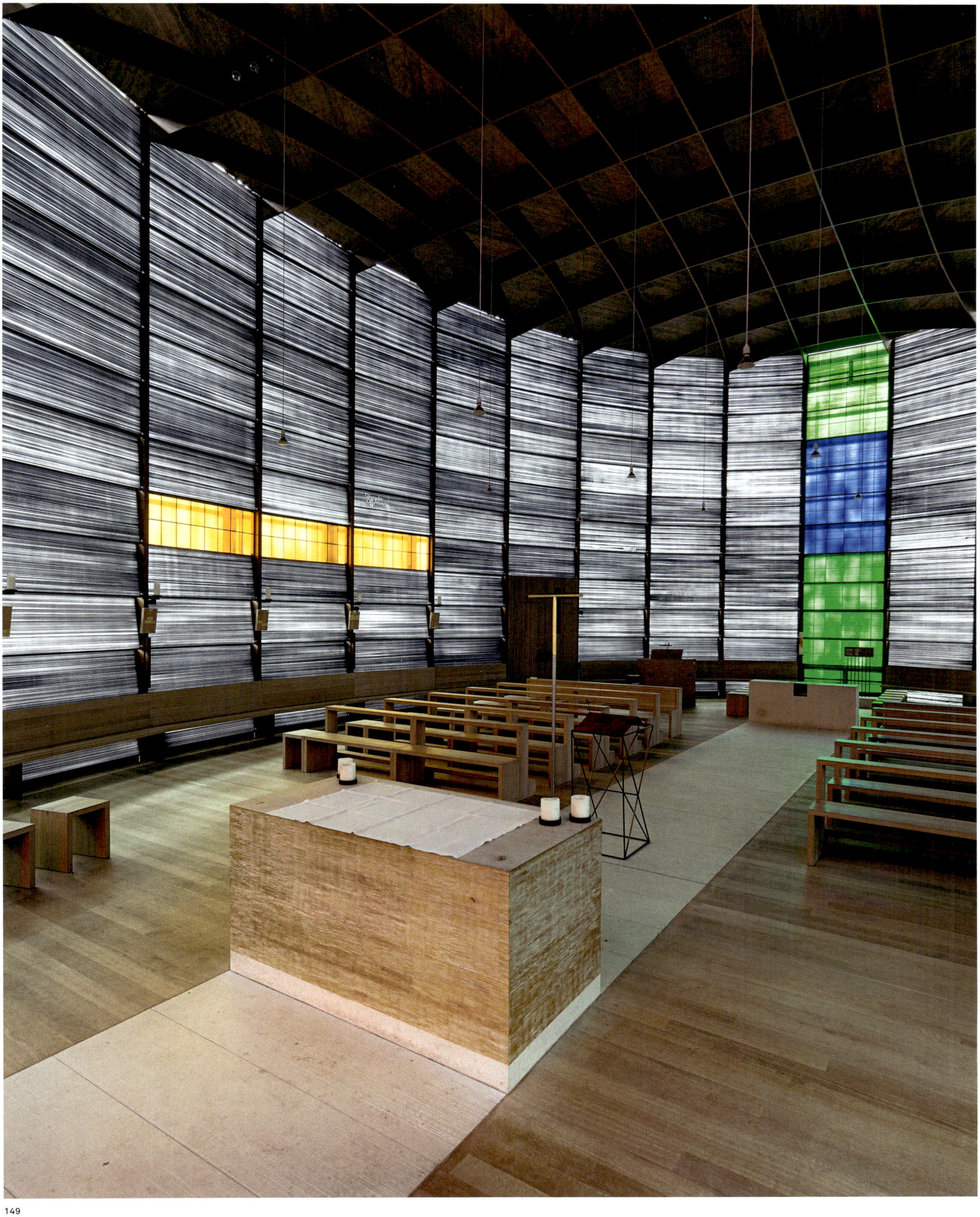

105

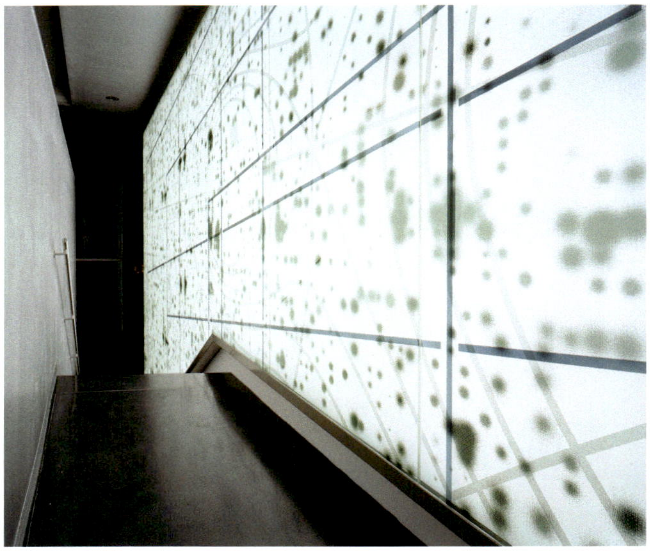

150

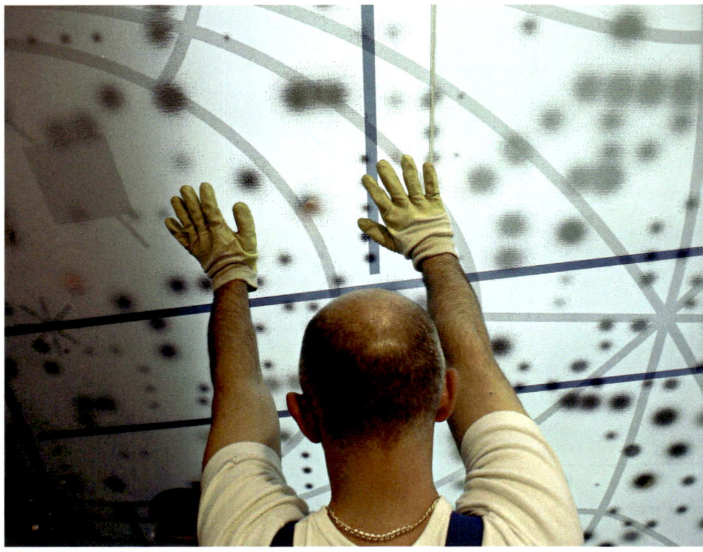

151

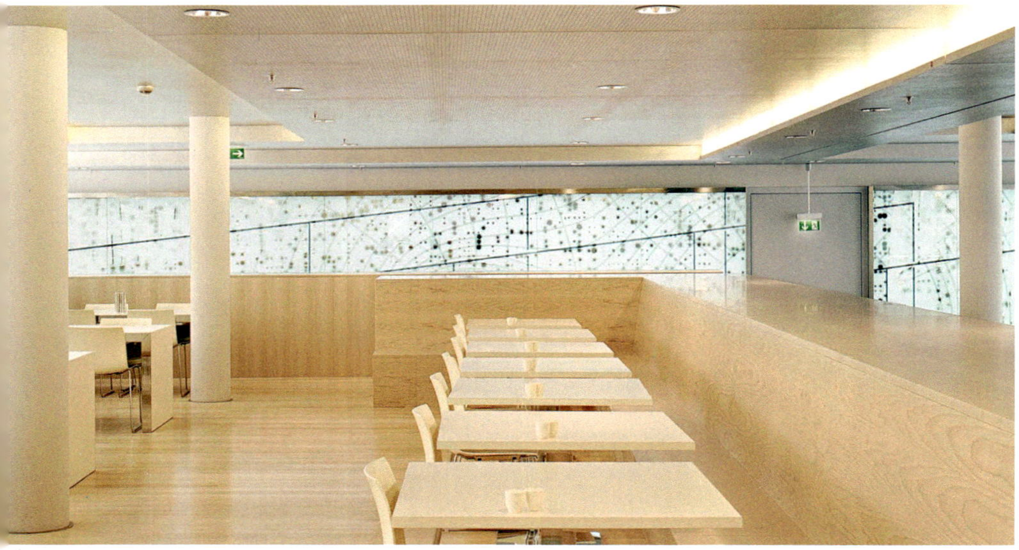

152

SIMULACRUM

150
A lateral view towards Horlitz's glass design at mid-level, behind the balustrade and towards the stairs.

151
During the installation of the art glass wall.

152
The section seen from the elevated restaurant level makes curious about the art, the space, and the light.

Andreas Horlitz / "Simulacrum" (E.ON) and "Polygramm" (Private Residence, Switzerland)

"Simulacrum" location: Casino E.ON Energie AG, Briennerstraße, Munich, DE / Adam Architects / **year:** 2006 / **technique:** float glass painting

"Polygramm" location: Private Residence in Switzerland / **year:** 2004 / **technique:** float glass painting, in part with mirrors

An artificially lit glass wall on the Casino's end wall in the new 2005 Munich edifice. The glass wall reaches to the floor of the mezzanine behind the wooden balustrade and then extends along the narrow staircase down to the street level. A coherent and harmonious interior design made of spatial depth, light, glass, and an artistic message.

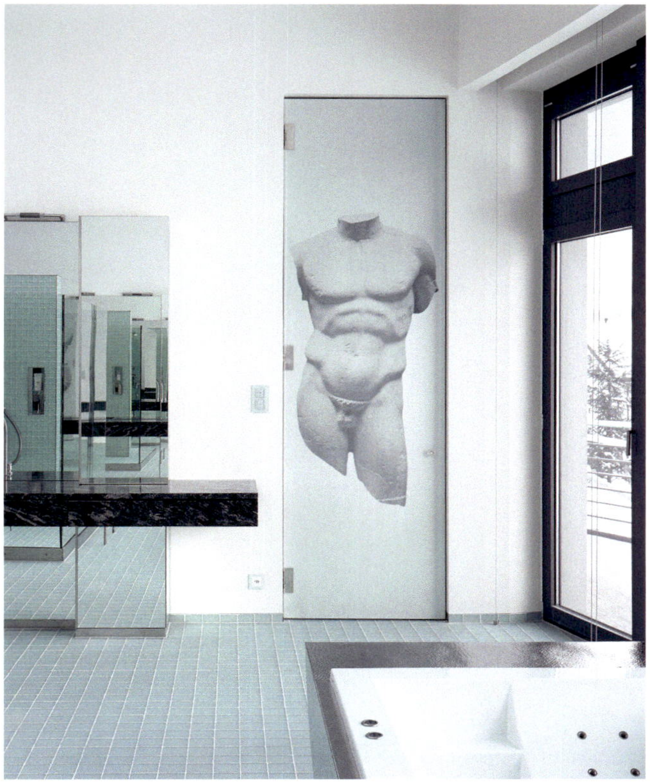

153

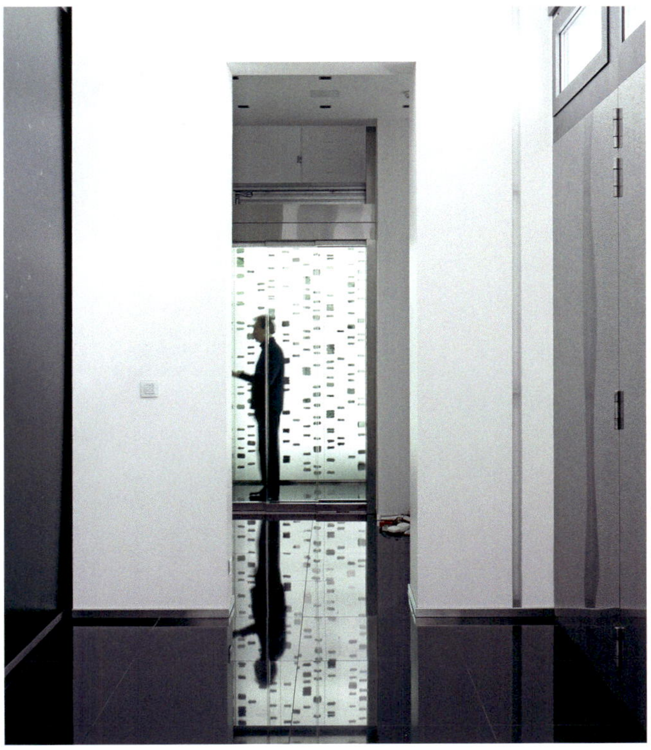

154

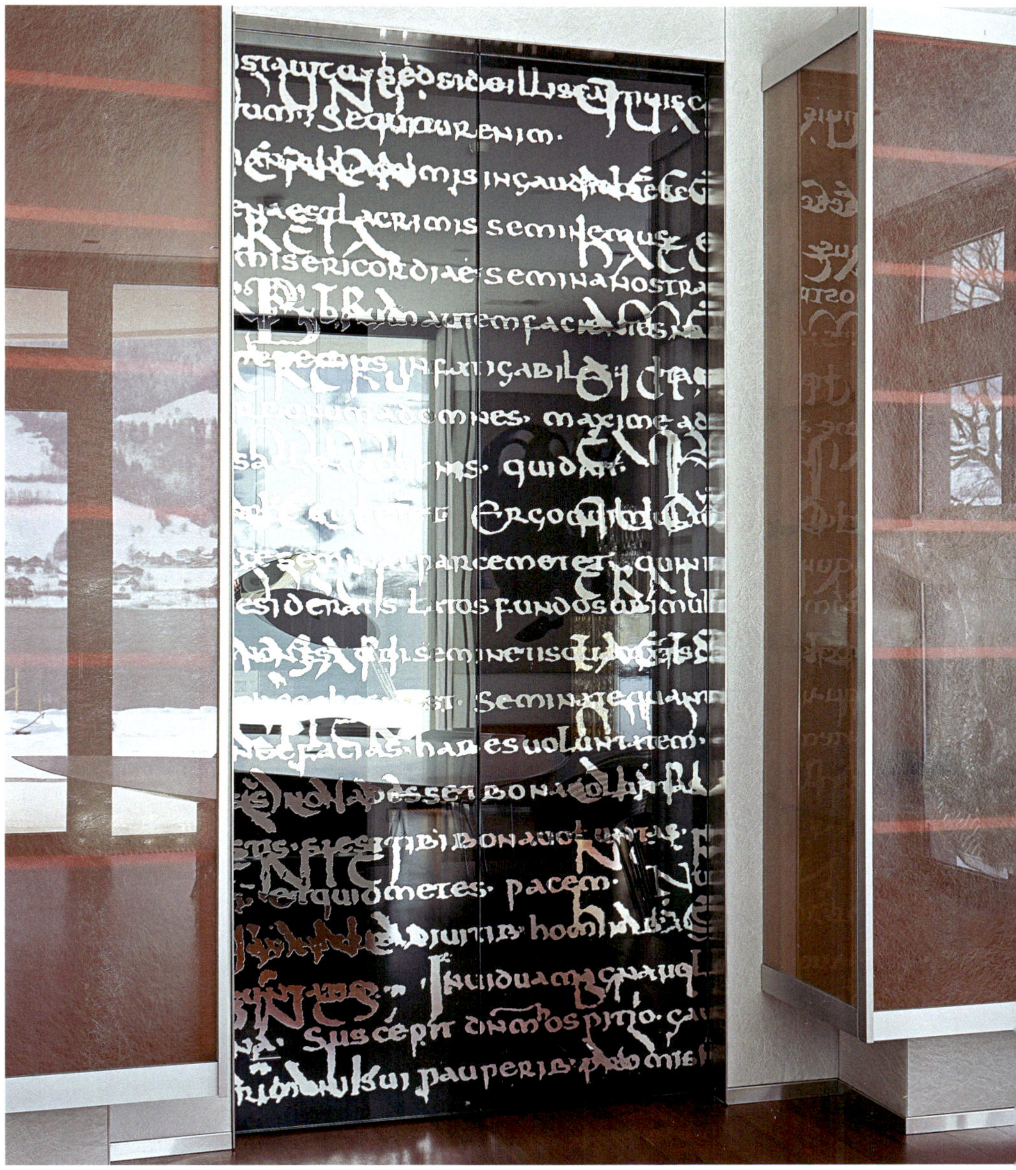

155

POLYGRAMM

153
The tall glass door with the Greek male torso towards the master bathroom

154
View towards the glass design of the elevator backwall

155
Bilateral mirror design at the door towards the library (Palimpsest).

It had been a special constellation at the "Polygramm" project: Client, studio and artist understood and complemented one another at best. This resulted in art glass and also steel works of cool sobriety and amazing diversity, which blended in the modern architecture of the building at the best.

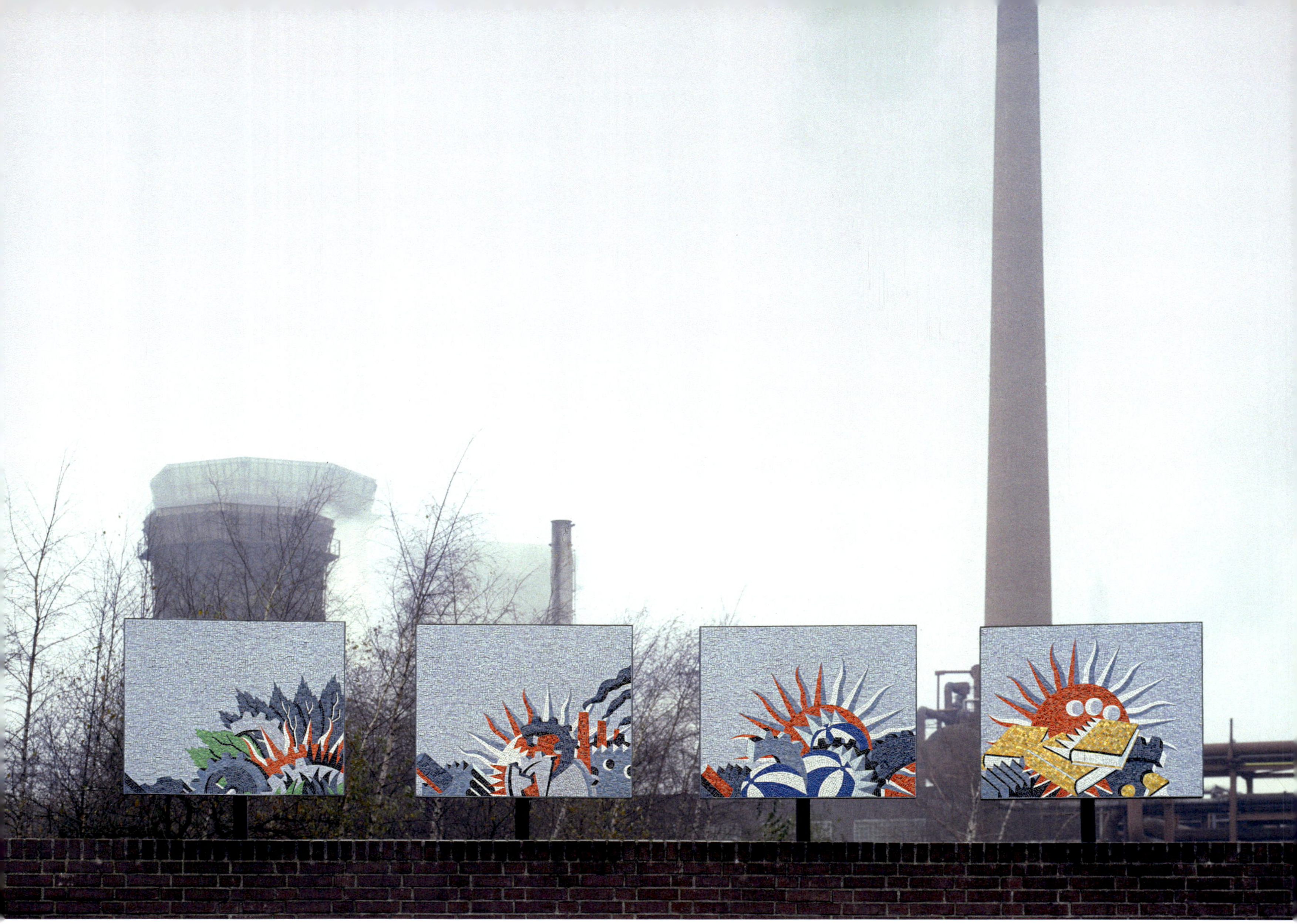

156
RED SUNS. Four mosaic panels on the factory wall of the Kokerei Zollverein – a memorial of the Ruhr Area's heyday – hope?

Stephan Huber / "Red Suns"

location: Kokerei Zollverein, Ruhrkohle AG, Essen, DE / **year:** 1987 / **technique:** glass mosaics

Four mosaic panels made of genuine Venetian color and gold smalti, hewn in the Byzantine manner, circa 10 × 10 × 6 millimeter; metal frames. Stephan Huber's first mosaic work.
The art project is part of the UNESCO World Heritage. In this part of town, in the north, there is only through traffic, no pedestrians. The entrance to the factory is also located elsewhere. The depiction of sequences of a sunrise is superimposed with cogwheel fragments. "With all power, up towards the light, emerges the age of industrialization."

TOWARDS ME

157
The two granite stelae with mirror images inserted as "micro photo mosaics."

158
The viewer who passes through the two mosaics is drawn into the aura of this fascinating woman and artist.

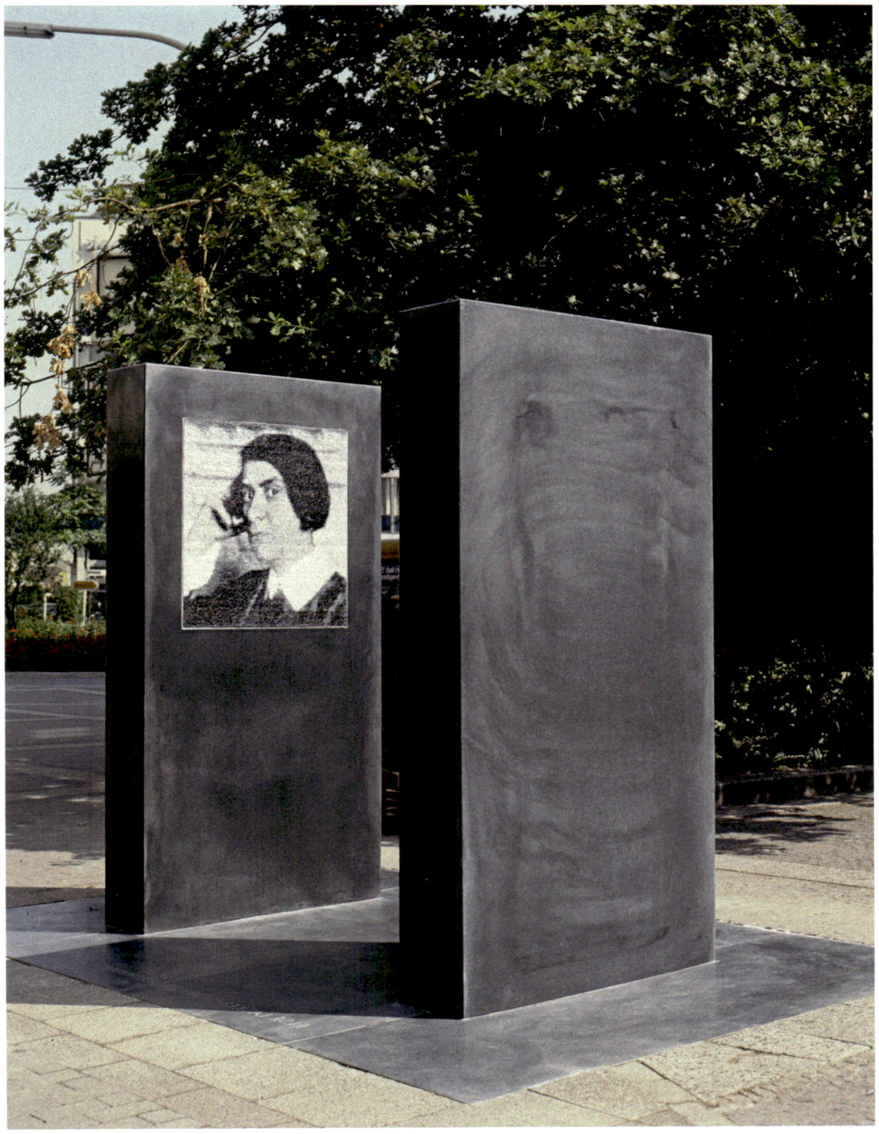

157

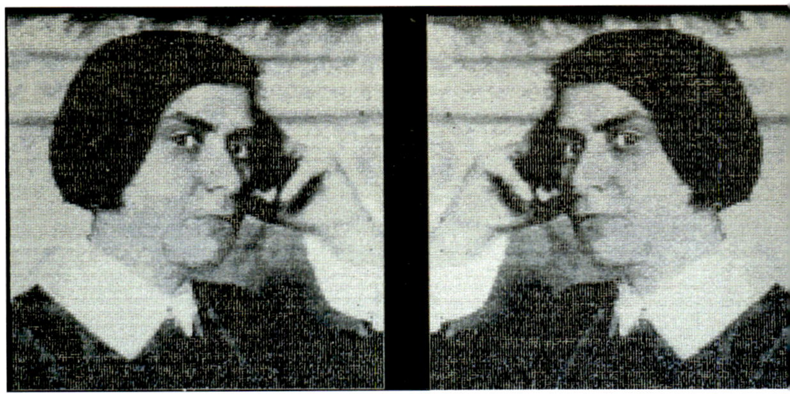

158

"Towards Me"

location: Memorial for Else Lasker-Schüler, Wuppertal, DE / **year:** 1989 / **technique:** glass mosaic and granite

Black granite stelae with mirror image mosaics of the poet: The important Jewish-German poet was an eminent representative of the avant-garde and Expressionism in German literature. Typical of Stephan Huber's later mosaic oeuvre, this first "photo" mosaic was made of Venetian glass smalti, hand-hewn to a size of roughly 5 × 5 × 5 millimeter; the tesserae were hand-placed using tweezers.

159
The "suspended fountain" with the large mosaic panel at Munich's Terminal 1 A.

Stephan Huber / "The Alps"

110

location: Terminal 1 A, Munich Airport, Munich, DE / Busso von Busse Architects / **year:** 1992 / **technique:** glass, mosaic, and water installation

This imposing artwork with motifs from the Alps, snow, and water extends over two floors. It creates, even for transit passengers, "identity" and for people from Munich references to home. The realistic black-and-white mosaic is made of minute, hand-hewn glass tesserae in a scale of circa twenty tonalities ranging from black to white. Glass is a frozen liquid, too.

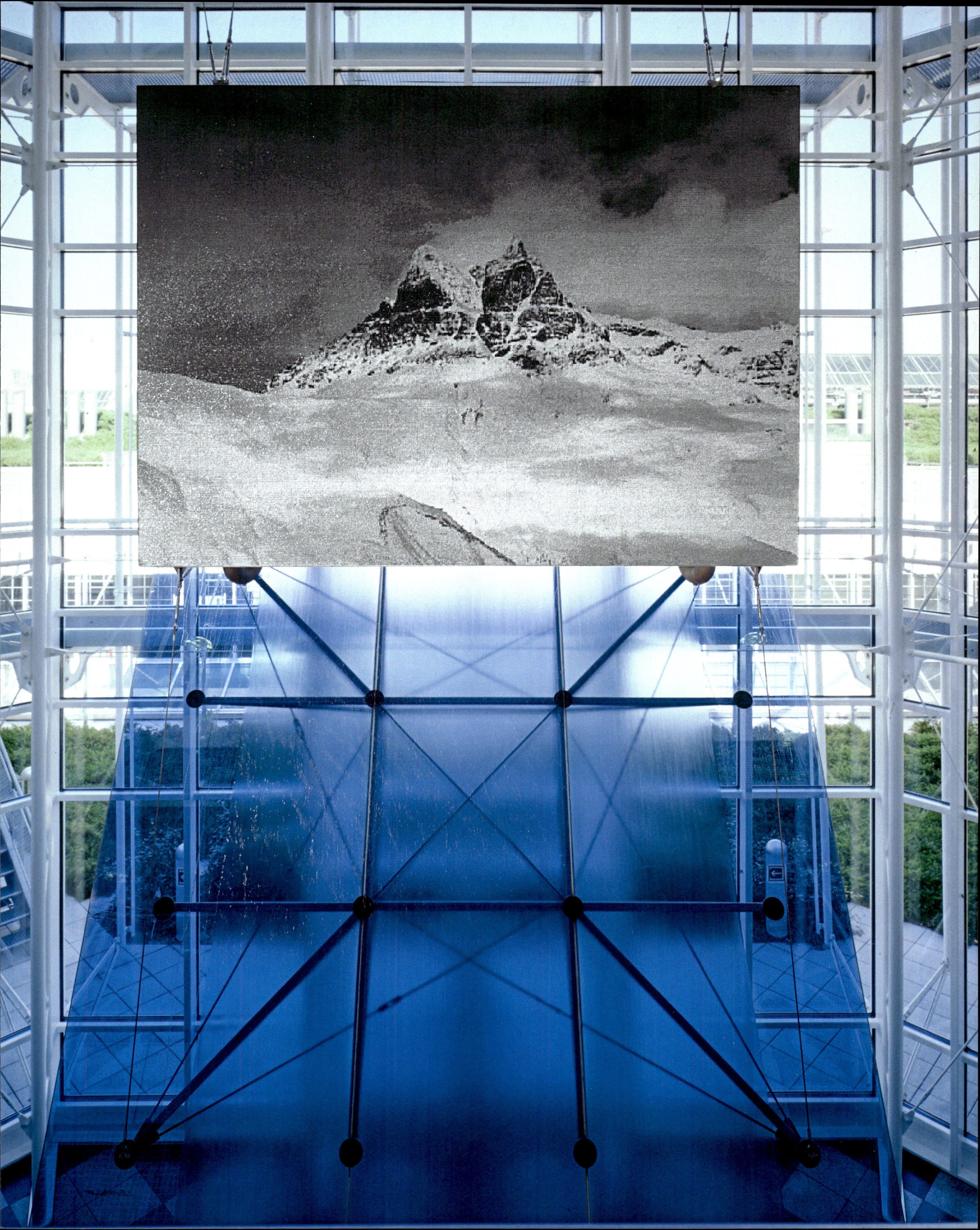

FRANKFURT STAIRS

160
56 public figures from the city of Frankfurt are gathered in this mosaic.

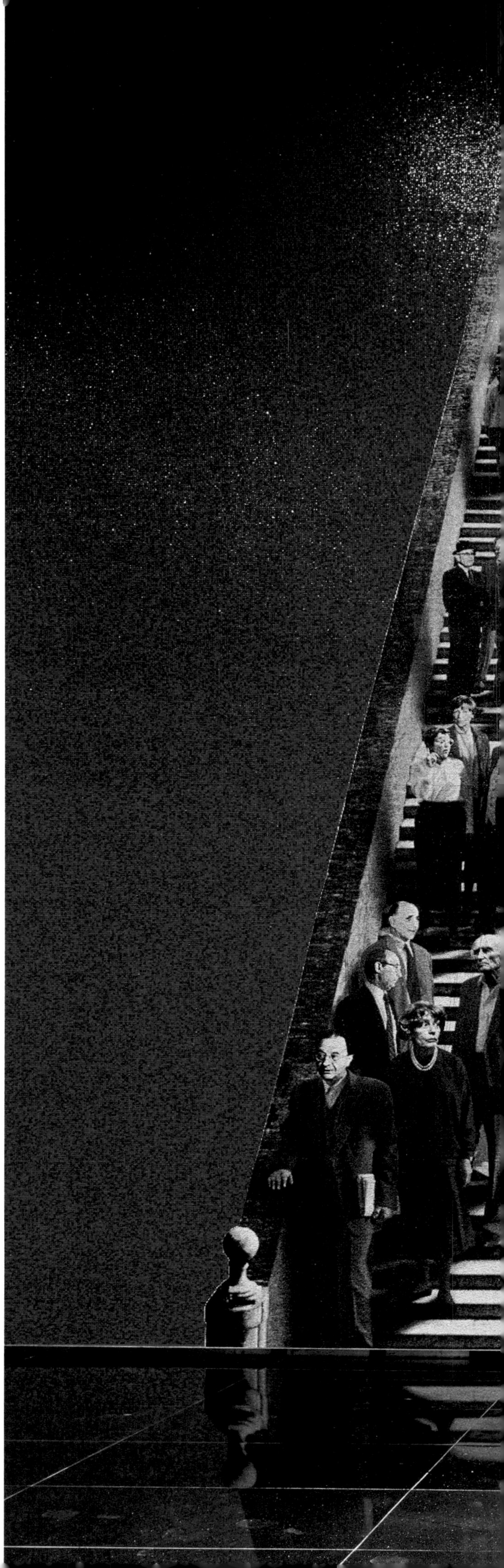

Stephan Huber / "Frankfurt Stairs"

location: Maintower, Hessische Landesbank, Frankfurt/Main, DE / Schweger + Partner Architects / **year:** 2000 / **technique:** glass mosaic

Hand-hewn and hand-placed glass smalti mosaic. The photorealistic area measures circa 430 square feet and consists of 5 millimeter glass smalti. The 650 square feet blue base area is made of 10 millimeter smalti.
"The result of combining the ancient technique from Ravenna with a contemporary, digitalized resolution and a linear laying method is an exciting rift. The effect of the mosaic as medium is opposite that of photography. Looking at the piece from a distance creates sharpness, from close-up, the image dissolves and blurs, turning into a moving, relief-like, painterly plane." (Stephan Huber)

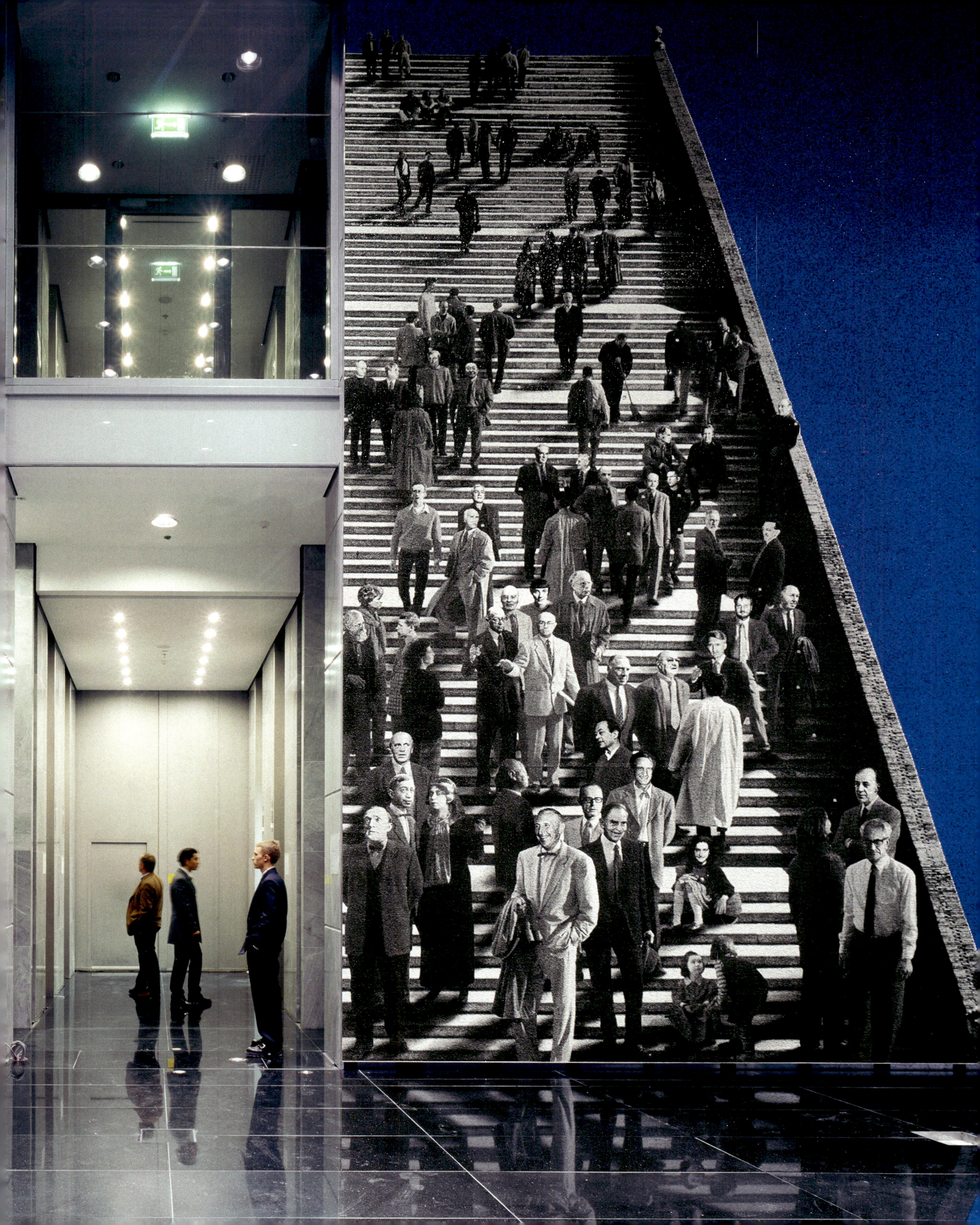

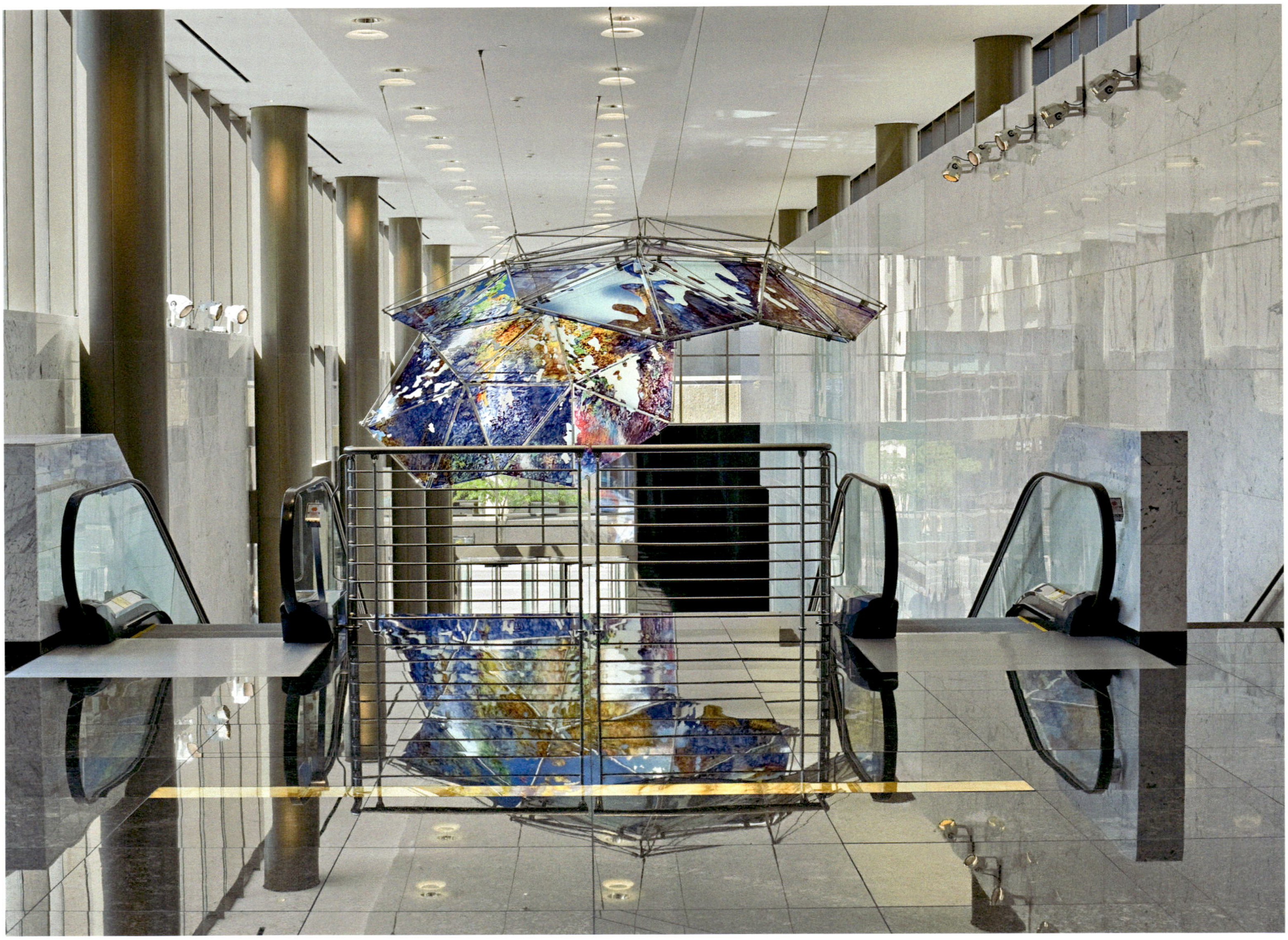

161

Reiner John / "Floating Mt. Evans Sky"

162

location: 1001 17th Street, Denver, CO, USA / Barber Architecture, Miller Global Properties / **year:** 2008 / **technique:** float glass painting, steel construction, and mosaic / steel construction: Peter Reich

Situations that need careful consideration when working on glass design include artificial light, daylight, interior and exterior views as well as proximity and distance. Apart from the real work, the studio task entails supporting the artist who might be unfamiliar with the technique and the effects in the architectural space. Transparency, translucency, and opacity must be mastered.

FLOATING MT. EVANS SKY

161
The glass sculpture seen in daylight from the vestibule.

162
The mosaic "carpet" and the suspended glass sculpture, installed between the escalators and seen in artificial light from the lower vestibule.

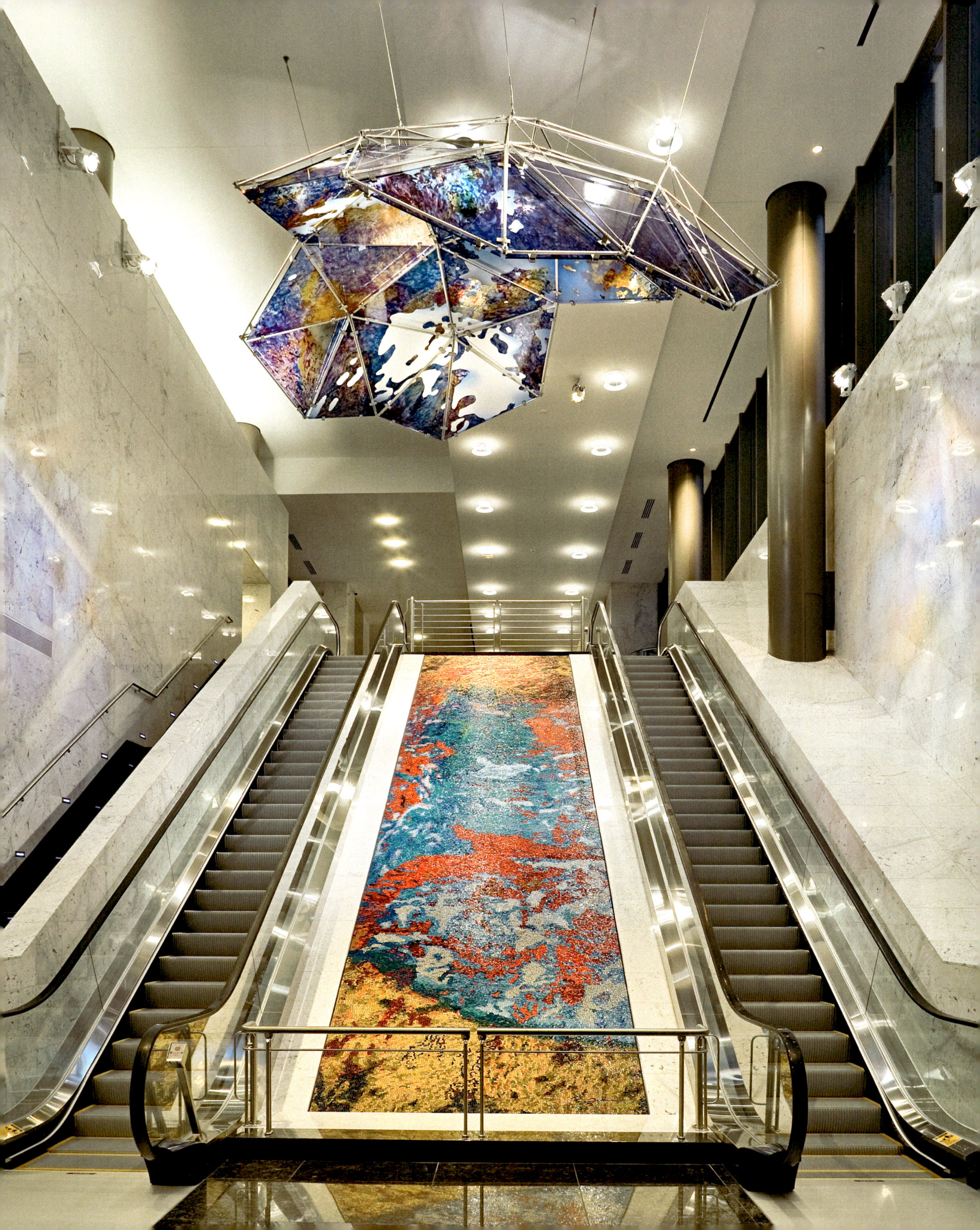

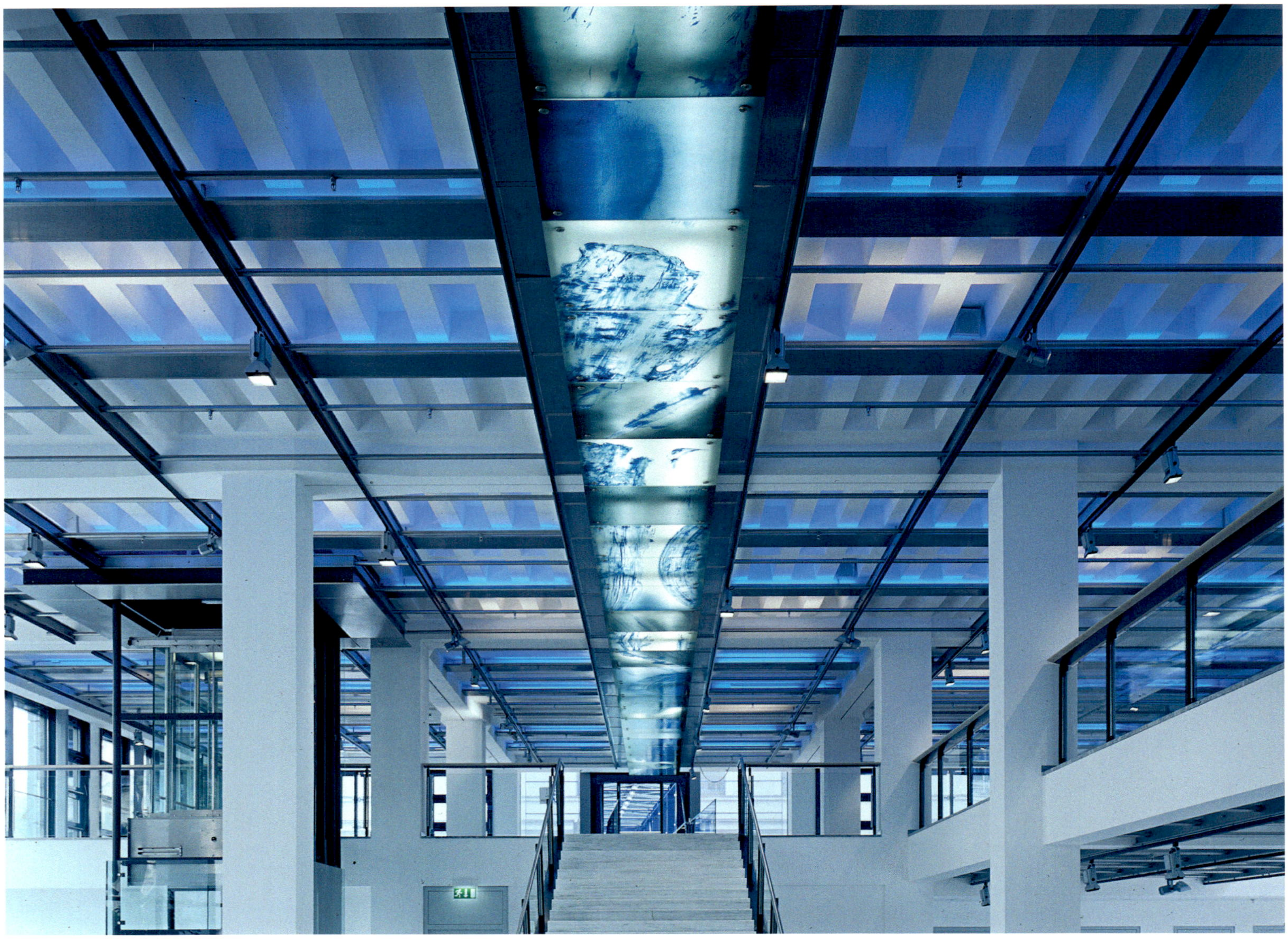

163
BLUE RIBBON OF GLASS. View of the two-story vestibule's light ceiling with the backlit ribbon of glass.

Reiner John / A Blue Ribbon of Glass

location: Bayerische Landesbank, Munich, DE / Achitect Peter Lanz / **year:** 1998 / **technique:** float glass painting

A glass band in float glass painting, some 110 feet long, is the dominant feature of the light ceiling. Ceramic glass melting colors are boldly applied by hand. It is appealing to combine the illumination of the coffered ceiling with indirect blue light and the backlit, spontaneous and gestural painted stripes of glass.

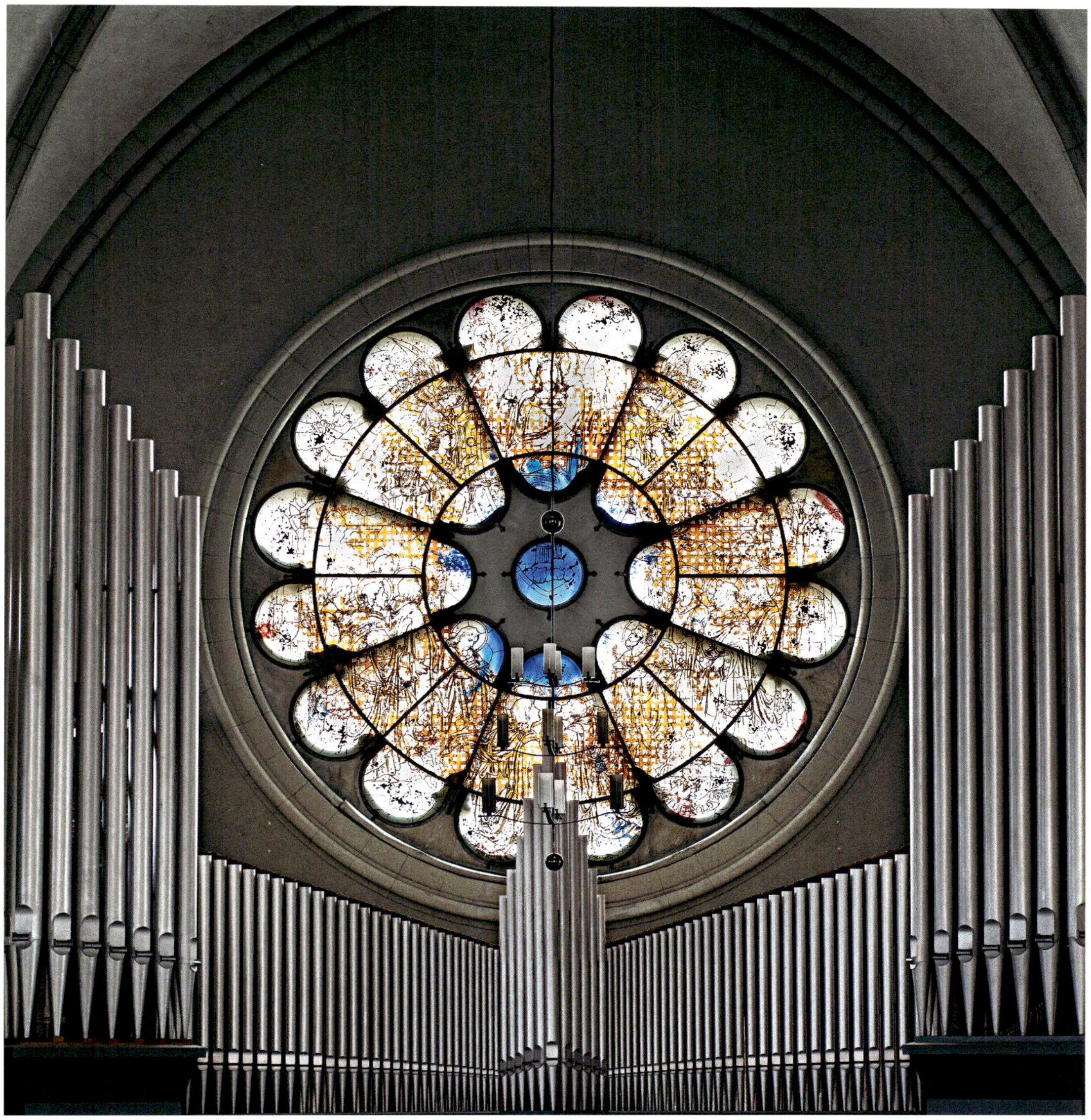

ROSE WINDOW

164
The new south rosette depicting the Ascension,after William Francis Dixon's original cartoon.

Rose windows in St. Luke's Church

location: Lutheran St. Lukaskirche, Munich, DE / Historic Church Building / Achitect Albert Schmidt, Kirchenbauamt des Dekanats Munich, Bayerisches Landesamt für Denkmalpflege / **year:** 1896/2008–09 / **technique:** float glass painting

Recreation of two rose windows by Franz Mayer of Munich, destroyed during World War Two. Dated 1896 and saved in Mayer's archives, one original full scale drawwing by British artist William Francis Dixon – a master student of Edward Burne-Jones – formed the basis for designing and executing this work.
Reiner John, the Hofkunstanstalt, and all involved managed to produce a contemporary, abstract solution without any loss of the graphic qualities of the original cartoon for the south rose windows and yet having to deal with the far inferior model saved of the north rosette.

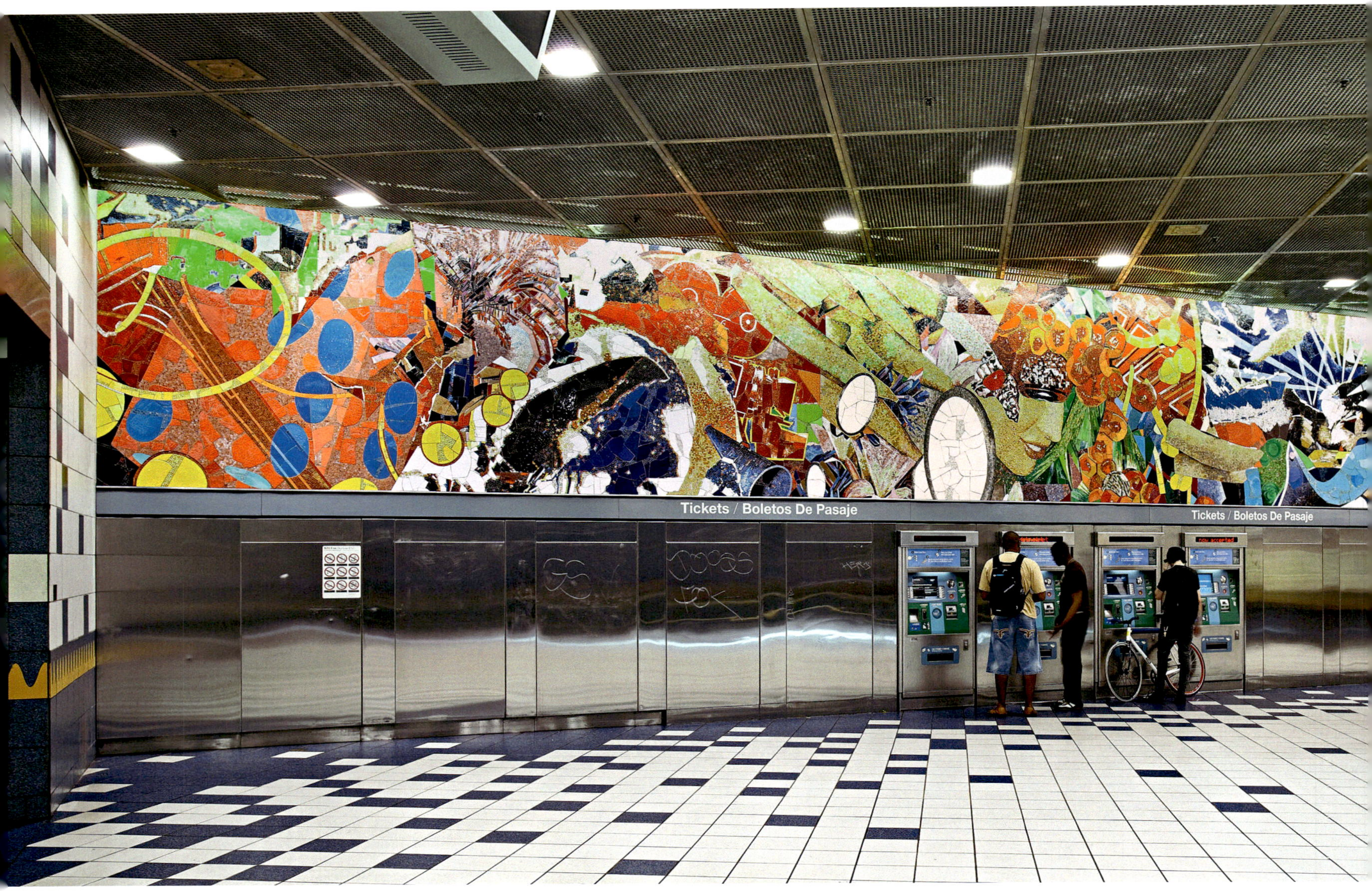

165

Stephen T. Johnson / "Universal Delights"

118

location: Universal City Metro Station, Los Angeles, CA., USA / Courtesy of LA County MTA (Metro) / **year:** 2010 / **technique:** glass mosaic

The artist's concept summary: Celebration of the film and television industry and their universal repercussions through an exuberant juxtaposition of colors, shapes, and familiar imagery.
"Absolutely Spectacular!!!
Gabriel, you have created one of the most glorious mosaics I have ever seen. You captured all the detail, subtlety and nuances as well as the overall punch and vitality of my collage. Simply stunning and I am so very, very proud and honored. If I were there in Munich I would give you all huge hugs, take you out for a celebratory dinner and jump up and down (you know me by now!!)" (Stephen T. Johnson)

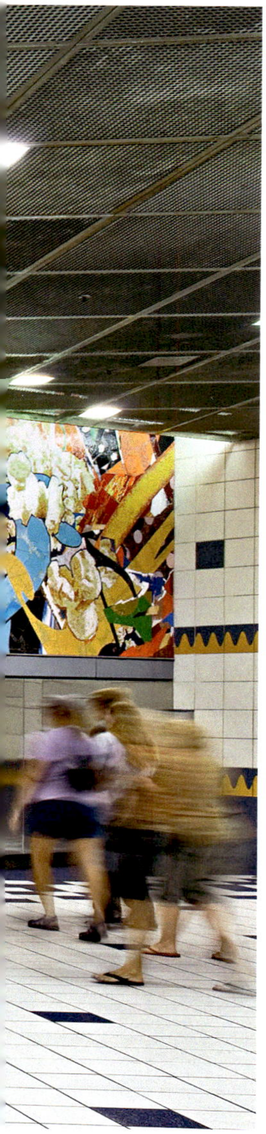

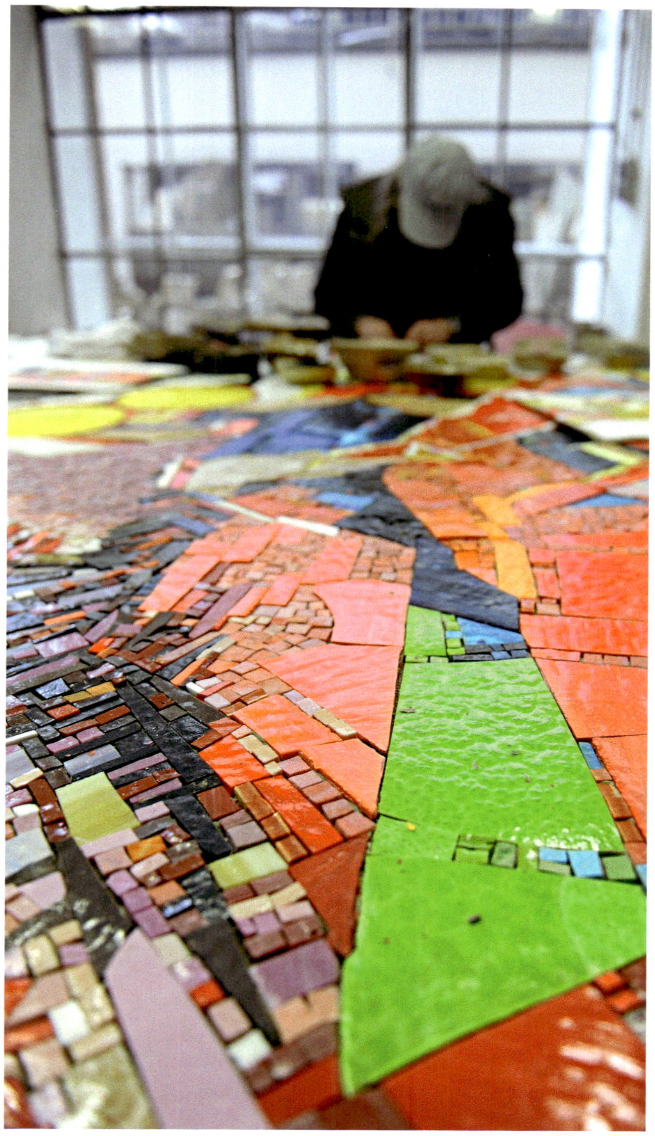

166

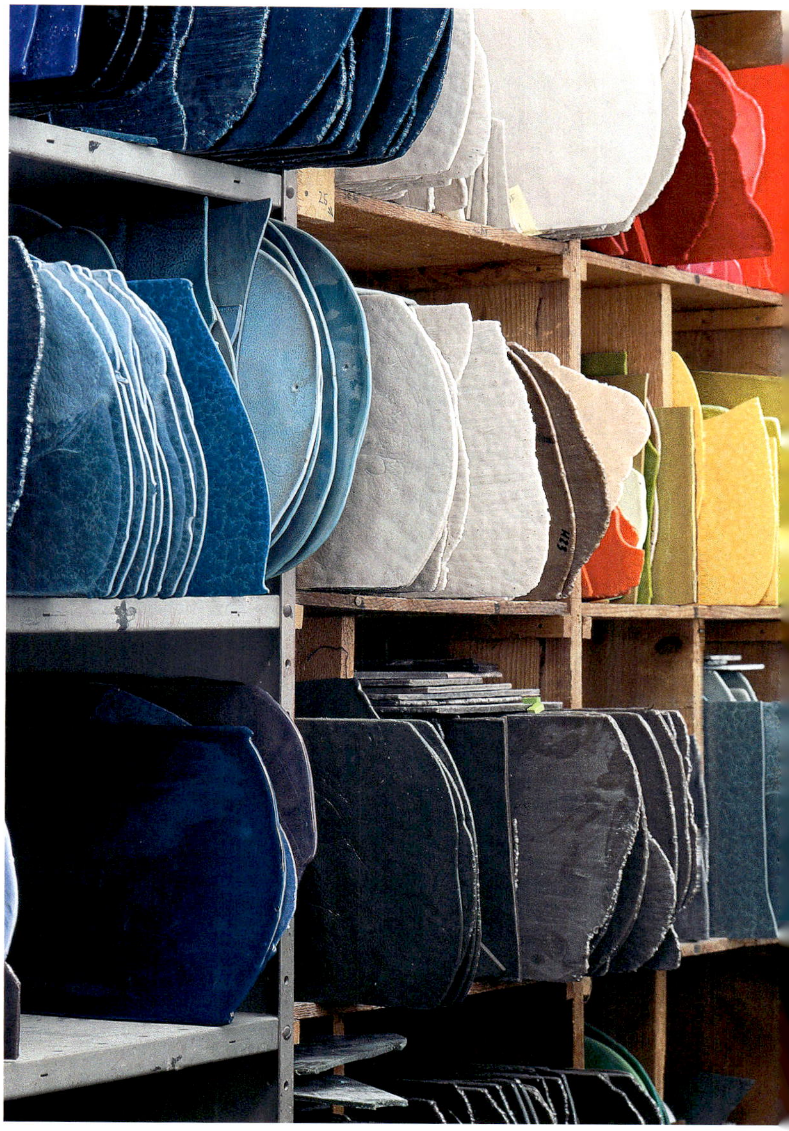

167

UNIVERSAL DELIGHTS

165
General view of North Hollywood's Main Station, serving, among others, the Universal City Studios, the CityWalk, and the future NBC Universal Operations.

166
Not a dull translation into mosaic – a new composition in color, material, form, and flow.

167
A small part of the Venetian glass cake storage.

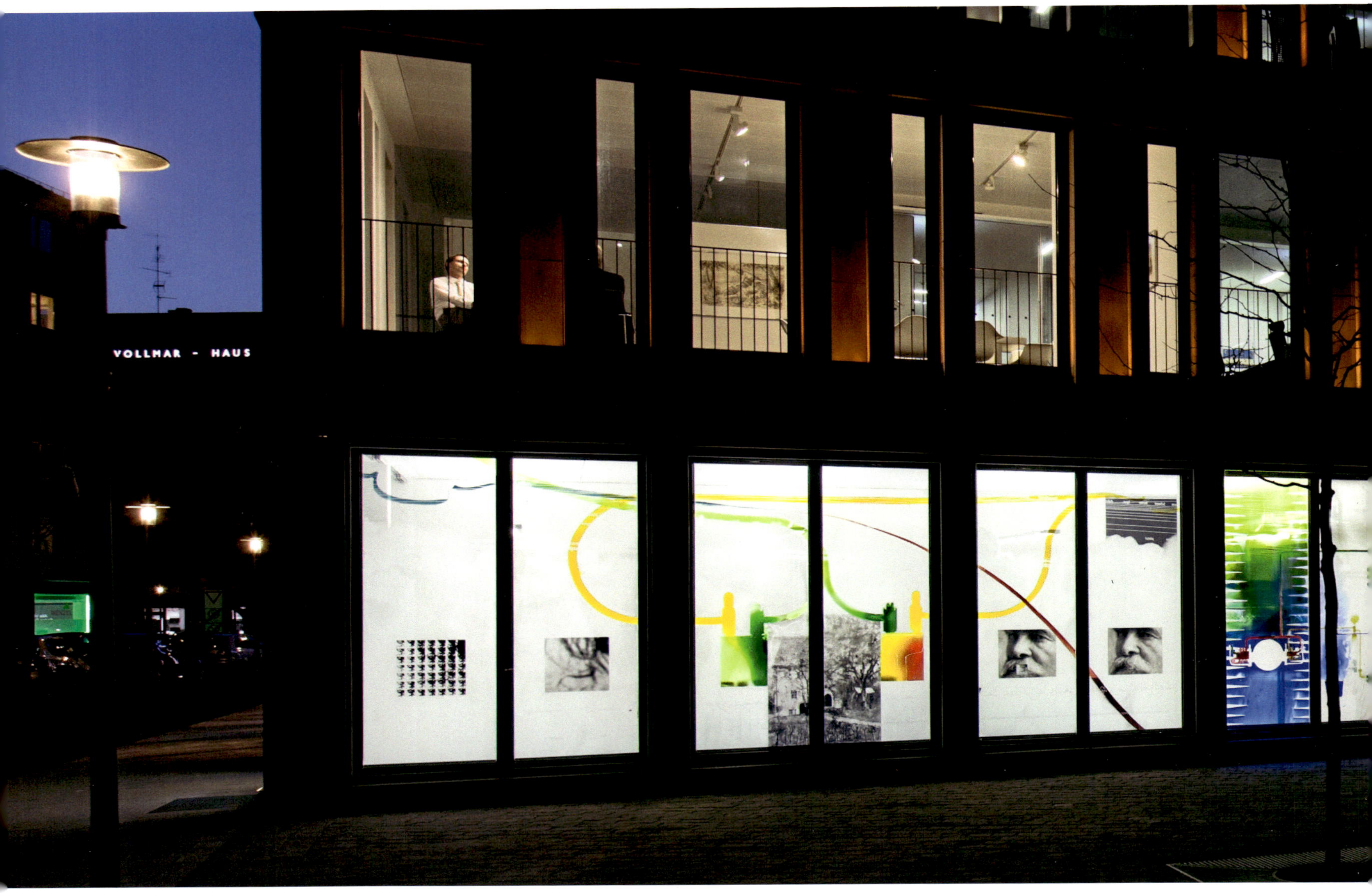

168

Joachim Jung / "Linde Score"

location: Carl von Linde Haus, Linde AG Headquarters, Angerhof Munich, DE / Steidle Architects / **year:** 2011 / **technique:** float glass painting

"Pour painting," hand painting, airbrush, photo-technical sandblasting, ceramic glass melting colors, float glass, tempered, and in parts laminated.
Joachim Jung translated records from the history of the Linde family and social documents into concrete and figurative painting. A temperature chart, sheet music for a piano sonata by Werner Linde, "anatomies" of refrigeration apparatuses, text fields, color atmospheres, and persons are intertwined, welded together and separated, forming contrasts, intervals, transitions, coherences and interferences. (Joachim Jung)

LINDE SCORE

168 Nocturnal view of the long row of windows seen from the street Unterer Anger. The glass design measures more than 260 feet long, reaching far into Klosterhofstraße.

169 Corner Klosterhofstraße / Unterer Anger.

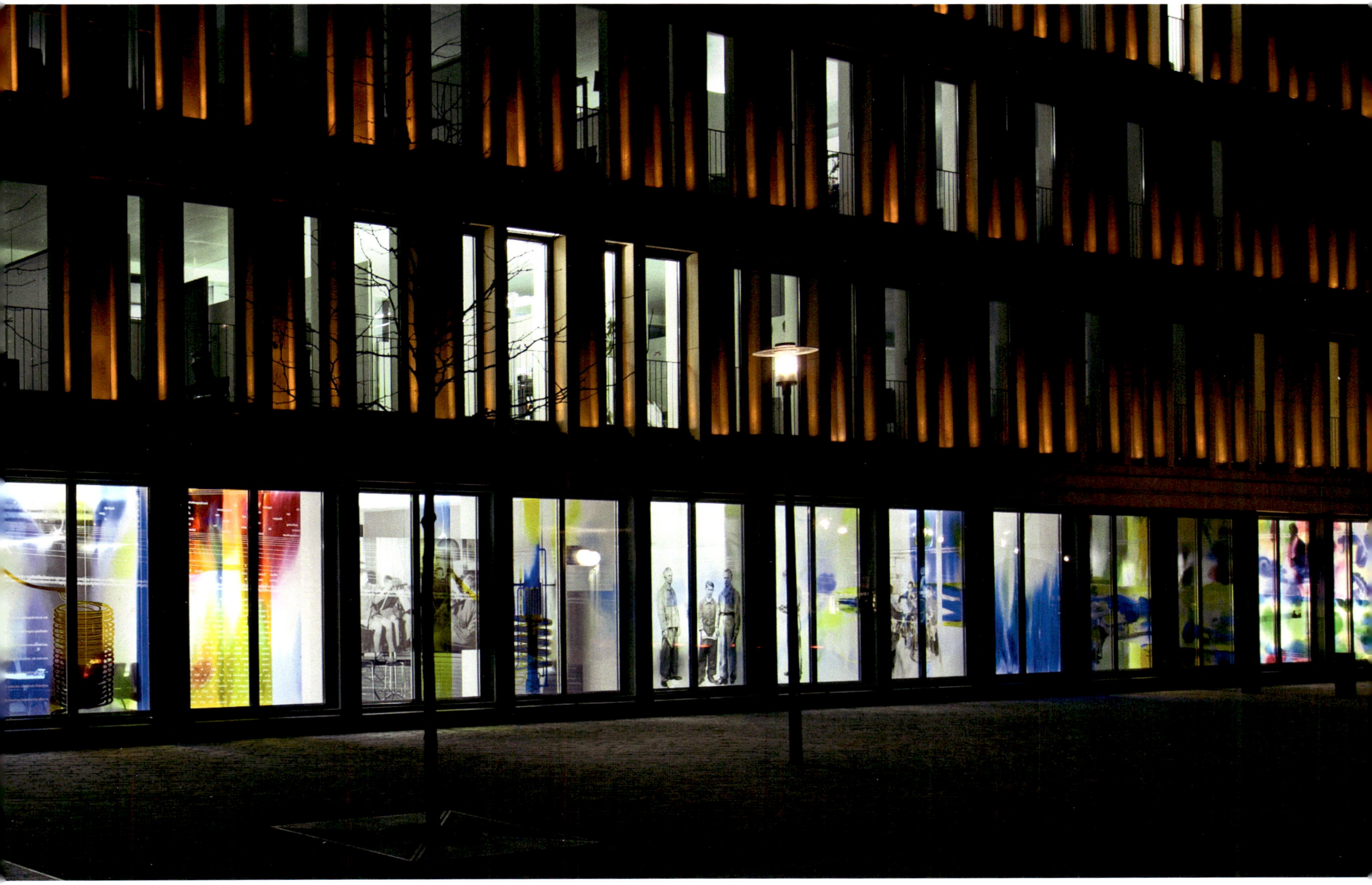

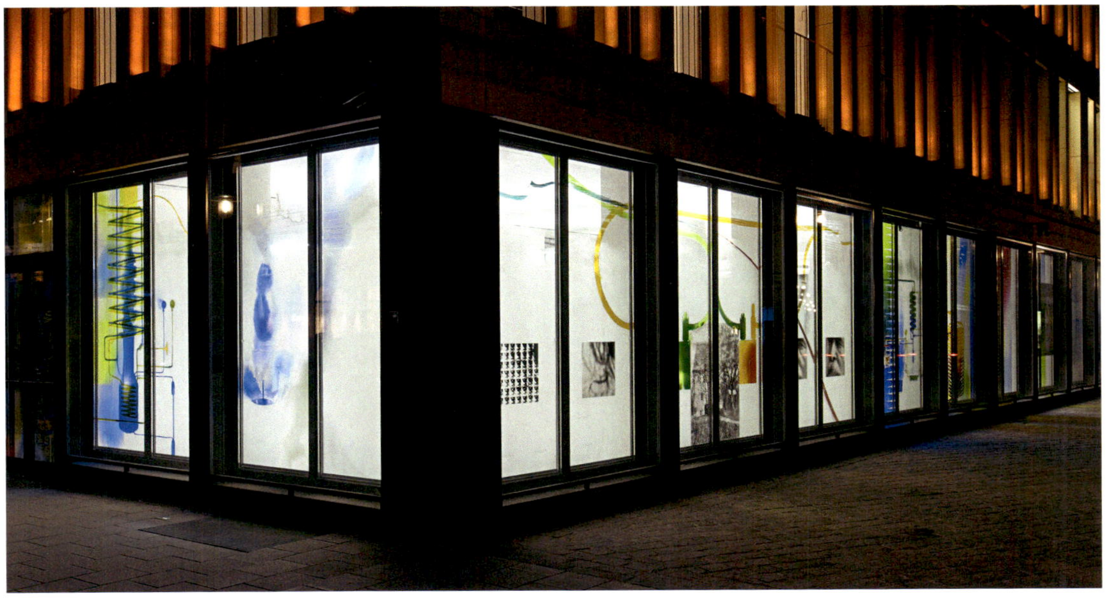

169

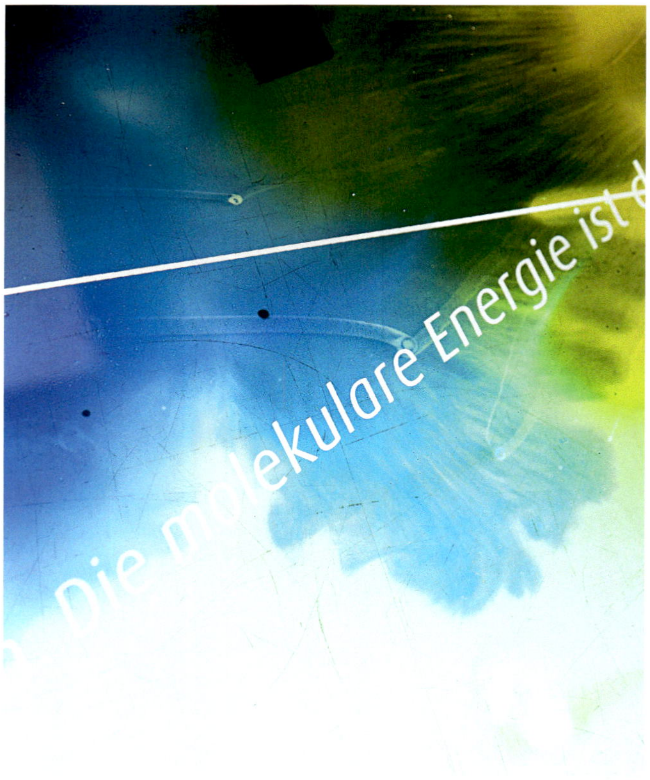

170

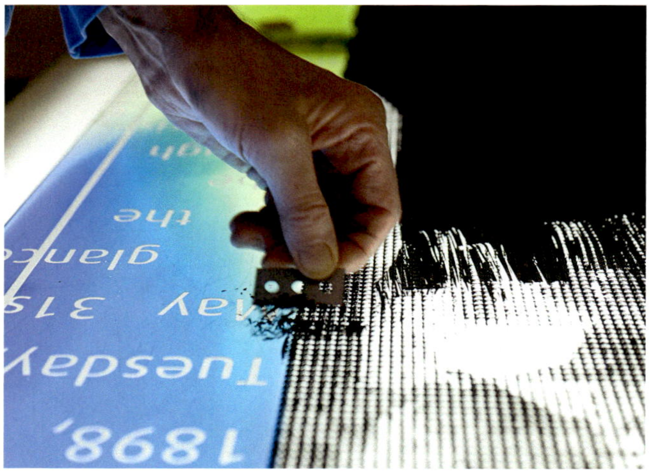

171

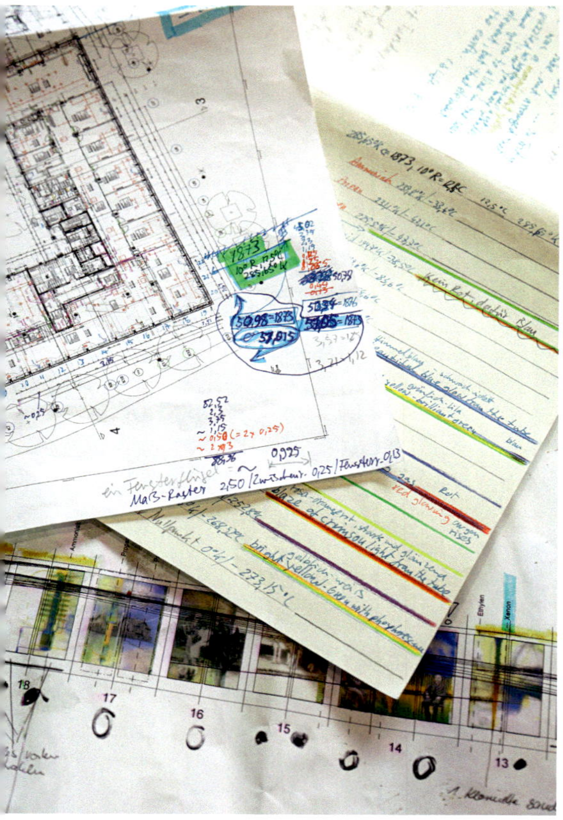

172

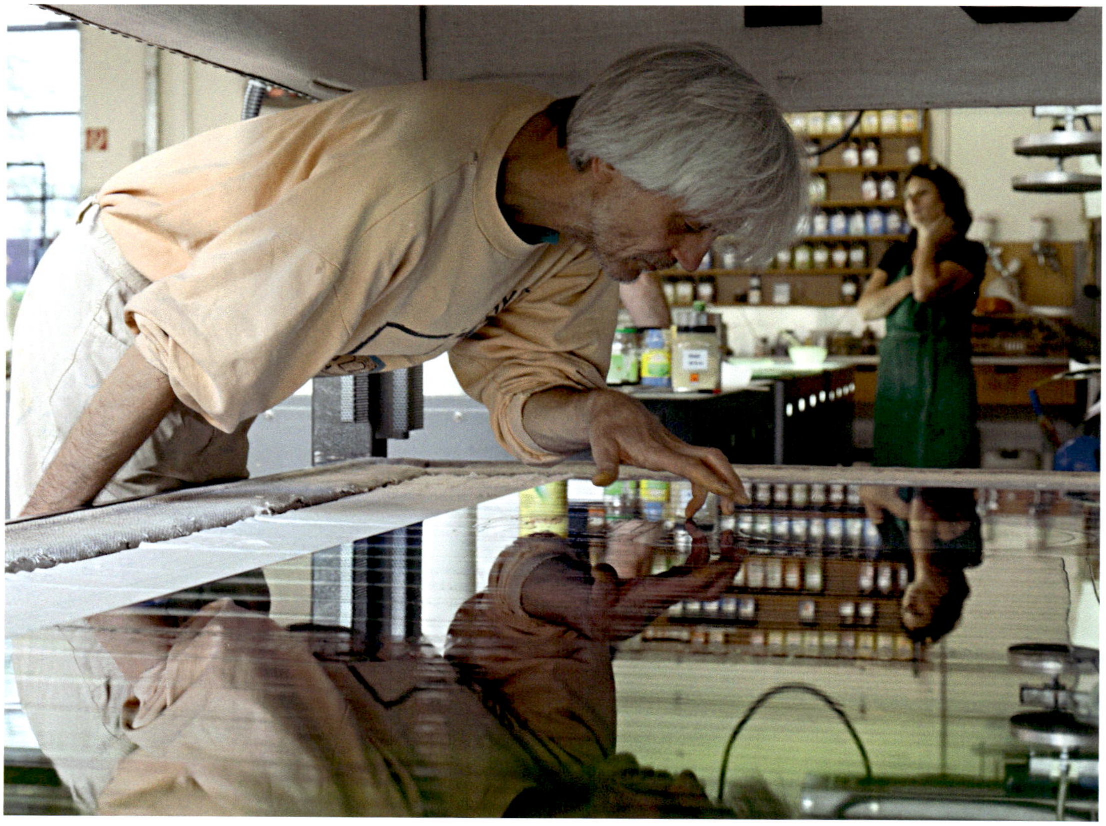

173

LINDE STUDIO

170
"Watercolor on glass" and sandblasted text.

171
The color is painted and fired; also the engravings are made; now, work with *Schwarzlot* will begin.

172
A still life – design, sketches, plans.

173
Checking the firing results – a first glance at the still hot kiln.

174 – 176
In the middle of the pouring and the painting process – artist and artisan "painting" with hose and paintbrush.

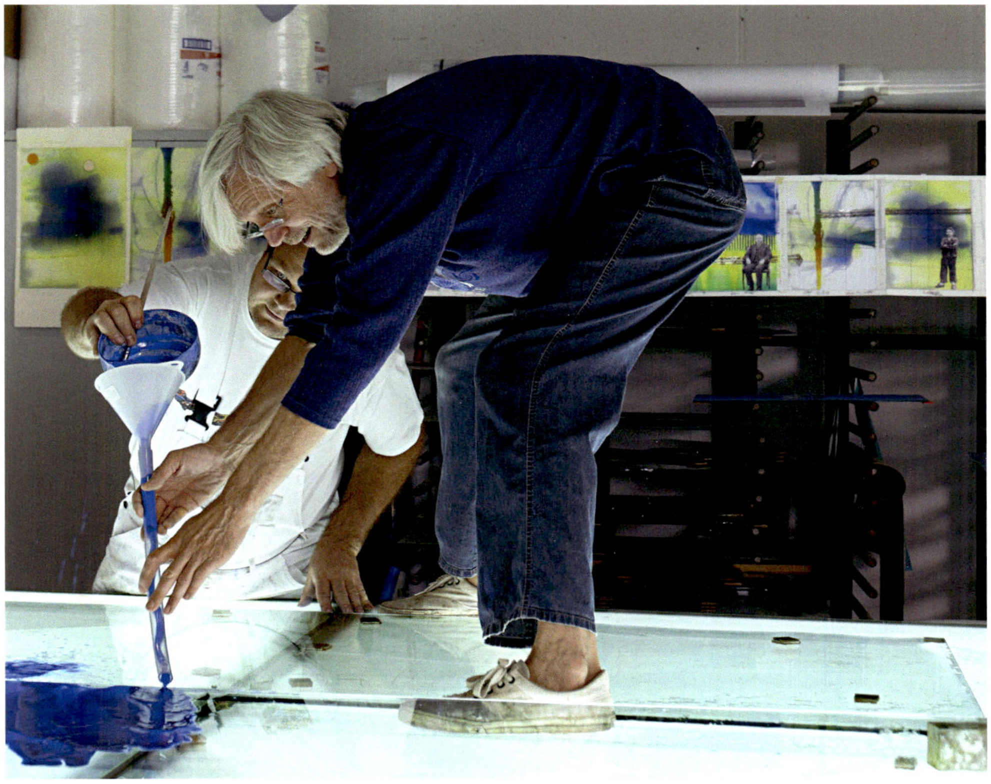

174

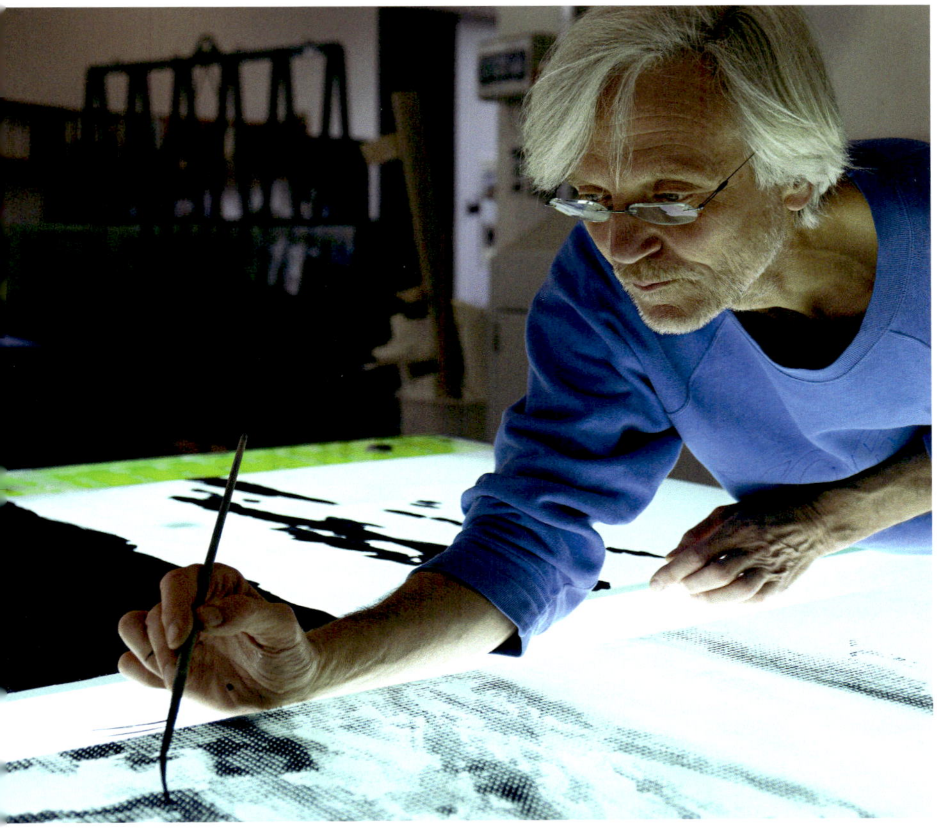

175

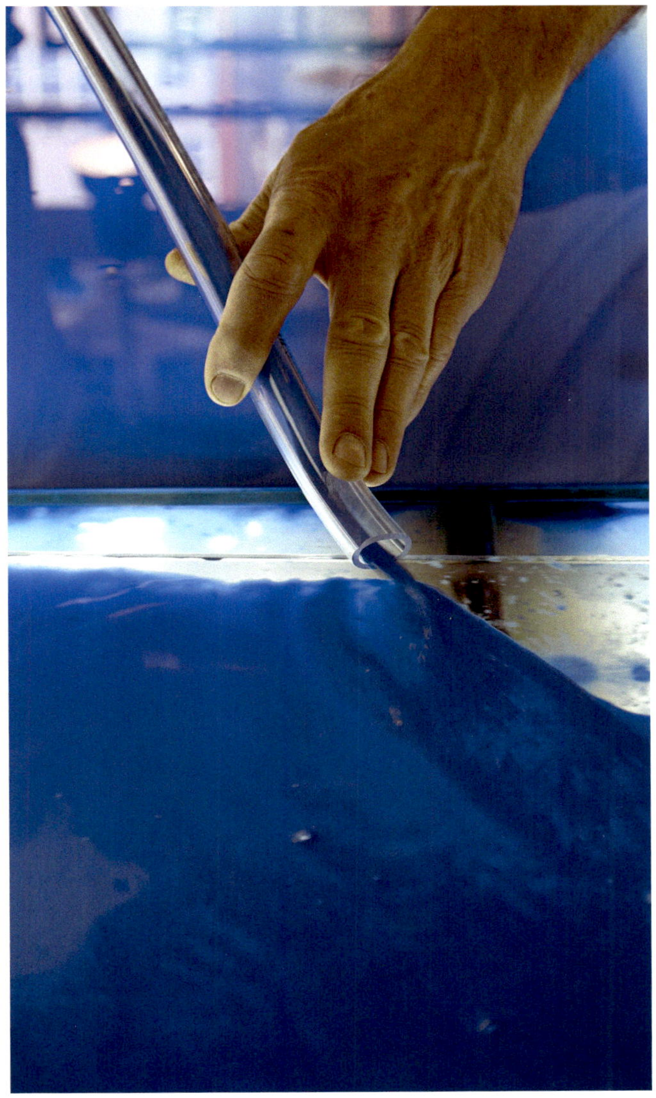

176

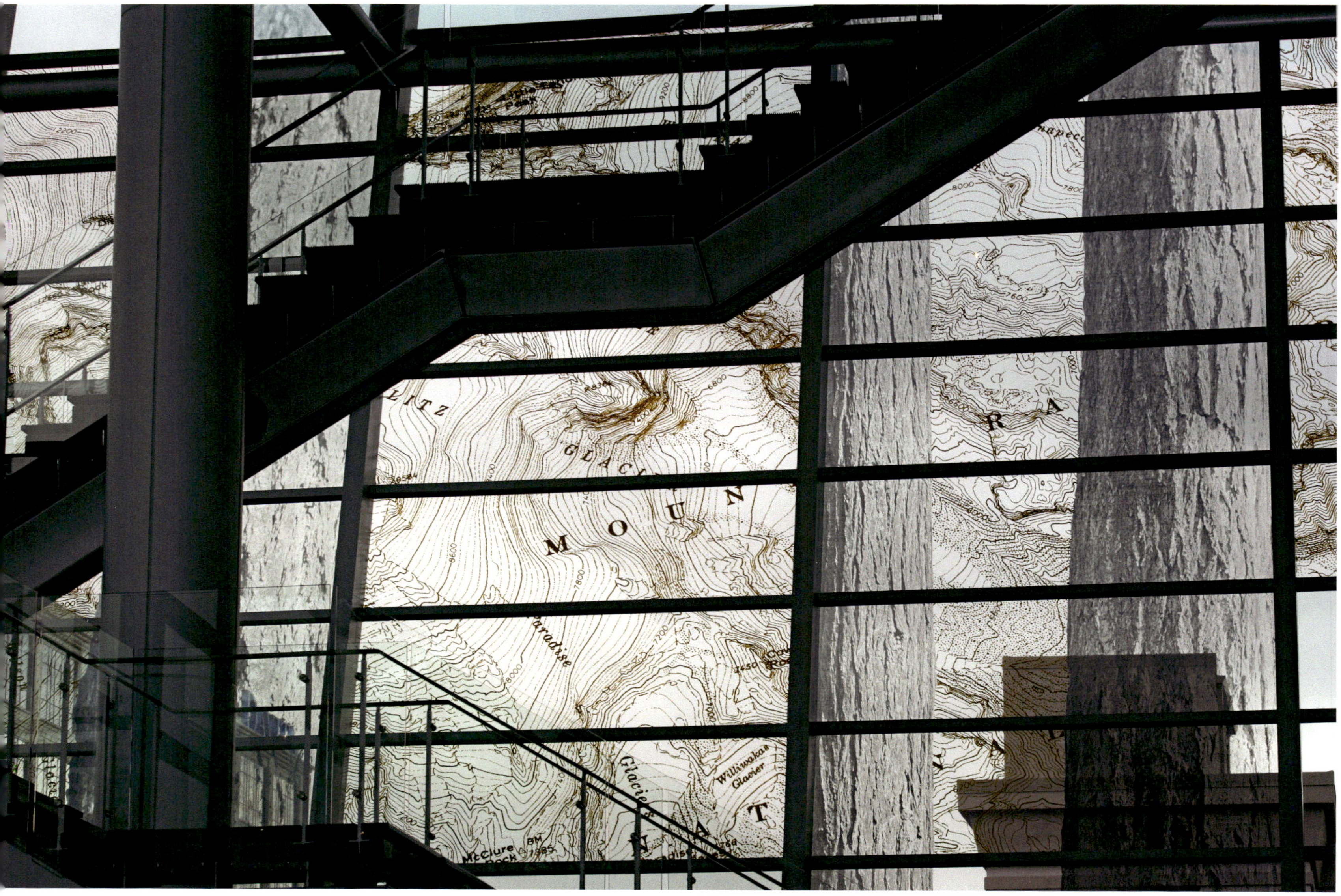

177

124

Stuart Keeler and Michael Machnic / “Apotheosis”

location: Greater Tacoma Convention and Trade Center, Tacoma, WA, USA / Merit Pardini Architects. City of Tacoma Public Art / **year:** 2004 / **technique:** float glass painting

2160 square feet of designed glass area. Different types of silkscreen print and airbrush, glass melting colors, IGUs for the protruding, slanted glass facade.
Humans threaten the enormous redwood trees – the “trees of mystery.” The artists refer to them with bulky beams in the stairwell and with “shadow trees” in the glass surfaces, and by topographic maps. 72 glass panels, each circa 3 × 10 feet, make up a significant portion of the glass facade, but they leave open a view to the outside and into the landscape.

APOTHEOSIS

177
A suspended staircase rising in front of the glass panels.

178
The “trees of mystery” appear like a transparent vision – surrounded by sepia colored maps.

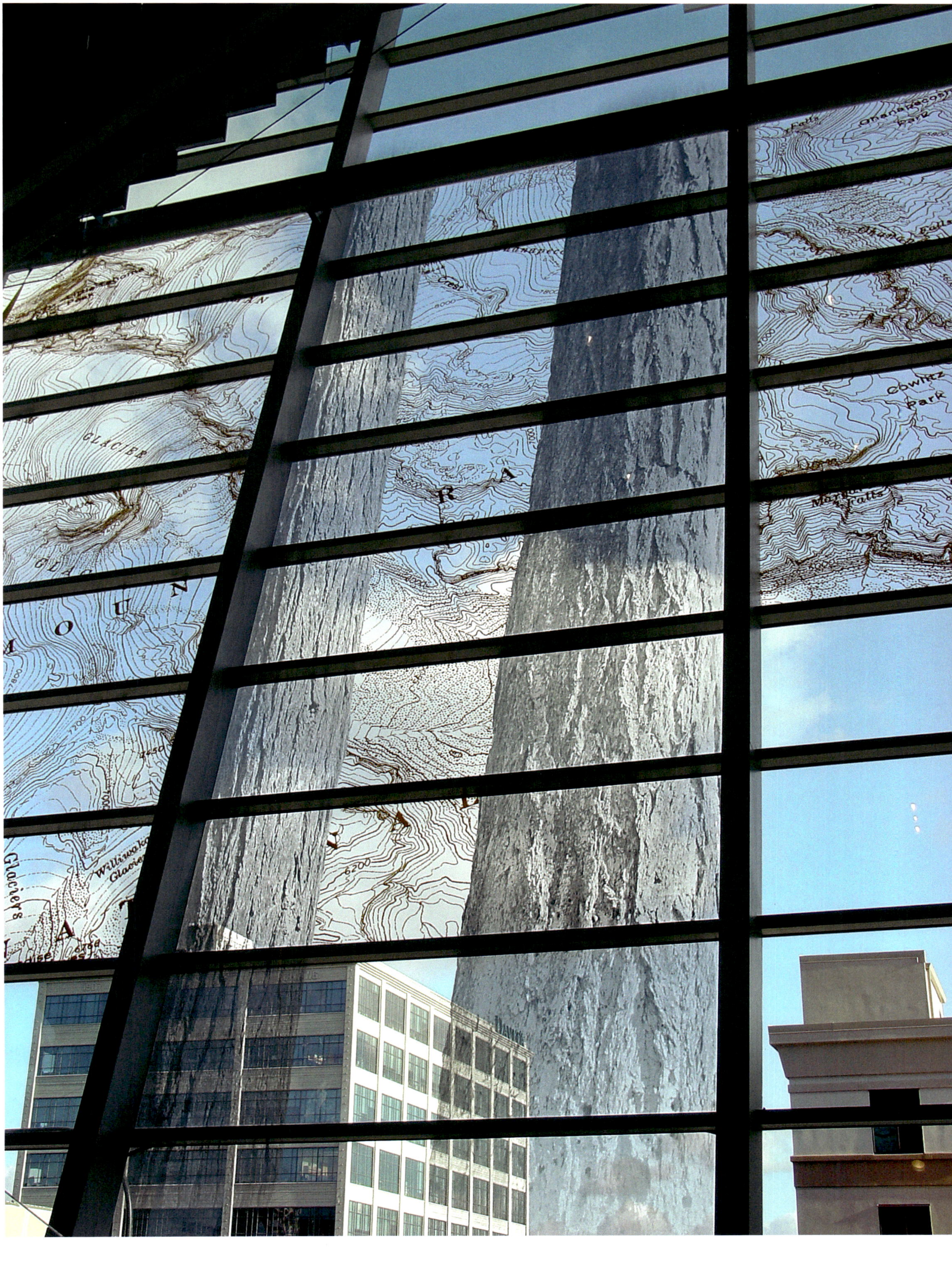
GLACIER
Cowlitz
Park
Glaciers

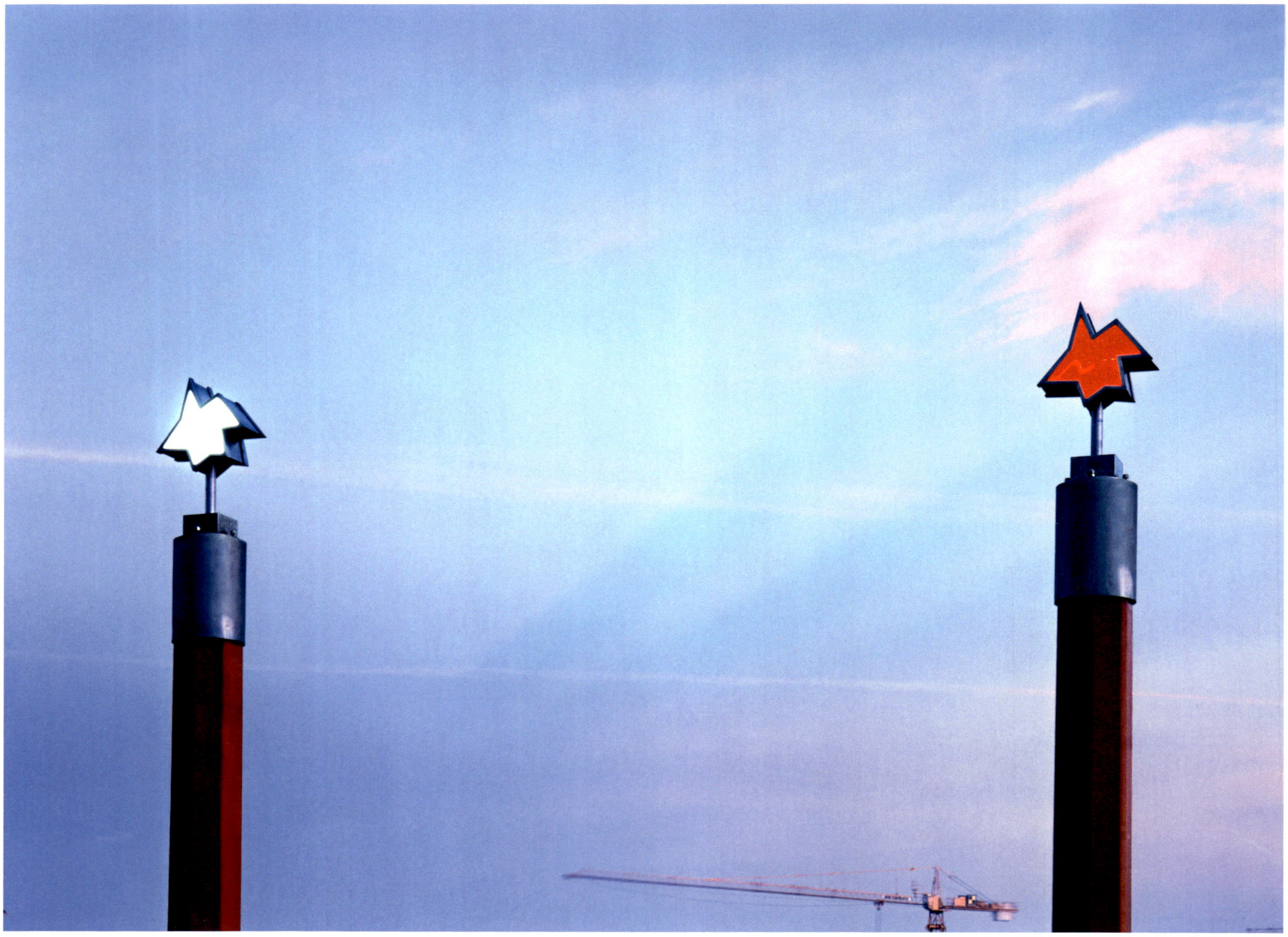

179

Imi Knoebel / "Children's Stars"

location: WWK Versicherungen Headquarters, Munich, DE / LAI Architects / **year:** 1999 / **technique:** colored glass, artificial light

Four oxidized metal pylons at the WWK Insurance Headquarter's main entrance; the "Children's Stars" may be found at the tips. Brightly lit around the clock, the stars are made of hand-blown colored glass in primary colors. This corporate artwork in public space is strong and convincing.

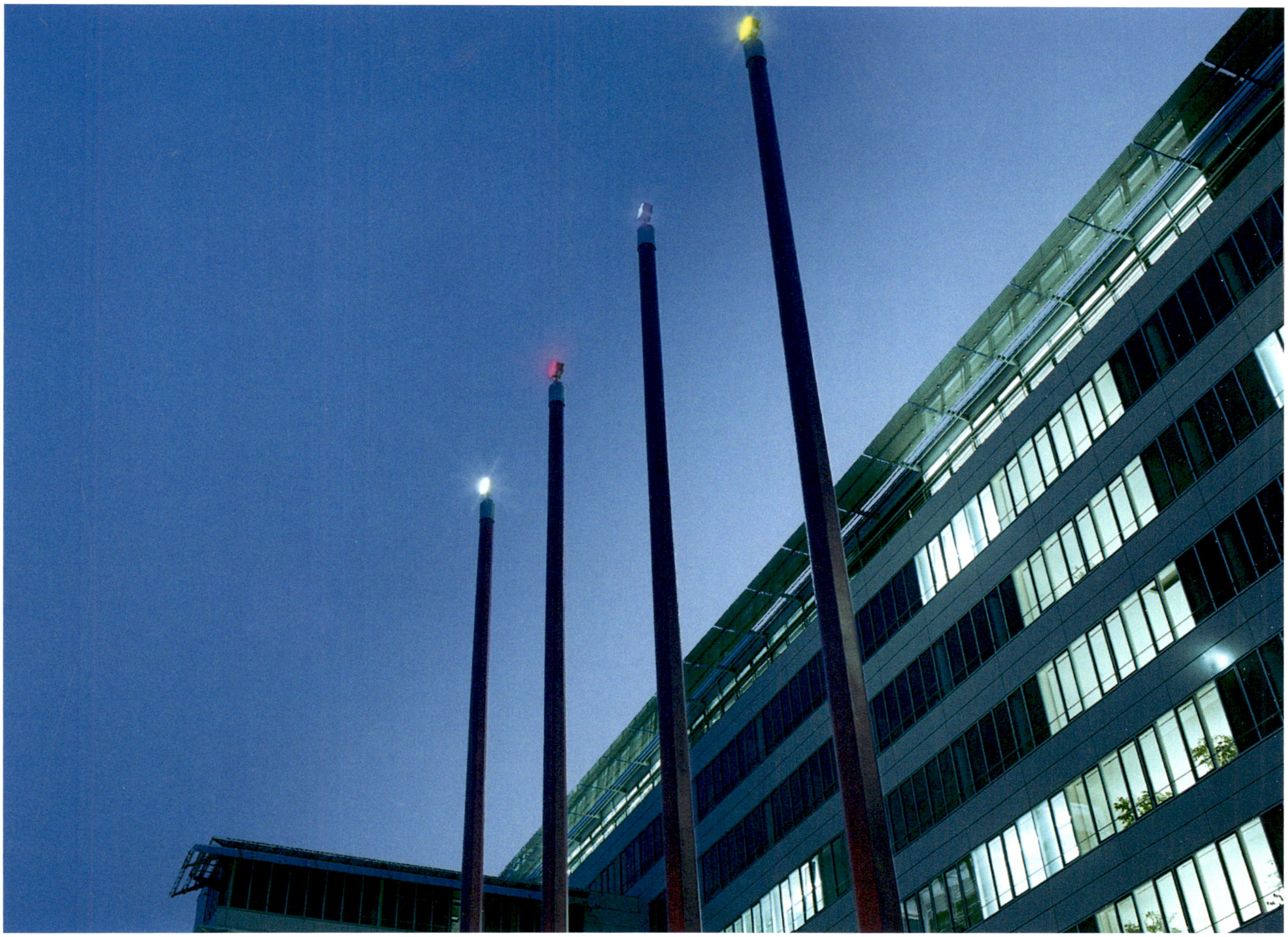

180

CHILDREN'S STARS

179
Highest tip of two of the "Children's Stars" pylons towards the sky.

180
View upwards from the entrance plaza to the pylons and the headquarter building.

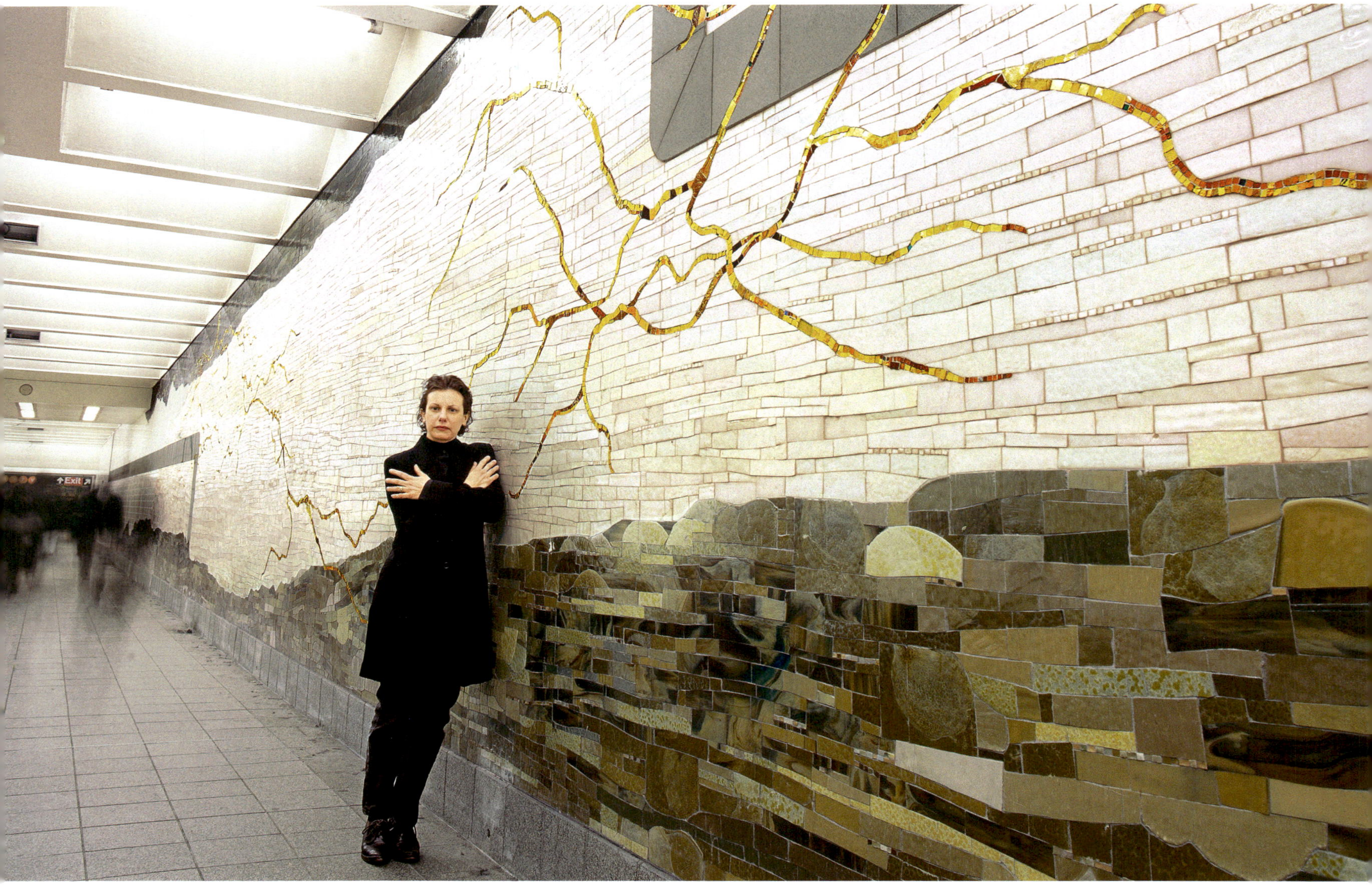

181

Samm Kunce / “Under Bryant Park”

location: Connecting cooridor between the east-west and north-south subway lines that intersect at the Avenue of the Americas and 42nd Street. New York, NY, USA / MTA Arts for Transit / **year:** 2002 / **technique:** glass mosaic and stone

Thanks to the courageous decision of New York’s MTA Arts for Transit’s Administration, environmental artist Samm Kunce was commissioned to design the tunnel walls in this central tunnel system located in Midtown Manhattan. This became one of the New York Subway system’s largest and most fascinating projects and was selected, along with works by Serra, Bourgeois, Dubuffet, Oldenburg, Plensa, and Kapoor, one of the 50 best “public art projects” in the US in the last fifty years.

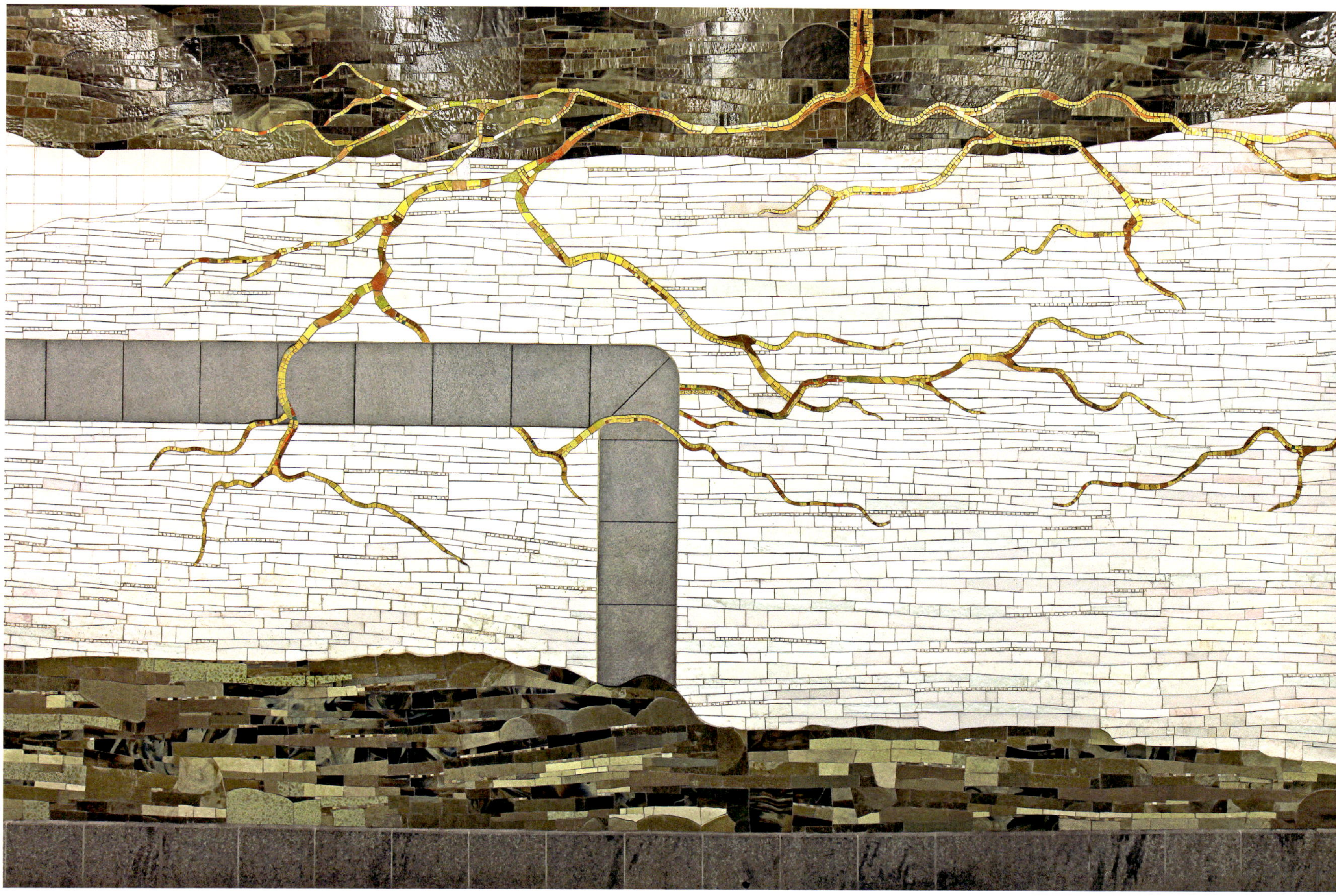

182

UNDER BRYANT PARK

181
Samm Kunce in front of one of the large mosaic walls. White and brown-violet colors dominate. The tangle of roots seems to penetrate the space from above and is made of gold tesserae. Granite text bands serve as accents.

182
Detail from the wall mosaics.

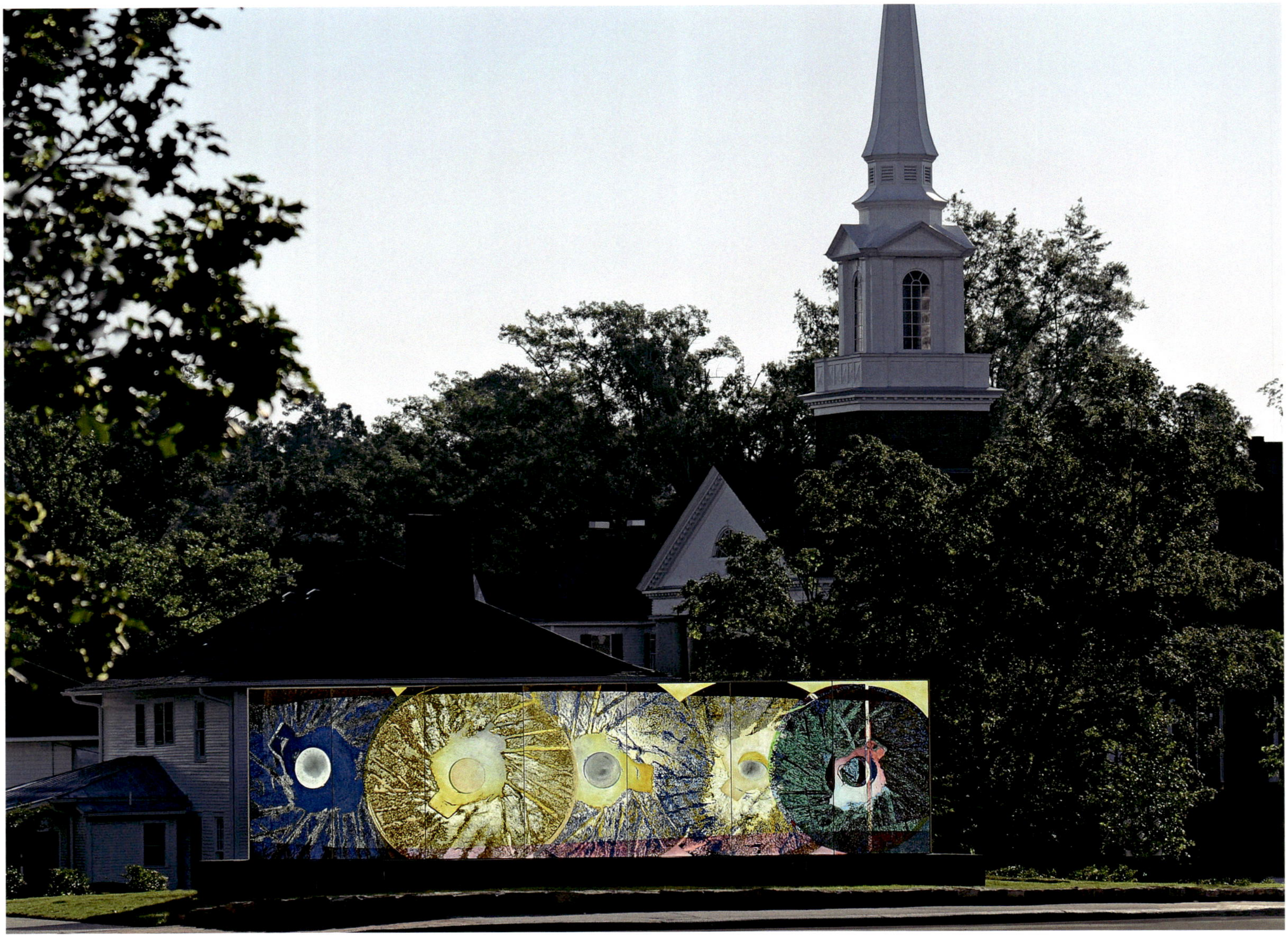

183
MILLING AROUND. In the morning sunlight, the glass wall seen against houses, the church, and trees still in shade.

Heidi Lippman / "Milling Around"

location: Glass sculpture, Downtown Clinton, NC, USA / Sampson Arts Council /
year: 2012 / **technique:** float glass painting

Located in a public square, this freestanding, colored glass wall in metal frames is made of transparent and opaque ceramic glass melting paints. The appearance of the slightly tilted glass wall is apparent from either side. The different light situations during the course of the day make the image appear different time and again. The object is illuminated at night. The abstracted millstones remind us of the mills and silos once located here.

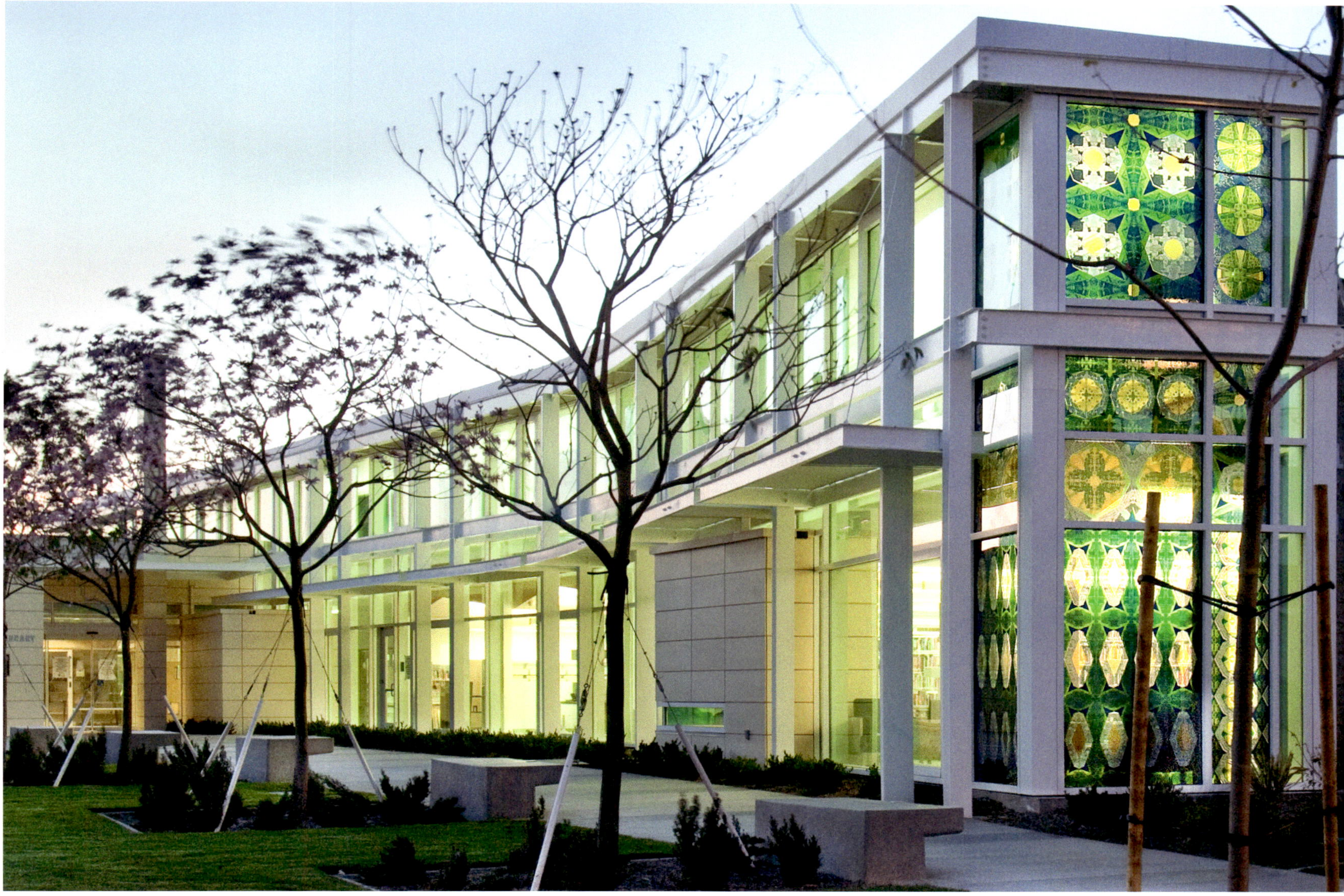

184
SUBDIVISIONS. Artistically designed, this glass wall extends over two floors and the corner of a building; seen here at dusk, the interior lit.

Anne Marie Karlsen / "Subdivisions"

location: Public Library, Lawndale, CA, USA / Gruen Associates Architects, Civic Art Program, Los Angeles and County Arts Commission / **year:** 2008 / **technique:** float glass painting

Transparent glass melting colors, silkscreen print, airbrush, worked in two layers, IGU panes. Public Art Award 2009.

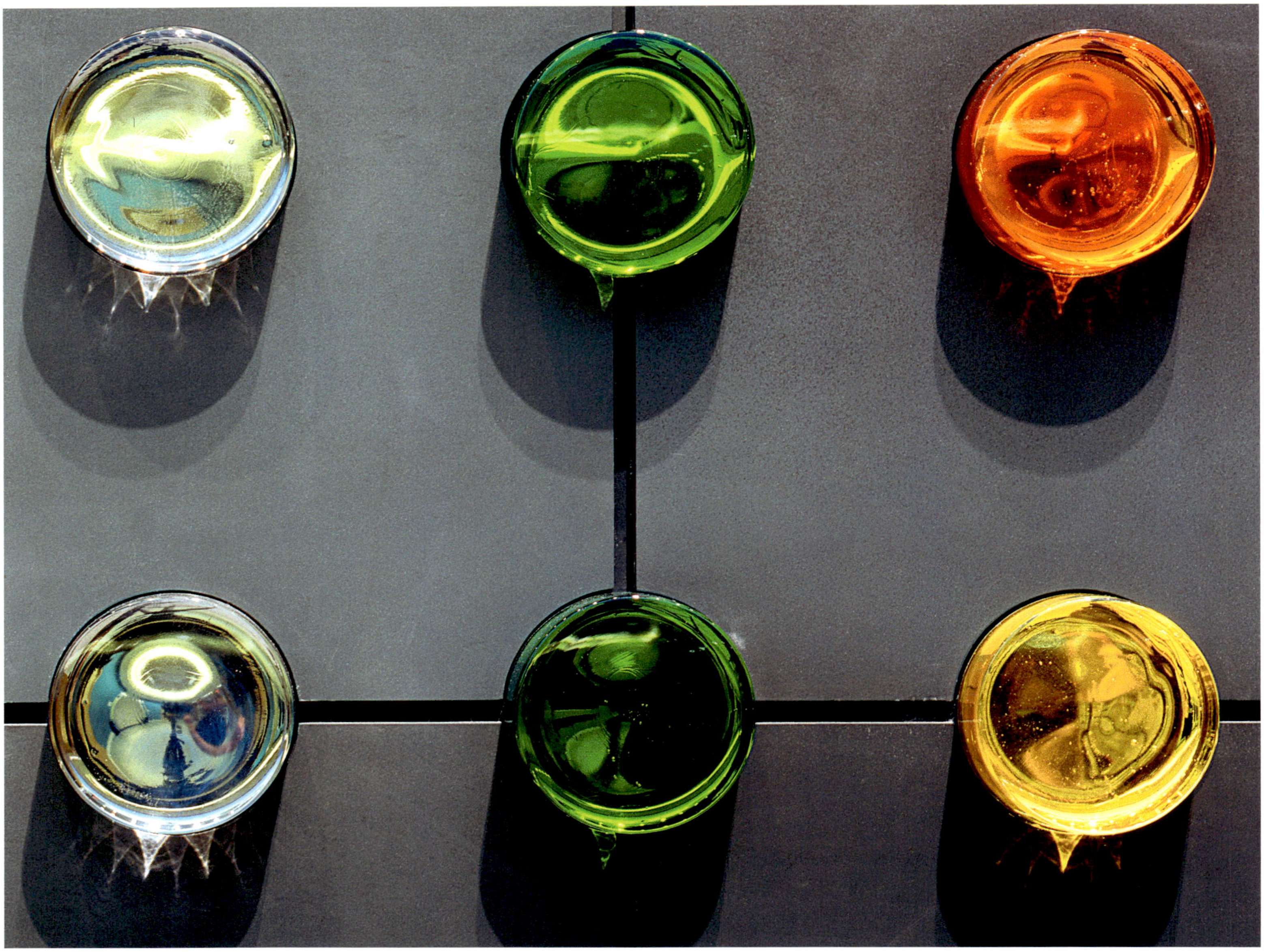

185

Iñigo Manglano-Ovalle / "Portrait of a Young Reader"

186

location: Bronx Library Center, New York, NY, USA / Dattner Architects, Public Art Project of the City of New York/ **year:** 2006 / **technique:** colored glass in steel panels

Round, very transparent colored glass discs, 32 millimeters thick, mounted in steel panels.
In 2007 Iñigo Manglano-Ovalle participated in Documenta XII and, in 2006, he designed the gene structure of "a young reader." Franz Mayer's primary task had been to find and to produce a specific mineral glass for the artist, which – even without being lit and when mounted into heavy, cut-out steel panels – possesed the greatest possible translucency and thus developed a radiance from "out of itself."

PORTRAIT OF A YOUNG READER

185 Detail of six colored glass discs within steel panel.

186 A section of the entire wall.

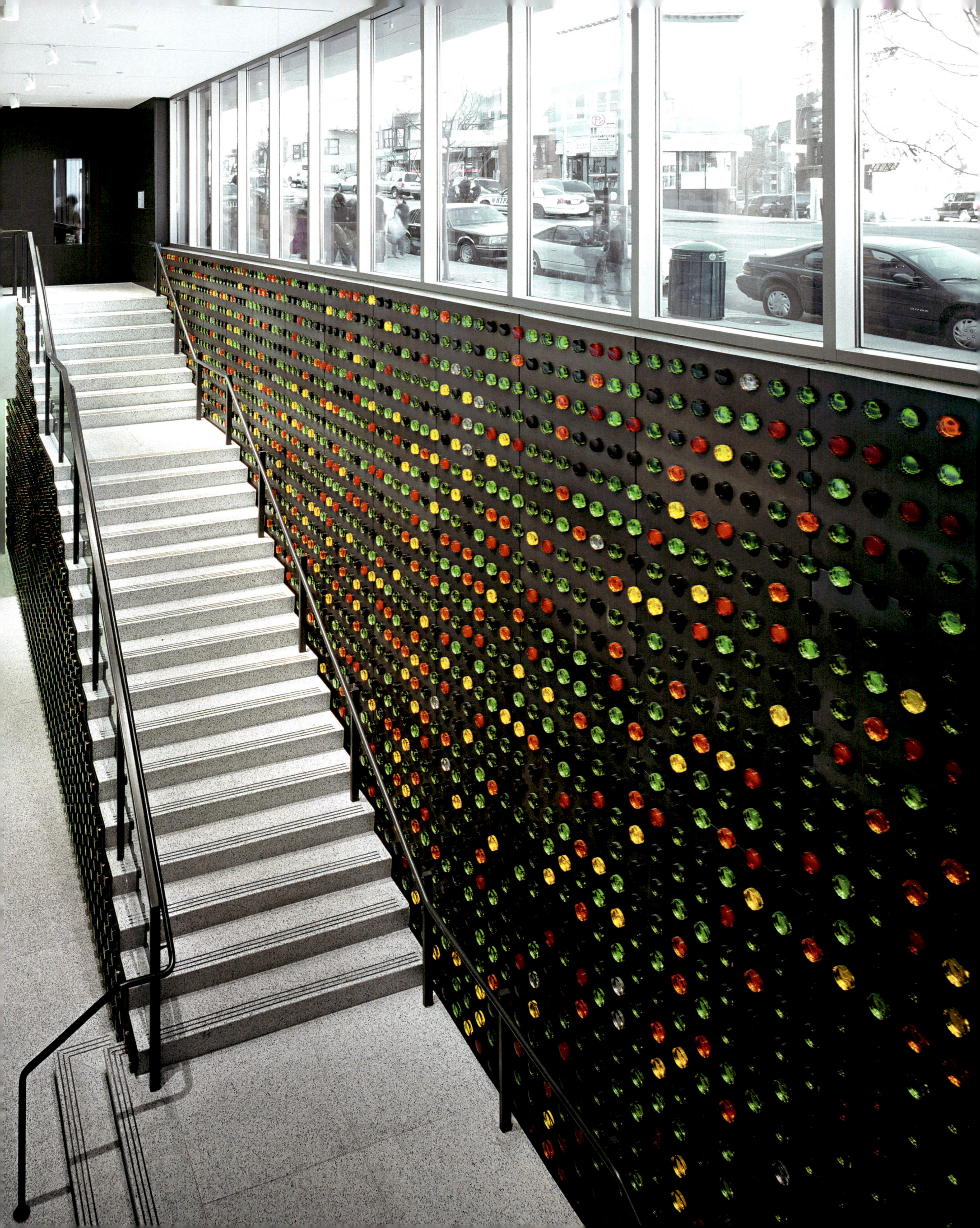

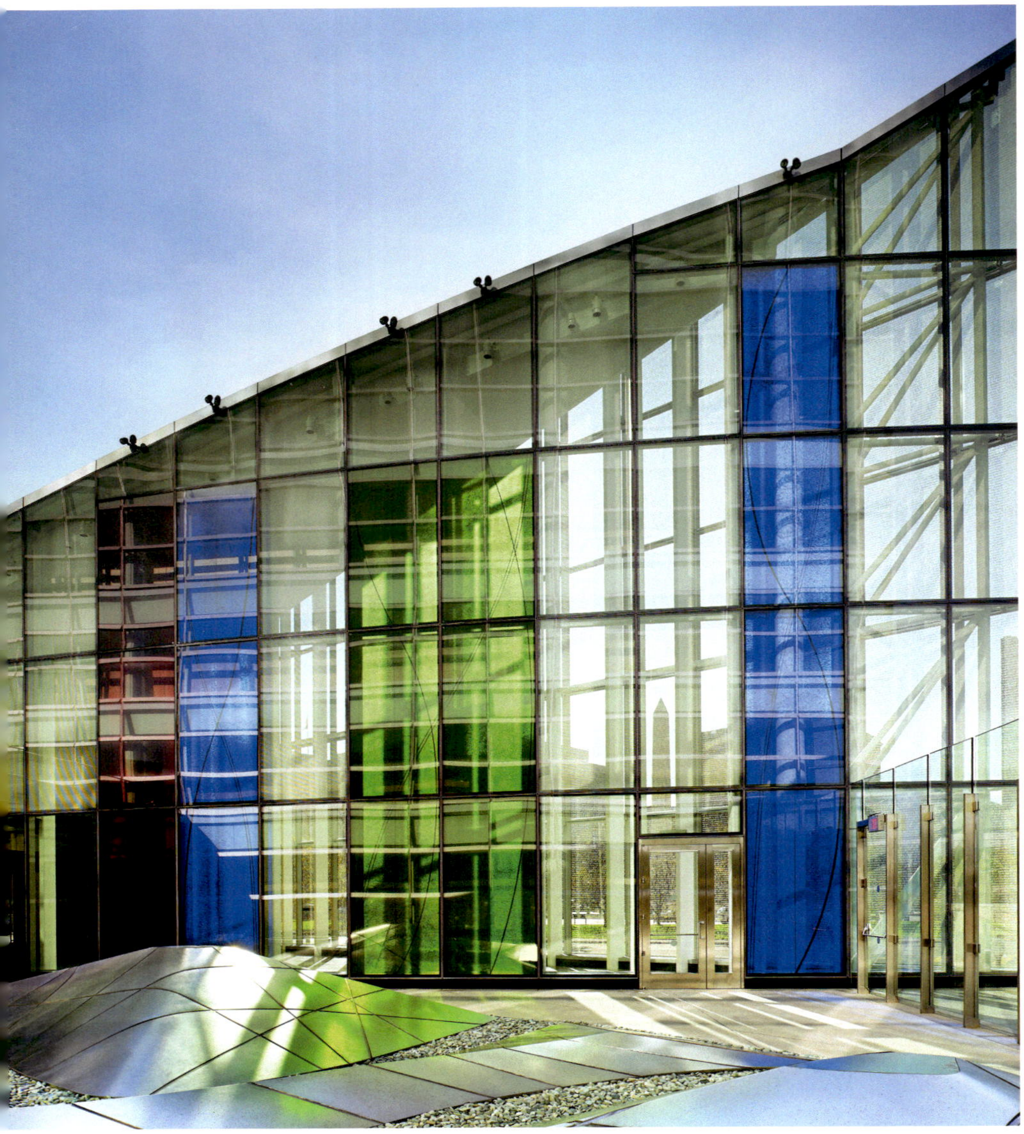

187

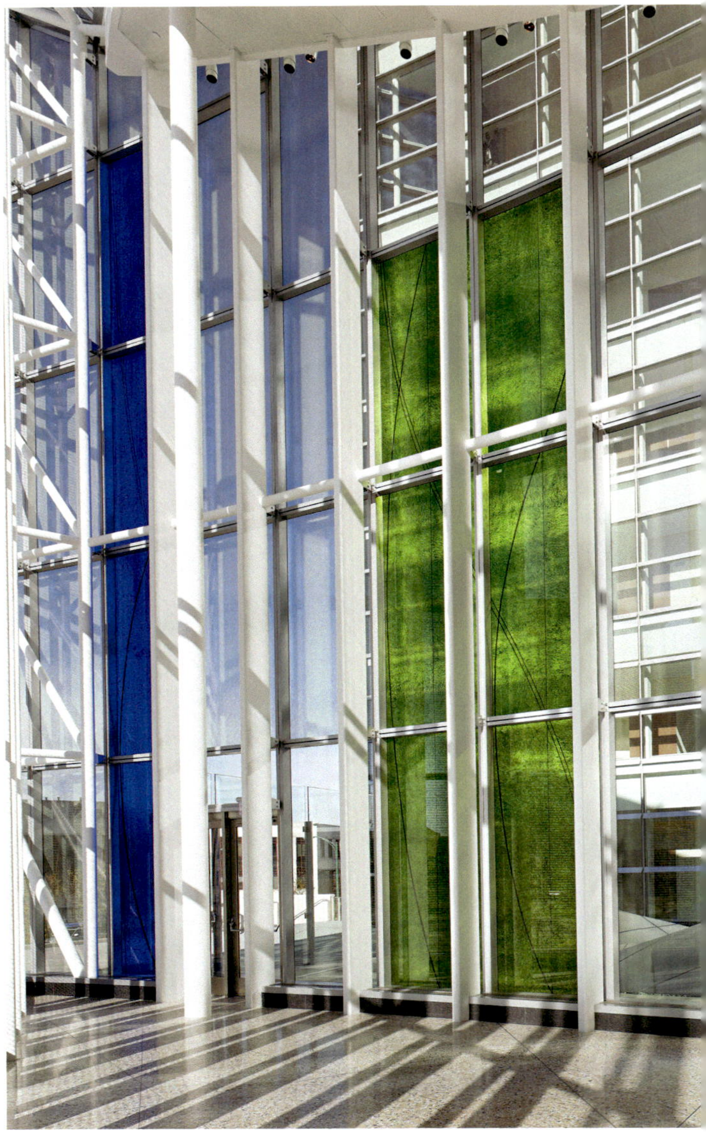

188

Robert Mangold / "Three Columns"

location: US Courthouse, Buffalo, NY, USA / Kohn Pedersen & Fox Architects, Art in Architecture Program US GSA / **year:** 2011 / **technique:** float glass painting

16 glass panels, on average 9 feet high and 4 ½ feet wide. Float glass painting, silkscreen print, and hand painting. Opaque and transparent ceramic glass melting colors. IGU glass units made of 10 millimeter art glass tempered and 12 millimeter laminated glass panels.

Robert Mangold's artwork for the new courthouse in Buffalo is a suite of monumental, tall, columnar stained glass windows for the courthouse's triangular entry pavilion. While the geometric imagery of Mangold's windows is totally abstract, the carefully balanced forms nonetheless relate well to the design, function, and symbolism of a

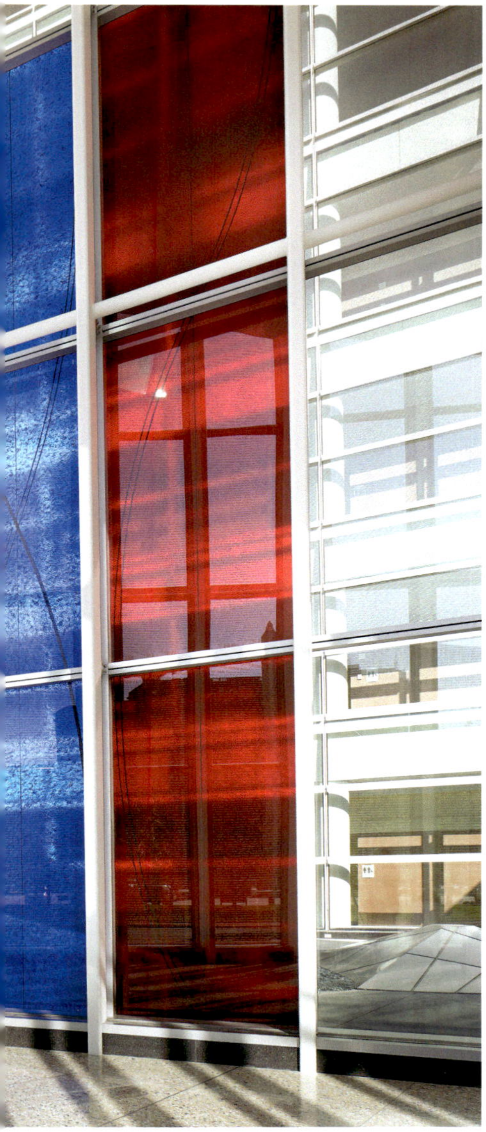

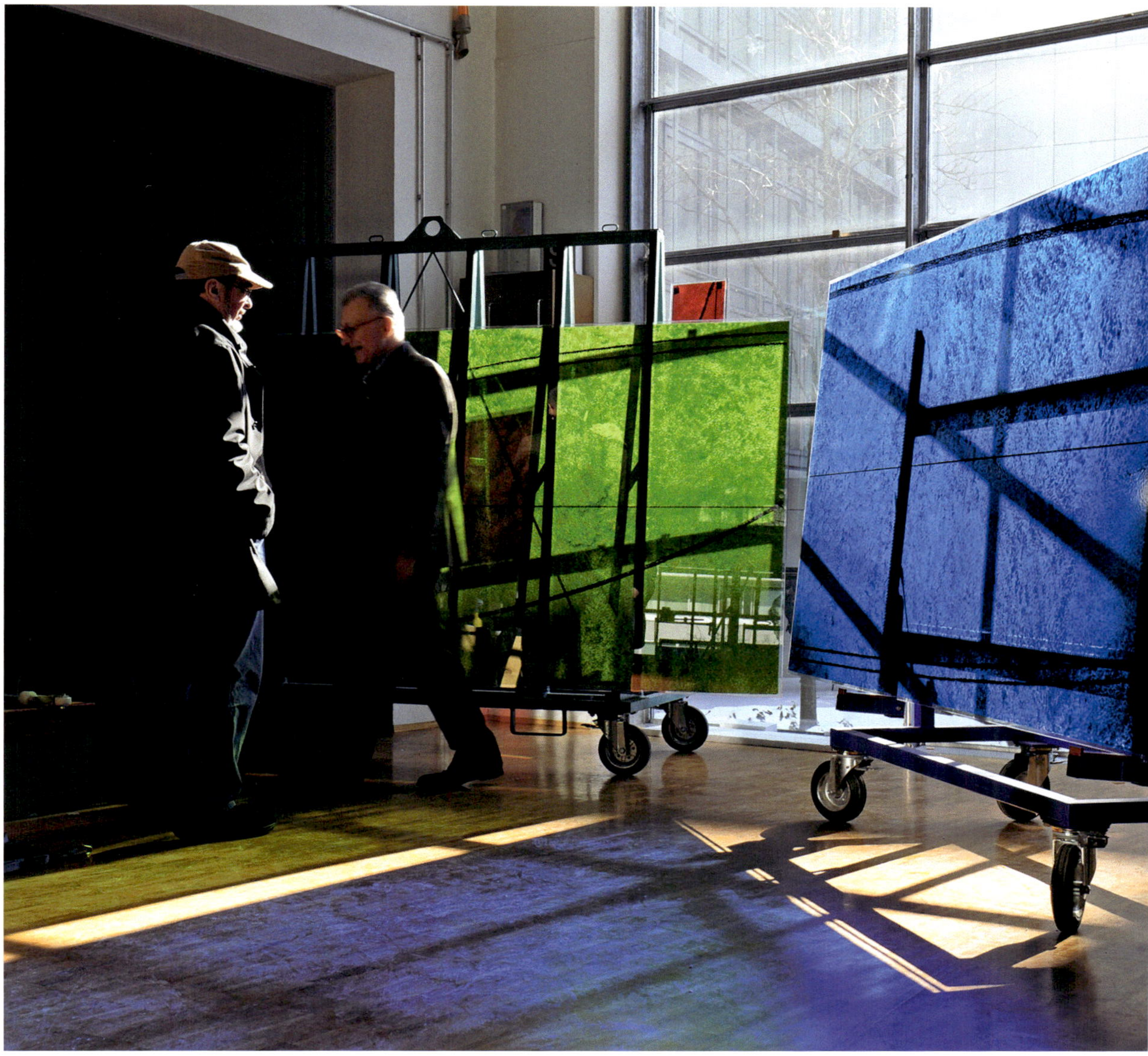

189

courthouse: Formally, the windows are about equilibration and resolution - as is the administration of law. For Mangold, it is important to maintain the hand-drawn quality of the lines, and the colors, which when translated into transparent glass melting colors, hold their structural and field qualities. He has worked closely with the Munich Studio to achieve this goal. For the Mayer studio it is always a pleasure and challenge to collaborate with the leaders in the art world.

THREE COLUMNS

187
The glass pavilion with Robert Mangold's glass painting seen from the main building.

188
View of the pavilion's inside towards the main building.

189
Robert Mangold (left) with Gabriel Mayer in the Munich studio.

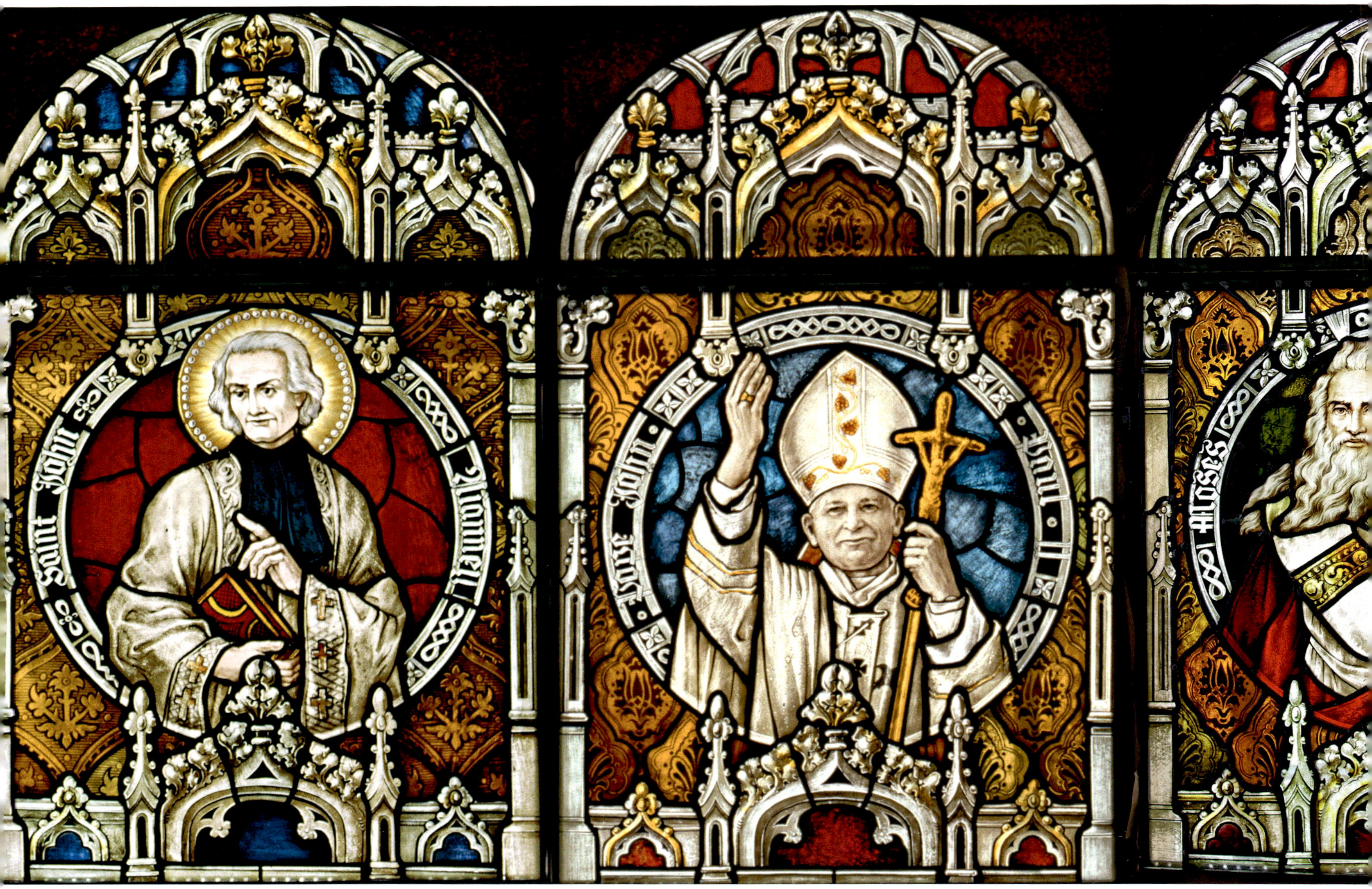

190 191 192

Fazl and Mahbuba Maqsoodi / “Munich Style”

location: St. Williams R.C. Church, Round Rock, TX, USA / **year:** 2008–11 / **technique:** traditional stained glass

32 new clerestory windows – designed and executed in traditional Munich style quality– to match and complete the series of circa 1911 Mayer of Munich windows. These had been purchased from a defunct orphanage in Philadelphia, PA and were installed in the lower nave of St. William's church.

The extraordinary graphic, painterly and pictorial qualities of the historic Munich style stained glass design had made Mayer of Munich and F. X. Zettler, the sister companies, two of

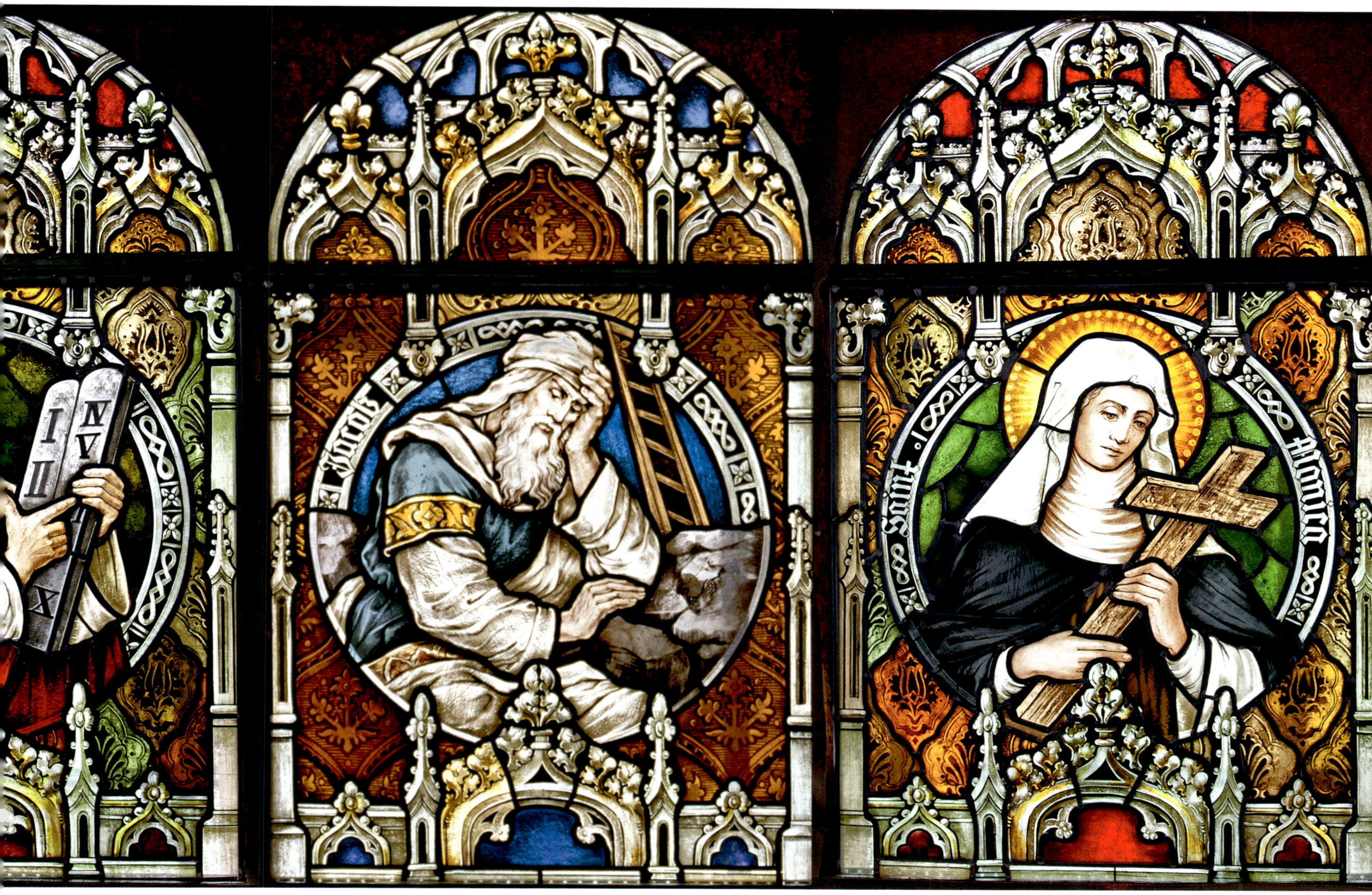

193

194

the leading studios worldwide in the realm of church art in the late 19th century. In recent years the Mayer studio and the Maqsoodis have made it a special goal to rediscover and recreate this very special quality of pictorial design and stained glass execution. With hard work, intense studies and thorough training they succeeded to nearly match the qualities of the Munich style of the 19th century. Contemporary and "modern" artists do benefit from these special design and painting skills.

"MUNICH STYLE"

Five of the 32 clerestory windows, designed and executed in the quality of the traditional Munich Style.

190 St. Jean-Marie Vienne.

191 Pope John Paul II.

192 Moses.

193 Jacob.

194 St. Monika.

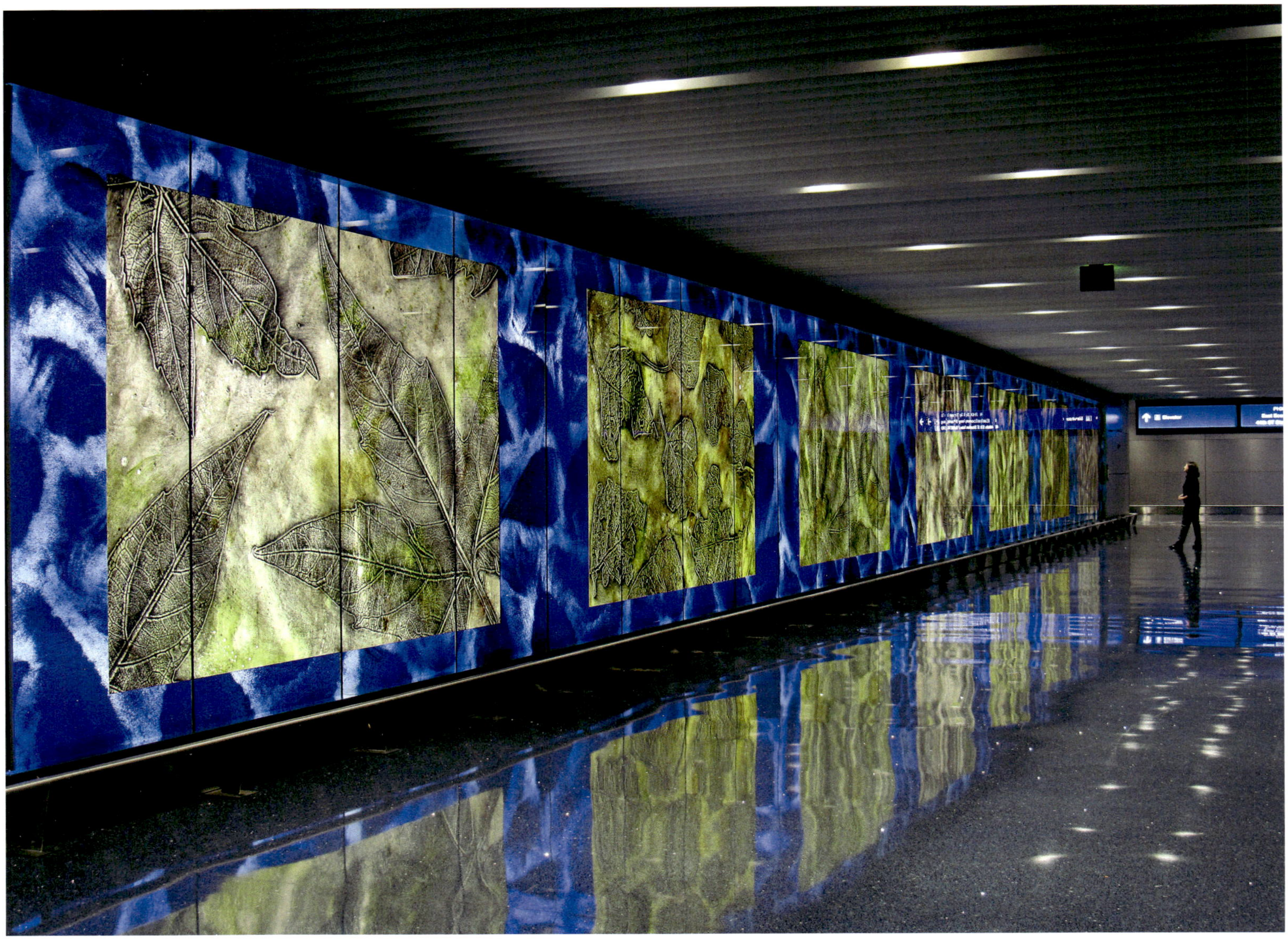

195

Daniel Mayer / "Trace Elements"

location: Sky Train Connector Bridges, Terminal 4, Phoenix Sky Harbor International Airport, AZ, USA / Phoenix Office of Arts and Culture – Public Art Program / **year:** 2011 / **technique:** float glass painting

A total of 56 laminated art glass panes, each 9'– 6" high and 4' – ½" wide. Two Connector Bridges, each 9'– 6" high and 113' wide, each bridge seven design fields. Artificial lighting.
Inspired by Arizona plant forms, small prints were made directly from their shapes through an etching press onto aluminum foils. Fourteen prints were scaled up for the two connector bridges and represent the need to observe our natural surroundings. The simplicity of peripheral vision is what enriches the path less taken. (Daniel Mayer)

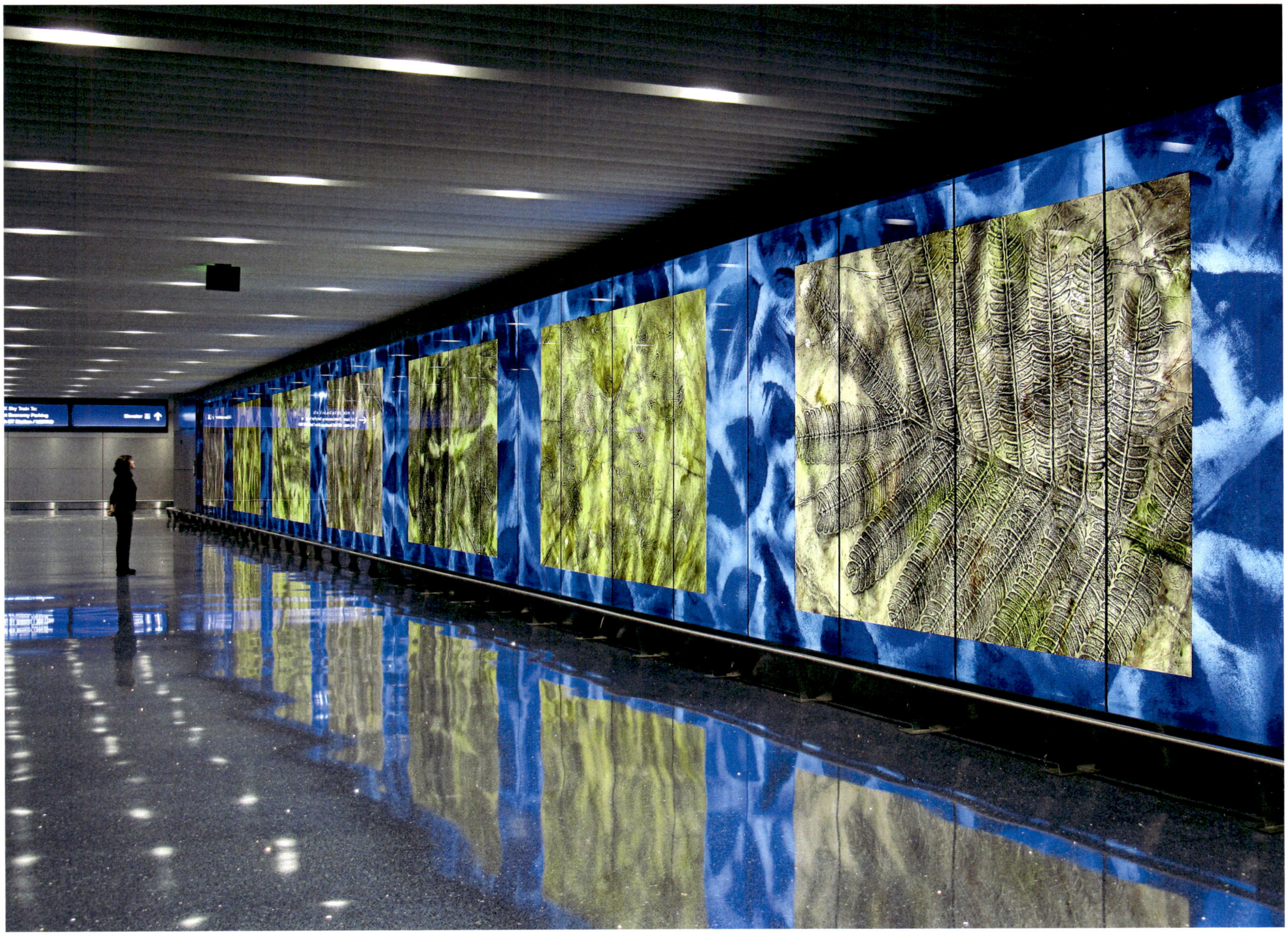

196

TRACE ELEMENTS

195 +
196

The two connector bridges run parallel from the train station to the terminal. Whatever direction one walks, the art glass walls are on the very outer sides of the two bridges. The inner sides have clear glass and allow to view the rather far away art glass of the opposite bridge.

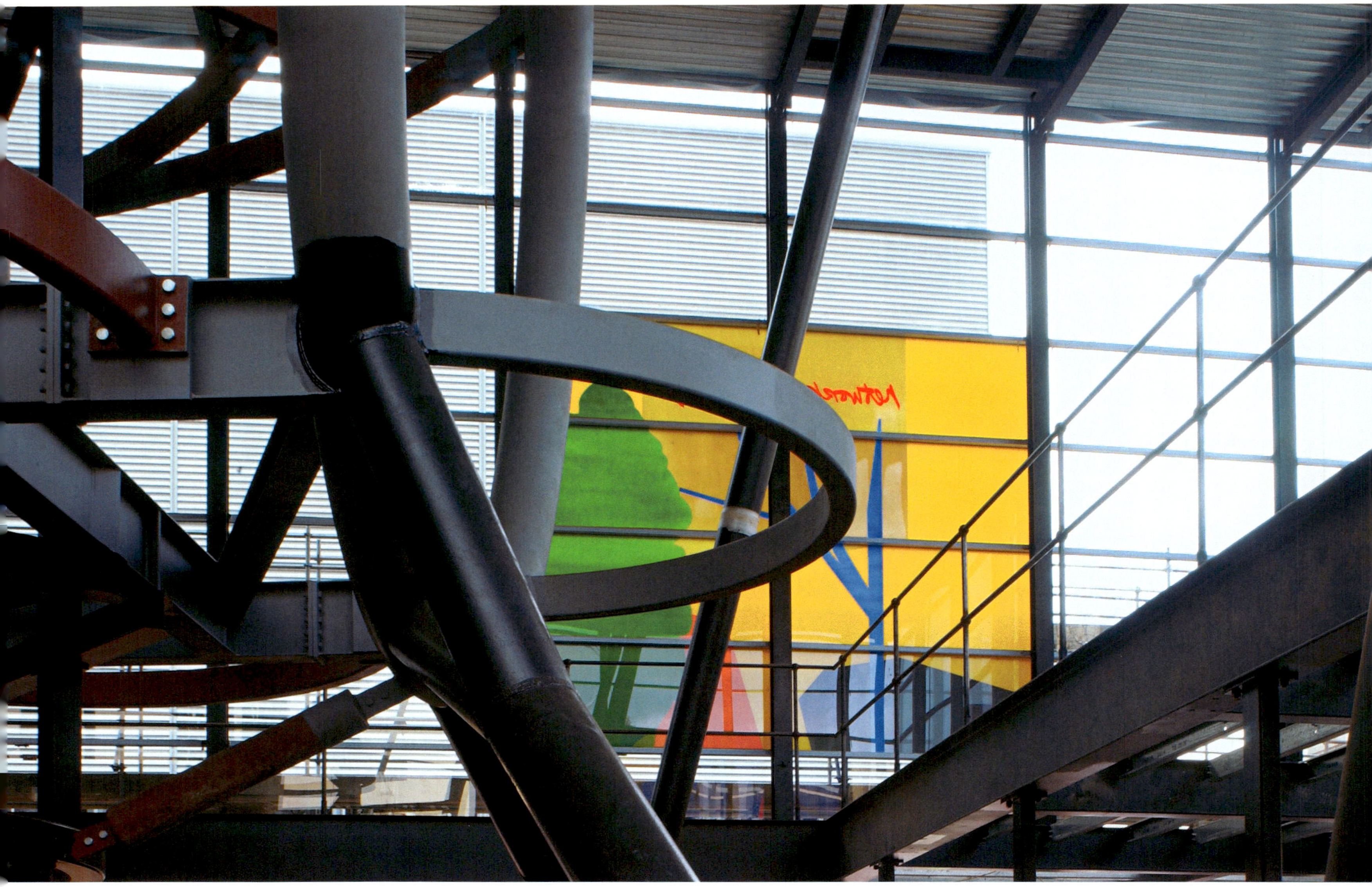

197

Bruce McLean / Medical University

location: Queen Mary University, New School of Medicine and Dentistry, London, GB / Alsop Architects / **year:** 2004 / **technique:** float glass painting

Nine powerful paintings on glass, on average measuring circa 270 square feet each, the area, roughly 2500 square feet, placed within the east and west curtain wall facades. Silkscreen print, sandblasting, airbrush; opaque ceramic glass melting colors. Laminated glass consisting of each two tempered and heat-soak-tested art glass panes.

Literally art in a "public space." You could also call these glass works "pictures on the street." The street turns into a museum. But at the same time, the glass pictures are also works of art for the "private" inner spaces.

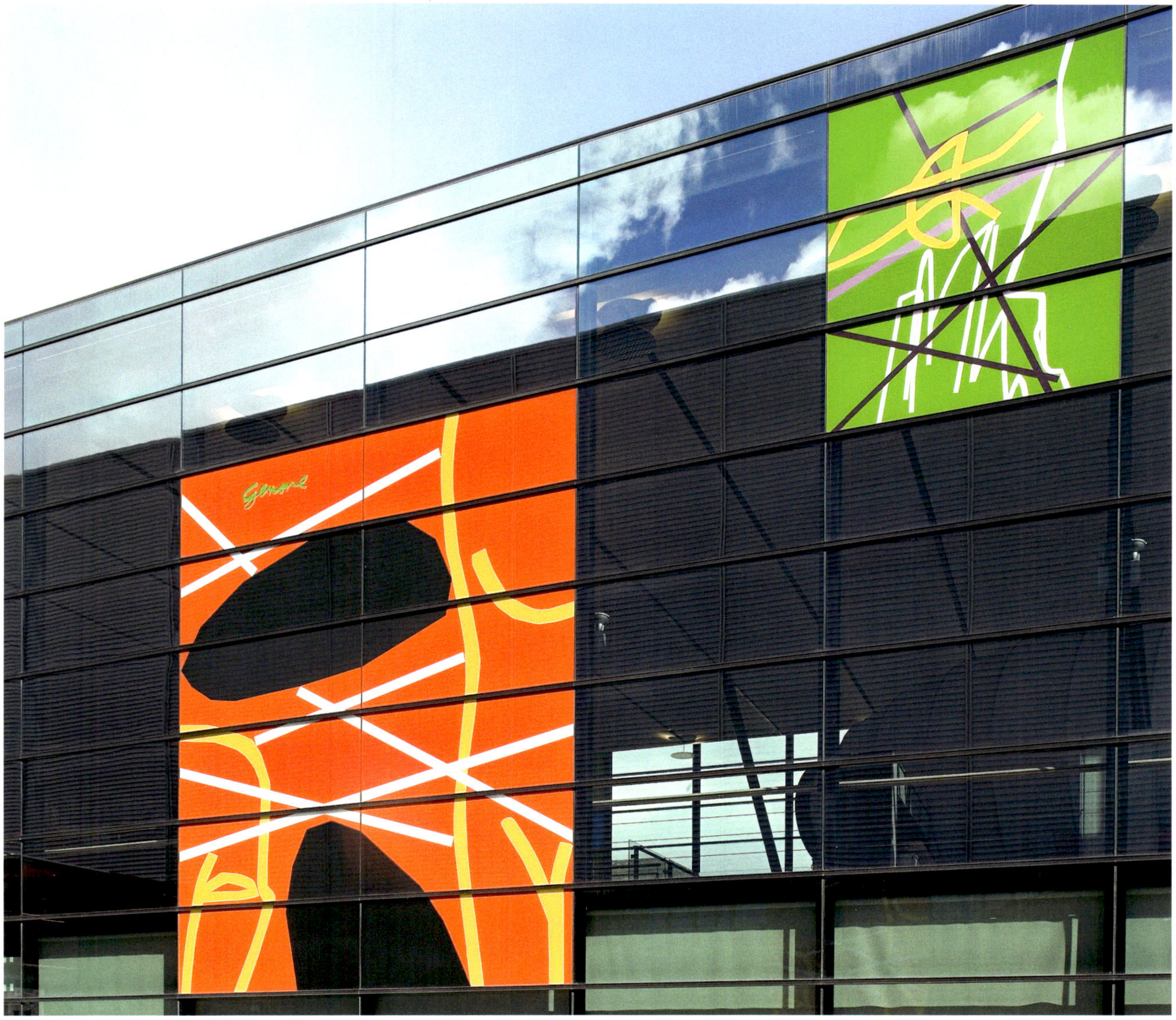

198

MEDICAL UNIVERSITY

197
The striking and strong color surfaces animate the interior spaces, both during the day and at night.

198
Monumental glass pictures, 18 and 9 feet high, seen from the outside.

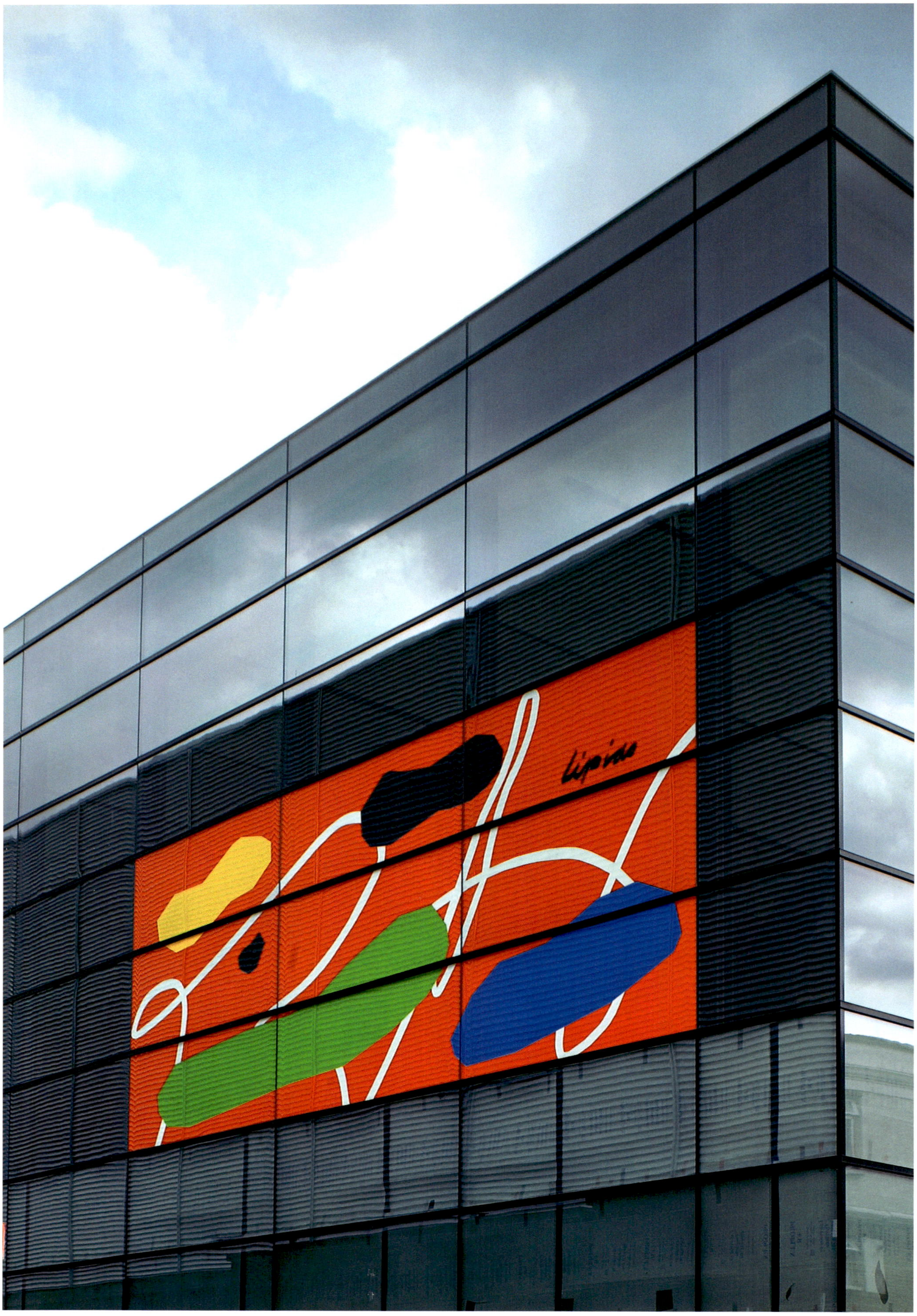

199

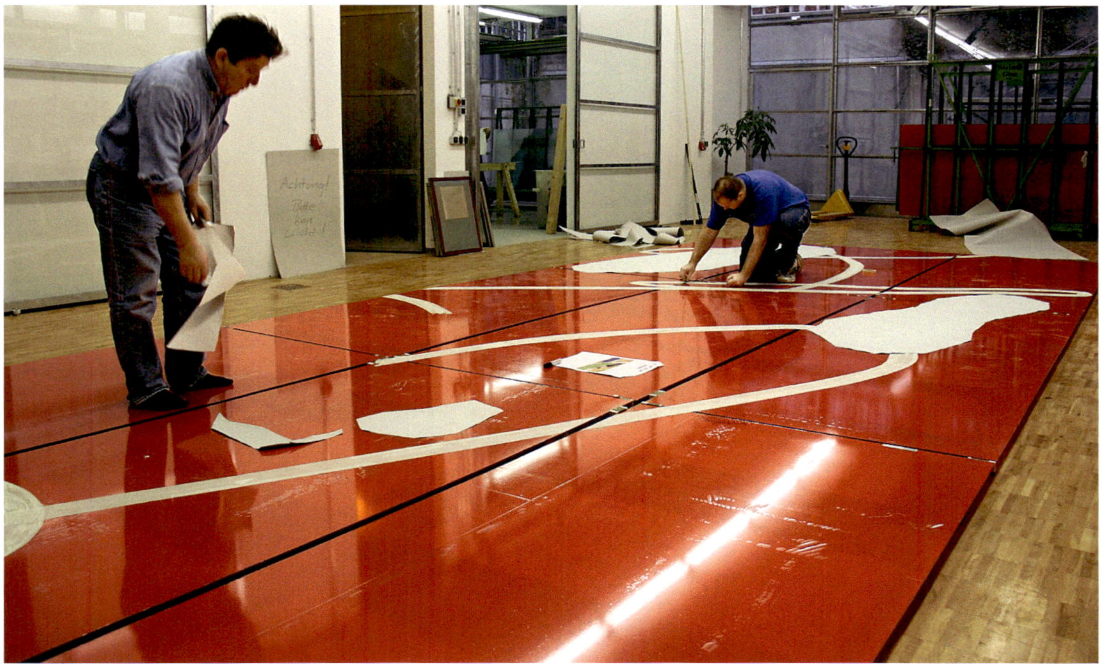

200

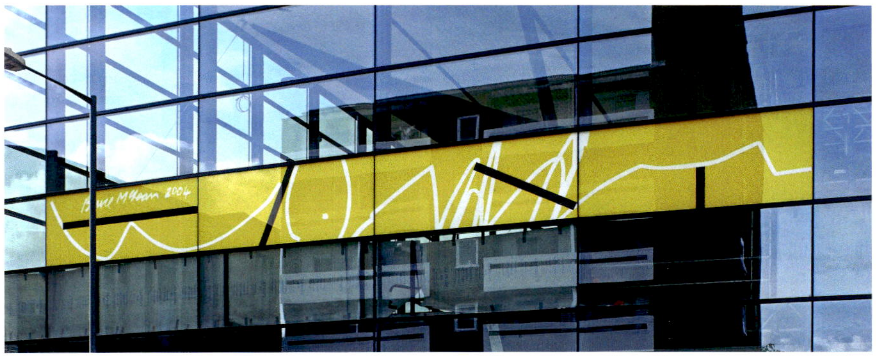

201

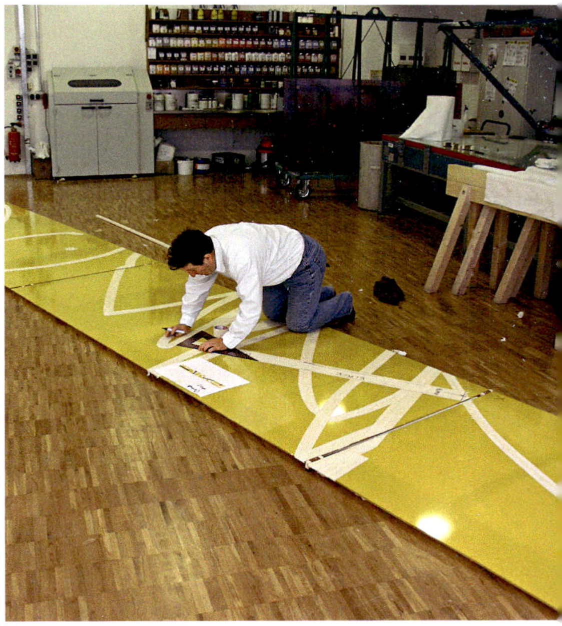

202

MEDICAL UNIVERSITY

199 +
201

Strong color accents for the exterior interplay with the reflective, translucent glass facade.

200 +
202

After the first color is fired, the glass pictures are placed on the studio floor for further treatment in the sandblasting machine and in the airbrush chamber.

FOLIAGE

203
The south facade of the university library ZBR in Hamburg with the transparent-translucent double glazing based on the ideas of the architects and the interpretation concept as well as execution by the Mayer studio.

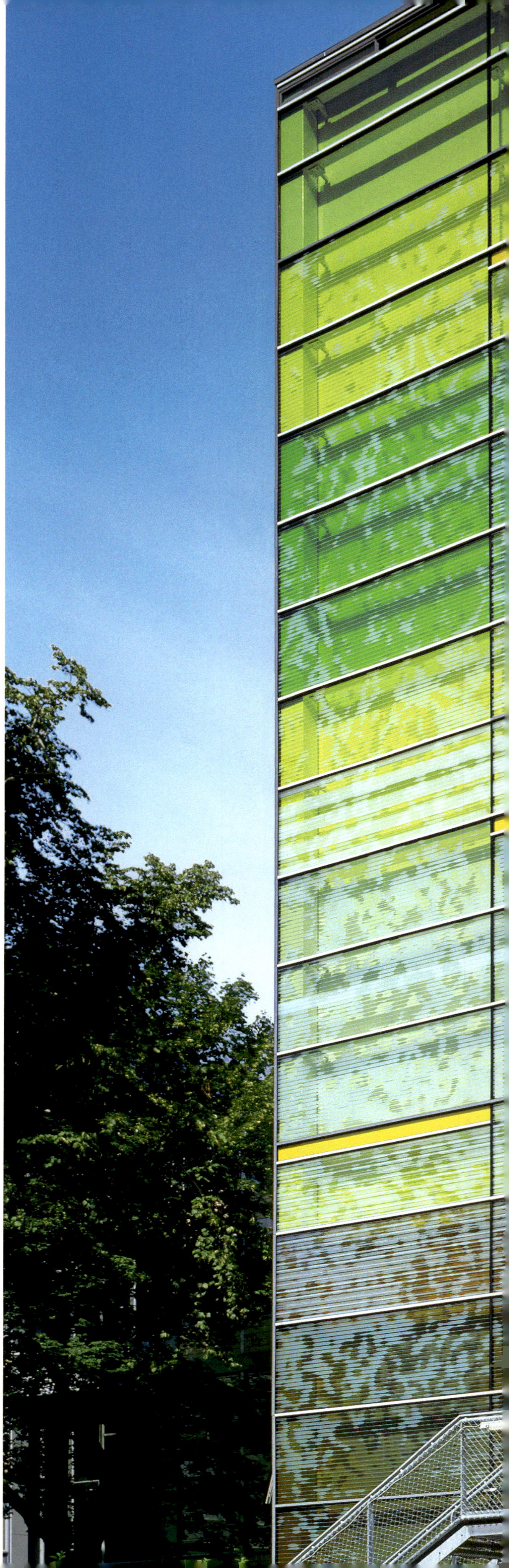

me di um Architekten / “Foliage”

144

location: Zentralbibliothek Recht, Universität Hamburg, Hamburg, DE / me di um Architekten / **year:** 2004 / **technique:** float glass painting

21,500 square feet of designed glass facades. A green suburbia, a landmark villa, a library tower for the university, 6 floors, the south wall made of concrete.
me di um Architekten wanted to “embed (the edifice) into the green,” and they envisioned foliage motifs for the south façade. The east and north facades were supposed to get accents in color and script. But most importantly: How to design the south facade? Printed foils? Opaque-printed glass? Back lighting?

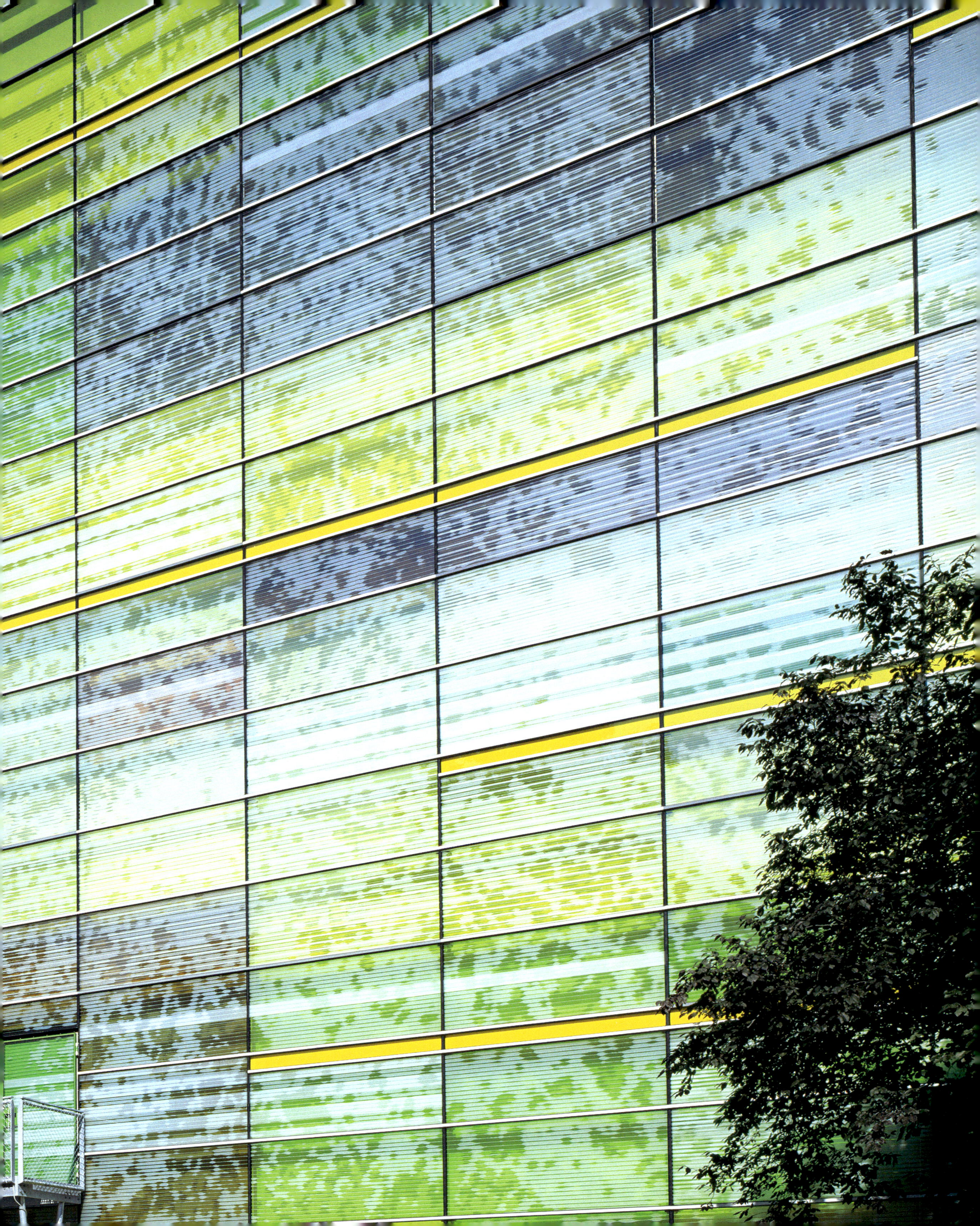

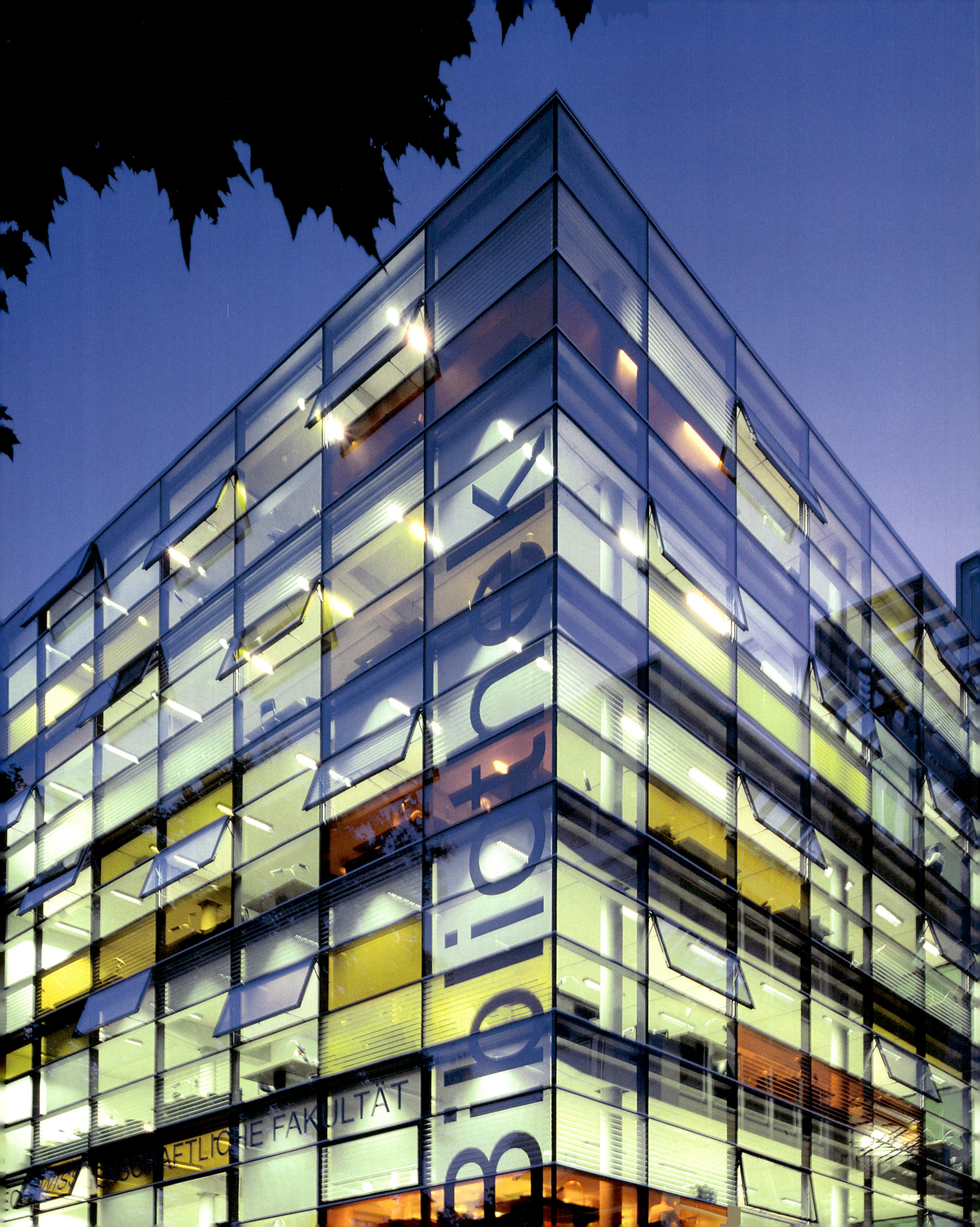
Bibliothek
SCHAFTLICHE FAKULTÄT

FOLIAGE

204
The north and east facades, facing the street, with large, single color panels, some with script, transparent ceramic glass melting color.

205
Detail of the south facade in the technique of double layered float glass painting.

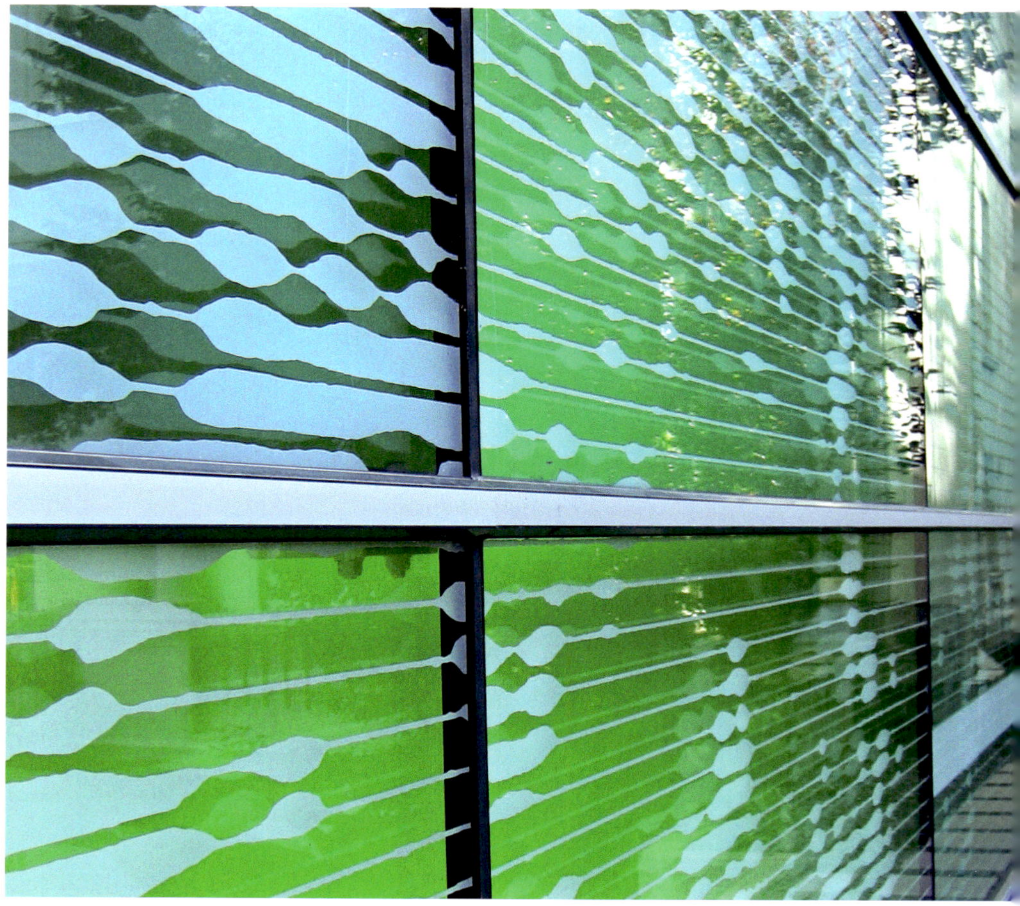

205

Printed foils? Insufficient light stability. Opaque-printed glass? Too graphic, also sterile. Back lighting? Artificial light cannot compete with natural daylight.
Especially the south facade: A natural challenge for the inventive and adventurous Munich workshop. Ultimately, the Hofkunstanstalt found a solution that is glassy and transparent and that "radiates" from within itself during daylight. A coherent solution, both when the sun shines and when it rains.

204

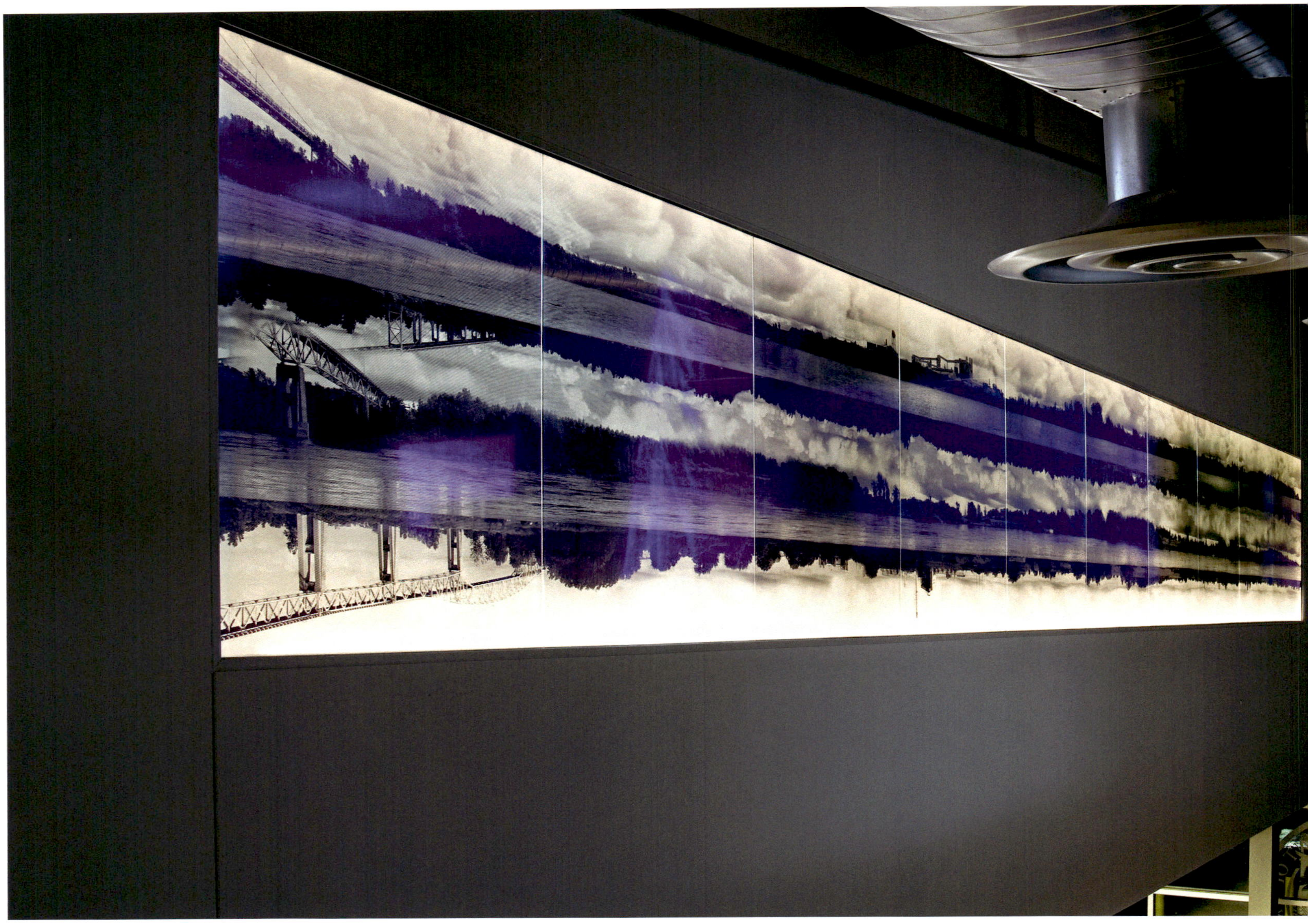

206
THIRD BANK OF THE RIVER. Alan Michelson's horizontal glass band above the control counters.

Alan Michelson / "Third Bank of the River"

location: Port of Entry, Massena, NY, USA / Smith-Miller+Hawkinson Architects. Art in Architecture Program US GSA. / **year:** 2009 / **technique:** float glass painting

Alan Michelson's "Third Bank of the River" art glass window panorama documents, in the form of the Two Row Wampum – a purple and white beaded belt signifying an early treaty of respectful coexistence between the Iroquois and Europeans – several miles of international shoreline of the St. Lawrence River at the complex local border between the United States, Akwesasne Mohawk Territory, and Canada. The work received the 2010 GSA Design Award, Citation in Art, and was also recognized in the 2010 Public Art Year in Review.

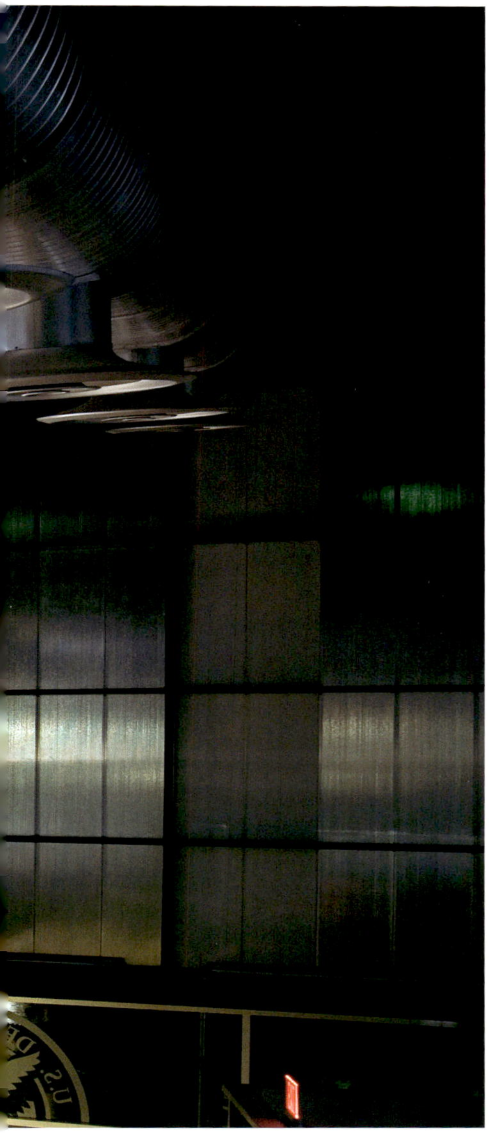

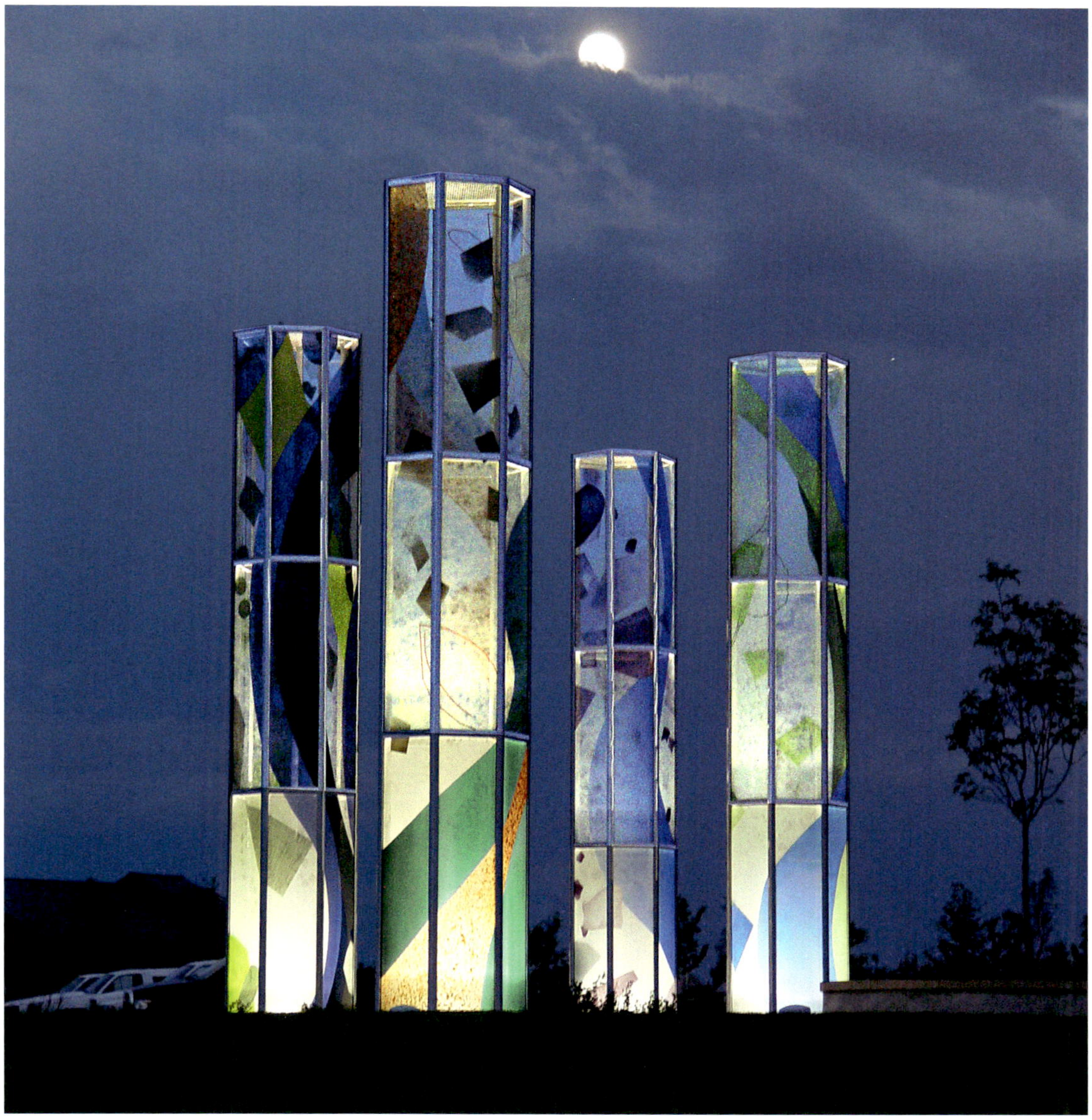

207
LUMINARIAS: THE SEASONS. Grygutis' Glass towers and sculpture in Colorado, at night and with the moon shining. Artificially lit.

Barbara Grygutis / "Luminarias: The Seasons"

location: Glass Towers, FunPlex, Twin Rivers Community Park, Greeley, CO, USA / **year:** 2006 / **technique:** float glass painting

The height of the four glass sculptures reaches circa 28 feet. Due to the use of both opaque and transparent glass melting colors the glass towers appear in translucent chromaticity during day and night and enrich the public space.

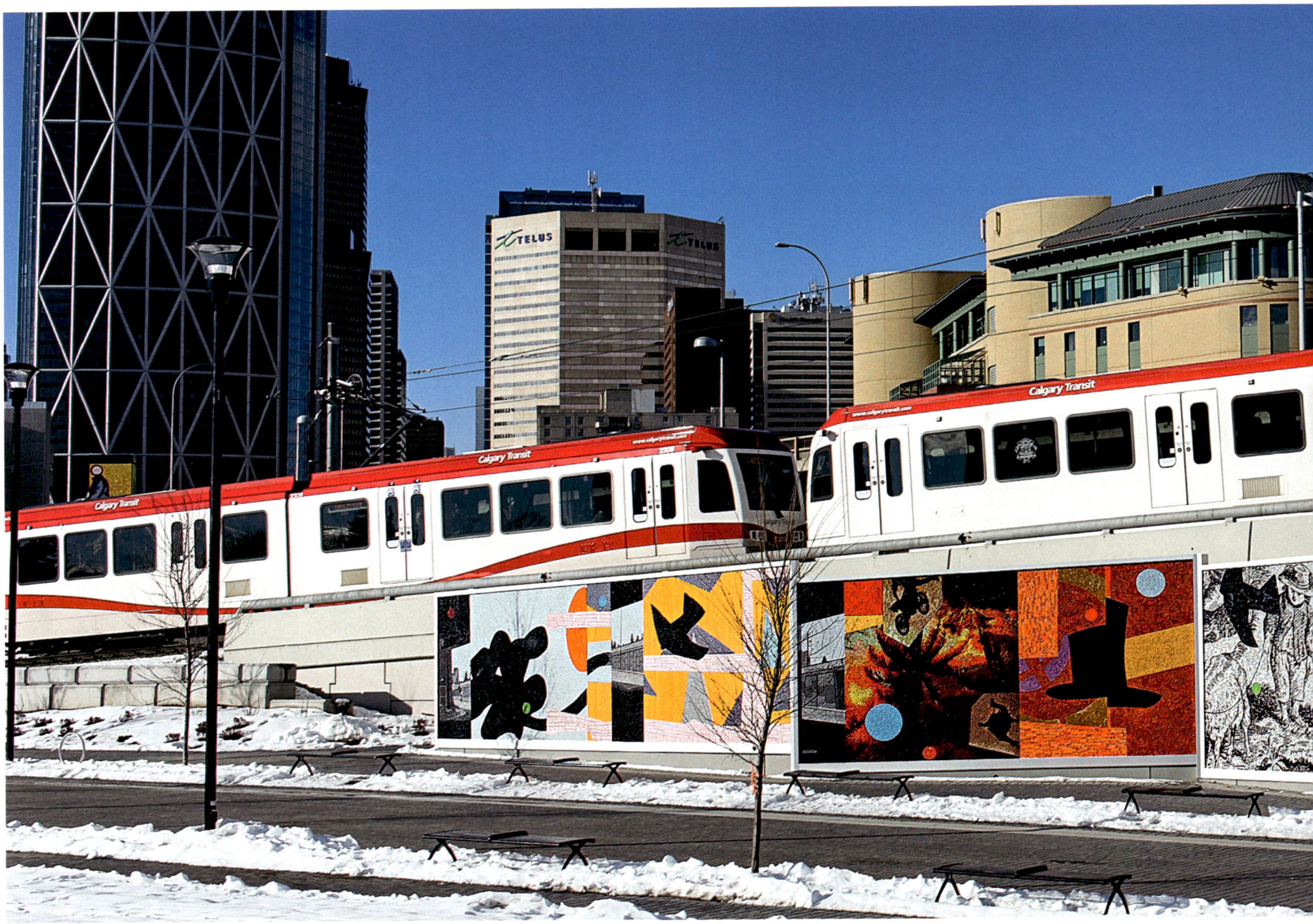

208

Ron Moppett / "THESAMEWAYBETTER / READER"

150

location: East Village re-development Project, River Walk Site, Calgary, Alberta, CAN / Calgary Municipal Land Corporation / **year:** 2012 / **technique:** glass and stone mosaic

Ron Moppett dedicated the work to the memory of Calgary Parks Dept. Superintendent, William Reader.
The "East Village" is the place where Calgary was founded. Today, the future of the center might unfold here. "East Village the newest, oldest, coolest, warmest place in town." (CMLC) – Ron Moppett's and Mayer's mosaic wall runs the length of 110 feet along the Riverfront Lane, Calgarys first pedestrian zone; the piece rises to a height of 12 feet. "It is the largest free-standing mosaic wall in Canada." (Nancy Tousley, News Calgary)

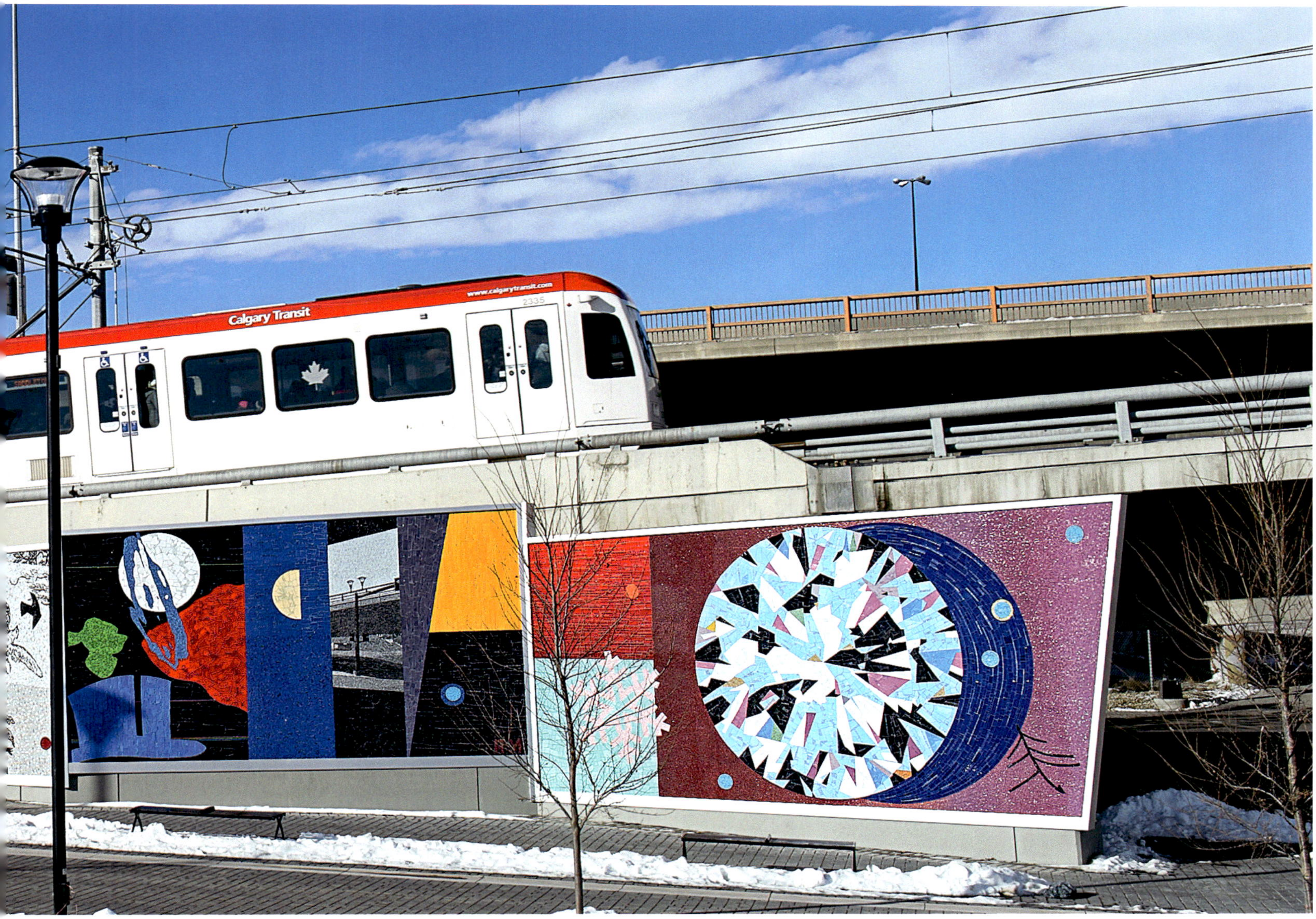

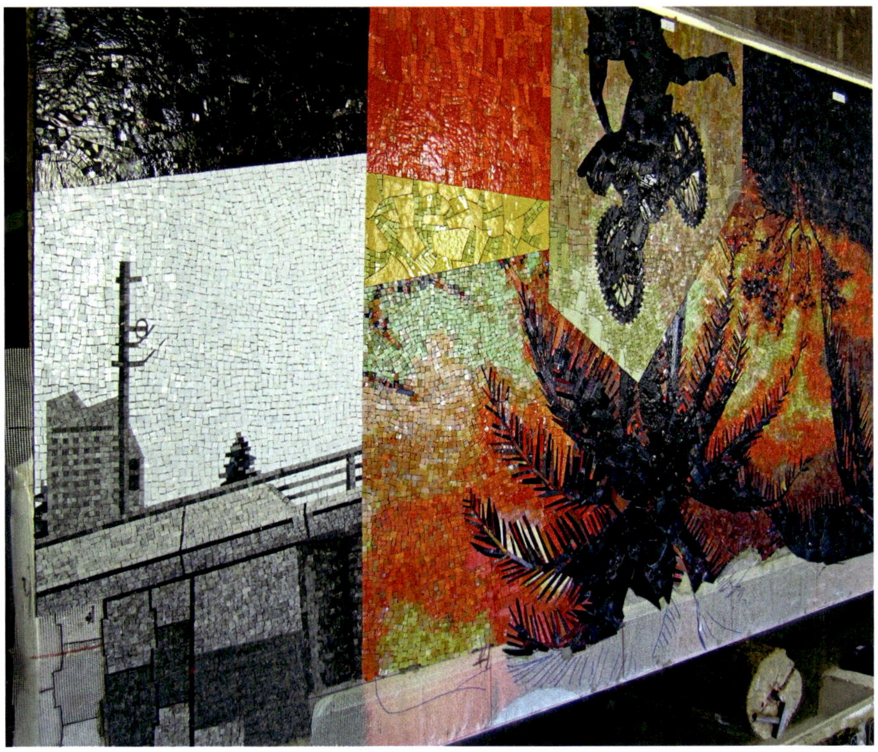

209

151

THESAMEWAYBETTER / READER

208
Complete view of the folded mosaic wall. Ron Moppett's work is located in an appealing redeveloped urban setting, leaning onto a slope along railway and bridge.

209
Detail from the second panel on the work table: The black-and-white photo of the former grey concrete slope that reappears four times is shown here on the edge of a colorfully exploding scene of palms and motorcyclist.

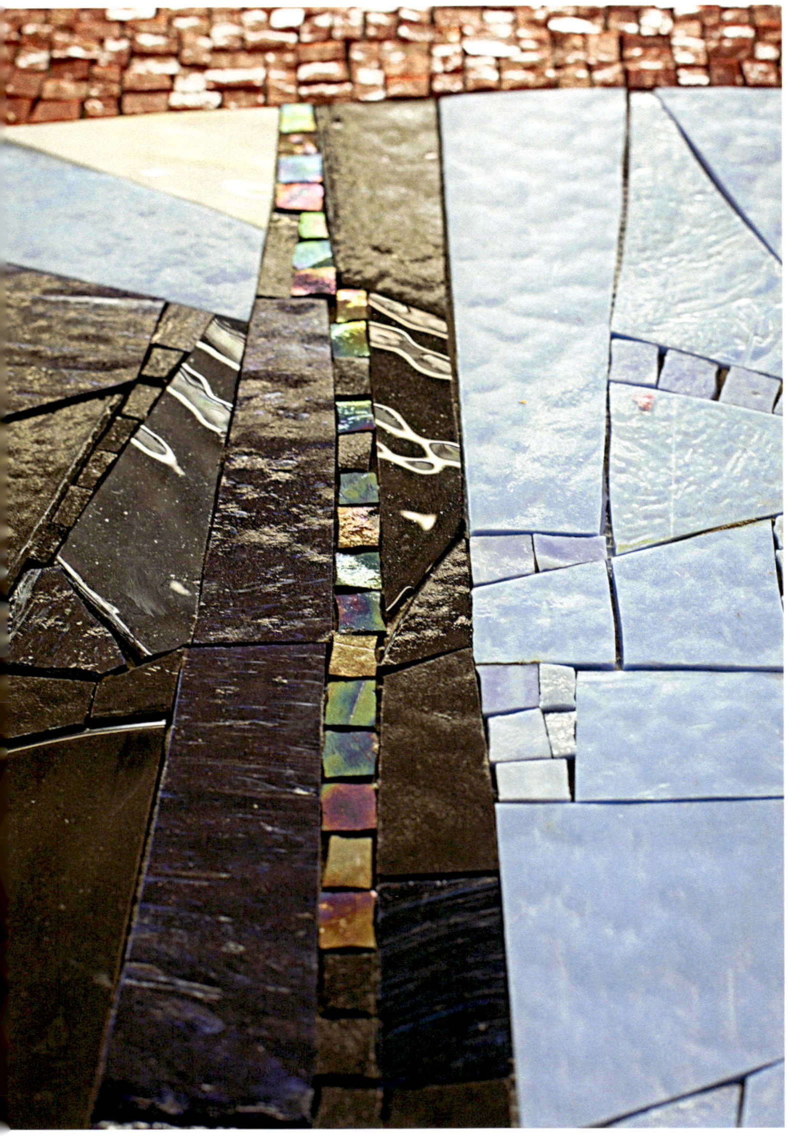

210

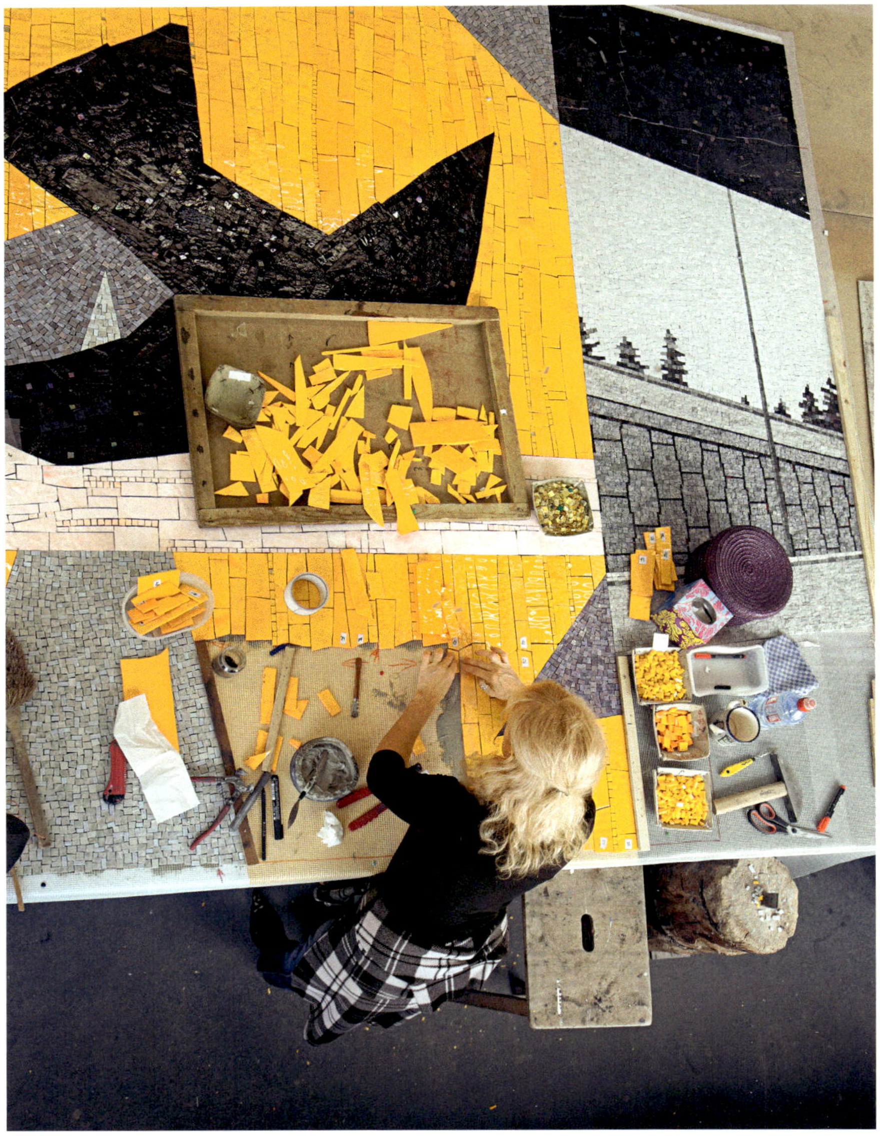

211

A large and visually complex, 'zip-line' of color that references Calgary as a dynamic multi-faceted narrative. The artist employs personal, representational, and abstract associations that conjure commentary and ambiguity.

"The 'East Village' was dominated by grey for such a long time, and I literally wanted to pour color into the great stream," says the artist and adds: "There are times when the artist wishes the colors were brighter ... The glass mosaic tesserae were magic ..."

(Ron Moppett)

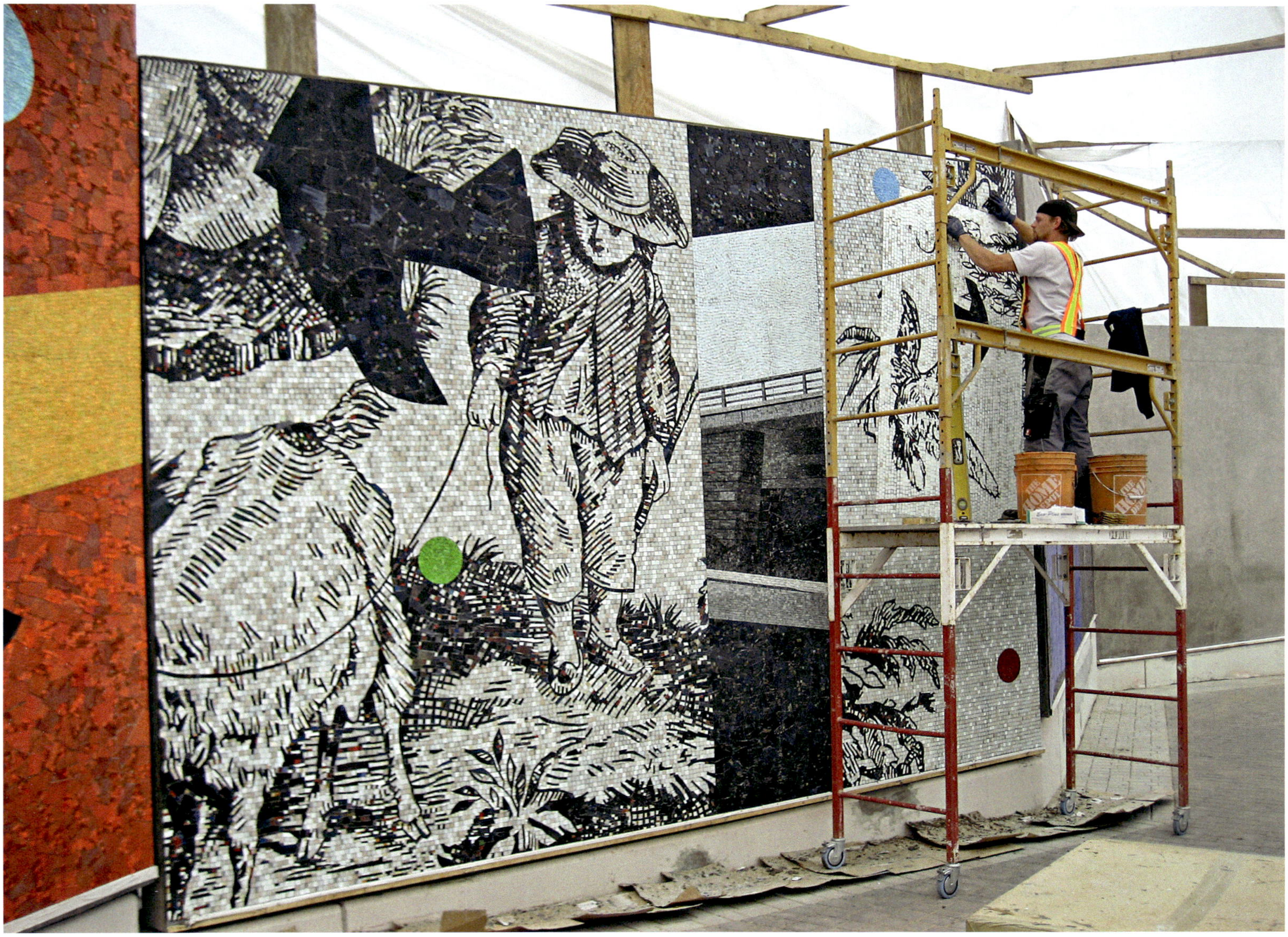

212

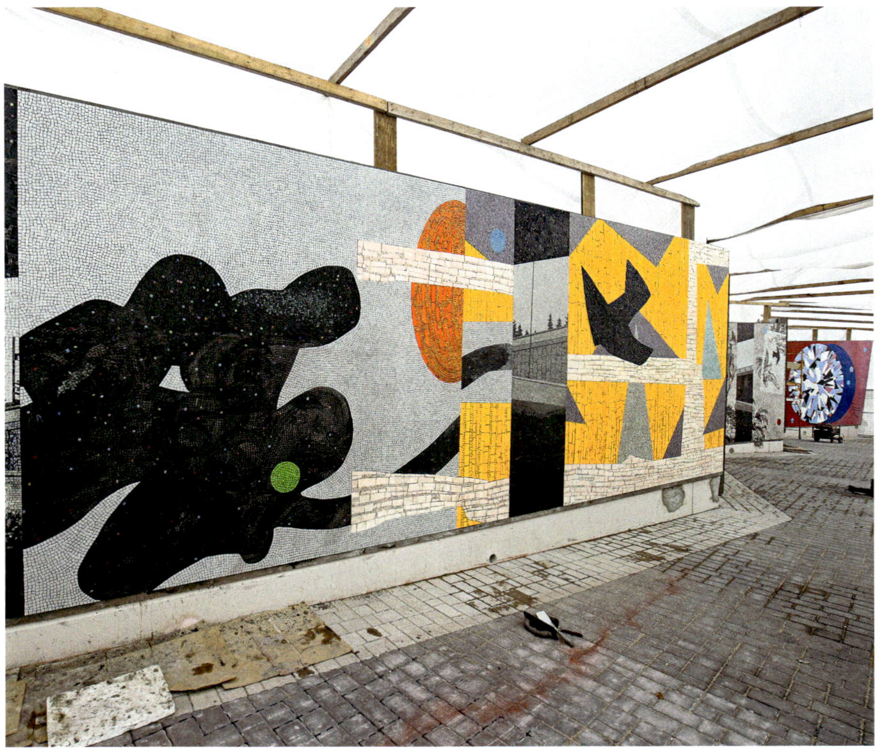

213

THESAMEWAYBETTER / READER

210
Detail from the mosaic: Composition with color, form, flow, and structure of the tesserae.

211
A view into the ceiling mirror during work in the studio; at right once more a photo image of the grey slope wall.

212
Installation of the third mosaic panel with the Baroque-Romantic shepherd in the meadow. The model of this was a woodcut.

213
The first mosaic panel on the left during installation and protected by a temporary tent. At the right side of the picture we see the folded mosaic wall continuing to the last circular mosaic with the ice crystals.

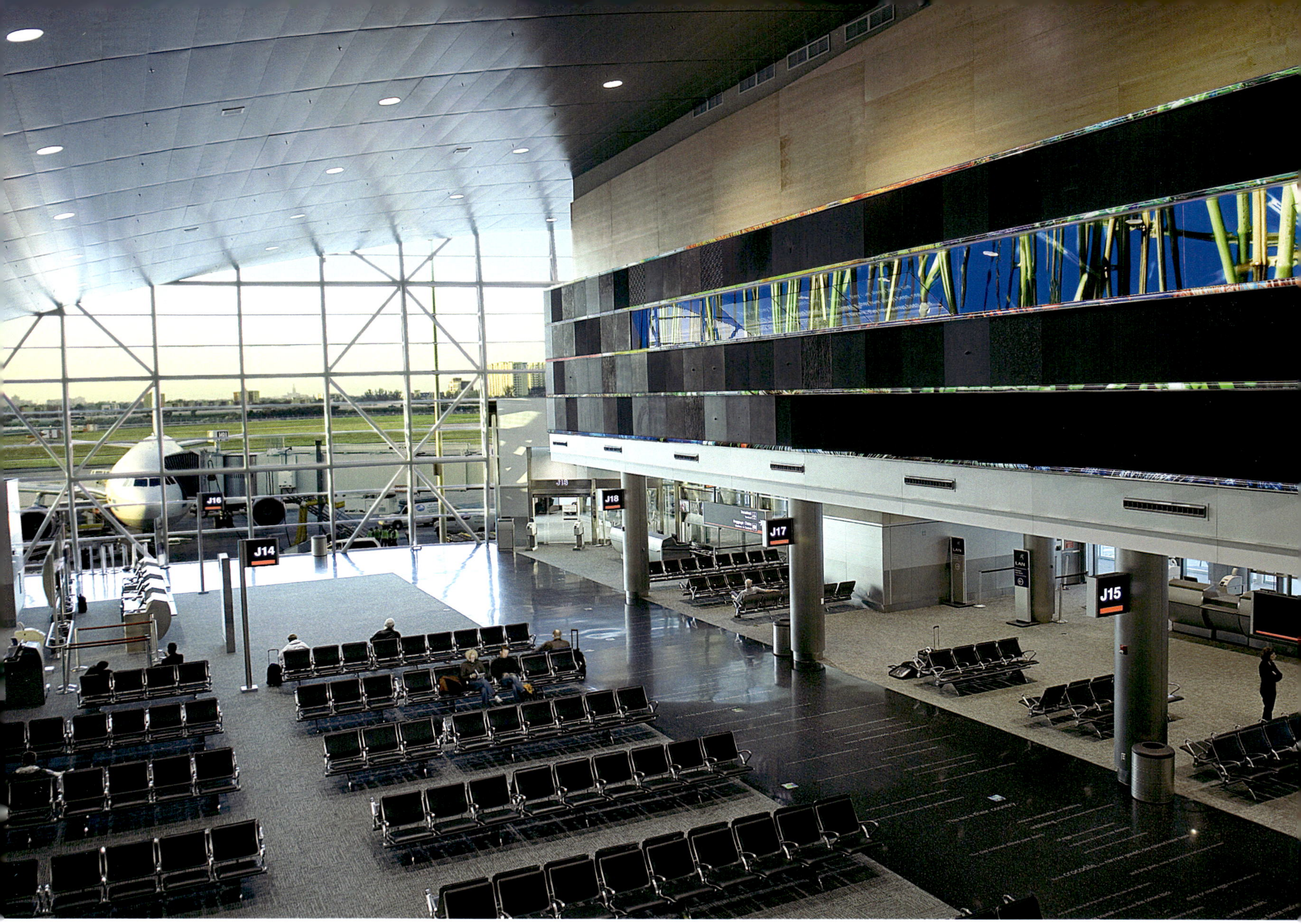

Barbara Neijna / "Foreverglades"

154

location: Miami International Airport, Terminal J, Miami, FL, USA / Thomas Carlson – MCHarry Associates. Miami Dade County Art in Public Places / **year:** 2007 / **technique:** float glass painting

For the new Terminal J at Miami Airport Barbara Neijna created an imposing, site specific *Gesamtkunstwerk* with seven glasswalls, stone panes, photo-prismatic bands and terrazzo floors; Mayer of Munich fabricated all of the glass walls with a total area of approximately 2500 square feet. Public art award 2008.

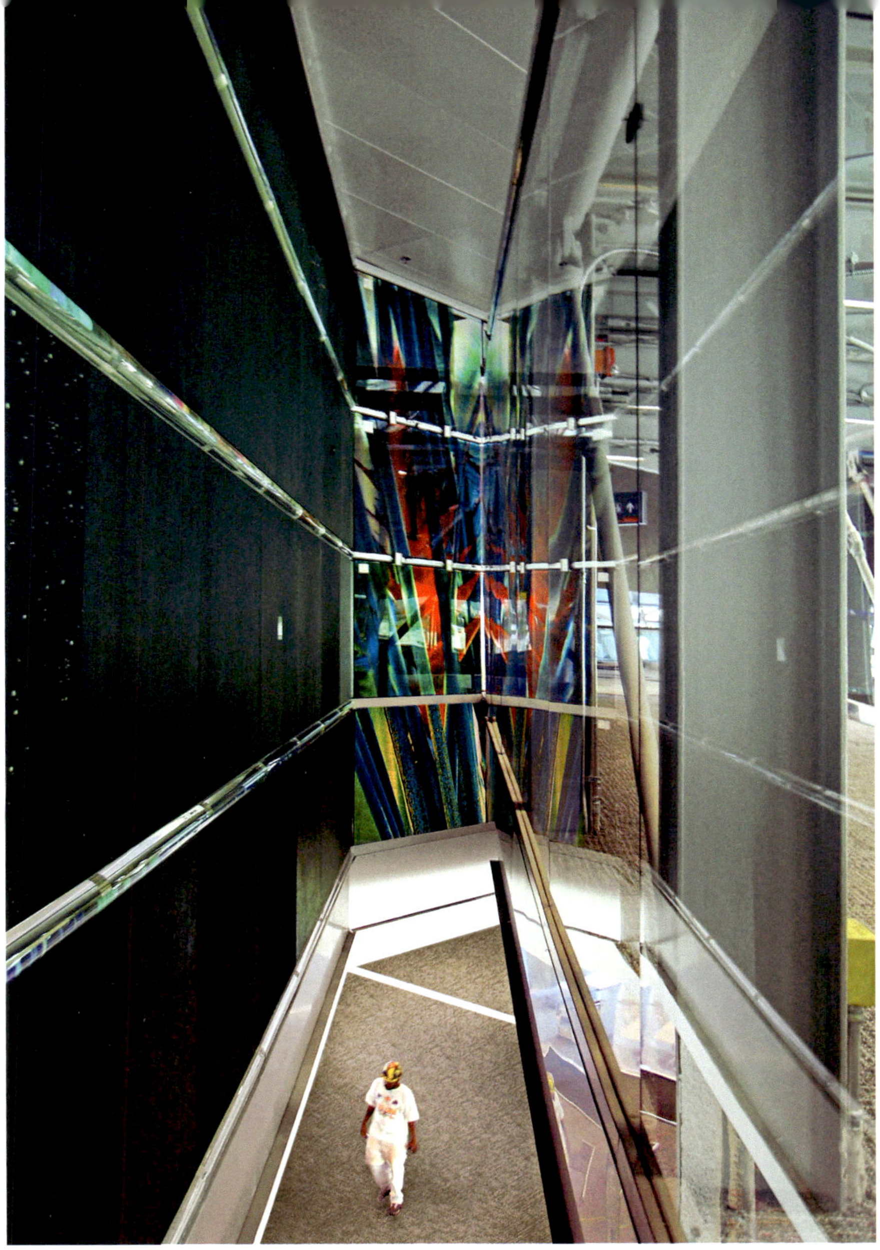

215

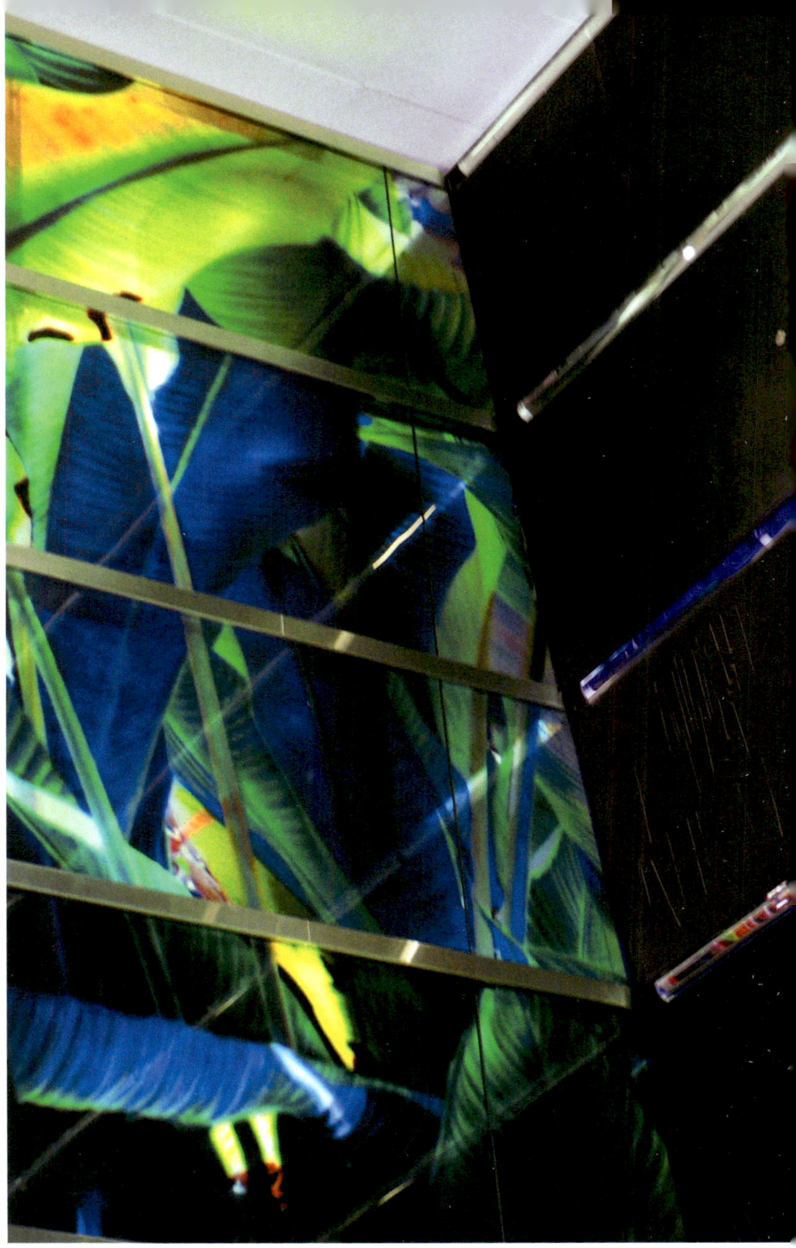

216

The artist wrote about her experiences with the Mayer studios on July 20th, 2010:
"The environment at the studio was one of complete collaboration. From the computer output of silkscreens ... to the exquisite hand painting ... and the oversight and direction ... the studio was nothing less than a unique opportunity to realize old world beauty and perfection. Working in this environment is nothing less than an artist's dream."

FOREVERGLADES

214 View from the south bridge to the runway with the blue "Ribbon Windows" on the right side; some of them with angularly mounted lettered glass. This image also shows the photo prisms, the black stone panels, and the texts in the terrazzo floors.

215 Partial view of the south bridge window on the west side.

216 Another detail of the glass on the west side.

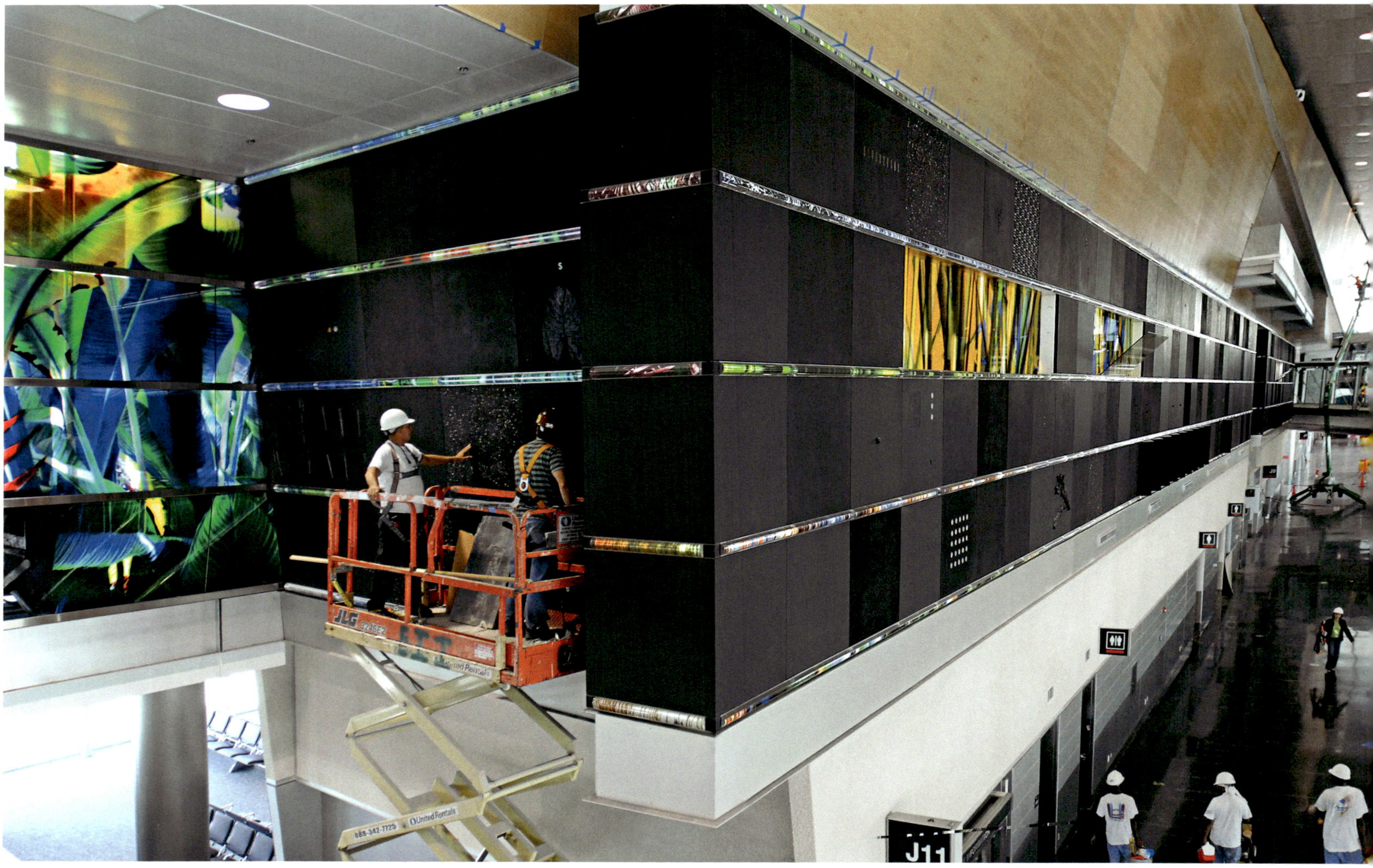

217

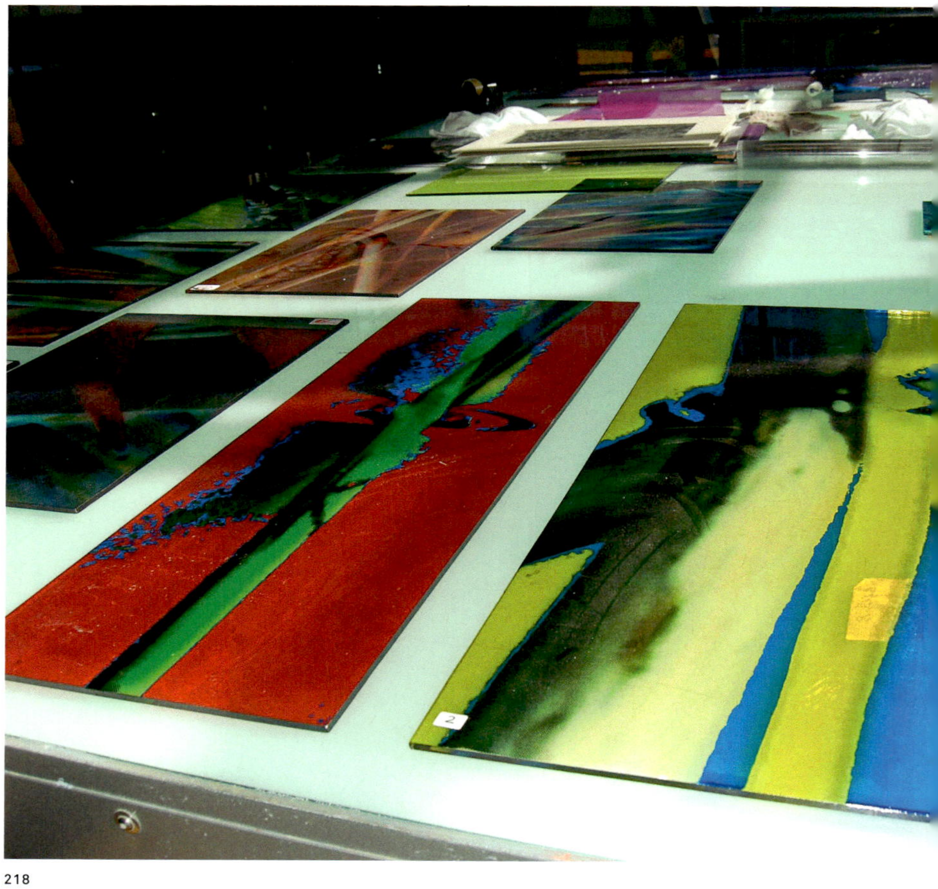

218

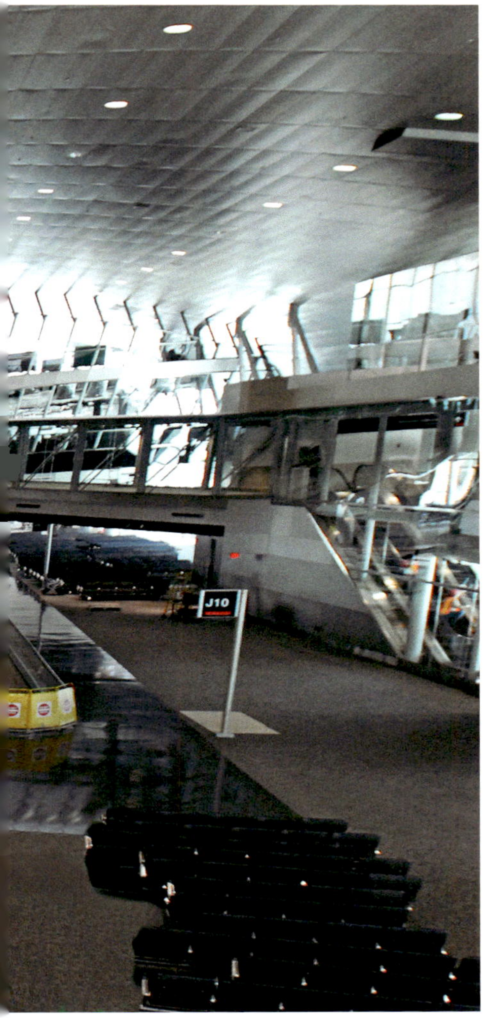

FOREVERGLADES

217

View from the south bridge into the northern section of the terminal with some of the glass designs, which only represent a part of the *Gesamtkunstwerk*.

218

A small excerpt from the many samples created at the studio, which helped to eventually develop the interpretation in glass.

219

View from the elevated west corridor to one of the glass bridges with the surrounding artglazing.

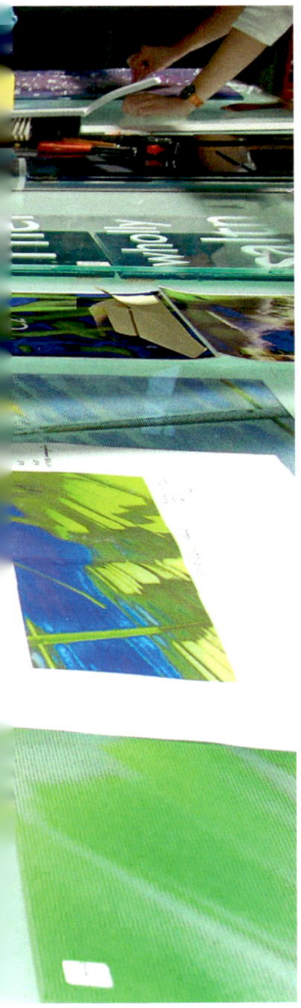

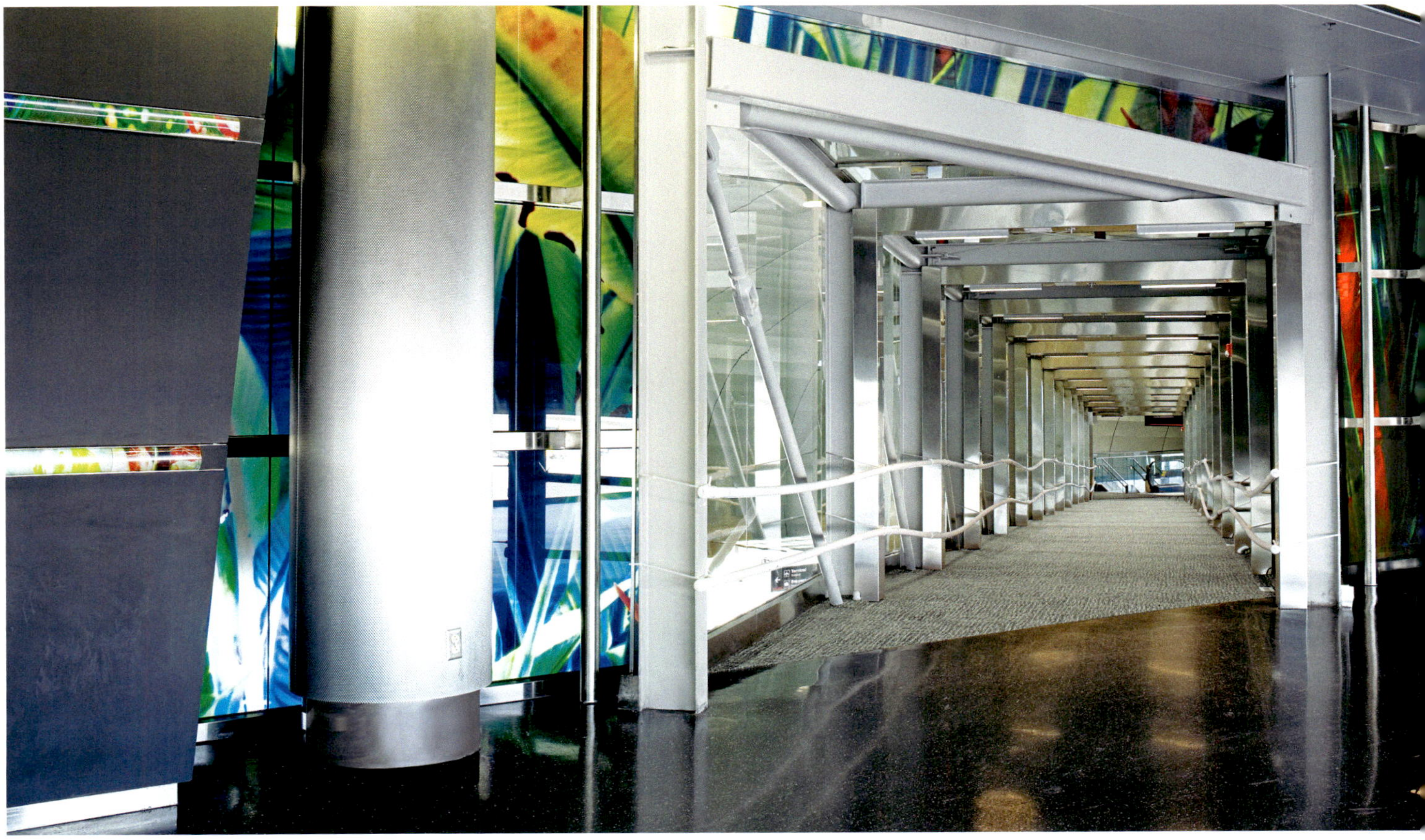

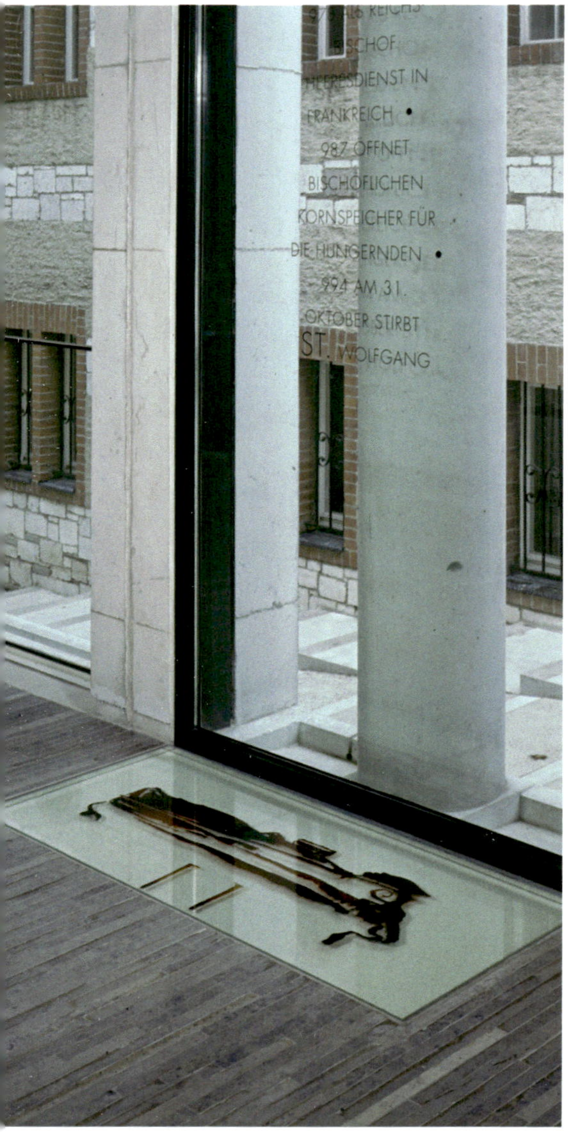

220

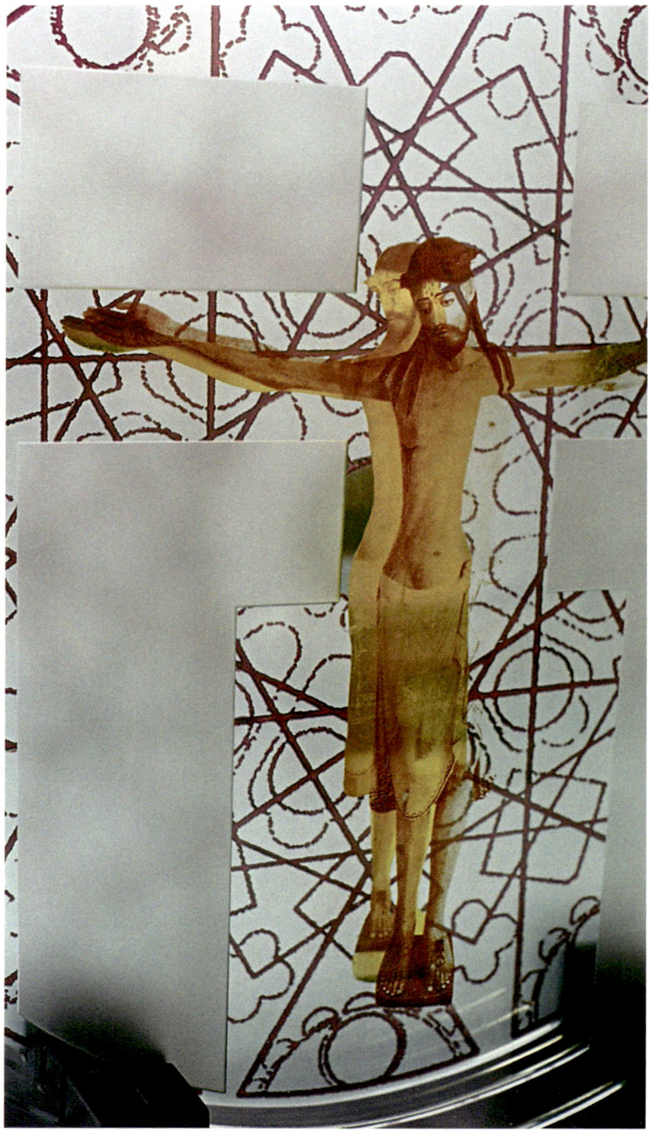

221

HEAVEN ON EARTH

220
Glass tomb slab of Saint Wolfgang's tomb, St. Wolfgang, Regensburg.

221
Multi-layered, circular glass slab with a Romanesque crucifixion motif.

222
The mirror installation "Heaven on Earth" from May 2006 in Munich's Asamkirche.

Bernd Nestler / "Heaven on Earth"

location: Asamkirche, Munich, DE / **year:** 2006 / **location:** glass tomb slab over the grave of Saint Wolfgang, St. Wolfgang Church, Regensburg, DE / **year:** 1997 / **technique:** float glass painting

The mirror installation "Heaven on Earth" from May 2006, installed on the benches of Munich's Asamkirche, the painted glass panel over the tomb of St. Wolfgang in Regensburg (in collaboration with the architect Peter Böhm), and the multi-panel glass crucifixion motif express Bernd Nestler's artistic sensitivity, his incredible sensation for spaces and materials, and his fantastic universe of ideas.

222

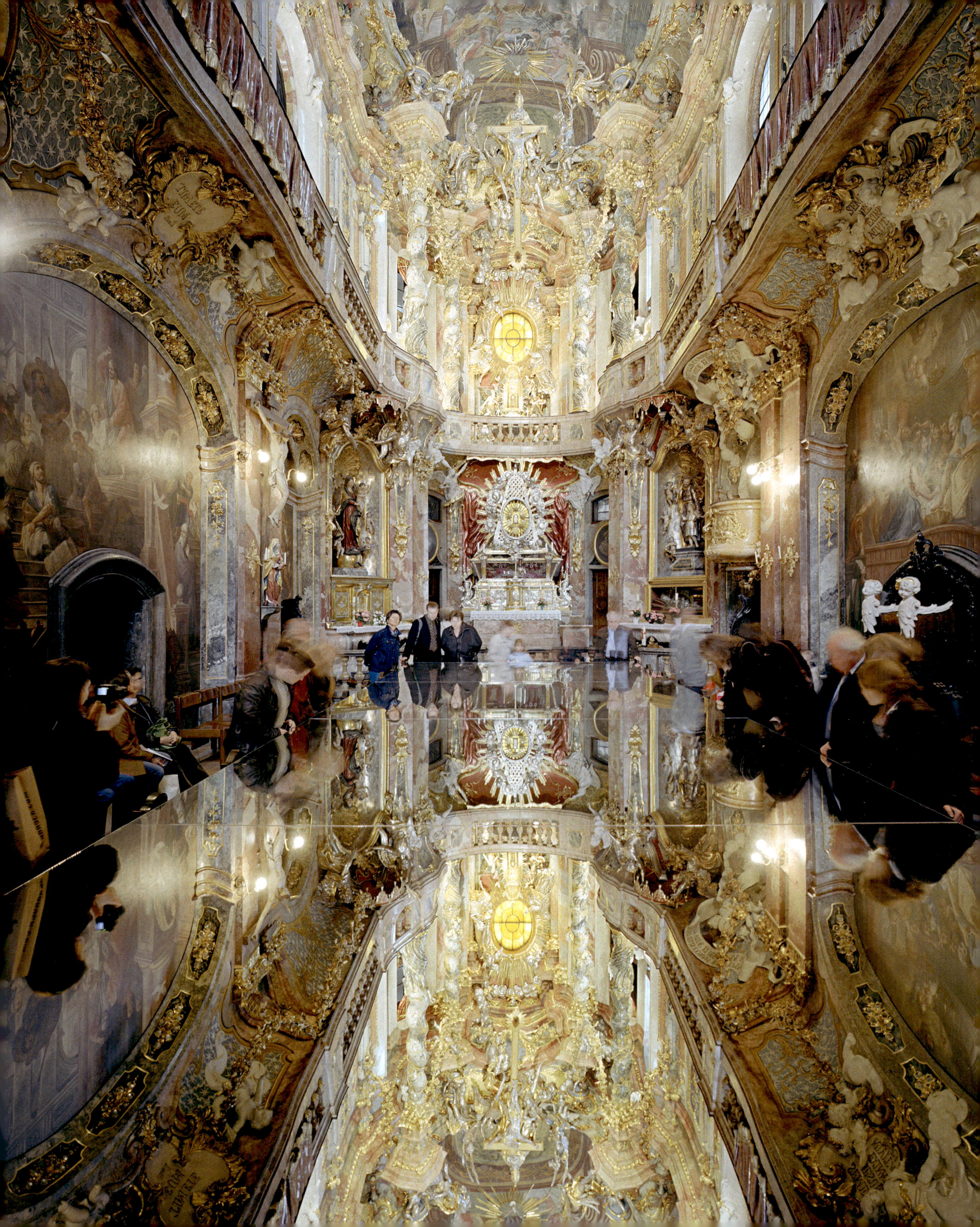

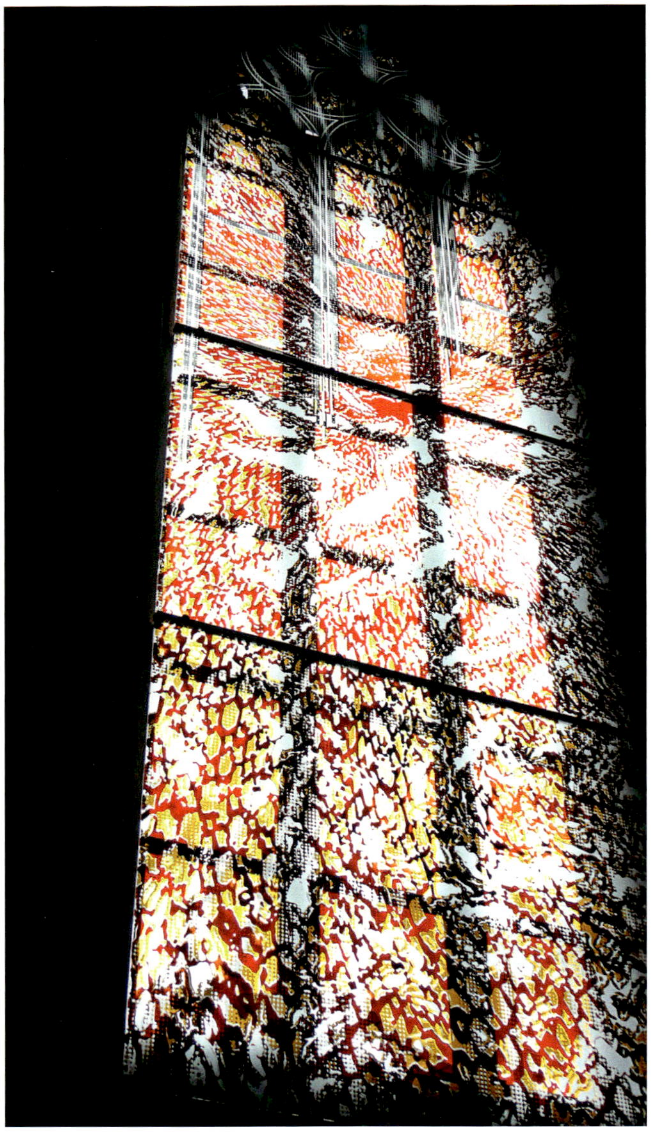

223

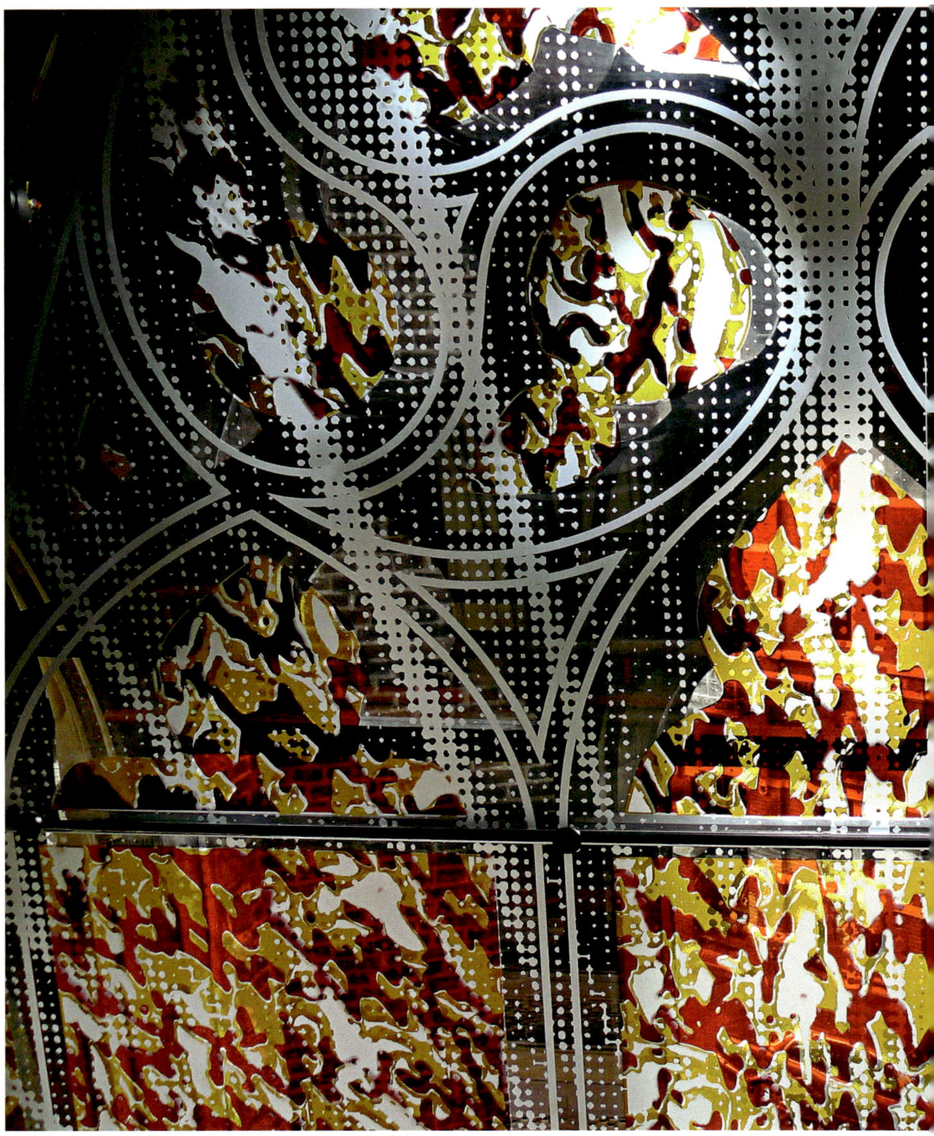

224

Bernd Nestler / "Lux Nova"

location: Cathedral of St. Christoffel, Roermond, NL / **year:** 2011 / **technique:** curtain type two layered float glass painting

In 2011, Bernd Nestler, who often used small formats when working in glass, won a prestigious competition for the design of a new glass window in the Romanesque-Gothic cathedral of St. Christoffel in Roermond from among 285 participating artists. He was rightfully selected, as the work shows, which the artist did in tandem with Mayer of Munich.

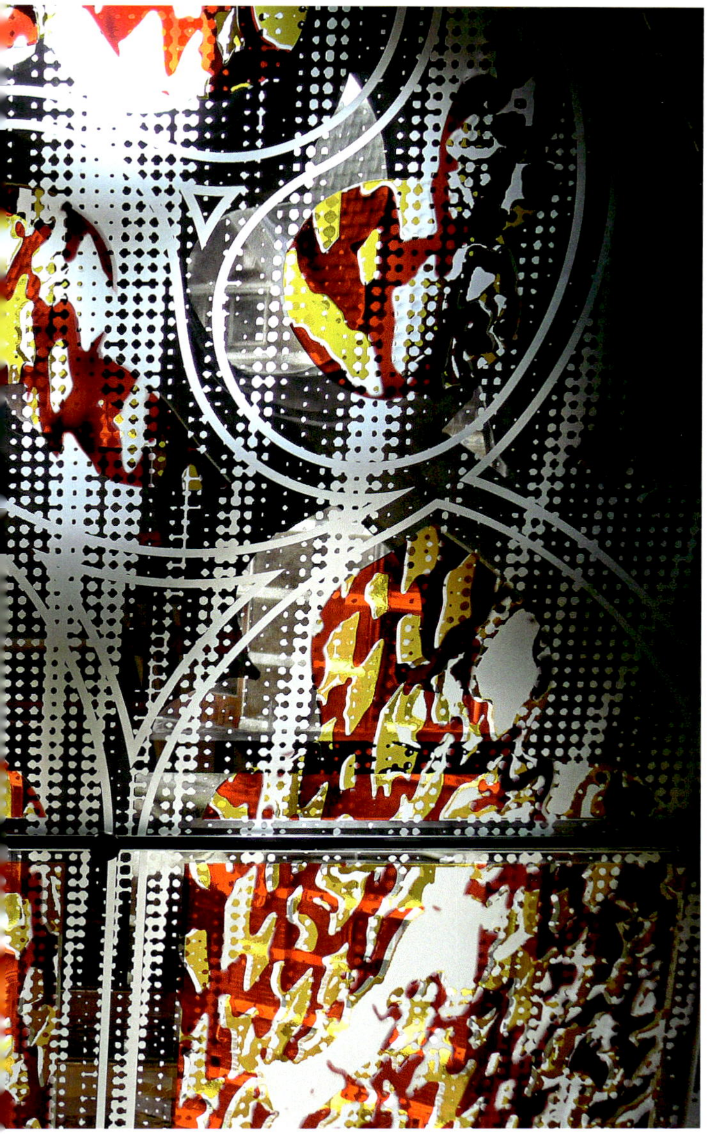

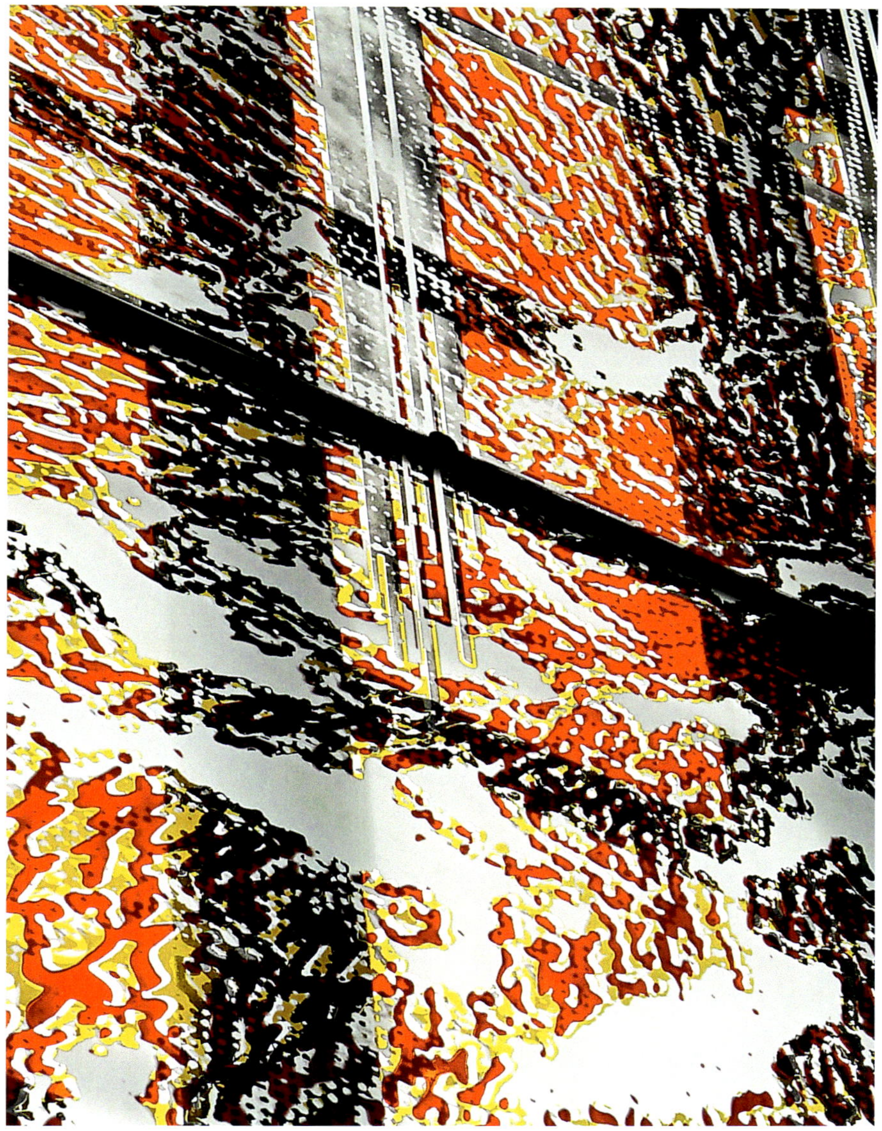

225

LUX NOVA

223 –
225
Numerous views and details of the installed window.

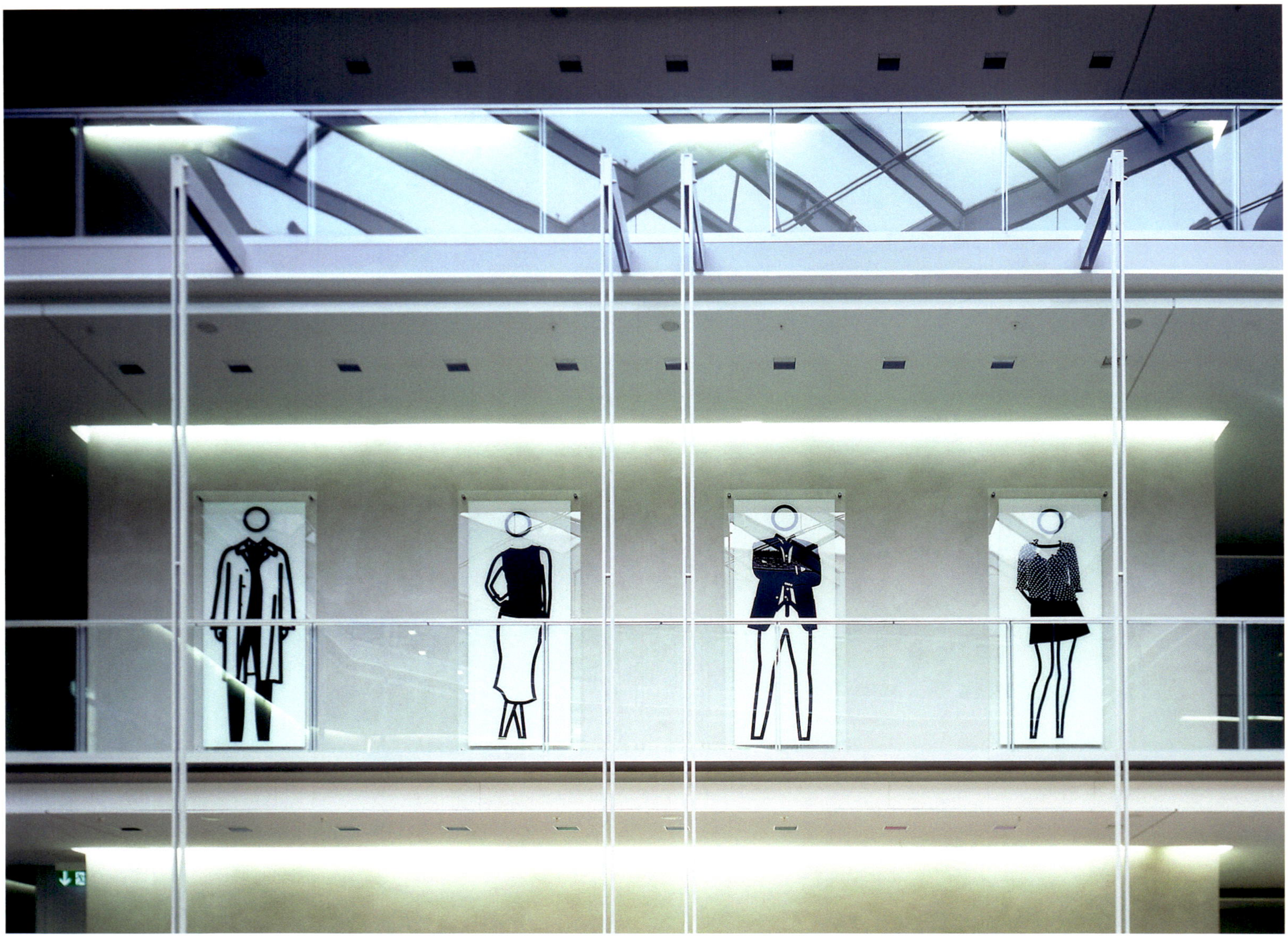

226

Julian Opie / "People" and "Portraits"

162

location: Headquarters of two Bavarian finance firms, Munich, DE / **year:** 2005 and 2000 / **technique:** float glass painting

With his work, Julian Opie checks out the borders of stylizations. Working with black contour lines and colorful monochrome backgrounds, he demands the utmost precision in execution. The materials, glass and ceramic enamel paints, get fired at circa 600 degrees Celsius, lending the works an almost unlimited light fastness and durability.

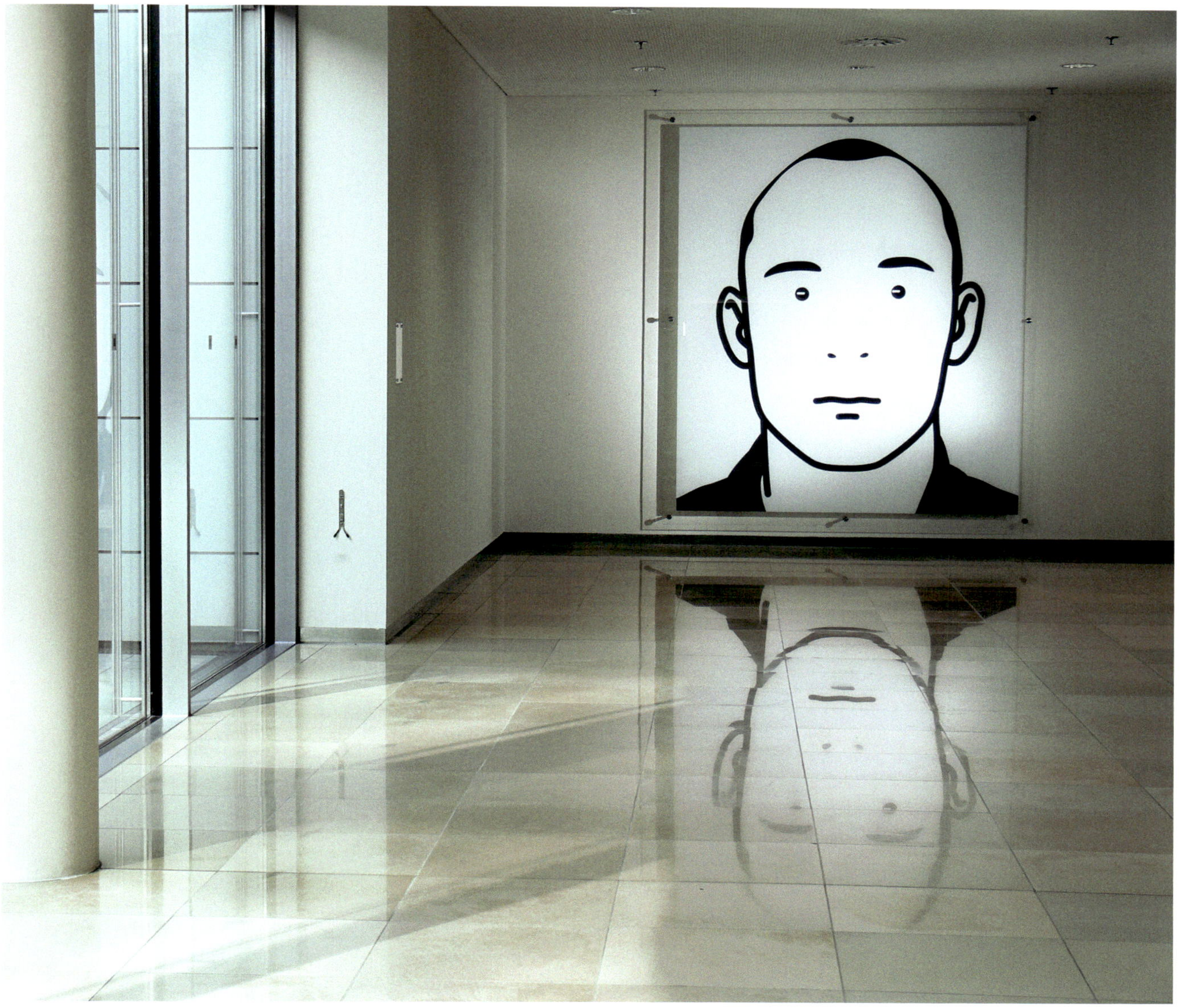

227

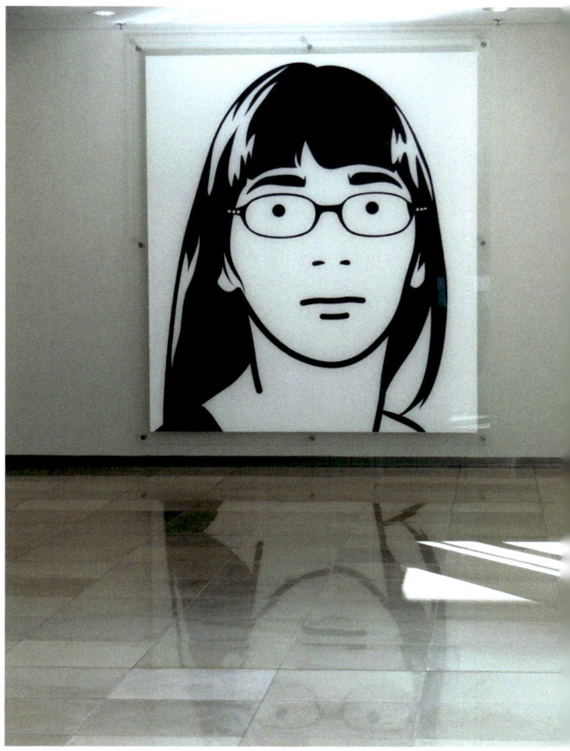

228

"PEOPLE" AND "PORTRAITS"

226
Julian Opie's four-part site specific installation "People," 2005, collection HypoVereinsbank, Kardinal-Faulhaber-Straße, Munich.

227 +
228
Two large glass panels in float glass painting, "Portraits," 2000, images of employees at the headquarters of WWK Versicherungen, Marsstraße, Munich.

Created in 1984–1985 this project probably is the first large and monumental work ever produced in the technique of float glass painting. This work was seminal and was likely the beginning of printing ceramic glass melting colors on architectural glass, so widespread today. Mayer of Munich not only triggered the first fundamental technical initiative of float glass painting, but has been and remains one of the leading studios for its further development and refinement.

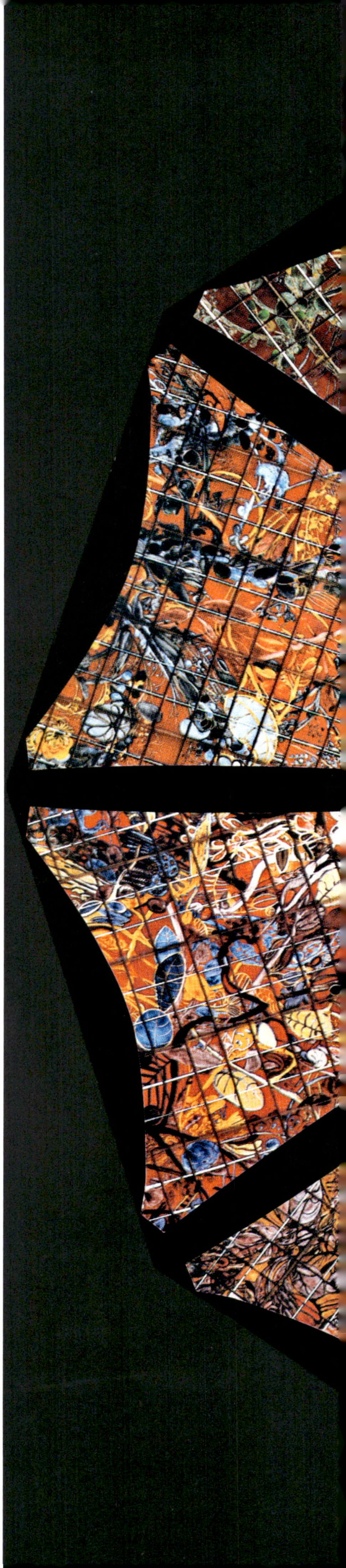

HEART TENT

229 Image constructed from the ten fanned-out segments of the glass tent roof – each individually mounted and photographed in Mayer of Munich's exhibition space.

Frei and Bettina Otto / "Heart Tent"

location: Diplomatic Club DQDC, Riyadh, SA / OHO Joint Venture (Frei Otto, Happold, Omrania) / **year:** 1985 / **technique:** float glass painting

In the mid-1980s, Frei Otto, one of the most important architects of the 20th c., was commissioned to build the Diplomatic Club for the new diplomatic quarter in Riyadh, Saudi Arabia. The building complex was conceived to simulate traditional stone fortifications in the desert. Numerous smaller tent groups were supposed to be placed in the garden compounds, scattered around the centrally located "Heart Tent", the main tent, symbolizing it and stressing the presence of the tribal chief. The concept picks up the tradition of painted sheiks' tents of nomadic peoples. Their colors, however, did fade quickly under the sun and had to be repainted again and again.

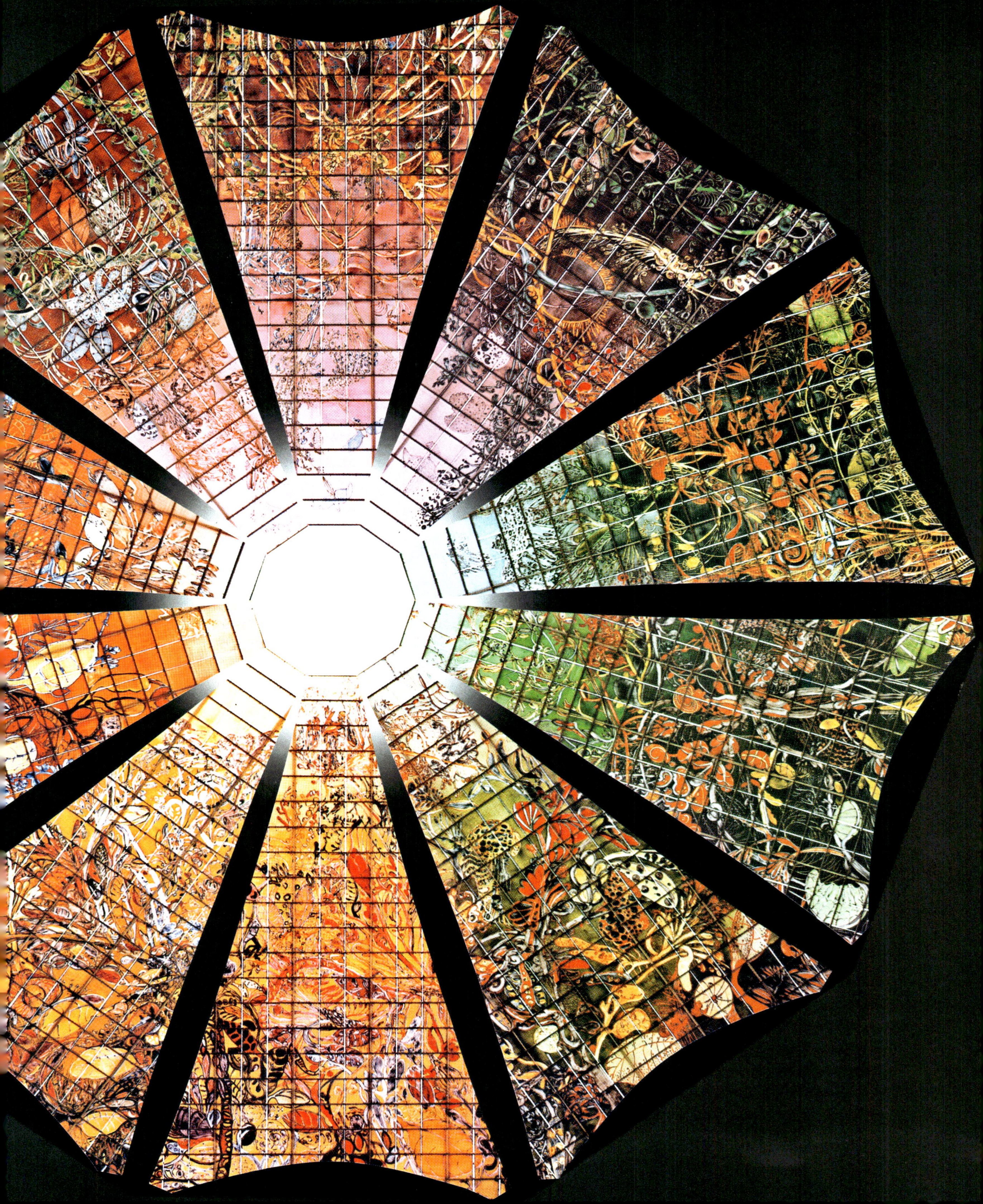

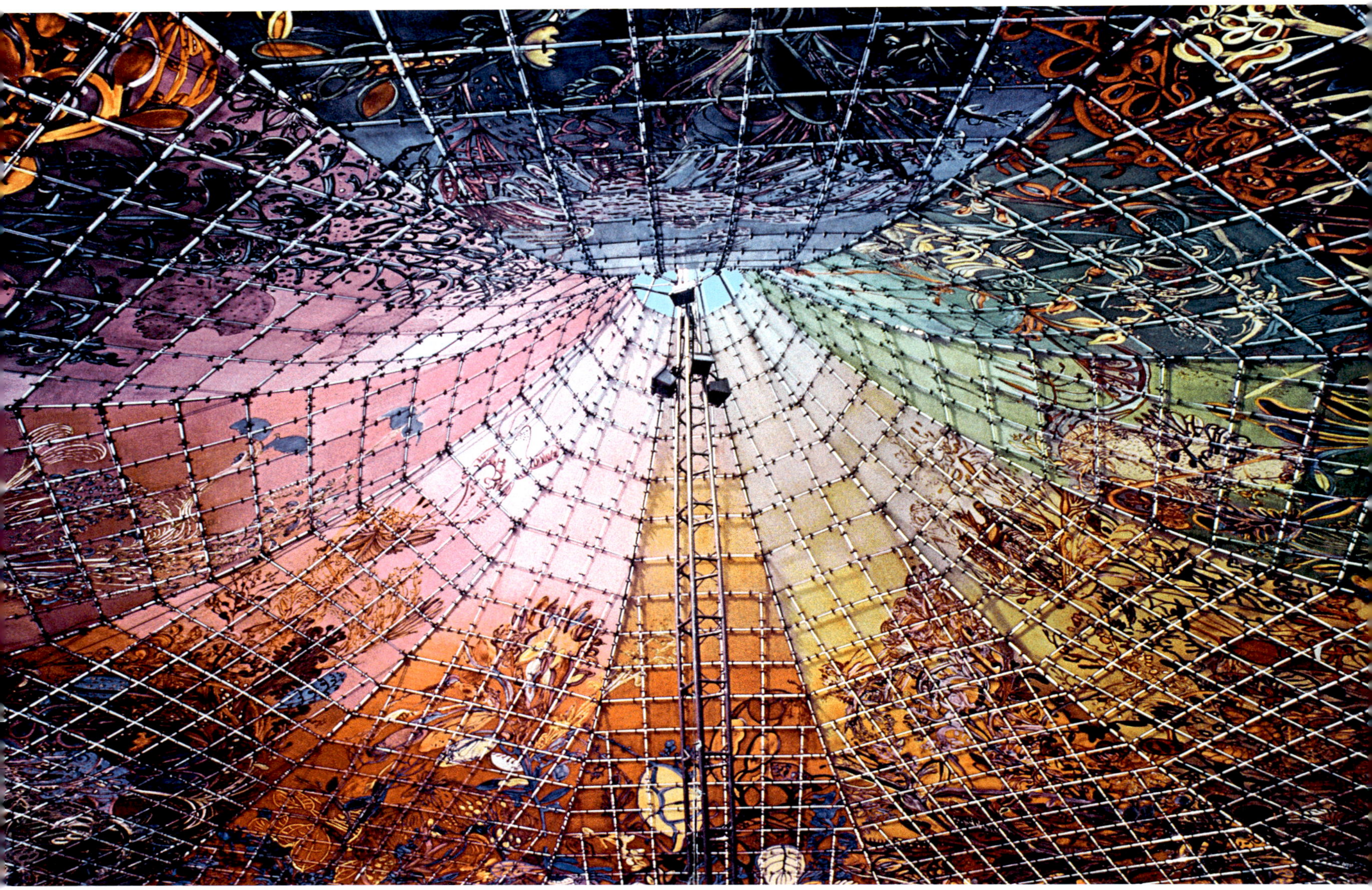

230

Bettina Otto, Frei Otto's daughter, studied with glass painter Gottfried von Stockhausen at the Akademie in Stuttgart. There were stacks of models of tent constructions in the paternal studio. As an artist, she was attracted to the task of rendering the tents in color, giving them artistic designs and longevity. Mayer of Munich and Gabriel Mayer felt utterly challenged by the project. Fantasy, experience as glass painters, and scholarly research, as well as practical and tough tests led to a solution, resulting in innovative glass painting techniques.

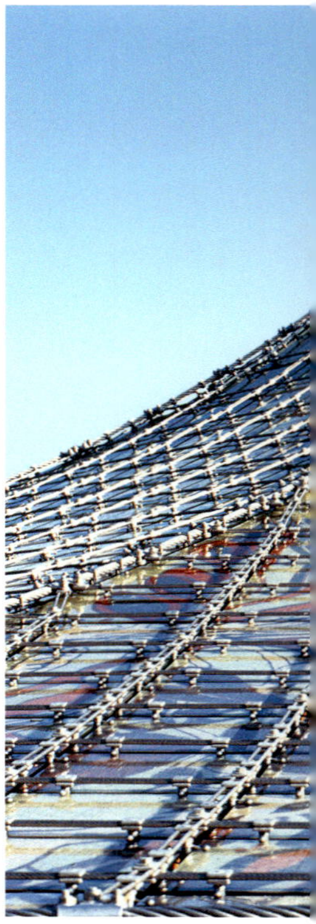

231

A technique was born. The Munich studio termed it "float glass painting," offering the most wonderful possibilities of designing glass.

Artistically designed "glass shingles" were suspended from a moveable steel net construction. The diameter of the glazed tent was circa 55 feet, height 25 feet, thickness of the float glass ³⁄₈ inches.
Unit size circa 1 foot in square and rhomboidal shape, open joints. Stained glass and etching technique, usage of ceramic glass melting colors. Even today, 27 years after its creation, the colors of the "glazed art tent" are still fresh in every respect. Despite the intense sunlight, there are no traces of fading. As far as the editor knows, there have also been no glass breakages.

HEART TENT

230
The artistic glazing of the "Heart Tent" after installation seen from below. The colors get increasingly bright towards the top, leading the gaze upwards. The joints between the glass pieces and the tip of the tent are open.

231
The steel net construction may also be seen from the outside. It is a fabulous engineering feat and fascinatingly beautiful. The stainless steel and lead glass brackets also profited from centuries of experience in stained glass.

232
The details of the tent borders are breathtaking, both from the point of view of aesthetics and construction.

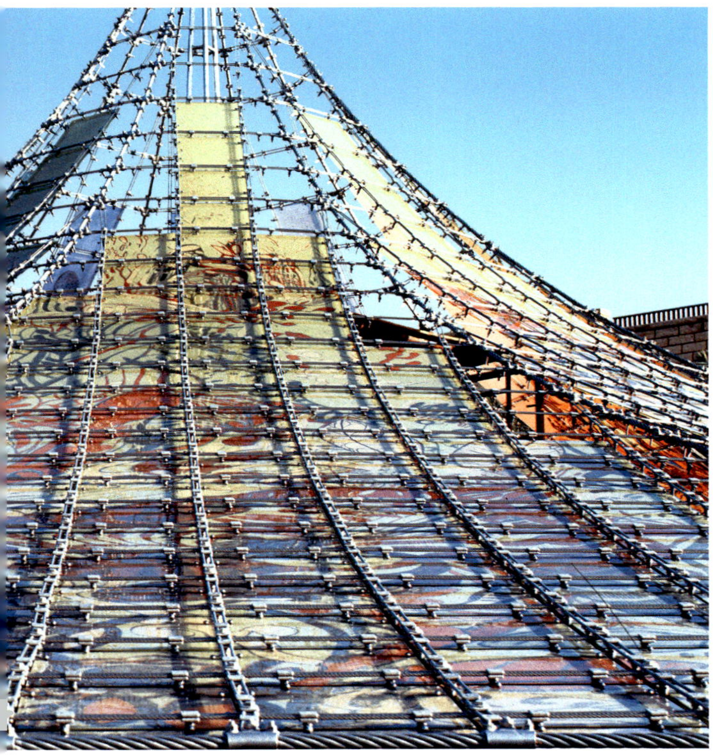

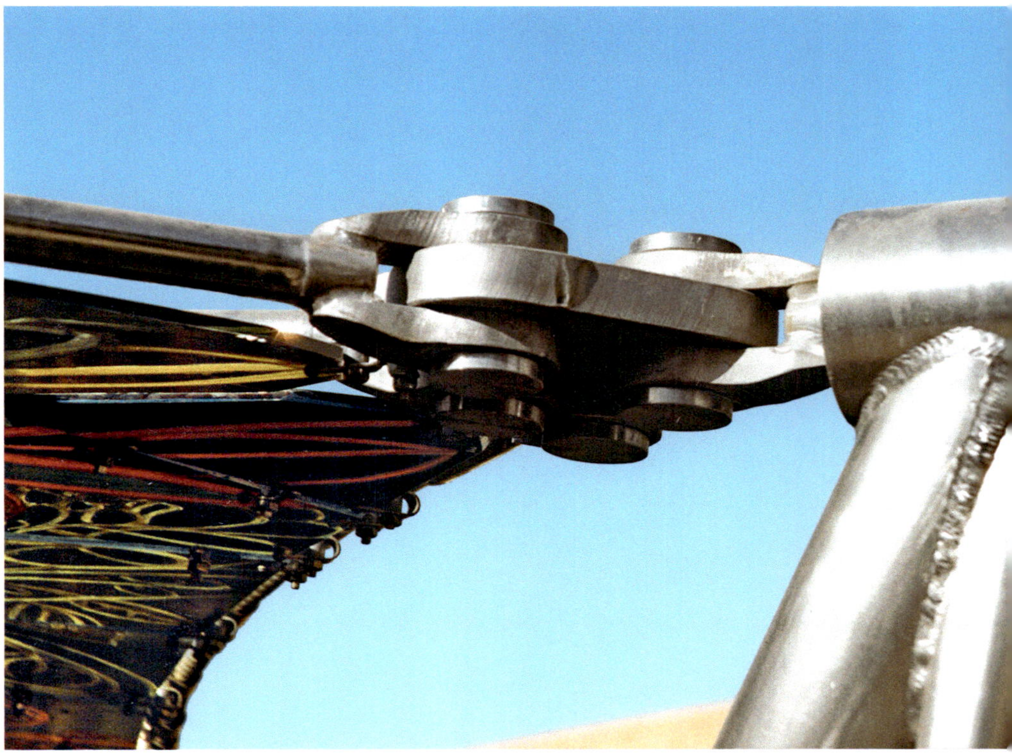

232

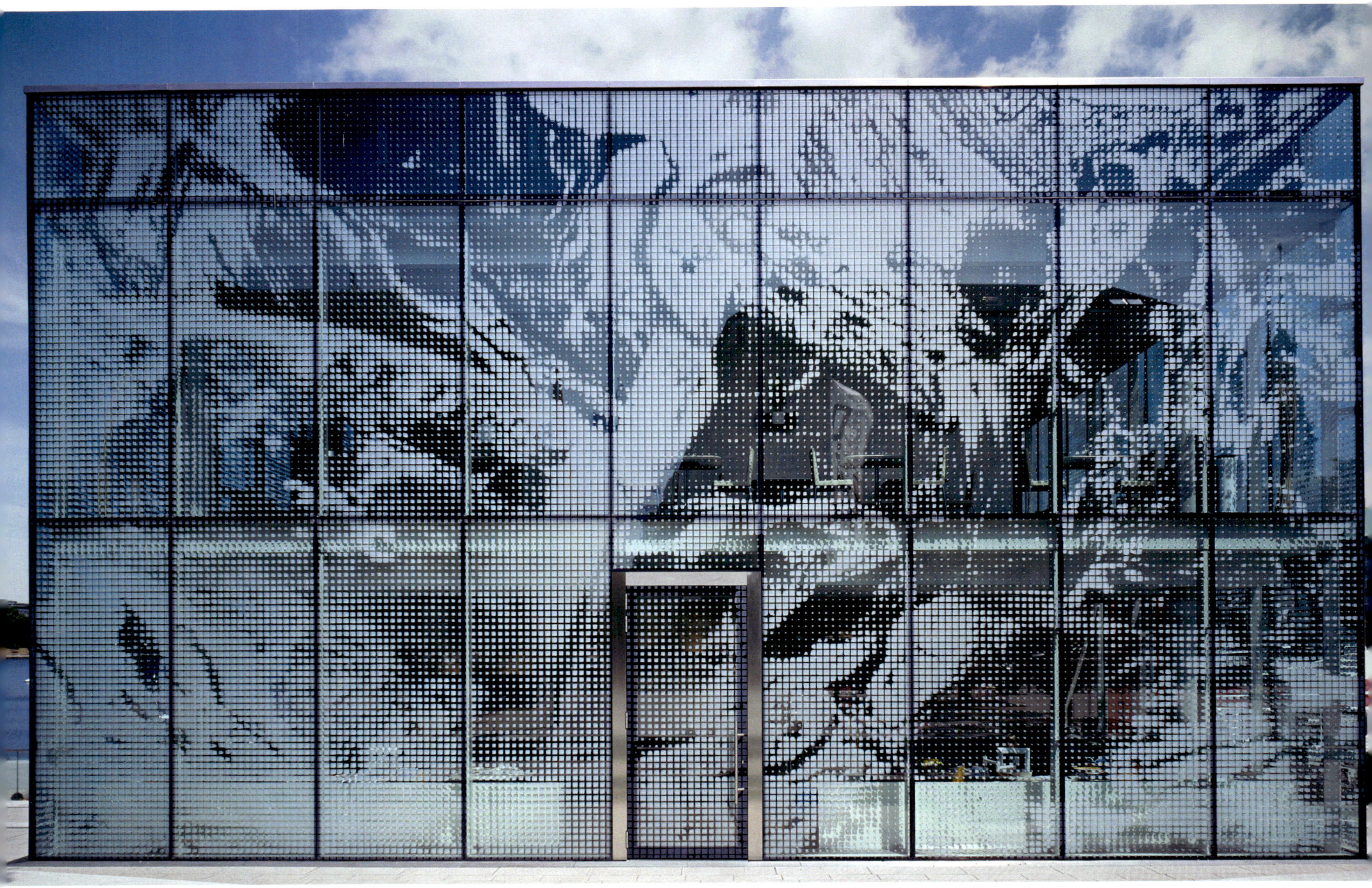

233

André Poitiers Architekten / Pavillon

168

location: Jungfernstieg-Pavillon and glass ceilings of the Hochbahn-Station, Hamburg, DE / André Poitiers architect / Sprinkenhof AG / **year:** 2009 / **technique:** float glass painting

IGU-glazing made of double laminated glass, design with sand blasting and individual silkscreen print with ceramic glass melting colors, including facade construction and execution.
The designed area of the glass facade measures 6000 square feet plus glass for the entrance to the elevated train measuring 2500 square feet.

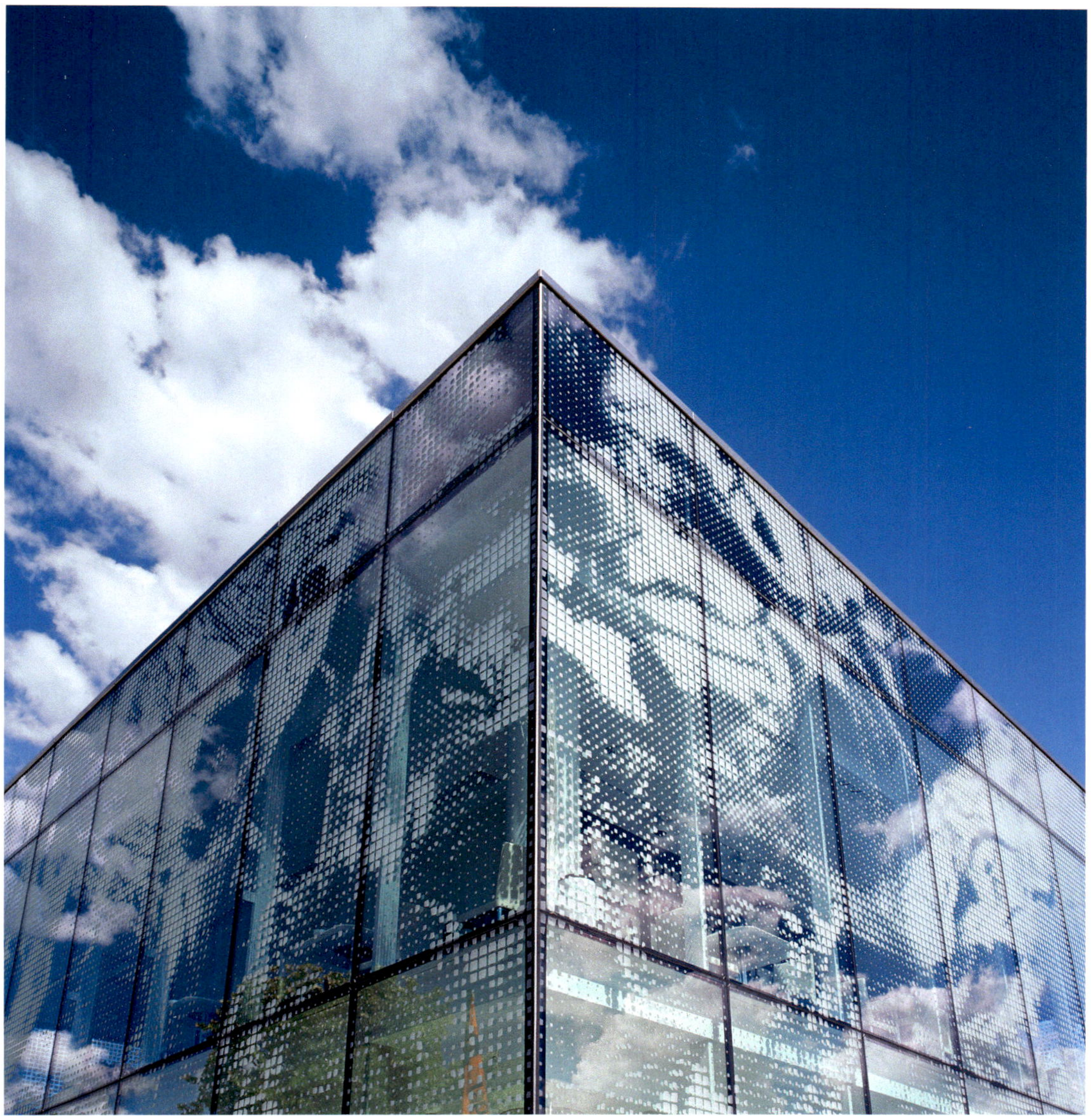

234

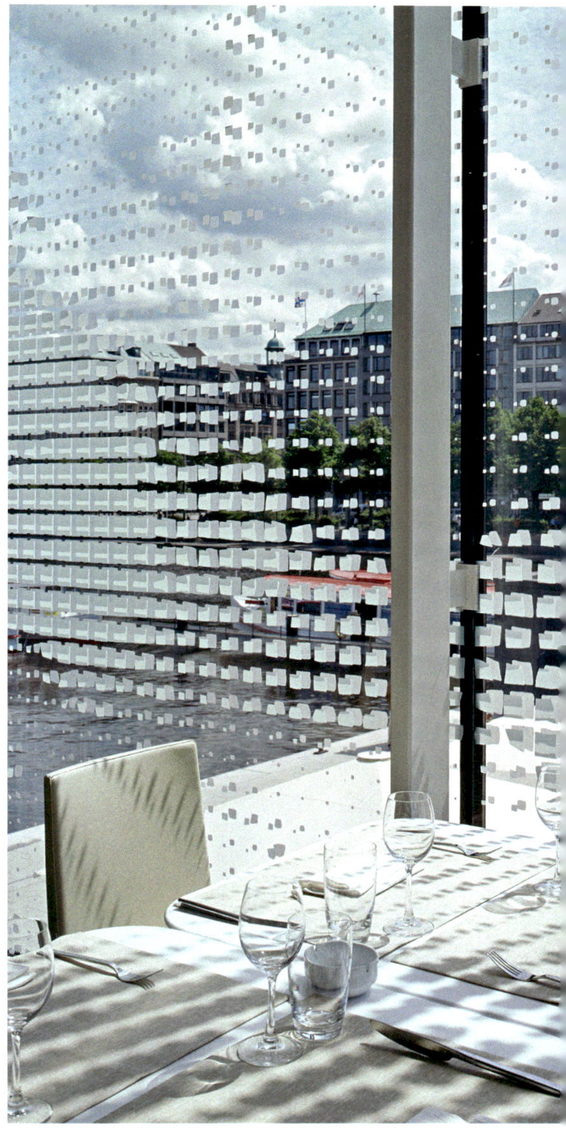

235

JUNGERNSTIEG PAVILLON

233 +
234

Two external views of the Pavillon with partly sun-lit glass facade.

235

Detail view of the glass from the inside in the restaurant.

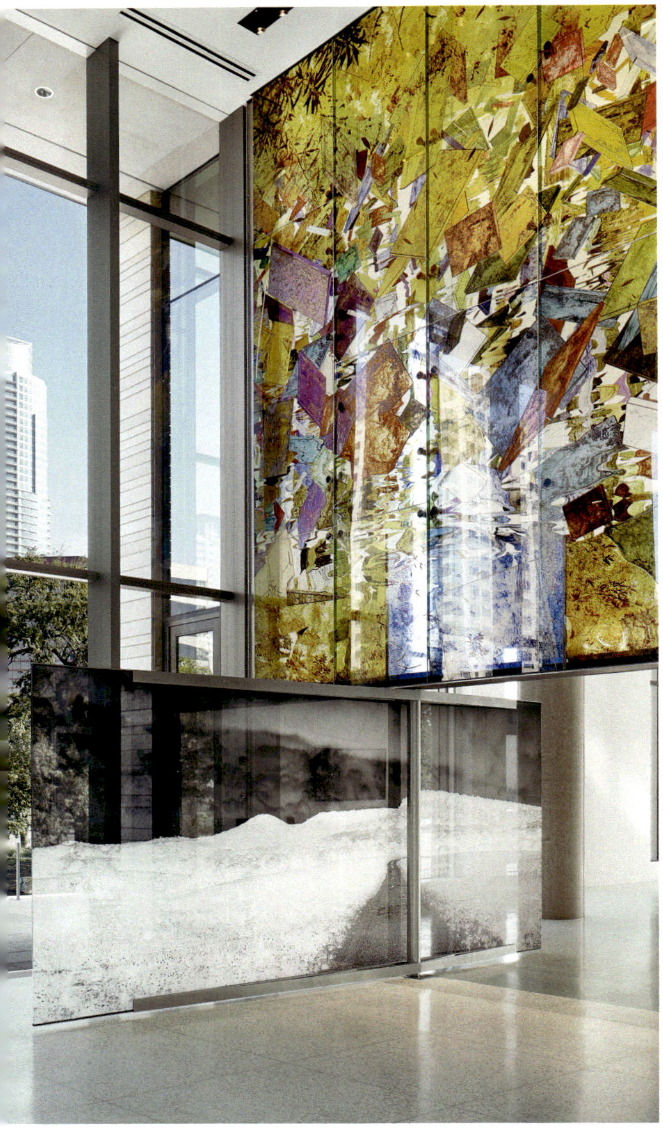

236

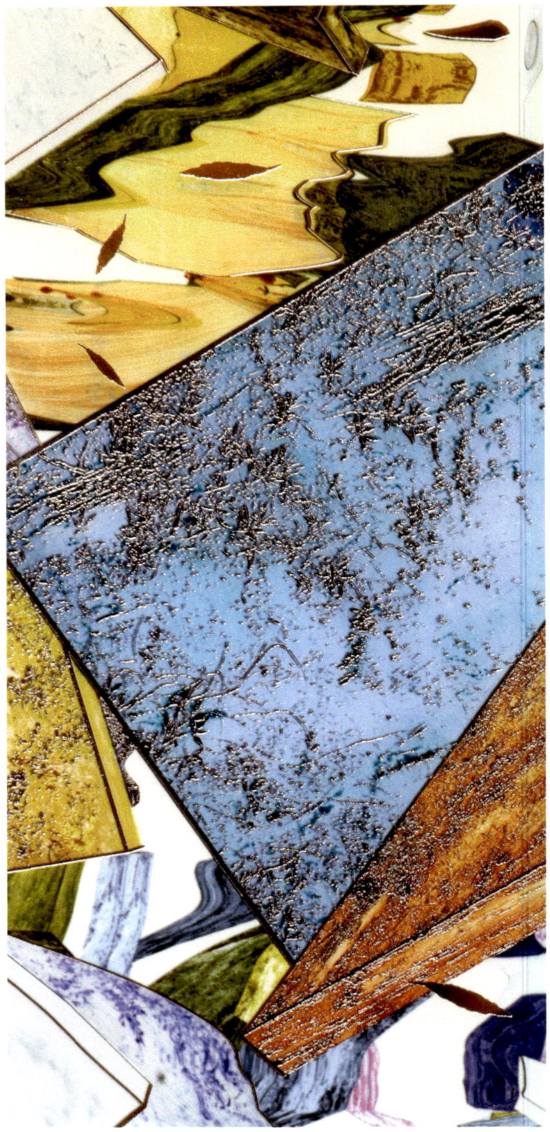

237

AUSTIN WALL

236
A detail of the massive hydraulically controlled glass doors and a section of the upper glass wall, here seen from the atrium side in the lower left part of the wall. The lower door section shows the basic motif of the Texan landscape in black and white and indicates the crisp sharpness and the richness in detail.

237
This glass detail shows an area rather close to the center. The colorful elements, called by the artist "Harmonia", dance all around the upper area of the art work and come from the black and white image from below.

238
The overall view of the art glass wall as seen from the atrium side. It is also the backside view from the smaller space of the jurors that amazes through artistic beauty, transparency and airiness.

Clifford Ross / "Austin Wall"

location: Federal Courthouse, Austin, TX, USA / Mack Scogin Merrill Elam Architects / Art in Architecture Program US GSA / **year:** 2012 / **technique:** float glass painting

Digital print with transparent ceramic glass melting colors, combined with silk screen print and sandblast, with airbrush and handpainting.

Ross' high-resolution photograph of the Texas Hill Country is the basis for the imagery of the 30' x 30' stained glass wall he has designed. The art glass piece represents the end wall of the atrium space and includes massive hydraulically controlled doors, which open to combine two large-scale interior spaces for public events. Sophisticated technology has been used for the realization of the art glass panes, but quite a bit of analysis, experiment, and effort has been used to create a reflecting back wall system, which allows best possible artificial lighting conditions.

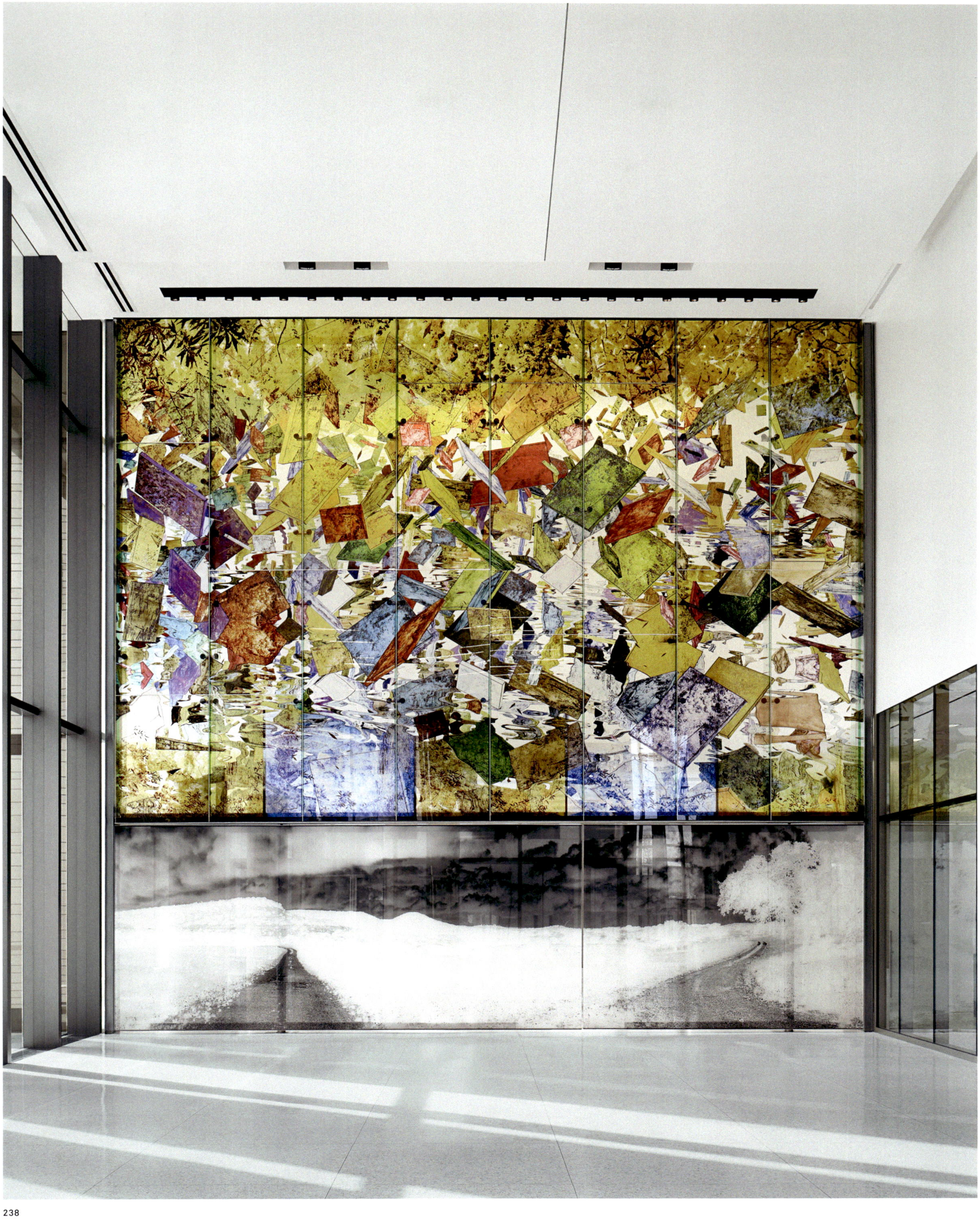

171

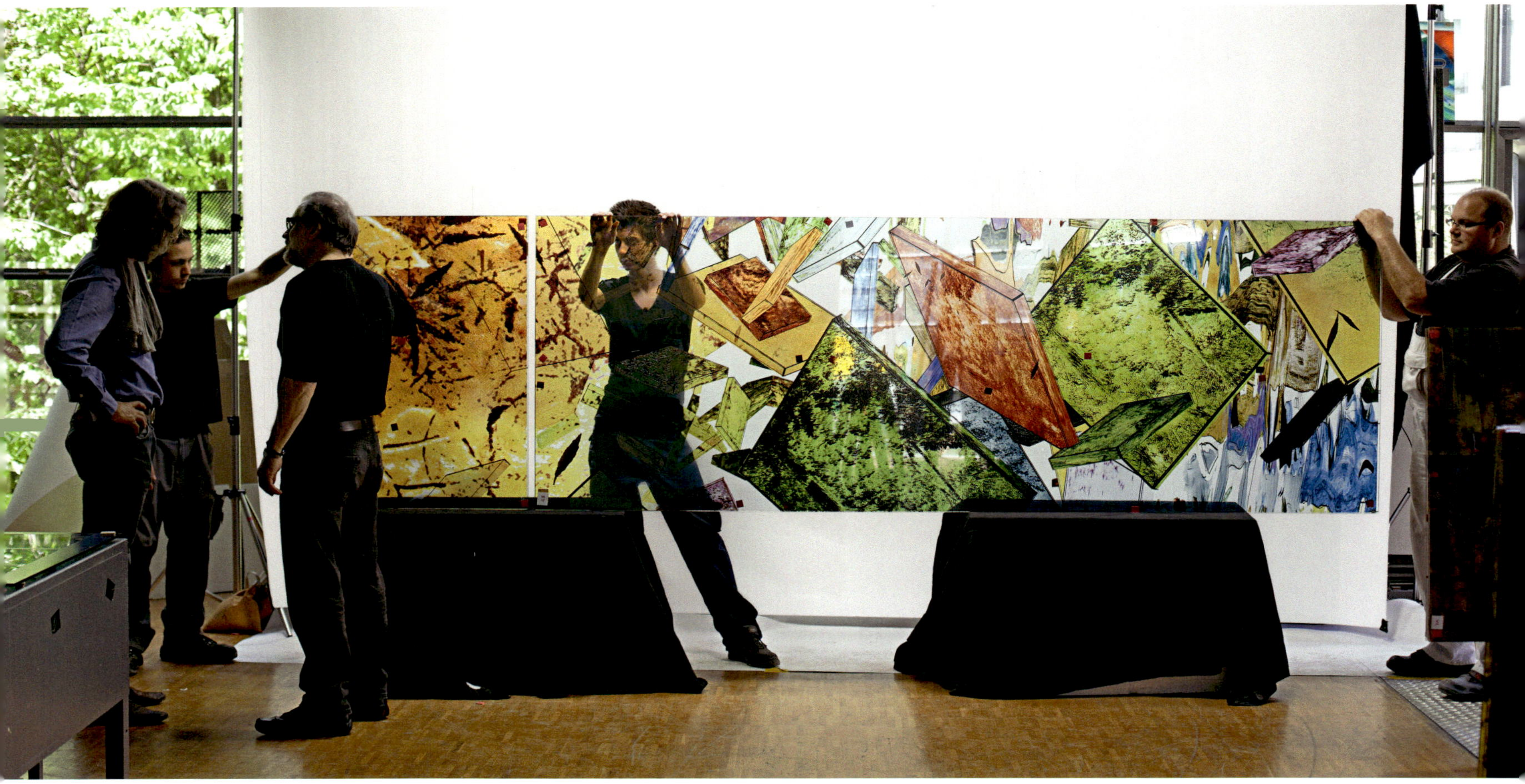

239

"One would expect the blending of centuries-old stained glass craftsmanship with 21st century digital technology to be fraught with difficulty, if not impossible – at an aesthetic level, and with regard to the temperament of the practitioners. Well, it's simply not the case. Franz Mayer proves it. Collaborating with Franz Mayer shows that imagery born of a Texas landscape, captured and transformed in pixel form by an American multimedia artist like myself, can find it's true expression in a 3½ ton, 81 square meter wall. Melted glass, brushes, the human wrist, and pixels. What a miraculous combination...." (Clifford Ross)

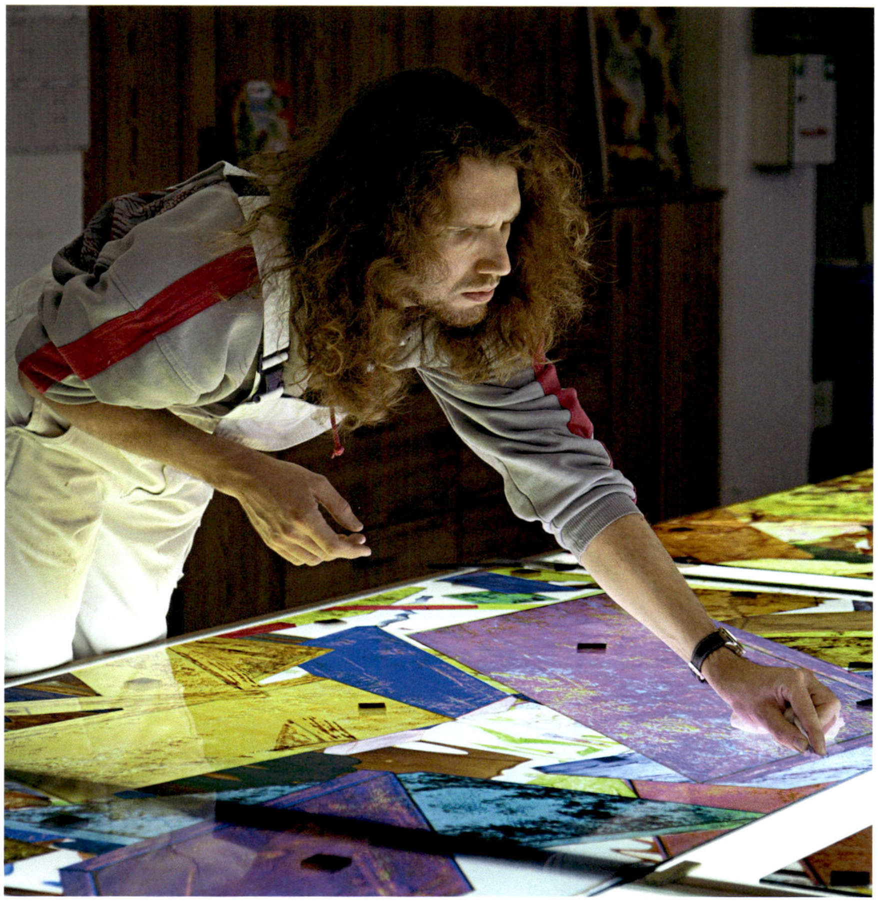

240

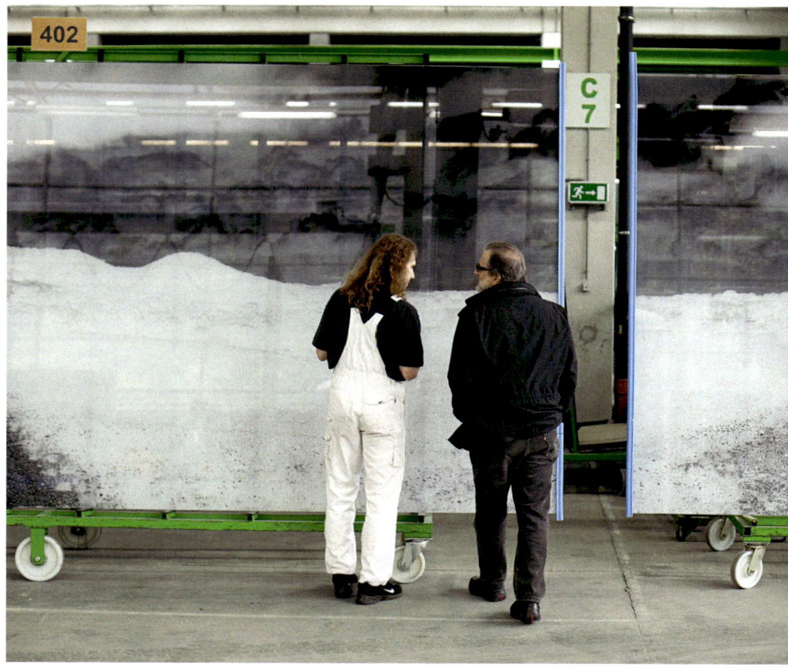

241

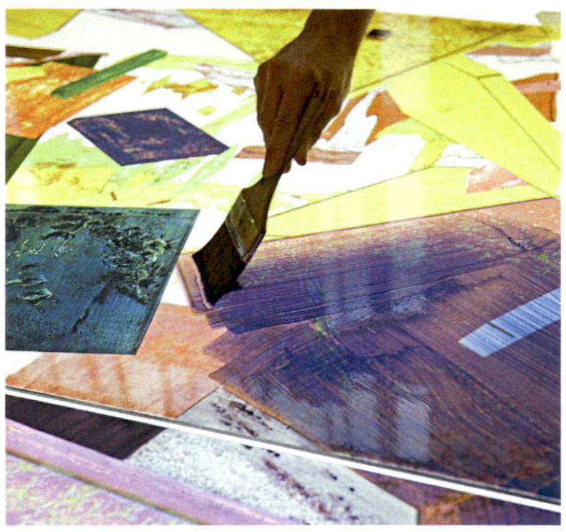

242

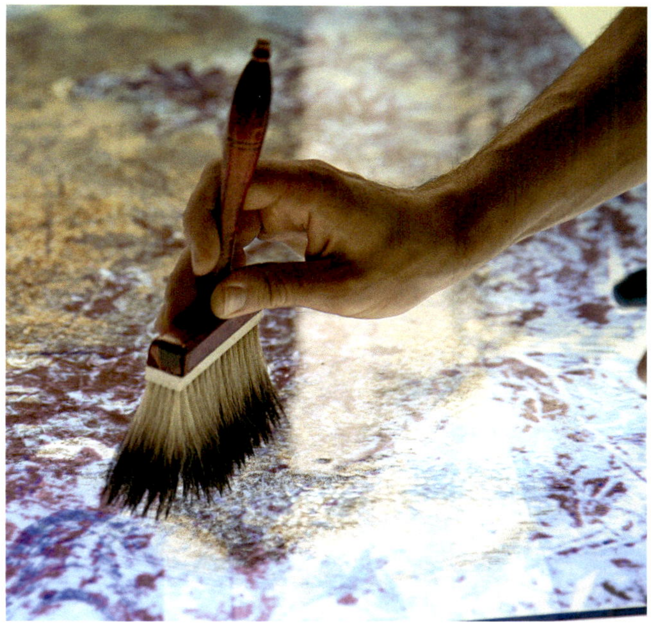

243

THE WORK IN MUNICH

239
Artist, Michael Mayer and artisan craftsmen of the studio checking all panels after completion in detail. The light situation has been created similar to the one expected at the site.

240
The highly skilled craftsman, who was responsible for the project, at work.

241
Artist and craftsman checking the huge and heavy lower glass panes after completion.

242 + 243
Hands and brushes.

RESURRECTIO

244

The Resurrection window on the altar side consists of 35 horizontal rectangular pieces, each measuring circa 4 feet in height and 8 feet in width. Some 400 holes had been drilled in total to receive the colorless Plexiglas rods, which are to bundle and conduct the light.

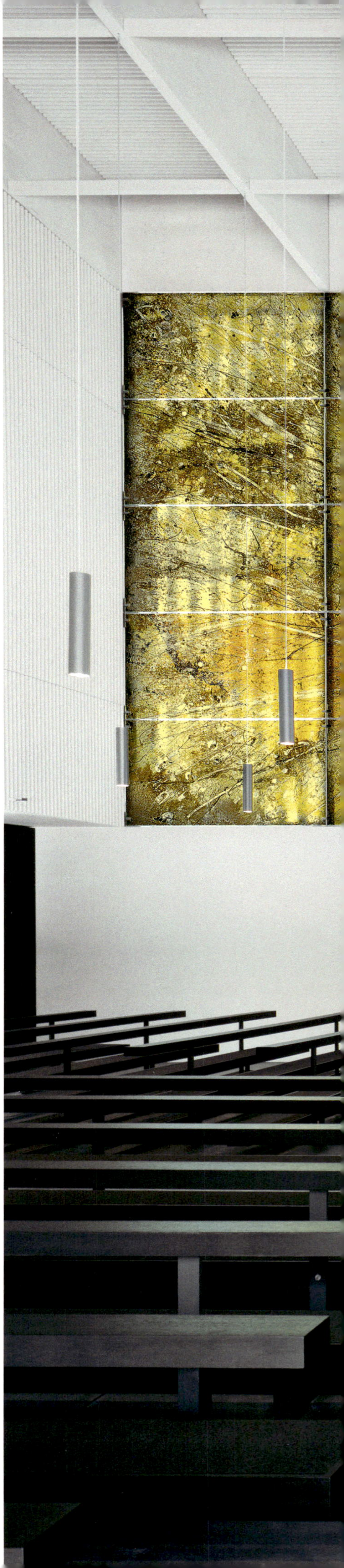

Hella Santarossa / “Resurrectio”

location: St. Florian Church, Munich-Riem, DE / Florian Nagler Architects / Archdiocese of Munich / **year:** 2005 / **technique:** float glass painting

57 × 22 feet, over 400 drill holes for the plexiglass light emitting rods.

This is “Action-Painting” in the truest sense of the word. The entire window was assembled horizontally and temporarily backlit first. A moveable, horizontal scaffold was built. The Mayer crew moved the artist over the glass surface and delivered the prepared colors for reflected and transmitted light. With her temperament and cutting-edge intentions the artist exceeded the materials’ capabilities and all of the glass had to be made twice. The ultimate result was fascinating: both the artist and Mayer of Munich can be proud.

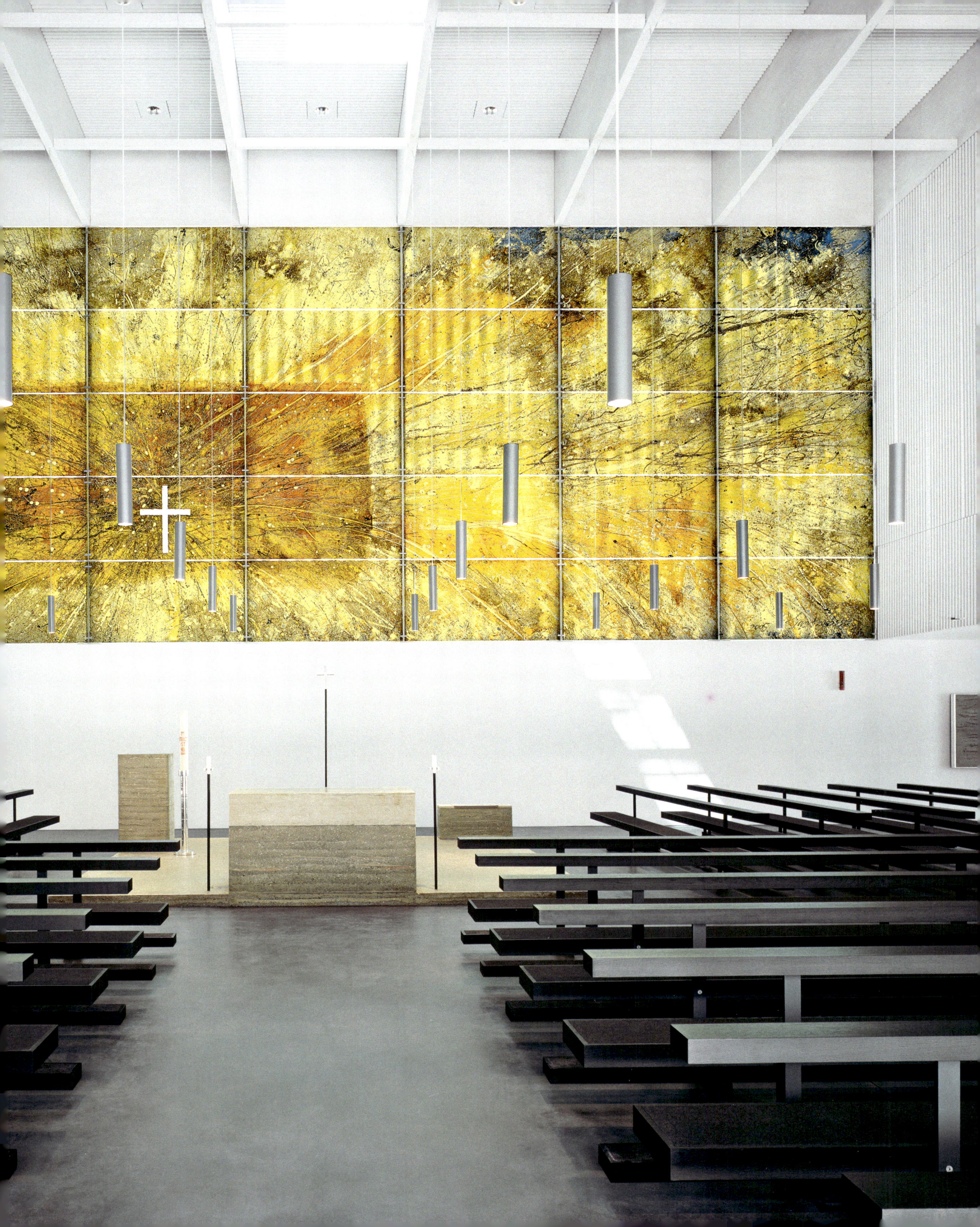

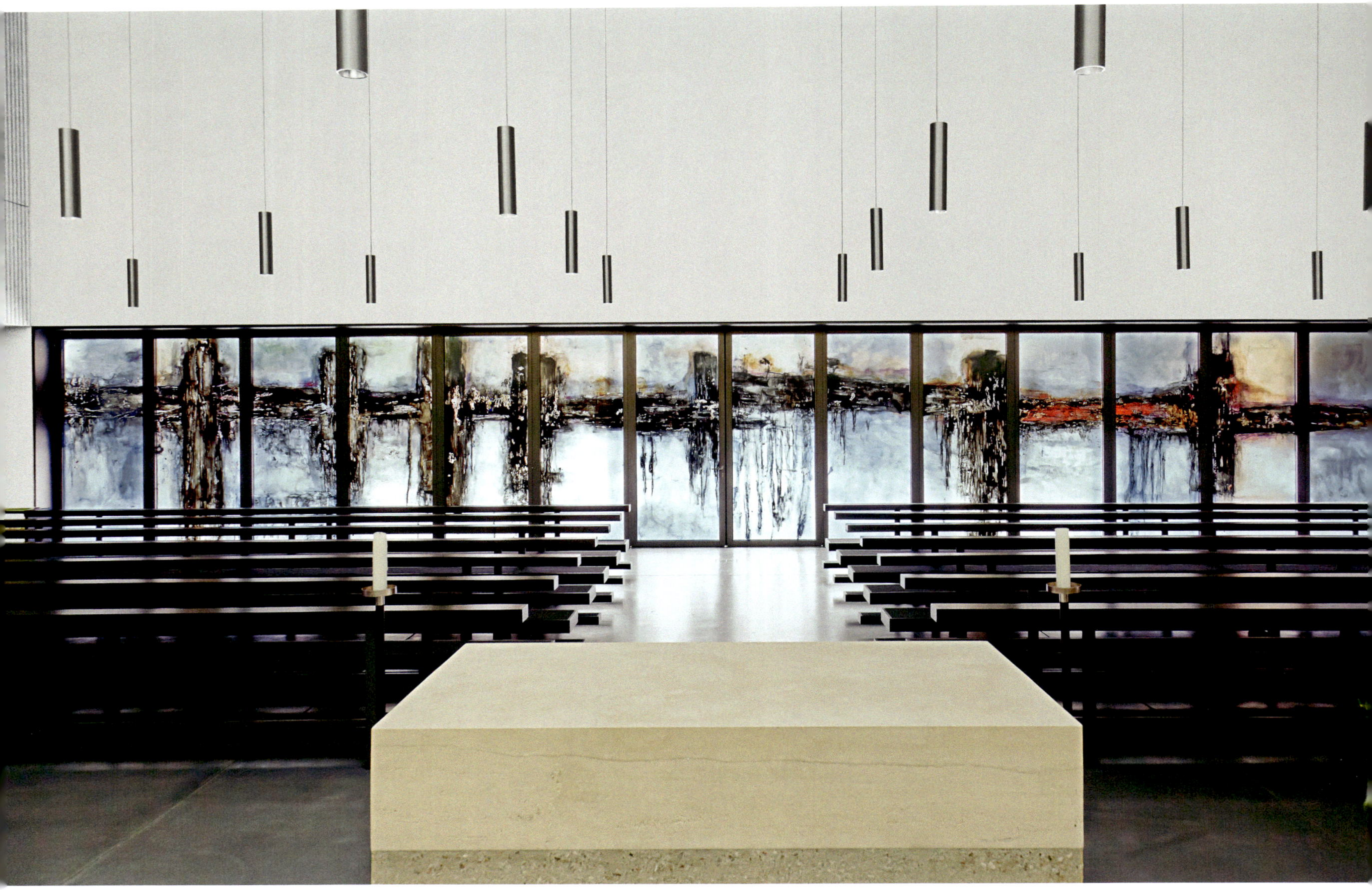

245

Horst Thürheimer / "Stations of the Cross"

176

location: St. Florian Church, Munich-Riem, DE / Florian Nagler Architects / Archdiocese of Munich / **year:** 2010 / **technique:** float glass painting

14 IGU-panes, each circa 9 × 3 feet, mostly painted by the artist himself.

Years after realizing Santarossa's Resurrection window in the altar wall (see above) the painter Horst Thürheimer and Mayer realized the 14 windows on the opposite backwall, which were to represent the Stations of the Cross. What a moving juxtaposition: The radiant yellow and bright Resurrection window behind the altar and the burdensome images of the Carrying of the Cross in its 14 stations.

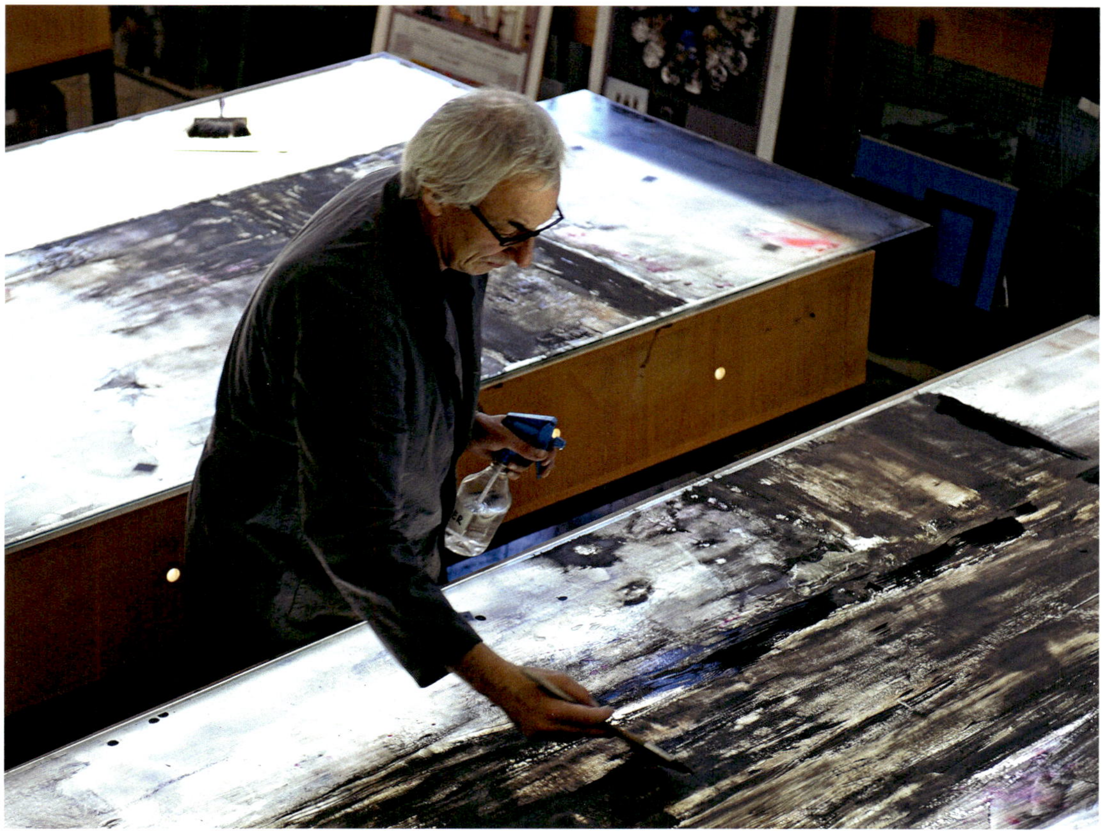

246

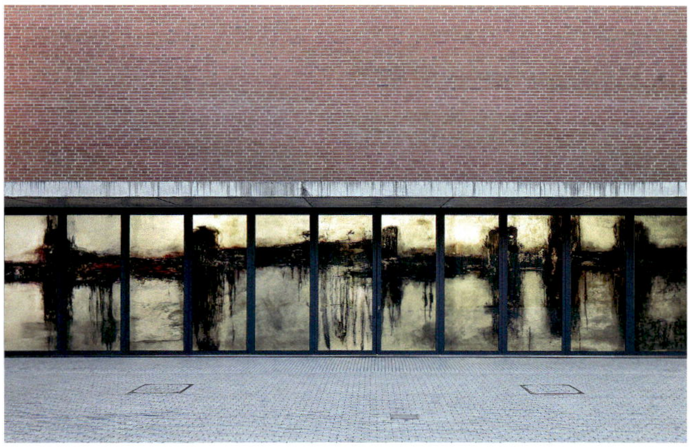

247

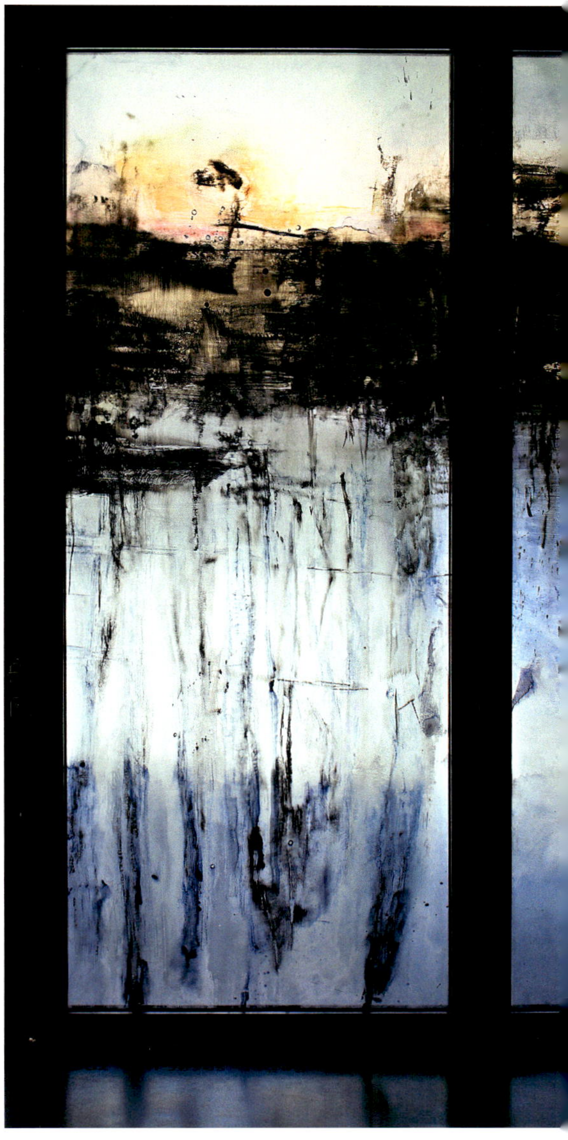

248

STATIONS OF THE CROSS

245
The 14 windows with the Stations of the Cross.

246
Horst Thürheimer painting in the Mayer studio.

247
The windows as night falls, seen from the exterior.

248
A detail showing the severe, heavy brushstrokes, the colors and the combination with sandblasting. The glass panes were fired again and again.

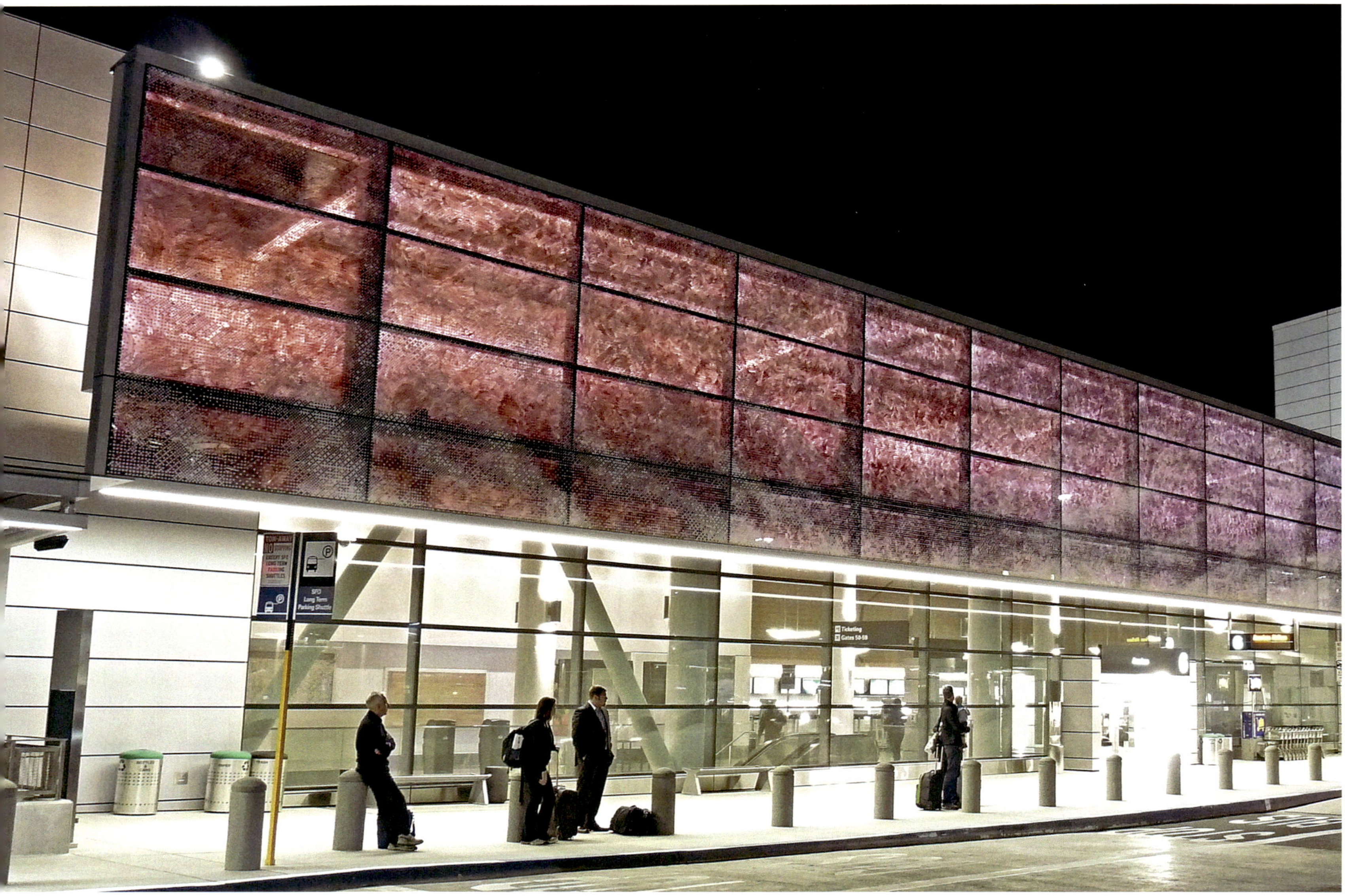

249

Norie Sato / "Air Over Under"

location: Terminal 2, San Francisco International Airport, CA, USA / Gensler Architects / City and County of San Francisco / **year:** 2011 / **technique:** float glass painting

120 pieces of laminated glass panels, two glass walls, 16 feet high and 300 feet wide in total, suspended circa 8 feet in front of the facades of both lateral wings of terminal 2.
A total of 4800 square feet of designed glass walls, Laminated glass made of heat strengthened/ tempered glass panes with printed and hand-painted glass, ceramic glass melting colors.
The combined effect is of a photographic image that, depending on the viewer's distance or point of view, either looks clear or more abstract and atmospheric. The colors are subtle and change gradually from blue to green on one side and from blue to purple on the other side.
Public Art Award PAN 2011

AIR OVER UNDER

249
Nocturnal view of the left glass wall from the outside.

250
The left end of same wall during the day, against the sky.

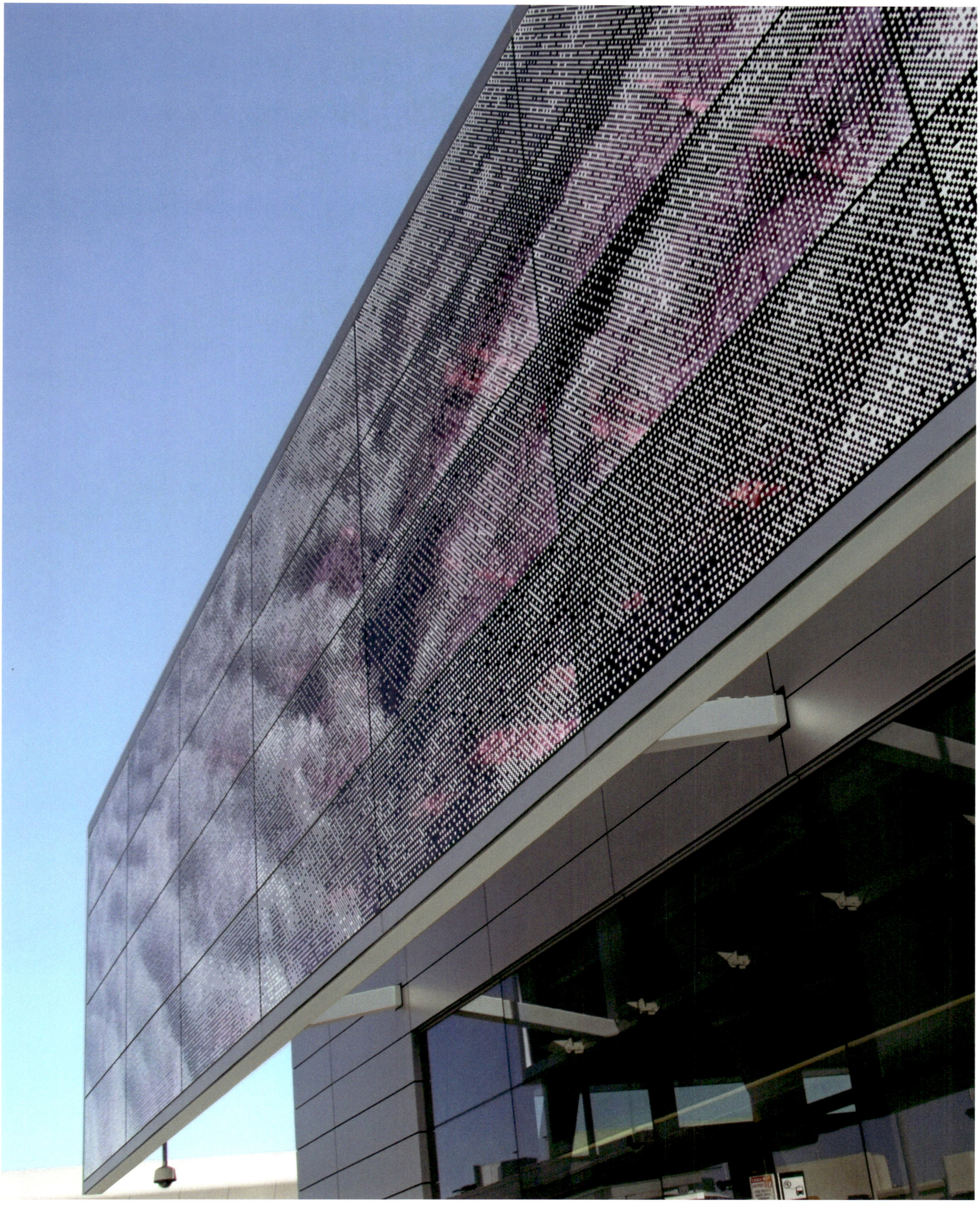

179

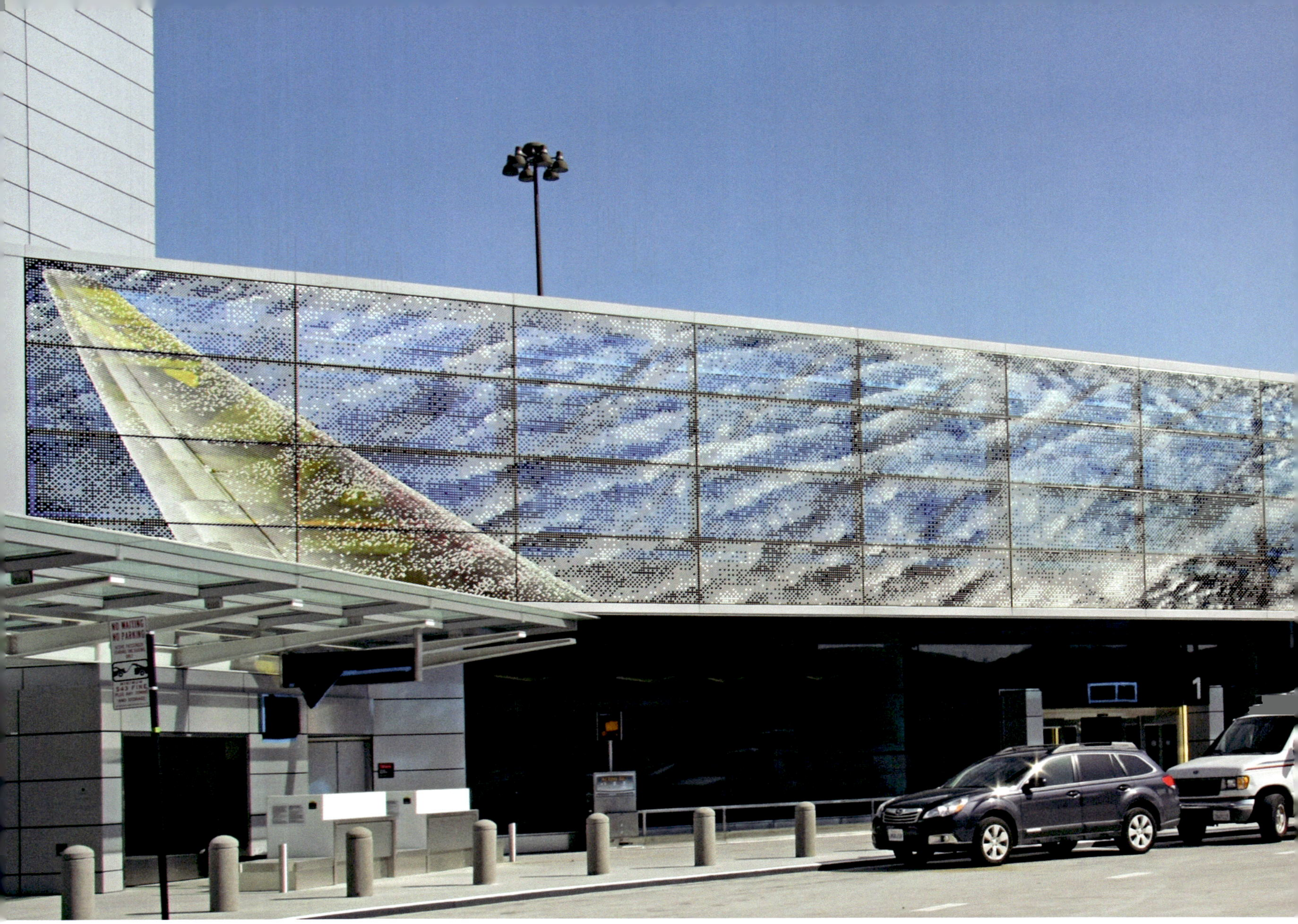

251

Norie Sato's imagery was inspired by our relationship to clouds and flight. Specifically, her work "Air Over Under" delves into some of flight's inherent qualities: ephemeral, abstract, pictorial, natural, man-made, symmetrical and changeable. The artwork depicts the dual experience of being under or over clouds when flying in a plane. According to the artist, "Air Over Under" is about perception, relativity and how our position and situations are never static.

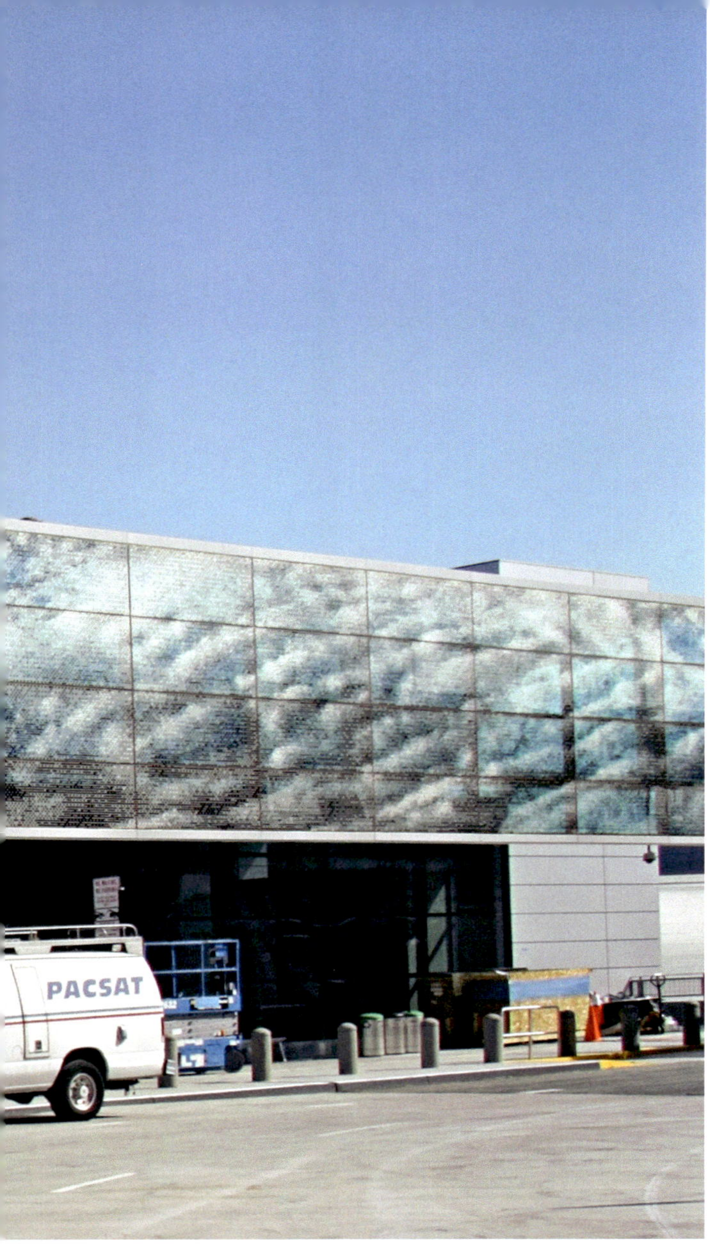

AIR OVER UNDER

251

The glass wall on the right of the lateral building with an airplane's pitch elevator (opposite, the wing of a bird is depicted. Not shown here).

252

In the Munich studio, days were spent with the artist discussing issues of different light, different vantage points, closeness and distance, interior and exterior, looking through and looking from above. Scaffolding was put up and moved; work was done during sunshine and rain, work and testing continued at night. "Light consulting" and "architectural consulting" are part of this studio's natural services.

253

The aircraft's pitch elevator with sunlight from behind.

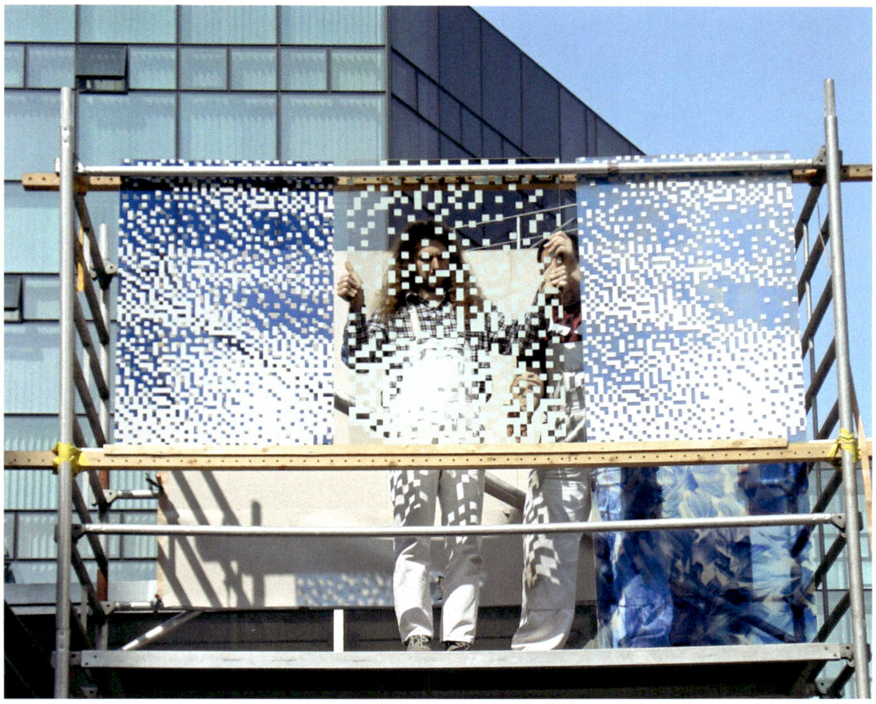

252

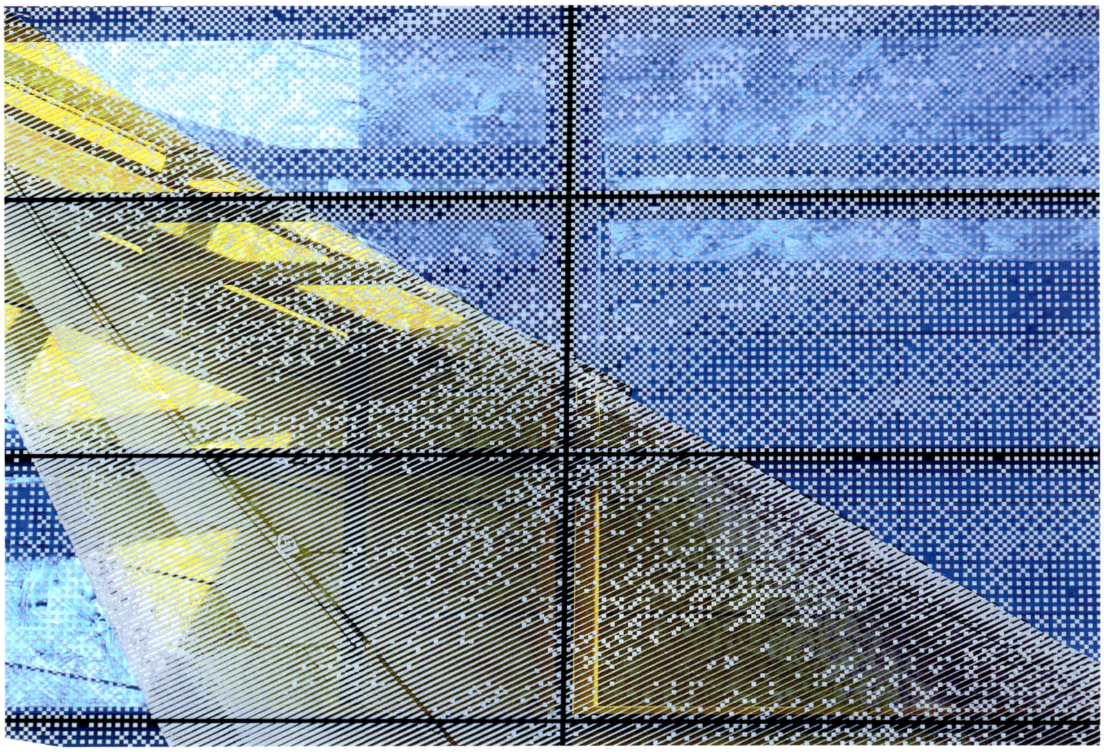

253

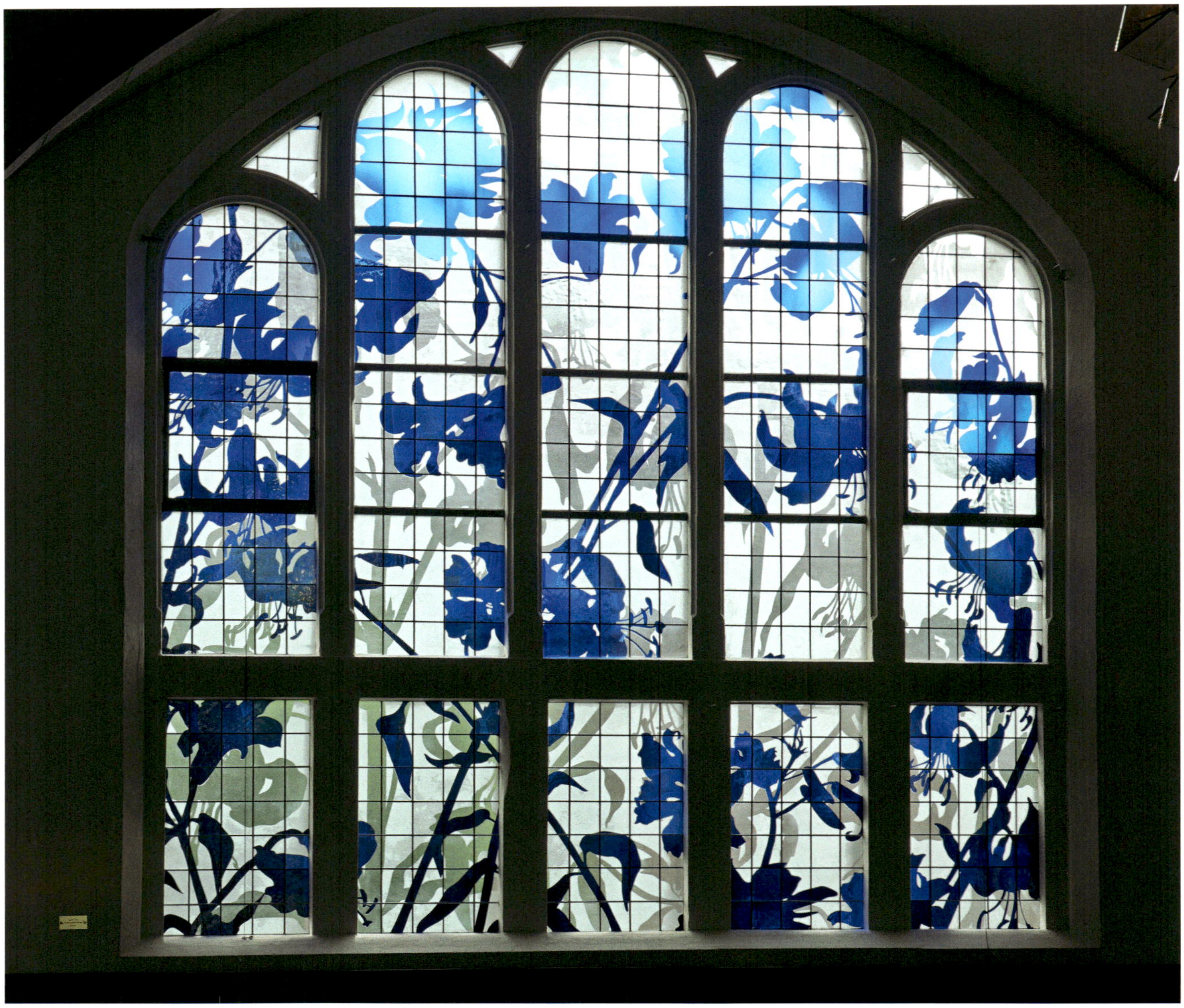

254

Saskia Schultz / “Color Space”

182

location: Lutheran Church (formerly garrison church), Saarlouis, DE / Ev.-luth. Church Community Saarlouis / **year:** 2010 / **technique:** traditional stained glass

Stained glass for the north, west, and east side of the church, flashed antique glass, sand blasting, acid etching, painting, firing and leading technique.

Stylistically, the garrison church in Saarlouis stands at the beginning of Art Nouveau. At the same time, it reveals a mix of stylistic elements derived from Romanesque and Gothic art, and Baroque elements. And yet, there is something “modern” about this church.

The basis for the design of the three main windows are three blossoms: Cherry, lily, and camellia and three colors: blue, red, and green. (Excerpts from the artist’s description)

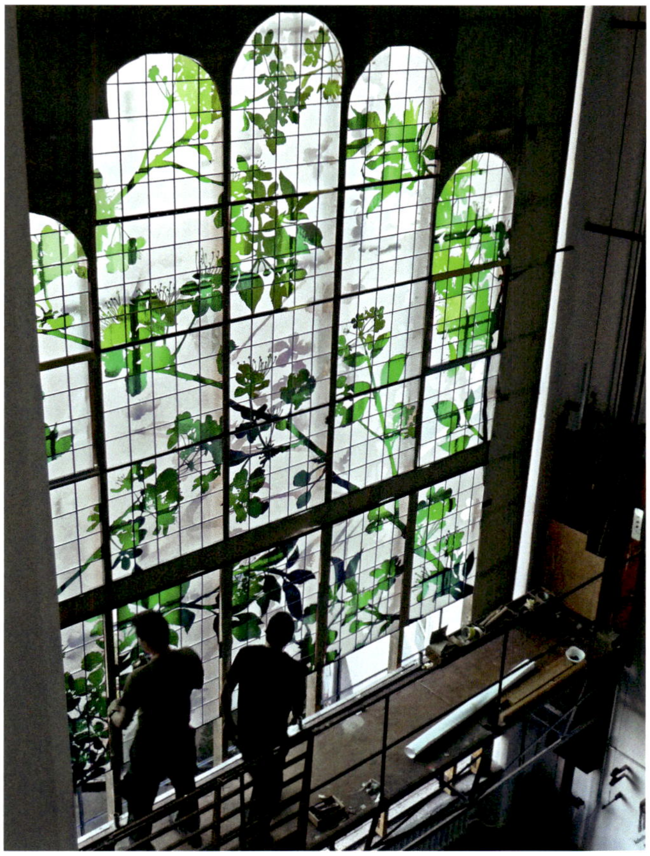

255

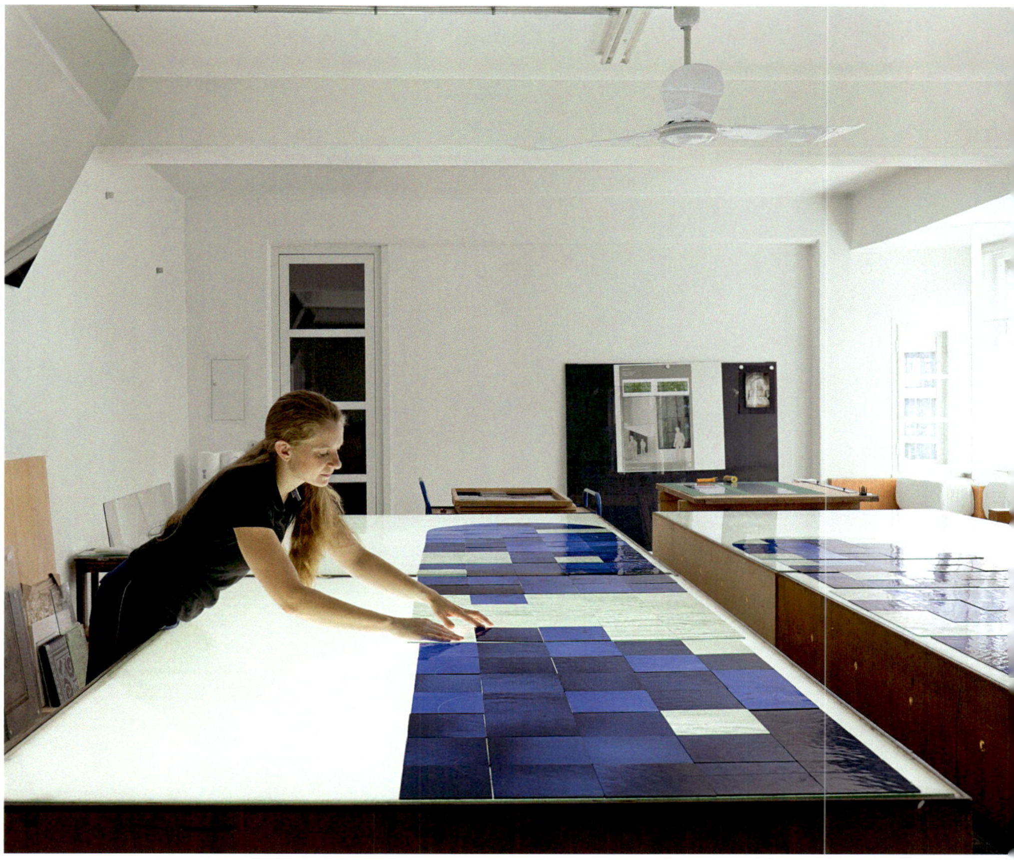

256

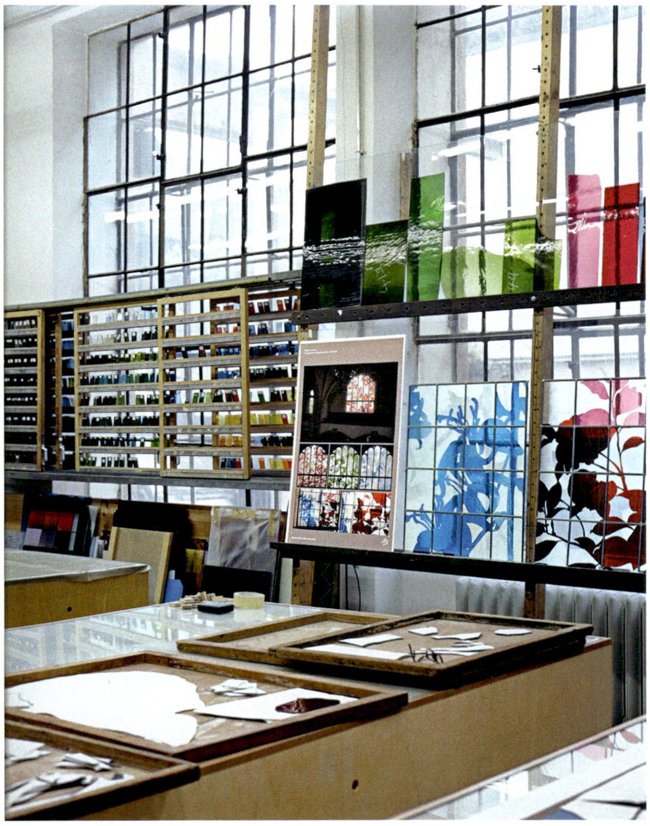

257

COLOR SPACE

254

The largest of the blue windows with the lily blossoms on the west side across from the altar.

255

The green and northern main window during installation in the exhibition space in Munich.

256

The blue flashed glass with its drifting colors is carefully selected.

257

The first color and work patterns: Green for the camellia blossoms window on the north side; rose-gold for the cherry blossoms of the south side, and blue – seen here in a brighter hue – for the window on the west side.

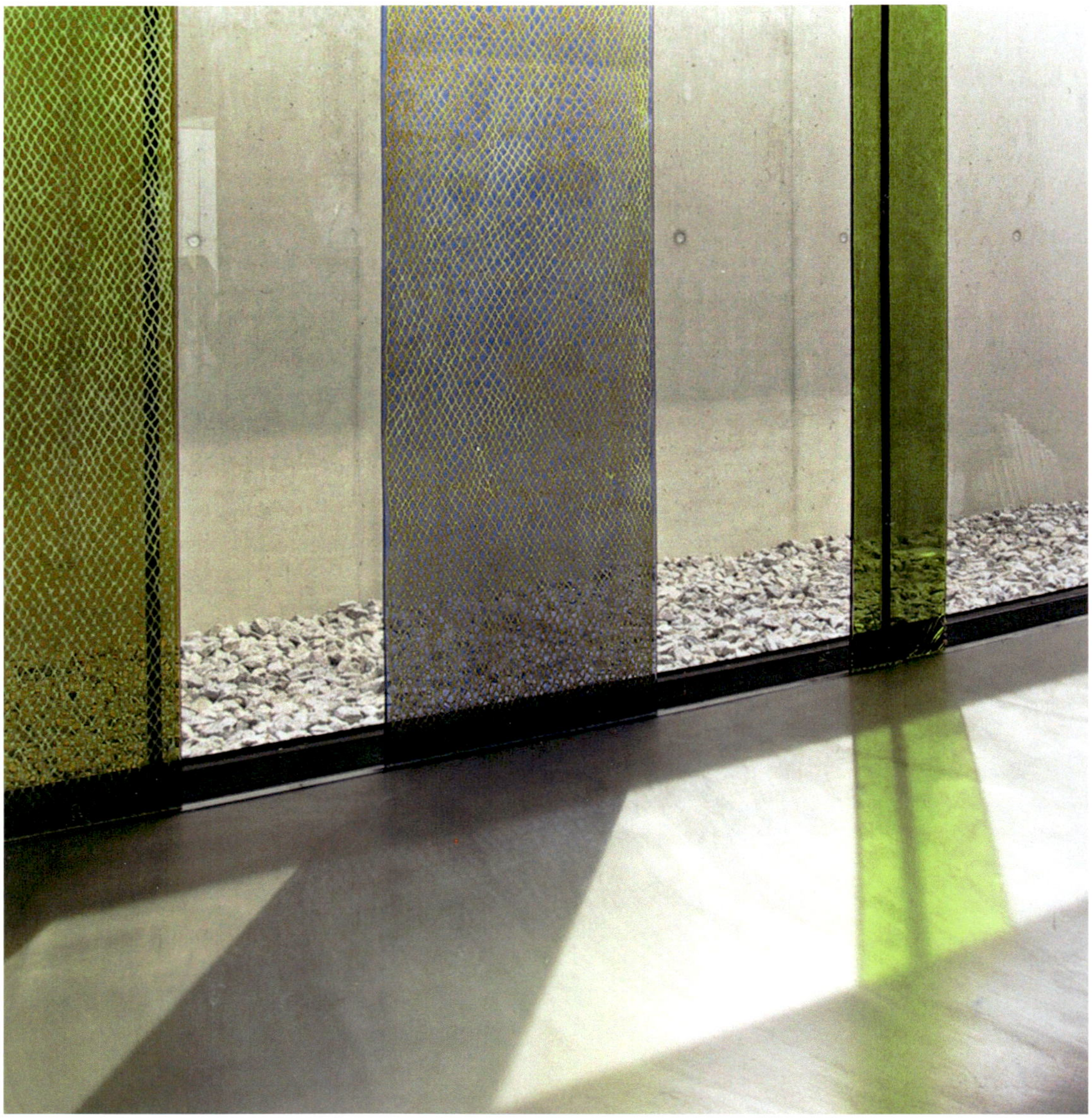

258

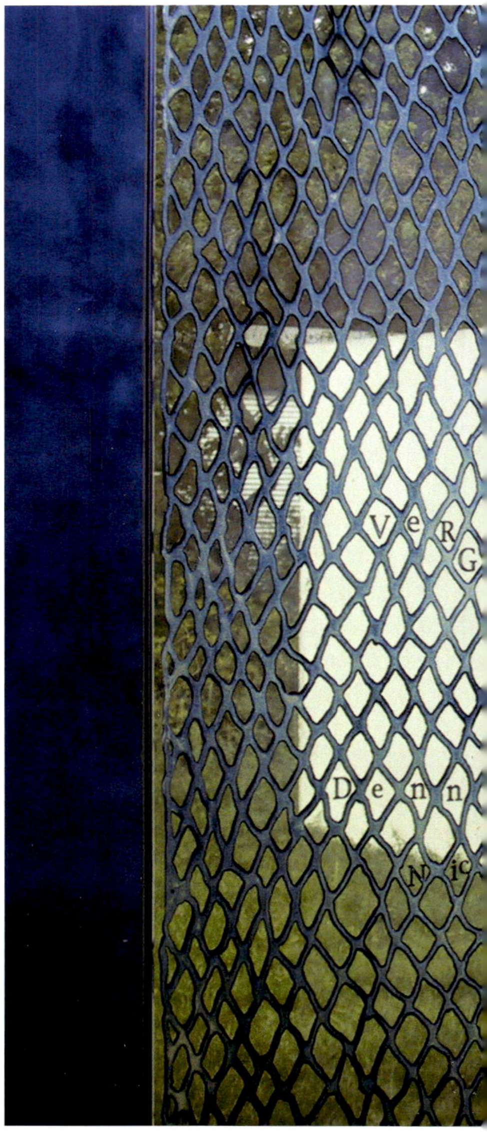

259

Saskia Schultz / “Protective Outlooks”

location: Glass design in the specialty clinic Ringgenhof in Wilhelmsdorf, DE / Architects Weinbrenner + Single / Zieglersche Anstalten / **year:** 2004 / **technique:** float glass painting

Transparent glass melting colors, airbrush, silk screen print, deep engravings and color fills, tempered float glass, sliding rails to move the glass.
The glass pictures surround the patients like tender curtains that let the light pass through, at the same time enclosing them like fences.

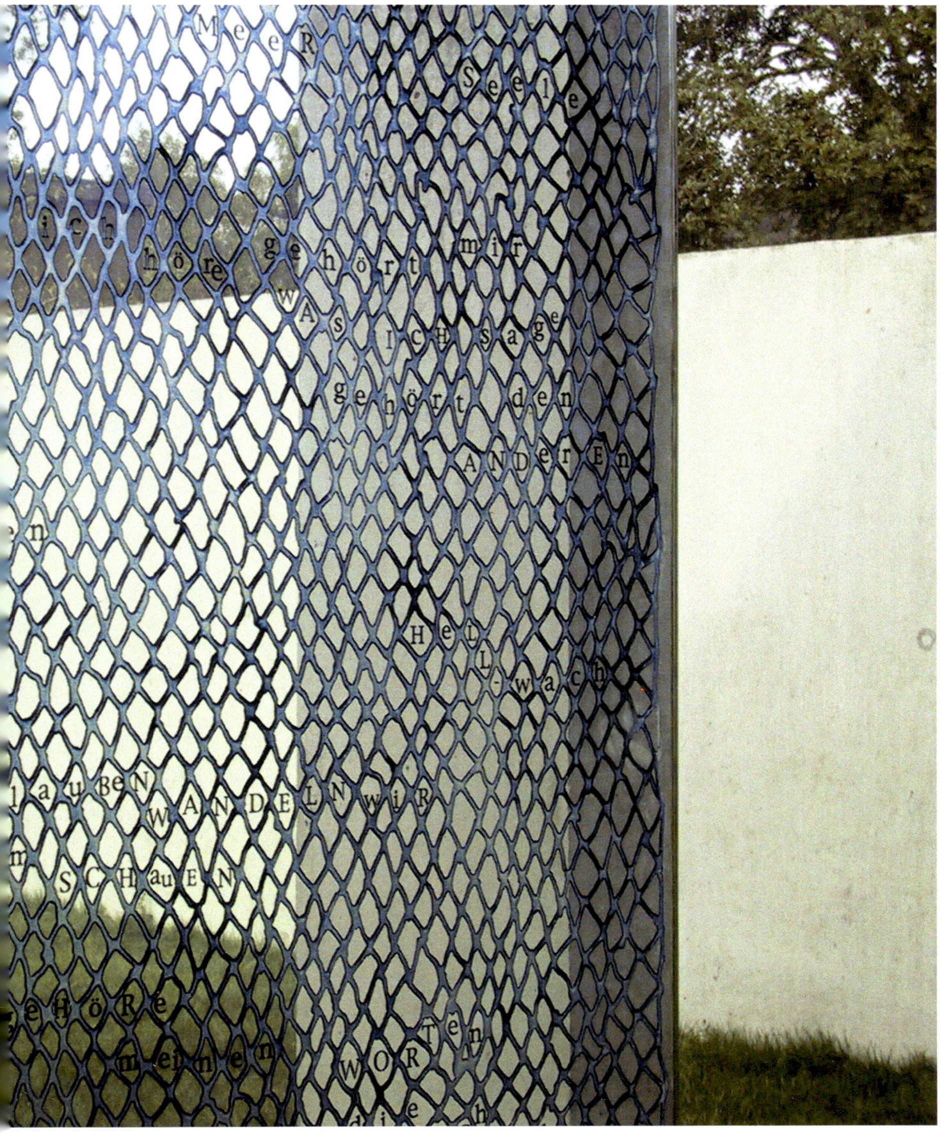

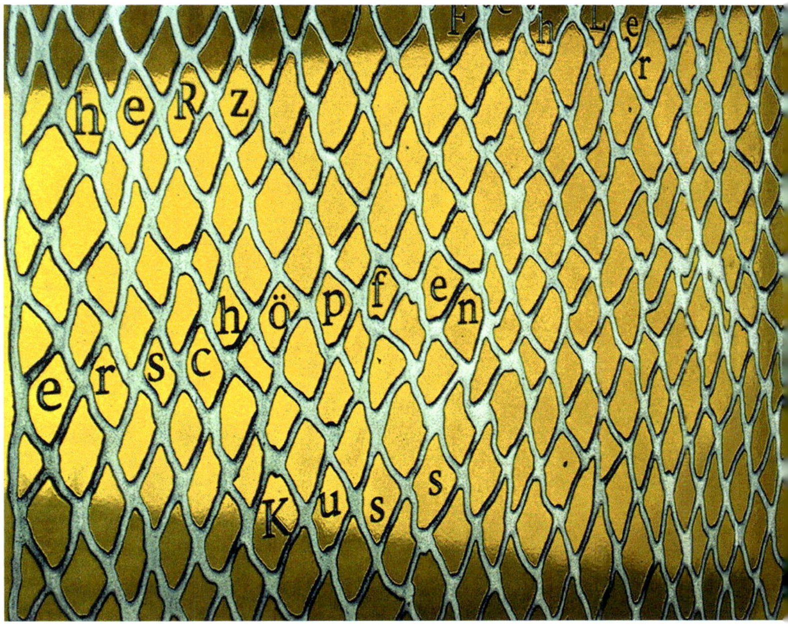

260

PROTECTIVE OUTLOOKS

258
Three of the very tender and transparent glass pictures and their projection on the ground. The glass can be moved, forming a casual separation between inside and outside.

259 +
260
Details: The transparent base colors, the silkscreened words, the deep engravings, and their color fills are clearly visible.

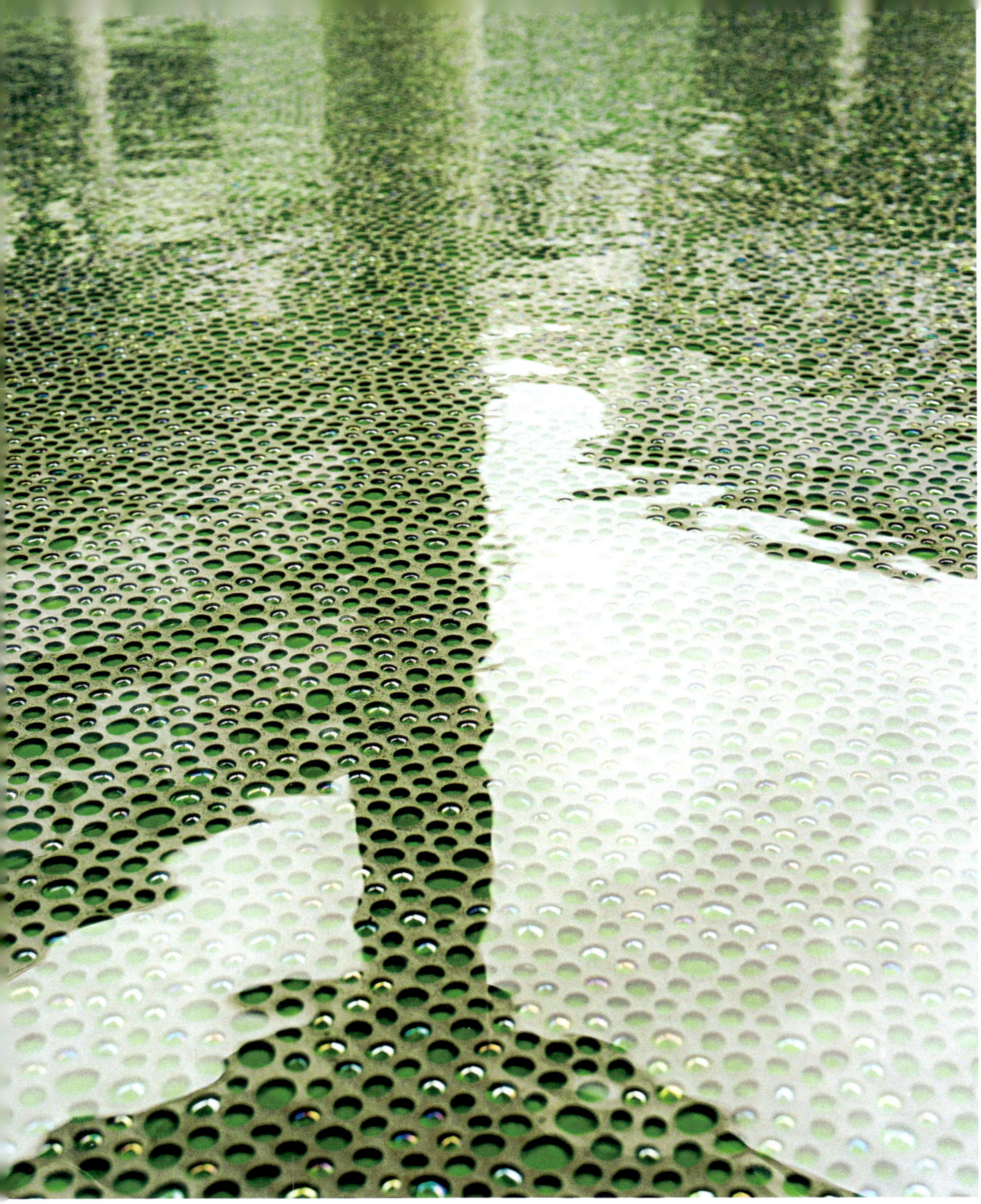

261

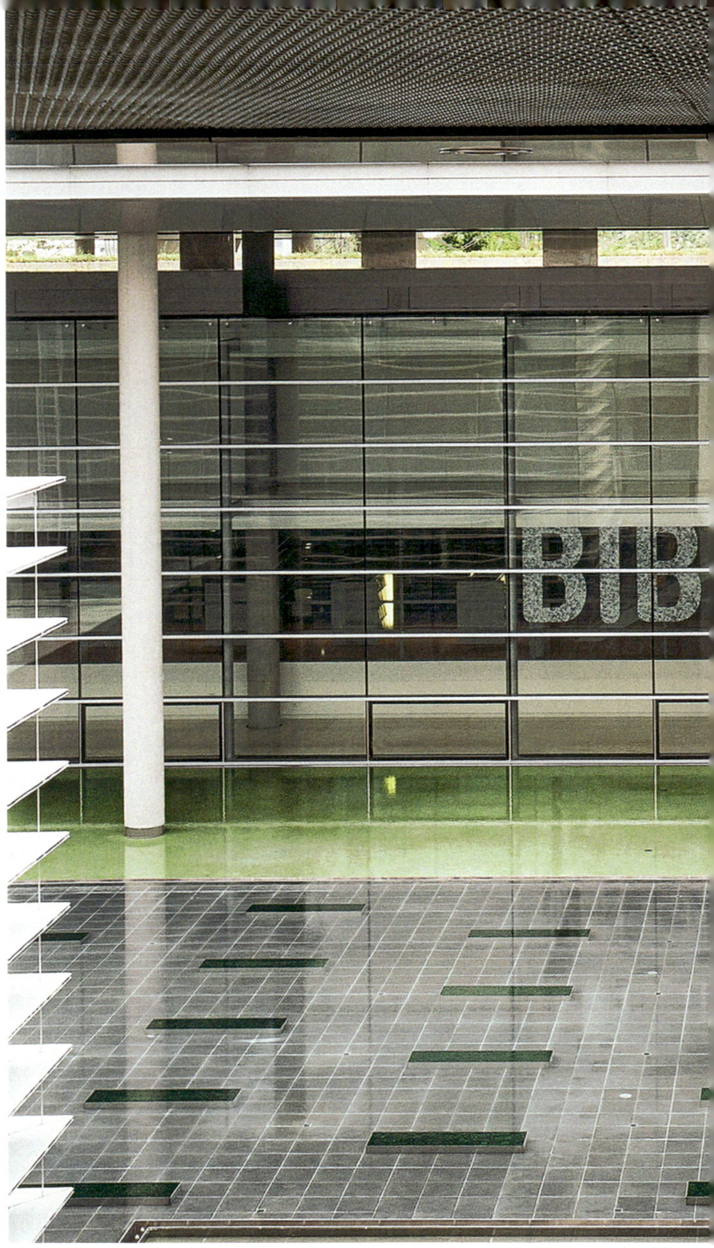

262

Martha Schwartz / “Pool – Underwater Landscape” and “Blue Cubes”

location: Swiss Re Germany AG, headquarters, Munich-Unterföhring, DE / BRT Bothe Richter Teherani Architects / Martha Schwartz with Peter Kluska landscape architects and designer. / **year:** 2002 / **technique:** glass mosaic, glass cubes

In the courtyard of Swiss Re’s German headquarter building, Martha Schwartz has created a mixture of landscape architecture and “outdoor art” that incorporates live plants. The result is an intermingling of landscape, architecture, plants, and artificial objects, which all come together in a large scale sculpture. Mayer of Munich contributed the blue, green, yellow, and red mosaics measuring 6500 square feet and the 115 blue glass cubes as “artificial objects”.

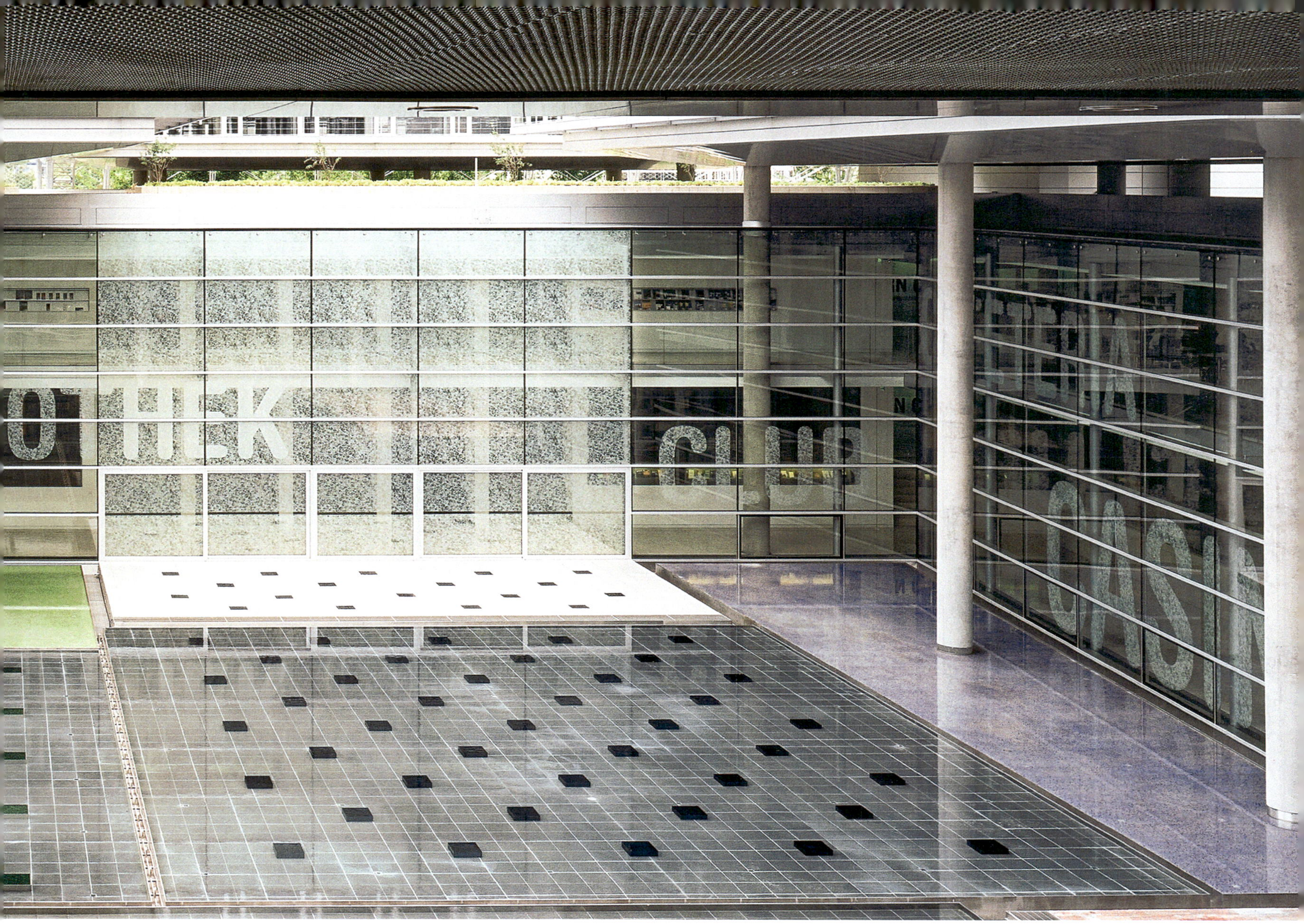

POOL – UNDERWATER LANDSCAPE

261
Detail of the green underwater “mosaic”-areas.

262
Section of the interior courtyard showing parts of the green and blue mosaics plus some of the small glass cubes.

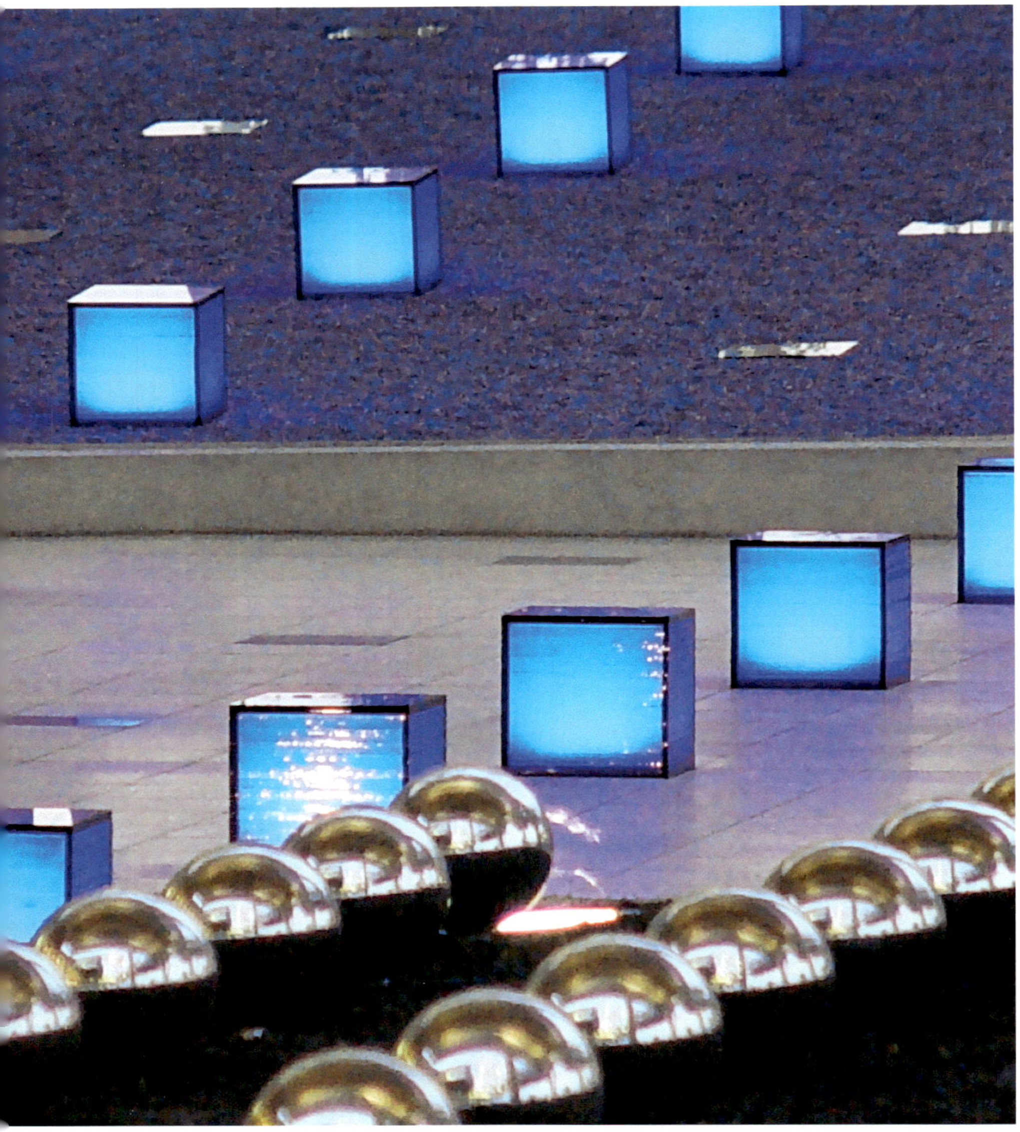

263

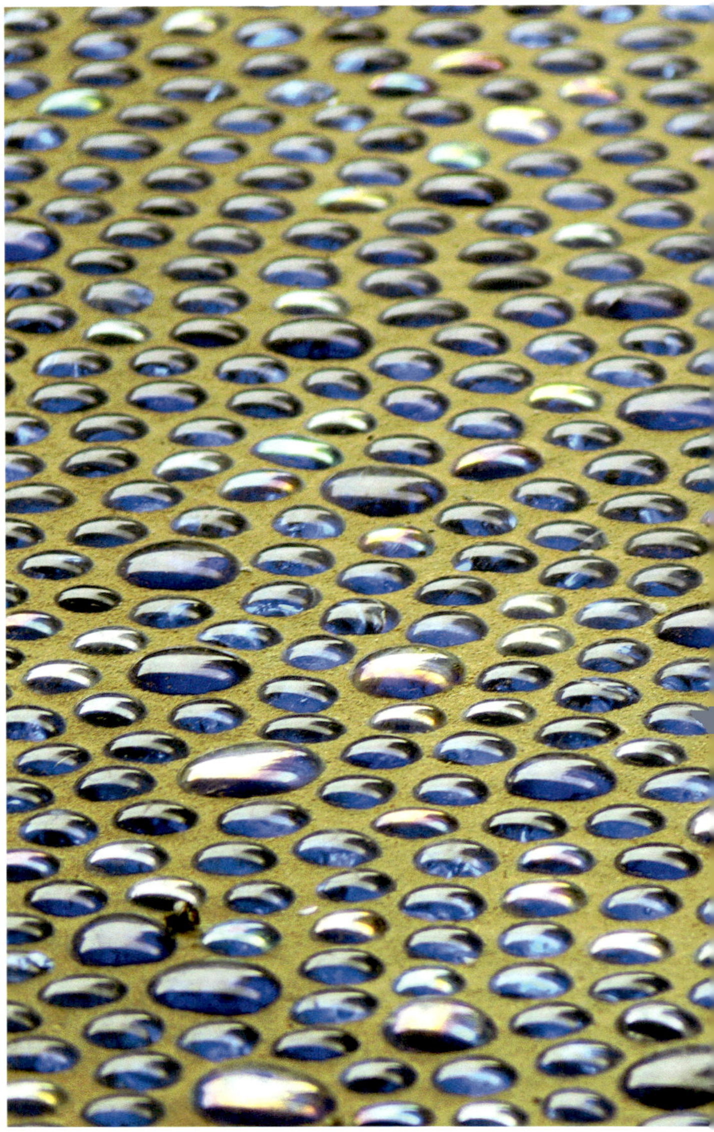

264

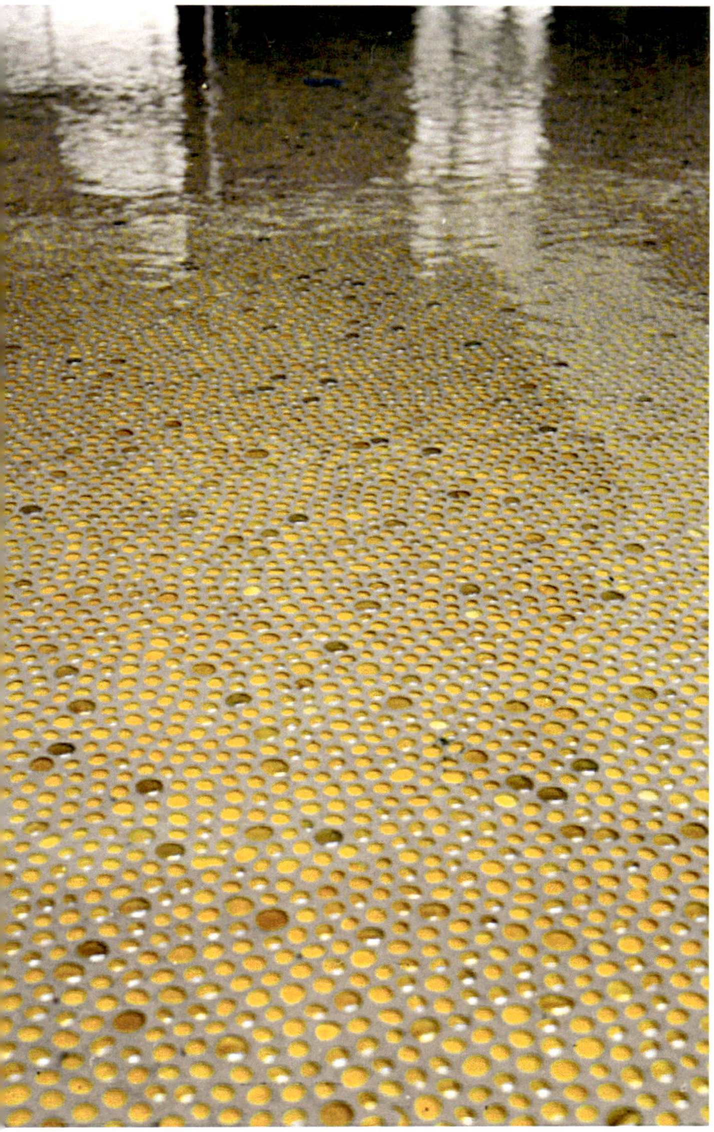

265

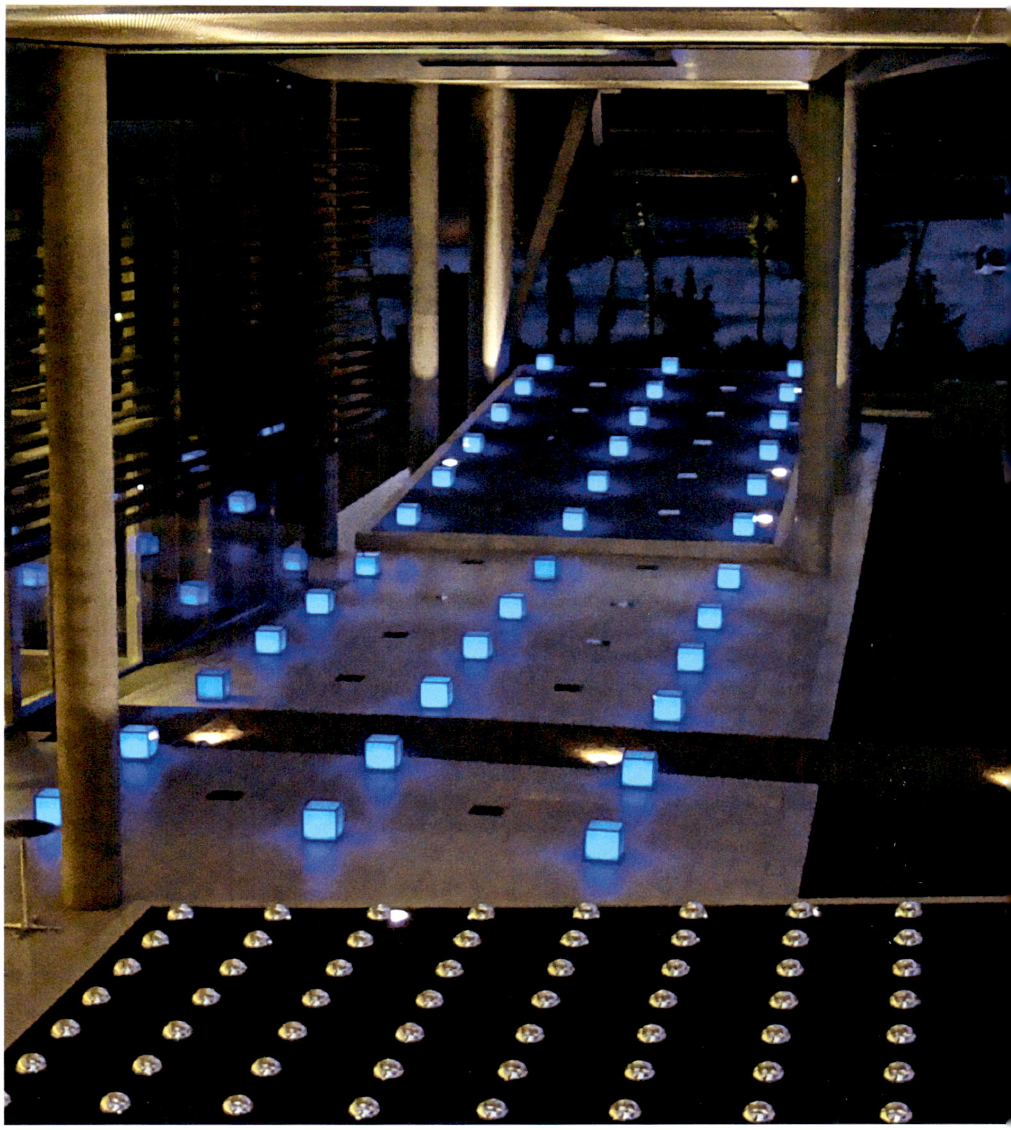

266

POOL – UNDERWATER LANDSCAPE BLUE CUBES

263
Detail of the blue cubes revealing the layering of the glass edges, cut by hand and water jet. In the foreground, the silvery glass balls may be seen.

264
Details of the blue, partly iridescent mosaics.

265
Section of the yellow mosaics.

266
The larger blue cubes – lit at night – in the outer garden.

INTERACTION STAIRCASE

267
A detail of the glass design from the corridor side: Glass melting color print in front of the mirror layers.

268
This is (almost) a full view of one of a total of 17 glass walls with the mirror and color forming a transparent network. They are beautiful if seen from the front corridor or the stairs.

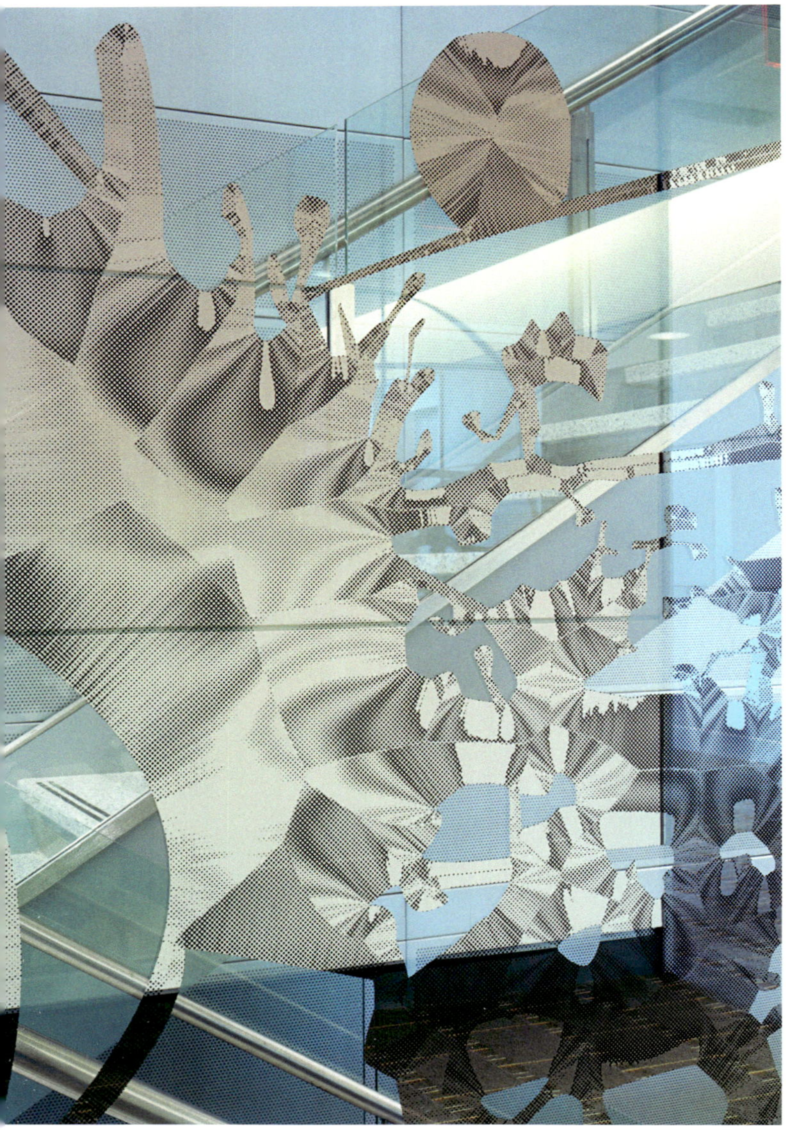

267

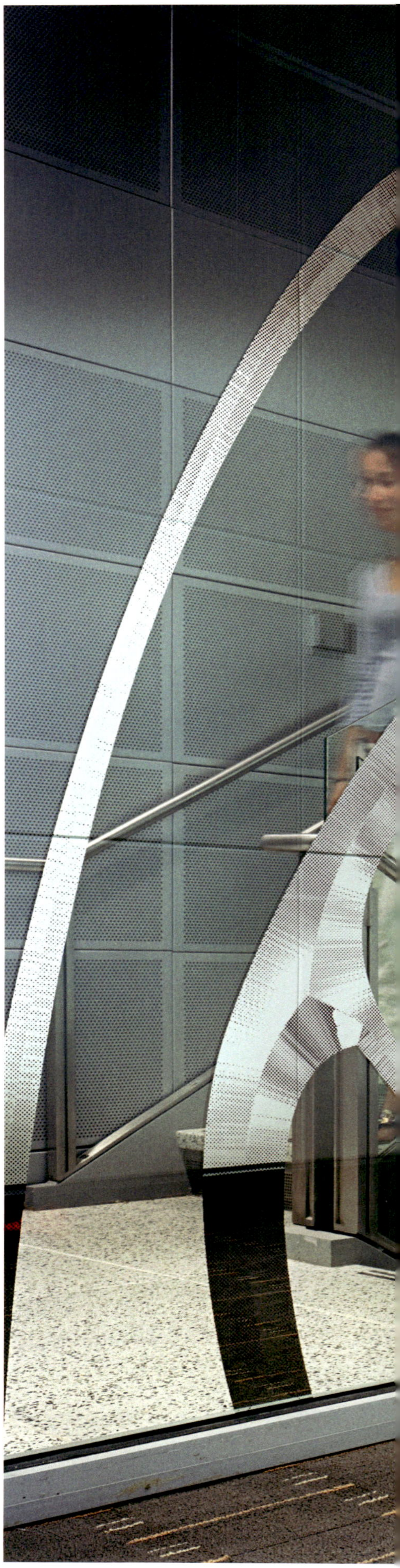

268

Alyson Shotz / "Transitional Objects in Two and Four Dimensions"

location: MSK – Zuckerman Research Center, New York, NY, USA / Architects SOM and ZGF / **year:** 2006 / **technique:** mirror, ceramic glass melting colors

17 glass walls and 2500 square feet of designed glass between the corridors and the stairwell from floors 4 to 9 and 11 to 21.

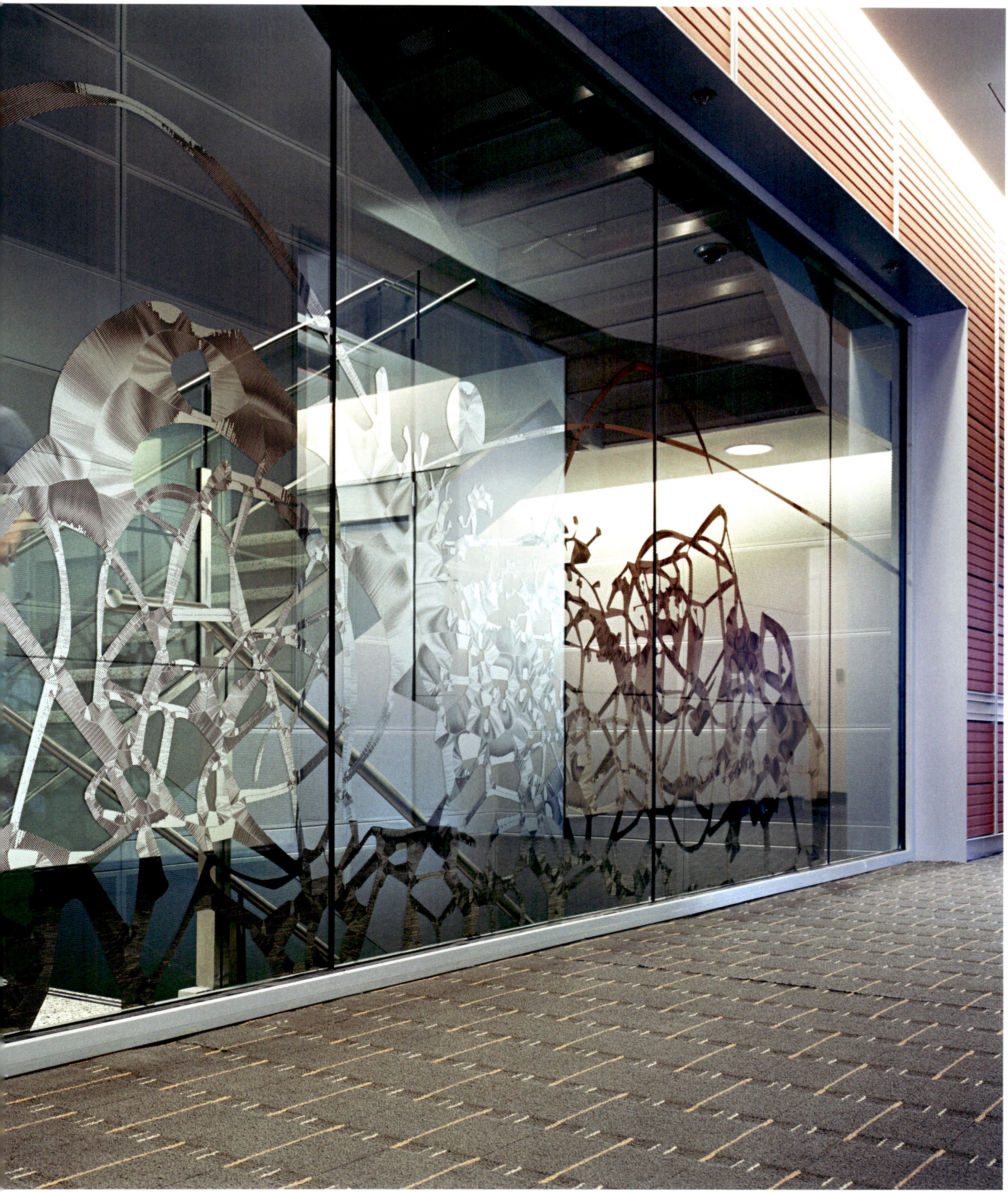

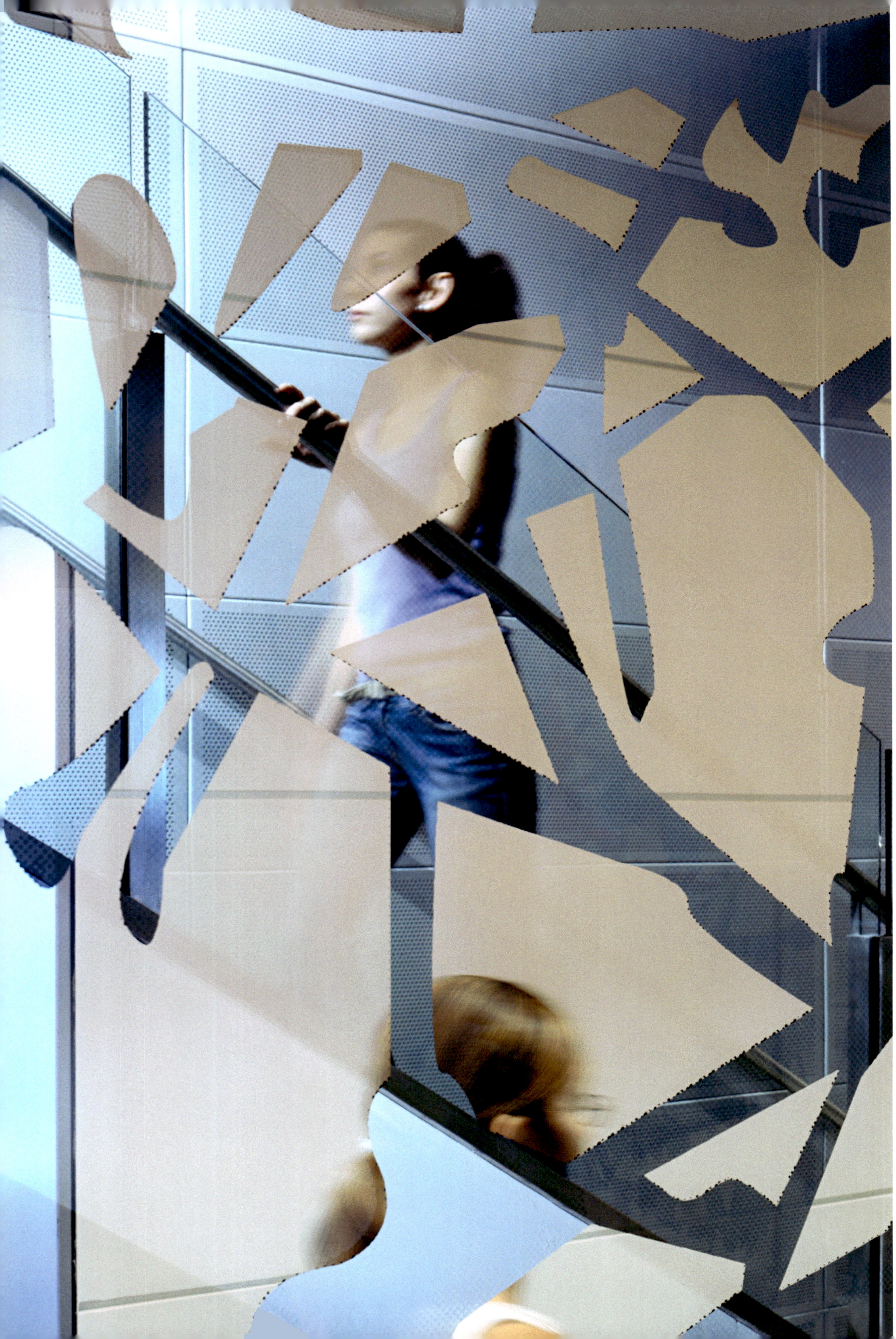

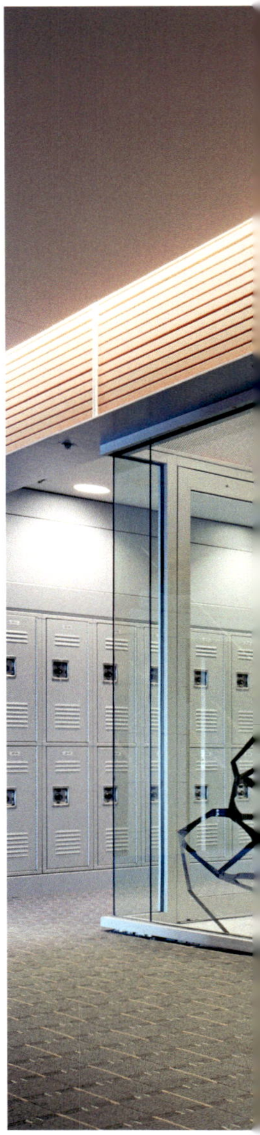

270

269

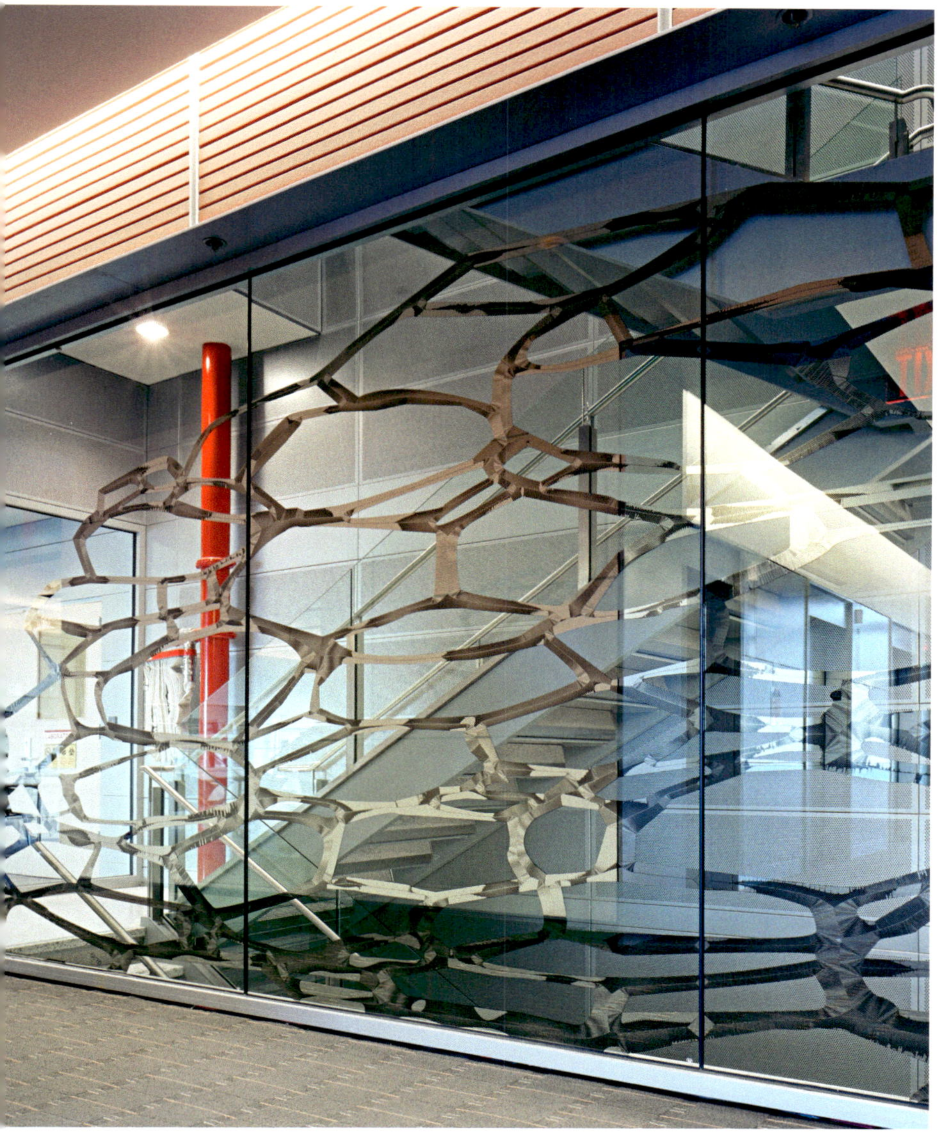

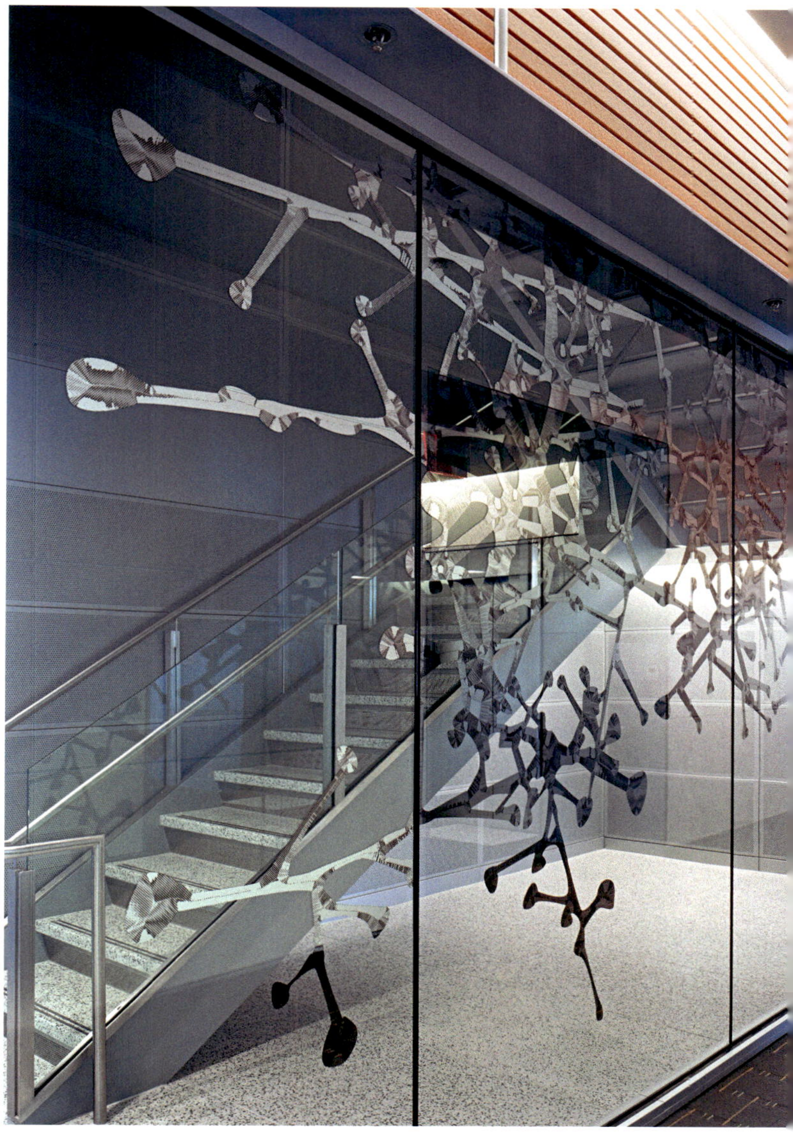

271

INTERACTION STAIRCASE

269
View through a network of mirrors and reflection.

270 + 271
Two different glass walls, each seen from the corridor.

Art that is drawn through 17 floors of one the leading US cancer research centers. The concept of the artist is to encourage a mutual exchange within one atmosphere of separated work. The intention was to create a permanent art installation that unfolds from one floor to the next: an "interaction staircase" (Alyson Shotz). Thanks to fantasy, knowledge, and experiment, high-quality art was created, which was, at the time, executed in the most innovative design technique. This was another "percent for art" project where Mayer of Munich's pioneering spirit in finding and applying the latest designing techniques could be sensed.

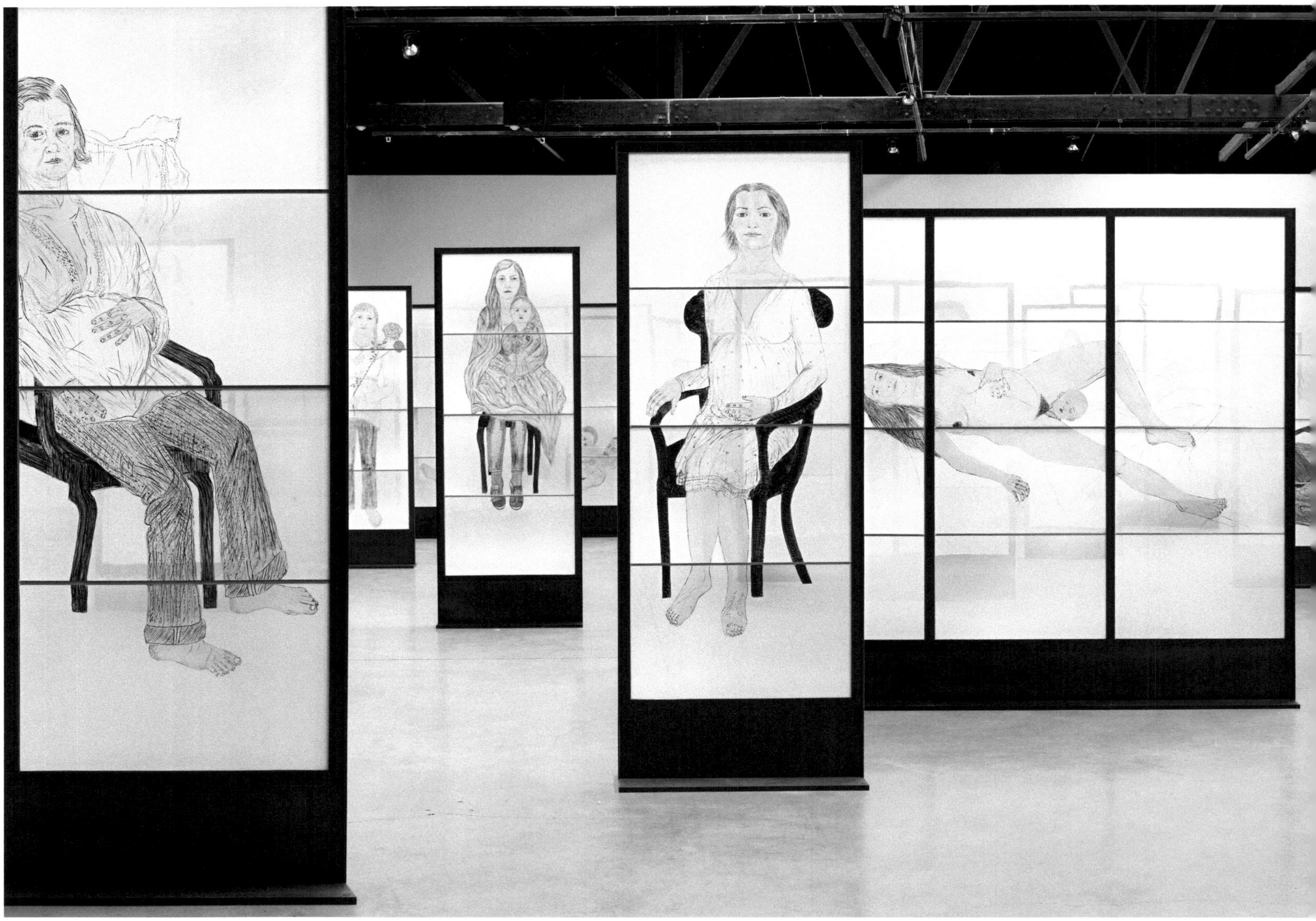

272

Kiki Smith / "Her Home" (Krefeld) and "Pilgrim" (Pace NYC)

location: Museums, among others Krefeld and Nuremberg, DE, Barcelona, ES, Brooklyn, and Pace Gallery, New York, NY, USA / Kiki Smith© / Courtesy: The Pace Gallery. Stained glass, Steel Frames / **year:** 2007–10 / **technique:** stained glass, steel frames

The artist herself painted the hand-blown opal flashed glass in the Munich studio; glass fired, leaded; stelae and pictures each circa 8 ¼ feet high and up to 11 feet wide (varying width).
Between 2007 and 2010, New York artist Kiki Smith and Mayer of Munich produced numerous glass paintings. The pieces were shown between 2008 and 2010 in various important museums like Krefeld, Nuremberg, Barcelona, and Brooklyn. The most comprehensive exhibition of the material (each year new glass paintings were added) happened in 2010 at the Pace Gallery in New York, where the steel-framed and leaded stained glass paintings were shown.

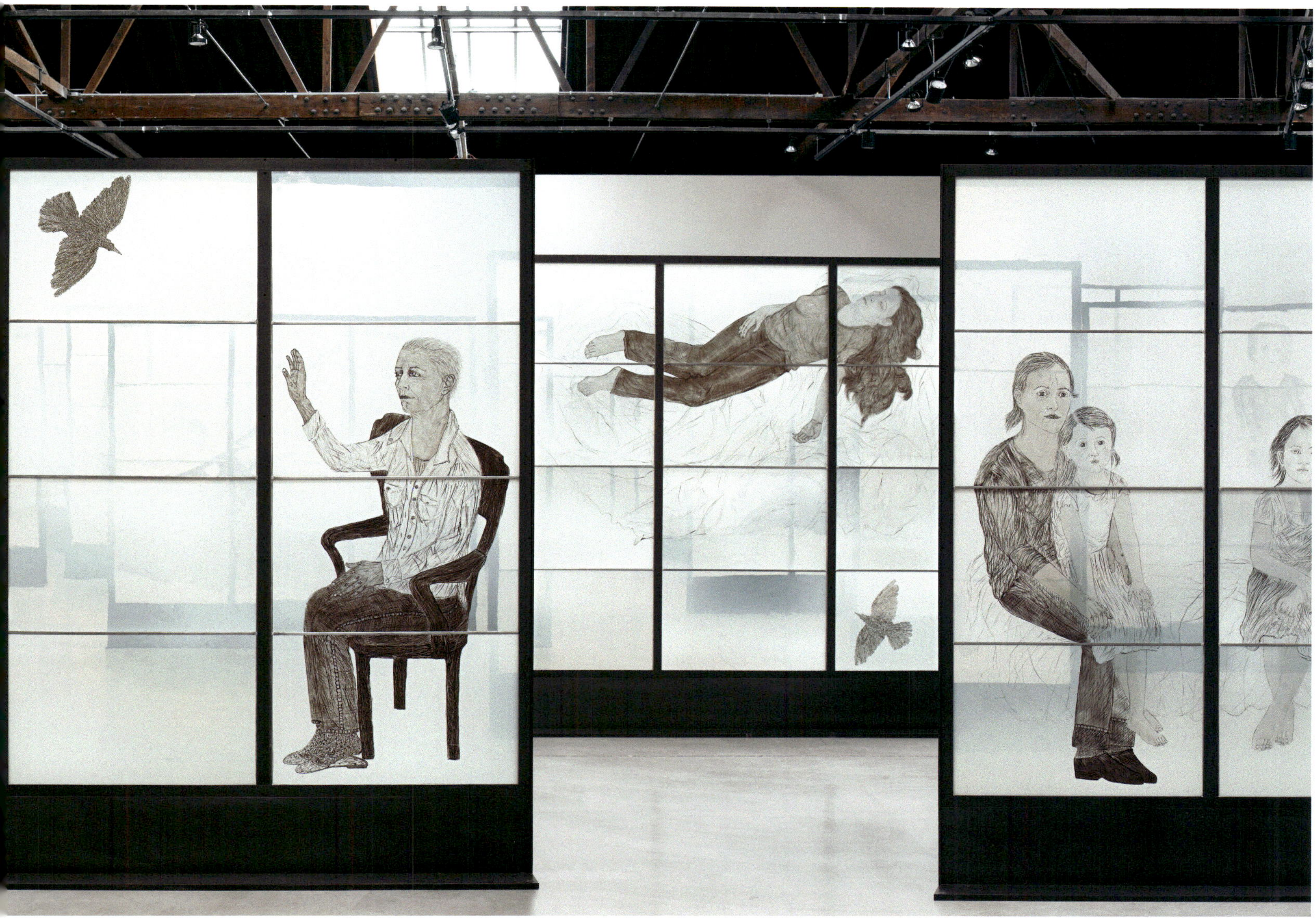

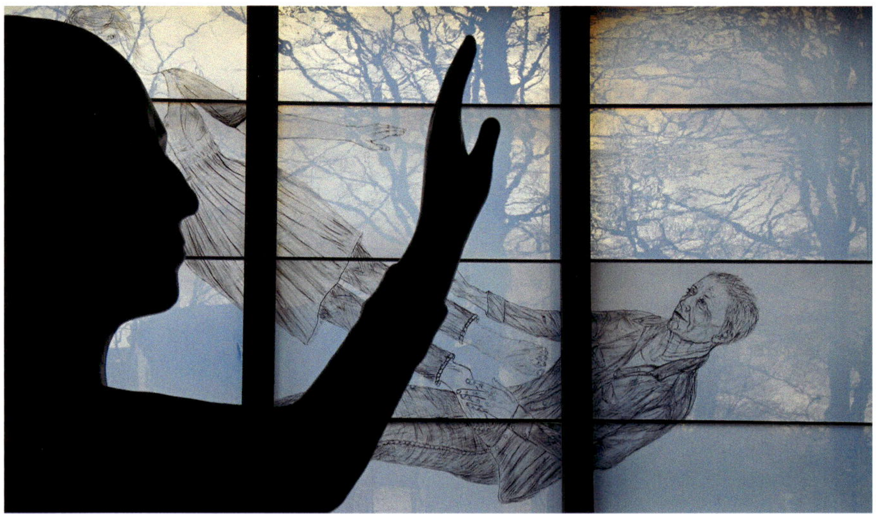

273

HER HOME
PILGRIM

272

A section of the exhibition at Pace Gallery, Chelsea, NYC 2010. This exhibition showed nearly all of the glass paintings, which were made between 2007 and 2010. They were steel-framed and freestanding in the interior space.

273

An image from the exhibition "Her Home" at the Museum Haus Esters in Krefeld, 2008. The sculpture in the foreground is an aluminum silhouette of a woman. Here, the stained glass was installed in the window frames.

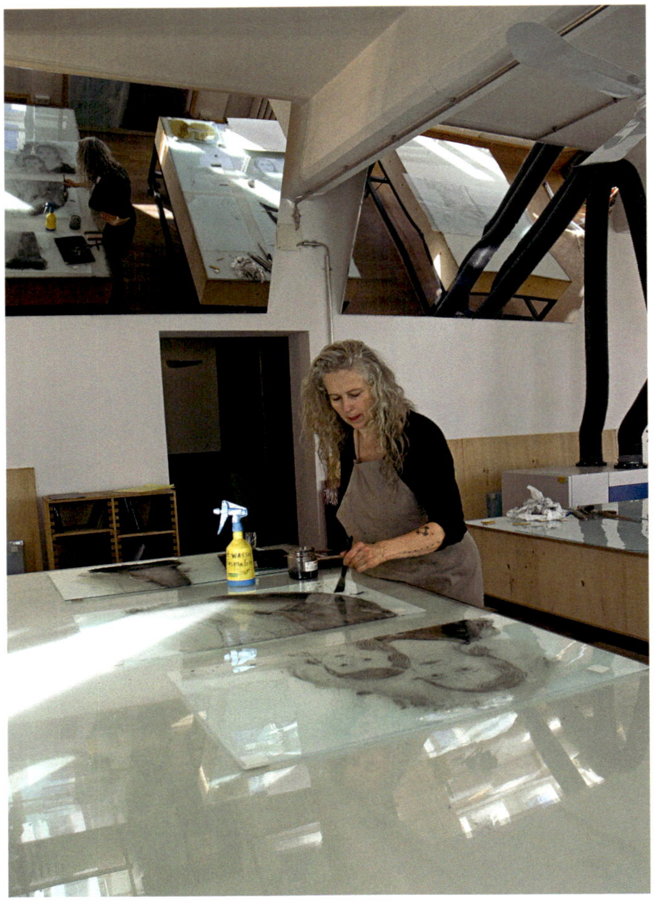

274

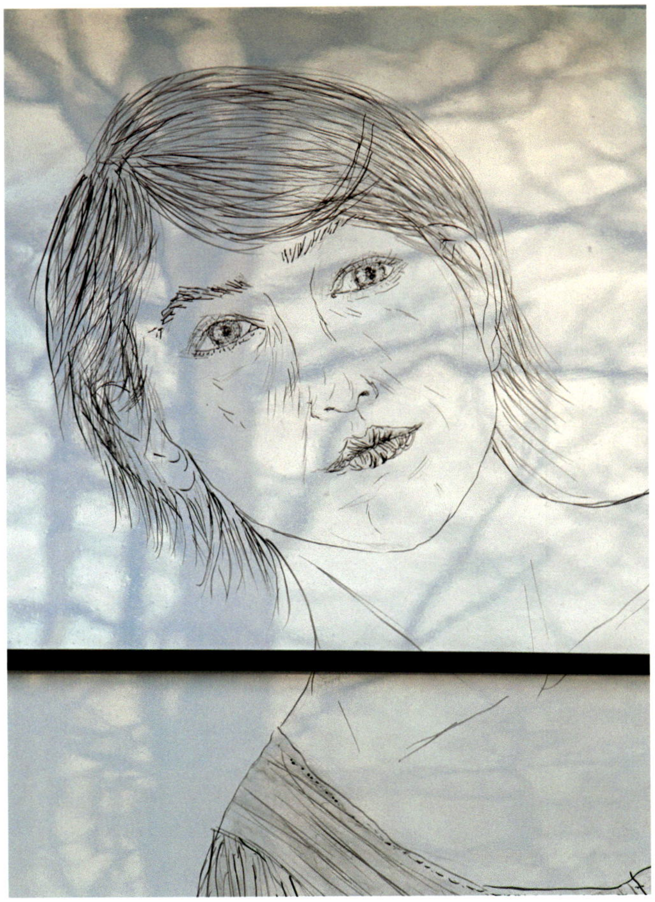

275

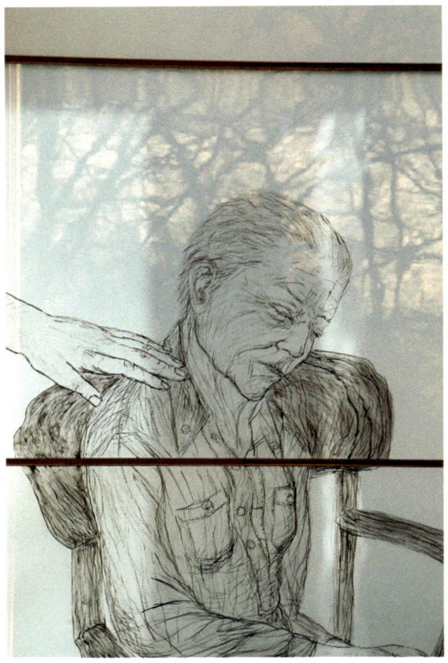

276

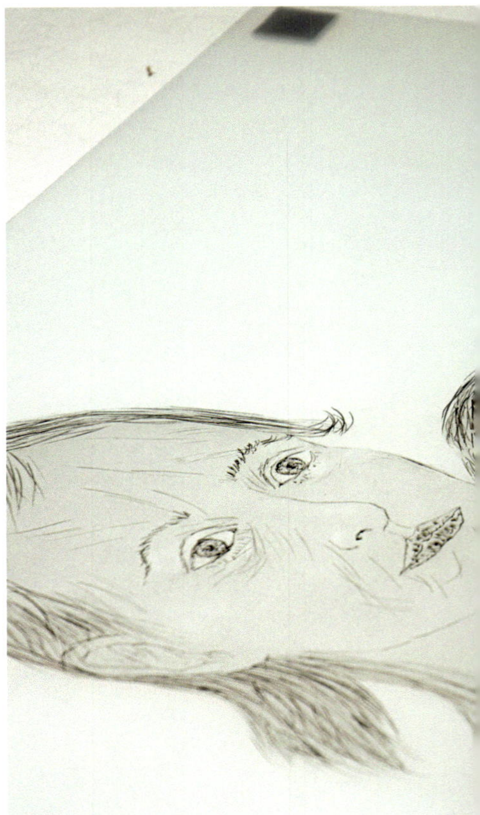

277

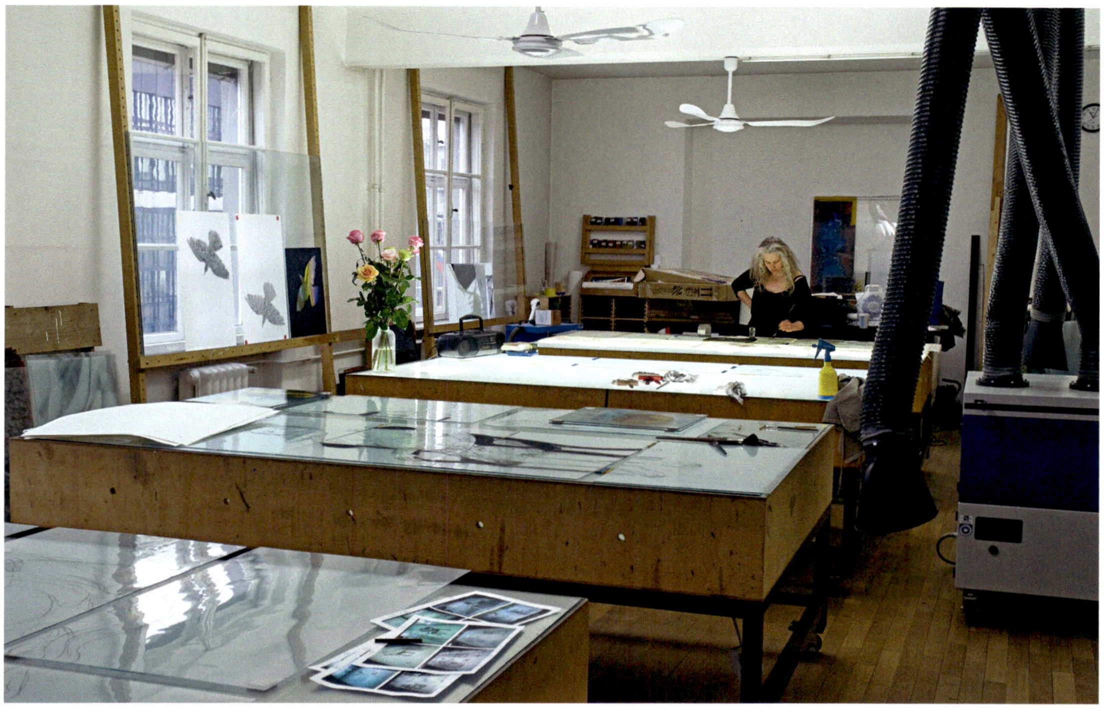

278

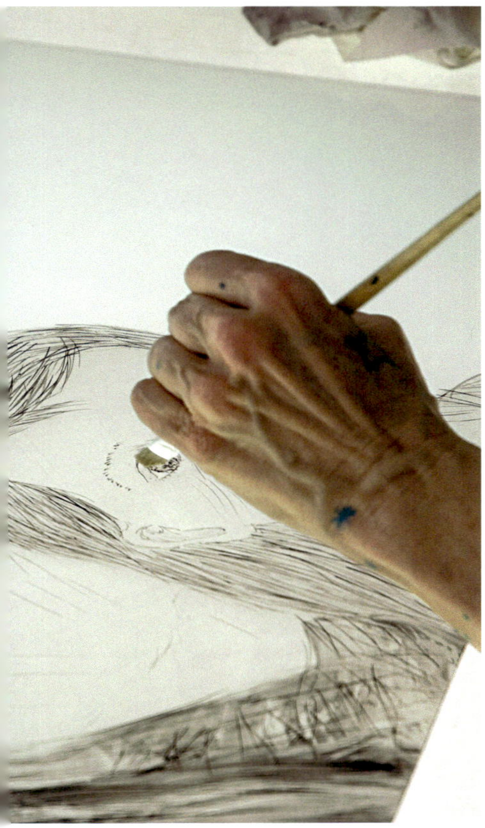

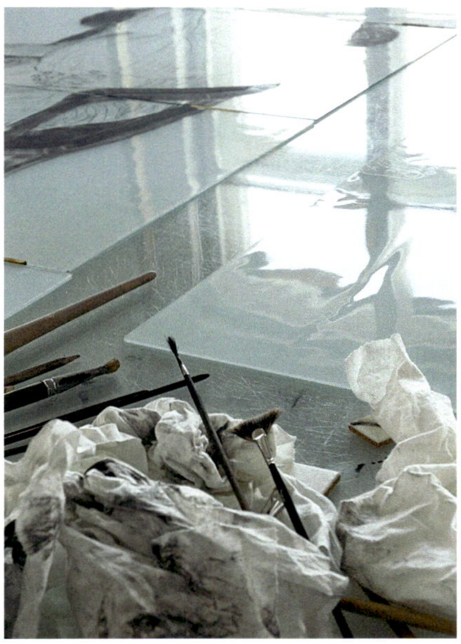

279

KIKI SMITH – WORKING IN MUNICH

274
At the Mayer studio, glass and light tables, mirrors.

275 + 276
Two details from the 2008 Krefeld show – at the time, the stained glass was installed in the window.

277
The hand during the painting process.

278
Kiki Smith often works until late at night in "her" studio at Mayer of Munich.

279
Still life.

Kiki Smith has used diverse materials during her career, including bronze, rice paper, and glass. She started the work with glass in 1985 at the New York Experimental Glass Workshop. Since 2005 she began to become fascinated by the glass.

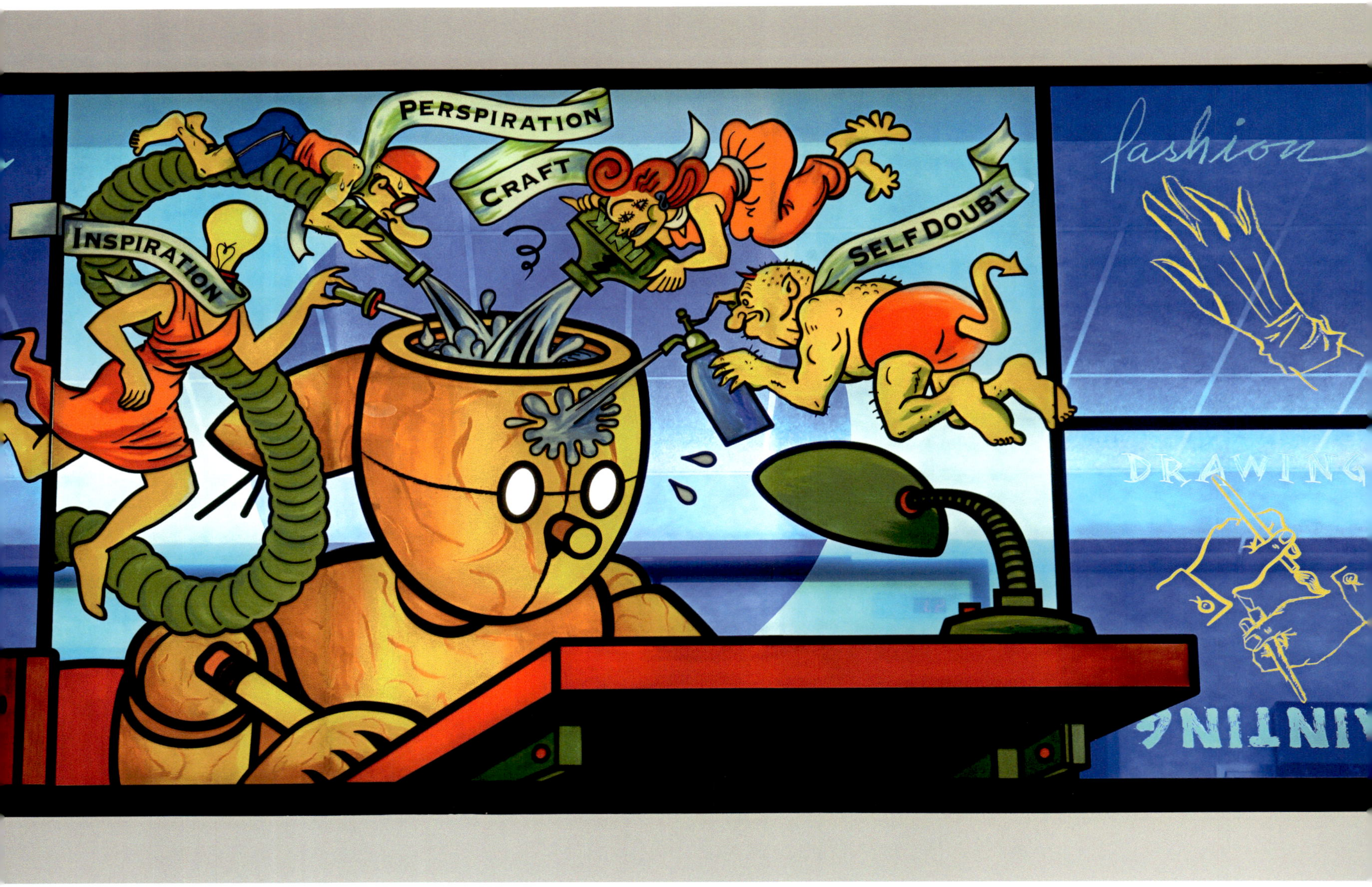

280

Art Spiegelman / "It was Today, only Yesterday"

198

location: High School of Art and Design, Manhattan, NY, USA / SOM Architects / NYC SCA, Public Art for Public Schools / **year:** 2012 / **technique:** float glass painting

Wall made of art glass 8 × 49 feet. Opaque and transparent glass melting colors, silkscreen, engraving, hand painting, laminated glass.
"Before this, I have never worked with images that were larger than 4 inches." In the summer of 2012, the Frankfurter Allgemeine Zeitung published a two-page article entitled "Genie in buntes Glas gefasst", i.e. Genius Set in Multi-Color Glass, about Art Spiegelman and the creation of the window for his former high school in Manhattan.

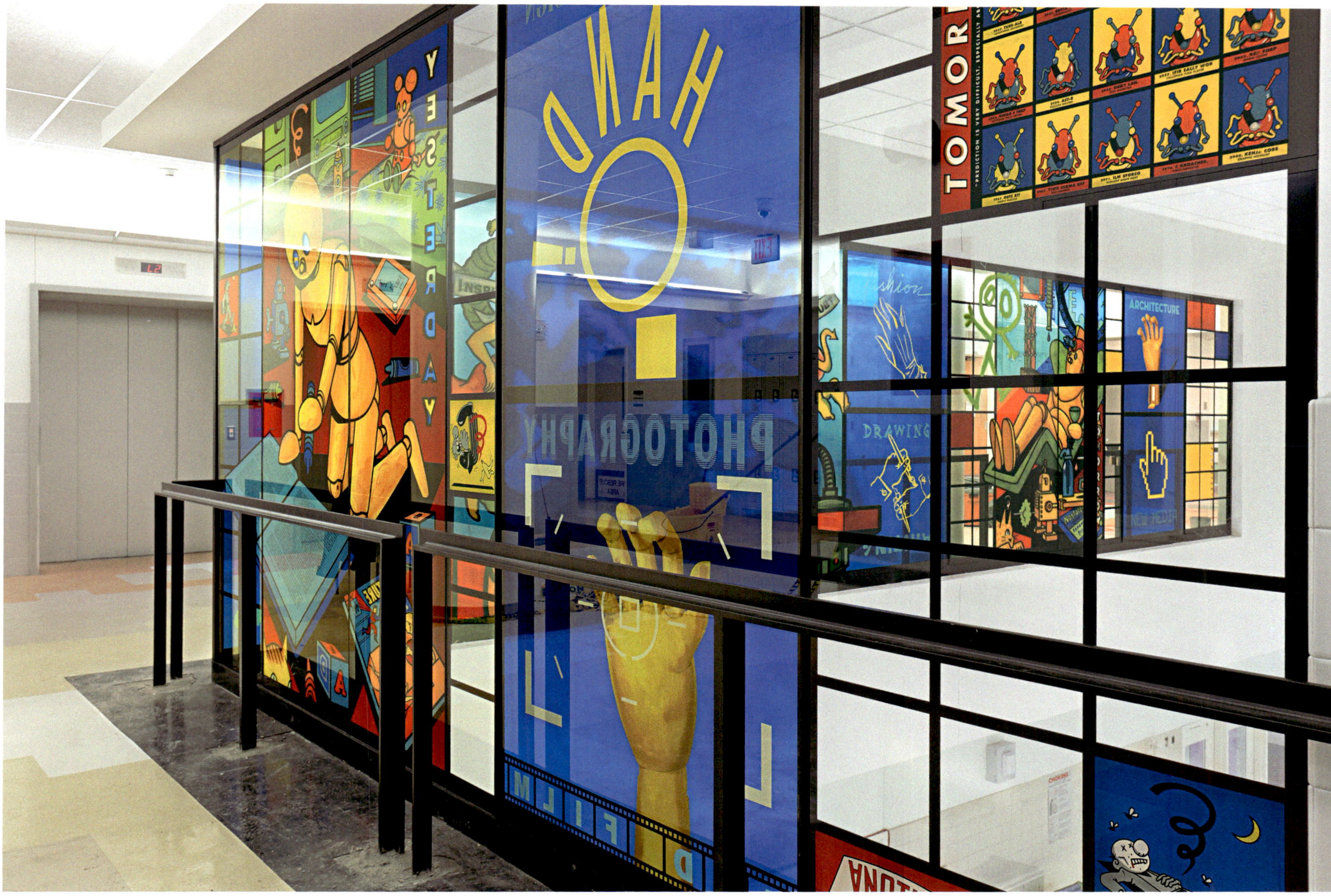

281

IT WAS TODAY, ONLY YESTERDAY

280
A section of the 8 feet high comic strip window in the two-story hall seen from below. Detail of the theme "Today:" "spirits" are filling the head of the student manikin – inspiration, perspiration, craft, self-doubt.

281
The windows extend along the front and side walls in the upper portion of the cafeteria hall. This is a view from the upper corridor into the hall. It is possible to see front and back of the glass and at the same time the mix of "reverse glass painting" and "stained glass" of the artwork.

Mayer of Munich transformed the "ideas of the maverick comic strip artist ... almost perfectly into the 'giant format' so unusual for him." Glass painter Marcela Teal was the "congenial artist". (Quoted from Andreas Platthaus: Art Spiegelmann, Frankfurter Allgemeine Zeitung, 24.1.2012)

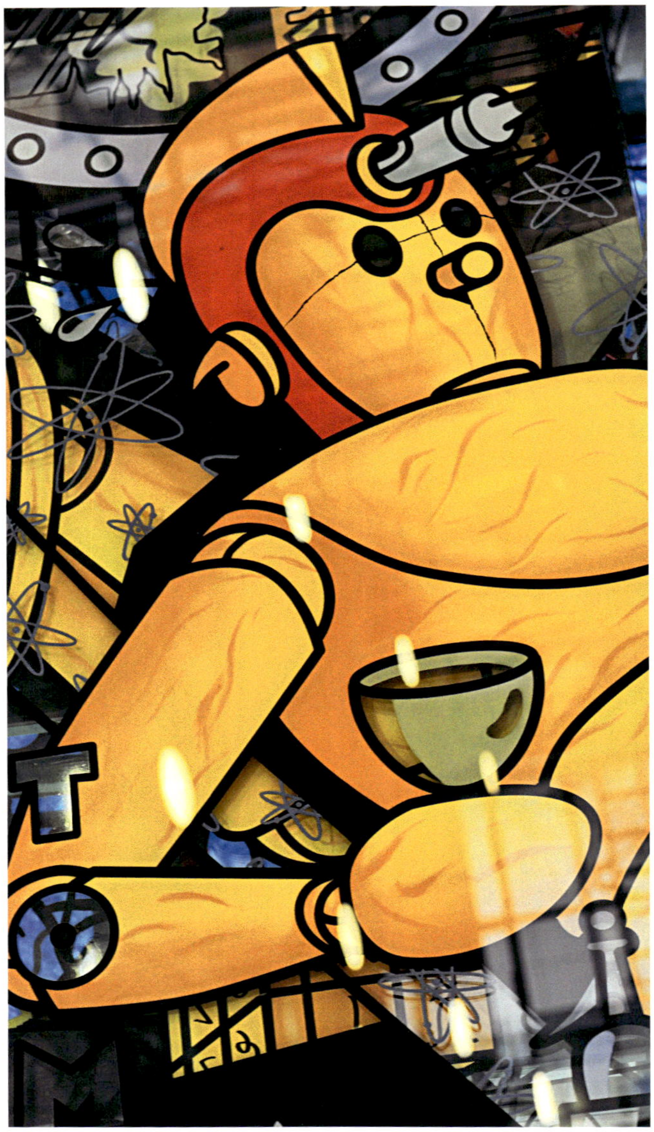

282

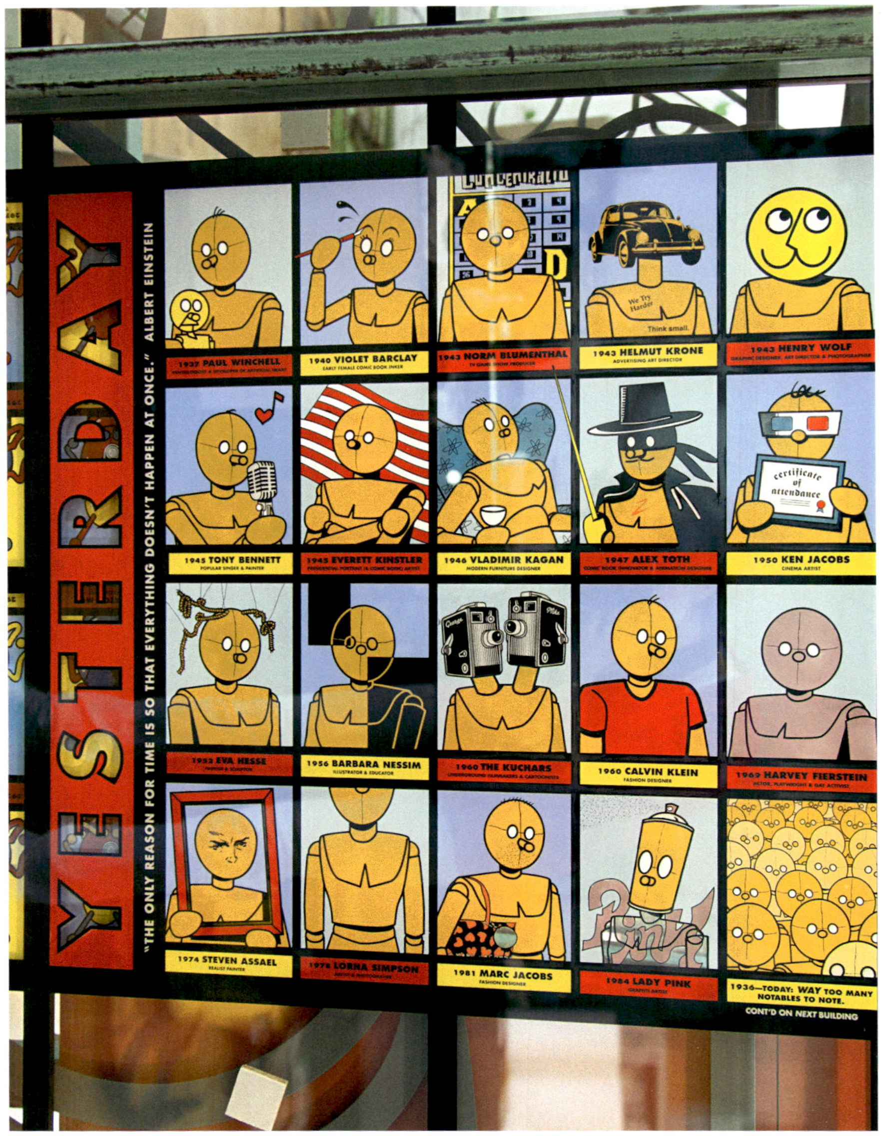

283

One of the challenges for the studio was to combine the reverse glass painting and traditional stained glass techniques. The effects of opaque ceramic color had to be merged with the transparent qualities. The graphic lines on the corridor side had to be done in silkscreen; the cafeteria side in engraving and color.

ART SPIEGELMAN –
STUDIO WORK IN MUNICH

282
Detail of the student manikin from "Tomorrow."

283
A small and very detailed panel from "Yesterday," towards the corridor side.

284
Marcela Teal painting.

285
Detail with hands.

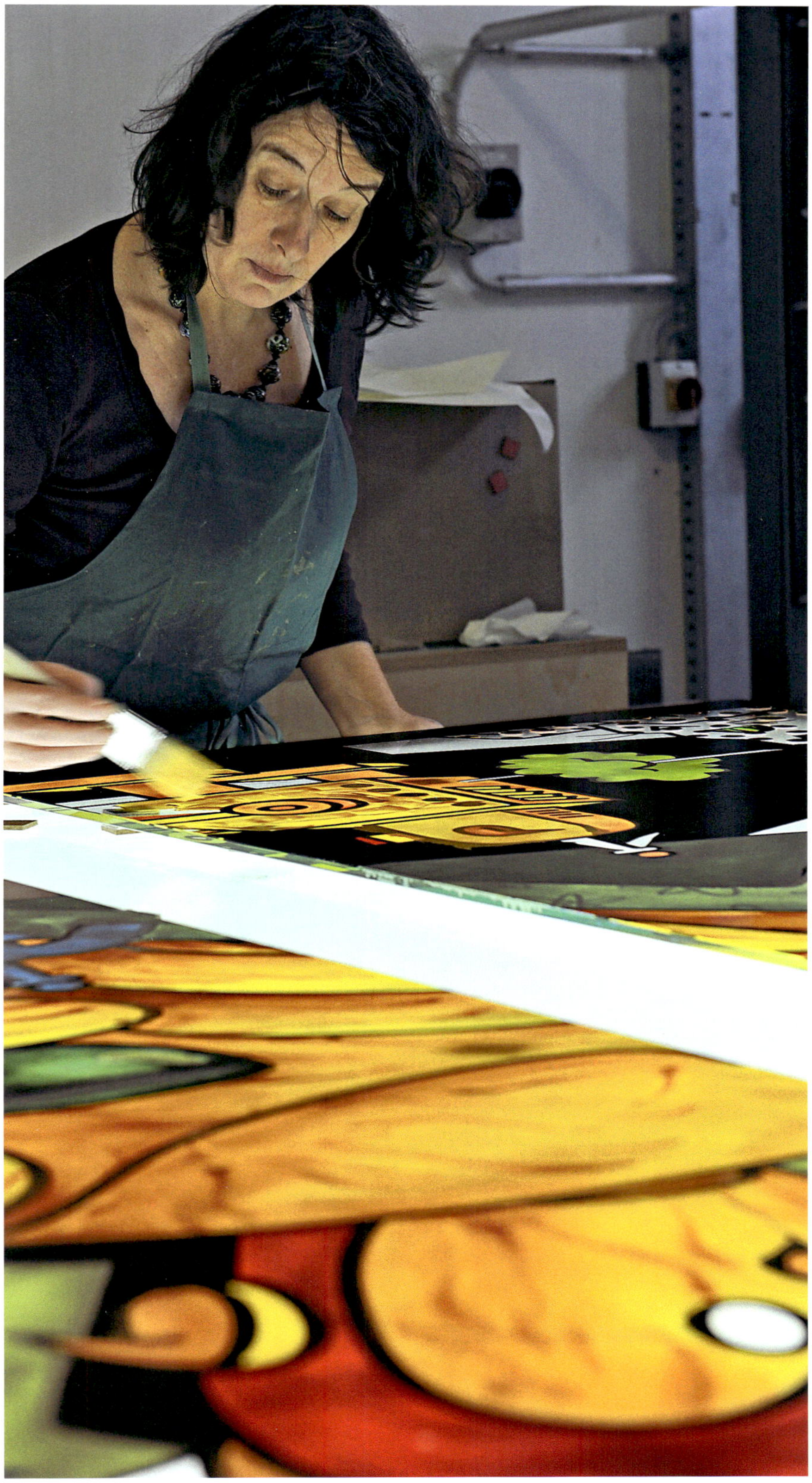

284

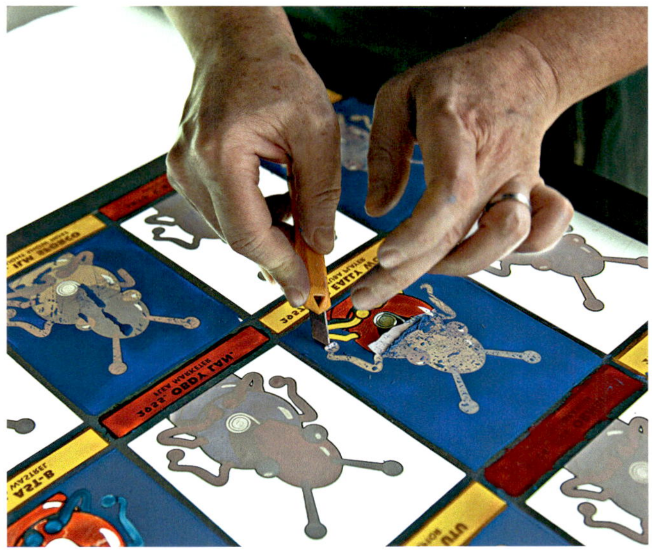

285

"I like the idea that my today in this high school was yesterday and for future students tomorrow will be today. Therefore the piece is called 'It Was Today, Only Yesterday'." (Spiegelman-Interview in Architectural Digest 5, 2012)

Commissioned by the NYC Department of Education and the NYC School Construction Authority Public Art for Public Schools Program, in collaboration with the NYC Department of Cultural Affairs Percent for Art Program.

286

The art glass piece in the central portion of the escalators. The glass panels, just under one inch thick, are mounted with invisible bolts onto a system of aluminum profiles placed behind the glass.

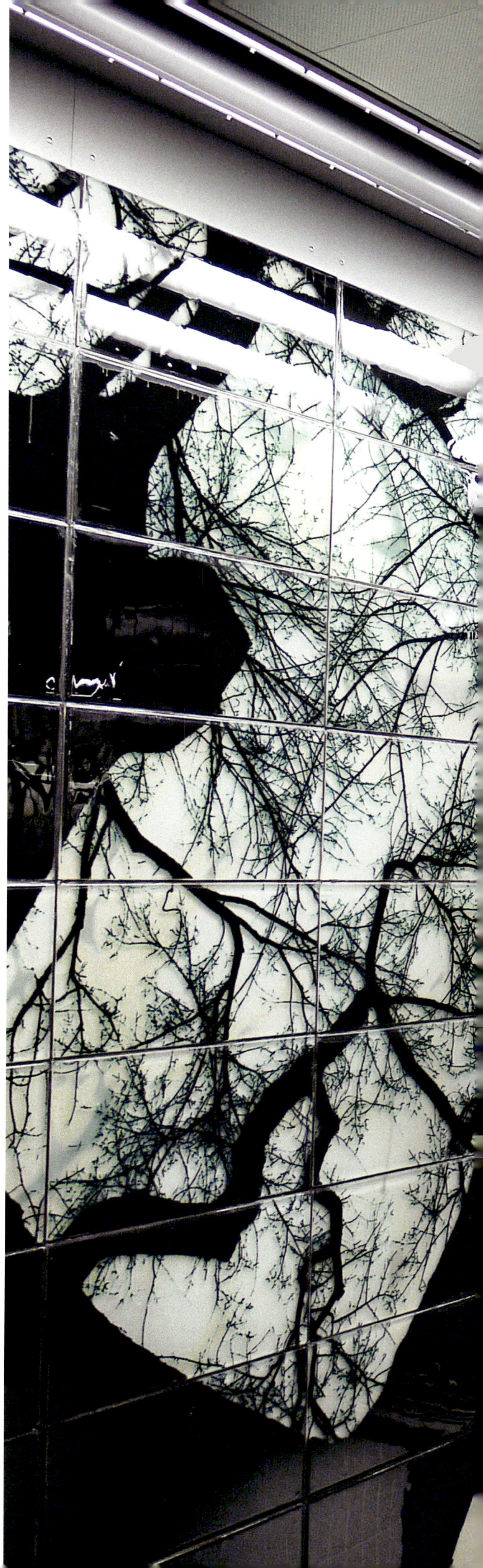

Mike and Doug Starn / "See it Split, See it Change"

location: South Ferry Station, New York City Transit, New York, NY, USA / MTA Arts for Transit / **year:** 2009 / **technique:** fused glass and marble mosaic

Thanks to the five-layered fusing glass technique – where the individual layers are worked quite differently – the studio and the artists managed to evoke the softness and the transparency of winter fog, behind which the sun can only be gathered, in a very beautiful way.

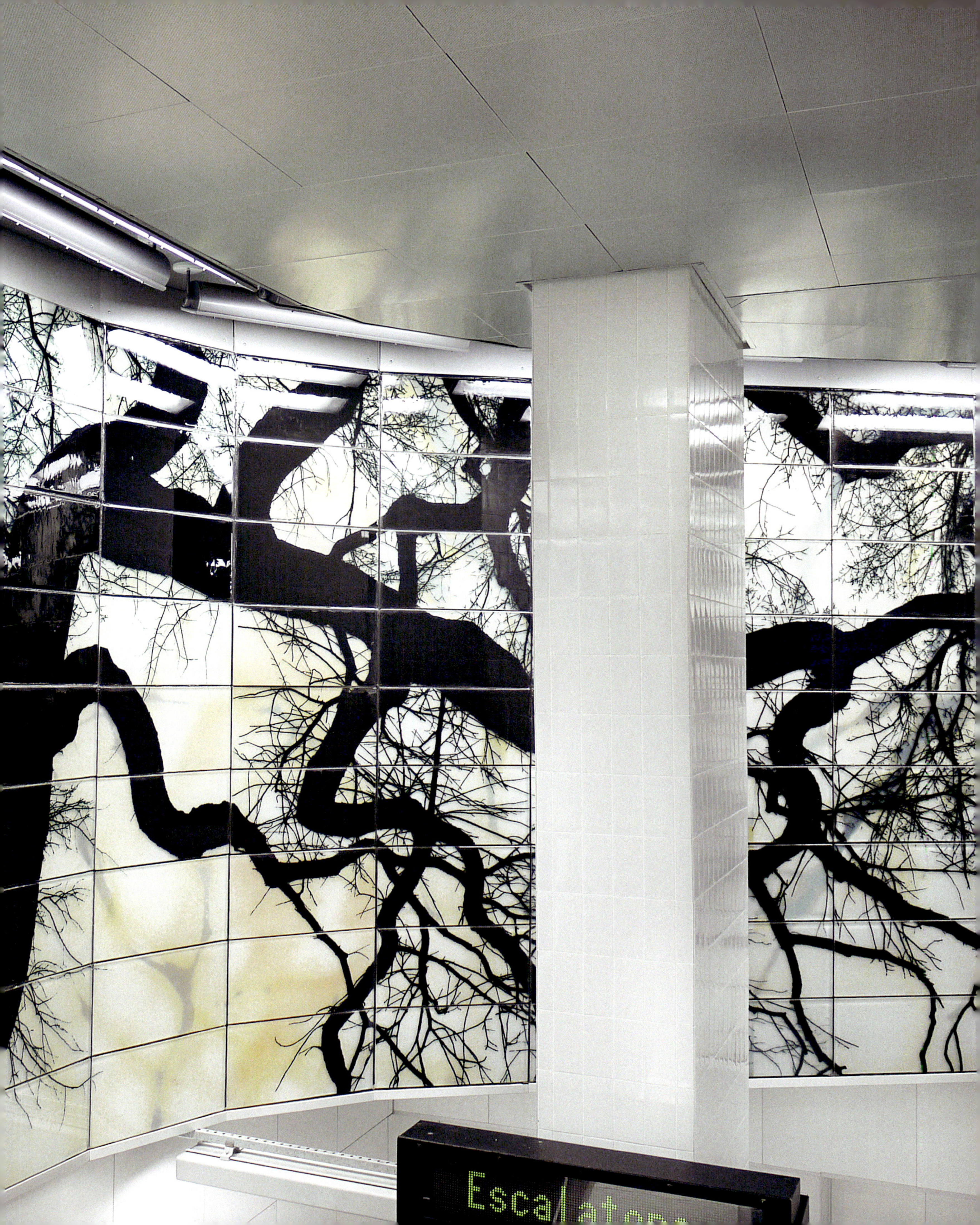
Escal

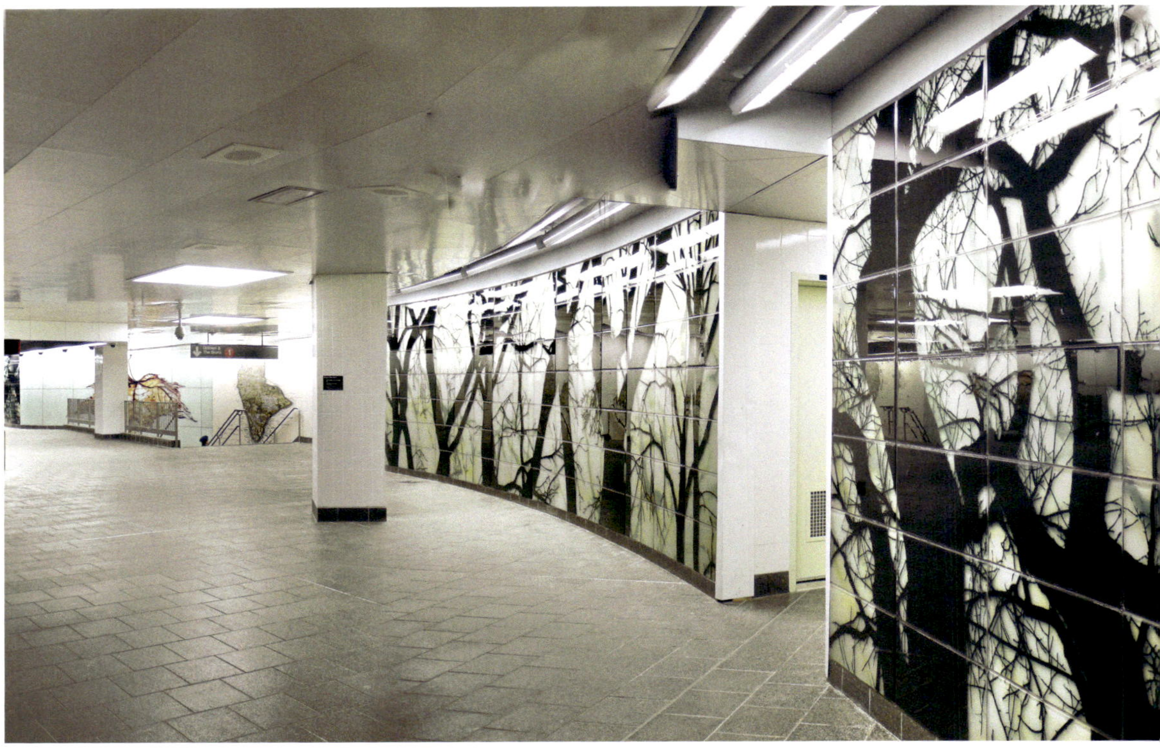

287

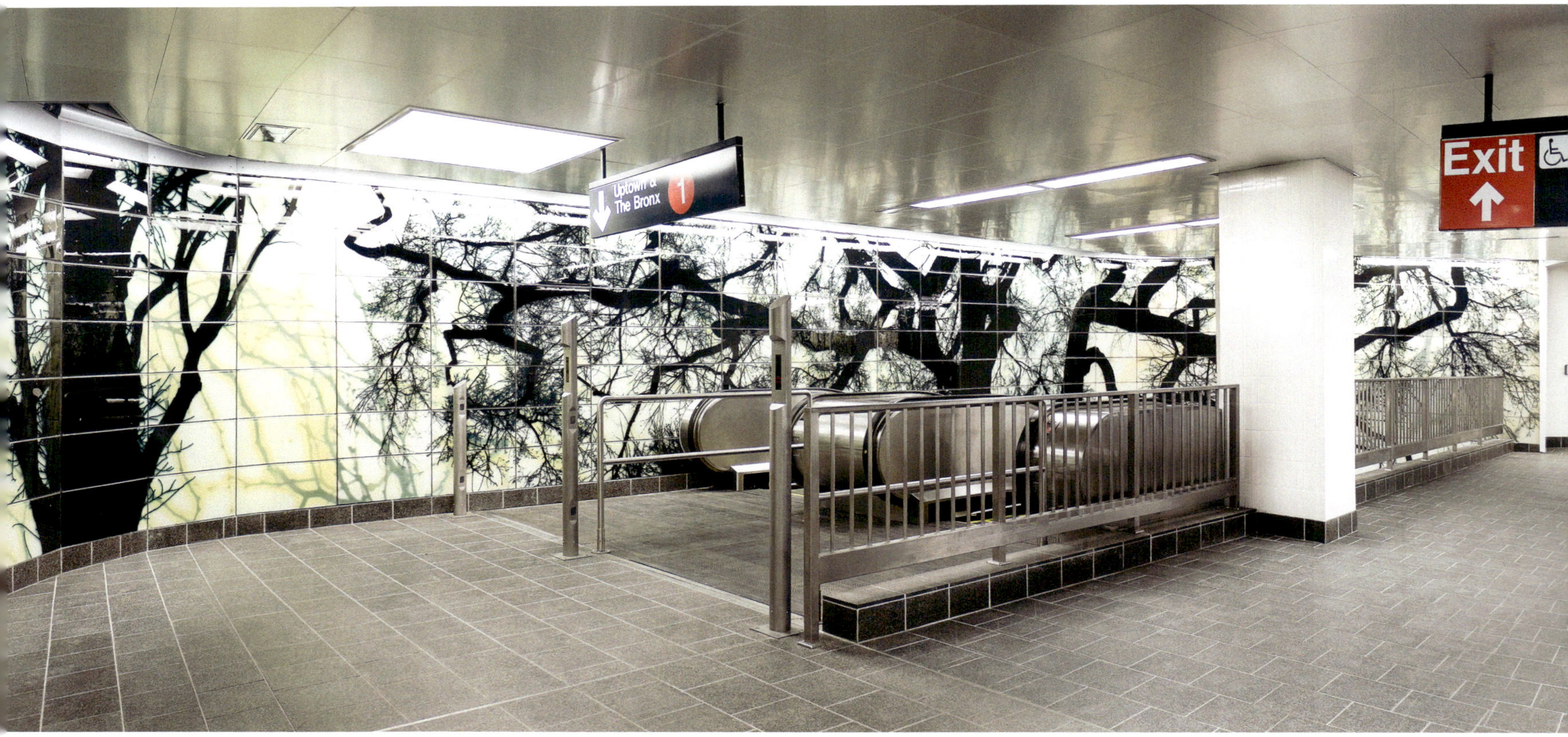

288

287 + 288
Two partial views of the long wall of the mezzanine.

289
The cartographic mosaic of Manhattan, set in "two-layer-technique."

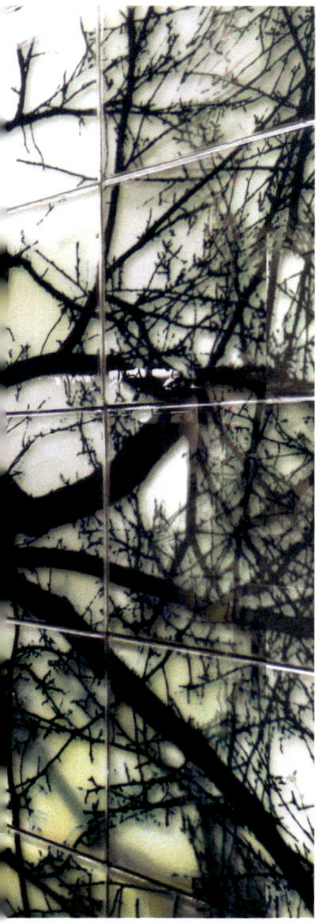

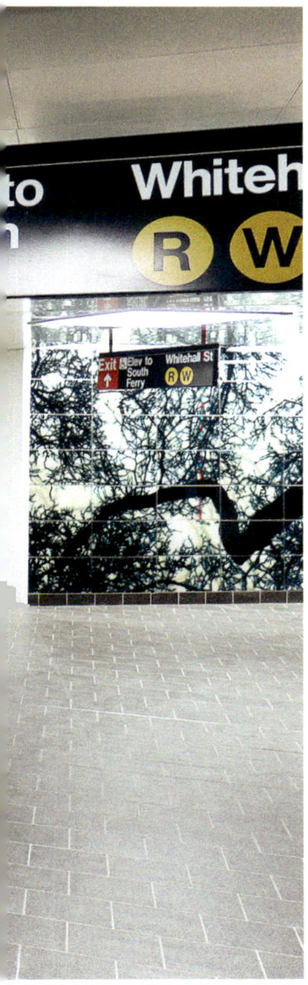

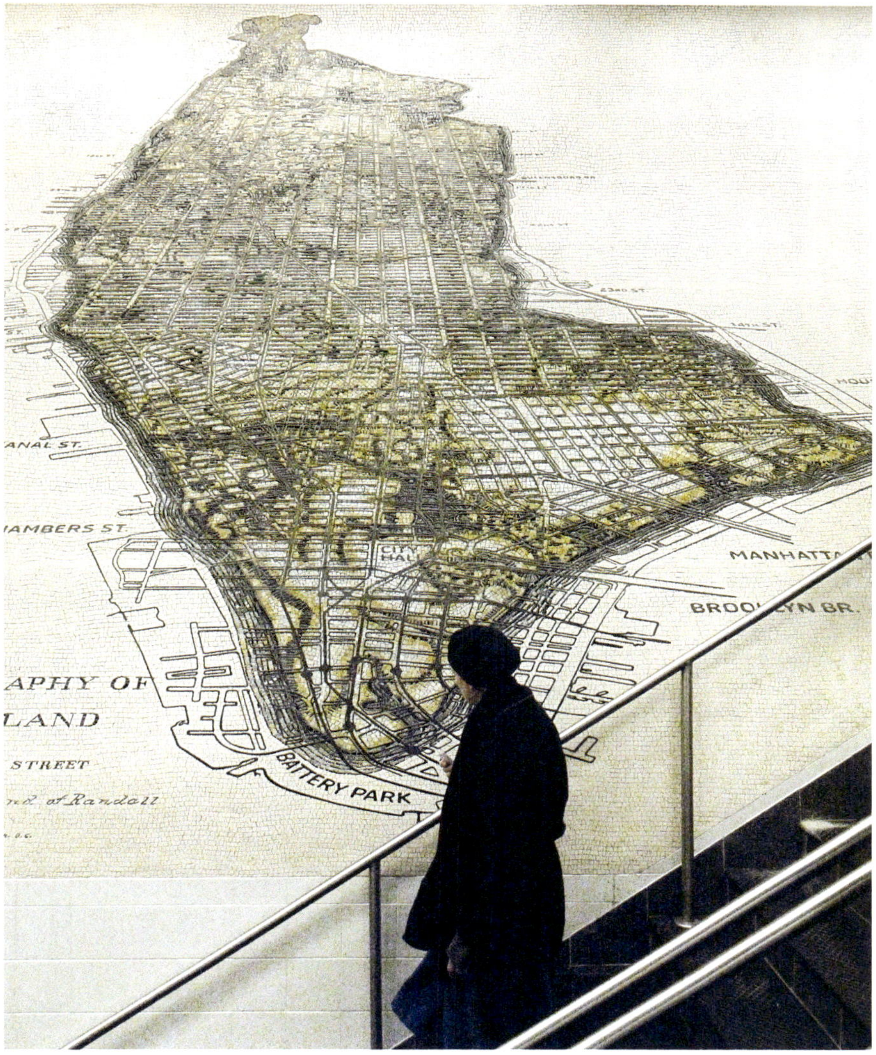

289

Approximately 300 feet long wall design, ceiling-height, five-layered fused glass using digital print, airbrush, and hand painting; mosaics made of chopped and grinded marble cubes, placed, in part, in a new "two-layer-technique."

Some skeptics or critics might feel that such a large and challenging project of public art is senseless or a waste of public funds. New York's MTA Arts for Transit, an office that is comparatively young by European standards, did indeed dare to undertake this and similar grand projects, to fight for it, and to realize it. New York's MTA Arts for Transit is a great office that uses fresh ideas and courage and believes in good art in public spaces. And it often reaches it goals.

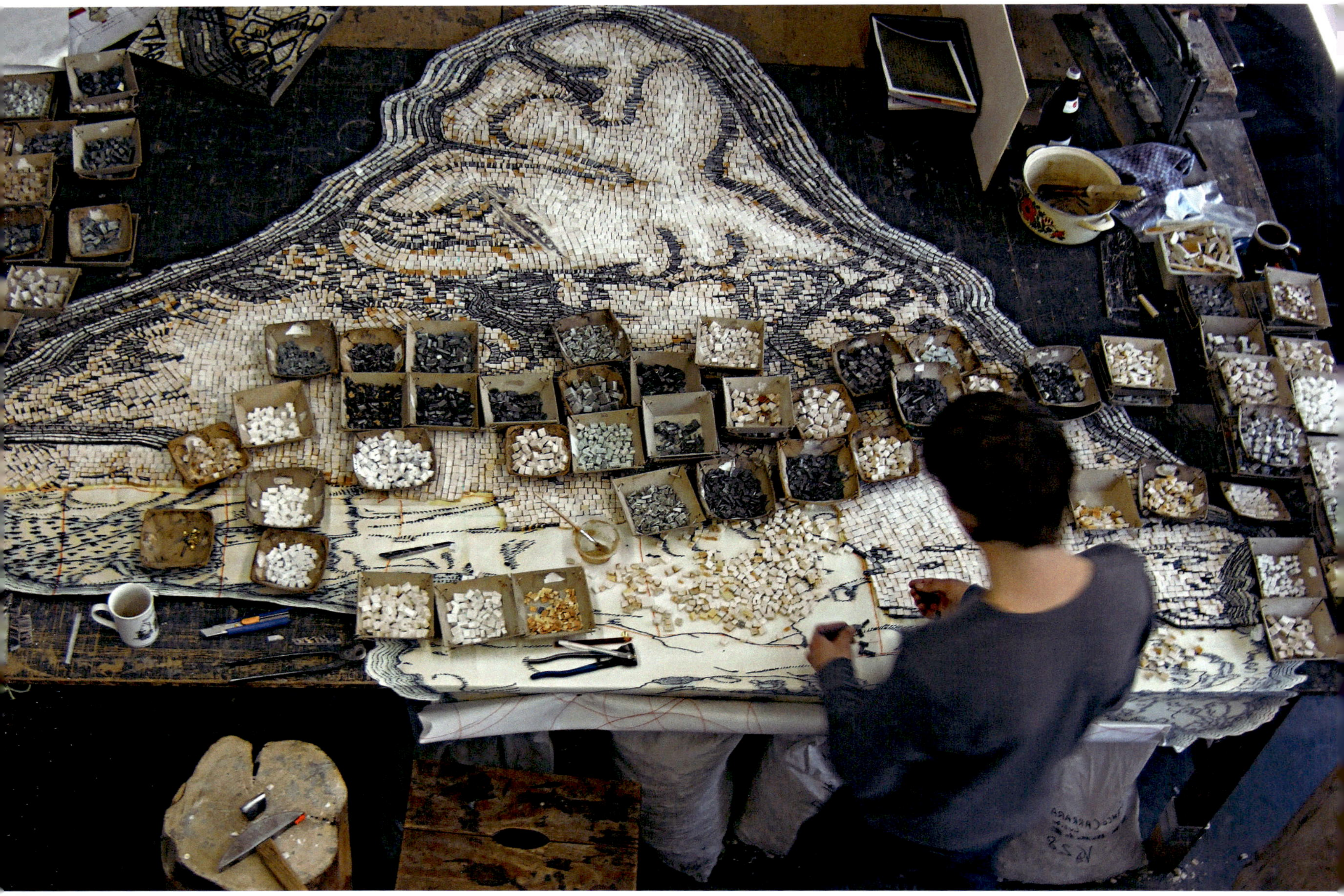

290

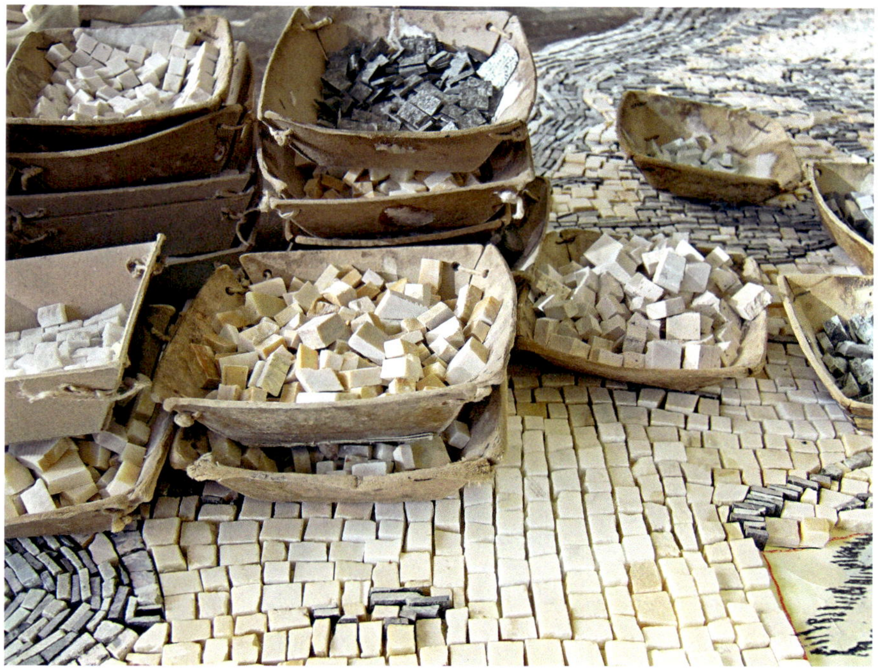

291

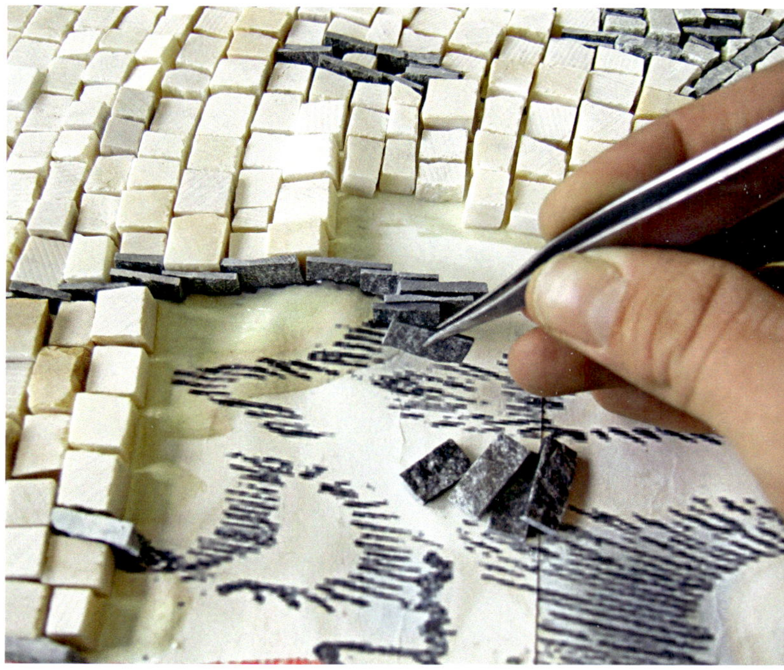

292

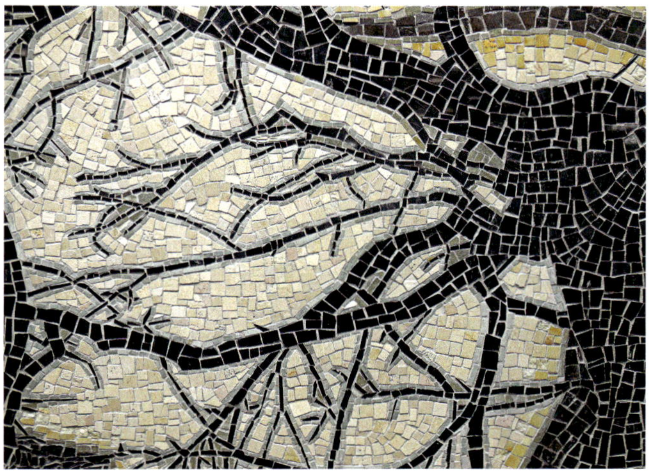

293

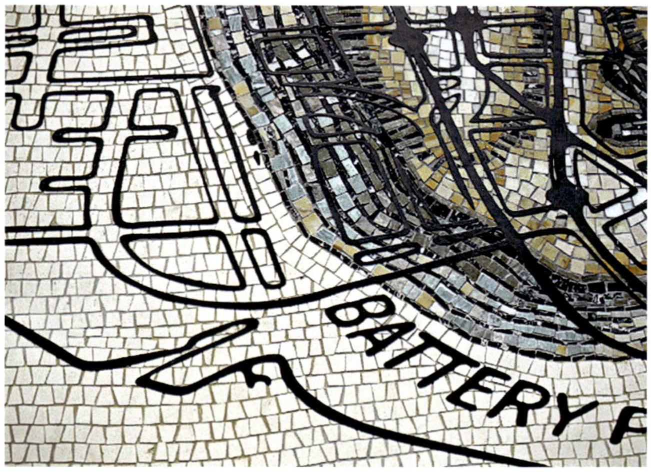

294

MIKE AND DOUG STARN – STUDIO

290
Working in the studio using the "two-layer-technique" on the cartographic mosaic of Manhattan. The studio images show how the two layers are created: The mosaic ground is the implementation of a historic map of Manhattan's southern tip. The second layer, the 20th c. street grid, is literally placed "over" the "archeological" base of the mosaic.

291 + 292
Details from the "Manhattan" base mosaic, some of it set in minute stones.

293
The bare winter trees in foggy sunlight are primarily made in fused glass technique. One of the winter tree motifs, however, is set in mosaic. In this case, as is customary for mosaic technique, only one layer was applied, stone beside stone. The dark branches and twigs are accompanied by shadows in order to emphasize the softness the light creates.

294
A detail from the completed two-layered Manhattan mosaic *(full view see fig. 289).*

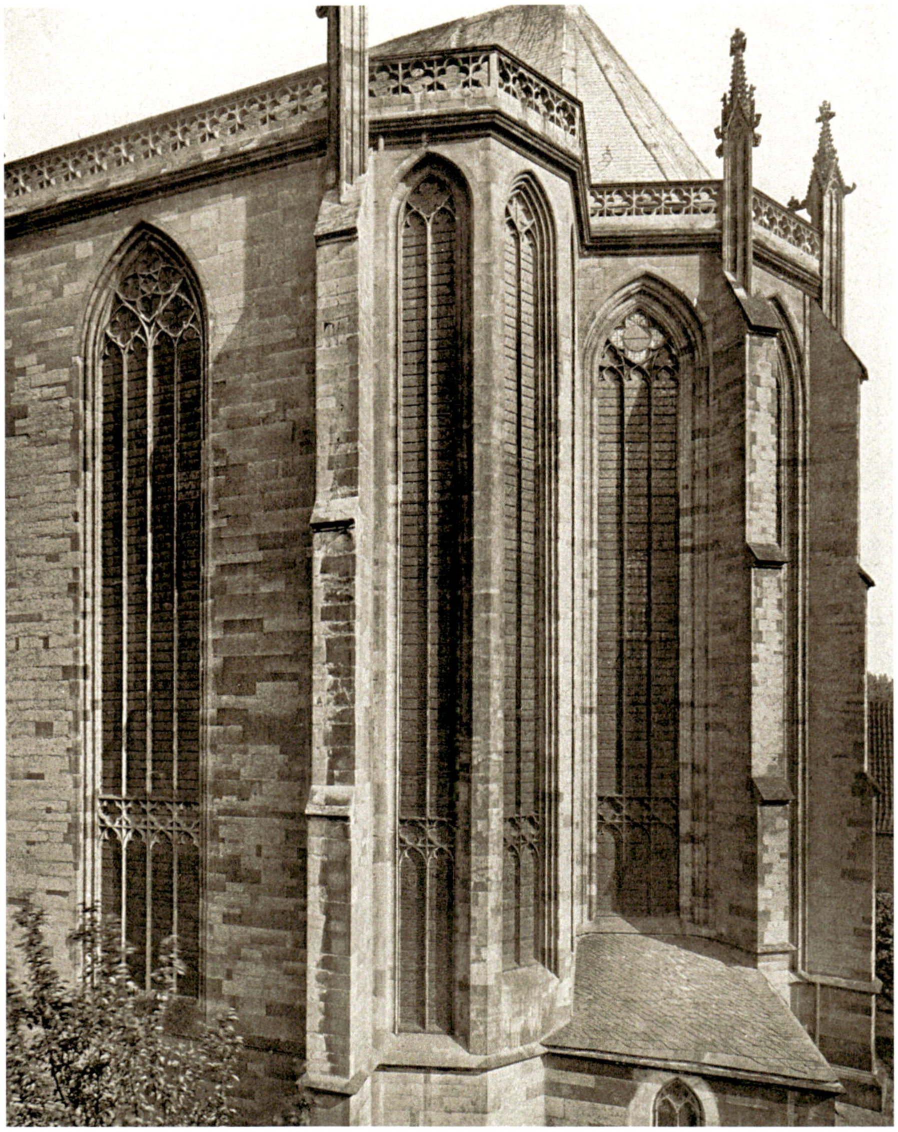

295

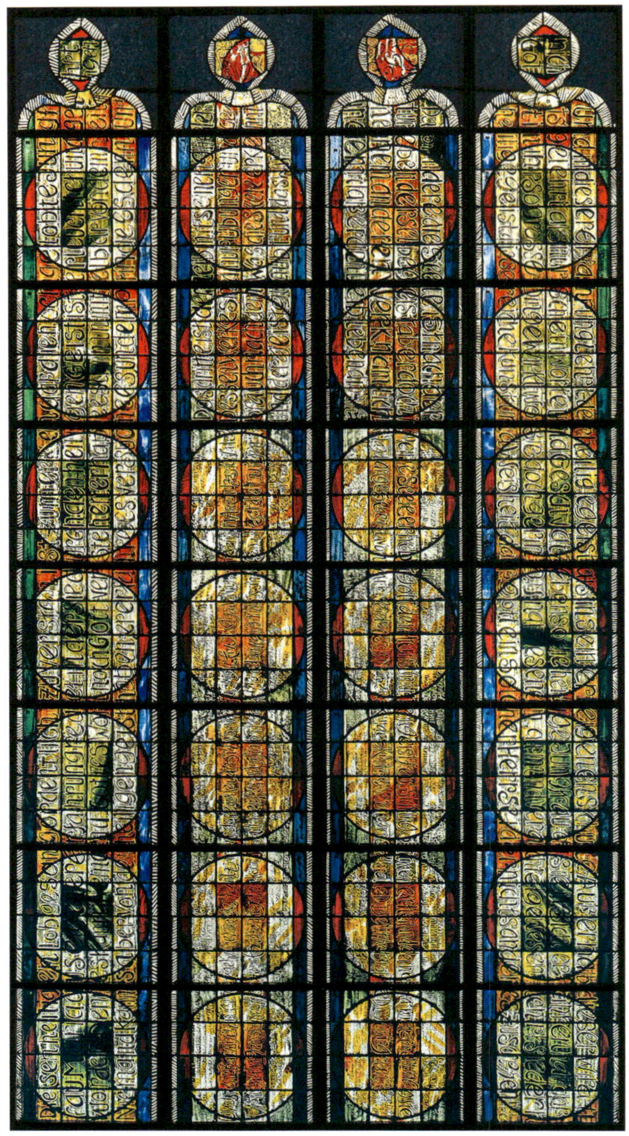

296

Hans Gottfried von Stockhausen / Wiesenkirche

location: St. Maria zur Wiese, Soest, DE / Gothic hall church / **year:** 2002 /
technique: stained glass

Multiple flashed glass, stained glass, leaded. Four 4-light, 60 feet high windows in the south nave of the Gothic Wiesenkirche.

Hans Gottfried von Stockhausen (1920–2010) was one of the great post-war glass artists and Mayer of Munich had the privilege to accompany and to cooperate amicably with this artist for over five decades. See also Bernhard Graf's History Chapter in this book, p. 29f.

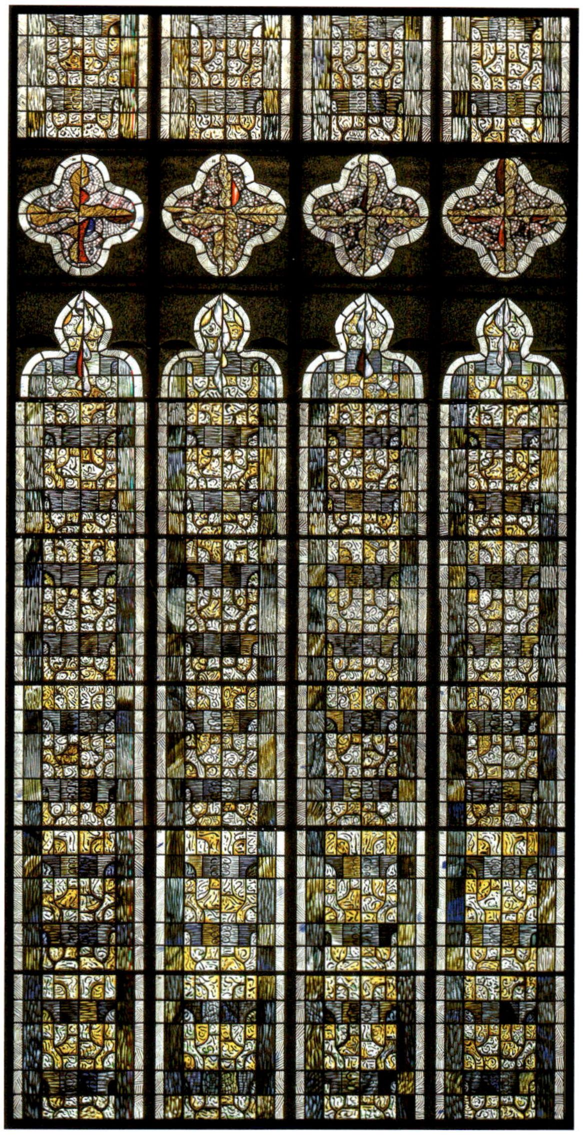

297

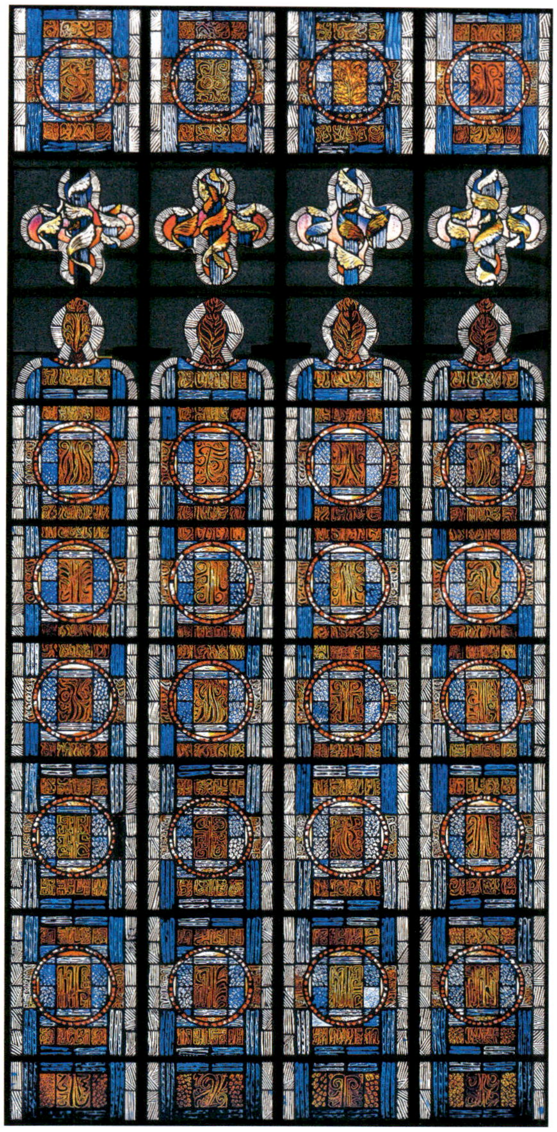

298

WIESENKIRCHE

295
Exterior view of the Wiesenkirche from southeast. On the left is the first of the 65 feet high, four-light windows in the south nave.

296 – 298
Each image shows the eight or nine lowest panel rows of the south nave windows; this only makes up a quarter of the total height of these Gothic windows that reach – while always maintaining the same diversity – all the way up to the tracery.

Between 1962 and 1970, Hans Gottfried von Stockhausen had been entrusted with comprehensive restoration works on the Gothic windows in the famous Wiesenkirche in Soest. Later – he was already well over 80 years old – he began, together with "his" studio, Mayer of Munich, the four last, tall, 4-light stained glass windows. He thereby managed to complete almost entirely the stained glass program of this sublime, light-filled church. Stockhausen was always concerned with the direction of light and its balance, especially in the great medieval churches. With these purely ornamental windows, using the paintbrush as his writing instrument, he executed a grand masterwork at an old age that will survive over time.

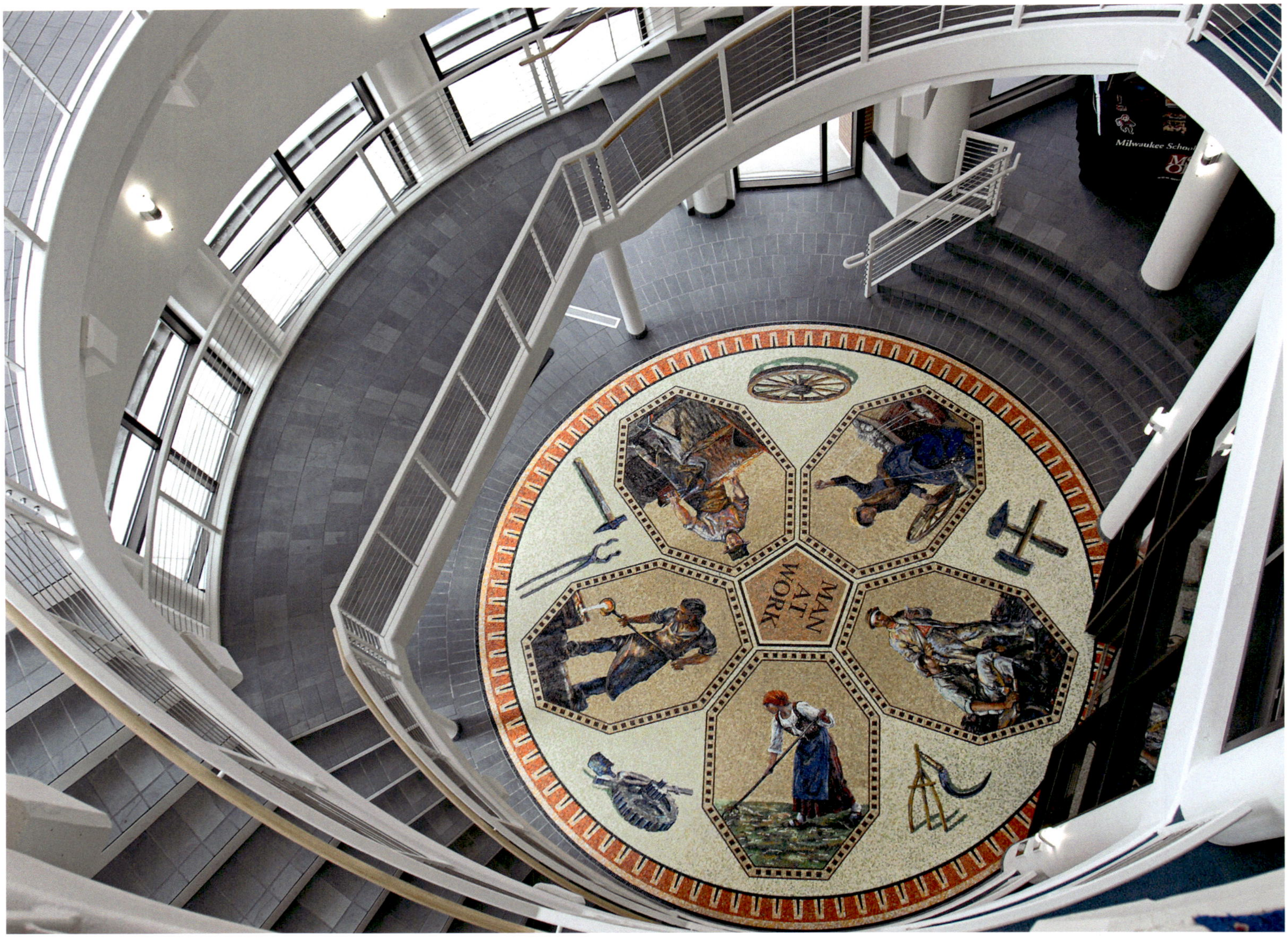

299

H. D. Tylle / "Man at Work"

300

location: MSOE Milwaukee School of Engineering. Eckhart G. Grohmann Collection, Milwaukee, WI, USA / **year:** 2007 / **technique:** floor mosaic

H. D. Tylle, works both in Germany and in the USA, painting in a powerful, late-expressionistic style. In the years 2009 to 2011 he took pictures of dozens of industrial plants and contemporary work situations as part of his "Deutschlandreise" or travels through Germany. In countries like Iceland, North Africa, or Japan, on the other hand, he is looking for extreme landscapes. The main emphasis of the Grohmann Museum at MSOE is "Man at Work". For this institution, he designed a glass mosaic with a 22 feet diameter to be placed on the floor of the entrance foyer. He also collaborated with Mayer on eight stained glass windows located in the attic.

MAN AT WORK

299 The floor mosaic in the entrance foyer seen from the upper floors.

300 The mosaic during its creation in the studio.

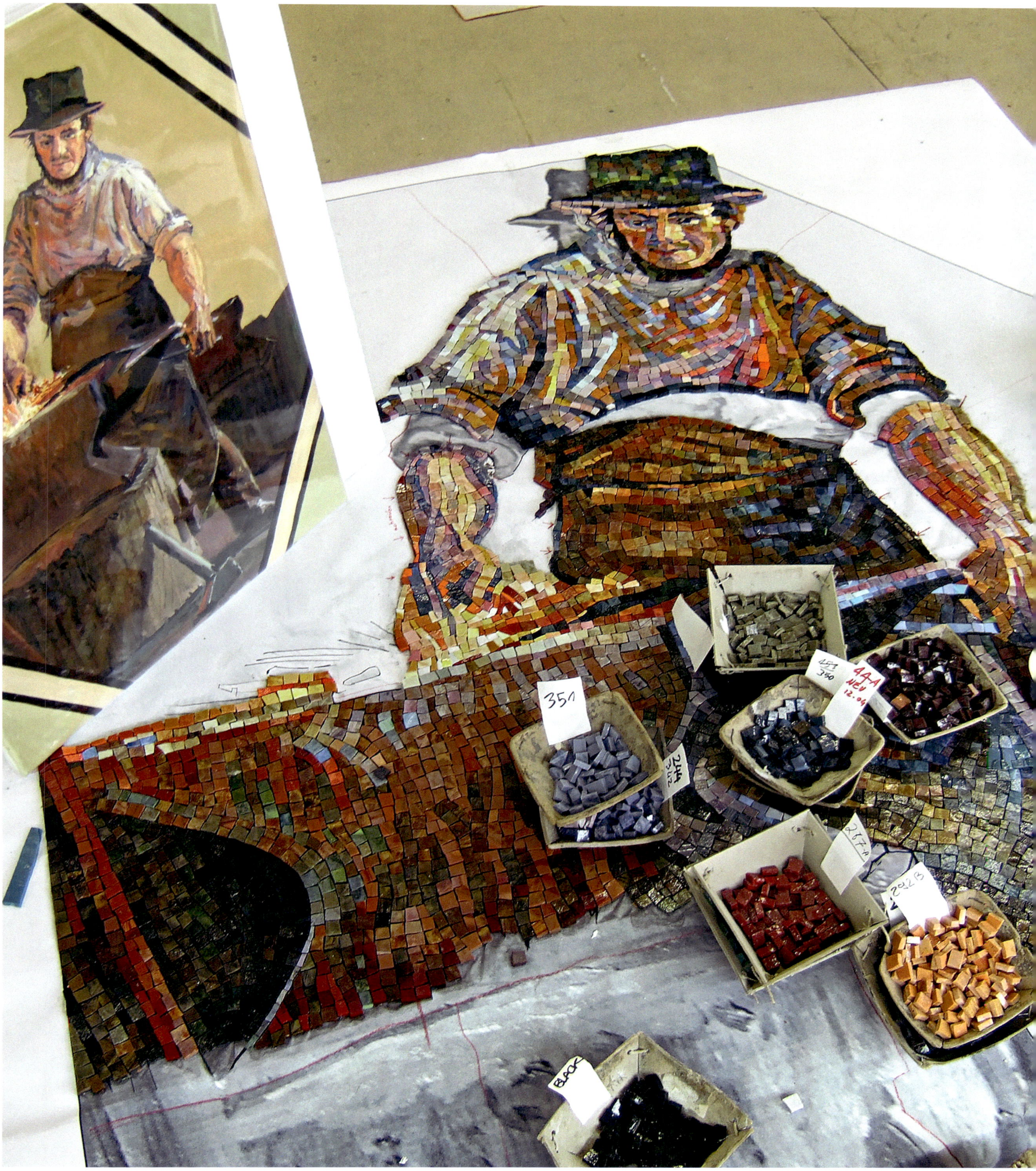
351

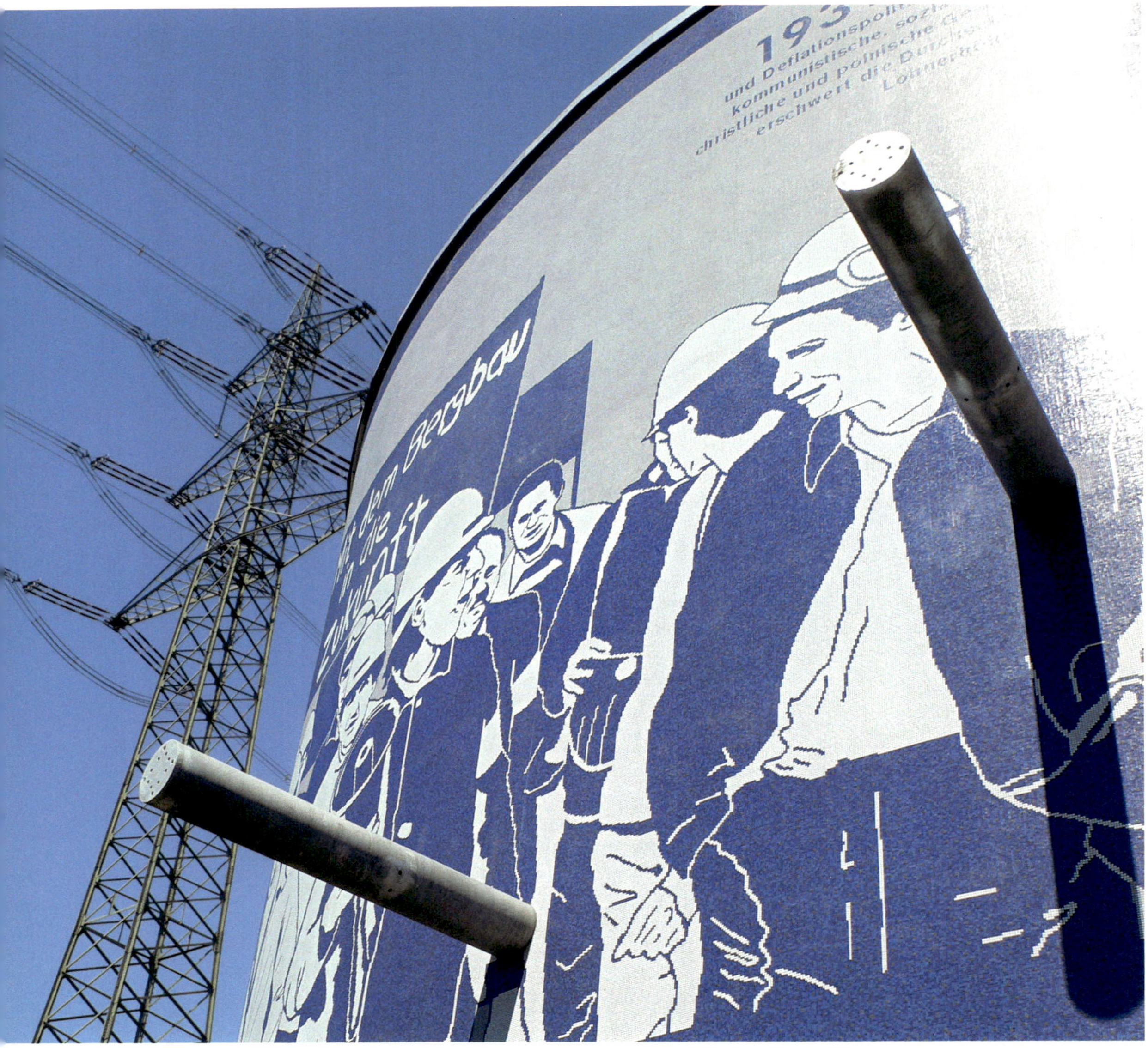

301

GOOD LUCK

301
A detail of the large mosaic on the south side.

302
Art in the industrial landscape of the Ruhr Area. View of the old sedimentation tank, the digester, and the mosaic.

Silke Wagner / "Good Luck. Protest of Miners in the Ruhr Area"

location: Digester of the former sewage plant Herne. EMSCHERKUNST – Projekt Kulturhauptstadt Europas RUHR 2010, DE / **year:** 2010 / **technique:** mosaic

A total of some 500,000 hand-set $\frac{3}{8} \times \frac{3}{8}$ inch industrial glass mosaic tesserae!
For the realization of her 6500 square feet mosaic, Silke Wagner has selected an unusual place: the digester of Herne's former sewage plant. Under the title "Good Luck. Protest of Miners in the Ruhr Area" she shows seminal historic mining scenes from the last 120 years. "I love and value such art!" (Gabriel Mayer)

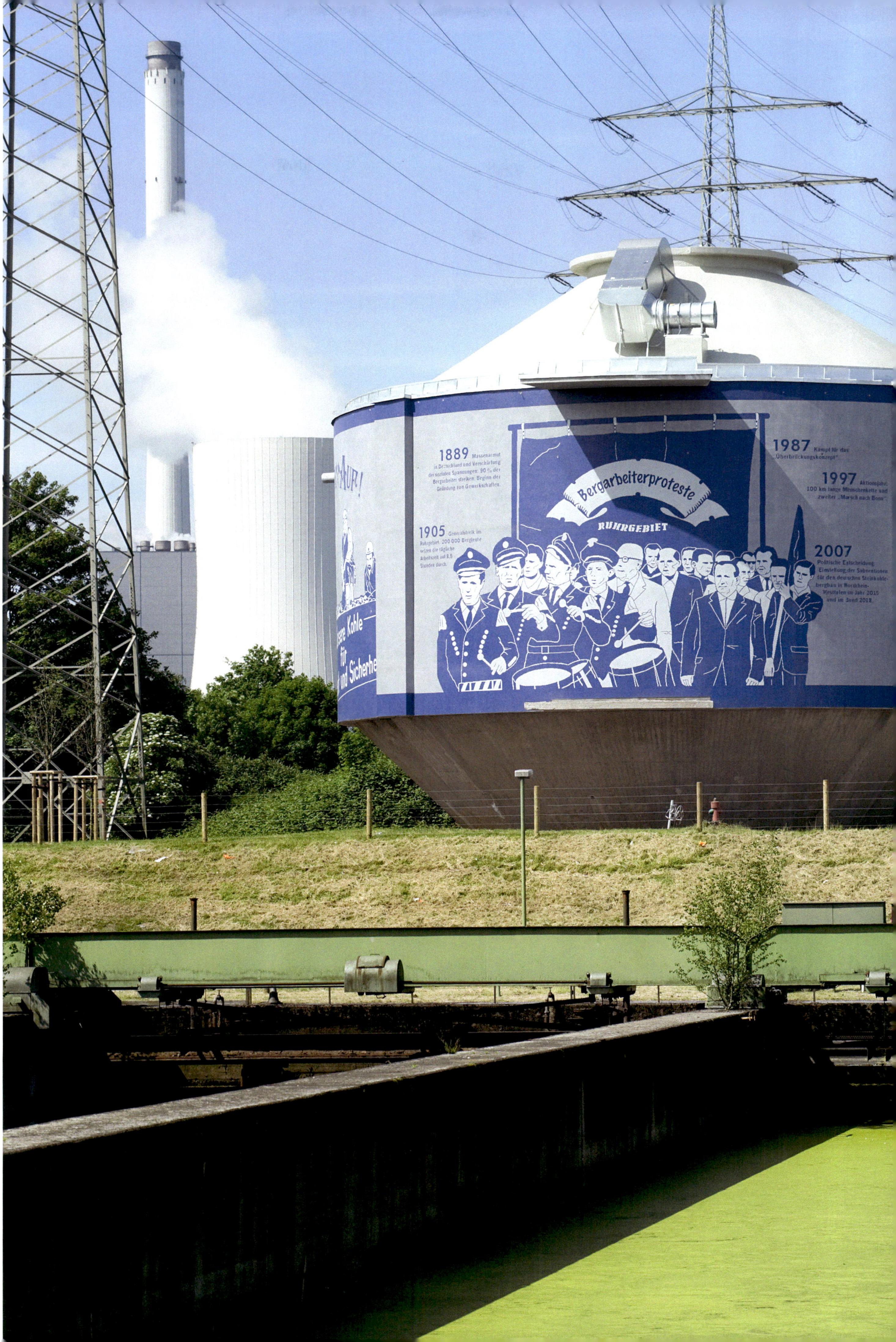
1889 Massenarmut in Deutschland und Verschärfung der sozialen Spannungen: 90 % der Bergarbeiter streiken. Beginn der Gründung von Gewerkschaften.
1905 Generalstreik im Ruhrgebiet. 200 000 Bergleute setzen die tägliche Arbeitszeit auf 8,5 Stunden durch.
Bergarbeiterproteste
RUHRGEBIET
1987 Kampf für das „Überbrückungskonzept".
1997 Aktionsjahr: 100 km lange Menschenkette und zweiter „Marsch nach Bonn".
2007

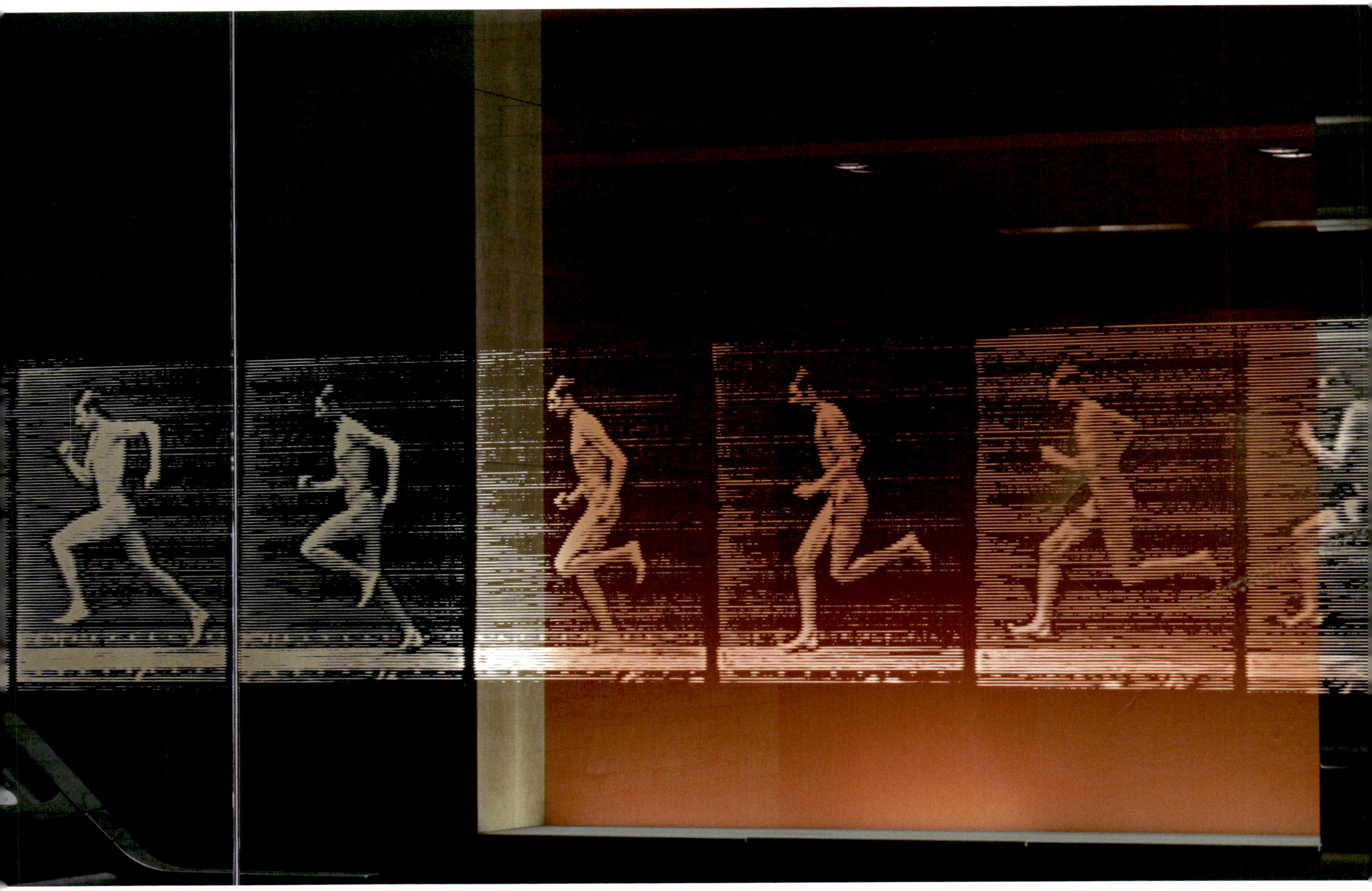

303

Felix Weinold / “Running Man” and “Satori”

location: Private residence South Germany / design associates / **year:** 2007 / **technique:** float glass painting

“Running Man:” The motif of a running man was sanded out of a semi-transparent mirror. Weinold used a seies of photographs by Eadweard Muybridge from “The Human Figure in Motion.” The glass wall separates and combines gym and swimming pool.

“Satori:” Sandblasting and silkscreen with glass melting color. The illustration of the greatly enlarged grass gives the impression of a Japanese rice paper wall. The fin structure further enhances this impression, and due to the exterior reflection, during the day the motif gets intertwined with the tree that stands in front of the facade.

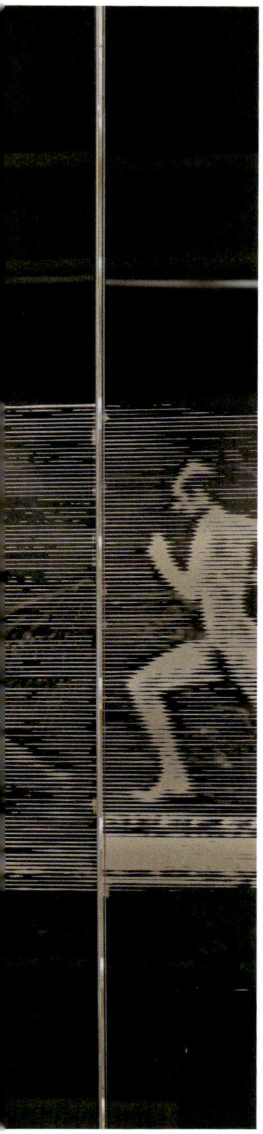

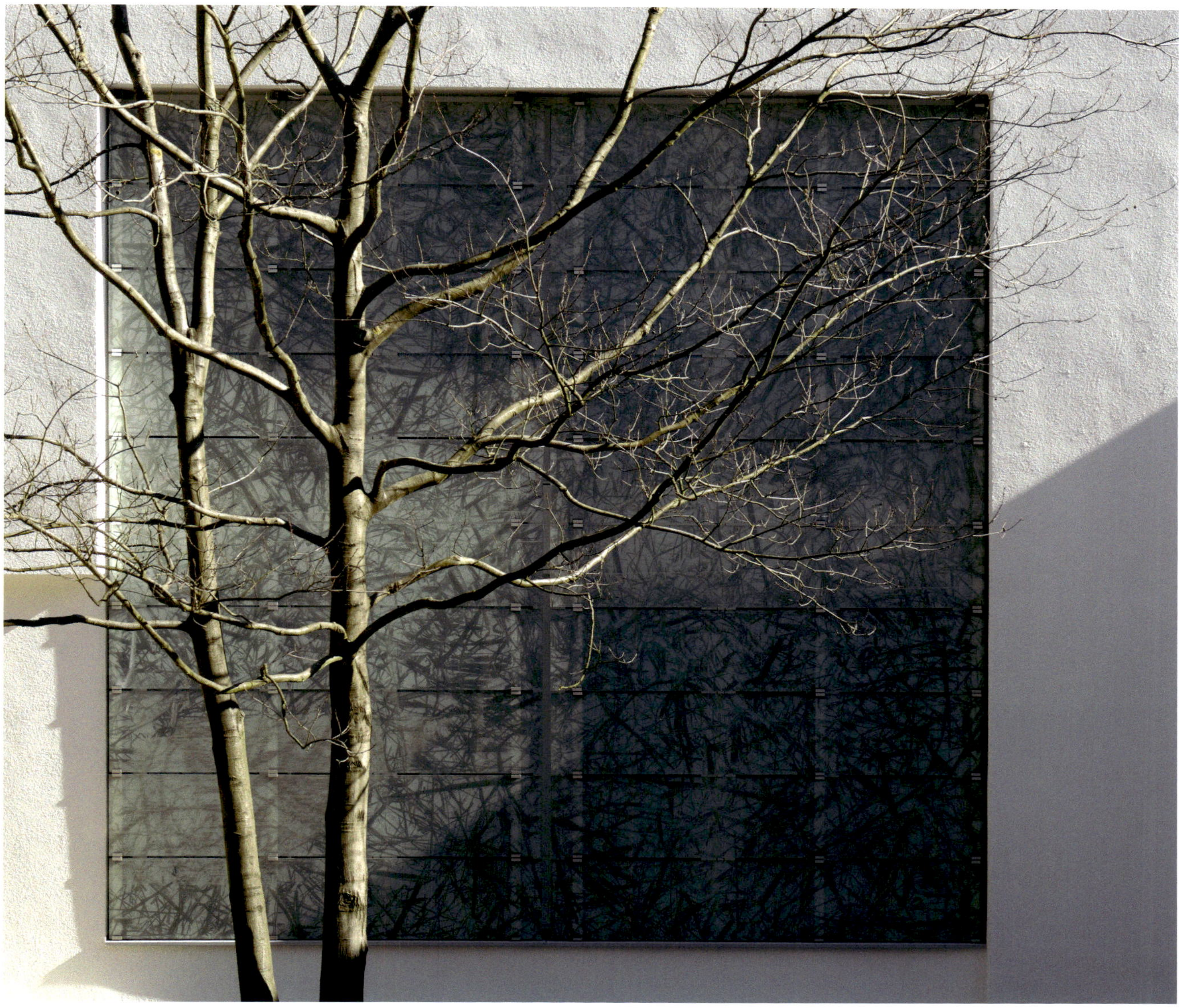

304

RUNNING MAN

303
Motion study from old photographs – wellness; mirror, sandblast.

SATORI

304
Grass structures in painting and engraving techniques on horizontal glass fins.

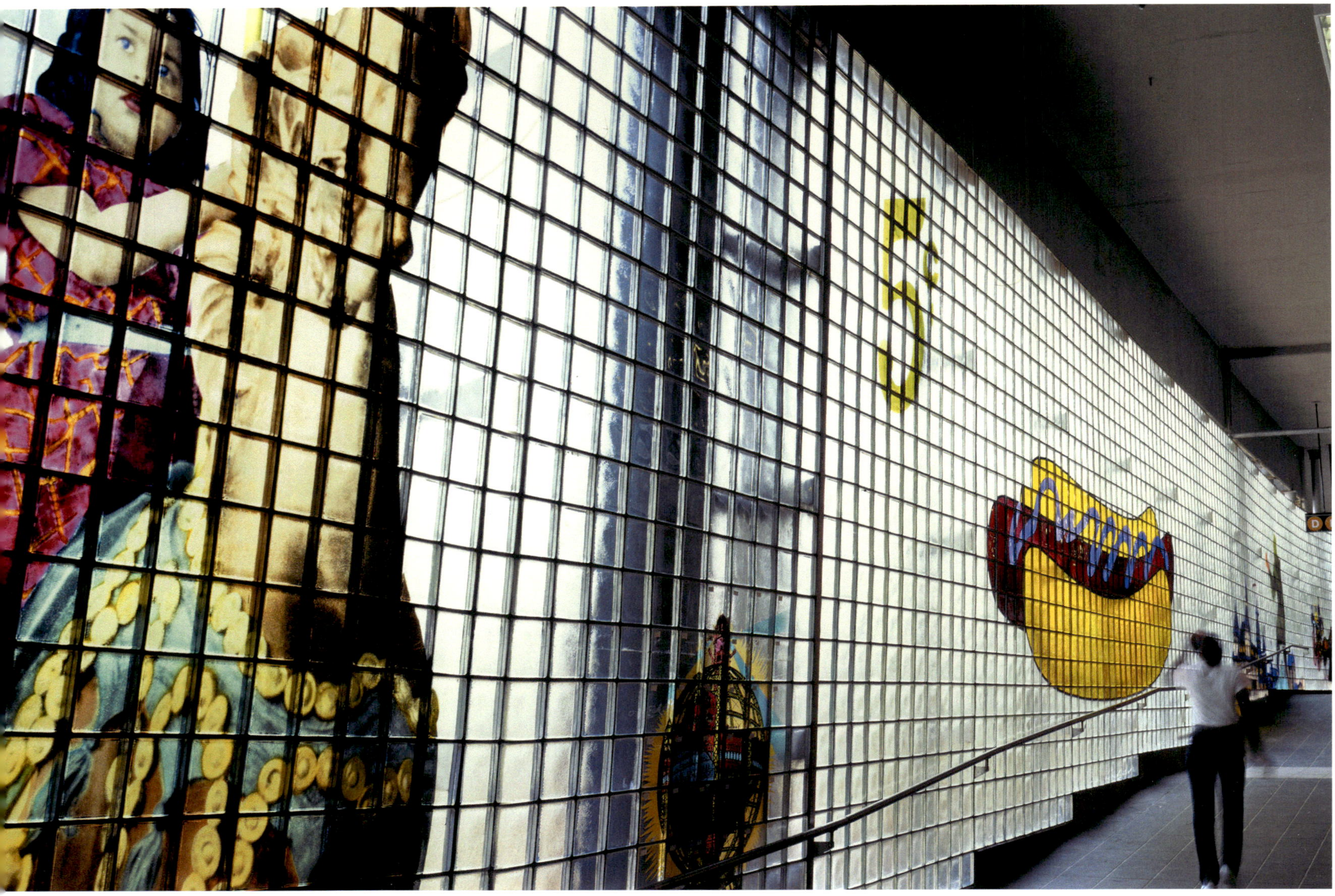

305

Robert Wilson / "My Coney Island Baby"

location: Stillwell Station, Coney Island, New York City Transit, NY, USA / MTA Arts for Transit / **year:** 2002 / **technique:** solid glass bricks, with color design

Robert Wilson is known throughout the world for his imaginative and fantastically colorful theater productions. New York's MTA Arts for Transit found the right man in him for the artistic design of their Stillwell Station in Coney Island. On glass walls that measure roughly 380 feet, the artist celebrates old Coney Island. In his bright and colorful designs, he uses archival photo images, which Mayer of Munich painted and printed on the interior of the heavy and solid glass bricks with ceramic glass colors. Two-layered, these stones are circa 3 ½ inches thick, requiring a long firing process and challenging lamination process.

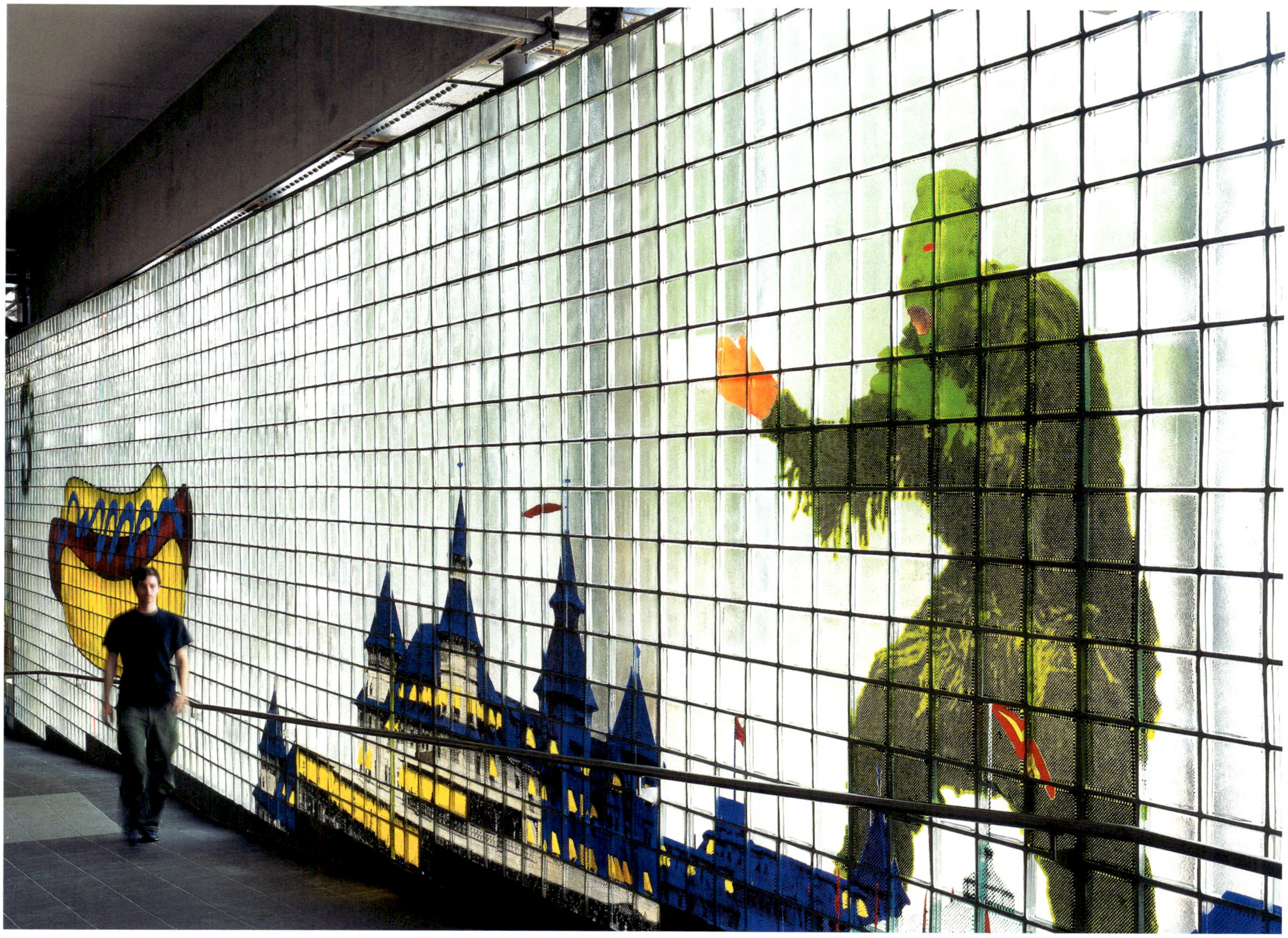

306

MY CONEY ISLAND BABY

305
On the left, a part of the 380 feet long glass wall: From the girl on a carousel horse to "Hot Dog" and more.

306
The central portion of the glass wall with the Coney Island Monster, the historic Subway Station, and the "Hot Dog."

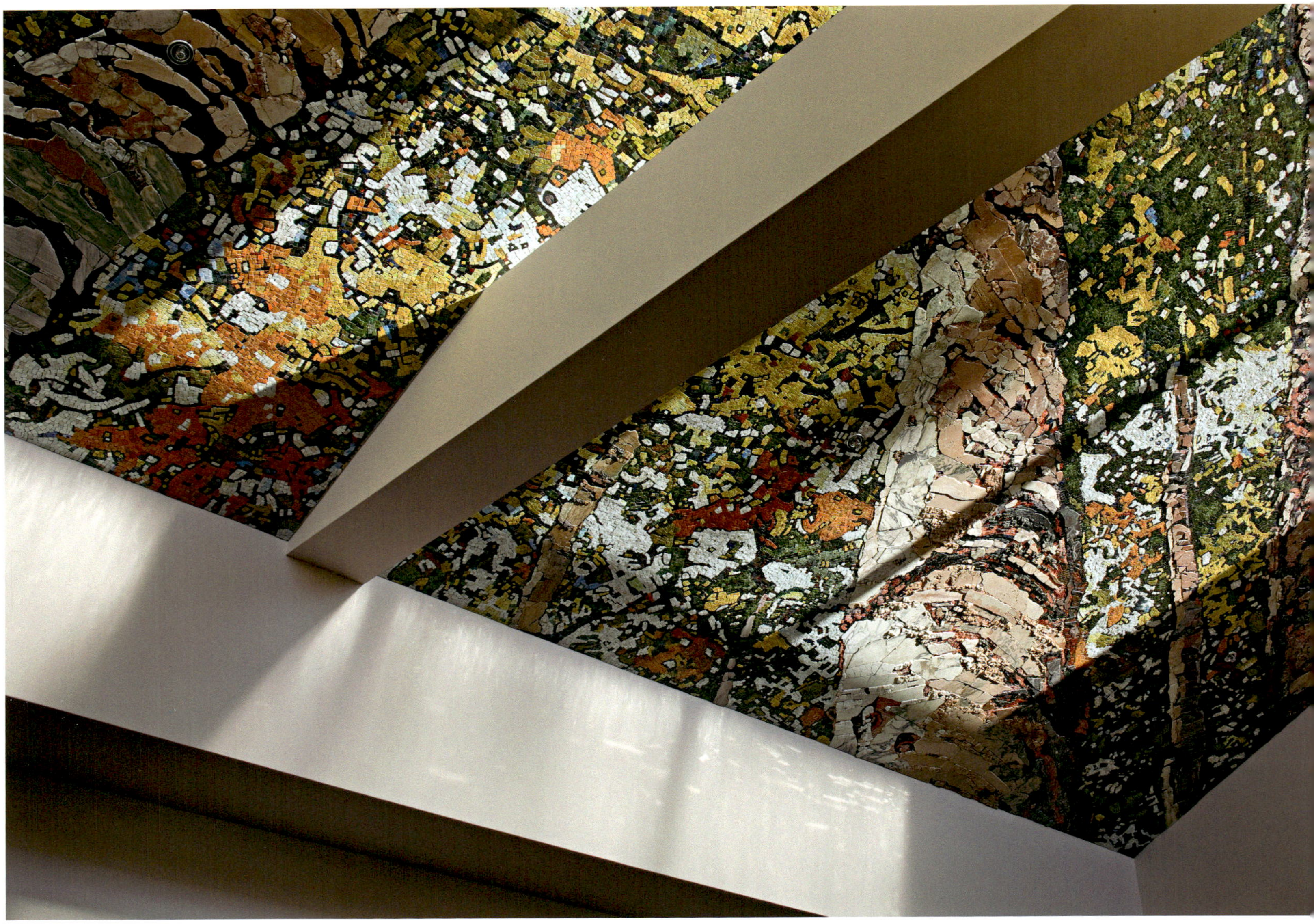

307

Sheila Wyne & Kesler Woodward / "Canopy"

218

location: Anchorage International Airport, AK, USA / James Dougherty, RIM-AK Architects / Alaska State Council on the Arts / **year:** 2009 / **technique:** glass mosaic

The column in the form of an abstracted birch trunk and the ceiling, which depicts a view looking up through a birch forest toward the sky are the result of a rather unique collaboration of two quite different Alaskan artists. Kesler Woodward is an artist whose fascination is with painterly surface, and the boreal forest. Sheila Wyne's strength is the facility for enlivening three-dimensional space and challenging the viewer. Franz Mayer of Munich eventually became the third player. The 680 square feet mosaic uses glass mosaic tesserae but also includes trunks of stone, marble and other materials.

CANOPY

307
A detail view into the canopy mosaic.

308
The mosaic canopy in the axis of the corridor becomes visible to the traveler only if he comes close to the mosaic. The column, however, visible at the right corner of the picture, can be seen from rather far away.

308

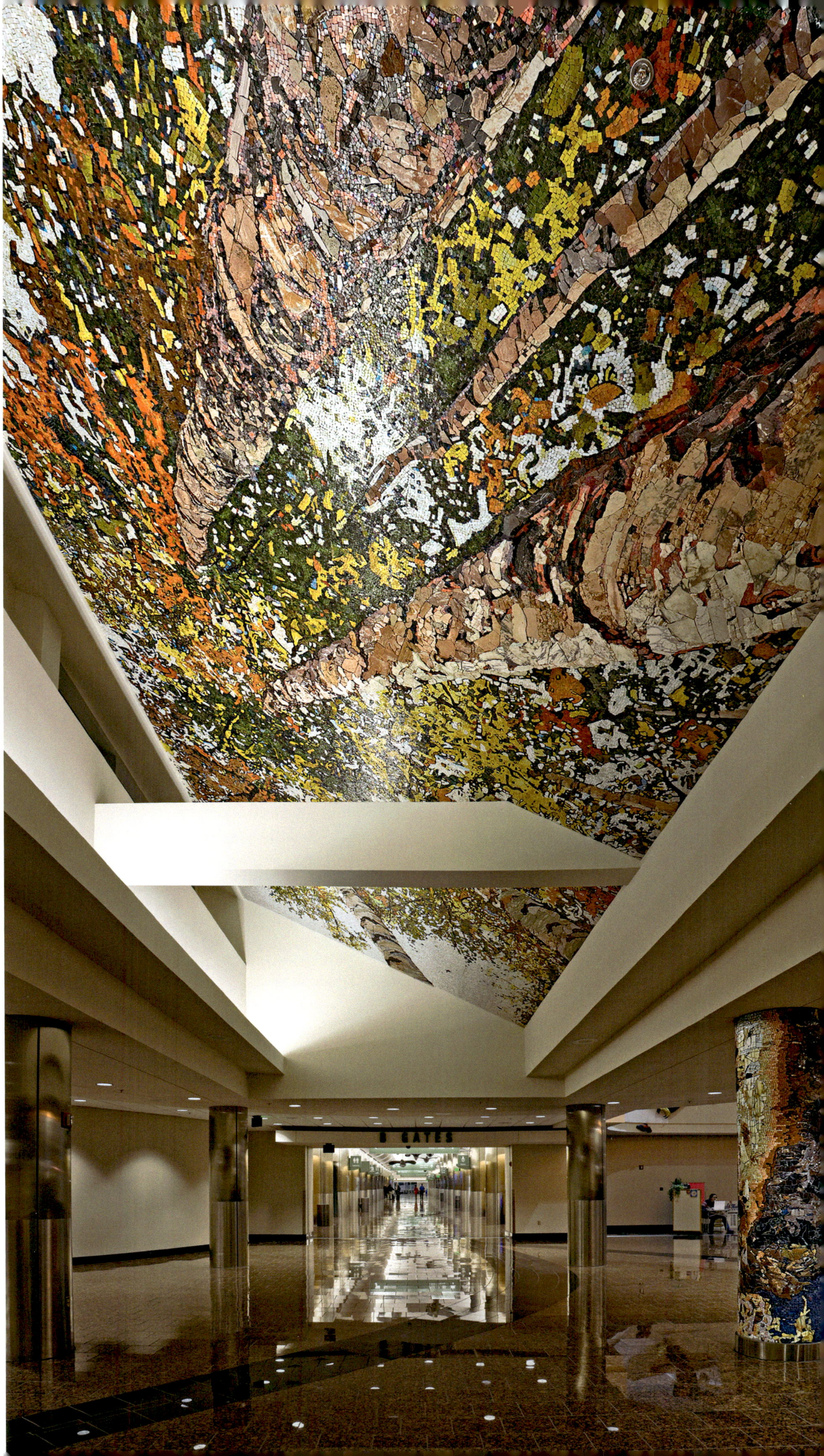

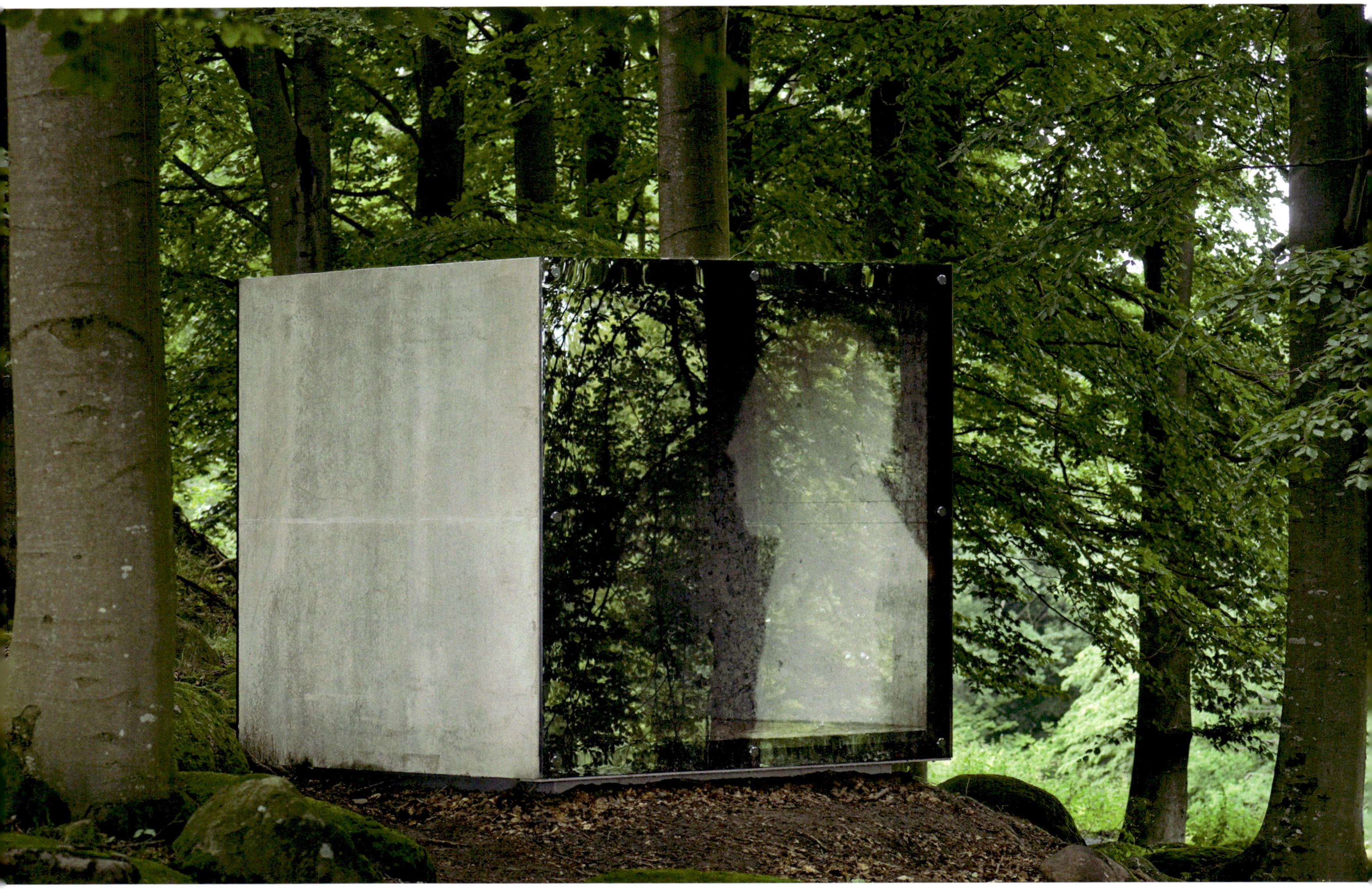

309
The concrete cube with the portrait of a man etched into the glass.

Tom Sandberg / Concrete and Glass Cube

location: Kivik Art Center, Österlen, SWE / Architects Snøhetta AS / **year:** 2007 /
technique: glass and concrete cube

Concrete, glass, art – man-made, man-invented – versus trees, nature: Metaphorical thoughts. Rather poetic, but not so easy to be noticed: The portrait of a man.

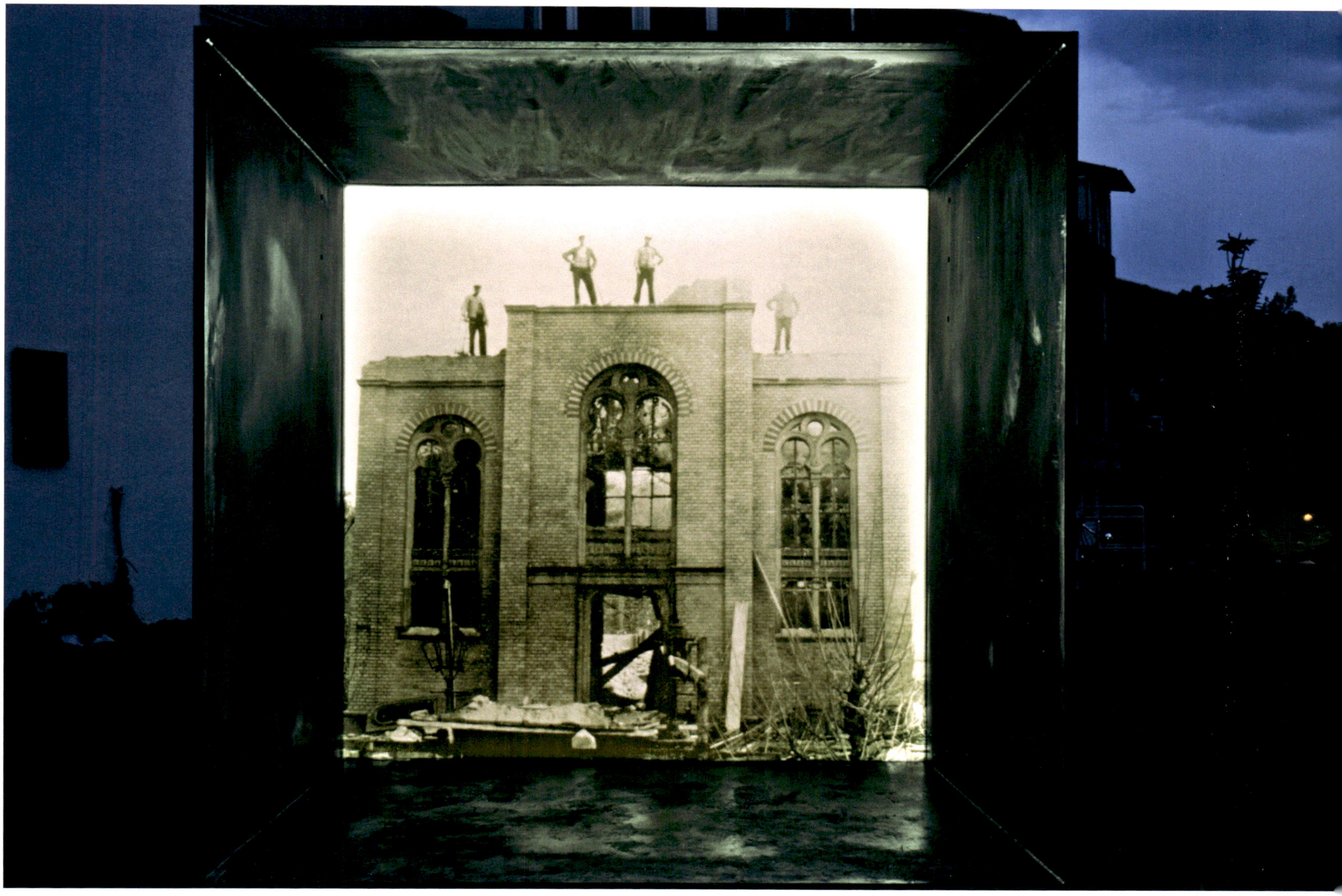

310
The memorial with the image of the synagogue, which was destroyed in November 1938.

Wandel Hoefer Lorch Architekten / Memorial

location: Memorial for the former synagogue, Bensheim, DE / Architects Wandel Hoefer Lorch and Hirsch / **year:** 2000 / **technique:** matte glass, ceramic glass melting color

The memorial consists of a “container” made of Corten steel with two “windows” showing two photos of the former synagogue. The first image was taken before the destruction. The second shows the synagogue during demolition after it was destroyed during *Kristallnacht* in 1938.

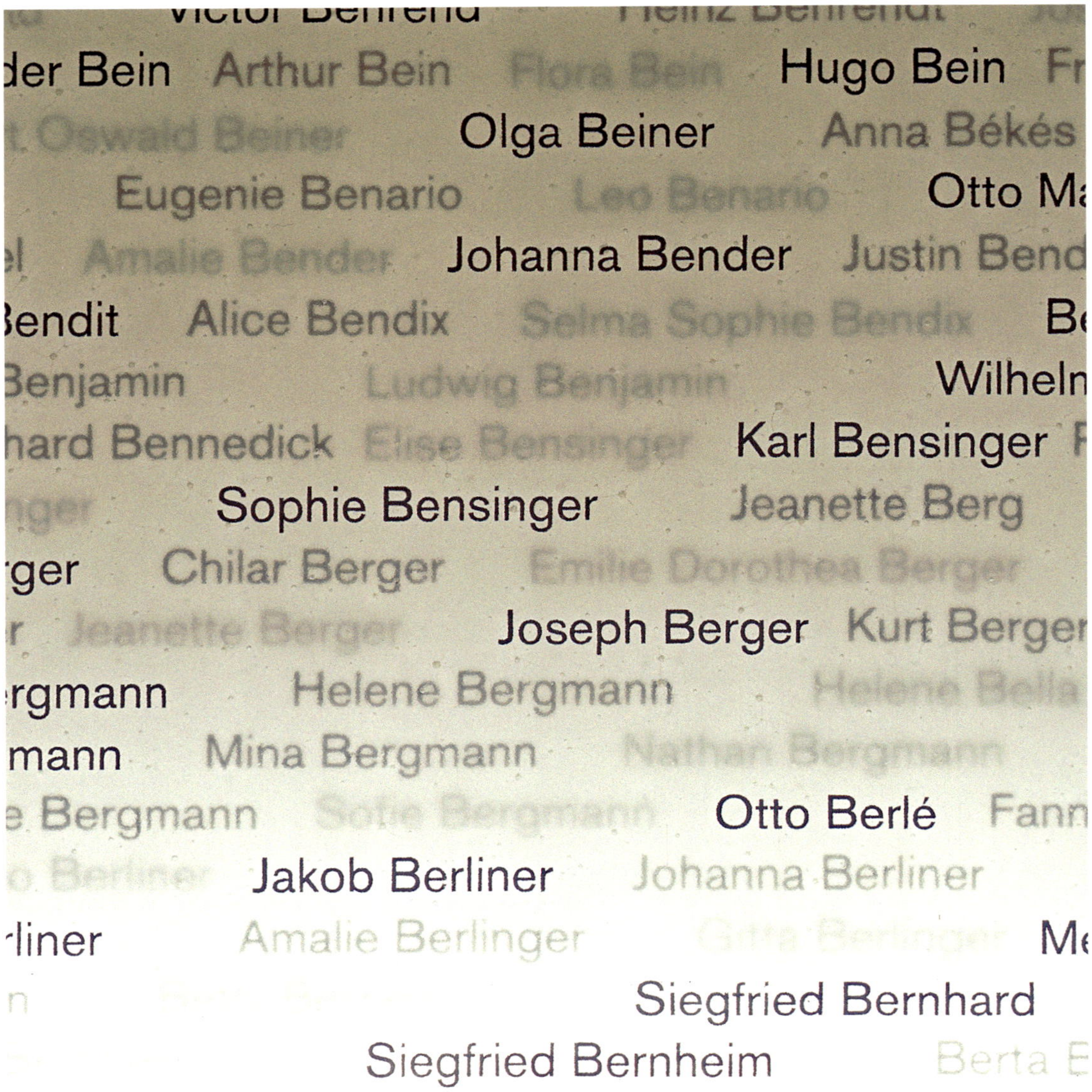

311

312

Wandel Hoefer Lorch / Georg Soanca-Pollak / "Path of Memory"

313

location: Jüdisches Zentrum, Munich, DE / Architects Wandel Hoefer Lorch and Hirsch /
year: 2006 / **technique:** six-layered enamel glass

The memorial wall consists of 32 glass panels with the names of those Munich Jews who were deported and killed during the Nazi regime. It was a great challenge both for the artist Georg Soanca-Pollak and Mayer of Munich to depict the 5000 names in a dignified manner. It took almost six months of trials with many aesthetic and artistic as well as technical alternatives and possibilities. Ultimately, the solution was found using six-layered fused glass panels showing the names on three different planes.

PATH OF MEMORY

311
A detail of the glass band in raking light.

312
A frontal view detail.

313
Looking through the "Path of Memory" located between the synagogue and the Jewish Center. On the right is the approximately 100 feet long glass memorial. The left wall shows the names of concentration camps engraved into the plaster.

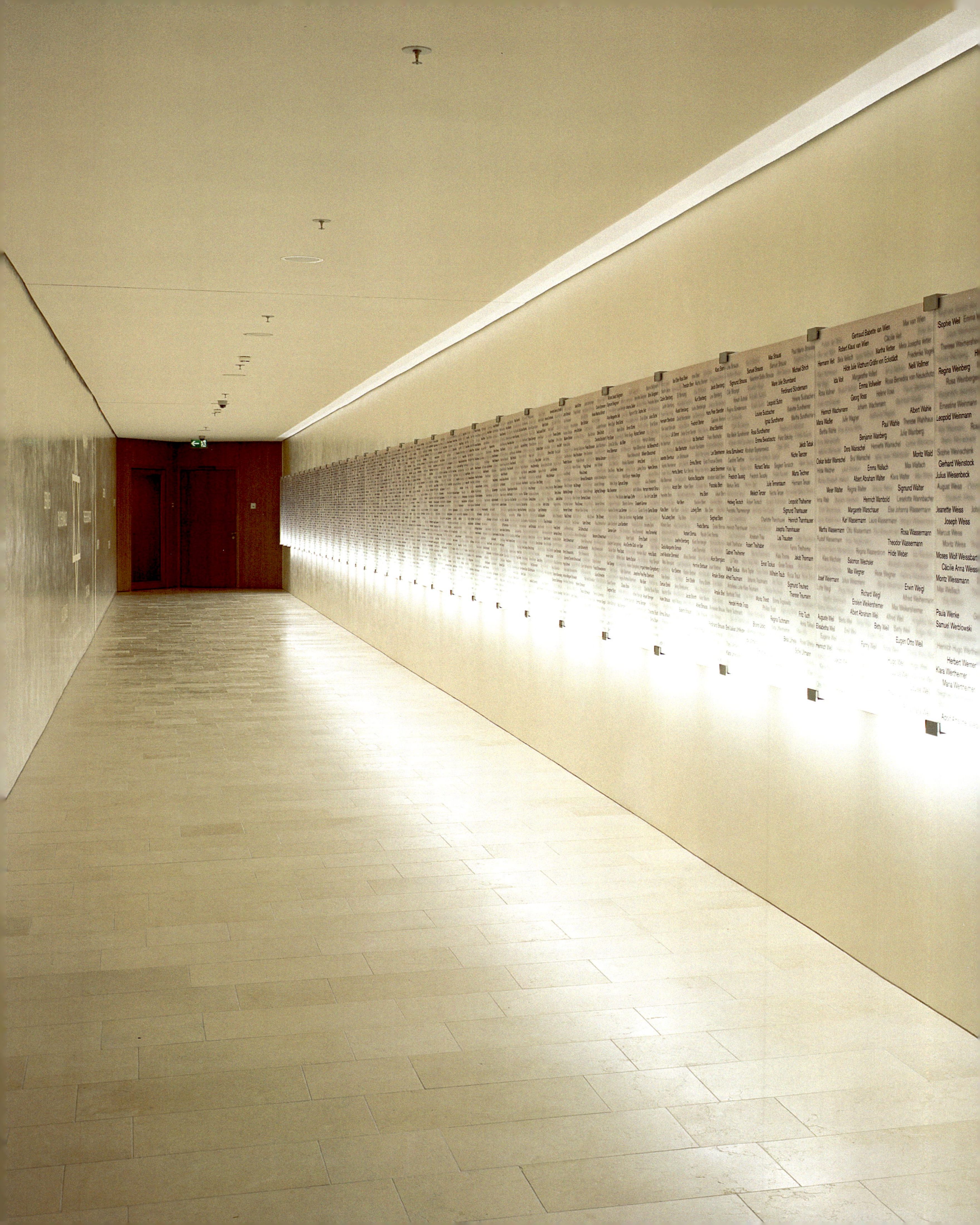

Artist Portrait Brian Clarke

224

* 1953. Lives and works in London. Independent Artist. Has collaborated with Mayer'sche Hofkunstanstalt, Franz Mayer of Munich since 1982 / Photography: Martin Booth

"It would be too easy to say that my works in stained glass express an optimistic view of our heroic innocence and my paintings a darker colder take of the contemptible baseness of who we are capable of being. Arcadia and Auschwitz are not so distant from each other. But it is not like that. I work in these two mediums not because I choose to, not on a whim but because it is by working with them in tandem that I have found a way to add something unique to this dialogue. Painting is seen by virtue of reflected light, stained glass by virtue of transmitted light. Using the two in tandem I try to explore the extremities of human experience through their distinct differences."
(Brian Clarke)

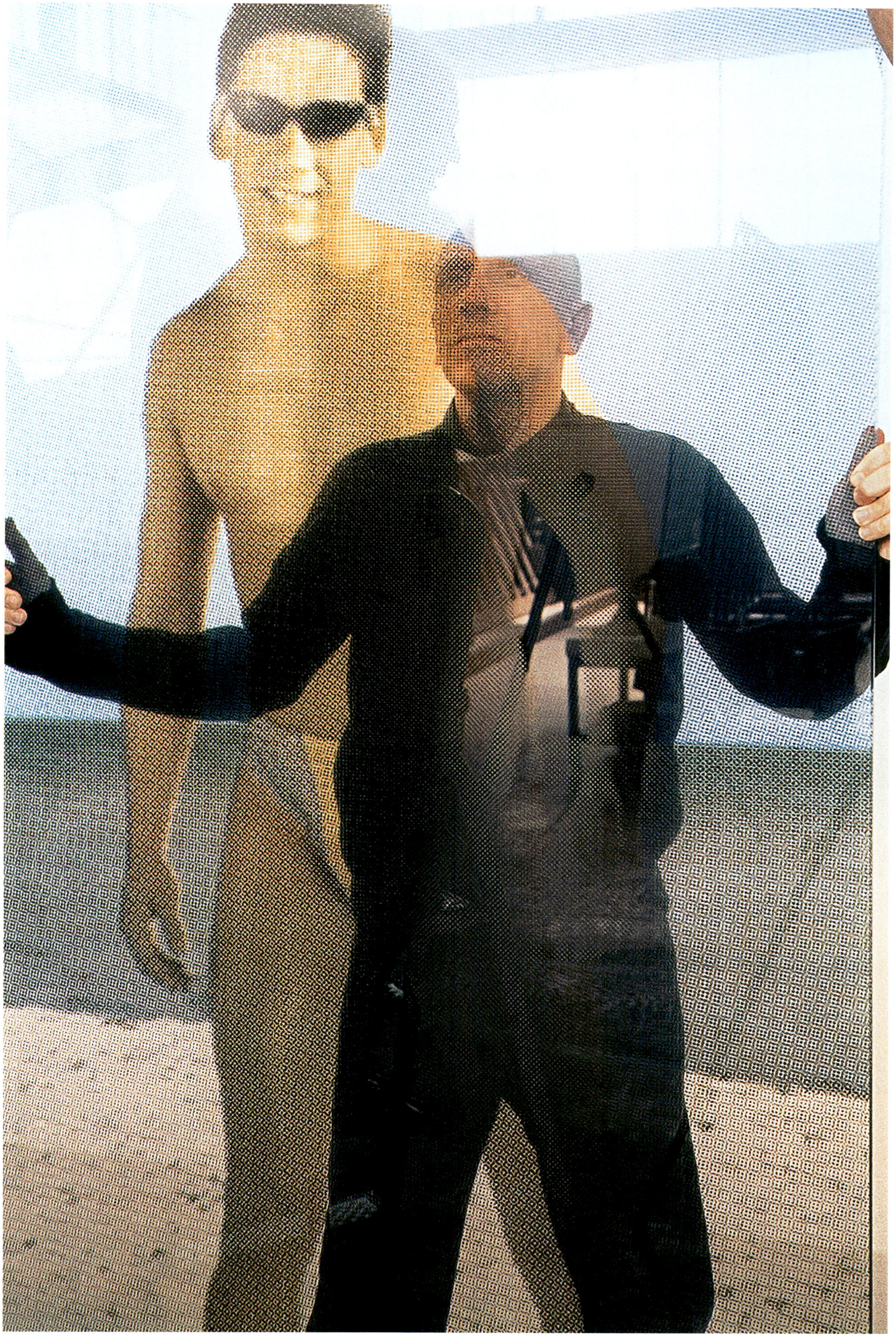

314
Brian Clarke on occasion of the studio check of a panel from the “Study for Atlantes,” 2002.

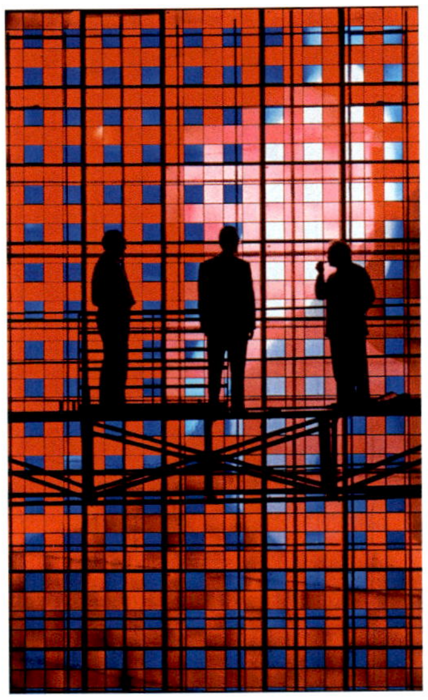

315

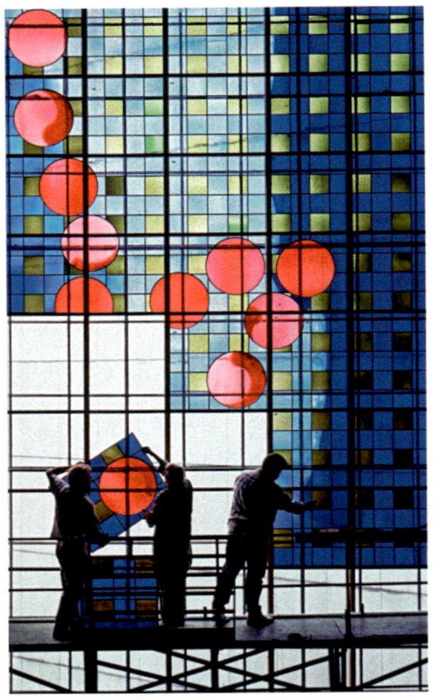

316

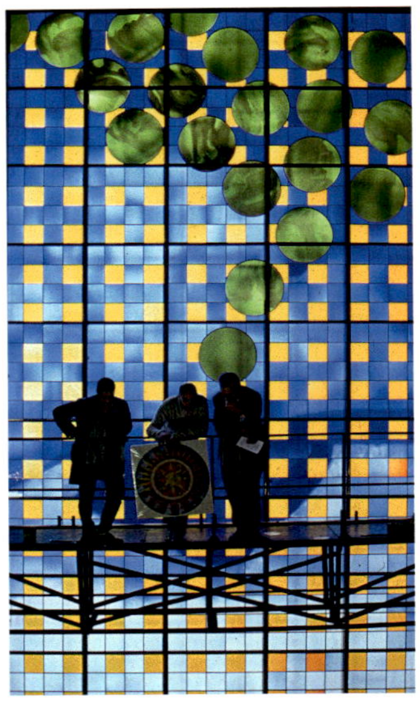

317

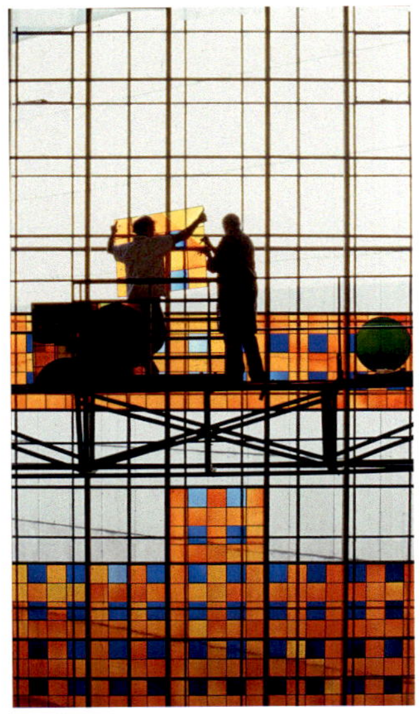

318

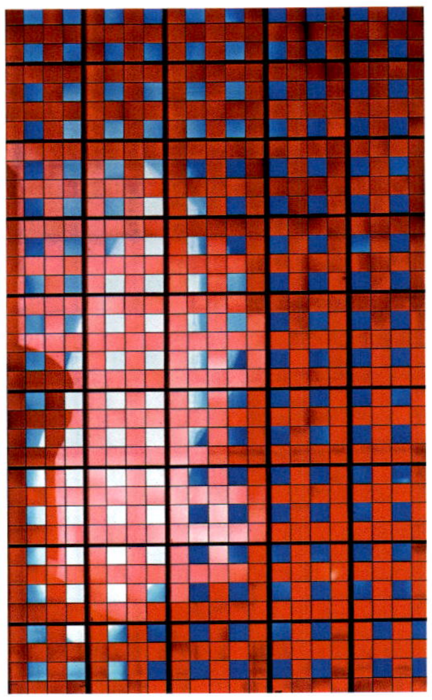

323

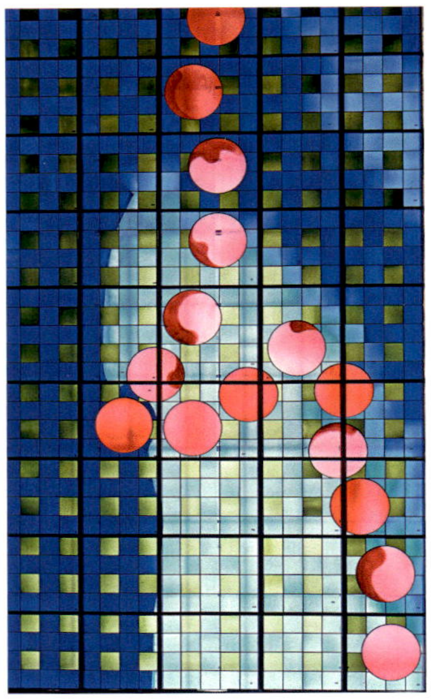

324

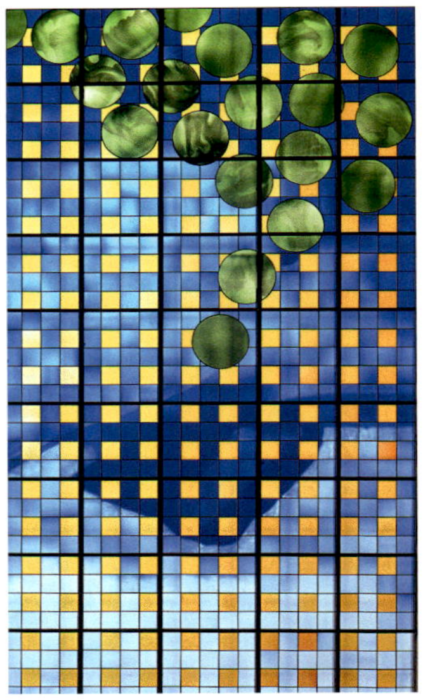

325

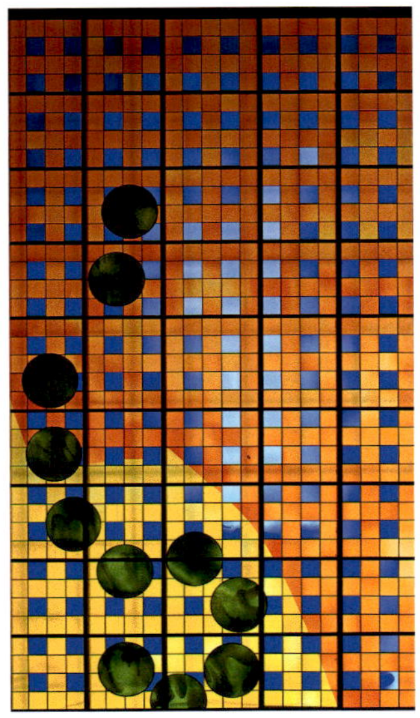

326

Brian Clarke / NorteShopping

location: Centre NorteShopping, Rio de Janeiro, BR / architect: LINDI / **year:** 1995-1997 / **technique:** leaded glass and mosaic

In total 11,000 square feet of stained glass skylights and 2200 square feet of ceiling and wall mosaics. Blown flashed glass, Venetian glass tesserae.
The majority of the glass skylights consist of longitudinal glass-segments throughout the extensive mall corridors. In addition there are numerous glass inlays in the ceilings in hexagonal, octagonal, circular or other forms. Strong stained glass design defines the canopy above the main entrance; and a very large and powerful mosaic ceiling dominates a two storied internal plaza.

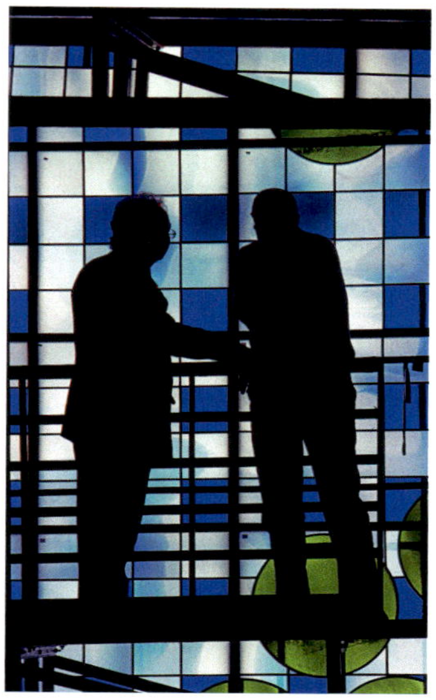

319

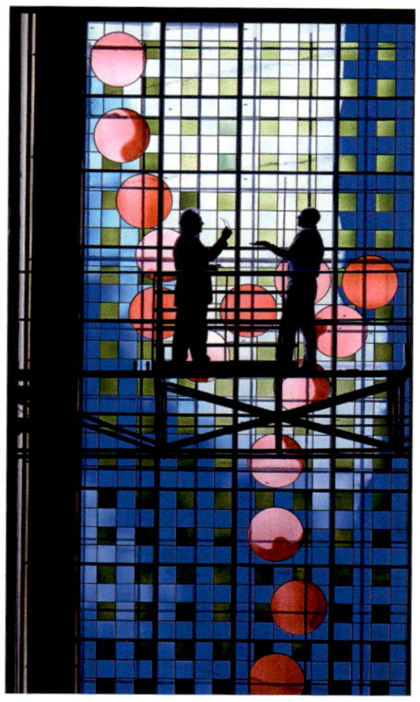

320

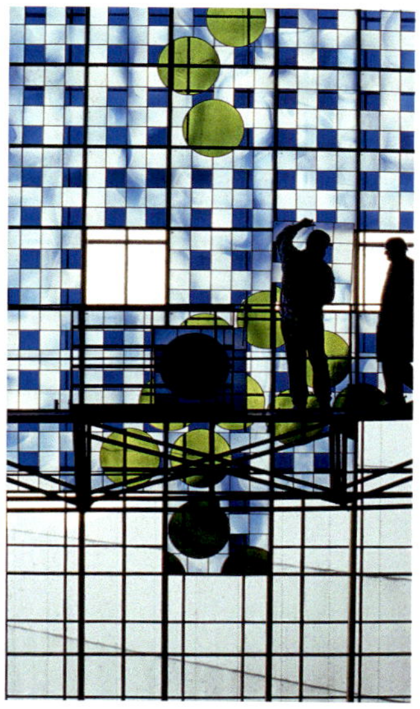

321

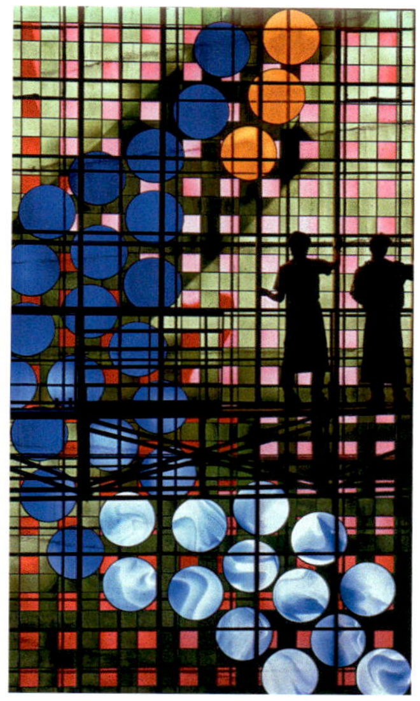

322

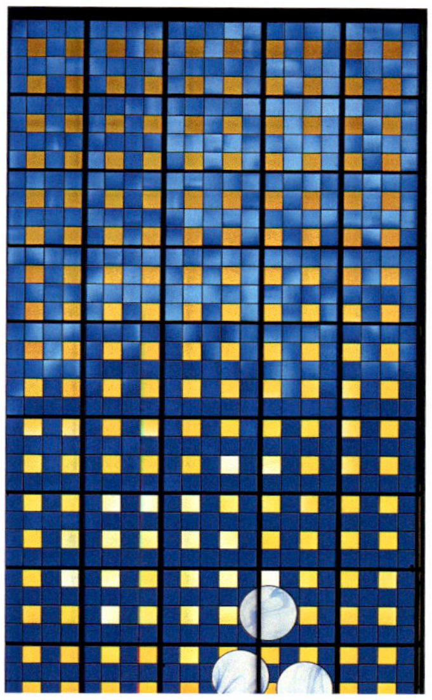

327

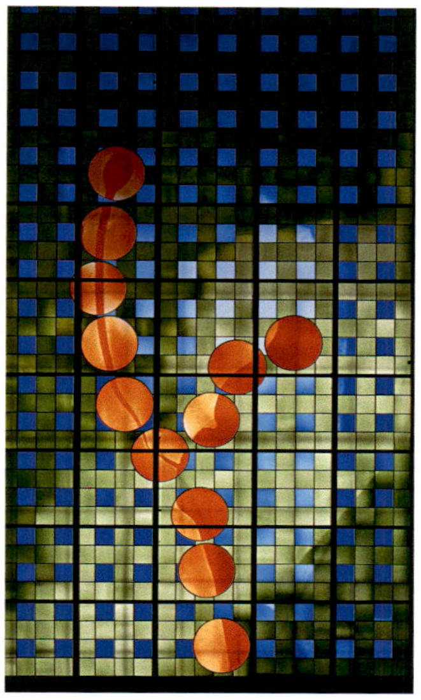

328

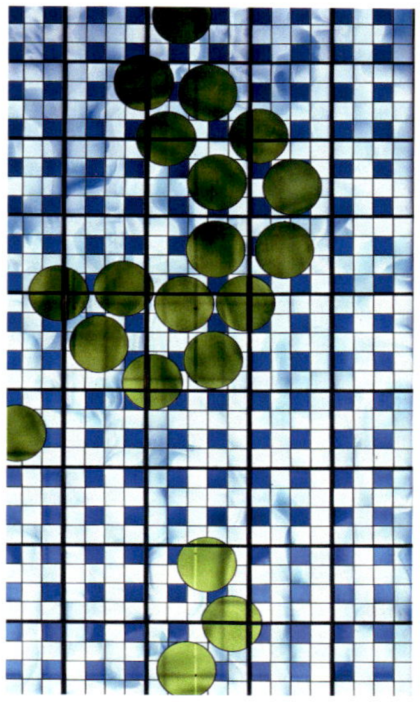

329

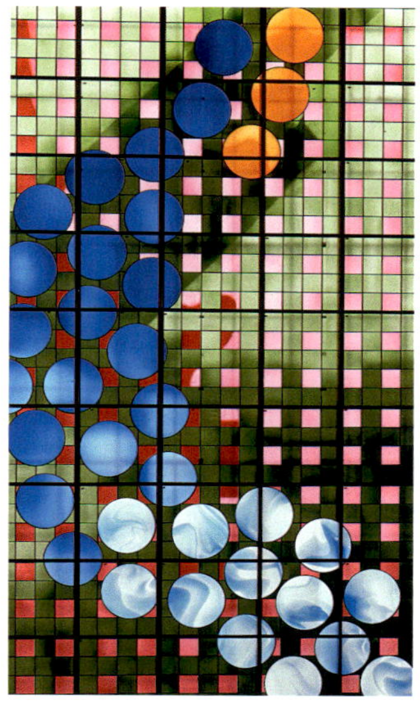

330

NORTESHOPPING

315 – 321

UPPER ROW:
Some of the longitudinal segments during the process of being temporarily built up at the exhibition window of the studio. Artist and artisans carefully check all details. Changes can be made at this point. – We see Brian Clarke, Tony Shafrazi, Gabriel Mayer, and craftsmen on the hoist.

323 – 330

LOWER ROW:
Completed longitudinal segments of the glass skylights above the extensive corridors of the mall still at the studio in Munich. Installed on site all these segments are accompanied by stripes of clear glass on both sides.

Circles of color in the roof light express an abstract narrative that moves down the mall like a Mardi Gras procession. When transmitted onto the floor, by the strong tropical sunlight, a colored footpath is formed, like vibrant stepping-stones. (Brian Clarke)

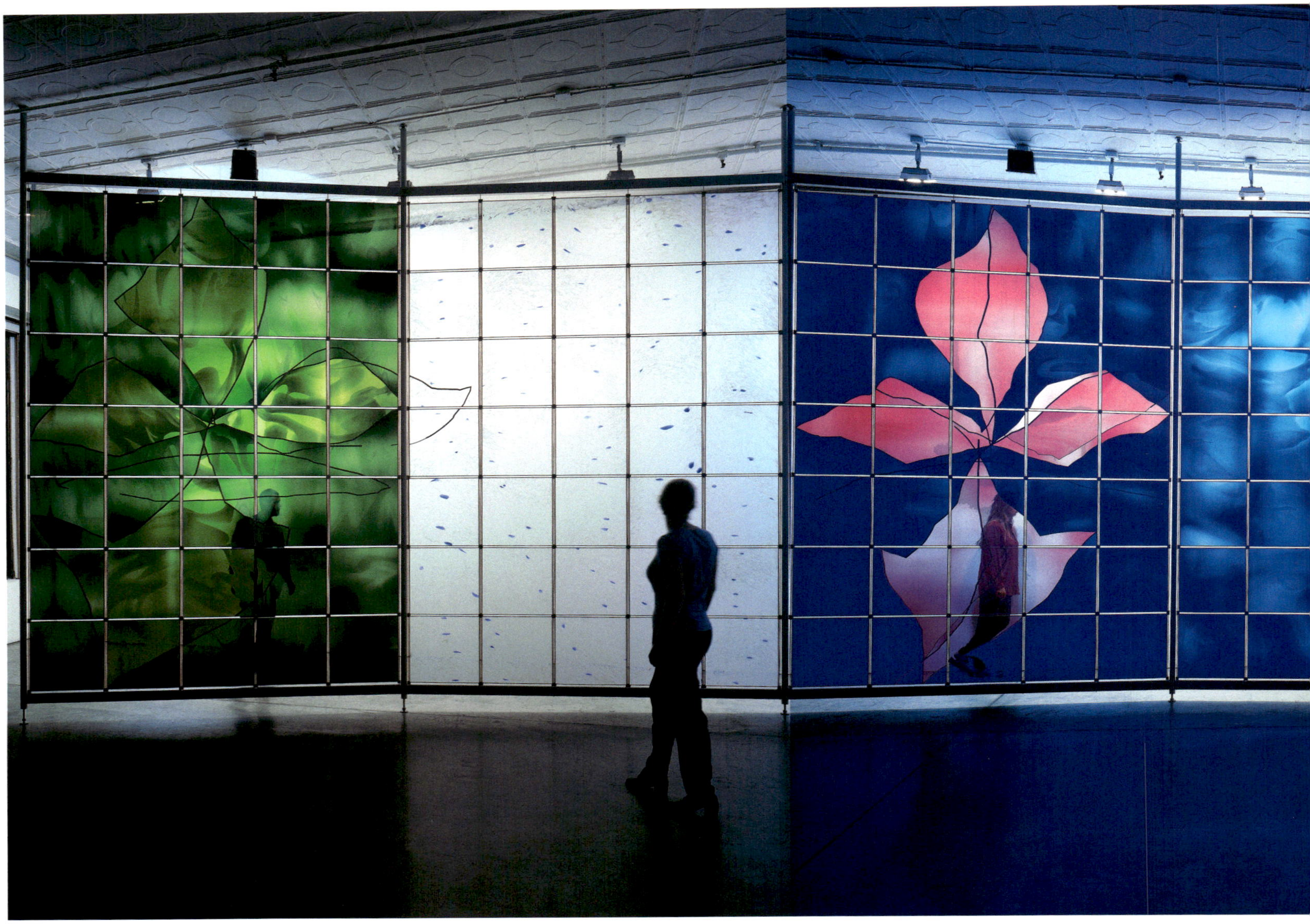

331

Brian Clarke / "The Glass Wall (Dedicated to Linda McCartney)"

location: Exhibition Tony Shafrazi Gallery, New York, NY, USA / **year:** June – September 1998 / Corning Museum of Glass, Corning, NY, USA / **technique:** stained glass, steel rods

Glasswall, 13 ½ × 70 feet. Blown glass, leaded. Frame system with steel rods
With this project Brian Clarke has stretched the limits of minimalistic and architectural stained glass and lead design, which lives from both the special glass and the few, most sensitively set lead lines. These are to be seen in diametric confrontation to Clarke's stained glass designs of later years, which – in parts – even consist of uninterrupted lead sheets *(see p. 243, fig. 358)*.

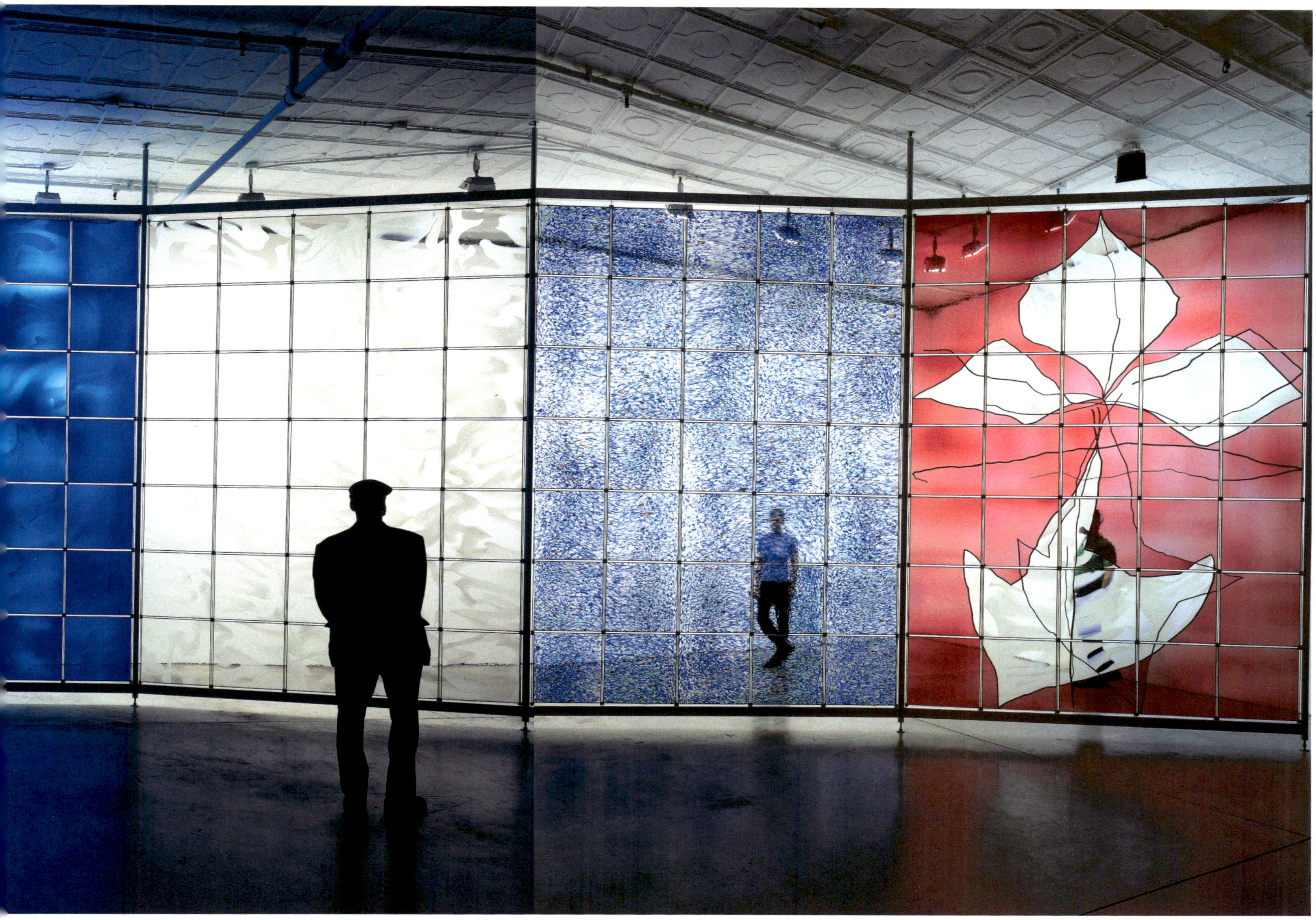

229

THE GLASS WALL

331
A wonderful "light" and transparent glass design. The viewers are standing in front of and behind the glass wall.

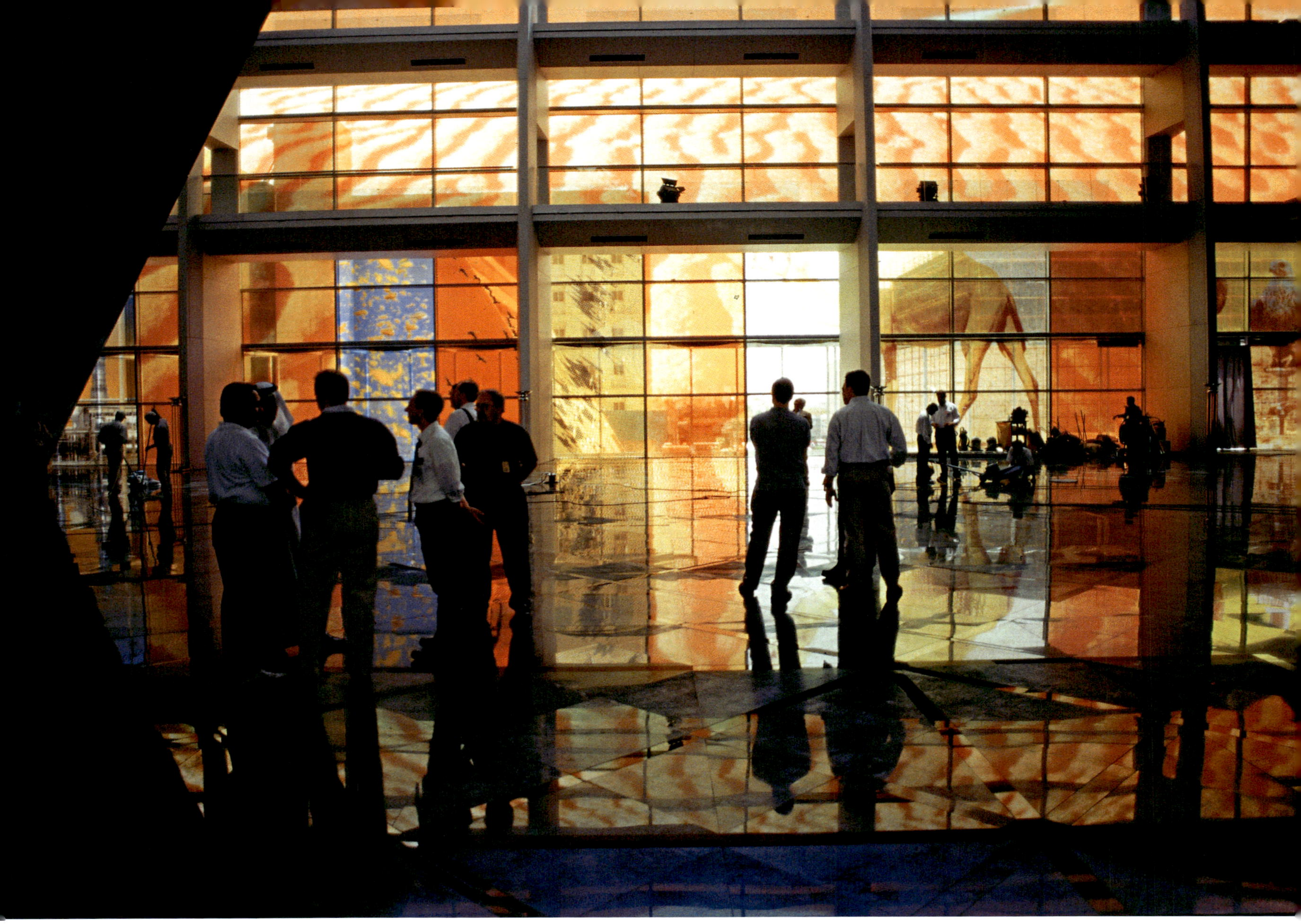

332

Brian Clarke / “Al Faisaliah Glass”

230

location: Glass wall Al Faisaliah Complex, Riyadh, SA / architects: Foster & Partners. King Faisal Foundation / **year:** 2000 / **technique:** float glass painting

80 feet high and 280 feet wide glass design. Transparent ceramic glass melting colors. 1- to 3-color silk screen print. Tempered glass.

21,750 square feet of stained glass make this project Brian Clarke’s largest architectural work to date and probably even nowadays the largest stained glass window in the world.

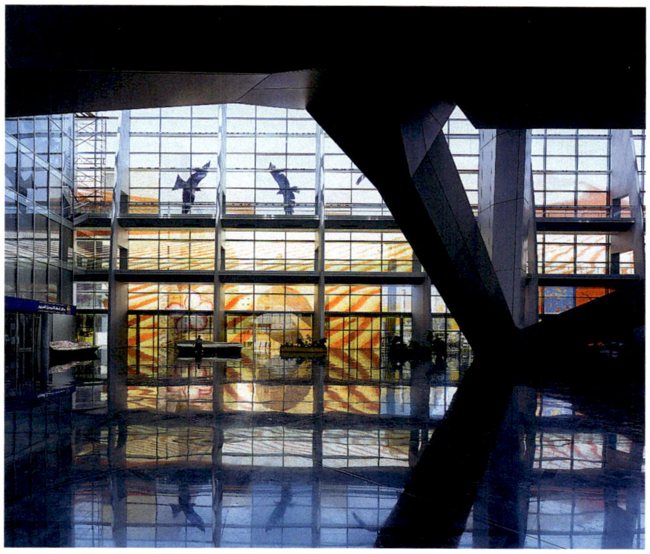

333

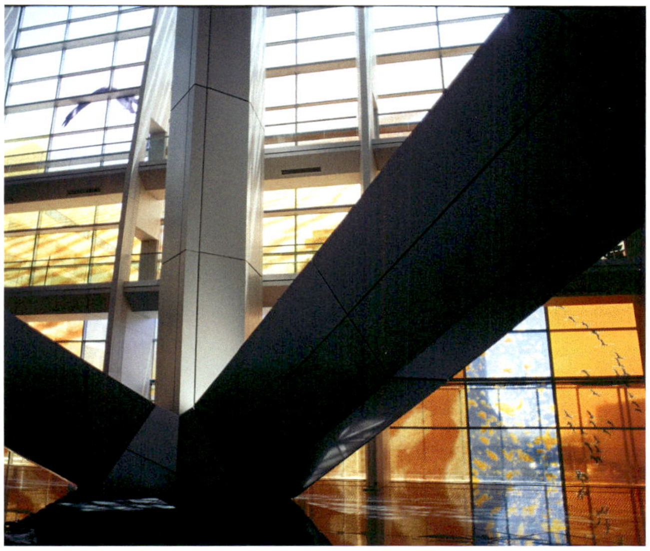

334

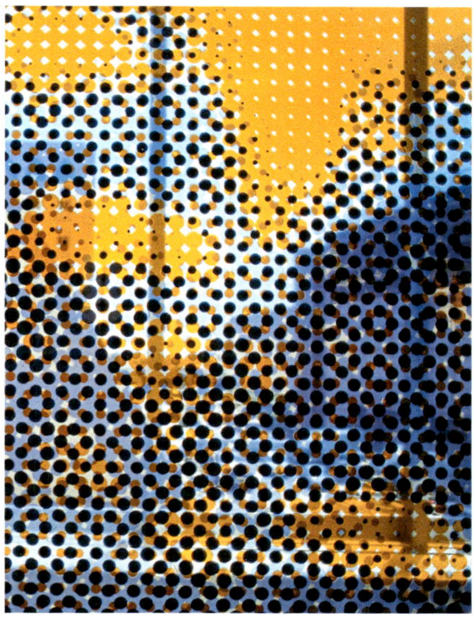

335

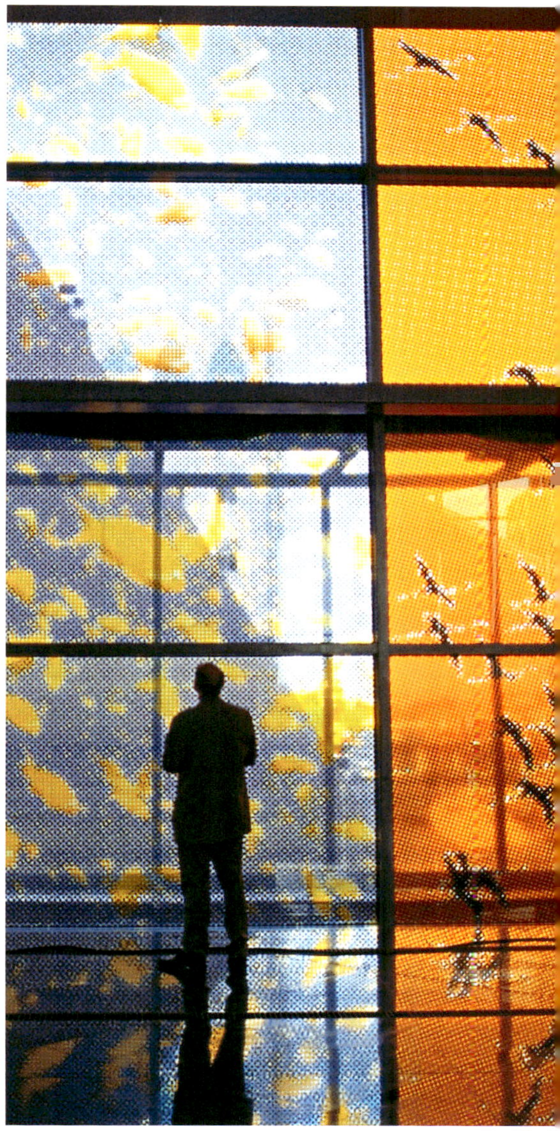

336

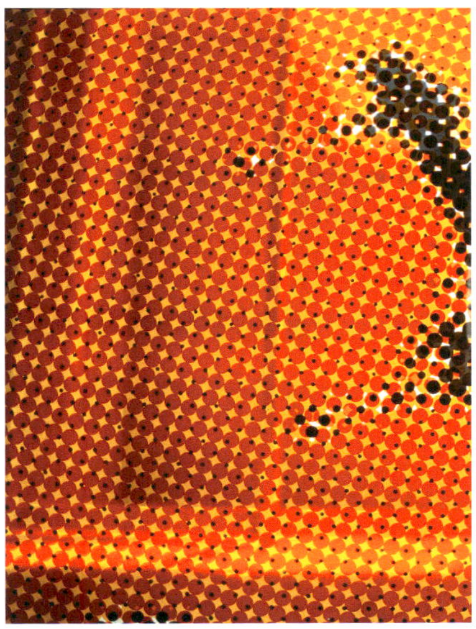

337

AL FAISALIAH GLASS

332

A portion of the window's lower half. The people in the background, placed near the stained glass wall, provide scale, indicating the enormous size of the piece.

333 + 334

The extraordinarily powerful architecture holds a dialogue with the window design.

335 – 337

The size of the silkscreen pixels makes the motifs appear fuzzy from close-up; from the distance they are clear.

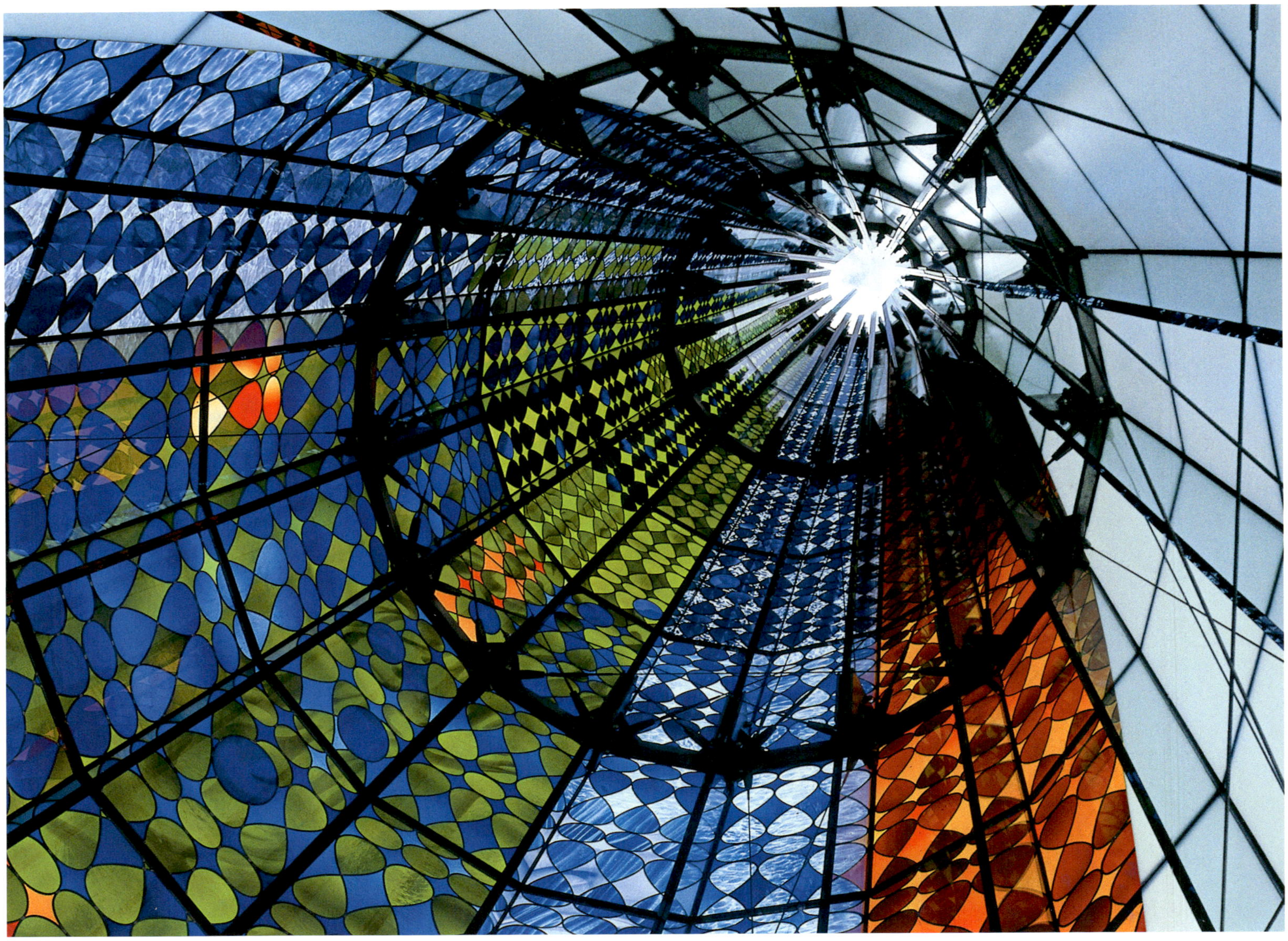

338

Brian Clarke / "The Swiss Bank Cone"

location: Swiss Banking Corporation, Stamford, CT, USA. / architects: Dewhurst McFarlane and Partners / **year:** 1999 / **technique:** stained glass; float glass painting

Leaded and stained glass, float glass painting. Triple insulated and structural glazing construction.

Brian Clarke says on the encounter with this work:

"The stained glass should create an effect like looking through leaves - layer upon layer of transparent color. Going inside is like entering into the center of a sapphire."

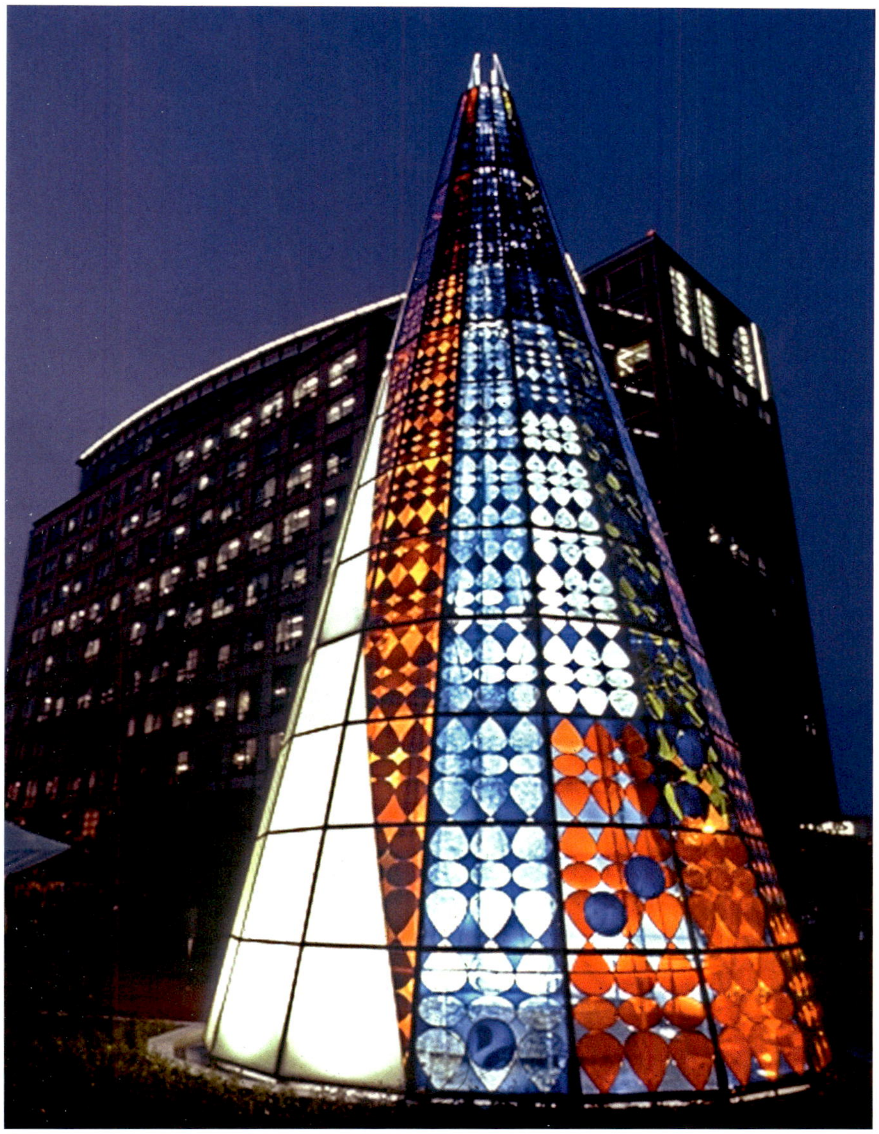

339

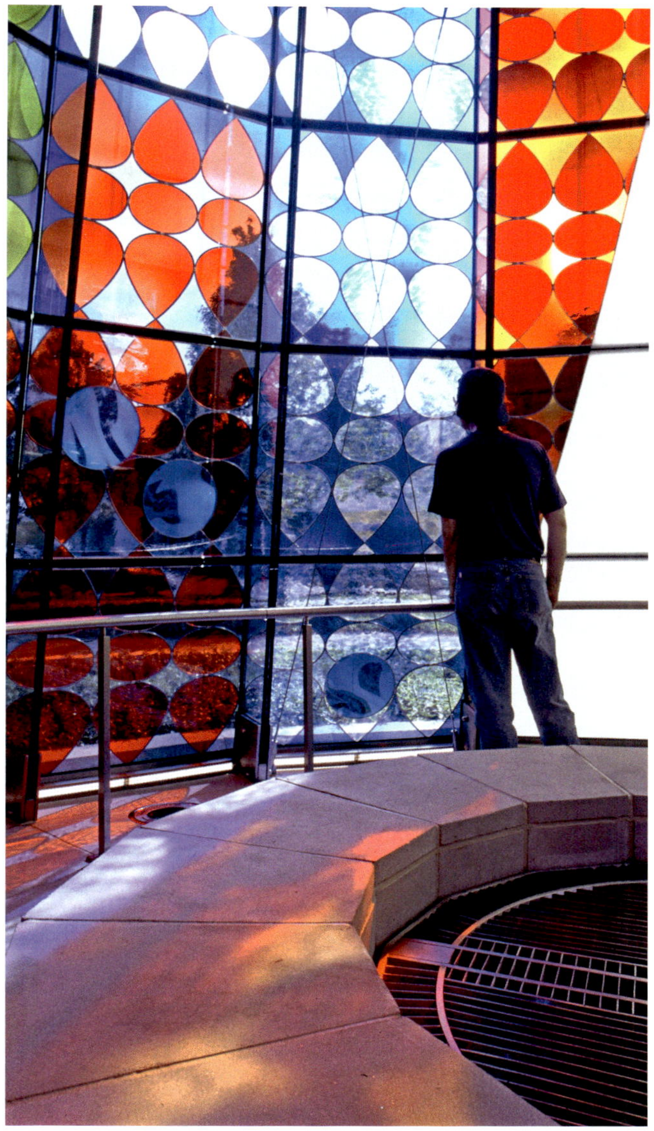

340

SWISS BANK CONE

338
Passers-by have access to the inside of the cone to view the artwork. They experience a burst of light and color.

339
At night the stained glass and the cone are visible by virtue of internally reflected lighting.

340
A detail inside of the cone.

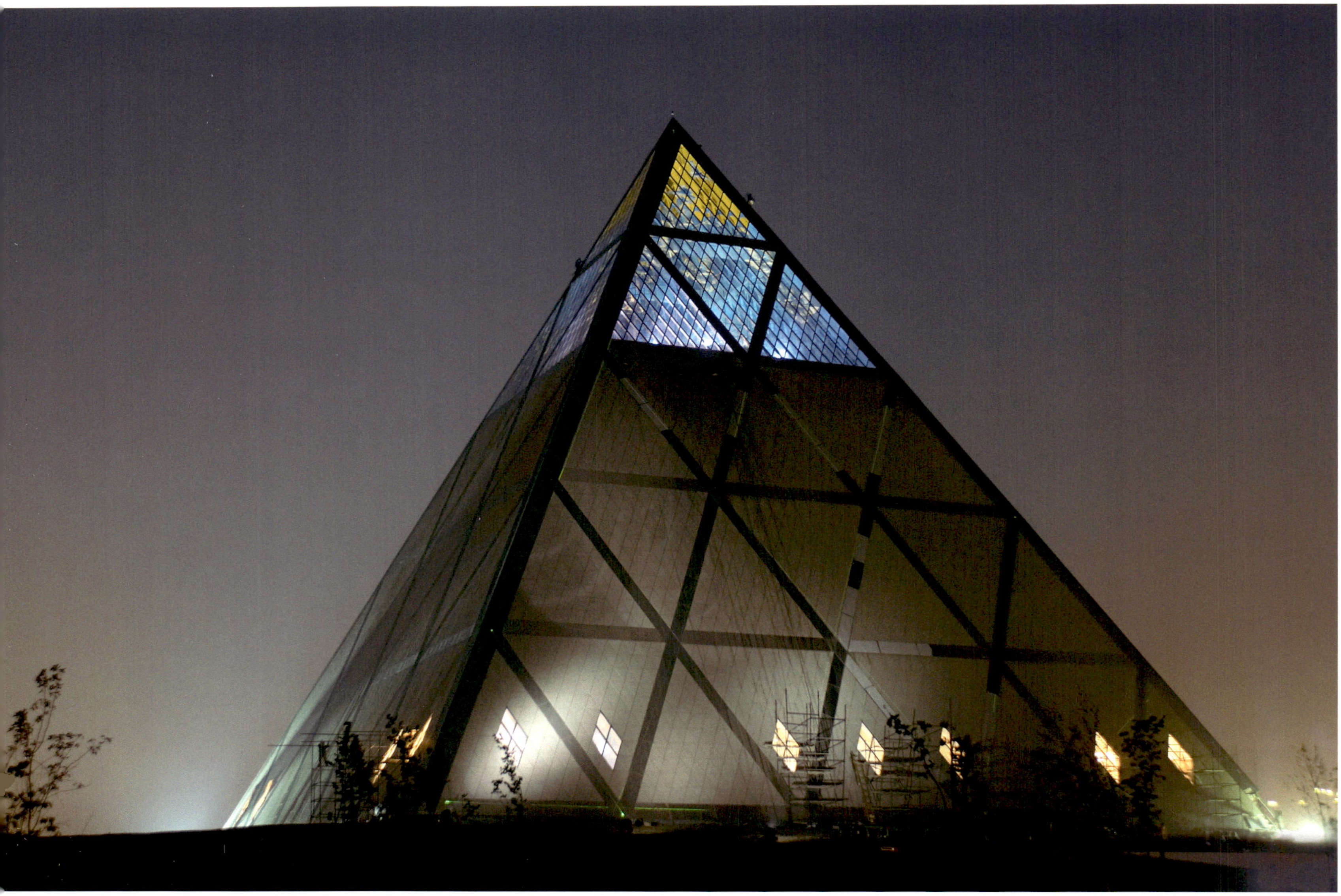

341

Brian Clarke / "Pyramid of Peace"

234

location: Apex, Pyramid of Peace, Astana, Kazakhstan / architects: Foster + Partners / **year:** 2006 / **technique:** stained glass; float glass painting

The pyramid has been designed to be a global centre for religious understanding, the renunciation of violence and the promotion of faith and human equality. In keeping with these aims Brian Clarke's 9700 square feet apex glass depicts a flock of white doves in flight set against a background field of vivid blue and gold.

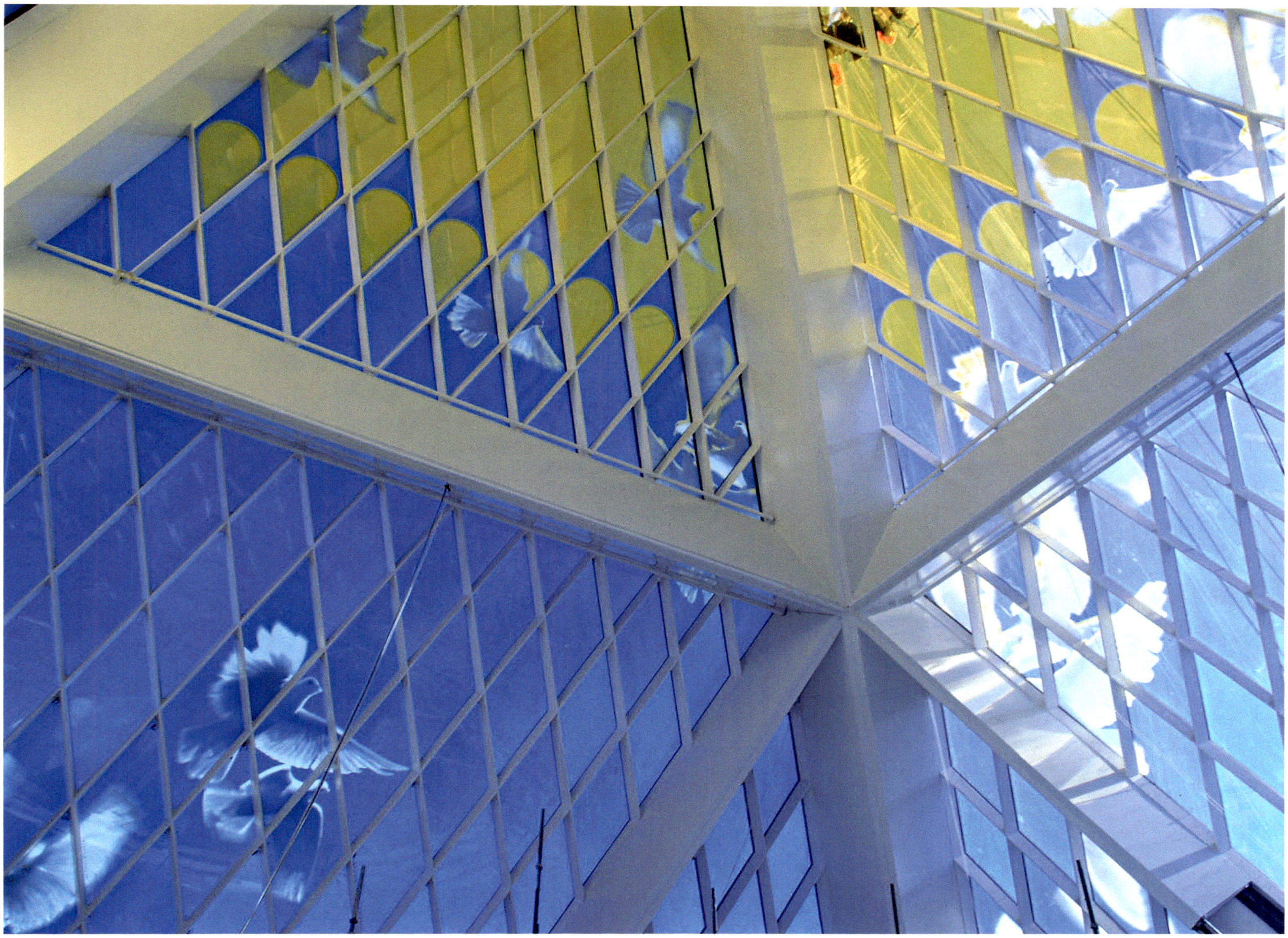

342

PYRAMID OF PEACE

341
The equal-sided pyramid at night with its glass tip illuminated. The scaffold in the lower portion indicates the scale of the work.

342
This view into the pyramid's inside makes it easy to see the swarm of white pigeons flying against a background of lively blue and gold – even against the bright day sky *(see also p. 44 + 45)*.

The composition uses artistic themes that Clarke has evolved through his work concerning the transillumination of light through naturally membranous materials such as petals, leaves, and feathers. Like these natural materials the glass and composition manifest the same emotive beauty with stunning effect.

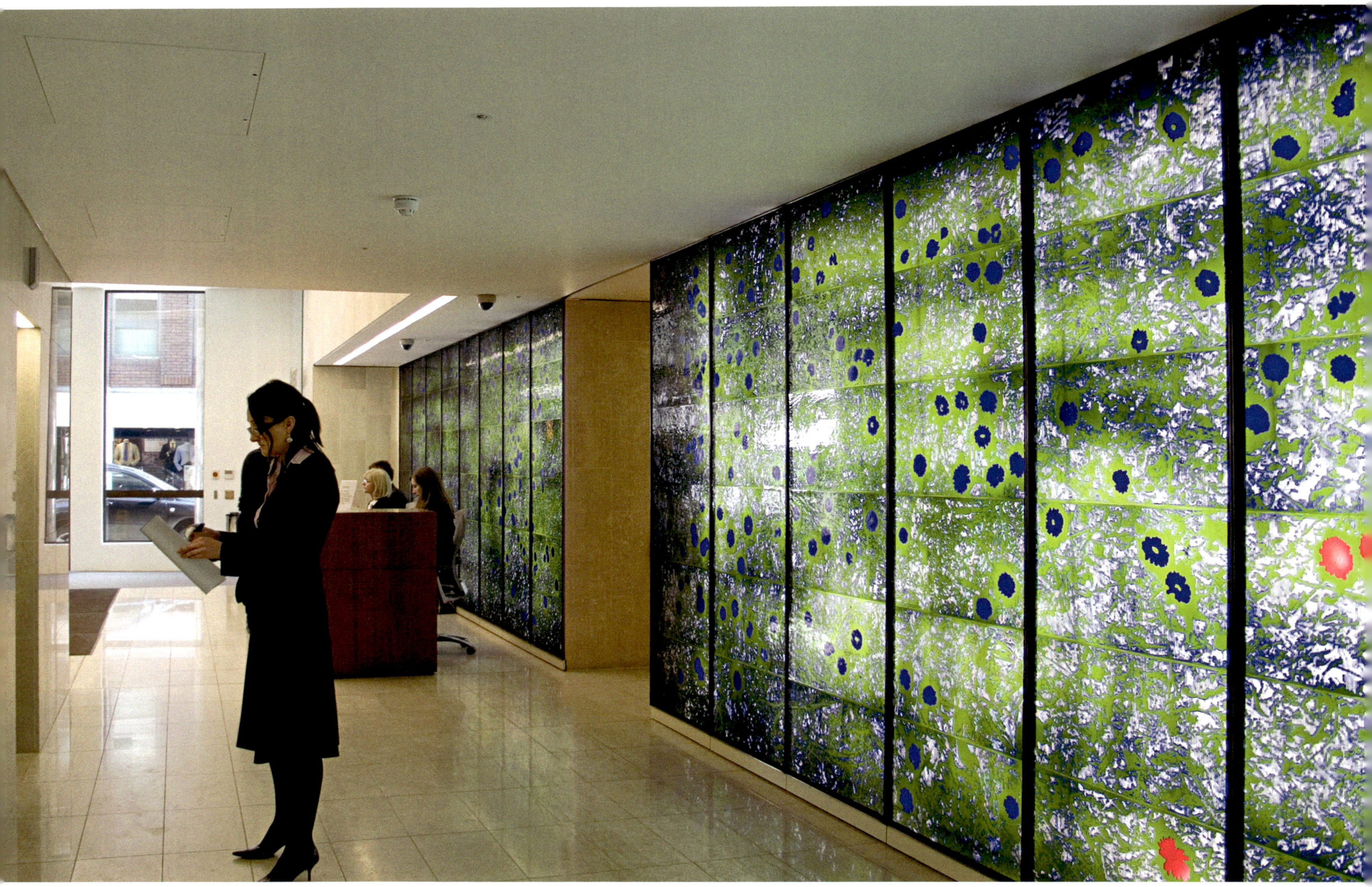

343

Brian Clarke / Apax – "Hovering There"

236

location: Administration Building, Apax Partners, London, GB / architect: Make / **year:** 2007 / **technique:** stained glass and oil on canvas

Flashed green glass, engraved, among others with blue/rose ceramic color infill and fired, glued onto laminated support glass, brass frames.

The work for this lobby includes the backlit stained glass screen and a large multi panel work on canvas entitled "Hovering There." Both are based on the shimmering color of an English Bluebell wood in May.

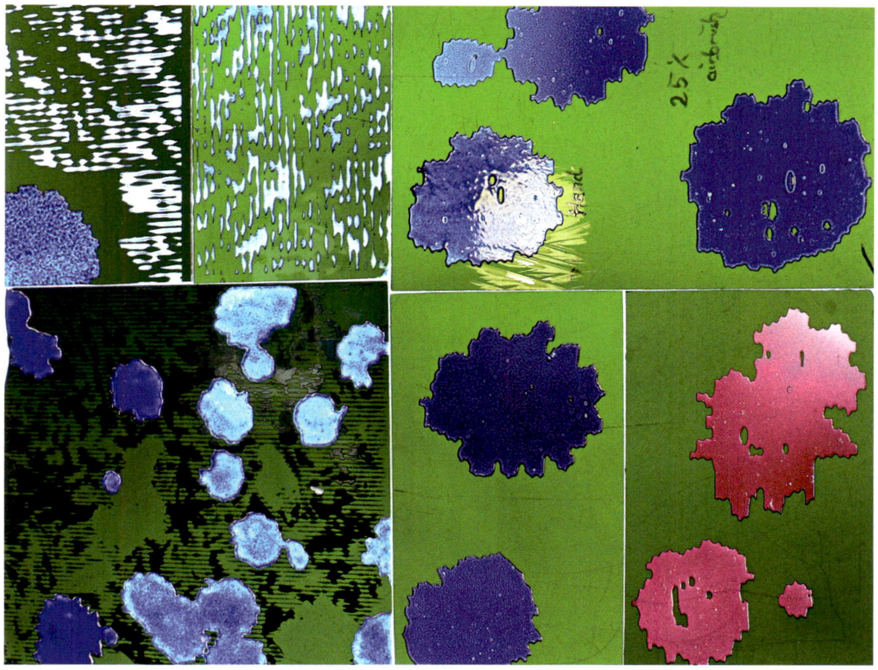

344

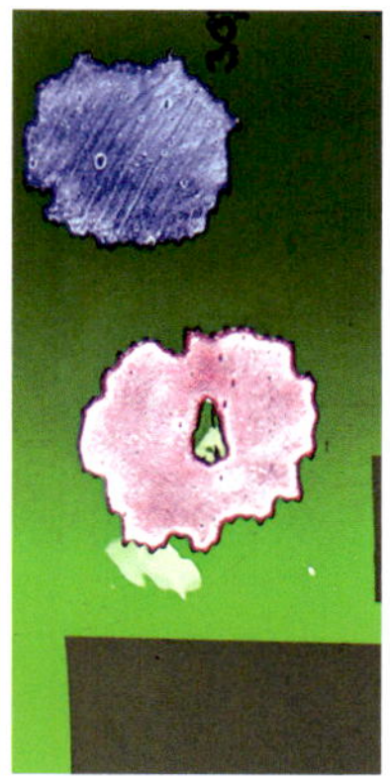

347

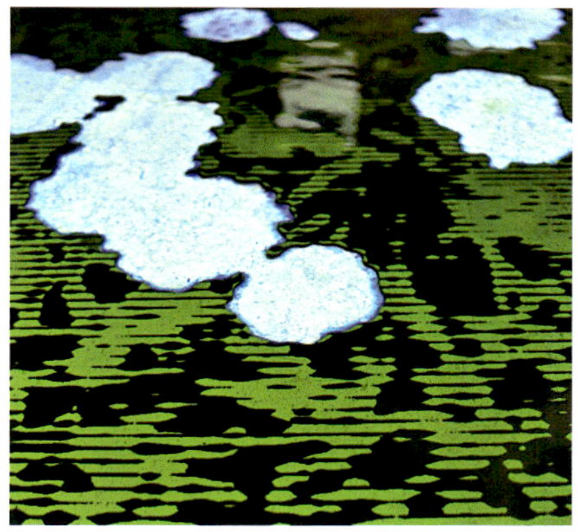

348

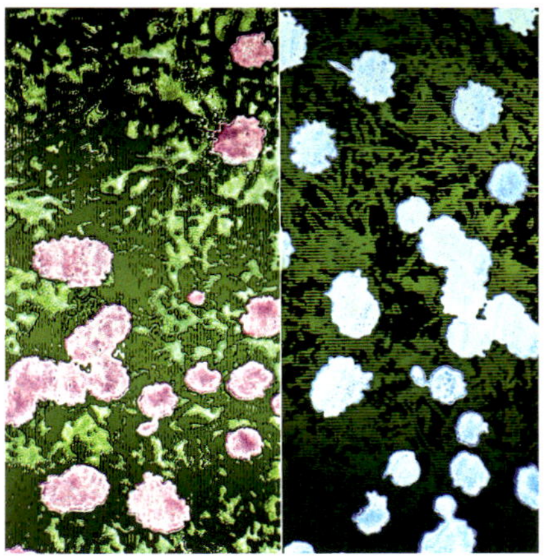

345

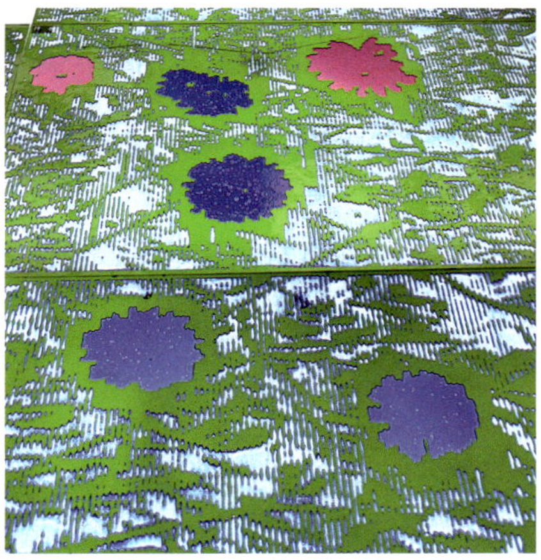

346

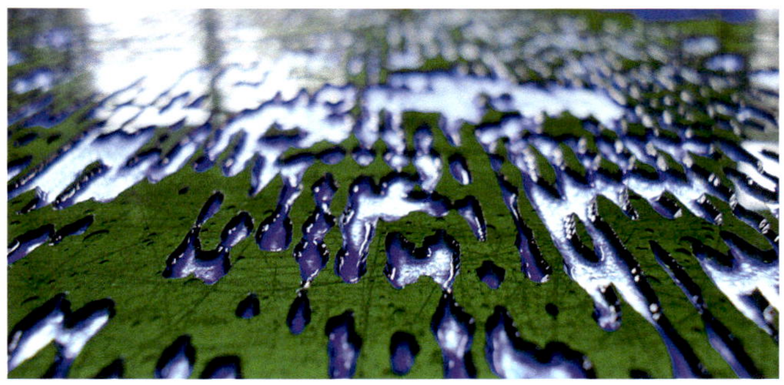

349

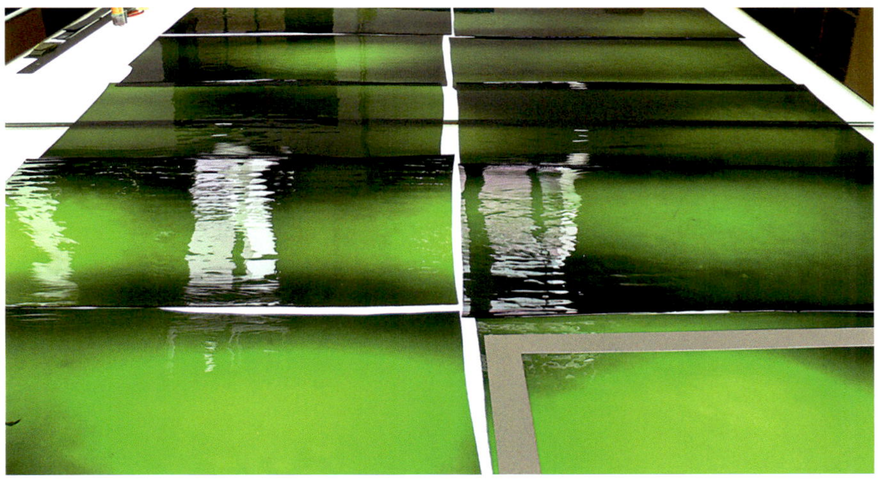

350

APAX – HOVERING THERE

343
The glass wall Brian Clarke designed extends from the entrance zone to the elevators and ends in a mirrored wall. The result is that from the opposite perspective the glass wall and the corridor are doubled.

344 –
350
The picture at the bottom shows flashed green glass plates, which considerably vary in intensity of color and are arranged according to the artist's wishes. The six smaller pictures show some of the steps of work, which slowly developed during the process of working.

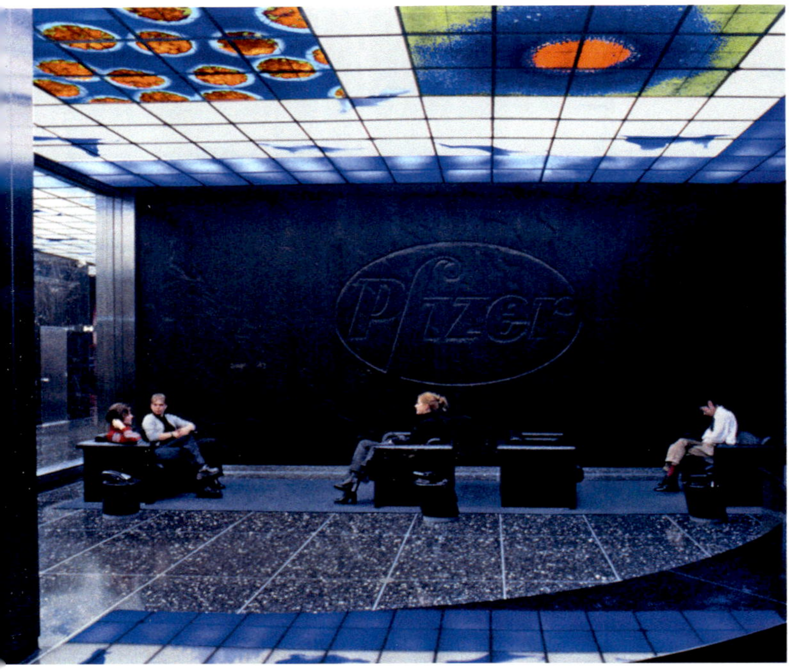

351

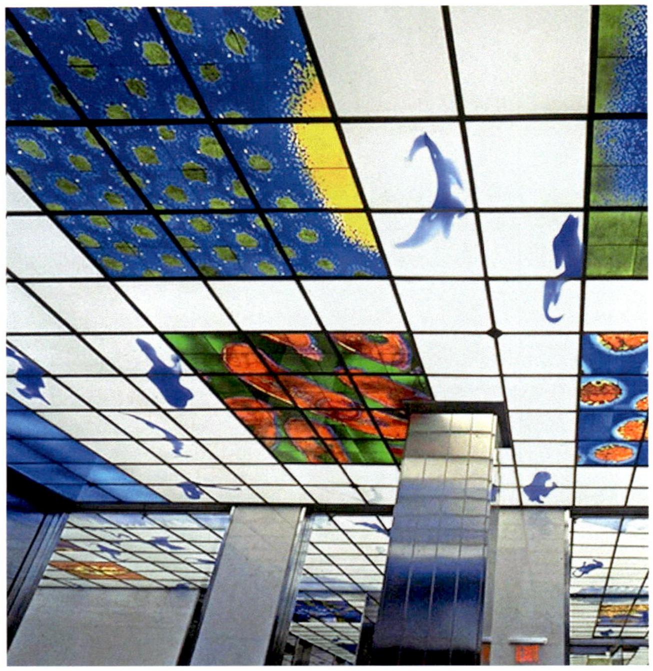

352

PFIZER PHARMACEUTICALS

351
Glass ceiling above the reception lounge

352 +
353
Differing impressions of the glass ceilings from various angles of view. The picture at right shows one of the elevator banks.

Brian Clarke / Pfizer Pharmaceuticals

location: Main entrance, lobby and street level façade, Pfizer Pharmaceutical WHQ, New York, NY, USA / Hixon Design Consultants / **year:** 1997 and 2001 / **technique:** stained glass, mosaic, float glass painting

Stained glass and mosaic in the inner lobby of the main entrance comprise an area of 6500 square feet; the glass facade at street level 3700 square feet.
While walking under the light and very painterly pattern of blue and white the viewer is confronted with fragments of modern science, embedded in an artistic and aesthetic structure - the grid. In 2001 Brian Clarke added to this suite of works another glass artwork for the street level facade on 42nd Street and 2nd Avenue. This work uses also the technique of float glass painting, which Clarke had used already for the Al Faisaliah Complex in Riyadh *(see pages 230–231)*.

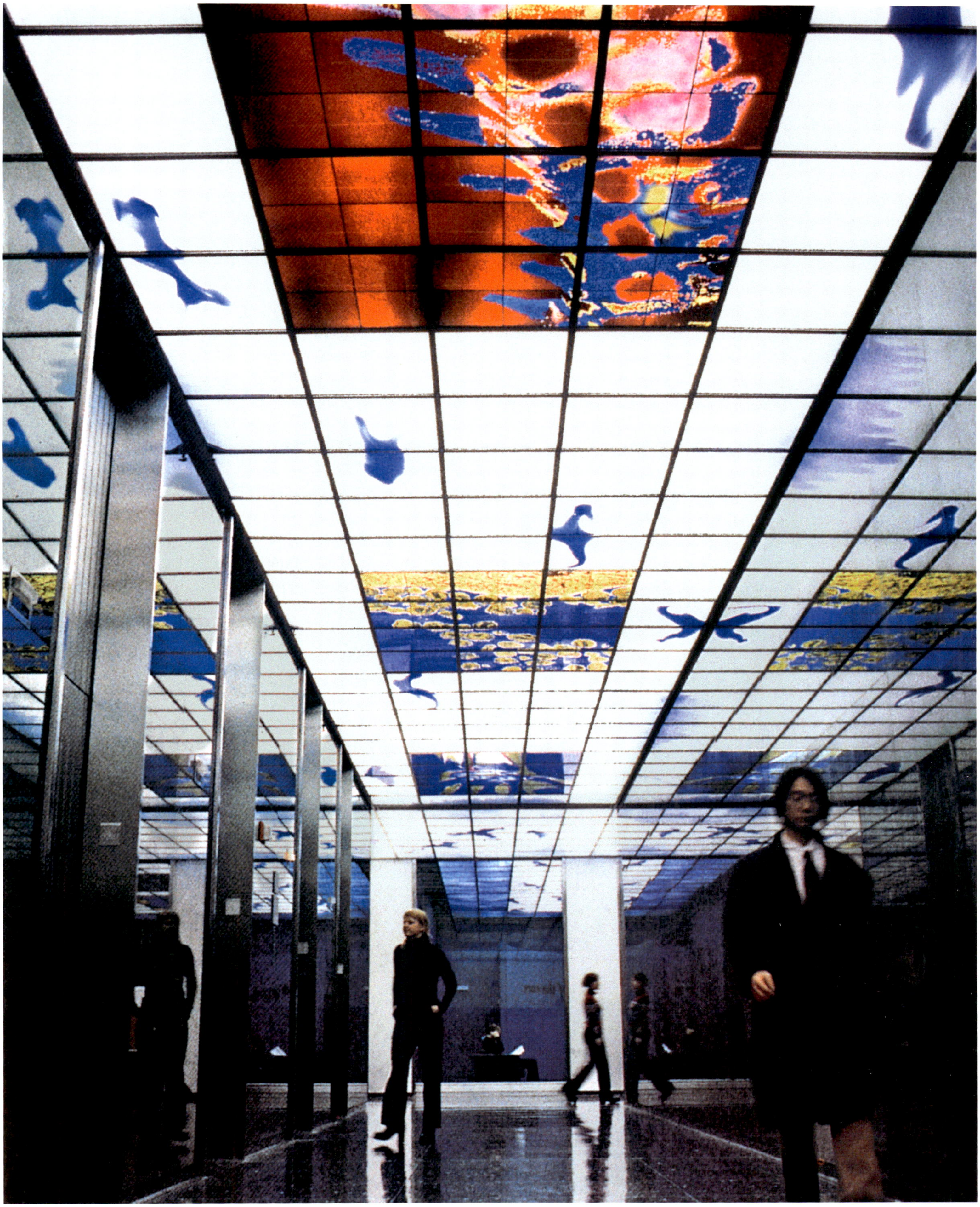

239

353

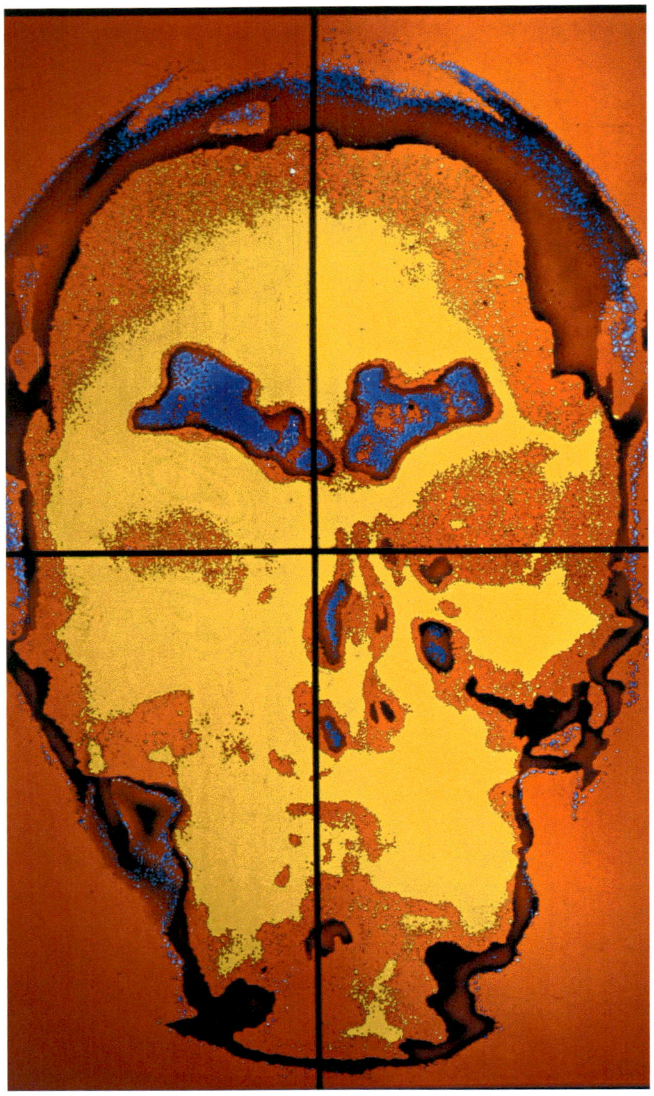

354

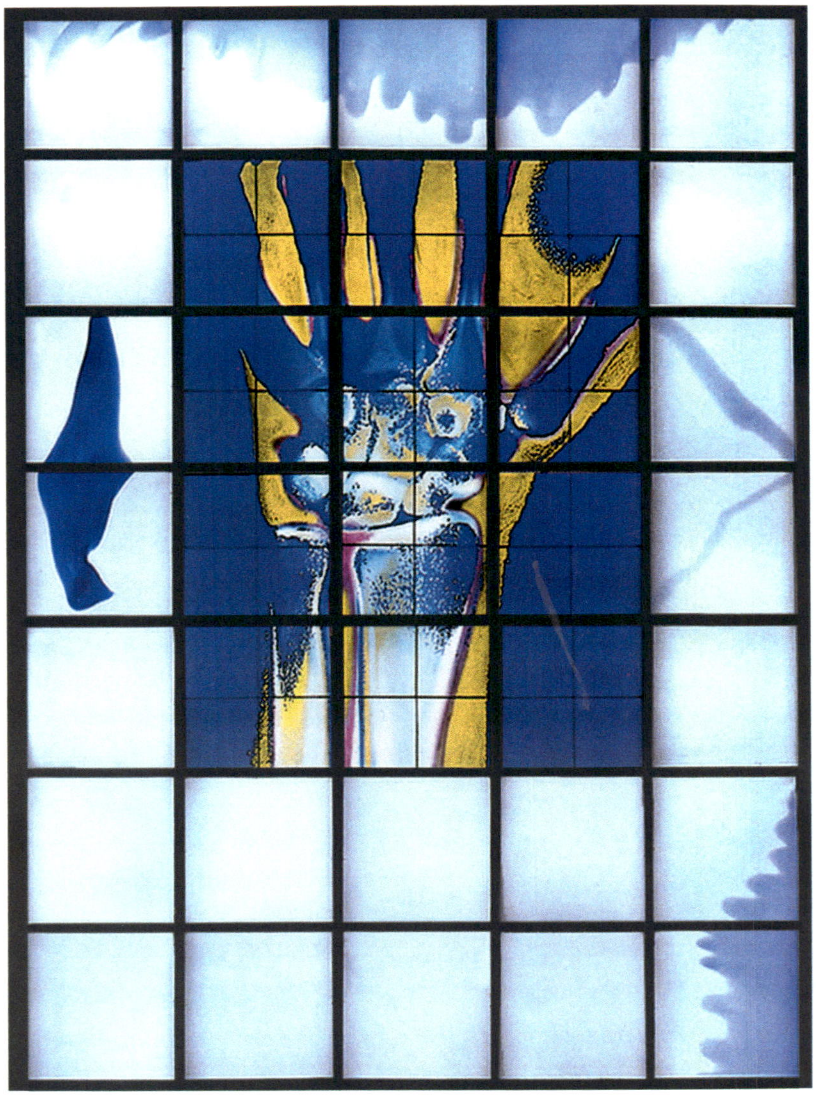

355

356

Brian Clarke matched the architectural situation (long aisles connecting the buildings and diverse functional spaces, a large lobby) by designing a composition that combines the openness and lightness of a space defined by shades of blue and white with contrapuntal images related to the “heart” of Pfizer’s enterprises.

This project, part of the refurbishment of Pfizer’s headquarters building, stretches over a whole block from 42nd to 43rd Street in Manhattan.

PFIZER PHARMACEUTICALS

Clarke called the motifs from Pfizer's areas of research predellas and embedded them into the bright and grid-like portions of the ceiling.

354
Detail of a glass predella. As can be seen here, this piece incorporates flashed glass, etching, and enamel paint.

355
This predella is embedded into the bright and painterly ceiling made of individually blown flashed glass pieces.

356
Detail of the external glass facade along 42nd Street and 2nd Avenue in Manhattan. Clarke adapted the amorphous blue motifs from the inner ceilings for the exterior space, realizing them with Mayer in float glass technique.

357
Two predellas and grid works done in the technique of glass mosaic. The long inner walkway towards 43rd Street is dominated by mosaic ceilings.

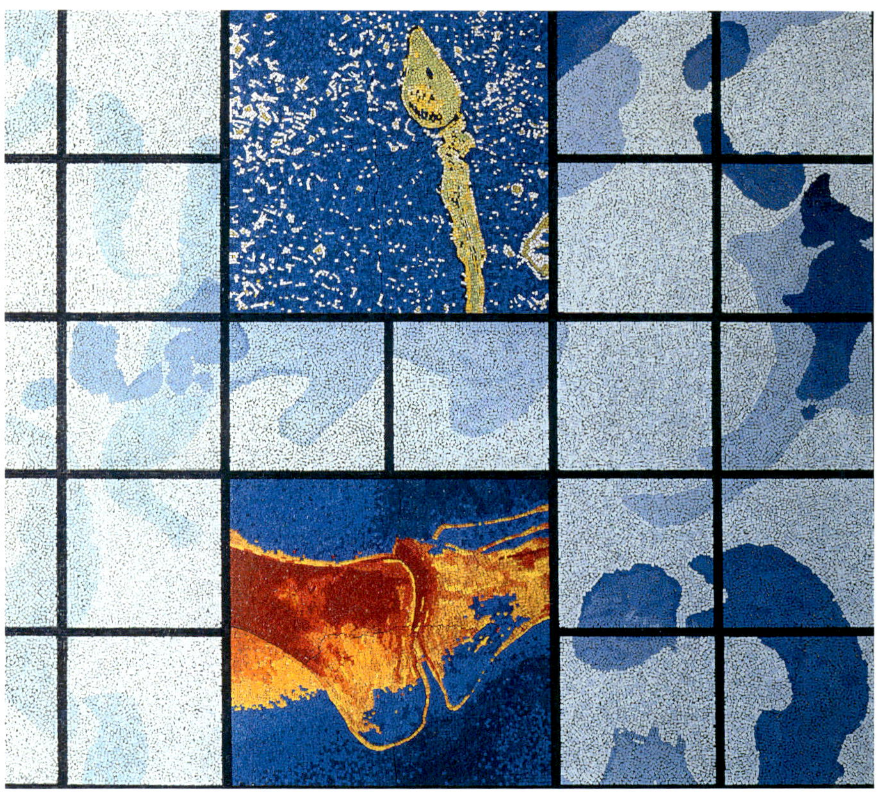

357

358
“Don’t Forget the Lamb,” a polyptych in seven panels, 93" × 166", stained glass, lead, painting on canvas, LED backlit.

359
Installation of thirteen freestanding stained glass panel artworks, each 82" × 36" (Studies for Atlantes) resp. 82" × 150" (Studies in Grisaille). The picture shows “Studies for Atlantes” at the right and Study in Grisaille II and III in the foreground and left background.

Brian Clarke / Exhibitions

“Don’t Forget the Lamb” Exhibition of stained glass, paintings, and leaded panels. Phillips de Pury, New York, NY / **year:** 2008

“Transillumination” Exhibition at Tony Shafrazi Gallery, New York, NY, USA / **year:** 2002 / **technique:** float glass painting

“Transillumination” as ‘glass without lead’ and “Don’t Forget the Lamb” as ‘lead without glass’ exemplify the extreme polarities of stained glass that Clarke has investigated in the last decade. They have stretched and completely redefined the medium.
(See article Martin Harrison, page 249).

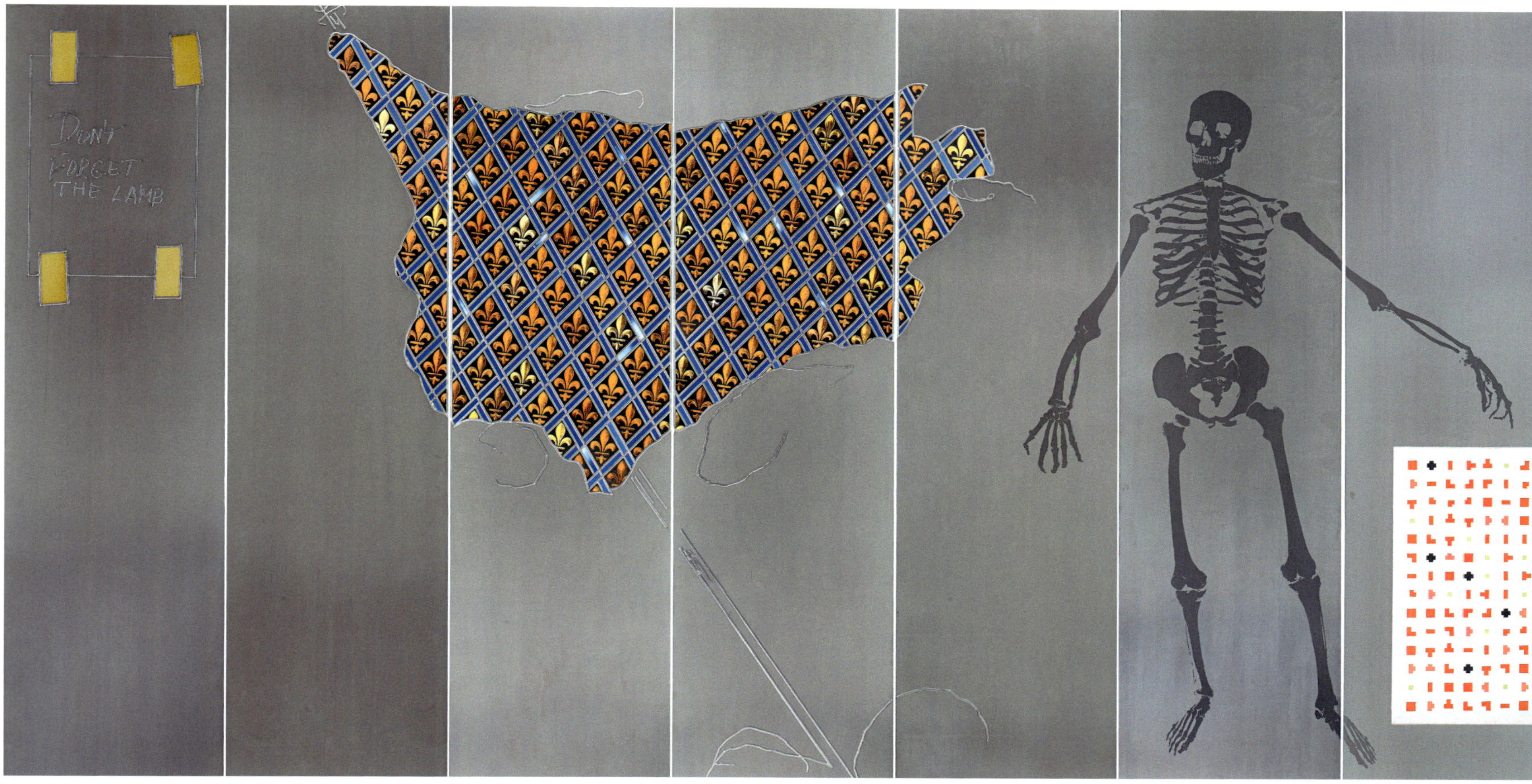

358

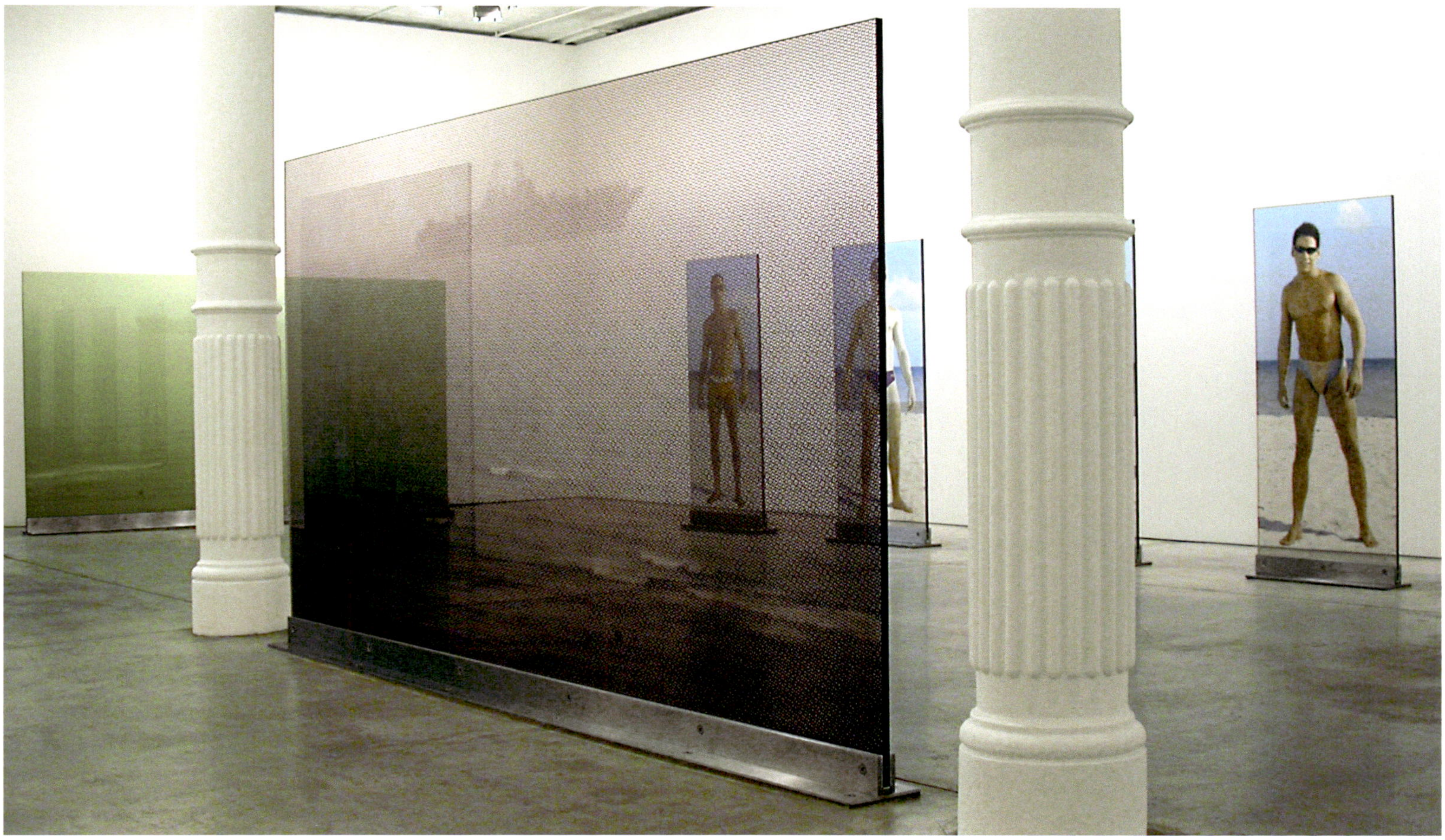

359

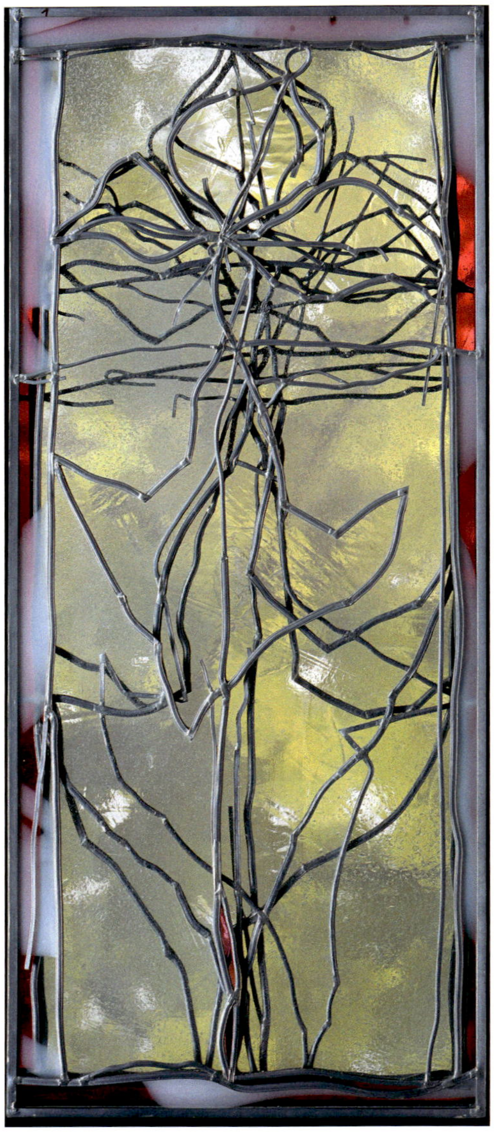

360

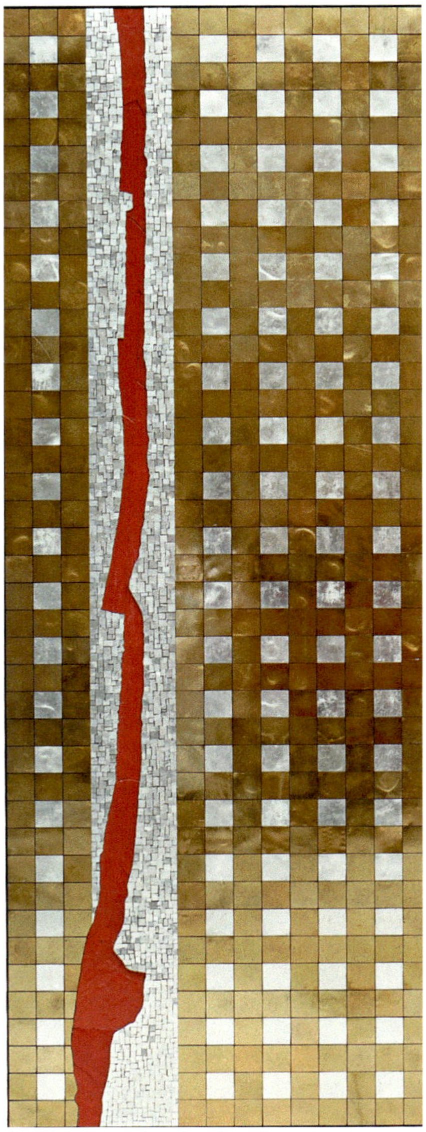

361

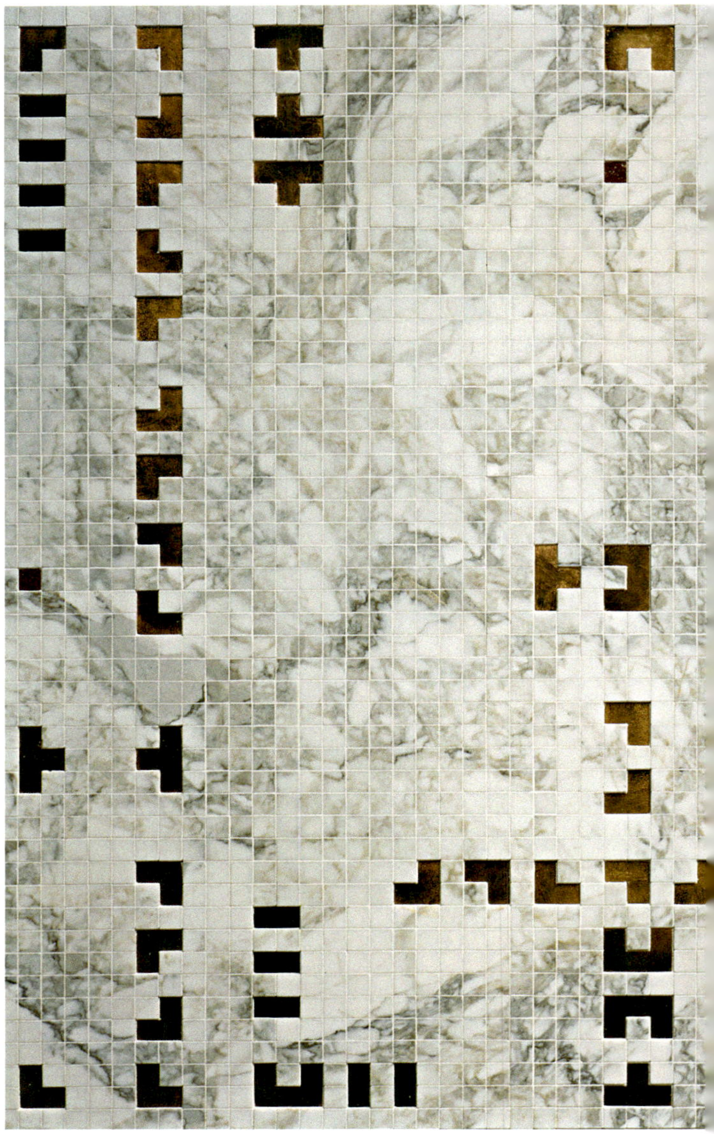

362

Brian Clarke / Museum, Gallery and Similar Work

Various places, years, techniques

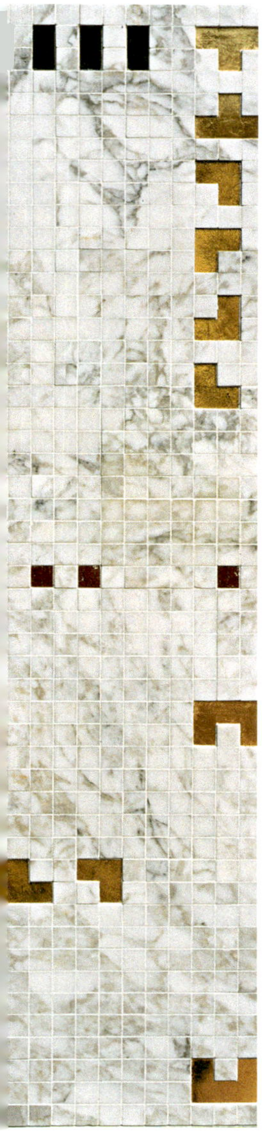

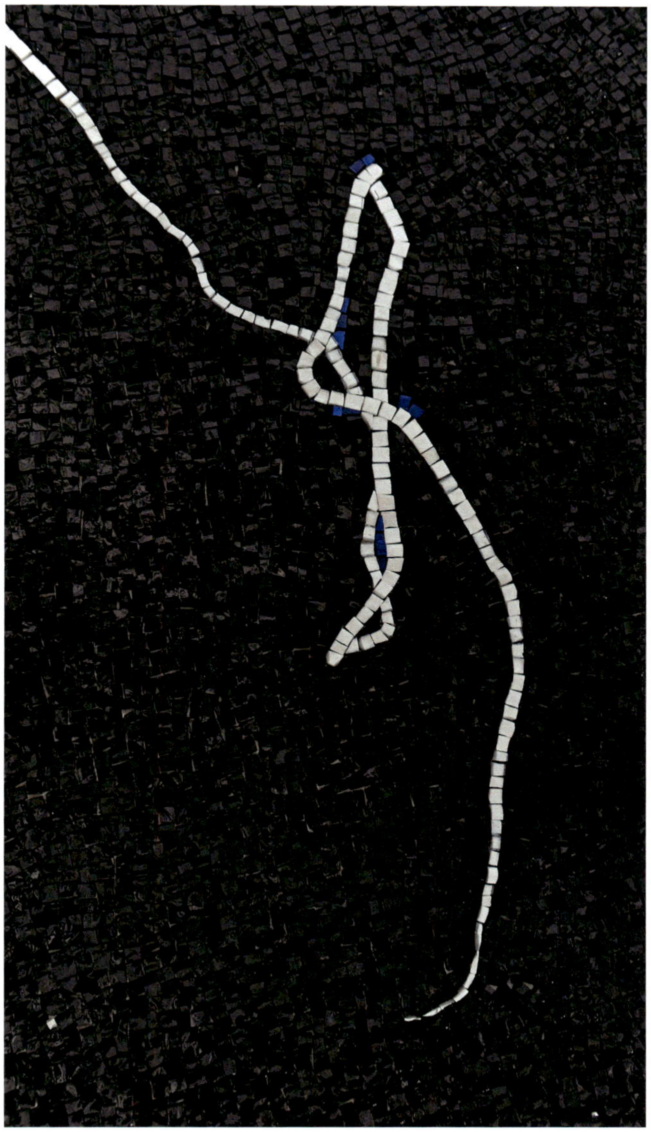

363

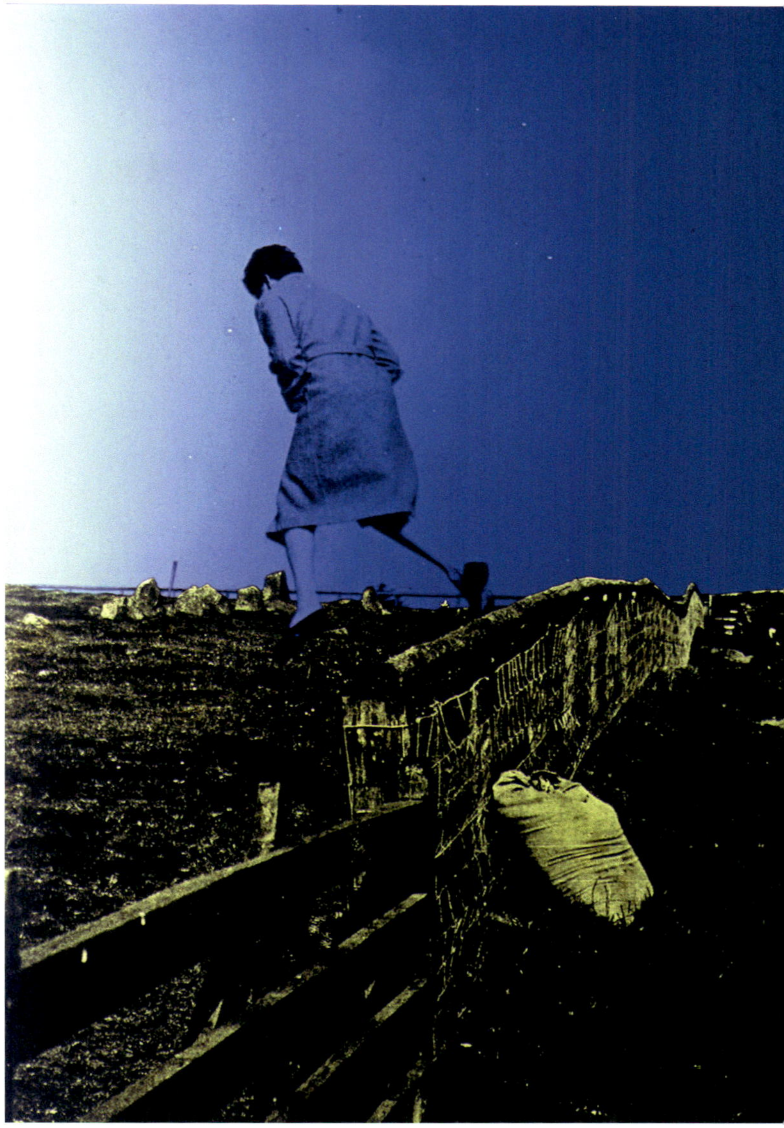

364

360
Untitled, stained glass and lead, three-layered 97 × 41 cm / 2003.

361
Mosaic for a complex modern building (one of two panels) / 235 × 87 cm, circa 1993.

362
"Mayer'sche Mosaic," marble, stone, and gold mosaic tesserae / 125 × 125 cm, 1982.

363
Detail of a mosaic floor for a private home, 2010.

364
Brian Clarke and Linda McCartney "Jumping off Fence," stained glass and photography, 65 × 43.5 cm, 1997.

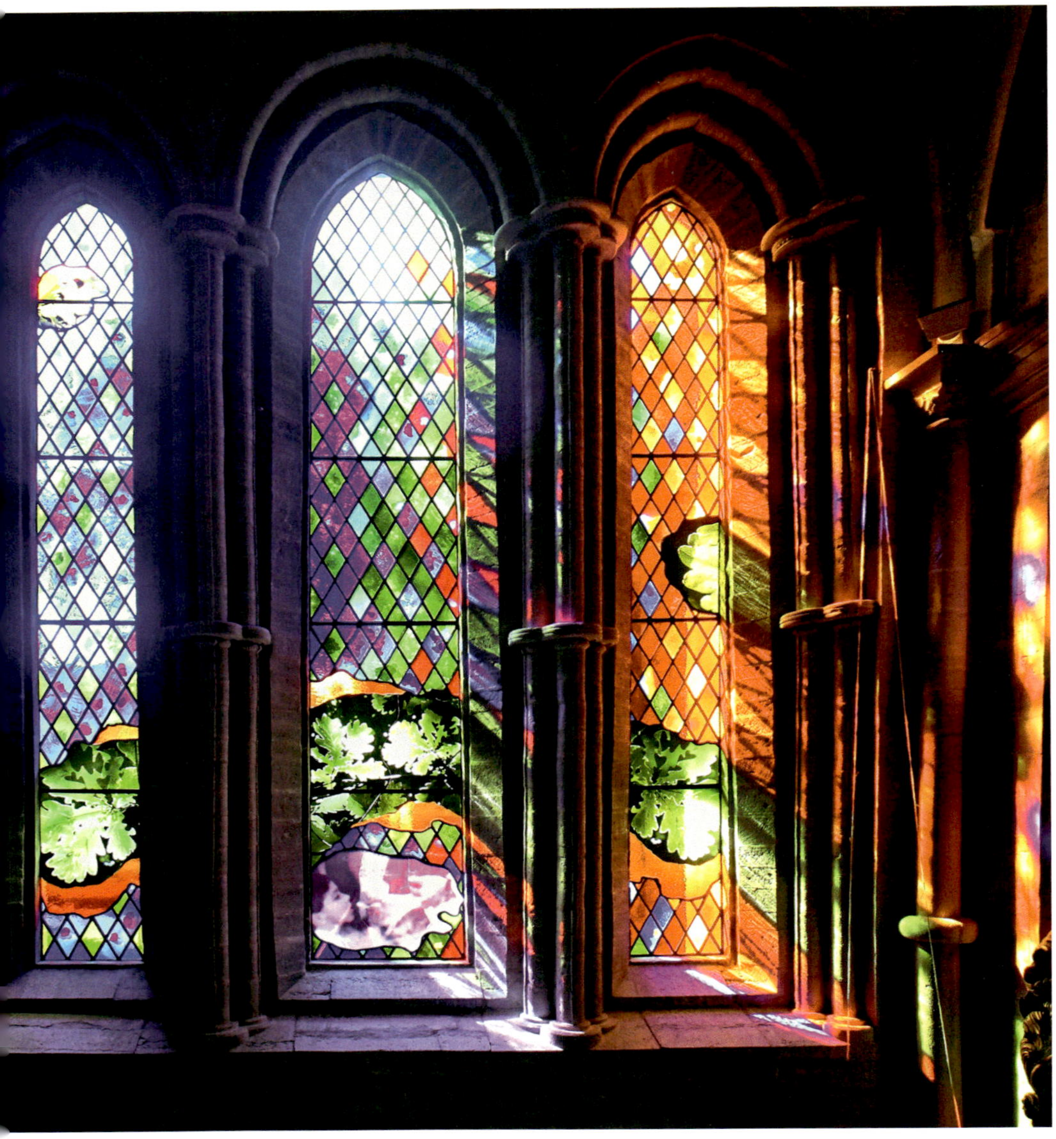

365

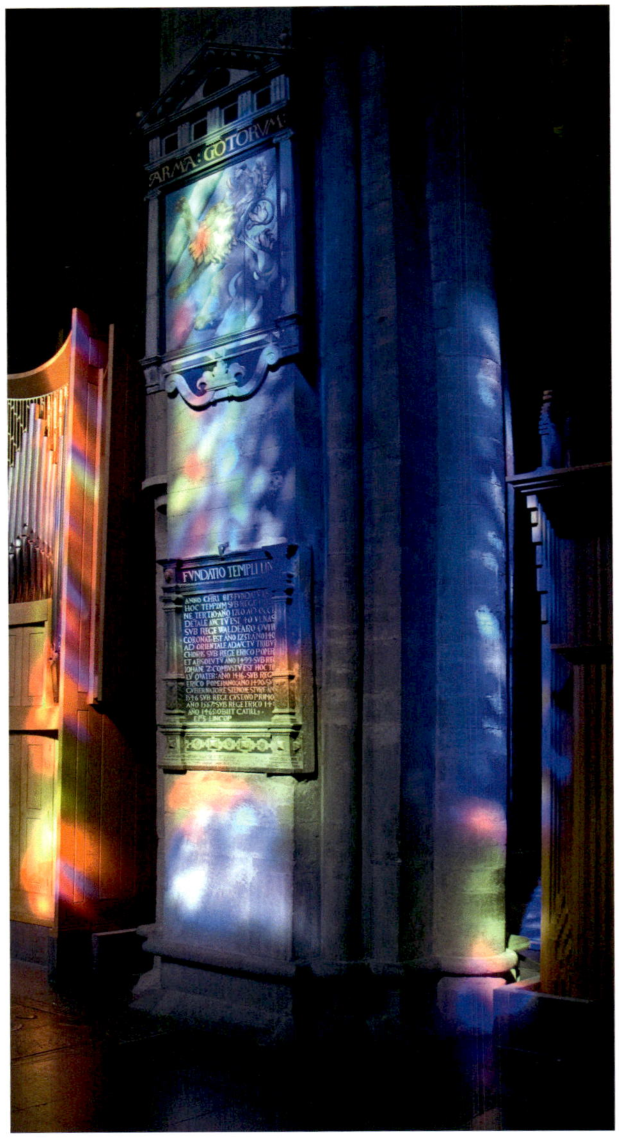

366

Brian Clarke / Linköpings Domkyrka und Romont

location: Linköpings Domkyrka, Gothic Cathedral Church, Linköping, SE / Cathedral Office and The Swedish National Heritage Board/ Riksantikvarieämbetet / **year:** 2010 / **technique:** stained glass

location: Romont, Medieval Chapel of the Abbaye Cistercienne de la Fille-Dieu, Romont, CH / **year:** 1997 / **technique:** stained glass

Blown and flashed antique glass, acid etched, painted, silkscreen print. Cast iron frame in rhombic and amorphic shapes.

Stained glass windows, distinctive and contemporary without compromise for medieval edifices and architectural jewels!

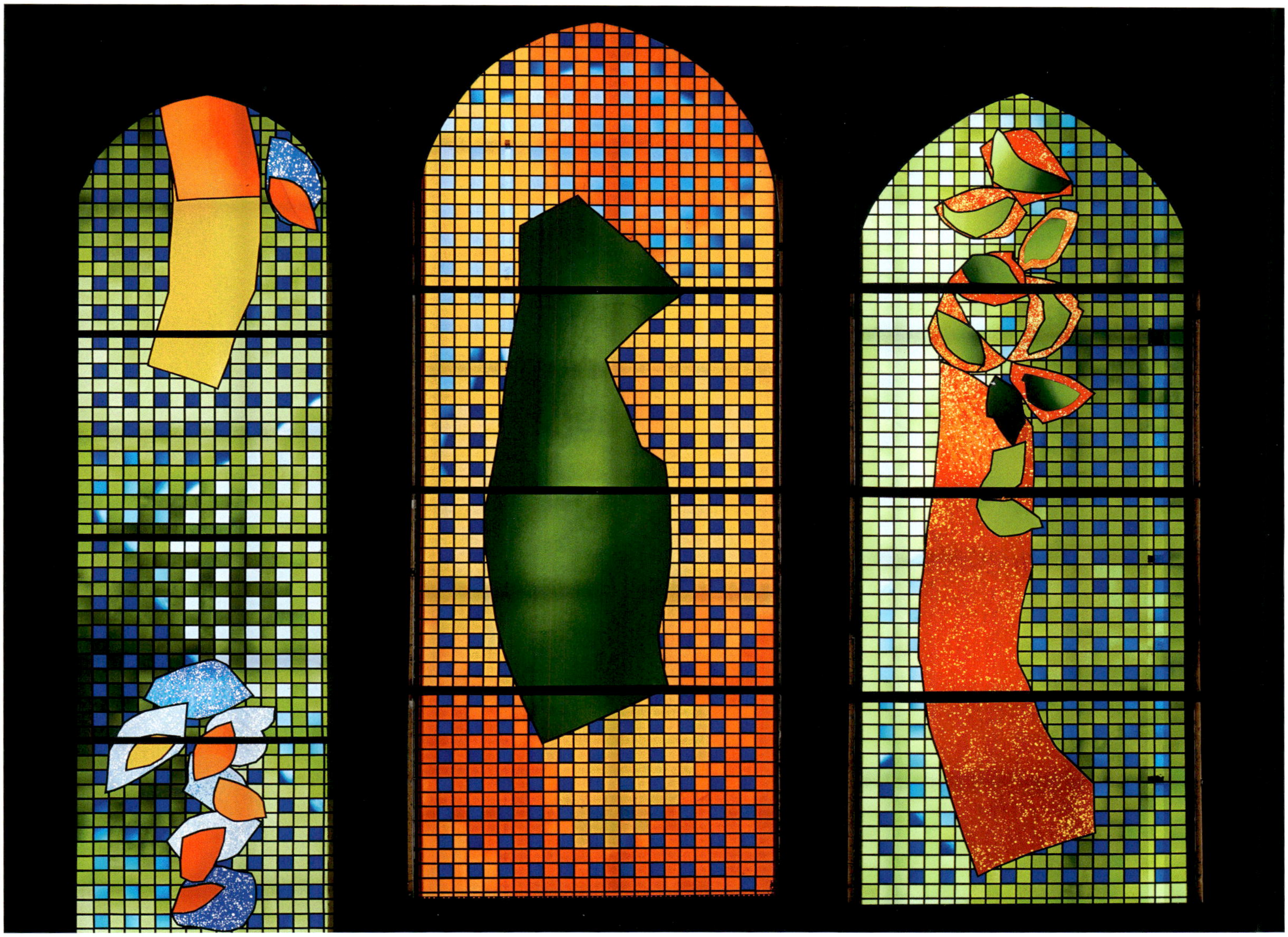

367

LINKÖPINGS DOMKYRKA

365
The three-light window at the south side. The rhombic structure of the historic cast iron frames was mostly conserved, yet changed in parts according to design.

366
Color and light reflections on medieval stone work.

ROMONT

367
Three windows from the south side.

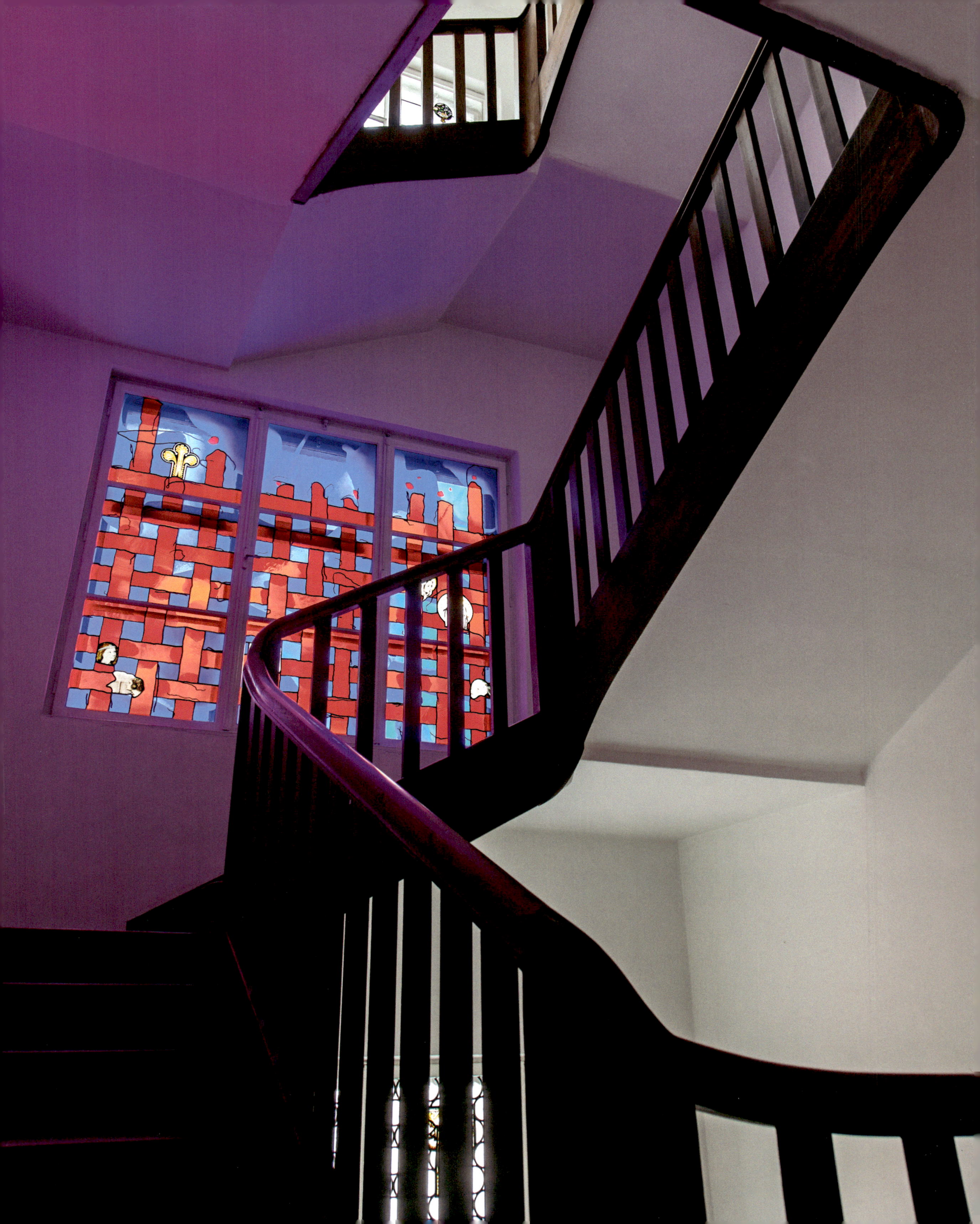

Mayer of Munich – A View from England

Martin Harrison

368
Brian Clarke, "Treppenhausfenster," stained glass including antique fragments, installed at the Mayer of Munich studio, Munich.

By a fortuitous chronological symmetry, the *Treppenhausfenster,* which was recently installed at the Franz Mayer studio in Munich, neatly encapsulates the main theme of this essay. Made in 2012, this visually arresting work of contemporary art simultaneously embodies the history and traditions of the Mayer'sche Hofkunstanstalt, founded over a century-and-a-half ago, in 1847. It accomplishes this by embracing the great tradition of medieval Gothic (in its bold primary colours and heraldic essence), Renaissance naturalism (the weaving of the vibrant ruby lattice-work, redolent in its three-dimensionality of Peter Hemmel's plant-form canopies) and by literally incorporating relics of Mayer stained glass dating from the 19th century, selected from Gabriel Mayer's archive of historical fragments. It exemplifies, too, the spirit of creative collaboration between artist and craftworker that typifies the Mayer studio of today: on the one hand experienced technicians appear to relish the challenge presented by the requirement to provide innovative solutions to the problems set by an artist whose conceptions demand levels of sophisticated interpretation; on the other, while the artist in this case has a consummate grasp of the parameters of the medium of lead and glass, he is conscious that he is continually stretching the boundaries of what is possible under the umbrella of 'stained glass', and that to achieve his aims he can rely on the entirely open-minded co-operation of Mayer's expert team of glaziers.

In realising his many large-scale architectural projects, as well as autonomous glass panels and installations, the artist who designed the *Treppenhausfenster,* Brian Clarke, has collaborated with Franz Mayer of Munich since 1982 and more or less exclusively since 1994. Shortly after this fruitful liaison began, float glass-painting was developed, a technology whose triumphant debut was marked by Frei Otto's beautiful stainless steel cable structure, the "Heart Tent" at Riyadh (1984-86), in which the glass canopy, hand-painted by the artist Bettina Otto, was executed in the Mayer studios. Many more artists have been drawn to Munich in order to have their visions realised, and one of the especially impressive aspects of the recent history of the Mayer studios has been their resourcefulness in translating designs as disparate stylistically as those of Alyson Shotz, Heidi Lippman, Stephan Huber or Daniel Buren, to say nothing of maintaining the family's long-standing tradition of manufacturing mosaics, which they have similarly reinvigorated (see, for example, the New York projects of Eric Fischl) .

Under the direction of Joseph Gabriel Mayer, and later Franz Borgias Mayer, the Mayer'sche Hofkunstanstalt established a world-wide reputation for its stained glass in the 19th century, its eminence founded principally, perhaps, on the unimpeachable technical prowess that was consistently bestowed on its products. In the early years of the firm these had followed the pattern set by the Königliche Glasmalereianstalt in the 1830s; it promoted a kind of Nazarene pictorialism that was the antithesis of medieval stained glass but which – albeit the surviving corpus is severely depleted – is rightly being reinstated in a position of high regard among scholars. From a British perspective there is a special interest in the work of the Mayer Studios in the period from 1880 onwards, since after that date many of the designs were provided by British artists. Working on a freelance basis, they would deliver their designs to the office in Grosvenor Street, London, that the Mayers had opened in 1865; these were then sent to Munich to be fabricated, although William Francis Dixon, arguably the most notable of the English artists, actually emigrated to Munich in 1894. The prolific and respected freelancer George Daniels also provided many designs in the period up to 1914, and took part, therefore, in an auspicious Anglo-German alliance that would be eventually re-engaged through Brian Clarke seventy years later. By the 1870s Mayer's stained glass was in demand throughout the world, as it is again today, and the vast amount of it exported to the USA necessitated the opening of a New York branch in 1888.

After 1918, however, the Mayer'sche Hofkunstanstalt underwent a radical transformation under the stewardship of the brothers Anton, Karl and Adalbert Mayer. One of the myriad paths to Modernism had been established by the revolutionary artists who initiated the Munich Secession in 1893, and their initiative was gradually manifested in profound changes in the approach to stained glass in Germany, which remained predominantly an architectural art, indeed an art form principally, though not exclusively, associated with religious buildings. In the 1920s the Mayer studios altered their modus operandi, no longer employing designers to follow a pre-ordained 'house style' but instead executing the designs of artists such as Karl Knappe, Albert Figel and Paul Thalheimer; all three worked in figurative styles, but in a manner that was diametrically opposed to those Mayer had produced before 1915. Any trace of linear or painterly over-elaboration was eliminated from stained glass that was fundamentally a radically simplified, pared-down modernist-primitivism.

Wilhelm Worringer's "Abstraction and Empathy" had been published in 1907, but Expressionism, with which Worringer was briefly identified, and the various modernisms that emerged subsequently, effectively left Britain behind as a potent force within the European stained glass avant-garde. Worringer's most influential follower in Britain was the anarchist, poet and art critic Herbert Read, whose interest in the German aesthetician coincided with his first book, "English Stained Glass" (1926). In 1927 Read made the first English translation of Worringer's "Formprobleme der Gotik" (1911), and in the following year he reviewed Hans Kiener's "Deutsche Glasmalkunst" (1927), which he concluded with the comment: 'The art of glass-painting is alive there. When will it revive again in England?'[1] In the sense that Read intended it did not begin to revive until the 1950s, for the muse had moved elsewhere, and not least to Germany. But twentieth-century stained glass has received little scholarly attention to date, and in Europe the fertile period between 1920 and 1940, sadly much decimated, awaits research and a process of retrieval: it will prove a deeply rewarding topic for those who seek to undertake it.

Partly as a consequence of its reconstruction programme and economic recovery after 1947, Germany again re-emerged as the epicentre of architectural stained glass; (although in France there were some significant exceptions designed by leading artists – the stained glass of Léger, Matisse, Braque and Le Corbusier for example – these remained relatively isolated occurrences). The designs of Meistermann, Wendling, and the

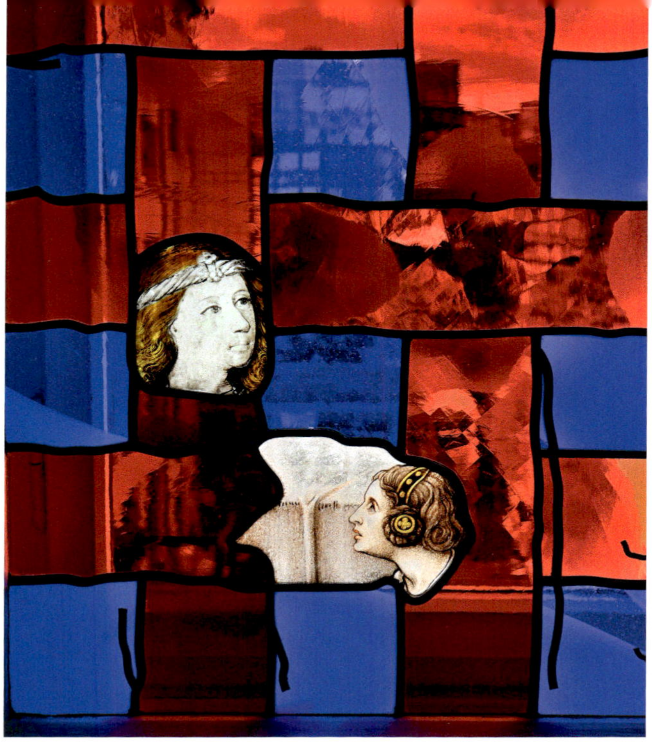

369
Brian Clarke, "Treppenhausfenster," detail.

later Rhenish School, Schaffrath and Schreiter, were first noticed by Robert Sowers and then by Brian Clarke, and their publications were instrumental in disseminating the message of Germany's important contributions to stained glass to a wider audience. During this period the Mayer studios were principally associated with figurative artists such as Hans Gottfried von Stockhausen, Josef Oberberger and Franz Nagel, but a major shift in direction occurred under the direction of Gabriel Mayer in the 1980s and later on intensely with Michael C. Mayer as Junior Partner. Henceforth the Mayer'sche Hofkunstanstalt was open to the widest range of experiment, an attitude that has attracted innumerable artists, confident that their designs would be interpreted with exemplary skill and sensitivity. I hope I will be forgiven if the highest testament I can pay to the Mayers' craftworkers concerns Brian Clarke, an artist who has also been my friend for more than thirty-five years. Clarke's autonomous works "Transillumination" and "Don't Forget the Lamb" exemplify the extreme polarities of 'stained glass' that he has investigated in the last decade, the one (executed in triple-laminated float glass) as 'glass without lead', the other 'lead without glass'. They have stretched and completely redefined the medium, and in achieving this Clarke has extracted some of the greatest performances in the long tradition of the Mayer'sche Hofkunstanstalt.

Martin Harrison was curator of the Stained Glass Museum, Ely Cathedral, from 1975–80. He is a Fellow of the Society of Antiquaries of London and has published widely on art, photography and stained glass. He is currently preparing the catalogue raisonné of the paintings of Francis Bacon.

[1] Journal of the British Society of Master Glass Painters, vol ii no 4, October 1928, p. 213–14.

DOCUMENTATION

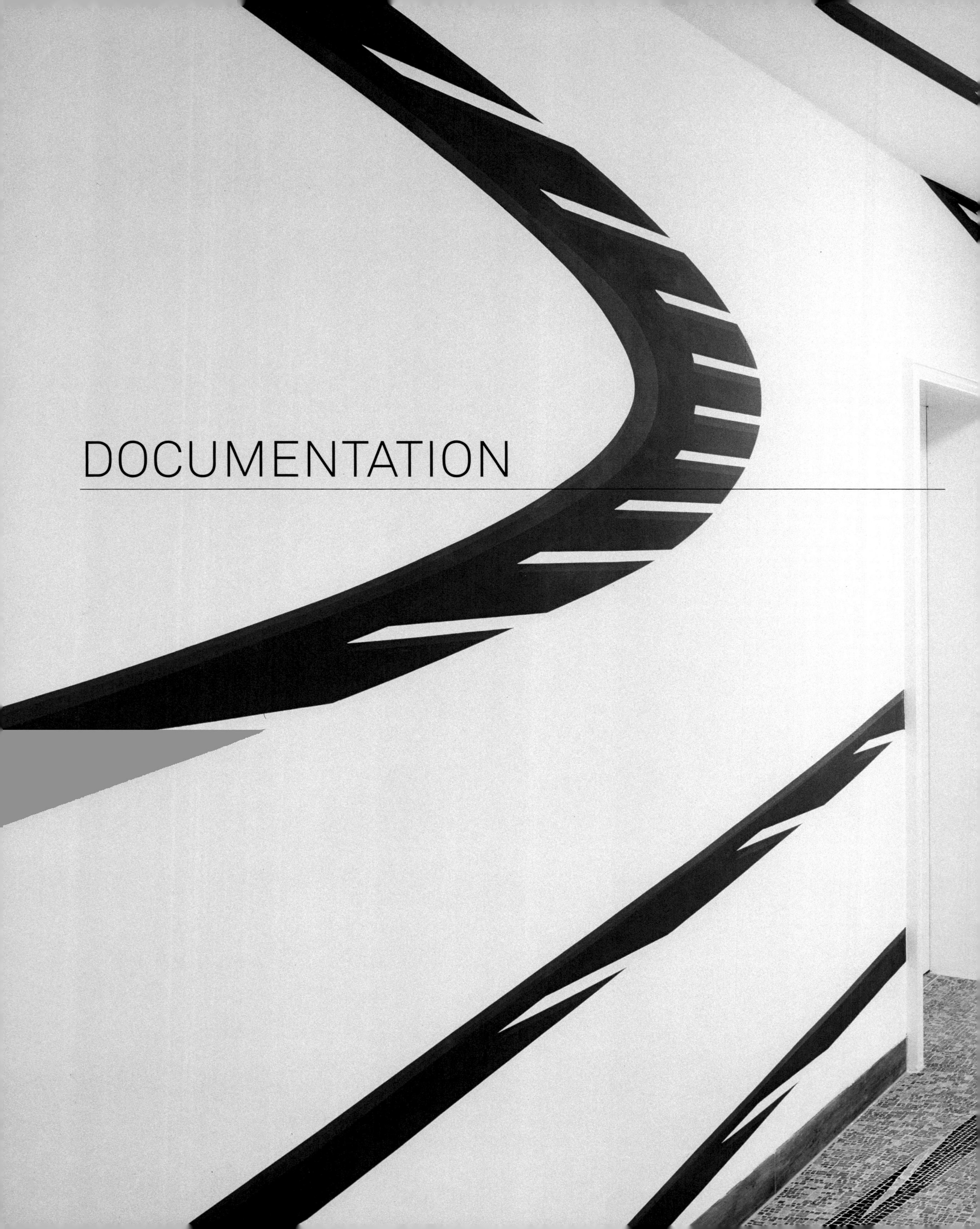

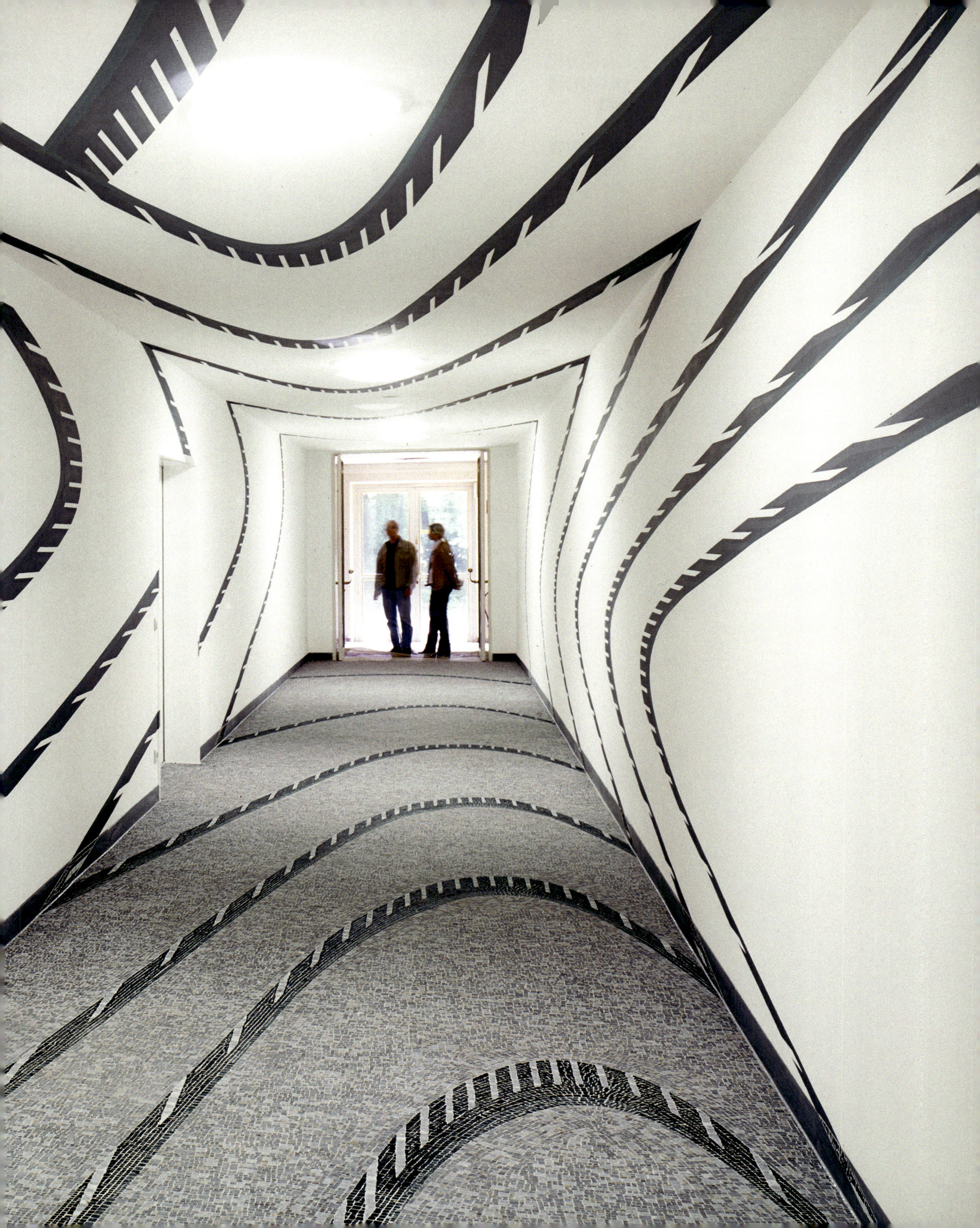

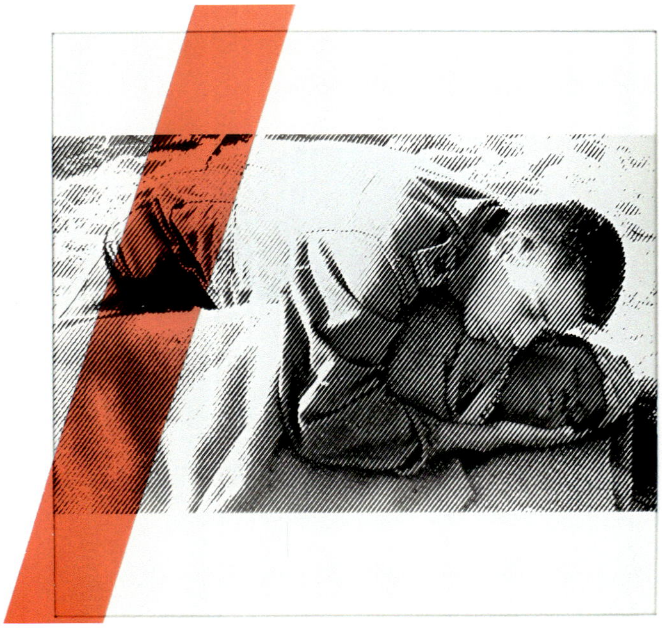

370

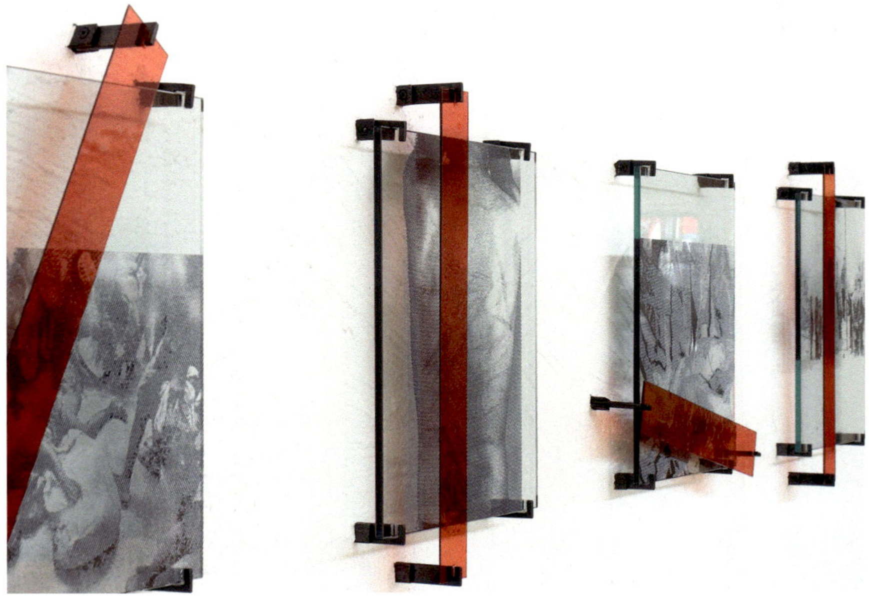

370 + 371
ATELIER ARNOLD + EICHLER / STATIONS OF THE CROSS / HERZ JESU KIRCHE, UFFENHEIM, DE / 2005 / FLOAT GLASS PAINTING

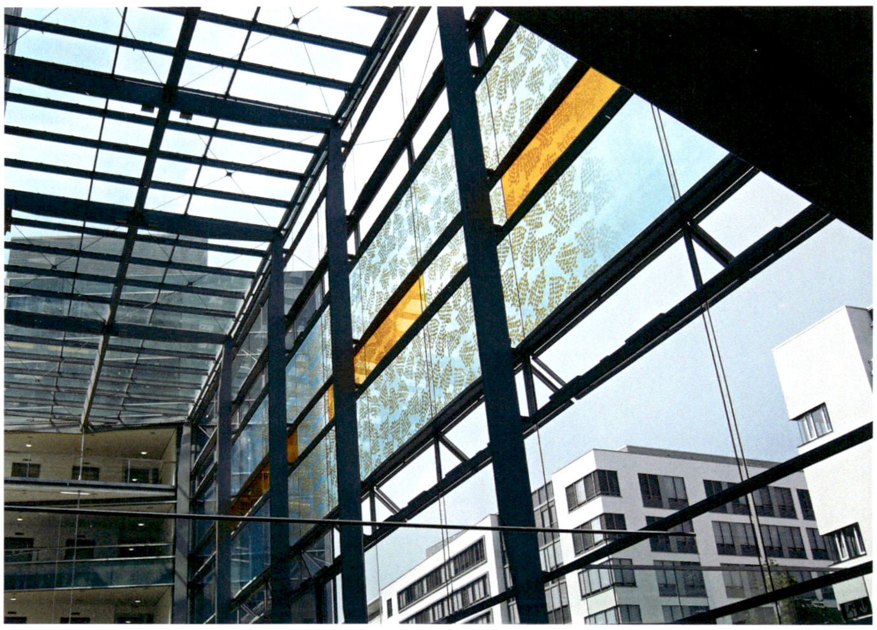

374
ALEXANDER BELESCHENKO / GLASS WALL / OFFICE BUILDING THEODOR-HEUSS-ALLEE 100, FRANKFURT/MAIN, DE / 2003 / FLOAT GLASS PAINTING

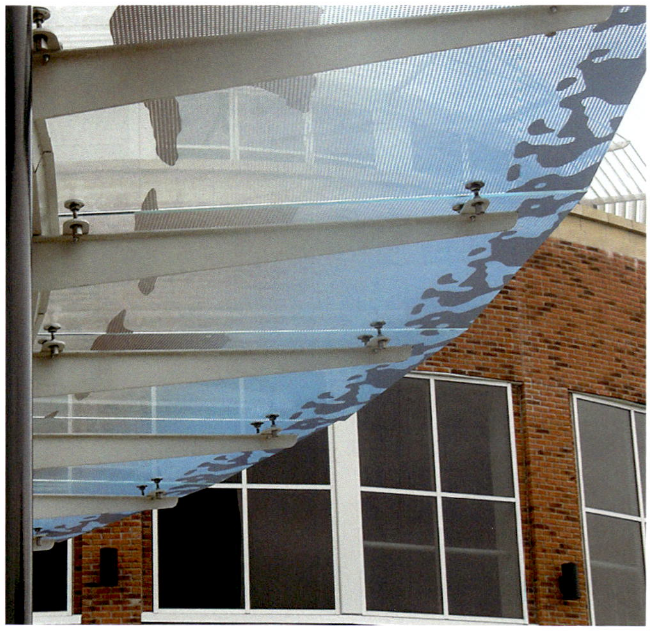

375–378
ALEXANDER BELESCHENKO / GLASS CANOPIES / CIRCA 2000 LINEAR FEET OF ARTISTICALLY DESIGNED INDIVIDUAL CANOPIES, SHOPPING MALL, WORKINGTON, GB / 2006 / FLOAT GLASS PAINTING

FIG. PAGE 252 + 253

Stefanie Zoche, Sabine Haubitz (Haubitz + Zoche) / "Eye of the Staircase" / Allianz Headquarters, Munich, DE / 2001 / marble mosaic floor

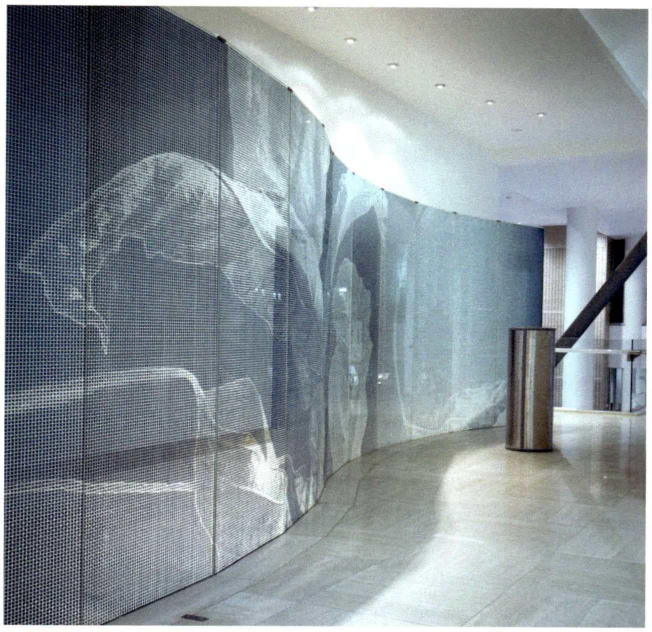

372
ALEXANDER BELESCHENKO / GLASS WALL / BRITISH EMBASSY, MOSCOW, RUSSIA / 1999 / FLOAT GLASS PAINTING

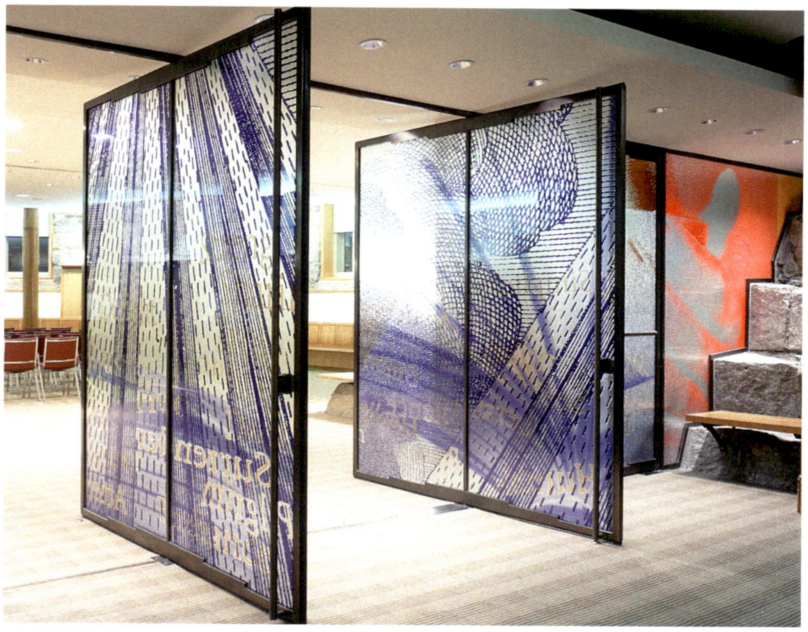

373
ALEXANDER BELESCHENKO / TWO DIVIDER GLASS WALLS / TRINITY CHURCH, BOSTON, MA, USA / 2005 / FLOAT GLASS PAINTING

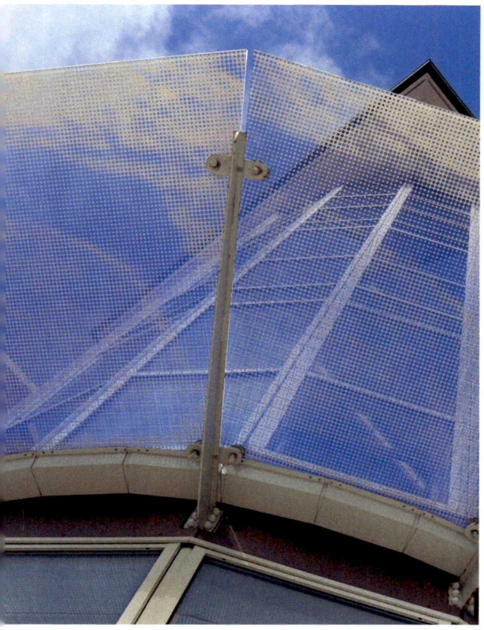

376

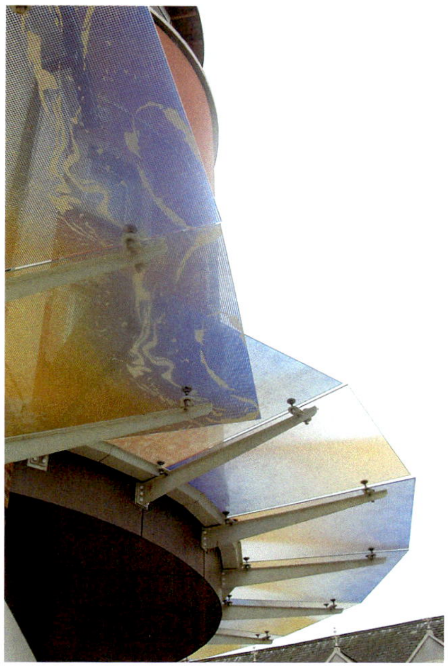

377

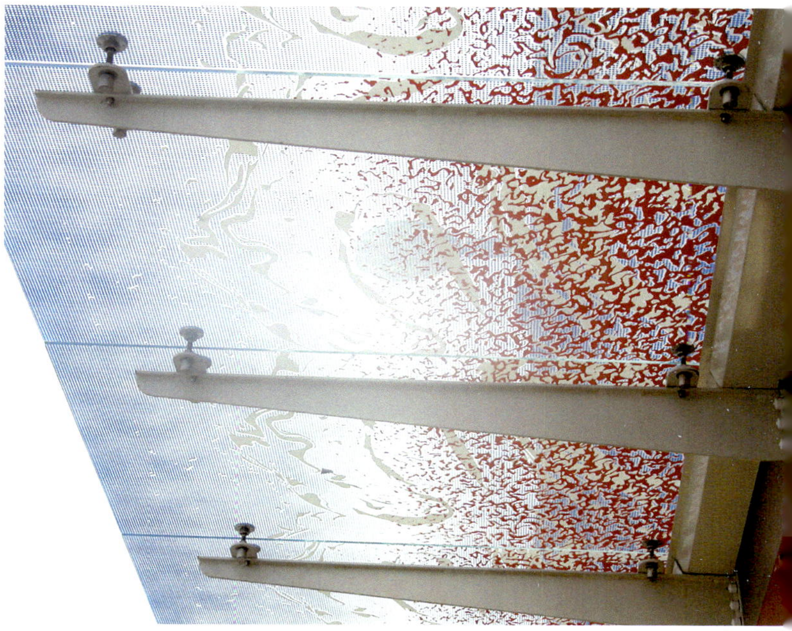

378

OF COURSE THERE ARE MANY MORE PROJECTS ...

A pictorial report on projects from the last 10 to 15 years would be incomplete if we did not attempt to report – at least briefly – also on the following projects. Regardless, this selection is bound to be both selective and subjective.

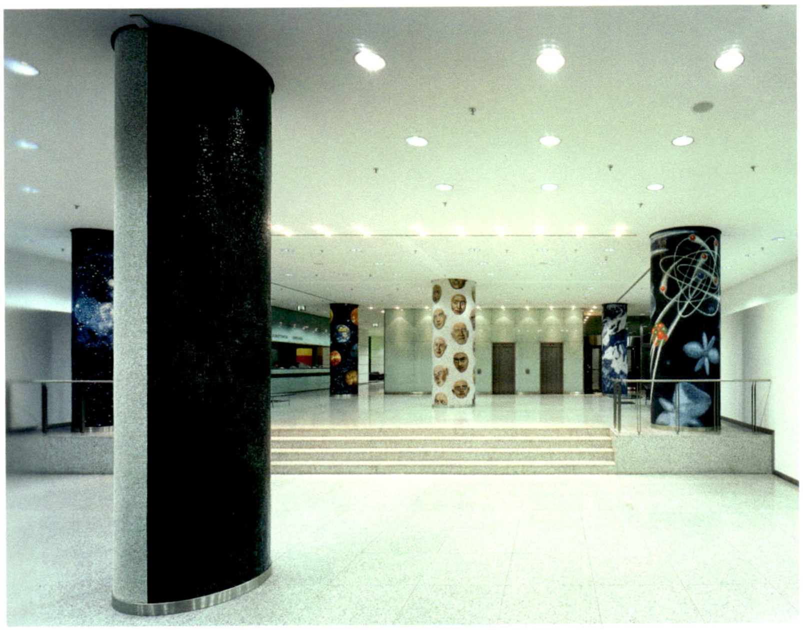

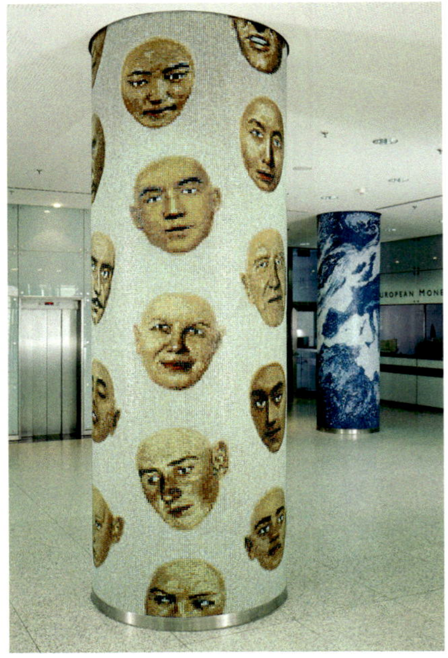

379 + 380
HEINER BLUM / "UNITS AND UNITIES" / SIX MOSAIC COLUMNS / EUROPEAN CENTRAL BANK, FRANKFURT/MAIN, DE / 1997 / GLASS MOSAIC

380

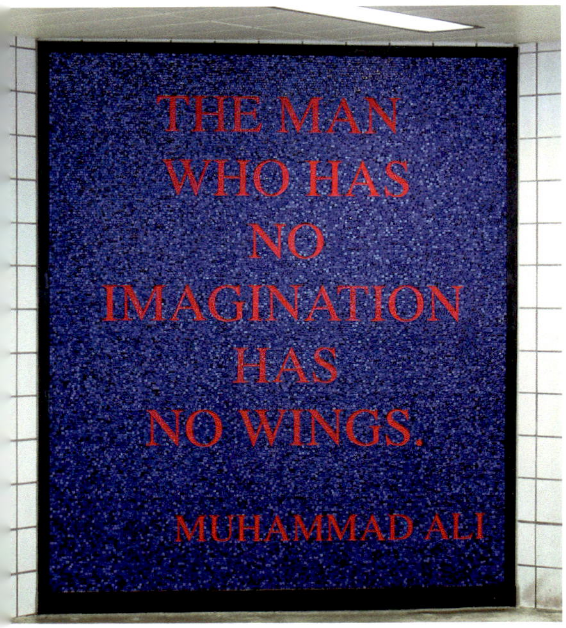

383–385
ADAM BROOKS / TEXT MOSAIC / PULASKI STATION, CHICAGO, IL, USA / 2004 / GLASS MOSAIC / CTA PUBLIC ART / CTA PUBLIC ART PROGRAM

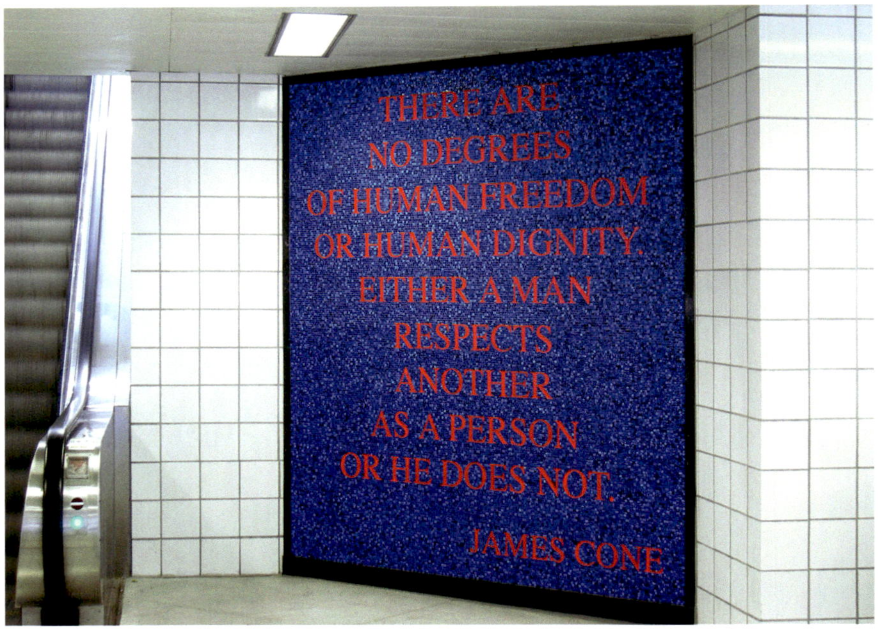

384

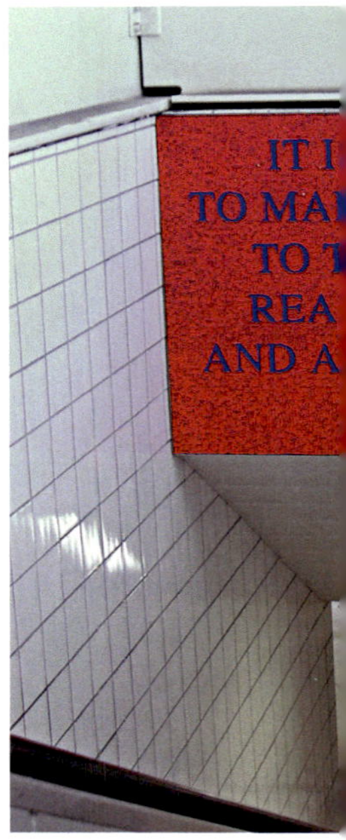

385

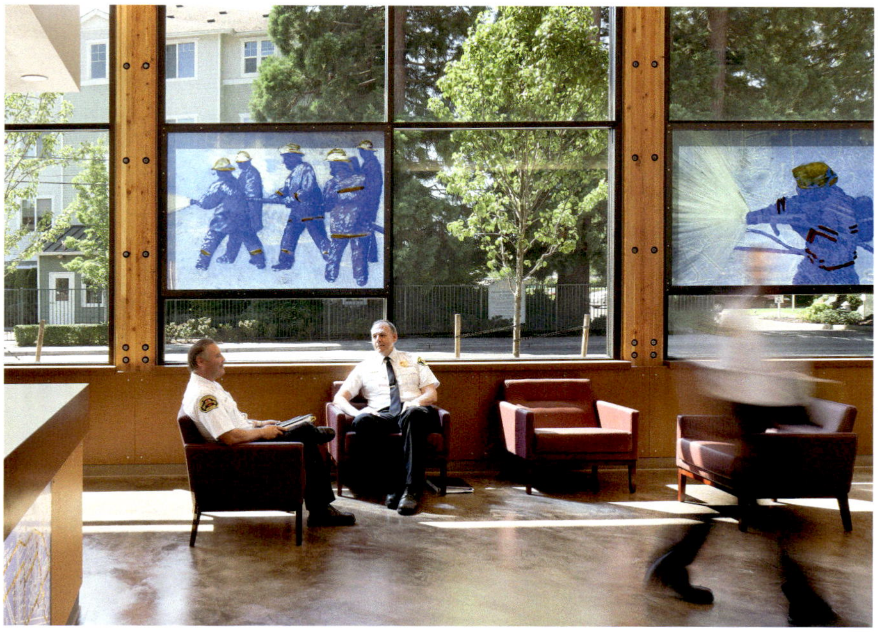

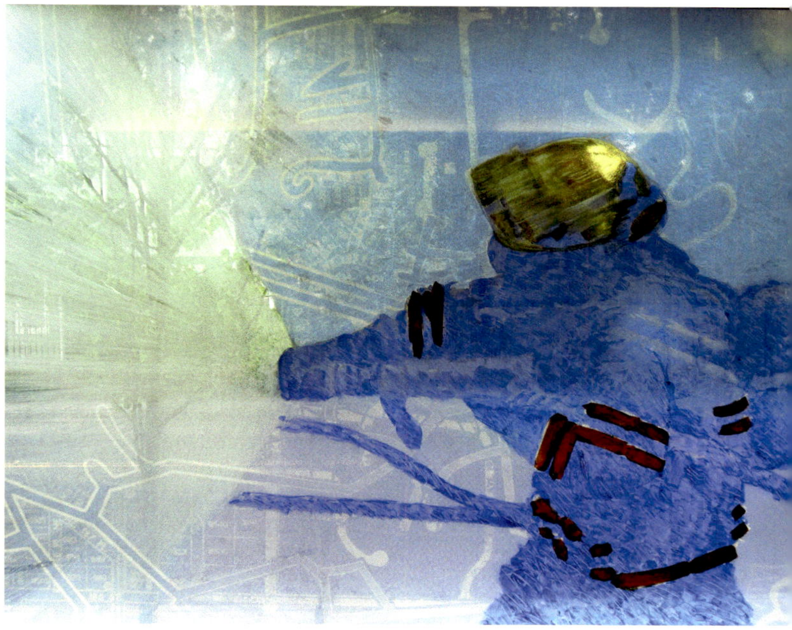

381 + 382
GLORIA BORNSTEIN / "UNDER THE HERON'S WING" / NORTHSHORE FIRE DEPARTMENT, KENMORE, WA, USA / 2010 / FLOAT GLASS PAINTING

382

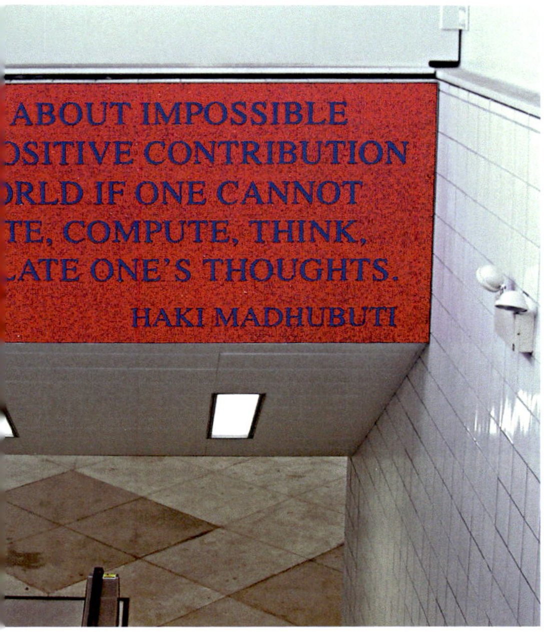

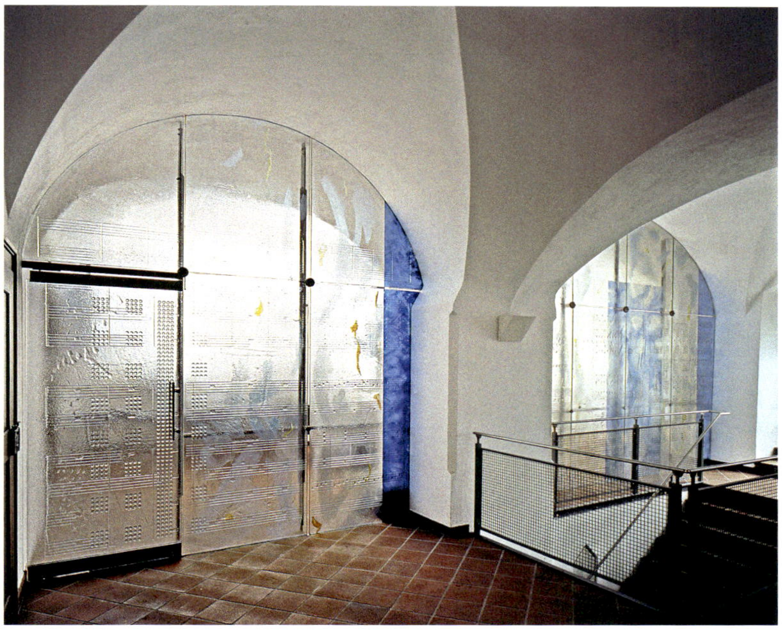

386
THIERRY BOISSEL / "DIE BERNAUERIN" / TWO GLASS PARTITION WALLS / FINANCE OFFICE, HERZOGSCHLOSS, STRAUBING, DE / 1996 / SLUMPED AND PAINTED GLASS

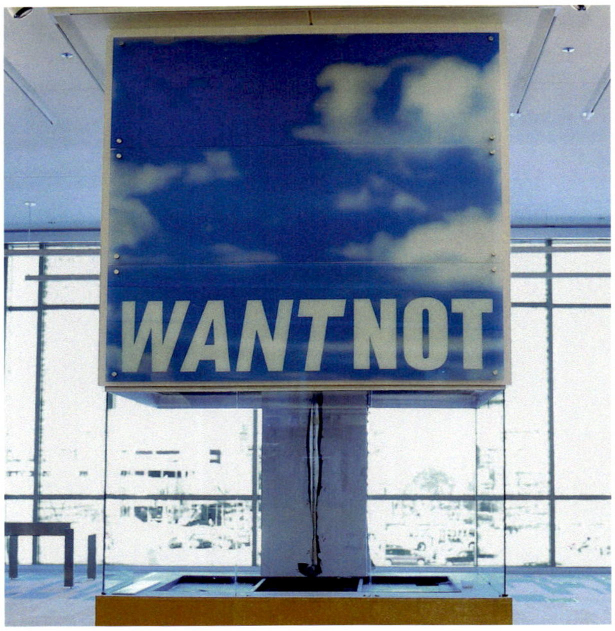

387
JACKIE CHANG / "WANTNOT" / MINNEAPOLIS CENTRAL LIBRARY, MINNEAPOLIS, MN, USA / CESAR PELLI ARCHITECTS / 2006 / FLOAT GLASS PAINTING

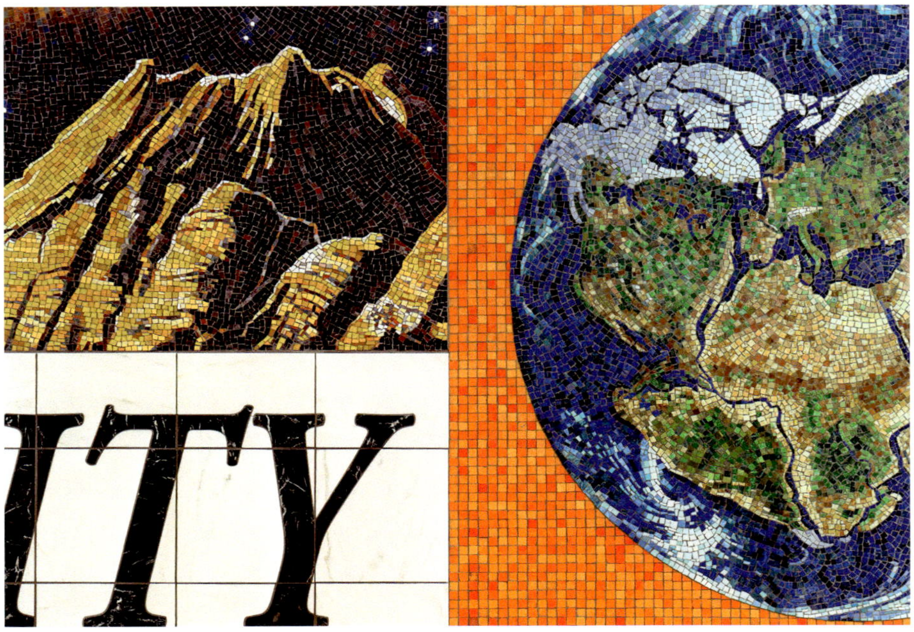

388 + 389
JACKIE CHANG / "IN OTHER WORDS" / PS 268 SCHOOL, JAMAICA, NEW YORK, NY, USA / 2002 / GLASS MOSAIC / NYC PUBLIC ART FOR PUBLIC SCHOOLS

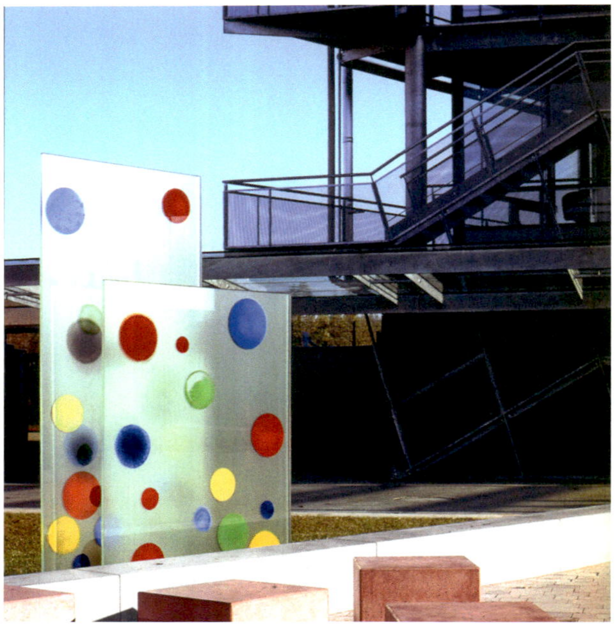

391
BODO BUHL / GLASS SCULPTURE / ELEMENTARY SCHOOL MARKGRAFENSTRASSE, MUNICH, DE / 2002 / FLOAT GLASS PAINTING

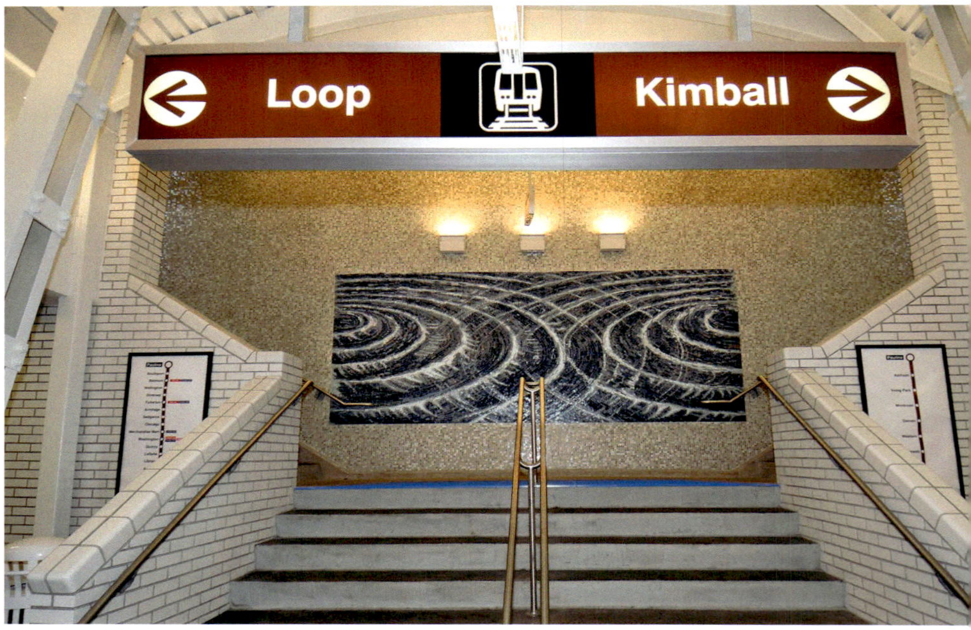

392 + 393
BARBARA COOPER / "TRANSITIONS" / PAULINA STATION, CHICAGO, IL, USA / 2007 / GLASS MOSAIC / CTA PUBLIC ART PROGRAM

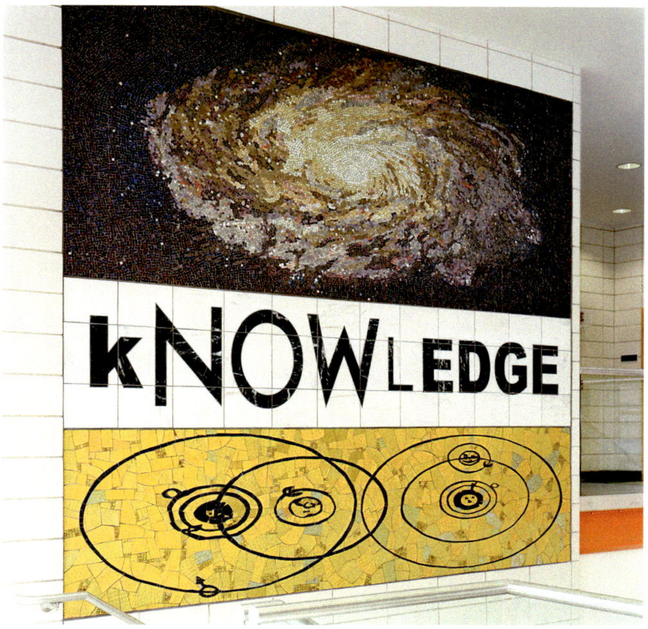

389

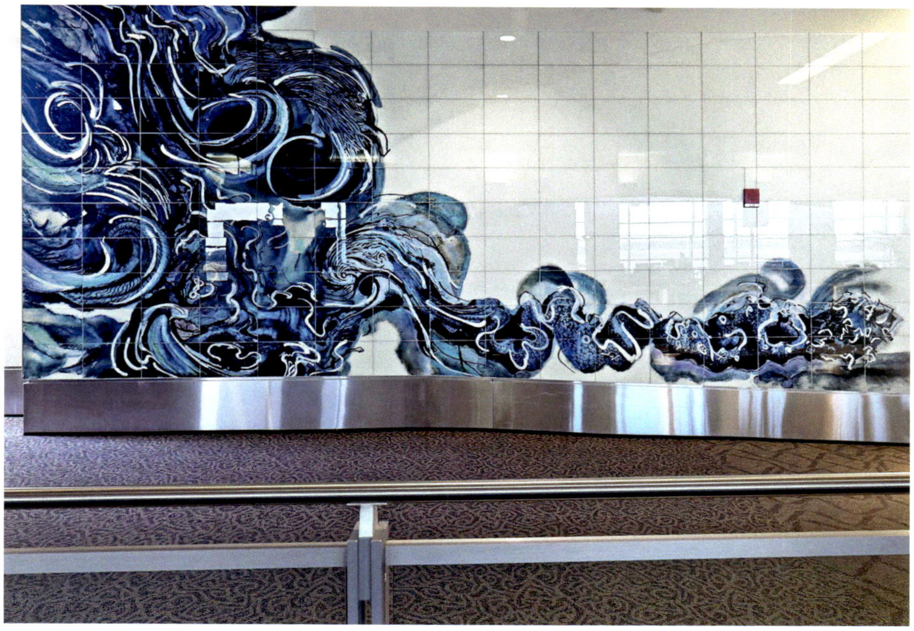

390

BARBARA COOPER / "INTERVAL" / T. F. GREEN AIRPORT, PROVIDENCE, RI, USA / 2009 / HANDPAINTED GLASS TILES / DETAIL

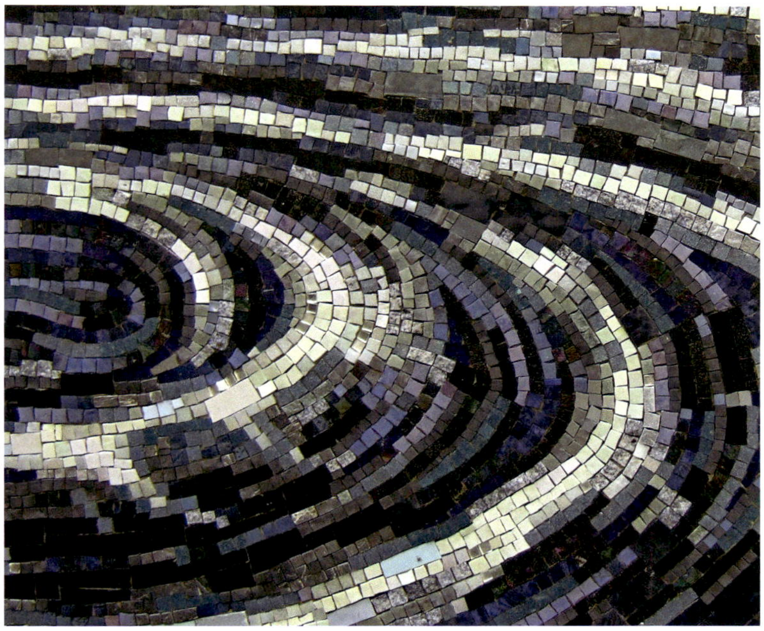

393

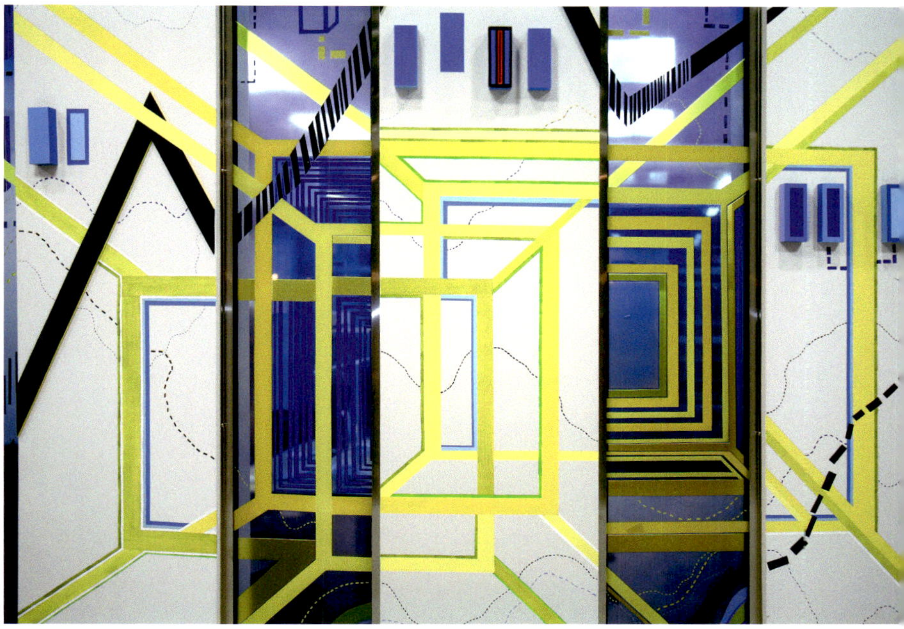

394

DIANA COOPER / "OUT OF THE CORNER OF MY EYE" / CSI HIGH SCHOOL FOR INTERNATIONAL STUDIES, STATEN ISLAND, NY, USA / 2008 / FLOAT GLASS PAINTING AND MIXED MEDIA WALL DESIGN / NYC PUBLIC ART FOR PUBLIC SCHOOLS

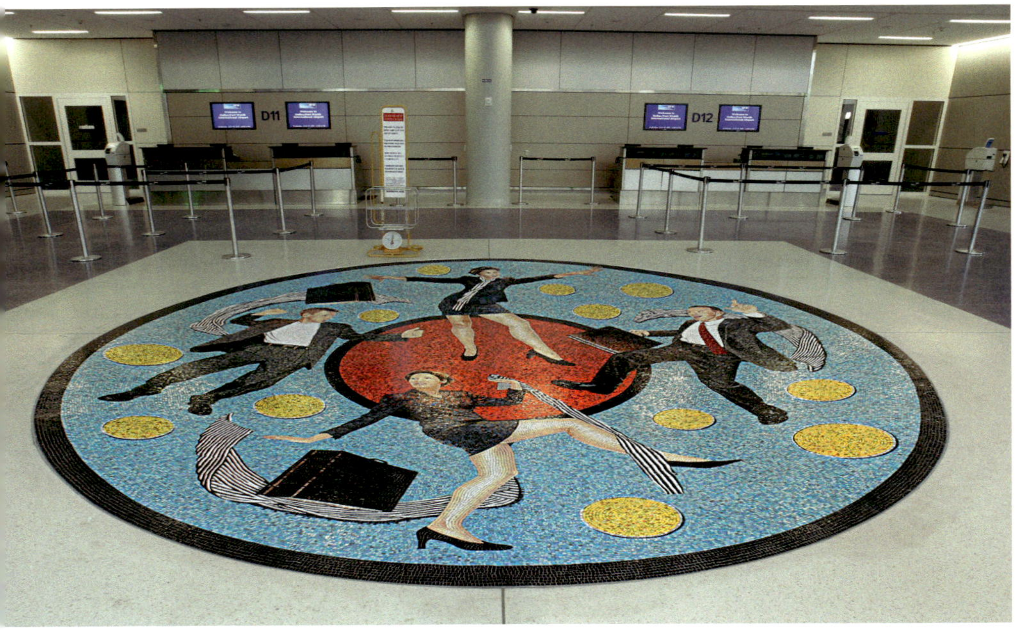

395

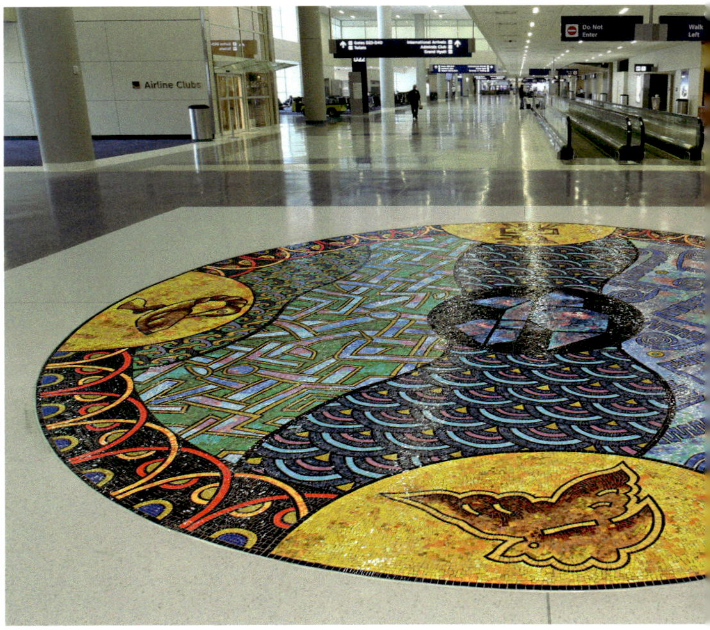

396

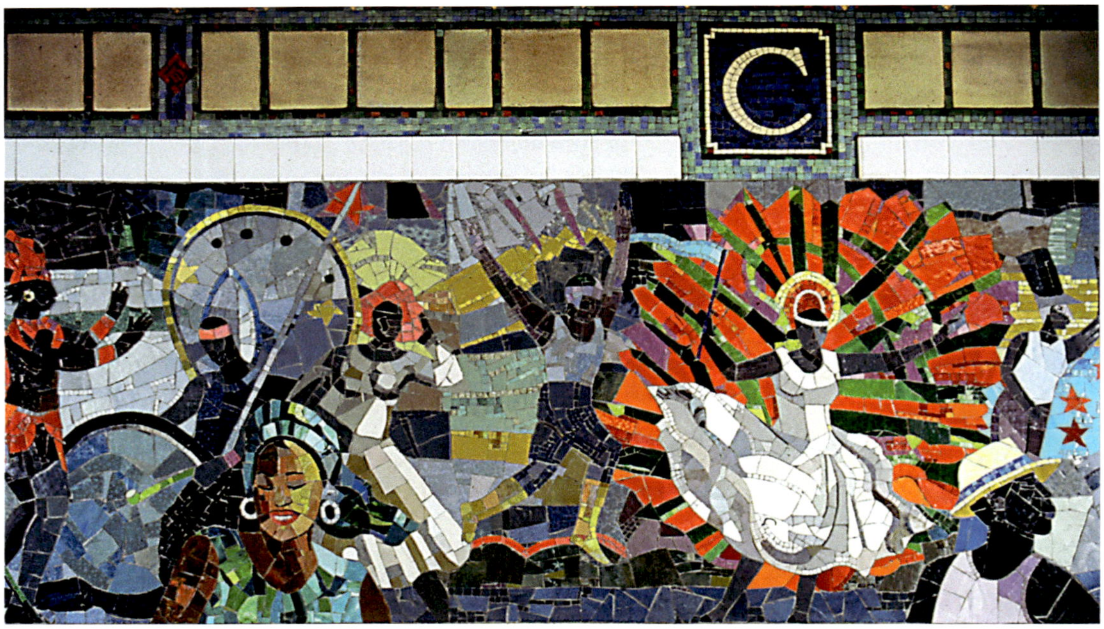

398

LOUIS DELSARTE / "TRANSITIONS" / CHURCH AVENUE SUBWAY STATION, BROOKLYN, NY, USA / 2001 / GLASS MOSAIC / MTA ARTS FOR TRANSIT

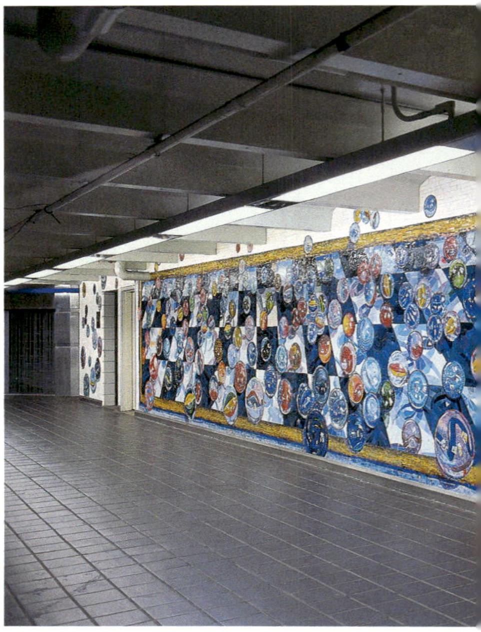

399

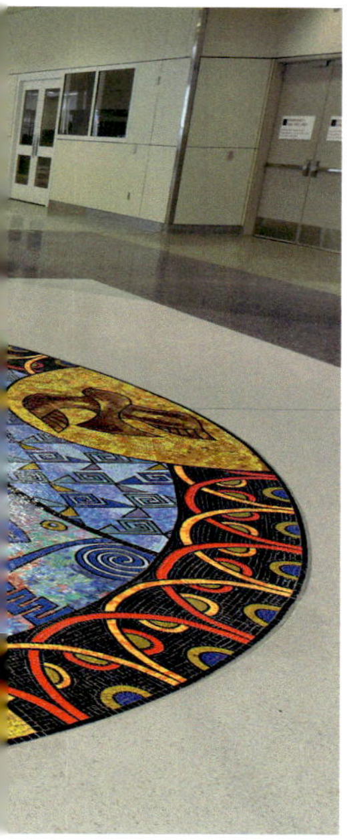

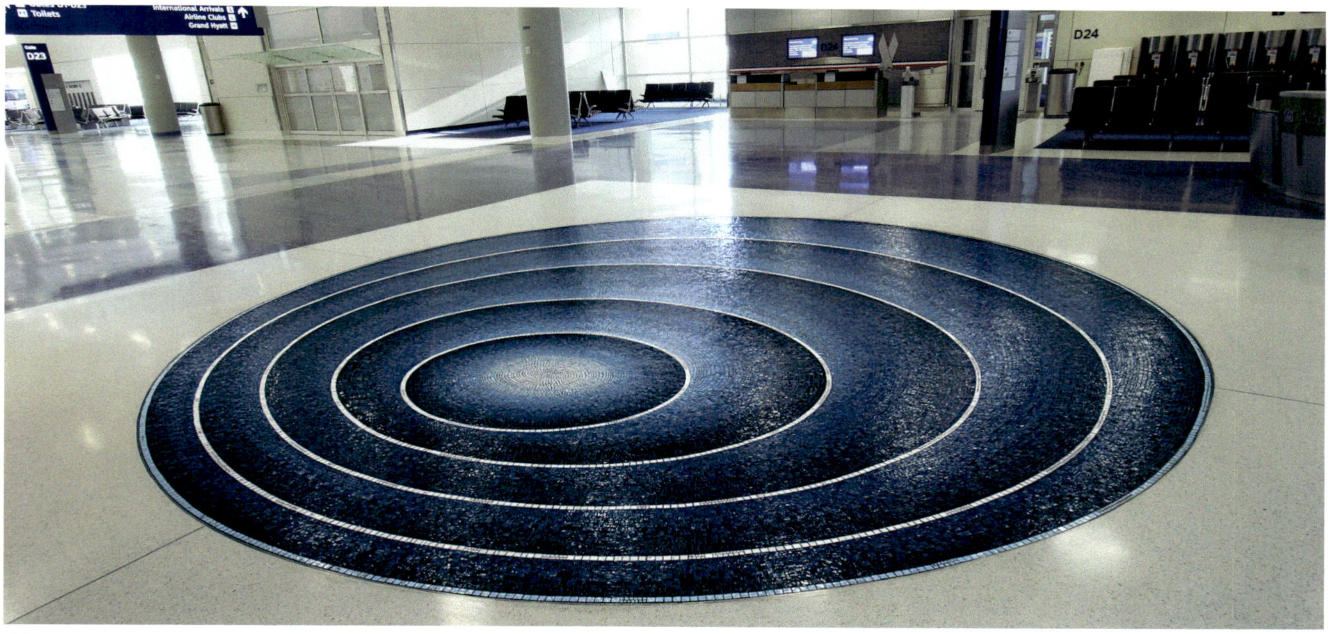

395–397

MULTIPLE ARTISTS / DALLAS - FORT WORTH INTERNATIONAL AIRPORT, TERMINAL D, TX, USA / ARCHITECTS HKS / SEVEN GLASS MOSAIC FLOOR INLAYS / 2005 / EACH CIRCA 18 FEET DIAMETER / FIG. 395: LINDA GUY / "DANCE! DON'T WALK" / FIG. 396: BEATRICE LEBRETON / "CELEBRATION" / FIG. 397: TED KINCAID / "UNTITLED"

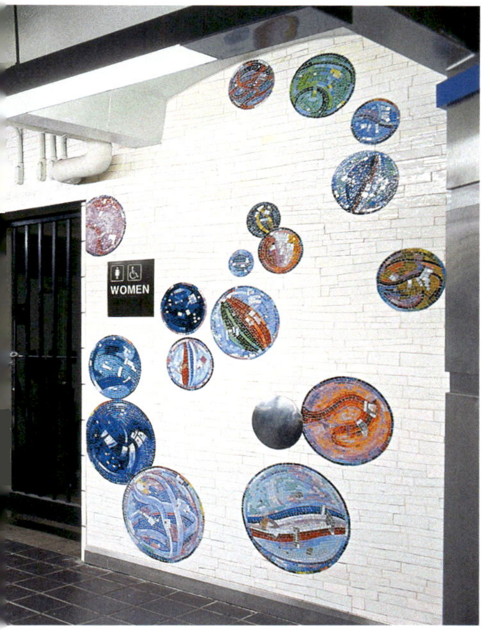

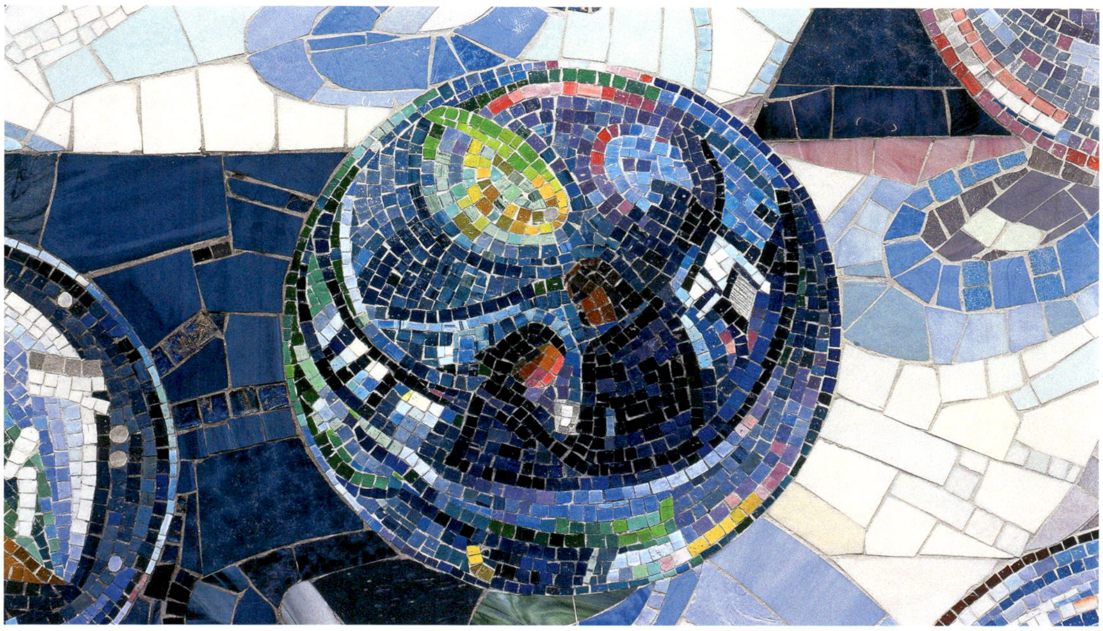

399 + 400

LISA DINHOFER / "LOSING MY MARBLES" / PORT AUTHORITY BUS TERMINAL, 42ND STREET, NEW YORK, NY, USA / 2003 / GLASS MOSAIC / MTA ARTS FOR TRANSIT

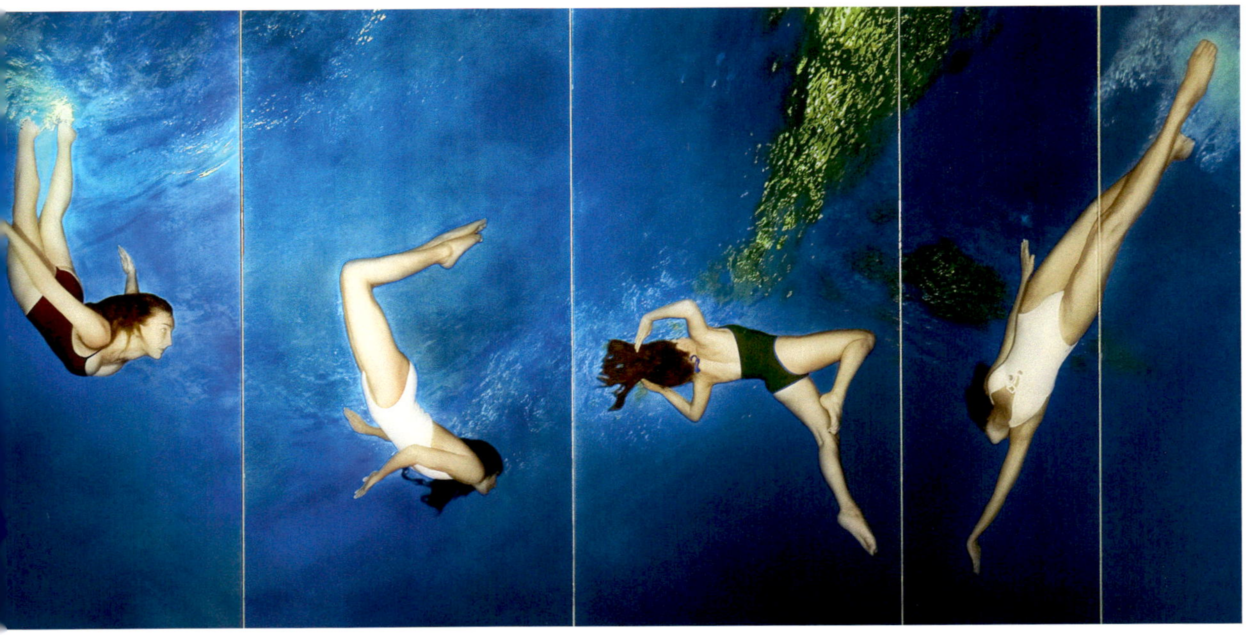

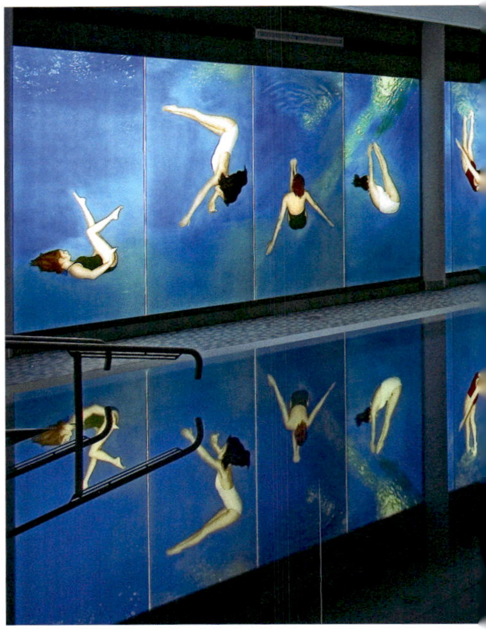

401 + 402
BERNHARD DRAZ / "NEREIDS AND OCEANIDS" / HEALTH CENTER LANGENAU, DE / 2008 / FLOAT GLASS PAINTING

402

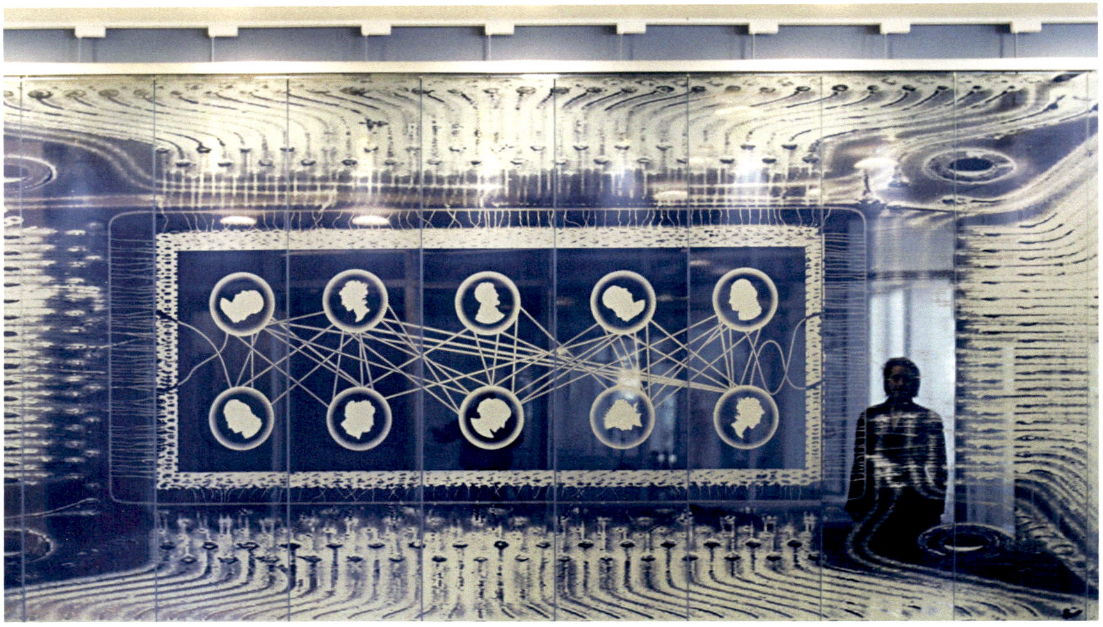

404
ELLEN DRISCOLL / "CIRCUITSTREAM" / BANK OF AMERICA, CHARLOTTE, NC, USA / 2000 / FLOAT GLASS PAINTING

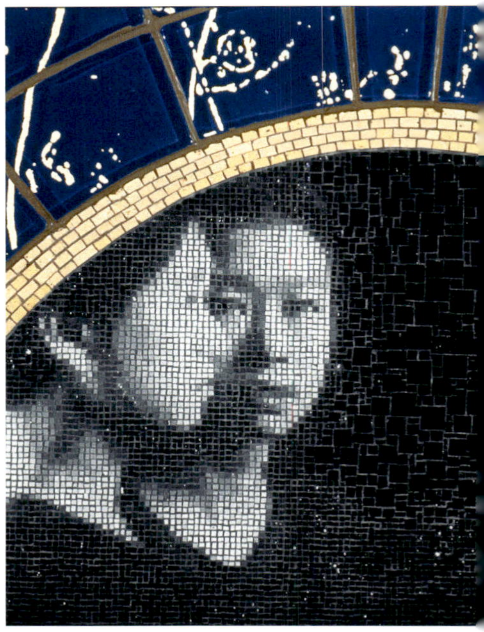

405–407
ELLEN DRISCOLL / "AS ABOVE, SO BELOW" / A TOTAL OF 13 WALL MOSAICS / GRAND CENTRAL TERMINAL, NORTH ACCESS, NEW YORK, NY, USA / 1998 / STONE AND GLASS MOSAIC / MTA ARTS FOR TRANSIT

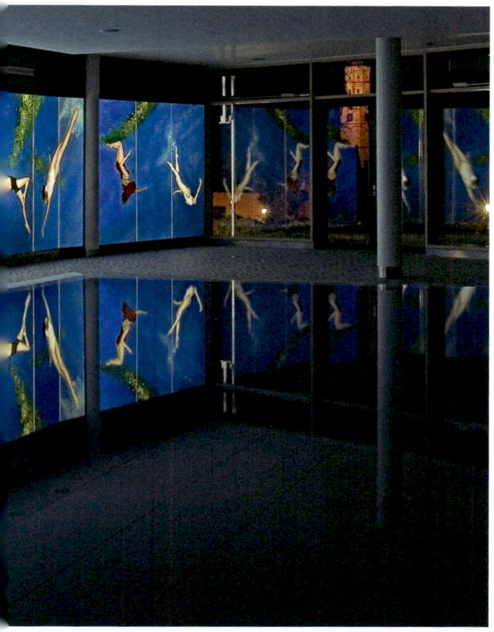

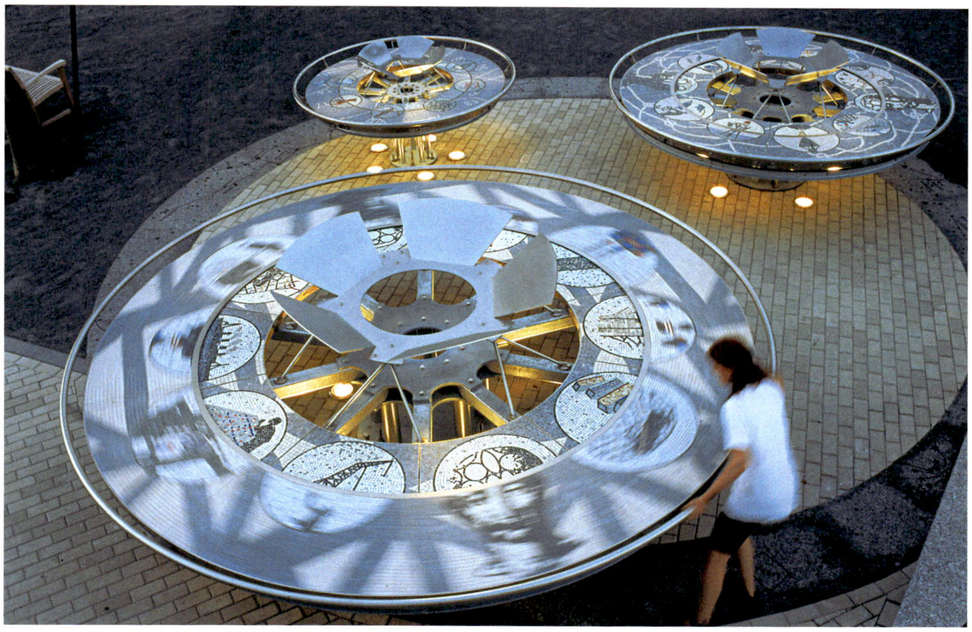

403

ELLEN DRISCOLL / “AQUEOUS HUMOUR” / SOUTH BOSTON MARITIME PARK, BOSTON, MA, USA / 2004 / MARBLE MOSAIC

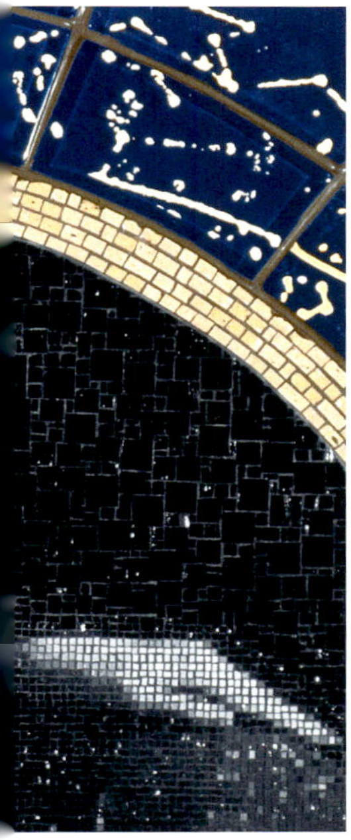

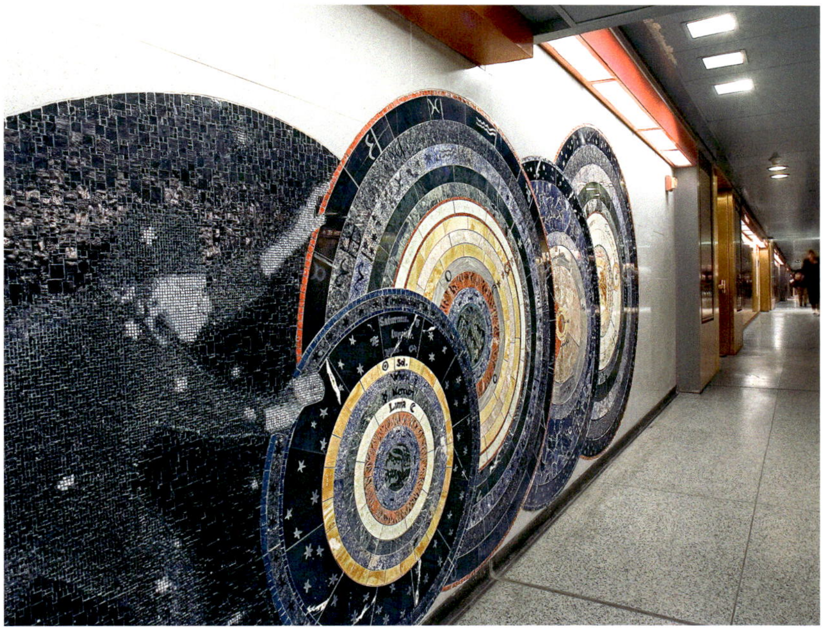

406

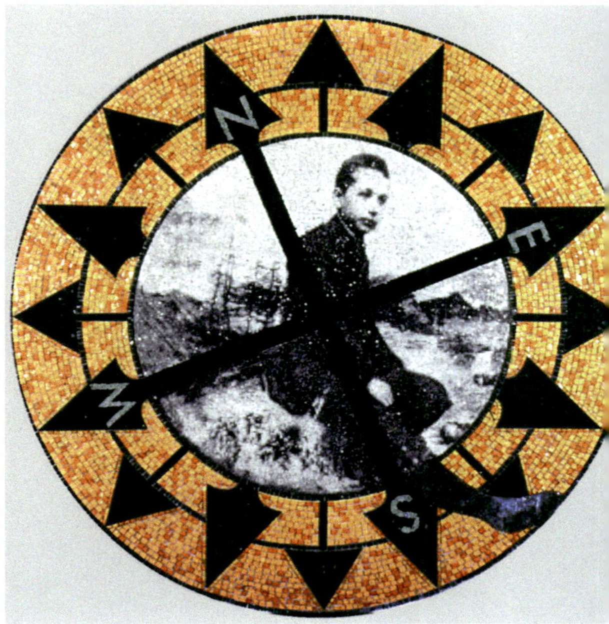

407

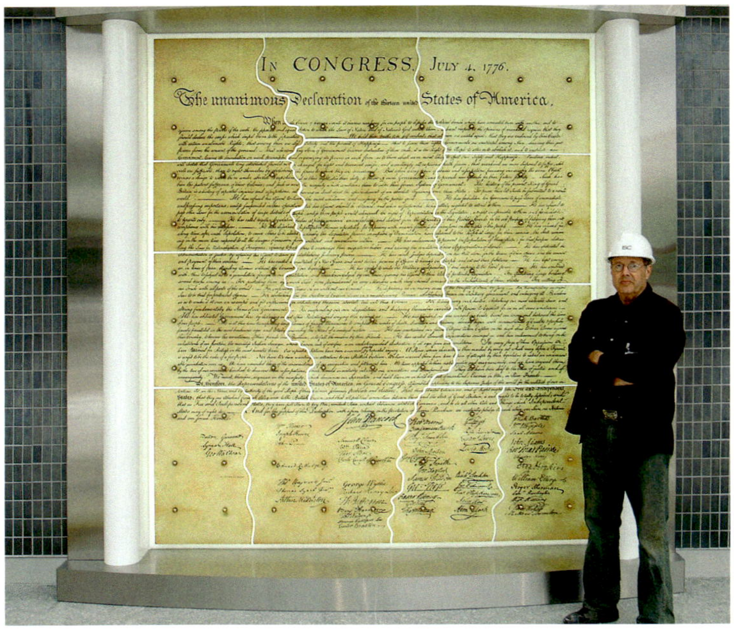

408

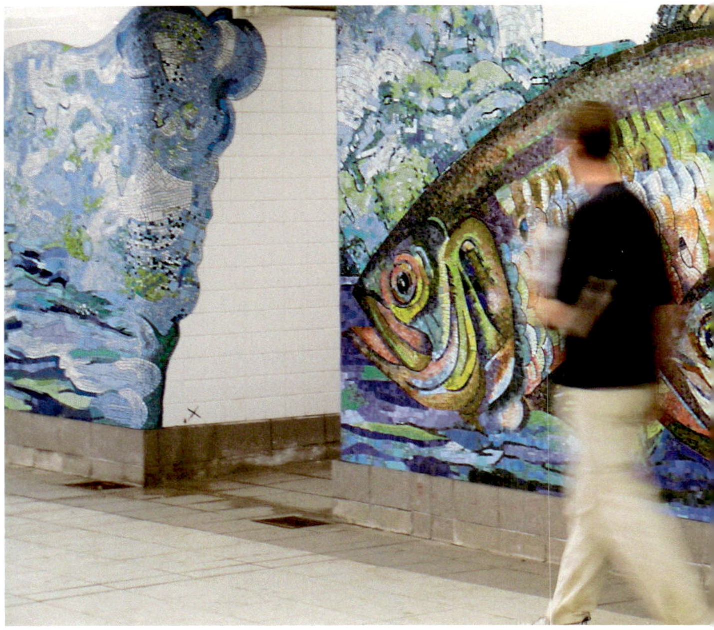

409

ROB FISHER / "DECLARATION" / US AIRWAYS TERMINAL, PHILADELPHIA INTERNATIONAL AIRPORT, PA, USA / 2003 / FLOAT GLASS PAINTING

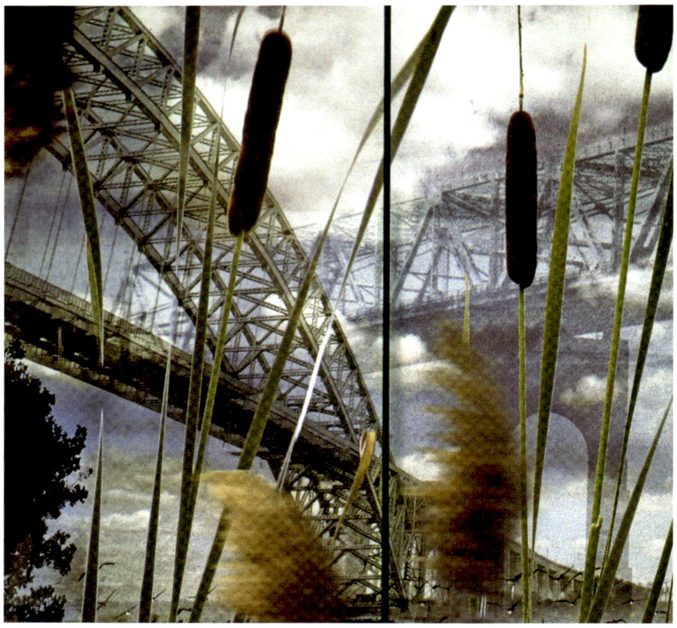

411 + 412

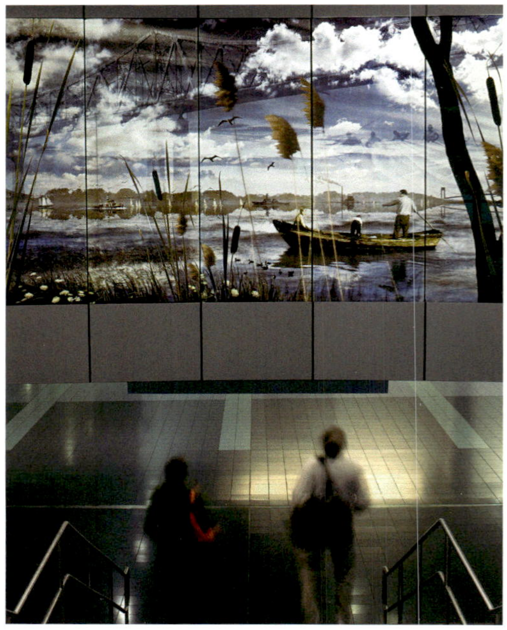

412

MICHAEL FALCO / "WHERE MARSH MEETS THE SEA" / STATEN ISLAND FERRY TERMINAL, NY, USA / 2007 / FLOAT GLASS PAINTING / NEW YORK CITY DEPARTMENT OF CULTURAL AFFAIRS

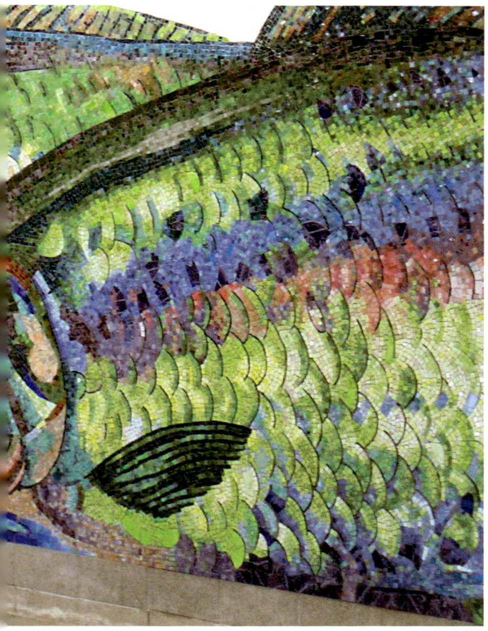

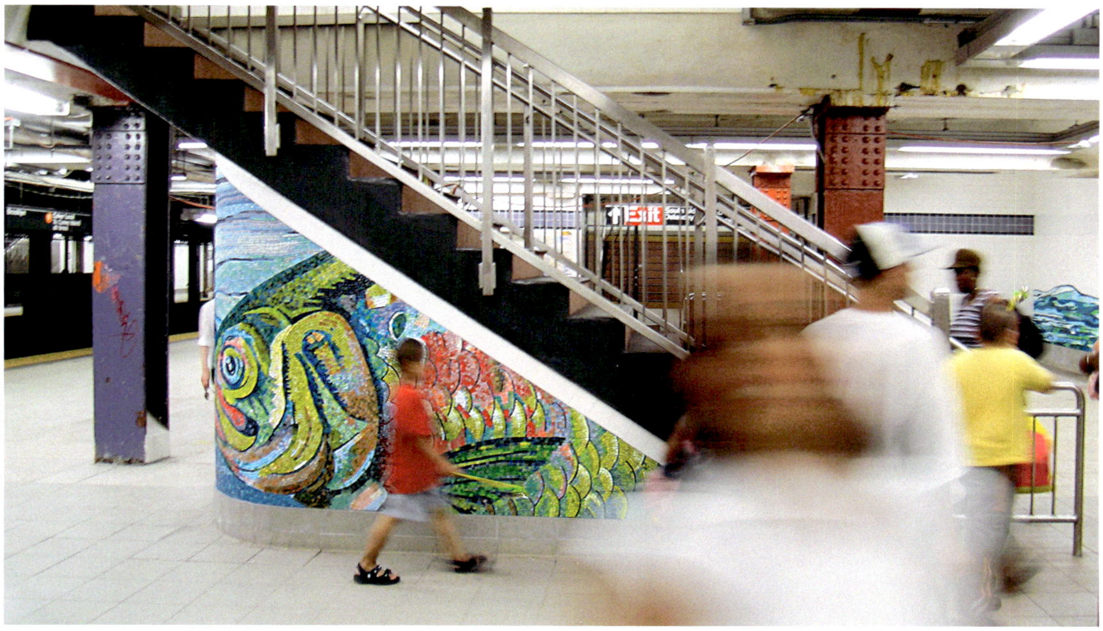

409 + 410
MING FAY / "SHAD CROSSING, DELANCEY ORCHARD" / DELANCEY/ESSEX STREET SUBWAY STATION, NEW YORK, NY, USA / 2004 / GLASS MOSAIC / MTA ARTS FOR TRANSIT

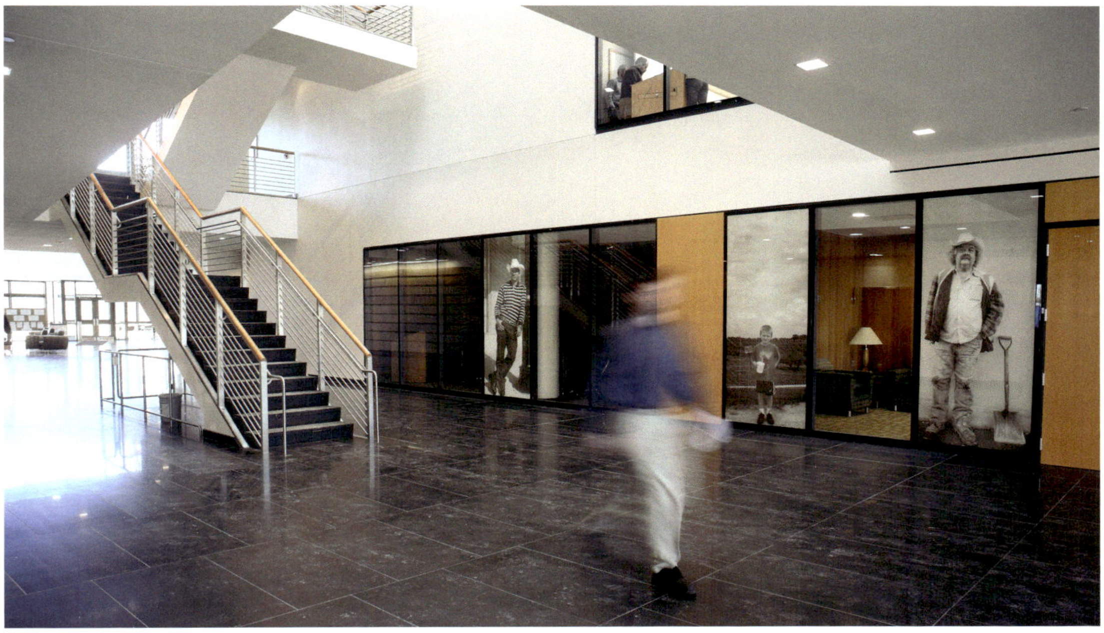

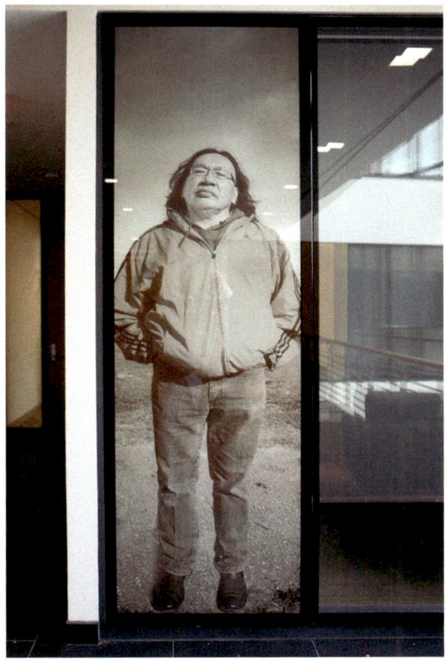

413 + 414
PETER FELDSTEIN / "OXFORD PROJECT" / COLLEGE OF PUBLIC HEALTH, THE UNIVERSITY OF IOWA, IOWA CITY, IA, USA / 2011 / FLOAT GLASS PAINTING

414

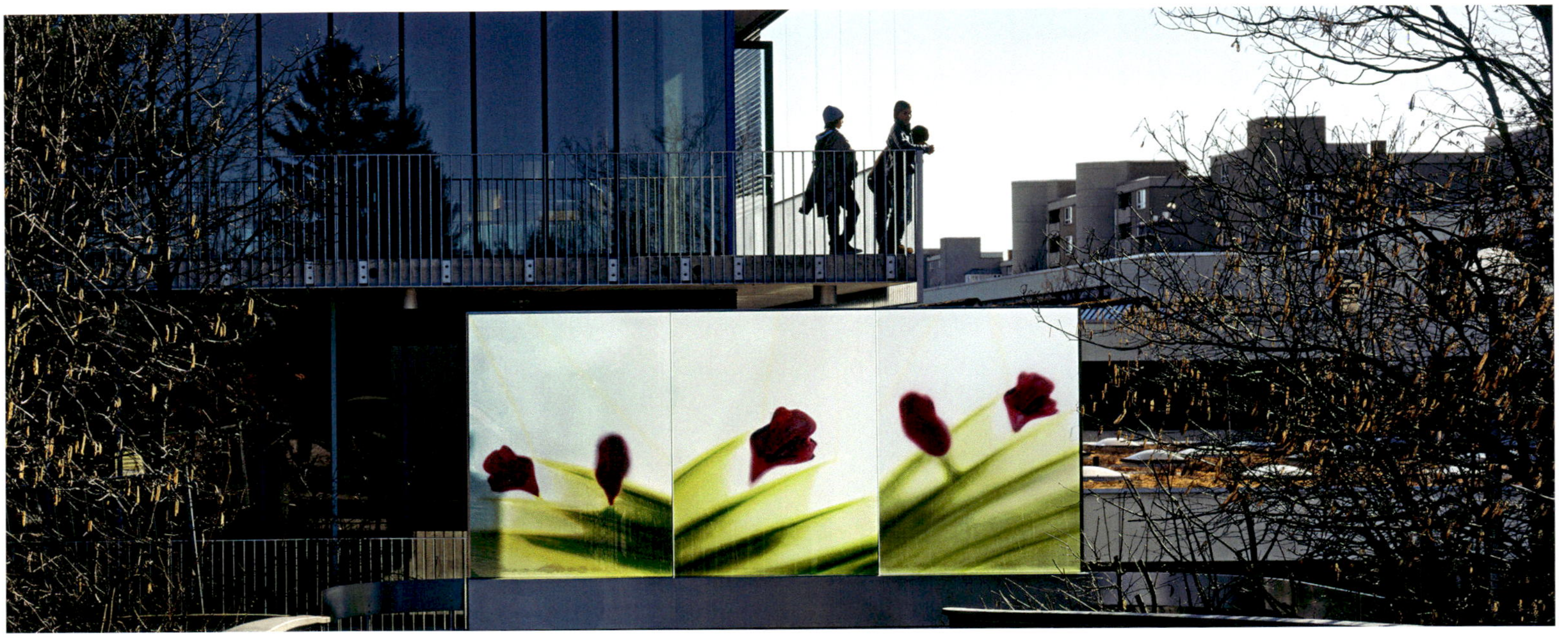

415
KLAUS VON GAFFRON / THREE-PART GLASS INSTALLATION / ERNST-MACH-GYMNASIUM HAAR, MUNICH, DE / 2007 / FLOAT GLASS PAINTING

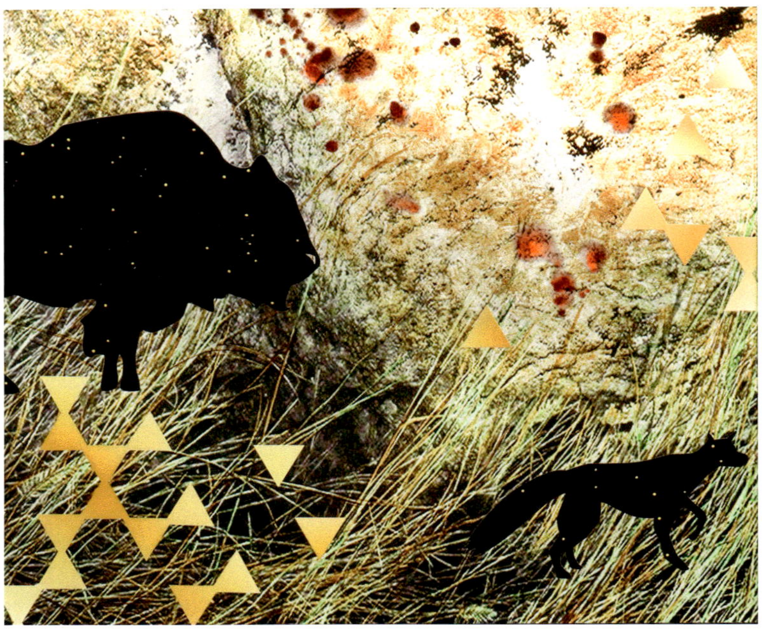

418

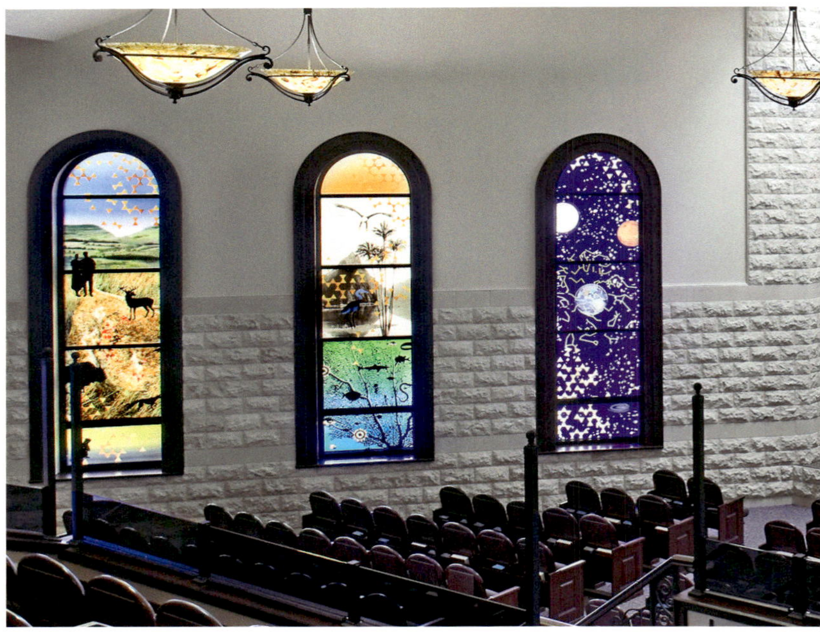

418 + 419
MIMI GELLMAN / SEVEN STAINED GLASS WINDOWS / LUBAVITCH SYNAGOGUE, TORONTO, ON, CAN / 2009 / FLOAT GLASS PAINTING, FIG. 418: DETAIL OF THE FAR LEFT WINDOW, FIG. 419: WINDOWS ON THE LEFT SIDE

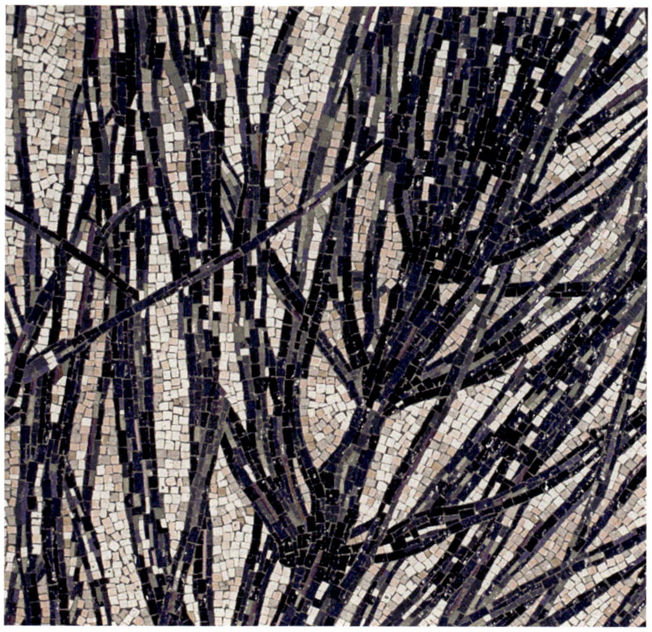

416

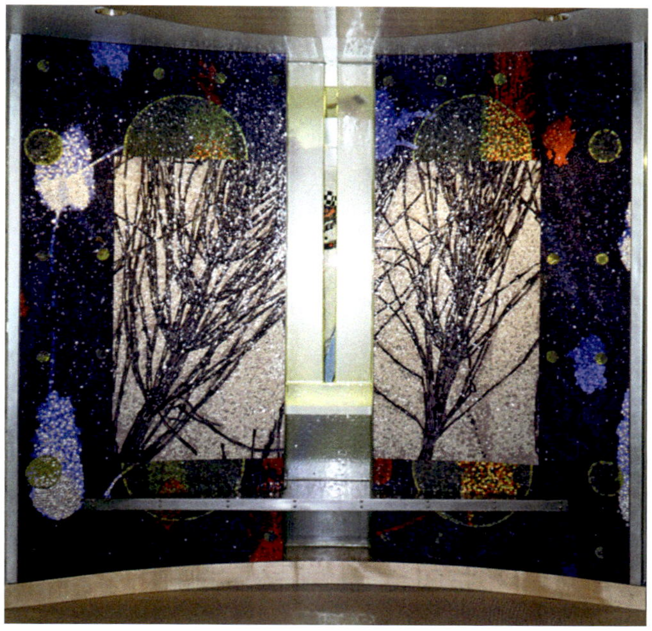

416 + 417
ANN GARDNER / "DAY AND NIGHT" / SWEDISH MEDICAL CENTER, SEATTLE, WA, USA / 2000 / STONE AND GLASS MOSAIC / FIG. 416: DETAIL

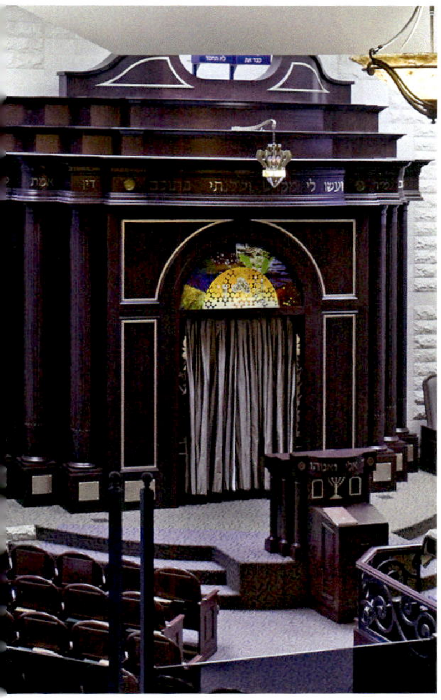

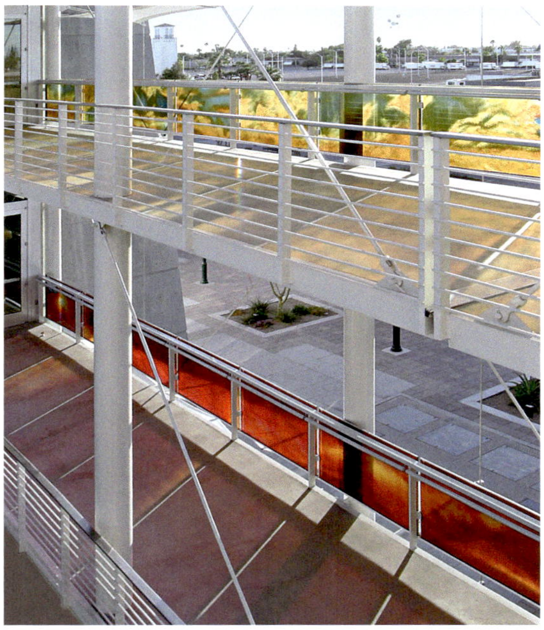

420
BETH GALSTON / "COLOR WALK" / MESA ARTS CENTER, MESA, AZ, USA / 2005 / FLOAT GLASS PAINTING

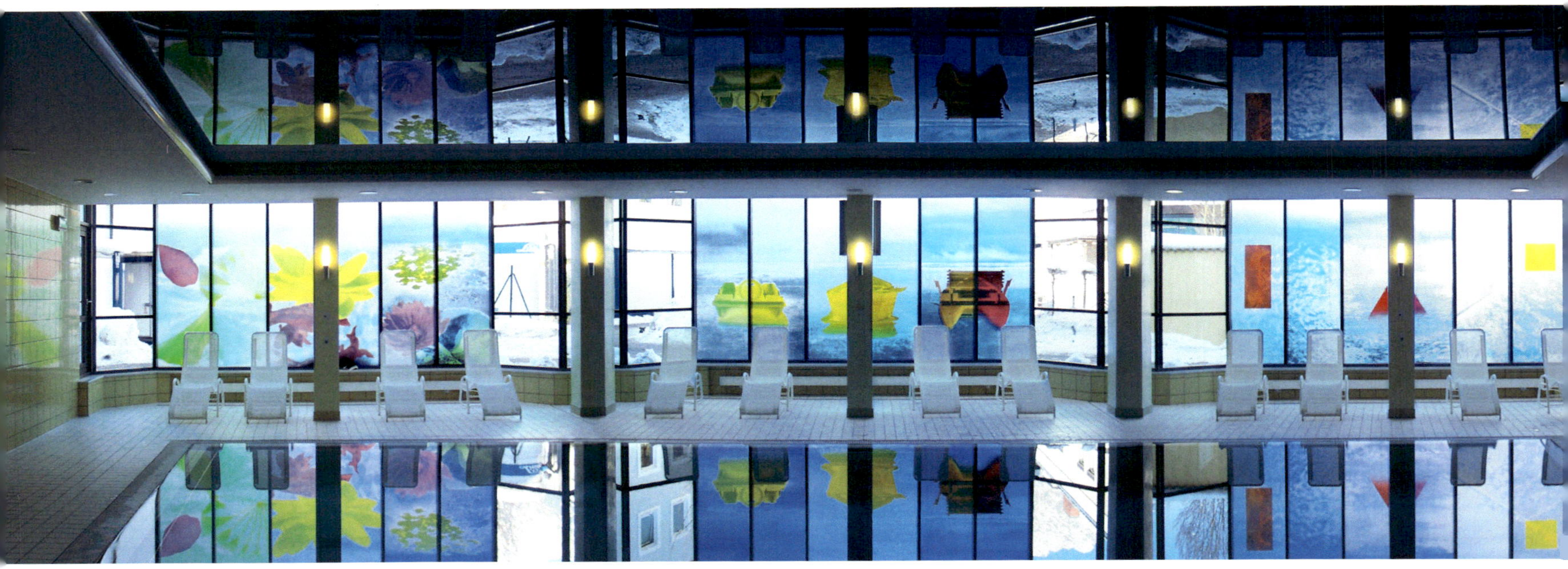

421
RAINER GOETZ / GLASS DESIGN INDOOR SWIMMING POOL / KLINIK BAD REICHENHALL, BAD REICHENHALL, DE / 2003 / ARCHITECTS AMBOS + WEIDENHAMMER / FLOAT GLASS PAINTING

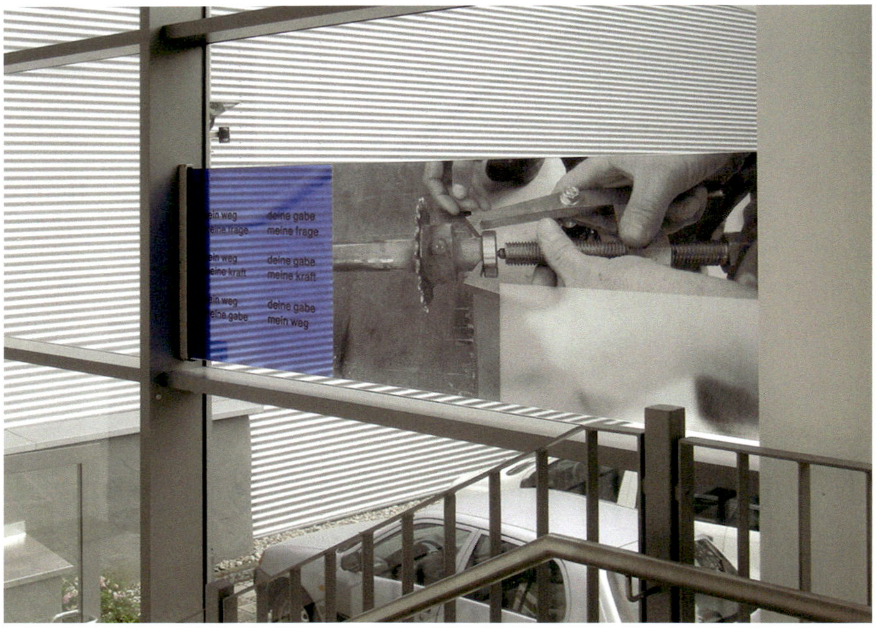

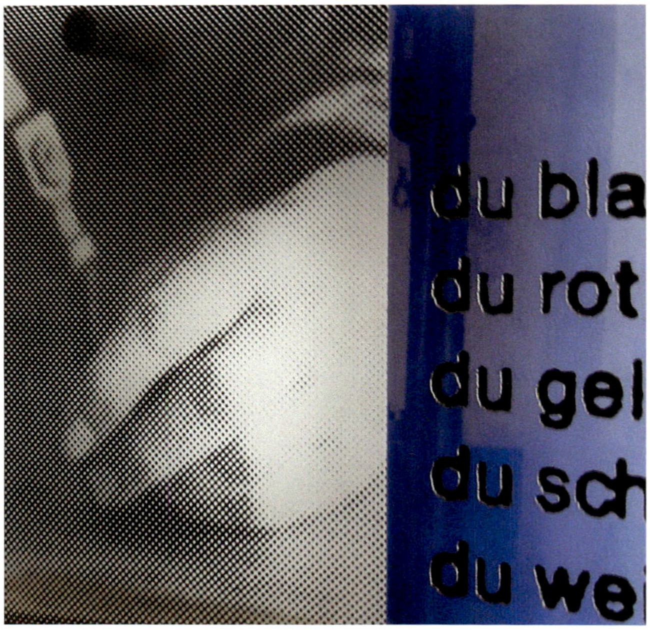

424 + 425
KLAUS GOTH / BENEDIKT-VON-NURSIA-BERUFSSCHULE, AUGSBURG, DE / 2008 / FLOAT GLASS PAINTING

425

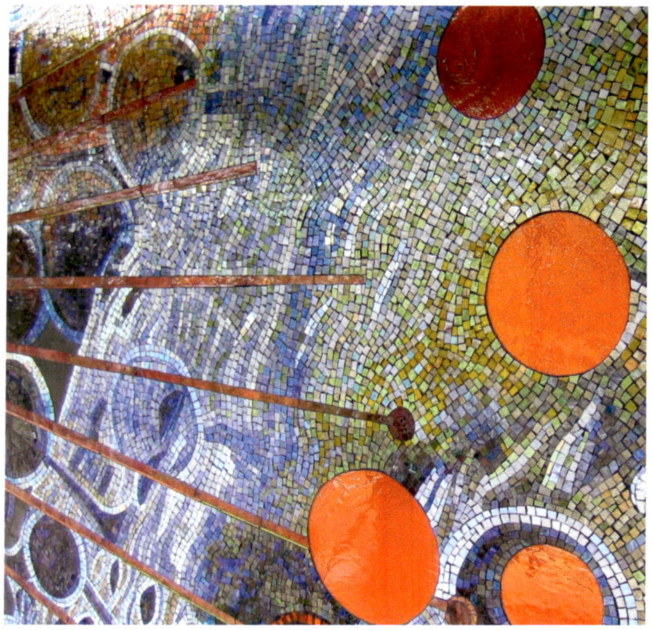

422

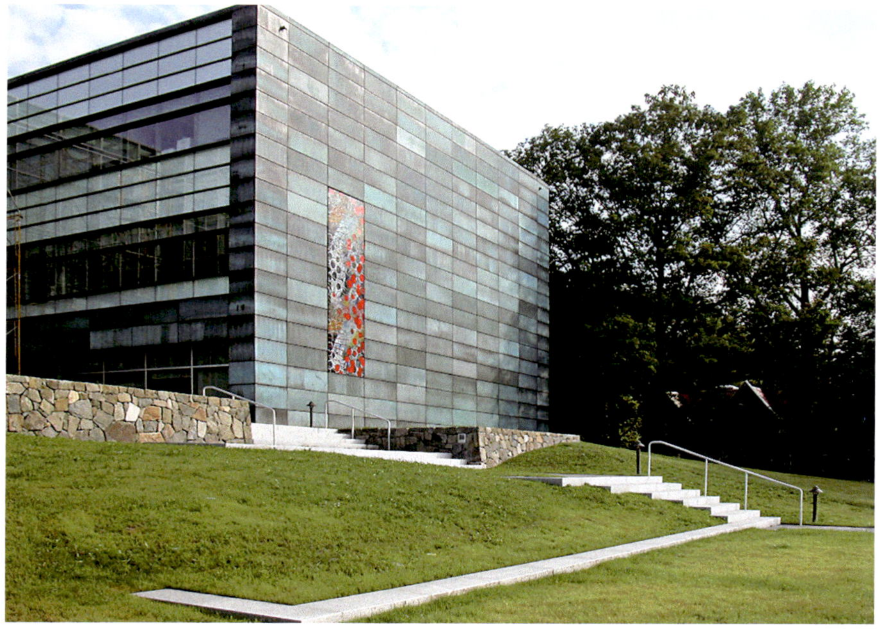

422 + 423

NICOLE GORDON / FACADE MOSAIC / NEW ENGLAND BIOLABS, IPSWICH, MA, USA / 2005 / GLASS MOSAIC

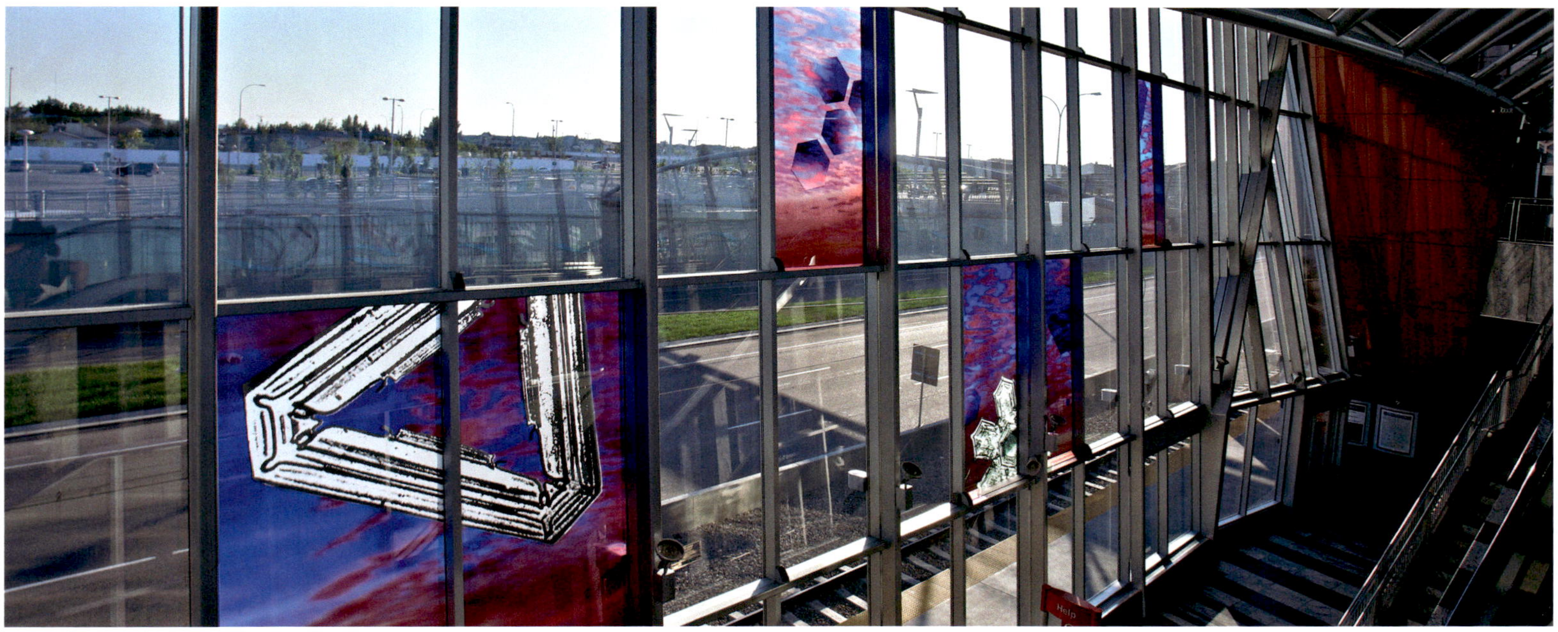

426

BARBARA GRYGUTIS / "THE COLOR OF SNOW" / NORTHWEST CROWFOOT LIGHT RAIL TRANSIT STATION / CALGARY, ALBERTA, CAN / 2008 / FLOAT GLASS PAINTING

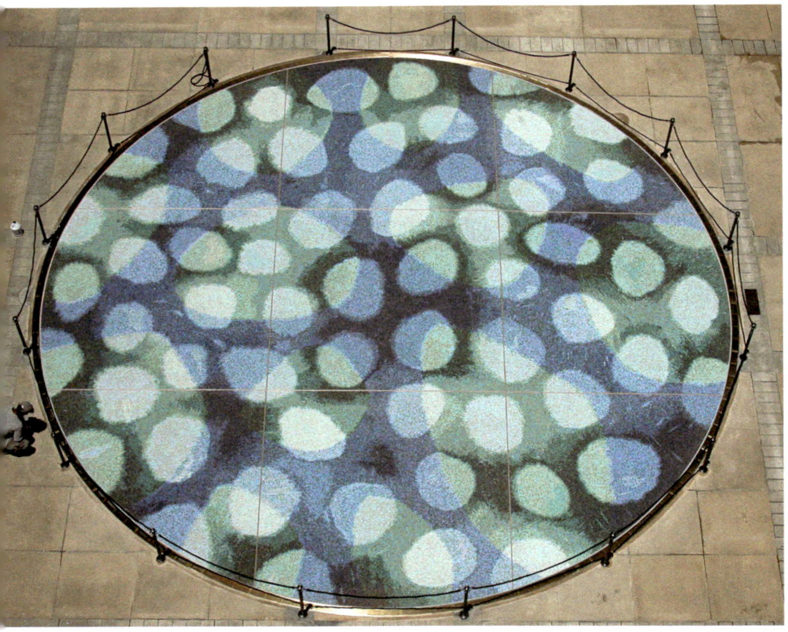

427

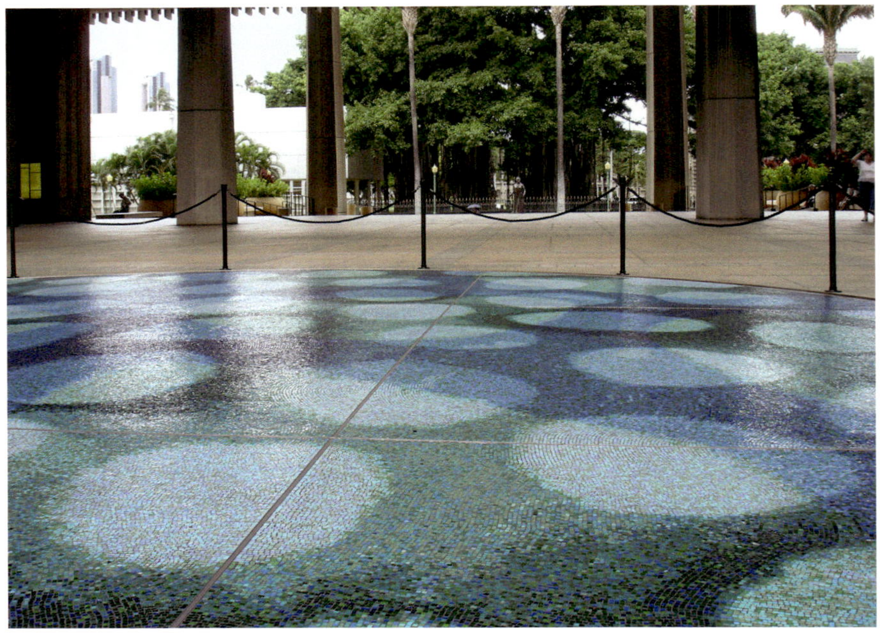

427 + 428
TADASHI SATO / "AQUARIUS" / MOSAIC FLOOR, HAWAII STATE CAPITOL, HONOLULU, HI, USA / ARCHITECTS HAWAII / HI STATE CULTURE + ARTS / 2009 / RECONSTRUCTION, GLASS MOSAIC

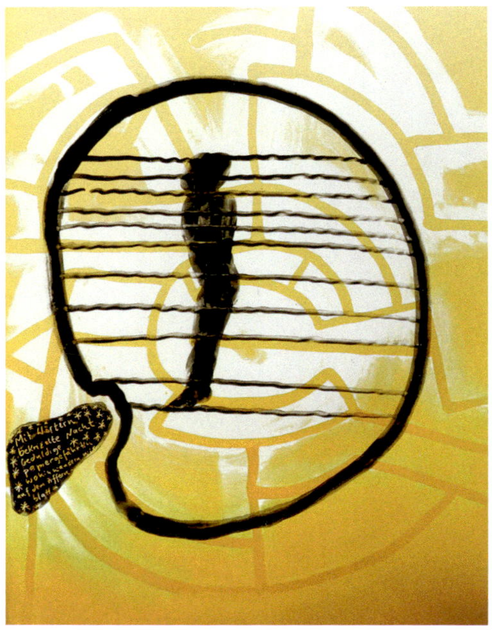

431 + 432
JOHANNES HEWEL / PRIVATE RESIDENCE, SOUTH GERMANY / 2001 / STAINED GLASS

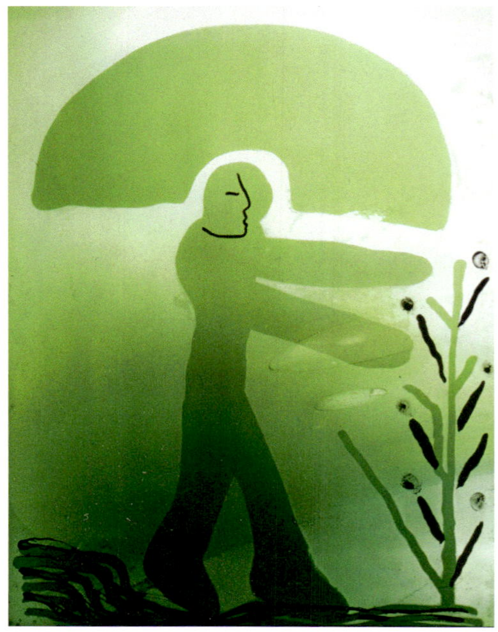

432

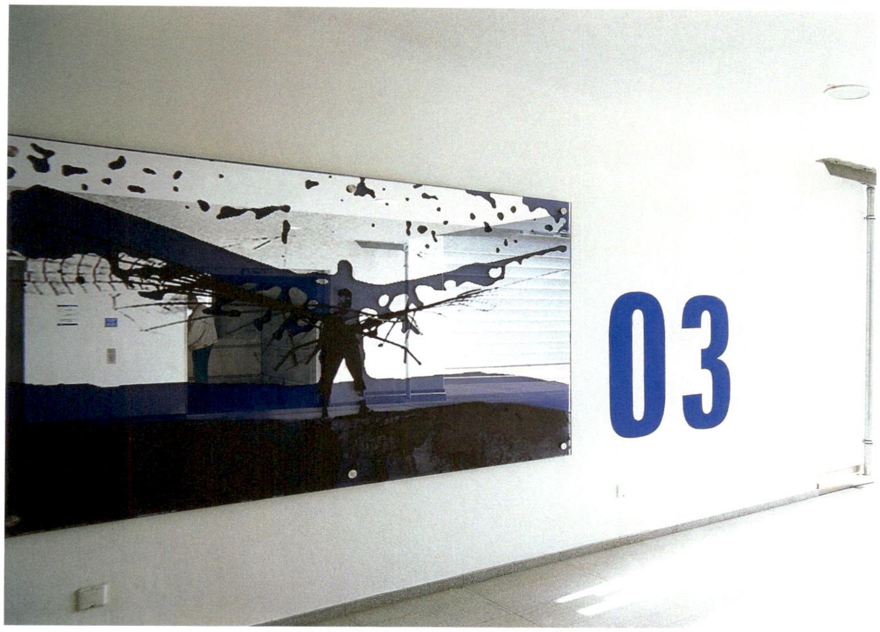

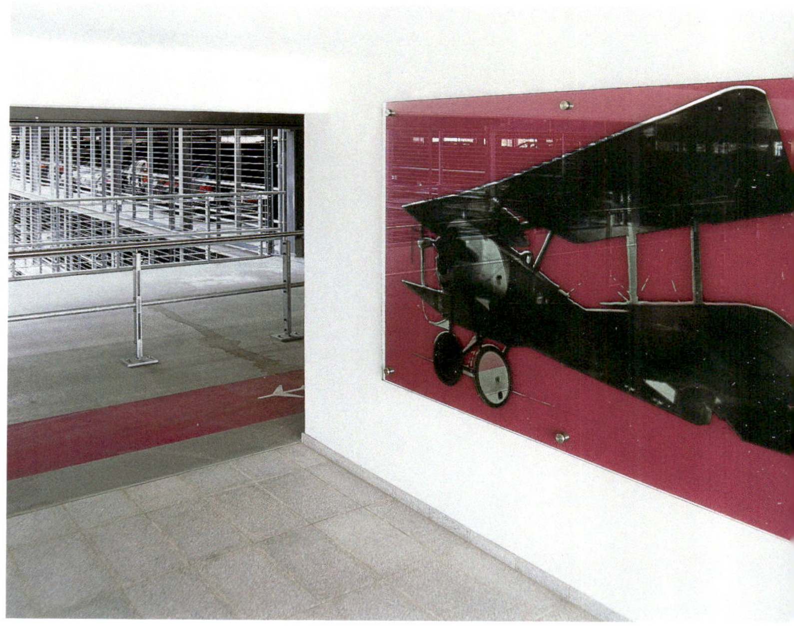

429 + 430
JOSEF HENSELMANN / EACH TWO ARCHITECTURAL ART GLASS PIECES FOR ALL LEVELS / PARKING GARAGE P20, TERMINAL 2, AIRPORT MUNICH, DE / ARCHITECTS KOCH + PARTNER / 2003 / FLOAT GLASS PAINTING

430

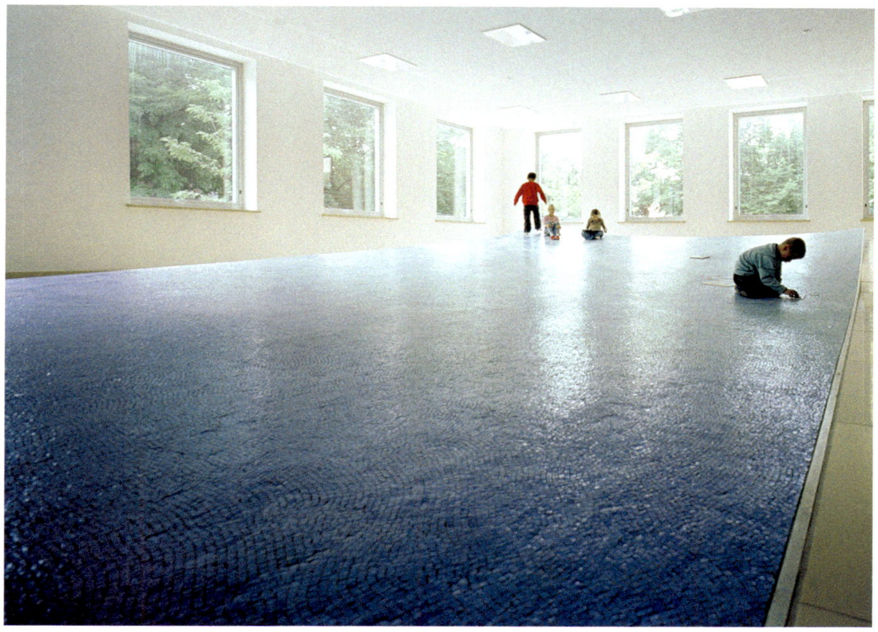

433
SABRINA HOHMANN / "ANTICIPATION" / THREE DIMENSIONAL MOSAIC FLOOR / STIELER-SCHULE, MUNICH, DE / 2006 / GLASS MOSAIC

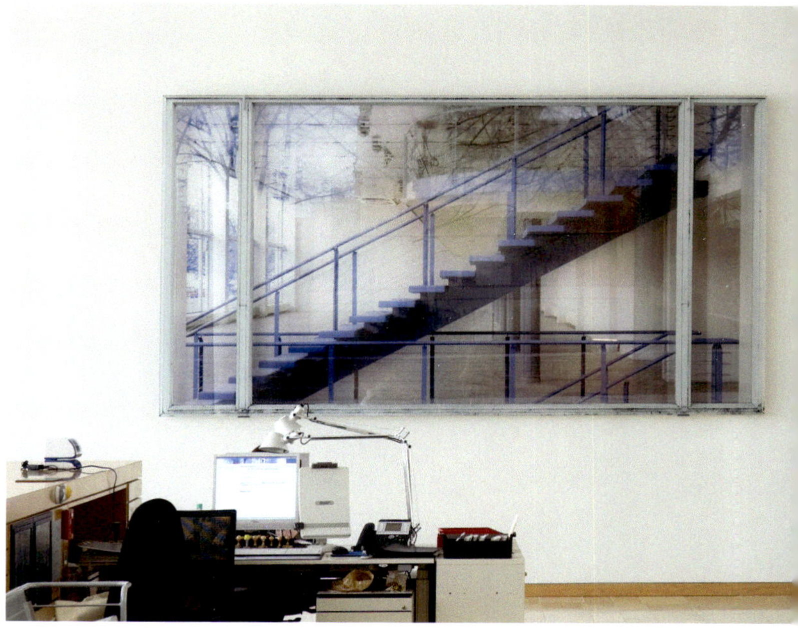

434
SABINE HORNIG / "WINDOW ON KARL MARX ALLEE" / DEUTSCHE BUNDESBANK, BERLIN, DE / 2010 / SILKSCREEN ON GLASS

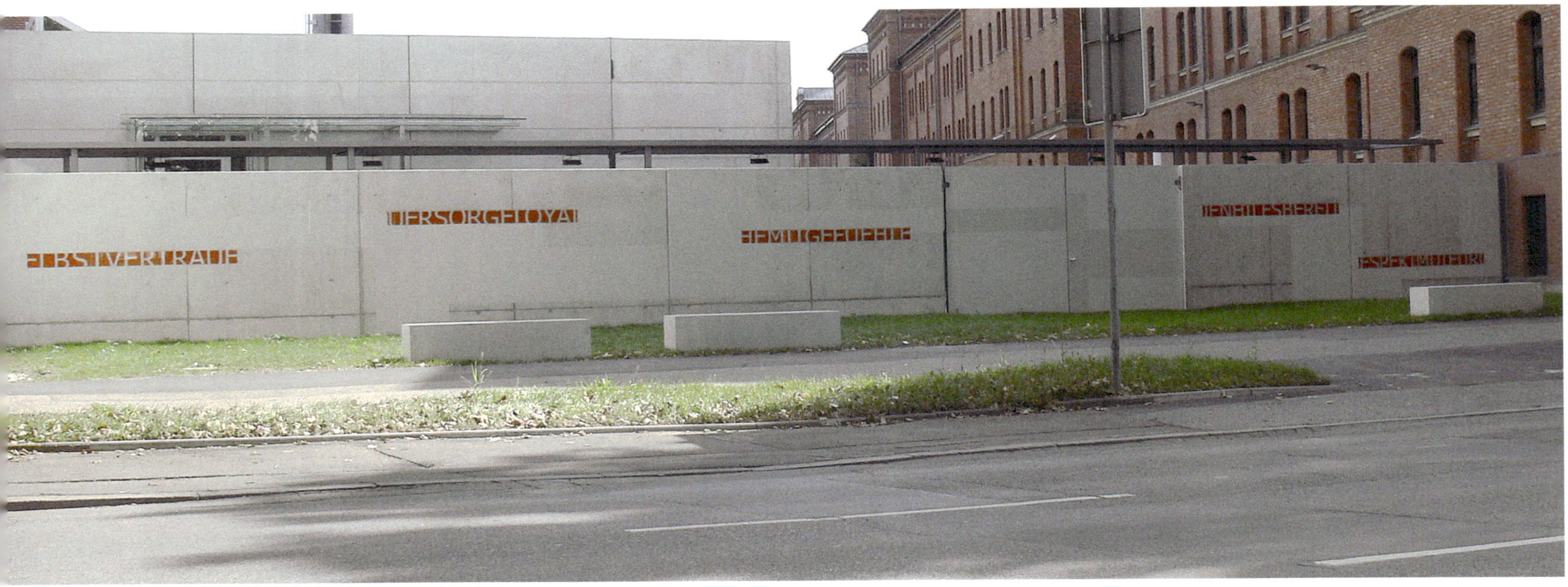

435+436
MONIKA HUBER / "IMAGES MADE OF LANGUAGE" / EXTERIOR AND INTERIOR ART GLASS, POLICE HEADQUARTERS, INGOLSTADT, DE / 2009 / FLOAT GLASS PAINTING

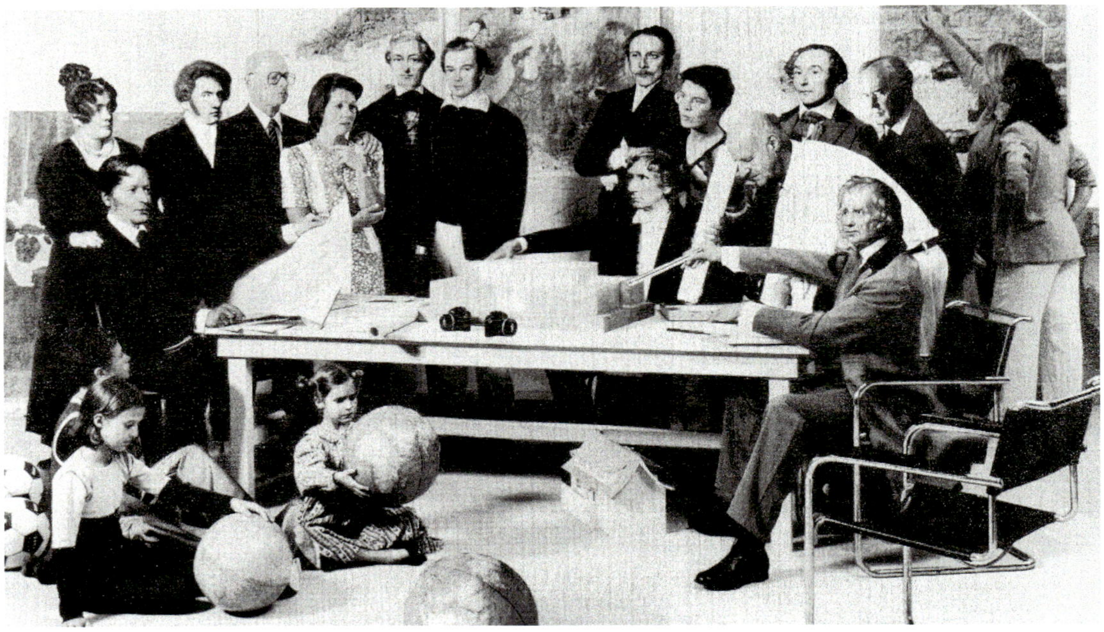

438
STEPHAN HUBER / "FOUNDERS' MOSAIC" / FOYER, MUSEUM DER BILDENDEN KÜNSTE, LEIPZIG, DE / 2004 / MICRO-GLASS MOSAIC

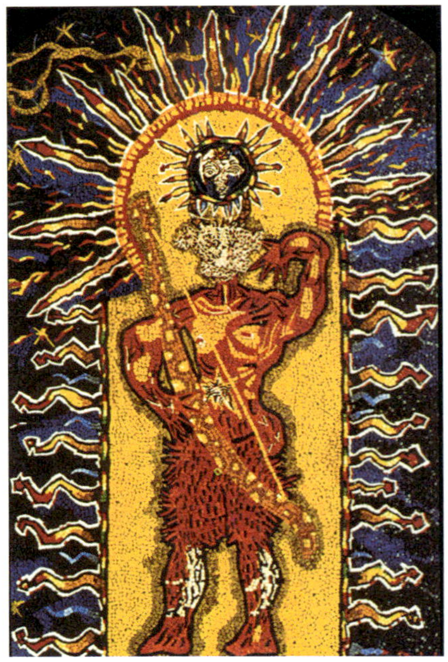

439
JOHN HUGHES / "RED MAN" FROM SERIES "RED - WHITE MAN" / PRIVATE HOME, DUBLIN, IRL / 1998 / GLASS MOSAIC

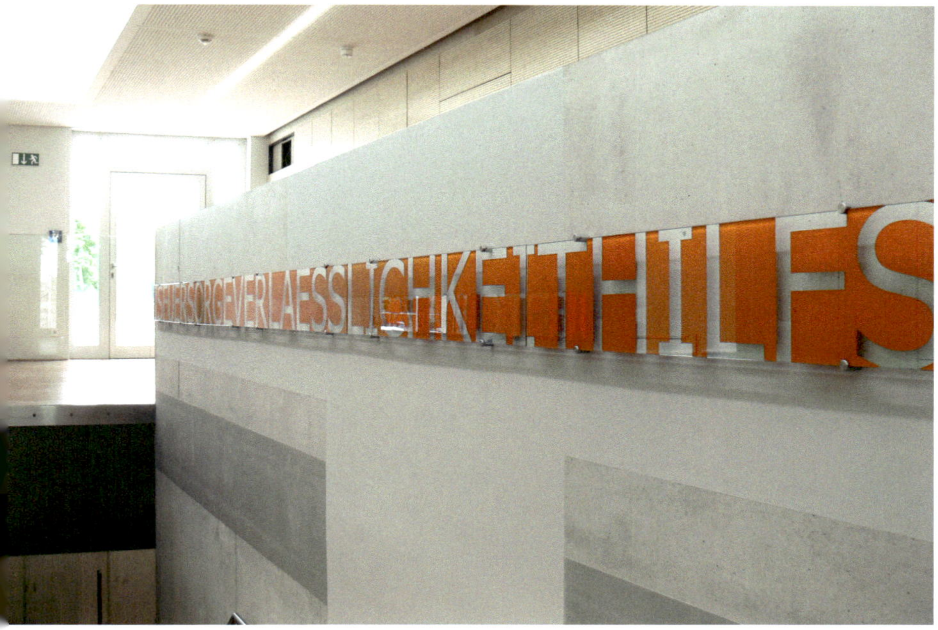

436

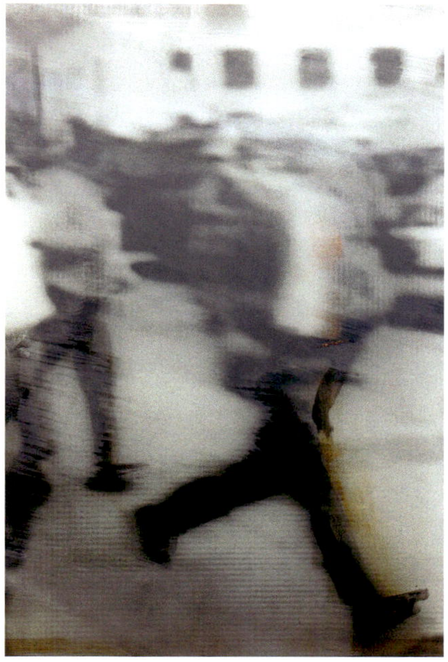

437

MONIKA HUBER / "ONE THIRTY" /
HAUS DER KUNST, MUNICH, DE / 2012 /
FLOAT GLASS PAINTING

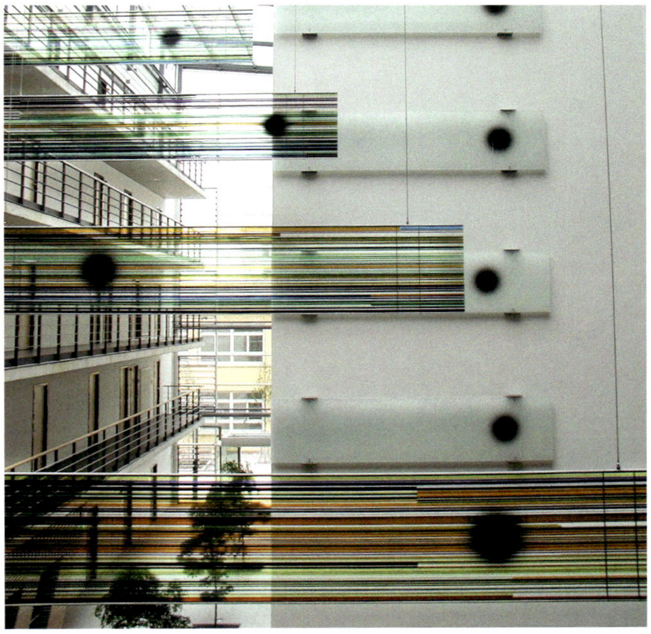

440

BERNHARD HUBER / "2 × 5 IMPULSE" / GÖPPINGEN, DE /
POLYTECHNIC / 2004 / FLOAT GLASS PAINTING

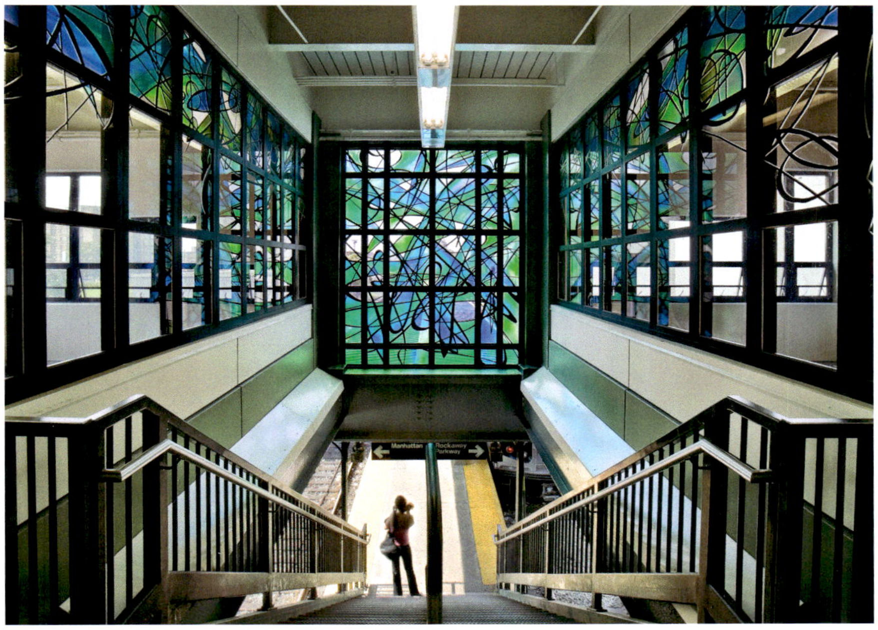

441

MICHAEL INGUI / "CRESCENDO" / SUBWAY STATION, EAST 105 STREET, NEW YORK, NY, USA /
MTA ARTS FOR TRANSIT / 2007 / FLOAT GLASS PAINTING

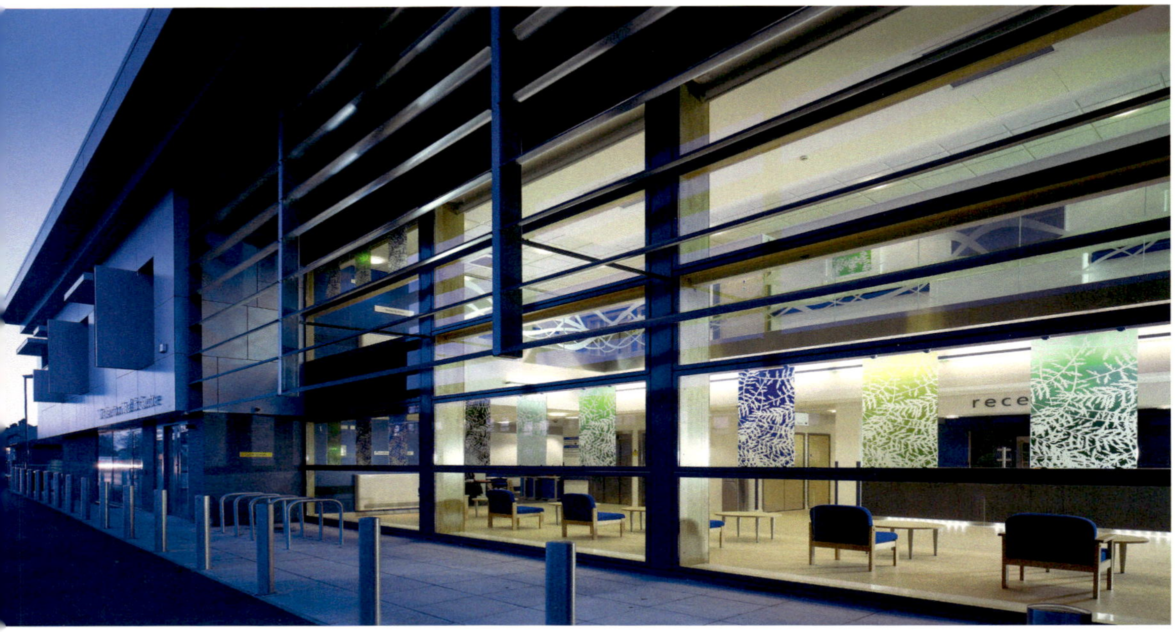

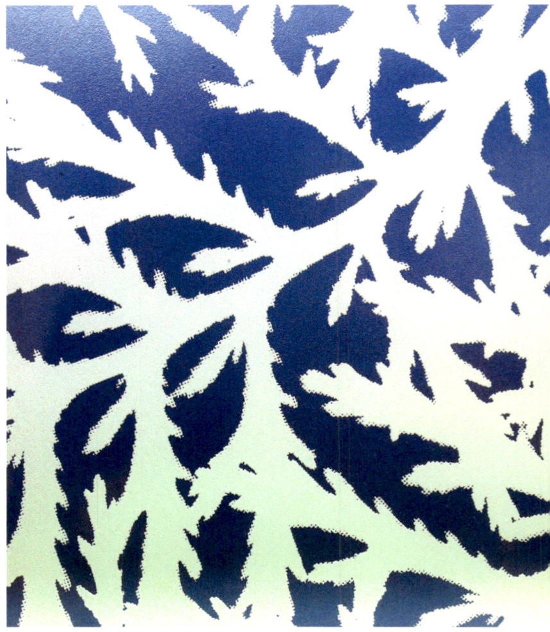

442 + 443

BRIDGET JONES / WREKENTON PRIMARY CARE CENTRE, GATESHEAD, GB / 2008 / FLOAT GLASS PAINTING / FIG. 443: DETAIL

443

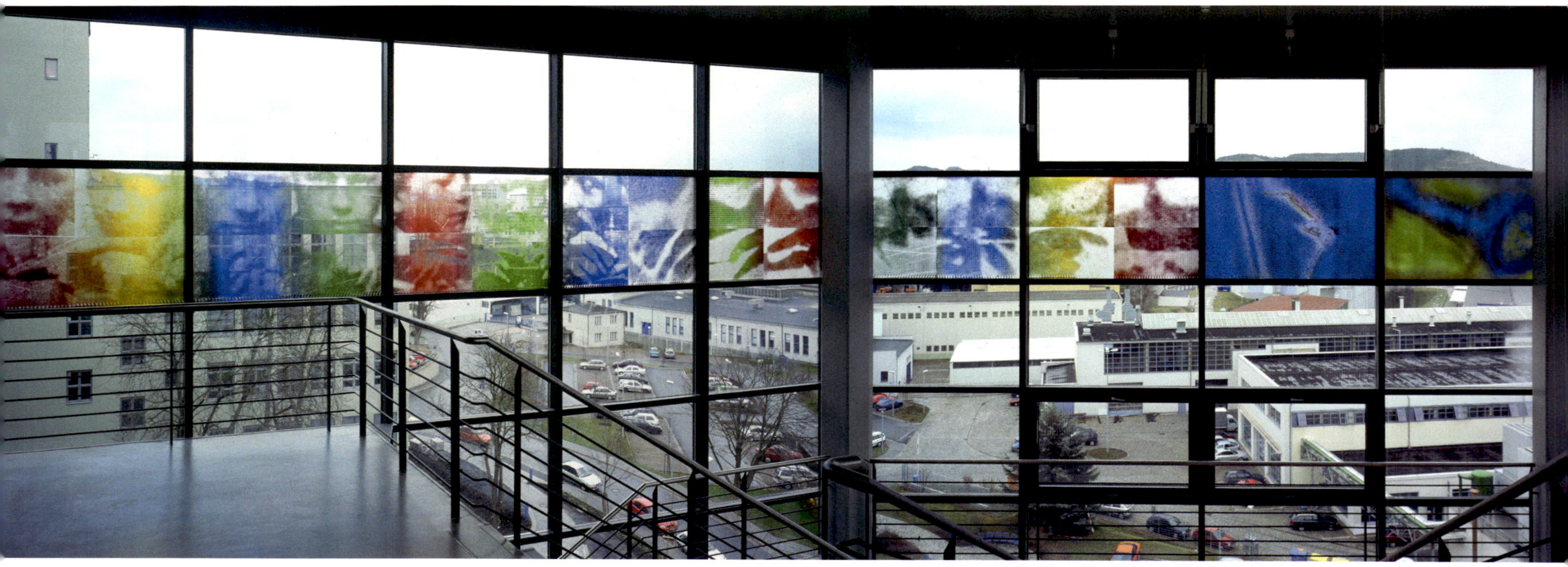

446 + 447

JOACHIM JUNG / "OPTICAL WORKSHOP CARL ZEISS 1864" / BUILDING 5, POLYTECHNIC COLLEGE, JENA, DE / 2001 / ARCHITECT: FALCO BAERENWALD / FLOAT GLASS PAINTING / FIG. 447: DETAIL FROM THIRD IMAGE LEFT

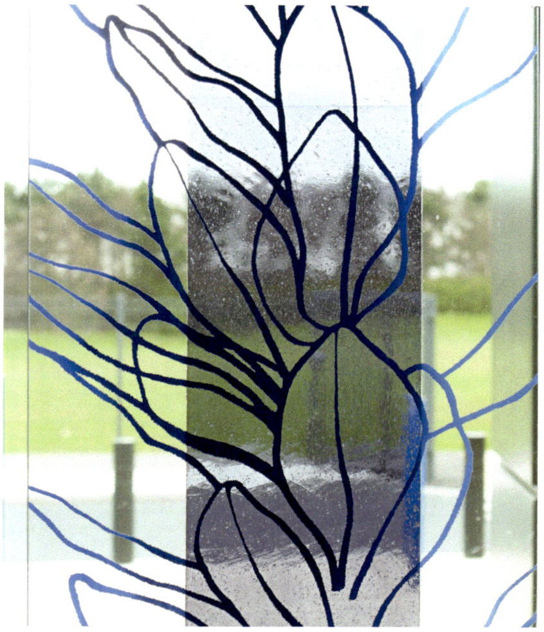

444
BRIDGET JONES / WASHINGTON PRIMARY CARE CENTRE, WASHINGTON, GB / 2008 / FLOAT GLASS PAINTING

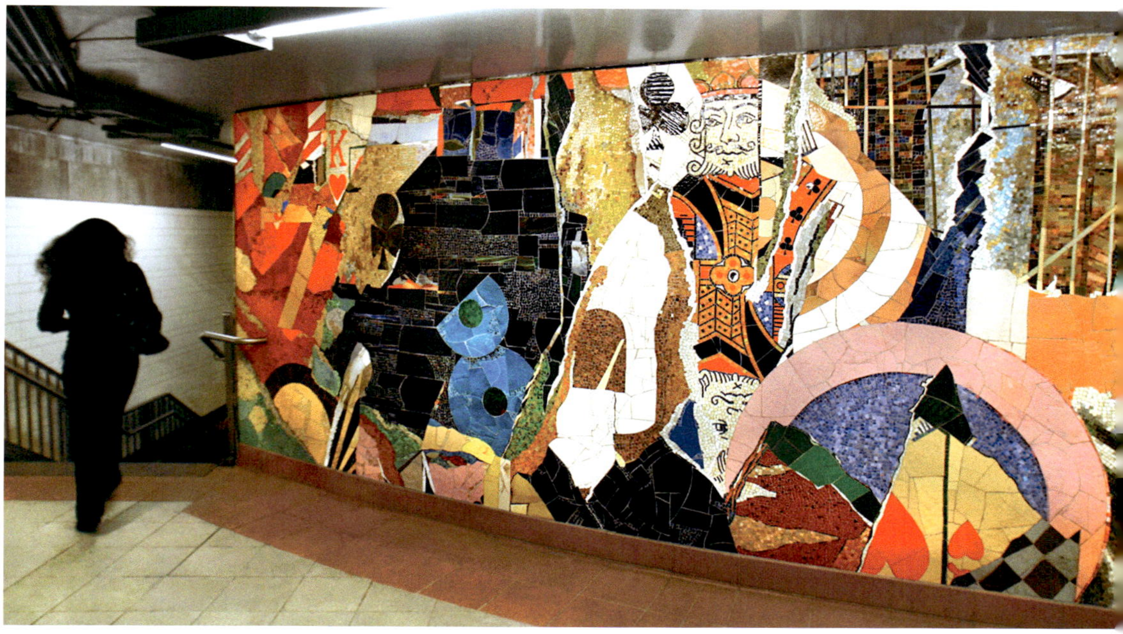

445
STEPHEN JOHNSON / “DEKALB IMPROVISATION” / DEKALB AVENUE SUBWAY STATION, BROOKLYN, NY, USA / MTA ARTS FOR TRANSIT / 2004 / GLASS MOSAIC

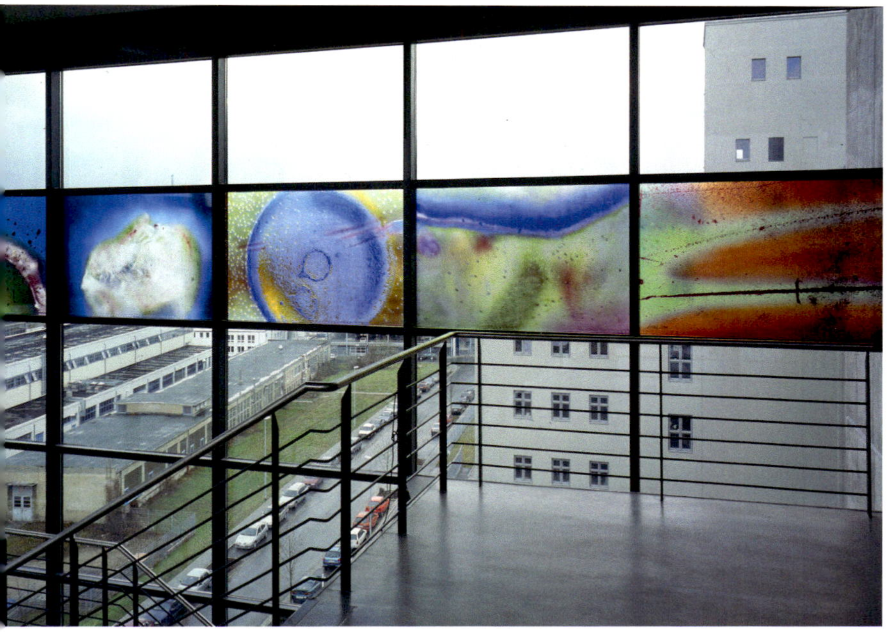

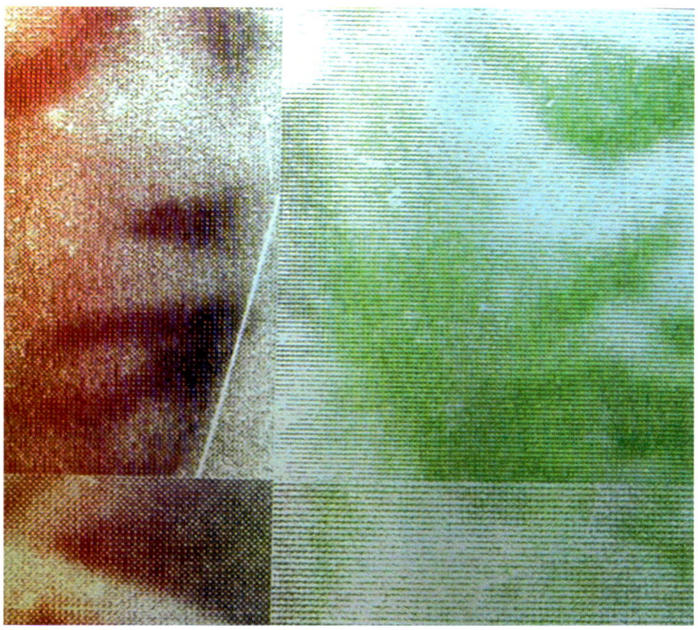

447

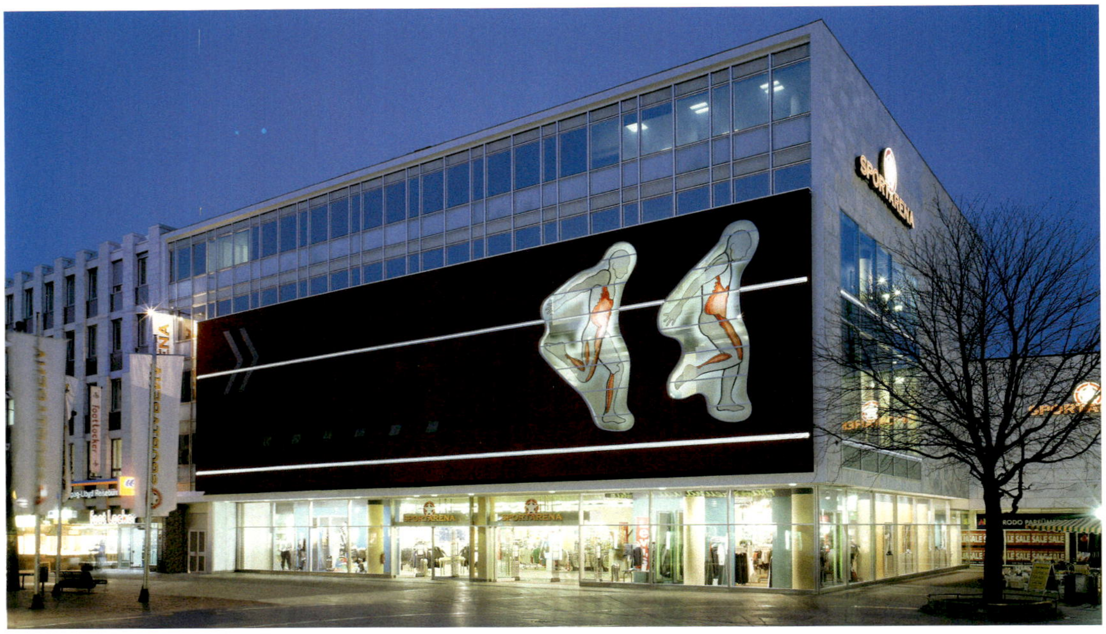

448

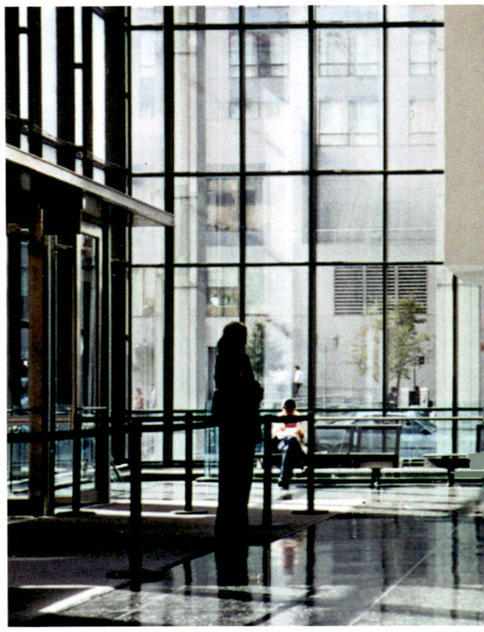

449

SABINE KAMMERL / “WALL RUNNER” / DEPARTMENT STORE, KÖNIGSTRASSE, STUTTGART, DE / 1999 / LEADED GLASS

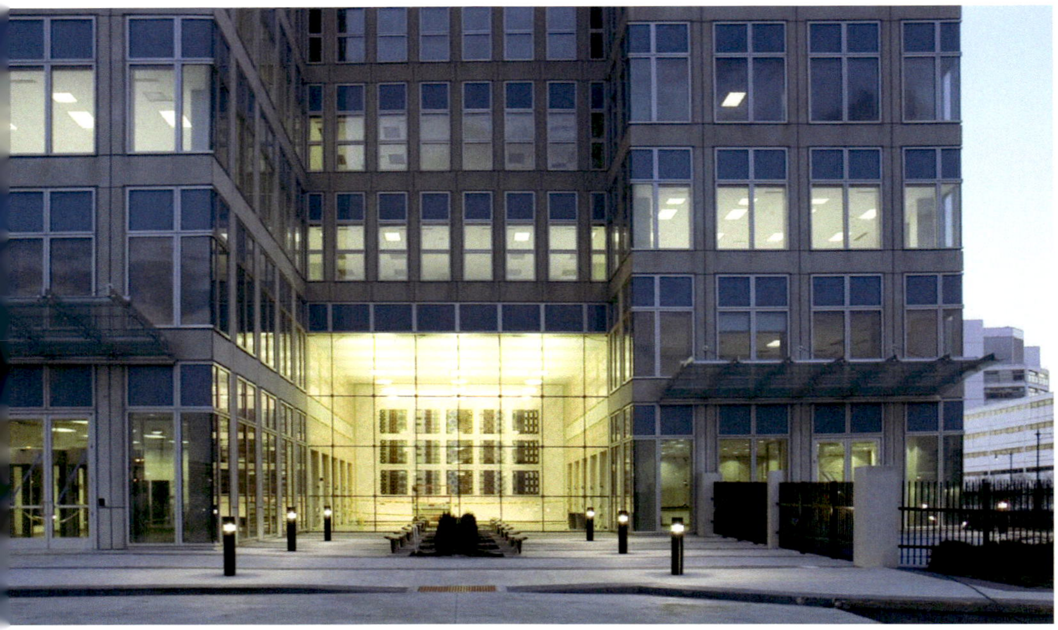

451

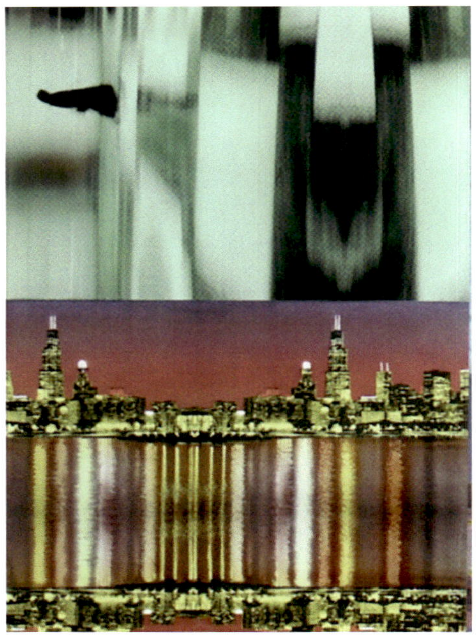

452

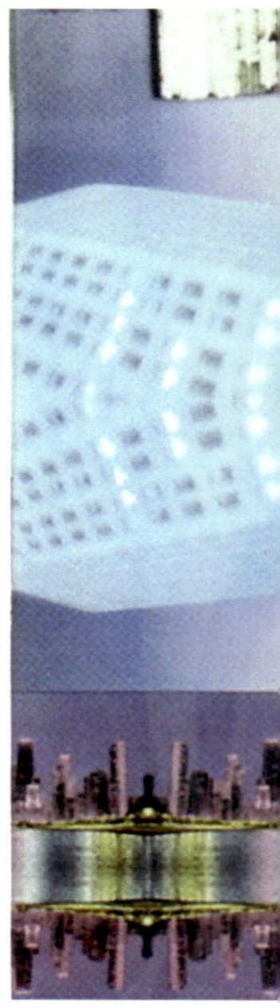

453

ANNE MARIE KARLSEN / “POINTS OF VIEW” / FBI HEADQUARTERS, CHICAGO, IL, USA / ARCHITECT: LOHAN ANDERSON / 2008 / FLOAT GLASS PAINTING

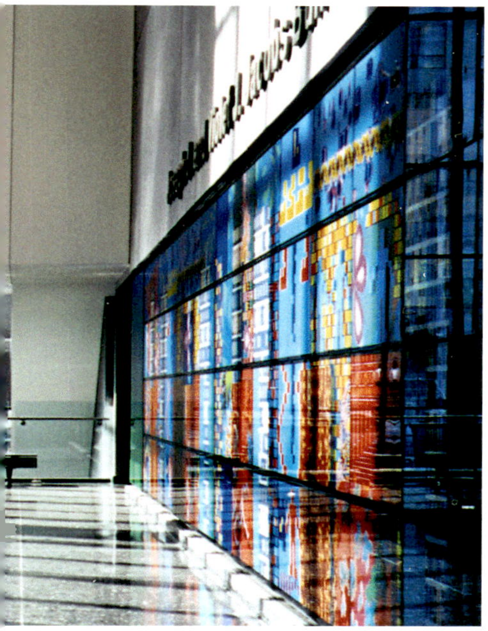

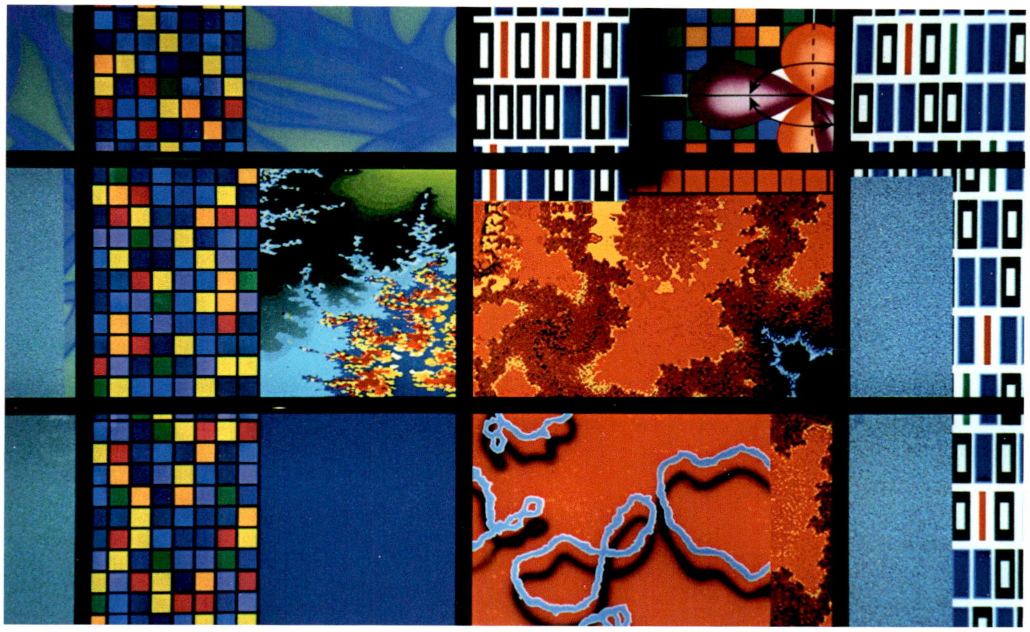

449 + 450
SUSAN KAPROV / "URBAN HELIX" / POLYTECHNIC INSTITUTE OF NEW YORK UNIVERSITY, BROOKLYN, NY, USA / 2002 / FLOAT GLASS PAINTING / FIG. 450: DETAIL

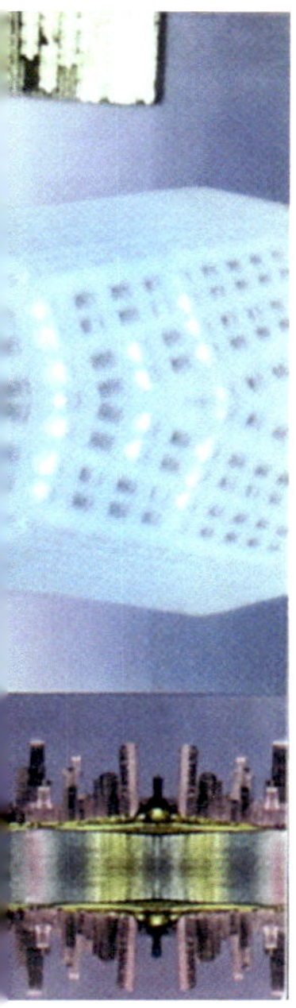

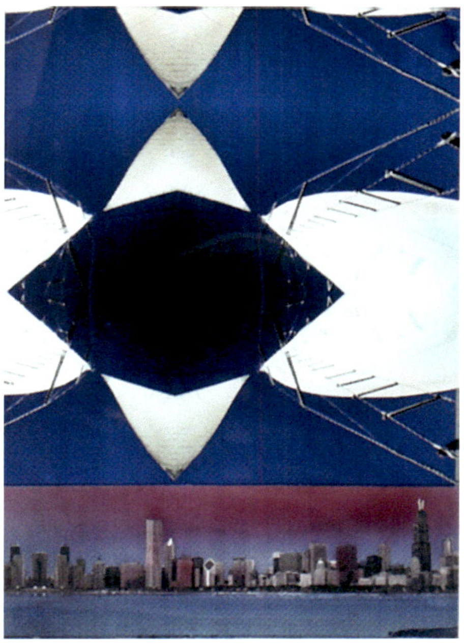

452–454
ANNE MARIE KARLSEN / "POINTS OF VIEW" / DETAILS

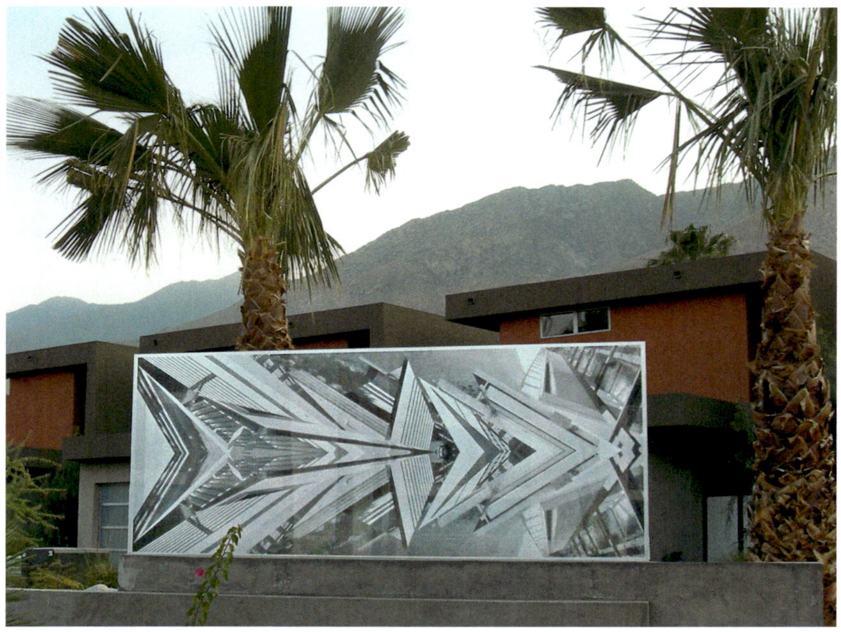

455
ANNE MARIE KARLSEN / "REVERB" / PALM SPRINGS, CA, USA / 2007 / FLOAT GLASS PAINTING

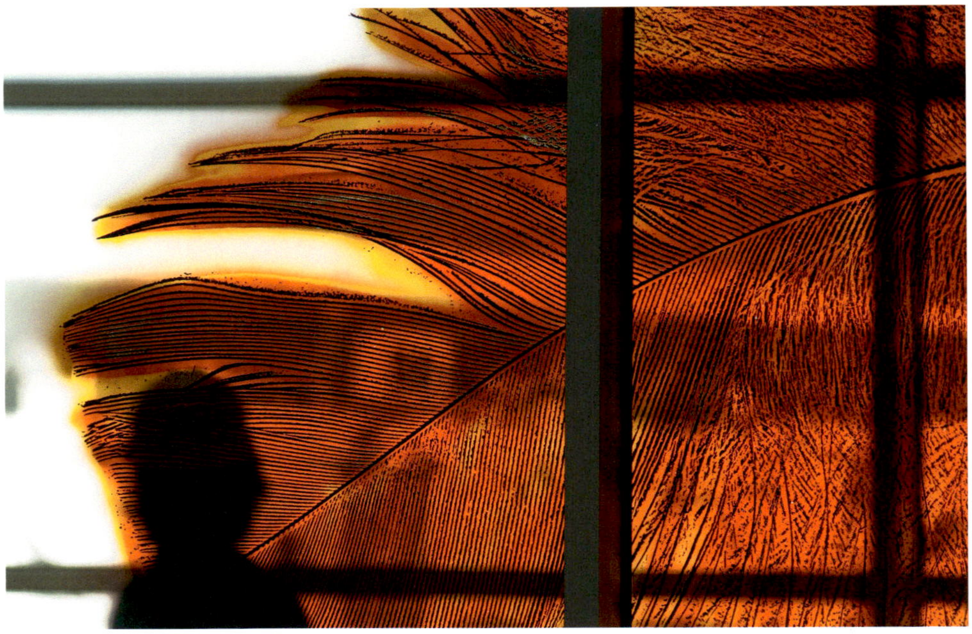

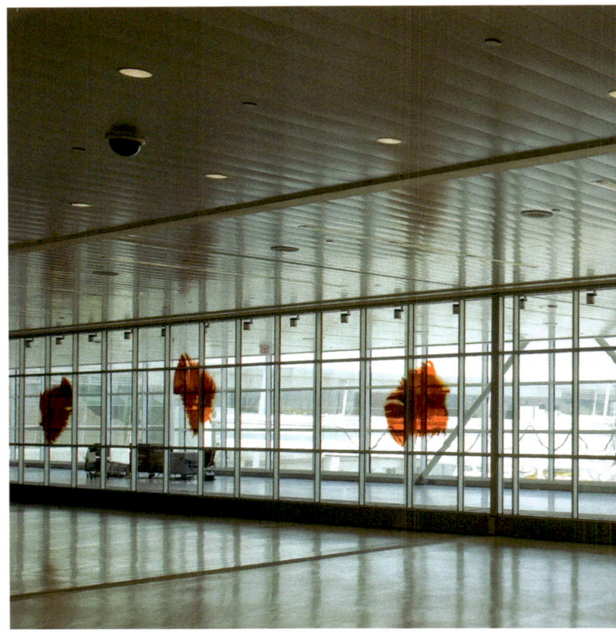

456 + 457
STUART KEELER, MICHAEL MACHNIC / "CARDINAL POINTS" / INDIANAPOLIS AIRPORT, IN, USA / HOK ARCHITECTS, BLACKBURN ARCHITECTS-ART ADMINISTRATORS / 2009 / FLOAT GLASS PAINTING

457

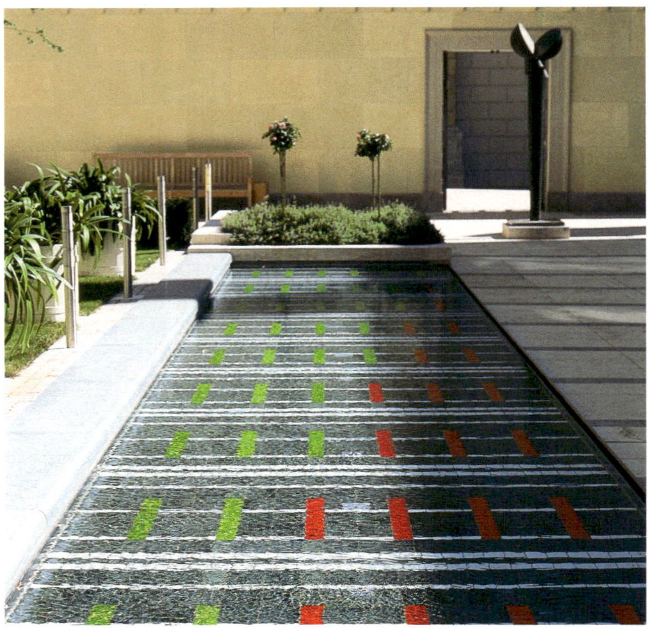

460
PETER KLUSKA / WATER BASIN / KABINETTGARTEN, RESIDENZ MUNICH, DE / 2003 / STONE AND GLASS MOSAIC

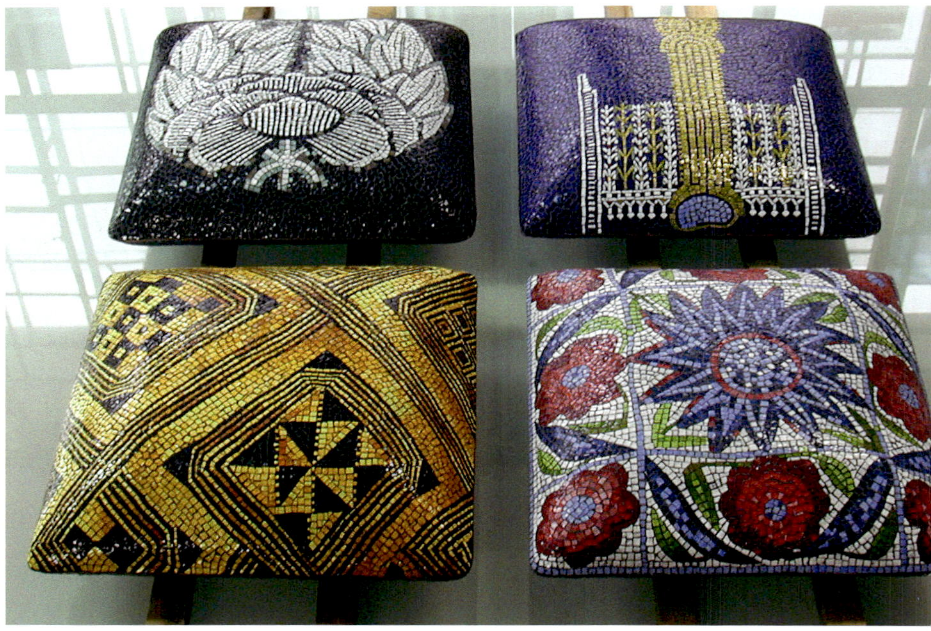

461
AIDA SAUL, LINDA KROFF / "THE SECRET GARDEN" / THE GREEN, CHARLOTTE, NC, USA / 2001 / GLASS MOSAIC ON POURED CONCRETE

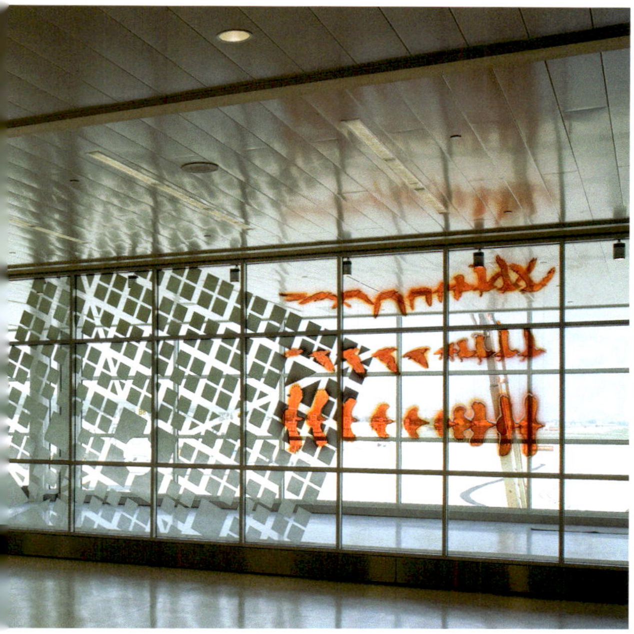

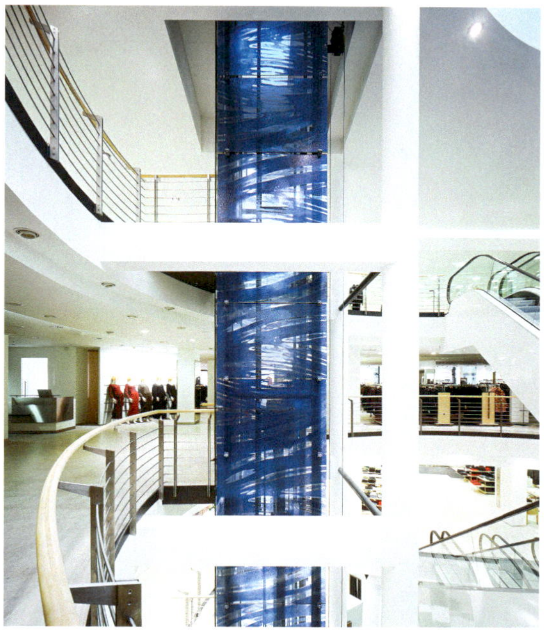

458 + 459
NIKOLAUS KOLIUSIS / “IN THE SAME WIND” / ELEVATOR MODEHAUS KAISER, FREIBURG I. BR., DE / 1999 / FLOAT GLASS PAINTING

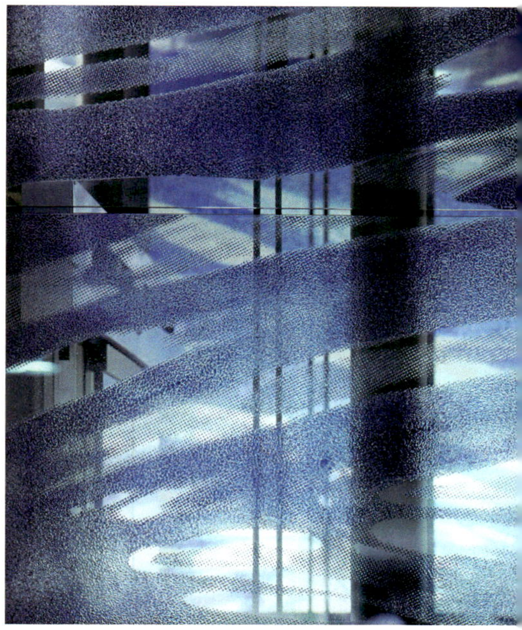

459

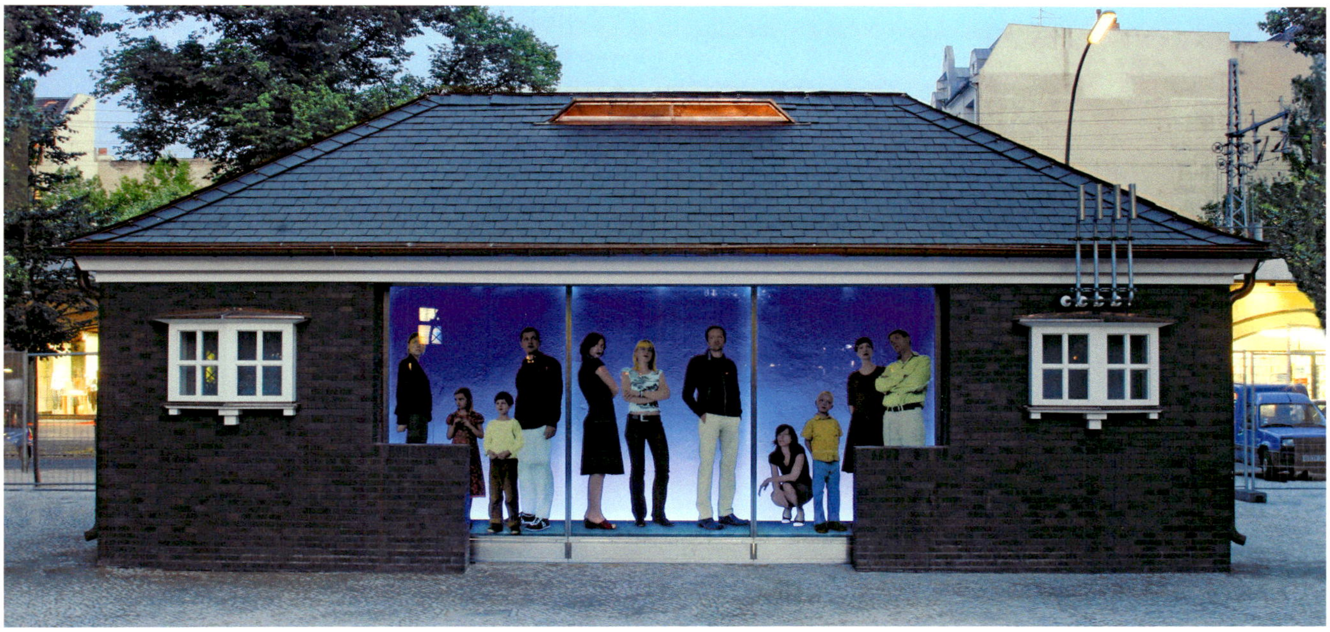

462
UTE LINDNER / “THROUGH THE LOOKING GLASS” / GASAG-PAVILION, SAVIGNYPLATZ, BERLIN, DE / 2007 / FLOAT GLASS PAINTING

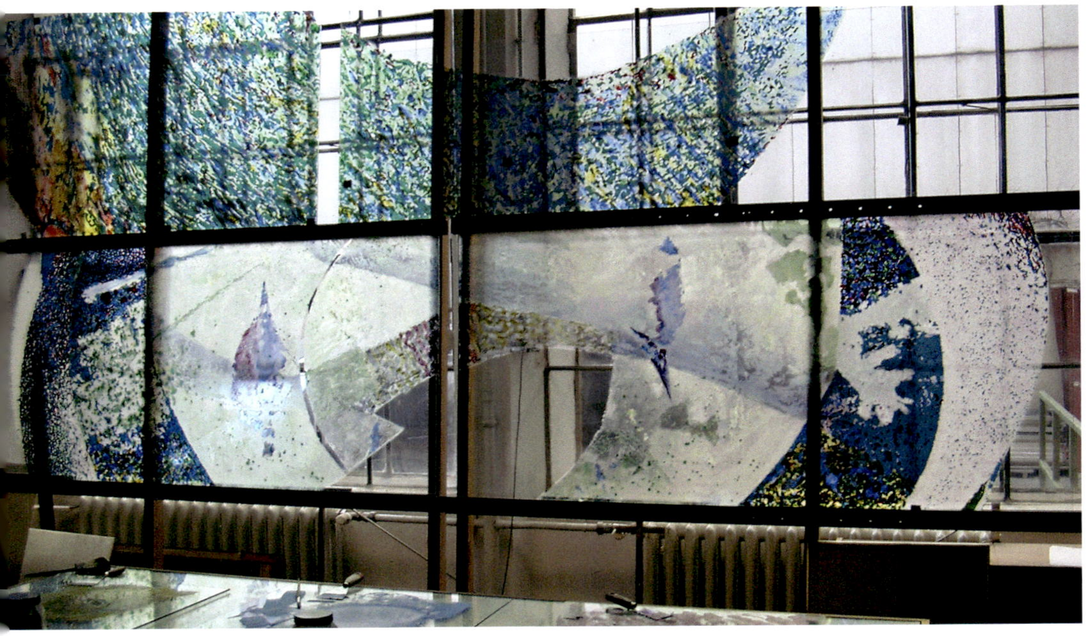

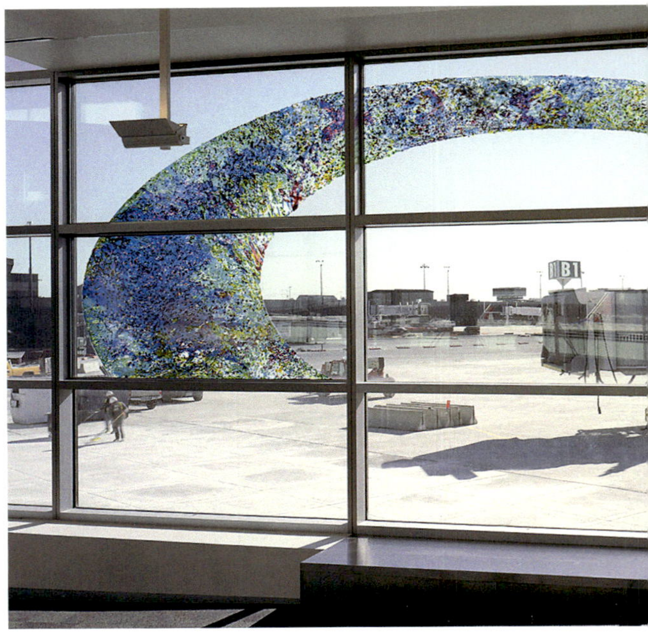

463 + 464
HEIDI LIPPMAN / "DEPARTURES: A QUINTET" / SW TERMINAL, BWI AIRPORT, BALTIMORE, MD, USA / ARCHITECT: MEDCO / 2004 / FLOAT GLASS PAINTING / FIG. 463: DETAILS AT STUDIO / FIG. 464: VIEW TOWARDS THE AIRFIELD

464

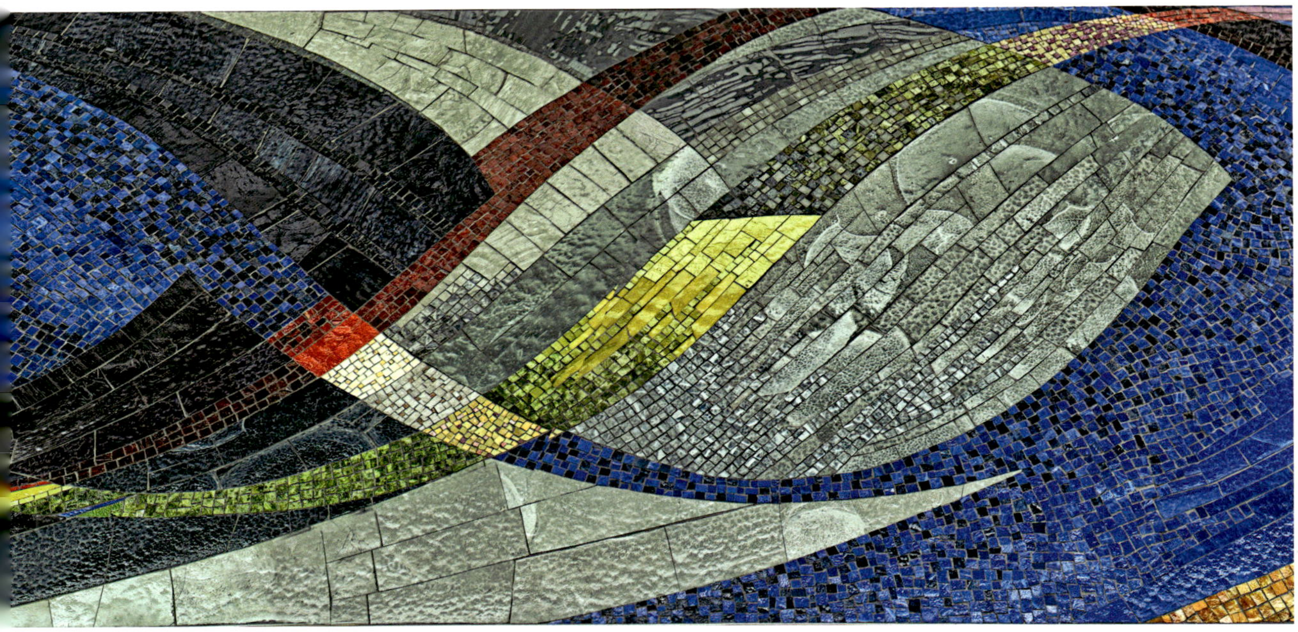

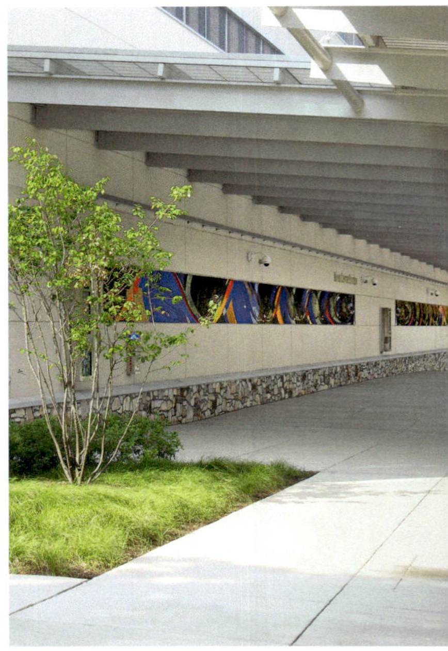

466 + 467
HEIDI LIPPMAN / "DOPPLER" / MARK CENTER, ALEXANDRIA, VA, USA / 2012 / GLASS MOSAIC / FIG. 466: DETAIL / FIG 467: THE LONG MOSAIC BAND, AN OVERALL VIEW

467

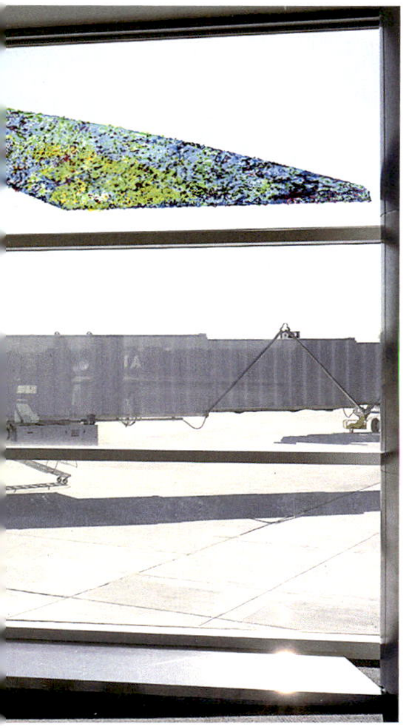

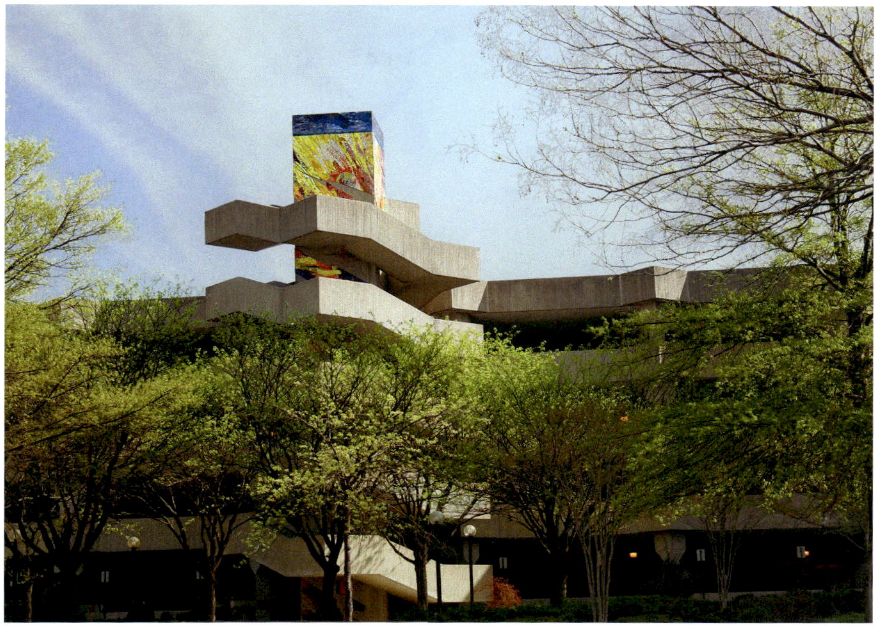

465
HEIDI LIPPMAN / "DAWN AND DUSK" / PARKING GARAGE, AMTRAK STATION, NEW CARROLTON, MD, USA / 1994 / GLASS MOSAIC ON FOUR STAIRWELL TOWERS

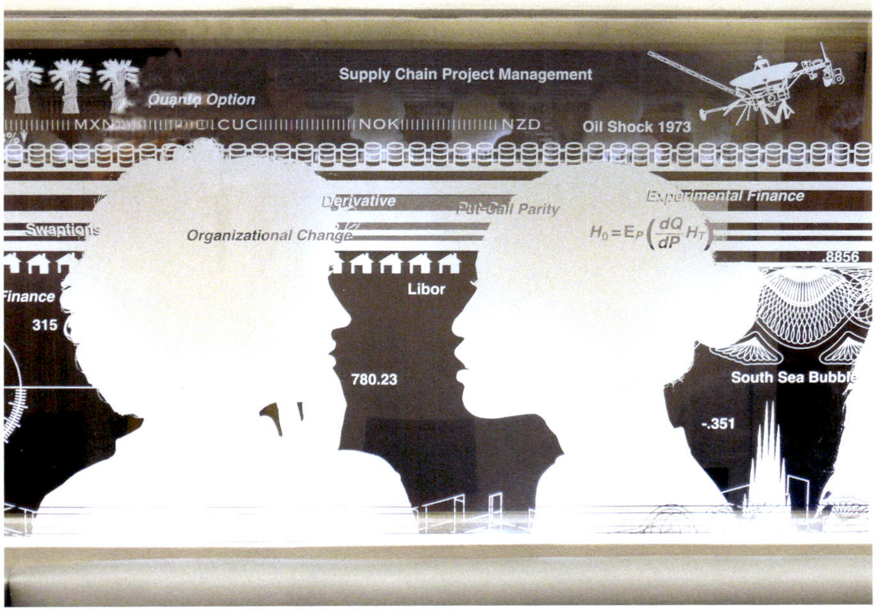

468
CLYDE LYNDS / NJT-STATION PLAUDERVILLE, GARFIELD, NJ, USA / 2010 / FLOAT GLASS PAINTING / DETAIL

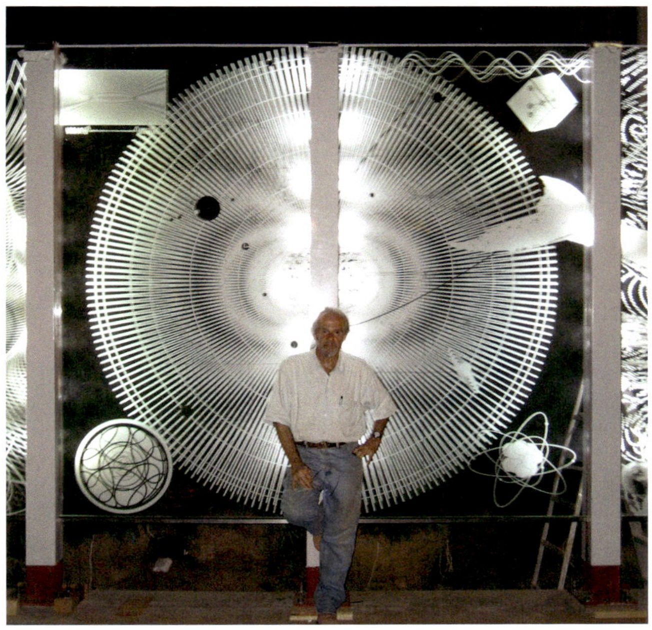

469
CLYDE LYNDS / "GATEWAY" / RUTGERS UNIVERSITY, CAMDEN, NJ, USA / NJ STATE COUNCIL ON THE ARTS / 2007 / FLOAT GLASS PAINTING / DETAIL

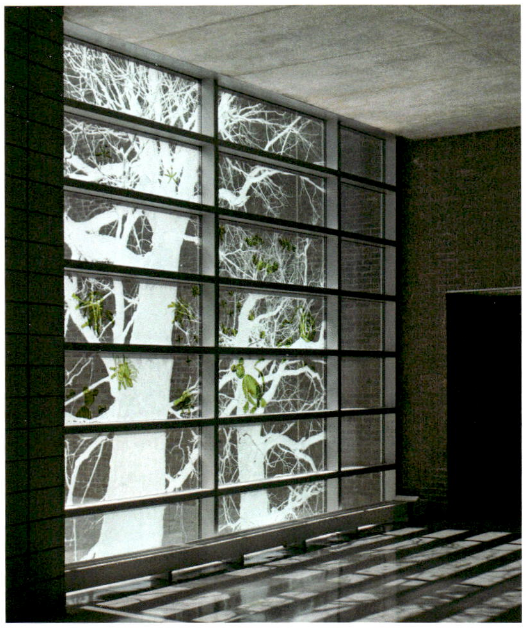

470

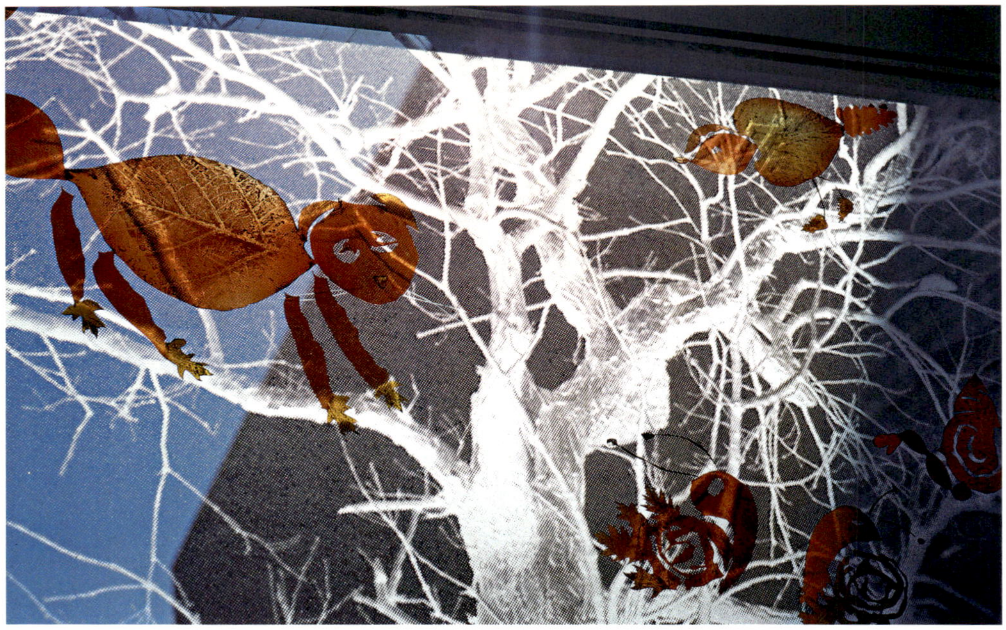

470 + 471

MARTHA MADIGAN / "OAK SEASONS" / PS IS 499 PUBLIC SCHOOL, QUEENS, NY, USA /NYC PUBLIC ART FOR PUBLIC SCHOOLS / 2004 / FLOAT GLASS PAINTING / FIG. 470: THE ART GLASS ON ONE OF THE FLOORS WITH GREEN LEAF ANIMALS / FIG. 471: DETAIL WITH RED LEAF CREATURES

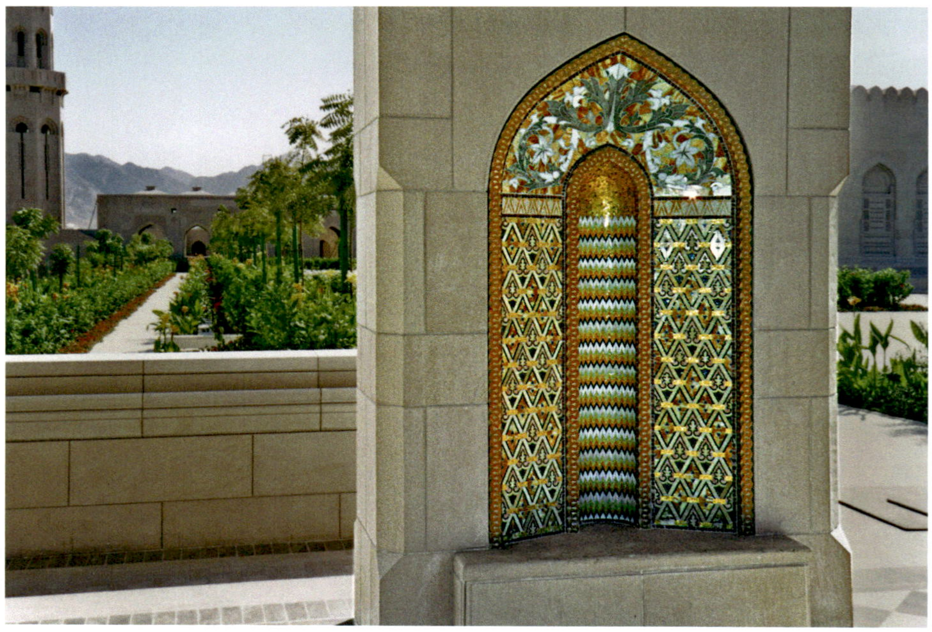

474–476

EDMAN O'AIVAZIAN / SULTAN QABOOS GRAND MOSQUE, MUSCAT, OMAN / 2001 / THREE OF THE MULTITUDINOUS GLASS, GOLD AND STONE MOSAICS

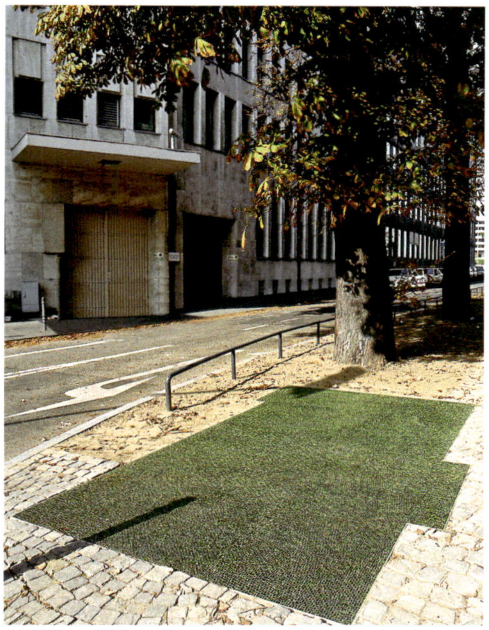

472
MARTIN MLECKO / "KIOSK" / COLOGNE, DE / 2004 / OUTDOOR GLASS MOSAIC FLOOR

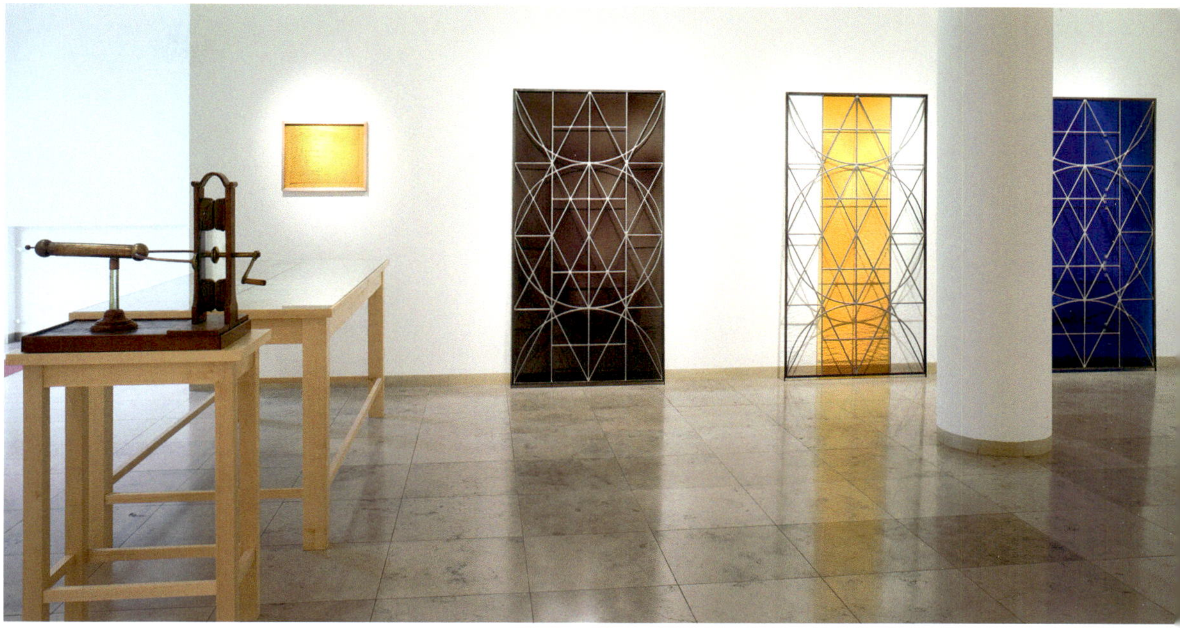

473
MATT MULLICAN / "LANGUAGE GLASS", "WORLD FRAMED GLASS", "WORLD UNFRAMED GLASS"/ 2010 / COURTESY GALERIE DANIEL BLAU, MUNICH, DE / THREE OF FIVE GLASS OBJECTS WITH LEAD GLAZING

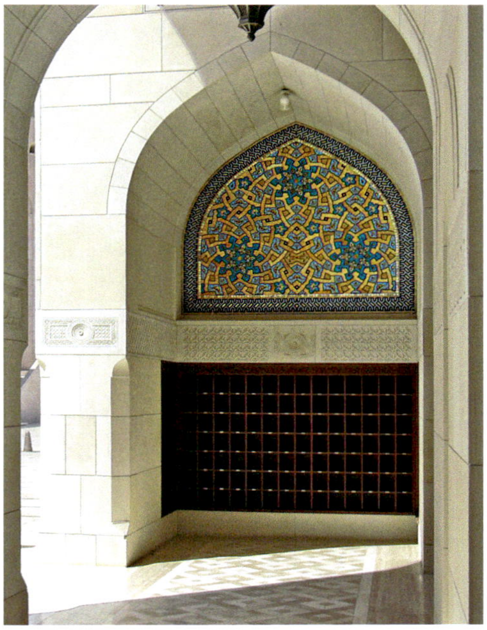

475

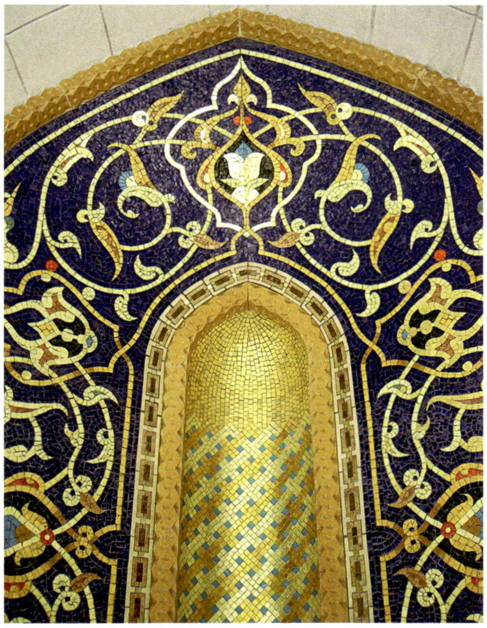

476

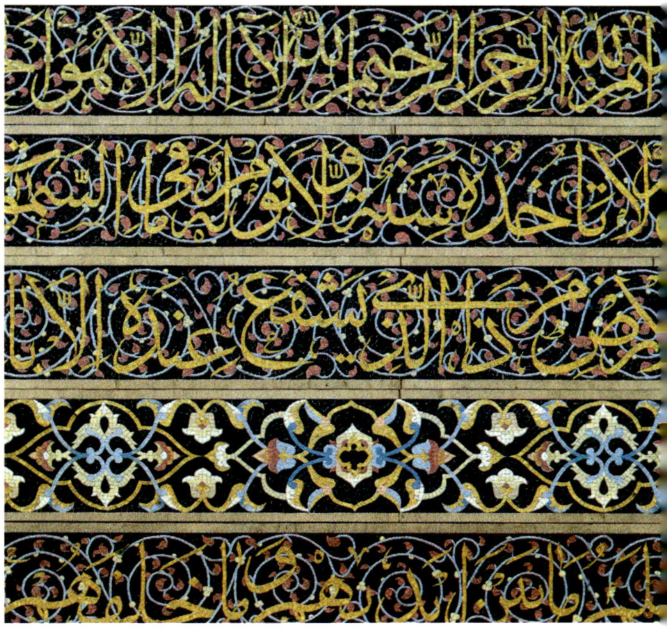

477
EDMAN O'AIVAZIAN / PRIVATE RESIDENCE, MUSCAT, OMAN / CALLIGRAPHY MOSAIC

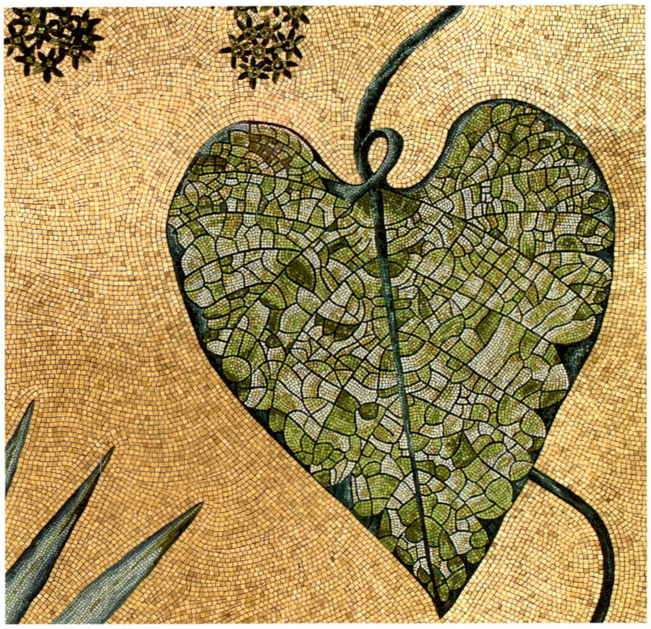

478

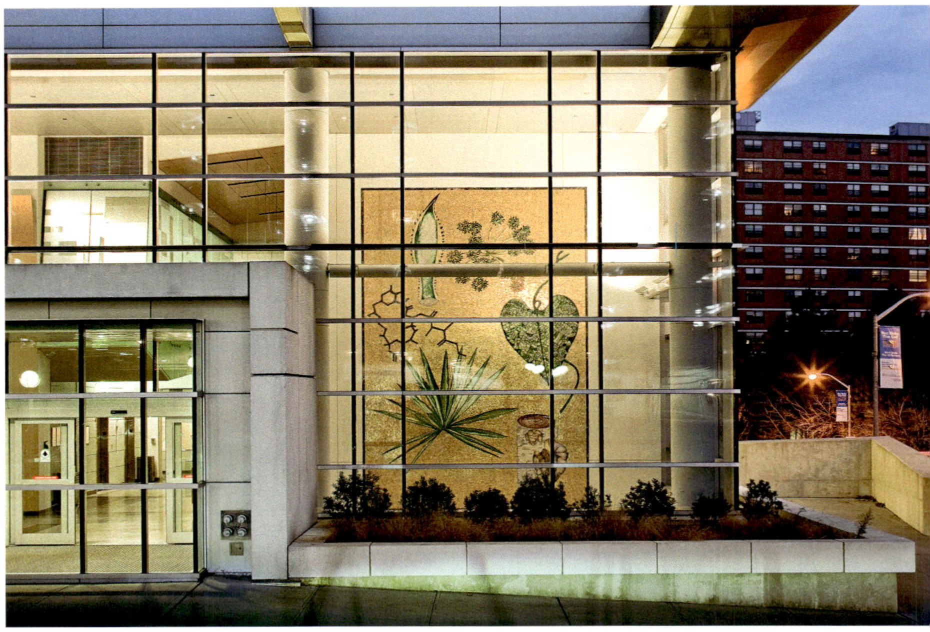

478 + 479

MICHELE OKA DONER / "HEALING PLANTS" / UNIVERSITY HOSPITAL CANCER CENTER, NEWARK, NJ, USA / 2009 / GOLD, GLASS, AND STONE MOSAIC

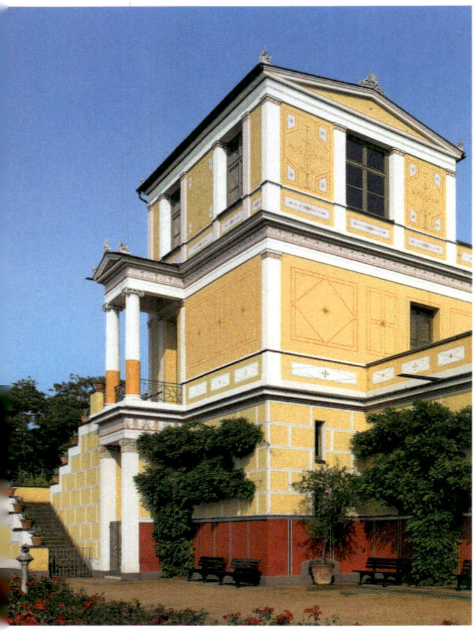

482

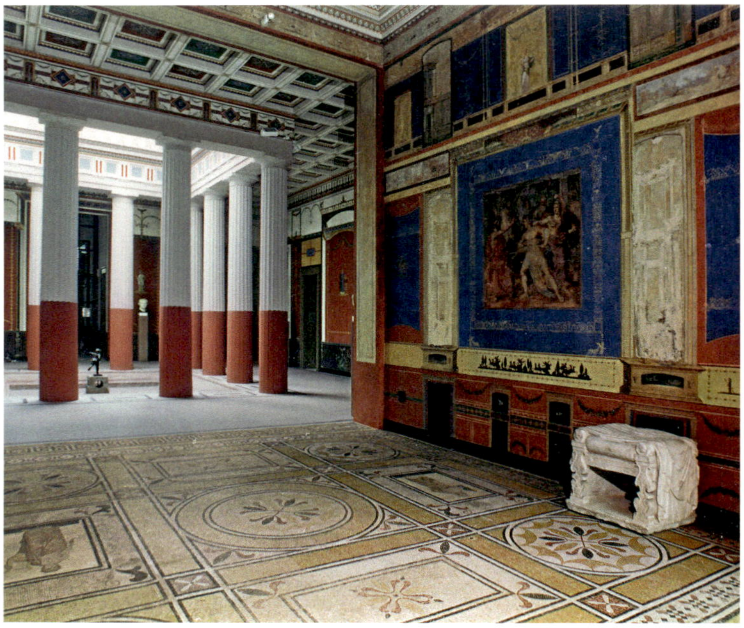

483

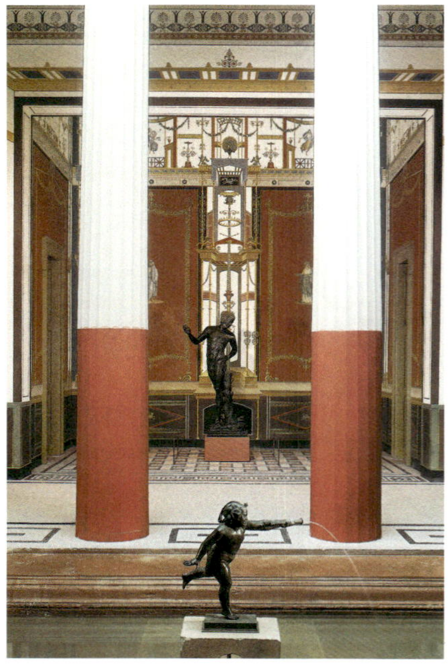

482–484

RESTORATION, RECONSTRUCTION OF ALL MOSAIC AND CRUSHED BRICK FLOORS / POMPEJANUM, ASCHAFFENBURG, DE / 1970s AND 1980s

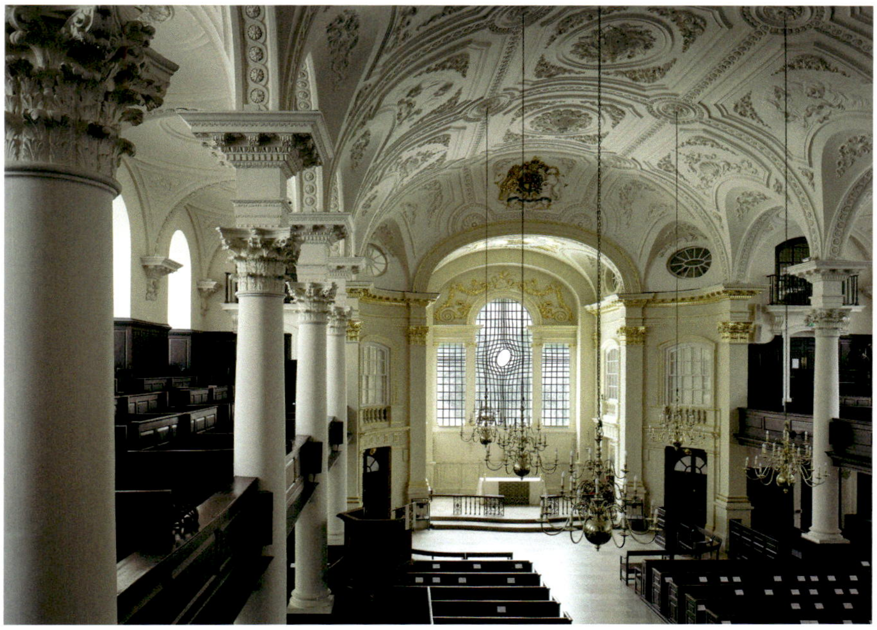

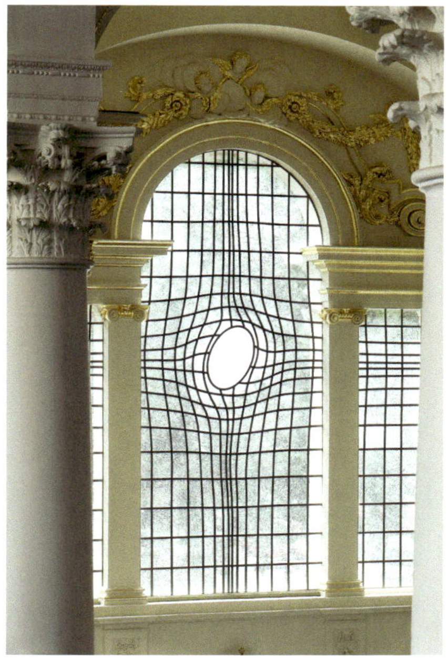

480 + 481

PHSTUDIO SHIRAZEH HOUSHIARY / EAST WINDOW / ST. MARTIN-IN-THE-FIELDS, LONDON, GB / 2008 / STAINED GLASS

481

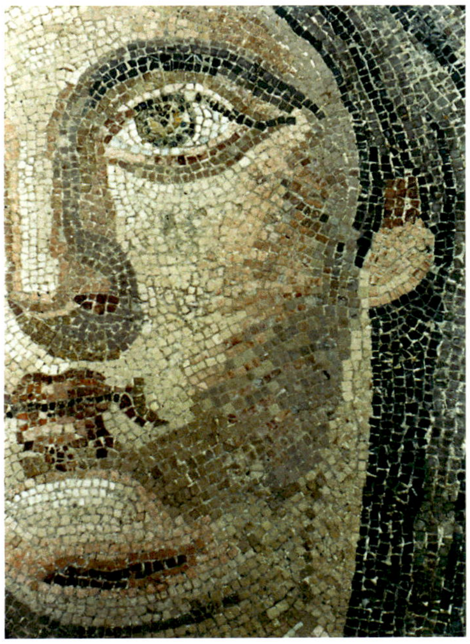

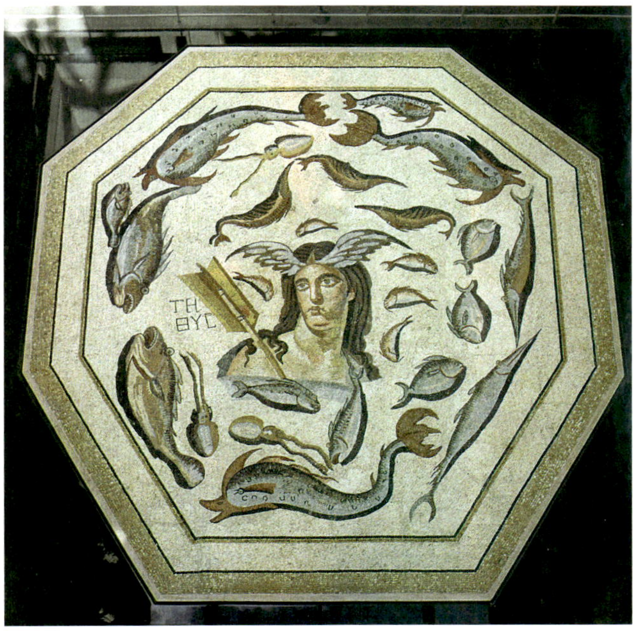

485

485 + 486

RESTORATION / CONSERVATION / ROMAN TETHYS MOSAIC / HARVARD UNIVERSITY, CAMBRIDGE, MA, USA / 1992

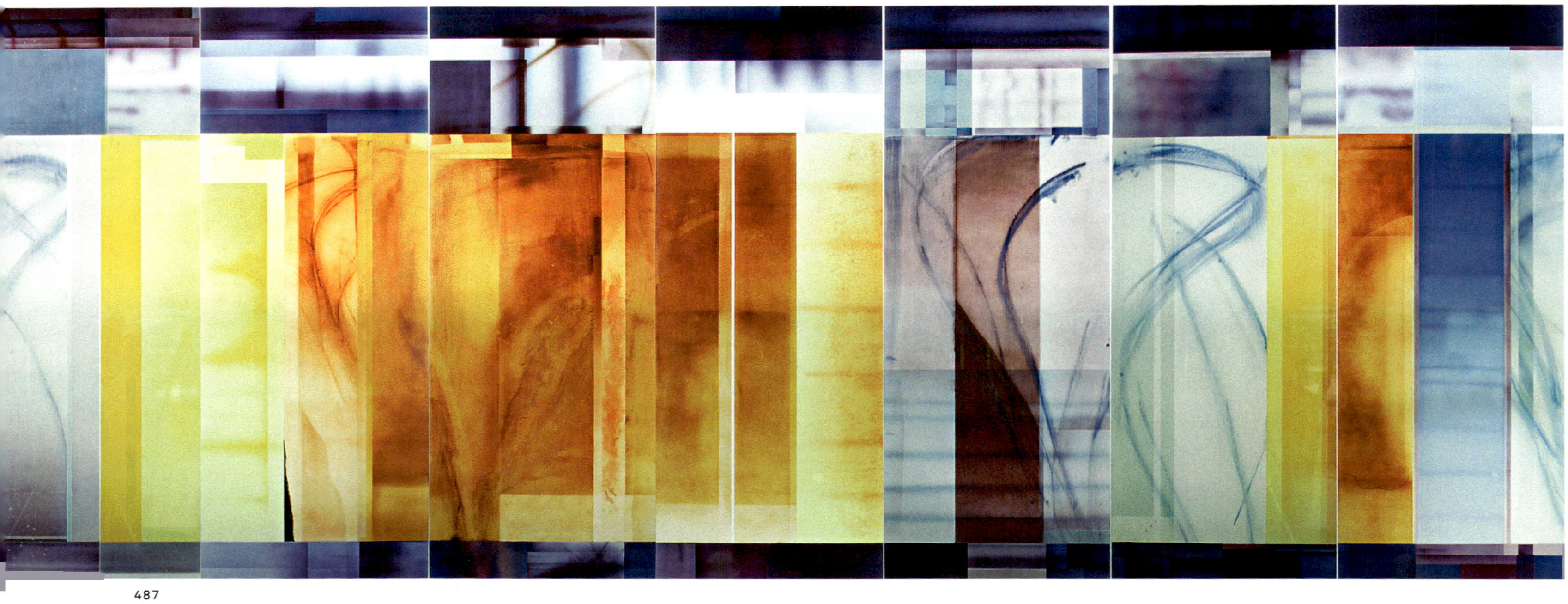

487
STUART REID / "LIQUID VEIL" / INTERCONTINENTAL HOTEL, TORONTO, ON, CANADA / 2003 / FLOAT GLASS PAINTING

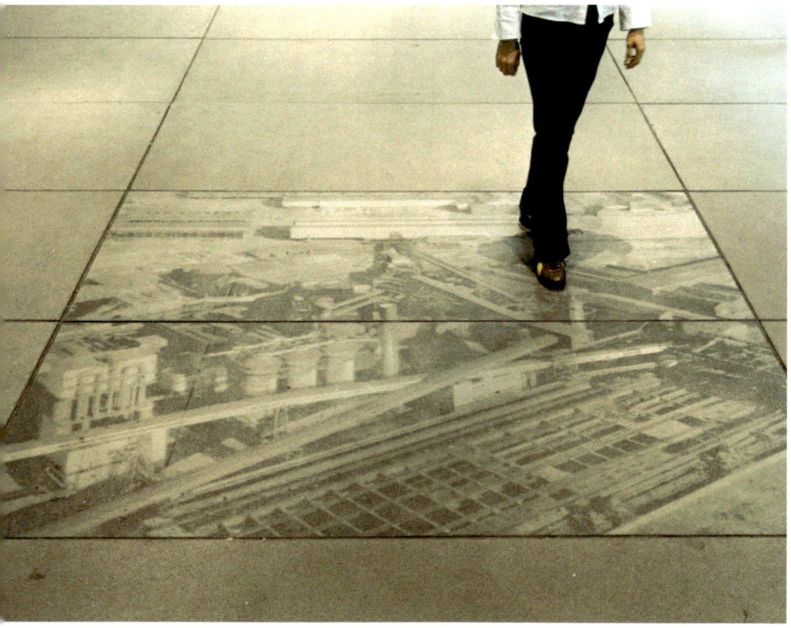

490
THOMAS RUFF / FÜNF HÖFE, MUNICH, DE / 2001 / CONCRETE FLOOR PANELS WITH PHOTOGRAPHIC IMAGES

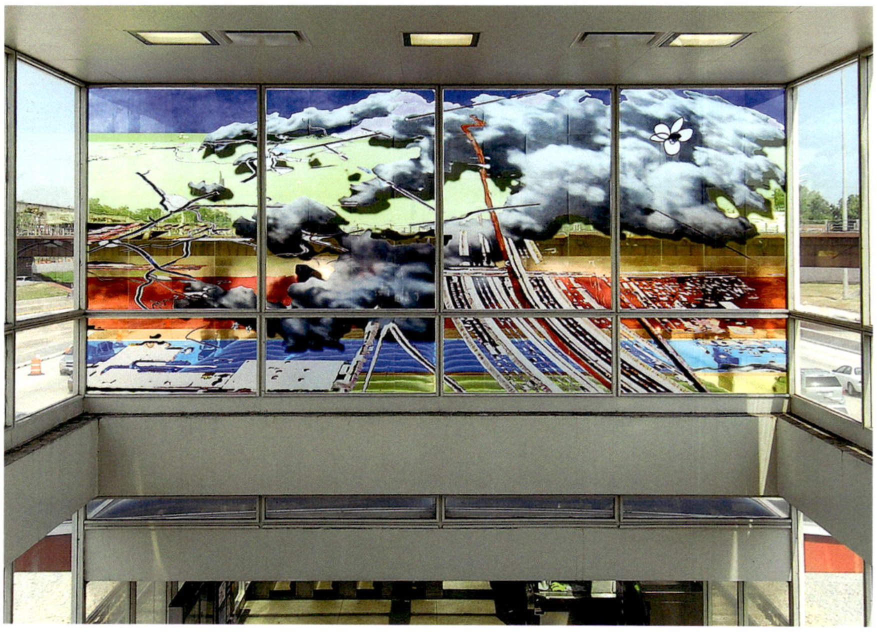

491
SABINA OTT / "A RED LINE AND A CLOUD" / 63RD STREET STATION, RED LINE, CHICAGO, IL, USA / CTA PUBLIC ART PROGRAM / 2006 / FLOAT GLASS PAINTING

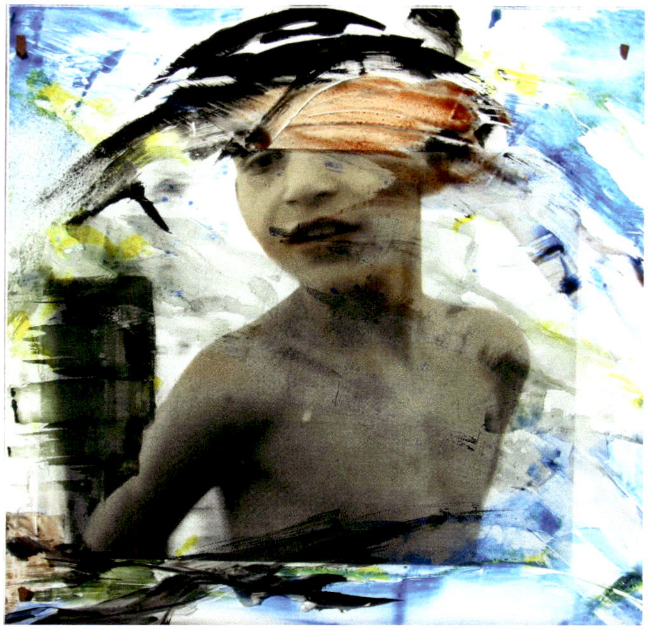

488
UDO REIN / "NADA"/ 2010 / FLOAT GLASS PAINTING

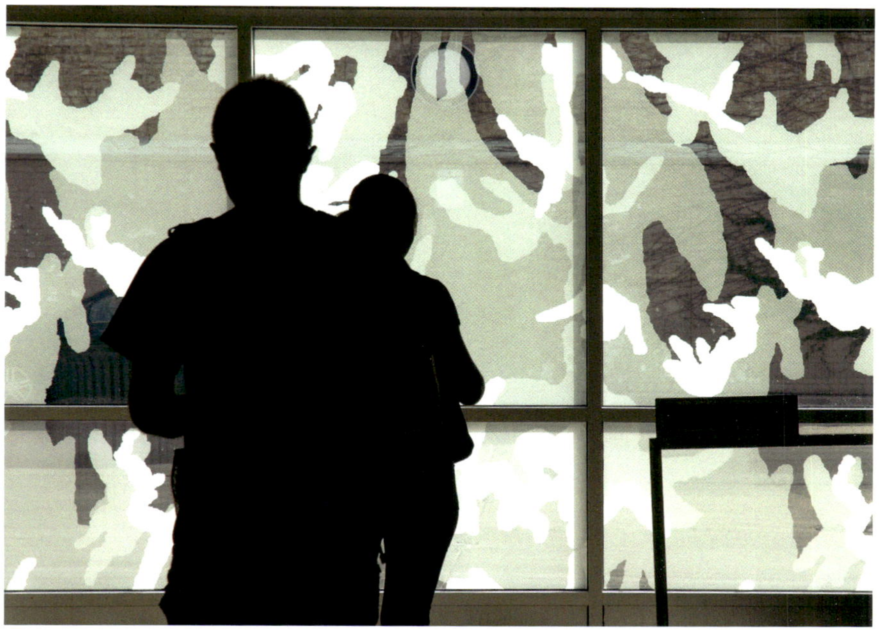

489
ELLEN ROTHENBERG / "CAMOUFLAGE SCREEN" / WESTERN AVENUE STATION, BROWN LINE, CHICAGO, IL, USA / 2007 / CTA PUBLIC ART PROGRAM

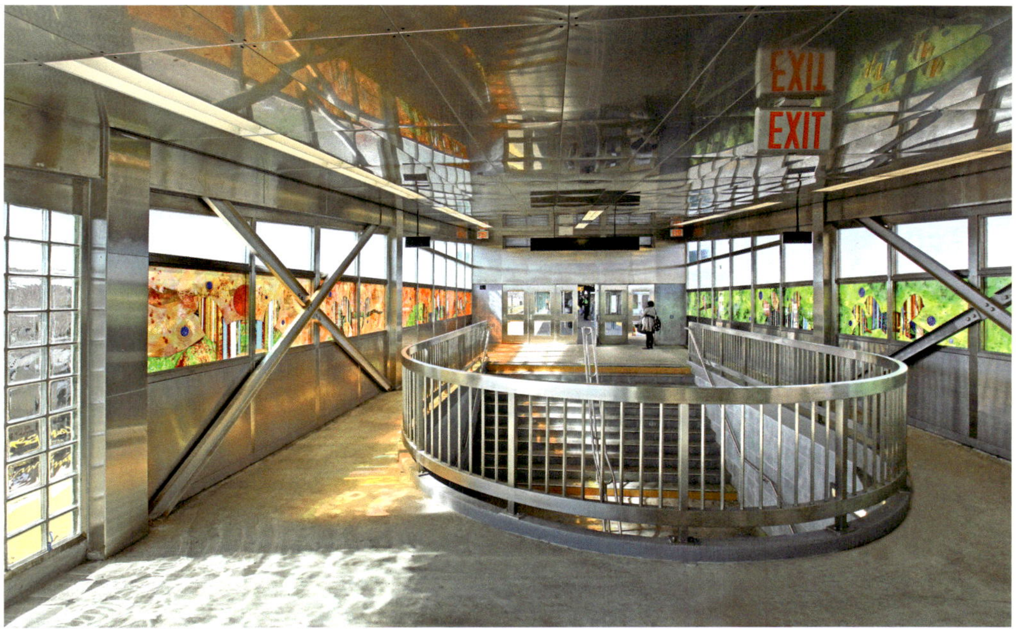

492
JASON ROHLF / "RESPITE" / FAR ROCKAWAY–MOTT AVENUE SUBWAY STATION, UPPER LEVEL SECTIONS, NEW YORK, NY, USA / MTA ARTS FOR TRANSIT / 2011 / FLOAT GLASS PAINTING

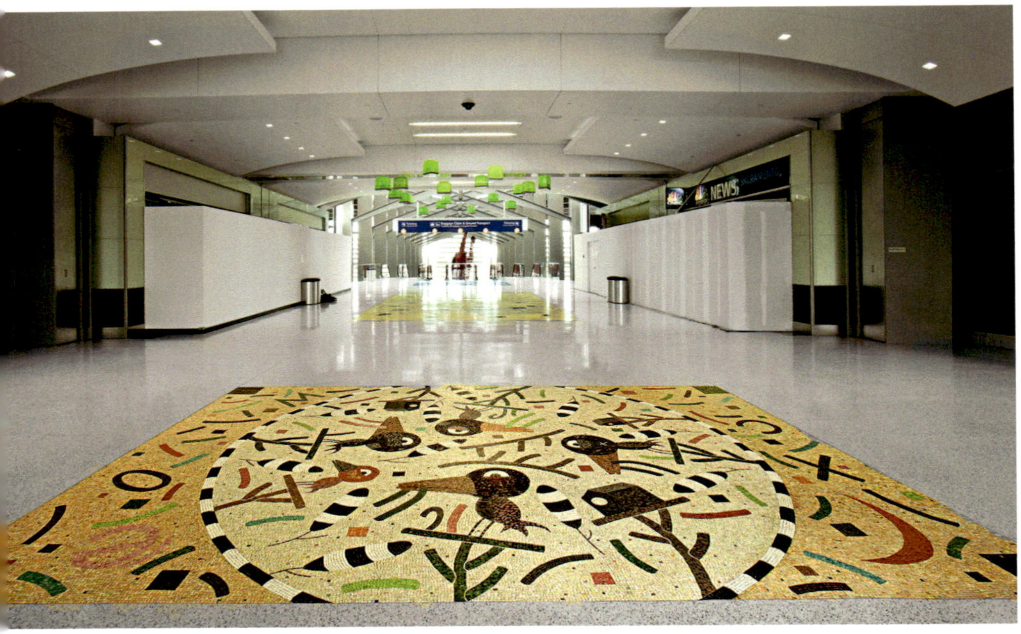

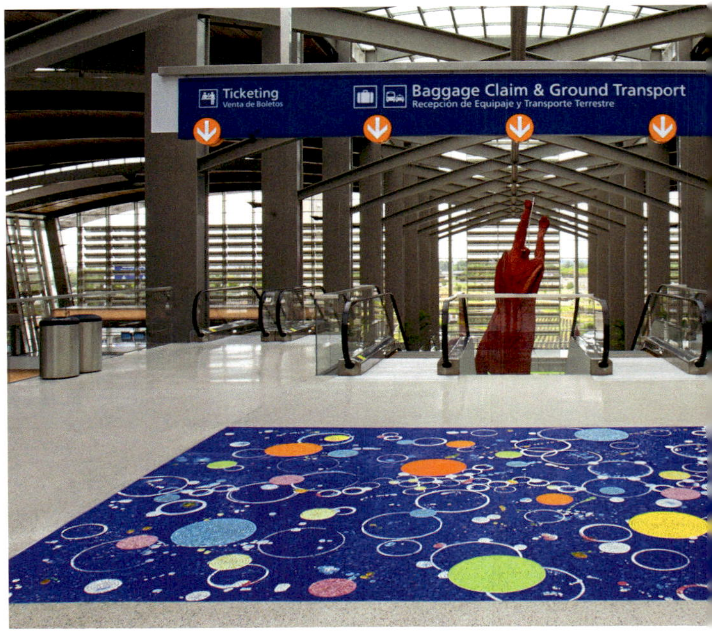

493 + 494
SACRAMENTO AIRPORT MOSAICS / SACRAMENTO INTERNATIONAL AIRPORT, CA, USA / SACRAMENTO METROPOLITAN ARTS COMMISSION / 2011 / GLASS MOSAIC FLOORS / FIG. 493: SUZANNE ADAN / "FLYING COLORS" / FIG. 494: JOAN MOMENT / "A FRAGMENT OF THE UNIVERSE"

494

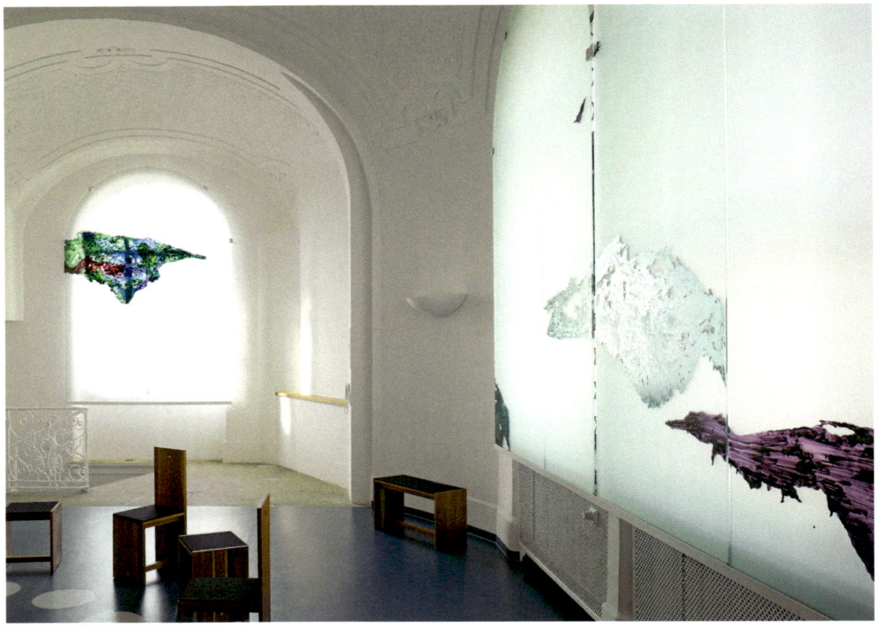

496
UWE SCHÄFER / ARCHITECTURAL ART GLASS / FRIEDENSKIRCHE, LUDWIGSBURG, DE / 2007 / FLOAT GLASS PAINTING

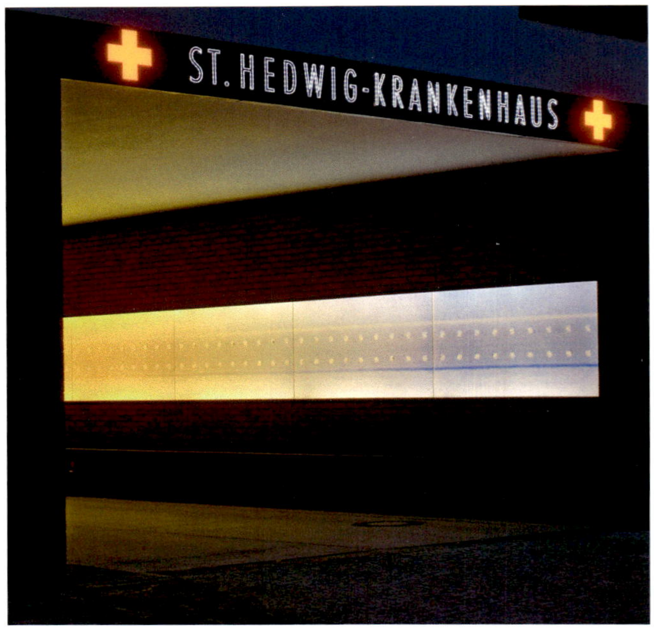

497
RALPH SCHMITT / "CONSOLATION BAND-AID" / ST. HEDWIG-KRANKENHAUS, BERLIN, DE / 2007 / FLOAT GLASS PAINTING

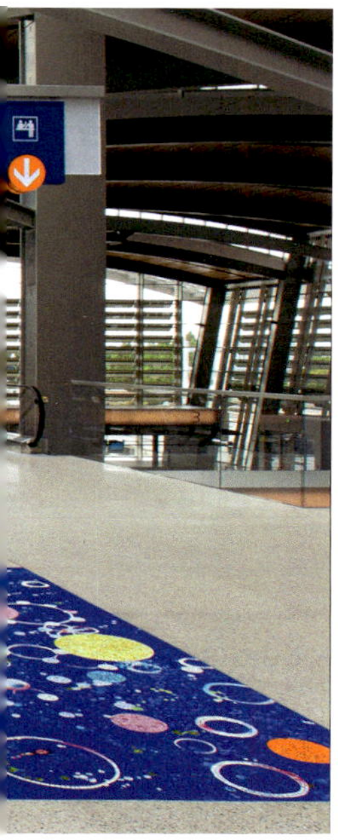

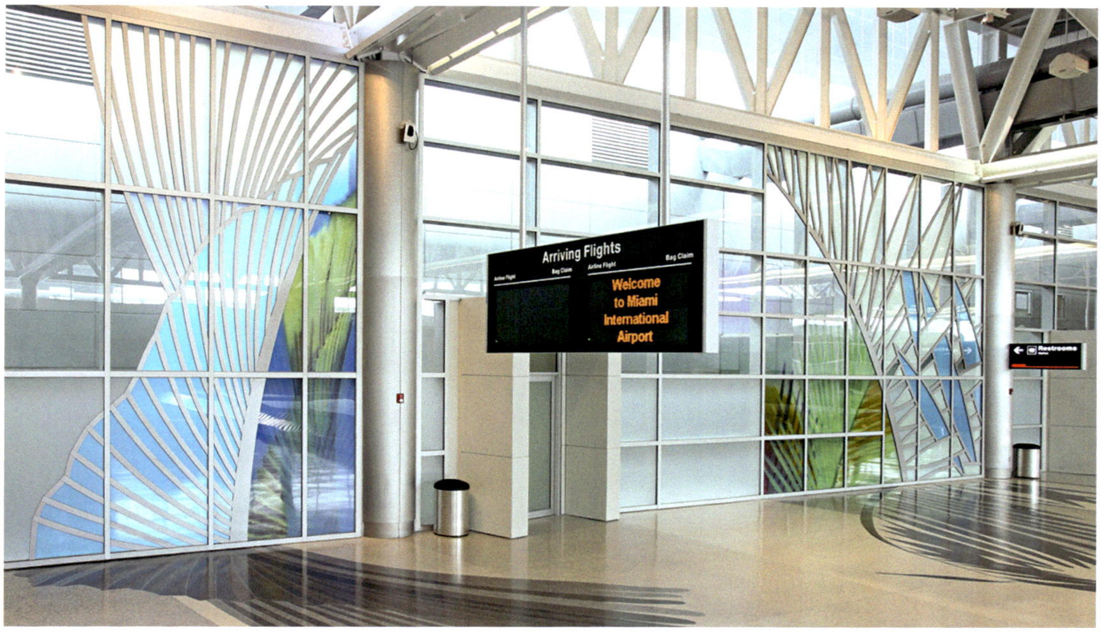

495

NORIE SATO / "GHOST PALMS" / BAGGAGE CLAIM, SOUTH TERMINAL, MIAMI INTERNATIONAL AIRPORT, FL, USA / MIAMI DADE ART IN PUBLIC PLACES / 2007 / FLOAT GLASS PAINTING AND OTHER ART FORMS

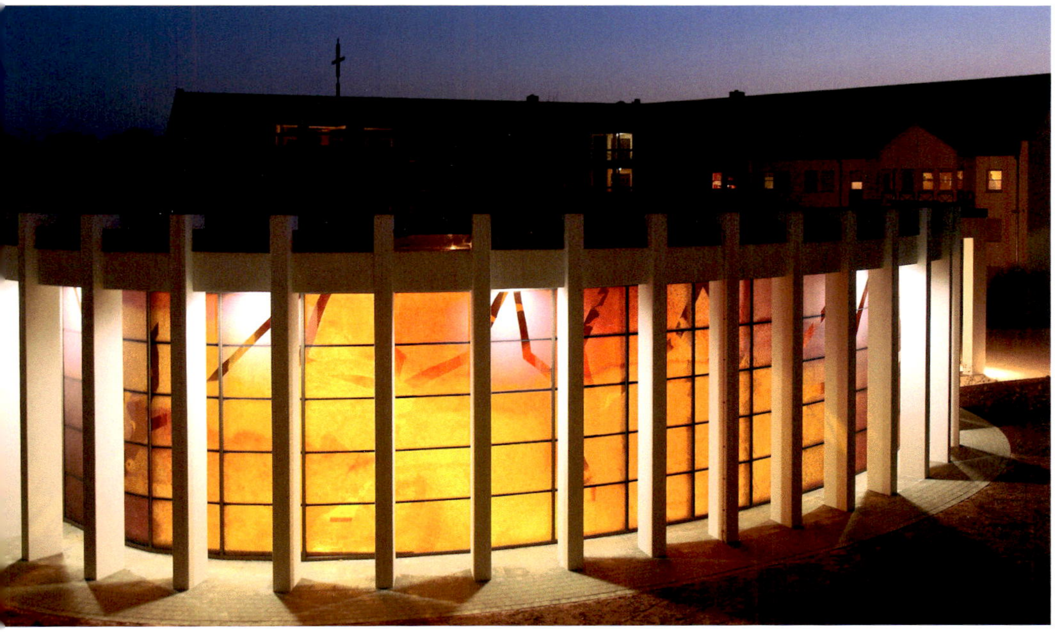

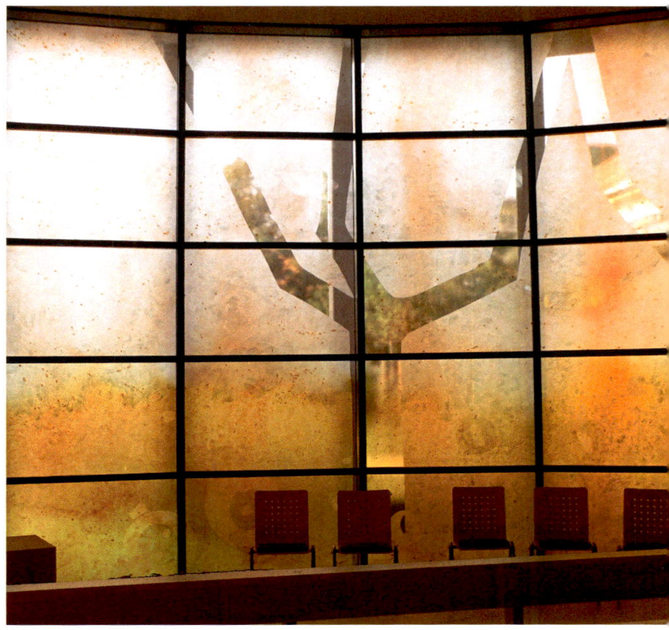

498 + 499

MARIO SCHOSSER / GLAZING PROGRAM / CHAPEL, KRANKENHAUS BARMHERZIGE BRÜDER, STRAUBING, DE / 2009 / FLOAT GLASS PAINTING / FIG. 130: SECTION SEEN FROM THE INTERIOR

499

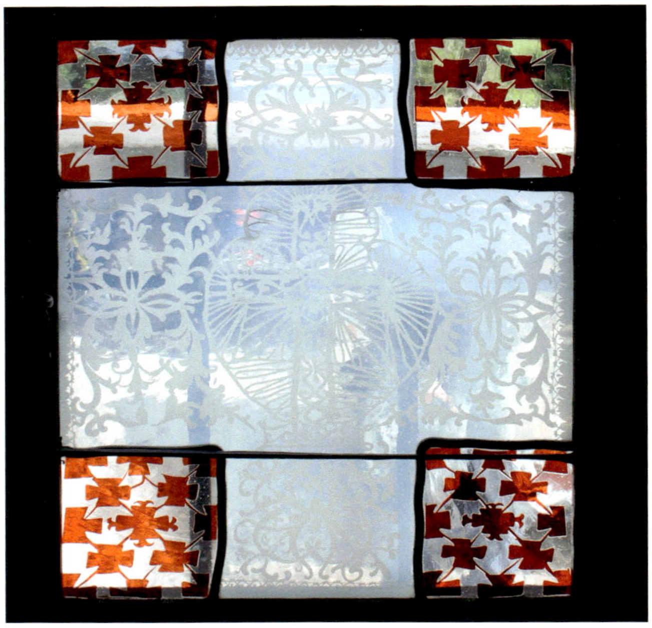

500
SASKIA SCHULTZ / CHAPEL "THE FOURTEEN HOLY HELPERS," FERNPASS, AT / 2008 / STAINED GLASS , DETAIL

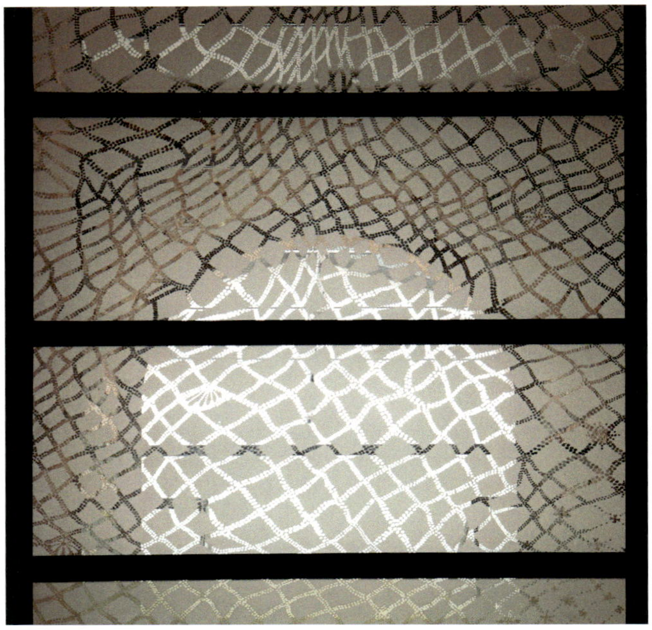

501
SASKIA SCHULTZ / ST. JAKOBSKIRCHE, FRANKFURT/MAIN, DE / 2004 / FLOAT GLASS PAINTING, DETAIL

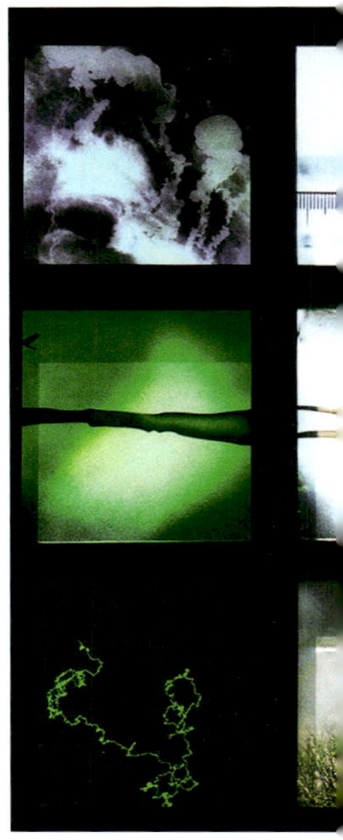

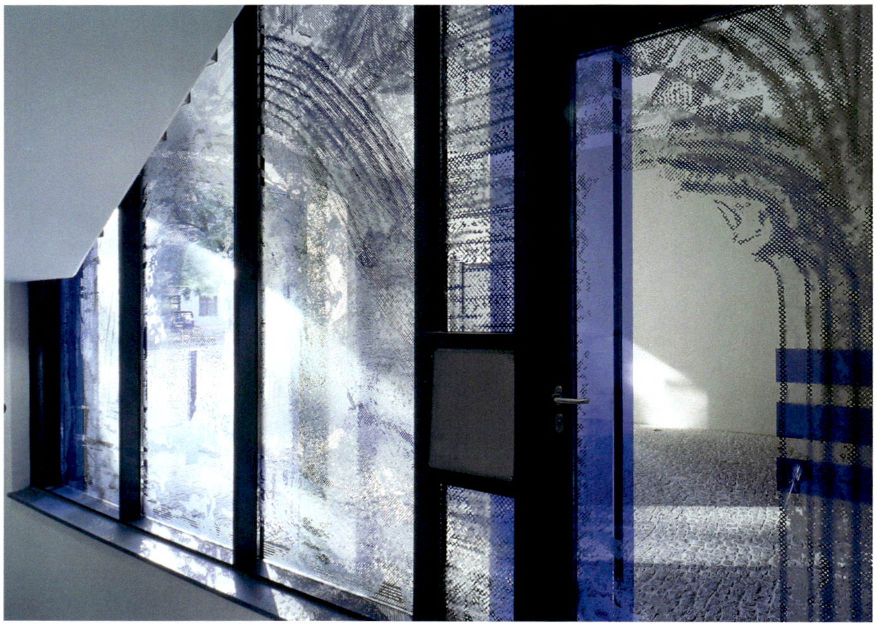

504
BRIGITTE SCHUSTER / GLASS PARTITION WALL / ALTER HOF, MUNICH, DE / 2004 / FLOAT GLASS PAINTING

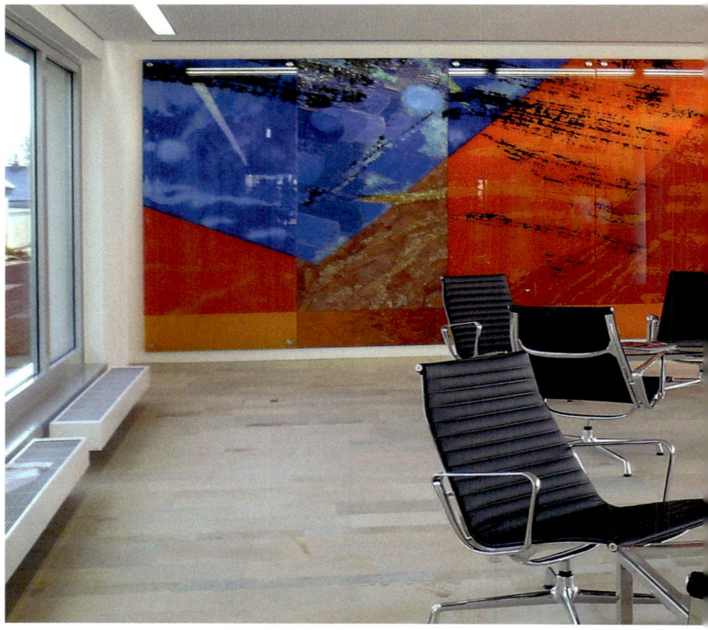

505
BRIGITTE SCHUSTER / "FORCES OF NATURE" / BAUER AG, SCHROBENHAUSEN, DE / 2007 / FLOAT GLASS PAINTING AND MOSAIC

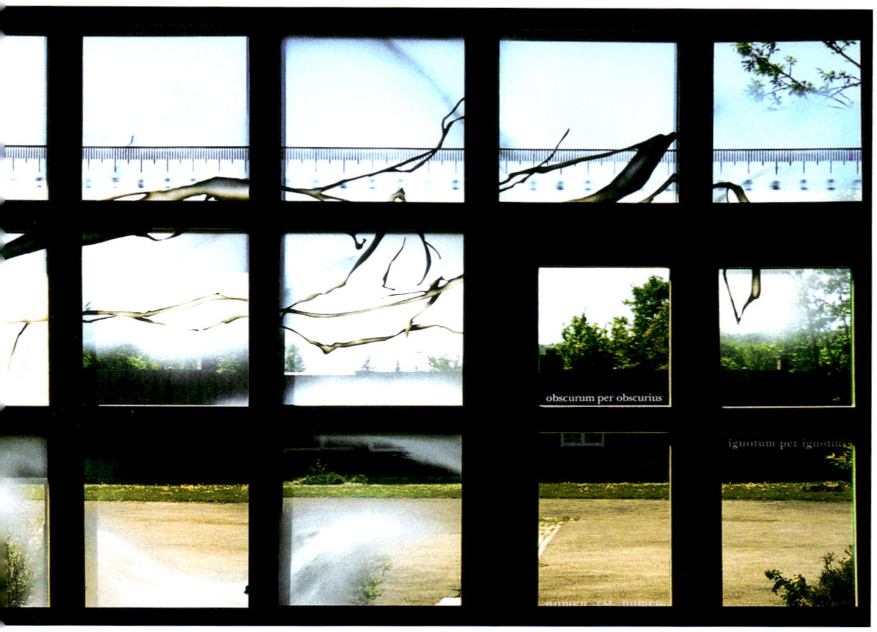

502
SASKIA SCHULTZ / LUTHERAN COMMUNITY CENTER / ALBSTADT-TAILFINGEN, DE / ARCHITECT CONCELMANN / 2003 / STAINED GLASS

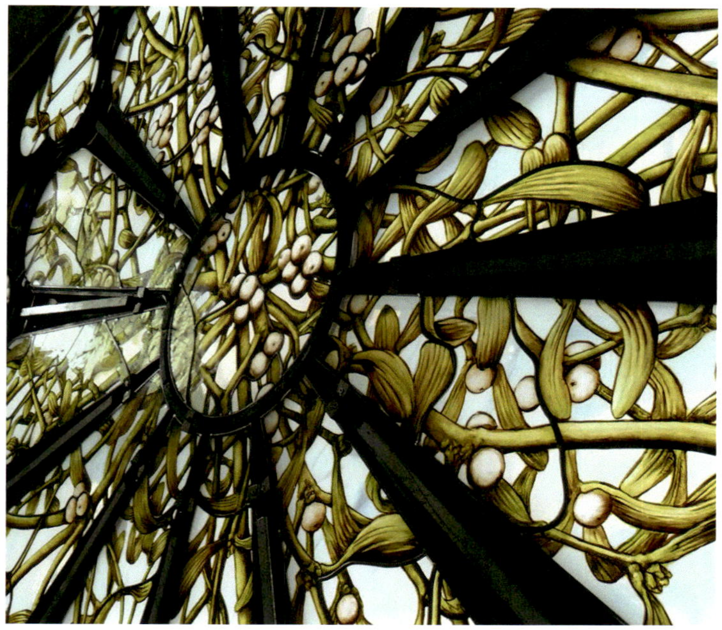

503
SASKIA SCHULTZ / ROSETTE GLAZING / MATTHÄUSKIRCHE, STUTTGART, DE / 2011 / STAINED GLASS, DETAIL

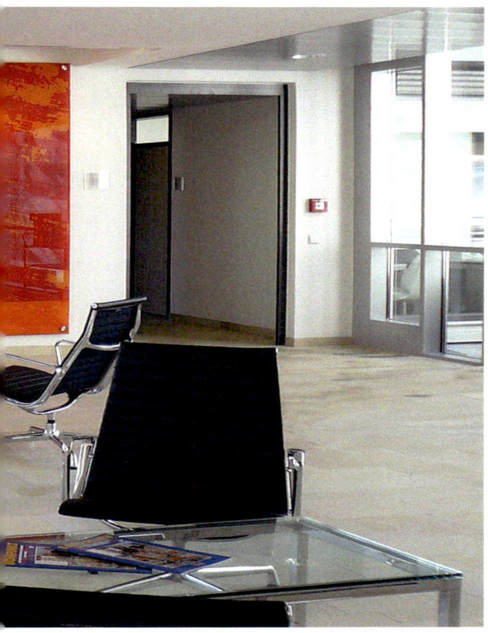

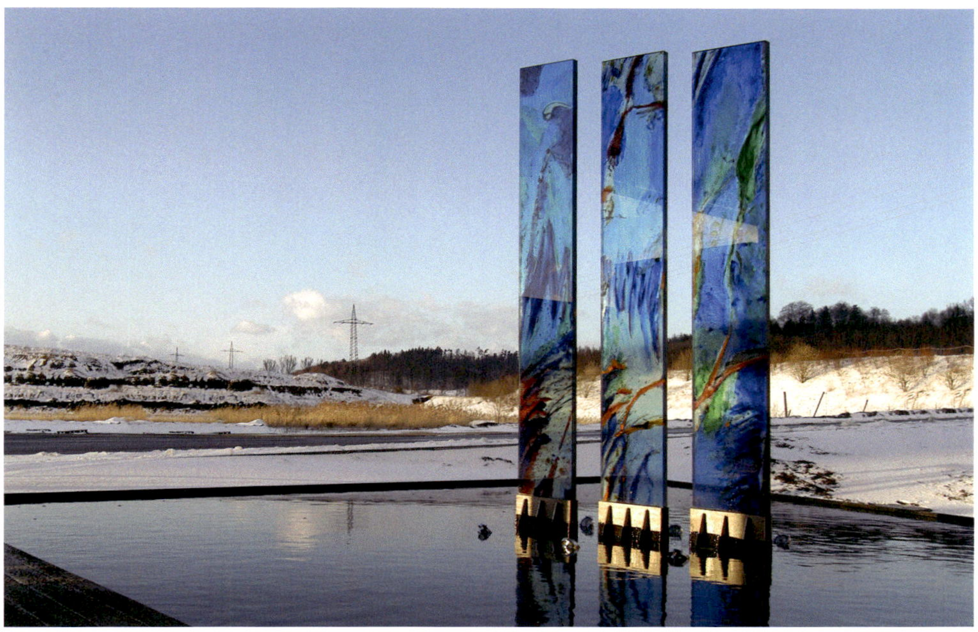

506
HELMUT SCHUSTER / GLASS STELES / SCHOLZ EDELSTAHL GMBH, ESSINGEN, DE / 2009 / FLOAT GLASS PAINTING

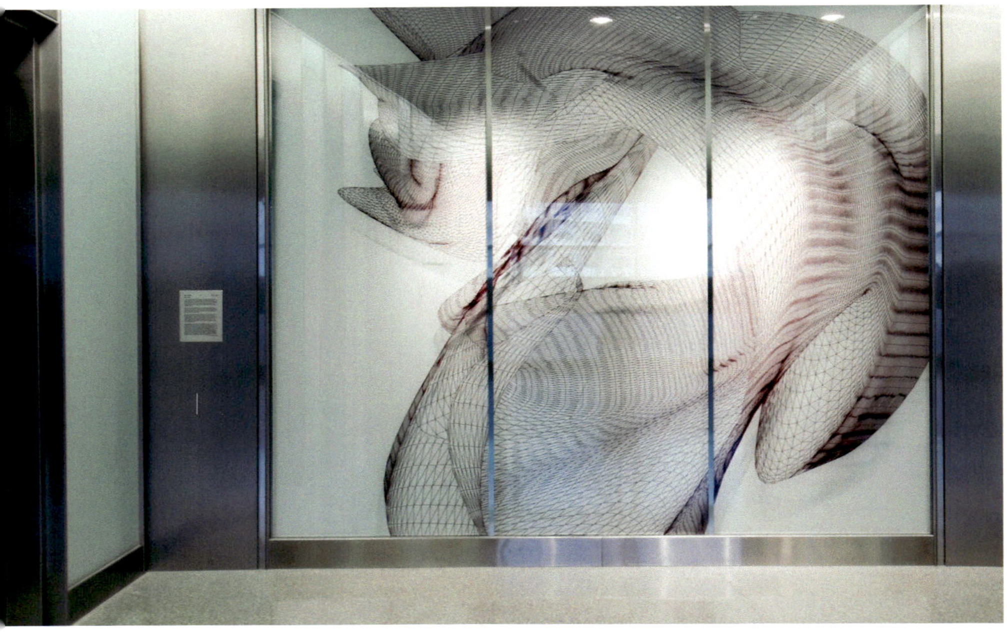

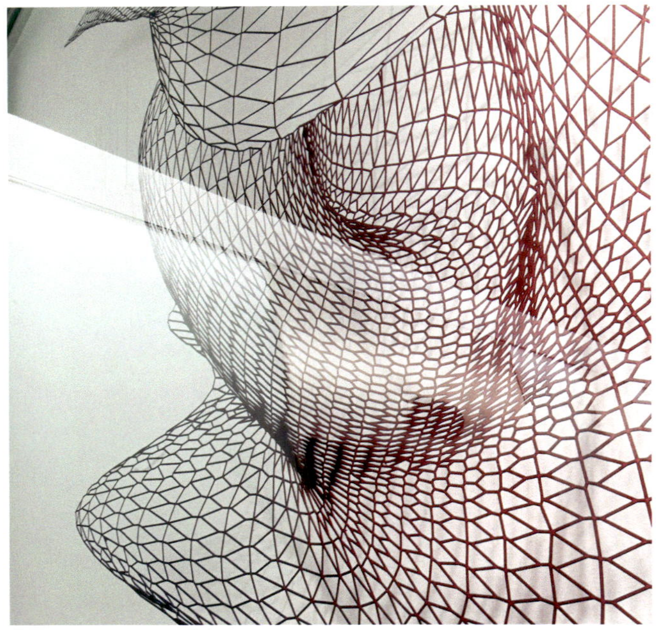

507 + 508
ALYSON SHOTZ / "EIGHT SPATIAL NETS" / GLASS WALLS EXTENDING OVER EIGHT FLOORS / CLEVELAND CLINIC, CLEVELAND, OH, USA / 2009 / FLOAT GLASS PAINTING

508

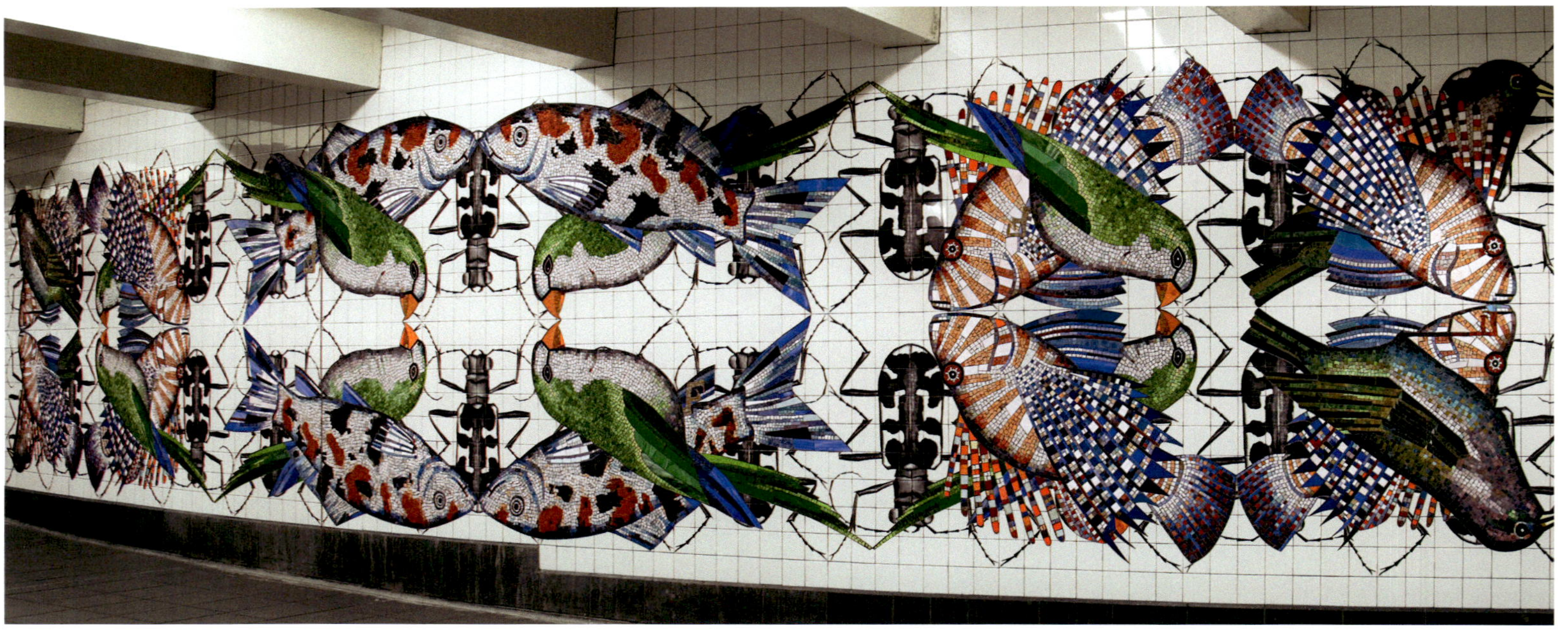

511 + 512
BEN SNEAD / "ARRIVALS AND DEPARTURES" / JAY STREET–BOROUGH HALL SUBWAY STATION, NEW YORK, NY, USA / MTA ARTS FOR TRANSIT / 2009 / GLASS MOSAIC AND TILES, PAINTED AND WATERJET CUT / FIG. 512: DETAIL

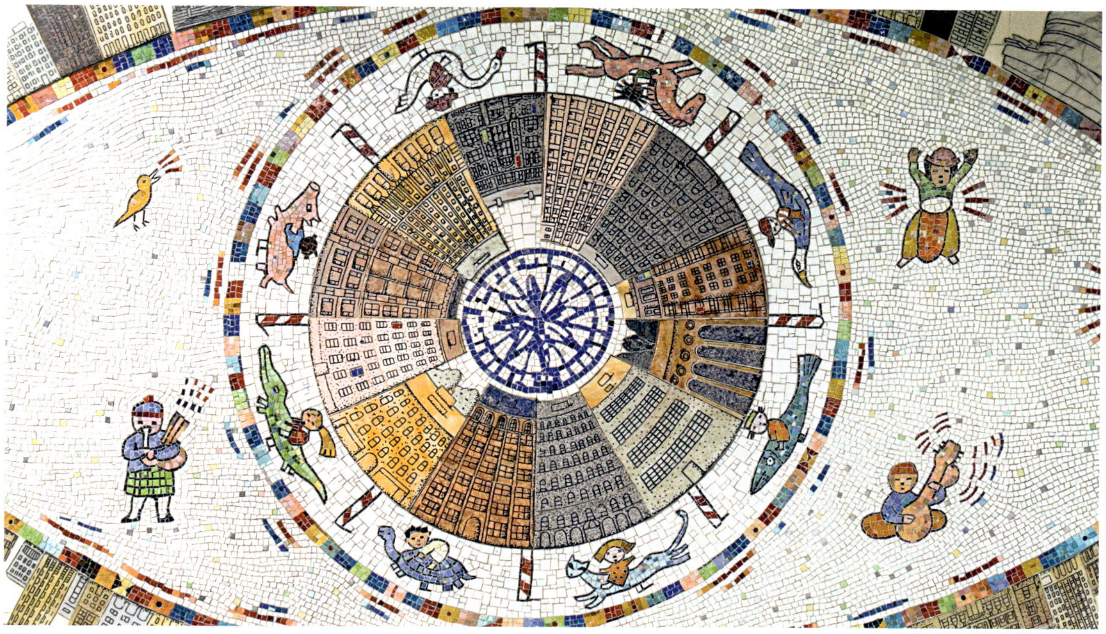

509 + 510

PETER SIS / "HAPPY CITY" / 86TH STREET–LEXINGTON AVENUE SUBWAY STATION, NEW YORK, NY, USA / 2004 / STONE AND GLASS MOSAIC / MTA ARTS FOR TRANSIT

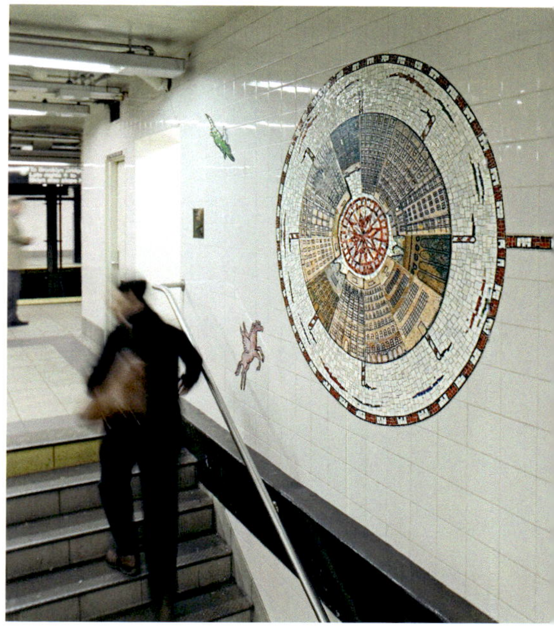

510

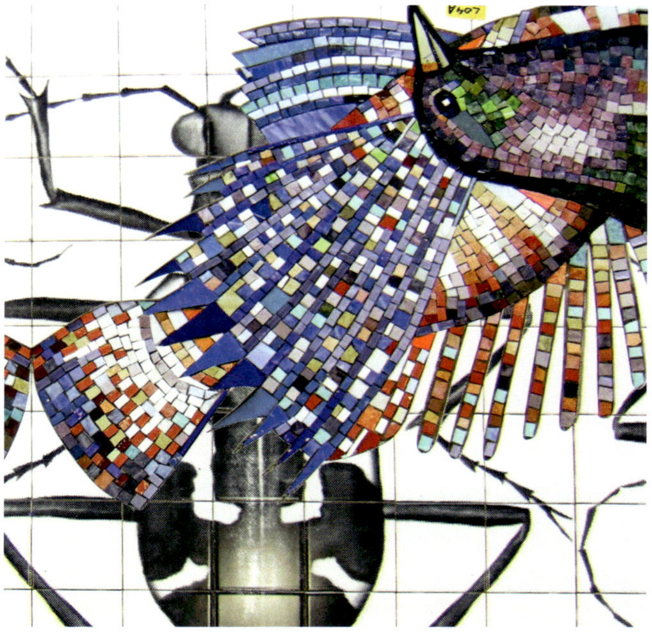

512

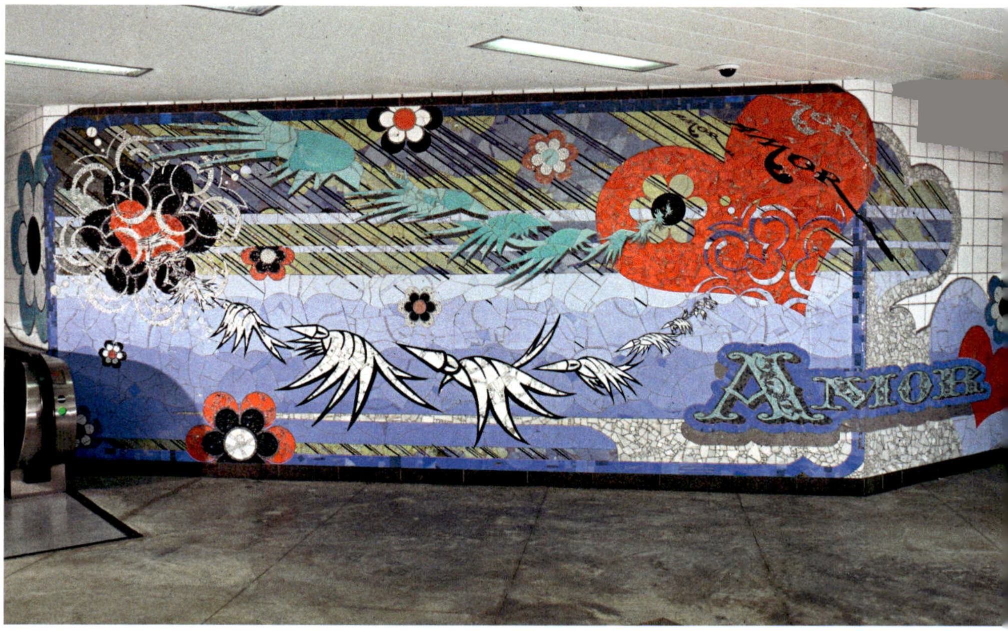

513

CHRIS SILVA / "AMOR" / CALIFORNIA STATION, PINK LINE, CHICAGO, IL, USA / CTA PUBLIC ART PROGRAM / 2004 / GLASS MOSAIC

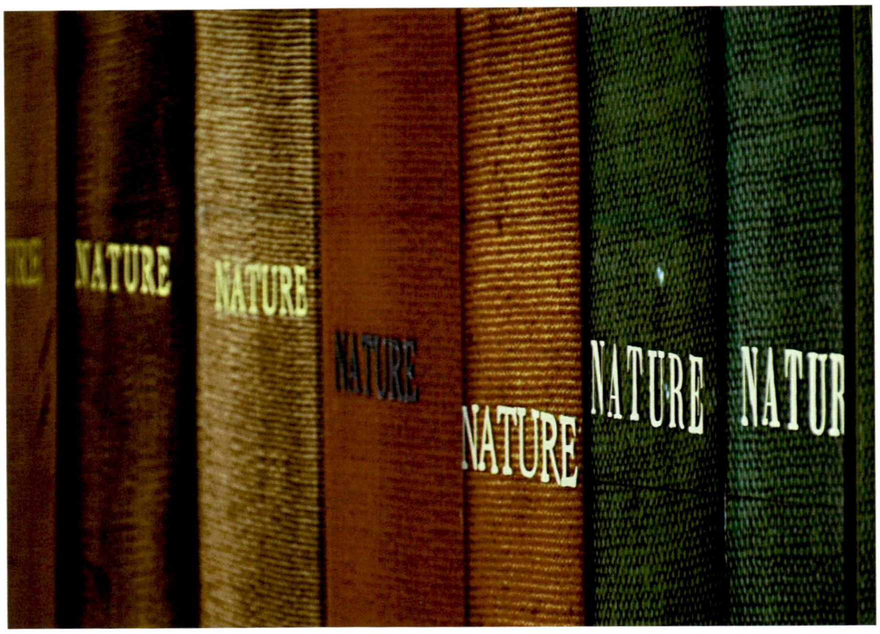

514

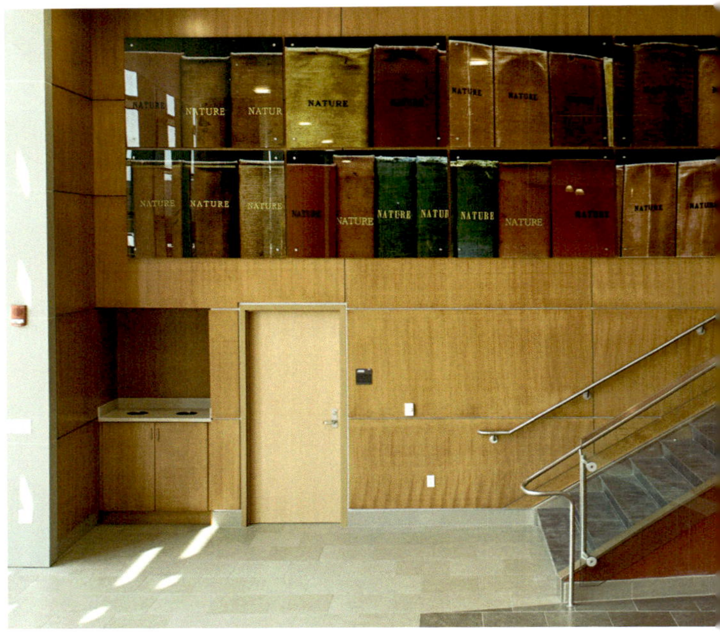

514 + 515
MICKEY SMITH / "COLLOCATION NO. 13 (NATURE)" / BIOMEDICAL SCIENCES BUILDING, UNIVERSITY OF FLORIDA, GAINESVILLE, FL, USA / 2009 / FLOAT GLASS PAINTING / FIG. 514: DETAIL

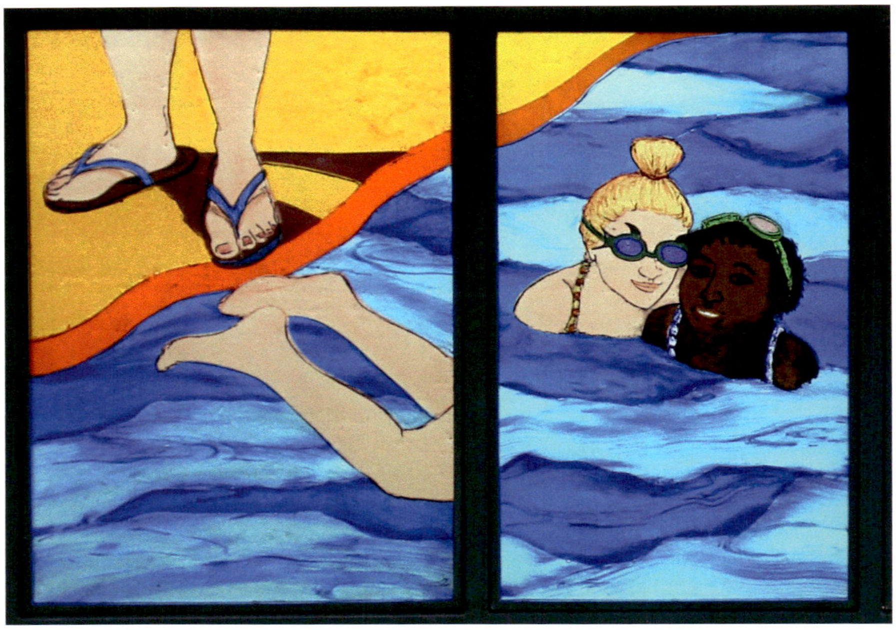

518

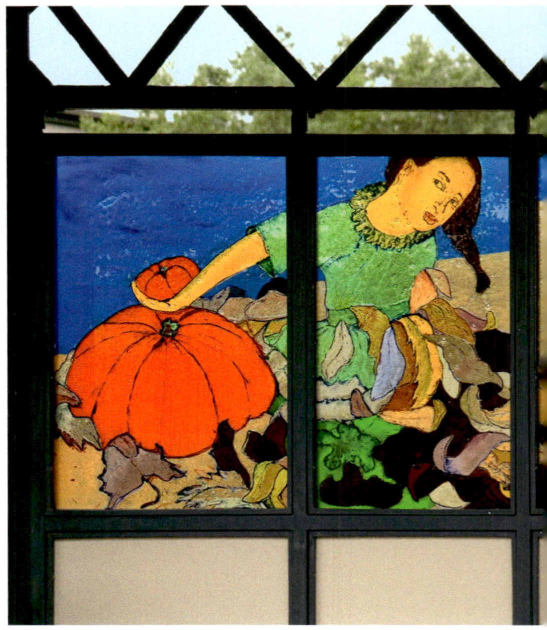

518 + 519
PHILEMONA WILLIAMSON / "SEASONS" / LIVONIA AVENUE SUBWAY STATION, NEW YORK, NY, USA / MTA ARTS FOR TRANSIT / 2007 / GLASS FUSING / FIG. 518: DETAIL LEFT "SUMMER," FIG. 519: ABOVE "AUTUMN"

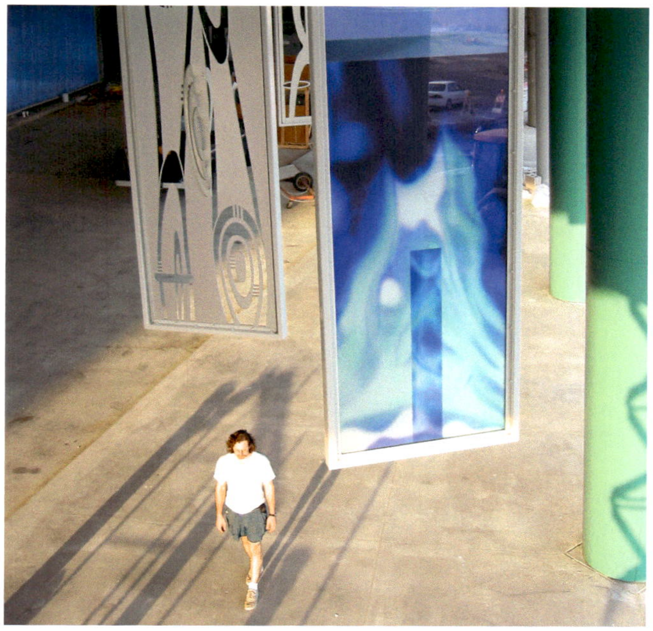

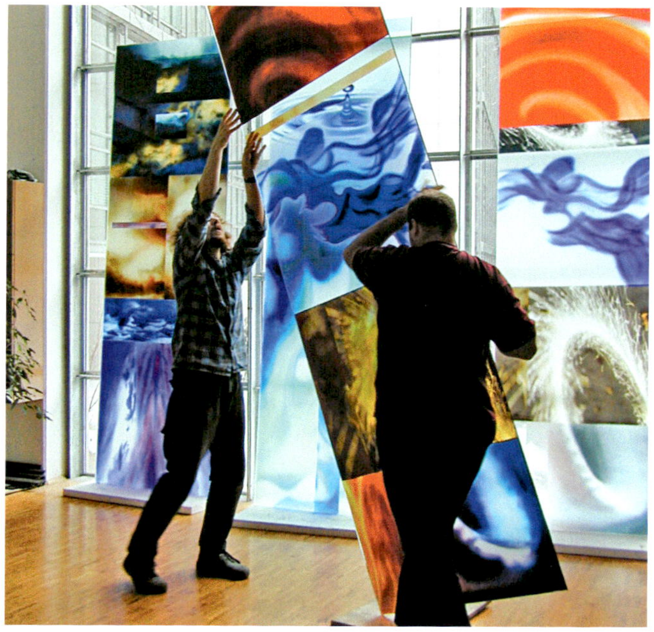

516 + 517

CATHERINE WOODS / "OASIS" / CLAYTON METRO BUS CENTER, ST. LOUIS, MO, USA / 2004 / FLOAT GLASS PAINTING / FIG. 517: GLASS PANES IN FABRICATION AT STUDIO

517

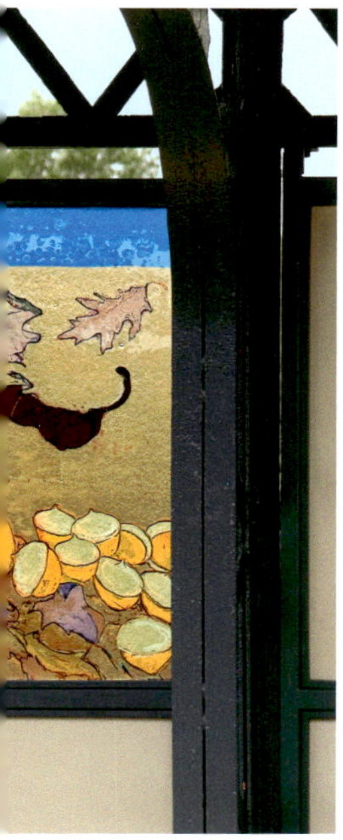

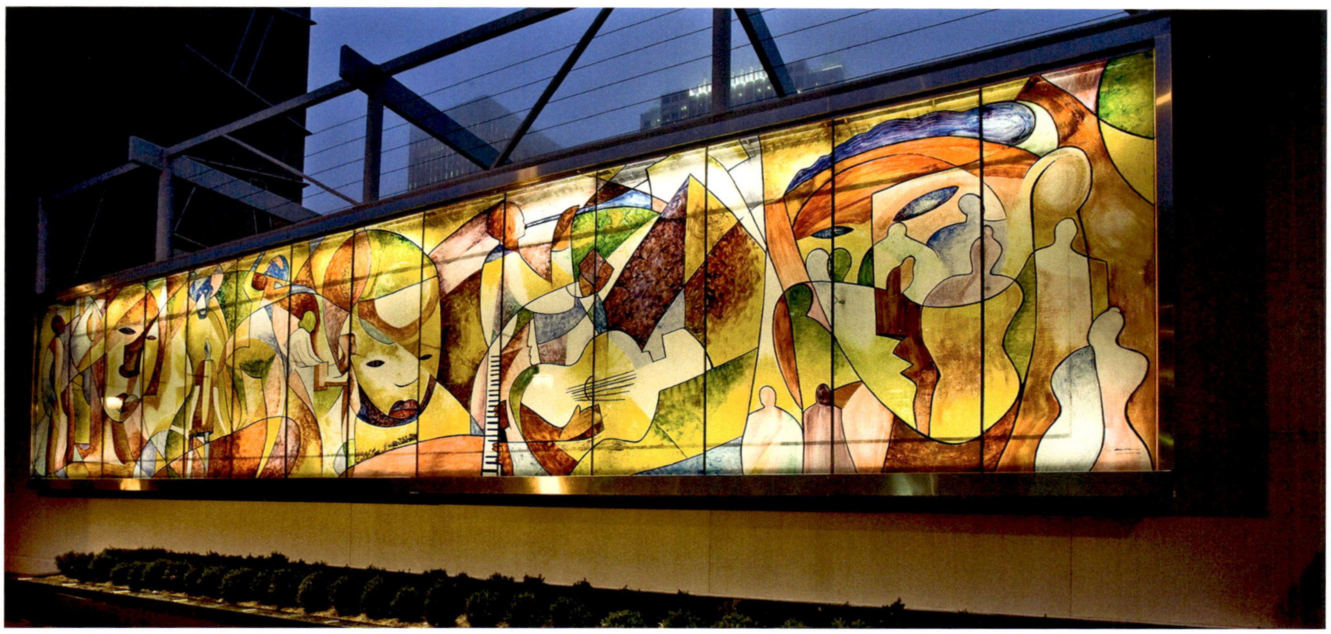

520

DAVID WILSON / WACHOVIA FIRST STREET CULTURAL CAMPUS, CHARLOTTE, NC, USA / 2009 / FLOAT GLASS PAINTING

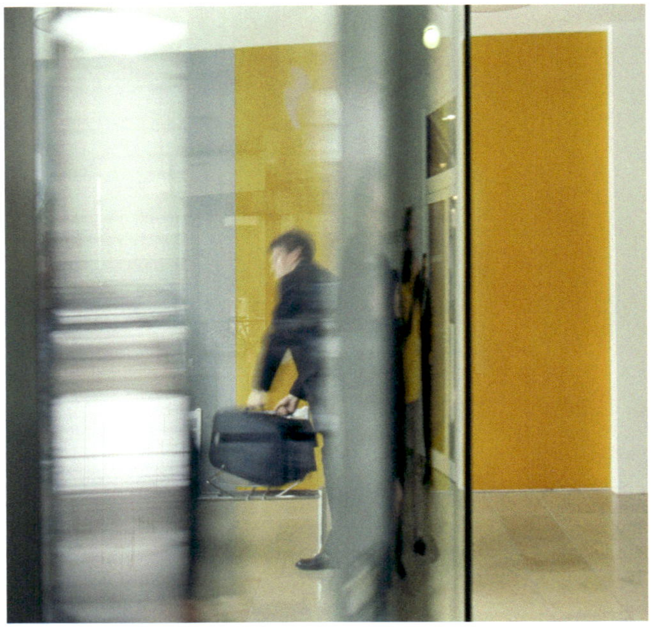

521
ERICH WIESNER / ESPLANADE, THERESIENHÖHE, MUNICH, DE / 2002 / FLOAT GLASS PAINTING

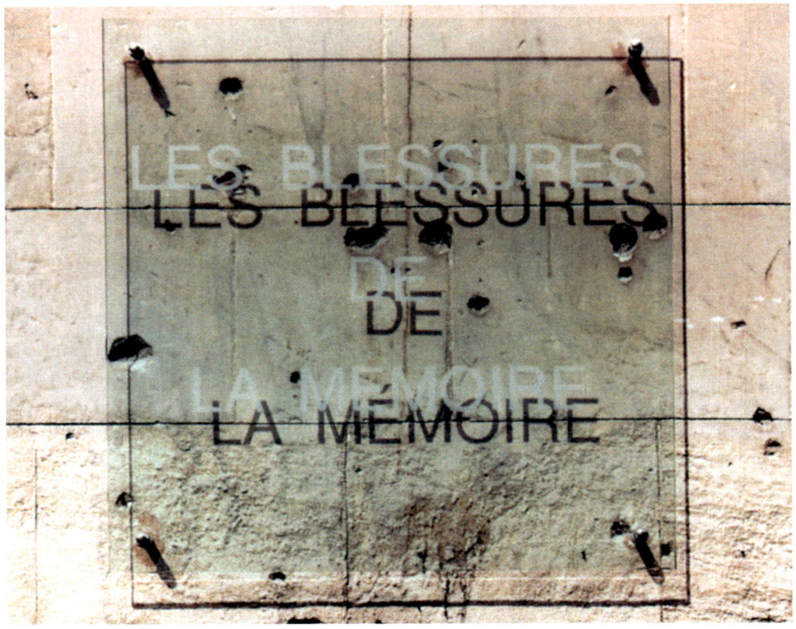

522
ANDREAS VON WEIZSÄCKER, BEATE PASSOW / "MEMORY WOUNDS" / EUROPEAN PROJECT, IN THIS CASE AVIGNON, FR / 1995 / FLOAT GLASS PAINTING

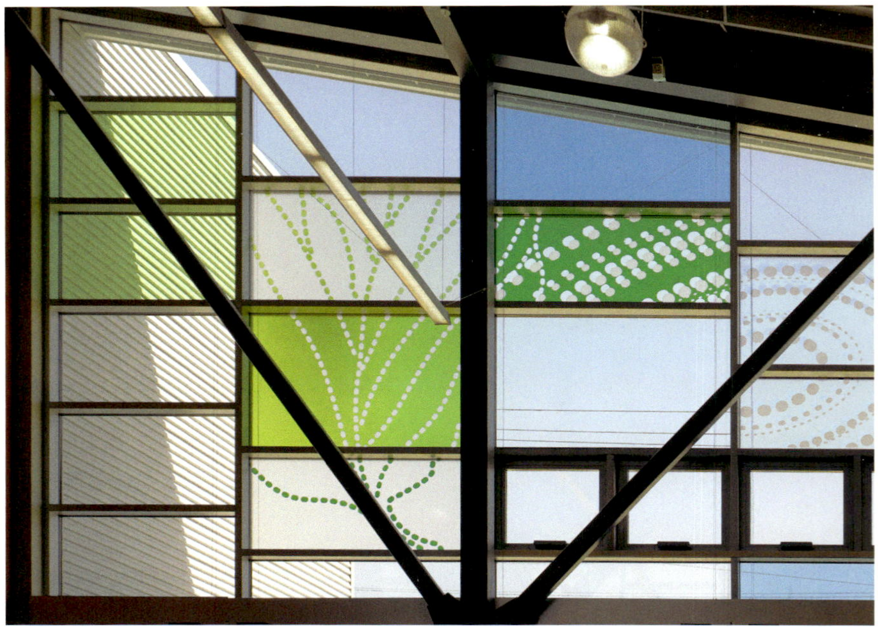

525 + 526
RENE YUNG / "OUR OAKLAND: EAST SIDE STORIES" / OAKLAND PUBLIC LIBRARY, 81ST AVENUE, OAKLAND, CA, USA / 2009 / FLOAT GLASS PAINTING / FIG. 526: DETAIL

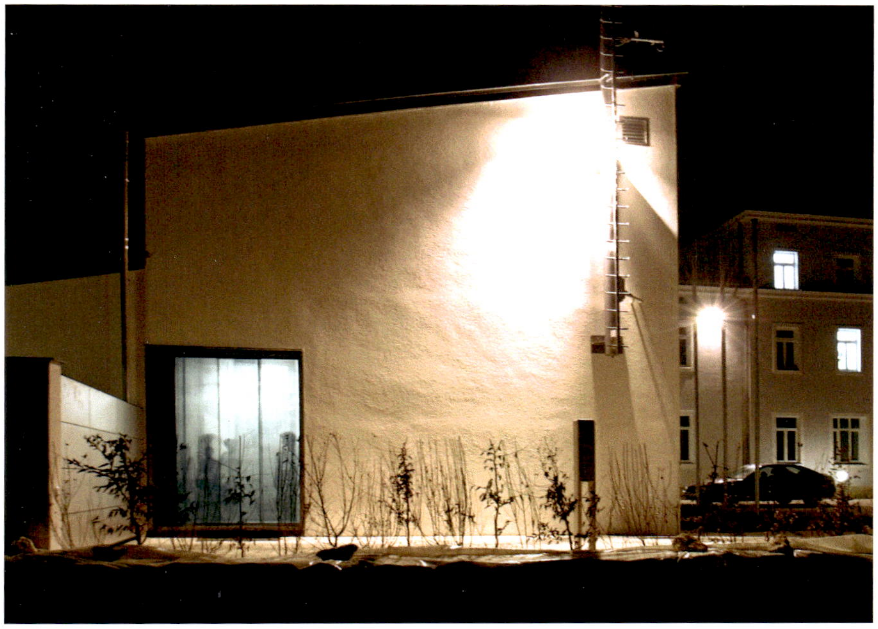

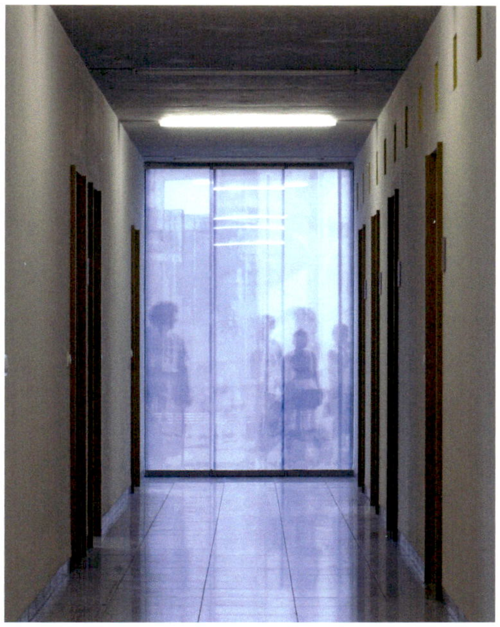

523 + 524

ROBERT M. WEBER / THREE-PART GLASS WORK / POLICE STATION KELHEIM, DE / 2001 / FLOAT GLASS PAINTING / FIG. 154: VIEW FROM OUTSIDE / FIG. 524: SAME GLASS PIECE FROM INSIDE

524

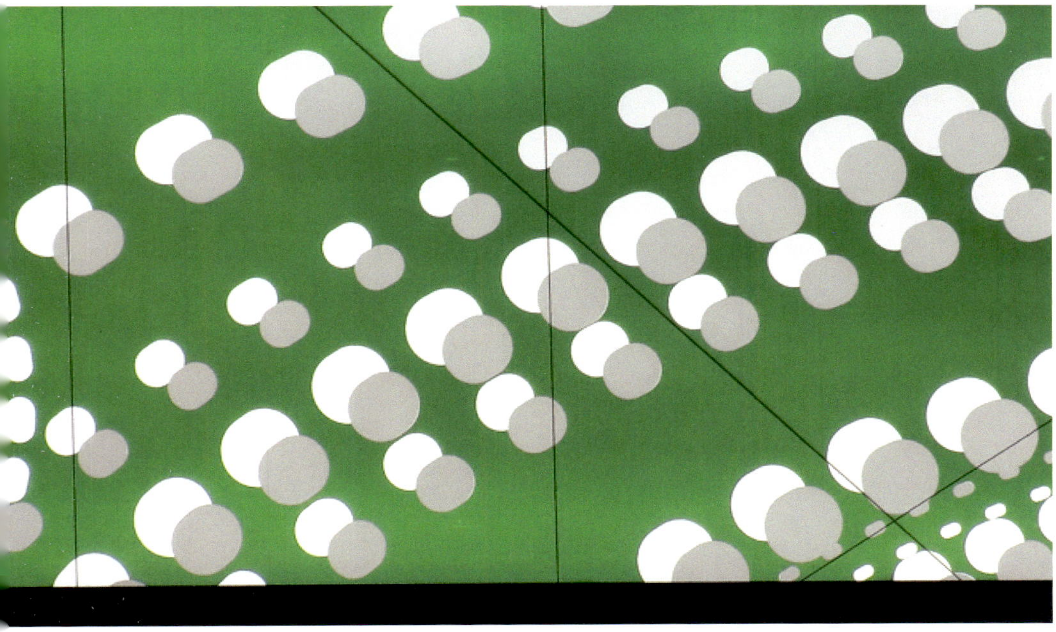

526

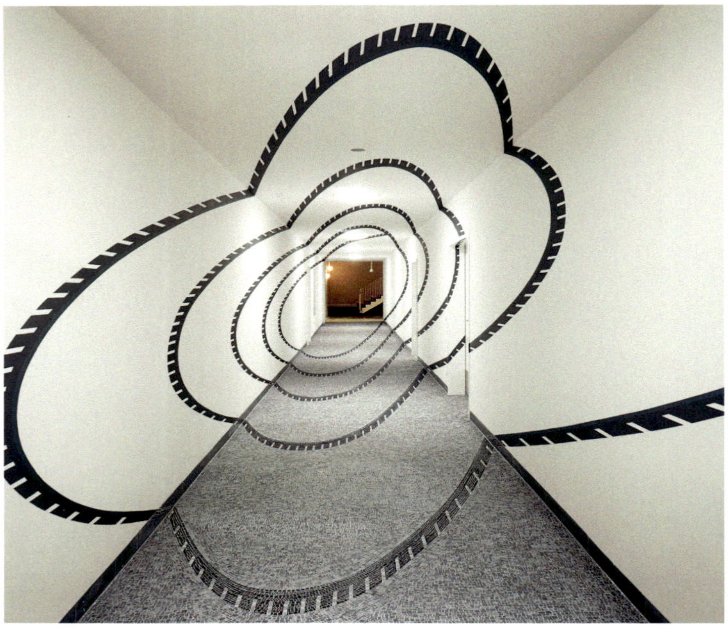

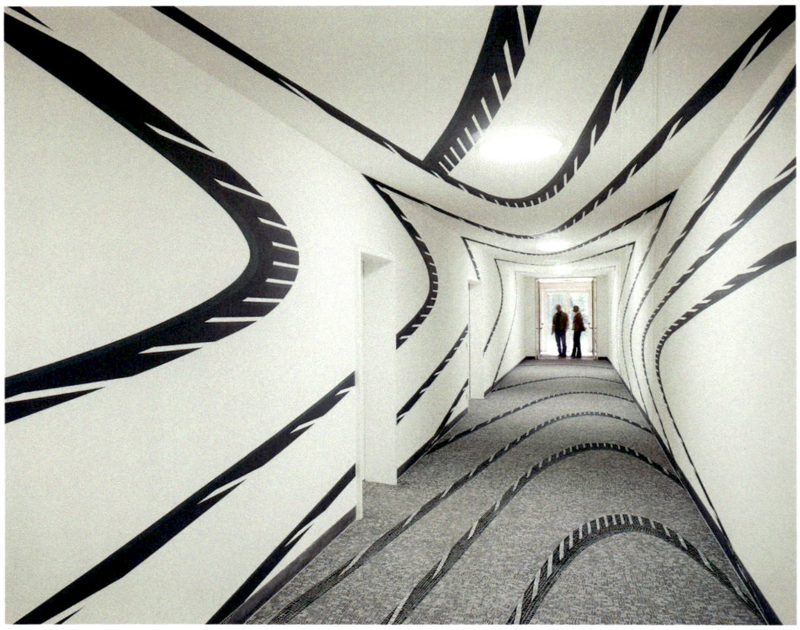

527 + 528
STEFANIE ZOCHE, SABINE HAUBITZ (HAUBITZ + ZOCHE) / "EYE OF THE STAIRCASE" / ALLIANZ HEADQUARTERS, MUNICH, DE / 2001 / MARBLE MOSAIC FLOOR

528

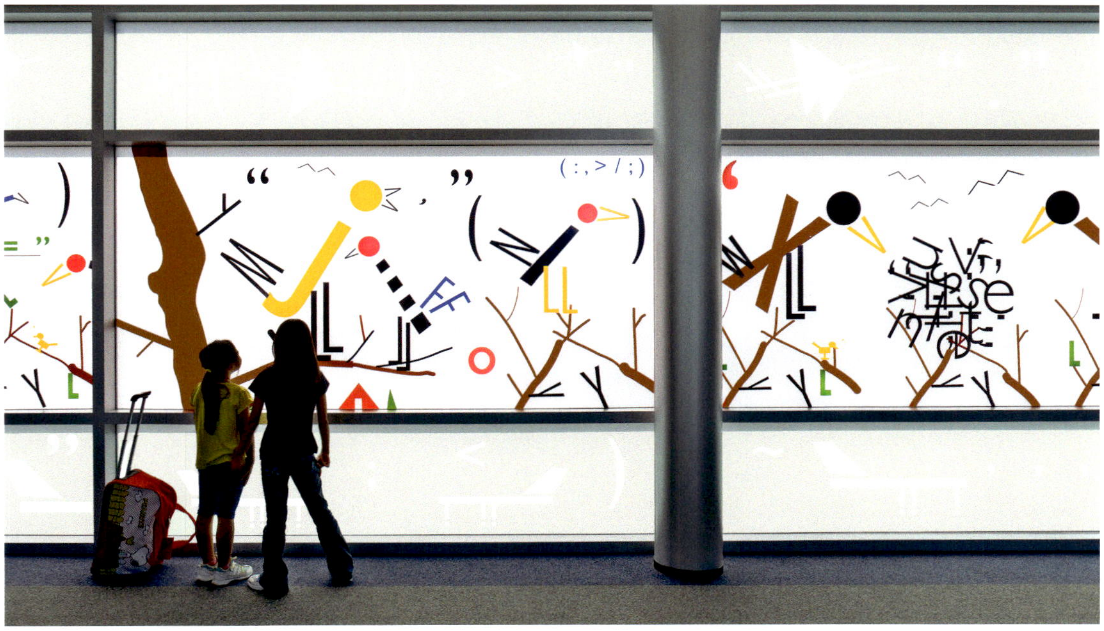

529

BOB ZOELL / "BFILRYD" (BIRD + FLY) / SAN FRANCISCO INTERNATIONAL AIRPORT, CA, USA / 2009 / FLOAT GLASS PAINTING

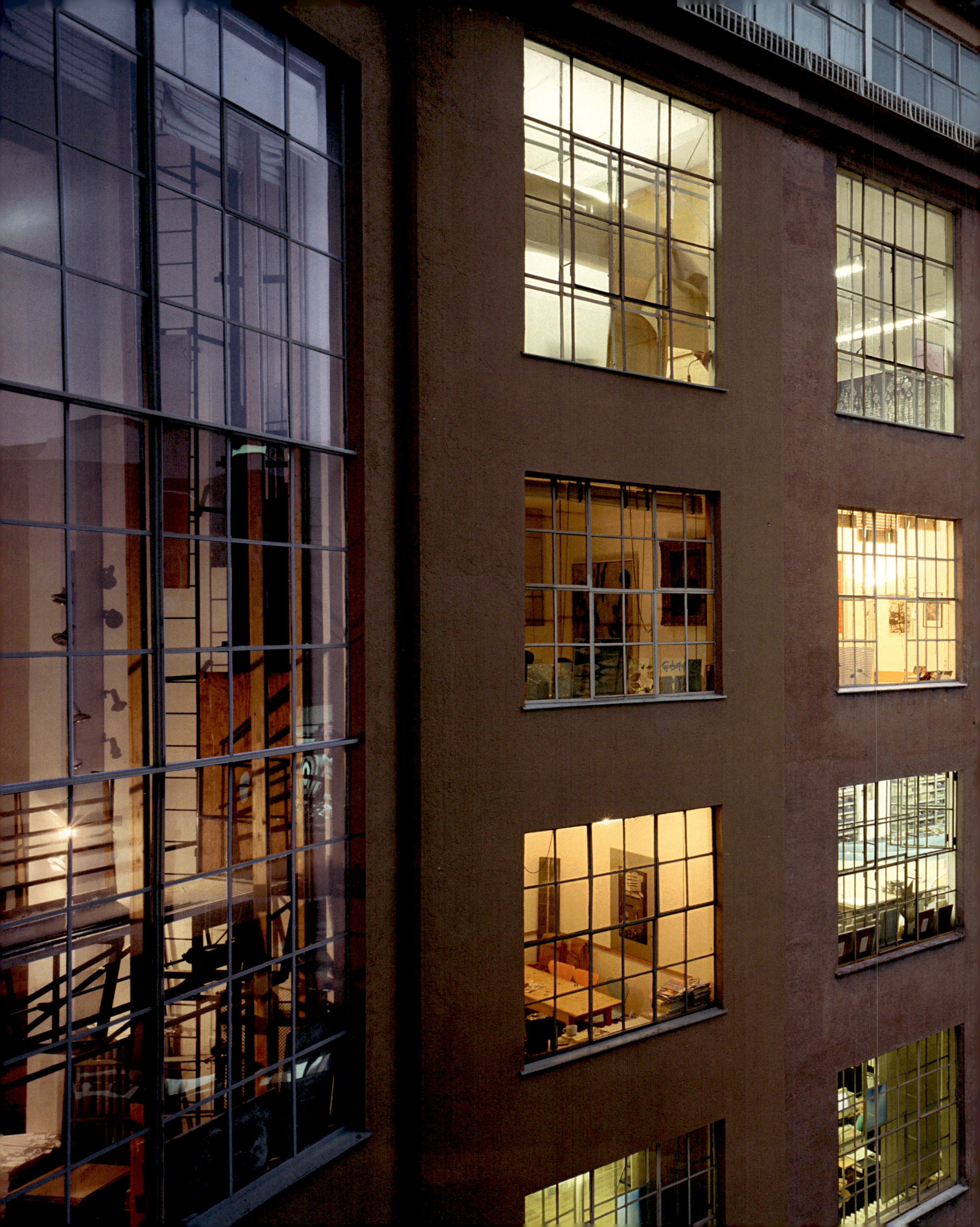

STUDIO, PROCESSES AND TECHNIQUES

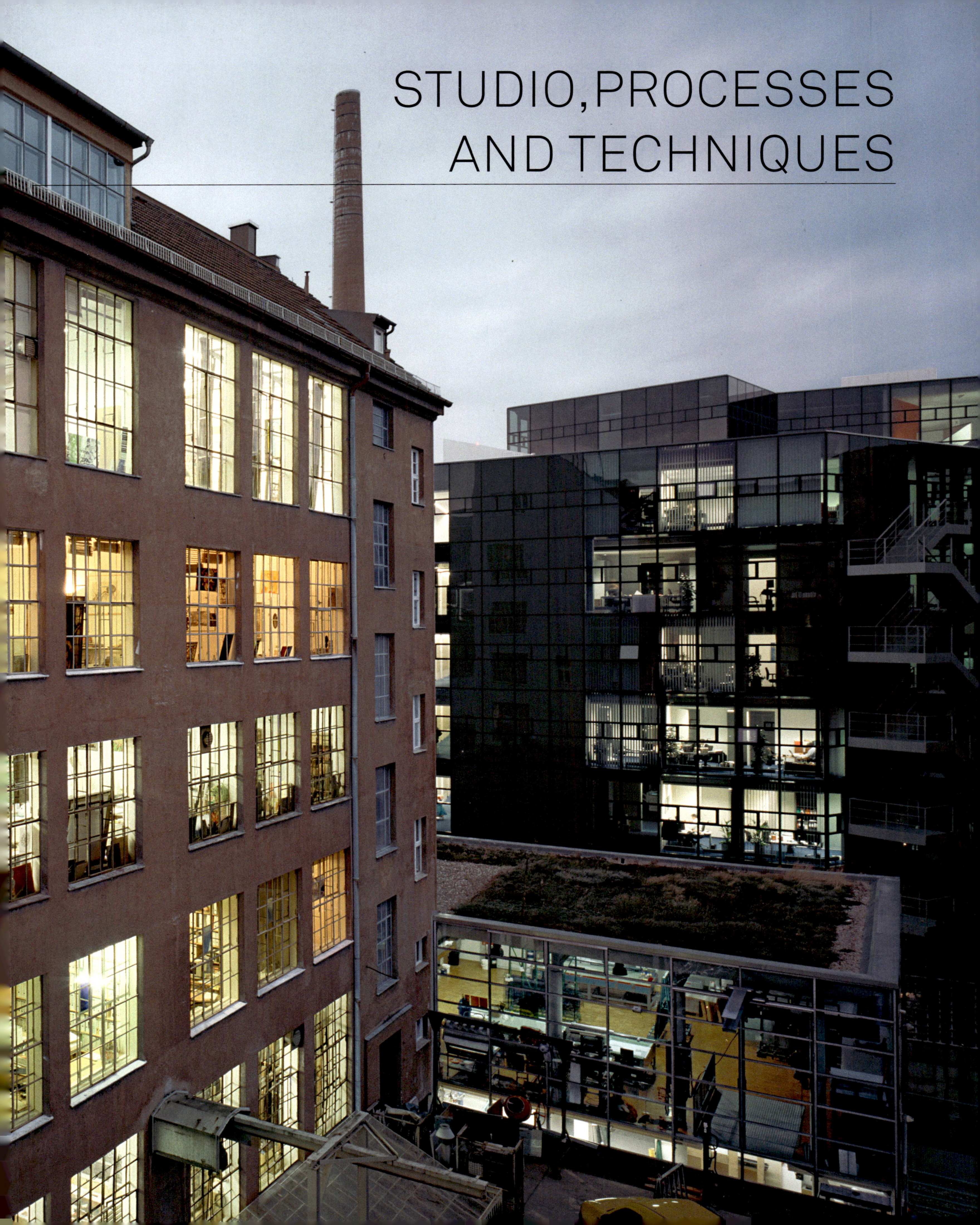

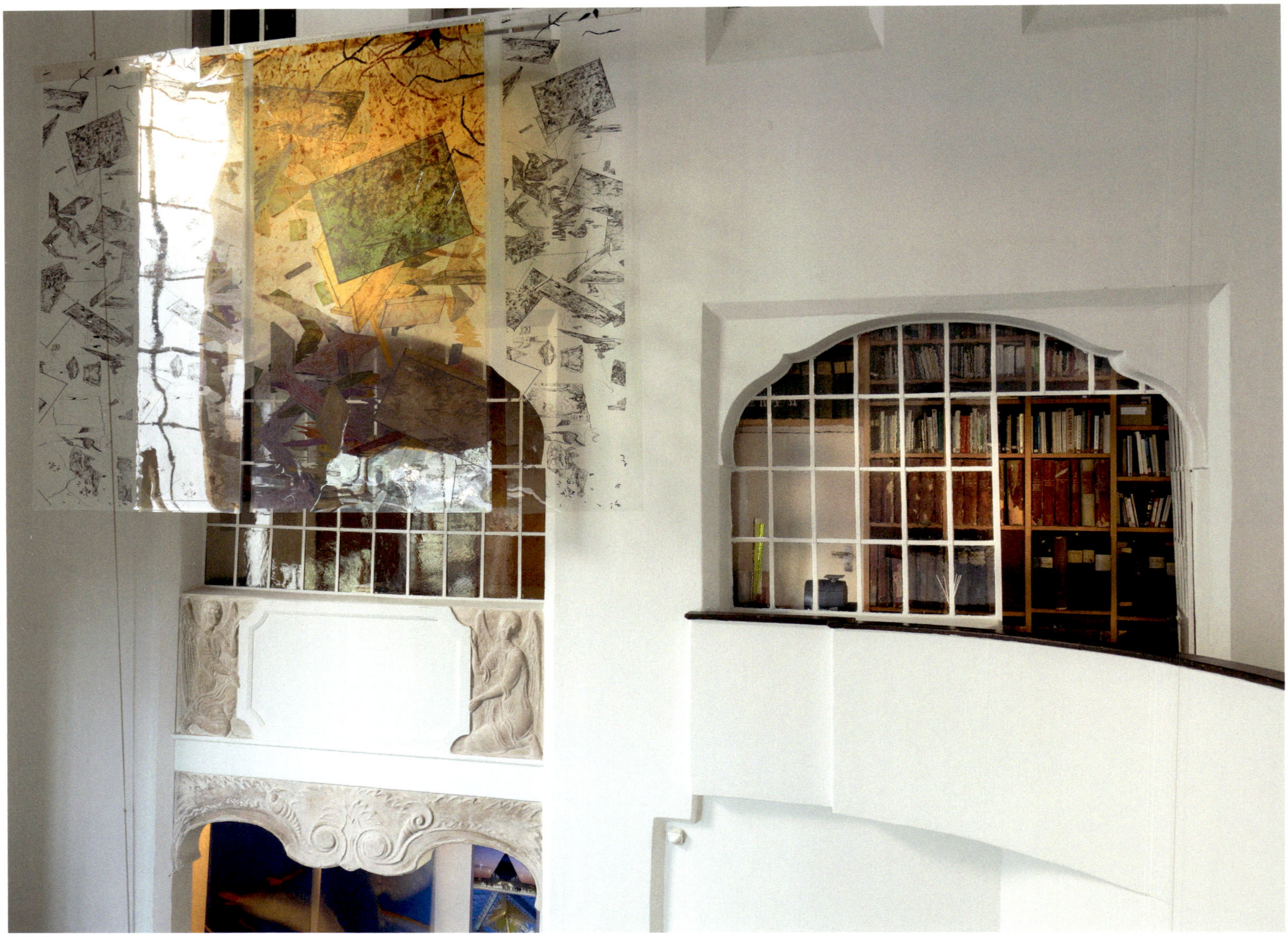

530

The Studio: A Workshop Environment

Creativity does not fall from the sky ...

A listed structure, Theodor Fischer constructed the distinctive workshop building on Stiglmaier-platz in 1923. Situated at the beginning of Munich's museum and art district, this lavish inner-city building features big and bright workshops, studios, offices, and exhibition spaces, as well as artist studios and the newly-added pavilion by Betz Architekten for float glass painting. The workshops and offices for creating artworks are spread out over some 32,000 square feet.

ENVIRONMENT

530
Image of the exhibition hall's fourth floor balustrade with a view into an historic archival space, onto film for digital print technology at a work-in-progress by Clifford Ross, historic bas-reliefs of angels, and other architectural details ...

531
View into the three-storey exhibition hall with lifting platform in front of the large window. Georg Baselitz's work for "Eagle 2011" is shown on the window *(s. p. 56 + 57)*, and a part of Ron Moppett's mosaic for Calgary *(s. p. 150–153)* on the floor.

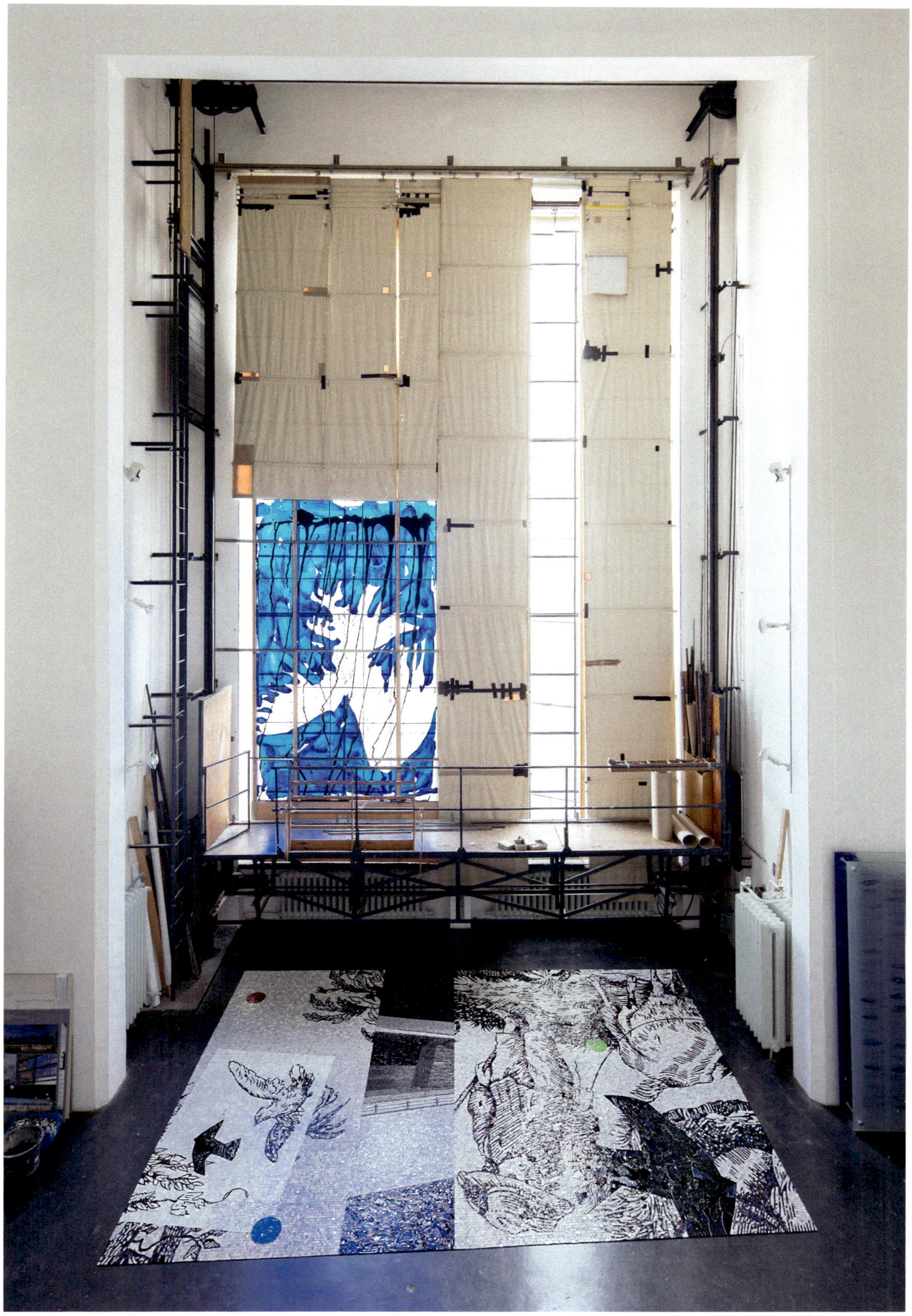

531

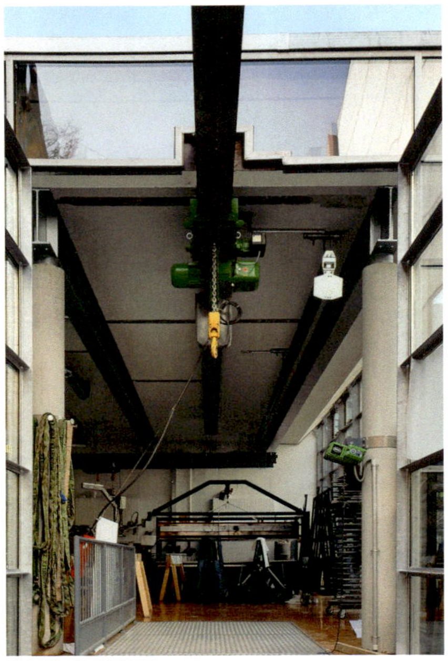

532

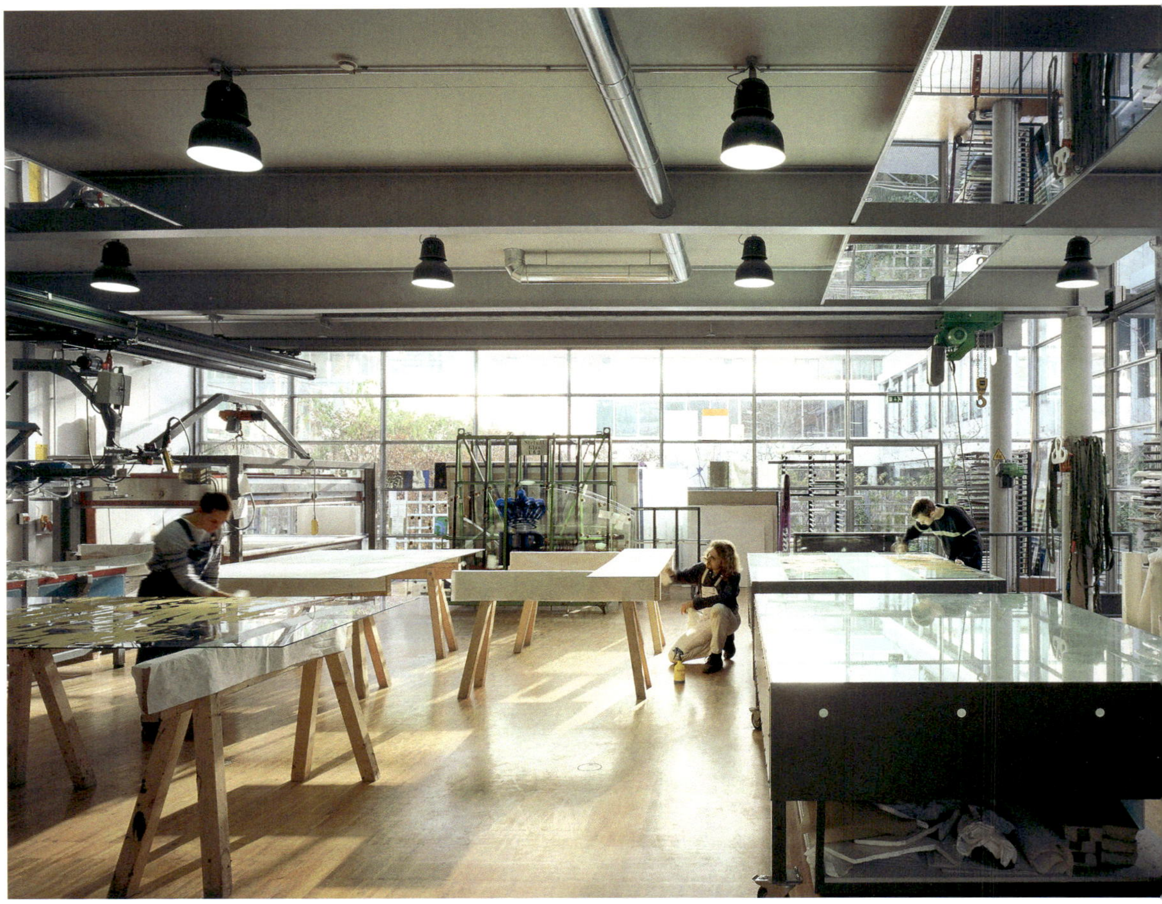

533

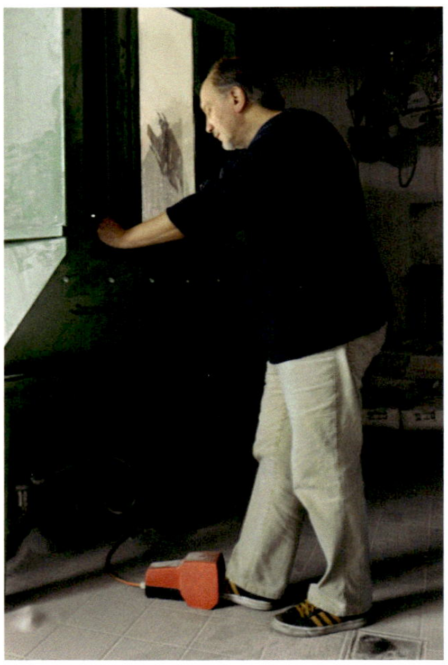

534

304

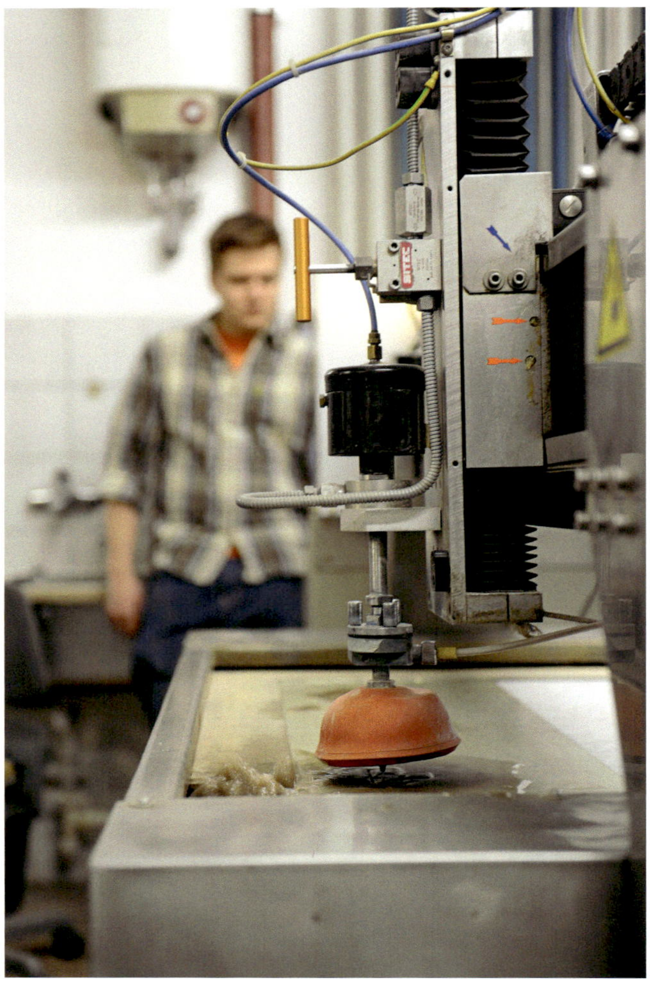

535

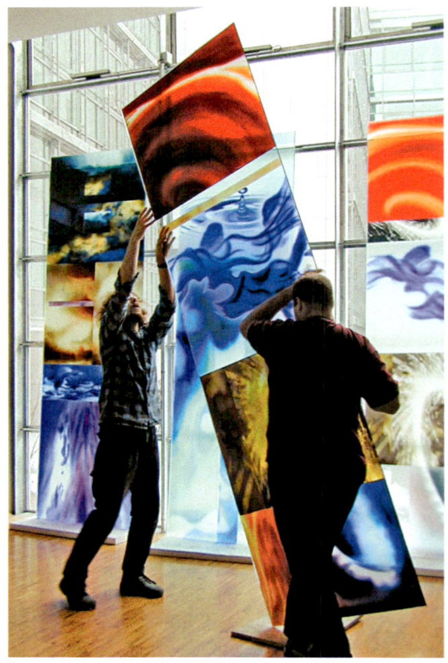

536

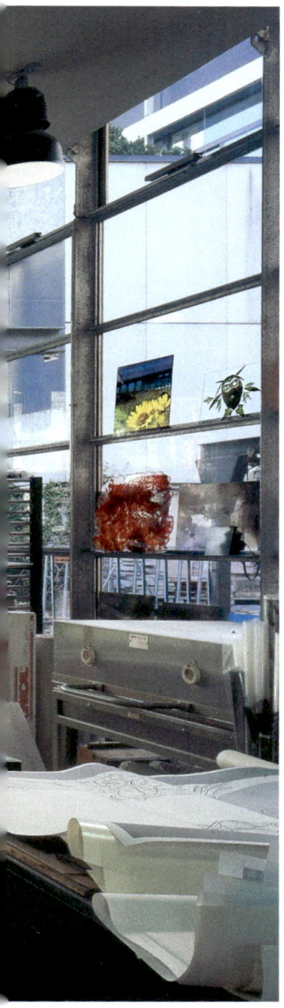

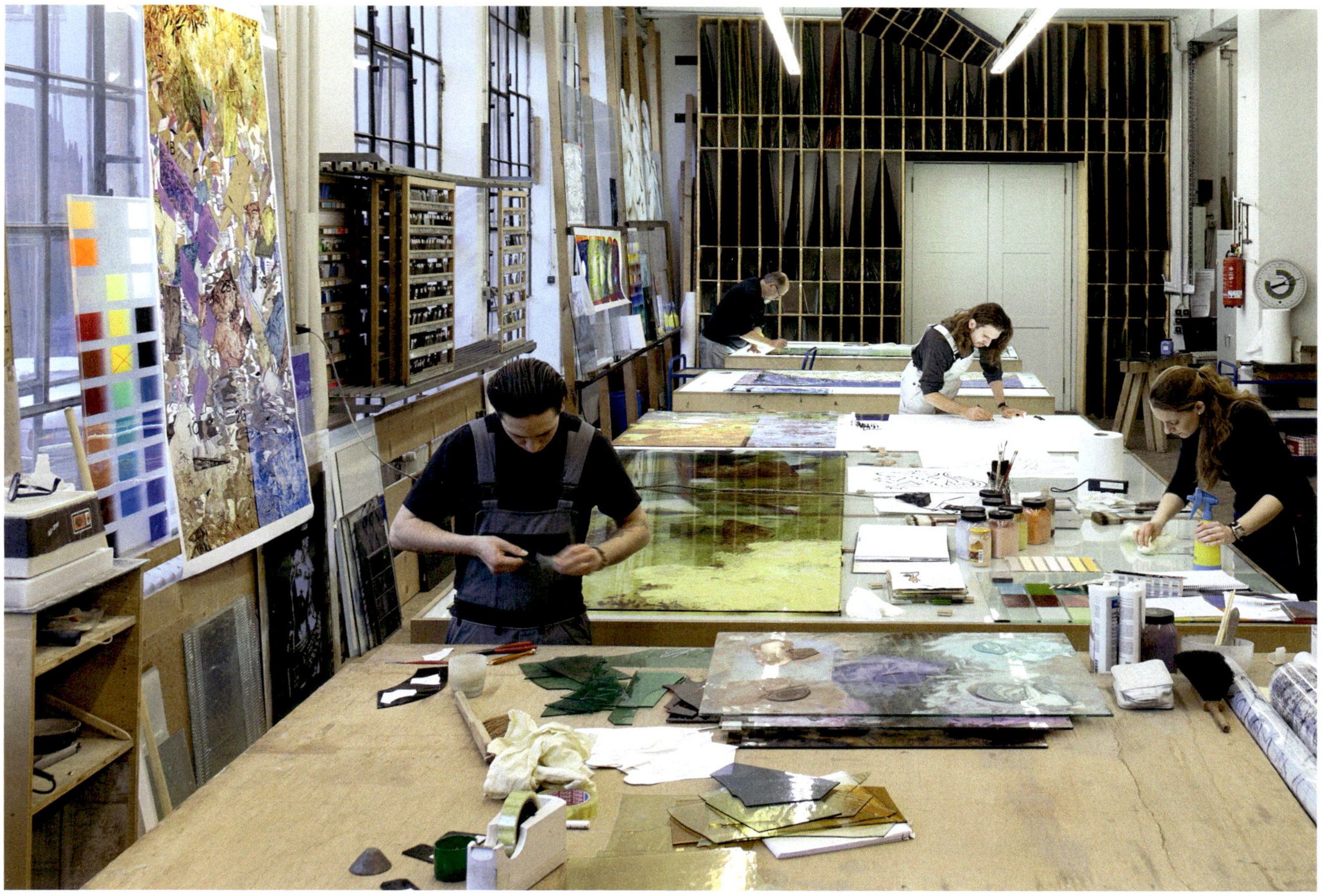

537

Workshop, Studio, Factory, Institution, Manufactory,
Handicraft Enterprise, Family Business – There are Many Names

ENVIRONMENT

532
Large gates, ceiling openings, cranes in the float glass department's new two-story structure.

533
Looking into the ground floor space for float glass painting: light tables, kilns, light cranes for especially developed plunger elevators.

534
A smaller sandblast device in the lower level.

535
The high-tech water-jet cutting device.

536
Painted glass panels from one of Catherine Wood's works are moved against the window.

537
High-ceiling room on the ground floor of the seven-story old workshop building: Cutting the glass and float glass painting.

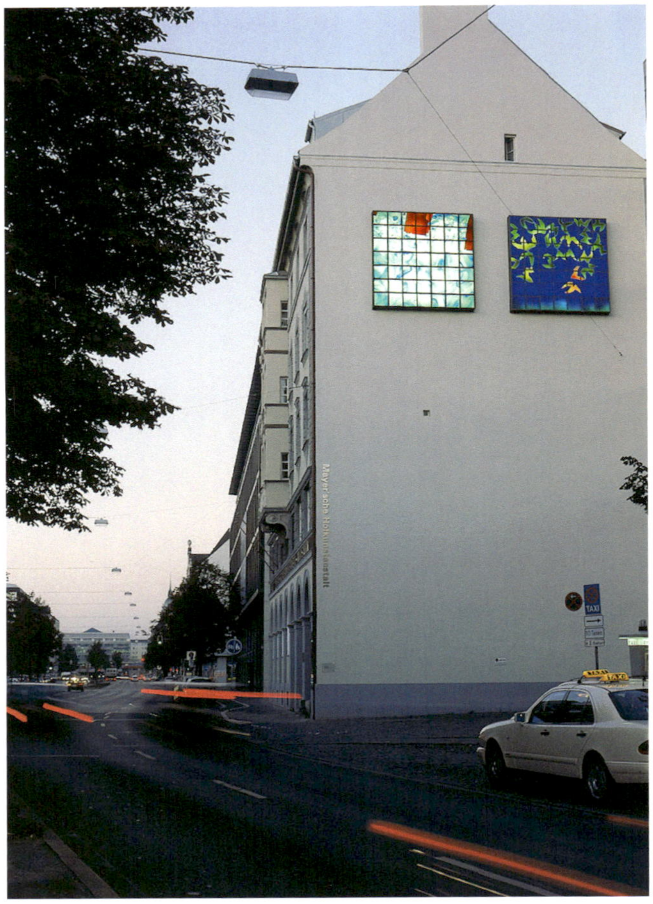

538

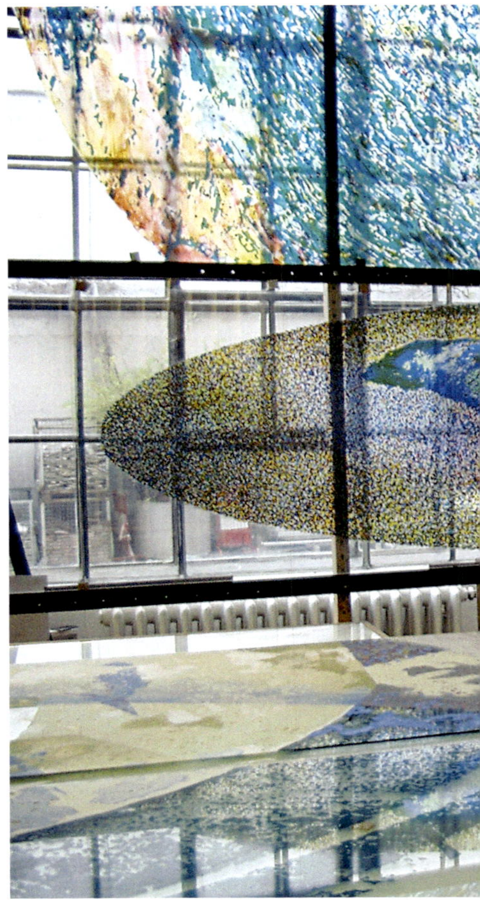

539

The workshop building is located about half a mile north of the main Railroad Station (Hauptbahnhof), two blocks from Lenbachhaus – the museum with the most beautiful "Blauer Reiter" collection, a new Norman Foster addition, and the Kunstbau – near the Glyptothek and the Pinakotheks. Good restaurants and beer gardens are found nearby.

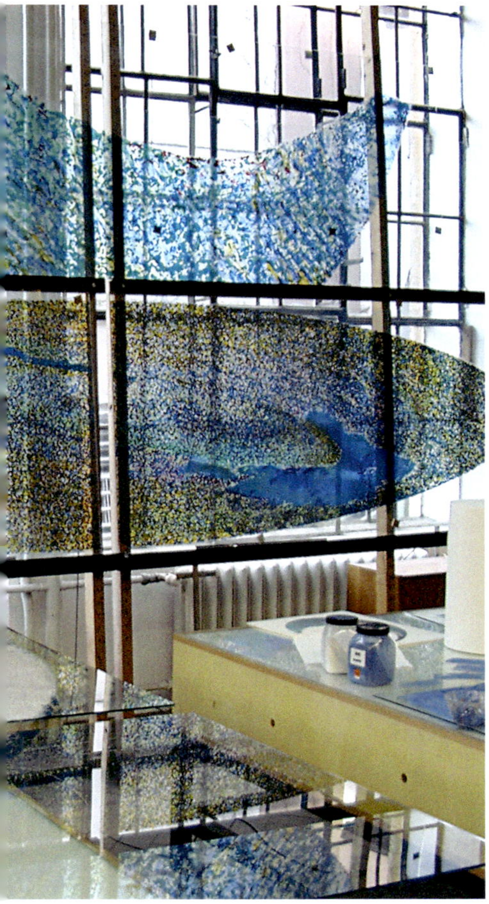

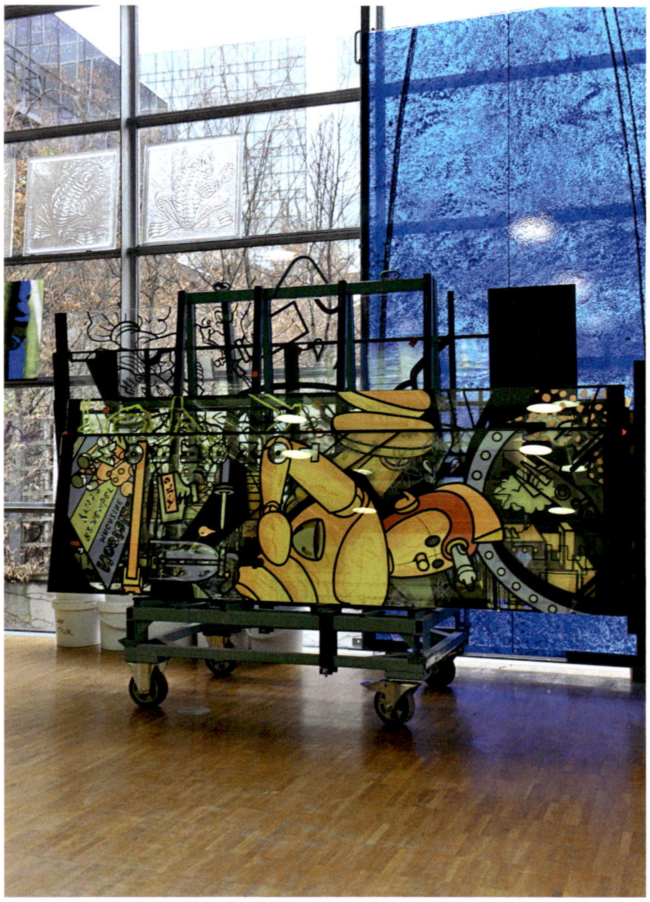

540

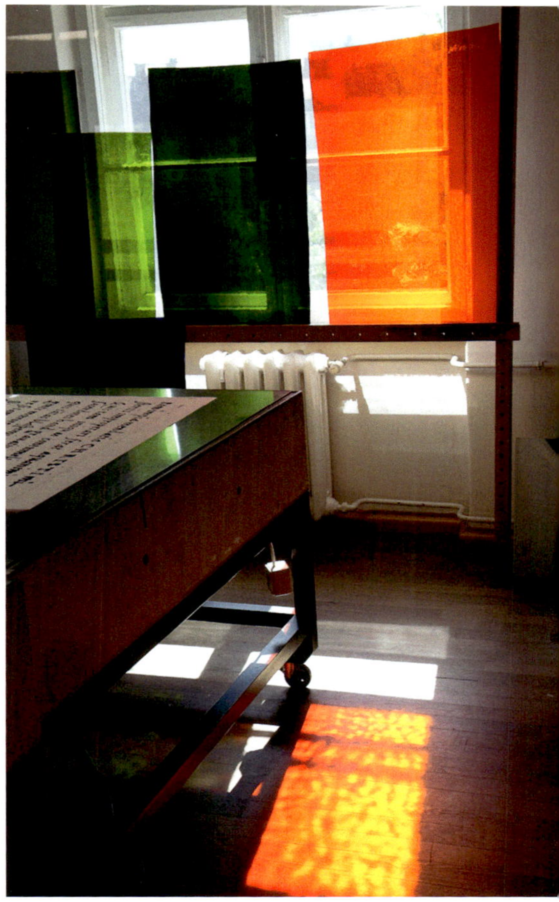

541

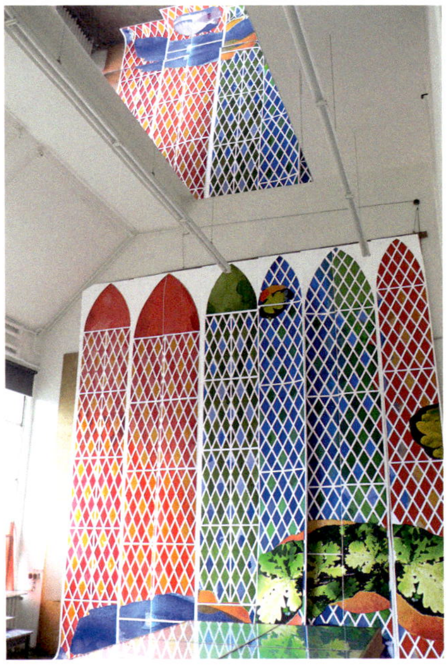

542

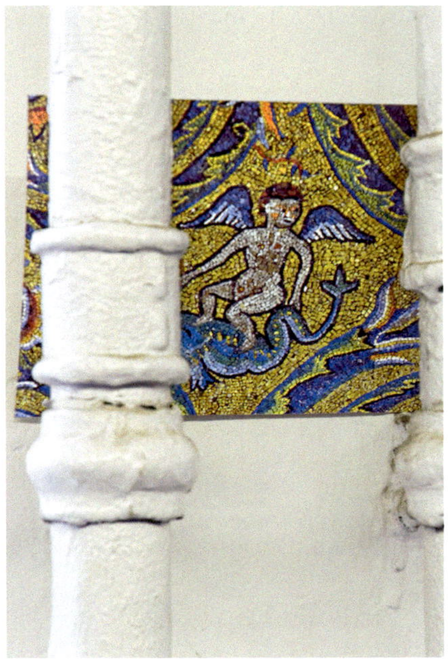

543

ENVIRONMENT

538
Brian Clarke's glass windows at the north gable of the front building, looking toward Stiglmaierplatz with taxi stand, subway, and tramway stop.

539
Panels from Heidi Lippman's BWI Airport work at the workshop window.

540
Panels from Art Spiegelman's and Robert Mangold's glass projects put on a cart and placed in front of a window.

541
Reflections of colored hand-blown glass in the sun.

542
Brian Clarke's color work drawings for the cathedral of Linköping, Sweden, seen in the big fifth floor painting studio.

543
An old mosaic pattern between pipes.

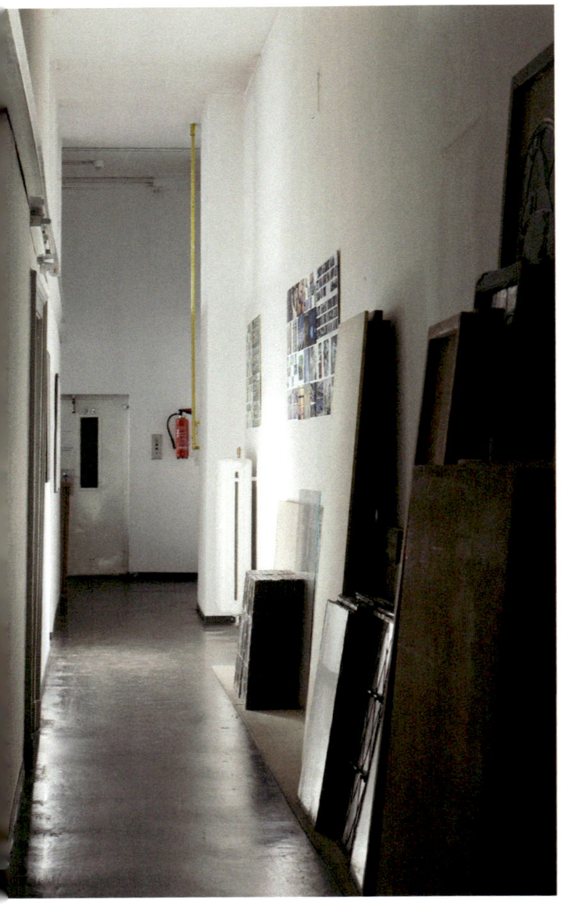
544

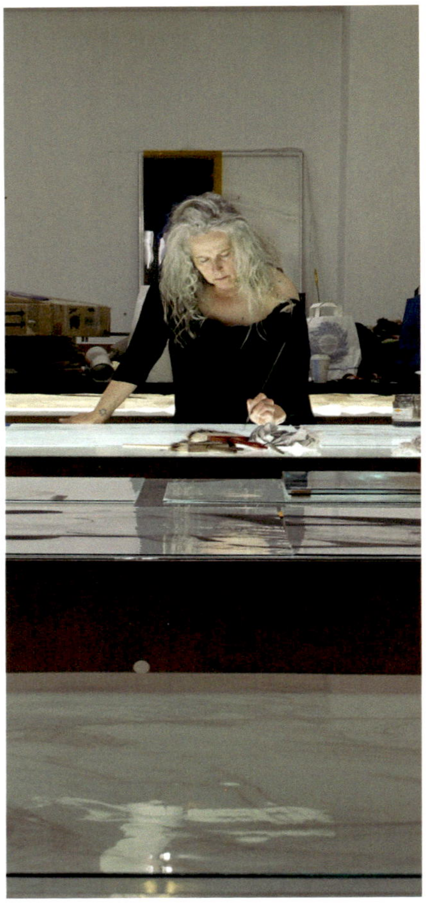
545

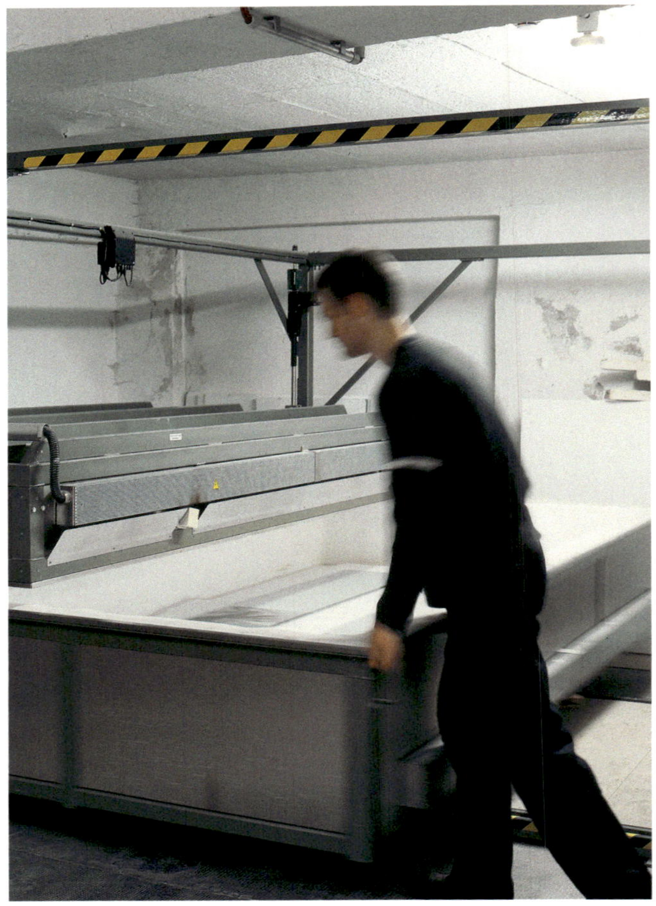
546

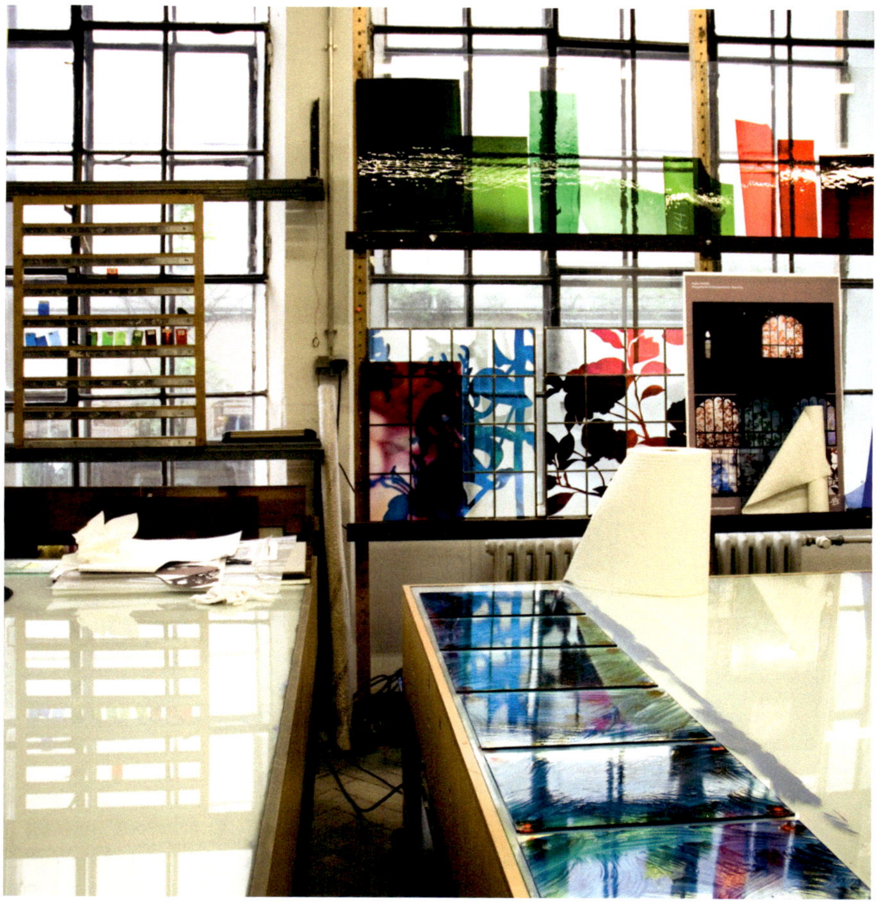

547

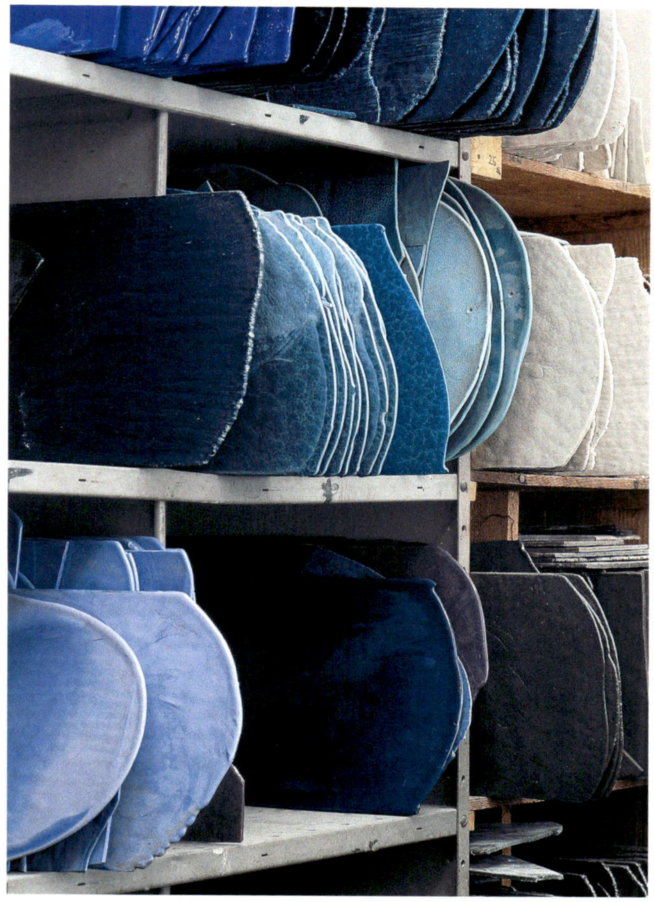

548

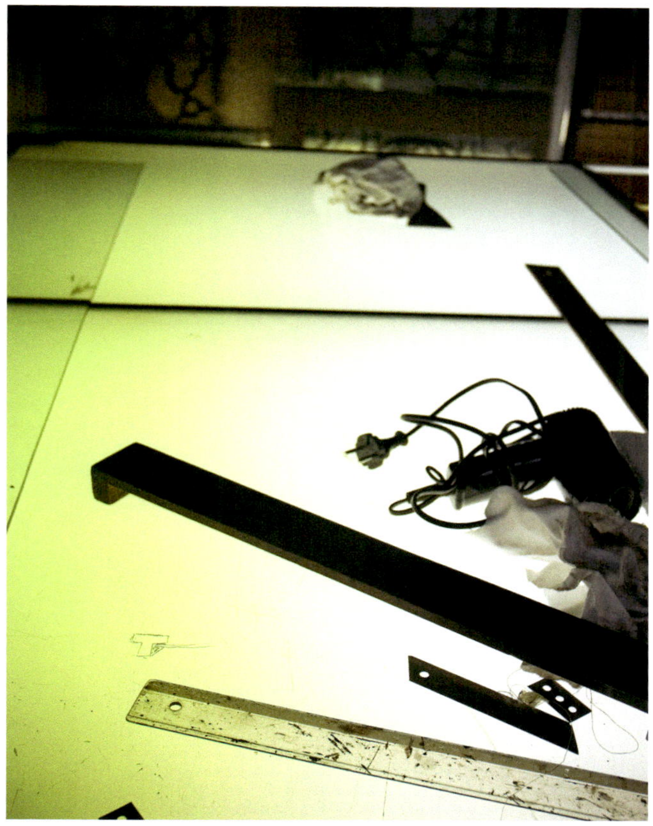

549

ENVIRONMENT

544
Fifth floor corridor.

545
Kiki Smith working at night in the eastern fifth floor painting studio.

546
Kiln on the lower floor.

547
Ground-floor impressions.

548
Venetian glass cakes in the third-floor mosaic spaces.

549
Tools.

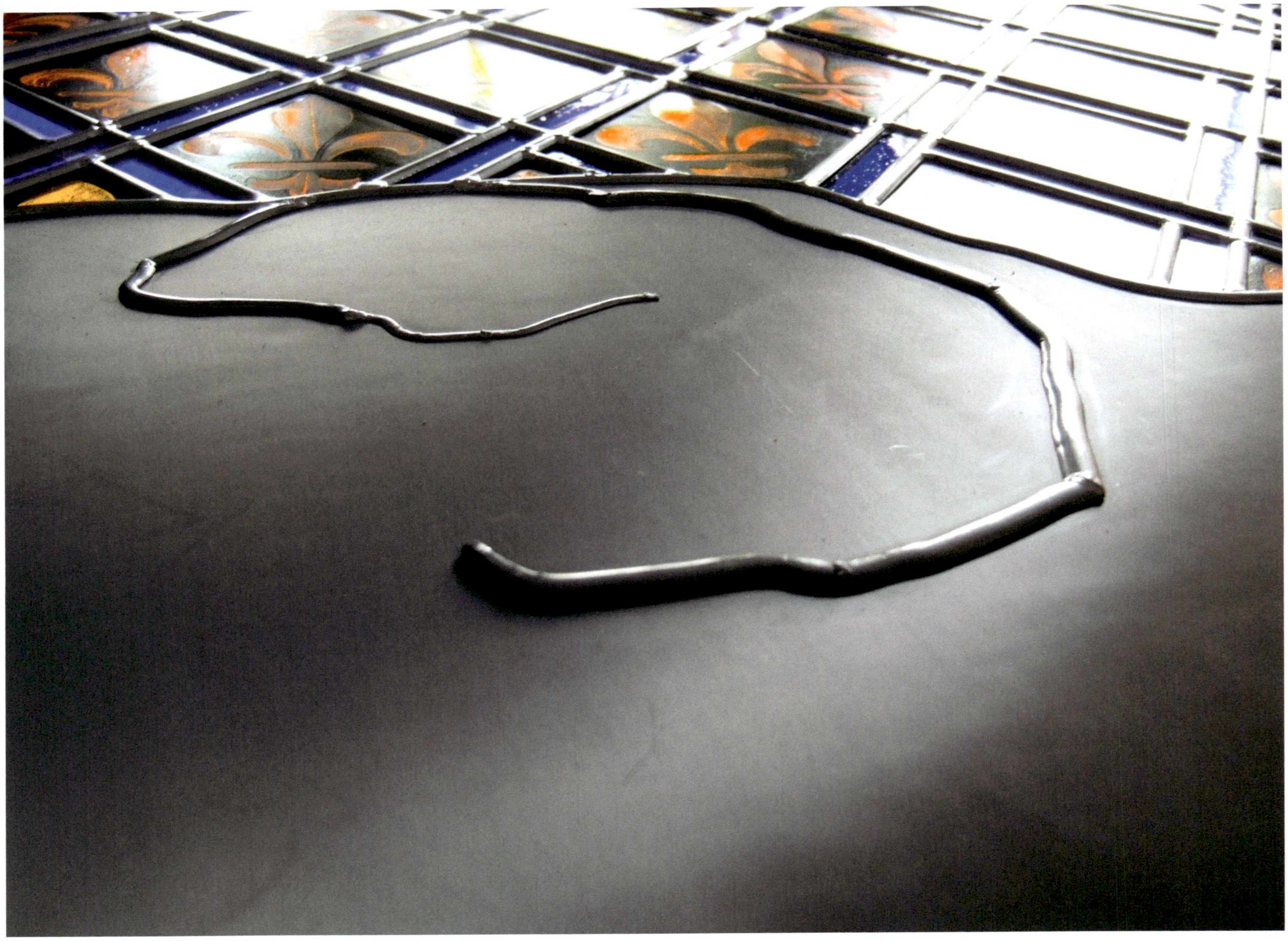

550

Glass Painting / Leading / Gluing

Working in the more traditional glass leading technique – the wonderful colored hand-blown glass

An increase in abstract designs and a decrease in painting on glass since World War Two has assigned a new role to lead cames, characterizing major parts of post-War stained glass: that of graphic design elements. Certainly, Johannes Schreiter is one of its main protagonists. For Brian Clarke, this graphic function of the line has also always been of major significance. However, with pieces like his "Glass Wall – Dedicated to Linda McCartney" from 1998, as well as with his most recent designs with lead sheet and his float glass paintings, he explores the qualities of lead and materials even further. – The pieces done in glass gluing technique were created to avoid the distracting lead lines.

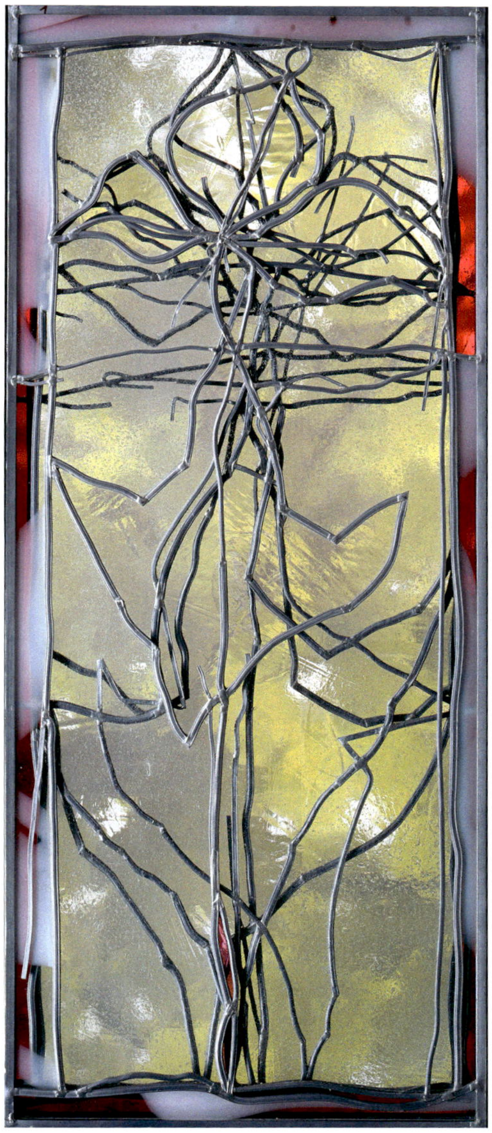

551

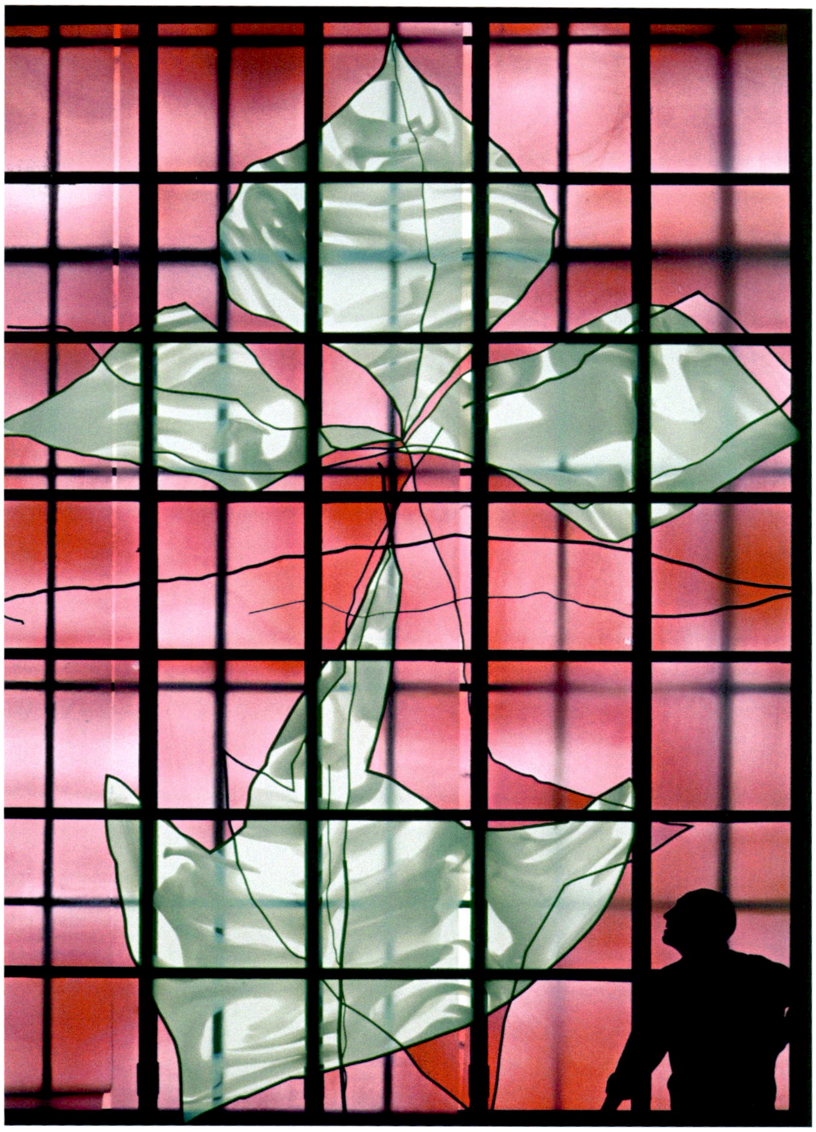

552

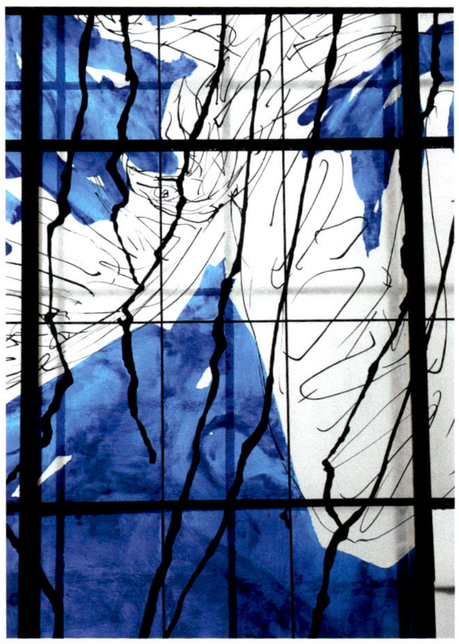

553

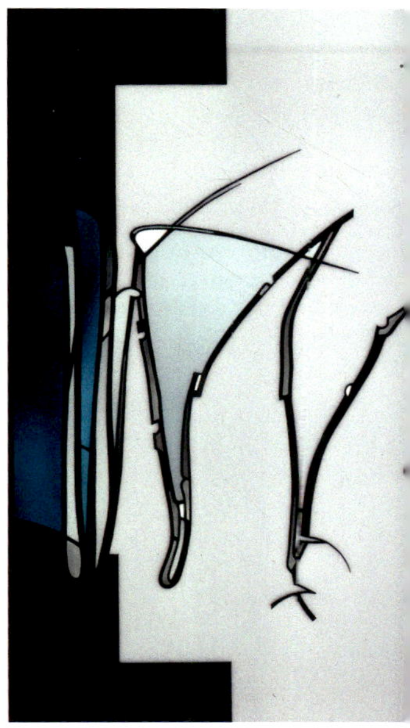

554

GLASS AND LEAD

550
This detail of Brian Clarke's "Don't Forget the Lamb" reveals lead sheet, lead cames as graphic lines, and glass painting in the old sense of the word.

551
Triple layers of leading lend the lead line a special effect; this is an example from Brian Clarke's 2003 series of small "Fleur-de-Lys."

552
The special quality of the colored glass and the rather rare lead lines distinguish this large 1998 "Fleur-de-Lys" motif by Brian Clarke. Section of his piece "Glass Wall – Dedicated to Linda McCartney" *(see p. 228–229)*.

553
Vertical and horizontal lead lines are chosen due to the painterly quality of a work by Georg Baselitz.

554
Lead as a graphic element: Detail from Johannes Schreiter's gorgeous 1979 lead and material piece of the glass wall for the city hall of Ludwigshafen.

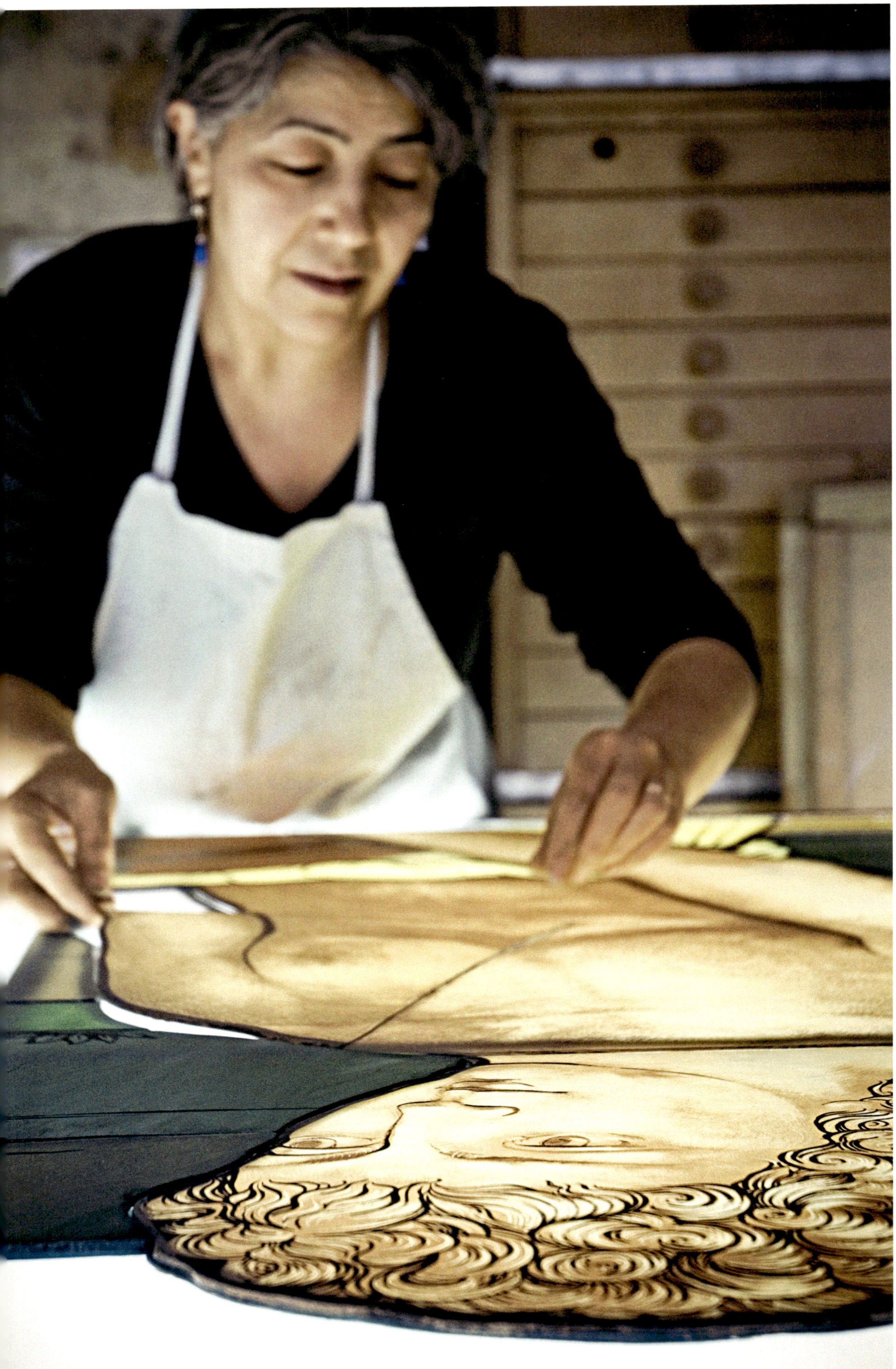

555

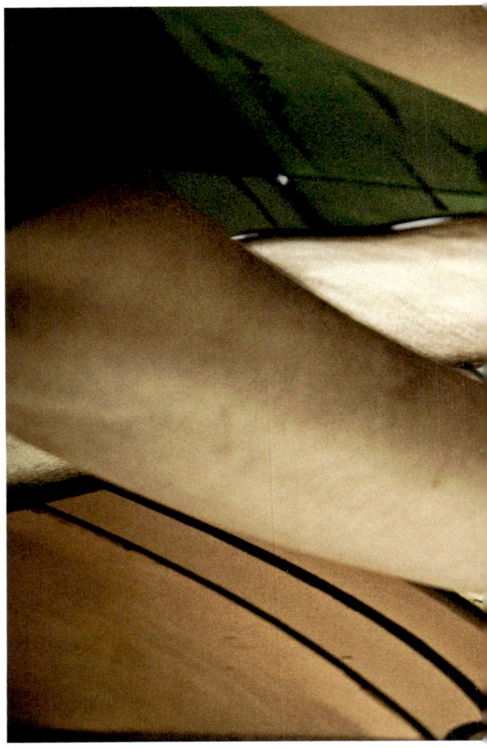

556

GLASS PAINTING

555 + 556
Traditional stained glass, 'musivic' assembly of glass, painting with *Schwarzlot* on glass, matting, etching, firing.

557
Timeless and modern figurative glass painting: Hans Gottfried von Stockhausen's head of the prophet Elijah from the "Israel window" in Ulm Minster.

558
Leading.

559
Paint brushes for the glass painters.

560
Selection of vivid blue flashed glass for etching.

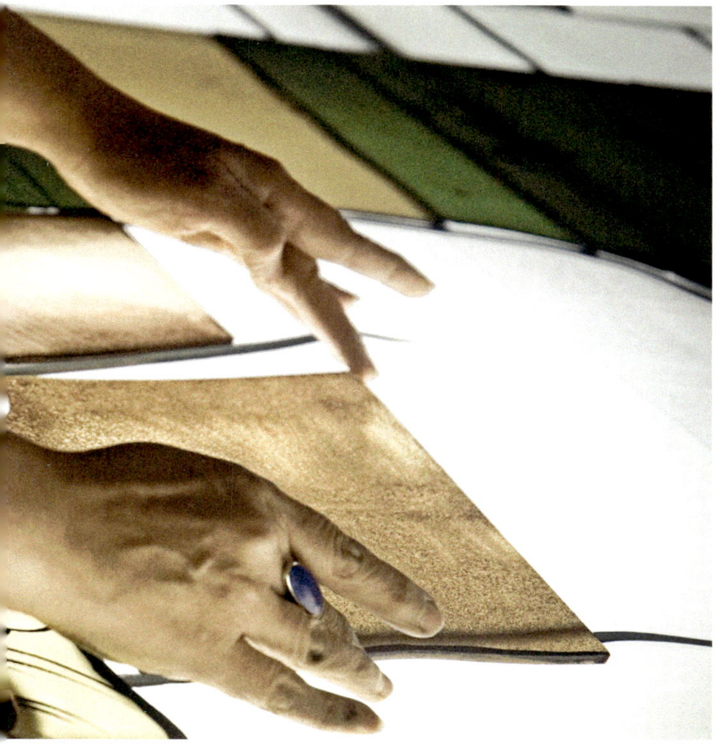

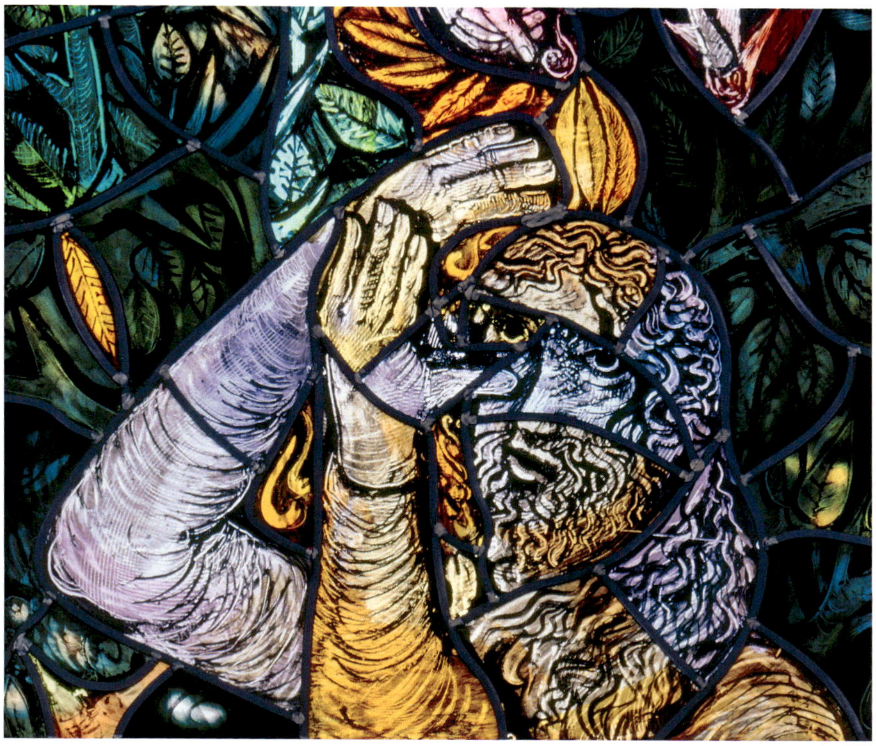

557

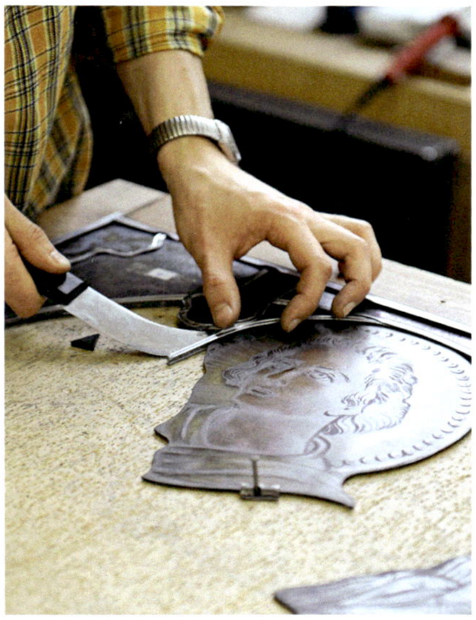

558

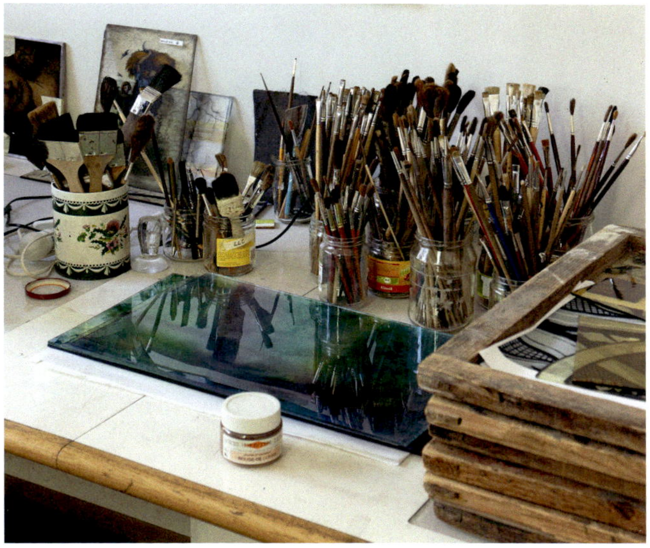

559

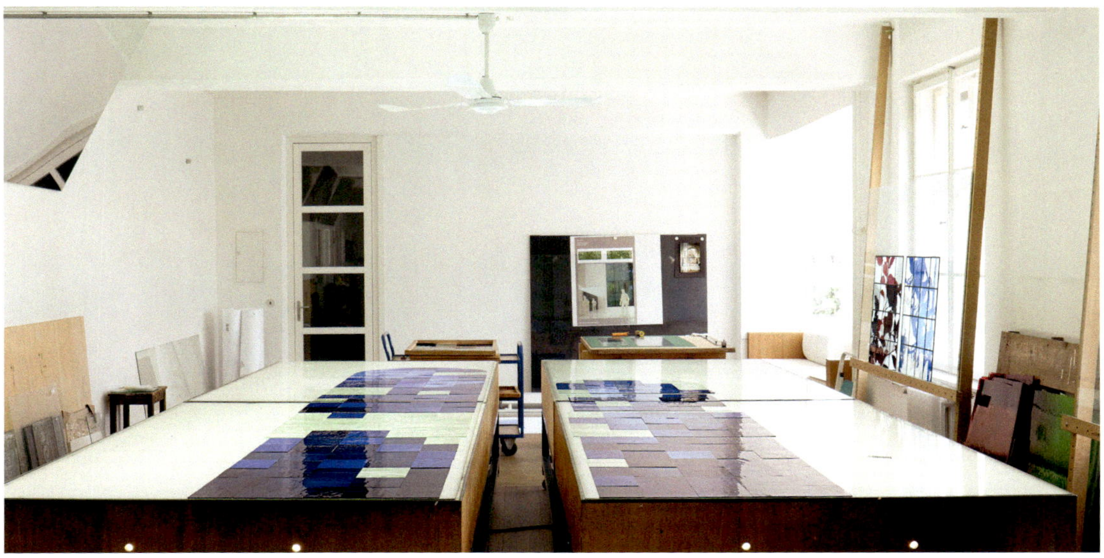

560

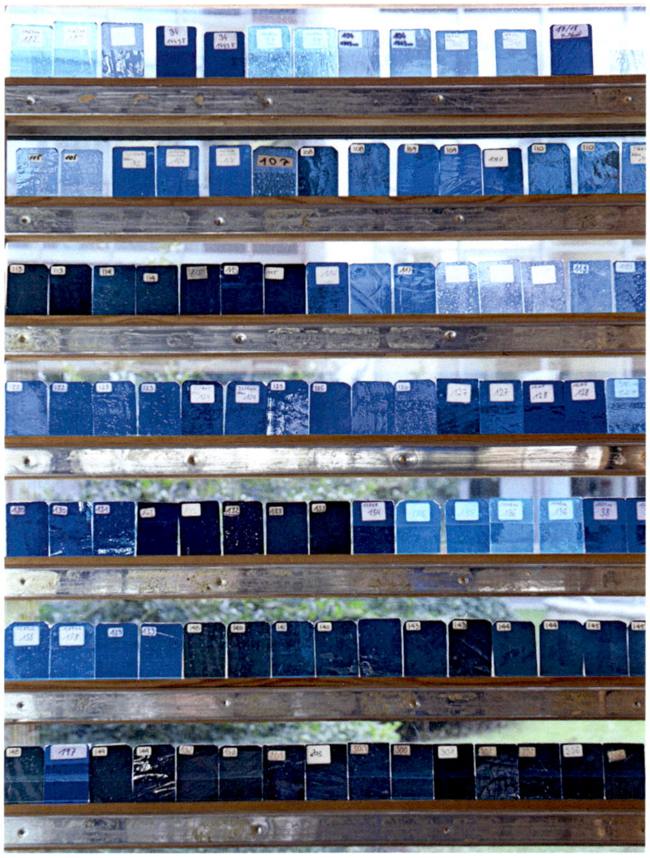
561

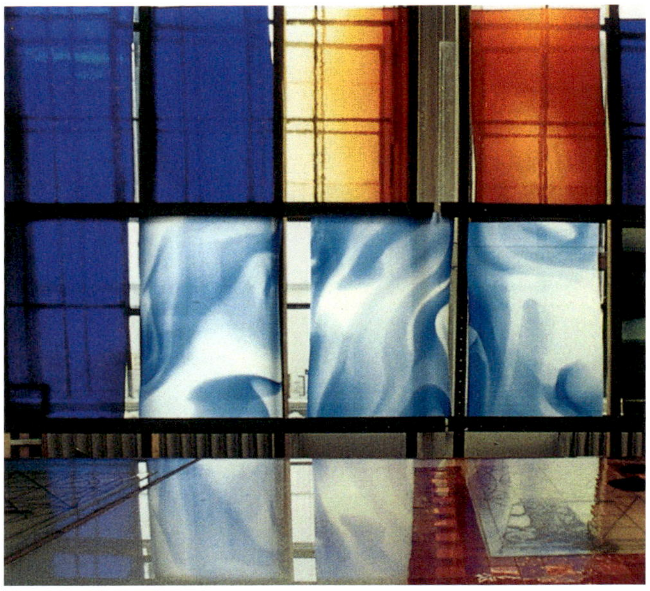
562

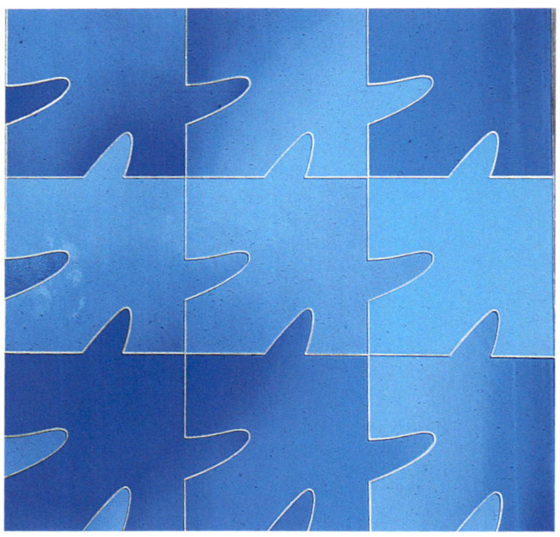
563

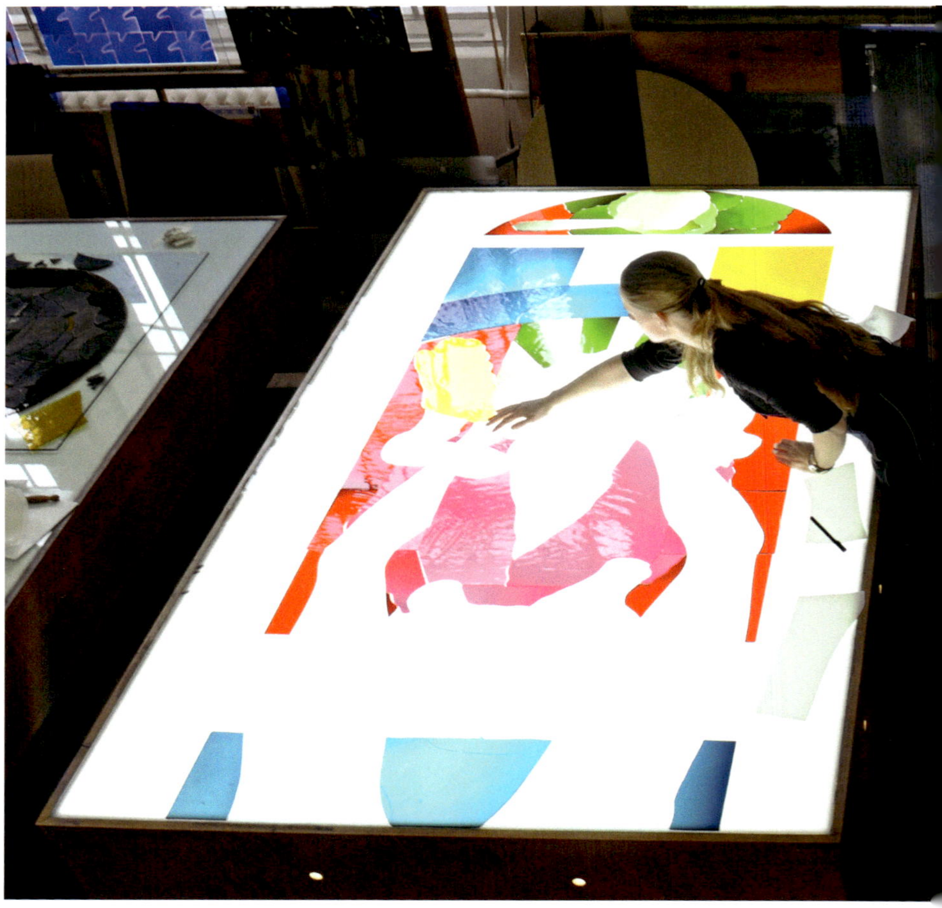
564

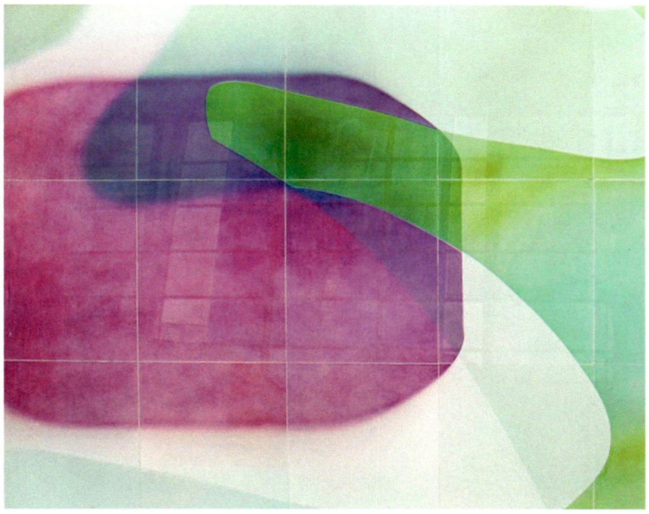

565

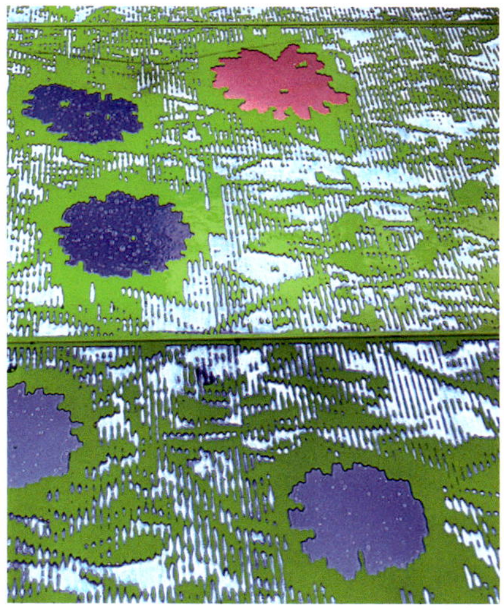

567

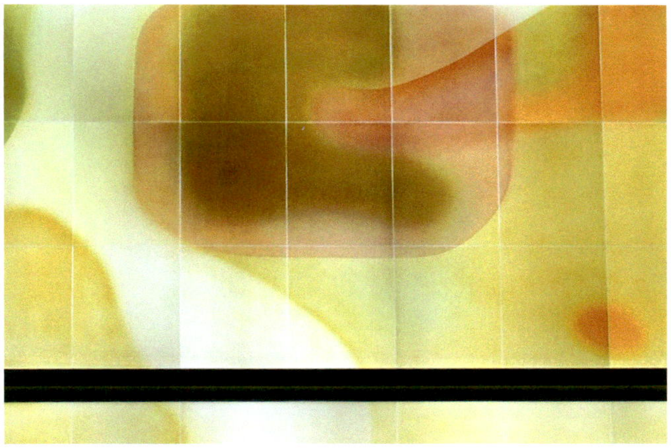

566

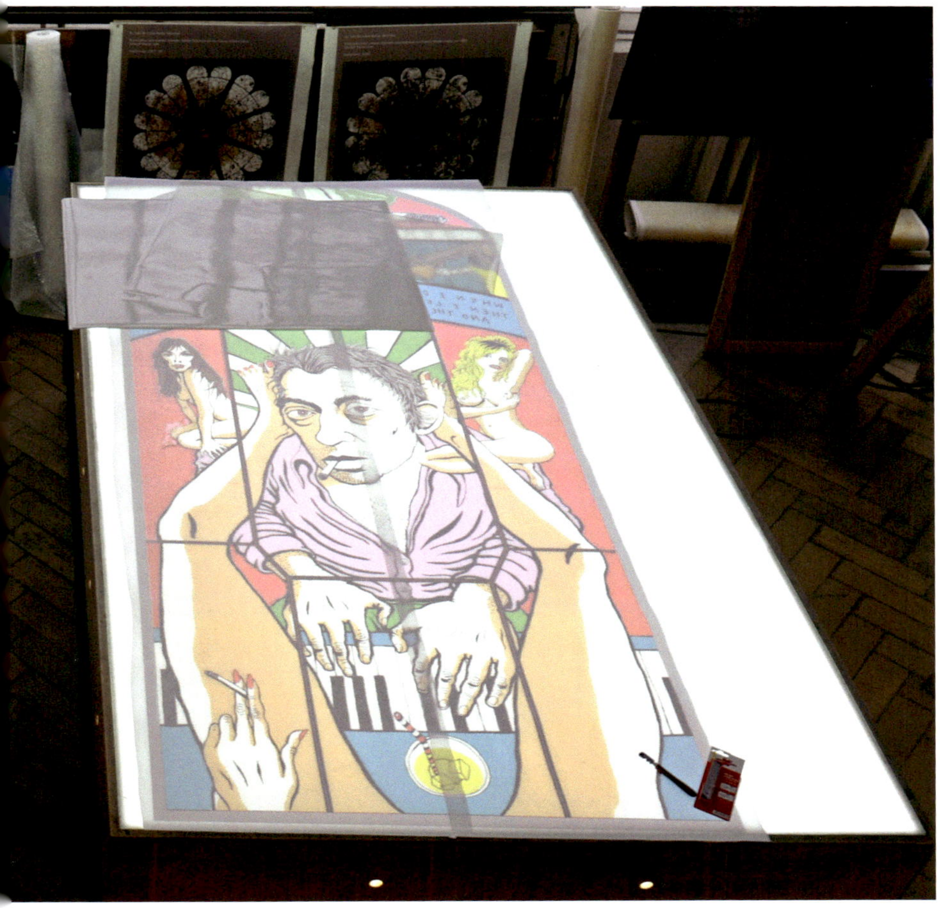

CUTTING, GLUING, ETCHING GLASS

561
A small selection of the color scale for the so-called genuine antique glass, the colored, hand-blown glass.

562
While selecting glass, larger panels in their original size are often placed in front of the windows.

563
Ornamental glass gluing: glass cut with a water-jet device and adhered to the carrier panel with transparent silicon glue.

564
Placing the cut panels on the light boxes – from Neal Fox's window series *(see p. 92–95)*.

565 + 566
Glass adhesion with etched and painted glass – soft and hard color transitions from Martin Donlin's windows *(see p. 80–81)*.

567
Sandblasted and etched green flashed glass, blue and pink melting colors from Brian Clarke's glass piece for the Apax administration in London *(see p. 236 +237)*.

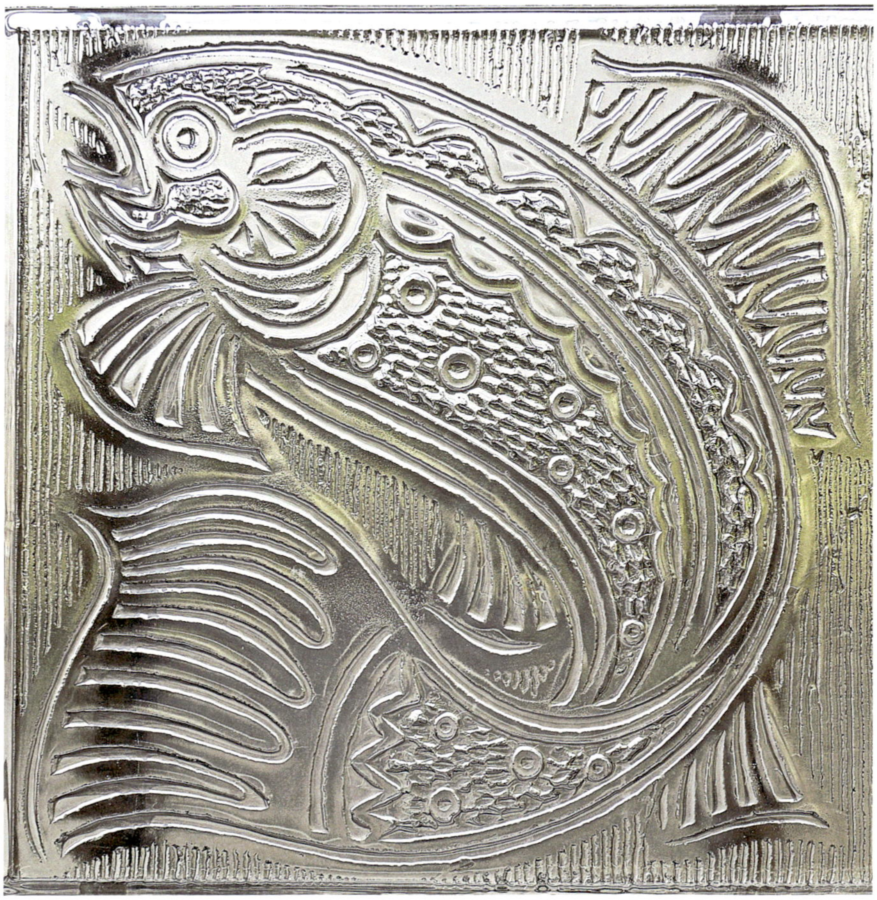

568

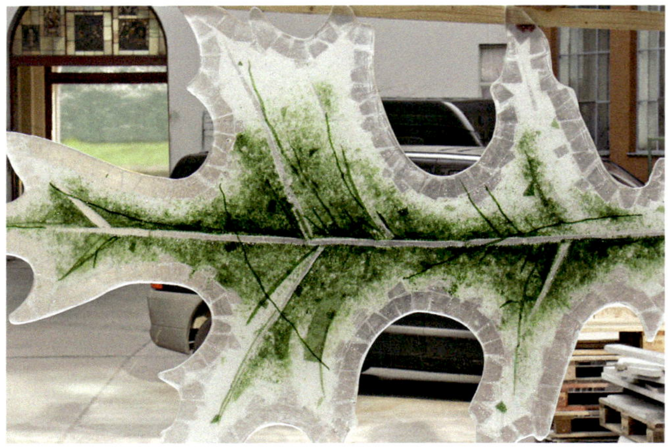

570

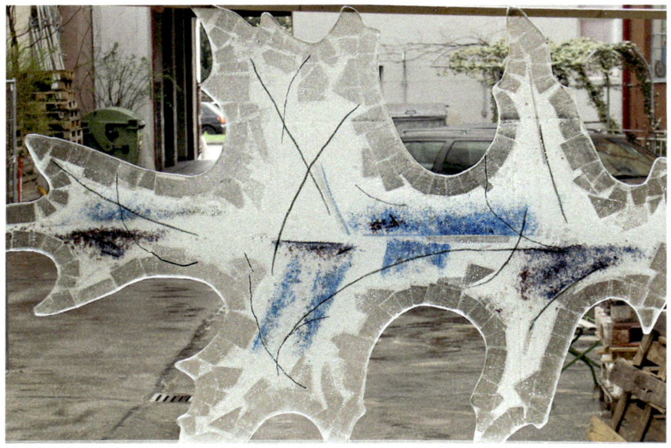

569

Faceted Glass / Slumped and Fused Glass / Stacked Glass

At 600 degrees centigrade glass begins to melt; at 1,460 degrees, it begins to flow

Thanks to surface deformations and the merging of different individually designed glass layers, slumping or fusing offer fascinating and subtle possibilities for glass design. In the 1950s and 60s, cast, thick faceted glass was very popular in Europe; then it was almost forgotten. While it often survives the buildings themselves, conserving or reconstructing such faceted glass windows in conjunction with modern glass architecture is utterly attractive. Stacking of glass panels or slats with their polished and cut edges also allows to create very special glass surfaces.

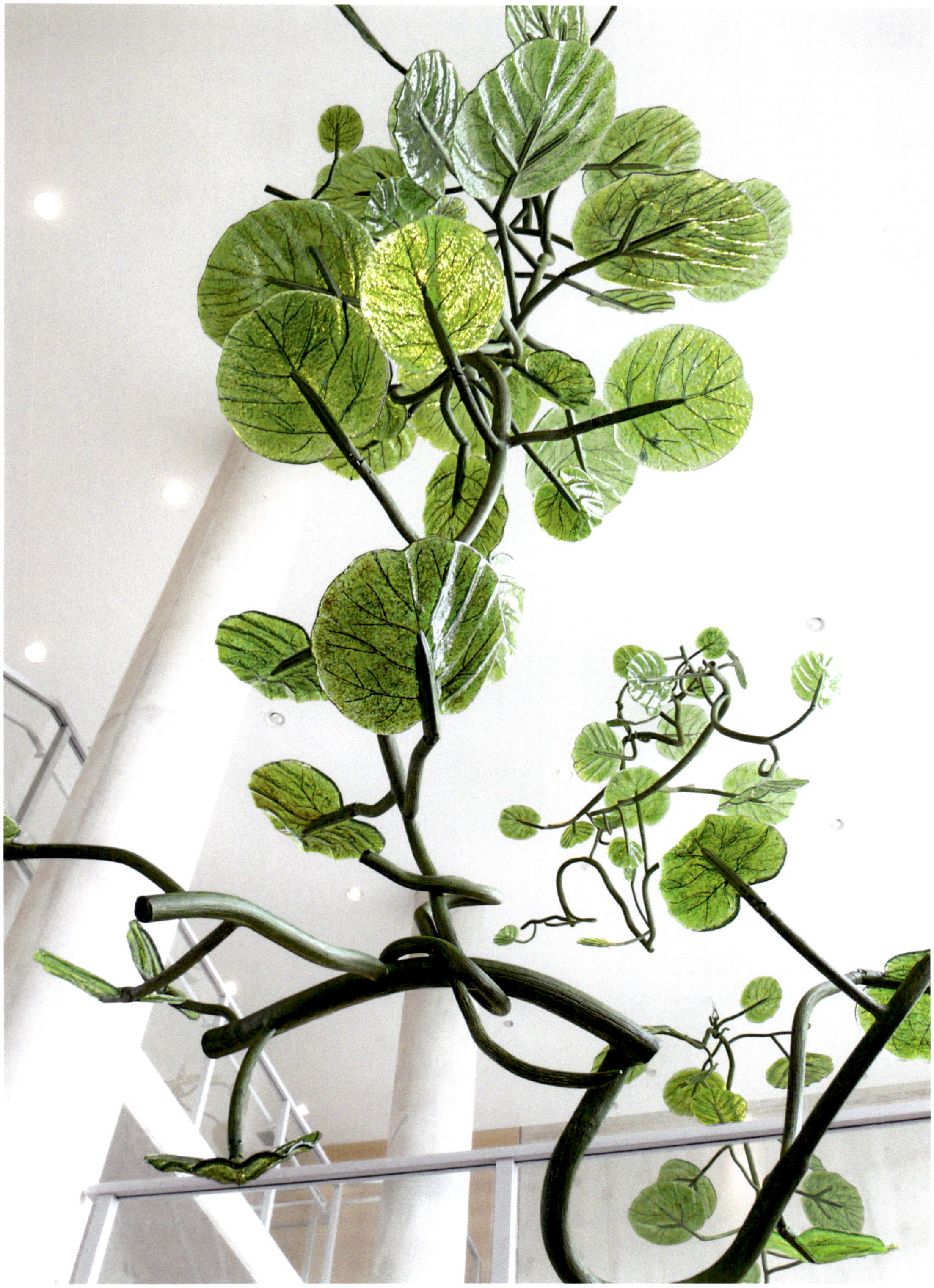

571

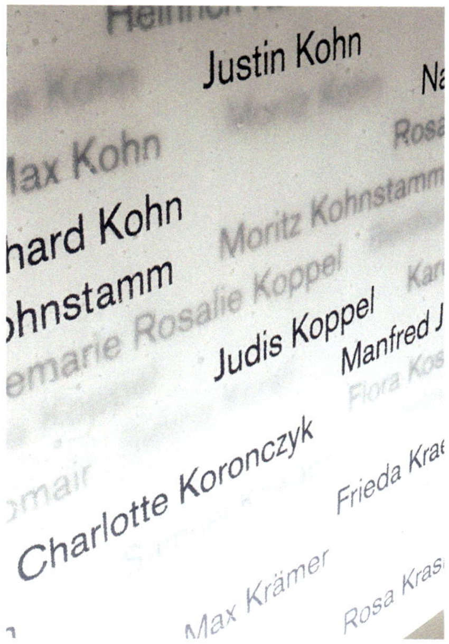

572

SLUMPED AND FUSED GLASS

568
For the large glass ceiling of the "Senate" stairwell in the New York State Capitol in Albany, 76 colorless slumped glass panels were fabricated according to in-house designs *(see p. 50–51)*.

569 + 570
Almost the size of a human, these maple leaves were made with Barbara Grygutis using fusing technique.

571
Ming Fay designed this structure of branches and leaves for a building in Philadelphia. The pieces of glass are up to 1 ½ feet long.

572
The possibility of fusing multiple layers of glass facilitated the creation of closeness, distance, and detachment in the many names remembered in the memorial of the New Synagogue in Munich *(see 222 + 223)*.

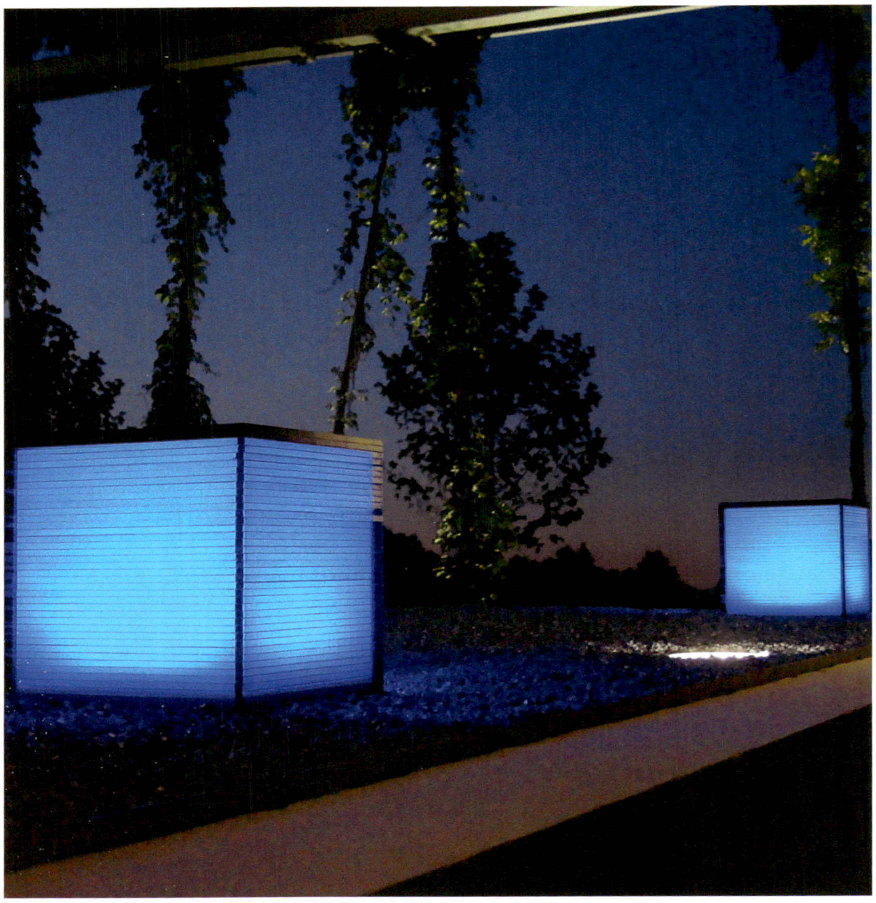

573

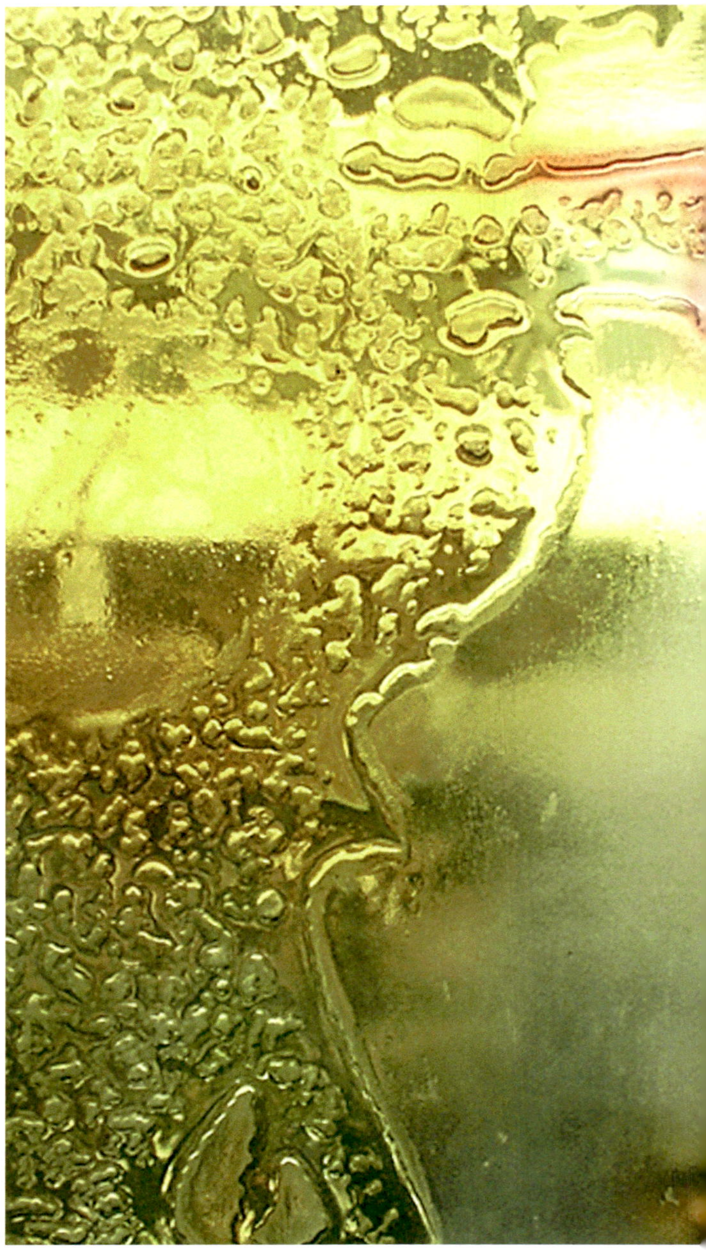

574

318

STACKED, SLUMPED, AND FUSED GLASS

573
Martha Schwartz's blue glass cubes with exterior broken and interior water-jet cut edges for the Munich headquarters of Swiss Re *(see p. 186–189)*.

574
This glass, fabricated for a project in the Netherlands, is very special due to its three-dimensional form, added color, transparency, and mattedness.

575
In this fused piece of artglass by Philomena Williamson drawing and color are placed on different levels *(see p. 294)*.

576
Distinguished by fusing and their curvature, these large glass rings are part of Sabine Kammerl's artwork for the Institut für Medizintechnik at the TU in Munich.

577
This design emphasizes the profundity of the transparent material: a detail of the fused piece by Mike and Doug Starn for New York City's South Ferry Station *(see p. 202–207)*.

578
Fusing, sawing, fusing – a detail.

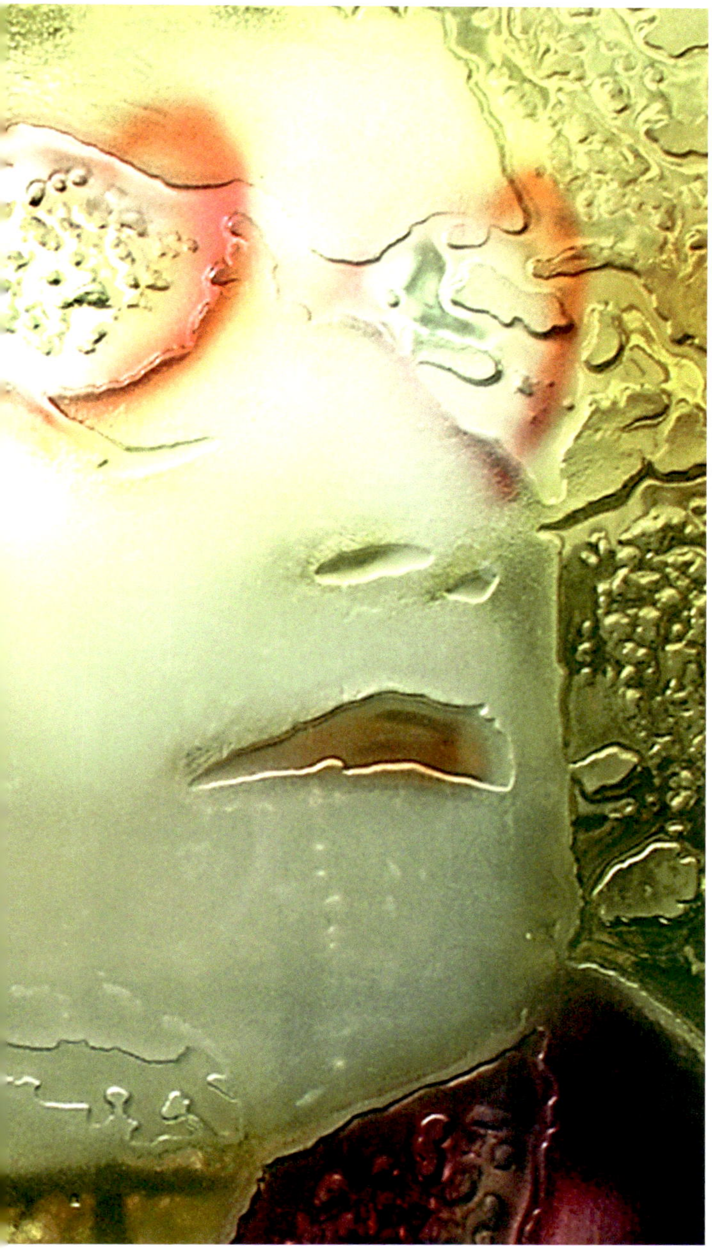

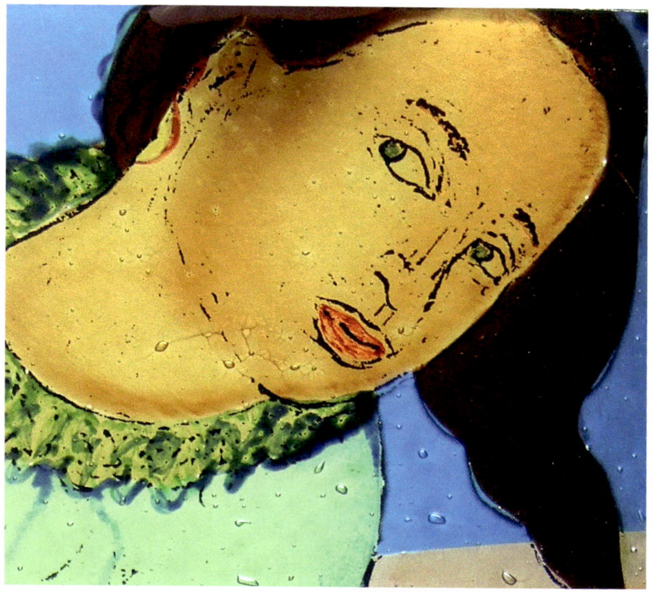

575

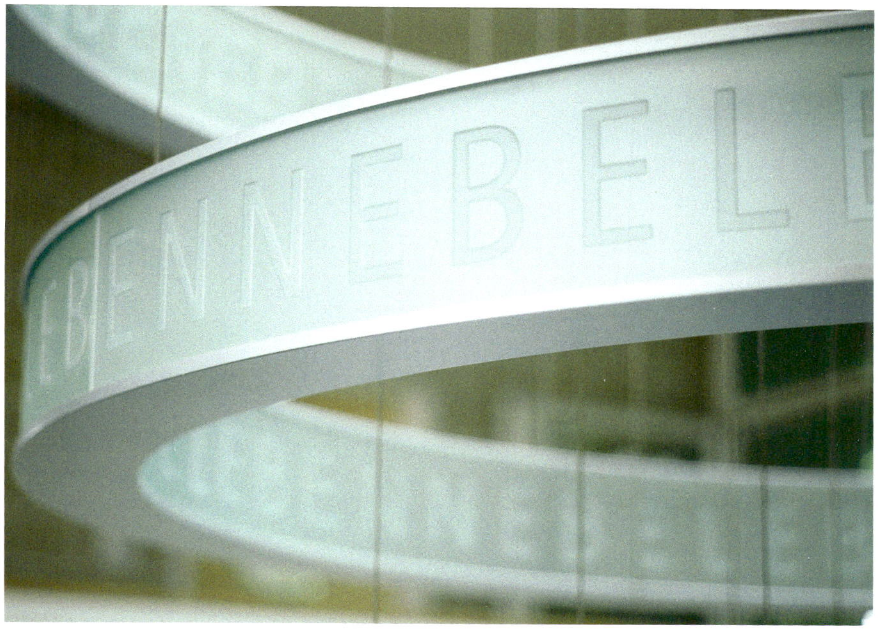

576

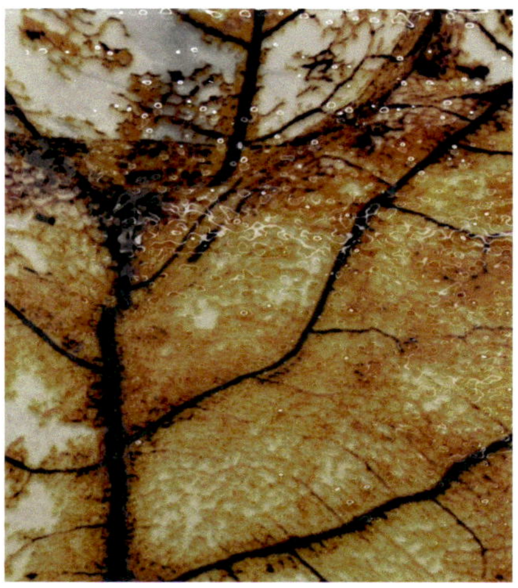

577

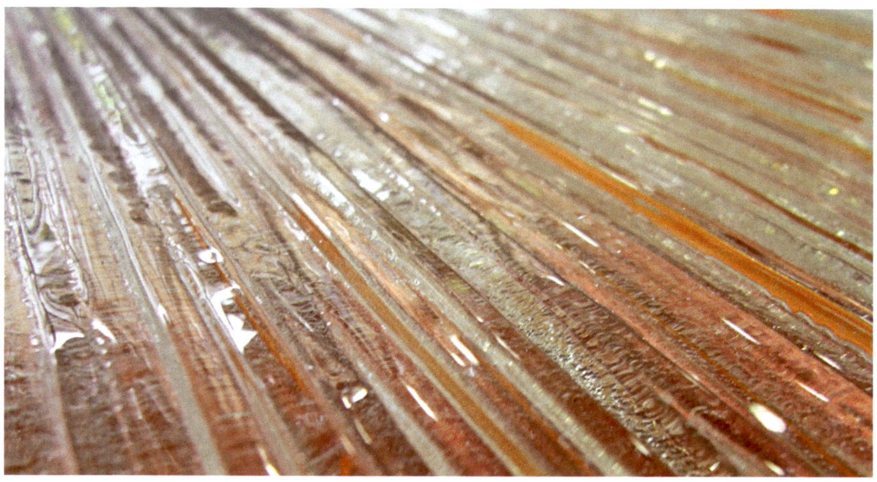

578

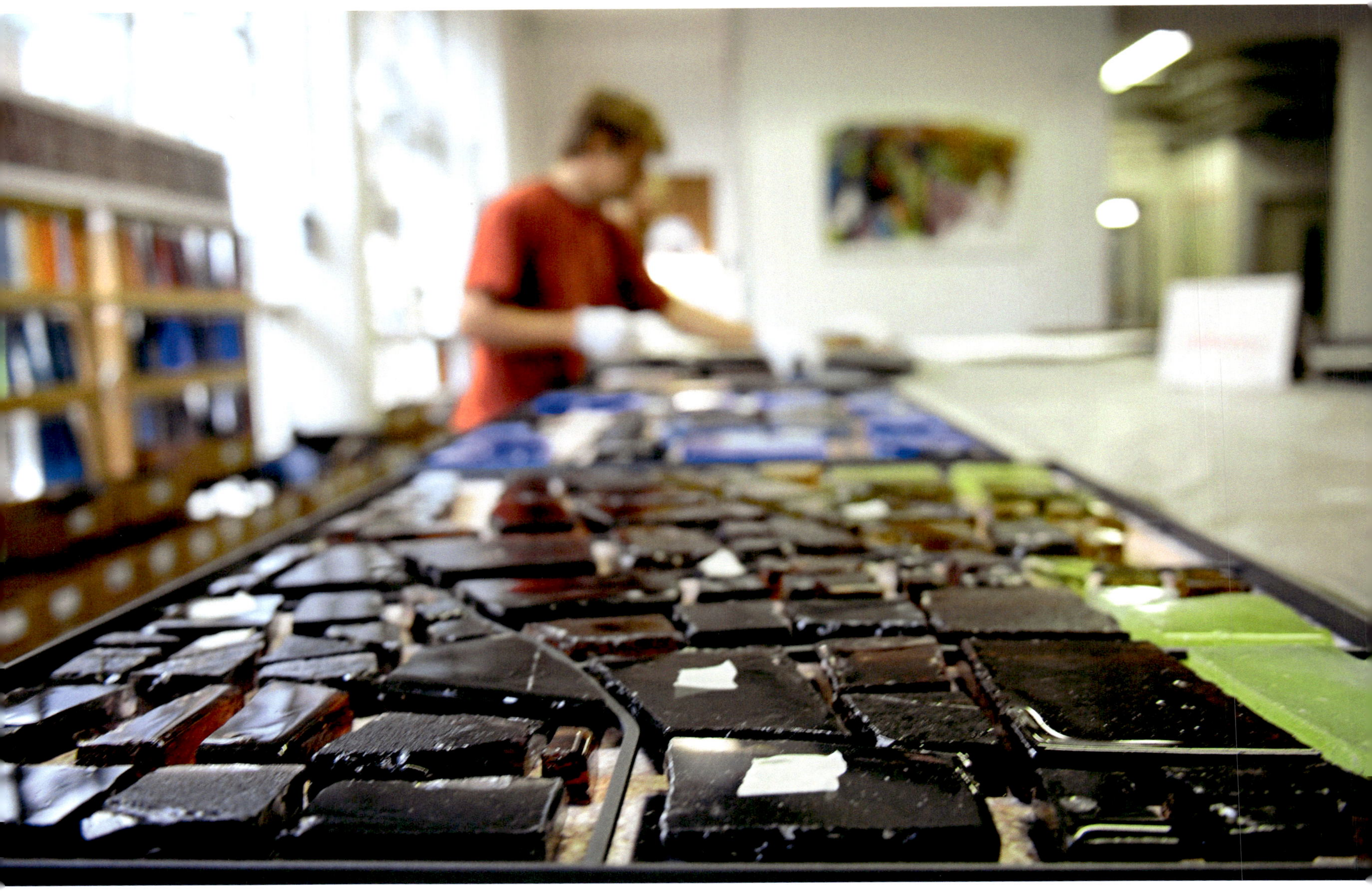

579

For many years so called faceted glass has been produced very rarely in Europe. Therefore, and the more it was exciting for the architects, the Hofkunstanstalt and their clients when at the EU Congress Center in Luxemburg the 130-feet-long faceted glass wall dating from the 1960's was rediscovered, restored, and reconstructed – resulting in a combination of 1960's art with contemporary glass technology. In New York City's Coney Island, Robert Wilson created monumental and gaudy glass brickwalls about 240 feet long. Also in New York, Mike and Doug Starn's glass walls near the South Ferry Station are about 350 feet long and executed using a fusing technique.

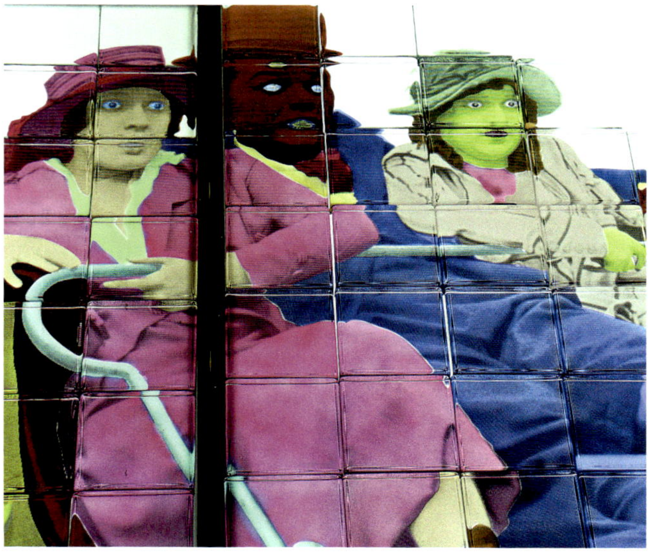

580

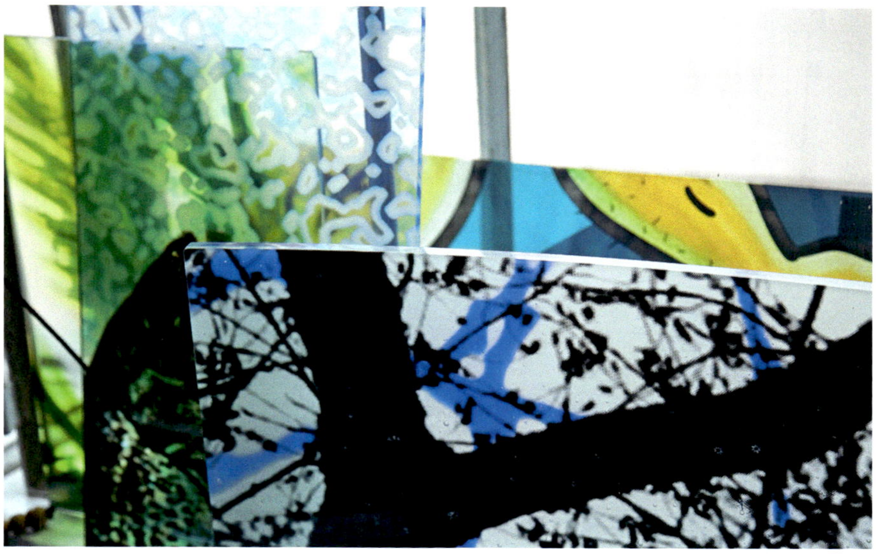

581

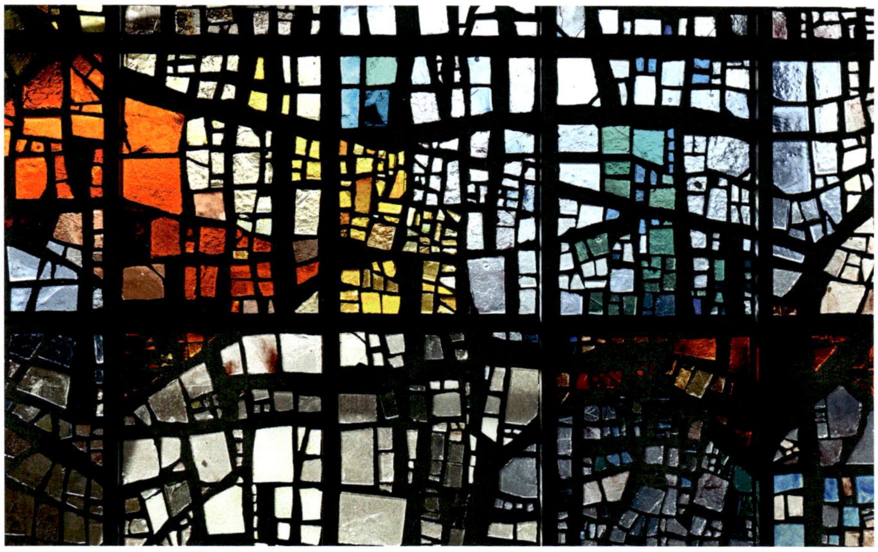

582

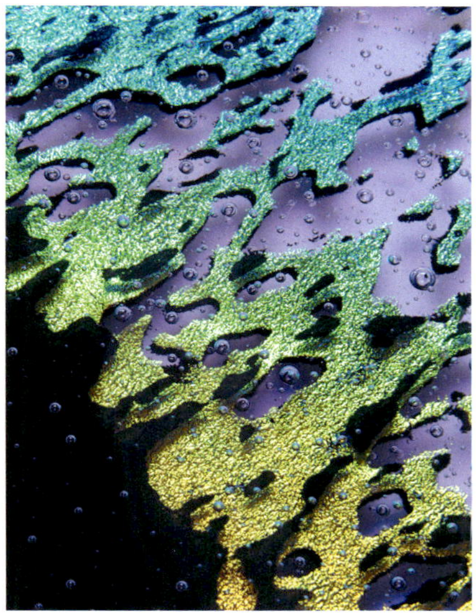

583

THICK GLASS SOLUTIONS

579 +
582

Thick glass pieces from the large Luxemburg faceted glass walls placed on the worktable: disassembled, cleaned, and repaired; and upon completion *(see p. 98 + 99)*.

580

Robert Wilson's windows, about 1½ inches thick, seen here after firing but before lamination.

581 +
583

Experimental fusing glass pieces from the Starns' project.

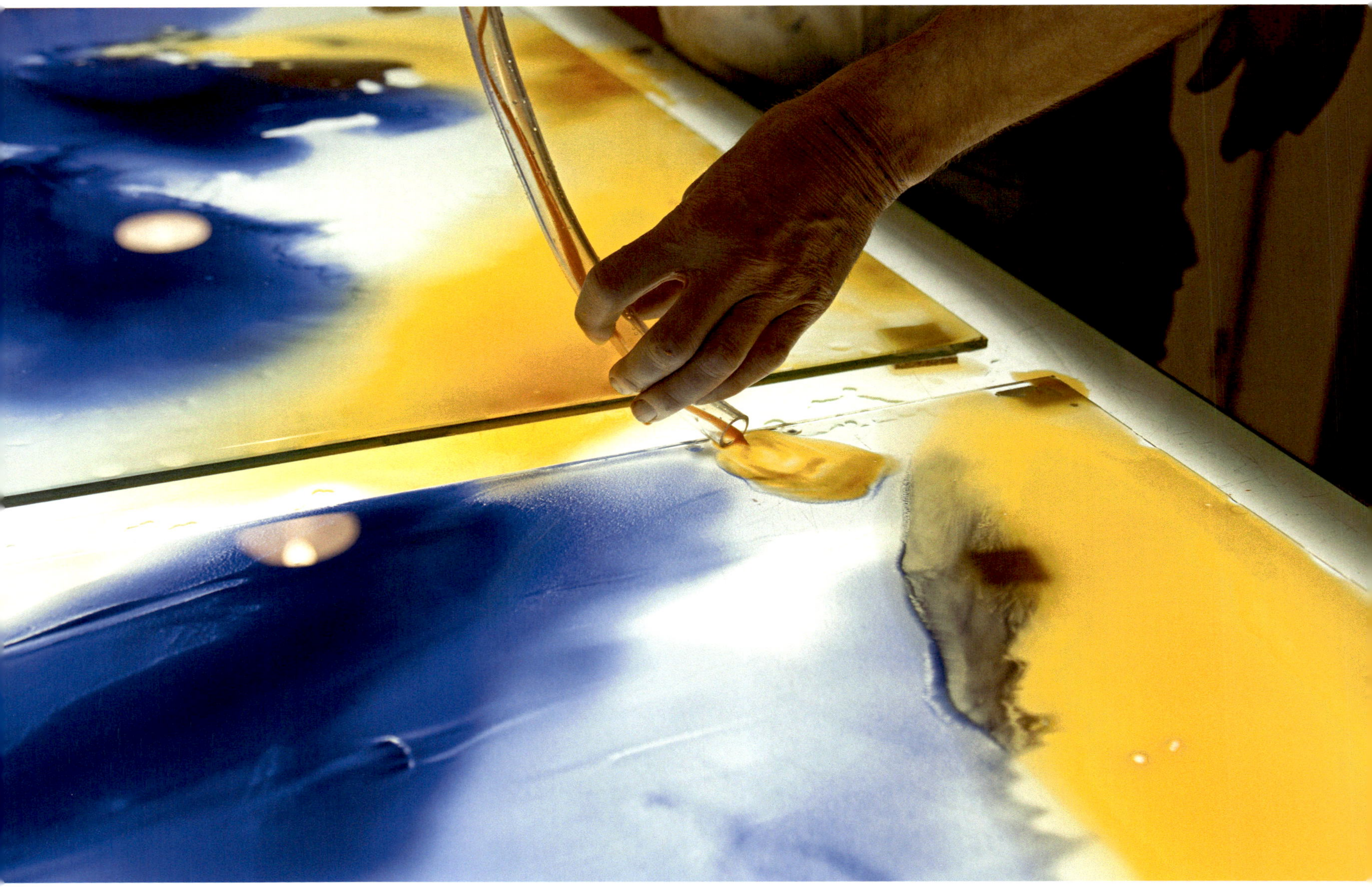

584

Float Glass Painting

A modern type of updated glass design in contemporary architecture

The Mayer'sche Hofkunstanstalt was involved in developing float glass painting. The first big project using this technique was realized in 1985. It was the so-called "artistic glass tent," based on ideas and designs of architect Frei Otto and his daughter, artist Bettina Otto-Matthes, and done in cooperation with them. Today it is customary to employ silkscreen and digital printing when working with ceramic glass melting colors; this is largely a result of the initial works produced by the Munich workshop. However, the Mayer'sche Hofkunstanstalt has developed the significance of float glass painting extensively since then. The plethora of illustrated projects may be seen as proof.

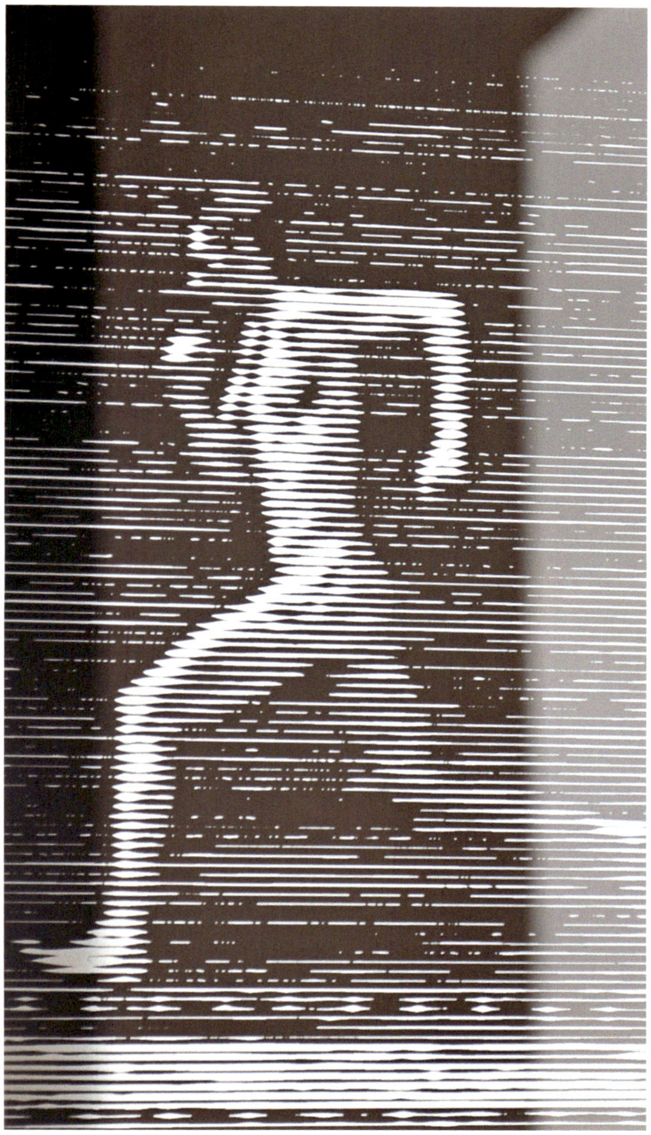

585

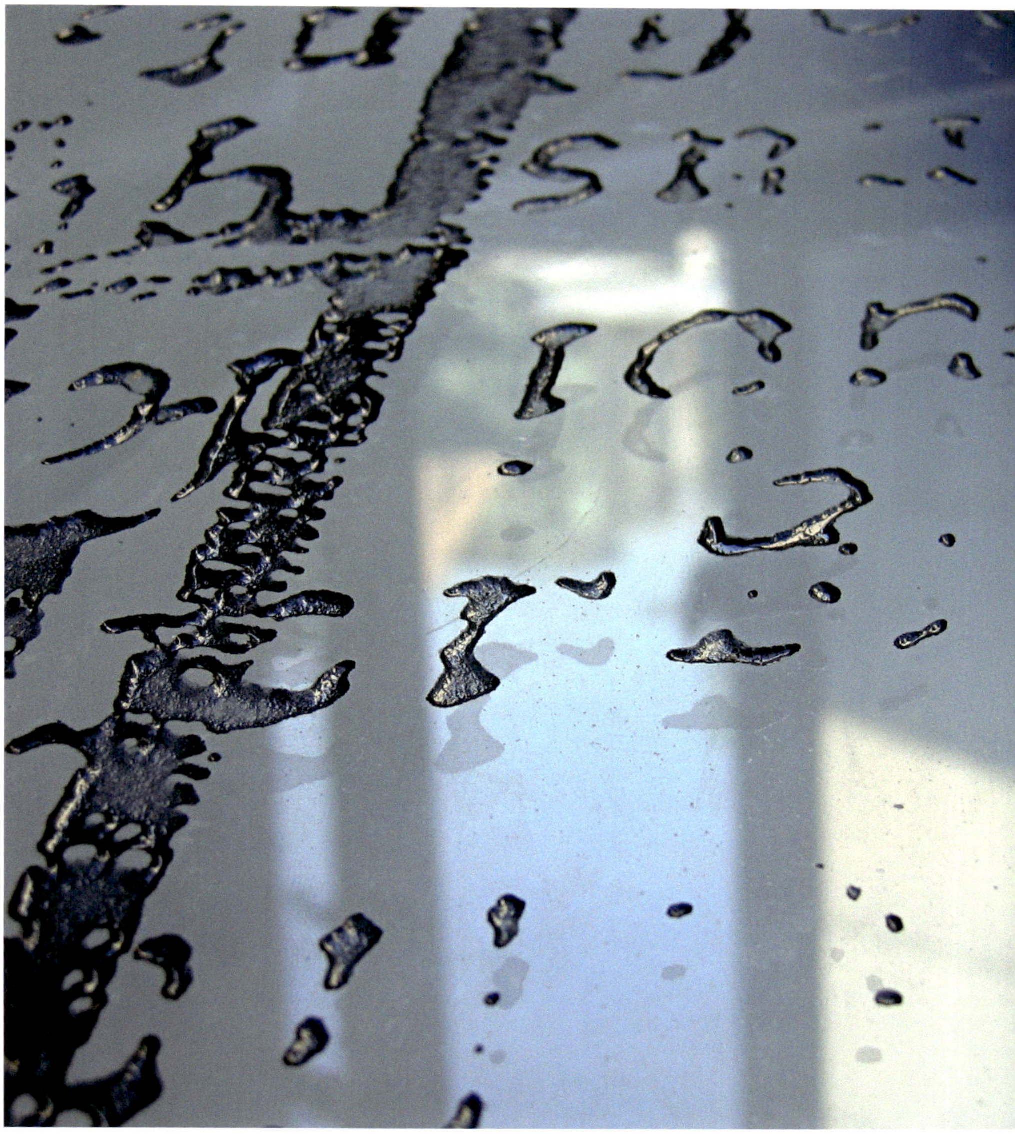

586

FLOAT GLASS PAINTING

584
Pouring of predominantly transparent enamel paints for Joachim Jung's project for the Munich headquarters of the Linde AG *(see p. 120–123)*.

585
Mirror plane, applied to the glass using a magnetron-sputter-process, surface sandblasting illustrated in a work by Felix Weinold *(see p. 214 + 215)*.

586
Ceramic color fired, engraving, and ceramic color infill.

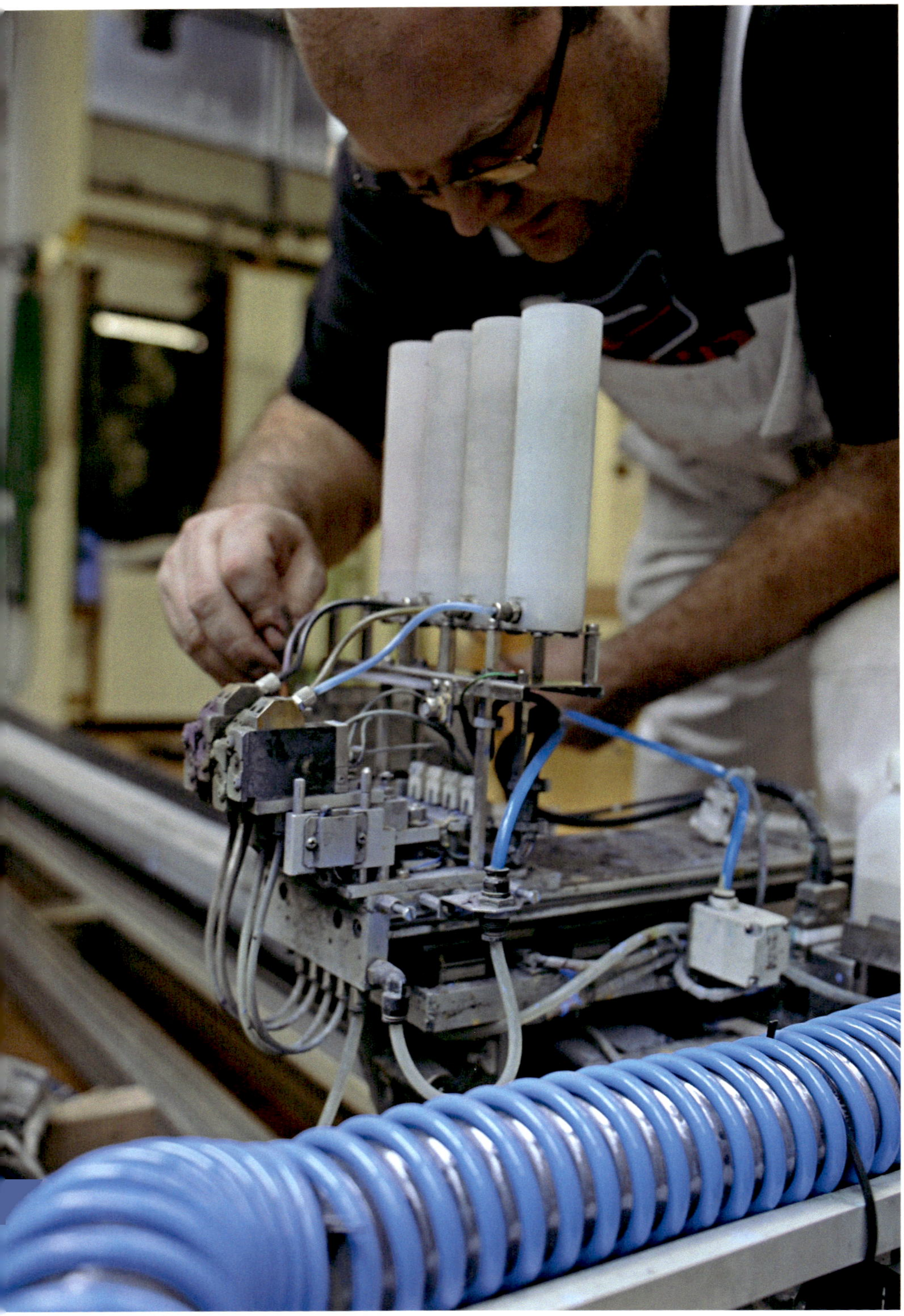

587

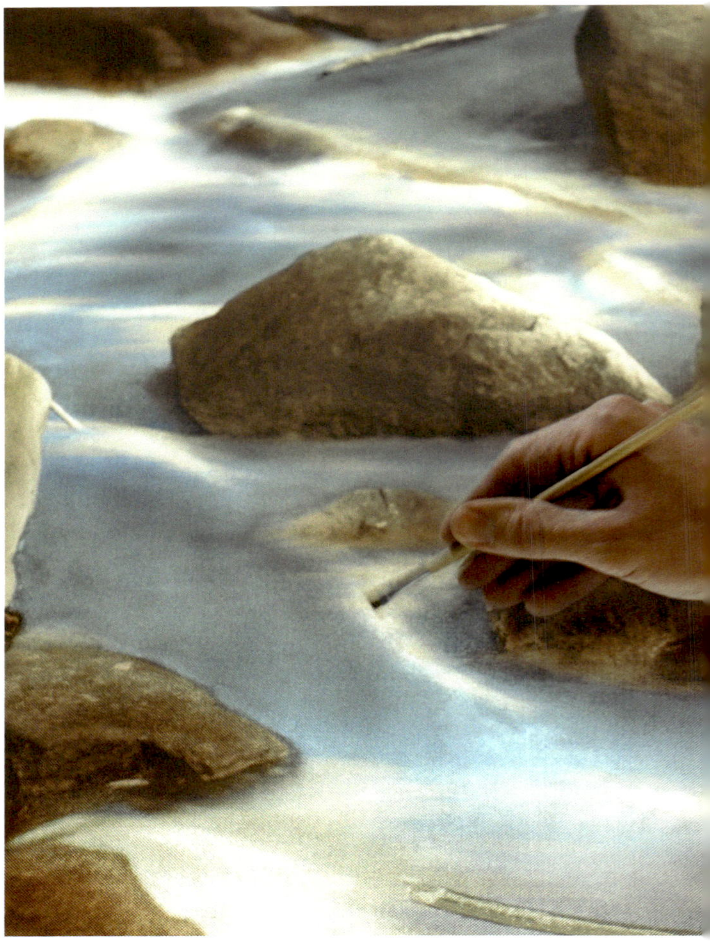

588

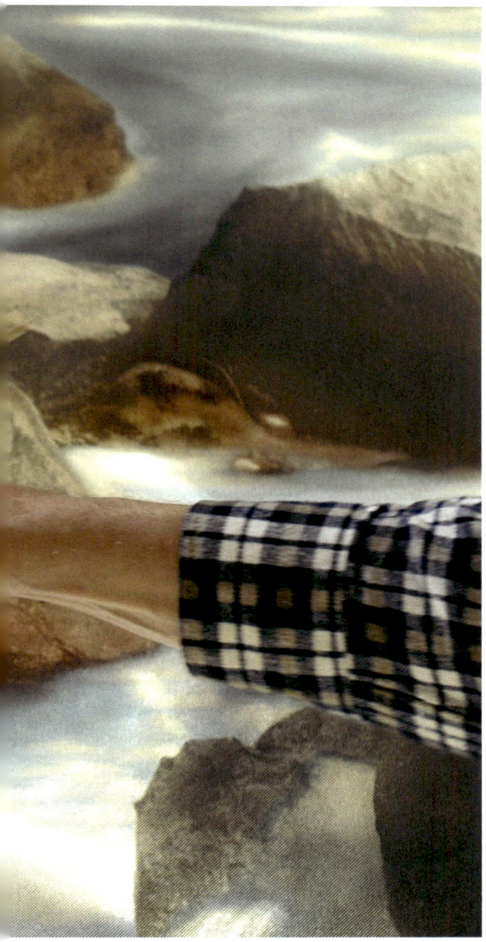

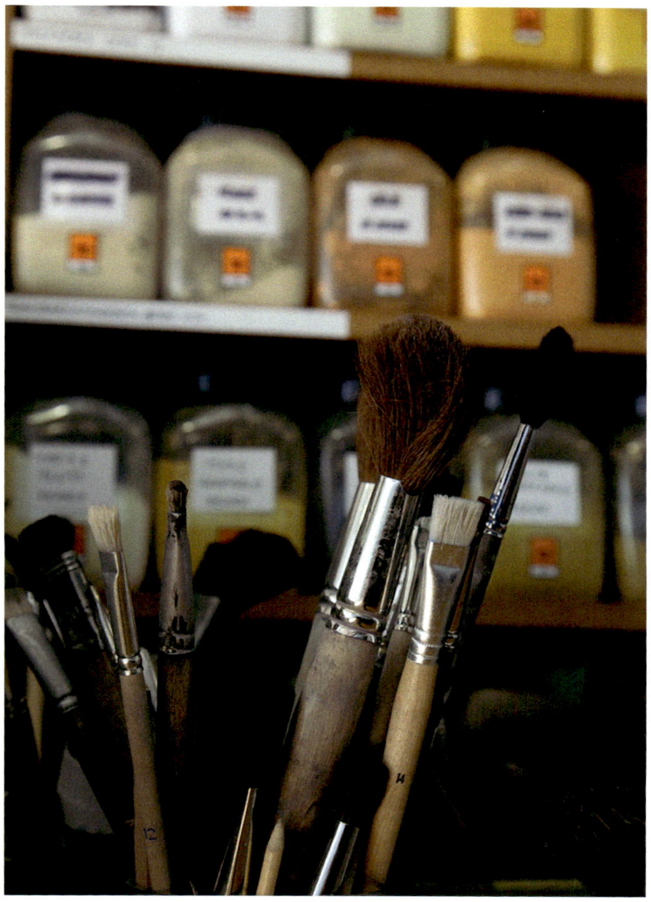

589

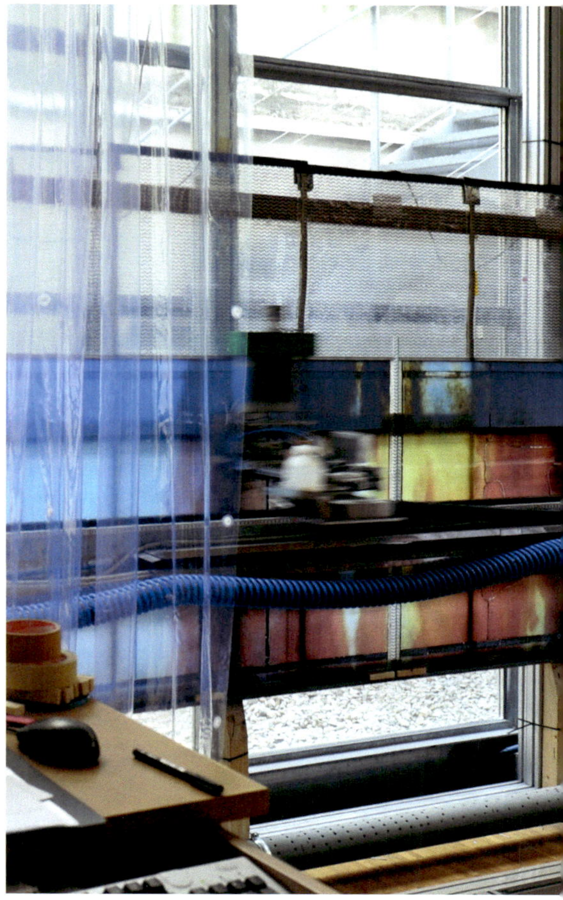

590

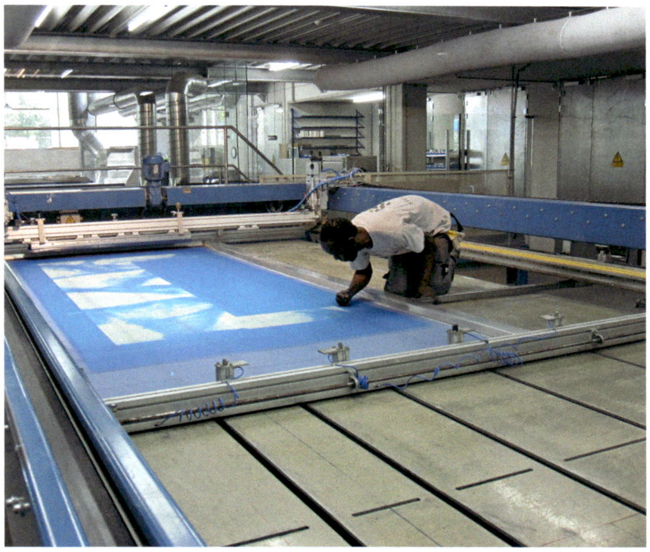

591

FLOAT GLASS PAINTING

587
The in-house digital printing machine is used among others to experiment with transparent glass melting colors.

588
Photographic float glass painting done by hand "like the coloring of the earliest black-and-white postcards" and using primarily transparent glass melting colors, printing, airbrush, and hand painting.

589
Ceramic glass melting colors, paint brushes.

590
Digital print with transparent ceramic colors.

591
Large silkscreen on glass, here seen at a partner's industrial plant.

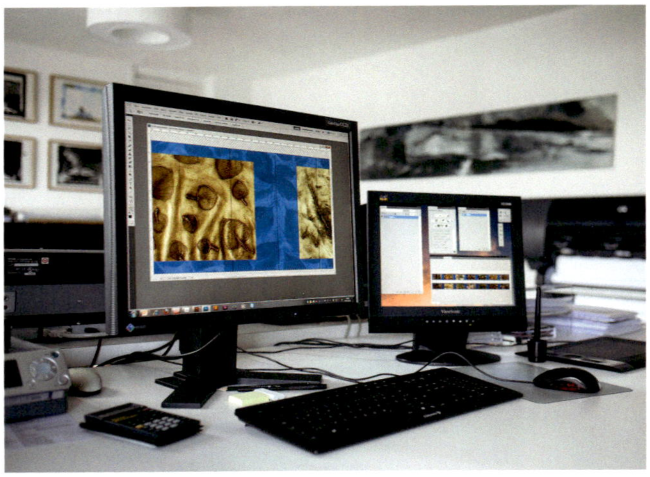

592

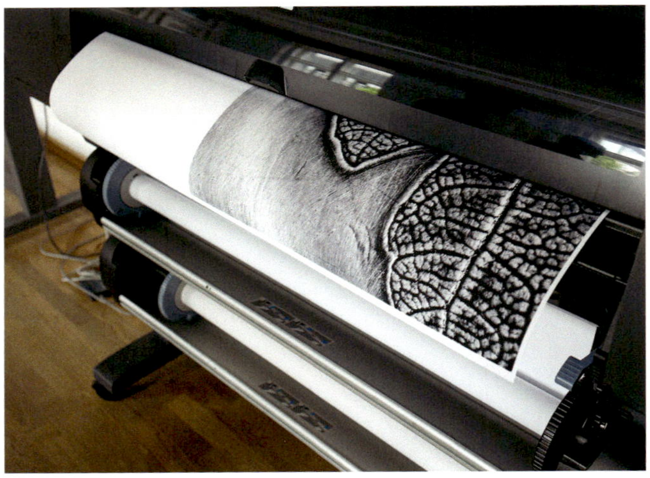

593

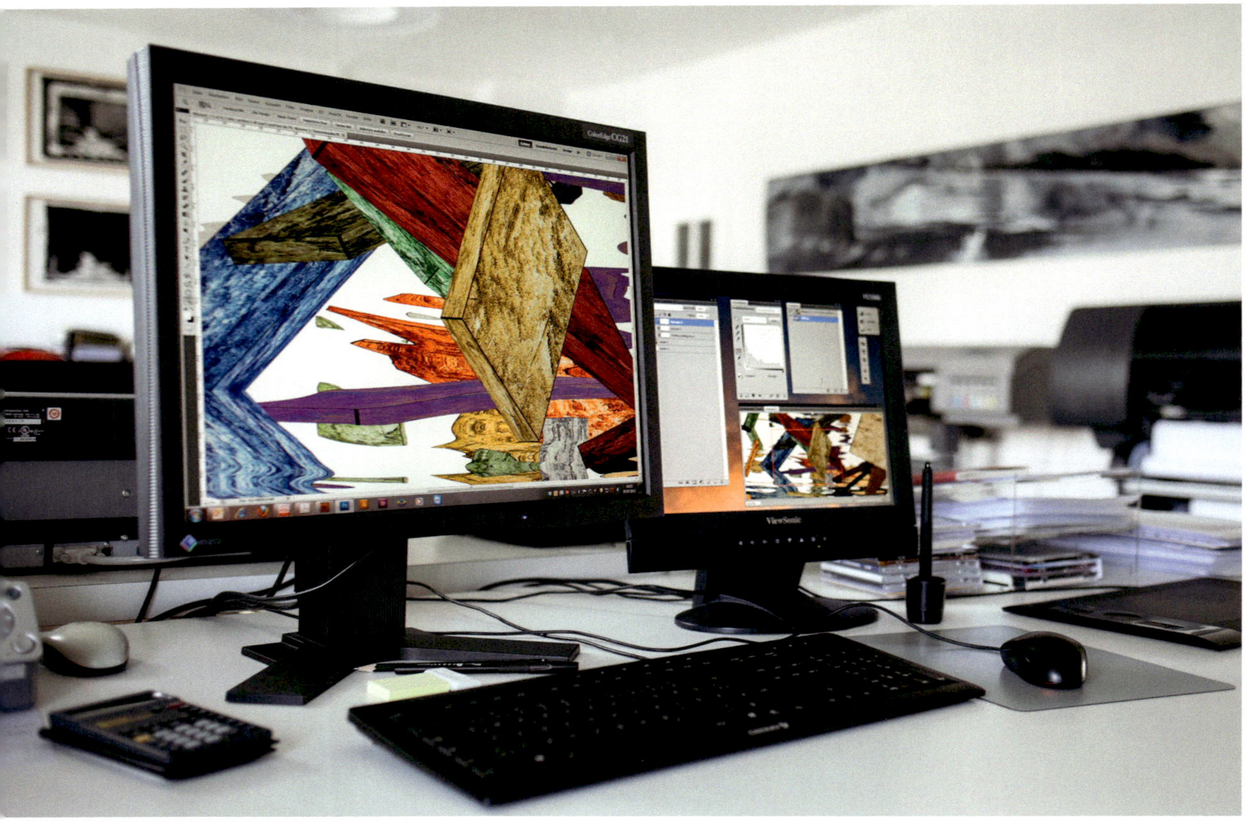

594

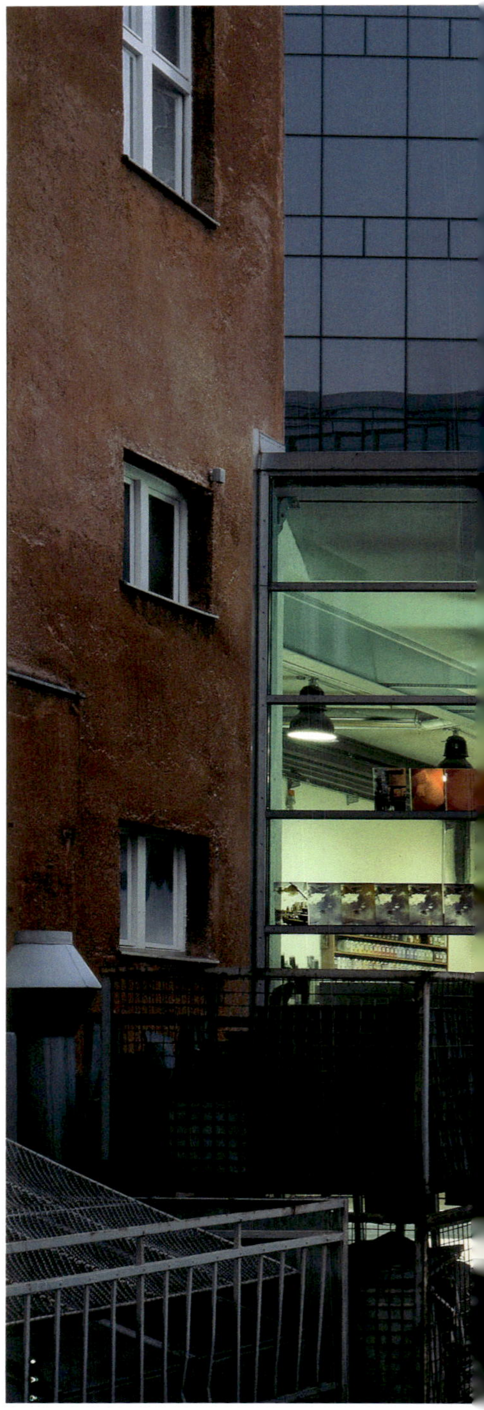

595

FLOAT GLASS PAINTING

592 – 594

"Computer still-life." Unlike traditional glass painting, float glass painting requires – apart from great hand-painting skills – advanced experience in computer technologies.

595

The new two-story building for float glass painting from 2001.

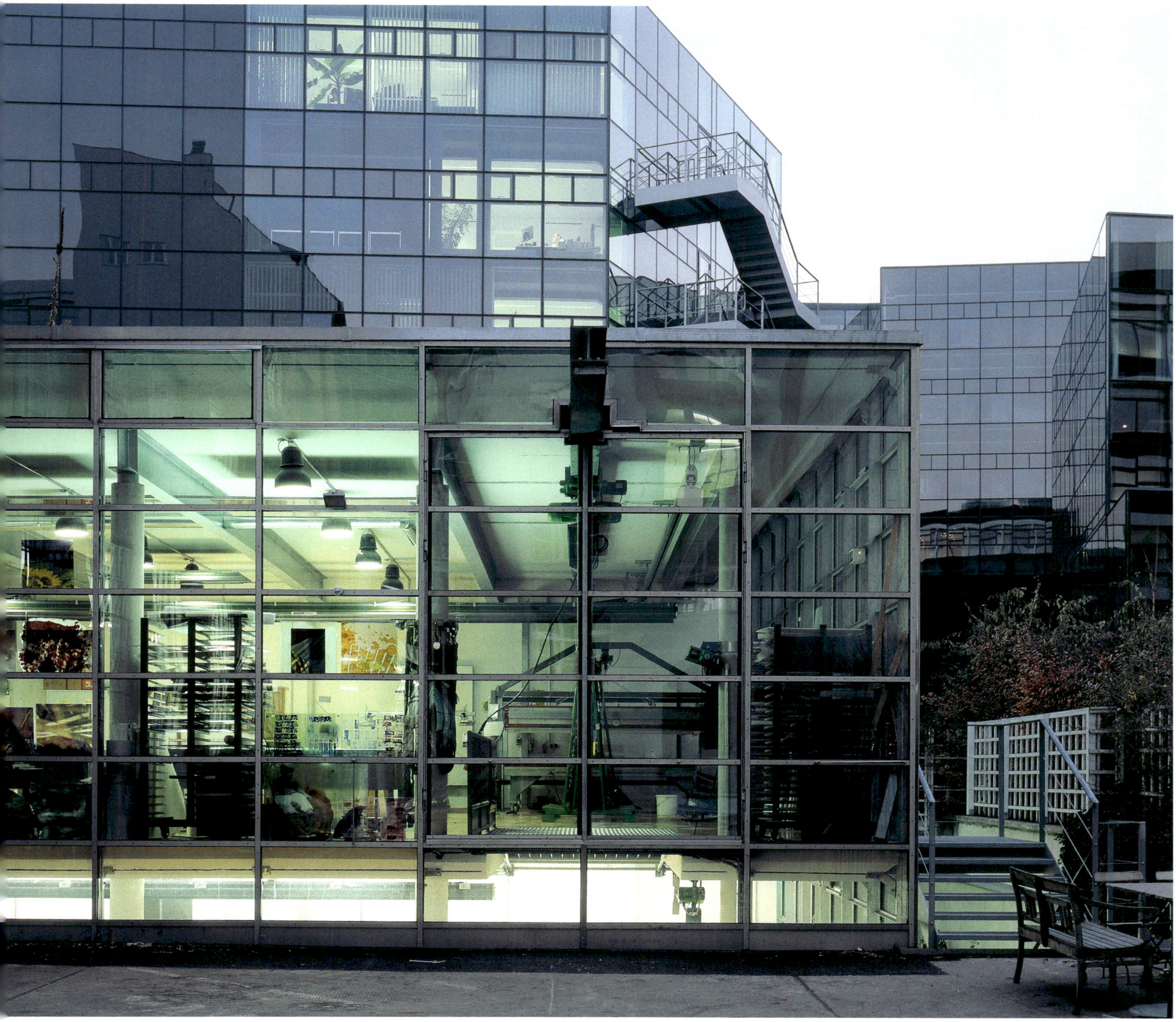

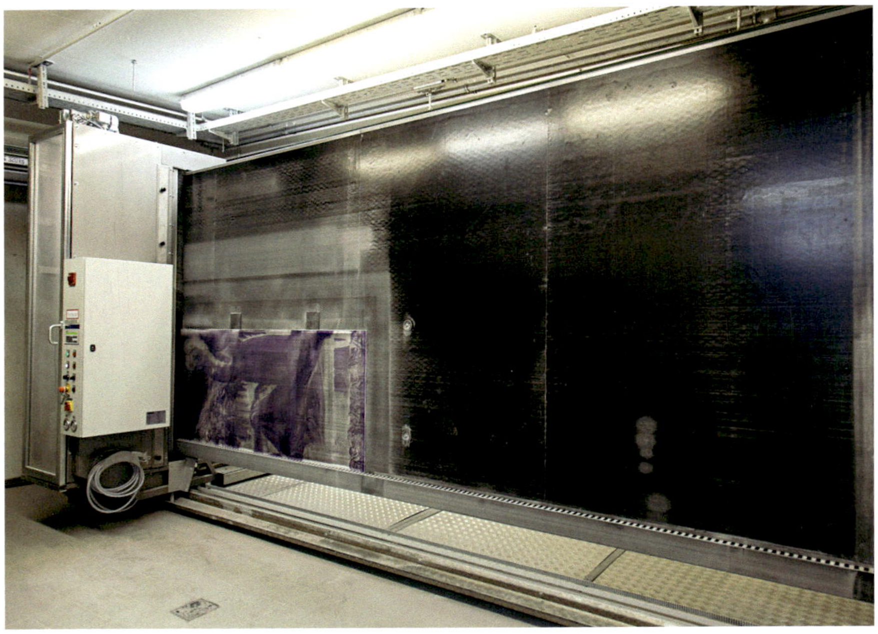
596

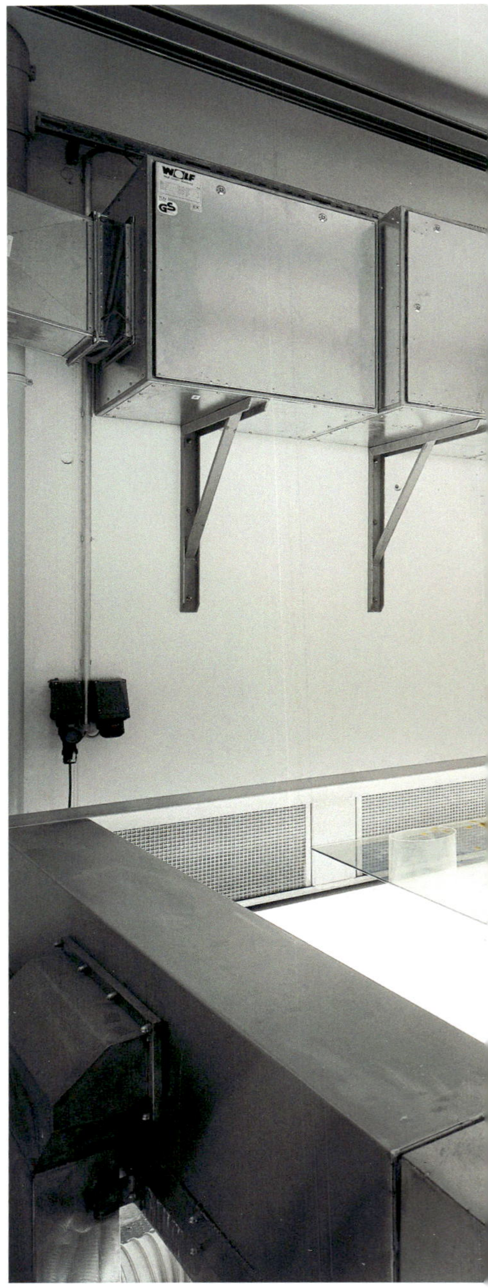

598

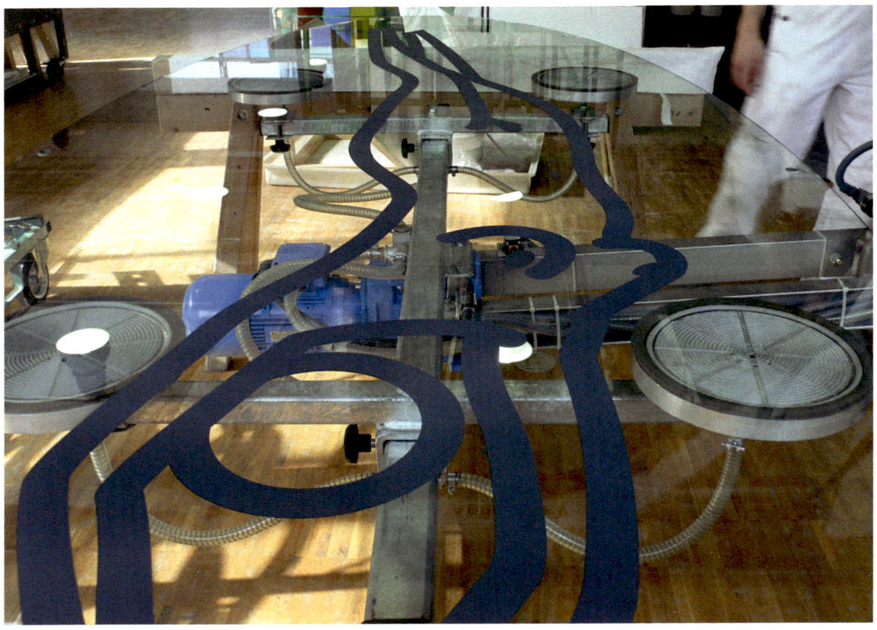
597

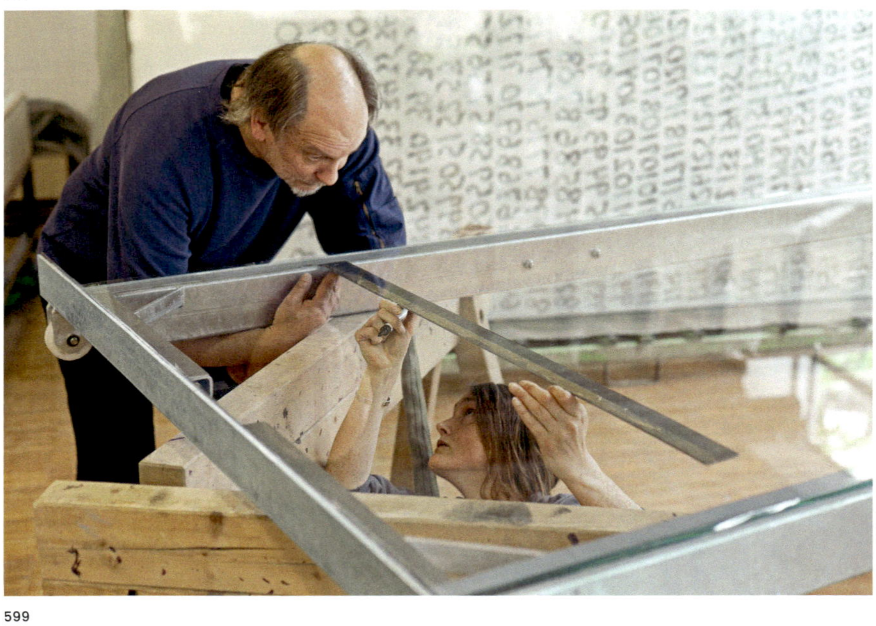
599

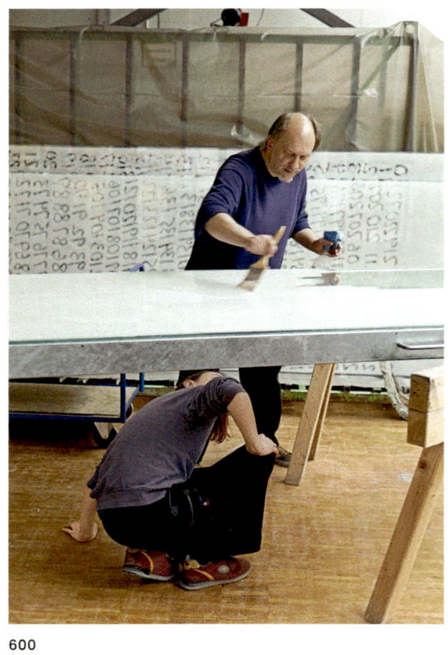
600

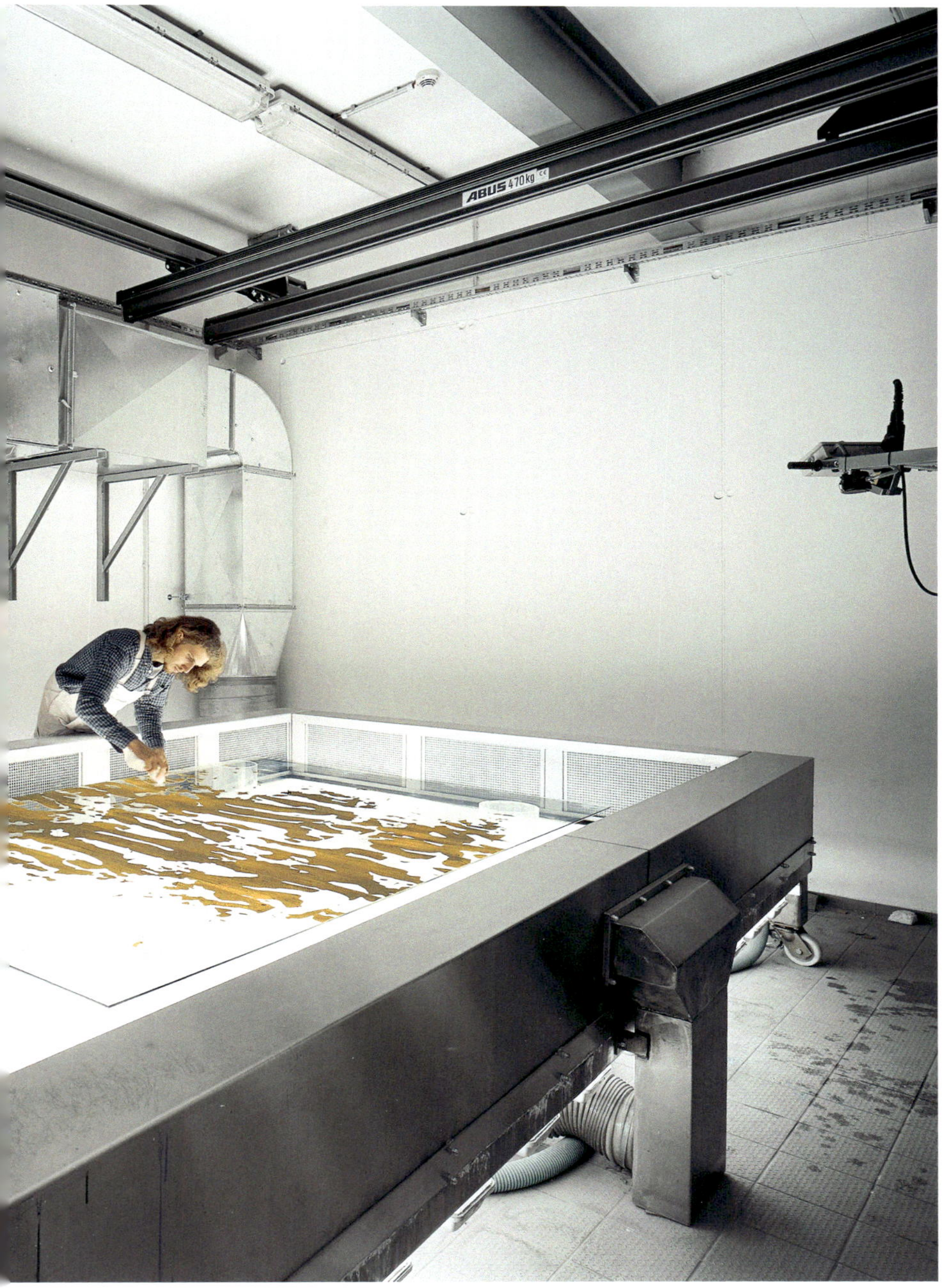

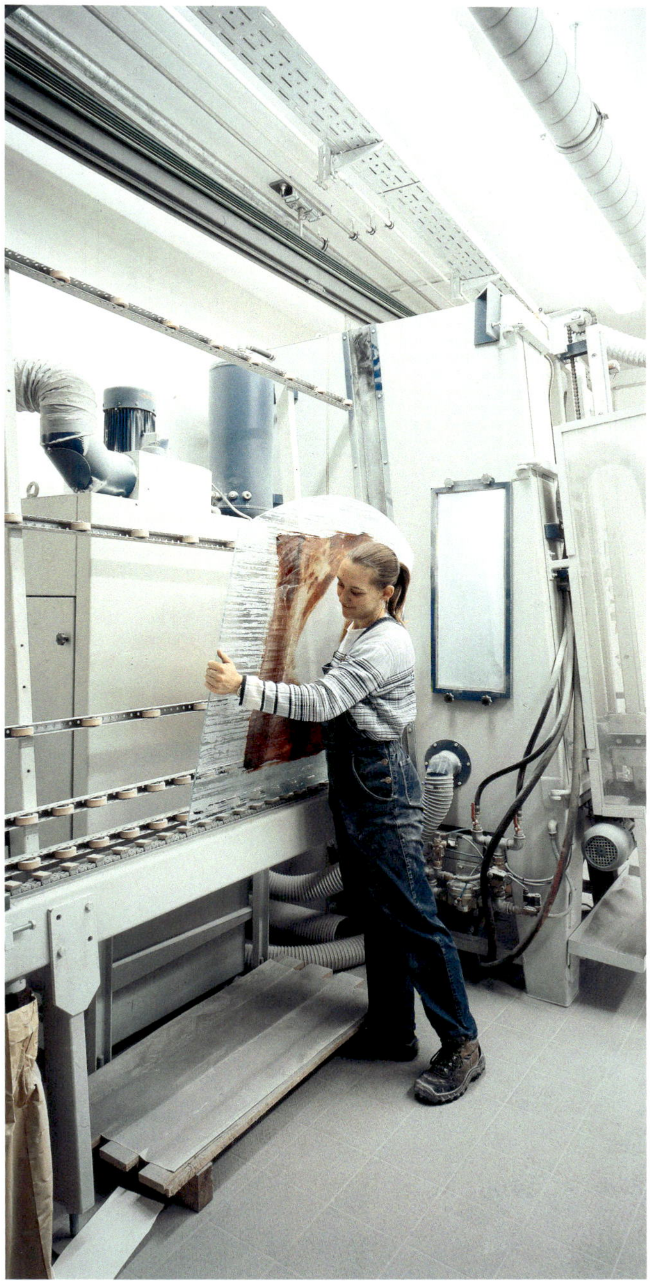

601

FLOAT GLASS PAINTING

596
Unusual for a stained glass enterprise: Large hi-tech devices such as this sand-blasting machine.

597
Glass vacuum cups for the underside of the glass panels are required because in many work processes the ceramic paint on the surface has not yet been burned-in (this piece is by Julian Opie).

598
The airbrush space with air vacuum and filters, light table, and lifting device.

599 + 600
Preparing the glass for Mel Bochner. Elaborate constructions were required to create a convenient work environment for the artist.

601
The "old" sandblasting device. The function of sandblasting in float glass painting is comparable to the etching or erasing used in traditional stained glass painting.

FLOAT GLASS PAINTING

602
Silkscreen, airbrush, matting – in a work by Klaus von Gaffron.

603
Printed script and blue masking in a work by Bridget Jones.

604
Engraving and color in-fills in a motif from the Hofkunstanstalt's archives.

605
"Elevated" and indirect silkscreen print with ceramic glass-melting paint – in one of Alexander Beleschenko's projects.

606
Solid hand painting in a project by Michelle Oka Dona.

607
(Nearly) photo-realistic rendering using print, airbrush, and hand painting applying primarily ceramic glass-melting colors.

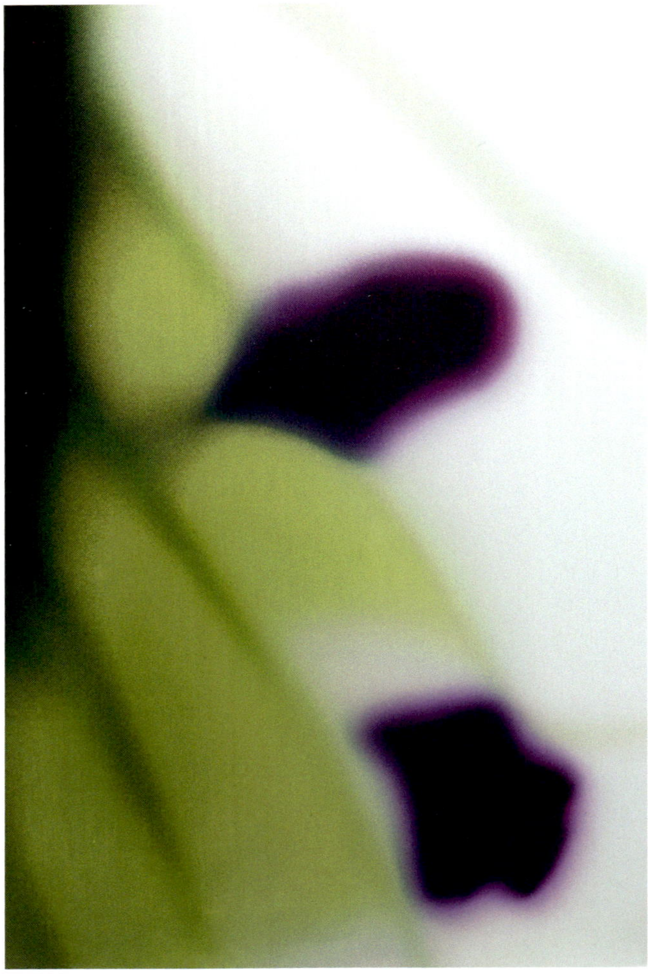

602

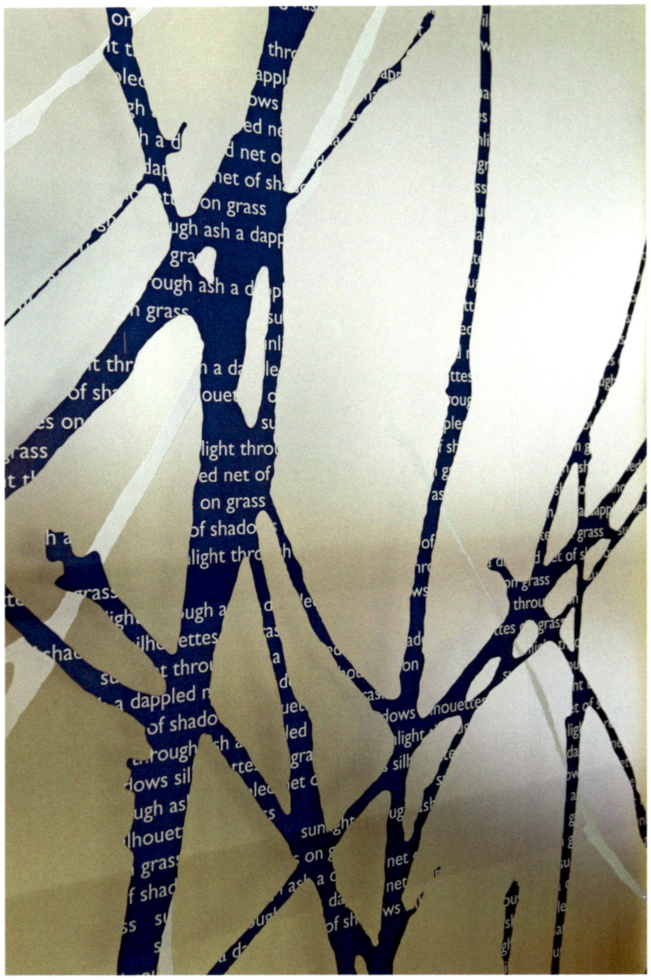

603

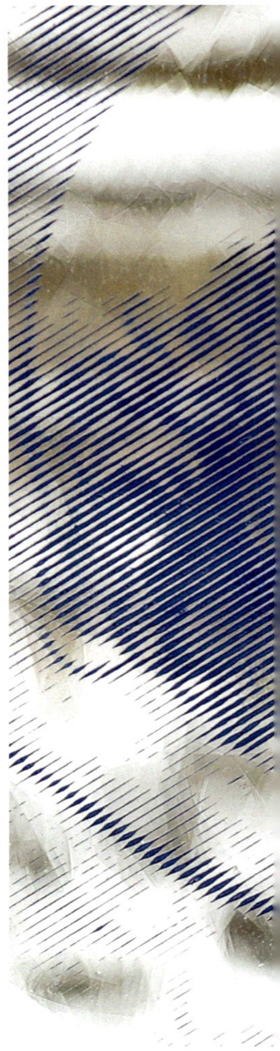

604

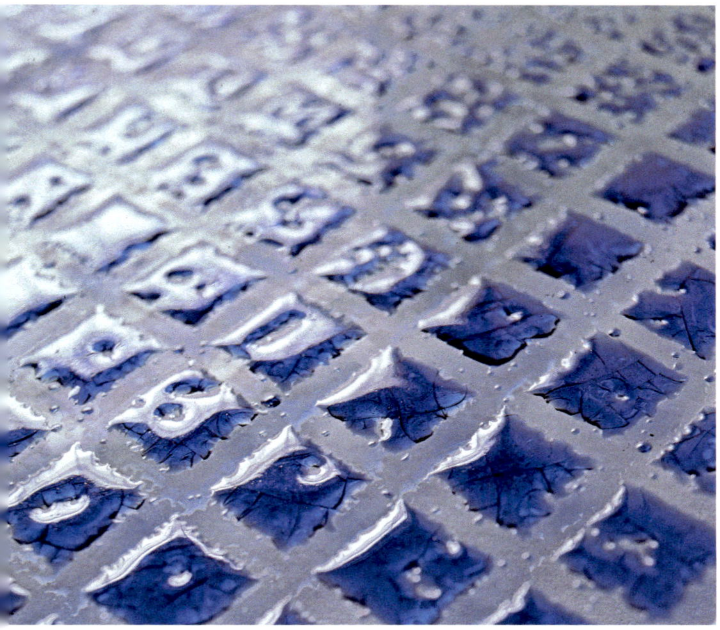

605

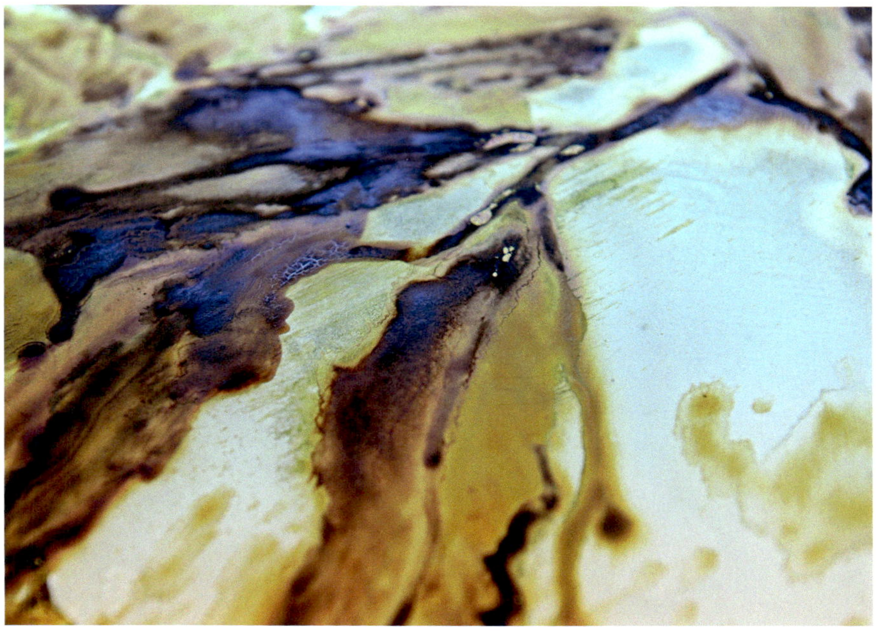

606

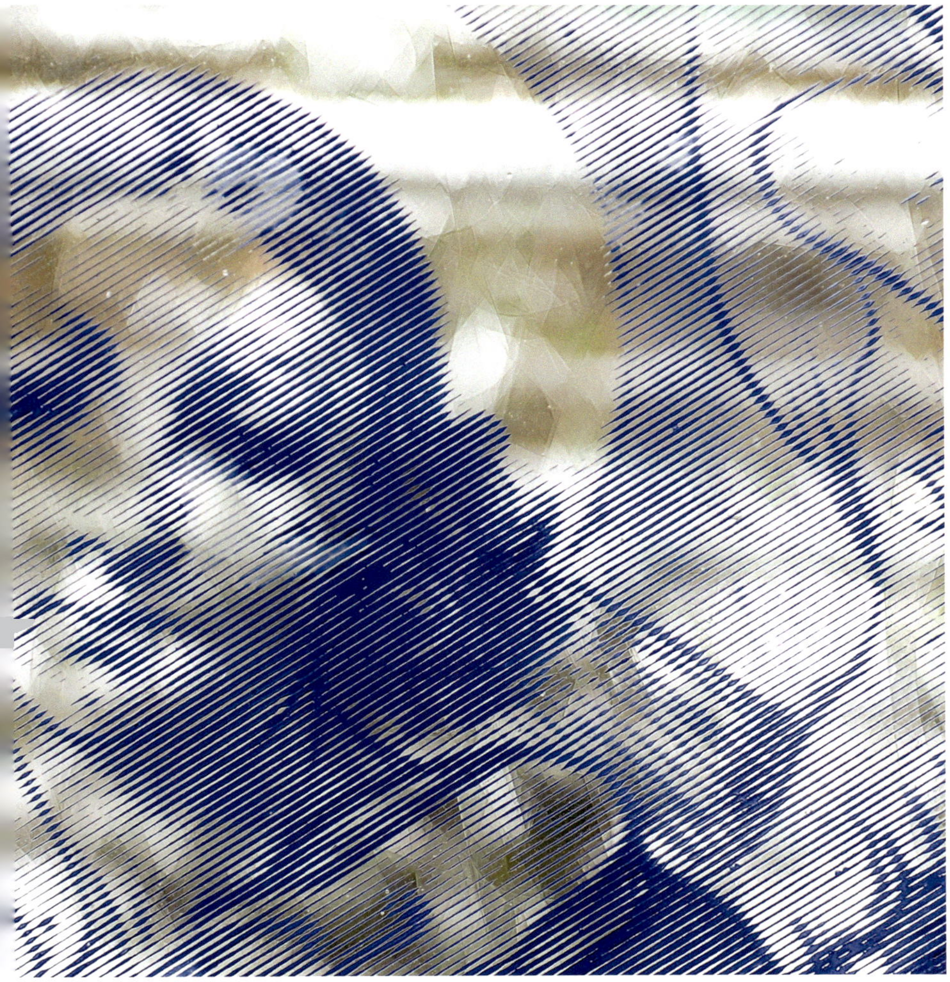

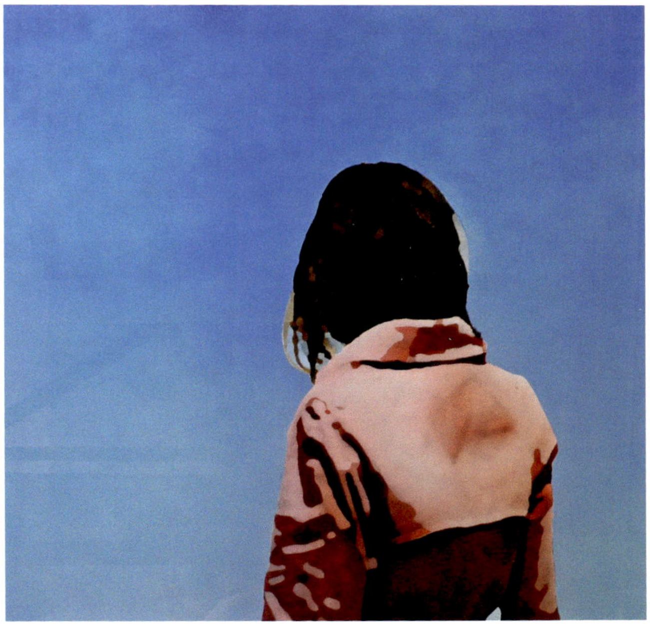

607

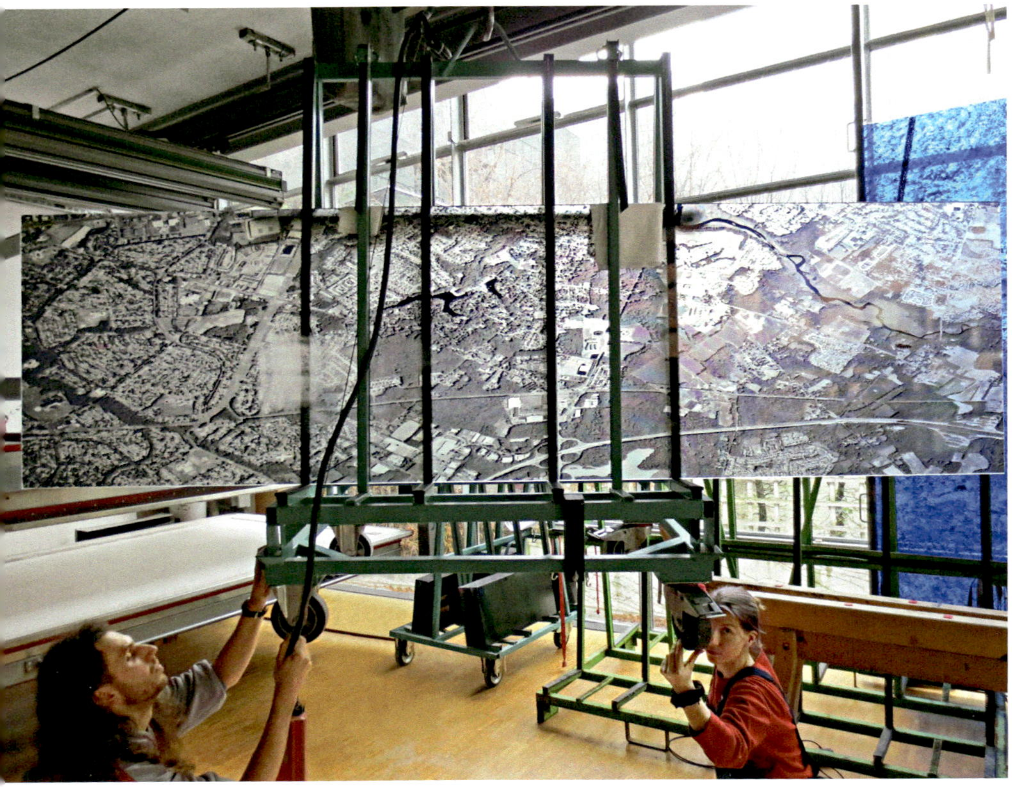

608

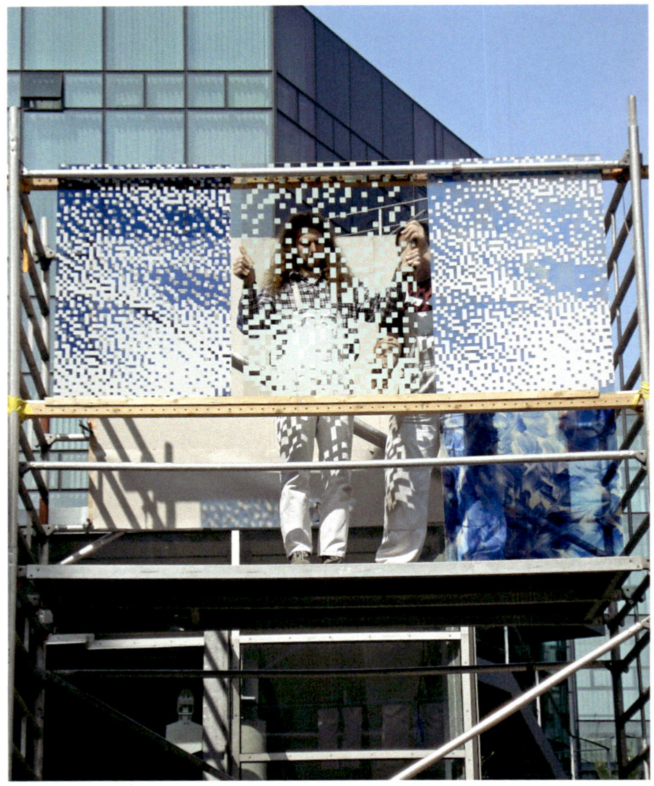

609

The Effects of Light and Space

Gothic glass paintings were incredibly innovative: they shaped architecture and space by using glass and light. These radiant paintings illustrated biblical contents and were intended to make imagining a divine sphere possible. Yet the gaze only went in one direction: from the inside to the outside – from darkness to light. Contemporary glass design applied in modern glass and steel architecture must do justice to any number of light and space constellations: Transmitted light – glass situated in front of bright daylight or placed before a dark background – glass with incident light, glass design supposed to be seen from two sides – glass painting with back, lateral, day, and artificial light sources – effects from close-up and from the distance.
Usually, the designs show an ideal. And it is exactly this supreme model that should become reality using fantasy, skill, diligence, and also passion. A major task. A good studio must also serve as consultant for light and space in an anticipated project. It must reflect all the influences light and space have on a situation, talk them through and even simulate them with the artist using experiments and mock-ups. The decision must be left to the artist. A good workshop must also help the artist to request and to attain appropriate on-site conditions.

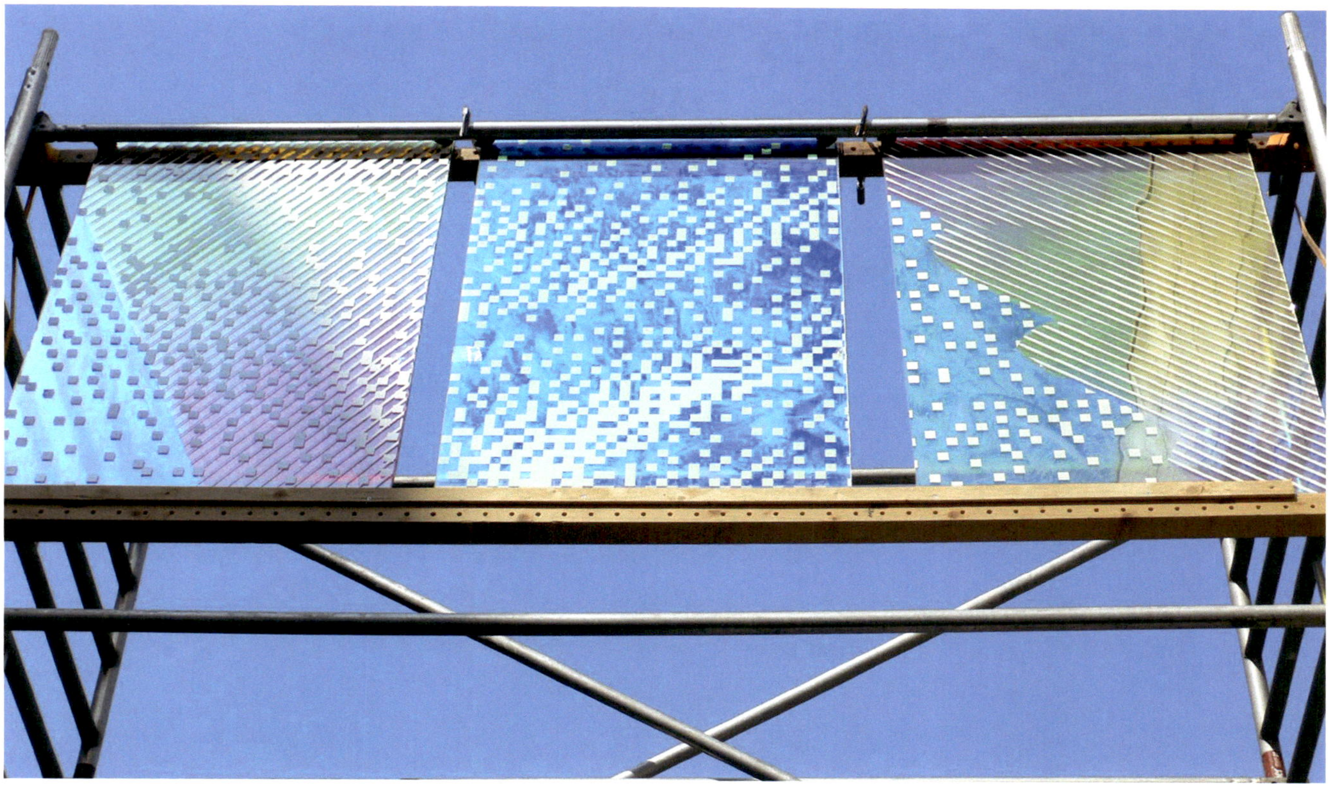

610

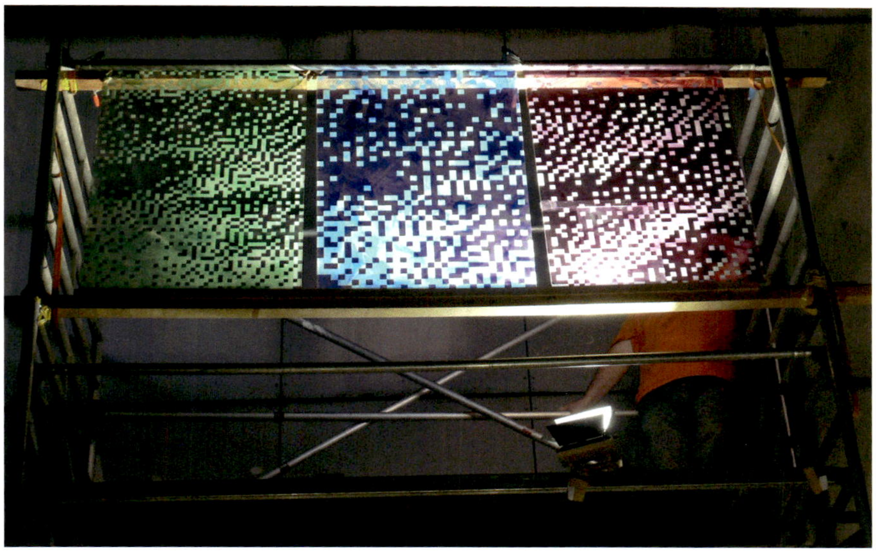

611

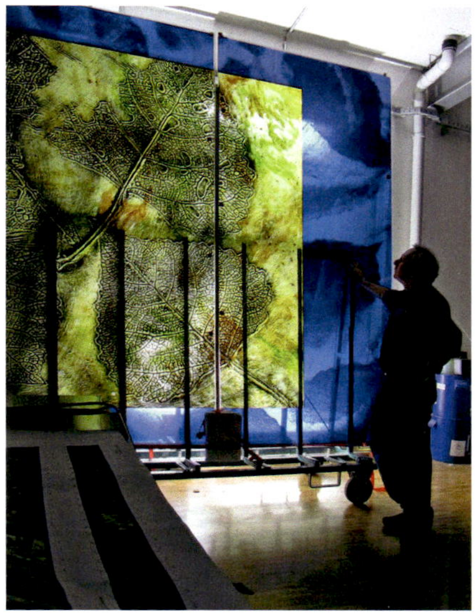

612

LIGHT'S INFLUENCE

608
Craftspeople lift up a pane from Jan Baracz's and Ellen Harvey's Philadelphia Airport project, creating a light situation similar to the site.

609 – 611
Outside and on scaffold: experiments with light for Norie Sato's glass project for the San Francisco International Airport *(see p. 178–181).*

609
The glass against the facade in the background.

610
Against the sky.

611
At night and with artificial light.

612
Artist and studio are thrilled because the last light test went well. The lighting system of Daniel Mayer's project for the Phoenix Sky Harbor was developed together and adjusted with the client (see p. *138 + 139*).

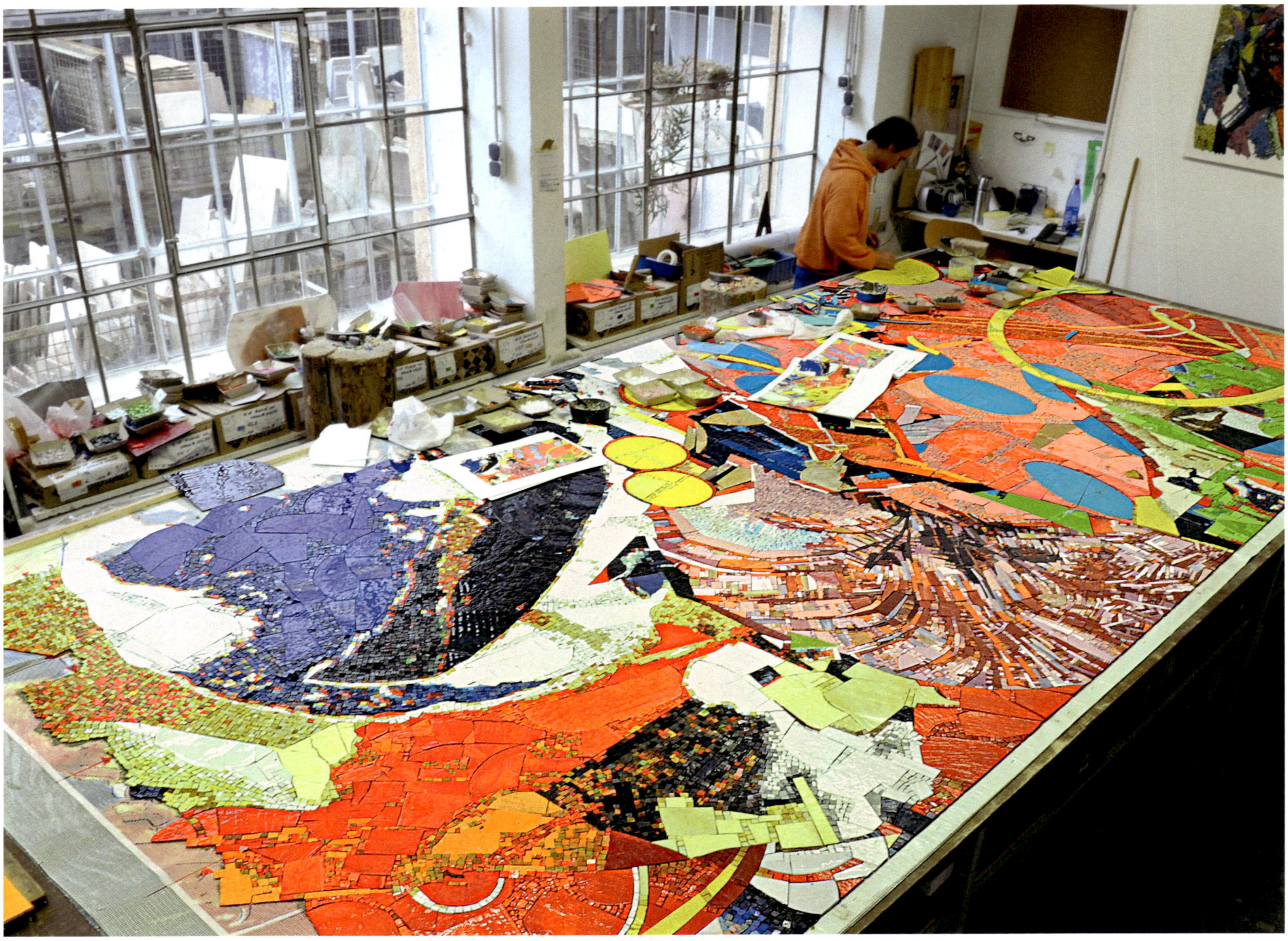

613

The Studio for Artistic Mosaic Design

Mosaic is among the oldest forms of architectural art

Rendering an artistic mosaic takes more than a certain versatility: It requires a special comprehension on the part of the contemporary artist as well as knowledge of how color and form are interrelated. Mosaic is an art form that is based upon the possibilities and the limitations of Impressionism and Pointillism; but it also shares characteristics with the collage. Each color dot is placed beside the next color dot; material beside material, form beside form. Contemporary artistic mosaic requires a rich stock of colors and types of mosaic materials.

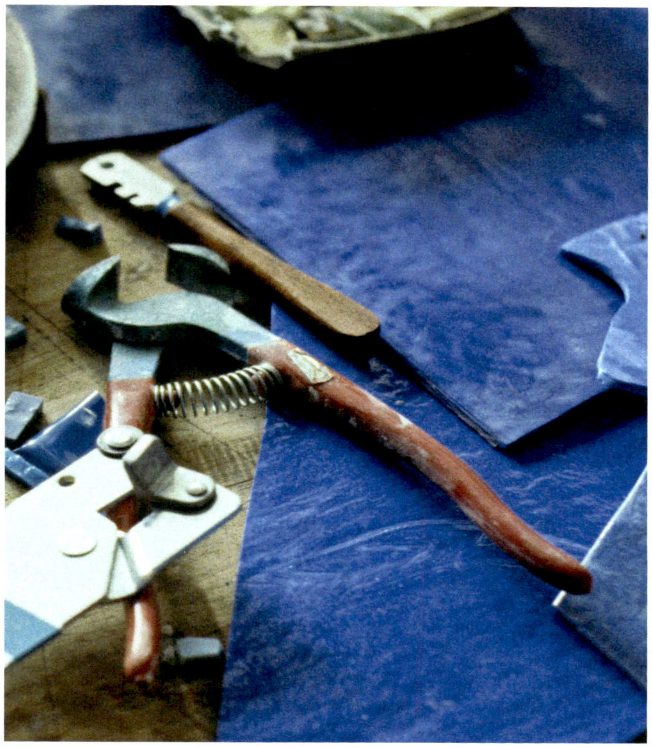

614

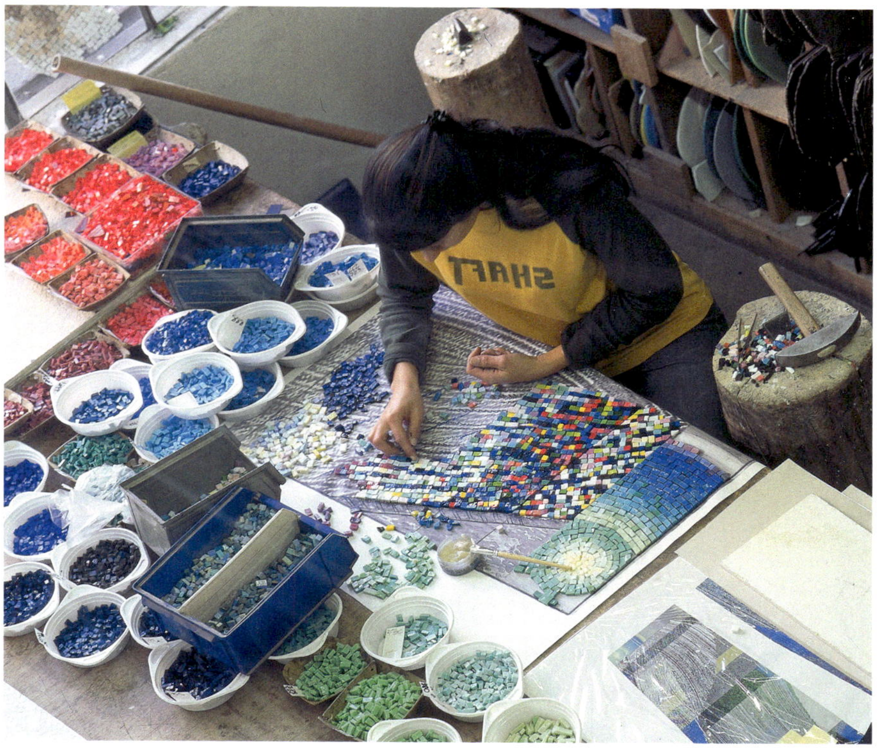

615

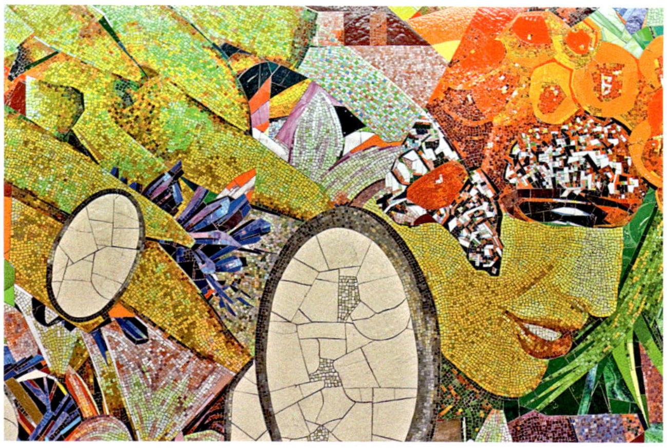

616

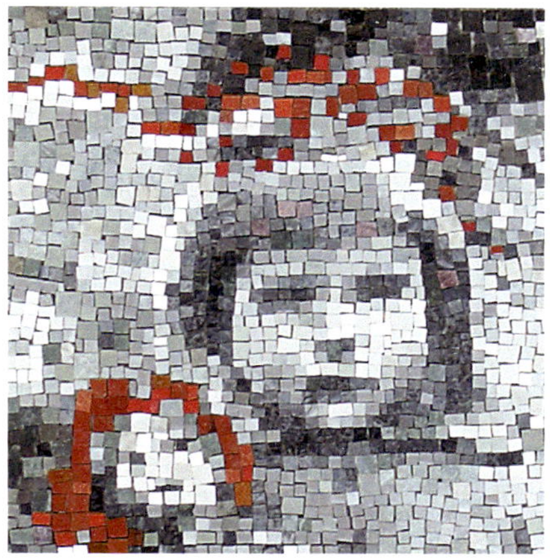

617

613
A major section of Stephen Johnson's work for the Universal City Metro Station in Los Angeles nearing completion on the worktable *(see p. 118 +119)*. When working on large-scale art mosaics the mosaicist must be able to see the composition in its entirety.

614
Venetian glass cake material and tools for cutting and breaking.

615
Detail from a mosaic by Heidi Lippman for the Holy Cross Hospital, Silver Spring, MD.

616
Another detail from Stephen Johnson's mosaic "Universal Delight:" the film diva, the mirrors, and the French fries.

617
Detail from a mosaic with a child's face and a doll from the mosaic bands by Ellen Driscoll for Kansas City *(see p. 82–83)*.

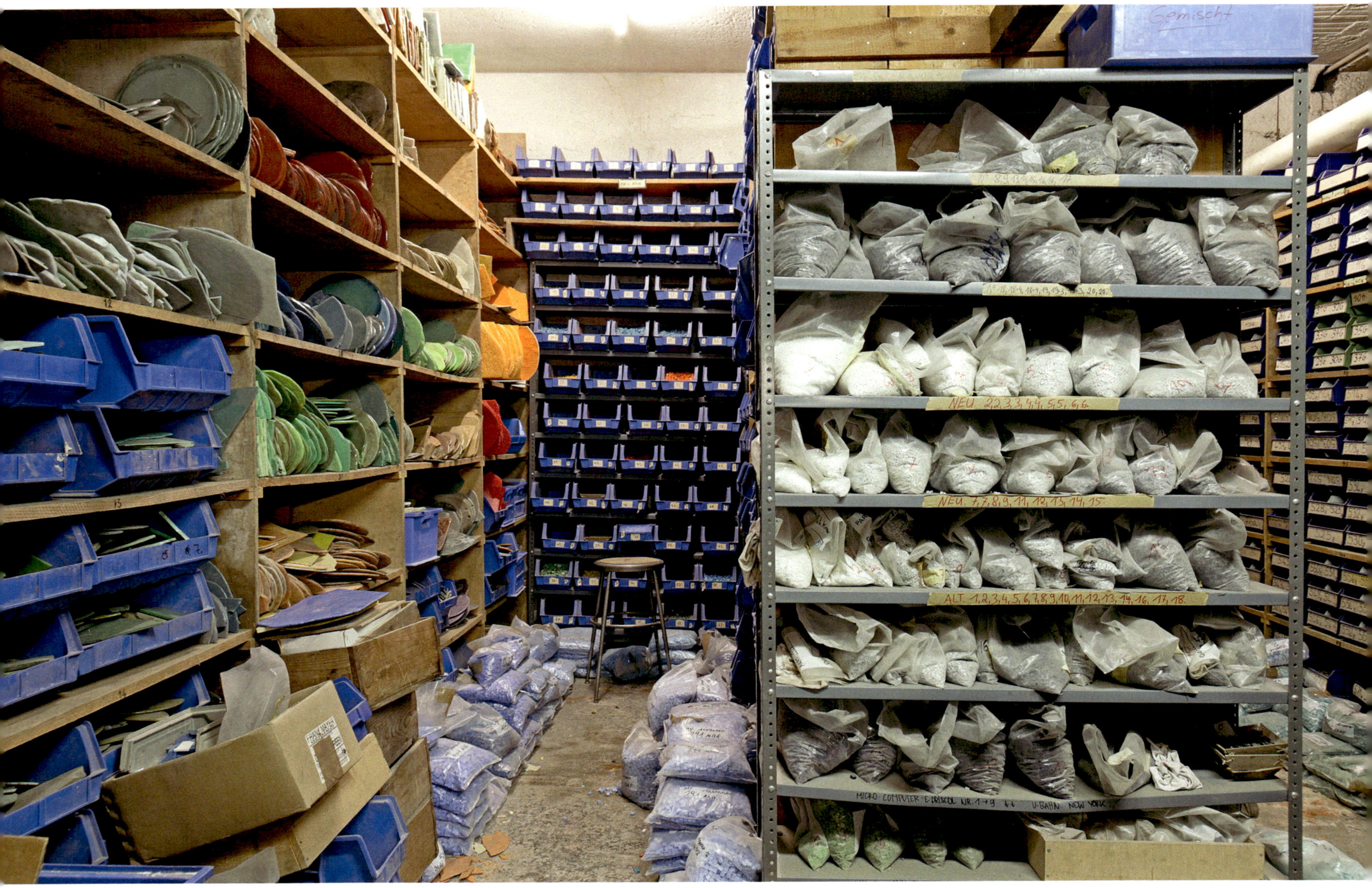

618

The Particular Importance of Richness and Complexity of Materials for Artistic Mosaics

The materials kept in storage are pivotal for mosaics. A good mosaic necessitates a wide range of supplies. A unicolor blue area may consist of numerous different hues of blue - “pure” blue, greenish, reddish, light or dark etc. Even if only one single shade of blue is selected, the choice ought to result from an affluence, not a paucity of supplies. The Mayer studio offers such affluence of mosaic colors and types of material in shelves of a length of some 300 feet, floor to ceiling.

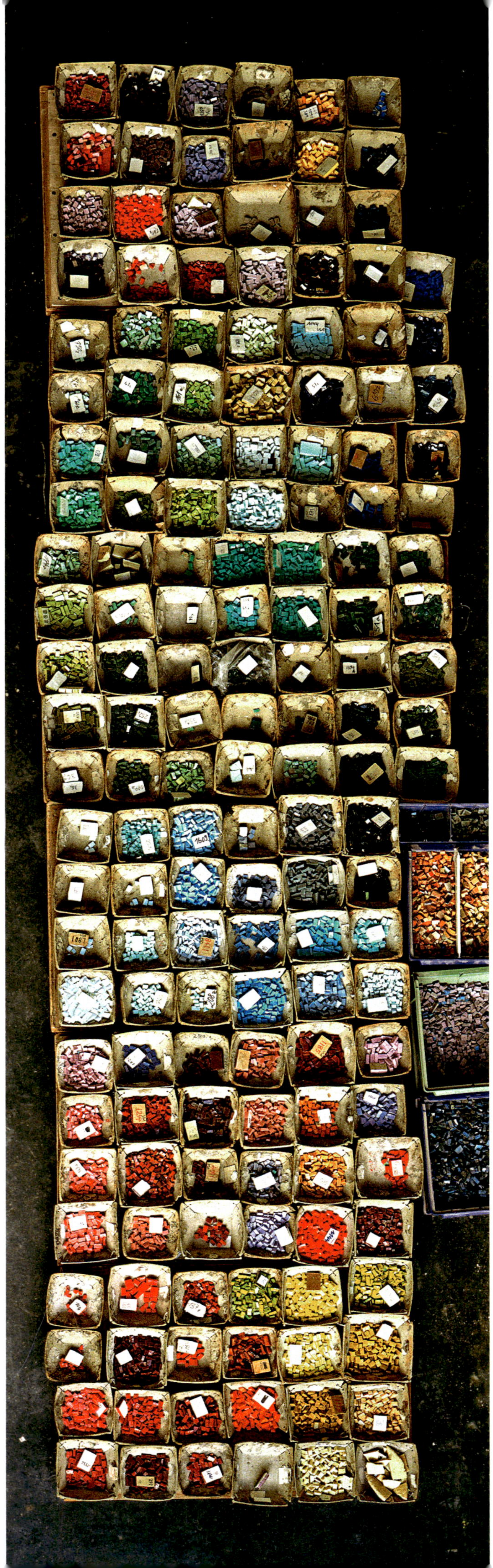

619

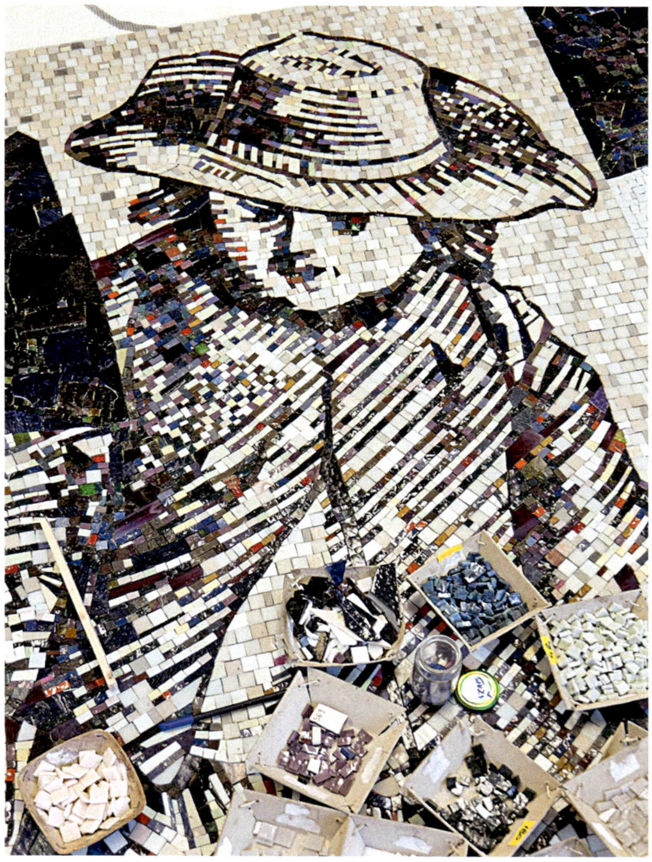

620

MATERIALS FOR MOSAICS

618
Glass mosaic smalti and cakes from Italy and Germany in a remote basement space.

619
Cardboard boxes with Italian glass smalti as they are used on the worktable.

620
Worktable detail of a mosaic by Ron Moppett for Calgary with mostly Mexican mosaic materials in Byzantine cut including many iridescent tonalities *(see p. 150–153)*.

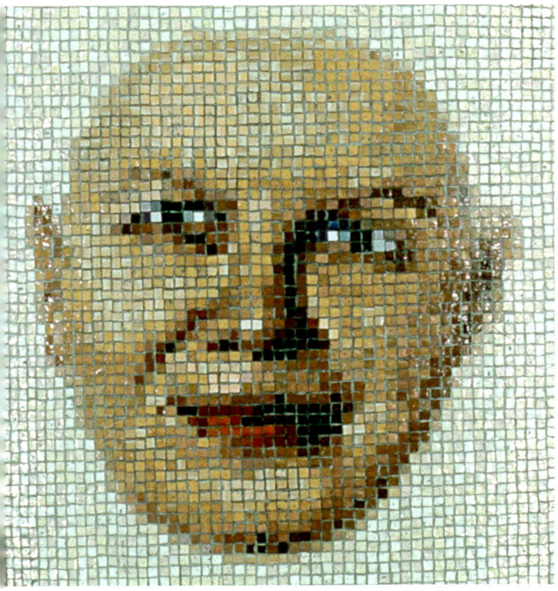

621

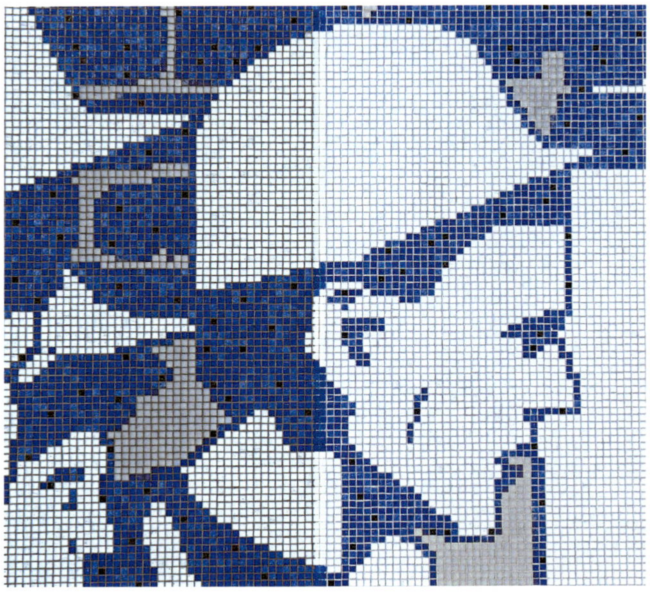

622

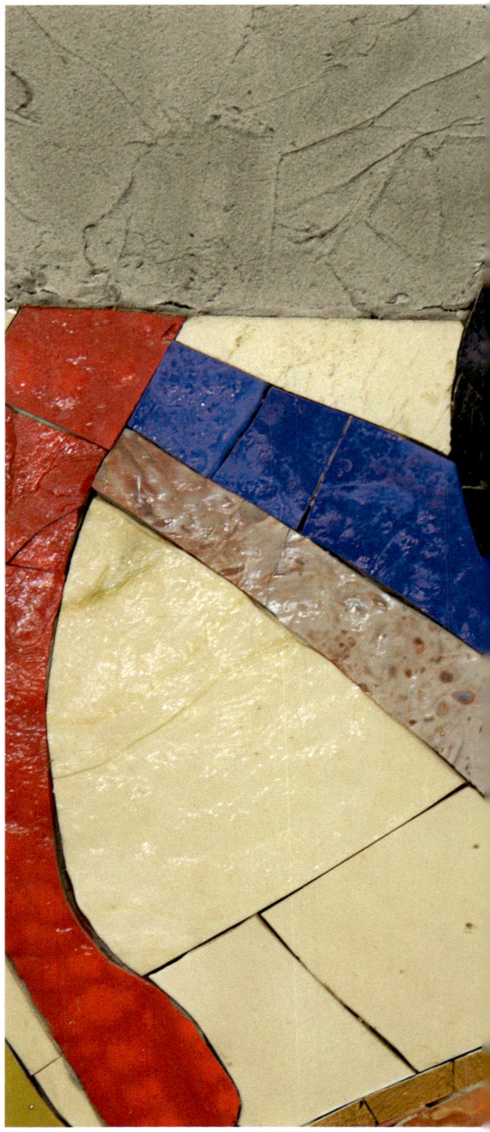

624

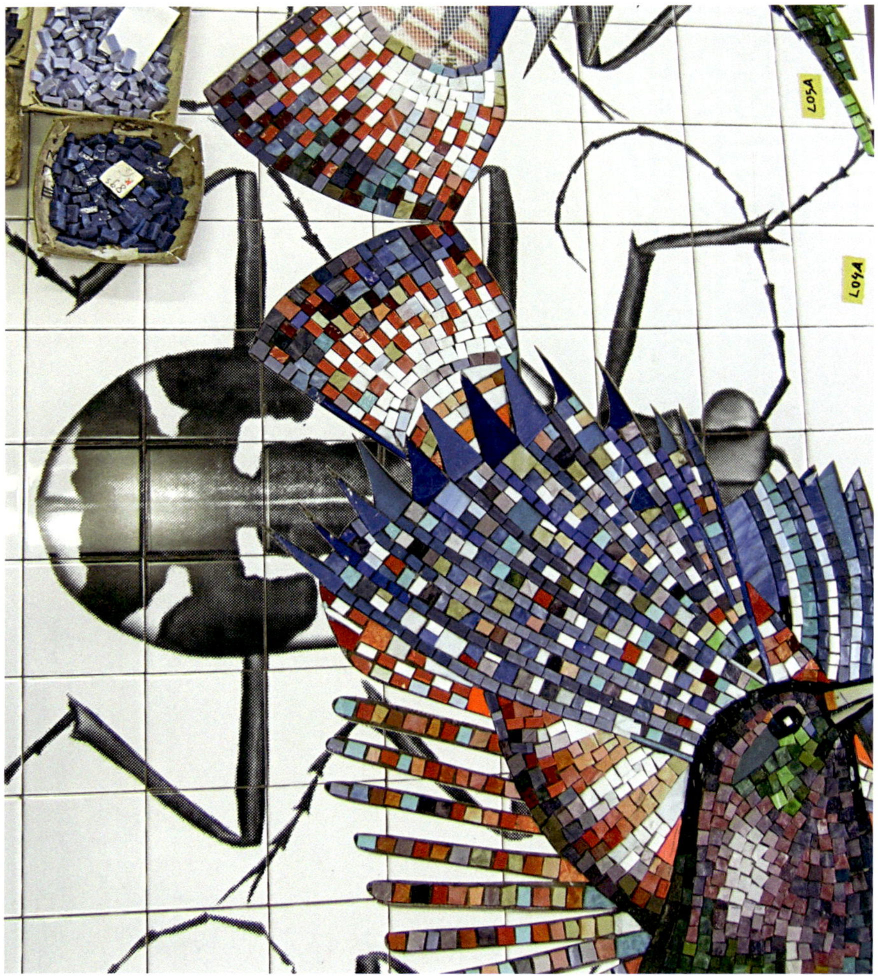

623

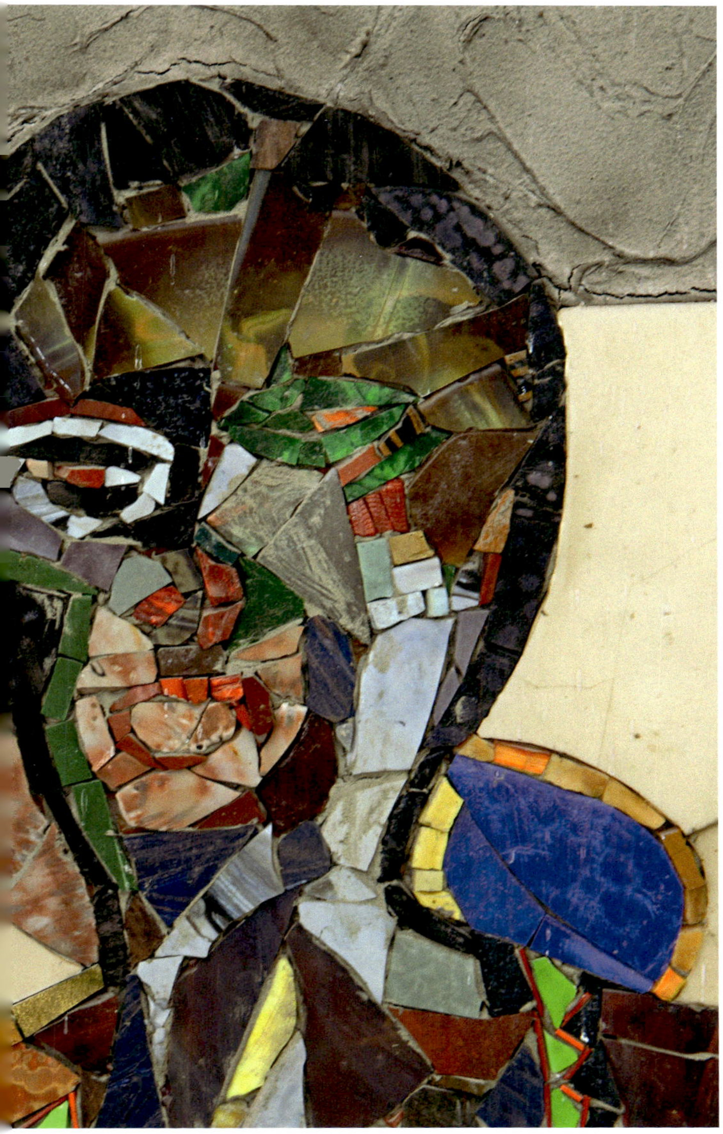

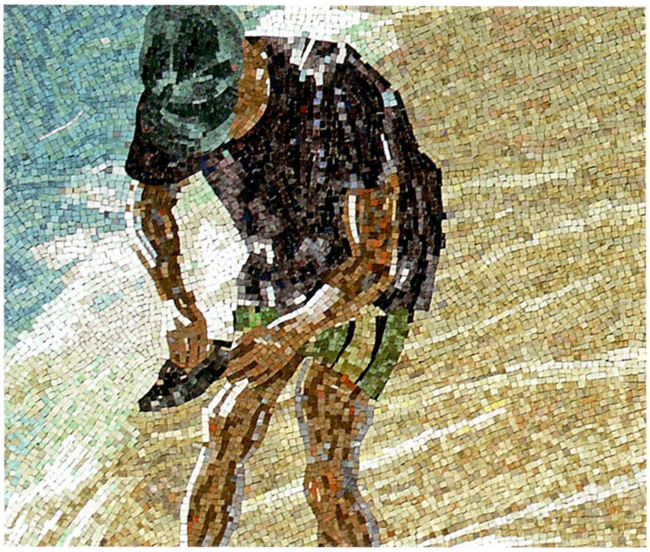

625

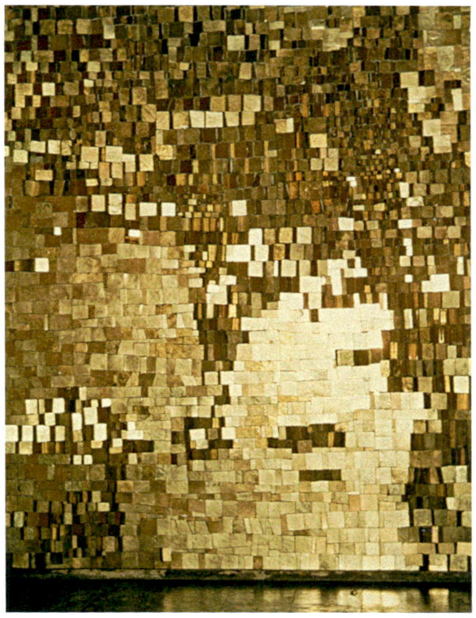

626

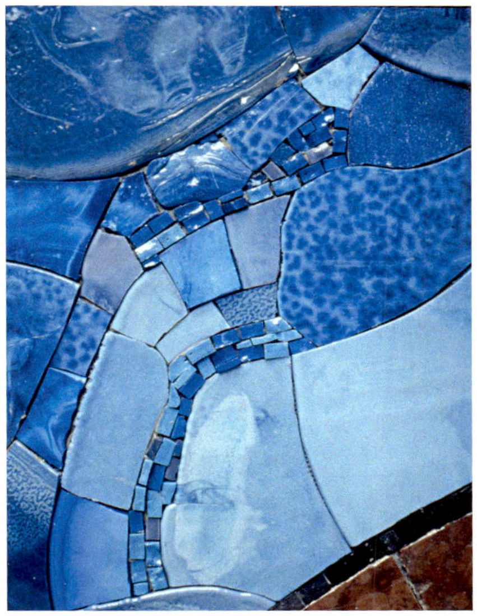

627

SETTING TYPES / MOSAIC FLOW

621
A mosaic head set in a grid, made of hand-hewn Byzantine glass smalti measuring just under ½ by ½ inch – from the work "Units and Unities" by Heiner Blum for the European Central Bank, Frankfurt/Main *(see p. 68 +69)*.

622
Head detail from industrially fabricated and hence consistently just under ½ by ½ inch glass mosaic stones – from the mosaic "Good Luck. Protest of miners in the Ruhr Area" by Silke Wagner for Herne *(see p. 212 + 213)*.

623
A detail from Ben Snead's wall mosaics for New York City's MTA Arts for Transit: Thanks to the aid of a complicated water-jet technique colored tesserae intertwine with specially printed tiles.

624
Collage of a head made of differently sized glass cakes and smalti beside a concrete foundation – from a mosaic work by Haralampi Count Oroschakoff.

625
Detail from a mosaic by Eric Fischl for a private residence in Los Angeles using irregular square Placetti mosaic supplies.

626
An almost linear-set wall mosaic with Venetian gold smalti placed on the plane and on edge from an eight feet high section of a wall mosaic by Leo Müllenholz.

627
Composition with small-scale mosaic dice and differently sized amorphous glass cake pieces: Color, form, size, and flow.

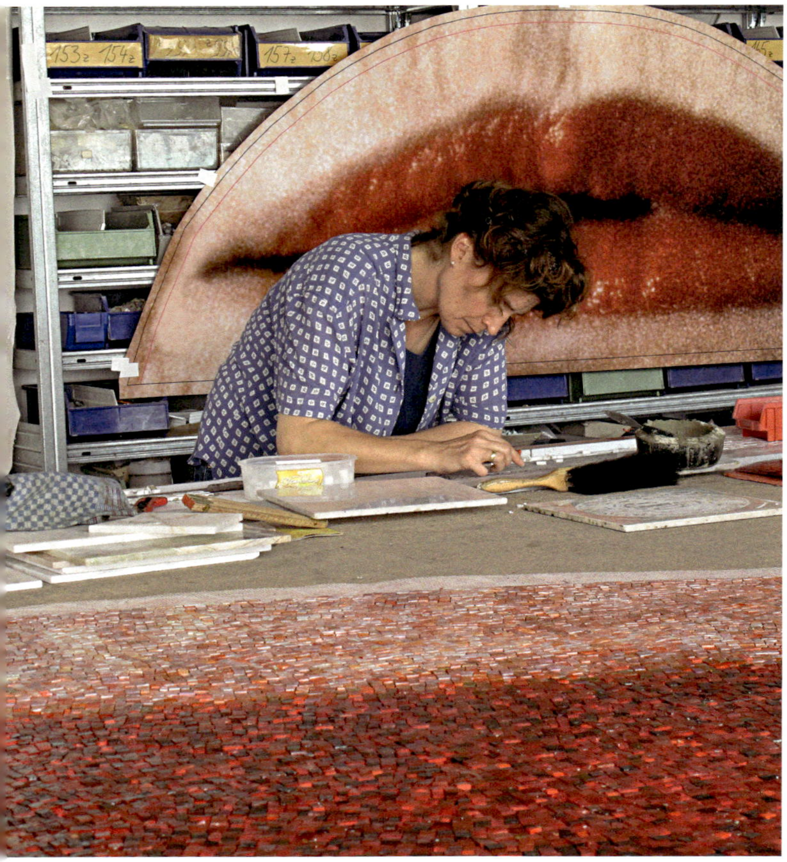

628

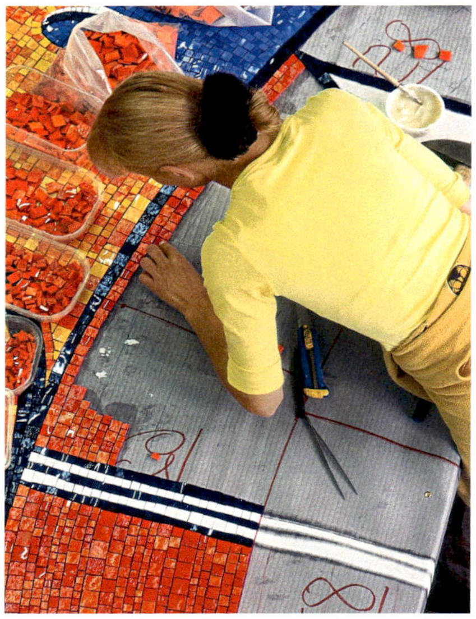

629

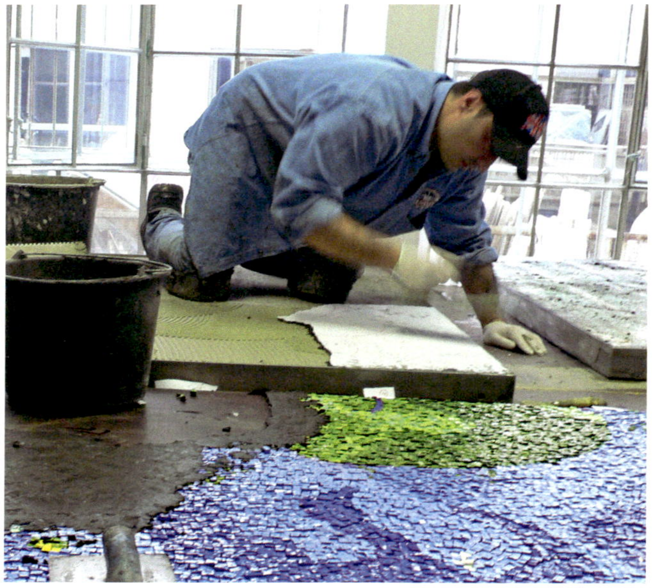

630

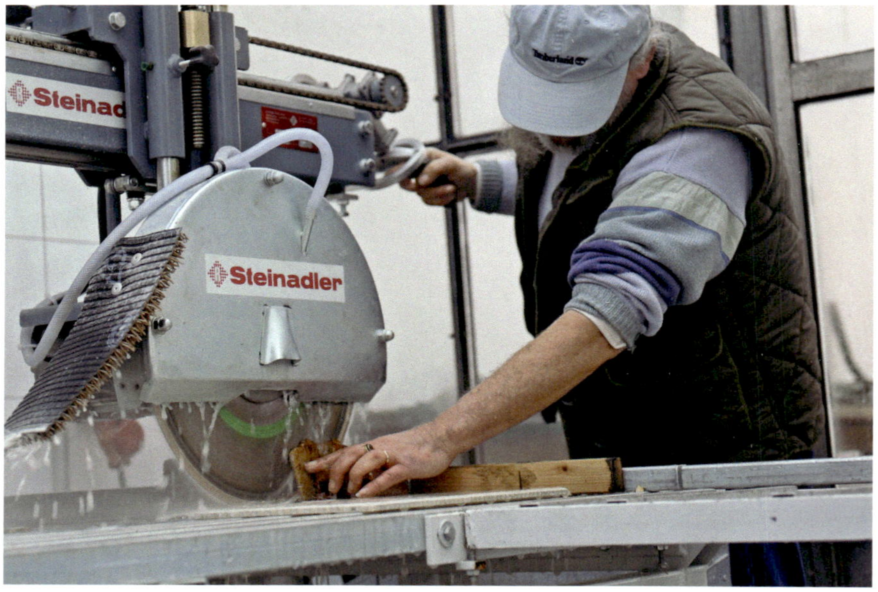

631

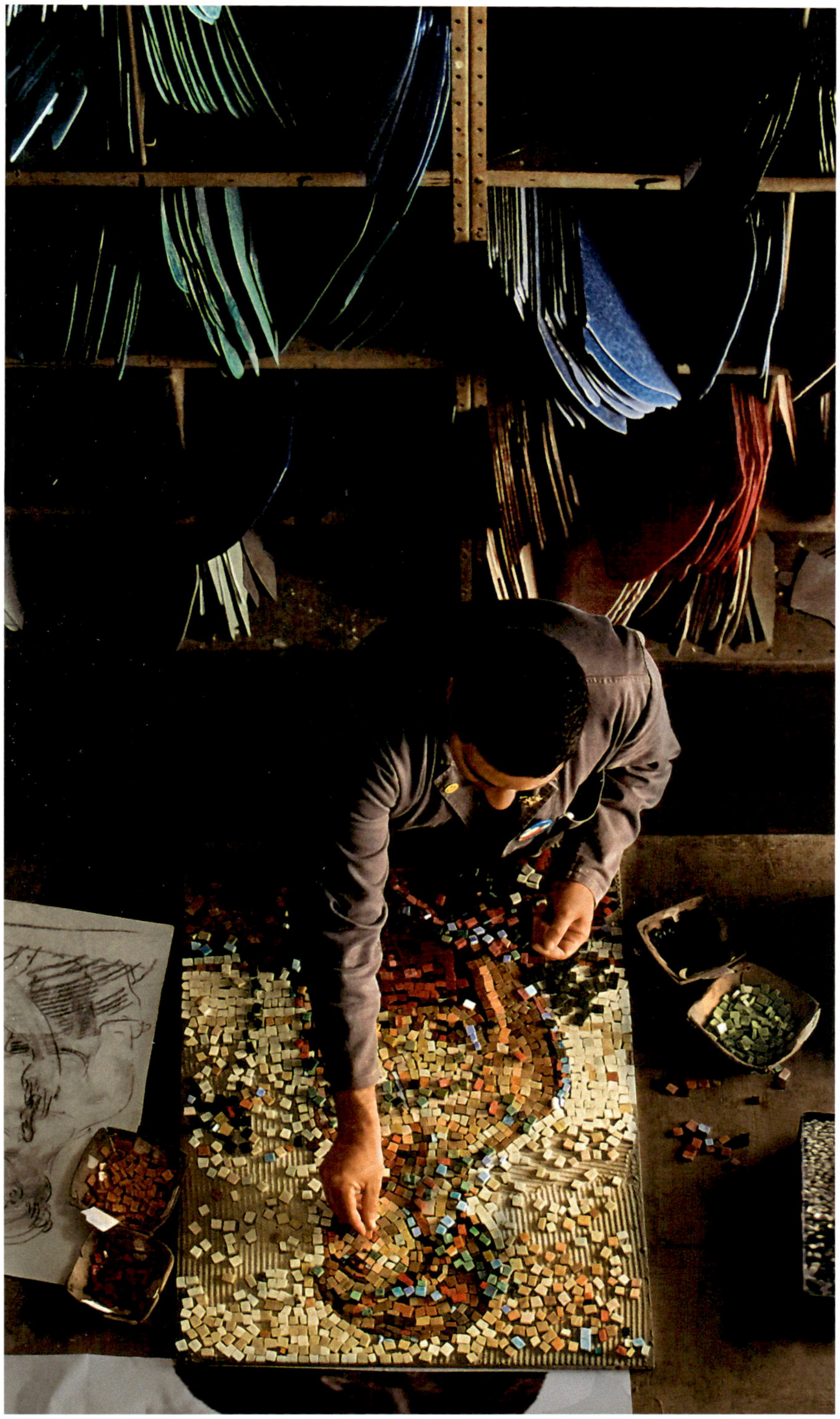

632

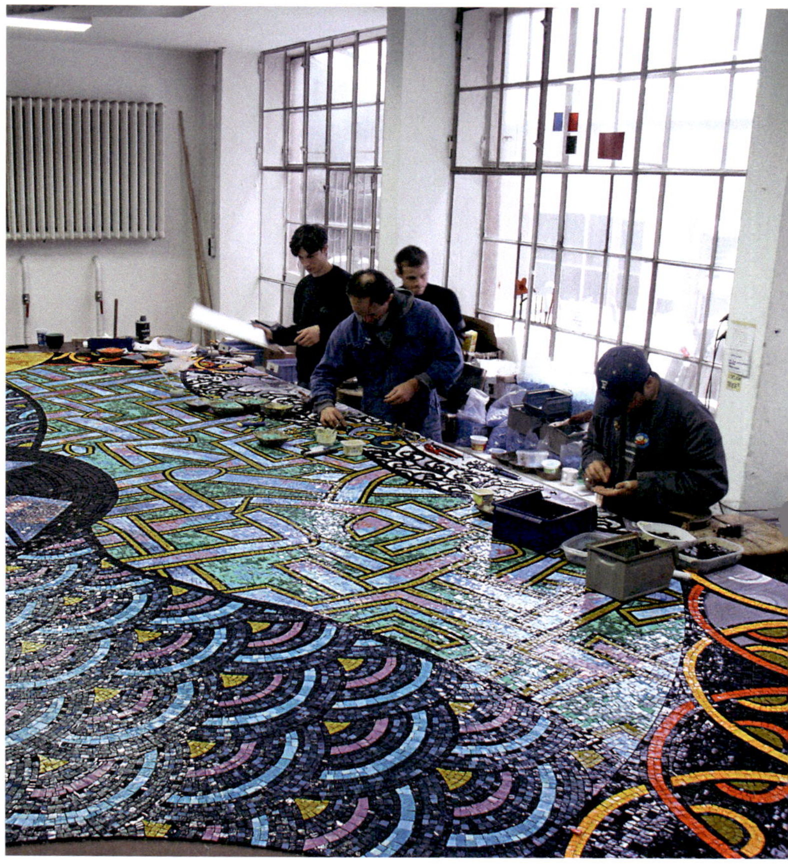

633

SETTING MOSAICS
THE WORK IN THE STUDIOS

628
Setting positive onto a fiberglass net: here Geneviève Cadieux's Metro mosaic for Paris *(see p. 78 + 79)*.

629
Setting negative on paper: here a floor mosaic of artist Viola Delgado for the DFW Airport.

630
Mounting a mosaic onto panels in the workshop.

631
At a stone and glass cutting machine.

632
A mosaicist begins to set an Expressionist figure.

633
Setting the artist Beatrice Lebreton's floor mosaic for the DFW Airport.

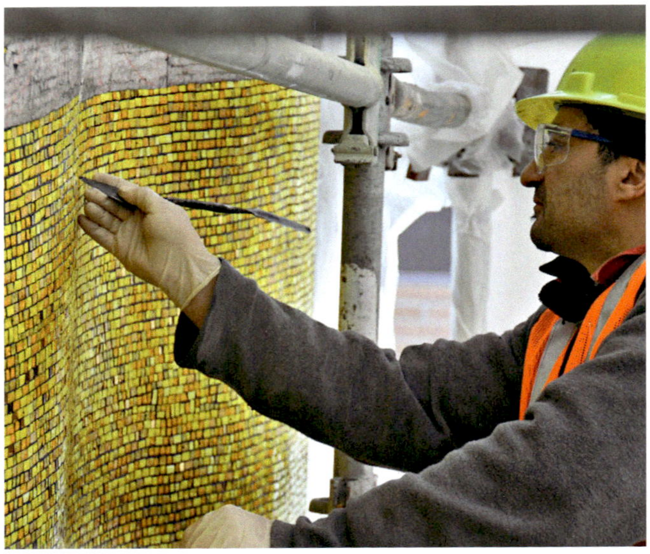

634

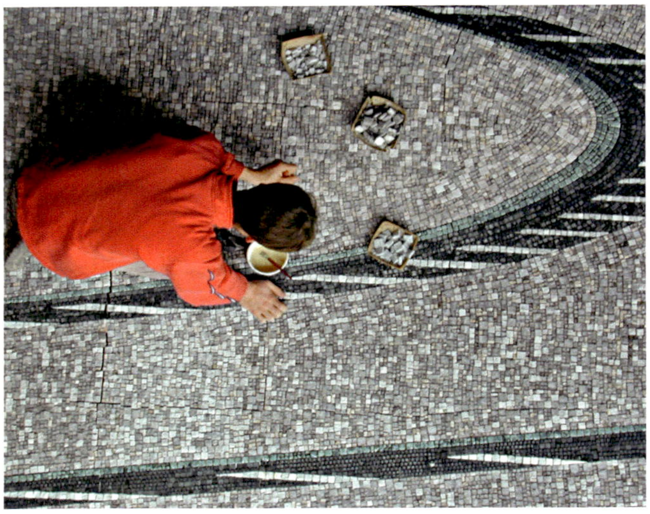

635

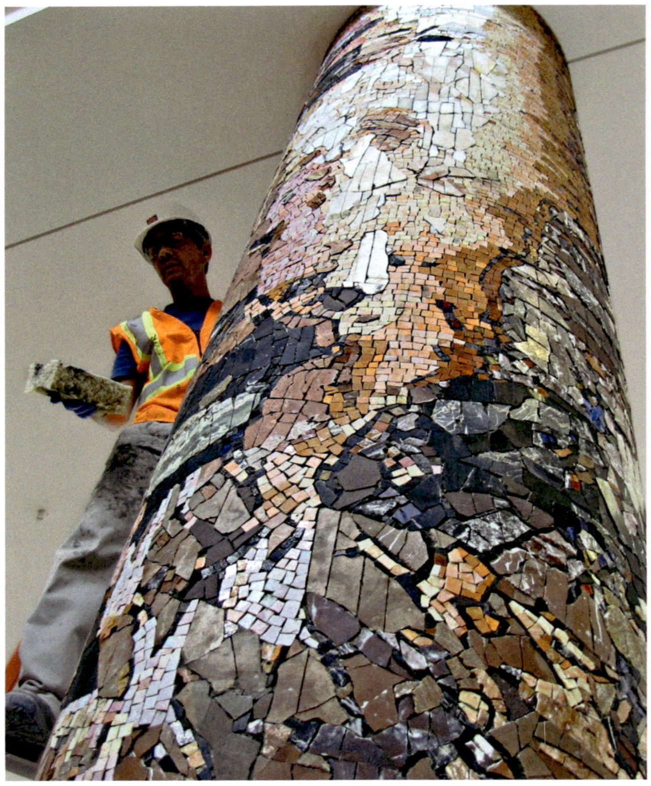

636

Installing artistic mosaics – regardless of whether they are set in the positive or the negative method, on the floor, underwater, an interior or exterior wall, or on the ceiling – requires plenty of experience and skill. The work's artistic value, its many little parts, the especially frail borders, the continous design lines, and other peculiarities of artistic mosaics frequently suggest the performance of the installation through or with at least the presence of mosaicists from Munich, even in far-away places.

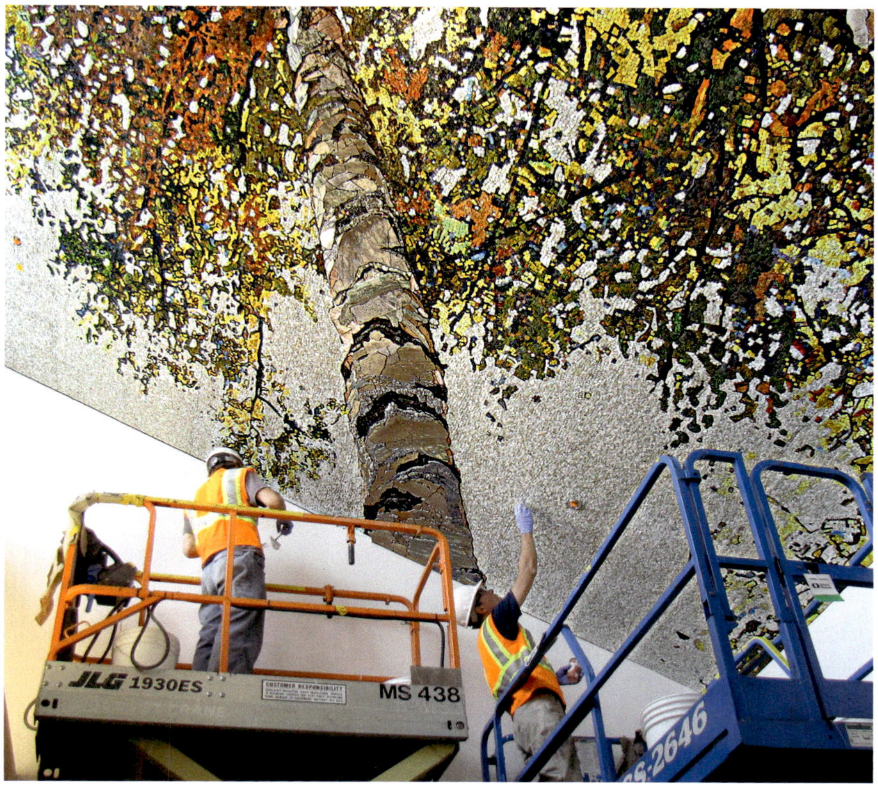

637

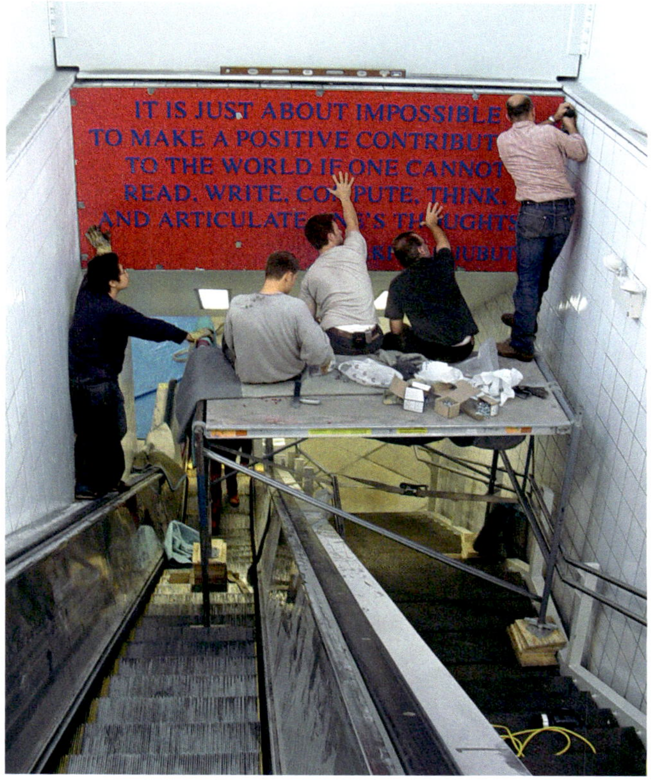

638

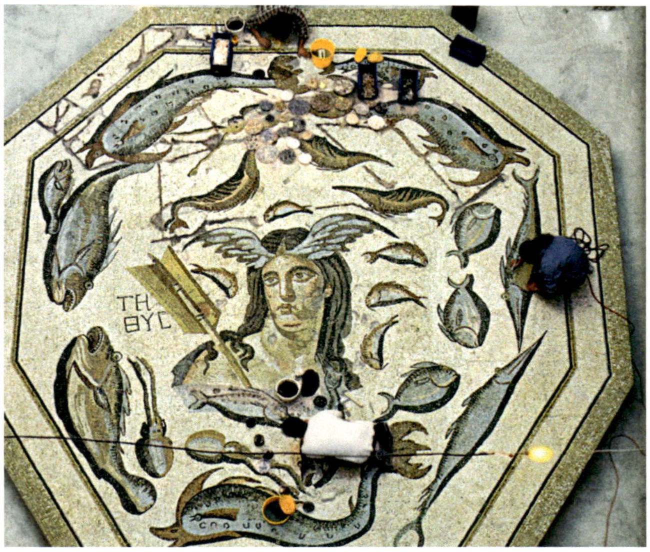

639

INSTALLING MOSAICS IN SITU
WITH MOSAICISTS FROM MUNICH

634
Regularity and cleanliness of the net of joints are important. The Munich mosaicist, assisted by a local craftsman, installs Ann Gardner's warped mosaic in Seattle *(see p. 97).*

635
Preparing the installation of the floor mosaic of Haubitz + Zoche in the Allianz headquarter building in Munich *(see p. 298).*

636 + 637
Installing the ceiling and column mosaics at Anchorage airport with the assistance of local workmen *(see p. 218 + 219).*

638
During the installation of Adam Brooks' text mosaics in Chicago, done in tandem with local aids. *(see p. 256).*

639
Conservation and reconstruction work on the Roman Thetis mosaic at Harvard University in Cambridge, MA, went on for months and required profound knowledge and experience. The largest ancient mosaic in the US, it originates from Antioch.

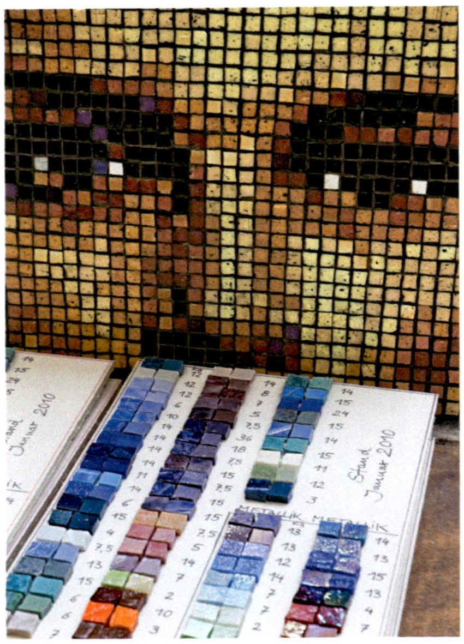

640

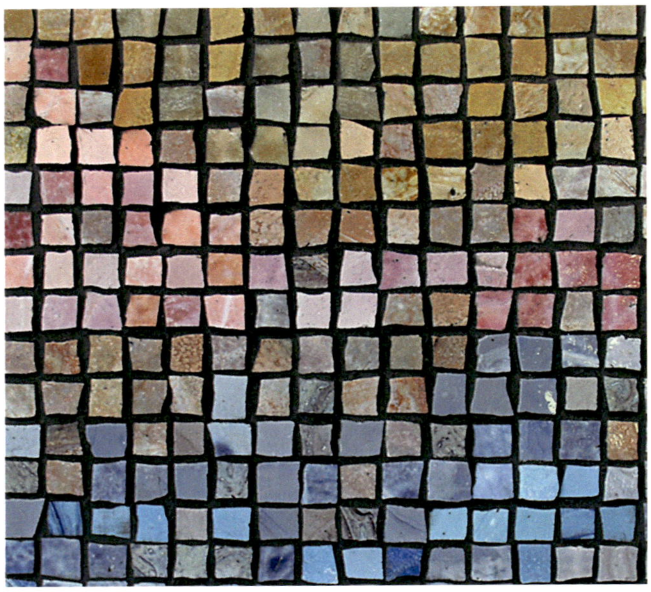

641

THE BEAUTY OF MOSAIC DETAILS

640
Color scales and mosaic face made of hand-cut, irregular, square tesserae.

641
In contrast to industrially made grid-mosaics, the hand-poured and hand-cut smalti offer plenty of nuances, and even in simple color gradients, the tesserae possess a particular beauty.

642
Head detail from a work of Juan Carlos Macias for the Chicago Transit Authority.

643
Water-jet cut letters made of Venetian glass cake in front of a blue background made from Byzantine-set glass smalti.

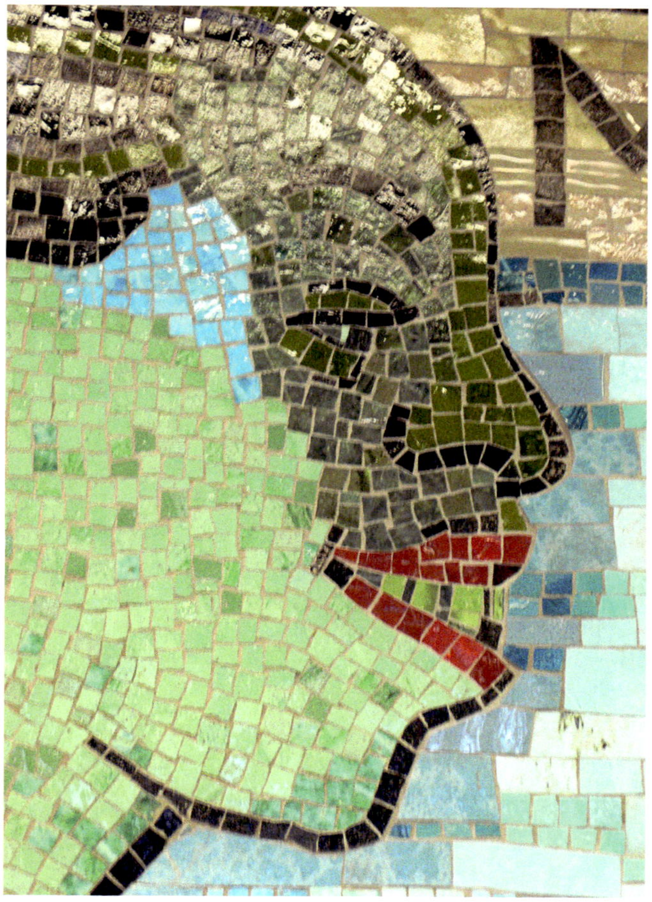

642

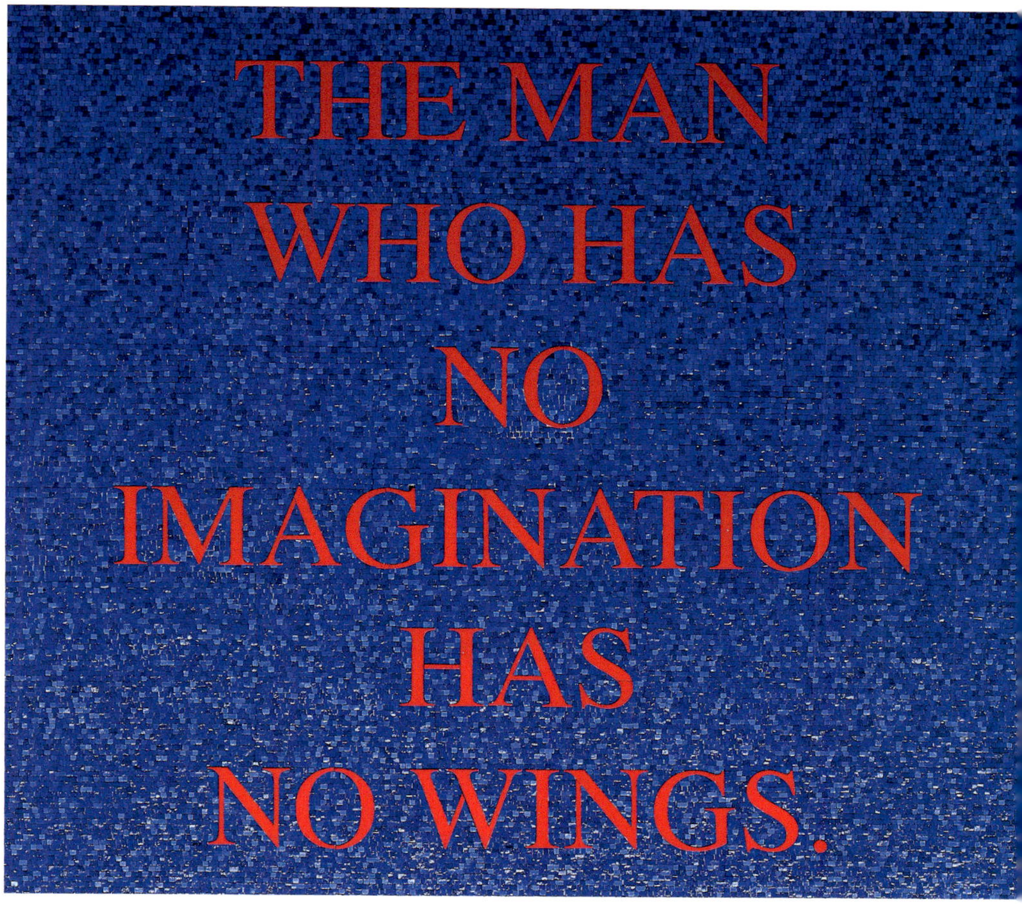

643

Editor's Epilogue

Gabriel Mayer

Accounting for 165 years of a firm's history by placing exemplary images from among countless works between two book covers is a real challenge. The history we – our Mayer family and generations of staff of the Mayer'sche Hofkunstanstalt – have experienced and shaped and our related works and projects are simply too multifaceted. We were able and privileged at the same time to realize all this with so many different artists. We feel an immense joy and simultaneous responsibility for our culturally important tasks. As we look back, we may also be proud of our achievements: As a private enterprise without any outside support, we have – thanks to our energy, endurance, plus our great love and passion for good art and architecture – managed to create culturally viable products, despite two world wars, times when our survival was at risk, and when what we did was considered "second or third rate, old fashioned," or "kitsch." Ultimately, perhaps this all had to be.

Two realizations have increasingly taken hold and have become the basis for our entire work: For us, quality comes first and we have always been and want to remain the studio for the artist, where the artist collaborates with us, develops concepts in an intense and creative process of give and take. In a joint effort, we strive for the best possible solutions. We know all too well about the risk of producing less-than-exciting artworks once this collaborative creative process falls victim to routine and might easily drown in hokum.

The Mayer'sche Hofkunstanstalt would not be what it is today (nor what it was yesterday) without the many artists who come to Munich from all over the world to collaborate with us. Without them this book could not have been produced. Therefore, I want to take this opportunity and thank all artists from the bottom of my heart for their trust and their appreciation. We are grateful that we could work together with them, and their art encouraged us. Seeing the limitations of this publication was a painful realization for us, and it was frustrating that we were forced to leave out so many artists and projects although we would love to have featured them. This book is the product of long discussions and difficult selections involving many individuals. Therefore, I want to especially thank those artists who could not be included in this documentation for their cooperation and their loyalty.

My thanks also go to the art agents and advisers, architects, private and public clients for their trust in us. The artistic visions could not have been realized without them. It is thanks to this group of people that projects such as the ones shown in this book can be realized at all. At the same time, I would like to ask you a favor: Keep considering public art that engages architecture in dialogues as art. Do not consider public art as mass-produced, decorative items, a sad tendency that may be observed time and again.

My thanks and my respect equally go to the studio and all our staff who – thanks to their enthusiasm for art, their technical skill, endurance, and eagerness for each and every single project – contribute to the successful production of artworks. Without them, the Mayer'sche Hofkunstanstalt would not be what it is today.

My son Michael has developed into a partner who values and nurtures the family tradition and our firm's vision: to be a professional and visionary studio for artists. I thank him especially for the shared years filled with creativity and inspiration, for his vision and his commitment to preserve the Mayer'sche Hofkunstanstalt as an attractive place for artistic exchanges and creations in the future.

This is the opportunity to extend special thanks to my wife, Renate, to whom I owe a special mention. I am incredibly grateful to her for all the decades during which she supported, encouraged, carried, and also tolerated me. Without her perpetual patience and her critical eye I would not be who I am today.

Index of Places

Index of Names

Photo Credits

IMAGE NO.

Abbott, Jon and Anne **84**

Albert, Judith **77, 80**

Alles, Pat **207**

Aperture Photography, Stepen Gould **395–397**

Baker, Keith **525, 526**

Baker, Pat **121**

Bako, Andrew **426**

Baracz, Jan **140–144**

Barros, Ricardo **478, 479**

Bartlett, Grace Kirsten **514, 515**

Beleschenko, Alexander **94, 375–378**

Bernhard, Manfred **498, 499**

Bernstein Assoc. Photographers, Laurie Donald **74, 75**

Blanchard, Tom **418, 419**

Blaukopf, Julia **79**

Brooks, Adam **383–385**

Brian Clarke Studio, Martin Booth **331–336, 338–340, 343, 359, 361–364**

Bunz, Achim **222**

Cadieux, Geneviève **108**

Cashin, Patrick **398**

Chong, Jerry **427, 428**

Christmas, G.R. **272**

Clements & Howcroft **403**

Costantini, Andre **206**

Coyne, Roderick **197, 199, 201**

Craig, Eric Studios **392, 393, 489, 491**

Damonte, Bruce **529**

Dee, James **399, 400**

Döhne, Volker **273, 275**

Donlin, Martin **110**

Draz, Bernhard **401, 402**

Dreßler, Roland **446, 447**

Dunn, Casey **236–238**

Durant, Peter **93**

Engelhardt/Sellin **89, 159**

Falco, Mike **305, 306, 409–412**

Fay, Ming **571**

Feldstein, Peter **413, 414**

Fisher, True **408**

Foster & Partners, Nigel Young **o. Nr. S. 44–45, 73, 341, 342**

Frahm, Klaus **203–205, 233–235**

Frajndlich, Abe **181**

Frossard, Etienene **280, 281**

Fuchs, Albrecht **132, 257, 564**

Gage, Hal **307, 308**

Galerie Daniel Blau **473**

Galston, Beth **420**

Gindroz, Rémy **76**

Gipe, Jim **115, 116**

Goetz, Rainer **421**

Gould, Eric **390**

Graf, Bernhard, Dr. **86–88, 146, 227, 228**

Günzel, Wolfgang **160**

Hanebeck, A. **433**

Hassos, Elias **99–103, 145, 148, 149, 164, 168–176, 226–228, 239–243, 245, 246, 282–285, 368, 490, 530, 531**

Havey Productions **161, 162**

Hellane, David **183, 466, 467**

Henrich, Biff **187, 188**

Hilbich, Markus **497**

Hill, Robin **495**

Hinz-Rosin, Peter **523, 524**

Hofmann, Rainer **163**

Holzherr, Florian **85, 311–313**

Hornig, Sabine **434**

Hyde, Joseph **464**

Indianapolis Airport Authority **111**

Jacoby, Lisa **133, 134**

James Ewing Photography **97–98**

Johansson, Gerry **309**

Johnson, Russel **135**

Jones, Jeremy **420**

Kamber, Mike **406, 407**

Kaprov, Susan **449, 450**

Karlsen, Anne Marie **451–454**

Kitzinger, Albert Dr. **220, 221**

Kleinbach, Frank **254**

Kluska, Peter **460**

LA County MTA (Metro) **165**

LaFleche, Collin **511, 512**

Laibarös, Ioni **370, 371**

Laurie Donald, Bernstein Assoc. **74, 75**

Lindner, Ute **462**

Lipa, Klaus 3**03, 304**

Lubarsky, David **388, 389**

Madigan, Martha **470, 471**

Mafford Spike Photography **177, 178**

Martinez, Marcos **214–217, 219**

Mayer, Daniel **195, 196**

Mayer, Gabriel **12**

McFarland, Rachael **387**

Mellenthin, Klaus J.A. **496**

Mensing, Roman **302**

Metropolitan Transportation Authority Arts for Transit **492**

Miebach, Bärbel **274, 277–279**

Miguletz, Norbert **310**

Miller, Joel **365, 366**

Moran MichaelPhotography Inc. **267–271**

Morris, James **480, 481**

Müller-Naumann, Stefan **244**

Myrzik + Jarisch **122, 261–265, 267, 573, 266**

Nestler, Bernd **223–225**

Peak Experience Imagery **208, 209, 212, 213**

Peirce, Peter **441**

Petzi, Wilfried **391**

Pfieffer, Erhard **455**

Ping-Weinberg Eli **185, 186**

Poon, Joe **333**

Portillo, Roberto **314, 359**

Punctum Fotografie **438**

Rau, Christoph **72**

Rehm, Dieter **386**

Rein, Udo **488**

Riehle, Tomas **458, 459**

Ries, Stan **394**

Reid, Stuart **487**

Rein, Udo **488**

COPYRIGHT VG BILD-KUNST, BONN 2013, IMAGE NO..

COPYRIGHTS ARTISTS

Colophon

Copy-editing: Alexander Langkals

Graphic design and typesetting: LIQUID | Agentur für Gestaltung, Augsburg

Production: Sabine Frohmader

Separations / Reproductions: Reproline mediateam

Printing and binding: Aumüller, Regensburg

Paper: GardaArt Matt 150g

The Deutsche Nationalbibliothek lists this publication in the Deutsche Nationalbibliografie; detailed bibliographic data are available on the Internet at http://dnb.d-nb.de

ISBN 978-3-7774-5251-7 (American Edition)

ISBN 978-3-7774-5601-0 (German Edition)

Hirmer Verlag

Nymphenburger Str. 84

D-80636 München

www.hirmerverlag.de

Cover illustration: Mel Bochner, "To Count: INTRANSITIVE", Private Residence, Dutchess County, NY, USA; view from the lower patio (s. p. 70–73)